MW00852457

THE EXPOSITOR'S BIBLE COMMENTARY

THE EXPOSITOR'S BIBLE COMMENTARY

in Thirteen Volumes

When complete, the Expositor's Bible Commentary will include the following volumes:

Volume 1: Genesis–Leviticus
Volume 2: Numbers–Ruth
Volume 3: 1 Samuel–2 Kings
Volume 4: 1 Chronicles–Job
Volume 5: Psalms
Volume 6: Proverbs–Isaiah
Volume 7: Jeremiah–Ezekiel
Volume 8: Daniel–Malachi
Volume 9: Matthew–Mark
Volume 10: Luke–Acts
Volume 11: Romans–Galatians
Volume 12: Ephesians–Philemon
Volume 13: Hebrews–Revelation

To see which titles are available, visit www.zondervan.com.

THE EXPOSITOR'S BIBLE COMMENTARY

REVISED EDITION

1 Samuel ~ 2 Kings

Tremper Longman III & David E. Garland
General Editors

ZONDERVAN

The Expositor's Bible Commentary: 1 Samuel–2 Kings

Requests for information should be addressed to:

Zondervan, *Grand Rapids, Michigan 49530*

Library of Congress Cataloging-in-Publication Data

The expositor's Bible commentary 1 Samuel–2 Kings/ [general editors], Tremper Longman III and David E. Garland.—Rev.
p. cm.
Includes bibliographical references.
IBSN 13: 978-0-310-23495-1
1. Bible. OT—Commentaries. I. Longman, Tremper. II. Garland, David E.
BS2341.53.E96 2005
220.7—dc22 2005006281

Interior design by Tracey Walker

Printed in the United States of America

12 13 14 15 16 17 18 19 20 • 30 29 28 27 26 25 24 23 22 21 20 19 18 17 16 15 14 13 12 11 10 9 8 7 6 5 4 3 2

CONTENTS

CONTRIBUTORS TO VOLUME THREE

1 and 2 Samuel: **Ronald F. Youngblood** (Ph.D., Dropsie College for Hebrew and Cognate Learning) has served as professor of Old Testament at Bethel Seminary in St. Paul, Wheaton Graduate School, Trinity Evangelical Divinity School, and Bethel Seminary in San Diego, and is currently serving in the same capacity at International College and Graduate School in Honolulu. He is an associate editor of the *NIV Study Bible* and serves on the committee for the NIV and TNIV translations.

1 and 2 Kings: **Richard D. Patterson** (Ph.D., University of California, Los Angeles) is distinguished professor emeritus, Liberty University, Lynchburg, Virginia. He has been involved in numerous Bible projects either as a translator, peer reviewer, or contributor. He was associate editor of the *New International Dictionary of Old Testament Theology and Exegesis* (Zondervan).

1 and 2 Kings: **Hermann J. Austel** (Ph.D. in ancient Near Eastern Languages, UCLA) has taught at Los Angeles Baptist College and Seminary and presently professor of Hebrew and Old Testament at Northwest Baptist Seminary in Tacoma, Washington.

General editor: **Tremper Longman III** (Ph.D., Yale University) is Robert H. Gundry professor of biblical studies at Westmont College in Santa Barbara, California.

General editor: **David E. Garland** (Ph.D., Southern Baptist Theological Seminary) is associate dean of academic affairs and William M. Hinson professor of Christian Scriptures at George W. Truett Seminary, Baylor University, in Waco, Texas.

PREFACE

Frank Gaebelein wrote the following in the preface to the original Expositor's Bible Commentary (which first appeared in 1979): "The title of this work defines its purpose. Written primarily by expositors for expositors, it aims to provide preachers, teachers, and students of the Bible with a new and comprehensive commentary on the books of the Old and New Testaments." Those volumes achieved that purpose admirably. The original EBC was exceptionally well received and had an enormous impact on the life of the church. It has served as the mainstay of countless pastors and students who could not afford an extensive library on each book of the Bible but who wanted solid guidance from scholars committed to the authority of the Holy Scriptures.

Gaebelein also wrote, "A commentary that will continue to be useful through the years should handle contemporary trends in biblical studies in such a way as to avoid becoming outdated when critical fashions change." This revision continues the EBC's exalted purpose and stands on the shoulders of the expositors of the first edition, but it seeks to maintain the usefulness of the commentary by interacting with new discoveries and academic discussions. While the primary goal of this commentary is to elucidate the text and not to provide a guide to the scholarly literature about the text, the commentators critically engage recent academic discussion and provide updated bibliographies so that pastors, teachers, and students can keep abreast of modern scholarship.

Some of the commentaries in the EBC have been revised by the original author or in conjunction with a younger colleague. In other cases, scholars have been commissioned to offer fresh commentaries because the original author had passed on or wanted to pass on the baton to the next generation of evangelical scholars. Today, with commentaries on a single book of the Old and New Testaments often extending into multiple volumes, the need for a comprehensive yet succinct commentary that guides one to the gist of the text's meaning is even more pressing. The new EBC seeks to fill this need.

The theological stance of this commentary series remains unchanged: the authors are committed to the divine inspiration, complete trustworthiness, and full authority of the Bible. The commentators have demonstrated proficiency in the biblical book that is their specialty, as well as commitment to the church and the pastoral dimension of biblical interpretation. They also represent the geographical and confessional diversity that characterized the first contributors.

The commentaries adhere to the same chief principle of grammatico-historical interpretation that drove the first edition. In the foreword to the inaugural issue of the journal *New Testament Studies* in 1954, Matthew Black warned that "the danger in the present is that theology, with its head too high in the clouds, may end by falling into the pit of an unhistorical and uncritical dogmatism. Into any new theological undertaking must be brought all that was best in the old ideal of sound learning, scrupulous attention to philology, text and history." The dangers that Black warned against over fifty years ago have not vanished. Indeed, new dangers arise in a secular, consumerist culture that finds it more acceptable to use God's name in exclamations than in prayer and that encourages insipid theologies that hang in the wind and shift to tickle the ears and to meet the latest fancy. Only a solid biblical foundation can fend off these fads.

The Bible was not written for our information but for our transformation. It is not a quarry to find stones with which to batter others but to find the rock on which to build the church. It does not invite us simply to speak of God but to hear God and to confess that his Son, Jesus Christ, is Lord to the glory of God the Father (Php 2:10). It also calls us to obey his commandments (Mt 28:20). It is not a self-interpreting text, however. Interpretation of the Holy Scriptures requires sound learning and regard for history, language, and text. Exegetes must interpret not only the primary documents but all that has a bearing, direct or indirect, on the grammar and syntax, historical context, transmission, and translation of these writings.

The translation used in this commentary remains the New International Version (North American edition), but all of the commentators work from the original languages (Hebrew and Greek) and draw on other translations when deemed useful. The format is also very similar to the original EBC, while the design is extensively updated with a view to enhanced ease of use for the reader. Each commentary section begins with an introduction (printed in a single-column format) that provides the reader with the background necessary to understand the Bible book. Almost all introductions include a short bibliography and an outline. The Bible text is divided into primary units that are often explained in an "Overview" section that precedes commentary on specific verses. The complete text of the New International Version is provided for quick reference, and an extensive "Commentary" section (printed in a double-column format) follows the reproducing of the text. When the Hebrew or Greek text is cited in the commentary section, a phonetic system of transliteration and translation is used. The "Notes" section (printed in a single-column format) provides a specialized discussion of key words or concepts, as well as helpful resource information. The original languages and their transliterations will appear in this section. Finally, on occasion, expanded thoughts can be found in a "Reflections" section (printed in a double-column format) that follows the Notes section.

One additional feature is worth mentioning. Throughout this volume, wherever specific biblical words are discussed, the Goodrick-Kohlenberger (GK) numbers have been added. These numbers, which appear in the *Strongest NIV Exhaustive Concordance* and other reference tools, are based on the numbering system developed by Edward Goodrick and John Kohlenberger III and provide a system similar but superior to the Strong's numbering system.

The editors wish to thank all of the contributors for their hard work and commitment to this project. We also deeply appreciate the labor and skill of the staff at Zondervan. It is a joy to work with them—in particular Jack Kuhatschek, Stan Gundry, Katya Covrett, Dirk Buursma, and Verlyn Verbrugge. In addition, we acknowledge with thanks the work of Connie Gundry Tappy as copy editor.

We all fervently desire that these commentaries will result not only in a deeper intellectual grasp of the Word of God but also in hearts that more profoundly love and obey the God who reveals himself to us in its pages.

David E. Garland, associate dean for academic affairs and William M. Hinson professor of Christian Scriptures, George W. Truett Theological Seminary at Baylor University

Tremper Longman III, Robert H. Gundry professor of biblical studies, Westmont College

ABBREVIATIONS

Bible Texts, Versions, Etc.

ASV	American Standard Version
AT	*The Complete Bible: An American Translation* (NT: E. J. Goodspeed)
Barclay	*The New Testament, A New Translation*
Beck	*New Testament in Language of Today*
BHK	*Biblia Hebraica Kittel*
BHS	*Biblia Hebraica Stuttgartensia*
CEV	Contemporary English Version
CSB	Christian Standard Bible
ESV	English Standard Version
GNB	Good News Bible (see also TEV)
GWT	God's Word Translation
JB	Jerusalem Bible
KJV	King James Version
Knox	*Holy Bible: A Translation from the Latin Vulgate*
MLB	Modern Language Bible
Moffatt	*A New Translation of the Bible*, James Moffatt
Montgomery	*Centenary Translation of the New Testament in Modern English*
NA^{27}	*Novum Testamentum Graece*, Nestle-Aland, 27th ed.
NAB	New American Bible
NASB	New American Standard Bible
NCV	New Century Version
NEB	New English Bible
NET	New English Translation (www.netbible.com)
NIV	New International Version
NJB	New Jerusalem Bible
NJPS	New Jewish Publication Society
NKJV	New King James Version
NLT	New Living Translation
Norlie	*New Testament in Modern English*
NRSV	New Revised Standard Version
Phillips	*New Testament in Modern English*, J. B. Phillips
REB	Revised English Bible
Rieu	*Penguin Bible*
RSV	Revised Standard Version
RV	Revised Version
Tanakh	Tanakh, a Jewish translation of the Hebrew Bible
TCNT	Twentieth Century New Testament
TEV	Today's English Version
TNIV	Today's New International Version
UBS^4	*The Greek New Testament*, United Bible Societies, 4th ed.
Weymouth	*New Testament in Modern Speech*, R. F. Weymouth
Williams	*The New Testament in the Language of the People*, C. B. Williams

Old Testament, New Testament, Apocrypha

Ge	Genesis
Ex	Exodus
Lev	Leviticus
Nu	Numbers
Dt	Deuteronomy
Jos	Joshua
Jdg	Judges
Ru	Ruth
1–2Sa	1–2 Samuel
1–2 Kgdms	1–2 Kingdoms (LXX)
1–2Ki	1–2 Kings
3–4 Kgdms	3–4 Kingdoms (LXX)
1–2Ch	1–2 Chronicles
Ezr	Ezra
Ne	Nehemiah
Est	Esther
Job	Job
Ps/Pss	Psalm/Psalms
Pr	Proverbs
Ecc	Ecclesiastes
SS	Song of Songs
Isa	Isaiah
Jer	Jeremiah
La	Lamentations
Eze	Ezekiel
Da	Daniel
Hos	Hosea
Joel	Joel
Am	Amos
Ob	Obadiah
Jnh	Jonah
Mic	Micah
Na	Nahum
Hab	Habakkuk
Zep	Zephaniah
Hag	Haggai
Zec	Zechariah
Mal	Malachi
Mt	Matthew
Mk	Mark
Lk	Luke
Jn	John
Ac	Acts
Ro	Romans
1–2Co	1–2 Corinthians
Gal	Galatians
Eph	Ephesians
Php	Philippians
Col	Colossians
1–2Th	1–2 Thessalonians
1–2Ti	1–2 Timothy
Tit	Titus
Phm	Philemon
Heb	Hebrews
Jas	James
1–2Pe	1–2 Peter
1–2–3Jn	1–2–3 John
Jude	Jude
Rev	Revelation
Add Esth	Additions to Esther
Add Dan	Additions to Daniel
Bar	Baruch
Bel	Bel and the Dragon
Ep Jer	Epistle of Jeremiah
1–2 Esd	1–2 Esdras
1–2 Macc	1–2 Maccabees
3–4 Macc	3–4 Maccabees
Jdt	Judith
Pr Azar	Prayer of Azariah
Pr Man	Prayer of Manasseh
Ps 151	Psalm 151
Sir	Sirach/Ecclesiasticus
Sus	Susanna
Tob	Tobit
Wis	Wisdom of Solomon

Dead Sea Scrolls and Related Texts

CD	Cairo Genizah copy of the *Damascus Document*	4QpPs	*Pesher Psalms* (texts from Qumran)
DSS	Dead Sea Scrolls	4Q44 (4QDt[q])	Deuteronomy (texts from Qumran)
1QapGen	*Genesis Apocryphon* (texts from Qumran)	4Q174	*Florilegium* (texts from Qumran)
1QH	*Hôdāyōt* or *Thanksgiving Hymns* (texts from Qumran)	4Q252	*Commentary on Genesis A*, formerly *Patriarchal Blessings* (texts from Qumran)
1QIsa	Isaiah (texts from Qumran)		
1QM	*Milḥāmāh* or *War Scroll* (texts from Qumran)	4Q394	*Miqṣat Maᶜaśê ha-Torah*[a] (texts from Qumran)
1QpHab	Pesher Habakkuk (texts from Qumran)	4Q400	*Songs of the Sabbath Sacrifice* (texts from Qumran)
1QS	*Serek hayyaḥad* or *Rule of the Community* (texts from Qumran)	4Q502	*Ritual of Marriage* (texts from Qumran)
1QSa	*Rule of the Congregation* (texts from Qumran)	4Q521	*Messianic Apocalypse* (texts from Qumran)
1QpMic	*Pesher Micah* (text from Qumran)	4Q525	*Beatitudes* (texts from Qumran)
4QpNa	*Pesher Nahum* (texts from Qumran)	11QPs[a]	*Psalms Scroll*[a]
		11Q13	*Melchizedek* (texts from Qumran)

Other Ancient Texts

ʾAbot R. Nat.	*ʾAbot of Rabbi Nathan*	*Ant. rom.*	*Antiquitates romanae* (Dionysius of Halicarnassus)
Abraham	*On the Life of Abraham* (Philo)		
Ad.	*Adelphi* (Terence)	*1 Apol.*	*First Apology* (Justin Martyr)
Aeth.	*Aethiopica* (Heliodorus)	*Apol.*	*Apologia* (Plato, Tertullian)
Ag.	*Agamemnon* (Aeschylus)	*Apos. Con.*	*Apostolic Constitutions*
Ag. Ap.	*Against Apion* (Josephus)	*Ascen. Isa.*	*Ascension of Isaiah*
Agr.	*De Lege agraria* (Cicero)	*As. Mos.*	*Assumption of Moses*
Alc.	*Alcibiades* (Plutarch)	*Att.*	*Epistulae ad Atticum* (Cicero)
Alex.	*Alexander the False Prophet* (Lucian)	*b. ᶜAbod. Zar.*	*ᶜAbodah Zarah* (Babylonian Talmud)
Amic.	*De amicitia* (Cicero)	*2–4 Bar.*	*2–4 Baruch*
An.	*De anima* (Tertullian)	*b. ᶜArak*	*ᶜArakin* (Babylonian Talmud)
Anab.	*Anabasis* (Xenophon)	*b. B. Bat.*	*Bava Batra* (Babylonian Talmud)
Ann.	*Annales* (Tacitus)	*b. B.Qam.*	*Baba Qamma* (Babylonian Talmud)
Ant.	*Antigone* (Sophocles)	*b. Ber.*	*Berakhot* (Babylonian Talmud)
Ant.	*Jewish Antiquities* (Josephus)	*b. Hag.*	*Hagigah* (Babylonian Talmud)

b. Hor.	*Horayot* (Babylonian Talmud)
b. Ker.	*Kerithot* (Babylonian Talmud)
b. Ketub.	*Ketubbot* (Babylonian Talmud)
b. Meg.	*Megillah* (Babylonian Talmud)
b. Menaḥ.	*Menaḥot* (Babylonian Talmud)
b. Mo'ed Qat.	*Mo'ed Qatan* (Babylonian Talmud)
b. Ned.	*Nedarim* (Babylonian Talmud)
b. Pesaḥ.	*Pesaḥim* (Babylonian Talmud)
b. Roš Haš.	*b. Roš Haššanah* (Babylonian Talmud)
b. Šabb.	*Šabbat* (Babylonian Talmud)
b. Sanh.	*Sanhedrin* (Babylonian Talmud)
b. Šebu.	*Shevu'ot* (Babylonian Talmud)
b. Soṭah	*Soṭah* (Babylonian Talmud)
b. Ta'an.	*Ta'anit* (Babylonian Talmud)
b. Yebam.	*Yebamot* (Babylonian Talmud)
b. Yoma	*Yoma* (Babylonian Talmud)
Bapt.	*De baptismo* (Tertullian)
Barn.	*Barnabas*
Ben.	*De beneficiis* (Seneca)
Bibl.	*Bibliotheca* (Photius)
Bibl. hist.	*Bibliotheca historica* (Diodorus Siculus)
Bride	*Advice to the Bride and Groom* (Plutarch)
Cels.	*Contra Celsum* (Origen)
Cic.	*Cicero* (Plutarch)
Claud.	*Divus Claudius* (Suetonius)
1–2 Clem.	*1–2 Clement*
Comm. Dan.	*Commentarium in Danielem* (Hippolytus)
Comm. Jo.	*Commentarii in evangelium Joannis* (Origen)
Comm. Matt.	*Commentarium in evangelium Matthaei* (Origen)
Corrept.	*De correptione et gratia* (Augustine)
Cyr.	*Cyropaedia* (Xenophon)
Decal.	*De decalogo* (Philo)
Decl.	*Declamationes* (Quintilian)
Def. orac.	*De defectu oraculorum* (Plutarch)
Deipn.	*Deipnosophistae* (Athenaeus)
Deut. Rab.	*Deuteronomy Rabbah*
Dial.	*Dialogus cum Tryphone* (Justin Martyr)
Diatr.	*Diatribai* (Epictetus)
Did.	*Didache*
Disc.	*Discourses* (Epictetus)
Doctr. chr.	*De doctrina christiana* (Augustine)
Dom.	*Domitianus* (Suetonius)
Ebr.	*De ebrietate* (Philo)
E Delph.	*De E apud Delphos* (Plutarch)
1–2 En.	*1–2 Enoch*
Ench.	*Enchiridion* (Epictetus)
Ep.	*Epistulae morales* (Seneca)
Eph.	*To the Ephesians* (Ignatius)
Epist.	*Epistulae* (Jerome, Pliny, Hippocrates)
Ep. Tra.	*Epistulae ad Trajanum* (Pliny)
Eth. nic.	*Ethica nichomachea* (Aristotle)
Exod. Rab.	*Exodus Rabbah*
Fam.	*Epistulae ad familiares* (Cicero)
Fid. Grat.	*De fide ad Gratianum* (Ambrose)
Flacc.	*In Flaccum* (Philo)
Flight	*On Flight and Finding* (Philo)
Fr. Prov.	*Fragmenta in Proverbia* (Hippolytus)
Gen. Rab.	*Genesis Rabbah*
Geogr.	*Geographica* (Strabo)
Gorg.	*Gorgias* (Plato)
Haer.	*Adversus Haereses* (Irenaeus)
Heir	*Who Is the Heir?* (Philo)
Hell.	*Hellenica* (Xenophon)
Hist.	*Historicus* (Polybius, Cassius Dio, Thucydides)
Hist.	*Historiae* (Herodotus, Tacitus)
Hist. eccl.	*History of the Church* (Eusebius)
Hist. Rome	*The History of Rome* (Livy)
Hom. Acts	*Homilies on Acts* (John Chrysostom)

Hom. Col.	*Homilies on Colossians* (John Chrysostom)
Hom. Jo.	*Homilies on John* (John Chrysostom)
Hom. Josh.	*Homilies on Joshua* (Origen)
Hom. Phil.	*Homilies on Philippians* (John Chrysostom)
Hom. Rom.	*Homilies on Romans* (John Chrysostom)
Hom. 1 Tim.	*Homilies on 1 Timothy* (John Chrysostom)
Hom. 2 Tim.	*Homilies on 2 Timothy* (John Chrysostom)
Hom. Tit.	*Homilies on Titus* (John Chrysostom)
Hypoth.	*Hypothetica* (Philo)
Inst.	*Institutio oratoria* (Quintilian)
Jos. Asen.	*Joseph and Aseneth*
Joseph	*On the Life of Joseph* (Philo)
Jub.	*Jubilees*
J.W.	*Jewish War* (Josephus)
Lam. Rab.	*Lamentations Rabbah*
L.A.E.	*Life of Adam and Eve*
Leg.	*Legum allegoriae* (Philo)
Legat.	*Legatio ad Gaium* (Philo)
Let. Aris.	*Letter of Aristeas*
Lev. Rab.	*Leviticus Rabbah*
Liv. Pro.	*Lives of the Prophets*
m. Bek.	*Bekhorot* (Mishnah)
m. Bik.	*Bikkurim* (Mishnah)
m. Giṭ.	*Giṭṭin* (Mishnah)
m. Mak.	*Makkot* (Mishnah)
m. Mid.	*Middot* (Mishnah)
m. Naz.	*Nazir* (Mishnah)
m. Ned.	*Nedarim* (Mishnah)
m. Nid.	*Niddah* (Mishnah)
m. Pesaḥ	*Pesaḥim* (Mishnah)
m. Šabb.	*Šabbat* (Mishnah)
m. Sanh.	*Sanhedrin* (Mishnah)
m. Šeqal.	*Šeqalim* (Mishnah)
m. Taᶜan.	*Taᶜanit* (Mishnah)
m. Tamid	*Tamid* (Mishnah)
m. Ṭehar.	*Ṭeharot* (Mishnah)
Magn.	*To the Magnesians* (Ignatius)
Mand.	*Mandate* (Shepherd of Hermas)
Marc.	*Adversus Marcionem* (Tertullian)
Mem.	*Memorabilia* (Xenophon)
Midr. Ps.	*Midrash on Psalms*
Migr.	*De migratione Abrahami* (Philo)
Mor.	*Moralia* (Plutarch)
Moses	*On the Life of Moses* (Philo)
Nat.	*Naturalis historia* (Pliny)
Num. Rab.	*Numbers Rabbah*
Onir.	*Onirocritica* (Artemidorus)
Or.	*Orationes* (Demosthenes)
Or.	*Orationes* (Dio Chrysostom)
Paed.	*Paedagogus* (Clement of Alexandria)
Peregr.	*The Passing of Peregrinus* (Lucian)
Pesiq. Rab.	*Pesiqta Rabbati*
Pesiq. Rab Kah.	*Pesiqta of Rab Kahana*
Phaed.	*Phaedo* (Plato)
Phil.	*To the Philippians* (Polycarp)
Phld.	*To the Philadelphians* (Ignatius)
Phorm.	*Phormio* (Terence)
Planc.	*Pro Plancio* (Cicero)
Plant.	*De plantatione* (Philo)
Pol.	*Politica* (Aristotle)
Pol.	*To Polycarp* (Ignatius)
Posterity	*On the Posterity of Cain* (Origen)
Praescr.	*De praescriptione haereticorum* (Tertullian)
Princ.	*De principiis* (Origen)
Prom.	*Prometheus vinctus* (Aeschylus)
Pss. Sol.	*Psalms of Solomon*
Pud.	*De pudicitia* (Tertullian)
Pyth.	*Pythionikai* (Pindar)
Pyth. orac.	*De Pythiae oraculis* (Plutarch)
Quaest. conv.	*Quaestionum convivialum libri IX* (Plutarch)

Quint. fratr.	*Epistulae ad Quintum fratrem* (Cicero)
Rab. Perd.	*Pro Rabirio Perduellionis Reo* (Cicero)
Resp.	*Respublica* (Plato)
Rewards	*On Rewards and Punishments* (Philo)
Rhet.	*Rhetorica* (Aristotle)
Rhet.	*Volumina rhetorica* (Philodemus)
Rom.	*To the Romans* (Ignatius)
Rosc. com.	*Pro Roscio comoedo* (Cicero)
Sacrifices	*On the Sacrifices of Cain and Abel* (Philo)
Sat.	*Satirae* (Horace, Juvenal)
Sera	*De sera numinis vindicta* (Plutarch)
Serm.	*Sermones* (Augustine)
Sib. Or.	*Sibylline Oracles*
Sim.	*Similitudes* (Shepherd of Hermas)
Smyrn.	*To the Smyrnaeans* (Ignatius)
S. ᶜOlam Rab.	*Seder ᶜOlam Rabbah*
Somn.	*De somniis* (Philo)
Spec.	*De specialibus legibus* (Philo)
Stat.	*Ad populum Antiochenum de statuis* (John Chrysostom)
Strom.	*Stromata* (Clement of Alexandria)
T. Ash.	*Testament of Asher*
T. Dan	*Testament of Dan*
T. Gad	*Testament of Gad*
T. Naph.	*Testament of Naphtali*
Tg. Neof.	*Targum Neofiti*
Tg. Onq.	*Targum Onqelos*
Tg. Ps.-J.	*Targum Pseudo-Jonathan*
Theaet.	*Theaetetus* (Plato)
t. Ḥul.	*Ḥullin* (Tosefta)
T. Jos.	*Testament of Joseph*
T. Jud.	*Testament of Judah*
T. Levi	*Testament of Levi*
T. Mos.	*Testament of Moses*
T. Naph.	*Testament of Naphtali*
Trall.	*To the Trallians* (Ignatius)
T. Reu.	*Testament of Reuben*
Tusc.	*Tusculanae disputationes* (Cicero)
Verr.	*In Verrem* (Cicero)
Virt.	*De virtutibus* (Philo)
Vis.	*Visions* (Shepherd of Hermas)
Vit. Apoll.	*Vita Apollonii* (Philostratus)
Vit. beat.	*De vita beata* (Seneca)
Vit. soph.	*Vitae sophistarum* (Philostratus)
y. ᶜAbod. Zar.	*ᶜAbodah Zarah* (Jerusalem Talmud)
y. Ḥag.	*Ḥagigah* (Jerusalem Talmud)
y. Šabb.	*Šabbat* (Jerusalem Talmud)

Journals, Periodicals, Reference Works, Series

AASOR	Annual of the American Schools of Oriental Research
AB	Anchor Bible
ABD	*Anchor Bible Dictionary*
ABR	*Australian Biblical Review*
AbrN	*Abr-Nahrain*
ABRL	Anchor Bible Reference Library
ABW	*Archaeology in the Biblical World*
ACCS	Ancient Christian Commentary on Scripture
ACNT	Augsburg Commentaries on the New Testament
AcT	*Acta theologica*
AIs	*Ancient Israel, by Roland de Vaux*
AJBI	*Annual of the Japanese Biblical Institute*
AJSL	*American Journal of Semitic Languages and Literature*
AnBib	Analecta biblica

ANEP	*The Ancient Near East in Pictures Relating to the Old Testament*
ANET	*Ancient Near Eastern Texts Relating to the Old Testament*
ANF	*Ante-Nicene Fathers*
AnOr	Analecta orientalia
ANRW	*Aufstieg und Niedergang der römischen Welt*
AOAT	Alter Orient und Altes Testament
AR	*Archiv für Religionssissenschaft*
ASORMS	American Schools of Oriental Research Monograph Series
ASTI	*Annual of the Swedish Theological Institute*
AThR	*Anglican Theological Review*
ATLA	American Theological Library Association
AuOr	Aula orientalis
AUSDDS	Andrews University Seminary Doctoral Dissertation Series
AUSS	*Andrews University Seminary Studies*
BA	*Biblical Archaeologist*
BAGD	Bauer, Arndt, Gingrich, and Danker (2d ed.). *Greek-English Lexicon of the New Testament and Other Early Christian Literature*
BAR	*Biblical Archaeology Review*
BASOR	*Bulletin of the American Schools of Oriental Research*
BBB	Bonner biblische Beiträge
BBR	*Bulletin for Biblical Research*
BDAG	Bauer, Danker, Arndt, and Gingrich (3d ed.). *Greek-English Lexicon of the New Testament and Other Early Christian Literature*
BDB	Brown, Driver, and Briggs. *A Hebrew and English Lexicon of the Old Testament*
BDF	Blass, Debrunner, and Funk. *A Greek Grammar of the New Testament and Other Early Christian Literature*
BEB	*Baker Encyclopedia of the Bible*
BECNT	Baker Exegetical Commentary on the New Testament
Ber	*Berytus*
BETL	Bibliotheca ephemeridum theologicarum lovaniensium
BGU	*Aegyptische Urkunden aus den Königlichen Staatlichen Museen zu Berlin, Griechische Urkunden*
BI	*Biblical Illustrator*
Bib	*Biblica*
BibInt	*Biblical Interpretation*
BibOr	Biblica et orientalia
BibS(N)	Biblische Studien (Neukirchen)
Bijdr	*Bijdragen: Tijdschrit voor filosofie en theologie*
BJRL	*Bulletin of the John Rylands University Library of Manchester*
BJS	Brown Judaic Studies
BKAT	Biblischer Kommentar, Altes Testament
BN	*Biblische Notizen*
BR	*Biblical Research*
BRev	*Bible Review*
BSac	*Bibliotheca sacra*
BST	The Bible Speaks Today
BT	*The Bible Translator*
BTB	*Biblical Theology Bulletin*
BWANT	Beiträge zur Wissenschaft zum Alter und Neuen Testament
BZ	*Biblische Zeitschrift*
BZAW	Beihefte zur Zeitschrift für die alttestamentliche Wissenschaft

BZNW Beihefte zur Zeitschrift für die neutestamentliche Wissenschaft
CAD *Assyrian Dictionary of the Oriental Institute of the University of Chicago*
CAH Cambridge Ancient History
CahRB Cahiers de la Revue biblique
CBC Cambridge Bible Commentary
CBQ *Catholic Biblical Quarterly*
CBQMS Catholic Biblical Quarterly Monograph Series
CGTC Cambridge Greek Testament Commentary
CH *Church History*
ChrT *Christianity Today*
CIG *Corpus inscriptionum graecarum*
CIL *Corpus inscriptionum latinarum*
CJT *Canadian Journal of Theology*
ConBNT Coniectanea biblica: New Testament Series
ConBOT Coniectanea biblica: Old Testament Series
COS *The Context of Scripture*
CTJ *Calvin Theological Journal*
CTM *Concordia Theological Monthly*
CTQ *Concordia Theological Quarterly*
CTR *Criswell Theological Review*
DDD *Dictionary of Deities and Demons in the Bible*
DJD Discoveries in the Judean Desert
DRev *Downside Review*
DukeDivR *Duke Divinity Review*
EA El-Amarna tablets
EBC Expositor's Bible Commentary
EBib *Études bibliques*
ECC Eerdmans Critical Commentary
EcR *Ecumenical Review*
EDNT *Exegetical Dictionary of the New Testament*
EgT *Eglise et théologie*
EGT Expositor's Greek Testament
EncJud *Encyclopedia Judaica*
ErIsr *Eretz-Israel*
ESCJ Etudes sur le christianisme et le judaisme (Studies in Christianity and Judaism)
EstBib *Estudios bíblicos*
ETL *Ephemerides theologicae lovanienses*
ETS Evangelical Theological Society
EuroJTh *European Journal of Theology*
EvJ *Evangelical Journal*
EvQ *Evangelical Quarterly*
EvT *Evangelische Theologie*
ExAud *Ex auditu*
Exeg *Exegetica*
ExpTim *Expository Times*
FF Foundations and Facets
FRLANT Forschungen zur Religion und Literatur des Alten und Neuen Testaments
GBS Guides to Biblical Scholarship
GKC *Genesius' Hebrew Grammar*
GNS *Good News Studies*
GR *Greece and Rome*
Grammar *A Grammar of the Greek New Testament; in the Light of Historical Research* (A.T. Robertson)
GRBS *Greek, Roman, and Byzantine Studies*
HALOT Koehler, Baumgartner, and Stamm. *The Hebrew and Aramaic Lexicon of the Old Testament*
HAR *Hebrew Annual Review*
HAT handbuch zum Alten Testament
HBD *HarperCollins Bible Dictionary*
HBT *Horizons in Biblical Theology*
Herm Hermeneia commentary series
HeyJ *Heythrop Journal*
HNT Handbuch zum Neuen Testament

HNTC	Harper's New Testament Commentaries
Hor	*Horizons*
HS	*Hebrew Studies*
HSM	Harvard Semitic Monographs
HSS	Harvard Semitic Studies
HTKNT	Herders theologischer Kommentar zum Neuen Testament
HTR	*Harvard Theological Review*
HTS	Harvard Theological Studies
HUBP	Hebrew Union Bible Project
HUCA	*Hebrew Union College Annual*
IB	*Interpreter's Bible*
IBC	Interpretation: A Bible Commentary for Teaching and Preaching
IBHS	*An Introduction to Biblical Hebrew Syntax*
IBS	*Irish Biblical Studies*
ICC	International Critical Commentary
IDB	*Interpreter's Dictionary of the Bible*
IDBSup	*Interpreter's Dictionary of the Bible: Supplement*
IEJ	*Israel Exploration Journal*
IJT	*Indian Journal of Theology*
Imm	*Immanuel*
Int	*Interpretation*
ISBE	*International Standard Bible Encyclopedia*, 2d ed.
IVPBBC	IVP Bible Background Commentary
IVPNTC	IVP New Testament Commentary
JAAR	*Journal of the American Academy of Religion*
JAARSup	JAAR Supplement Series
JANESCU	*Journal of the Ancient Near Eastern Society of Columbia University*
JAOS	*Journal of the American Oriental Society*
JAOSSup	Journal of the American Oriental Society Supplement Series
JBL	*Journal of Biblical Literature*
JBMW	*Journal for Biblical Manhood and Womanhood*
JBQ	*Jewish Biblical Quaterly*
JBR	*Journal of Bible and Religion*
JCS	*Journal of Cuneiform Studies*
Jeev	*Jeevadhara*
JE	*Jewish Encyclopedia*
JETS	*Journal of the Evangelical Theological Society*
JNES	*Journal of Near Eastern Studies*
JNSL	*Journal of Northwest Semitic Languages*
JPOS	*Journal of the Palestine Oriental Society*
JQR	*Jewish Quarterly Review*
JRS	*Journal of Roman Studies*
JSNT	*Journal for the Study of the New Testament*
JSNTSup	JSNT Supplement Series
JSOT	*Journal for the Study of the Old Testament*
JSOTSup	JSOT Supplement Series
JSP	*Journal for the Study of the Pseudepigrapha*
JSS	*Journal of Semitic Studies*
JSSEA	*Journal of the Society for the Study of Egyptian Antiquities*
JTC	*Journal for Theology and the Church*
JTS	*Journal of Theological Studies*
K&D	Keil and Delitzsch, *Biblical Commentary on the Old Testament*
KB	Koehler-Baumgartner, *Hebräisches und Aramäisches Lexicon zum Alten Testament* (first or second edition; third edition is *HALOT*)

KEK	Kritisch-exegetischer Kommentar über das Neue Testament
KTU	*Die keilalphabetischen Texte aus Ugarit*
L&N	Louw and Nida. *Greek-English Lexicon of the New Testament: Based on Semantic Domains*
LCC	Library of Christian Classics
LCL	Loeb Classical Library
LEC	Library of Early Christianity
LS	*Louvain Studies*
LSJ	Liddell, Scott, and Jones. *A Greek-English Lexicon*
LTP	*Laval théologique et philosophique*
MM	Moulton and Milligan. *The Vocabulary of the Greek Testament*
MSJ	*The Master's Seminary Journal*
NAC	New American Commentary
NBC	*New Bible Commentary*, rev. ed.
NBD	*New Bible Dictionary*, 2d ed.
NCBC	New Century Bible Commentary
Neot	*Neotestamentica*
NewDocs	*New Documents Illustrating Early Christianity*
NIBC	New International Biblical Commentary
NICNT	New International Commentary on the New Testament
NICOT	New International Commentary on the Old Testament
NIDNTT	*New International Dictionary of New Testament Theology*
NIDOTTE	*New International Dictionary of Old Testament Theology and Exegesis*
NIGTC	New International Greek Testament Commentary
NIVAC	NIV Application Commentary
NIVSB	Zondervan NIV Study Bible
Notes	*Notes on Translation*
NovT	*Novum Testamentum*
NovTSup	Novum Testamentum Supplements
NPNF	*Nicene and Post-Nicene Fathers*
NTC	New Testament Commentary (Baker)
NTD	Das Neue Testament Deutsch
NTG	New Testament Guides
NTS	*New Testament Studies*
NTT	New Testament Theology
NTTS	New Testament Tools and Studies
OBO	Orbis biblicus et orientalis
OJRS	*Ohio Journal of Religious Studies*
OLA	Orientalia lovaniensia analecta
Or	*Orientalia* (NS)
OTE	Old Testament Essays
OTG	Old Testament Guides
OTL	Old Testament Library
OTS	Old Testament Studies
OtSt	*Oudtestamentische Studien*
PEGLMBS	*Proceedings, Eastern Great Lakes and Midwest Bible Societies*
PEQ	*Palestine Exploration Quarterly*
PG	Patrologia graeca
PL	Patrologia latina
PNTC	Pillar New Testament Commentary
Presb	*Presbyterion*
PresR	*Presbyterian Review*
PRSt	*Perspectives in Religious Studies*
PTMS	Pittsburgh Theological Monograph Series
PTR	*Princeton Theological Review*
RB	*Revue biblique*
RBibLit	*Review of Biblical Literature*
RefJ	*Reformed Journal*
RelSRev	*Religious Studies Review*
ResQ	*Restoration Quarterly*
RevExp	*Review and Expositor*
RevScRel	*Revue des sciences religieuses*

RHPR	*Revue d'histoire et de philosophie religieuses*
RTR	*Reformed Theological Review*
SAOC	Studies in Ancient Oriental Civilizations
SBB	Stuttgarter biblische Beiträge
SBJT	*Southern Baptist Journal of Theology*
SBLDS	Society of Biblical Literature Dissertation Series
SBLSP	*Society of Biblical Literature Seminar Papers*
SBLWAW	Society of Biblical Literature Writings from the Ancient World
SBT	*Studies in Biblical Theology*
ScEccl	*Sciences ecclésiastiques*
ScEs	*Science et esprit*
ScrHier	Scripta hierosolymitana
SE	*Studia evangelica*
SEG	Supplementum epigraphicum graecum
Sem	*Semitica*
SJLA	Studies in Judaism of Late Antiquity
SJT	*Scottish Journal of Theology*
SNT	Studien zum Neuen Testament
SNTSMS	Society for New Testament Studies Monograph Series
SNTSU	Studien zum Neuen Testament und seiner Umwelt
SP	Sacra Pagina
SR	*Studies in Religion*
ST	*Studia theologica*
Str-B	Strack, H. L., and P. Billerbeck, *Kommentar zum Neuen Testament aus Talmud und Midrasch*
StudBT	*Studia biblica et theologica*
SUNT	Studien zur Umwelt des Neuen Testaments
SVF	*Stoicorum veterum fragmenta*
SVT	Studia in Veteris Testamenti
SwJT	*Southwestern Journal of Theology*
TA	*Tel Aviv*
TBT	*The Bible Today*
TDNT	Kittel and Friedrich. *Theological Dictionary of the New Testament*
TDOT	Botterweck and Ringgren. *Theological Dictionary of the Old Testament*
TF	*Theologische Forschung*
THAT	*Theologisches Handwörterbuch zum Alten Testament*
Them	*Themelios*
ThEv	*Theologia Evangelica*
THKNT	Theologischer Handkommentar zum Neuen Testament
ThTo	*Theology Today*
TJ	*Trinity Journal*
TLNT	*Theological Lexicon of the New Testament*
TLOT	*Theological Lexicon of the Old Testament*
TNTC	Tyndale New Testament Commentaries
TOTC	Tyndale Old Testament Commentaries
TQ	*Theologische Quartalschrift*
TS	*Theological Studies*
TWOT	*Theological Wordbook of the Old Testament*
TynBul	*Tyndale Bulletin*
TZ	*Theologische Zeitschrift*
UBD	*Unger's Bible Dictionary*
UF	*Ugarit-Forschungen*
UT	*Ugaritic Textbook*
VE	*Vox evangelica*
VT	*Vetus Testamentum*
VTSup	Supplements to Vetus Testamentum
WBC	Word Biblical Commentary

WBE	*Wycliffe Bible Encyclopedia*	*ZAW*	*Zeitschrift für die alttestamentliche Wissenschaft*
WMANT	Wissenschaftliche Monographien zum Alten und Neuen Testament	*ZNW*	*Zeitschrift für die neutestamentliche Wissenschaft und die Kunde der älterern Kirche*
WTJ	*Westminster Theological Journal*		
WUNT	Wissenschaftliche Untersuchungen zum Neuen Testament	*ZPEB*	*Zondervan Pictorial Encyclopedia of the Bible*
YCS	*Yale Classical Studies*	*ZWT*	*Zeitschrift für wissenschaftliche Theologie*
ZAH	*Zeitschrift für Althebräistik*		

General

AD	*anno Domini* (in the year of [our] Lord)	Lat.	Latin
		lit.	literally
Akkad.	Akkadian	LXX	Septuagint (the Greek OT)
Arab.	Arabic	MS(S)	manuscript(s)
Aram.	Aramaic	MT	Masoretic Text of the OT
BC	before Christ	n(n).	note(s)
ca.	*circa* (around, about, approximately)	n.d.	no date
		NS	New Series
cf.	*confer*, compare	NT	New Testament
ch(s).	chapter(s)	OT	Old Testament
d.	died	p(p).	page(s)
diss.	dissertation	par.	parallel (indicates textual parallels)
ed(s).	editor(s), edited by, edition		
e.g.	*exempli gratia*, for example	para.	paragraph
esp.	especially	repr.	reprinted
et al.	*et alii*, and others	rev.	revised
EV	English versions of the Bible	Samar.	Samaritan Pentateuch
f(f).	and the following one(s)	s.v.	*sub verbo*, under the word
fig.	figuratively	Syr.	Syriac
frg.	fragment	Tg.	Targum
Gk.	Greek	TR	Textus Receptus (Greek text of the KJV translation)
GK	Goodrick & Kohlenberger numbering system	trans.	translator, translated by
Heb.	Hebrew	v(v).	verse(s)
ibid.	*ibidem*, in the same place	vs.	versus
i.e.	*id est*, that is	Vul.	Vulgate
JPS	Jewish Publication Society		

1, 2 SAMUEL

RONALD F. YOUNGBLOOD

Introduction

1. TITLE

In the Jewish canon the two books of Samuel were originally one. There is no break in the Masoretic text (MT) between 1 and 2 Samuel; the Masoretic notes at the end of 2 Samuel give a total of 1,506 verses for the entire corpus and point to 1 Samuel 28:24 as the middle verse of the "book" (*spr*, singular). Like Kings and Chronicles, each of which is slightly longer than Samuel, the scroll of Samuel was too unwieldy to be handled with ease and so was divided into two parts in early manuscripts of the Septuagint (LXX). Not until the fifteenth century AD was the Hebrew text of Samuel separated into two books, and the first printed Hebrew Bible to exhibit the division is the Bomberg edition published in Venice in 1516/17.

It is understandable that the ancient Hebrew title of the book was *šᵉmûʾēl* since the prophet Samuel is the dominant figure in the early chapters. A major theme of the work, however, led the LXX translators to group Samuel together with *mᵉlākîm* ("Kings") and to refer to them collectively as *Bibloi Basileiōn* ("Books of Kingdoms"). Jerome modified the title slightly to *Librī Rēgum* ("Books of Kings") so that Samuel and Kings, each divided into two parts, became known as 1, 2, 3, and 4 Kings respectively. To this day Catholic commentators and translators often refer to 1 and 2 Samuel as "1 and 2 Kings" (cf. the version by Ronald Knox), a practice that has caused no end of confusion, even if only temporary, to non-Catholic users of their works. Protestants have uniformly reverted to labeling the books after their ancient Hebrew name.

2. AUTHORSHIP AND DATE

According to the Babylonian Talmud, "Samuel wrote the book that bears his name" (*b. B. Bat. 14b*). The same Talmud also asserts that the first twenty-four chapters of 1 Samuel were written by Samuel himself (chs. 25 and beyond being excluded, since 1Sa 25:1 reports his death) and that the rest of the Samuel corpus was the work of Nathan and Gad (*b. B. Bat. 15a*). First Chronicles 29:29 is doubtless the source of the latter rabbinic assessment: "As for the events of King David's reign, from beginning to end, they are written in the records of Samuel the seer, the records of Nathan the prophet and the records of Gad the seer." Samuel, Nathan, and Gad may not have been the authors of the "records" that bear their names, however; and, in any event, 1 Chronicles 29:29 appears to be listing sources used by the Chronicler and therefore should not be understood as having anything to say about the authorship of the canonical books of Samuel. Although the priests Ahimaaz (cf. 2Sa 15:27, 36; 17:17, 20; 18:19, 22–23, 27–29) and Zabud (cf. 1Ki 4:5), among others, have been proposed as possible candidates, arguments in their favor fail to convince. In sum, we must remain content to leave the authorship of Samuel—and, for that matter, of other OT books such as Joshua, Judges, Kings, and Chronicles—in the realm of anonymity. Ultimately, of course, the Holy Spirit is the Author who prompted the inspired narrator and gave his work the "omniscient" quality often remarked upon.[1]

Although the statement that "Ziklag ... has belonged to the kings [plural] of Judah ever since" (1Sa 27:6) implies that Samuel was not written until after the division of the kingdom of Israel following the death of Solomon in 931 BC, the possibility of a modest number of later editorial updatings and/or modernizations of the original work cannot be ruled out. In any case, "one imagines the writer of Samuel or the Chronicler as authors, not redactors, rather much as one might assume that any anonymous text, whatever its history might have been, implies an 'author' and a 'reader' whose narrative strategies and response may be inferred from the 'work.'"[2] With respect to the date of the books of Samuel, all that can be said for certain is that since they report "the last words of David" (2Sa 23:1), they could not have been written earlier than the second quarter of the tenth century BC (David having died ca. 970). On the basis of historical and archaeological data as well as literary analysis, Baruch Halpern concludes that "the composition of Samuel cannot be placed later than the 9th century, and probably should be dated in the 10th century, shortly after David's death,"[3] "in Solomon's day."[4]

3. HISTORICAL CONTEXT

Because of its setting during the period of the judges, the book of Ruth was inserted between Judges and Samuel at least as early as the translation of the LXX and continues to occupy that position in most versions to the present time. In the Jewish canon, however, Ruth is one of the five festal "scrolls" (*m^egillôt*) and therefore appears closer to the end of the Hebrew Bible in a section called *k^etûbîm* ("Writings"). When Ruth is thus displaced, Samuel follows immediately upon Judges.

After the conquest of Canaan by Joshua, the people of Israel experienced the normal range of problems that face colonizers of newly occupied territory. Exacerbating their situation, however, was not only

1. Cf. Shimon Bar-Efrat, "Literary Modes and Methods in the Biblical Narrative in View of 2 Samuel 10–20 and 1 Kings 1–2," *Imm* 8 (Spring 1978): 20.
2. Burke O. Long, "Framing Repetitions in Biblical Historiography," *JBL* 106/3 (1987): 386.
3. Baruch Halpern, *David's Secret Demons: Messiah, Murderer, Traitor, King* (Grand Rapids: Eerdmans, 2001), 112.
4. Ibid., 298. For his useful summary of archaeological evidence that bears on the reign of David (as well as that of Solomon), see 427–78.

the resilience of the conquered but also the failures—moral and spiritual, as well as military—of the conquerors. Their rebellion against the covenant that God had established with them at Sinai brought divine retribution, and the restoration that resulted from their repentance lasted only until they rebelled again (cf. Jdg 2:10–19; Ne 9:24–29). The dreary cycle of rebellion–retribution–repentance–restoration–rebellion is repeated over and over again throughout the book of Judges, which in many respects rehearses the darkest days of Israel's long history.

By the end of Judges the situation in the land had become intolerable. Israel was *in extremis* and anarchy reigned: "Everyone did as he saw fit" (Jdg 17:6; 21:25). A series of judges, upon whom the Spirit of the Lord "came" (3:10; 6:34; 11:29) with energizing "power" (14:6, 19; 15:14), provided little more than a holding action against Israel's enemies within and without, who were both numerous and varied. More than three centuries of settlement (cf. 11:26) did not materially improve Israel's position, and thoughtful people must have begun crying out for change.

If theocracy implemented through divine charisma was the hallmark of the period of the judges (cf. Jdg 8:28–29), theocracy mediated through divinely sanctioned monarchy would characterize the next phase in the history of the Israelites. In the days of the judges "Israel had no king" (17:6; 18:1; 19:1; 21:25), and it was becoming apparent to many that she desperately needed one. Judgeship did not end with Samson, however. The priest Eli and the prophet Samuel both served as judges (cf. 1Sa 4:18; 7:6, 15, 17). Not until the accession of Saul did the people have a king in the truest sense of the word—and even then they expected him to "judge" them (cf. 8:5–6, 20).

Edwin R. Thiele has succeeded in establishing 931/30 BC as the year when the division of the monarchy took place following Solomon's death.[5] If we interpret the biblical figures literally, Solomon reigned from 970 to 931 (forty years, 1Ki 11:42), David from 1010 to 970 (forty years and six months, 2Sa 5:5), and Saul from 1052 to 1010 (forty-two years, 1Sa 13:1). Assuming that Samuel was about thirty years old when he anointed Saul as king of Israel, we arrive at the approximate dates of 1080 (the birth of Samuel) to 970 BC (the death of David) as the time span covered in the books of Samuel.

4. LITERARY CONTEXT AND UNITY

Joshua, Judges, Samuel, and Kings constitute the first half of *n^{e}bîʾîm* ("Prophets"), the middle section of the Jewish canon. As the so-called Former Prophets, these four books present a carefully selected series of narratives that summarize the history of God's people during a period spanning well over eight centuries: from the beginning of the conquest of Canaan (ca. 1405 BC) to the end of the monarchy and beyond (ca. 561 BC, "the thirty-seventh year of the exile of Jehoiachin king of Judah" [2Ki 25:27]). Told from

5. Edwin R. Thiele, *A Chronology of the Hebrew Kings* (Grand Rapids: Zondervan, 1977), 15, 31. Although he objects to certain aspects of Thiele's overall tour de force, William Hamilton Barnes settles on 932 BC as the most likely year for the beginning of the divided monarchy; see his *Studies in the Chronology of the Divided Monarchy of Israel* (HSM 48; Atlanta: Scholars, 1991), 153–54. It becomes more and more doubtful that arguments in favor of an earlier (e.g., 945 BC; cf. E.W. Falstich, *History, Harmony, and the Hebrew Kings* [Spencer, Ia.: Chronology, 1986], 202–3) or later date (e.g., 927 BC; cf. John H. Hayes and Paul K. Hooker, *A New Chronology for the Kings of Israel and Judah and Its Implications for Biblical History and Literature* [Atlanta: John Knox, 1988], 18–19) will succeed in winning the day.

a prophetic viewpoint (cf. 2Ki 18:13, 17–37; 19:1–20:19 = Isa 36:1–38:8; 39:1–8; cf. 2Ki 25:27–30 = Jer 52:31–34), the story proclaims the central truth that Israel could anticipate the Lord's blessing only so long as she remained faithful to the stipulations of the Sinaitic covenant and to the laws and decrees that explicated them.

It has long been recognized that the four books of the Former Prophets expand the paraenetic exhortations of Moses enshrined in the book of Deuteronomy, itself a covenant-renewal document of the first order.[6] That the Lord rewards the righteous and punishes the wicked is only to be expected in the light of the covenantal blessings and curses detailed in Deuteronomy 27:9–28:68. One of the many interrelationships shared by the five books is a theology of monarchy, well summarized by Raymond B. Dillard: "Deuteronomy also provided for the day that the people would want a king (17:14–20), so the [Deuteronomic] historian reports what life was like both without a king (Joshua, Judges) and with a king (Samuel, Kings); it is largely a record of the disobedience of the people and the faithfulness of God."[7]

Building on the impressively "Deuteronomic" qualities of Joshua, Judges, Samuel, and Kings, Martin Noth concluded that Deuteronomy should be detached from the Pentateuch (the remaining four books—Genesis, Exodus, Leviticus, Numbers—thus their constituting a "Tetrateuch") and added to Joshua through Kings, thus forming a five-part continuous work that he called the "Deuteronomistic History" and that he claimed was compiled during the exilic period.[8] Its author made use of a number of independent literary units (including Deuteronomy itself), which he interwove with his own contributions to produce the finished product. Strictly speaking, the term "Deuteronomic" refers to the writer(s) of Deuteronomy, and the term "Deuteronomistic" applies to the compiler(s) of the great historical narrative that stretches from Deuteronomy through 2 Kings. Since the second term is cumbersome, however, the first is often used in both senses and will be thus employed throughout this commentary.

How are we to evaluate Noth's theory? Undoubted similarities among the various books make it attractive indeed. Even the casual reader cannot fail to observe that Joshua begins with "After the death of Moses," Judges with "After the death of Joshua," and 2 Samuel with "After the death of Saul," and that 2 Kings begins similarly, although the corresponding phrase sits differently in its context and is therefore rendered in a slightly different way: "After Ahab's death." It would therefore appear that the narrator

---

6. Cf. especially Meredith G. Kline, *Treaty of the Great King: The Covenant Structure of Deuteronomy: Studies and Commentary* (Grand Rapids: Eerdmans, 1963).

7. Raymond B. Dillard, "David's Census: Perspectives on II Samuel 24 and I Chronicles 21," in *Through Christ's Word: A Festschrift for Dr. Philip E. Hughes*, ed. W. Robert Godfrey and Jesse L. Boyd III (Phillipsburg, N.J.: Presbyterian and Reformed, 1985), 100; cf. also Gerald Eddie Gerbrandt, *Kingship according to the Deuteronomic History* (SBLDS 87; Atlanta: Scholars, 1986), 189–94.

8. Martin Noth, *Überlieferungsgeschichtliche Studien*, 2nd ed. (Tübingen: Max Niemeyer, 1957), 1–110; English translation: *The Deuteronomistic History* (JSOTSup 15; Sheffield: JSOT Press, 1981). For helpful critiques of Noth as well as useful discussions of the scholarly debates that continue unabated concerning the putative sources of the books of Samuel, see Walter Dietrich and Thomas Naumann, "The David-Saul Narrative," in *Reconsidering Israel and Judah: Recent Studies in the Deteronomistic History*, ed. Gary N. Knoppers and J. Gordon McConville [Winona Lake, Ind.: Eisenbrauns, 2000), 276–318; Raymond B. Dillard and Tremper Longman III, *An Introduction to the Old Testament* (Grand Rapids: Zondervan, 1994), 137–40.

deliberately signaled to his readers as sharp a break at 2 Samuel 1:1 and at 2 Kings 1:1 (breaks later confirmed by whoever divided the scrolls of Samuel and Kings into two books each) as he had at Joshua 1:1 and Judges 1:1. Numerous other stylistic, linguistic, and thematic features are shared by the books of Deuteronomy through Kings so that references to the "Deuteronom(ist)ic historian" are *de rigueur* in scholarly discussion, no matter what the theological persuasion of the participants.

A word of caution is in order, however. My use of the term "Deuteronomic" does not imply a late date for Deuteronomy (which I believe to have come essentially from the hand of Moses) or an exilic date for Joshua, Judges, or Samuel (which I believe to have been written relatively soon after the events that they record). Whether there was in fact a "Deuteronomic" historian who lived during the exile and who gathered together the books of the Former Prophets, collating them into a continuous narrative and adding his own editorial touches to reflect the Mosaic theology enshrined in the book of Deuteronomy, remains moot. In the following commentary, therefore, "Deuteronomic" is used descriptively rather than prescriptively.[9]

In the Jewish canon the Latter Prophets (Isaiah, Jeremiah, Ezekiel, the Twelve [Minor Prophets]) follow immediately after the historical narratives known as the Former Prophets and strengthen the rabbinic tradition that Joshua, Judges, Samuel, and Kings were written from a prophetic perspective (see above). The translators of the LXX, by contrast, placed Chronicles immediately after the Former Prophets. In so doing they honored the fact that the Chronicler, writing late in the fifth century BC during the era of restoration following exile, summarized the narratives of Genesis through Kings in much briefer detail. Greater attention, however, is paid by the Chronicler to the period of the monarchy, especially to those aspects of the Davidic dynasty that he considered admirable. Among the literary sources used extensively by Chronicles were the books of Samuel and Kings. The chapters of 1 Chronicles most indebted to Samuel are 3, 10–11, 13–15, and 17–21. Comparisons between the two parallel accounts will be noted in the commentary.[10]

5. PURPOSE

From the beginning of the book of Joshua to its end, Joshua and the Israelites are commanded to obey the "Book of the Law" (Jos 1:8; 23:6), probably Deuteronomy (cf. esp. Jos 8:31, where Dt 27:5–6 is cited along with Ex 20:25; also Jos 14:9, which echoes Dt 1:36). Although the conqueror of Canaan, Joshua knows full well that the Lord gives the victory (cf. Jos 1:2–3, 5, 9, 11, 13, 15; 2:9–11, 14, 24; 3:10 et al.). He thus prefigures the coming monarchy, whose kings are to submit to divine leadership as they rule over Israel under God.

---

9. Cf. similarly Dillard, "David's Census," 99 and n. 15; David M. Howard Jr., "The Case for Kingship in the Old Testament Narrative Books and the Psalms," *TJ* 9 (1988): 19 and n. 2; idem, "The Case for Kingship in Deuteronomy and the Former Prophets. Review of Kingship According to the Deuteronomistic History, by G. E. Gerbrandt," *WTJ* 52 (1990): 101 and n. 3, 103 and n. 5.

10. For detailed comparisons between the Hebrew text of Samuel and its parallels in 1 Chronicles and Psalm 18 (as well as elsewhere in the OT), cf. especially Abba Bendavid, *Parallels in the Bible* (Jerusalem: Carta, 1972), 31–70; for detailed comparisons in English, cf. William Crockett, *A Harmony of the Books of Samuel, Kings, and Chronicles* (London: Revell, 1897), 106–41; James D. Newsome Jr., ed., *A Synoptic Harmony of Samuel, Kings, and Chronicles with Related Passages from Psalms, Isaiah, Jeremiah, and Ezra* (Grand Rapids: Baker, 1986), 23–79.

Judges is permeated by the same theme: When Israel was oppressed by the enemy and cried out to God for help, the Lord delivered them by raising up "judges, who saved them out of the hands of these raiders" (Jdg 2:16). When "the kings of Canaan fought" against the people (5:19), they were no match for Israel's God: "From the heavens the stars fought, from their courses they fought against Sisera" (5:20). Because the enemies of Israel were also the enemies of the Lord, their doom was sealed (cf. 5:31). Like Joshua, the judges therefore also foreshadow the kings who would succeed them.

In the books of Samuel, monarchy becomes a reality. Three dominant figures—Samuel the kingmaker, Saul the abortive king, David the ideal king—highlight its agonies as well as its ecstasies.

According to the Deuteronomist the political success or failure of a king was entirely dependent upon the degree to which Israel obeyed the covenant. Political success could thus only be achieved by a king through fulfilling his responsibility as covenant administrator. Given this view, it is also clear that military success was not a major accomplishment of a king, but the act of Yahweh in his role as protector of the people. The king's role in this was to trust Yahweh to deliver, and then to be obedient to his word.[11]

A major purpose of Samuel, then, is to define monarchy as a gracious gift of God to his chosen people. Their desire for a king (1Sa 8:5) was not in itself inappropriate, despite Samuel's initial displeasure (v.6). Nor were they necessarily wrong in wanting a king like "all the other nations" had (vv.5, 20). Their sin consisted in the fact that they were asking for a king "to lead us and to go out before us and to fight our battles" (v.20). In other words, they refused to believe that the Lord would grant them victory in his own time and according to his own good pleasure (contrast 2Sa 8:6, 14). They were willing to exchange humble faith in the protection and power of "the LORD Almighty" (1Sa 1:3) for misguided reliance on the naked strength of "the fighting men of Israel" (2Sa 24:4).

> The messianic aspiration has always been a mixed blessing for Israel and Judah and their descendants, but a Davidic legacy that, for better or worse, has affected the lives of millions, influenced the Jewish community, its character and quality of life, and shaped and directed the Christian movement. Variously reformulated, it is the vehicle of constant renewal, of faith and confidence in the purposes of God for the establishment of his kingdom.[12]

6. LITERARY FORM

Justifiable concern for the inspired truth and moral excellence of Scripture should not be permitted to blind us to its consummate beauty. For the most part the books of Samuel are composed of prose narratives that serve well in presenting a continuous, historical account of the advent, establishment, and consolidation of monarchy in Israel. It is possible to isolate various literary units within the larger whole—ark narratives (1Sa 4:1b–7:17), rise of Saul (chs. 8–12), decline of Saul (chs. 13–15), rise of David (16:1–28:2), David's accession to kingship (over Judah, 2Sa 1:1–3:5; over Israel, 3:6–5:16), David's powerful reign (5:17–8:18), David's court history (chs. 9–20), epilogue (chs. 21–24)—although debate is vigorous concerning the parameters of many of them.

---

11. Gerbrandt, *Kingship*, 194.
12. David Noel Freedman, *History and Religion* (Grand Rapids: Eerdmans, 1997), 313.

In recent years various sections of the books of Samuel have been subjected to close reading in order to uncover aspects of Samuel's exquisite literary structure. While manufacturing chiasms where there are none is a constant temptation that the exegete must avoid at all costs, the author of Samuel seems to have used the technique on numerous occasions. A clear example is the epilogue, in which the Song of David (2Sa 22) and David's last words (23:1–7) nestle between two warrior narratives (21:15–22; 23:8–39) that are framed in turn by reports of divine wrath against the people of God (21:1–14; ch. 24).

Second Samuel 1–20 displays a four-part architectonic structure that is impressive indeed. David's accession to kingship over Judah (1:1–3:5) ends with a four-verse listing of the sons born to David in Hebron (3:2–5); David's accession to kingship over Israel (3:6–5:16) ends with a four-verse listing of the children born to him in Jerusalem (5:13–16); David's powerful reign (5:17–8:18) and David's court history (chs. 9–20) each end with a four-verse roster of his officials (8:15–18; 20:23–26). A symmetrical literary edifice of such magnitude can hardly be accidental. Similar examples, for many of which I am indebted to the monographs listed in the Bibliography as well as to other books and articles, are noted in the commentary.[13]

When poetry punctuates the corpus here and there, it does so in memorable and striking ways. David's lament for Saul and Jonathan (2Sa 1:17–27) not only underscores his genuine esteem for Saul and his heartfelt love for Jonathan but also serves as a means of opening the second book of Samuel on a poignantly lyrical note. The Song of Hannah and the Song of David—the first near the beginning of the work (1Sa 2:1–11) and the second near its end (2Sa 22)—remind us that the two books were originally one by framing their main contents, by opening and closing in similar ways, and by highlighting the messianic horizons of the Davidic dynasty through initial promise (1Sa 2:10) and eternal fulfillment (2Sa 22:51).

7. CANONICITY AND TEXT

> The three sections of the [Hebrew Bible] have a descending order of sanctity. The Torah was believed to be the direct word of God, spoken to Moses on top of Mount Sinai.... The books of the prophets [*sic*] were believed to have been revealed to them in the "spirit of prophecy." The message is from God, but the words are the prophet's own words. The Writings were believed to have been written in the "holy spirit." They were inspired by God but had a human authorship.... The books of the Prophets and the Writings exist for inspirational purposes, but actual Jewish law and practice is derived solely from the five books of the Torah.[14]

Despite Judaism's trilevel theory of inspiration, the canonicity of the books of Samuel has rarely if ever been disputed by Jews or Christians. Although 1 Samuel is not quoted in the NT, and although citations from 2 Samuel appear there only a few times (cf. 2Sa 7:8, 14 in 2Co 6:18; 2Sa 7:14 in Heb 1:5; 2Sa 22:50 in Ro 15:9), Samuel and David in particular are mentioned frequently in its pages. In addition the OT stories about Hannah and Peninnah, Samuel and Eli, Saul and David, David and Jonathan, David and Goliath, Samuel and the medium at Endor, David and Bathsheba, Amnon and Tamar, David and Absalom, and numerous other pericopes have proven to be rich resources for countless sermons, lectures, and lessons throughout the centuries.

13. Cf. John A. Martin, "Studies in 1 and 2 Samuel. Part 1: The Structure of 1 and 2 Samuel," *BSac* 141/1 (1984): 28–42.

14. Stephen M. Wylen, *Settings of Silver: An Introduction to Judaism* (Mahwah, N.J.: Paulist, 1989), 12.

For reasons unknown, the MT of Samuel has suffered more in scribal transmission than any other OT book.[15] Fortunately the Dead Sea Scrolls (DSS), the Lucianic recension of the LXX (together with proto-Lucianic versions), the LXX itself (especially the Vaticanus manuscript), and parallels in 1 Chronicles and Psalm 18 are often helpful in attempts to recover the original text. When two or more non-MT readings agree as over against the MT, careful attention should be paid to the evidence they present.

In Cave 1 at Qumran, only one very fragmentary manuscript of Samuel (1Q7) was found. Cave 4, however, yielded three priceless manuscripts: (1) 4QSamuel[b], dating from the middle of the third century BC and containing fragments of 1 Samuel; (2) 4QSamuel[c], from the early first century BC and containing fragments of 1 Samuel 25; 2 Samuel 14–15; (3) 4QSamuel[a]—the best-preserved of the biblical manuscripts from Cave 4—a large scroll dated in the third quarter of the first century BC and containing fragmentary parts of about 15 percent of the text of 1 and 2 Samuel. Indeed, 1 Samuel 13 is the only chapter not represented at all in the DSS. Since all four manuscripts are a thousand years older than any previously known Hebrew manuscript, their value for the textual criticism of Samuel is obvious. Although the technical literature on the Samuel DSS is extensive,[16] the release of photographs of all unpublished DSS for scholarly examination several years ago has greatly enhanced DSS research through provision of materials that until recently had been granted to only a privileged few. The official publication of the 4Q Samuel manuscripts is now available.[17]

With respect to the various manuscripts and recensions of the LXX (including the Lucianic), the notes of the BH and BHS are not always trustworthy. Since the text edited by Alfred Rahlfs is incomplete,[18] for serious Septuagintal textual research with respect to the books of Samuel one must use *The Old Testament in Greek According to the Text of Codex Vaticanus.*[19]

All things considered, resource materials for textual criticism of 1 and 2 Samuel have never been more abundant or accessible. Their judicious use can assist scholars in making substantial strides toward restoring the original Hebrew text. Caution remains the watchword, however, and changes should always and only

---

15. In almost fifty separate instances in the books of Samuel, the NIV's footnotes indicate preference for a reading other than that of the MT.

16. See Frank Moore Cross Jr., "The Contribution of the Qumran Discoveries to the Studies of the Biblical Text," in *Qumran and the History of the Biblical Text*, ed. Frank Moore Cross and Shemaryahu Talmon (Cambridge, Mass.: Harvard Univ. Press, 1975), 278–92; "The History of the Biblical Text in the Light of Discoveries in the Judaean Desert," in *Qumran and the History of the Biblical Text*, 177–95; idem, "The Oldest Manuscripts from Qumran," *JBL* 74/3 (1955): 147–72; idem, "The Ammonite Oppression of the Tribes of Gad and Reuben: Missing Verses from 1 Samuel 11 Found in 4QSamuel[a]," in *History, Historiography and Interpretation: Studies in Biblical and Cuneiform Literatures*, ed. H. Tadmor and M. Weinfeld (Leiden: Brill, 1984), 148–58; idem, "II: Original Biblical Text Reconstructed from Newly Found Fragments," *BRev* 1/3 (1985): 26–35; Ralph W. Klein, *Textual Criticism of the Old Testament: The Septuagint after Qumran* (Philadelphia: Fortress, 1974); Eugene Charles Ulrich Jr., "4QSam[c]: A Fragmentary Manuscript of 2 Samuel 14–15 from the Scribe of the *Serek Hay-yaḥad* (1QS)," *BASOR* 235 (Summer 1979): 1–25; *The Qumran Text of Samuel and Josephus* (HSM 19; Missoula, Mont.: Scholars, 1978).

17. See *Qumran Cave 4 XII: 1–2 Samuel*, ed. Frank Moore Cross (DJD 17; Oxford: Clarendon, 2005).

18. Alfred Rahlfs, ed., *Septuaginta*, 2 vols. (Stuttgart: Württembergische Bibelanstalt, 1962).

19. *The Old Testament in Greek According to the Text of Codex Vaticanus. Volume II: The Later Historical Books*, Part I: I and II Samuel, ed. Alan England Brooke and Norman McLean with Henry St. John Thackeray (Cambridge: Cambridge Univ. Press, 1927).

be suggested on a case-by-case basis. The observation of Carlson is both typical and apropos: "The LXX text of the Books of Samuel is of outstanding value, though emendation and correction of the Masoretic text demands careful and thorough consideration."[20]

8. THEOLOGICAL VALUES

In terms of the political scene, Israel at the beginning of 1 Samuel was a loosely organized federation of anemic tribal territories scarcely able to keep the Philistines and other enemies at bay. By the end of 2 Samuel, however, Israel under David had become the most powerful kingdom in the eastern Mediterranean region, strong at home and secure abroad. As far as the religious picture is concerned, the opening chapters of 1 Samuel find Israel worshiping at a nondescript shrine presided over by a corrupt priesthood. The last chapter of 2 Samuel, however, records David's purchase of a site in Jerusalem on which the temple of Solomon, one of the most magnificent buildings in the ancient world, would soon be erected. Sweeping change, then, is a hallmark of the Samuel narratives—change guided and energized by the Lord himself through fragile vessels of the likes of Samuel, Saul, and David.

"Perhaps God's major act in 1 and 2 Samuel is his electing or choosing."[21] The Lord's elective purposes embraced Samuel (cf. 1Sa 1:19–20), Saul (cf. 10:20–24), and David (cf. 16:6–13). As the theological centerpiece of the Deuteronomic corpus, 2 Samuel 7 describes the choice of the Davidic dynasty, through which the future kings of Judah (including the Messiah) would come. In 2 Samuel 7, kingship and covenant kiss each other.

Reversal of fortune as an index of divine sovereignty is another significant motif. The Song of Hannah is programmatic in this regard:

> The LORD brings death and makes alive;
>   he brings down to the grave and raises up.
> The LORD sends poverty and wealth;
>   he humbles and he exalts.
> He raises the poor from the dust
>   and lifts the needy from the ash heap;
> he seats them with princes
>   and has them inherit a throne of honor. (1Sa 2:6–8)

---

20. R. A. Carlson, *David the Chosen King: A Traditio-Historical Approach to the Second Book of Samuel* (Stockholm: Almqvist and Wiksell, 1964), 37. Cf. also J. Barton Payne, "The Sahidic Coptic Text of I Samuel," *JBL* 72/1 (1953): 60–62; Bruce M. Metzger, "Lucian and the Lucianic Recension of the Greek Bible," *NTS* 8/3 (1962): 193–200; Gleason L. Archer, "A Reassessment of the Value of the Septuagint of 1 Samuel for Textual Emendation, in the Light of the Qumran Fragments," in *Tradition and Testament: Essays in Honor of Charles Lee Feinberg*, ed. John S. and Paul D. Feinberg (Chicago: Moody, 1981), 234–40; cf. esp. Stephen Pisano, *Additions or Omissions in the Books of Samuel: The Significant Pluses and Minuses in the Massoretic, LXX, and Qumran Texts* (OBO 57; Göttingen: Vandenhoeck & Ruprecht, 1984), 1–16, 283–85; Emanuel Tov, "The Composition of 1 Samuel 16–18 in the Light of the Septuagint Version," in *Empirical Models for Biblical Criticism*, ed. Jeffrey H. Tigay (Philadelphia: Univ. of Pennsylvania Press, 1985); Karen H. Jobes and Moisés Silva, *Invitation to the Septuagint* (Grand Rapids: Baker, 2000), 177–80.

21. John A. Martin, "Part 4: The Theology of Samuel," *BSac* 141/4 (1984): 309.

A formerly barren woman (cf. 1Sa 1:5–6) becomes the mother of six children (cf. 2:21); men of privilege (cf. 2:12–16), Eli's sons, die in shame (cf. 4:11); an unheralded donkey wrangler (cf. 9:2–3) and an obscure shepherd boy (cf. 16:11) are anointed as the first two rulers of Israel (cf. 10:1; 16:13). The overall structure of each of the books of Samuel makes its contribution in this respect as well. Just as the literary and theological midpoint of 1 Samuel foresees the divinely energized transition from Saulide to Davidic rule (cf. 1Sa 16:13–14), so also does the prophetic rebuke at the literary and theological crux of 2 Samuel besmirch David's kingship with an indelible stain (cf. 2Sa 12:9–10).

A key theme of the ark narratives (1Sa 4–7) is that God refuses to be manipulated. Carrying the ark into battle does not guarantee an Israelite victory (cf. 4:3–11), placing the ark in a Philistine temple does not ensure divine blessing (cf. 5:1–6:12), and looking into the ark brings death (cf. 6:19; also 2Sa 6:6–7). If the ark's exile at Kiriath Jearim (cf. 1Sa 6:21–7:2) coincided with the end of the period of the judges, its triumphal entry into Jerusalem (cf. 2Sa 6:16) confirmed that a new day had dawned for God's people.

As repository of the tablets of the covenant, the ark reminded the Israelites of God's demands on their lives. The priesthood, however, continued to preside over the divine oracles, the lots known as Urim and Thummim, to which penitents and supplicants alike resorted in time of need. Oracular inquiry brought Saul to the people's attention (cf. 1Sa 10:20–24), determined the best time for military attack (cf. 14:36–37; 23:1–4; 30:8; 2Sa 2:1; 5:19–25), and provided assistance for David (cf. 1Sa 22:9–15). Forsaken by dreams, Urim, and prophets, the desperate Saul resorted to a medium for guidance (cf. 28:6–25).

In one sense, the offices of king and prophet arose simultaneously in Israel. Saul, the first king (cf. 1Sa 10:24), was anointed by Samuel, who stands at the head of the prophetic line (cf. 9:6–10, 19; Ac 3:24; 13:20; Heb 11:32) as promised to Moses (cf. Dt 18:15–18), who himself was the paradigmatic prophet (Nu 12:6–8; Dt 18:15, 18; 34:10). If the task of the king was to obey and administer the covenant (cf. Dt 17:18–20), that of the prophet was to interpret its demands (cf. 2Ki 22:11–20). In matters relative to God's will as revealed through his word, the submission of kings to prophets was self-understood (cf. 1Sa 13:13; 15:22–23; 2Sa 12:7–14). To the end of the monarchy, the prophets protected with holy zeal their divinely authorized claims over kingship.

Theocracy through monarchy was an ideal that fared better in proclamation than in practice. What Samuel had warned about (cf. 1Sa 8:10–18), the people continued to lust after (cf. vv.19–20). In any event, Saul's failure brought about not a new dispensation but a different king, a man "better than" him (15:28), a man after God's own heart (cf. 13:14). To the extent that David understood that his role as human king was to implement the mandates of the divine King, blessing would follow (cf. 2Sa 6:11–15, 17–19; and esp. 7:27–29). When he deliberately flouted God's will, however, he could count equally on the fact that he would be under the curse (cf. 12:1–18). And so it would be with his descendants on the throne: if the Davidic covenant was eternal in the sense that his line would continue forever (cf. 7:12–16, 25–29; 23:5; Ps 89:27–29, 33–37), it was also conditional in that individual participants in it would be punished when they sinned (cf. 1Ki 2:4; 8:25; 9:4–5; Pss 89:30–32; 132:12).[22]

"Uneasy lies the head that wears a crown," wrote William Shakespeare (*King Henry IV* 2.3.1). Royal perquisites are often overbalanced by seemingly intractable problems. When enemies lift the siege, family

---

22. Cf. similarly Howard, "The Case for Kingship in Deuteronomy and the Former Prophets," 102, 113–14.

members engage in betrayal; when voyeurism ceases to beckon and panic subsides, ambitious sons rebel. At such times begging for God's mercy becomes a daily exercise, and psalms of petition and lament are written and sung. And when all is said and done, the towering figure of David continues alternately to attract and repel.[23] He is the Lord's anointed, and therefore we pay him rightful homage; he is insulated from mundane matters and oblivious to his people's needs, but because of his divine appointment we fault him for not following the highest possible standard.

> O hard condition,
> Twin-born with greatness, subject to the breath
> Of every fool, whose sense no more can feel
> But his own wringing! What infinite heart's-ease
> Must kings neglect, that private men enjoy![24]

9. BIBLIOGRAPHY

Commentaries

Ackroyd, Peter R. *The First Book of Samuel.* Cambridge Bible Commentary on the New English Bible. Cambridge: Cambridge University Press, 1971.

Alter, Robert. *The David Story: A Translation with Commentary of 1 and 2 Samuel.* New York: Norton, 1999.

Anderson, A. A. *2 Samuel.* Word Biblical Commentary 11. Dallas: Word, 1989.

Baldwin, Joyce G. *1 & 2 Samuel.* Downers Grove, Ill.: InterVarsity Press, 1988.

Brueggemann, Walter. *First and Second Samuel.* Interpretation: A Bible Commentary for Teaching and Preaching. Louisville: John Knox, 1990.

Campbell, Antony F. *1 Samuel.* The Forms of the Old Testament Literature 7. Grand Rapids: Eerdmans, 2003.

---

23. Biographies of David, which for the most part treat his negative as well as his positive traits and activities in an evenhanded way, are already legion and show no signs of abating. Recent examples of note include Baruch Halpern, *David's Secret Demons*, and Steven L. McKenzie, *King David: A Biography* (New York: Oxford Univ. Press, 2000), see esp. 191–92, 212–29 for useful lists of biographies of David and bibliographies relating to various aspects of David's life. Halpern is especially strong in matters of biblical and ancient Near Eastern history, archaeology, and geography; McKenzie's forte is in the areas of art and literature. While both authors strongly affirm that David was a real person who reigned over Israel in the tenth century BC, both read the text of Samuel through a critical lens that discounts its affirmations at numerous points. For his part, McKenzie, 44, adopts "two major principles as guidelines" for interpretation: skepticism ("when some aspect of the biblical story fits a literary or ideological theme we should be skeptical about its historical value") and analogy ("the past was basically analogous to the present and to what is known of similar societies and circumstances.... people of all time [*sic*] have the same basic ambitions and instincts"). Such an approach, however, not only pronounces the text of Samuel guilty until proven innocent but also tends to homogenize life experiences and thus disallow uniqueness. Halpern, although approaching the task with characteristic humor as well as exegetical insight, nevertheless uses source-critical methodology in ways that skew the biblical picture of David in a number of areas (see, e.g., Halpern, 277–87). For a trenchant critique of both volumes that at the same time assesses all the evidence in a manner emphasizing the plausibility of the biblical account, see V. Philips Long, "The Early Monarchy," in *A Biblical History of Israel*, ed. Iain Provan, V. Philips Long, and Tremper Longman III (Louisville: Westminster John Knox, 2003), esp. 215–38; cf. also the fine and balanced summary of David A. Bosworth, "Evaluating King David: Old Problems and Recent Scholarship," *CBQ* 68/2 (2006): 191–210.

24. William Shakespeare, *King Henry V*, Act 4, Scene 1, lines 250–54.

———. *2 Samuel*. The Forms of the Old Testament Literature 8. Grand Rapids: Eerdmans, 2005.

Driver, S. R. *Notes on the Hebrew Text and the Topography of the Books of Samuel*. 2nd ed. Rev. and enl. Oxford: Clarendon, 1913.

Eslinger, Lyle M. *Kingship of God in Crisis: A Close Reading of 1 Samuel 1–12*. Bible and Literature 10. Sheffield: Almond, 1985.

Fokkelman, Jan P. *Narrative Art and Poetry in the Books of Samuel: A Full Interpretation Based on Stylistic and Structural Analyses*. 4 vols. Assen: Van Gorcum, 1981–86.

Goldman, S. *Samuel: Hebrew Text and English Translation with an Introduction and Commentary*. London: Soncino, 1951.

Gordon, Robert P. *I and II Samuel: A Commentary*. Grand Rapids: Zondervan, 1986.

Hertzberg, Hans Wilhelm. *I and II Samuel: A Commentary*. Old Testament Library. Philadelphia: Westminster, 1964.

Keil, C. F., and F. Delitzsch. *Biblical Commentary on the Books of Samuel*. Grand Rapids: Eerdmans, 1956.

Kirkpatrick, A. F. *The First Book of Samuel*. Cambridge Bible for Schools and Colleges. Cambridge: Cambridge University Press, 1880.

———. *The Second Book of Samuel*. Cambridge Bible for Schools and Colleges. Cambridge: Cambridge University Press, 1891.

Klein, Ralph W. *1 Samuel*. Word Biblical Commentary 10. Waco, Tex.: Word, 1983.

Mauchline, John. *1 and 2 Samuel*. New Century Bible. London: Oliphants, 1971.

McCarter, P. Kyle, Jr. *I Samuel: A New Translation with Introduction, Notes and Commentary*. Anchor Bible 8. Garden City, N.Y.: Doubleday, 1980.

———. *II Samuel: A New Translation with Introduction, Notes and Commentary*. Anchor Bible 9. Garden City, N.Y.: Doubleday, 1984.

Miscall, Peter D. *1 Samuel: A Literary Reading*. Bloomington, Ind.: Indiana University Press, 1986.

Patrick, Symon. *A Commentary upon the Two Books of Samuel*. London: Chiswell, 1703.

Smith, Henry Preserved. *A Critical and Exegetical Commentary on the Books of Samuel*. International Critical Commentary. Edinburgh: T&T Clark, 1904.

General Works

Ackerman, James S. "Knowing Good and Evil: A Literary Analysis of the Court History in 2 Samuel 9–20 and 1 Kings 1–2." *Journal of Biblical Literature* 109/1 (1990): 41–64.

Ackroyd, Peter R. "The Verb Love—ʾĀhēb in the David–Jonathan Narratives—A Footnote." *Vetus Testamentum* 25/2 (1975): 213–14.

Aharoni, Yohanan. *The Land of the Bible*. Rev. ed. Philadelphia: Westminster, 1979.

Albright, William F. *Archaeology and the Religion of Israel*. Fifth ed. Baltimore: Johns Hopkins University Press, 1956.

Alter, Robert. *The Art of Biblical Narrative*. New York: Basic, 1981.

———. *The Art of Biblical Poetry*. New York: Basic, 1985.

Archer, Gleason L. *Encyclopedia of Bible Difficulties*. Grand Rapids: Zondervan, 1982.

Avigad, Nahman. *Hebrew Bullae from the Time of Jeremiah: Remnants of a Burnt Archive*. Jerusalem: Israel Exploration Society, 1986.

Bailey, Randall C. *David in Love and War: The Pursuit of Power in 2 Samuel 10–12*. Journal for the Study of the Old Testament Supplement Series 75. Sheffield: JSOT, 1990.

Barrick, W. Boyd, and John R. Spencer, eds. *In the Shelter of Elyon: Essays on Ancient Palestinian Life and Literature in Honor of G. W. Ahlström*. Journal for the Study of the Old Testament Supplement Series 31. Sheffield: JSOT, 1984.

Barthélemy, Dominique, et al., eds. *Historical Books*. Vol. 2 of *Preliminary and Interim Report on the Hebrew Old Testament Project*. Edited by Dominique Barthélemy et al. New York: United Bible Societies, 1979.

Bellefontaine, Elizabeth. "Customary Law and Chieftainship: Judicial Aspects of 2 Samuel 14:4–21." *Journal for the Study of the Old Testament* 38 (1987): 47–72.

Ben-Barak, Zafrira. "The Mizpah Covenant (1 Samuel 10:25)—The Source of the Israelite Monarchic Covenant." *Zeitschrift für die alttestmentliche Wissenschaft* 91/1 (1979): 30–43.

Berlin, Adele. "Characterization in Biblical Narrative: David's Wives." *Journal for the Study of the Old Testament* 23 (1982): 69–85.

———. *Poetics and Interpretation of Biblical Narrative*. Sheffield: Almond, 1983.

Blenkinsopp, Joseph. "Kiriath-jearim and the Ark." *Journal of Biblical Literature* 88/2 (1969): 143–56.

Boogaart, T. A. "History and Drama in the Story of David and Goliath." *Reformed Review* 38 (1985): 204–14.

Bosworth, David A. "Evaluating King David: Old Problems and Recent Scholarship." *Catholic Biblical Quarterly* 68/2 (2006): 191–210.

Brettler, Marc Z. "Biblical Literature as Politics: The Case of Samuel." Pages 71–92 in *Religion and Politics in the Ancient Near East*, ed. Adele Berlin. Bethesda, Md.: University of Maryland Press, 1996.

Brueggemann, Walter. *David's Truth in Israel's Imagination and Memory*. Philadelphia: Fortress, 1985.

———. *In Man We Trust: The Neglected Side of Biblical Faith*. Atlanta: John Knox, 1972.

———. "Of the Same Flesh and Bone [Gn 2,23a]." *CBQ* 32/4 (1970): 532–42.

———. "On Coping with Curse: A Study of 2 Sam 16:5–14." *CBQ* 36/2 (1974): 175–92.

———. "On Trust and Freedom: A Study of Faith in the Succession Narrative." *Interpretation* 26/1 (1972): 3–19.

Camp, Claudia V. "The Wise Women of 2 Samuel: A Role Model for Women in Early Israel?" *Catholic Biblical Quarterly* 43/1 (1981): 14–29.

Campbell, Antony F. *The Ark Narrative [1 Samuel 4–6; 2 Samuel 6]: A Form-Critical and Traditio-Historical Study*. Missoula, Mont.: Scholars, 1975.

Carlson, R. A. *David the Chosen King: A Traditio-Historical Approach to the Second Book of Samuel*. Stockholm: Almqvist and Wiksell, 1964.

Ceresko, Anthony R. "A Rhetorical Analysis of David's 'Boast' [1 Samuel 17:34–37]: Some Reflections on Method." *Catholic Biblical Quarterly* 47/1 (1985): 58–74.

Clements, Ronald E. *Abraham and David: Genesis 15 and Its Meaning for Israelite Tradition*. Studies in Biblical Theology Second Series 5. London: SCM, 1967.

Clines, D. J. A. "X, X *Ben* Y, *Ben* Y: Personal Names in Hebrew Narrative Style." *Vetus Testamentum* 22/3 (1972): 266–87.

Conroy, Charles. *Absalom, Absalom! Narrative and Language in 2 Samuel 13–20*. Analecta Biblica 81. Rome: Pontifical Biblical Institute, 1978.

Cross, Frank Moore. "The Ammonite Oppression of the Tribes of Gad and Reuben: Missing Verses from 1 Samuel 11 Found in 4QSamuel[a]." Pages 148–58 in *History, Historiography and Interpretation: Studies in Biblical and Cuneiform Literatures*. Edited by H. Tadmor and M. Weinfeld. Leiden: Brill, 1984.

———. *Canaanite Myth and Hebrew Epic: Essays in the History of the Religion of Israel*. Cambridge, Mass.: Harvard University Press, 1973.

———. "The Oldest Manuscripts from Qumran." *Journal of Biblical Literature* 74/3 (1955): 147–72.

———. "II: Original Biblical Text Reconstructed from Newly Found Fragments." *Bible Review* 1/3 (1985): 26–35.

Cross, Frank Moore, and David Noel Freedman. "A Royal Song of Thanksgiving: II Samuel 22 = Psalm 18." *Journal of Biblical Literature* 72/1 (1953): 15–34.

———. *Studies in Ancient Yahwistic Poetry*. Society of Biblical Literature Dissertation Series 21. Missoula, Mont.: Scholars, 1975.

Curtis, John Briggs. "'East Is East....'" *Journal of Biblical Literature* 80/4 (1961): 355–63.

Del Olmo Lete, G. "David's Oracle [2 Samuel xxiii 1–7]: A Literary Analysis." *Vetus Testamentum* 34/4 (1984): 414–37.

Delitzsch, Franz. *Old Testament History of Redemption*. Trans. Samuel I. Curtiss. Peabody, Mass.: Hendrickson, repr. 1988 (1881).

De Moor, Johannes C. *An Anthology of Religious Texts from Ugarit*. Leiden: Brill, 1987.

Dillard, Raymond B. "David's Census: Perspectives on II Samuel 24 and I Chronicles 21." Pages 94–107 in *Through Christ's Word: A Festschrift for Dr. Philip E. Hughes*. Edited by W. Robert Godfrey and Jesse L. Boyd III. Phillipsburg, N.J.: Presbyterian and Reformed, 1985.

Edelman, Diana. "Saul's Rescue of Jabesh-Gilead (1 Sam 11:1–11): Sorting Story from History." *Zeitschrift für die alttestmentliche Wissenschaft* 96/2 (1984): 195–209.

———. "Saul's Battle against Amaleq [1 Sam. 15]." *Journal for the Study of the Old Testament* 35 (1986): 71–84.

Eskhult, Mats. *Studies in Verbal Aspect and Narrative Technique in Biblical Hebrew Prose*. Stockholm: Almqvist and Wiksell, 1990.

Eslinger, Lyle. *House of God or House of David: The Rhetoric of 2 Samuel 7*. Journal for the Study of the Old Testament Supplement Series 164. Sheffield: JSOT, 1994.

Eslinger, Lyle, and Glen Taylor, eds. *Ascribe to the Lord: Biblical and Other Studies in Memory of Peter C. Craigie*. Journal for the Study of the Old Testament Supplement Series 67. Sheffield: JSOT, 1988.

Fauna and Flora of the Bible. (No designated author.) London: United Bible Societies, 1972.

Fokkelman, Jan P. "Saul and David: Crossed Fates." *Bible Review* 5/3 (1989): 20–32.

Fontaine. Carole. "The Bearing of Wisdom on the Shape of 2 Samuel 11–12 and 1 Kings 3." *Journal for the Study of the Old Testament* 34 (1986): 61–77.

Fox, Michael V. "*Ṭôb* as Covenant Terminology." *Bulletin of the American Schools of Oriental Research* 209 (1973): 41–42.

Freedman, David Noel. *History and Religion*. Vol. 1 of *Divine Commitment and Human Obligation. Selected Writings of David Noel Freedman*. Edited by John R. Huddlestun. Grand Rapids: Eerdmans, 1997.

———. "Divine Names and Titles in Early Hebrew Poetry." Pages 55–107 in *Magnalia Dei: The Mighty Acts of God. Essays on the Bible and Archaeology in Memory of G. Ernest Wright*. Edited by Frank Moore Cross, Werner E. Lemke, and Patrick D. Miller Jr. Garden City, N.Y.: Doubleday, 1976.

———. "The Refrain in David's Lament over Saul and Jonathan." Pages 115–26 in *Ex Orbe Religionum: Studia Geo. Widengren*. Part 1. Leiden: Brill, 1972.

Fretheim, Terence E. "Divine Foreknowledge, Divine Constancy, and the Rejection of Saul's Kingship." *Catholic Biblical Quarterly* 47/4 (1985): 595–602.

Garsiel, Moshe. *The First Book of Samuel: A Literary Study of Comparative Structures, Analogies, and Parallels*. Ramat-Gan: Revivim, 1985.

Gerbrandt, Gerald Eddie. *Kingship According to the Deuteronomic History*. Society of Biblical Literature Dissertation Series 87. Atlanta: Scholars, 1986.

Gevirtz, Stanley. *Patterns in the Early Poetry of Israel*. Studies in Ancient Oriental Civilizations 32. Chicago: University of Chicago Press, 1963.

Gileadi, Avraham. *Israel's Apostasy and Restoration: Essays in Honor of Roland K. Harrison*. Grand Rapids: Baker, 1988.

Gordon, Robert P. "David's Rise and Saul's Demise." *Tyndale Bulletin* 31 (1980): 37–64.

———. "Who Made the Kingmaker? Reflections on Samuel and the Institution of the Monarchy." Pages 255–69 in *Faith, Tradition, and History*. Edited by A. R. Millard et al. Winona Lake, Ind.: Eisenbrauns, 1994.

Graffy, Adrian. "The Literary Genre of Isaiah 5, 1–7." *Biblica* 60/3 (1979): 400–409.

Gunn, David M. "David and the Gift of the Kingdom [2 Samuel 2–4, 9–20, 1 Kings 1–2]." *Semeia* 3 (1975): 14–45.

———. *The Fate of King Saul: An Interpretation of a Biblical Story*. Journal for the Study of the Old Testament Supplement Series 14. Sheffield: JSOT, 1980.

———. *The Story of King David: Genre and Interpretation*. Journal for the Study of the Old Testament Supplement Series 6. Sheffield: JSOT, 1978.

———. "Traditional Composition in the 'Succession Narrative.'" *Vetus Testamentum* 26/2 (1976): 214–29.

Haley, John W. *An Examination of the Alleged Discrepancies of the Bible*. Grand Rapids: Baker, repr. 1958.

Halpern, Baruch. *David's Secret Demons: Messiah, Murderer, Traitor, King*. Grand Rapids: Eerdmans, 2001.

Hauer, Christian E., Jr. "Foreign Intelligence and Internal Security in Davidic Israel." *Concordia Journal* 7/3 (1981): 96–99.

Herzog, Chaim, and Mordechai Gichon. *Battles of the Bible*. New York: Random House, 1978.

Hill, Andrew E. "A Jonadab Connection in the Absalom Conspiracy?" *Journal of the Evangelical Theological Society* 30/4 (1987): 387–90.

Hoffner, Harry A., Jr. "A Hittite Analogue to the David and Goliath Contest of Champions?" *CBQ* 30 (1968): 220–25.

Hoftijzer, J. "David and the Tekoite Woman." *Vetus Testamentuam* 20/4 (1970): 419–44.

Holladay, William L. "Form and Word-Play in David's Lament over Saul and Jonathan." *Vetus Testamentum* 20/2 (1970): 153–89.

Howard, David M., Jr. "The Case for Kingship in the Old Testament Narrative Books and the Psalms." *Trinity Journal* 9 (1988): 19–35.

———. "The Transfer of Power from Saul to David in 1 Samuel 16:13–14." *Journal of the Evangelical Theological Society* 32/4 (1989): 473–83.

Hubbard, David A. "The Song of Hannah: A Bible Study." *Theology, News and Notes* 20 (1974): 12–14.

Humphreys, W. Lee. "From Tragic Hero to Villain: A Study of the Figure of Saul and the Development of 1 Samuel." *Journal for the Study of the Old Testament* 22 (1982): 95–117.

Ishida, Tomoo, ed. *Studies in the Period of David and Solomon and Other Essays.* Winona Lake, Ind.: Eisenbrauns, 1982.

Jackson, Jared J. "David's Throne: Patterns in the Succession Story." *Canadian Journal of Theology* 11/3 (1965): 183–95.

Jobling, David. "Saul's Fall and Jonathan's Rise: Tradition and Redaction in 1 Sam 14:1–46." *Journal of Biblical Literature* 95/3 (1976): 367–76.

Jones, Gwilym H. *The Nathan Narratives.* Journal for the Study of the Old Testament Supplement Series 80. Sheffield: JSOT, 1990.

Kaiser, Walter C., Jr. *Toward an Old Testament Theology.* Grand Rapids: Zondervan, 1978.

———. *Hard Sayings of the Old Testament.* Downers Grove, Ill.: InterVarsity Press, 1988.

———. "The Blessing of David: The Charter for Humanity." Pages 298–319 in *The Law and the Prophets: Old Testament Studies Prepared in Honor of Oswald Thompson Allis.* Edited by John H. Skilton. Nutley, N.J.: Presbyterian and Reformed, 1974.

———. "The Unfailing Kindnesses Promised to David: Isaiah 55:3." *Journal for the Study of the Old Testament* 45 (1989): 91–98.

Kitchen, Kenneth A. *On the Reliability of the Old Testament.* Grand Rapids: Eerdmans, 2003.

———. *Ancient Orient and Old Testament.* Downers Grove, Ill.: InterVarsity Press, 1966.

Koehler, Ludwig. "Problems in the Study of the Language of the Old Testament." *Journal of Semitic Studies* 1/1 (1956): 3–24.

Kruse, Heinz. "David's Covenant." *Vetus Testamentum* 35/2 (1985): 139–64.

Kuntz, J. Kenneth. "Psalm 18: A Rhetorical-Critical Analysis." *Journal for the Study of the Old Testament* 26 (1983): 3–31.

Laato, Antti. "Second Samuel 7 and Ancient Near Eastern Royal Ideology." *Catholic Biblical Quarterly* 59/2 (1997): 244–69.

Labuschagne, C. J. *The Incomparability of Yahweh in the Old Testament.* Leiden: Brill, 1966.

Lasine, Stuart. "Melodrama as Parable: The Story of the Poor Man's Ewe-Lamb and the Unmasking of David's Topsy-Turvy Emotions." *Harvard Annual Review* 8 (1984): 101–24.

Lawlor, John I. "Theology and Art in the Narrative of the Ammonite War." *Grace Theological Journal* 3/2 (1982): 193–205.

Lawton, Robert B. "1 Samuel 18: David, Merob, and Michal." *Catholic Biblical Quarterly* 51/2 (1989): 423–25.

Lemos, T. M. "Shame and Mutilation of Enemies in the Hebrew Bible." *Journal of Biblical Literature* 125/2 (2006): 225–41.

Leonard, Jeanne Marie. "La femme de Teqoa et le fils de David: étude de 2 Samuel 14:1–20." *Communio viatorum* 23/3 (1980): 135–48.

Levenson, Jon D. "I Samuel 25 as Literature and History." Pages 220–242 in vol. 2 of *Literary Interpretations of Biblical Narratives.* Edited by Kenneth R. R. Gros Louis. Nashville: Abingdon, 1982.

Levenson, Jon D., and Baruch Halpern. "The Political Import of David's Marriages." *Journal of Biblical Literature* 99/4 (1980): 507–18.

Lewis, Theodore J. *Cults of the Dead in Ancient Israel and Ugarit.* Harvard Semitic Monographs 39. Atlanta: Scholars, 1989.

Linafelt, Tod. "Taking Women in Samuel: Readers/Responses/Responsibility." Pages 91–113 in *Reading between Texts: Intertextuality in the Hebrew Bible.* Edited by Danna Nolan Fewell. Louisville: Westminster John Knox, 1992.

Long, Burke O. "Framing Repetitions in Biblical Historiography." *Journal of Biblical Literature* 106/3 (1987): 385–99.

Long, V. Philips. "The Early Monarchy." Pages 193–238 in *A Biblical History of Israel.* Edited by Iain Provan, V. Philips Long, and Tremper Longman III. Louisville: Westminster John Knox, 2003.

———. *The Reign and Rejection of King Saul: A Case for Literary and Theological Coherence.* Society of Biblical Literature Dissertation Series 118. Atlanta: Scholars, 1989.

Mabee, Charles. "David's Judicial Exoneration." *Zeitschrift für die alttestmentliche Wissenschaft* 92/1 (1980): 89–105.

Malamat, Abraham. "The Kingdom of David and Solomon in Its Contact with Egypt and Aram Naharaim." *Biblical Archaeologist* 21/4 (1958): 96–104.

Martin, John A. "Studies in 1 and 2 Samuel. Part 1: The Structure of 1 and 2 Samuel." *Bibliotheca Sacra* 141/1 (1984): 28–42; "Part 2: The Literary Quality of 1 and 2 Samuel," *Bibliotheca Sacra* 141/2 (1984): 131–45; "Part 4: The Theology of Samuel," *BSac* 141/4 (1984): 303–14.

Mazar, Benjamin. "The Aramean Empire and Its Relations with Israel." *Biblical Archaeologist* 25/4 (1962): 98–120.

———. "The Military Elite of King David." *Vetus Testamentum* 133 (1963): 310–20.

McCarter, P. Kyle, Jr. "'Plots, True or False': The Succession Narrative as Court Apologetic." *Interpretation* 35/4 (1981): 355–67.

———. "The Apology of David." *Journal of Biblical Literature* 99/4 (1980): 489–504.

McCarthy, Dennis J. "The Inauguration of Monarchy in Israel: A Form-Critical Study of I Samuel 8–12." *Interpretation* 27 (1973): 410–12.

———. "II Samuel 7 and the Structure of the Deuteronomistic History." *Journal of Biblical Literature* 84 (1965): 131–38.

McKane, William. *Prophets and Wise Men.* Studies in Biblical Theology 44. Naperville, Ill.: Allenson, 1965.

Mendelsohn, I. "Samuel's Denunciation of Kingship in the Light of the Akkadian Documents From Ugarit." *Bulletin of the American Schools of Oriental Research* 143 (1956): 17–22.

Merrill, Eugene H. *Kingdom of Priests: A History of Old Testament Israel.* Grand Rapids: Baker, 1987.

Mettinger, Tryggve N. D. *In Search of God: The Meaning and Message of the Everlasting Names.* Philadelphia: Fortress, 1988.

Meyers, Carol L., and M. O'Connor, eds. *The Word of the Lord Shall Go Forth: Essays in Honor of David Noel Freedman in Celebration of His Sixtieth Birthday.* ASOR special vol. series 1. Winona Lake, Ind.: Eisenbrauns, 1983.

Millard, Alan. "The Armor of Goliath." Pages 337–43 in *Exploring the Long Durée: Essays in Honor of Lawrence E. Stager.* Edited by J. David Schloen. Winona Lake. Ind.: Eisenbrauns, 2009.

Miller, J. Maxwell. "Saul's Rise to Power: Some Observations concerning 1 Sam 9:1–10:16; 10:26–11:15; and 13:2–14:46." *Catholic Biblical Quarterly* 36/2 (1974): 157–74.

Miller, Patrick D., Jr., Paul D. Hanson, and S. Dean McBride, eds. *Ancient Israelite Religion: Essays in Honor of Frank Moore Cross.* Philadelphia: Fortress, 1987.

Miller, Patrick D., Jr., and J. J. M. Roberts. *The Hand of the Lord: A Reassessment of the "Ark Narrative" of 1 Samuel.* Baltimore: Johns Hopkins University Press, 1977.

Neufeld, Edward. "Hygiene Conditions in Ancient Israel [Iron Age]." *Biblical Archaeologist* 34/2 (1971): 42–66.

North, Robert. "David's Rise: Sacral, Military, or Psychiatric?" *Biblica* 63/4 (1982): 524–44.

Olyan, Saul. "Zadok's Origins and the Tribal Politics of David." *Journal of Biblical Literature* 101/2 (1982): 177–93.

Perdue, Leo G. "'Is There Anyone Left of the House of Saul ...?': Ambiguity and the Characterization of David in the Succession Narrative." *Journal for the Study of the Old Testament* 30 (1984): 67–84.

Polzin, Robert. "*HWQYᶜ* and Covenantal Institutions in Early Israel." *Harvard Theological Review* 62 (1969): 227–40.

———. "On Taking Renewal Seriously: 1 Samuel 11:1–15." Pages 493–507 in *Ascribe to the Lord: Biblical and Other Studies in Memory of Peter C. Craigie.* Journal for the Study of the Old Testament Supplement Series 67. Edited by Lyle Eslinger and Glen Taylor. Sheffield: JSOT, 1988.

———. *Samuel and the Deuteronomist.* San Francisco: Harper, 1989.

———. "Curses and Kings: A Reading of 2 Samuel 15–16." Pages 201–26 in *The New Literary Criticism and the Hebrew Bible.* Edited by J. Cheryl Exum and David J. A. Clines. Sheffield: JSOT Press, 1993.

Porter, J. R. "The Interpretation of 2 Samuel VI and Psalm CXXXII." *Journal of Theological Studies* 5 (1954): 161–73.

Preston, Thomas R. "The Heroism of Saul: Patterns of Meaning in the Narrative of the Early Kingship." *Journal for the Study of the Old Testament* 24 (1982): 27–46.

Rasmussen, Carl G. *Zondervan NIV Atlas of the Bible.* Grand Rapids: Zondervan, 1989.

Ridout, George P. *Prose Compositional Techniques in the Succession Narrative [2 Samuel 7:9–20; 1 Kings 1–2].* Ann Arbor, Mich.: University Microfilms, 1985.

Rosenberg, Joel. *King and Kin: Political Allegory in the Hebrew Bible.* Bloomington, Ind.: Indiana University Press, 1986.

Rost, Leonhard. *The Succession to the Throne of David.* Translated by Michael D. Rutter and David M. Gunn. Sheffield: Almond, 1982.

Roth, Wolfgang M. W. "A Study of the Classical Hebrew Verb *skl.*" *Vetus Testamentum* 18/1 (1968): 69–78.

———. "The Deuteronomic Rest Theology: A Redaction-Critical Study." *Biblical Research* 21 (1976): 5–14.

———. "You Are the Man! Structural Interaction in 2 Samuel 10–12." *Semeia* 8 (1977): 1–13.

Sacon, Kiyoshi K. "A Study of the Literary Structure of 'The Succession Narrative.'" Pages 27–54 in *Studies in the Period of David and Solomon and Other Essays*. Winona Lake, Ind.: Eisenbrauns, 1982.

Sarna, Nahum M. "The Interchange of the Prepositions *Beth* and *Min* in Biblical Hebrew." *Journal of Biblical Literature* 78/4 (1959): 310–16.

Segal, J. B. "Numerals in the Old Testament." *Journal of Semitic Studies* 10/1 (1965): 2–20.

Segal, M. H. *The Pentateuch: Its Composition and Its Authorship and Other Biblical Studies*. Jerusalem: Magnes, 1967.

Sellers, Ovid R. "Musical Instruments of Israel." *Biblical Archaeologist* 4/3 (1941): 33–47.

Shea, William H. "Chiasmus and the Structure of David's Lament." *Journal of Biblical Literature* 105/1 (1986): 13–25.

———. "David's Lament." *Bulletin of the American Schools of Oriental Research* 221 (1976): 141)44.

Simon, Uriel. "The Poor Man's Ewe-Lamb: An Example of a Juridical Parable." *Biblica* 48/2 (1967): 207–42.

Snaith, Norman H. *Notes on the Hebrew Text of 2 Samuel xvi–xix*. London: Epworth, 1945.

Stek, John. "The Former Prophets: A Syllabus." 1985.

Sternberg, Meir. *The Poetics of Biblical Narrative: Ideological Literature and the Drama of Reading*. Bloomington, Ind.: Indiana University Press, 1987.

Talmon, Shemaryahu. *King, Cult, and Calendar in Ancient Israel: Collected Studies*. Jerusalem: Magnes, 1986.

Thompson, J. A. "The Significance of the Verb *Love* in the David–Jonathan Narratives in 1 Samuel." *Vetus Testamentum* 24/3 (1974): 334–38.

Tidwell, N. L. "The Philistine Incursions into the Valley of Rephaim." Pages 190–212 in *Studies in the Historical Books of the Old Testament*. Ed. J. A. Emerton. Vetus Testamentum Supplements 30. Leiden: Brill, 1979.

Trible, Phyllis. *Texts of Terror: Literary-Feminist Readings of Biblical Narratives*. Philadelphia: Fortress, 1984.

Tromp, Nicholas J. *Primitive Conceptions of Death and the Nether World in the Old Testament*. Rome: Pontifical Biblical Institute, 1969.

Ulrich, Eugene Charles, Jr. *The Qumran Text of Samuel and Josephus*. Harvard Semitic Monographs 19. Missoula, Mont.: Scholars, 1978.

Unger, Merrill F. "Archaeology and the Reign of David." *Bibliotheca Sacra* 111/441 (1954): 11–26.

Vanderkam, James. "Davidic Complicity in the Deaths of Abner and Eshbaal: A Historical and Redactional Study." *Journal of Biblical Literature* 99/4 (1980): 521–39.

Vannoy, J. Robert. *Covenant Renewal at Gilgal*. Cherry Hill, N.J.: Mack, 1978.

Vogels, Walter. "David's Greatness in His Sin and Repentance." *The Way* 15/4 (1975): 243–54.

Walters, S. D. "The Light and the Dark." Pages 567–89 in *Ascribe to the Lord: Biblical and Other Studies in Memory of Peter C. Craigie*. Ed. Lyle Eslinger and Glen Taylor. Journal for the Study of the Old Testament Supplement Series 67. Sheffield: JSOT, 1988.

Watson, Wilfred. "Shared Consonants in Northwest Semitic." *Biblica* 50/4 (1969): 525–33.

Weinberg, Werner. "Language Consciousness in the OT." *Zeitschrift für die alttestmentliche Wissenschaft* 92/2 (1980): 185–200.

Weinfeld, M. "The Covenant of Grant in the Old Testament and in the Ancient Near East." *Journal of the American Oriental Society* 90/2 (1970): 184–203.

Wharton, James A. "A Plausible Tale: Story and Theology in 2 Samuel 9–20, 1 Kings 1–2." *Interpretation* 35/4 (1981): 341–54.

Whybray, R. N. *The Succession Narrative: A Study of II Sam. 9–20 and I Kings 1 and 2*. Studies in Biblical Theology 9. London: SCM, 1968.

Willis, John T. "The Song of Hannah and Psalm 113." *Catholic Biblical Quarterly* 25/2 (1973): 139–54.

Wiseman, D. J. "'Is It Peace?'—Covenant and Diplomacy." *Vetus Testamentum* 32/3 (1982): 313–24.

Wiseman, D. J., ed. *Peoples of Old Testament Times*. Oxford: Clarendon, 1973.

Yadin, Yigael. *The Art of Warfare in Biblical Lands in the Light of Archaeological Discovery*. London: Weidenfeld & Nicolson, 1963.

Youngblood, Ronald F. *The Amarna Correspondence of Rib-Haddi, Prince of Byblos (EA 68–96)*. Ann Arbor, Mich.: University Microfilms, 1973.

———. *The Book of Genesis*. 2nd ed. Eugene, Ore.: Wipf and Stock, 2000.

10. OUTLINE

1 Samuel

- I. Prelude to Monarchy in Israel (1:1–7:17)
  - A. The Childhood of Samuel (1:1–4:1a)
    1. The Birth and Dedication of Samuel (1:1–28)
    2. The Song of Hannah (2:1–11)
    3. The Wicked Sons of Eli (2:12–26)
    4. The Oracle against the House of Eli (2:27–36)
    5. The Call of Samuel (3:1–4:1a)
  - B. The Ark Narratives (4:1b–7:17)
    1. The Capture of the Ark (4:1b–11)
    2. The Death of Eli (4:12–22)
    3. The Lord's Affliction of the Philistines (5:1–12)
    4. The Return of the Ark (6:1–7:1)
    5. Samuel the Judge (7:2–17)
- II. Advent of Monarchy in Israel (8:1–15:35)
  - A. The Rise of Saul (8:1–12:25)
    1. The Demand for a King (8:1–22)
    2. The Anointing of Saul (9:1–10:16)
    3. The Choice of Saul by Lot (10:17–27)
    4. The Defeat of the Ammonites (11:1–11)
    5. The Confirmation of Saul as King (11:12–12:25)
  - B. The Decline of Saul (13:1–15:35)
    1. The Rebuke of Saul (13:1–15)
    2. The Struggle against the Philistines (13:16–14:23)
    3. The Cursing of Jonathan (14:24–46)
    4. Further Wars of Saul (14:47–52)
    5. The Rejection of Saul (15:1–35)
- III. Establishment of Monarchy in Israel (16:1–31:13)
  - A. The Rise of David (16:1–28:2)
    1. The Anointing of David (16:1–13)
    2. The Arrival of David in the Court of Saul (16:14–23)
    3. The Death of Goliath (17:1–58)
    4. The Jealousy of Saul (18:1–30)
    5. David the Refugee (19:1–24)
    6. Jonathan's Friendship (20:1–42)
    7. David and the Priest of Nob (21:1–9)
    8. David the Fugitive: Gath, Adullam, Mizpah (21:10–22:5)

9. The Slaughter of the Priests of Nob (22:6–23)
10. The Rescue of Keilah (23:1–6)
11. The Pursuit of David (23:7–29)
12. Sparing Saul's Life (24:1–22)
13. David, Nabal, and Abigail (25:1–44)
14. Sparing Saul's Life Again (26:1–25)
15. Achish the Philistine (27:1–28:2)

B. The End of the Reign of Saul (28:3–31:13)
1. Saul and the Medium at Endor (28:3–25)
2. The Dismissal of David (29:1–11)
3. The Defeat of the Amalekites (30:1–31)
4. The Death of Saul and Jonathan (31:1–13)

2 Samuel

I. Consolidation of Monarchy in Israel (1:1–20:26)

A. David's Accession to Kingship over Judah (1:1–3:5)
1. The Death of Saul and Jonathan (1:1–16)
2. David's Lament for Saul and Jonathan (1:17–27)
3. David Anointed King over Judah (2:1–7)
4. War between Saul's House and David's House (2:8–3:1)
5. Sons Born to David in Hebron (3:2–5)

B. David's Accession to Kingship over Israel (3:6–5:16)
1. Abner's Defection to David (3:6–21)
2. The Murder of Abner (3:22–39)
3. The Murder of Ish-Bosheth (4:1–12)
4. David Anointed King over Israel (5:1–5)
5. David's Conquest of Jerusalem (5:6–12)
6. Children Born to David in Jerusalem (5:13–16)

C. David's Powerful Reign (5:17–8:18)
1. The Philistines Defeated (5:17–25)
2. The Ark Brought to Jerusalem (6:1–23)
3. The Lord's Covenant with David (7:1–17)
4. David's Prayer to the Lord (7:18–29)
5. David's Enemies Defeated (8:1–14)
6. David's Officials (8:15–18)

D. David's Court History (9:1–20:26)
1. Kindness to Mephibosheth (9:1–13)
2. The Ammonites Defeated (10:1–19)

3. David's Sin against Bathsheba (11:1–5)
4. The Murder of Uriah (11:6–27)
5. Nathan's Rebuke (12:1–25)
6. The Ammonites Defeated (12:26–31)
7. Amnon's Sin against Tamar (13:1–22)
8. The Murder of Amnon (13:23–39)
9. The Wise Woman of Tekoa (14:1–20)
10. Absalom's Return to Jerusalem (14:21–33)
11. Absalom's Conspiracy (15:1–12)
12. David's Flight (15:13–37)
13. Kindness to Ziba (16:1–4)
14. Shimei's Curse (16:5–14)
15. The Advice of Hushai and Ahithophel (16:15–17:29)
16. Absalom's Death (18:1–18)
17. David's Mourning for Absalom (18:19–19:8)
18. David's Return to Jerusalem (19:9–43)
19. Sheba's Rebellion (20:1–22)
20. David's Officials (20:23–26)

II. Epilogue (21:1–24:25)
A. The Lord's Wrath against Israel (21:1–14)
B. David's Heroes (21:15–22)
C. David's Song of Praise (22:1–51)
D. David's Last Words (23:1–7)
E. David's Mighty Men (23:8–39)
F. The Lord's Wrath against Israel (24:1–25)

Text and Exposition

FIRST SAMUEL

I. PRELUDE TO MONARCHY IN ISRAEL (1:1–7:17)

OVERVIEW

The theme of the books of Samuel is the beginning of Israel's monarchy in the eleventh century BC. Recognizing this theme, the LXX's translators titled the books *Basileiōn* ("Concerning Kingdoms"), a title that includes the books of the Kings. First Samuel introduces us to Israel's last two judges (Eli, a failure; Samuel, a success) and first two kings (Saul, a failure; David, a success).

A. The Childhood of Samuel (1:1–4:1a)

OVERVIEW

Appropriately, the story of Israel's monarchy begins with an account of the early life of Samuel: prophet, priest, judge and, most significantly, kingmaker. God chose Samuel to anoint both Saul and David, Israel's first two kings. Each was to be the "leader" (*nāgîd*) over his people (10:1; 13:14; 16:13).

1. The Birth and Dedication of Samuel (1:1–28)

1There was a certain man from Ramathaim, a Zuphite from the hill country of Ephraim,
whose name was Elkanah son of Jeroham, the son of Elihu, the son of Tohu, the son of
Zuph, an Ephraimite. 2He had two wives; one was called Hannah and the other Peninnah.
Peninnah had children, but Hannah had none.
3Year after year this man went up from his town to worship and sacrifice to the LORD
Almighty at Shiloh, where Hophni and Phinehas, the two sons of Eli, were priests of the
LORD. 4Whenever the day came for Elkanah to sacrifice, he would give portions of the meat
to his wife Peninnah and to all her sons and daughters. 5But to Hannah he gave a double
portion because he loved her, and the LORD had closed her womb. 6And because the LORD
had closed her womb, her rival kept provoking her in order to irritate her. 7This went on
year after year. Whenever Hannah went up to the house of the LORD, her rival provoked her
till she wept and would not eat. 8Elkanah her husband would say to her, "Hannah, why are

you weeping? Why don't you eat? Why are you downhearted? Don't I mean more to you
than ten sons?"
[9]Once when they had finished eating and drinking in Shiloh, Hannah stood up. Now
Eli the priest was sitting on a chair by the doorpost of the LORD's temple. [10]In bitterness of
soul Hannah wept much and prayed to the LORD. [11]And she made a vow, saying, "O LORD
Almighty, if you will only look upon your servant's misery and remember me, and not
forget your servant but give her a son, then I will give him to the LORD for all the days of his
life, and no razor will ever be used on his head."
[12]As she kept on praying to the LORD, Eli observed her mouth. [13]Hannah was praying in her heart, and her lips were moving but her voice was not heard. Eli thought she
was drunk [14]and said to her, "How long will you keep on getting drunk? Get rid of your
wine."
[15]"Not so, my lord," Hannah replied, "I am a woman who is deeply troubled. I have not
been drinking wine or beer; I was pouring out my soul to the LORD. [16]Do not take your
servant for a wicked woman; I have been praying here out of my great anguish and
grief."
[17]Eli answered, "Go in peace, and may the God of Israel grant you what you have asked
of him."
[18]She said, "May your servant find favor in your eyes." Then she went her way and ate
something, and her face was no longer downcast.
[19]Early the next morning they arose and worshiped before the LORD and then went back
to their home at Ramah. Elkanah lay with Hannah his wife, and the LORD remembered her.
[20]So in the course of time Hannah conceived and gave birth to a son. She named him
Samuel, saying, "Because I asked the LORD for him."
[21]When the man Elkanah went up with all his family to offer the annual sacrifice to
the LORD and to fulfill his vow, [22]Hannah did not go. She said to her husband, "After the
boy is weaned, I will take him and present him before the LORD, and he will live there
always."
[23]"Do what seems best to you," Elkanah her husband told her. "Stay here until you have
weaned him; only may the LORD make good his word." So the woman stayed at home and
nursed her son until she had weaned him.
[24]After he was weaned, she took the boy with her, young as he was, along with a three-
year-old bull, an ephah of flour and a skin of wine, and brought him to the house of the
LORD at Shiloh. [25]When they had slaughtered the bull, they brought the boy to Eli, [26]and
she said to him, "As surely as you live, my lord, I am the woman who stood here beside you
praying to the LORD. [27]I prayed for this child, and the LORD has granted me what I asked of
him. [28]So now I give him to the LORD. For his whole life he will be given over to the LORD."
And he worshiped the LORD there.

COMMENTARY

1–2 In the MT the beginning of the description of Samuel's father, Elkanah, is identical to that of Samson's father, Manoah, in Judges 13:2. Each description begins with the statement, "There was a certain man," followed by the name of his hometown, his own name, the tribe he comes from or is living with, and a reference to his marital status. The strong similarity between the two passages is probably intentional and highlights Samson's and Samuel's dedication to the Lord as Nazirites from birth (see below).

The word "Ramathaim"—the name of the town of Samuel's birth, official residence, and burial—is dual in form and appears to mean "Two Heights." It is probably not intended as a grammatical dual, however, but rather possesses locative force (cf. Aharoni, 120). Elsewhere the town is called simply Ramah (1:19; 2:11; 7:17 et al.). Of the several Israelite towns bearing that name, Ramah ("height") of Ephraim (mentioned in the Bible more often than any other Ramah) is perhaps to be identified with the NT Arimathea (Mt 27:57; Jn 19:38) and the modern Rentis, sixteen miles east of Joppa on the western slope of the hill country of Ephraim.

Samuel's Ramah is probably not to be equated with the Ramah of Joshua 18:25, since the latter is specifically located in the tribal territory of Benjamin (Jos 18:21, 28). Nebi Samwil (Arabic for "Prophet Samuel"), visible from the outskirts of Jerusalem high on the horizon to the northwest, is the traditional site of Samuel's tomb; but there is no certain basis for this identification.

Samuel's father is called a Zuphite, doubtless because of his descent from Zuph (v.1). The same family line (with minor variations) is recorded twice in 1 Chronicles 6 (vv.26–27, 34–35 [in reverse order]). The Chronicles genealogies identify Samuel as a member of the Kohathite branch of the tribe of Levi and an ancestor of tabernacle and temple musicians (1Ch 6:16, 22, 31–33). The reference to Samuel's father as an Ephraimite, then, relates to the territory where he lived rather than to his tribal origin. Allotted no patrimony of their own, the Levites lived among the other tribes. (See Jos 21:20–22, where, however, Ramah is not specifically mentioned as a Levitical town.)

In ancient Israel "Elkanah" was a popular name shared by at least five different OT men (two of whom were ancestors of Samuel's father; see 1Ch 6:22–27). The name means "God has created [a son]"—tantalizingly prophetic of what is soon to occur in Hannah's womb.

Elkanah must have been a man of some means, for he is the only commoner in the books of Samuel and Kings specifically mentioned as having more than one wife (cf., e.g., J. S. Grabowski, "Covenantal Sexuality," *EgT* 27 [1996]: 238 n. 28). Although polygamy was not God's intention for humankind (cf. the singular "wife" and "one flesh" in Ge 2:24; also Mal 2:15), having "two wives" (v.2) accords with the polygamous culture of the ancient world (cf. *AIs*, 24–26). Lamech, the seventh descendant in the line of Cain, is the first-mentioned polygamist in the Bible (Ge 4:19). Although polygamy is never explicitly condemned in Scripture, its complications and unsavory results are everywhere apparent.

Hannah (*ḥannâ*, lit., "Grace") initially has pride of place in v.2, probably because she was Elkanah's favorite. Later in the same verse, however, Peninnah (*pᵉninnâ*, lit., "Ruby") is mentioned first, no doubt because she was a prolific childbearer (cf. v.4, "all her sons and daughters"). Barrenness in ancient times was the ultimate tragedy for a married woman, since her husband's hopes and dreams depended on her providing him with a son to perpetuate his name and inherit his estate (cf. Ge 11:30; 15:2–4; 16:1–2; 17:15–16; 21:1–2; 25:5; Dt 25:5–6).

3–8 Three times each year all Israelite men were required to be at the central or most important sanctuary to offer sacrifices in observance of the main religious festivals (Ex 34:23; Dt 12:5–7; see also Lk 2:22–24, 41). Elkanah was no exception (vv.3, 21; 2:19). For some time Shiloh (modern Seilun, sixteen miles east of Ramah) had been the location of the tabernacle and the ark of the covenant (4:3–4; cf. Jos 18:1; Jdg 18:31) as well as the site where one of the annual festivals was celebrated (Jdg 21:19; the time gap between Judges 21 and 1 Samuel 1 remains uncertain). Eli ("Exalted is [the Lord]"), the priest at Shiloh (v.9; 2:11) and a judge in Israel (4:18; cf. NIV margin), was descended from Aaron's son Ithamar, if the Ahimelech who was Eli's great-grandson and successor (14:3; 22:20) is the one mentioned in 1 Chronicles 24:3. Each of Eli's two reprobate sons—unfortunately also priests—had an Egyptian name: Hophni ("Tadpole") and Phinehas ("The Nubian"). The latter should not be confused with his earlier, godly namesake, a son of Aaron's son Eleazar (Ex 6:25; Nu 25:11).

The festival in view here is probably the Feast of Tabernacles (as also in Jdg 21:19–21), celebrated in the fall. Sacrifices were offered to "the LORD Almighty" (v.3; *yhwh ṣᵉbāʾôt*, lit., "the LORD of hosts"; GK 3378, 7372). This is the first time in the OT that "Almighty/hosts" appears as added to a divine name. One connotation of the title is that he is "the God of the armies of Israel" (17:45; in this case the Hebrew word for "armies" is different from that for "hosts"). Since, however, "hosts" can mean not only human armies (Ex 7:4, "divisions"; cf. the use of the plural and singular renderings of *ṣābāʾ* in Isa 13:4: "The LORD of Armies is assembling his army for battle" [GWT]; "The LORD of Hosts is mustering a host for war" [Tanakh]) but also celestial bodies (Dt 4:19, "array") or heavenly creatures (Jos 5:14), the NIV everywhere translates the word as "Almighty" in the sense of "he who is sovereign over all the 'hosts' (powers) in heaven and on earth, especially over the 'hosts' (armies) of Israel" (NIV preface). It is noteworthy that this majestic name for God, appearing at the inception of the Israelite monarchy, describes him in a way that is much more royal than military (cf. J. P. Ross, "Jahweh *Ṣᵉbāʾōt* in Samuel and Psalms," *VT* 17/1 [1967]: 76–92).

Festival celebrations were times of rejoicing in God's blessings, especially that of a bountiful harvest. Elkanah distributed portions of sacrificial meat (cf. Ex 29:26; Lev 7:33; 8:29) to Peninnah and her children, since family members shared in certain of the sacrificial offerings brought to the Lord (cf. Dt 12:17–18; 16:13–14). Elkanah provided Hannah with a double portion because of his love for her. He perhaps also knew—along with the narrator—that his wife's barrenness was by divine providence (vv.5–6; cf. Ge 15:3; 16:2; 20:18; 30:2).

Hannah's sterility likely prompted Elkanah to take Peninnah as his second wife (cf. the actions of Sarai in Ge 16:2; Rachel in 30:3; and Leah in 30:9). Peninnah thus became Hannah's "rival" (*ṣārâ* [GK 7651], v.6; *ṣar* ["adversary, enemy"] was used in this sense as early as the time of Moses [Lev 18:18] and as late as the intertestamental period [Sir 37:11]). She "kept provoking" (v.6) Hannah—activity that culminated in "grief" (v.16; the repetition of the root *kʿs* underscores the connection). Peninnah intended to "irritate" (*rāʿam*, lit., to "thunder against"; GK 8307) Hannah (cf. 2:10, where Hannah declares that the Lord will "thunder against" [*rāʿam*] all who oppose him, doubtless including Peninnah). The devout Hannah, in the spirit of Deuteronomy 32:35, is content to allow the Lord to avenge the wrong committed against her (cf. David's statement in 2Sa 3:39).

Elkanah's family "went up" (in the technical sense of journeying to a sacred place; cf. v.3; Ex 34:24) yearly to the "house of the LORD" (v.7). This term refers to the tabernacle but apparently also includes more permanent auxiliary structures that had doors (3:15) and therefore doorposts (v.9). These sacred buildings are called "the LORD's temple" (cf. 3:3). Hannah's rival took special delight in using the annual pilgrimage to Shiloh as an occasion for continued provocation, badgering Hannah to the point of tears.

Elkanah, mindful of Hannah's grief, asked her, "Why are you downhearted?" (v.8). More literally the question is, "Why is your heart bad?" The only other precise OT parallel for this phrase is Deuteronomy 15:10: "Do so without a grudging heart" (lit., "May your heart not be bad when you do so!" [i.e., when you give generously to the Lord]). To do something "with a bad heart" means to do it resentfully (or grudgingly; so the NIV on Dt 15:10). Thus Elkanah is not so much asking Hannah why her heart is sad ("Why are you downhearted?") but why her heart is bad ("Why are you resentful?"). Are you angry or full of spite because you do not have children? "Don't I"—your husband, who loves you very much—"mean more to you than ten sons?" (ten, like seven, represents completeness or fullness; note the Ten Commandments; cf. Ex 26:1, 16; 34:28 et al.; also 2:5; Ru 4:15; Edward F. Campbell Jr., *Ruth* [AB 7; Garden City, N.Y.: Doubleday, 1975], 164; M. H. Pope, *IDB*, 3:565–66).

9–11 Hannah's misery peaked at Shiloh during an annual pilgrimage. Eli, "the LORD's priest in Shiloh" (14:3), the chief religious official, was sitting on "a chair" (lit., "the chair," in the sense of "his chair"; cf. 4:13, 18; also Jdg 3:20) near the worship complex (which included the tabernacle; cf. NIV note). The earlier Sumerian cognate of the word translated "temple" also means "palace" (Sumerian É.GAL [lit., "large house"] > Akkad. *ēkallu* > Heb. *hêkāl*) and thus reminds us that the tabernacle and temple in the Israelite theocracy were residences symbolically inhabited by the divine King.

Hannah's sadness and "bitterness of soul" (v.10 and a favorite concept of Job [see Job 3:20; 7:11; 10:1; 21:25]; see also "discontented" in 1Sa 22:2) led her to pray and make a vow to the Lord. On behalf of her hoped-for son, she made "a special vow, a vow of separation to the LORD" (Nu 6:2). The Nazirite vow included (1) abstaining from the use of grapes in any form, (2) not shaving the hair on one's head, and (3) avoiding dead bodies (Nu 6:3–7). Although the term "Nazirite" is absent in the MT of 1 Samuel, it is surely presupposed. The text states that "no razor will ever be used on his head" (v.11), an expression used elsewhere only of the Nazirite Samson (Jdg 13:5; 16:17; see also Nu 6:5, which, however, renders a different Hebrew phrase). The LXX inserts "and he will not drink wine or any intoxicating beverage" (cf. the similar description of John the Baptist in Lk 1:15).

DSS fragment 4QSamuel[a] states at the end of verse 22: "[I g]ave him (to be) a Nazirite forever all the days of [his life]" (for a photograph of the Hebrew text, see Frank M. Cross Jr., "A New Qumran Biblical Fragment Related to the Original Hebrew Underlying the Septuagint," *BASOR* 132 [1953]: 17; cf. also Cross's transcription on p. 18 and in context on p. 26, col. I, lines 3–4). Samuel is described in the Apocrypha as "a Nazirite of the LORD in the prophetic office" (Sir 46:13 [Heb.]). As Robert P. Gordon ("Who Made the Kingmaker?" 265) observes, Amos 2:11–12 "links prophets and Nazirites in poetic parallelism and implies a close connection between the two groups." Josephus (*Ant.* 5.347 [10.3]) states that Samuel drank only water. The Mishnah argues that Samuel was indeed a Nazirite (*Nazir* 9.5). The Nazirite vow was not usually taken by proxy and was rarely lifelong; the only other biblical parallels to Samuel's Naziriteship are Samson (Jdg 13:5) and perhaps John the Baptist (Lk 1:15).

Hannah humbly calls herself "your servant" (v.11), a submissive way of referring to oneself in the presence of a superior in ancient Near Eastern culture (cf. v.16; 3:9–10). Her request that God "look upon [her] misery" recalls Leah's grateful response after the birth of her firstborn son, Reuben (Ge 29:32; see NIV note). David later uses the same expression in a time of crisis (2Sa 16:12). Hannah's plea to the Lord to "remember" her was soon answered (v.19). God's remembrance is not a matter of recalling to mind but of paying special attention to or lavishing special care on one (cf. Ps 8:4, where the same Hebrew verb is rendered "are mindful of" in parallelism with "care for"). Hannah recognizes that children are always a gift of God, the Great Enabler of conception and childbirth (cf. Ru 4:13). If he will "give" her a son, in gratitude she will "give" him back to the Lord—which in a broader sense was covenantally required of every Israelite mother (Ex 22:29).

12–18 Hannah's prayer reveals her conscious, intimate relationship with God. She prays "to" (*lipnê*, lit., "in the presence of"; cf. 1Ki 8:28 ["in your presence"]) the Lord (v.12); she prays "in her heart" (i.e., to herself [v.13]; cf. Abraham's servant in Ge 24:45); and she prays silently. Hannah is a woman of prayer; indeed, she is the first and only woman in the Bible "to utter a formal, spoken prayer, and have her prayer quoted in the text for us to read" (Trevor Dennis, *Sarah Laughed* [Nashville: Abingdon, 1994], 124). Eli, observing that Hannah's "lips were moving but her voice was not heard" (v.13), misunderstood what she was doing. Prayer in the ancient world was almost always audible (cf. Pss 3:4; 4:1; 6:9 [and throughout Psalms, the prayerbook of ancient Israel]; Da 6:10–11), and drunkenness was not an uncommon accompaniment of festal occasions (including esp. the Feast of Tabernacles [cf. *AIs*, 496] and perhaps also Pentecost [Ac 2:13]).

Eli—who, after all, was the chief priest at Shiloh—can hardly be excused for his spiritual insensitivity. He should have realized that Hannah's moving lips signified earnest prayer rather than intoxicated mumbling. He therefore mistakenly rebukes her: "How long will you make a drunken spectacle of yourself?" (v.14, my translation).

Hannah justly protests that she has been drinking neither wine nor beer—which, when imbibed in sufficient quantities, produce drunkenness (Isa 28:7). Far from pouring herself too many drinks, she had been "pouring out [her] soul to the LORD" (v.15), a vivid idiom for praying earnestly (cf. Pss 42:4; 62:8; La 2:19). She declares herself to be "deeply troubled" (*qᵉšat-rûaḥ*, lit., "burdened in spirit"; cf. Job 7:11); and under no circumstances does she want Eli to mistake her for a "wicked woman" (*bat-bᵉlîyāʿal*, lit., "daughter of worthlessness," v.16; cf. the description of Hophni and Phinehas as "wicked men"—*bᵉnê-bᵉlîyāʿal* [lit., "sons of worthlessness"]—in 2:12).

Satisfied with Hannah's explanation, Eli tells her to "go in peace" (v.17), a common biblical expression of farewell (cf. 25:35; Mk 5:34). Eli's hope that God would grant Hannah's request is soon fulfilled in the birth of Samuel (v.27; cf. 2:20). Godly Hannah, God's willing servant (v.18; cf. Dt 10:12; Mic 6:8), will receive the desire of her heart from God's gracious hand. Being assured by Eli's response, she breaks her self-imposed fast, and her face is "no longer downcast" (*lōʾ-hāyû-lāh ʿôd*, lit., "no longer to her [as it had been previously]").

19–20 The next day Elkanah's family worshiped the Lord, an experience with special meaning for Hannah this time. After their return from Shiloh to Ramah, Elkanah "lay with" (*wayyēdaʿ* [GK 3359], lit., "and he knew," a common OT euphemism for sexual intimacy; cf. Ge 4:1, 17, 25) Hannah. The

Lord, as she had earnestly prayed (v.11), "remembered her" (v.19; see comment on v.11)—just as he had remembered her ancestor Rachel (Ge 30:22)—by enabling her to bear a son. Hannah called him Samuel (lit., "name of God") and then punned on the name (a common ancient practice; cf. NIV note at Ge 11:9; Ex 2:10) by saying that she had "asked" the Lord for him (interestingly, all three consonants in Hebrew *š'l*, "ask," are found in the same order in *šmw'l*, "Samuel").

21–23 After Samuel was born, Elkanah continued his custom of taking his family with him annually to Shiloh to sacrifice to the Lord (1:3; 2:19). On at least one occasion he had the additional purpose of fulfilling a "vow" (v.21), perhaps in support of Hannah's earlier vow (v.11)—although it was not unusual for sacrifice and vow to accompany each other (Dt 12:11). In any case, Hannah decided not to make the trip to Shiloh this time (v.22). She preferred to wait until Samuel was weaned. Then she could leave him there to serve the Lord at the tabernacle for the rest of his life, as she had promised.

In the ancient world a child was breast-fed for two or three years (cf. 2 Macc 7:27) before being considered old enough to spend extended periods of time away from home. After Samuel's weaning, Hannah intended to "present him before the LORD" (v.22; see Notes). Elkanah agreed with his wife's desire to follow through with her vow (v.23).

24–28 The big day finally arrived, and Hannah was ready. We are not told whether the family waited for an official annual festival. For the trip from Ramah to Shiloh, they took ample provisions with them (v.24). The three-year-old bull, in the prime of life, was doubtless meant to be sacrificed to the Lord (v.25). The purpose of the flour and wine, however, remains obscure. The Hebrew word for "flour" used here (*qemaḥ*) occurs in a sacrificial context only once in the OT—and that in a special situation unaccompanied by the sacrifice of an animal (Nu 5:15). It is possible, therefore, that the flour here was to be baked into loaves or cakes of unleavened bread (cf. 28:24; Jdg 6:19) and used as food, along with the wine. ("Skin[s] of wine" always refers only to food [10:3; 25:18; 2Sa 16:1; Jer 13:12].)

When "they" (doubtless the official slaughterers at the tabernacle; the Hebrew for "they had slaughtered the bull" should be construed as an impersonal passive; namely, "the bull had been slaughtered") had sacrificed the bull, "they" (in this case, Hannah and Elkanah) brought Samuel before Eli the priest (v.25). In addressing Eli, Hannah uses a common oath formula: "As surely as you live" (*ḥê napšᵉkā*, lit., "By the life of your soul" = "By your life," v.26; cf. 20:3; see also 17:55; 25:26; 2Sa 11:11; 14:19). She thus solemnly affirms that she is indeed the same woman he first had met a few years earlier and that the boy Samuel, given in answer to her prayers, is now to be given back to the Lord for the rest of his life. Her words to Eli in v.27 echo his to her in v.17, the main difference being that Eli referred to Hannah's benefactor as "the God of Israel" while she used his more intimate, covenantal name: "the LORD." Eli responds to Hannah's brief remarks by worshiping the God whom they both served (v.28).

NOTES

1 צוֹפִים (*ṣôpîm*) is interpreted by the NIV as "Zuphite" (*ṣûpî*) with reference to Elkanah's descent from a man named Zuph. The *m* on *ṣôpîm* must thus be understood either (1) as dittography (from the following word, which in Hebrew begins with *m*) or (2) as an example of the so-called enclitic *m*, which is not infrequently appended to words in several Semitic languages, including Hebrew. The NIV note suggests the less plausible (because grammatically difficult) reading "Ramathaim Zuphim," understanding the phrase as a compound proper name that would relate the town of Ramah to the "district of Zuph" (1Sa 9:5). For additional details concerning the location of Ramah/Ramathaim, see J. Albright, "Ramah," *BI* 9/4 (1983): 23–26; R. A. Spencer, "Arimathea," *BI* 10/3 (1984): 77–78.

קָנָה (*qānâ*; GK 7865), the verbal root underlying the name Elkanah, occurs in the OT as early as Genesis 4:1 ("brought forth"), where it puns on the name "Cain," קַיִן (*qayin*). The verb also appears in Genesis 14:19, 22, where "God Most High" (*ʾēl ʿelyôn*) is called "Creator [קֹנֵה, *qōnēh*] of heaven and earth." Similar titles were also frequently applied to El, the chief Canaanite deity, in ancient times (for details cf. M. H. Pope, *El in the Ugaritic Texts* [VTSup 2; Leiden: Brill, 1955], 50–54).

אֶלְקָנָה (*ʾelqānâ*, "Elkanah"; see Ronald Youngblood, "Elkanah," *ABD*, 2:475–76) appears on an unpublished seal decorated with the figure of an ibex (see Avigad, in Miller, Hanson, and McBride, 200, fig. 4). Two other seals mentioned by Avigad and containing the same verbal root are pertinent here: (1) *qnyw*, "Yahweh has created"; and especially (2) *mqnyw*, "the creation of Yahweh" (ibid., 197–98). The latter name is the same as that of Mikneiah (1Ch 15:18), who, like Elkanah's descendants, was a tabernacle/temple musician (1Ch 15:21). It has long been recognized (BDB, 888–89) that the root *qny* in various Semitic languages often means "create," especially when a deity is its subject; cf. KB, 843; N. Habel, "'Yahweh, Maker of Heaven and Earth': A Study in Tradition Criticism," *JBL* 91 (1972): 321–37; U. Cassuto, *Biblical and Oriental Studies* (Jerusalem: Magnes, 1975), 2:55; P. D. Miller Jr., "El, the Creator of Earth," *BASOR* 239 (1980): 43–46; Joseph Aistleitner, *Wörterbuch der Ugaritischen Sprache* (Berlin: Akademie, 1963), 229. Contrast, however, B. Vawter, "Yahweh: Lord of the Heavens and the Earth," *CBQ* 48 (1968): 461–67.

2 The names "Hannah" and "Peninnah" appear only in the first two chapters of 1 Samuel in the OT. A Hebrew seal from the Lachish area dating to the period of 725–675 BC, however, displays the name Hannah (*ḥnh*); cf. J. R. Bartlett, "The Seal of *Ḥnh* from the Neighbourhood of *Tell ed-Duweir*," *PEQ* 108 (1976): 59–60. In the NT a prophetess named Hannah is mentioned in Luke 2:36. Unfortunately the KJV's spelling "Anna" in that verse has become traditional; the only recent English versions that spell the name correctly (and therefore maintain continuity with the OT counterpart) are those of Lamsa, Moffatt, and Smith-Goodspeed (cf. NASB note). The apocryphal book of Tobit includes a Hannah (also spelled "Anna" in most English versions) who, like Hannah in 1 Samuel 1–2, is connected with procreation, as her three extended conversations with her husband Tobit demonstrate (Tob 2:13–14; 5:17–21; 10:4–7). In addition 4Q215, a fragment of the Hebrew text of *T. Naph.*, tells a story about still another Hannah, one of Laban's female servants, who is said to have mothered Zilpah and Bilhah, Jacob's two female servants.

The name "Peninnah" may be related to a similar Arabic word meaning "woman with luxuriant hair" (cf. KB 2:768). But it is perhaps better to assume it to be the feminine singular form of the masculine plural פְּנִינִים (*pᵉnînîm*), which means something like "coral(s)" or "rubies." The latter is the consistent translation of the NIV (cf. Job 28:18; Pr 3:15; 8:11; 20:15; 31:10; La 4:7). With the exception of Proverbs 20:15, all the other texts describe something or someone as being better than rubies. Similarly, Hannah ("Grace")—at least in Elkanah's eyes—was better than Peninnah ("Ruby"; cf. 1Sa 1:5; see Ronald Youngblood, "Hannah," *ABD*, 3:51–52; "Peninnah," *ABD*, 5:222).

3 The tabernacle's location at Shiloh was probably on a flat rock surface about 160 yards north of the summit of the tell of modern Seilun (for details see A. S. Kaufman, "Fixing the Site of the Tabernacle at Shiloh," *BAR* 14/6 [1988]: 49).

5 Although clearly a dual noun, אַפָּיִם (*ʾappāyim*, "double") elsewhere always means either "face" ("nose, nostril" in the singular) or "anger." On the basis of LXX's evidence, it is often emended here to אֶפֶס (*ʾepes*) and, combined with the following כִּי (*kî*), translated as "nevertheless, although" (for details and the resulting understanding of v.5, see Driver, 8). David Aberbach retains the consonantal MT (*ʾpym*) but interprets it as *pym* (a measure of weight; see comment on 13:21) prefixed by prosthetic *aleph* and thus interprets the gift Elkanah gave to Hannah as "one portion, a *pim* in value" ("מנה אחת אפים [1 Sam. I 5]: A New Interpretation," *VT* 24/3 [1974]: 350–53). Ferdinand Deist successfully criticizes Aberbach, but his own proposal—to emend the already emended *ʾepes* to *ʾabûs(â)* ("fattened") and to understand the resulting phrase as "one portion (of) fattened (meat)" but to translate it as "one selected portion" on the basis of a targum on Samuel—heaps conjecture on conjecture and therefore fares no better ("*ʾAppayim* [1 Sam. I 5] < **pym*?" *VT* 27/2 [1977]: 205–9).

Preferable is the suggestion of Barthélemy et al., 2:146, who state that the literal meaning of *ʾappāyim* ("face") designates Hannah's portion as one that "was particularly large and honourable." They would therefore translate the phrase as "a worthy portion." But the NIV's "double" remains the best rendering of *ʾappāyim*. The word is after all a dual—"two nostrils, two sides of the face"—and in this context would mean simply "two times." I have argued elsewhere that "overwhelmingly in Hebrew a part of the body is used to represent 'time' in this sense" (Youngblood, *The Amarna Correspondence*, 17). The entire phrase in v.5 should thus be translated "one portion two times," hence "a double portion."

9 The word translated "doorpost," מְזוּזָה (*meᵉzûzâ*), is rendered "doorframe" in Exodus 12:7; Deuteronomy 6:9; 11:20. The last two of these passages is the basis for the Jewish tradition of placing a small wooden, metal, or glass case, called a *mezuzah*, about five feet from the floor to the right of the entrance on the doorframe of the home. Inside the *mezuzah* is a tiny parchment on which are written the words of Deuteronomy 6:4–9 (the *Shema*, Judaism's confession of faith, proclaiming God's unity; see Dt 11:13–21). On entering their homes, devout Jews touch the *mezuzah* and are thereby reminded of their belief in the sanctity of the house in which they live.

15 שֵׁכָר (*šēkār*) is the etymological and semantic equivalent of the Akkadian *šikaru* ("beer"). The Hebrew word was rendered almost exclusively as "strong drink" in earlier English versions; the NIV, however, translates the word correctly as "beer" or "fermented drink" throughout. For a thorough treatment of the Akkadian materials, see especially L. F. Hartman and A. L. Oppenheim, "On Beer and Brewing Techniques in Ancient Mesopotamia," JAOSSup 10 (Baltimore: Johns Hopkins Univ. Press, 1950).

16 The etymology of בְּלִיַּעַל (*beᵉlîyaᶜal*; GK 1175), translated here as "wicked," has long been disputed. Modern scholars tend to derive it from the root *blᶜ* ("to swallow"), referring to personified Death or Sheol as the Great Swallower (e.g., Pr 1:12); cf. D. Winton Thomas, *Biblical and Patristic Studies*, ed. J. N. Birdsall and R. W. Thomson (New York: Herder, 1963), 11–19; Mitchell Dahood, *Psalms I* (AB; Garden City, N.Y.: Doubleday, 1965), 105 n. 5. The most transparent etymology is *beᵉlî* + *yaᶜal*, "without value, worthless(ness)" (so BDB, 116). Another attractive possibility, however, is to understand the second element in the word, *yᶜl*, as an imperfect/jussive form of the root *ᶜly* ("to go/come up") and to translate "[the place from which] none comes up," a euphemism for Sheol expressing a motif not unknown in the OT (cf. Job 7:9; 10:21; 16:22; Cross and Freedman, "A Royal Song," 22 n. 16). *Ben bᵉlîyaʿal* would then mean "son of perdition, hellion." In any case, although its etymology remains uncertain, the word came into the NT as "Belial," a proper name virtually synonymous with "Satan," the very personification of wickedness (2Co 6:15).

20 The NIV note on the name Samuel, although superficially true, has little if anything to do with the argument of the text itself. שׁמע (*šmʿ*, "hear") is found only once in 1 Samuel 1 (v.13, "heard"), but not in connection with the birth, naming, or dedication of the child. On the other hand, שׁאל (*šʾl*, "ask") is found seven times in 1 Samuel 1 (v.17, "request" ["what," NIV]; v.17, "asked"; v.20, "asked"; v.27, "request" ["what," NIV]; v.27, "asked"; v.28, "give"; v.28, "given")—each time in connection with the birth, naming, or dedication of the child. Although שְׁמוּאֵל (*šᵉmûʾēl*) means "name of God" on the analogy of other proper nouns such as Penuel or Peniel ("face of God," cf. Ge 32:30–31; also NIV note), Reuel ("friend of God," Ex 2:18), and Jeruel (perhaps "foundation of God," 2Ch 20:16), the narrator chose to pun on the name by using the verb *šʾl* ("ask") rather than to connect it in any way with the verb *šmʿ* ("hear") or the noun *šm* ("name").

Those scholars (for example, Ackroyd; McCarter, *I Samuel*) who see in the frequent use of *šʾl* in 1 Samuel 1 an attempt to explain the origin of the name Saul (the last of the seven occurrences—*šāʾûl*, "given," in v.28—is precisely the Hebrew spelling of "Saul") would do better to reckon with the likelihood that the continued association of the root of Saul's name, not with Saul but with Samuel, is the narrator's subtle way of reminding us that throughout most of Saul's reign the Lord's will for his people was channeled through Samuel the kingmaker, not Saul the king, who soon demonstrated his inability to rule over Israel under God. Only the "name of God"—that is, the divine presence—was to be sovereign over his people. This fact diminishes W. J. Martin's suggestive proposal that the name Samuel "was probably part of a sentence spoken by Hannah at his birth. The full sentence would have been in some such form as: 'I asked for him *a godly name*'" (W. J. Martin, *NBD*, 1134). The word "name" in "name of God" refers to God's name, not Samuel's.

22 וְנִרְאָה אֶת־פְּנֵי יהוה (*wᵉnirʾâ ʾet-pᵉnê yhwh*, lit., "and he will appear before the LORD") is a technical expression used in reference to the requirement of all male Israelites to attend the three annual religious festivals at the central sanctuary (cf. Ex 34:23–24; Dt 16:16; 31:11).

23 The NIV's note reads "your" (instead of "his") from the DSS and the LXX (the Syriac reading probably derives from the LXX). More specifically, 4QSamuel[a] and the LXX read "what goes forth from your mouth" instead of the MT's "his word." Since no divine word has been mentioned thus far in 1 Samuel, 4QSamuel[a] (dutifully followed by the LXX) is probably trying to smooth out a difficulty by equating the word with Hannah's vow. Earlier commentators (e.g., K&D) resolved the problem by referring the divine word to the statement of Eli in v.17, who presumably was speaking on God's behalf. There, however, the birth of Samuel is in view—and by v.23 Samuel has already been born (v.20). At the same time, why would a scribe change an original "your (word)" to "his (word)"? It seems best to assume an earlier word of the Lord not recorded in our text. Interestingly, the JB reads "your" in v.23, but the NJB (commendably) reverts to the MT's "his."

24 For over a century most commentators have read פר משלש (*pr mšlš*, "a three-year-old bull") with the LXX (cf. also Ge 15:9) instead of the MT's פר[י]ם שלשה (*pr[y]m šlšh*, "three bulls"), assuming that the *m* on *pr[y]m* was misplaced. The LXX's reading has now been confirmed by 4QSamuel[a]: *[pr bn] bqr mšlš*. For parallel usage at Nuzi, where (as here and in Ge 15:9) the animal's age specifies maturity for purposes of sacrifice, see E. A. Speiser, "The Nuzi Tablets Solve a Puzzle in the Books of Samuel," *BASOR* 72 (1938): 15–17.

27–28 Near the end of 1 Samuel 1, the narrator clusters four of the seven times he uses the root שׁאל (*šʾl*, "ask") as a pun on the name "Samuel" (שׁמואל, *šmwʾl*). Twice in v.27 it has its usual meaning ("a/the request," translated as "what" and "asked" in the NIV). Twice in v.28, however, it bears the derived meaning "allow to ask, lend on request," hence "give." The son Hannah requested God gave, and she gratefully gives her gift back to the Giver.

2. The Song of Hannah (2:1–11)

1Then Hannah prayed and said:

"My heart rejoices in the LORD;
in the LORD my horn is lifted high.
My mouth boasts over my enemies,
for I delight in your deliverance.

2"There is no one holy like the LORD;
there is no one besides you;
there is no Rock like our God.

3"Do not keep talking so proudly
or let your mouth speak such arrogance,
for the LORD is a God who knows,
and by him deeds are weighed.
4"The bows of the warriors are broken,
but those who stumbled are armed with strength.
5Those who were full hire themselves out for food,
but those who were hungry hunger no more.
She who was barren has borne seven children,
but she who has had many sons pines away.

6"The LORD brings death and makes alive;
he brings down to the grave and raises up.
7The LORD sends poverty and wealth;
he humbles and he exalts.
8He raises the poor from the dust
and lifts the needy from the ash heap;
he seats them with princes
and has them inherit a throne of honor.

"For the foundations of the earth are the LORD's;
upon them he has set the world.
9 He will guard the feet of his saints,
but the wicked will be silenced in darkness.

"It is not by strength that one prevails;
10 those who oppose the LORD will be shattered.
He will thunder against them from heaven;
the LORD will judge the ends of the earth.

"He will give strength to his king
and exalt the horn of his anointed."

11 Then Elkanah went home to Ramah, but the boy ministered before the LORD under Eli the priest.

COMMENTARY

1–2 Although 1 Samuel 2:1–10 is a prayer, as v.1 indicates and the NIV section head acknowledges, it is commonly referred to as the "Song of Hannah" because of its lyrical qualities and similarities to other ancient OT hymns (e.g., the Song of Moses and Miriam [Ex 15:1–18, 21]; the Song of Moses [Dt 32:1–43]; the Song of Deborah [Jdg 5]; and esp. the Song of David [2Sa 22]). Robert Lowth, eighteenth-century doyen of Hebrew poetic structure, called it a "thanksgiving ode" (*Lectures on the Sacred Poetry of the Hebrews* [London: Chadwick, 1847], 216). Sigmund Mowinckel, calling it a psalm of thank offering, stated that it was sung in celebration of victory over enemies (*Samuelsboken* [Oslo: Aschehoug, 1936], 152). Like the Song of Hannah, Jonah's song of thanksgiving (though much later) is also called a prayer (Jnh 2:1, 7, 9).

John T. Willis, 139–54, has shown that the Song of Hannah is a royal song of victory/triumph that is to be classified among the other ancient hymns listed above, all of which reflect traditional combat motifs, are composed in the first person singular, and emphasize the Lord's everlasting and universal power and sovereignty. In terms of poetic style, all contain repetitive parallelism in both bicola and tricola, exhibit a staccato effect, and tend to repeat important words in sequence (see Notes on v.3). Characteristic expressions and ideas also recur in these victory hymns; those that appear in both 2:1–10 and 2 Samuel 22 will be especially noted in the commentary. First Samuel 2:1–10 may have originated as a song of triumph at the Shiloh sanctuary in connection with Israel's victory over an enemy. Such songs would then have been taught to worshipers, and this one perhaps became a personal favorite of Hannah. Therefore, when she brought Samuel to Shiloh to dedicate him to the Lord, she sang it as a means of expressing her gratitude and praise to the Giver of life (cf. esp. v.5).

The Song of Hannah appears near the beginning of 1 Samuel, and the Song of David appears near the end of 2 Samuel. These two remarkably similar hymns of praise thus constitute a kind of inclusio framing the main contents of the books and reminding us that the two books were originally one. (For a convenient comparison of the songs' similarities see Polzin, *Samuel and the Deuteronomist*, 33–34.) Both hymns begin by using "horn" (1Sa 2:1; 2Sa 22:3) as a metaphor for "strength," referring to God as the "Rock," and reflecting on divine "deliverance/salvation" (1Sa 2:1–2; 2Sa 22:2–3). Both end by paralleling "his king" with "his anointed" (1Sa 2:10; 2Sa 22:51).

It may well be that Hannah's song served as the seed plot for Mary's Magnificat (Lk 1:46–55; cf. also the Song of Zechariah in vv.68–79). The two hymns begin similarly, and certain themes in the Song of Hannah recur in the Song of Mary (cf. 1Sa 2:4, 7–8 with Lk 1:52; 1Sa 2:5 with Lk 1:53; notice also that Lk 1:48a—"for he has been mindful of the humble state of his servant"—is obviously dependent on 1Sa 1:11 LXX: "if you will only look upon the humble state of your servant"). Both Hannah and Mary became pregnant miraculously (though admittedly in quite different ways), in due course each presented her firstborn son to the Lord at the central sanctuary (1:22; Lk 2:22), and both sang a hymn of thanksgiving and praise (Hannah after the birth of Samuel [1Sa 2:1–10], Mary before the birth of Jesus [Lk 1:46–55]). Further parallels between the two hymns, as well as expansions and reappropriations of Hannah's song in Pseudo-Philo's *Liber antiquitatum biblicarum* (first century AD) and the *Targum of the Prophets* (second century AD), are offered in Joan E. Cook, "Hannah's Later Songs: A Study in Comparative Methods of Interpretation," in *The Function of Scripture in Early Jewish and Christian Tradition*, ed. C. A. Evans and J. A. Sanders (JSNTSup 154; Sheffield: Sheffield Academic, 1998), 241–61. Compare further D. J. Harrington's translation of and introduction to Pseudo-Philo in *The Old Testament Pseudepigrapha*, ed. J. H. Charlesworth (Garden City, N.Y.: Doubleday, 1985), 2:297–377, esp. 365–66.

The songs of Hannah and Mary, together with their contexts, have in turn influenced a second-century-AD pseudepigraphal work known as the *Protevangelium of James*. It tells the story of Mary's elderly parents independently praying for a child. The old woman vows that the child will be "a gift to the Lord my God" (cf. 1Sa 1:11). Mary is born in response to the prayers, and at the age of three she is presented by her parents to the priests in the temple at Jerusalem. The name of Mary's aged mother—Anna—is the same as that of Samuel's aged mother, Hannah.

The Song of Hannah begins on a note of grateful exuberance: "Heart, strength, mouth—all that she thinks and does and says is centered in the great act of God on her behalf" (Hubbard, 13). Like that of the psalmist (Ps 9:1–2; cf. also 5:11), Hannah's heart rejoices in the Lord—and in his deliverance (or salvation) as well (see Pss 9:14; 13:5; 35:9; Isa 25:9). The metaphor of one's horn being lifted high (see also Pss 89:17, 24; 112:9) perhaps comes from the animal world, where members of the *Cervidae* family (deer et al.) use their antlers in playful or mortal combat (cf. Dt 33:17; Ps 92:10). "Horn" thus symbolizes strength (see NIV note). Whereas here Hannah is grateful that her own "horn" is lifted high (i.e., that Samuel has been born—cf. 1Ch 25:5 NIV note; so McCarter, *I Samuel*), in 2 Samuel 22:3 David refers to God himself as "the horn of my salvation."

For Hannah, the Lord is holy, unique, and mighty (v.2). She therefore celebrates God's holiness, his otherness, in righteous victory (as in Ex 15:11; Ps 99:3, 5, 9; Isa 5:16). She then connects his uniqueness with the metaphor of the "Rock," exactly as David later does (2Sa 22:32). However rocklike others—human or divine—may consider themselves, "their rock is not like our Rock" (Dt 32:31). God as the Rock is one of the most recognizable and familiar images of divine refuge and strength, not only in the OT (cf. Ge 49:24; Dt 32:4; Isa 26:4; Hab 1:12; frequently in the Psalms) but also in Christian hymnody ("Rock of Ages," "O Safe to the Rock That Is Higher Than I," et al.).

3–8d After describing God in his majesty and power, Hannah warns all (the verbs in v.3 being plural) who would vaunt themselves in their pride (including, of course, Peninnah). In the light of all that God is and does, arrogance is both foolish and futile (Pss 31:18; 75:4; 138:6; Isa 5:15–16). Using the same verb used earlier of her (*rby*), Hannah contrasts the fact that she "kept" praying (1:12) with her rebuke to Peninnah (among others) not to "keep" talking so proudly. The doubling of *g*[e]*bōhâ* ("proudly"), rendered "so proudly" in the NIV, is a literary feature characteristic of the most ancient Hebrew poetry and helps us date the Song of Hannah early rather than late. God, who knows the heart, judges and weighs it rather than external appearances (16:7; 1Ki 8:39; Pr 16:2; 21:2; 24:12).

The informal contrasts here presented by Hannah prepare us for the series of seven formal contrasts in vv.4–7 (v.8a–d simply expands the two contrasts in v.7): (1) strong and weak, (2) full and hungry, (3) barren and fertile, (4) dead and alive, (5) sick and well, (6) poor and rich, and (7) humble and exalted. So classic and striking are these opposing qualities and characteristics that Robert Lowth uses them as a paradigm for what he calls antithetic parallelism (*Lectures on the Sacred Poetry of the Hebrews* [London, Tegg, 1835], 215–16). As Hubbard, 13, puts it, God "turns losers into winners and winners into losers."

The "broken" bows of v.4 are echoed by the "shattered" opponents of v.10, since the Hebrew root (*ḥtt*) is the same. And if the verb translated "bend" (*niḥat*) in 2 Samuel 22:35 is derived from the same root (as one Hebrew manuscript indicates), we have yet another connection between the Song of David and the Song of Hannah. In any case, the phrase "armed with strength" in v.4 reappears in 2 Samuel 22:40 as well as in a Qumran text of 22:33 (see NIV note at 22:33). Making the strong weak and the weak strong is what God does in Hebrews 11:32–34, a text that includes both Samuel and David as the recipients of divine deliverance.

The last half of v.5 had special meaning for Hannah. Like the mother of Samson, another lifelong Nazirite, the mother of Samuel had once been barren (cf. Jdg 13:2–3). "Seven" here means simply "many" (cf. Ru 4:15), as the parallel line shows and as numerous extrabiblical texts attest (cf., e.g., W. G. Lambert, "DINGIR.ŠA.DIB.BA Incantations," *JNES* 33 [1974]: 283–85; for a similar phenomenon, cf. comment on 1Sa 1:8). At the same time, seven—as a number symbolizing completion—also represents the ideal (cf. Job 1:2; 42:13). Just as she who has had many "pines away" (*ʾumlālâ*), so also the mother of seven will "grow faint" (Jer 15:9; same Hebrew word). The formerly barren Hannah eventually had a total of six children (v.21)—one short of the ideal.

Verses 6–8 make explicit what was only implicit in vv.4–5: The sovereign God, according to his own good pleasure, ultimately blesses some and curses others (cf. vv.9c–10c). Verse 6a contrasts death with life, and possibly v.6b does too (so McCarter, *I Samuel*). However, v.6b may refer rather to rescue from the brink of death after a serious illness and therefore contrast sickness with health. Deuteronomy 32:39 and 2 Kings 5:7 have the same two sets of contrasts (death/life, sickness/health). In addition, bringing up from the grave in Psalm 30:2–3 clearly refers to healing rather than resurrection.

The Lord can—and does—reverse the fortunes of poor and rich (Zec 9:3–4), of the humble and the proud (Job 5:11; Ps 75:7; and esp. 2Sa 22:28). He can lift a Baasha "from the dust" and later consume him (1Ki 16:2–3); he can ensconce a Job on an ash heap (Job 2:8) and later restore him (Job 42:10).

The MT of the first three lines of v.8 is almost identical to that of Psalm 113:7–8a. If (as seems likely) Psalm 113 is later than Hannah's song, the psalmist has added an exquisite touch in the light of Hannah's situation: "He [the LORD] settles the barren woman in her home as a happy mother of children" (113:9).

8e–10 Though the underlying Hebrew text is different, 2 Samuel 22:16 also makes reference to the "foundations of the earth." There, as here and elsewhere (cf. similarly Job 38:4; Pss 75:3; 82:5; 104:5; Isa 24:18; 48:13; 51:13, 16), such phrases refer pictorially to the firmness and stability of God's creation—which, however, is always under his sovereign control, for good or ill. How much more is he able to protect his people (Pr 3:26) and confound his (and their) enemies (Dt 32:35)!

The word *ḥāsîd* (GK 2883), often translated "saint" (as in v.9), means "one to whom the Lord has pledged his covenant love," his *ḥesed*. As here, it frequently appears in the Psalms in opposition to the wicked: cf. Psalms 12:1 ("godly"), 8; 50:5 ("consecrated ones"), 16; 97:10 ("faithful ones"); 145:10 (for discussion cf. Willis J. Beecher, *The Prophets and the Promise* [Grand Rapids: Baker, 1963], 313–43; for messianic implications in the present passage, cf. esp. 325). The final destiny of the ungodly, however, is the silence of Sheol, the grave, the netherworld, where all is darkness (Job 10:21–22; 17:13; 18:18; Ps 88:12; Pr 20:20; cf. also Mt 8:12; for further details, cf. Ronald F. Youngblood, "Qoheleth's 'Dark House' [Eccl 12:5]," *JETS* 29/4 [1986]: 397–410).

Hannah learned that in the battles of life it is not physical strength that brings victory (cf. also Ps 33:16–17; Jer 9:23). Had Moses depended on such resources against the Amalekites, he would not have defeated them. ("Winning" in Ex 17:11 is from the same Hebrew root as "prevails" here [*gbr*].) But whether through human agency or directly, God always shatters the enemy (v.10; cf. Ex 15:6; Ps 2:9). Peninnah may have "thundered against" (see comment on 1:6 above) Hannah, but never mind: Hannah knows full well that the Lord will ultimately "thunder against" Peninnah and all others who oppose him (v.10; 2Sa 22:14), including Israel's inveterate enemies, the Philistines (1Sa 7:10).

The Song of Hannah ends as it began, concluding the inclusio by again using the word "horn" metaphorically in the sense of "strength" (as the parallel in the preceding line demonstrates). Hannah voices the divine promise of strength to the coming "king"—initially David, who will found a dynasty with messianic implications. ("King" is used in a messianic sense in, e.g., Ps 2:6; Isa 32:1; Jer 23:5; Eze 37:22, 24; Hos 3:5; Zec 9:9.) The king—the "anointed" one—will rule by virtue of God's command and will therefore belong to him body and soul. The king will be "his" (v.10; 2Sa 22:51).

11 With Samuel's dedication and Hannah's song complete, the family returned to Ramah—except for Samuel, who began what was to be a continuing ministry (so the verb forms imply; cf. Driver, 28, 151) as a priest (2:18; 3:1; so *šrt* intends when "the LORD" is its grammatical object; see BDB, 1058).

NOTES

3 4QSamuel[a] reads דעת (*dʿt*, singular) instead of the MT's דעות (*dʿwt*, plural), thus describing God simply as a God of "knowledge." But the Qumran text also has חתה (*ḥth*, singular) instead of the MT's חתים (*ḥtym*, plural) in v.4, thereby exhibiting a tendency toward the singular in this hymn. It would therefore seem best to read אֵל דֵּעוֹת (*ʾēl dēʿôt*) with the MT here and to translate something like "the all-knowing God" (so BDB, 42).

5 The MT underlying the translation "hunger no more" is fraught with difficulties. The meaning of the verb is uncertain, its connection with the following particle is unclear, and the Masoretic punctuation is suspect. But since the verb חדל (*ḥdl*) in several other places (for example, Jdg 20:28; Jer 40:4; Eze 2:5, 7; 3:11; Zec 11:12) seems to mean "not to do something," where the "something" is the preceding verb in question (so NIV in all the passages), it is perhaps best to translate the first two lines of v.5 as follows: "Those who were full hire themselves out for food, but the hungry do not do so anymore." This was the solution of several early Jewish exegetes and has been argued forcefully by Theodore J. Lewis, "The Songs of Hannah and Deborah: *HDL*–II ('Growing Plump')," *JBL* 104/1 (1985): 105–8.

6 שְׁאוֹל (*še*ʾ*ôl*; GK 8619) is usually translated "the grave" in the NIV (cf. R. Laird Harris in *The NIV: The Making of a Contemporary Translation*, ed. Kenneth L. Barker (Grand Rapids: Zondervan, 1986], 58–71). In a few instances, however, it is rendered "the realm of death" or the equivalent (e.g., Dt 32:22) as a vivid image of the netherworld, the place of the departed spirits of the dead (cf. Tromp, 10, 70, 129–51, 167–96). The two concepts are not mutually exclusive since the grave, a literal tomb, can also be viewed figuratively as the portal through which the deceased gains admission to the afterlife.

10 In the common expression "ends of the earth," אַפְסֵי (*ʾapsê*, "ends of") derives ultimately from the Sumerian *ab.zu* via the Akkadian *apsû* ("fresh water"), referring to the fresh waters that were believed to surround the earth in ancient cosmology. The Sumerian word is also the origin of the Greek ἀβύσσος (*abyssos*), the "Abyss" of Luke 8:31; Revelation 9:1–2, 11; 11:7; 17:8; 20:1, 3.

The NIV rightly scans v.10b–c as a couplet, but the translation "against them" is highly suspect at best. One would not expect "the LORD" in the second line to be paralleled by "he" in the first line (the reverse would be the normal pattern). The parallel passage in 2 Samuel 22:14 is helpful at this point: "The LORD thundered from heaven; the voice of the Most High resounded." More literally the second line reads: "The Most High gave his voice"—that is, "the Most High" is the subject of the second line, paralleling "the LORD" as the subject of the first. "Most High" here is עֶלְיוֹן (*ʿelyôn*). Some seventy years ago H. S. Nyberg observed that the alternate forms על/עלי/עלו (*ʿl/ʿly/ʿlw*) were used as a divine name cognate to *ʿelyôn* and also meaning "Most High" in several OT poetic passages as well as elsewhere in the ancient Near East (cf. "Studien zum Religionskampf im Alten Testament," *AR* 35 [1938]: 329–87). The NIV acknowledges this usage in 2 Samuel 23:1; Psalm 7:8, 10; and Hosea 7:16; 11:7. עלו (*ʿlw*) should be translated "Most High" in 1 Samuel 2:10 as well (as Nyberg already recognized): "The Most High will thunder from heaven / the LORD will judge the ends of the earth." The Hebrew name is formally similar to that of "Eli," which (as indicated above in the comment on 1:3) means something like "Exalted is [the LORD]" or "The Most High [is the LORD]." For additional details see Mitchell Dahood, "The Divine Name *ʿĒlî* in the Psalms," *TS* 14/3 (1953): 452–57; Freedman, "Divine Names and Titles," 55–107.

מָשִׁיחַ (*māšîaḥ*, "anointed"; GK 5431) underlies our word "Messiah" and reminds us that great David's greater Son, Jesus the Christ—Greek *Christos* ("anointed")—would some day culminate David's royal line (cf. this typological, eschatological use of "anointed" here as well as in v.35; 2Sa 22:51; 2Ch 6:42; Pss 2:2; 89:38, 51; 132:10, 17). For a fine summary statement of this interpretation, see Delitzsch, 79; for the possibility that v.10 originally had in mind a local "king" of an Israelite city-state or tribe, and that therefore the Song of Hannah comes from a promonarchic circle of the premonarchic period who felt that the Lord's kingship was not jeopardized by an earthly king, see Willis, 148–49.

The Song of Hannah is commonly dated during the period of the monarchy (tenth century BC or later) because of the reference to a future king in v.10. On the basis of stylistic phenomena, however, W. F.

Albright (cited in Freedman, "Divine Names and Titles," 55, 96) dated it to the late eleventh century (i.e., only slightly later than the time of Hannah herself); and on the basis of divine names and titles, Freedman himself places it in the eleventh or tenth century. When all is said and done, then, there would seem to be no insuperable reason not to assume that Hannah's song is contemporary with her. Her celebration of the Lord's victory (v.1), uniqueness (v.2), power (vv.3–8), and judgment (vv.9–10; Hubbard, 12–14) demonstrates her earnest desire to praise God for blessings past, present, and future.

3. The Wicked Sons of Eli (2:12–26)

[12]Eli's sons were wicked men; they had no regard for the LORD. [13]Now it was the practice of the priests with the people that whenever anyone offered a sacrifice and while the meat was being boiled, the servant of the priest would come with a three-pronged fork in his hand. [14]He would plunge it into the pan or kettle or caldron or pot, and the priest would take for himself whatever the fork brought up. This is how they treated all the Israelites who came to Shiloh. [15]But even before the fat was burned, the servant of the priest would come and say to the man who was sacrificing, "Give the priest some meat to roast; he won't accept boiled meat from you, but only raw."

[16]If the man said to him, "Let the fat be burned up first, and then take whatever you want," the servant would then answer, "No, hand it over now; if you don't, I'll take it by force."

[17]This sin of the young men was very great in the LORD's sight, for they were treating the LORD's offering with contempt.

[18]But Samuel was ministering before the LORD—a boy wearing a linen ephod. [19]Each year his mother made him a little robe and took it to him when she went up with her husband to offer the annual sacrifice. [20]Eli would bless Elkanah and his wife, saying, "May the LORD give you children by this woman to take the place of the one she prayed for and gave to the LORD." Then they would go home. [21]And the LORD was gracious to Hannah; she conceived and gave birth to three sons and two daughters. Meanwhile, the boy Samuel grew up in the presence of the LORD.

[22]Now Eli, who was very old, heard about everything his sons were doing to all Israel and how they slept with the women who served at the entrance to the Tent of Meeting. [23]So he said to them, "Why do you do such things? I hear from all the people about these wicked deeds of yours. [24]No, my sons; it is not a good report that I hear spreading among the LORD's people. [25]If a man sins against another man, God may mediate for him; but if a man sins against the LORD, who will intercede for him?" His sons, however, did not listen to their father's rebuke, for it was the LORD's will to put them to death.

[26]And the boy Samuel continued to grow in stature and in favor with the LORD and with men.

COMMENTARY

12–17 This account of the sin of Eli's sons is followed immediately by a statement concerning Samuel's ministry before the Lord (v.18), as is the subsequent account (vv.27–36) of the prophecy against Eli's house (3:1). Thus the narrator highlights the sharp contrast between Eli and his sons on the one hand, and Samuel on the other. In addition, the reference to Hophni and Phinehas as "wicked men" (v.12) contrasts them with Hannah, who did not consider herself a "wicked woman" (1:16)—as Eli himself acknowledged (1:17). Finally, the sons of Eli "had no regard for" (*lōʾ yādᵉʿû*, lit., "did not know") the Lord—unlike Samuel, who "did not yet know" (3:7) the Lord (implying that he would come to know him in the future).

Attempts are often made to distinguish the priestly practice/custom described in vv.13–14 from the obvious priestly violation depicted in vv.15–16 (e.g., Eslinger; McCarter, *I Samuel*). But by comparing vv.13–14 with Deuteronomy 18:3, Garsiel, 38–39, has shown that "the 'ordinance of the priests' here, like the 'ordinance of the king' later on (8:11)," is an ironic opening "whose point is the antithesis between the actual and the desirable, or (to put it differently) between the murky reality and the requirements of the law." Not content with the specified portions of the animals that the sacrificer was to "give" (see Dt 18:3) to the priests (cf. also Lev 7:34), Eli's sons would take for themselves "whatever the fork brought up" (v.14).

Not only that, "even [*gam*] before the fat was burned" (v.15), as the law mandated (Lev 7:31), Hophni and Phinehas demanded raw meat. In fact, on occasion they even preferred roasted meat to boiled—as though in mockery of the necessarily hasty method of preparing the first Passover feast (Ex 12:8–11). They wanted their unlawful portion before the Lord received what was rightfully his (cf. K&D, Driver, Hertzberg, Klein). Their rebellion, impatience, and impudence (v.16) are described as a "very great" sin (v.17). Like their postexilic counterparts (Mal 1:6–14), these premonarchic priests treated the Lord's offerings with contempt. Such conduct, especially when practiced by God's ministers, can only lead to disaster (cf. Nu 16:30–32).

18–26 Even as a young apprentice priest under Eli's supervision, Samuel wore the linen ephod characteristic of that ministry. Anthony Phillips ("David's Linen Ephod," *VT* 19/4 [1969]: 487), primarily on the basis of 2 Samuel 6:14, attempted to prove that Samuel's ephod "is not to be understood as a special priestly garment but a brief loincloth suitable for young children." But Phillips fails to explain why David (2Sa 6:14) would wear a child's garment, and he resorts to the LXX's omission of "linen" in 1 Samuel 22:18 to confirm his belief that the eighty-five priests slaughtered by Doeg are not described there as "wearing" ephods but as "carrying" an "oracular instrument" (another meaning for *ʾēpōd*). N. L. Tidwell ("The Linen Ephod: 1 Sam. II 18 and 2 Sam. VI 14," *VT* 24/4 [1974]: 505–7) rightly criticizes Phillips' view in favor of the traditional interpretation: "Linen ephod" always refers to a priest's garment, whether worn by a youth or by an adult. Indeed, the little "robe" that Samuel's mother made for him annually as he was growing up (v.19) may well have been an example of the "robe of the ephod" mentioned in Exodus 28:31 (the Hebrew word for "robe" being the same in both passages). Although David is not described as wearing such a robe in 2 Samuel 6:14, he is so depicted in the parallel text of 1 Chronicles 15:27.

The use of *šʾl* twice in v.20 (here translated "the one she prayed for/gave") echoes its sevenfold use in ch. 1 (see Notes on 1:20) and reminds us of Hannah's vow. By providing Hannah with additional children, the Lord continued to be gracious to her, as he had been to her ancestor Sarah centuries earlier (Ge 21:1). The narrator's description of Samuel's continued growth in the Lord's presence (v.21), as well as in stature and in favor with God and human beings (v.26), is echoed in Luke's portrayal of Jesus' youth (Lk 2:40, 52; cf. also Lk 1:80a with respect to John the Baptist). The narrator's description also frames the account of further sinful activity by Eli's sons (vv.22–25) and thus extends the contrast between them and Samuel.

The hapless Eli, whose advanced age is stressed in the text from this point on (v.22; 4:15, 18), was unable to restrain the sinful conduct of his sons. To their earlier callous treatment of their fellow Israelites (vv.13–16) they added sexual promiscuity—and with the women who served at the tabernacle (cf. Ex 38:8) at that. Such ritual prostitution (if indeed it was; Eslinger, 122–23, expresses doubts), though common among Israel's Canaanite neighbors, was specifically forbidden to the people of God (Nu 25:1–5; Dt 23:17; Am 2:7–8). Eli's rebuke, justified in the light of widespread and public reports of his sons' evil deeds, fell on deaf ears. His theological arguments, weak at best, were to no avail, especially since God had already determined to put Hophni and Phinehas to death (v.25).

The most familiar and notable case of divine judicial hardening against defiant refusal to repent is that of the pharaoh of the oppression (Ex 4:21–14:17); for a summary explanation, see Ronald F. Youngblood, *Exodus* (Chicago: Moody Press, 1983), 45–46. Numerous sensitive discussions (cf. Matitiahu Tsevat, "The Death of the Sons of Eli," *JBR* 32/4 [1964]: 355–58; Eslinger, 126–27), while admirable, do not materially advance our understanding beyond the traditional view (cf. K&D). What is eminently clear is that God's decision to end the lives of Eli's sons was irrevocable. Hannah had already expressed her willingness to leave such decisions within the sphere of divine sovereignty (2:6)—and so must we.

NOTES

13 Three-pronged forks, dating to the Late Bronze Age and apparently used as sacrificial implements, have been excavated at Gezer (cf. Neufeld, 53–54).

20 This verse contains two excellent examples of how Qumran readings may confirm earlier suggestions for changes in the MT. 4QSamuel[a] reads ישלם (*yšlm*, "restore, repay") instead of the MT's יָשֵׂם (*yśm*, "give, grant"), thus reinstating the idiom שִׁלֵּם תַּחַת (*šillēm taḥat*, "repay in exchange for") as in Exodus 21:36. The purpose of Eli's blessing is that the Lord might restore children to Elkanah in exchange for the loss of Samuel, whom Hannah had given to the Lord in faithfulness to her vow (cf. similarly Eslinger, 121). 4QSamuel[a] also reads the more grammatically correct השאיל[ה] (*hš*ʾ*yl[h]*, "she gave") instead of the MT's שָׁאַל (*š*ʾ*l*, "he asked"). Both readings were proposed eighty years ago, partly on the basis of the LXX, in BDB (964, 982).

25 As the NIV note indicates, we cannot always be sure whether אֱלֹהִים (ʾ*ᵉlōhîm*; GK 466) means "God" or "(the) judges" in certain contexts. In Exodus 21:6 and 22:8–9, the NIV places "judges" in the text, "God" in the text note; in 22:28 the situation is reversed. In Psalms 82:1, 6; 138:1, however, the NIV renders "gods" (in quotation marks) to bring out the idea of prideful self-deification on the part of arrogant rulers. Here in v.25, and in the Exodus passages, it is perhaps best to leave the question moot, since in any case the "judges" (if such they be) are viewed as God's representatives who reflect his will and carry out his desires.

4. The Oracle against the House of Eli (2:27–36)

[27]Now a man of God came to Eli and said to him, "This is what the LORD says: 'Did I not
clearly reveal myself to your father's house when they were in Egypt under Pharaoh?
[28]I chose your father out of all the tribes of Israel to be my priest, to go up to my altar, to
burn incense, and to wear an ephod in my presence. I also gave your father's house all the
offerings made with fire by the Israelites. [29]Why do you scorn my sacrifice and offering that
I prescribed for my dwelling? Why do you honor your sons more than me by fattening
yourselves on the choice parts of every offering made by my people Israel?'
[30]"Therefore the LORD, the God of Israel, declares: 'I promised that your house and your
father's house would minister before me forever.' But now the LORD declares: 'Far be it from
me! Those who honor me I will honor, but those who despise me will be disdained. [31]The
time is coming when I will cut short your strength and the strength of your father's house,
so that there will not be an old man in your family line [32]and you will see distress in my
dwelling. Although good will be done to Israel, in your family line there will never be an
old man. [33]Every one of you that I do not cut off from my altar will be spared only to blind
your eyes with tears and to grieve your heart, and all your descendants will die in the
prime of life.
[34]"'And what happens to your two sons, Hophni and Phinehas, will be a sign to
you—they will both die on the same day. [35]I will raise up for myself a faithful priest, who
will do according to what is in my heart and mind. I will firmly establish his house, and
he will minister before my anointed one always. [36]Then everyone left in your family line
will come and bow down before him for a piece of silver and a crust of bread and plead,
"Appoint me to some priestly office so I can have food to eat."'"

COMMENTARY

27–36 After the contrasting and transitional v.26 (see above), the chapter concludes by expanding the Lord's intention to put Eli's sons to death (v.25). The prophetic oracle to (and against) Eli uses the messenger formula ("This is what the LORD says") and mediates the divine word through a "man of God" (v.27). The term "man of God" occasionally refers to an angel (cf. Jdg 13:3, 6, 8–9), but it is usually employed as a synonym for "prophet" (cf. esp. 1Sa 9:9–10). In the ancient world it was used in extrabiblical literature as well; for example, a seal of a prophet of the god Melqart reads: "Belonging to Baal-yaton, the man of God, who depends on Melqart" (see Walter Beyerlin, ed., *Near Eastern Religious Texts Relating to the Old Testament* [Philadelphia: Westminster, 1978], 247).

Though almost always identified by name, in v.27 the man of God is anonymous. He reminds Eli that God had revealed himself to his ancestor Levi's house (in Aaron; see Ex 4:14–16) before the exodus. Indeed, Aaron had been the object of special divine election (v.28) to serve the Lord as the first in a long line of priests (Ex 28:1–4). Aaron would go up "to" the Lord's altar (or, perhaps better, "upon" one or more steps leading up to it, since archaeologists have frequently unearthed ancient stepped altars in Israel; cf. also Lev 9:22) and would wear the ephod in the course of his divinely ordained work (v.28; cf. Lev 8:7). Recipients of such privilege, Eli and his sons (see NIV note; DSS and LXX use a singular verb here, but cf. "yourselves" later in the verse) nevertheless "scorn" the Lord's prescribed sacrifices (v.29).

The verb translated "scorn" here (*bāᶜaṭ*, v.29; GK 1246) means literally "to kick" and is found only once elsewhere in the OT: "Jeshurun [a poetic name for Israel; cf. Isa 44:1–2] grew fat and kicked; filled with food, he became heavy and sleek" (Dt 32:15). Although the Hebrew words for "fat" and "heavy" are different there from the word for "fattening" here, the parallel is striking: Like Israel centuries earlier, the house of Eli has "kicked at" the Lord's offerings by gorging themselves on the best parts of the sacrifices brought by the Israelites (vv.13–17). By condoning the sin of Hophni and Phinehas (however reluctantly), Eli has demonstrated that he loves his sons more than he loves God and that he is therefore unworthy of the Lord's continued blessing (see Mt 10:37). Was Eli's participation in his sons' gluttony one of the reasons why, at the time of his death, he had become "heavy" (4:18; yet a fourth Hebrew root)?

The Lord had promised that Aaron's descendants would always be priests (v.30; cf. Ex 29:9), and he had confirmed that promise on covenantal oath (Nu 25:13). They would "minister before"—*hithillēk*, literally, "walk (back and forth) before" (as did Enoch [Ge 5:22, 24], Noah [6:9], and Abraham [17:1])—the Lord forever. But because of flagrant disobedience, the house of Eli, like the house of Saul later (13:13–14), would be judged by God. Although the Aaronic priesthood was perpetual, individual priests who sinned could thereby forfeit covenantal blessing. The Lord honors (*kābēd*, lit., "makes heavy"; GK 3877) those who honor him, but he disdains (*qālâ*, lit., "makes light"; GK 7829) those who despise him. Eli had honored his sons (v.29) more than he honored God (v.30). The description of divine judgment in v.31, when translated literally, is vivid indeed: "I will chop off your arm and the arm of your father's house" (*zᵉrōaᶜ*, "arm," being often used as a metaphor for "strength" in the OT). Eli will be the last "old man" in his family line, because God's fulfillment of his death sentence will be swift and sure (4:11, 18; 22:17–20; 1Ki 2:26–27).

Examples of the predicted distress in God's "dwelling" (v.32; the tabernacle is meant) are the capture of the ark by the Philistines (4:11) and the destruction of Shiloh (cf. Jer 7:12, 14; 26:6, 9). Although in Eli's line there would "never" (lit., "not ... all the days") be an old man, in the line that would replace his there would "always" (lit., "all the days," v.35) be a faithful priest. The only member of Eli's line to "be spared" (v.33) was Abiathar, and in any case he was removed from the priesthood (1Ki 2:26–27).

Hophni and Phinehas will die "on the same day" (v.34; fulfilled in 4:11), a prophetic sign to Eli not only of his own impending death but also of the fulfillment of the other components in the oracle of the man of God. The Lord will bring a "faithful" priest on the scene, who will be privy to the very thoughts of God and obedient to him (v.35).

Neʾᵉmān ("faithful," v.35; GK 586) contrasts strongly with the rebellion of Eli's sons and plays an important role in the succeeding context, both near and remote. In this same verse the Lord says, "I will firmly establish his house"—literally, "I will build for him a faithful house" (cf. 2Sa 7:27 with respect to David's dynasty)—in which "firmly" translates the same Hebrew word (*neʾᵉmān*). In 25:28 "lasting dynasty" (lit., "faithful house") is used of David, and 1 Chronicles 17:23 records a similar promise concerning David and his house, where "established" is *yēʾāmēn*. In the present context the faithful priest whose house the Lord would firmly establish refers initially to Samuel (3:1; 7:9; 9:12–13; cf. esp. 3:20, where it states that all Israel knew that Samuel "was attested"—*neʾᵉmān*—as a prophet). Later, however, the line of Zadok son of Ahitub would replace that of Abiathar, Eli's descendant (2Sa 8:17; 15:24–29; 1Ki 2:35), a replacement that would constitute a greater fulfillment of the oracle of the man of God. Zadok and his descendants would thus "always" minister before the Lord's "anointed one"—David's son Solomon (1Ki 2:27, 35) and his descendants. Nevertheless, "the prophecy of the man of God was fulfilled in Zadok and Solomon, but was not exhausted" there (Delitzsch, 79).

Ultimate fulfillment would come only in Jesus the Christ, the supremely Anointed One, "designated by God to be high priest" (Heb 5:10) "forever, in the order of Melchizedek" (6:20), the ancient priest-king of Jerusalem (Ge 14:18; Heb 7:1). Although Zadok and Melchizedek were clearly two different people, the obvious connection between their names may not be unintentional. In his high-priestly office, Jesus brings the ministry of both men to full fruition.

As for the members of Eli's house, once fattened on priestly perquisites (v.29), soon not even the least benefit of priestly office would be theirs (v.36). The magnificent chiastic structure of 1 Samuel 2 must not be missed:

- A The song of Hannah, concluding with reference to the Lord's anointed (2:1–10)
  - B Samuel ministers before the Lord (2:11)
    - C The sins of Eli's sons (2:12–17)
      - D Samuel ministers before the Lord (2:18–19)
        - E Eli blesses Samuel's parents (2:20–21a)
      - D' Samuel grows in the Lord's presence (2:21b)
    - C' The sins of Eli's sons (2:22–25)
  - B' Samuel grows in the Lord's presence (2:26)
- A' The oracle of the man of God, concluding with reference to the Lord's anointed (2:27–36)

At the center of the chiasm is Eli's blessing of Elkanah and Hannah, who now disappear from the narrative. The blessing is framed by references to the ministry and growth of their son and Eli's successor, which in turn prepare us for references to Samuel's ministry (3:1) and growth (3:19) in the next chapter. For a similar analysis and additional details, see Michael Fishbane, "I Samuel 3: Historical Narrative and Narrative Poetics," in *Literary Interpretations of Biblical Narratives*, ed. Kenneth R. R. Gros Louis and J. S. Ackerman (Nashville: Abingdon, 1982), 2:194–96.

NOTES

29 BDB, 733, pronounces מָעוֹן (*māʿôn*) in vv.29 and 32 "unintelligible." But the ancient versions provide no variants by way of help, and Barthélemy, 2:153–55, declares the translation "dwelling" to be one of three possible, acceptable renderings in both verses (cf. also K&D).

33 The Hebrew form of the verb translated "to grieve," לַאֲדִיב (*laʾᵃdîb*), is morphologically suspect; and in any case its root, אדב (*ʾdb*), is unique in the OT. Leviticus 26:16 reads in part מְכַלּוֹת עֵינַיִם וּמְדִיבֹת נָפֶשׁ

(*mᵉkallôt ʿênayim ûmᵉdîbōt nāpeš*, "destroy your sight and drain away your life"), providing an excellent parallel to the phrase here: לְכַלּוֹת אֶת־עֵינֶיךָ וְלַאֲדִיב אֶת־נַפְשֶׁךָ (*lᵉkallôt ʾet-ʿêneykā wᵉlaʾᵃdîb ʾet-napšekā*, "to blind your eyes with tears and to grieve your heart"). It is therefore advisable to assume a scribal error in v.33 and to change the incorrect form *laʾᵃdîb* to *lᵉhādîb* (לְהָדִיב), Hiphil infinitive construct of דּוּב (*dûb*), just as מְדִיבֹת (*mᵉdîbōt*) is a Hiphil feminine plural participle from the same root (cf. similarly Driver, 39). The 1 Samuel passage could just as well be translated, to conform with the Leviticus passage, as "to destroy your sight and drain away your life" (perhaps to be understood figuratively). Such, in any case, was to be Eli's literal fate (4:15, 18).

36 אֲגוֹרָה (*ʾᵃgôrâ*, "piece") is found only here in the OT. Its obvious reference to a very small amount of silver made it suitable to serve as the modern Hebrew word to denote the smallest Israeli coin.

5. The Call of Samuel (3:1–4:1a)

OVERVIEW

The literary genre of 1 Samuel 3 has usually been considered a prophetic-call narrative in the grand tradition of Exodus 3 (Moses), Isaiah 6, Jeremiah 1, and the like. Recently, however, on the basis of ancient Near Eastern parallels, Robert Gnuse, in *The Dream Theophany of Samuel: Its Structure in Relation to Ancient Near Eastern Dreams and Its Theological Significance* (Lanham, Md.: Univ. Press of America, 1984) has theorized that 1 Samuel 3 is best analyzed as an auditory message dream theophany. Although he sometimes tilts the evidence in his direction (e.g., he translates *šākab* as "sleep" in vv.2–3 but is content to render it in its more common sense of "lie down" in the rest of the chapter), his arguments are impressive. (See his p. 249 for the summary of ten characteristics that Samuel's experience shares with accounts of other ancient Near Eastern dreams.) In any event, the literary genre in this case is not destructive of the historicity of the event being narrated (contrary to Gnuse; cf. 219–23, 250). Of course, the genre could turn out to be a blend of both types (a not uncommon feature of OT literature)—prophetic-call narrative plus auditory message dream theophany. But the advantage of Gnuse's analysis is that it deals adequately with the fact that the Lord speaks to Samuel at night—a matter not handled convincingly by the theory that 1 Samuel 3 is a prophetic-call narrative and nothing more.

[1]The boy Samuel ministered before the LORD under Eli. In those days the word of the
LORD was rare; there were not many visions.
[2]One night Eli, whose eyes were becoming so weak that he could barely see, was lying
down in his usual place. [3]The lamp of God had not yet gone out, and Samuel was lying
down in the temple of the LORD, where the ark of God was. [4]Then the LORD called Samuel.
Samuel answered, "Here I am." [5]And he ran to Eli and said, "Here I am; you called me."

But Eli said, "I did not call; go back and lie down." So he went and lay down.
6Again the LORD called, "Samuel!" And Samuel got up and went to Eli and said, "Here I
am; you called me."
"My son," Eli said, "I did not call; go back and lie down."
7Now Samuel did not yet know the LORD: The word of the LORD had not yet been
revealed to him.
8The LORD called Samuel a third time, and Samuel got up and went to Eli and said, "Here
I am; you called me."
Then Eli realized that the LORD was calling the boy. 9So Eli told Samuel, "Go and lie down,
and if he calls you, say, 'Speak, LORD, for your servant is listening.'" So Samuel went and lay
down in his place.
10The LORD came and stood there, calling as at the other times, "Samuel! Samuel!"
Then Samuel said, "Speak, for your servant is listening."
11And the LORD said to Samuel: "See, I am about to do something in Israel that will make
the ears of everyone who hears of it tingle. 12At that time I will carry out against Eli everything I spoke against his family—from beginning to end. 13For I told him that I would
judge his family forever because of the sin he knew about; his sons made themselves
contemptible, and he failed to restrain them. 14Therefore, I swore to the house of Eli, 'The
guilt of Eli's house will never be atoned for by sacrifice or offering.'"
15Samuel lay down until morning and then opened the doors of the house of the LORD.
He was afraid to tell Eli the vision, 16but Eli called him and said, "Samuel, my son."
Samuel answered, "Here I am."
17"What was it he said to you?" Eli asked. "Do not hide it from me. May God deal with
you, be it ever so severely, if you hide from me anything he told you." 18So Samuel told him
everything, hiding nothing from him. Then Eli said, "He is the LORD; let him do what is good
in his eyes."
19The LORD was with Samuel as he grew up, and he let none of his words fall to the
ground. 20And all Israel from Dan to Beersheba recognized that Samuel was attested as a
prophet of the LORD. 21The LORD continued to appear at Shiloh, and there he revealed himself to Samuel through his word.
4:1And Samuel's word came to all Israel.

COMMENTARY

1 This introductory verse informs us of the rarity of special revelation in the days of the judges. There were not "many" visions in the sense that the few visions that did exist were not widely known. (In 2Ch 31:5 the same Hebrew root speaks of an order that "went out"—i.e., it was disseminated far and wide.) Amos 8:11–12 tells of similar days of spiritual famine that were soon to come, a prophecy fulfilled not only as a result of the disaster of 722 BC but also in the exilic and postexilic periods (Ps 74:9; Eze 7:26). The word "vision(s)" is a technical term for "divine revelation mediated through a seer." (*Ḥôzeh*, one of the two Hebrew words for "seer," has the same root as that for "vision," *ḥāzôn* [GK 2606]; *marʾâ* [GK 5261], the other word for "vision" in this chapter [v.15], also is used in the sense of "vision as a means of divine revelation" and has the same root as *rôʾeh*, the other word for "seer.") *Ḥāzôn* appears in the title verse of three OT prophetic books (Isaiah, Obadiah, Nahum).

2 "In that day" is used here in the general sense of "at that time," justifying the NIV's contextual rendering "One night." Eli's aging eyes were so "weak" (contrast Moses in Dt 34:7) that he could barely "see." (He would eventually go completely blind [cf. 4:15].) How different from Samuel, whose eyes saw clearly in a physical and a spiritual sense (v.15)!

3 The lamps on the seven-branched lampstand (Ex 25:31–37) were filled with olive oil, lit at twilight (30:8), and kept burning "before the LORD from evening till morning" (27:20–21; cf. Lev 24:2–4; 2Ch 13:11). Thus Samuel's encounter with the Lord on his bed in the tabernacle compound (v.3; cf. comment on 1:7 above) took place during the night, since the "lamp of God had not yet gone out."

4–10 Although "Samuel did not yet know" (v.7) that it was the Lord who was speaking to him (v.7), his answer was typical of the servant who hears and obeys the divine call: "Here I am" (v.4; see Ge 22:1, 11; Ex 3:4; Isa 6:8). Samuel's openness to serving God would soon enable him to know the Lord (v.7) in a way that Eli's sons never did (2:12). Although the word of the Lord had not yet been revealed to Samuel, that would take place very soon (v.11); and as God continued to speak to Samuel through the years (v.21), the Lord's word would so captivate him that it would be virtually indistinguishable from "Samuel's word" (4:1). Samuel the priest, God's minister, would become Samuel the prophet (v.20), God's spokesman.

Samuel—on that fateful night—thought that Eli was calling him. Twice Eli told Samuel to go back to bed, but the third time it finally dawned on the aged priest that it must be God who was calling the boy (vv.5–8). He therefore told Samuel that he should respond the next time by saying, "Speak, LORD, for your servant is listening" (v.9).

That this time the Lord "came and stood there" (v.10) suggests Samuel could see him as well as hear him (cf. similarly Ge 18:22 and NIV note). Again the Lord called out Samuel's name—this time twice, imparting a sense of urgency and finality (cf. Ge 22:11; Ex 3:4; Ac 9:4). Samuel responded as Eli had instructed, repeating Eli's words verbatim—with one notable exception: he left out the word "LORD" (whether through caution, ignorance, or accident, it is impossible to say; cf. again v.7).

11–14 The Lord's word to Samuel, like the man of God's oracle to Eli (2:27–36), not only had immediate reference to Eli's house but also pointed forward to the more remote future. The disaster that would overcome Eli and his sons (including the destruction of Shiloh, the location of the central sanctuary) would "make the ears of everyone who hears of it tingle" (v.11)—a striking expression used only here (at the beginning of the monarchy) and in 2 Kings 21:12; Jeremiah 19:3 (at the end of the monarchy, when Jerusalem and the central sanctuary were destroyed). The Lord would carry out his judgment against Eli and his sons "from beginning to end" (v.12), an idiom implying the accomplishment of his full purpose (BDB, 320). Death was the penalty for showing contempt for the priesthood (Dt 17:12) as well as for disobeying one's parents (Dt 21:18–21), and Eli was implicated because he did not restrain Hophni and Phinehas (v.13).

If the NIV note gives the correct reading (as seems likely [the MT reading being grammatically difficult]), the sins of Eli's sons are compounded: Blaspheming the divine name was always a capital sin (Lev 24:11–16, 23). The house of Eli had committed blatant sins against God and showed no signs of remorse. Having passed the point of no return, they were subject to the divine death sentence (2:25; cf. Heb 12:16–17); no sacrifice or offering could atone for their guilt (v.14). Centuries later the same fate, and for much the same reasons, would overtake Jerusalem (Isa 22:14).

15–18 When Samuel arose in the morning, he opened the doors of the tabernacle compound (v.15) and doubtless busied himself with other tasks to avoid telling Eli what he had seen and heard. The aged priest was not to be denied, however, and demanded a full report (vv.16–17). Indeed, he swore an oath of imprecation (cf. 2Sa 3:35), calling down God's judgment on Samuel if the boy refused to tell everything he knew. The chiastic structure of v.17 focuses our attention on Eli's oath:

A "The word that he spoke to you,
  B you hide from me;
    C (the oath)
  B' you hide from me,
A' the word that he spoke to you" [my translation].

(See Wilfred G. E. Watson, "The Structure of 1 Samuel 3," *BZ* 29/1 [1985]: 93.)

The narrator, in describing Samuel's obedient response to Eli (v.18), echoes key words from v.17 (my translation): "Samuel told him all the words; he did not hide [anything] from him." Eli's reaction is both devout and submissive (like that of Job in Job 2:10): "Let him do [better, 'he does,' since the verb is imperfect rather than jussive and is identical to the form translated 'deal' in v.17] what is good in his eyes" (v.18). Eli resigns himself to divine sovereignty, for he realizes it would be futile to do otherwise.

3:19–4:1a As the Lord's presence would later be with David (16:18; 18:12), so the Lord was with Samuel (v.19), a fact evident to all the Israelites (v.20). That God "let none of [Samuel's] words fall" (v.19) means that he made sure everything Samuel said with divine authorization came true (the idiom is translated "Do not neglect anything you have recommended" in Est 6:10); the same idea is expressed differently in 9:6. Although earlier God's word had not been revealed to Samuel (v.7), it now was; and as the Lord had appeared to him earlier (vv.10–14), so he "continued to appear at Shiloh" (v.21). As stated above, the Lord's word (v.21) became equivalent to "Samuel's word" (4:1), which is here introduced with the same formula that appears throughout the books of the Prophets with respect to the word of the Lord: It "came" to its recipients (cf. Jer 1:2, 4, 11, 13; Hos 1:1; Mic 1:1).

The expression "from Dan to Beersheba" (v.20) represents the northern and southern boundaries respectively of the united monarchy under David and Solomon (1Ki 4:25). This expression occurs frequently in the narratives about David (2Sa 3:10; 17:11; 24:2, 15).

It is demonstrable, not only contextually but also by the fact that many Hebrew manuscripts of 1 Samuel display a section interval after "Israel," that the literary unit under consideration here ends at 4:1a. The entire unit (3:1–4:1a) is arranged in chiastic fashion:

A Absence of divine oracles (3:1)
  B Eli's fading powers (3:2)
    C Three divine calls to Samuel (3:3–9)
      D A divine oracle to Samuel (3:10–15)
    C' Eli's request for Samuel's report (3:16–18)
  B' Samuel's growing stature (3:19a)
A' Return of divine oracles (3:19b–4:1a)

(cf. similarly Fishbane, "I Samuel 3," 193).

The focus of the section is thus the Lord's sentence of judgment against the house of Eli. The boy Samuel, having become a "man of God" (vv.19–20; 9:6–14), has confirmed in no uncertain terms the prophecy earlier proclaimed by the anonymous "man of God" (2:27–36).

NOTE

20 Yohanan Aharoni suggests that two impressive city gates having the same basic plan, one excavated at the ancient site of Dan and the other at Beersheba, should be dated to the time of David. He further proposes that since the external limits of the land had been fortified by David, it was necessary for Solomon to fortify only certain strategically located internal cities (Hazor, Gezer, Megiddo, Jerusalem, et al.; cf. 1Ki 9:15–19). For a summary of Aharoni's position (not shared by Avraham Biran, Dan's excavator—although his date differs from that of Aharoni by scarcely fifty years), see his article "King David as Builder" (*BAR* 1/1 [1975]: 13–14).

B. The Ark Narratives (4:1b–7:17)

OVERVIEW

Research carried out over the past several decades has questioned the proper parameters of the narratives about the ark of the covenant in the books of Samuel. More than eighty years ago, L. Rost, esp. 6–34, implied that 1 Samuel 4:1b–7:1 and 2 Samuel 6 were the only remaining excerpts from a longer and continuous ark narrative. At first his theory was widely accepted; indeed, Antony F. Campbell has vigorously defended Rost's basic thesis. In a study titled "Chronological Sequence in Two Hebrew Narratives," *BT* 29/3 (1978), esp. 317, Robert Dorn also takes for granted the demarcations of Rost and Campbell.

Two other careful studies of the matter, however, have attracted considerable attention. Franz Schicklberger (*Die Ladeerzählungen des ersten Samuel-Buches: Eine literaturwissenschaftliche und theologiegeschichtliche Untersuchung* [Würzburg: Echter, 1973]) wants to limit the ark narratives to 4:1–6:16, while Patrick D. Miller Jr. and J. J. M. Roberts (*The Hand of the Lord*) opt for 2:12–17, 22–25, 27–36; 4:1b–7:1. These in turn provoked a spirited response from Antony F. Campbell ("Yahweh and the Ark: A Case Study in Narrative," *JBL* 98/1 [1979]: 31–43), who rightly points out that the delimiting of the extent of the text is strongly dependent on estimates of its theological intention.

In any case, John Willis ("An Anti-Elide Narrative Tradition from a Prophetic Circle at the Ramah Sanctuary," *JBL* 90 [1971]: 288–308) has argued for the essential integrity of the first seven chapters of 1 Samuel as an overall literary unit, without precluding the possibility of subunits within those chapters. Since the debate continues without a resolution in sight, I advance the proposal, which I attempt to justify in the ensuing comments, that the ark narrative begins at 4:1b with the first of the Israelite-Philistine wars and ends at 7:17 with the brief notice of Samuel's judgeship following the last of the Israelite-Philistine wars before Israel's demand for a king. It is impossible for us to know whether 2 Samuel 6, which resumes the story of what happened to the ark after David became king, was at one time part of a longer narrative.

1. *The Capture of the Ark (4:1b–11)*

Now the Israelites went out to fight against the Philistines. The Israelites camped at
Ebenezer, and the Philistines at Aphek. [2]The Philistines deployed their forces to meet
Israel, and as the battle spread, Israel was defeated by the Philistines, who killed about
four thousand of them on the battlefield. [3]When the soldiers returned to camp, the elders
of Israel asked, "Why did the LORD bring defeat upon us today before the Philistines? Let
us bring the ark of the LORD's covenant from Shiloh, so that it may go with us and save us
from the hand of our enemies."

[4]So the people sent men to Shiloh, and they brought back the ark of the covenant of
the LORD Almighty, who is enthroned between the cherubim. And Eli's two sons, Hophni
and Phinehas, were there with the ark of the covenant of God.

[5]When the ark of the LORD's covenant came into the camp, all Israel raised such a great
shout that the ground shook. [6]Hearing the uproar, the Philistines asked, "What's all this
shouting in the Hebrew camp?"

When they learned that the ark of the LORD had come into the camp, [7]the Philistines
were afraid. "A god has come into the camp," they said. "We're in trouble! Nothing like
this has happened before. [8]Woe to us! Who will deliver us from the hand of these mighty
gods? They are the gods who struck the Egyptians with all kinds of plagues in the desert.
[9]Be strong, Philistines! Be men, or you will be subject to the Hebrews, as they have been to
you. Be men, and fight!"

[10]So the Philistines fought, and the Israelites were defeated and every man fled to his
tent. The slaughter was very great; Israel lost thirty thousand foot soldiers. [11]The ark of God
was captured, and Eli's two sons, Hophni and Phinehas, died.

COMMENTARY

1b The Philistines, inveterate enemies of Israel during the latter half of the period of the judges and the early years of the Israelite monarchy, are mentioned nearly 150 times in 1 and 2 Samuel alone. They were so entrenched and dominant in the coastal areas and the foothills of Canaan that they eventually gave their name (Palestine) to the entire land. Although their connections with various Aegean cultures have been verified through decades of intensive research, their origins remain somewhat obscure (cf., e.g., R. K. Harrison, "Philistine Origins: A Reappraisal," in Eslinger and Taylor, 11–19). The OT relates them to Caphtor (Ge 10:14 = 1Ch 1:12; Jer 47:4; Am 9:7), which is probably Crete. The aggressive, expansionist ancestors of the Philistines of the time of Samuel apparently arrived in Canaan shortly after 1200 BC. For details see especially Trude Dothan, *The Philistines and Their Material Culture* (New Haven, Conn.: Yale Univ. Press, 1982), 13–16, 21–24, 289–96; "What We Know about the Philistines," *BAR* 8/4 (1982): 20–44; Rodger Dalman, "Egypt and Early Israel's Cultural Setting: A Quest for Evidential Possibilities," *JETS* 51/3 (2008): 481–88.

It is impossible to say who the aggressor was in this first-recorded battle between Israel and the Philistines. The Philistines camped at Aphek (modern Ras el-Ain, in the plain of Sharon ten miles east and slightly north of Joppa), an important site inhabited during the entire biblical period. (In NT days it was called "Antipatris"; see Ac 23:31.) Ebenezer, where the Israelites camped, is probably to be identified with modern Izbet Sartah, about two miles east of Aphek on the road to Shiloh. Izbet Sartah, a primitive Israelite outpost, was occupied for only about two centuries (ca. 1200–1000 BC; see Moshe Kochavi and Aaron Demsky, "An Israelite Village from the Days of the Judges," *BAR* 4/3 [1978]: 19–21; "An Alphabet from the Days of the Judges," *BAR* 4/3 [1978]: 23–30). Although the Ebenezer in 7:12 may not be the same as the one in 4:1, the presence of the name in both verses is surely not accidental and helps us to identify the parameters of the overall literary unit known as the ark narratives (4:1b–7:17). Aphek is mentioned again in the books of Samuel only in 1 Samuel 29:1.

2–3 The Israelites were defeated not once but twice in this chapter (vv.2, 10). Not until 7:10–11 did they defeat the Philistines on the battlefield and then only (as always) with divine help. The Israelites lost "four thousand" men (v.2), a terrible tragedy no matter how that number is understood. J. B. Segal, 12, observes that the numbers 400, 4,000, and 40,000 are sometimes "associated with flight and with battles." In addition to being a round number, then, "four thousand" here is perhaps a metaphor for "a large number of military casualties."

Another complicating factor is that *ʾelep* ("thousand") is often used in a more general sense in reference to a military "unit" (cf. 17:18; 29:2; 2Sa 18:4). Perhaps "four thousand" here means "four units of soldiers." Thus a measure of uncertainty often obtains when the word for "thousand" or "unit" is used in a military context in the OT. (See Ronald Allen's extensive discussion of the problem of large numbers in his introduction to the book of Numbers, *EBC* 2:680–91 [1st ed.].) "Soldiers" (v.3) translates *ʿam*, the common word for "people" (as in v.4). The NIV frequently and correctly renders it "soldiers" or "troops" in military settings.

The Israelite elders (who make their next appearance at the beginning of the following literary unit; see 8:4) are puzzled by the debacle on the battlefield (v.3). Their solution is to bring the ark of the covenant into the camp to guarantee the Lord's presence with his people. Clearly the ark is a significant thematic element in this section; of the sixty-one occurrences of the word "ark" in the books of Samuel, all but twenty-five appear in 1 Samuel 4:1b–7:2.

The elders doubtless remembered the account of Joshua's victory over Jericho, in which the ark was a highly visible symbol of divine help and strength (Jos 6:2–20; cf. also Nu 10:35). It would accompany Israel's army on at least one other occasion in the future as well (2Sa 11:11). What the elders failed to understand, however, was that the ark was neither an infallible talisman nor a military palladium that would ensure victory. If God willed defeat for his people, a thousand arks would not bring success. Marten H. Woudstra has well stated concerning attempts to manipulate the ark: "The offenses against the ark as pledge of Yahweh's presence appear to be mainly of two kinds: (1) a misplaced reliance on the ark, and (2) an irreverent disregard for the ark"

(*The Ark of the Covenant from Conquest to Kingship* [Philadelphia: Presbyterian & Reformed, 1965], 55). The elders understood clearly that if God was not "with" them, defeat was inevitable (Nu 14:42; Dt 1:42). They mistakenly assumed, however, that wherever the ark was, the Lord was.

4–9 So men were sent to Shiloh from the Israelite camp at Ebenezer (vv.4–5; 5:1) to bring back the ark, here impressively described as "the ark of the covenant of the LORD Almighty [see comment on 1:3], who is enthroned between the cherubim" (cf. 2Sa 6:2; 2Ki 19:15 = Isa 37:16; 1Ch 13:6; Pss 80:1; 99:1). More than seventy years ago W. F. Albright demonstrated that cherubim were winged sphinxes—i.e., winged lions with human heads ("What Were the Cherubim?" *BA* 1/1 [1938]: 1–3). In ancient Near Eastern art a king was often pictured as sitting on a throne supported on each side by a cherub. It appears, then, that one function of the ark of the covenant was to serve as the symbolic cherub-throne of the invisible Great King. If so, the two cherubim on the ark stood parallel to each other, with faces turned slightly inward (Ex 25:20).

By comparing v.4 with 2 Samuel 6:2, 1 Chronicles 13:6, and Isaiah 37:16, Albright further suggests that "[Name of] Yahweh of Hosts, Enthroned on the Cherubim" was the official name given to the ark. He visualizes Hezekiah's prayer in Isaiah as having been "addressed to the invisible Presence which hovered above" the ark inside the Most Holy Place in the temple (W. F. Albright, review of B. N. Wambacq, *L'épithète divine Jahvé Sᵉbaʾôt: étude philologique historique et exégétique* [Bruges: Desclée, 1947], in *JBL* 67 [1948]: 377–81, esp. 379). While such a name would certainly have been appropriate during the period of the monarchy, Albright's theory remains unproven.

The ark, accompanied by Hophni and Phinehas, caused a great commotion upon reaching the Israelite camp (v.5). The people gave a loud shout, reminiscent of the battle cry at Jericho's demise (Jos 6:5, 20). The uproar aroused the Philistines camped nearby, and their superstitious response echoed that of the Israelite elders (vv.6–8). They believed that the arrival of the ark heralded the coming of whatever god (v.7) or gods (v.8) its owners worshiped. To avoid being enslaved by the Hebrews, as the Hebrews had been by them (cf. Jdg 13:1), they encouraged one another to be strong and fight like men (v.9).

10–11 The result of the ark's presence was another Israelite defeat, this one far more severe than the previous and described as a *makkâ* ("slaughter," v.10)—echoing the same word used of the Egyptian "plague(s)," whose memory had so impressed the Philistines (v.8). The Philistines' own turn would come (14:13; 19:8; 23:5), but in the meantime Israel suffered heavy losses. The sins of Eli's sons produced appalling casualties among Israel's foot soldiers (cf. Dt 28:15, 25). As foretold by the man of God (2:34), Hophni and Phinehas died (v.11). The elders' folly was revealed as the Philistines captured the ark (a doleful refrain occurring in vv.17, 19, 21–22), and the destruction of Shiloh—and perhaps the tabernacle itself—was not far behind (cf. Ps 78:56–64; Jer 7:12, 14; 26:6, 9).

NOTES

1 In 1976 an ostracon containing a five-line inscription dating from the twelfth or eleventh century BC was recovered from an Early Iron Age storage pit in the ruins of Izbet Sartah. The fifth line was soon identified as an alphabet. The most intriguing attempt to read the first four lines as a connected text is that of William H. Shea: "Unto the field we came, (unto) Aphek from Shiloh. The Kittim took (it [the ark of the covenant] and) came to Azor, (to) Dagon lord of Ashdod, (and to) Gath. (It returned to) Kiriath Jearim. The companion of the foot soldiers, Hophni, came to tell the elders, 'A horse has come (and) upon (it was my) brother for us to bury'" ("The ʿIzbet Sartah Ostracon," *AUSS* 28/1 [1990]: 62). Shea, 81, observes that eleven of the key words in the inscription appear in the parallel account of the capture of the ark in chs. 4–6: "Aphek" (4:1), "field" (4:2), "elders" (4:3), "Shiloh" (4:3–4), "Hophni" (4:4, 11, 17), "foot soldiers" (4:10), "take/capture" (4:11 ff.), "tell" (4:13), "Ashdod" (5:1–7), "Gath" (5:8), "Kiriath Jearim" (written "Jearim Kiriah"; 6:21).

Shea's reading, however, is beset by numerous difficulties that at present seem insurmountable (for details see L. J. Mykytiuk, "Is Hophni in the ʿIzbeṭ Sartah Ostracon?" *AUSS* 36/1 [1998]: 69–80; Mykytiuk concludes that "the present degree of knowledge of second-millennium B.C.E. Northwest-Semitic inscriptions does not permit us to *demonstrate* [the ostracon] to be anything more than a penmanship exercise written by someone practicing the Proto-Canaanite alphabet" [80; italics his]).

2 The verbal root in the difficult phrase וַתִּטֹּשׁ הַמִּלְחָמָה (*wattiṭṭōš hammilḥāmâ*, "and as the battle spread") is נָטַשׁ (*nāṭaš*), which means "leave, abandon." Mitchell Dahood suggests that the verb is a by-form of לָטַשׁ (*lāṭaš*, "sharpen") and translates the phrase "and when the clash grew sharp" (cf. "Hebrew-Ugaritic Lexicography VI," *Bib* 49/3 [1968]: 361–62). The interchange of the dentals *n* and *l* occurs elsewhere in Hebrew, and the root *lṭš* is used figuratively in Job 16:9: "My opponent fastens on me his piercing eyes."

3 The origin of the word בְּרִית (*bᵉrît*, "covenant"; GK 1382) is disputed. Likely it derives from the Akkadian *birīt* ("between"), emphasizing the indispensable quality of relationship that inheres in every covenant (see Ronald F. Youngblood, "The Abrahamic Covenant: Conditional or Unconditional?" in *The Living and Active Word of God: Essays in Honor of Samuel J. Schultz*, ed. Morris Inch and Ronald Youngblood [Winona Lake, Ind.: Eisenbrauns, 1983], 34–35).

The NIV text's "it" and its margin "he" should probably be reversed. God, not the ark, is "with" his people to avert defeat in Numbers 14:42 and Deuteronomy 1:42. God, not the ark, "saves" his people "from the hand of" the enemy; see Judges 6:14 and 2 Kings 16:7 where, as here, the Hebrew idiom is הוֹשִׁיעַ מִכַּף (*hôšîaʿ mikkap*, "save from the hand of").

4 For representative examples of cherubim in ancient Near Eastern iconography, see Elie Borowski, "Cherubim: God's Throne?" *BAR* 21/4 (1995): 36–41.

2. The Death of Eli (4:12–22)

[12]That same day a Benjamite ran from the battle line and went to Shiloh, his clothes torn and dust on his head. [13]When he arrived, there was Eli sitting on his chair by the side of the road, watching, because his heart feared for the ark of God. When the man entered the town and told what had happened, the whole town sent up a cry.

[14]Eli heard the outcry and asked, "What is the meaning of this uproar?"
The man hurried over to Eli, [15]who was ninety-eight years old and whose eyes were set
so that he could not see. [16]He told Eli, "I have just come from the battle line; I fled from it
this very day."
Eli asked, "What happened, my son?"
[17]The man who brought the news replied, "Israel fled before the Philistines, and the
army has suffered heavy losses. Also your two sons, Hophni and Phinehas, are dead, and
the ark of God has been captured."
[18]When he mentioned the ark of God, Eli fell backward off his chair by the side of the
gate. His neck was broken and he died, for he was an old man and heavy. He had led Israel
forty years.
[19]His daughter-in-law, the wife of Phinehas, was pregnant and near the time of delivery.
When she heard the news that the ark of God had been captured and that her father-in-
law and her husband were dead, she went into labor and gave birth, but was overcome
by her labor pains. [20]As she was dying, the women attending her said, "Don't despair; you
have given birth to a son." But she did not respond or pay any attention.
[21]She named the boy Ichabod, saying, "The glory has departed from Israel"—because
of the capture of the ark of God and the deaths of her father-in-law and her husband.
[22]She said, "The glory has departed from Israel, for the ark of God has been captured."

COMMENTARY

12–18 No sooner was the second battle with the Philistines over than the tragic news of Israel's defeat reached Shiloh. The apprehensive question, "What happened?" (*meh-hāyâ haddābār*, v.16), occurs elsewhere only in 2 Samuel 1:4 and telegraphs the narrator's intention to compare this account and the one that begins 2 Samuel. Here a Benjamite (v.12) reports Israel's flight from and slaughter by the Philistines as well as the death of two prominent Levites (v.17); there an Amalekite (2Sa 1:8) reports Israel's flight from and slaughter by the Philistines as well as the death of two prominent Benjamites (2Sa 1:4). In both cases (v.12; 2Sa 1:2) the messenger arrives with "his clothes torn and (with) dust on his head" (the identical Hebrew phrase appearing in both places), a sign of anguish and distress (cf. Jos 7:6; Ne 9:1).

Eli is as he was when we first met him (1:9), and there he will be when he dies: sitting on his chair by the wayside (v.13), near an entrance to the Lord's house (v.18; see 1:9 and commentary). Whether or not at his advanced age Eli still considered himself to be the priest he once was, he nevertheless trembled with fear (v.13; for this nuance of the verb, cf. Jdg 7:3) for the ark's safety.

The messenger first told his story to the townspeople at Shiloh, who "sent up a cry" (v.13) when they learned that the ark had not brought them victory and was no longer with them. The later reaction of the Ekronites was similar but for the opposite reason: Philistine possession of the ark was causing an epidemic of tumors among the people (5:9–12). Mere possession of the ark enabled neither Israelite nor Philistine to manipulate the God whose presence it symbolized.

Hearing the uproar in the town, Eli wanted to know its meaning. Ninety-eight years old, obese (v.18), and totally blind (v.15; the Hebrew phrase translated "eyes were set" occurs again only in 1Ki 14:4 [Ahijah's "sight was gone"]), Eli was probably unable to go into town without considerable help. In any event, the messenger continued on his northward journey through the town and arrived at the tabernacle site (v.14; see Note on 1:3 for the probable location of the Shiloh tabernacle). The verb *bāśar* (v.17, "bring news"; GK 1413) and its cognate noun *b*[e]*śōrâ* ("news") almost always connote news that is good—or at least neutral. In v.17, however, the verb is used in the sense of bringing bad news, the only such case in the OT. The news is bad indeed, and the messenger concludes by reporting that the ark of God has been captured.

The news that Hophni and Phinehas were dead did not seem to faze Eli, who may have already given them up as hopeless. But the shock of hearing that the ark had been captured was too much for him. He "fell" off his chair, broke his neck, and died (v.18), a tragic parody of the results of Israel's second encounter (v.10) with the Philistines (lit., "thirty thousand foot soldiers fell"; same Hebrew verb). The corpulence that contributed to Eli's death may have been partly due to his participation in the gluttony of his sons (see comment on 2:30). The tragedy of Eli's life thus matches that of Saul: sometimes serving God faithfully, other times not measuring up to even the most moderate of standards. Priest at Shiloh for most of his adult life, he had judged (cf. NIV note) Israel for forty years. Following him as both priest and judge (7:6, 15–17) was his young protégé, Samuel.

19–22 Eli's death did not end the tragedy, even in his own family. The message of Eli's and Phinehas's deaths, combined with the report of the ark's capture (given pride of place in v.19; cf. also v.22), caused Phinehas's pregnant wife to go into premature labor. As a disturbing vision would later cause Daniel to be "overcome with anguish" (Da 10:16), so a distressing report caused her to be "overcome by her labor pains" (same Hebrew expression). In her case, however, the combination was fatal—she died in childbirth. The narrator patterns the account after that of Rachel's death. (The Hebrew for "Don't despair" here is more literally translated "Don't be afraid" in Ge 35:17.)

Before she died, Phinehas's wife named her newborn son "Ichabod" (lit., "no glory," v.21 [NIV note]; cf. 14:3). Verse 21 gives a general reason for the naming, but v.22 is more specific: "The glory [*kābôd*; GK 3883] has departed [lit., 'has gone into exile'; so also v.21] from Israel, for the ark of God has been captured." After the exodus the Lord promised to consecrate the tabernacle by his glory (Ex 29:43); after it was set up, his glory filled it and the cloud covered it (Ex 40:34–35). The term "glory" represents the presence of God dwelling—*škn*—in the tabernacle (Ps 26:8; cf. also Ex 25:8; 29:44–46), giving rise to the later theological term *š*[e]*kînâ* and sometimes called the "Shek(h)inah Glory." Hebrews 9:5 clarifies the connection between the ark and the divine Presence: "Above the ark were the cherubim of the Glory, overshadowing the atonement cover." Perhaps the wife of Phinehas, in her dying hour, spoke better than she knew. R. Gane ("The End of the Israelite Monarchy," *Journal of the Adventist Theological Society* 10/1–2 [1999]: 339 n. 8) comments further on the additional implications of her words:

> In the time of Samuel, the last judge, the ark was captured and the glory (*kābôd*) departed from Israel (1Sa 4:22). In the time of Zedekiah, the last king,

the glory (*kābôd*) left the temple (Eze 9:3; 10:4, 18–19) and the temple was destroyed. Jeremiah explicitly referred to a parallel between the late monarchy and the late period of the judges when he prophecied [*sic*] that the temple would become like Shiloh (Jer 26:6; cp. vs. 9).

NOTES

18 J. B. Segal, 11, remarks: "40 years represents the period of a complete generation.... The rule of Eli, of David, and of Solomon each lasted 40 years; so also did the rule of Saul.... But it is, of course, the 40 years of Israel's wanderings in the Wilderness that left the most vivid mark on the Old Testament." In at least a few of these cases "forty years" should be understood as a rough approximation or perhaps even as a figure of speech for a generation, as Segal suggests (cf. also Ps 95:10).

21 אִי־כָבוֹד (*ʾî-kābôd*, "no glory") uses a rare form of the Hebrew negative particle, the only other clear case occurring in Job 22:30 ("not innocent"). The same particle, however, is used more frequently in Ugaritic and Phoenician. Since *zbl* ("Prince") is an epithet of Baal in Ugaritic, it is quite likely that the Hebrew form of the name of the Phoenician princess Jezebel, אִיזֶבֶל (*ʾîzebel*), means "No Prince" in reference to the myth of Baal's death (e.g., as recorded in the epic literature of Ugarit). The Ugaritic text CTA 6:III–IV:29, 40 reads as follows: *iy zbl bʿl arṣ*, "There is no prince, lord [= Baal] of the earth" (cf. Cyrus H. Gordon, *Ugaritic Textbook* [AnOr 38; Rome, Pontifical Biblical Institute, 1965], 356). Another possibility is to read *iy* as the interrogative "Where?" and to translate *iy zbl* as "Where is the prince?" (cf. Baruch Margalit, *A Matter of "Life" and "Death": A Study of the Baal-Mot Epic [CTA 4–5–6]* [Neukirchen-Vluyn: Neukirchener, 1980], 169). In either case *iy zbl* (= Jezebel) would imply the (at least temporary) nonexistence of "Prince" Baal.

3. The Lord's Affliction of the Philistines (5:1–12)

[1]After the Philistines had captured the ark of God, they took it from Ebenezer to
Ashdod. [2]Then they carried the ark into Dagon's temple and set it beside Dagon. [3]When
the people of Ashdod rose early the next day, there was Dagon, fallen on his face on the
ground before the ark of the LORD! They took Dagon and put him back in his place. [4]But
the following morning when they rose, there was Dagon, fallen on his face on the ground
before the ark of the LORD! His head and hands had been broken off and were lying on the
threshold; only his body remained. [5]That is why to this day neither the priests of Dagon
nor any others who enter Dagon's temple at Ashdod step on the threshold.

[6]The LORD's hand was heavy upon the people of Ashdod and its vicinity; he brought devastation upon them and afflicted them with tumors. [7]When the men of Ashdod saw what
was happening, they said, "The ark of the god of Israel must not stay here with us, because
his hand is heavy upon us and upon Dagon our god." [8]So they called together all the rulers
of the Philistines and asked them, "What shall we do with the ark of the god of Israel?"

They answered, "Have the ark of the god of Israel moved to Gath." So they moved the ark of the God of Israel.

[9]But after they had moved it, the LORD's hand was against that city, throwing it into a
great panic. He afflicted the people of the city, both young and old, with an outbreak of
tumors. [10]So they sent the ark of God to Ekron.

As the ark of God was entering Ekron, the people of Ekron cried out, "They have
brought the ark of the god of Israel around to us to kill us and our people." [11]So they called
together all the rulers of the Philistines and said, "Send the ark of the god of Israel away;
let it go back to its own place, or it will kill us and our people." For death had filled the city
with panic; God's hand was very heavy upon it. [12]Those who did not die were afflicted with
tumors, and the outcry of the city went up to heaven.

COMMENTARY

1–5 From the battlefield at Ebenezer, the Philistines took the ark of the covenant to Ashdod (v.1), apparently the chief city of their pentapolis (6:17). Ashdod, the only extensively excavated Philistine capital, was located three miles from the Mediterranean coast about thirty miles southwest of Ebenezer. The ark was brought into the temple of Dagon, the Philistine national deity (v.2), and placed near a large idol representing him. The next day the statue of Dagon had fallen facedown, vanquished by Israel's God (as the Philistine champion Goliath would later be defeated by David; see 17:49) and prostrate before the ark in a posture of worship. The people of Ashdod put the idol back in its "place." (The people of Ekron, filled with panic, would soon demand that the ark be returned to "its own place" [see v.11].) The next morning Dagon was again facedown before the ark—this time with its head and hands "broken off" (v.4), just as Goliath's head would later be "cut off" by David (17:51; same Hebrew verb).

In the ancient world severed heads (cf. Goliath; see also 29:4) and hands (cf. Jdg 8:6) were battlefield trophies that assisted the victor in establishing the correct body count (see Campbell, *1 Samuel*, 86 n. 1). The Lord had therefore vanquished Dagon in his own temple, a premonition of things to come. At the temple of Dagon in Gaza, the power of God—symbolized by the hair on Samson's head and the strength in his earlier hands—had defeated the Philistines and their god (Jdg 16:21–30). On yet another occasion, however, the Philistines enjoyed a notable victory: They hung up the severed head of Israel's king Saul in a temple of Dagon (1Ch 10:10), perhaps at Beth Shan (cf. 1Sa 31:10).

The head and hands of Dagon's statue landed on the temple threshold, thus rendering it sacred (in the minds of his worshipers) and therefore untouchable (v.5). Zephaniah describes "idolatrous priests" (Zep 1:4) and their followers as those who "avoid stepping on the threshold" (v.9). They, like the superstitious Philistines before them, were ripe for punishment.

6–12 With the reference to Dagon's hands being rendered helpless, the narrator introduces a major motif in the account: the hand of the Lord. This motif is so thematic within the ark narratives that P. D. Miller and J. J. M. Roberts, 48, have perceptively used it as the title of their monograph on the subject. They find it (or its equivalent) eight times in the narrative: 4:8; 5:6, 7, 9, 11; 6:3, 5, 9 (their ninth citation [5:4] admittedly relates to the hands of Dagon's statue). Because they end the ark narratives at 7:1, they omit from their list of citations the important reference in 7:13, which summarizes the theme.

The first reference here to the hand of the Lord comes from the lips of the Philistines, who related the divine hand to the plagues of Egypt (4:8)—and rightly so (see Ex 9:3; cf. also Jer 21:5–6). They did not take lightly the possibility that the fate of the Egyptians might befall them also (6:6). In the ancient world, sickness and plague were often specifically described as the baleful effects of the "hand" of a god (cf. J. J. M. Roberts, "The Hand of Yahweh," *VT* 21/2 [1971]: 244–51). In addition, every characteristic expression relating to the hand of the Lord in the ark narratives has a strikingly similar Akkadian parallel (cf. ibid., 248–49 n. 6).

Tumors were one of the many potential curses that would be inflicted on the Israelites if they disobeyed God (Dt 28:58–60). Here that affliction descended on the Philistines (v.6), who realized that the hand of the Lord was heavy on them (v.7; cf. v.11). Their five rulers (6:18) advised them to get rid of the ark (v.8)—which all recognized as the visible surrogate for the Israelite deity and therefore the cause of the plague—by moving it to Gath (modern Tell es-Safi, about twelve miles east-southeast of Ashdod). Thus the Lord's hand was against Gath (v.9; cf. 7:13) and brought "an outbreak of tumors" on its inhabitants. The Hebrew word for "outbreak" is found only here and was apparently interpreted by the LXX as "groin," thus yielding the translation "tumors in the groin" (see NIV note)—a common symptom of bubonic plague.

The ark was quickly shipped to Ekron (modern Khirbet el-Muqanna, about six miles due north of Gath; for a survey of recent archaeological discoveries at Ekron during its peak of development in the time of Samuel, see Trude Dothan, "Ekron of the Philistines. Part I: Where They Came From, How They Settled Down, and the Place They Worshiped In," *BAR* 16/1 [1990]: 26–36). But the arrival of the ark in Ekron had the same effect there as the news of its capture had in Shiloh: The people sent up a cry for help (vv.10, 12; see 4:13–14), fearful that the God of Israel would "kill" them—a power he certainly possessed (cf. 2:6, 25). As the pharaoh's officials had urged him to let the Israelites go in order to stop the series of plagues engulfing them (Ex 10:7; cf. 12:31–33), so also the people of Ekron told their rulers to send the ark away (v.11). Even those who did not die were afflicted with tumors (v.12); no one escaped the dreaded plague.

The lesson of chs. 4 and 5 is clear: Neither Israelites nor Philistines—not even Dagon himself—can control or resist the will of the sovereign Lord, whose Presence, though enthroned between the cherubim surmounting the ark of the covenant, is not limited by that location and therefore cannot be manipulated by the whim of whoever happens to be in possession of it at any particular time.

NOTES

2 The older etymology of דָּגוֹן (*dāgôn*) from דָּג (*dāg*, "fish")—assuming either that Dagon was a fish god or that he was the god of a maritime people—has now been almost universally abandoned in favor of a derivation from דָּגָן (*dāgān*, "grain"; for details, see, for example, V. Orel, "The Great Fall of Dagon," *ZAW* 110/5 [1998]: 428 and nn. 6–12). Ugaritic epic literature claims that Dagon was the father of Baal, the storm god of fertility, a paternity compatible with his role as a grain god. From early times he was worshiped widely by the Semitic peoples of the Levant. Numerous towns were named after him, including Beth Dagon in Judah (Jos 15:41) and Beth Dagon in Asher (Jos 19:27), neither of which has been located.

4 Archaeological discoveries provide instructive parallels to the bizarre scene described in vv.2–4. A chalk stela from Early Bronze Arad pictures a god (Dagon?) with a wheat-shaped head and raised arms in two postures: standing upright and lying down. In the second posture his head and hands are situated on a straight line that may represent a threshold. (For a drawing of the stela and a detailed explanation of its features, see Orel, "The Great Fall of Dagon," 430–31.) And in the ruins of Late Bronze Hazor were found the remains of several statues, including "the largest Canaanite statue of human form ever found in Israel"—with head and hands missing, "apparently cut off by the city's conquerors" (A. Ben-Tor and M. T. Rubiato, "Did the Israelites Destroy the Canaanite City?" *BAR* 25/3 [1999]: 22).

5 The phrase עַד הַיּוֹם הַזֶּה (*ʿad hayyôm hazzeh*, "to this day"), here and elsewhere in Samuel (e.g., 6:18; 27:6 ["ever since"]; 30:25; 2Sa 4:3; 6:8; 18:18), indicates that the narrator lived some time later than the events he recorded.

6 "Tumors" (vv.6, 9, 12; 6:4–5, 11, 17; cf. also Dt 28:27) translates two different words in the MT (often marginal readings): עֳפָלִים (*ʿŏpālîm*, "swellings") and טְחֹרִים (*ṭᵉḥōrîm*, perhaps "hemorrhoids"; hence KJV, "emerods"). Of the numerous suggested identifications of the specific malady that struck the Philistines, bubonic plague remains the most likely: "It is a disease characterized by an epidemic occurrence, by the appearance of tumours, by the production of panic amongst the affected population, by a high mortality rate, and by an association with mice or rats" (John Wilkinson, "The Philistine Epidemic of I Samuel 5 and 6," *EvT* 88/5 [1977]: 137). The attempt of John B. Geyer ("Mice and Rites in 1 Samuel V–VI," *VT* 31/3 [1981]: 293–304) to resurrect the theory that the plague was dysentery and that the tumors were a late symptom uses hopelessly tortuous arguments, makes questionable textual choices, and finds no causal connection between the plague and the rats (and also seems not to have been aware of Wilkinson's fine article). The LXX's addition to v.6 (see NIV note), which makes the connection, doubtless rests on reliable tradition, and the guilt offering described in ch. 6 demonstrates that the Philistines were aware of the link as well.

The causal connection between rats and plague was not conclusively demonstrated until 1908 (Wilkinson, "The Philistine Epidemic," 139). That fleas, hosted by rats, are the actual transmitters of plague is now widely known (for details, see Nicole Duplaix, "Fleas: The Lethal Leapers," *National Geographic* 173/5 [1988]: 672–94). In 1630–31 French artist Nicolas Poussin produced a remarkable painting titled "The Plague at Ashdod" (for a reproduction see Robert R. Stieglitz, "Ancient Records and the Exodus Plagues," *BAR* 13/6 [1987]: 48). Whether 1 Samuel 5–6 records the first occurrence of bubonic plague in history is impossible to say. Accounts of earlier plagues abound (cf. Ronald F. Youngblood, "Amorite Influence in a Canaanite Amarna Letter [EA 96]," *BASOR* 168 [1962]: 24–27), but information concerning whether they were bubonic is lacking. A recent article by Aren M. Maeir ("Did Captured Ark Afflict Philistines with E. D.?" *BAR* 34/3 [2008]: 46–51), adducing archaeological evidence, suggests that "swellings" refers to an affliction of the male sexual organ. It may be noted here that such a possibility is at least hinted at in the LXX of v.9 ("tumors in the groin"; cf. NIV note).

8 סֶרֶן (*seren*, "ruler"), used in the OT only of Philistine rulers, is perhaps related to τύραννος (*tyrannos*), from which "tyrant" is derived, and/or to the Hittite *tarwanas* "judge" (see K. A. Kitchen, "The Philistines," in Wiseman, *Peoples of OT Times*, 67, 77 n. 110).

10 In the summer of 1996 a royal dedicatory inscription referring to "Achish ... the ruler of Ekron" was found in the ruins of the sanctuary at Khirbet el-Muqanna/Tel Miqne, thus confirming the identification of the site as Ekron of the Philistines. For a convenient summary of the results of fourteen excavation seasons conducted between 1981 and 1996 see Seymour Gitin, "The Philistines: Neighbors of the Canaanites, Phoenicians and Israelites," in *100 Years of American Archaeology in the Middle East*, ed. Douglas R. Clark and Victor H. Matthews (Boston: ASOR, 2003), 57–76. Gitin documents the remarkable staying power of Philistine culture at Ekron down to the end of the seventh century BC.

11 "For death had filled the city with panic" (lit., "For a panic of death [i.e., a most severe panic] was throughout the city") provides a fine example of *māwet* ("death") used with superlative force (D. Winton Thomas, " צַלְמָוֶת in the Old Testament," *JSS* 7 [1962]: 196).

4. The Return of the Ark (6:1–7:1)

[1]When the ark of the LORD had been in Philistine territory seven months, [2]the Philistines
called for the priests and the diviners and said, "What shall we do with the ark of the LORD?
Tell us how we should send it back to its place."
[3]They answered, "If you return the ark of the god of Israel, do not send it away empty,
but by all means send a guilt offering to him. Then you will be healed, and you will know
why his hand has not been lifted from you."
[4]The Philistines asked, "What guilt offering should we send to him?"
They replied, "Five gold tumors and five gold rats, according to the number of the Philistine rulers, because the same plague has struck both you and your rulers. [5]Make models
of the tumors and of the rats that are destroying the country, and pay honor to Israel's
god. Perhaps he will lift his hand from you and your gods and your land. [6]Why do you
harden your hearts as the Egyptians and Pharaoh did? When he treated them harshly, did
they not send the Israelites out so they could go on their way?
[7]"Now then, get a new cart ready, with two cows that have calved and have never been
yoked. Hitch the cows to the cart, but take their calves away and pen them up. [8]Take the
ark of the LORD and put it on the cart, and in a chest beside it put the gold objects you are
sending back to him as a guilt offering. Send it on its way, [9]but keep watching it. If it goes
up to its own territory, toward Beth Shemesh, then the LORD has brought this great disaster
on us. But if it does not, then we will know that it was not his hand that struck us and that
it happened to us by chance."
[10]So they did this. They took two such cows and hitched them to the cart and penned
up their calves. [11]They placed the ark of the LORD on the cart and along with it the chest

containing the gold rats and the models of the tumors. 12Then the cows went straight up
toward Beth Shemesh, keeping on the road and lowing all the way; they did not turn to
the right or to the left. The rulers of the Philistines followed them as far as the border of
Beth Shemesh.

13Now the people of Beth Shemesh were harvesting their wheat in the valley, and when
they looked up and saw the ark, they rejoiced at the sight. 14The cart came to the field of
Joshua of Beth Shemesh, and there it stopped beside a large rock. The people chopped
up the wood of the cart and sacrificed the cows as a burnt offering to the LORD. 15The
Levites took down the ark of the LORD, together with the chest containing the gold objects,
and placed them on the large rock. On that day the people of Beth Shemesh offered burnt
offerings and made sacrifices to the LORD. 16The five rulers of the Philistines saw all this and
then returned that same day to Ekron.

17These are the gold tumors the Philistines sent as a guilt offering to the LORD—one
each for Ashdod, Gaza, Ashkelon, Gath and Ekron. 18And the number of the gold rats was
according to the number of Philistine towns belonging to the five rulers—the fortified
towns with their country villages. The large rock, on which they set the ark of the LORD, is a
witness to this day in the field of Joshua of Beth Shemesh.

19But God struck down some of the men of Beth Shemesh, putting seventy of them to
death because they had looked into the ark of the LORD. The people mourned because
of the heavy blow the LORD had dealt them, 20and the men of Beth Shemesh asked, "Who
can stand in the presence of the LORD, this holy God? To whom will the ark go up from
here?"

21Then they sent messengers to the people of Kiriath Jearim, saying, "The Philistines
have returned the ark of the LORD. Come down and take it up to your place." 7:1So the men
of Kiriath Jearim came and took up the ark of the LORD. They took it to Abinadab's house
on the hill and consecrated Eleazar his son to guard the ark of the LORD.

COMMENTARY

1–6 Chapter 4 tells of the capture of the ark, ch. 5 of its movement from place to place in Philistia, and ch. 6 of its return to Israel after being in Philistine territory for several months (v.1; "seven" is perhaps a figurative number or an approximation, as "three" is in a similar situation in 2Sa 6:11). The Philistines, eager to rid themselves of the ark and its sinister influence, and not possessed of the same scruples concerning divination as the Israelites were (cf. Dt 18:14; Isa 2:6), sought supernatural guidance as to the best way of sending the ark back to "its [proper] place" (v.2). "Tell us [*hôdiʿunû*, lit., 'make known to us'; see 'you will know,' v.3, *w^{e}nôdaʿ lākem*, lit., 'it will be made known to you,' from the same Hebrew root, *ydʿ*] how," they said to their pagan counselors.

Ancient religious protocol prohibited the worshiper from approaching his god(s) empty-handed (cf. Ex 23:15; Dt 16:16). Thus the Philistine priests and diviners advised that a guilt offering (which, in Israel at least, served as payment to atone for unintentional sins; see Lev 5:14–19) accompany the ark back to Israel (v.3). Although such an offering was normally an animal sacrifice, occasionally money or other valuables were acceptable (even in Israel; see 2Ki 12:16). If the Lord accepted the Philistines' offering, their people would be healed; then they would know that his hand had been responsible for their misery (see also v.9).

Verse 4, by linking tumors, rats, and plague, strengthens the theory that the tumors were symptoms of bubonic plague spread by an infestation of rats, which, like human invaders, were capable of destroying a country (v.5; cf. Jer 36:29; Da 11:16). The Philistine advisers recommended gold models of tumors and rats to serve as the guilt offering to placate the God of Israel. Perhaps the Philistines intended the models to function in the realm of sympathetic magic also, so that by sending them out of their land the genuine articles would depart as well. Apart from the present context, the only other references to rats/mice in the OT are Leviticus 11:29 and Isaiah 66:17, where they are numbered among ceremonially unclean animals.

That the Hebrew word for "plague" (*maggēpâ*, v.4) is also used to describe the Egyptian plagues in Exodus 9:14 further heightens the parallel between the earlier disaster and this one (cf. again v.6). The lesson is clear: Hardening one's heart (the same Hebrew expression as in Ex 8:15, 32; 9:34) only brings divine retribution, resulting in the victory of God's people over their enemies (Ex 12:31–32). The Philistines are thus well advised to cut their losses as soon as possible.

7–12 A new cart (as in 2Sa 6:3) pulled by two cows "that have calved and have never been yoked" (translating *ʿālôt ʾᵃšer lōʾ-ʿālâ ʿᵃlêhem ʿōl*—a remarkable example of assonance; v.7) was to be used to transport the ark. The cows would later be sacrificed by the Israelites (v.14) in faint reminiscence of the slaughter of the red heifer by Eleazar (Nu 19:2–3; cf.—coincidentally?—the Eleazar consecrated to guard the ark at the end of its long journey [7:1]; further Dt 21:1–9). The Philistines were to "take" the calves from their mothers (v.7), "send" the gold objects as a guilt offering to the Lord (vv.8, 17), and "return" the ark to him and his people (v.21; the verbs are all forms of the same stem of the same Hebrew verb *šûb*).

The first destination of the ark was Beth Shemesh (modern Tell er-Rumeileh, about nine miles east-southeast of Ekron), just inside Israelite territory. Listed among the priestly cities (Jos 21:13–16; 1Ch 6:57–59), Beth Shemesh had a pagan past (its name meaning "Temple of the Sun God"). Large quantities of Philistine pottery found in its ruins attest to Philistine cultural influence there during the period of the judges. The Philistines of Samuel's day, however, acknowledged that Beth Shemesh was under Israelite control. They hoped that the cows would take the ark there, reasoning that if cows new to the yoke would desert their newborn calves—even temporarily—to pull a cart all the way to Beth Shemesh, their doing so would be a supernatural sign that the divine owner of the ark had sent the plague. But if the ark did not reach Beth Shemesh, they would take that fact as proof that the Lord's hand had not struck them (v.9; for the same expression see Job 1:11; 2:5; 19:21) and that mere chance was responsible. (For the biblical distinction between divine providence and pagan belief in chance, see Gustav Friedrich Oehler, *Theology of the Old Testament*, 4th ed. [New York: Funk & Wagnalls, 1883], 121–22.)

Against nature ("lowing all the way" because their calves were not with them [v.12]) and under divine compulsion (not turning "to the right or to the left"—that is, staying on the main road; see

Dt 2:27), the cows pulled the cart straight to Beth Shemesh (vv.11–12a). The five Philistine rulers, following the cows to the border, stayed only long enough to make sure the ark was securely in Israelite hands (vv.12b, 16).

6:13–7:1 The ark arrived at Beth Shemesh in June, during wheat harvest (v.13), after the spring rains (cf. 12:16–18). Rejoicing to see the ark, the people decided to use the cart for fuel and to sacrifice the cows as a burnt offering. They "chopped up the wood" (v.14), a phrase that also describes the preliminaries for another memorable burnt offering a thousand years earlier (Ge 22:3; "cut enough wood" is the same Hebrew expression). (The idiom "sacrifice/offer up a burnt offering" appears also in 7:9–10, another indication that the ark narratives continue through to the end of ch. 7.)

A large rock in a field belonging to Joshua of Beth Shemesh (not to be confused with Joshua son of Nun, Moses' successor) became the temporary locale for the ark (vv.14–15, 18). The Levites, who alone were permitted to handle the ark (cf. Jos 3:3; 2Sa 15:24), had removed it from the cart and set it on the rock (v.15), which served as a witness of the ark's homecoming until at least the time of the narrator ("to this day," v.18).

Meanwhile, the five Philistine rulers returned to their pentapolis (v.17), all five cities of which are mentioned elsewhere only in Joshua 13:3. Gaza, the southernmost of the five, was located about three miles from the Mediterranean coast and about twenty-two miles southwest of Ashdod, while Ashkelon was on the coast about halfway between Ashdod and Gaza (for Ekron's location, see comment on 5:10). Each of the five fortified towns was supported by a number of nearby "country villages" (v.18; cf. similarly Dt 3:5 ["unwalled villages"]; Est 9:19 ["rural ... villages"]).

Divine retribution continued to overtake those who misused the ark. This time some men of Beth Shemesh "looked into" the ark (v.19), a sin punishable by instant death (Nu 4:5, 20; cf. also 2Sa 6:6–7). The mourners sensed that the ark symbolized the presence of a "holy God" (v.20; cf. Lev 11:44–45), whose sanctity they could not approach. They therefore hoped he would depart from them. (The unexpressed subject of "go up" could be either "the ark" or "God"; perhaps both are intended.)

Kiriath Jearim (v.21; modern Deir el-Azar, about ten miles northeast of Beth Shemesh) was the ark's location for the next twenty years (7:2; for details see Blenkinsopp, 143–56). More specifically, it resided at "Abinadab's house on the hill" (7:1; 2Sa 6:3; cf. also NIV note on 2Sa 6:4). Eleazar (whose name has perhaps survived in the modern Arabic name of Kiriath Jearim, namely, Deir el-Azar) son of Abinadab was then consecrated to guard it. The downgraded status of the ark may have been partially due to the Philistines' destruction of Shiloh (not referred to in this context but presupposed by Ps 78:60; Jer 7:12, 14; 26:6, 9) and perhaps the tabernacle as well (which would then have been rebuilt later), ca. 1050 BC. Not until David's accession as king in Jerusalem would the ark once again be restored to its rightful place of honor (2Sa 6).

NOTES

3 The NIV's translation of the last sentence of this verse makes good sense of the relationship between the two clauses; cf. similarly Aelred Cody's review of Miller and Roberts' *The Hand of the Lord* (see *CBQ* 40 [1978]: 98), which provides a convincing parallel with the Hittite Plague Prayers of Mursilis.

5 "Models" renders a plural form of צֶלֶם (*ṣelem*; GK 7512), which is normally translated as "image" and whose most frequent meaning refers to a physical image, as here (cf., e.g., Ge 5:3; Nu 33:52; Eze 16:17). The expression "image of God" (found only in Ge 1:27; 9:6; cf. also 1:26), which has traveled a long and rocky road in the history of interpretation (cf. conveniently K. Mulzac, "Genesis 9:1–7: Its Theological Connections with the Creation Motif," *Journal of the Adventist Theological Society* 12/1 [2001]: 75 n. 54), is now increasingly understood in the physical sense as the result of the discovery in 1979 of a ninth-century BC bilingual inscription on a statue of Hadad-yithʿi, a local ruler, at Tell Fekheriyeh in northeast Syria. There "the Akkadian word *ṣalmu*, 'image/statue,' is rendered into Aramaic as *ṣalma* in lines 12 and 16 and as *dĕmûta* in lines 1 and 5" (E. M. Curtis, "Image of God," *ABD*, 3:391). This observation suggests that the Hebrew cognates *ṣelem* ("image") and *dᵉmût* ("likeness") in Genesis 1:26; 5:3 are synonyms with no appreciable difference in meaning. Just as the corresponding Aramaic terms both stress the idea that Hadad-yithʿi's statue is a "representation/image/likeness" of the physical presence of the man himself, so also the "image of God" (Ge 1:27; 9:6) is first and foremost a "representation of God's presence" in individual human beings, who have collectively been mandated to rule over the rest of creation (Ge 1:28) as God's vicegerents. See further R. S. Hess, "Eden—a Well-Watered Place," *BRev* 7/6 (1991): 28–33.

"Pay honor" and "harden" (v.6) are renderings of the root כבד (*kbd*, "heavy"), and "lift" (v.5) translates the root קלל (*qll*, "light"). This coupling echoes the same pair of roots in 2:30 ("honor" and "disdain" respectively; see comment there) and highlights the ironic contrast between the refusal of two Aaronic (and therefore legitimate) priests to obey God and the willingness of Philistine (and therefore illegitimate) priests to do everything necessary to placate God.

8 אַרְגָּז (*ʾargaz*, "chest"; elsewhere only in vv.11, 15) is a word "possibly of southwestern Anatolian, Cilician, or Illyrian origin" (Dothan, *The Philistines and Their Material Culture* [New Haven, Conn.: Yale Univ. Press, 1982], 23) and was therefore probably brought to the Canaanite mainland by the Philistines.

18 The main difference between the text and the marginal reading is the reading אֶבֶן (*ʾeben*, "rock"; see vv.14–15), with a few Hebrew manuscripts, as opposed to אָבֵל (*ʾābēl*, apparently to be understood as a proper name), with most Hebrew manuscripts. The latter reading may have arisen due to the occurrence of the same root in the next verse ("mourned"). For the possibility that "Great Mourning" is in fact the correct reading and had become a name for the large rock, see Campbell, *The Ark Narrative*, 117 n. 2.

19 The reading in the NIV note, "50,070," is attested in all the major ancient versions and is therefore textually secure. The number is far too large, however, to have constituted only "some" of the men of Beth Shemesh; at the same time, the death of "seventy" would hardly be described as a "heavy blow," especially in the light of 4:10 (where "thirty thousand" men died in a "slaughter" that was "very great" [excluding "very," the Hebrew is the same as that for "heavy blow"]). A suggested solution is to change ויך בעם שבעים איש חמשים אלף איש (*wyk bʿm šbʿym ʾyš ḥmšym ʾlp ʾyš*, "He struck down among the people seventy men [and] fifty thousand men") to read ויך בעם שבע ים איש חמש ים אלף איש (*wyk bʿm šbʿ ym ʾyš ḥmš ym ʾlp ʾyš*, "He struck down the people for seven days, men for five days, a thousand men") (cf. R. Althann, "Consonantal *ym*: Ending or Noun in Isaiah 3:13; Jeremiah 17:16; 1 Samuel 6:19," *Bib* 63/4 [1982]: 563–65). The number slain at Beth Shemesh then becomes a "thousand" rather than "seventy" or "50,070." Although the proposal is attractive, the resulting Hebrew text is awkward and difficult grammatically, even in the poetic format in which Althann casts it.

5. Samuel the Judge (7:2–17)

OVERVIEW

Although it is generally assumed that 7:1 concludes the ark narratives (at least the 1 Samuel portion of them), I have argued in the foregoing pages that the account continues to the end of ch. 7 (see esp. the comment on 4:1b–7:17). To summarize: Mention of the ark and Kiriath Jearim links v.2 tightly to v.1; the thematic word "hand" appears throughout (vv.3, 8, 13–14 [in the last verse "power" is the same Hebrew word]); "rulers of the Philistines" occurs in v.7 (and not again until 29:2); "burnt offering" (vv.9–10) reprises 6:14–15; the Philistines continue to attack Israel (vv.10–11) but are defeated in a decisive campaign that rounds out this series of battles (v.13); the memorial stone in v.12 recalls the large rock in 6:14–15, 18; and Ebenezer (v.12), even if it represents a different place, echoes Ebenezer in 4:1; 5:1 (the only other two places in the Bible where the name occurs).

An attempt to parallel 1 Samuel 7 with Exodus 17 (J. Ernest Runions, "Exodus Motifs in First Samuel 7 and 8," *EvQ* 52/3 [1980]: 130–31) collapses when the details of the alleged similarities are carefully compared. Runions's comments concerning Samuel's career and role as generally analogous to those of Moses, however, are helpful indeed.

[2]It was a long time, twenty years in all, that the ark remained at Kiriath Jearim, and all
the people of Israel mourned and sought after the LORD. [3]And Samuel said to the whole
house of Israel, "If you are returning to the LORD with all your hearts, then rid yourselves
of the foreign gods and the Ashtoreths and commit yourselves to the LORD and serve him
only, and he will deliver you out of the hand of the Philistines." [4]So the Israelites put away
their Baals and Ashtoreths, and served the LORD only.

[5]Then Samuel said, "Assemble all Israel at Mizpah and I will intercede with the LORD for
you." [6]When they had assembled at Mizpah, they drew water and poured it out before the
LORD. On that day they fasted and there they confessed, "We have sinned against the LORD."
And Samuel was leader of Israel at Mizpah.

[7]When the Philistines heard that Israel had assembled at Mizpah, the rulers of the
Philistines came up to attack them. And when the Israelites heard of it, they were afraid
because of the Philistines. [8]They said to Samuel, "Do not stop crying out to the LORD our
God for us, that he may rescue us from the hand of the Philistines." [9]Then Samuel took a
suckling lamb and offered it up as a whole burnt offering to the LORD. He cried out to the
LORD on Israel's behalf, and the LORD answered him.

[10]While Samuel was sacrificing the burnt offering, the Philistines drew near to engage
Israel in battle. But that day the LORD thundered with loud thunder against the Philistines
and threw them into such a panic that they were routed before the Israelites. [11]The men of

Israel rushed out of Mizpah and pursued the Philistines, slaughtering them along the way to a point below Beth Car.

[12]Then Samuel took a stone and set it up between Mizpah and Shen. He named it Ebenezer, saying, "Thus far has the LORD helped us." [13]So the Philistines were subdued and did not invade Israelite territory again.

Throughout Samuel's lifetime, the hand of the LORD was against the Philistines. [14]The towns from Ekron to Gath that the Philistines had captured from Israel were restored to her, and Israel delivered the neighboring territory from the power of the Philistines. And there was peace between Israel and the Amorites.

[15]Samuel continued as judge over Israel all the days of his life. [16]From year to year he went on a circuit from Bethel to Gilgal to Mizpah, judging Israel in all those places. [17]But he always went back to Ramah, where his home was, and there he also judged Israel. And he built an altar there to the LORD.

COMMENTARY

2–4 The "twenty years" that the ark remained at Kiriath Jearim (v.2) may be figurative for "half a generation" (cf. J. B. Segal, 11 n. 14), during which time the "people" (lit., "house," as in v.3, in the sense of "family, community") of Israel "mourned" (the Heb. verb *nāhâ*, different from the far more common one represented in 6:19 [*ʾābal*], occurs only twice elsewhere: Eze 32:18 ["wail"] and Mic 2:4 ["taunt"]), apparently with sincere remorse. They were bemoaning the reduced status of the ark, no longer housed in a tabernacle. Samuel encouraged them to repent and to serve the Lord wholeheartedly (v.3), as he himself would again (12:20, 24).

Like Jacob (Ge 35:2, 4) and Joshua (Jos 24:14, 23) before him, Samuel urged the people to get rid of the foreign gods (idols) they were so prone to worship (cf. also Dt 12:3; Jdg 10:16; 2Ch 19:3; 33:15). "Foreign gods and ... Ashtoreths" (v.3) is essentially synonymous with "Baals and Ashtoreths" (v.4; 12:10; Jdg 2:13; 10:6), as the people's response in v.4 to Samuel's counsel in v.3 indicates. Baal and Ashtoreth (or, alternatively, Asherah; cf. Jdg 3:7) were the chief god and goddess, respectively, in the Canaanite pantheon during this period; so the phrases in vv.3–4 signify "gods and goddesses" (cf. the corresponding Akkadian expression *ilū u ištarātu*). Local manifestations (idols) of such deities in hundreds of Canaanite towns and villages provide yet another reason for the frequent use of their names in the plural.

Baal, god of fertility and the storm, was believed to be the son of Dagon, god of grain (see Notes on 5:2). Ashtoreth, goddess of love and fertility, vied for supremacy with Asherah, mother goddess and consort of El (the creator god in the earlier Canaanite pantheon but now displaced by Baal). The association of Baal, Asherah, and Ashtoreth with fertility, particularly as expressed in depraved sexual ritual at Canaanite shrines, made them especially abominable in the Lord's eyes. The name "Baal" was often linked with *bōšet* ("shame[ful]") in the biblical text (cf. Jer 11:13; Hos 9:10), and the two words occasionally interchanged in proper names (for example, Ish-Bosheth in 2Sa 2:8 = Esh-Baal in 1Ch 8:33

[see NIV note]). The name "Ashtoreth" (originally "Ashtart[u]") has been revocalized to rhyme with *bōšet* and thus stigmatize her with Baal's shame.

Samuel's plea is light years away from the depraved paganism of Canaanite religion: "Commit yourselves [lit., 'your hearts'; cf. earlier in the same verse] to the LORD" (v.3). God's people are to serve him exclusively (vv.3–4; see esp. Dt 6:13, quoted by Jesus in Mt 4:10 = Lk 4:8).

5–6 The assembly of "all Israel" (v.5) did not necessarily include every single Israelite living in the land but probably consisted of representatives from all the tribal territories. A common phrase in the books of Samuel, it is of course sometimes used in an all-inclusive way (cf. 3:20) as determined by context. Convocations at Mizpah (probably either modern Tell en-Nasbeh [see Jeffrey R. Zorn, "Mizpah: Newly Discovered Stratum Reveals Judah's Other Capital," *BAR* 23/5 (1997): 28–38, 66], about eight miles north of Jerusalem, or modern Nebi Samwil [see Yitzhak Magen, "Nebi Samwil: Where Samuel Crowned Israel's First King," *BAR* 34/3 (2008): 36–45, 78–79], about five miles northwest of Jerusalem) were not uncommon in the days of the judges and early monarchy (cf. 10:17; Jdg 20:1; 21:8).

At Mizpah Samuel prayed for the people (for Samuel as a man of prayer see also vv.8–9; 8:6; 12:19, 23; 15:11; Jer 15:1), and there they "poured ... out [water] before the LORD" (v.6). Although the meaning of this latter act is somewhat uncertain (the expression is unique, and BDB, 1049, is perhaps correct in calling it a "symbol of contrition" in this setting), David later "poured out" water before the Lord (2Sa 23:16, but with a different Heb. verb) as a libation in the context of the heroism of his three companions.

The notice of Samuel's judgeship (v.6; see NIV note) is followed immediately by a report of Philistine intention to attack Israel. We are thus reminded that the function of a "judge" during this period was more executive than judicial. "Judge" often paralleled "ruler" or "prince" in contemporary Canaanite literature as well as in the OT itself (cf. Ex 2:14), and one of the most common roles of the judge was to repel invaders (v.8; Jdg 2:16, 18).

7–9 Cowed by Philistine might, Israel typically reacted with fear to news of impending warfare with them (v.7; 17:11; 28:5). But when the Philistines "came up" to attack, Samuel prayerfully "offered ... up" (v.9; in both cases the same Heb. root [*ʿālâ*]) a burnt offering to the Lord (for Samuel as priest, cf. 9:12; 11:14–15; 16:2; Ps 99:6). The sacrificial animal was a suckling lamb at least eight days old (cf. Lev 22:27).

10–12 While the sacrifice was still in progress, the Philistine troops marched forward. Before the battle could be joined, however, the Lord "thundered" against the enemy (v.10; see 2:10; 2Sa 22:14–15). In so doing he demonstrated that he, not the Philistine Dagon, not the Canaanite Baal son of Dagon, was truly the God of the storm, the only one able to control the elements whether for good or ill (cf. 12:17–18). The NIV's translation, "with loud thunder," for the more literal, "with a great voice" (v.10), highlights the vivid OT image of thunder as the voice of God (see Ps 29:3–9).

The ensuing panic in the Philistines' ranks (cf. 2Sa 22:14–15) drove them into full retreat, enabling the Israelites to pursue and slaughter them (v.11). The location of Beth Car (perhaps meaning "House of the Lamb"; cf. 15:9) is unknown, as is that of Shen ("Tooth," v.12). The best suggestion for the latter is that of Delitzsch (cf. also Klein), who reads it as a common noun referring to the sharp overhang of a cliff (as in 14:4–5; Job 39:28). Another possibility, although hardly necessary, is to emend *haššēn* ("The Tooth") to *yᵉšānâ* ("The Old One") on the basis of readings in the ancient versions (cf. also 2Ch 13:19). In either case the Ebenezer of v.12 is almost certainly not the Ebenezer of 4:1 and 5:1, since the latter is too far to the northwest for Mizpah to be used as a benchmark for its location.

The stone set up by Samuel is reminiscent of other commemorative stelae (cf. Ge 35:14; Jos 4:9; 24:26; for details see Carl F. Graesser, "Standing Stones in Ancient Palestine," *BA* 35/2 [1972]: 34–63). *ʾEben hāʿāzer* ("The Stone of [Divine] Help"; see NIV note) pays tribute to Israel's God, apart from whom victory is inconceivable.

13–17 These verses echo "the formulae which mark the end of the story of a judge (cf. Judg. 3:30; 8:28)" (Dennis J. McCarthy, "The Inauguration of Monarchy," 402). A new paragraph should therefore start at the beginning of v.13, not in the middle (as in the NIV). At the same time the second half of the verse assumes continued Philistine pressure (though greatly reduced) against Israel and thus cautions us not to understand the first half as meaning that the Philistines no longer bothered the Israelites in any way (cf. esp. 9:16). The Amorites (the Heb. term being cognate to Akkadian *amurrû*, "westerner"), who preferred to live in the hilly regions of the land (cf. Nu 13:29; Dt 1:7) as compared to the Philistines who lived along the coast, were also relatively nonbelligerent during this period (v.14; cf. further 2Sa 21:2). The Hebrew for the phrase "peace between" (*šālôm bên*) occurs only twice elsewhere (Jdg 4:17 ["friendly relations between"]; 1Ki 5:12 ["peaceful relations between"]); the latter text suggests that the Israelites and Amorites had signed a mutual nonaggression pact.

The circuit of Samuel's judgeship (v.16) was relatively restricted: Bethel (perhaps modern Beitin), Gilgal (perhaps modern Khirbet el-Mefjer), and Mizpah (for possible location, see comment on v.5) were all within a few miles of one another. All three towns served as shrine centers at one time or another, as did Ramah, Samuel's hometown (cf. the mention of the altar in v.17). The latter was not far from the other three (about fourteen miles northwest of Mizpah). The narrator reminds us again of the local nature of judgeship in ancient Israel to subtly introduce us to the need—however ambiguous and contradictory—for a king "such as all the other nations have" (8:5, 20).

NOTES

4 Gordon J. Hamilton, in "New Evidence for the Authenticity of *bšt* in Hebrew Personal Names and for Its Use as a Divine Epithet in Biblical Texts" (*CBQ* 60 [1998]: 228–50), mounts an impressive series of arguments in favor of rendering the Hebrew noun *bōšet* as "protective spirit" (rather than as "shame") as its original meaning in all such cases, based primarily on the admitted meaning of the Akkadian cognate noun *baštu* in Amorite personal names. But Hamilton's attempts to translate *bōšet* as "protective spirit" instead of "shame(ful god/idol)" where it refers to Baal in texts such as Jeremiah 11:13 and Hosea 9:10, are tortuous if not tendentious, and his reluctance to deal with the widely accepted transfer of the vowel pattern *ō-e* of *bōšet* to the names of various other pagan gods and practices referred to in the OT (e.g., Asht*o*r*e*th, M*o*l*e*ch, T*o*ph*e*t; cf. Hamilton, 229 n. 4) considerably weakens his overall thesis. On balance, then, "shame" is to be preferred in all such cases.

9 טָלֶה (*ṭāleh*, "lamb") occurs only twice elsewhere (Isa 40:11; 65:25) and emphasizes the young age of the animal. The Aramaic cognate means not only "young lamb" but also "young boy"; Jesus uses the feminine form of the word in the story of the resurrection of a twelve-year-old girl (Mk 5:41).

II. ADVENT OF MONARCHY IN ISRAEL (8:1–15:35)

OVERVIEW

Monarchy was a significant factor in God's plans for his people from the days of Abraham (Ge 17:6, 16). The blessing of Jacob hints at the establishment of a continuing dynasty (Ge 49:10). Israel was to be "a kingdom of priests and a holy nation" (Ex 19:6). Balaam's fourth oracle refers to monarchical rule (Nu 24:17–19), and Moses outlines the divine expectations Israel's kings were to meet (Dt 17:14–20).

From the earliest days, however, it was recognized that ultimately God himself was King (Ex 15:18; Nu 23:21; Dt 33:5); he alone possessed absolute power and authority (Ex 15:6, 11; Jdg 5:3–5; cf. also Jdg 8:22–23). Any king of Israel would have to appreciate from the outset that he was to rule over Israel but under God. Indeed, "kingship is God's central image in the OT" (A. J. Schmutzer, "A Theology of Sexual Abuse: A Reflection on Creation and Devastation," *JETS* 51/4 [2008]: 790 n. 14; "God is the Great King over all, the One to whom all things are subject" (J. H. Stek, "Psalms: Introduction: Theology: Major Themes: 1.," *NIV Study Bible* [fully revised; ed. K. L. Barker [Grand Rapids: Zondervan, 2002]). Only on the basis of this fundamental theological premise can the narratives of the advent of monarchy in Israel be properly understood. Those narratives consist of the accounts of the rise (8:1–12:25) and decline (13:1–15:35) of Saul, Israel's first king.

A. The Rise of Saul (8:1–12:25)

OVERVIEW

Many commentators routinely assert that chs. 8–12 are a literary pastiche of diametrically opposed promonarchical and antimonarchical source materials. The claim is often made that the former originated in preexilic times and that the latter arose in the bitterness and disappointment of exile some time (whether sooner or later) after the destruction of Jerusalem in 586 BC. The chapters therefore do not provide reliable historical information but constitute a mixture of contradictory tracts for different times. It is becoming increasingly clear, however, that the account of the beginnings of Israel's monarchy is partly a reflection of the ambiguity toward kingship in general in the light of the excesses that characterized monarchy among Israel's neighbors (cf. Mendelsohn, 17–22). "Israel failed in so far as she sought earthly power and political influence, and succeeded only in so far as she realized her divine destiny" (Hugh J. Blair, "Kingship in Israel and Its Implications for the Lordship of Christ Today," *EvQ* 47/2 [1975]: 71).

Many of the nations surrounding Israel considered their kings to be gods, whether by divine adoption or through self-deification (cf. Isa 14:4, 13–14; Eze 28:2, 6, 9). In Israel such a claim was unthinkable since the king possessed neither deity nor absolute authority (2Ki 5:7), but the temptation and danger were ever present. To be sure, Israel's king was to exercise "political and military power, but he stood under the authority and judgment of God" (Waylon Bailey, "The King and the Sinai Covenant," *BI* 10/3 [1984]: 39). Finally, discussion of monarchy among God's people must take into account God's will. J. Barton Payne's comments are helpful in this regard ("Saul and the Changing Will of God," *BSac* 129 [1972]: 323):

> It *was not* God's will for Israel to have a king in the way they were asking for it. Still, God's resultant precept, what His "permissive will" came to be, was to direct Samuel to anoint Saul as king out of the tribe of Benjamin.... Three important distinctions are here to be observed. (1) God changed His preceptive will, but only because men had changed (cf. 8:3–5). In fact, it was because God's standard of righteousness had not changed that His precept had to change.... (2) God performed the very act that men wanted; but, while their motive was wrong and in this act they became guilty, God's motive was right and in the very same act He did not become guilty.... (3) God was grieved over men's apostasy (v.7); and their act called forth His divine love. In spite of the sin-inspired situation of Saul, and in fact through it, God ministered a number of deliverances (1 Sam. 9:16; 10:9, 24; 11:13). Saul had thus been a part of God's decree from the first, and He used the wrath of men to praise Him (Ps 76:10).

Ronald E. Clements ("The Deuteronomistic Interpretation of the Founding of the Monarchy in I Sam. VIII," *VT* 24/4 [1974]: 406–7) summarizes:

> The sharpness of the criticism of the kingship expressed here is not in order to reject the institution altogether, which would make nonsense of the sequel in Yahweh's acceding to the request. Rather it is to condemn the precipitate action of the people in pressing their desire, when Yahweh himself was able to do all that was necessary in order to ensure the people's salvation, as the preceding Deuteronomistic narrative of the victory won by Samuel over the Philistines illustrates.

Clearly chs. 8–12 constitute a literary unit, for they are immediately preceded by the formula that marks the end of the story of a judge (7:13–17) and immediately followed by the formula that marks the beginning of the account of a reign (13:1; cf. McCarthy, "The Inauguration of Monarchy," 402). The divisions of the unit (as determined here) alternate between negative and positive attitudes toward monarchy (not as contradictory but as complementary): 8:1–22, negative; 9:1–10:16, positive; 10:17–27, negative; 11:1–11, positive; 11:12–12:25, negative (cf. McCarthy, ibid., 401–2, who characterizes the alternating sections as "reports" and "stories"; for a full discussion of the entire problem, see Vannoy, 197–239).

1. The Demand for a King (8:1–22)

[1]When Samuel grew old, he appointed his sons as judges for Israel. [2]The name of his
firstborn was Joel and the name of his second was Abijah, and they served at Beersheba.
[3]But his sons did not walk in his ways. They turned aside after dishonest gain and
accepted bribes and perverted justice.

[4]So all the elders of Israel gathered together and came to Samuel at Ramah. [5]They said
to him, "You are old, and your sons do not walk in your ways; now appoint a king to lead
us, such as all the other nations have."

[6]But when they said, "Give us a king to lead us," this displeased Samuel; so he prayed
to the LORD. [7]And the LORD told him: "Listen to all that the people are saying to you; it is not
you they have rejected, but they have rejected me as their king. [8]As they have done from
the day I brought them up out of Egypt until this day, forsaking me and serving other
gods, so they are doing to you. [9]Now listen to them; but warn them solemnly and let them
know what the king who will reign over them will do."
[10]Samuel told all the words of the LORD to the people who were asking him for a king.
[11]He said, "This is what the king who will reign over you will do: He will take your sons and
make them serve with his chariots and horses, and they will run in front of his chariots.
[12]Some he will assign to be commanders of thousands and commanders of fifties, and
others to plow his ground and reap his harvest, and still others to make weapons of war
and equipment for his chariots. [13]He will take your daughters to be perfumers and cooks
and bakers. [14]He will take the best of your fields and vineyards and olive groves and give
them to his attendants. [15]He will take a tenth of your grain and of your vintage and give it
to his officials and attendants. [16]Your menservants and maidservants and the best of your
cattle and donkeys he will take for his own use. [17]He will take a tenth of your flocks, and
you yourselves will become his slaves. [18]When that day comes, you will cry out for relief
from the king you have chosen, and the LORD will not answer you in that day."
[19]But the people refused to listen to Samuel. "No!" they said. "We want a king over us.
[20]Then we will be like all the other nations, with a king to lead us and to go out before us
and fight our battles."
[21]When Samuel heard all that the people said, he repeated it before the LORD. [22]The LORD
answered, "Listen to them and give them a king."
Then Samuel said to the men of Israel, "Everyone go back to his town."

COMMENTARY

1–3 Although Samuel's death is not recorded until 25:1, the narrator begins here to refer to his advanced age (vv.1, 5; 12:2). The old order (of the judges) is passing, the new (of the monarchy) is dawning. That the root *špṭ* ("judge"; GK 9149) appears frequently in this chapter (v.1, "judges"; v.2, "served"; v.3, "justice"; vv.5–6, 20, "lead" ["judge," NIV note]; vv.9, 11, "what ... will do") further strengthens the chapter's function as transitional, as well as linking judgeship closely to the coming monarchy. While Samuel continued as judge at Ramah and nearby towns (7:15–17), he appointed his two sons to serve in the same capacity at Beersheba (v.2) on the southern boundary of the land (cf. 3:20). Their actions and reputations (v.5) belied their names—Joel ("The LORD is God"), Abijah ("My [Divine] Father is the LORD")—but at least their geographical distance from Samuel (Beersheba being about fifty-seven miles south-southwest of Ramah) absolved him from any direct complicity in their evil deeds (so Eslinger, 252).

Whether Samuel should have appointed his sons as judges in the first place is highly questionable, since judgeship was usually a divine charisma (cf. Jdg 2:16, 18; 3:10, 15; 6:12; 11:29; 13:25). In any event, they did not follow in their father's footsteps (v.3). "Turned aside" and "perverted" are identical in the Hebrew text and tie the three sins—"dishonest gain and accepted bribes and perverted justice"—together. Failing to emulate their father (12:3–4) or their God (Dt 10:17), Joel and Abijah accepted bribes, a crime inseparable from the perversion and denial of justice (Pr 17:23). Moses condemned these common offenses again and again (Ex 23:6, 8; Dt 16:18–19; 24:17; 27:19; cf. also Ps 15:5; La 3:35; Am 2:7). Ironically, Samuel's two sons were as wicked in their own way as were Eli's two sons.

4–9 Old men ("elders," v.4) confront an old man (Samuel, v.4) and—perhaps unwittingly—remind him of the cruel parallel between himself and the aged (and now deceased) Eli, Samuel's predecessor as priest and judge (v.5; cf. 2:22). Because of Samuel's age, and because they want nothing to do with a dynastic succession that will include his rebellious sons, the elders in their collective wisdom decide that a king will best suit their needs. "Samuel experiences what Moses, the prophets, and even Jesus experience: 'We do not want this man to reign over us' (Lk 19.14)" (Hertzberg, 72). Samuel had "appointed" his sons as "judges" (v.1); the elders want him to "appoint" a king to "judge" (see NIV note) Israel (v.5). Samuel's reluctant compliance with their request will—ironically—twice include the Hebrew verb "appoint," but in a harsher sense: "make them serve" (v.11), "assign" (v.12).

The elders want a king "such as all the other nations have" (v.5). Verse 20 reveals their hidden agenda: The king will "go out before us and fight our battles." As Robert P. Gordon ("Who Made the Kingmaker?" 257) observes, "in the biblical text it is principally the external pressure exerted by the Philistines to the west, with some Ammonite input from the east, that brings the monarchical question to the fore (8:20; 9:16; 10:1 [LXX], 5–7, and 27)." Israel's elders are looking for a permanent military leader who will build a standing army powerful enough to repulse any invader. Moses clearly foresaw the elders' demand (Dt 17:14) and warned of the grave dangers involved in pursuing such a course of action (Dt 17:15–17). Samuel, fully aware of those dangers, is "displeased" with the elders' request (v.6)—and he is convinced that the Lord too is displeased (12:17; cf. also 15:11).

Nevertheless, Samuel, seeking God's mind in the matter, is doubtless surprised when the Lord tells him to "listen to" (lit., "obey"; vv.7, 9, 22) the people's request mediated through their elders. As in the desert centuries earlier (Ex 16:8), Israel is not rejecting the Lord's chosen leader but the Lord himself (v.7; see also 10:19). Since the days of the exodus—that mighty act of corporate and personal redemption—the people had consistently preferred other gods and other leaders to God himself and his chosen servants (v.8).

But why does the Lord exclude Samuel from the people's rejection in v.7 and then include him in it in v.8? K&D assert that by rejecting Samuel (God's representative), the people are in effect rejecting God himself. That is clearly not the most obvious meaning of the passage, however. Scott L. Harris ("1 Samuel VIII 7–8," *VT* 31/1 [1981]: 79–80) proposes *gm-mlk* ("also a king") instead of *gm-lk* ("also to you") at the end of v.8. The MT error would have occurred by simple haplography (writing once what should have been written twice) of the *m*, and the new reading yields the translation "so they are also making a king." The "now" (*wᵉᶜattâ*) that begins the next verse is then reprised in 10:19b ("so now") and 12:13, both times in contexts that begin—as here—with a rehearsal of Israel's sins during the days of the exodus and conclude with their impetuous demand for a king (10:18–19a; 12:6–12). Although Harris's suggestion lacks textual evidence, the conjectural emendation has much to commend it in the overall context of the larger unit (chs. 8–12).

God, graciously condescending to the people's desire (a desire not in itself wrong but sullied by the motivation behind it), tells Samuel to warn them what the "regulations of the kingship" (10:25; cf. the almost identical phrase in vv.9, 11 ["what the king ... will do"]) will demand of them. The phrase "will reign over them" (vv.9, 11) highlights the loss of freedom in (absolute) monarchy and is a sad commentary on Israel's renunciation of their divine King.

10–18 The "regulations of the kingship" described by Samuel (with God's prompting and approval, v.10) are totally bereft of redeeming features and consist only of oppressive requirements. Among the latter is the corvée (forced labor), including compulsory induction ("make them serve," v.11) of both raw recruits (cf. Saul's policy, 14:52) and laborers in field and foundry (v.12). Although common in the ancient world generally, the corvée was unknown in Israel during the time of the judges and was introduced there under the monarchy (cf. Mendelsohn, 21 n. 33; "On Corvee Labor in Ancient Canaan and Israel," *BASOR* 167 [1962]: 33).

The palace-to-be would acquire horses in great numbers (contrary to Dt 17:16), and the king's chariots would need advance runners (v.11; cf. the practice of Absalom [2Sa 15:1] and Adonijah [1Ki 1:5]). Reference (v.12) to commanders "of thousands and ... of fifties" (probably shorthand for "thousands, hundreds, fifties and tens"; cf. Ex 18:21, 25; Dt 1:15) implies a huge standing army. The term "weapons of war" (v.12) would become so immediately recognizable that David would be able to use it as a figure of speech in his elegy for Saul and Jonathan (2Sa 1:27). Women would not be exempt from conscription into royal service (v.13). Even in desperate times the king would always get his share (Am 7:1)—a minimum of 10 percent of the income from field and flock (vv.15, 17).

Key words in the "regulations of the kingship" are "take" (vv.11, 13–17) and "best" (vv.14, 16). By nature royalty is parasitic rather than giving, and kings are never satisfied with the worst. Although Israelite rulers were prohibited from expropriating family property (cf. Eze 46:18), no such scruples applied to Canaanite rulers—as Ahab learned in the sordid case of Naboth's vineyard (1Ki 21:7). Garsiel, 69–70, observes that although the king "takes" everything, Samuel reminds the people that he himself has "taken" nothing (12:3–4).

Samuel's "regulations of the kingship," which would not benefit the average Israelite, followed contemporary semifeudal Canaanite society. "In view of the evidence from the Akkadian texts from Ugarit it seems obvious that the Samuel summary of 'the manner of the king' does not constitute 'a rewriting of history' by a late opponent of kingship but represents an eloquent appeal to the people by a contemporary of Saul not to impose upon themselves a Canaanite institution alien to their own way of life" (Mendelsohn, 22). Various aspects of the "regulations" would be implemented by Saul (22:6–19) and Absalom (2Sa 15:1–6)—although Solomon would become the most notable offender. In the light of Samuel's own record of fairness and honesty during his judgeship (cf. esp. 12:3–5), it is no wonder that he was alarmed at the prospect of setting up a typical oriental monarchy in Israel.

If the "regulations of the kingship" attained full authority, the average Israelite would soon be little more than a chattel at the disposal of his monarch. The frequent occurrence of *ʿebed* ("servant, slave"; GK 6269) thus sounds an especially ominous note (vv.14–15, "attendants"; v.16, "menservants"; v.17, "slaves"). In v.17 Samuel warned the people that they would "become" their king's "slaves," terminology employed elsewhere of bondage imposed by a conqueror (17:9, "become ... subjects"; 27:12, "be ... servant"; 2Sa 8:2, 6, "became subject to"). Too late the Israelites would cry out to a God who would not answer (v.18)—unlike the days when Samuel was judge (7:8–9).

19–22 Samuel's best efforts were futile. Despite his totally negative delineation of the royal "regulations," the people refused to "listen to" (i.e., "obey," v.19; see comment on v.7) him. They wanted a king—a demand that Samuel hurled back in their teeth twice in the context of their rejection of divine rule (10:19; 12:12). They clung doggedly to their original request (v.5): "We [emphatic in Heb.] will be like all the other [pagan] nations" (v.20). The implicit military component of their idea of monarchy now becomes explicit: Their king will "fight our battles"—although a godly Israelite king would know from the outset that it was the Lord's joyful duty to do just that for his people (2Ch 32:8).

As the Lord had told Samuel earlier (v.7), so he tells him now: "Listen to [= obey] them and give them a king" (v.22). On that negative (for Samuel) note this chapter ends and Samuel's farewell oration to Israel begins (12:1).

The eight speeches in ch. 8 constitute a remarkable chiasm in which the second element in each pair reverses the roles of speaker and addressee:

- A The people to Samuel (v.5)
  - B Samuel to the Lord (v.6)
    - C The Lord to Samuel (vv.7–9)
      - D Samuel to the people (vv.10–18)
      - D' The people to Samuel (vv.19–20)
    - C' Samuel to the Lord (v.21)
  - B' The Lord to Samuel (v.22a)
- A' Samuel to the people (v.22b)

Eslinger, 258–59, helpfully notes:

> At the centre of this inversion we see that the opposition between two groups is really between Samuel and the people—not between the people and Yahweh as would be expected. The structural opposition supports and confirms a fact that appears during the course of the unfolding dialogue: Yahweh, though not liking the request, does not deny it; instead, he simply subverts it.

NOTES

2 The names of Samuel's two sons occur again only in 1 Chronicles 6:28, 33 (both in v.28, Joel alone in v.33). In 1 Chronicles 6:28 the word יוֹאֵל (*yôʾēl*, "Joel") was omitted in Hebrew manuscripts (see NIV note) after the word שְׁמוּאֵל (*šᵉmûʾēl*, "Samuel") due to the scribal error known as *homoioteleuton* ("same ending").

6 Except for the change of verb, "Give us a king to lead us" is a verbatim citation of "Appoint a king to lead us" (v.5). The Bible often follows the practice, common in the ancient world, of approximating direct quotations instead of citing *ipsissima verba*.

16 In the context, "cattle" rather than "young men" (see NIV note) is clearly the better reading. The MT's בַּחוּרֵיכֶם הַטּוֹבִים (*baḥûrêkem haṭṭôbîm*, "the best of your young men") perhaps arose under the influence of בָּחוּר וָטוֹב (*bāḥûr wāṭôb*, "an impressive young man," 9:2). The word "best" modifies only "cattle/young men" in the MT; the NIV's extension to "donkeys" is contextually apt.

2. The Anointing of Saul (9:1–10:16)

[1]There was a Benjamite, a man of standing, whose name was Kish son of Abiel, the son of Zeror, the son of Becorath, the son of Aphiah of Benjamin. [2]He had a son named Saul, an impressive young man without equal among the Israelites — a head taller than any of the others.

[3]Now the donkeys belonging to Saul's father Kish were lost, and Kish said to his son Saul, "Take one of the servants with you and go and look for the donkeys." [4]So he passed through the hill country of Ephraim and through the area around Shalisha, but they did not find them. They went on into the district of Shaalim, but the donkeys were not there. Then he passed through the territory of Benjamin, but they did not find them.

[5]When they reached the district of Zuph, Saul said to the servant who was with him, "Come, let's go back, or my father will stop thinking about the donkeys and start worrying about us."

[6]But the servant replied, "Look, in this town there is a man of God; he is highly respected, and everything he says comes true. Let's go there now. Perhaps he will tell us what way to take."

[7]Saul said to his servant, "If we go, what can we give the man? The food in our sacks is gone. We have no gift to take to the man of God. What do we have?"

[8]The servant answered him again. "Look," he said, "I have a quarter of a shekel of silver. I will give it to the man of God so that he will tell us what way to take." [9](Formerly in Israel, if a man went to inquire of God, he would say, "Come, let us go to the seer," because the prophet of today used to be called a seer.)

[10]"Good," Saul said to his servant. "Come, let's go." So they set out for the town where the man of God was.

[11]As they were going up the hill to the town, they met some girls coming out to draw water, and they asked them, "Is the seer here?"

[12]"He is," they answered. "He's ahead of you. Hurry now; he has just come to our town today, for the people have a sacrifice at the high place. [13]As soon as you enter the town, you will find him before he goes up to the high place to eat. The people will not begin eating until he comes, because he must bless the sacrifice; afterward, those who are invited will eat. Go up now; you should find him about this time."

[14]They went up to the town, and as they were entering it, there was Samuel, coming toward them on his way up to the high place.

[15]Now the day before Saul came, the LORD had revealed this to Samuel: [16]"About this time tomorrow I will send you a man from the land of Benjamin. Anoint him leader over my people Israel; he will deliver my people from the hand of the Philistines. I have looked upon my people, for their cry has reached me."

17When Samuel caught sight of Saul, the LORD said to him, "This is the man I spoke to
you about; he will govern my people."
18Saul approached Samuel in the gateway and asked, "Would you please tell me where
the seer's house is?"
19"I am the seer," Samuel replied. "Go up ahead of me to the high place, for today you are
to eat with me, and in the morning I will let you go and will tell you all that is in your heart.
20As for the donkeys you lost three days ago, do not worry about them; they have been
found. And to whom is all the desire of Israel turned, if not to you and all your father's
family?"
21Saul answered, "But am I not a Benjamite, from the smallest tribe of Israel, and is not
my clan the least of all the clans of the tribe of Benjamin? Why do you say such a thing
to me?"
22Then Samuel brought Saul and his servant into the hall and seated them at the head
of those who were invited—about thirty in number. 23Samuel said to the cook, "Bring the
piece of meat I gave you, the one I told you to lay aside."
24So the cook took up the leg with what was on it and set it in front of Saul. Samuel said,
"Here is what has been kept for you. Eat, because it was set aside for you for this occasion,
from the time I said, 'I have invited guests.'" And Saul dined with Samuel that day.
25After they came down from the high place to the town, Samuel talked with Saul on
the roof of his house. 26They rose about daybreak and Samuel called to Saul on the roof,
"Get ready, and I will send you on your way." When Saul got ready, he and Samuel went
outside together. 27As they were going down to the edge of the town, Samuel said to
Saul, "Tell the servant to go on ahead of us"—and the servant did so—"but you stay here
awhile, so that I may give you a message from God."
10:1Then Samuel took a flask of oil and poured it on Saul's head and kissed him, saying,
"Has not the LORD anointed you leader over his inheritance? 2When you leave me today,
you will meet two men near Rachel's tomb, at Zelzah on the border of Benjamin. They will
say to you, 'The donkeys you set out to look for have been found. And now your father
has stopped thinking about them and is worried about you. He is asking, "What shall I do
about my son?"'
3"Then you will go on from there until you reach the great tree of Tabor. Three men
going up to God at Bethel will meet you there. One will be carrying three young goats,
another three loaves of bread, and another a skin of wine. 4They will greet you and offer
you two loaves of bread, which you will accept from them.
5"After that you will go to Gibeah of God, where there is a Philistine outpost. As you
approach the town, you will meet a procession of prophets coming down from the high
place with lyres, tambourines, flutes and harps being played before them, and they will be
prophesying. 6The Spirit of the LORD will come upon you in power, and you will prophesy

with them; and you will be changed into a different person. [7]Once these signs are fulfilled,
do whatever your hand finds to do, for God is with you.
[8]"Go down ahead of me to Gilgal. I will surely come down to you to sacrifice burnt offerings and fellowship offerings, but you must wait seven days until I come to you and tell
you what you are to do."
[9]As Saul turned to leave Samuel, God changed Saul's heart, and all these signs were fulfilled that day. [10]When they arrived at Gibeah, a procession of prophets met him; the Spirit
of God came upon him in power, and he joined in their prophesying. [11]When all those who
had formerly known him saw him prophesying with the prophets, they asked each other,
"What is this that has happened to the son of Kish? Is Saul also among the prophets?"
[12]A man who lived there answered, "And who is their father?" So it became a saying: "Is
Saul also among the prophets?" [13]After Saul stopped prophesying, he went to the high place.
[14]Now Saul's uncle asked him and his servant, "Where have you been?"
"Looking for the donkeys," he said. "But when we saw they were not to be found, we
went to Samuel."
[15]Saul's uncle said, "Tell me what Samuel said to you."
[16]Saul replied, "He assured us that the donkeys had been found." But he did not tell his
uncle what Samuel had said about the kingship.

COMMENTARY

1–2 Scholarly studies of Saul, the first king of Israel, have depicted him as (among other things) villain, tragic figure, flawed ruler, naive farm boy, degenerate madman, fate-driven pawn, reluctant king—the list goes on and on. Such characterizations are at least partially true; Saul is surely one of the most complex persons described in Scripture.

Notice that almost all the above portrayals are decidedly negative. Historically, writers have focused on the darker side of Saul's nature. While not wishing to deny that side, I am sympathetic with those scholars (still in the minority, to be sure) who attempt to portray Saul more fairly by means of a closer reading of the text itself. Fresh winds are blowing in Saulide scholarship, and Israel's first king is undergoing a long-overdue rehabilitation. Although at times moody, impulsive, suspicious, violent, insincerely remorseful, out of control, and disobedient to God, at other times he was kind, thoughtful, generous, courageous, very much in control, and willing to obey God. My commentary from this point to the end of 2 Samuel 1, while by no means neglecting Saul's undoubted negative qualities and actions, will nevertheless praise him wherever justified.

Humphreys, 95–117, outlines the biblical story of Saul as a drama in three acts: Saul becomes king (essentially chs. 9–14), Saul is rejected (essentially chs. 15–27), and denouement (essentially chs. 28–31). The progressive deterioration in Saul's character and career, clear enough in the basic outline, becomes even more evident as the parallel scenes in each act unfold (the divisions and basic titles are essentially those of Humphreys, 98; the elaborations are mine):

Act I, Scene 1: Saul meets Samuel, who anoints him (9:3–10:16)
Act II, Scene 1: Saul meets Samuel, who condemns him (ch. 15)
Act III, Scene 1: Saul meets Samuel, who dooms him (ch. 28)
Act I, Scene 2: Success in battle, with the help of God (ch. 11)
Act II, Scene 2: Success in battle, with the help of David (chs. 17–18)
Act III, Scene 2: Suicide in battle (ch. 31)
Act I, Scene 3: Saul's failure, before Samuel and Jonathan (chs. 13–14)
Act II, Scene 3: Saul's failure, before David (chs. 19–26)

For Humphreys' fuller summary, see his p. 98.

As Samuel's father, Elkanah, was given a formal and stereotyped introduction in 1:1 (see comment there), so Saul's father, Kish, is introduced in a strikingly similar way in 9:1. To highlight the comparison even further, a few Hebrew manuscripts add *ʾeḥād* ("certain"; see 1:1) before "Benjamite." David is later given a similar formal introduction, though much abbreviated (17:12). Kish is called a "man of standing," a characteristic title used also of Boaz (Ru 2:1) and Jeroboam I (1Ki 11:28). The term often has military connotations and is translated "brave man" in Saul's servant's description of David (16:18). It is nowhere used of Saul himself. The names of the ancestors of Kish are undistinguished; most are not found elsewhere, the only exception being Abiel (see 1Ch 11:32). The family line is from Benjamin, the smallest of the tribes. Israel's first king came from these humble origins.

The Hebrew root for the name "Saul," which means "Asked (of God)," occurs in 8:10, where the people were "asking" for a king (cf. Notes on 1:20 concerning "given" in 1:28). "Though God actually appointed Saul, Saul did not in the final analysis represent God's choice, but the people's choice.... The Israelites ... wanted ... one who was grand in appearance and in whom they could rejoice with fleshly pride (1Sa 8:20). So God picked for them the man who in all Israel came nearest to fulfilling their idea of what a king should be" (G. Coleman Luck, "The First Glimpse of the First King of Israel," *BSac* 123 [1966]: 61). As another Saul (Ac 13:9) later summarized: "The people asked for a king, and [God] gave them Saul son of Kish" (Ac 13:21). A name closely related to that of Saul is Shealtiel ("I Have Asked of God"), a descendant of David and ancestor of Jesus (Mt 1:12).

Saul is introduced as an "impressive young man" (v.2). The Hebrew adjective is *ṭôb* ("good"), translated "handsome" with respect to David when he is introduced into the narrative (16:12). It is also used of the baby Moses ("fine") at his introduction (Ex 2:2).

In v.2 *ṭôb* is used again of Saul: He was "without equal" (lit., there was "none better than he") among the Israelites. That would eventually change, however; his kingdom would be torn from him and given to "one better than" he—to David (15:28). Since the word originally meant "good" in general and "good-looking" only by extension, it is a "two-faced epithet. Does Saul owe his election to his being the best or the best-looking of the Israelites? Since the two possibilities are compatible ... the question remains submerged for the time being" (Sternberg, 355).

Saul was also "a head taller" than his fellow Israelites (v.2), a characteristic noteworthy enough to be mentioned again (10:23–24). Of regal stature, he had the potential of being every inch a king. Saul's subsequent failure as king makes the well-known divine admonition in 16:7 all the more poignant: "Do not consider his appearance or his height, for I have rejected him." An attractive appearance is desirable, of course, especially in leaders (cf. Ge 39:6 of Joseph; 2Sa 14:25 of Absalom). Luck observes ("First Glimpse," 63) that another Saul (also from Benjamin), though lacking the externals (2Co 10:10), possessed the internal, spiritual qualities that made him one of the greatest men who ever lived.

3–14 The Lord used straying donkeys, of all things, to bring Saul into contact with Samuel. The first and last occurrences of the donkeys in this context (v.3; 10:16) serve as a frame for the larger literary unit. A gentle irony: Just as Saul son of Kish was sent to "look for" donkeys that temporarily could not be "found" (vv.3–4, 20; 10:2, 14, 16), so also the people intent on making him king "looked for" the bashful and reluctant Saul son of Kish, who temporarily could not be "found" (10:21; for additional examples of *māṣāʾ* [GK 5162], "find," as a *Leitwort* in chs. 9–10, see M. White, "'The History of Saul's Rise'; Saulide State Propaganda in 1 Samuel 1–14," in *"A Wise and Discerning Mind": Essays in Honor of Burke O. Long*, ed. S. M. Olyan and R. C. Culley [Providence, R.I.: Brown Univ. Press, 2000], 284–85).

Searching for the lost donkeys, Saul and his servant crisscrossed the borderlands between Benjamin and Ephraim, but to no avail (v.4). The locations of Shalisha and Shaalim remain uncertain; the connection, if any, between Shalisha and Baal Shalishah (2Ki 4:42) is equally obscure. Aharoni, 244, suggests that Shaalim and Shalisha are related respectively to Shual and Shilshah, the names of Asherite clans (1Ch 7:30, 36–37) "associated with the border districts of Benjamin and Ephraim" (for a region named Shual, cf. also 13:17). It is also possible that the names of two relatively unknown regions were chosen because of their euphony with the name *šāʾûl* ("Saul").

Because the "hill country of Ephraim" (v.4) was a relatively large area, we cannot be sure of the route taken by Saul and the servant. But they began and ended their search there since the "district of Zuph" (v.5; better, "district of the Zuphite clan"; for details see R. Callaway, "The Name Game: Onomastic Evidence and Archaeological Reflections on Religion in Late Judah," *Jian Dao* 11 [1999]: 27) is associated with the hill country of Ephraim in 1:1 (see Notes there). The unnamed town in v.6 is therefore probably Ramah.

Saul, not wishing to cause his father needless worry, wants to give up the search and return to Benjamin (v.5). The servant, however, points out that there is a "man of God" nearby who might be able to tell them which route to take to complete their mission (v.6). The servant appears to be more persistent and imaginative than Saul himself (cf. also v.8)—a fact that may not speak well for Saul's future attempts at leadership. Although the man of God is not named at first (probably to heighten suspense), we are later informed that he is indeed Samuel (v.14).

The term "man of God," common in the OT, is also found occasionally elsewhere in the ancient Near East (see comment on 2:27). Generally in Israel (but cf. its application to David in 2Ch 8:14) it is synonymous with "prophet" or "seer" (e.g., Moses [Dt 33:1]; Elijah [1Ki 17:18]; Elisha [2Ki 4:16]), as in vv.9–10. The true man of God can be characterized as a man of virtue (he is "highly respected" [v.6], a description applied to David in 22:14; cf. the sarcastic use of the same Heb. verb by Michal in 2Sa 6:20 ["has distinguished himself"], followed by David's devastating reply to her in v.22, concluding with the same verb: "I will be held in honor"). The true man of God is also, equally appropriately, a man of victory ("everything he says comes true," v.6; cf., with respect to Samuel, 3:19: The Lord "let none of his words fall to the ground").

Saul continued to protest (v.7), reminding the servant that they had no gift for the prophet; their "sacks" (lit., "vessels"; the word *kᵉlî* usually refers to solid containers, less frequently to bags or sacks [e.g., 17:40, 49; Ge 42:25]) were empty. When consulting a prophet, it was common courtesy to bring a gift (Am 7:12), whether modest (1Ki 14:3) or lavish (2Ki 8:8–9). The prophet, of course, reserved the right to refuse it (2Ki 5:15–16). Obviously the custom suffered considerable abuse (Jer 6:13; 8:10; Eze 22:25 [see NIV note]; Mic 3:5, 11).

The servant responded that he had "a quarter of a shekel of silver" to give to the prophet (v.8). Although coinage was not invented until the seventh century BC, it is likely that much earlier there were pieces of silver of fixed weight (in this case, about three grams; see NIV note) for use in trade and commerce (cf. Baruch Kanael, "Ancient Jewish Coins and Their Historical Importance," *BA* 26/2 [1963]: 39).

Verses 9–10 bring together in one place the three main terms to describe the prophetic office: "seer," "prophet," "man of God." The narrator has chosen an especially appropriate context for doing so, since Samuel is often (and fittingly) called the "last of the judges and first of the prophets"—the latter in the sense that the formal office of prophet began with the monarchy and ended shortly after the monarchy did (for Samuel's unique role, cf. 2Ch 35:18; Ps 99:6; Jer 15:1; and esp. Ac 3:24; 13:20; Heb 11:32).

Verse 9 has been called the only example in the OT of semantic change (explanatory substitution of one word for another): "The prophet of today used to be called a seer"; cf. Weinberg, 185–86. The word "seer" translates two different Hebrew words: *rōʾeh* as here, and *ḥōzeh*. Although the latter appears to be the more technical synonym for "prophet" (its cognate nouns are used almost exclusively in the sense of "[divine communication through] vision/revelation"), the two words for "seer" are used interchangeably (cf. esp. Isa 30:10, where they appear in parallel lines and where, to avoid redundancy in English, *ḥōzîm* is rendered "prophets"). *Rōʾeh* was not completely replaced by "prophet" (cf. the MT of Isa 30:10). In addition to the present context, Samuel is called a seer also in 1 Chronicles 9:22; 26:28; and *ḥōzeh* and "prophet" both describe Gad in 2 Samuel 24:11.

"Seer" means just what its Hebrew (and English) root implies: one who sees—but with spiritual eyes—beneath the surface of the obvious, focusing on the divine dimension. A seer was a man of (spiritual) vision (cf. Isa 1:1; 6:1–5; Jer 1:11–19; Am 7:7–9; 8:1–2; Zec 1:7–6:8).

The word "prophet" (*nābîʾ*; GK 5566) occurs more than three hundred times in the OT. The prophet, more specifically, was "called" in the sense of being "summoned by God to be a spokesman for God" (cf. Ex 7:1–2, where Aaron is called Moses' "prophet" just as Moses is God's prophet [who says everything God commands him to say], and Ex 4:16, where it is said of Aaron: "He will speak to the people for you, and it will be as if he were your mouth and as if you were God to him"). The prophet was to be God's "mouth"; that was his "calling." In other words, the prophet, as God's spokesman, was a man (or woman, several prophetesses being attested in the OT) of vocation. Prophecy was by calling, not by choice. It is therefore not surprising that prophetic-call narratives play such a prominent role in the Bible (e.g., Ex 3:1–4:17, Moses; 1Sa 3:4–18; Isa 6; Jer 1:4–19; Eze 1–3; Hos 1:2–3:5; Am 7:14–15; Jnh 1:1–2; 3:1–2).

Saul and his servant went "up the hill" (v.11) to the town (likely Ramah, which means "height"). It was early evening, since some girls were coming out to the well to draw water (see Ge 24:11;

cf. also v.19). When asked whether the seer was there, they informed the men that he had arrived only recently to participate in a sacrificial ritual at the *bāmâ* ("high place," v.12). Almost always on conspicuous elevations and often located outside town (vv.14, 25), high places were open-air sanctuaries, sometimes with shrines or other buildings (v.22), where worship was conducted. The Lord was occasionally worshiped there (as here; cf. also 1Ki 3:2, 4–5), but their habitual use for idolatry and other pagan practices (1Ki 12:31–32) brought them under divine condemnation (1Ki 13:1–2). Kings of the divided monarchy were often judged by whether they had destroyed the high places (cf. 2Ki 12:1–3; 14:1–4; 18:1–4; 23:4–15). The association of high places with idolatry had contributed to the divine rejection of Shiloh and the capture of the ark (Ps 78:58–61).

Verses 12–13 are charged with urgency: "He's ahead of you. Hurry now; he has just come.... Go up now." The same is true of 13:8–9, where Saul's impatience compels him to act precipitously. Then, just as "he finished making the offering, Samuel arrived" (13:10). Gunn (*The Fate of King Saul*, 62) astutely observes: "Saul's haste in the one scene leads to success, in the other to disaster. In chapter 13 he decides to wait no longer for the prophet. The remark in chapter 9 comes back to haunt us: 'for the people will not eat till he comes, since he must bless the sacrifice.'"

H. Mowvley ("The Concept and Content of 'Blessing' in the Old Testament," *BT* 16 [1965]: 78) sees an act of consecration in v.13: "In blessing the sacrifice Samuel set it apart for divine use." Baruch M. Bokser ("*Maᶜal* and Blessings over Food: Rabbinic Transformation of Cultic Terminology and Alternative Modes of Piety," *JBL* 100/4 [1981]: 557) more appropriately understands the expression to refer to a blessing said before eating food that happened to be part of a sacrificial animal about to be offered to the Lord. Such thanksgiving prayers became more common during the intertestamental period and are reflected in the NT as well (Mt 26:26–27; Mk 6:41; 8:6–7; Lk 24:30).

15–24 Bruce C. Birch ("The Development of the Tradition on the Anointing of Saul in I Sam 9:1–10:16," *JBL* 90/1 [1971]: 55–68) believes that v.15 begins a modified version of the formal literary structure known as the "call narrative" (often used to describe the calls of the classical prophets). The elements in this case are (1) divine confrontation (v.15); (2) introductory word (vv.16–17); (3) objection (v.21); (4) commission (10:1); (5) sign (10:1 [reading with the LXX; cf. NIV note], 5–7a; (6) reassurance (10:7b). The divine encounter with Saul was mediated through Samuel, to whom the Lord had "revealed" (lit., "uncovered the ear of," as though to speak in secret; v.15) his will (the same idiom used of David in 2Sa 7:27; 1Ch 17:25).

As Birch points out, the language of 10:1 (if the longer LXX reading is followed; cf. NIV note) is largely paralleled in 9:16–17, which constitute the introductory word of the call narrative. As an act of gracious condescension to the people's request (Ac 13:21), the Lord would send an obscure Benjamite to Samuel (v.16), emphasizing the divine initiative in the matter. Samuel was to "anoint" him (with olive oil; cf. 10:1; also 15:1, 17; with respect to David, see 16:3, 12–13; 2Sa 2:4, 7; 3:39; 5:3, 17; 12:7); the verb is *māšaḥ* from which *māšîaḥ* ("anointed [one], messiah") is derived.

Anointing was by prophet and/or people, both acting as agents of the Lord (cf. in David's case 16:12–13; 2Sa 2:4; 5:3). It symbolized the coming of the Holy Spirit in power (16:13; Isa 61:1–3). (For a thorough study see E. Kutsch, *Salbung als Rechtsakt im Alten Testament und im alten Orient* [BZAW 88; Berlin: Topelmann, 1963].) Especially at the beginning of the monarchy, anointing was to the office of *nāgîd* ("leader, ruler") rather than *melek* ("king";

cf. v.16; 10:1; of David, cf. 13:14; 25:30; 2Sa 5:2; 6:21; 7:8). Beyond the likelihood that it represents Samuel's understandable reluctance to establish a full-fledged kingship (with all its negative implications; cf. again 8:10–18), the term *nāgîd* (lit., "[one] given prominence, [one] placed in front") might have been a title for "king-designate, king-elect" (cf. 2Ch 11:22) with military connotations (v.16).

Communicated in language strongly reminiscent of the exodus (v.16), God had looked on the people of Israel (cf. Ex 2:25), whose cry had reached him (cf. Ex 3:9). The new leader would have the potential of delivering Israel from the Philistines (cf. the earlier flawed strategy of the elders, 4:3)—although some (troublemakers, to be sure) seriously doubted that Saul would be able to accomplish that formidable task (10:27). Blenkinsopp, 145, notes that the Philistines were not subdued during the rest of Samuel's lifetime (7:13; 10:5; 13:3–22; 14:46) and beyond (31:1–10).

The verb *rāʾâ* ("to see"; GK 8011) is prominent in these verses. Samuel the "seer" (vv.18–19) "caught sight of" Saul (v.17), raised up as leader because God had "looked upon" his people (v.16). "This is the man," the Lord said to Samuel (v.17), in a scene that would be replayed with only modest variations a few years later, this time with David as the subject (16:12). The string of parallels can be extended to Isaiah 42:1–4 ("Here is my servant") and John 19:5 ("Here is the man"), 14 ("Here is your king"), all of which refer to Jesus the "Christ," the "Anointed One" par excellence, who neither disappoints nor fails and whose kingdom has no end (Luck, "First Glimpse," 66).

The Lord identified Saul for Samuel (v.17), who then identified himself to Saul (vv.18–19). As the Lord had promised to "send" (v.16) Saul to Samuel, so Samuel would soon "let" Saul "go" (lit., "send" him on his way, v.19, as in v.26; same Heb. root) after his divine commissioning (10:9). Samuel the seer authenticated his prophetic role by revealing Saul's inmost thoughts and relieved Saul's mind by informing him that his father's donkeys had been found (vv.19–20). He then told Saul that all Israel was eagerly awaiting his benevolent reign.

In the manner of Moses (Ex 3:11; 4:10) and Jeremiah (Jer 1:6), Saul respectfully demurs (v.21). He points out that Benjamin, his tribe, was the smallest in all Israel (doubtless due to the terrible massacre decades earlier; cf. Jdg 20:46–48) and that, like Gideon (Jdg 6:15), his clan was the weakest in his tribe. Saul's humility, here and elsewhere (cf. 10:22), was thus in the grand tradition of prophets and judges.

Samuel, however, knowing that Saul was God's choice, brushed aside his objections and led him and his servant into a "hall" in a building on the high place outside Ramah (v.22). The Hebrew word for "hall" (*liškâ*) almost always denotes a room in a sanctuary or temple. Such rooms were normally used as apartments for sanctuary personnel or as storerooms (cf. Ne 10:39; Jer 35:2, 4). The hall at Ramah was large enough to seat thirty people, a figure J. B. Segal, 19, suggests is used to express "minimum decemplurality"—that is, an approximate number in the low tens (cf. Jdg 14:11; 2Sa 23:13, 24; the LXX reads "seventy" here, a somewhat larger approximation).

Saul and his servant, guests of honor, were seated at the head of the table. The special "piece of meat" (v.23) brought to Saul was perhaps the "share" of the sacrifice normally reserved for priests (cf. Lev 7:33, same Heb. word [*mānâ*]; "leg" in v.24 and "thigh" in Lev 7:33 both translate *šôq*). If so, Samuel may have been treating Saul as though he were a fellow priest. It was a special "occasion" (lit., "appointed time," v.24) indeed, a time for celebration—unlike a future "set time" (13:8, 11) when Saul's impatience and disobedience would initiate his downfall (13:13–14).

25–27 After what must have been a sumptuous if solemn meal, eaten in a house of worship on a sacred site, Samuel, Saul, and Saul's servant retired to Ramah and conversed for a while on the "roof" of Samuel's house (v.25). Fateful events, also with profound implications for monarchical rule, would later take place on the "roof" of David's palace (2Sa 11:2; 16:22). But for now Samuel was preparing Saul for his divine commissioning as ruler of Israel. Sleeping overnight on the roof of a house (v.26) is a common practice even today in the Middle East. In ancient times wealthy householders occasionally constructed a small bedroom on the roof to provide comfort, privacy, and protection for their guests (2Ki 4:10).

The following morning Samuel told Saul to dismiss his servant temporarily (v.27; see 10:14). Saul himself, however, was to stay briefly at Ramah (10:2) to receive a communication from God (v.27) and to be anointed leader over the Lord's inheritance (10:1).

10:1–8 Saul's rise to kingship over Israel took place in three distinct stages: He was (1) anointed by Samuel (9:1–10:16), (2) chosen by lot (10:17–27), and (3) confirmed by public acclamation (11:1–15; for a virtually identical analysis, arrived at independently of mine, see V. Philips Long, "How Did Saul Become King? Literary Reading and Historical Reconstruction," in *Faith, Tradition, and History*, ed. A. R. Millard, James K. Hoffmeier, and David W. Baker [Winona Lake, Ind.: Eisenbrauns, 1994], 276–78). Scholarly proclivity to fragment longer texts into shorter ones in a search for earlier documents has tended to parcel out these three accounts into two or more sources. Such a procedure is unnecessary here, however, since the accounts describe three separate actions that are complementary rather than contradictory.

Christian E. Hauer Jr. ("Does 1 Samuel 9:1–11:15 Reflect the Extension of Saul's Dominions?" *JBL* 86/3 [1967]: 306–10) tantalizingly suggests that the stories themselves reflect the successive extensions of Saul's dominion, whether by enthusiastic public approval or by conquest. Corresponding to the above three stages, in Hauer's view the expansion would have been from (1) Gibeah of God to (2) Mizpah to (3) Gilgal (the latter including modest acquisitions in Transjordan as a result of the defeat of the Ammonites). Although one might quibble over details, Hauer's theory has the advantage of being paralleled in the similar successive accessions of David to kingship (Ziklag to Hebron to Jerusalem), involving clear territorial increments.

The Lord had told Samuel to anoint Saul as leader over his people Israel (9:16). Samuel now proceeded to fulfill that command, being careful to inform Saul that the anointing was from the Lord (v.1). The Israelites are here called the Lord's "inheritance" (see also 26:19; 2Sa 20:19; 21:3) in the sense that they inhabited his territorial patrimony and belonged uniquely to him as Creator, Redeemer, and Conqueror (Dt 4:20; 9:26; 32:8–9; Ps 78:70–71). The anointing oil that Samuel poured on Saul's head was a distinctive formula, not to be used for any other purpose (Ex 30:23–33); it was "sacred" oil (Ps 89:20). Samuel also kissed Saul as an act of respect and in recognition of his new role as ruler of Israel (cf. Ps 2:11–12).

Zafrira Ben-Barak, 38, has helpfully summarized various aspects and features of the anointing ritual: (1) The anointer of the chosen one is either a prophet or a priest (or both, as here; cf. 16:13; 1Ki 1:39; 2Ki 9:1–6; 11:12); (2) the chosen one was sometimes anointed privately (9:25–10:1; 2Ki 9:6), with public acclaim coming only later; (3) *nāgîd* ("ruler, leader") was often the title conferred by this act (v.1; 13:14; 2Sa 5:2–3; 1Ki 1:35); (4) the anointing oil was poured from a flask or horn (v.1; 16:13; 1Ki 1:39; 2Ki 9:1).

The expansionist LXX text of 10:1 (see NIV note) calls for a "sign" (singular) confirming the Lord's choice of Saul as authenticated by his anointing. Verses 7 and 9, however, speak of "signs" (plural)—of which there were three. The first (v.2) was the promise that Saul would "meet" (the root is *māṣāʾ* [GK 5162], which figures prominently throughout the rest of this section: "found" [v.2]; "meet" [v.3]; "finds" [v.7]; cf. also the comment on "found" at 9:3) two men who would verify that Kish's donkeys had indeed been found and that therefore Saul's father could now devote his attention to his son's welfare.

The second sign (vv.3–4) was that three men would meet Saul and offer him two loaves of bread, which he would accept. Like Moses before them (Ex 19:3), the men were "going up to God" to worship and commune with him. On their way they would "greet" Saul (lit., "ask concerning" his "well-being/welfare," the same idiom used in 17:22; 30:21; 2Sa 8:10; cf. 25:5–6). The verbal root is *šāʾal* ("ask"), yet another example of the familiar pun on the name *šāʾûl* ("Saul").

The third and final sign (vv.5–7), because of its significance, is described at greater length. Whereas the first sign involved two men and the second involved three men, the third focused on a "procession"—a larger band or group—of prophets (vv.5, 10). Saul would meet them outside "Gibeah of God" (v.5), so-called perhaps because a high place was nearby. The location of a "Philistine outpost" there identifies it with Geba in Benjamin (13:3), modern Jeba, about five miles north-northeast of Jerusalem (cf. Aharoni, 275, 286, 317 n. 2; for an unsuccessful attempt to locate "Gibeah of God" at Gibeon, cf. Aaron Demsky, "Geba, Gibeah, and Gibeon—An Historico-Geographic Riddle," *BASOR* 212 [1973]: 26–31).

The beginnings of the Israelite monarchy witnessed the emergence of a prophetic movement known as (lit.) "the sons of the prophets" (cf. 1Ki 20:35). "Sons" is used here in the sense of "members of a group," and the NIV therefore often translates this Hebrew idiom as "company of the prophets" (cf. 2Ki 2:3, 5, 7, 15). They served as a refreshing counterpoise to the potential despotism of the monarchy and the tendency toward formalism in the priesthood. The bands or companies (vv.5, 10; 19:20; 2Ki 2:15–17) were often large in number ("fifty," 2Ki 2:7; "one hundred," 1Ki 18:4, 13; 2Ki 4:43). They were frequently associated with time-honored places, often at or near shrines, such as Ramah (19:18–20), Bethel (2Ki 2:3), Jericho (2:5), and Gilgal (4:38).

The characteristic activity of the prophetic bands was "prophesying" (v.5), usually interpreted in these contexts to mean "uttering ecstatic praises/oracles" or the like (BDB, 612; cf. also K&D, Klein). A strong case can be made in vv.5–13 and 19:20–24, however, for the meaning "being in" or "falling into a possession trance":

> In the first passage the behavior is accompanied, perhaps fostered, by music. It is interpreted as a radical transformation of the personality, and may confer extraordinary powers on the person so affected. According to the second it may entail stripping off one's clothes, and may issue in a coma. In both its onset is described as an invasion, or at least as visitation, by a divine spirit. It is a group behavior and is contagious. It seems clear that we have to do with some kind of trance state, or altered state of consciousness. (Simon B. Parker, "Possession Trance and Prophecy in Pre-exilic Israel," *VT* 28/3 [1978]: 272)

In the same article, Parker, 274, notes that studies of similar phenomena in other cultures, both ancient and modern, have shown that possession trance can be either personal/compensatory (as here) or mediumistic (involving communication between God and man or between persons). A classic example of mediumistic possession trance in the eleventh century BC (contemporary with Samuel) is that witnessed by the Egyptian official Wenamun at Byblos in Phoenicia (cf. Hans Goedicke, *The Report of Wenamun* [Baltimore: Johns Hopkins Univ. Press, 1975], 53–57).

Parker ("Possession Trance," 275–78) further observes that possession by "the Spirit of the Lord" (v.6), in whose name Saul has just been anointed leader over Israel (v.1), confirms and legitimates that appointment—a function of possession trance attested elsewhere in the OT (Nu 11:16–17, 24–29) as well as in other cultures. To ask "Is Saul also among the prophets [*nᵉbîʾîm*]?" (vv.11–12), then, is to question his qualifications and legitimacy as Israel's ruler. The denominative verbs *nibbāʾ*/ *hitnabbēʾ* ("act like a prophet or ecstatic"—*nābîʾ*) therefore means either "prophesy" or "be in" or "fall into" a "possession trance," depending on the context.

As in v.5, the actions and activities of prophetic bands elsewhere were sometimes accompanied by music or minstrels (1Ch 13:8; 25:1, 6; Ps 33:2). "Lyres" and "harps" (see also 16:16, 23) render the words *nēbel* (the same word also refers to a "skin" of wine, as in v.3) and *kinnôr* respectively, although some scholars think the English definitions of the two Hebrew words should be reversed. The ancient lyre was a three-to-twelve-stringed instrument played with the fingers or a plectrum, while the harp was much larger, a ten-to-twenty-stringed instrument usually played without a plectrum. The ancient tambourine or timbrel was typically played by women (and therefore not used in temple worship in Israel). It almost certainly did not have small metal disks or rings attached to its frame (cf. David W. Music, "Tabrets," *BI* 10/3 [1984]: 79–81). The flute (or, more precisely, single or double clarinet, oboe, or shawm) had one or more mouthpieces and was played with its shaft(s) extended straight ahead rather than to the side. (For details on these and other instruments, cf. Sellers, 33–47.) All four musical instruments are mentioned in Isaiah 5:12 in a context of drunken banqueting; three of them (plus two more) appear in 2 Samuel 6:5 in a context of joyful celebration before the Lord. As always music could be used for good or ill, which is true of other phenomena associated with prophecy.

Individual or group prophesying, ecstatic or not, was often induced when the Spirit of the Lord came on a person in power (v.6; 19:20, 23; Nu 11:25, 29). At such times the prophet would experience an altered state of consciousness and would be "changed into a different person" (cf. also v.9). Such ecstasy was often contagious (v.10; 19:20–24). Similar ecstatic phenomena, though in a negative sense, were sometimes induced when an "evil" or "injurious" spirit came on a person (18:10; cf. also 16:14–16, 23). Members of prophetic bands were often young (2Ki 5:22; 9:4); they frequently lived together (2Ki 6:1–2), ate together (2Ki 4:38), and were supported by the generosity of their fellow Israelites (2Ki 4:42–43). Such characteristics led the church father Jerome to refer to them as the "monks of the OT"—although celibacy was not a requirement for membership (2Ki 4:1). Samuel provided guidance and direction for the movement in its early stages, as Elijah and Elisha did later. At the head of a particular group of prophets would be the "father" (v.12; 2Ki 2:12) or "leader" (19:20).

The "sons of the prophets" and their distinguished mentors performed yeoman service for their fellow Israelites. They served as counselors of kings, historians of the nation, and instructors of the people (2Ki 4:13; 6:9; 1Ch 29:29). Although they have left us no readily identifiable written legacy, they were the precursors of the classical canonical prophets (Isaiah through Malachi).

Samuel told Saul that after three signs had been fulfilled, he was to do what(ever) his hand found to do (for a staunch defense of "what" instead of the NIV's "whatever" in v.7, see V. Philips Long, "How Did Saul Become King," 275–80), a sound bit of advice strongly recommended by the Teacher (Qoheleth) as well (Ecc 9:10). Samuel assured Saul that God was with him, implying that therefore he could not fail (cf. Jos 1:5).

Then came a sober warning: At a later time Samuel would meet Saul at Gilgal (about eleven miles east-northeast of Gibeah of God) in the Jordan Valley (and therefore "down" with respect to Gibeah; v.8). A preliminary meeting would first be held there to reaffirm Saul's kingship (11:14–15), with the appropriate fellowship offerings and accompanying celebration. Then on a later occasion Samuel would meet Saul again at Gilgal, this time to sacrifice burnt offerings (cf. Lev 1:3–17; 6:8–13) and fellowship offerings (cf. Lev 3:1–17; 7:11–21). On this latter occasion Saul was to wait seven days, until Samuel came and told him what to do. Saul faithfully fulfilled the former obligation (13:8), but impatience got the better of him. He failed to await Samuel's arrival with further instructions, and his act of disobedience was the beginning of the end for his kingdom (13:9–14).

9–16 Meanwhile, however, Saul was open to Samuel's instructions and the Lord's leading. He "turned" to leave (v.9)—literally, "turned his shoulder" to leave, a symbol of having reached the point of no return, whether in resoluteness or retreat (cf. the similar idiom in Ps 21:12, where the Hebrew word for "shoulder" is translated "backs" in context). When he did so, God "changed Saul's heart" (v.9), as Samuel had predicted would happen in connection with the fulfillment of the third sign (v.6). The arrival of Saul and his servant ("they," v.10) at Gibeah of God (cf. v.5) was followed by the Spirit of God's coming on Saul in power, resulting in his joining the prophetic band in their ecstatic behavior. The same powerful accession of God's Spirit would later energize Saul to lead his troops into battle against the Ammonites (11:6).

Gibeah of God (more commonly called Geba, modern Jeba) was scarcely four miles northeast of Gibeah of Saul (more commonly called Gibeah in Benjamin or simply Gibeah, modern Tell el-Ful), the hometown of the new Israelite ruler. When his fellow townsmen learned of Saul's arrival, they turned out in force to see what had happened to the "son of Kish" (v.11). Since the peculiar way of referring here to Saul follows a pattern sometimes used in a disparaging or contemptuous sense (cf. "son of Jesse" used of David [20:27]; "sons of Zeruiah" used of Joab and Abishai [2Sa 16:10]; "son of Remaliah" used of Pekah [Isa 7:4]), Saul's acquaintances may have been insulting him by calling him "son of Kish" (so perhaps BDB). It is more likely, however, that they, longtime residents of the area, knew the young Saul primarily as the son of his father (cf. the detailed discussion of Clines, 282–85). A thousand years later another Prophet, the "carpenter's son," would be similarly criticized by his fellow citizens and would declare himself to be "without honor"—and that "in his hometown and in his own house" (Mt 13:53–57).

In any case, the following sentence—"Is Saul also among the [ecstatic] prophets?" (v.11)—is surely to be understood as a rhetorical question demanding a negative answer. The Spirit of the Lord, coming on Saul in power, authenticated him as Israel's next ruler and produced the visible evidences of ecstatic behavior (see comment on v.5). To question the genuineness of that behavior was to question Saul's legitimacy in his new office. John Sturdy's suggestion ("The Original Meaning of 'Is Saul Also Among the Prophets?' [1 Samuel x 11, 12; xix 24]," *VT* 20/2 [1970]: 206–13) that the saying represents later Davidic propaganda against Saul is based on its supposedly late and legendary setting and is thus unverifiable conjecture.

A. S. Herbert ("The 'Parable' [*Māšāl*] in the Old Testament," *SJT* 7/2 [1954]: 182–83) points out that the "saying" (*māšāl*, "proverb, parable," v.12) reported here and in 19:24 is not a typical example of popular wisdom. It is a scornful phrase and should be understood as such. Other popular proverbs used in similarly mocking or despondent ways are recorded in Ezekiel 12:22–23 and 18:2–3.

In terms of literary structure, the use of this particular proverb in vv.11–12 and then later in 19:24 brackets the narrative at the descriptions of Saul's first and last encounters with the Spirit of God. "The first comes just before he attains kingship, the last just before his full descent from kingship into madness and death" (Humphreys, 97 n. 41).

"And who is their father?" (v.12) was asked to find out the identity of the leader of the "procession of prophets" (vv.5, 10; cf. 2Ki 2:12). Although perhaps prompted by the reference to Saul as "son of Kish" (v.11), the question was not so banal as to be requesting information about Saul's physical paternity (despite ancient versional support for the reading "his" instead of "their"—in which case the inquirer would still have been asking about the identity of Saul's spiritual father).

Verses 14–16 conclude the theme of Kish's concern for Saul's whereabouts and welfare (see v.2; 9:5). Saul's "uncle" (v.14; the word specifically means "father's brother") was doubtless seeking information for Kish and himself. Although the uncle is not identified by name here, he may have been Ner the father of Abner, later the commander of Saul's army (14:50–51). The story of finding Kish's lost donkeys is once again related, but Saul did not tell his uncle anything about Samuel's view of kingship or his own participation in it (v.16; cf. 8:6–22). Rule over Israel would soon be his in truth (11:14), but it would not be long before he would be convinced that he was about to lose it to a man after God's own heart (18:8).

NOTES

7 תְּשׁוּרָה (*tᵉšûrâ*, "gift") is not found elsewhere; its meaning has been determined by context. Mitchell Dahood suggests "food for a journey," deriving it from Hebrew-Ugaritic *š(w)r* ("to travel"; "Hebrew-Ugaritic Lexicography XI," *Bib* 54/3 [1973]: 354; "Hebrew-Ugaritic Lexicography XII," *Bib* 55/3 [1974]: 392–93). Shalom M. Paul ("1 Samuel 9:7: An Interview Fee," *Bib* 59/4 [1978]: 542–44), agreeing with several earlier Jewish commentators that the word is derived from שׁוּר (*šûr*, "to see") and therefore means "interview fee," substantiates that derivation by comparing Akkadian *nāmurtu/tāmartu* ("audience fee, interview present") from *amāru* ("to see"). Since the Akkadian noun had that meaning in the twelfth century BC, the comparison with its Hebrew semantic equivalent is especially appropriate.

9 Although we cannot be certain, the Hebrew word נָבִיא (*nābîʾ*, "prophet"; GK 5566) may be a Qal passive participle from a verbal root cognate to Akkadian *nabû* ("to summon, call a person [to exercise a function], to appoint a person to an office"; *CAD* 11/1 [1980]: 35–37). The Akkadian adjective *nabû/nabīu* means simply "called" (*CAD* 11/1 [1980]: 31). Recently published texts from Mari and Emar in second-millennium-BC Syria, however, provide evidence that the Hebrew word may be a Qal active participle, yielding the meaning "speaker, spokesperson, one who invokes the name of" or the like (for details see Daniel E. Fleming, "The Etymological Origins of the Hebrew *nābîʾ*: The One Who Invokes God," *CBQ* 55/2 [1993]: 217–24). John Briggs Curtis ("A Folk Etymology of *Nābîʾ*" *VT* 29/4 [1979]: 491–93) had suggested that v.7, where נָבִיא (*nābî*ʾ) is a Hiphil first person plural imperfect ("we bring/give") of בּוֹא (*bô*ʾ, "to enter"), provides us with a folk etymology of its homograph in v.9. *Nābî*ʾ in the sense of "prophet" would then have popularly meant something like a "person to whom we bring gifts to obtain oracles." It is much more likely, however, that the form in v.7 resulted from the narrator's indulging his love of wordplay or punning, a common phenomenon in the OT (cf. 25:25; for selected examples see Weinberg, 198–200).

24 הֶעָלֶיהָ (*heʿāleyhā*, "what was on it") is a grammatical anomaly, being the only known OT instance of a preposition preceded by a definite article functioning as a relative pronoun (BDB, 209). The form is therefore commonly emended to הָאַלְיָה (*hāʾalyâ*, "the fat tail"). Every occurrence of the latter, however (Ex 29:22; Lev 3:9; 7:3; 8:25; 9:19), is in a sacrificial context; the fat tail was always offered to the Lord, never eaten as part of a meal. 4QSamuel[a] reads [ה]עלינה (*[h]ʿlynh*, "the upper"; McCarter, *I Samuel*, 170), which could conceivably modify the preceding הַשּׁוֹק (*haššôq*, "the thigh," a feminine noun; see Lev 7:33). But since the "upper thigh" is not attested as a cut of meat elsewhere, it is best to read with the MT here.

10:1 In 1988 archaeologists uncovered in the bottom of a three-foot-deep pit near Qumran, at the northwestern end of the Dead Sea, a five-inch-diameter clay flask wrapped in a nest of palm fibers and containing a small amount of well-preserved reddish oil, probably distilled from balsam. Dating from the first century AD, the oil may be the only surviving sample of its kind and may be similar to that used to anoint ancient Israelite kings (cf. provisionally *Los Angeles Times*, San Diego edition, 16 [1989], Part I: 11; *National Geographic* 176/4 [1989]: 562; and especially Joseph Patrich, "Hideouts in the Judean Wilderness," *BAR* 15/5 [1989]: 34–35).

2 The location of Zelzah, the site of Rachel's tomb, is unknown. Rachel, who died in childbirth, was buried "on the way to Ephrath (that is, Bethlehem)" (Ge 35:19; cf. also 48:7), a reference that describes the location only generally. Jeremiah 31:15 offers no help, since the word "Rachel" there is used metaphorically and Ramah is merely a representative town where some of the exiles were living (Jer 40:1). The shrine enclosing Rachel's tomb on the road northwest of Bethlehem dates only to the Crusader period and in any case is simply a guess as to the tomb's location. Attempts to equate Zelzah with Zela (2Sa 21:14), the site of the tomb of Kish (Saul's father), are philologically unconvincing.

3 Similarly, the location of אֵלוֹן תָּבוֹר (*ʾēlôn tābôr*, "the great tree of Tabor") is unknown. It is tempting to identify it with אַלּוֹן בָּכוּת (*ʾallôn bākût*, "Oak of Weeping" [Ge 35:8, see NIV note), where Rebekah's nurse Deborah (דְּבֹרָה, *d*ᵉ*bōrâ*) was buried, and also with תֹּמֶר דְּבוֹרָה (*tōmer d*ᵉ*bôrâ*, "The Palm of Deborah" [Jdg 4:5]; cf. the punning proximity of הַר תָּבוֹר [*har tābôr*, "Mount Tabor"] in the next verse). As their contexts suggest, all three trees were near Bethel. Proposed connections between any two of the sites, however, are tenuous at best.

5 In 1969 Moshe Dothan excavated a tenth-century BC pottery stand at Ashdod in the first post-Philistine stratum at the site. The stand is decorated with five figures: (1) a tambourine player, (2) a flute player, (3) a lyre player, (4) a woman (musician?), and (5) a male (musician?). Although the interpretation of the last two figures remains uncertain because they are partially destroyed, Dothan immediately noticed the striking relationship between this scene and the one depicted in v.5 (cf. Bathja Bayer, "The Finds That Could Not Be," *BAR* 8/1 [1982]: 32).

14 Except for the poorly supported reading of one or two manuscripts in 27:10 (see BHS there for details), אָן (*ʾān*, "where") is anomalous in v.14. Elsewhere אָנָה (*ʾānâ*) is the normal word used to express "where" in the sense of "whither" (cf. 2Sa 2:1; 13:13). If the vocalization of the MT is incorrect in v.14, one could account for the consonantal text by assuming defective writing of the final long vowel in the original word. It is also possible that the consonantal text simply exhibits the phenomenon of shared consonants, in this case the ה (*h*) at the beginning of the next word doing double duty by being assumed at the end of the MT's אָן (*ʾān*; cf. Watson, 531).

3. The Choice of Saul by Lot (10:17–27)

17Samuel summoned the people of Israel to the Lord at Mizpah 18and said to them, "This
is what the Lord, the God of Israel, says: 'I brought Israel up out of Egypt, and I delivered
you from the power of Egypt and all the kingdoms that oppressed you.' 19But you have
now rejected your God, who saves you out of all your calamities and distresses. And you
have said, 'No, set a king over us.' So now present yourselves before the Lord by your tribes
and clans."
20When Samuel brought all the tribes of Israel near, the tribe of Benjamin was chosen.
21Then he brought forward the tribe of Benjamin, clan by clan, and Matri's clan was chosen.
Finally Saul son of Kish was chosen. But when they looked for him, he was not to be found.
22So they inquired further of the Lord, "Has the man come here yet?"
And the Lord said, "Yes, he has hidden himself among the baggage."
23They ran and brought him out, and as he stood among the people he was a head
taller than any of the others. 24Samuel said to all the people, "Do you see the man the Lord
has chosen? There is no one like him among all the people."
Then the people shouted, "Long live the king!"
25Samuel explained to the people the regulations of the kingship. He wrote them down
on a scroll and deposited it before the Lord. Then Samuel dismissed the people, each to
his own home.
26Saul also went to his home in Gibeah, accompanied by valiant men whose hearts God
had touched. 27But some troublemakers said, "How can this fellow save us?" They despised
him and brought him no gifts. But Saul kept silent.

COMMENTARY

17–24 We have observed that the major literary units comprising the narrative of the rise of Saul (chs. 8–12) alternate between negative (8:1–22; 10:17–27; 11:12–12:25) and positive (9:1–10:16; 11:1–11), the former being antimonarchical and the latter promonarchical. Verses 17–27, though mostly negative, contain certain positive elements (esp. in vv.20–24; cf. Bruce C. Birch, "The Choosing of Saul at Mizpah," *CBQ* 37/4 [1975]: 447–57). Birch, 452–54, appropriately analyzes the literary structure of vv.17–19 as follows: (1) call to assembly (v.17); (2) messenger formula (v.18a); (3) recitation of saving acts (v.18b); (4) accusation (v.19a); (5) announcement (v.19b).

Assembling the Israelites at Mizpah (for probable location, see comments at 7:5), the site of other noteworthy convocations, Samuel addresses them (v.18) in words strongly reminiscent of those of the unnamed prophet in Judges 6:8–9a. The messenger formula identifies the Lord, in expansive terms, as specifically the God of his chosen people Israel. The Lord then speaks in the first person, using the emphatic pronoun "I" (v.18) in strong contrast to the emphatic "But you" of v.19. The familiar exodus-redemption formula is followed by a reminder that God delivered his people not only from Egypt but also from the "kingdoms" (such as Bashan, Nu 32:33; Dt 3:4, 10, 13; cf. also Dt 3:21; 28:25; Jos 11:10) that "oppressed" them (such as Egypt itself [Ex 3:9]; Canaan [Jdg 4:3]; Sidon, Amalek, Maon [Jdg 10:12]; cf. Jdg 2:18).

Although the Lord has saved them out of all their "calamities and distresses" (v.19; for the same Hebrew expression, see Dt 31:17, 21, "disasters and difficulties"; Ps 71:20, "troubles many and bitter"), they have rejected him (echoing 8:7; cf. also Nu 11:20). The Israelites continued to insist in no uncertain terms that they wanted a king (see 8:5, 19)—a demand not outside God's will (Dt 17:14–15) but one sinfully motivated. Samuel, reluctantly acquiescing, told the people to present themselves before the Lord (cf. the assembly at Shechem after Joshua's conquest of Canaan [Jos 24:1]) by their tribes and clans.

The procedure of casting sacred lots, here to pinpoint Saul as Israel's king (vv.20–21; cf. also 14:41–42), was used earlier to isolate Achan as the thief of Israel's plunder (Jos 7:14–18; the Hebrew verb translated "chosen" here is rendered "taken" there). The lots, known as Urim ("Curses," providing negative responses) and Thummim ("Perfections," providing positive responses), were stored in the breastplate attached to the ephod of the high priest (Ex 28:28–30) and were brought out and cast whenever a simple "yes" or "no" would suffice (as here, where the process of elimination could be used effectively; cf. also 23:2, 4, 9, 11–12; Nu 27:21). Although casting lots was perhaps not unlike throwing dice, the results were not left to chance since God himself guided the decisions (Pr 16:33). Verses 20–21 show that Benjamin was chosen by lot from the twelve tribes, Matri (unknown elsewhere) from the Benjamite clans, and Saul—God's man for this season—from the Matrite families. Ironically, like the lost donkeys that had earlier consumed so much anxious time for their searchers (9:3–5, 20; 10:2, 14–16), "when they looked for [Saul], he was not to be found" (v.21).

Another divine oracle was therefore necessary, but this time the question demanded more than a "yes" or "no" answer. So in a more direct way the people "inquired" (the root is *šā'al*, another example of the familiar pun on Saul's name) of the Lord to discover Saul's whereabouts. The reluctant "leader" was subsequently found hiding among the "baggage" (v.22; the Heb. word in this specific sense is elsewhere translated "supplies," always in a military context, perhaps hinting at the major task that the people hoped Saul would enthusiastically assume; cf. 17:22; 25:13; 30:24; Isa 10:28).

Anxious to hail their new king, the people ran to bring him out from his hiding place (v.23). He came out and "stood"—presented himself—in their midst (the verbal root being the same as that translated "present yourselves" in v.19). Saul's impressive height is again stressed, as it had been earlier (9:2)—but the fact that he was "a head taller than any of the others" (v.23) had not kept him from trying to hide himself "among the baggage" (v.22). Samuel reminded the Israelites that the Lord had "chosen" Saul (the Heb. verb is different from that used in vv.20–21, distinguishing direct and personal divine choice from the indirect and impersonal decisions of Urim and Thummim). The verb "choose" in similar contexts is used most often of God's choice of David (16:8–10; 2Sa 6:21; 1Ki 8:16; 1Ch 28:4; 2Ch 6:5–6; Ps 78:70). "Like Saul (10:17–26), David (16:1–13) is selected by Yahweh even though he seems the least likely candidate" (Humphreys, 107).

C. J. Labuschagne (*The Incomparability of Yahweh in the Old Testament* [Leiden: Brill, 1966], 10) has noted that the vocabulary of incomparability to describe a newly appointed king of Israel was significant because only he—to the exclusion of all others—had a claim to the throne (cf. Solomon [1Ki 3:12–13; Ne 13:26]; Hezekiah [2Ki 18:5]; Josiah [2Ki 23:25]). At the same time, of course, such language is most appropriate to the incomparable God himself, as David recognized (2Sa 7:22).

The public acclamation—"Long live the king!" (v.24, used also of the pretenders Absalom [2Sa 16:16] and Adonijah [1Ki 1:25] as well as of kings David [1Ki 1:31], Solomon [1Ki 1:34, 39], and Joash [2Ki 11:12 = 2Ch 23:11])—has survived virtually to modern times. It represents now, as it did then, the enthusiastic hopes of the citizenry that their monarch may remain hale and hearty in order to bring their fondest dreams to fruition. The people of Saul's day "shouted" their approval—and the verb the narrator uses to describe their praise surfaces in Zechariah 9:9, where the prophet advises Jerusalem to "shout" in recognition of the coming of a righteous and saving king (ultimately the Messiah, the Christ; see Mt 21:4–5; Jn 12:12–15).

25–27 After the people's acclamation of Saul as their king, Samuel outlines for them the "regulations of the kingship" (*mišpaṭ* [GK 5477] *hamm*[e]*lukâ*, v.25), a phrase equivalent to "what the king ... will do" (*mišpaṭ hammelek*) in 8:9, 11 (see comments on 8:10–18). Some commentators (e.g., Vannoy, 229–33) contend that the two phrases must be distinguished from each other and have different referents. Others (e.g., Eslinger, 352–55) agree but prefer to extend the distinction still further by giving "what the king ... will do" a different nuance in 8:9 ("manner of the king"—i.e., how a [benevolent] king should conduct himself) from that in 8:11 ("custom of the king"—i.e., how a [despotic] king will conduct himself). This latter position usually assumes that God told Samuel to instruct—and warn—the Israelites about what they could expect if they persisted in their demand to have a king (8:9), but that when Samuel relayed the divine word to them he either deliberately skewed it in a decidedly negative direction or at least selectively emphasized the obvious problems inherent in monarchy while omitting or downplaying its potential benefits (8:11–18; cf. Polzin, *Samuel and the Deuteronomist*, 86–88, in a section that Polzin suggestively titles, "Why Samuel's *Mišpaṭ* Is Only Half the Story").

It is difficult, however, to maintain a distinction between 8:9 and 8:11, especially considering 8:10: "Samuel told *all* the words of the LORD to the people" (emphasis mine). Furthermore, insisting on the equation of 8:9, 11 with 10:25 is at least as old at the LXX, which reads *to dikaiōma tou basileōs* ("the regulation[s]/requirement[s] of the kingship") in all three verses. Hertzberg, 90, however, is doubtless correct in observing that the written document in 10:25 "was not intended to contain just the complicating factors mentioned as a warning to the people in chapter 8" (cf. also Polzin, *Samuel and the Deuteronomist*, 86, who correctly asserts that "both the rights *and* the duties of the king appear to be what Samuel would have 'written in a book and laid before the LORD' [10:25]; surely one without the other would have ill-served both God and the community" [emphasis his]).

Talmon, 53–67, in an extended discussion of "The Rule of the King," insists on the virtual identity of the *mišpaṭ* mentioned in 8:9, 11 with that in 10:25: "Samuel's speech was political in tone in the interests of persuasion, his remarks addressed only to controversial issues. Only later, after the anointing ceremony had taken place, was the 'Rule of the King' presented in complete form and properly formulated. Then Samuel 'told the people of the rule of the kingdom, and wrote it in a book, and laid it up before the Lord' (1 Sam 10:25)" (Talmon, 61). Talmon writes: "There is no distinction between משפט המלך [*mšpṭ hmlk*] and משפט המלוכה [*mšpṭ hmlwkh*]; they are not to be set up as separate concepts" (cf. also Smith, 74; *AIs*, 94, 98).

I heartily agree with such assessments. The "kingship" of 10:25 is the same as the "kingship" of 10:16, the negative aspects of which Samuel warns the people about in ch. 8. That the description in 10:25 implies a somewhat fuller document than is warranted in Samuel's earlier summary is clear enough, but to claim that the two sets of regulations are completely different is not justified by either the language or the context. Smith, 74, expresses the relationship well here: "The *custom of the king* already recited in 8:9–18 ... was threatened as the penalty of the people's choice. As they have persisted in their choice, the threat will be carried out. The document is laid up before Yahweh as a testimony, so that when they complain of tyranny they can be pointed to the fact that they have brought it upon themselves."

Eslinger, 355, translates *mišpaṭ hammᵉlukâ* as "monarchic constitution," while the title of Ben-Barak's study, "The Mizpah Covenant (1 Sam 10:25)—the Source of the Israelite Monarchic Covenant," attempts to define it even more precisely. But "constitution," with all its modern connotations, is an overtranslation of *mišpaṭ*; and despite Ben-Barak's best efforts to elicit comparisons between this document and the covenants of Exodus 19–24 and Joshua 24, he surely extracts more from a single verse than could have been found there were it not for the fuller Exodus and Joshua "parallels." Ben-Barak, 33, himself admits that the 10:25 document is not called a *bᵉrît* ("covenant") in the OT. It is perhaps best to be content with the more modest rendering of the NIV: "regulations of the kingship" (which included, but were not restricted to, those mentioned in 8:11–18). The closest parallel is the "law and ... decrees" of the king(dom) outlined in Deuteronomy 17:14–20 (cf. esp. v.19). For a possible relationship between ch. 8 and 10:17–27, and Deuteronomy 17:14–20, see S. R. Driver, *A Critical and Exegetical Commentary on Deuteronomy* (ICC; Edinburgh: T&T Clark, 1895), 212–13, and esp. Gerbrandt, 108.

After Samuel explained to the people the monarchic regulations (v.25), he wrote them down on a scroll, a common method used throughout the OT period to record important matters (Ex 17:14; Jos 18:9) in perpetuity (Job 19:23–24; Isa 30:8). He deposited the scroll in a safe place "before the LORD"—that is, in the tabernacle, which was probably located at Mizpah at this time (cf. v.17)—in order (1) that it might be preserved for future reference (cf. similarly 2Ki 22:8) and (2) that it might serve as a witness against the king and/or people should its provisions ever be violated (cf. similarly Dt 31:26; Jos 24:26–27).

Samuel then permitted all the people to return to their homes (v.25). Saul, the recently anointed king, went to his home in Gibeah (v.26; see also 14:2; 22:6; 26:1), also known as Gibeah of Saul (11:4; 15:34) and Gibeah in Benjamin (13:2, 15; 14:16) to distinguish it from other towns bearing the same name ("Gibeah" means "hill"). The site, modern Tell el-Ful, is three miles north of Jerusalem, whose modern skyline is clearly visible from the tell. Tell el-Ful was excavated by William F. Albright, who in 1922 and 1933 cleared the remains of what might possibly be Saul's citadel. Though little survived, at the time of its discovery the site was the "oldest datable Israelite fortification of Iron I" (*The Archaeology of Palestine* [Harmondsworth: Penguin, 1949], 120; cf. also 121 fig. 30, updated in Yohanan Aharoni, *The Archaeology of the Land of Israel* [Philadelphia: Westminster, 1982], 191 fig. 56).

With the formal festivities over, two opposing reactions to Israel's new leader surface: "valiant men" (v.26), apparently eager to affirm God's choice ("whose hearts God had touched"; cf. v.24), accompany Saul to Gibeah, while "troublemakers" (v.27; the same Heb. expression is translated "wicked men" in 2:12) despise him. The latter group unwittingly echoes to Saul the earlier words of Gideon about himself: "How can I save Israel?" (Jdg 6:15). Neither Gideon nor the troublemakers understood—at least not at first—that it is God, not human beings, who can and will save (Jdg 6:16; 1Sa 10:19).

In contemptible violation of ancient custom about seeking the favor or help of prophet (9:7–8) or king (1Ki 10:25; 2Ch 17:5), the troublemakers, despising Saul, "brought him no gifts" (v.27). Saul, however, always reticent, kept his silence (as he had before; cf. v.16).

NOTES

19 אֶלֶף (*ʾelep*, lit., "thousand") is infrequently used in the metaphorical sense of "clan" (as here; cf. also 23:23; Jos 22:14; Jdg 6:15; Mic 5:2). Numbers 31:5 is especially instructive in this connection, for there the Hebrew word is appropriately translated both as "thousand" and as "clan."

26 "Valiant men" translates הַחַיִל (*haḥayil*, "valor") by synecdoche. 4QSamuel[a], however, reads בני החיל (*bny hḥyl*, "sons/men of valor"; cf. also the LXX's υἱοὶ δυνάμεων [*huioi dynameōn*]), probably correctly, since it forms a better parallel with בְּנֵי בְלִיַּעַל (*b^{e}nê b^{e}lîyaʿal*, "sons/men of worthlessness") in v.27.

27 Based on 4QSamuel[a] and the LXX, many read the last two Hebrew words of verse 27—וַיְהִי כְּמַחֲרִישׁ (*way^{e}hî k^{e}maḥ^{a}rîš*, lit., "and/but he was like one being silent")—as וַיְהִי כְּמוֹ חֹדֶשׁ (*way^{e}hî k^{e}mô ḥādāš*, lit., "and it was about a month [later]"; for the idiom and construction, cf. Ge 38:24) and attach it to the beginning of ch. 11 (cf. the similar suggestion of BDB, 294, long before the DSS were discovered). Barthélemy, 2:168, however, prefers to retain the MT, rendering the phrase "and he was as one who imposed silence on himself" (cf. the NIV's "But Saul kept silent"). Since the MT is contextually appropriate (see commentary on v.27 above), there is no compelling reason to abandon it here.

4. The Defeat of the Ammonites (11:1–11)

1 Nahash the Ammonite went up and besieged Jabesh Gilead. And all the men of
Jabesh said to him, "Make a treaty with us, and we will be subject to you."
2 But Nahash the Ammonite replied, "I will make a treaty with you only on the condition
that I gouge out the right eye of every one of you and so bring disgrace on all Israel."
3 The elders of Jabesh said to him, "Give us seven days so we can send messengers
throughout Israel; if no one comes to rescue us, we will surrender to you."

4When the messengers came to Gibeah of Saul and reported these terms to the people,
they all wept aloud. 5Just then Saul was returning from the fields, behind his oxen, and he
asked, "What is wrong with the people? Why are they weeping?" Then they repeated to
him what the men of Jabesh had said.
6When Saul heard their words, the Spirit of God came upon him in power, and he
burned with anger. 7He took a pair of oxen, cut them into pieces, and sent the pieces by
messengers throughout Israel, proclaiming, "This is what will be done to the oxen of anyone who does not follow Saul and Samuel." Then the terror of the LORD fell on the people,
and they turned out as one man. 8When Saul mustered them at Bezek, the men of Israel
numbered three hundred thousand and the men of Judah thirty thousand.
9They told the messengers who had come, "Say to the men of Jabesh Gilead, 'By the
time the sun is hot tomorrow, you will be delivered.'" When the messengers went and
reported this to the men of Jabesh, they were elated. 10They said to the Ammonites,
"Tomorrow we will surrender to you, and you can do to us whatever seems good to you."
11The next day Saul separated his men into three divisions; during the last watch of the
night they broke into the camp of the Ammonites and slaughtered them until the heat of
the day. Those who survived were scattered, so that no two of them were left together.

COMMENTARY

1–2 "If any chapter of 1 Samuel gives even the most conservative reader cause for textual emendation of the MT, it is chap. 11" (Polzin, "On Taking Renewal Seriously," 493). For "But Saul kept silent" in 10:27, 4QSamuel[a]—the most fully preserved of the biblical scrolls from Qumran cave 4—substitutes the following extensive passage: "[Na]hash king of the Ammonites sorely oppressed the Gadites and the Reubenites, and he gouged out the right [e]ye of ea[ch] of them and struck ter[ror and dread] in [I]srael. Not a man was left among the Israelites bey[ond Jordan who]se right eye had no[t been go]uged out by Naha[sh king] of the [A]mmonites, except that seven thousand men [had fled from] the Ammonites and entered [J]abesh Gilead. About a month later"—at which point the scroll continues with "Nahash the Ammonite went up" (11:1 MT).

Obviously 4QSamuel[a] contains valuable background information and provides a helpful rationale for what otherwise is an abrupt and vicious threat by the Ammonite king against the inhabitants of Jabesh Gilead. Cross points out that the vengeful punishment insisted on by Nahash is best explained by the 4QSamuel[a] additional paragraph—namely, the Jabeshites were giving aid and comfort to Ammon's ancestral enemies, the Reubenites and Gadites, who occupied territory traditionally claimed by the Ammonites; therefore the Jabeshites should receive the same harsh treatment earlier meted out to the Reubenites and Gadites (cf. Cross, "The Ammonite Oppression," 148–58; "II. Original Biblical Text Reconstructed," 26–35). Josephus's account of Nahash's aggression (*Ant.* 6.68–72 [5.1]) also presupposes some such prologue as described in the 4QSamuel[a] paragraph.

The above considerations, and others like them (cf. Terry L. Eves, "One Ammonite Invasion or Two? 1 Samuel 10:27–11:2 in the Light of 4QSam[a]," *WTJ* 44 [1982]: 308–26, esp. 318–21—but notice the assumptions that Eves, 324, is forced to make about how the MT's reading arose), have led the NRSV, NLT (2nd ed.), GWT, and The Message to include it in their text of 1 Samuel 10:27 (although several others have preserved it in a footnote).

The Qumran addition, however, should not be accorded primacy simply because of its contextual attractiveness. OT narrative often appears inexplicably terse—especially from our modern perspective. Indeed, 4QSamuel[a] strips the standardized account of its leanness and elegance. As Polzin admits: "Although providing important background for the key events of this chapter, 4QSam[a] adds little else to the esthetic and ideological dimensions of the story as found in the MT" (Polzin, "On Taking Renewal Seriously," 493 n. 1). Furthermore, why would Nahash's mutilation of the Jabeshites suddenly "bring disgrace on all Israel" (v.2) if he had been mutilating Reubenites and Gadites all along? And why could not the "background" information provided by 4QSamuel[a] be just as easily an indication of its secondary character—inserted later to "explain" the abruptness of Nahash's actions—as of its originality? "The wise course for the present, therefore, is to reserve judgement on the status of these additional lines in 4QSam[a]" (Gordon, *I and II Samuel*, 64; cf. further Alexander Rofé, "The Acts of Nahash According to 4QSam[a]," *IEJ* 32 [1982]: 129–33; Karen H. Jobes and Moisés Silva, *Invitation to the Septuagint* [Grand Rapids: Baker, 2000], 179–80).

As for the broader historical context of 1 Samuel 11, commentators have long recognized the resemblance between a tribal call to arms represented by Saul's dismembering of a pair of oxen and the disposition of the pieces (v.7) and the dismemberment of the Levite's concubine and the disposition of the parts (Jdg 19:29). The similarities between Judges 19–21 and 1 Samuel 11 are even more extensive, as Polzin ("On Taking Renewal Seriously," 500–501) observes:

1. Jabesh Gilead is paired with Gibeah in Benjamin in both passages. In Judges, Jabesh Gilead refuses to join Israel's call against sinful Gibeah; in Samuel, Saul at Gibeah issues Israel's call to deliver besieged Jabesh.
2. The narrative in Judges is framed by emphatically premonarchic statements—"In those days Israel had no king" (Jdg 19:1; 21:25)—while in Samuel the account is embellished by distinctively monarchic statements: "Then Samuel said to the people, 'Come, let us go to Gilgal and there reaffirm the kingship.' So all the people went to Gilgal and confirmed Saul as king in the presence of the LORD" (11:14–15).
3. The ubiquitous Benjamin (*binyāmin*, "right son") in the Judges account sends forth "paronomastic rays" (Polzin's suggestive term) to the Samuel narrative, where Nahash threatens (v.2) to gouge out every "right eye" (*ʿên yāmîn*) of the Jabeshites, who later respond to the Ammonites (v.10): "Do to us whatever seems good to you" (lit., "good in your eyes")—a phrase in turn reminiscent of the conclusion of Judges 21: "Everyone did as he saw fit" (lit., "did what was fitting in his eyes," v.25).
4. The phrase *tᵉnû hāʾanāšîm ûnᵉmîtēm* occurs in the entire OT only in 11:12 ("Bring these men ... and we will put them to death") and in Judges 20:13 ("Surrender those ... men ... so that we may put them to death").

Polzin concludes ("On Taking Renewal Seriously," 503), "That the men of Jabesh-Gilead had earlier refused to honour their tribal obligations at Mizpah makes their present treachery in offering covenantal peace to Ammon without a fight (v. 1) simply characteristic." However, it also must be pointed out that by liberating Jabesh Gilead from Ammonite oppression, Saul gained the support and gratitude of Israel's Transjordanian regions. In particular, the people of Jabesh remained loyal to Saul even after his death, risking their own lives at the hands of the Philistines to rescue the bodies of Saul and his sons and to give them proper burial (31:11–13; cf. 2Sa 21:11–14). Saul's successor, David, recognizing the strategic importance of Transjordan, courted the favor of the men of Jabesh by implying that he would protect them just as Saul had done (2Sa 2:4–7; for additional details, see Curtis, 356–57).

During the time of the judges, the Ammonites, descendants of Lot's son Ben-Ammi (Ge 19:36–38), encroached on Israelite territory on more than one occasion (Jdg 3:13; 10:6–9; 11:4). Their belligerence against Jabesh Gilead ("Dry [Soil] of Gilead")—either modern Tell el-Maqlub (Aharoni, 127–28; the nearby Wadi Yabis preserves the element "Jabesh" in the ancient name), located about twelve miles southeast of Beth Shan, or Tell Abu al-Kharaz ("A Guide to '99 Digs," *BAR* 25/1 [1999]: 48), about nine miles east of Beth Shan—in the days of Saul was thus not unexpected.

The royal name Nahash (v.1), although usually (and not inappropriately) taken to mean "Snake" (*nāḥāš*), is understood by Cross ("II: Original Biblical Text Reconstructed," 26) to be an abbreviation of *nḥš ṭwb* ("Good Luck"; the verbal root *nḥš* means "to practice divination" or "to look for omens," as in Ge 44:5, 15). "Nahash" appears elsewhere in the OT only in the books of Samuel and in a parallel passage in 1 Chronicles (1Sa 12:12; 2Sa 10:2 [with which cf. 1Ch 19:1–2]; 17:27 [cf. also v.25]). Apart from 1 Samuel 12:12, we cannot know for certain whether the other men named Nahash are the same as the Nahash of 1 Samuel 11 since the name may have been an Ammonite dynastic title.

The Ammonite threat directed at Jabesh Gilead produced a conciliatory response in its inhabitants. They asked Nahash to "make a treaty" (lit., "cut a covenant," v.1) with them, as a result of which they would recognize him as their suzerain and become his vassals (cf. similarly 2Sa 3:12–21; Eze 17:13–14; further Jdg 9:6–15). The phrase "cut a covenant" is almost universally understood to refer to the sacrifice ("cutting") of one or more animals as an important element in covenant solemnization ceremonies in ancient times. That "cut" in the formula harks back to the method of slaughtering an animal can hardly be denied (cf. Jer 34:18: "The men who ... have not fulfilled the terms of the covenant they *made* [lit., 'cut'] ... I will treat like the calf they *cut* in two and then walked between its pieces" [italics mine], in which the two occurrences of "cut" are identical in Hebrew). Polzin ("Covenantal Institutions in Early Israel," 227–40), however, proposes an alternative interpretation, namely, that "cut," "kill," "dismember," and similar verbs in covenantal contexts vividly refer to acting out the fulfillment of the self-maledictory curse spoken by participants in covenants rather than to a ritual sacrifice.

Although, of course, the two interpretations are not necessarily mutually exclusive, Polzin's suggestion is attractive. As Polzin himself observes, Saul's threat in v.7 ("This is what will be done to the oxen [i.e., cutting them into pieces] of anyone who does not follow Saul and Samuel") "brings to mind the conditional curse oaths of treaty ratification ceremonies" (Polzin, "Covenantal Institutions in Early Israel," 240). Upon receiving the pieces of Saul's oxen brought to them by messengers, the various Israelite tribes are to honor the mutual-protection clauses of their covenant in defense of Jabesh Gilead. (The theory of Diana Edelman, "Saul's

Rescue," esp. 205, that Jabesh Gilead was not Israelite during the days of Saul can be maintained only at the unacceptable expense of claiming that several verses in 1 Samuel 11 are later additions; recall also that the Jabeshites were numbered among the Israelites at least as early as the time of the judges [Jdg 21:8].)

Cross ("The Ammonite Oppression," 156–57 and n. 23) sees an additional implication as well. Nahash's threat to gouge out the right eye of every Jabeshite (v.2) may imply their rebellion against a previously established overlordship (at least as understood from Nahash's perspective), especially considering such texts as Numbers 16:13–14; Judges 16:21; 2Ki 25:7 (cf. Jer 39:6–7; 52:10–11); and Zechariah 11:17. In the ancient Near East, physical mutilation and the resultant "disgrace" (v.2) could be expected as the inevitable penalty for treaty violation (cf. esp. Lemos, 229–32, 241). Thus "make" (= "cut," v.1), "gouge out" (v.2), and "cut ... into pieces" (v.7) all belong to what Cross calls a "single ideological complex" (*Canaanite Myth and Hebrew Epic*, 266).

3 Nahash's threat (v.2) received a plaintive response from the elders of Jabesh, who functioned in their normal responsibility as representatives of the community (cf. 4:3; 8:4; 16:4). They tried to buy some time: "Give us seven days" (lit., "Leave us alone [for] seven days"; cf. the same Heb. verb in 2Ki 4:27) to send for help. Although the text is silent about Nahash's reaction, the implication is that he acceded to the elders' request, apparently not only sure of his own military superiority but perhaps also hoping to avoid the necessity of following through on his threat to mount a siege against the city.

The language of the elders' plea uses two key verbal roots that are thematic throughout the rest of the chapter. The first is *yšʿ* (GK 3828), translated "rescue[d]" here and in v.13 and "delivered" in v.9. Human rescue is desperately yearned for in v.3, but Saul recognizes the coming of that hoped-for deliverance as deriving from God himself (v.13; its origin is [deliberately?] ambiguous in v.9; in 19:5 and 2Sa 23:10, 12, the same root is rendered "victory," the source of which is clearly stated to be divine). Although human beings are often deputized to fight God's battles in the OT, the victory—whether mediated through human agency or not—is always his and his alone (cf. Ex 15:1–10; Jdg 5:20; 2Sa 8:6, 14; Pss 60:12; 144:10; Pr 21:31; Isa 10:5; Jer 51:20–23).

The second verbal root is *yṣʾ* ("to go out"; GK 3655). Here and in v.10 it is translated "surrender" (namely, to the Ammonites; cf. similarly 2Ki 18:31 = Isa 36:16; Jer 38:17, 21), while in v.7 it is rendered "follow" (Saul and Samuel) and "turned out" (as one man). For the Israelites generally and the Jabeshites specifically, doing nothing was not an option. They would either "go out" to the enemy in defeat and humiliation or "go out" in victory under the divinely authorized leadership of Saul and Samuel.

4 When the Jabeshite messengers arrived at Gibeah of Saul (modern Tell el-Ful, three miles north of Jerusalem) with the terms of Nahash's demands, its people "wept aloud" (lit., "raised their voice[s] and wept"), a common Israelite display of helplessness, grief, distress, or remorse (cf. Jdg 2:4; 1Sa 24:16; 2Sa 3:32; 13:36). Apparently Saul's fellow citizens in his own hometown despaired of leadership at this critical juncture in their history.

5–6 But at that very moment, Saul was returning from plowing in the fields, and he asked two questions: "What is wrong with the people? Why are they weeping?" (v.5). Upon hearing the Jabeshites' report, Saul was energized by a powerful accession of God's Spirit (v.6). He had already experienced a similar accession earlier, enabling him to "prophesy" (10:6–10). This time, however, in the tradition of the judges from Othniel (Jdg 3:10) to Samson (Jdg 14:19), the Spirit of God filled Saul with divine indignation ("he burned with anger"; cf. Jdg 14:19) and empowered him as a military leader. Although the earlier accession had been temporary, this one was somewhat more permanent, apparently lasting until Samuel anointed David to replace Saul as king (16:13–14; cf. Leon J. Wood, *The Holy Spirit in the Old Testament* [Grand Rapids: Zondervan, 1976], 50, 60–63). The pouring out of the Holy Spirit in the OT often symbolized and accompanied the anointing of the recipient to an important position of leadership, whether as prophet, army commander, king (16:1, 13), or preacher/proclaimer (Isa 61:1).

7 Rallying the troops to defend a covenantal suzerain, vassal, or brother was a common stipulation in ancient treaties. Like the Levite before him who had issued a call to arms by cutting up his dead concubine and sending the parts to each of the various Israelite tribes (Jdg 19:29; 20:6), Saul cut two of his oxen into pieces and sent them throughout Israel as a graphic illustration of what would happen to any tribe that failed to commit a contingent of troops (cf. Jdg 21:5, 10). As Elisha the plowman slaughtered a pair of oxen and served a meal to his friends at the time of his prophetic call (1Ki 19:21), so Saul the plowman slaughtered a pair of oxen as a means of rallying the people to his side at the onset of his service as their king. The "terror of the LORD" that here fell on the people is not to be understood as fear of divine punishment. K&D, 112, well summarizes its true intent: "In Saul's energetic appeal the people discerned the power of Jehovah, which inspired them with fear, and impelled them to immediate obedience."

8 The mustering or counting of the troops (cf. 13:15; 14:17; 2Sa 24:2, 4) took place at Bezek (modern Khirbet Ibziq, about seventeen miles west of Jabesh Gilead), which is mentioned elsewhere in the Hebrew text of the OT only in Judges 1:4–5. There, at the beginning of the period of the judges, two tribes cooperated to rout the Canaanites and Perizzites at Bezek; here, at the beginning of the Israelite monarchy, Bezek becomes a staging ground for a united Israelite attack that will lead to the defeat of the Ammonites.

As in 4:2, 10, so also here in v.8 we cannot be sure whether *ʾelep* means "thousand" or is used in a more general sense to refer to a military "unit" (as in 17:18; 29:2; 2Sa 18:4; see comment on 1Sa 4:2). Nor can the possibility of hyperbole be discounted (cf. 18:7; 21:11). In any case, the numbers in this verse represent substantial contingents of troops. Their being listed separately as "men of Israel" and "men of Judah" either anticipates the eventual division of the kingdom into north and south (a division perhaps already incipient in earlier times) or reflects authorship (or later modest editorial updating) of this section of the books of Samuel in the days of the divided monarchy (that is, after 931 BC; cf. similarly the implications of the reference to "all Israel from Dan to Beersheba" in 3:20).

9 Saul and his troops told the messengers to return to Jabesh Gilead and inform its frightened citizens that divine deliverance (cf. v.13; also 19:5; 2Sa 23:10, 12) would come to them the very next day. It would take place "by the time the sun is hot" (for this expression, cf. Ex 16:21 ["when the sun grew hot"]; Ne 7:3), a phrase that almost surely refers to high noon, the hottest and brightest time of day (cf. similarly Ps 37:6; Am 8:9; and esp. v.11 with 2Sa 4:5). The messengers' report caused the men of Jabesh to become "elated," an emotion experienced also by those who gathered at Gilgal after the Ammonite defeat to confirm Saul as king in recognition of his military prowess under God's direction (v.15; "held a ... celebration" translates the same Heb. verb as "were elated" in v.9).

10 Confident of victory, the Jabeshites—tongue in cheek—promised the Ammonites that they would surrender to them the following day and that the Ammonites would then be free to do "whatever seems good to you" (lit., "whatever seems good in your eyes," the narrator's ironic pun on Nahash's earlier threat to gouge out the right eye of any rebellious Jabeshite; cf. the same idiom in 14:36).

11 Saul wasted no time in deploying "his men" (lit., "the people," a noun often meaning "troops" in OT military contexts) for the attack on Ammon. "The next day" probably refers to the evening of the day on which Saul's message reached the Jabeshites (v.9), since among the Israelites each new day began after sunset (rather than after midnight as in the modern Western world). Saul, following a military strategy common in those days (see 13:17–18; Jdg 7:16; 9:43; 2Sa 18:2), divided his men into three groups: Offensively, it gave the troops more options and greater mobility, while defensively it lessened the possibility of losing everyone to a surprise enemy attack. The Israelites under Saul's leadership broke into the Ammonite camp "during the last watch of the night," reminiscent of the beginning of the end for another of Israel's ancient enemies as well (see Ex 14:24, the only other place where the phrase in quotation marks is used).

The Mesopotamian practice of dividing the night into three "watches" (first [cf. La 2:19], middle [Jdg 7:19], and last), each about four hours long, was followed throughout western Asia in the pre-Christian period; the last or morning watch included the transition from darkness to dawn. Saul's attack obviously caught the Ammonites by surprise, and—as promised (v.9)—by high noon God had defeated them and delivered his people, routing the enemy survivors by scattering them in every direction (cf. also Nu 10:35; Ps 68:1).

NOTES

5 The second question—"Why are they weeping?"—contains an example of the relatively infrequent use of כִּי (*kî*) as an interrogative particle following the more common interrogatives, such as מַה־ (*mah-*) and מִי (*mî*). Since *kî* is often causal, it is usually translated "that" (here and in similar sequences), especially in the KJV tradition (cf. ASV, RSV, NASB, NKJV). When a *kî* clause occurs after an interrogative clause that demands the reason for an exceptional event or situation, however, it often functions as a logical (and not necessarily causal) follow-up question itself (cf. Ge 20:9; Ex 3:11; 32:21; Nu 11:12–13; 16:13; 22:28; Jdg 9:28; 11:12; 1Sa 17:26; 18:18; Isa 36:5; cf. similarly Anneli Aejmelaeus ["Function and Interpretation of כִּי in Biblical Hebrew," *JBL* 105/2 (1986): 201–2], who tends to "regard these cases as a special group within the causal function of כִּי"). In any event, the emotion-freighted contexts in which the above examples occur seem to demand vigorous, staccato-like sequences of short questions rather than the bland, question-plus-causal-statement renderings usually encountered in English translations—including the NIV (except here and in Nu 11:12; 16:13).

9 In vv.9–11, in several places where the MT has plural verbal forms, one or more manuscripts of the LXX use singular forms: "They told" (v.9), LXX "He told"; "they broke into" (v.11), LXX "he broke into"; "[they] slaughtered" (v.11), LXX "he slaughtered." Although the plural form in v.9 could conceivably be understood as an impersonal passive in terms of its meaning, the forms in the MT of v.11 obviously have Saul's troops as their subject. The LXX's singular renderings, then, are perhaps intended to highlight Saul's leadership by attributing the victory over the Ammonites to him personally.

A similar phenomenon may be observed in vv.12–15, but this time its effect is to stress Samuel's role, especially in the confirmation of Saul as king: "Bring [pl.]" (v.12), LXX "Bring [sing.]"; "Saul said" (v.13), LXX "Samuel said"; "[they] confirmed" (v.15), LXX "Samuel confirmed"; "they sacrificed" (v.15), LXX "he sacrificed"; "Saul and all the Israelites" (v.15), LXX "Samuel and all the Israelites." In all these cases in vv.9–15, however, it seems evident that the LXX's renderings represent not so much a translation as a commentary or interpretation.

5. The Confirmation of Saul as King (11:12–12:25)

[12]The people then said to Samuel, "Who was it that asked, 'Shall Saul reign over us?'
Bring these men to us and we will put them to death."
[13]But Saul said, "No one shall be put to death today, for this day the LORD has rescued
Israel."
[14]Then Samuel said to the people, "Come, let us go to Gilgal and there reaffirm the
kingship." [15]So all the people went to Gilgal and confirmed Saul as king in the presence of
the LORD. There they sacrificed fellowship offerings before the LORD, and Saul and all the
Israelites held a great celebration.
[12:1]Samuel said to all Israel, "I have listened to everything you said to me and have set a
king over you. [2]Now you have a king as your leader. As for me, I am old and gray, and my
sons are here with you. I have been your leader from my youth until this day. [3]Here I stand.
Testify against me in the presence of the LORD and his anointed. Whose ox have I taken?
Whose donkey have I taken? Whom have I cheated? Whom have I oppressed? From whose
hand have I accepted a bribe to make me shut my eyes? If I have done any of these, I will
make it right."
[4]"You have not cheated or oppressed us," they replied. "You have not taken anything
from anyone's hand."
[5]Samuel said to them, "The LORD is witness against you, and also his anointed is witness
this day, that you have not found anything in my hand."
"He is witness," they said.
[6]Then Samuel said to the people, "It is the LORD who appointed Moses and Aaron and
brought your forefathers up out of Egypt. [7]Now then, stand here, because I am going to
confront you with evidence before the LORD as to all the righteous acts performed by the
LORD for you and your fathers.
[8]"After Jacob entered Egypt, they cried to the LORD for help, and the LORD sent Moses and
Aaron, who brought your forefathers out of Egypt and settled them in this place.
[9]"But they forgot the LORD their God; so he sold them into the hand of Sisera, the commander of the army of Hazor, and into the hands of the Philistines and the king of Moab,
who fought against them. [10]They cried out to the LORD and said, 'We have sinned; we

have forsaken the LORD and served the Baals and the Ashtoreths. But now deliver us from
the hands of our enemies, and we will serve you.' 11Then the LORD sent Jerub-Baal, Barak,
Jephthah and Samuel, and he delivered you from the hands of your enemies on every
side, so that you lived securely.
12"But when you saw that Nahash king of the Ammonites was moving against you, you
said to me, 'No, we want a king to rule over us'—even though the LORD your God was your
king. 13Now here is the king you have chosen, the one you asked for; see, the LORD has set
a king over you. 14If you fear the LORD and serve and obey him and do not rebel against
his commands, and if both you and the king who reigns over you follow the LORD your
God—good! 15But if you do not obey the LORD, and if you rebel against his commands, his
hand will be against you, as it was against your fathers.
16"Now then, stand still and see this great thing the LORD is about to do before your eyes!
17Is it not wheat harvest now? I will call upon the LORD to send thunder and rain. And you
will realize what an evil thing you did in the eyes of the LORD when you asked for a king."
18Then Samuel called upon the LORD, and that same day the LORD sent thunder and rain.
So all the people stood in awe of the LORD and of Samuel.
19The people all said to Samuel, "Pray to the LORD your God for your servants so that we
will not die, for we have added to all our other sins the evil of asking for a king."
20"Do not be afraid," Samuel replied. "You have done all this evil; yet do not turn away
from the LORD, but serve the LORD with all your heart. 21Do not turn away after useless idols.
They can do you no good, nor can they rescue you, because they are useless. 22For the
sake of his great name the LORD will not reject his people, because the LORD was pleased
to make you his own. 23As for me, far be it from me that I should sin against the LORD by
failing to pray for you. And I will teach you the way that is good and right. 24But be sure to
fear the LORD and serve him faithfully with all your heart; consider what great things he has
done for you. 25Yet if you persist in doing evil, both you and your king will be swept away."

COMMENTARY

12–15 Saul's gracious refusal to execute his erstwhile internal enemies seems to tie v.13 (and therefore also v.12) more closely with vv.14–15 (and ch. 12) than with vv.1–11 (see NIV sectional heading at v.12). Vannoy, however, considers 11:14–12:25 to be a single literary unit, as the subtitle of his work shows. I fully agree that ch. 12 describes a covenant-renewal ceremony (cf. also Klaus Baltzer, *The Covenant Formulary* [Philadelphia: Fortress, 1971], 66–68; William J. Dumbrell, *Covenant and Creation* [Nashville: Nelson, 1984], 135; Eslinger, 37, 383–428 passim) at Gilgal. I nevertheless see no compelling reason not to begin the major compositional unit at 11:12 rather than at v.14. In any case, the conjunctions the NIV uses—correctly, I believe ("But," v.13; "Then," v.14; "So," v.15)—obviously tie vv.12–15 together as a coherent section within the larger compositional unit of 11:12–12:25 and do not commend a sharp break at v.14.

The substance of v.12 finds an eerie echo at the end of Jesus' parable of the ten minas: "'But those enemies of mine who did not want me to be king over them—bring them here and kill them in front of me'" (Lk 19:27). Saul's troops and the people of Jabesh Gilead, having witnessed God's victory over Ammon under Saul's leadership, demanded from Samuel the death penalty (v.12) for all the trouble-makers who had questioned his ability to save them from foreign rule (10:27).

Saul, however, showing how magnanimous he could be when given the opportunity, asserted that the divine deliverance was a cause for gratitude, not vengeful retribution (v.13). Perhaps Jonathan's later rebuke of his father, Saul, in a somewhat similar situation, was inspired by the events recorded here, and perhaps Saul's ready agreement to what his son was saying (19:1–6) came because he then remembered his own earlier statesmanlike declaration of generosity. In any event, Saul's words would later echo in a rhetorical question asked by his successor, David, with the result that the life of the miserable Shimei was spared: "Should anyone be put to death in Israel today?" (2Sa 19:22).

Saul's demonstration of the leadership qualities necessary to be Israel's king led Samuel to convoke an important meeting at Gilgal (v.14), perhaps modern Khirbet el-Mefjer (about thirty-eight miles southwest of Jabesh Gilead and eight miles north of the Dead Sea west of the Jordan). Vannoy, 82–83, points out that Gilgal was an appropriate site for such a meeting because of its covenant-renewal associations at the beginning of the conquest period (Jos 4–5). The OT records three meetings of Samuel and Saul at Gilgal, each fateful for Saul: (1) In the flush of his victory over Ammon, Saul was reaffirmed as king (11:14–15); (2) because of his impatience while awaiting Samuel's arrival, Saul was rebuked by his spiritual mentor (13:7–14); and (3) because of his disobedient pride after the defeat of the Amalekites, Saul was rejected as king (15:10–26).

The purpose of the first meeting is to "reaffirm the kingship" (v.14) of Saul, who had already been anointed at Ramah (10:1) and chosen by lot at Mizpah (10:17–25). The reaffirmation of Saul's kingship is a confirmation by public acclamation (v.15) and is the last of the three stages comprising his rise to monarchy over Israel. The verb *ḥdš* (GK 2542) in the Piel, appropriately translated "reaffirm" in the NIV, means "make new, renew" and is perhaps used here to "refer to the initiation of the final stage of the coronation process—an 'inauguration' in the sense of launching the third and final stage of the kingship rite" (Edelman, "Saul's Rescue," 199).

Samuel's invitation to the people to reaffirm Saul as king was greeted with enthusiasm (v.15). "In the presence of the LORD" they confirmed their earlier choice, and "before the LORD" (same Heb. expression) they brought their sacrifices. As in an earlier ceremony of covenant ratification (Ex 24:5), so also here fellowship offerings were the appropriate response of the people of Israel, who by sacrificing them were expressing their desire to rededicate themselves to God in covenantal communion and allegiance. Saul's ascent to the throne is now complete, and the "great celebration" that accompanied the sacrificial ritual more than matched Israel's earlier elation upon their receiving the messengers' report of the imminent doom of the Ammonites (v.9).

12:1 Chapter 12 concludes the account of the rise of Saul to kingship over Israel, a story that began in ch. 8 with the people's demand for a king. In the broader sweep of the Deuteronomic presentation, however, ch. 12 is appropriately included among those passages that "stand at the turning points of Israel's history: the beginning and the end of the conquest, of the era of the judges, and of the monarchy" (McCarthy, "II Samuel 7," 131). McCarthy, 137, rightly observes that in the total scheme of things, the Deuteronomic history provides three programmatic chapters and then uses six of its key passages "to show how these programs worked or failed in subsequent history ... as follows" (slightly modified):

A. Moses commands the conquest and distribution of the land (Deut 31).	A_1. Joshua undertakes the conquest (Josh 2). A_2. Joshua conquers and prepares the distribution (Josh 11–13).
B. Joshua commands the covenant, the program for life in the land (Josh 23).	B_1. The people break the covenant (Judg 2). B_2. The people reject the Lord for a human king (1 Sam 12).
C. Nathan's promise (2 Sam 7).	C_1. The promise fulfilled in Solomon (1 Kings 8). C_2. Final failure of the kingship (2 Kings 17).

It is immediately evident that 1 Samuel 12 plays a prominent role in the Deuteronomic formulation of Israel's history from the Mosaic period through the end of the monarchy (for additional details, see Kaiser, *Toward an Old Testament Theology*, 64–66, 123–24). McCarthy's schema is moderately deficient, however, in failing to include Joshua 24 together with Joshua 23 as the two-chapter ending of the conquest period. That Joshua 24 should be included becomes clear when one observes (1) that Judges 2:6–9 reprises Joshua 24:28–31 and (2) that Joshua 23–24, like 1 Samuel 12, constitutes the farewell of an Israelite leader combined with a covenant-renewal ceremony. Thus Joshua 23–24 describes covenant renewal, Judges 2 summarizes covenant violation, and 1 Samuel 12 describes covenant renewal again. Joshua 23–24 and 1 Samuel 12 serve as a literary frame for the narrative of the judges. The prophet Samuel, the "last of the judges," here at Gilgal delivers *apologia pro vita sua* in the context of covenant renewal (cf. Baltzer, *The Covenant Formulary*, 66–68; Gerbrandt, 143; Vannoy, 131) and formally (if grudgingly) ushers in the period of the monarchy, which begins with the formulaic description of the length of Saul's reign in 13:1.

Literary analysis enables us to divide ch. 12 into four roughly equal parts, arranged chiastically, with v.13 serving as the hinge:

A Samuel vindicates his covenantal faithfulness before the people as witnessed by the Lord and his newly anointed king (vv.1–5)
  B Samuel summarizes the righteous acts of the Lord during the periods of the exodus and the judges to demonstrate divine reign through human leaders (vv.6–12)
    C Samuel observes that the Lord has granted the people's selfish and apostate desire for a king (v.13)
  B' Samuel summarizes the prospect of blessing for covenantal obedience and of curse for covenantal disobedience, confirming the ominous side of that prospect by a divinely sent miracle (vv.14–19)
A' Samuel calls the people, the king, and himself to continued covenantal faithfulness (vv.20–25)

Although Vannoy, 131, outlines vv.14–25 differently, his isolation of v.13 as a separate unit calls attention to its central importance in the chapter (cf. ibid., 41 n. 95: "I Sam. 12:13 with its juxtaposition of the people's request and Yahweh's response points to the resolution of the kingship issue which has been the focal point of the narratives of 1 Sam. 8–12").

As ch. 12 opens, Samuel begins his *apologia* by reminding the people of Israel that he has "listened to" them and has set a king over them. The phrase "listened to" (in the sense of "obeyed"; cf. vv.14–15) echoes 8:7, 9, 22 and highlights Samuel's commitment to God's will despite his own personal reservations. After all, Saul is "the man the LORD has chosen," the king affirmed by public acclamation (10:24).

2 However reluctantly, Samuel formally acknowledges the transfer of Israel's leadership from himself to Saul. Although Samuel has been the recognized "leader" of the people from his youth until the present (cf. 3:10; 3:19–4:1; 7:15–17), King Saul is now their "leader." Both "as ... leader" and "have been ... leader" translate the common idiom "walk before" (cf. Ge 17:1), an expression that can mean, among other things, "to minister before" (as in 2:35) and "to walk in front of as leader" (as here)—that is, in this context "living in the public eye, under constant scrutiny" (Baldwin, 99). Samuel's reference to himself as "old and gray" is probably a modest claim to wisdom (cf. Job 15:9–10), which was often an expectation attaching to elders' years of experience. His mention of his sons emphasizes the length of time it has been his privilege to serve the people of Israel—and perhaps also provides them with an unwelcome reminder of their earlier refusal to allow his sons to succeed him as judge (8:5).

3 The NIV's "Here I stand" (reminiscent—though with a different nuance and in a different situation—of Martin Luther's reputed *Hier stehe/bin ich*) translates *hin^e nî*, which is literally "Here I am," and echoes an important servant motif (e.g., Ge 22:1, 11) in Samuel's first recorded words (cf. 3:4–6, 8, 16). Samuel invites the people to "testify against" him about covenantal stipulations he may have violated. As though in a courtroom, the inquiry takes place "in the presence of" Samuel's heavenly and earthly superiors: "the LORD and his anointed" (Saul, cf. 10:1; for the entire phrase in reference to God and the king, cf. the NIV note on Ps 2:2).

Aware that testifying on his own behalf could well result in self-incrimination (cf. 2Sa 1:16), Samuel nevertheless launches a brief series of protestations of innocence. The key verb is "taken" ("accepted" renders the same Heb. word), which Samuel consciously uses as a powerful means of contrasting his admirable behavior with the potentially oppressive demands of a (despotic) king he had earlier warned about (8:11, 13–17; cf. Eslinger, 388; Garsiel, 69–70; Vannoy, 16). Doubtless alluding to the covenantal stipulations of Exodus 20:17, Samuel challenges the people to accuse him of having taken from any of them so much as an ox or a donkey (contrast 8:16; 22:19; 27:9). His claim of exemplary conduct in this regard may be compared to that of Moses (Nu 16:15) and Paul (Ac 20:33).

Samuel goes on to affirm that he has neither "cheated" nor "oppressed" anyone (v.3). The parallel use of these two verbs in the poetry of Amos 4:1, where they are translated "oppress" and "crush" respectively (cf. also Hos 5:11, "oppressed ... trampled"; Dt 28:33, where the NIV translates the two verbs as a hendiadys: "cruel oppression"), shows that they are approximately synonymous. Samuel's refusal to cheat/oppress others looks back to his specific denial of having engaged in bribery. The Book of the Covenant in Exodus 23:8 (repeated almost verbatim in Dt 16:19) issues a general warning against accepting bribes, pointing out that doing so "blinds" (distorts) a judge's ability to make fair and just decisions.

Although in v.3 the word for "bribe" is different from that used in the Covenant Code and means literally "ransom, price for life" (the same word being translated "bribes" in Am 5:12; Sir 46:19), and although "make me shut my eyes" is a different expression from "blinds" in the Covenant Code, the intent there and here is virtually identical. Accepting bribes is universally condemned in Scripture, and Samuel carefully distances himself from a practice that has already made his own sons infamous (8:3; cf. further Ps 15:5; Am 5:12). "If I have done any of these," though not in the MT, is necessary in English to prepare for Samuel's conclusion: "I will make it right" (lit., "I will restore to you"; cf. 2Sa 9:7).

4 The people readily accepted and agreed with Samuel's declaration. Like Elisha after him (2Ki 5:16–17)—and unlike Elisha's servant Gehazi (2Ki 5:20)—Samuel declared his determination not to make merchandise of the prophetic office (cf. further Mic 2:6–11; 3:11).

5 After solemnly affirming his innocence of any wrongdoing, Samuel—using characteristic covenant-renewal terminology (cf. Jos 24:21–22, 27)—declares that the Lord and Saul (cf. v.3) are witnesses to the truthfulness of his words. As Achish would later absolve David of any fault attributed to him by his detractors (29:3, 6; cf. David's concurrence in v.8), so Samuel here denies—under implied oath—that he is guilty of crimes against his fellow Israelites. The people's response, "He is witness," could refer either to the Lord or to Saul and may be intentionally ambiguous. Less likely, though not impossible, would be the translation "They are witness[es]" (so Vannoy, 18).

6 Joshua 24:2–15, in proper covenant-renewal fashion, summarizes the history of God's people from the time of Abraham through the conquest of Canaan, stressing divine leadership and the people's idolatrous disloyalty while challenging them to covenantal faithfulness. Similarly vv.6–12 summarize the history of Israel from the time of Moses and the exodus through the period of the judges and their sinful request for a king, stressing divine leadership and Israel's idolatrous disloyalty while challenging them to the same covenantal faithfulness (for a brief analysis of these and other similar passages, cf. W. Gordon Robinson, "Historical Summaries of Biblical History," *EvQ* 47/4 [1975]: 195–207). Such historical prologues are common features in suzerainty covenant documents throughout the Near East in the second millennium BC (cf. George E. Mendenhall, "Law and Covenant in Israel and the Ancient Near East," *BA* 17/3 [1954]: 58).

By highlighting the name Yahweh from the outset (v.6), Samuel leaves no doubt that, in the final sense, Israel's leader has always been "the LORD." The NIV's "appointed" attempts to translate *ʿāśâ ʾet*—a difficult phrase in this context. The best solution is "worked with" (cf. BDB, 794, which compares 14:45 [where the semantic equivalent *ʿāśâ ʿim-* obviously has that sense; cf. the NIV's "did this ... with God's help"]). The meaning is then that God, working through and in concert with Moses and Aaron, freed his people from Egyptian bondage (cf. Ex 6:13, 26–27; for the same idea, cf. the NIV note on Ro 8:28: "God works together with those who love him to bring about what is good"; cf. also the expression "God's fellow workers" in 1Co 3:9).

The exodus of Israel from Egypt during the days of Moses was remembered as the greatest of all divine acts of redemption for the nation. "I am the LORD your God, who brought you out of Egypt, out of the land of slavery" stands in Exodus 20:2 as the elegantly brief preamble-plus-historical-prologue that precedes the Ten Commandments—the covenantal stipulations to be obeyed unquestioningly by God's people—and its modified form therefore serves here as an appropriate opening to Samuel's summary (cf. also v.8). Kaiser (*Toward an Old Testament Theology*, 59) estimates that similar formulaic reminders of the exodus redemption occur throughout the OT "about 125 times."

7 Samuel continues to use the language of the courtroom as he commands the people to "stand" at attention and in anticipation before the bar of

God's justice (cf. v.16 and Ex 14:13). He intends to "confront [them] with evidence" (lit., "enter into judgment/litigation with/against" them, using the niphal of *špṭ* followed by *ʾēt*; cf. Pr 29:9, "goes to court with") of God's blessing on their history, all the more casting their apostasy in darker relief. The contrast is heightened by using *ʾittᵉkem* twice, first as a particle of disadvantage ("confront you" [NIV], lit., "against you") and then as a particle of advantage ("for you"; see Theophile J. Meek, "Translating the Hebrew Bible," *BT* 16 [1965]: 144). Samuel's evidence is "the righteous acts performed by the LORD" (*ṣidqôt yhwh*; cf. Jdg 5:11; Da 9:16; Mic 6:5; further, Rev 15:4), virtually synonymous with the *magnalia Dei*, the "mighty acts" of God for his people (cf. Ex 6:6; 7:4; Pss 106:2; 145:4, 12; 150:2 ["acts of power"]; and esp. Ps 71:16, 24).

8 Verses 8–12 recapitulate and expand 8:6–8. In 12:8 "Jacob" refers not only to the patriarch himself but also, by extension, to the nation of Israel (as often in the OT). The Lord (cf. also v.10) graciously answered (Ex 2:25) their cry for help (Ex 2:23–24). He sent his servants Moses (Ex 3:10) and Aaron to lead Israel out of Egypt (cf. 1Sa 10:18)—a fact acknowledged even by their enemies (1Sa 6:6)—and to bring them to the borders of the Promised Land.

9 The language of vv.9–11 is heavily dependent on terminology characteristic of the book of Judges. The dreary cycle of rebellion–retribution–repentance–restoration described throughout that book (cf. also the summary in Ne 9:26–31) is reprised here: rebellion (v.9a), retribution (v.9b), repentance (v.10), and restoration (v.11).

Rebelling against their God, the Israelites "forgot" (v.9; cf. Jdg 3:7) what he had done for them in the past and ignored him personally as they worshiped other gods (cf. v.10). In response to his people's apostasy and in retribution against them for their sin, the Lord "sold them" (cf. Jdg 2:14; 3:8)—as though on the slave market—"into the hand[s] [i.e., 'power'] of" their enemies, including Sisera (Jdg 4:2; cf. Ps 83:9), the commander of the army of the city of Hazor (modern Tell el-Qedah, about nine miles north of the Sea of Galilee; cf. Ronald F. Youngblood, "Hazor," in *Major Cities of the Biblical World*, ed. R. K. Harrison [Nashville: Nelson, 1985], 119–29), the Philistines (Jdg 3:31; 10:7; 13:1), and Eglon, king of Moab (Jdg 3:12–14).

10 Verse 10, part of which summarizes Judges 10:15–16, describes repentant Israel sporadically throughout the period of the judges. Although they often forsook the Lord and violated his covenant with them by serving the Baals (male deities; cf. comment on 7:4; also Jdg 2:11; 3:7; 10:6, 10) and the Ashtoreths (female deities; also Jdg 2:13; 10:6), they pled for his deliverance and promised to serve him alone if only he would release them from the shackles of enemy oppression.

11 God did restore the Israelites to their former covenantal relationship by sending judges to their rescue. Jerub-Baal, another name for Gideon (cf. NIV note), is perhaps mentioned first (1) because he is the central figure in the book of Judges and arguably the most important of the judges themselves, (2) because his very name (cf. Jdg 6:32 and NIV note there) means "Let Baal contend" and thus explicitly contradicts the Israelite tendency to worship the shameful god Baal (cf. 2Sa 11:21, where Gideon is called Jerub-Besheth, a scornful scribal variant that means "Let shame contend"; and cf. v.10), and (3) because he specifically refused to establish dynastic as opposed to divine rule over his countrymen (Jdg 8:22–23)—for which refusal he must surely have been one of Samuel's heroes (cf. v.13).

Reference is next made to Barak, Deborah's general in the successful war against Sisera's Canaanite army (Jdg 4:6–7). Barak is followed by Jephthah (Jdg 11:1), victor over the Ammonites—who had been aided and abetted by the Philistines to establish hegemony over Israel in Transjordan (Jdg 10:7–8). (One would have expected Samuel to refer also to Ehud, the judge who led Israel's troops against the "king of Moab" [v.9; cf. Jdg 3:26–30], but perhaps allusion to the implied defeat of "the gods of Moab" alongside "the gods of the Ammonites and the gods of the Philistines" in the Jephthah narratives [Jdg 10:6] was considered sufficient.)

Finally, Samuel mentions himself as the last of the judges as well as the most recent victor over the Philistines (7:6, 11–15). He then summarizes the Lord's triumphant deliverance of his people, through his chosen leaders, from "your enemies on every side, so that you lived securely" (v.11; the underlying Hebrew is a clear echo—and here a fulfillment—of the divine promise recorded in Dt 12:10, which the NIV translates, "your enemies around you so that you will live in safety").

12 Three times in these chapters the antithetical negative *lōʾ kî* (lit., "no, but"; for details cf. GKC, sec. 163) is used to stress the people's determination not to have God as their king but rather to have a human king like "all the other nations" (8:5–7): (1) after Samuel's earlier warning about the dangers inherent in their demand (8:19–20), (2) during the public assembly at Mizpah (10:19), and (3) in the face of the Ammonite threat (12:12). Later in v.12 the poignancy of Samuel's sadness is brought out even more starkly by the syntax, as Daniel Lys observes: "The *waw* connecting the two parts of this verse indicates a strong opposition: 'when [whereas, even though] the Lord your God was your king'" ("Who Is Our President? From Text to Sermon on 1 Samuel 12:12," *Int* 21/4 [1967]: 410). Their sinful demand proved them to be totally unlike Jerub-Baal/Gideon (Jdg 8:23), the paradigmatic judge (v.11).

13 Serving as the hinge of the chapter, this verse focuses once again on the gracious, permissive will of God, who has "given" (lit.; "set," NIV; cf. Ge 41:41, "put ... in charge") his people the king they "asked for" (*šʾl*; yet another pun on the name "Saul," *šāʾûl*; cf. also vv.17, 19). Over and over Israel had requested—yea, demanded—a king (e.g., 8:5–6, 22; 10:19; 12:1), and Saul in successive stages had acceded to that office. The Lord's eventual rejection of the very king the people demanded is eerily echoed later in a similar situation in Hosea 13:10–11 (cf. esp. v.11: "In my anger I gave you a king, and in my wrath I took him away").

14–15 Certain key phrases in v.14 ("fear the Lord and serve," "both you and the king who reigns over you") are echoed in vv.24–25 ("fear the Lord and serve," "both you and your king") and frame the last half of the chapter (vv.14–25).

Verses 14–15 represent the blessings and curses sections respectively that were part of ancient suzerainty covenants. As such the structure of each balances and parallels that of the other—but not as usually thought. The NIV sides with most translations and commentators, who assume an aposiopesis (here a suppressed apodosis) at the end of v.14, which must then be contextually supplied to complete the sense (hence the NIV's "good!" for which there is no equivalent in the Heb.). However, Vannoy, 42, points out that "the two verses display a remarkably close parallelism in wording and structure, and because the apodosis is introduced in verse 15 with והיתה [*whyth*], the parallelism strongly supports beginning the apodosis of verse 14 with והיתם [*whytm*]." The resulting translation of vv.14–15 would then be: "If you fear the Lord and serve and obey ... and do not rebel ... then both you and the king who reigns over you will follow the Lord your God. But if you do not obey the Lord, and if you rebel ... then his hand will be against you, as it was against your fathers." Vannoy, 44, summarizes this new understanding of v.14 thus: "Israel must not replace her loyalty to Yahweh by loyalty to her human ruler.... If Israel fears Yahweh ... then she will show that even though human kingship has been introduced into the structure of the theocracy, she continues to recognize Yahweh as her sovereign" (cf. similarly Antony F. Campbell, *The Study Companion to Old Testament Literature: An Approach to the Writings of Pre-Exilic and Exilic Israel* [Wilmington, Del.: Michael Glazer, 1989], 156–57 and n. 15).

The blessings-and-curses terminology of Deuteronomy and Joshua permeates vv.14–15. To "fear the LORD and serve" him (v.14; Jos 24:14) brings his blessing; to "rebel against his commands" (v.15; Dt 1:26, 43; 9:23; Jos 1:18) brings his curse. "Fear of God/the LORD" (*yirʾat ʾelōhîm/yhwh*), a common expression in OT wisdom literature (cf. Job 28:28; Pr 1:7; 9:10), was the generic term for "religion" in ancient Israel; the Akkadian phrase *puluḫti ili* ("fear of God") is the semantic equivalent. As is well known, in the OT fearing God had more the connotation of reverence and awe (cf. Dt 17:19) than of terror or dread—although the latter was not totally lacking. To "serve" means not only to work and minister but also to worship (cf. already 7:3–4). If Israel and her new king will fear, serve, and obey God (v.14) by carefully following his law, they will receive his blessing (for the king, see Dt 17:18–20). Disobedience and rebellion "against his commands" (v.15), however—including especially forgetting or forsaking him and serving other gods (cf. Dt 8:19; Jos 24:20)—will result in his curse (symbolized by his powerful "hand") against them in the future (cf. 1Ki 13:21–26; La 1:18) as it had been against their "fathers" in the past (cf. Nu 20:24–26; 27:12–14).

16 Verses 16–19 continue the theme of covenantal curse established in v.15. Earlier (v.7) Samuel had told the people to "stand" before the bar of divine justice and be confronted with the evidence of God's righteous acts in the past in their behalf. Now (v.16) he commands them to "stand" and be awed by divine omnipotence, to "see this great thing the LORD is about to do before your eyes" (cf. also Ex 14:31). The divine act then results in what Raymond C. van Leeuwen ("Proverbs 30:21–23 and the Biblical World Upside Down," *JBL* 105/4 [1986]: 604) appropriately calls a "cosmic inversion": "Rain and thunder appear during the dry season of wheat harvest." In that part of the world not only is "rain in harvest ... not fitting" (Pr 26:1), it is so totally unexpected that it could easily be interpreted as a sign of divine displeasure.

17 "Thunder" is literally "voices" (cf. also Ex 9:33–34), a metaphor that represents thunder as the loud and powerful voice of God manifested in storms (cf. 7:10; also esp. Ps 29:3–9). The narrator's use of "voices" in the sense of "thunder" (NIV) might well have been intended to echo its use in the account of the establishment of the Sinaitic covenant (Ex 19:16; 20:18; cf. similarly Vannoy, 51 and n. 118). The driving rain that often accompanied such thunder could be especially destructive to crops (Pr 28:3), and when it occurred unseasonably, it could leave those who depended on it destitute. By destroying Philistine grain during wheat harvest, Samson had understood fully that he could inflict serious harm on his enemies (Jdg 15:1–5). Before the exodus, a plague of hail accompanied by thunder and rain devastated a recalcitrant pharaoh's fruit trees, flax, and barley (Ex 9:22–32).

Thus Samuel's rhetorical question—"Is it not wheat harvest now [lit., 'today']?"—served as an ominous reminder to the people that all their hard work had the potential of being wiped out in an equally brief period of time. In any event, the display of divine power in the rainstorm would force the people to "realize" (lit., "know and see"; the same Heb. phrase echoes later in Saul's desire to "find out" [14:38] what sin had been committed) how evil their motives had been when they had "asked" (a pun on the name "Saul"; also v.19) for a king.

18–19 Samuel's prayer for a storm out of season was answered "that same day," and all the people "stood in awe" (lit., "feared"; same Heb. root in v.14) of both God and Samuel (v.18). A similar statement in Exodus 14:31 pairs God and Moses as the objects of Israel's fear and trust after the miracle at the Sea of Reeds. The reputation of Moses and Samuel as being especially close to God's counsel (Jer 15:1) was justly deserved: Although the Hebrew verbs are different, the people's plea to Samuel—"Pray to the LORD" (v.19)—is a clear echo of a pharaoh's cry to Moses (and Aaron) centuries earlier in a similar situation (Ex 9:28). That the people should ask Samuel to pray to the Lord "your" God (rather than "our" God) may be an index of their perception of their own apostate condition. Reflecting Samuel's words in v.17, they admit that asking for a king was an evil that "added to" (v.19)—and thus perhaps superseded—all their other sins (cf. similarly 2Ch 28:13; Job 34:37; Isa 30:1).

The people's concern that they should not die—in the broad context of the entire chapter but especially in the narrow context of unseasonable thunder and rain that might be expected to destroy their wheat before it could be harvested—prompted Tremper Longman III to propose correctly that vv.16–19 should be interpreted "as the outworking of a covenant curse which motivates the Israelites to repent of their past sin and to keep the sanctions which had just been presented to them by Samuel" ("1 Samuel 12:16–19: Divine Omnipotence or Covenant Curse?" *WTJ* 45 [1983]: 171). Longman, 170–71, observes that covenantal curses due to general apostasy are often described elsewhere in the OT in terms of drought, famine, and the like (cf. Lev 26:19–20; Dt 28:22–24, 38–42).

20 The literary coherence of vv.20–25 (cf. also McCarthy, "II Samuel 7," 135) is established by key words and phrases in the MT of vv. 20 and 24–25 to frame it: "be afraid" (v.20); "fear" (v.24); "you" (emphatic; vv.20, 24 [second occurrence in Hebrew]); "evil" (vv.20, 25); and especially "serve ... with all your heart" (vv.20, 24). Samuel concludes his address to the people of Israel by encouraging them to do good (vv.20–24) and warning them not to do evil (v.25).

Samuel reminds the people that they (emphatic "you," *ʾattem*, v.20) were the ones who asked for—indeed, demanded—a king (cf. v.19); thus they have only themselves to blame if Saul proves to be either weak or despotic. Not all is lost, however, if only the people will acknowledge that their true King is the Lord himself: "Do not [*ʾal*] turn away." Samuel further urges Israel to "serve the LORD with all your heart," an often expressed covenantal requirement (e.g., Dt 10:12–13; 11:13–14; cf. also 30:9–10).

21 By contrast, says Samuel, the people are not to follow "useless" (*tōhû* [GK 9332], the word rendered "formless" in Ge 1:2) things/people. Although idols are described as *tōhû* in Isaiah 41:29 ("confusion," NIV; cf. also 44:9, "nothing")—hence the NIV's "useless idols" here—the reference in this context is perhaps broader and denotes any defection from serving the Lord, including, of course, preference for a human king (so Eslinger, 418–19; cf. similarly Vannoy, 55). Only God can do the people good; no one else can "rescue" (cf. the NIV's "deliver[ed]" in vv.10–11; 10:18).

22 The Lord's elective purposes for his people will not be denied. His intention to make Israel his own covenantal people (Ex 19:5; cf. 1Pe 2:9) is not because of any merit on their part (Dt 7:6–7). Far from it, he has chosen them because of his love for them and in order to fulfill the oath he had sworn to their forefathers (Dt 7:8–9; cf. Ge

15:4–6, 13–18; 22:16–18). In addition, and perhaps most important of all, he has chosen them "for the sake of his great name" (cf. also Jos 7:9–11, where the Lord's "great name" is linked to the Sinaitic covenant)—that is, based on the integrity of his self-revelation (cf. Vannoy, 56). In this last clause of v.22, says McCarthy, "the problems raised in the pericope are finally solved. The kingship has been integrated into the fundamental relationship between Yahweh and the people and that relationship reaffirmed" ("The Inauguration of Monarchy," 412; cf. further V. Philips Long, *The Reign and Rejection of King Saul*, 176–83).

23 Taking his rightful place among such giants of intercession as Moses (Ex 32:30–32), Daniel (Da 9:4–20), Paul (Ro 1:9–10; Col 1:9; 1Th 3:10; 2Ti 1:3), and Jesus (Isa 53:12; Ro 8:34; Heb 7:25), Samuel declares his unwillingness to sin against God (cf. Saul's command in 14:33–34) by failing to pray for Israel (cf. also v.19; 7:5, 8–9; 8:6; 15:11; Jer 15:1). To help the people live a life pleasing to God, Samuel promises to "teach" (the Heb. root is *yrh*, the same as in *tôrâ*, "instruction, law") them "the way that is good and right" (cf. also 1Ki 8:36 = 2Ch 6:27; Pss 25:8; 32:8; Pr 4:11).

24–25 The rest is up to the people themselves; thus, ch. 12 ends with encouragement to faith and obedience (v.24, which summarizes Dt 10:20–21) and with warning against the consequences of disobedience (v.25) appropriate to a covenant-renewal document. Samuel's admonition in v.24a is strikingly similar to that of "the Teacher, son of David, king in Jerusalem" (Ecc 1:1): "Here is the conclusion of the matter: Fear God and keep his commandments" (Ecc 12:13). After all, the Lord had done "great things" for his people (v.24b), which should have been a cause for rejoicing on their part (Ps 126:2–3; Joel 2:21).

Samuel feels constrained to remind them, however, that pursuing their penchant for evil will surely result in their destruction: "You and your king will be swept away" (v.25). The verbal root is *sph*, which appears again in 26:10, where David predicts that the Lord will cause Saul's demise, that perhaps Saul will go into battle and "perish"—and so it happened (31:1–5). Thus the final words of Samuel's address and the final days of Saul's kingship, passages that frame the account of Saul's reign (chs. 13–31), are suffused with the stench of death.

NOTES

14–15 Vannoy, 61–82, in a lengthy and carefully reasoned argument, insists that מְלוּכָה (*m*[e]*lûkâ*, "kingship," v.14) here refers to God's kingdom rather than to human monarchy and that v.15 is the first reference in 1 Samuel to Saul's actually becoming king as but one aspect of Israel's continued recognition of the kingship of God over his people. The immediate context of v.14, however, uses the root מלך (*mlk*), not of God, but of Saul ("reign," v.12; "confirmed ... as king," v.15; "set a king," 12:1; "king," 12:2). Furthermore, of the twenty-four times that the word *m*[e]*lûkâ* occurs in the OT, it refers to divine kingship only twice at best (Ps 22:28; Ob 21)—as Vannoy (76 n. 44) himself acknowledges. Fifteen of the twenty-four occurrences are in Samuel and Kings, and in all fifteen cases—unless v.14 is the exception—it means human rather than divine kingship (cf. 10:16, 25; 14:47; 18:8). Although there can be no doubt that Saul was supposed to rule under God's direction, divine superintendence of Israel's monarchy should not be read into the word *m*[e]*lûkâ* in v.14.

12:3 Sirach 46:13–20, a passage that praises Samuel, includes a summary of 1 Samuel 12:1–5 in 46:19, in which the MT's אַעְלִים (*ʾaʿlîm*, "make me shut") is replaced by נעל[י]ם (*nʿl[y]m* "[pair of] sandal[s]"). The Hebrew text of Sirach 46:19 thus reads, in part: "From whom have I accepted a bribe, even so much as a [pair of] sandal[s]?" (i.e., the most trifling bribe; cf. Ge 14:23; Am 2:6; 8:6). The LXX's ὑποδημα[των] (*hypodēma[tōn]*, "sandal[s]") dutifully follows this reading (or a similar Hebrew variant) in both 1 Samuel and Sirach. But the MT idiom העלים עיני (*hʿlym ʿyny*, "shut/close [one's] eyes"), in the sense of "refuse to help/protest/get involved," is well established in the OT (Lev 20:4; Pr 28:27; Eze 22:26) and fits admirably in the present context.

5 The NIV's "they said" at the end of this verse either translates the plural verb found in many Hebrew manuscripts (also in the LXX) or else understands the MT singular form as a collective, with "people" as the implied subject (cf. v.6).

11 Three of the four proper names in this verse deserve further comment. The narrator's explanation of the name Jerub-Baal in Jdg 6:32—"Let Baal contend"—may be, as often in the Bible, a wordplay, considering the context. Names such as Ireba-Adad ("Adad substitutes") and Rib-Haddi ("The compensation of Hadad"), rulers of Assyria and Byblos, respectively, during the Amarna age, might well lead to the conclusion that "Baal substitutes" was the original meaning of Jerub-Baal—especially when it is recognized that Hadad and Baal were two different names for the same god (*hd* and *bʿl* being often parallel to each other in Ugaritic; cf. *UT*, II AB vii:35–37). Jerub-Baal would thus be an *Ersatzname*, one of a class of names that indicates the previous loss of a child in the family. Although there is no evidence for the meaning "substitute" or "compensate" for the verb רִיב (*rîb*) in the OT, since proper names tend to preserve archaic usages it may well be that a name such as Jerub-Baal (and, for that matter, Jeroboam) is an *Ersatzname* survival from an earlier era (for additional details, see Youngblood, *The Amarna Correspondence*, 5–8).

"Barak" is the reading in some LXX manuscripts and also in the Syriac; the MT has "Bedan," Hebrew בְּדָן (*bᵉdān*; cf. NIV note). Attempts to equate Bedan with Samson (understanding *bdn* to be an abbreviation for "son of Dan, Danite") or with the minor judge Abdon (Jdg 12:13, 15) are rightly rejected by Y. Zakovitch, " יפתח = בדן," *VT* 22/1 (1972): 123–24. His own solution, however (124–25)—namely, that Bedan is another name for Jephthah based on an argument derived from the occurrence of the name Bedan in 1 Chronicles 7:17—depends on the unlikely suggestion that later scribes twice emended the text to insert Jephthah's name smoothly into it. Nor does the proposal of Vannoy (33 n. 66), who accepts the suggestion that Bedan is another name for Barak, fare any better, since there is no evidence to support it. The best solution remains that of most commentators: The versional "Barak" is correct, and the MT's בדן (*bdn*) is an early transcriptional error for ברק (*brq*). Confusion between *d* and *r* and between *n* and *q* was not of infrequent occurrence in the ancient West Semitic scripts, especially in the tenth to ninth centuries BC. In any case, the sequence "Jerub-Baal, Barak, Jephthah and Samuel" (v.11) appears alluded to in Hebrews 11:32: "Gideon, Barak ... Jephthah ... Samuel."

The Syriac and Lucianic reading "Samson" for the Hebrew "Samuel" as the final name in the list (cf. NIV note) may have been intended to protect Samuel from the accusation of pride. Such third-person references to oneself are not uncommon in the OT, however, and were a frequent narrative device. Furthermore, that Samuel would mention himself in his roles as the last of the judges and the most recent conqueror of the Philistines is not at all unexpected.

B. The Decline of Saul (13:1–15:35)

OVERVIEW

Although the story of Saul's decline begins in ch. 13 and is highlighted in chs. 13–15, it continues sporadically to the end of 1 Samuel and is inextricably intertwined with the story of David's rise (16:1–28:2). The entire account of the interaction between the two processes as recorded in chs. 13–31 is aptly termed "the crossing fates" by Jan P. Fokkelman (*Narrative Art and Poetry*, vol. 2). Elsewhere Fokkelman states, "As one man's fate goes down, the other's goes up" ("Saul and David," 25).

Chapters 13–15, which constitute a separate unit apart from the preceding and following chapters, focus our attention on Saul's reign after the problem of kingship is resolved in chs. 8–12. Chapter 13 (the only chapter of 1 and 2 Samuel, as it turns out, that is not found in the four Dead Sea Scrolls manuscripts of Samuel) begins with the typical Deuteronomic formula for introducing the reign of a southern Israelite king (see below for details); ch. 15 ends with a final breach between Samuel and Saul; and ch. 16 begins with God's command to Samuel to anoint a son of Jesse of Bethlehem to replace Saul as king. Gerbrandt, 158, summarizes: "The narrative in 1 Samuel 13–15 thus performs the important function of being a bridge between 1 Samuel 8–12 and 1 Samuel 16 ff, and also provides the Deuteronomist with the opportunity to emphasize some key elements of his understanding of the role of the king in this new era."

Chapters 13–15 may be outlined as follows.

A. The Rebuke of Saul (13:1–15)
B. The Struggle against the Philistines (13:16–14:23)
C. The Cursing of Jonathan (14:24–46)
D. Further Wars of Saul (14:47–52)
E. The Rejection of Saul (15:1–35)

Samuel's initial rebuke of Saul (A) parallels God's final rejection of Saul (E); Saul's victory against the Philistines (B) parallels his victories against various enemies, including the Philistines (D). The hinge of the section is Saul's determination, however reluctant, to execute his firstborn son, Jonathan, heir to the throne (C).

1. The Rebuke of Saul (13:1–15)

[1]Saul was ⌞thirty⌟ years old when he became king, and he reigned over Israel ⌞forty-⌟ two years.

[2]Saul chose three thousand men from Israel; two thousand were with him at Micmash and in the hill country of Bethel, and a thousand were with Jonathan at Gibeah in Benjamin. The rest of the men he sent back to their homes.

[3]Jonathan attacked the Philistine outpost at Geba, and the Philistines heard about it. Then Saul had the trumpet blown throughout the land and said, "Let the Hebrews hear!"
[4]So all Israel heard the news: "Saul has attacked the Philistine outpost, and now Israel

has become a stench to the Philistines." And the people were summoned to join Saul at
Gilgal.
[5]The Philistines assembled to fight Israel, with three thousand chariots, six thousand
charioteers, and soldiers as numerous as the sand on the seashore. They went up and
camped at Micmash, east of Beth Aven. [6]When the men of Israel saw that their situation
was critical and that their army was hard pressed, they hid in caves and thickets, among
the rocks, and in pits and cisterns. [7]Some Hebrews even crossed the Jordan to the land of
Gad and Gilead.

Saul remained at Gilgal, and all the troops with him were quaking with fear. [8]He waited
seven days, the time set by Samuel; but Samuel did not come to Gilgal, and Saul's men
began to scatter. [9]So he said, "Bring me the burnt offering and the fellowship offerings.'"
And Saul offered up the burnt offering. [10]Just as he finished making the offering, Samuel
arrived, and Saul went out to greet him.
[11]"What have you done?" asked Samuel.

Saul replied, "When I saw that the men were scattering, and that you did not come at
the set time, and that the Philistines were assembling at Micmash, [12]I thought, 'Now the
Philistines will come down against me at Gilgal, and I have not sought the LORD's favor.' So
I felt compelled to offer the burnt offering."
[13]"You acted foolishly," Samuel said. "You have not kept the command the LORD your
God gave you; if you had, he would have established your kingdom over Israel for all
time. [14]But now your kingdom will not endure; the LORD has sought out a man after his
own heart and appointed him leader of his people, because you have not kept the LORD's
command."
[15]Then Samuel left Gilgal and went up to Gibeah in Benjamin, and Saul counted the
men who were with him. They numbered about six hundred.

COMMENTARY

1 The RSV's rendering of this verse might be the most courageous translation of a biblical verse ever made: "Saul was ... years old when he began to reign; and he reigned ... two years over Israel." (Footnotes inform the reader that the lacunae represent numbers that have dropped out during the course of transmitting the text.) Although the KJV tried to make the best of a bad situation by translating the Hebrew as it stood ("Saul reigned one year; and when he had reigned two years over Israel," followed by the main clause beginning v.2), scholars generally agree that since "something has happened to the Hebrew text of 1 Samuel 13:1, the length of Saul's reign can only be estimated" (Kitchen, *Ancient Orient*, 75). In any event, omission (whether accidental or not) of year-dates from official regnal documents was not uncommon in ancient times (cf. ibid., n. 65).

Verse 1 is doubtless the defective remnant of the formal introduction of Saul's reign. Such formulas are common in later portions of the Deuteronomic history but—beginning with David in 2 Samuel 5:4—always and only concerning southern kings: Rehoboam (1Ki 14:21); Jehoshaphat (22:42); Jehoram (2Ki 8:17); Ahaziah (8:26); Joash (11:21–12:1); Amaziah (14:2); Azariah/Uzziah (15:2); Jotham (15:33); Ahaz (16:2); Hezekiah (18:2); Manasseh (21:1); Amon (21:19); Josiah (22:1); Jehoahaz (23:31); Jehoiakim (23:36); Jehoiachin (24:8); and Zedekiah (24:18). Each of the above kings from Rehoboam through Zedekiah is honored by a similar formula in 2 Chronicles; none of the northern Israelite kings beginning with Jeroboam I—who are considered both illegitimate and apostate—is so honored in either history. It is not immediately apparent why the 2 Samuel 5:4 formula for David is not repeated in 1 Chronicles; nor can we be sure why neither Abijah nor Asa, the second and third southern kings during the divided monarchy—not to mention Solomon, son of David—was recognized by such a formula.

Two notable exceptions to the southern orientation of the regnal formula must be mentioned: that of Saul in v.1 and that of Ish-Bosheth, son of Saul (2Sa 2:10). The latter verse is especially suggestive since it ends as follows: "The house of Judah, however, followed David." After the murder of Ish-Bosheth (2Sa 4), the regnal formula is reserved exclusively for southern kings. As for Saul, the mutilated condition (whether deliberate or accidental) of v.1 may reflect later scribal antipathy or indifference toward him.

The two NIV footnotes to v.1 summarize the text-critical reasons for the numbers the NIV restores there. Other attempts to solve the problem of the lacunae are numerous, and none is more certain than any other. (For full treatment of the various options, see especially V. Philips Long, *The Reign and Rejection of King Saul*, 71–75; cf. also conveniently Michael Kuykendall, "I Samuel 13:1: A Chronological Conundrum," *Bible Editions & Versions* 9/2 [2008]: 19.) In the light of the above discussion, however, all attempts based on the supposed integrity of the present Hebrew text are doomed to failure. (Compare the suggestion of Edward A. Niederhiser to the effect that Saul spent one year exercising his kingship and two years being officially anointed king ["One More Proposal for 1 Samuel 13:1," *HS* 20 [1979]: 44–46.)

2–10 The background of v.2 appears to be an occasion when Saul was dispersing the mustered troops of Israel (J. Maxwell Miller, 161). The people had "chosen" a king to lead them into battle (8:18–20), and now their king obliged them: Saul "chose" three thousand Israelite men (v.2) to serve in his standing army (cf. Samuel's warning in 8:11–12). Two thousand were under his command at Micmash (modern Mukhmas) and in the high country at Bethel (modern Beitin), while one thousand were at Gibeah in Benjamin (his hometown, modern Tell el-Ful, three miles north of Jerusalem) under the command of his son Jonathan (which means "The LORD has given," with v.2 containing the first mention of Jonathan in the Bible). Micmash was almost five miles southeast of Bethel and about four miles northeast of Gibeah. Apparently feeling confident in the size of his two military units, Saul sent the rest of the men home.

The smaller unit under Jonathan started a war against the Philistines by attacking their outpost at Geba in Benjamin (v.3), modern Jeba (called "Gibeah of God" in 10:5), about five miles north-northeast of Jerusalem. Saul, ultimately responsible for the attack (v.4) and realizing that the main Philistine army had heard about it, entertained second thoughts about his own troop strength. He therefore had the ram's-horn trumpet blown throughout Israel to summon additional men (cf. Jdg 3:27;

6:34). The verb "hear[d]," used three times in vv.3–4, heightens narrative suspense as it stresses the awareness of all the antagonists who have a stake in the upcoming hostilities. Since "Hebrew" was commonly used by non-Israelites as a synonym for "Israelite" (cf. 4:5–10), it is understandable that the two terms should alternate throughout the narratives of the Philistine wars in chs. 13–14.

To state that Israel had now become a "stench to the Philistines" (v.4) is tantamount to affirming that Philistia would muster her troops to fight Israel (cf. 2Sa 10:6 = 1Ch 19:6; Ge 34:30; Ex 5:21)—and so she did (v.5). In the meantime, Saul's call to arms (v.3) was answered by the "people" (v.4; ʿ*am* is used here in the technical sense of "soldiers, [fighting] men," as in vv.2, 5). They assembled at Gilgal, perhaps modern Khirbet el-Mefjer (about eleven miles east-northeast of Geba).

The Philistines were feared far and wide for their wooden chariots armed with iron fittings at vulnerable and strategic points. Although there is no mention of Philistine chariots or charioteers in the account of Saul's death in ch. 31, the Amalekite who reported the event to David introduced them into his story (2Sa 1:6), presumably to enliven it and to impress David with his own courage in the face of enemy fire. Similarly, the present account (v.5) uses hyperbole to emphasize the magnitude of the Philistine threat. Besides being able to put three thousand two-man chariots into the field, the enemy had summoned troops "as numerous as the sand on the seashore"—a simile not only familiar to a believing community who traced their allegiance to the Lord back to the Abrahamic covenant (Ge 22:17; cf. also 1Ki 4:20–21), but also useful in describing huge numbers of fighting men (2Sa 17:11; Jos 11:4) and their animals (Jdg 7:12).

Since the Philistines set up camp at Micmash, Saul either hastily retreated to Gilgal or perhaps had earlier decided to make his headquarters there (vv.4, 7). Beth Aven ("Temple of Wickedness"), although elsewhere used as a pejorative nickname for Bethel ("Temple of God"; cf. Hos 4:15; 5:8; 10:5; and NIV note to those verses), here in v.5 (and 14:23) refers to a site (possibly Tell Maryam) just west of Micmash. This Beth Aven (perhaps originally vocalized as Beth On, "Temple of Strength"; cf. the name of the Benjamite town Ono in 1Ch 8:12; Ezr 2:33; Ne 7:37; 11:35) is distinguished from Bethel in Joshua 18:12–13 and is said in Joshua 7:2 to be east of Bethel.

The Philistine deployment at Micmash caused mass desertions in the Israelite army. Like their ancestors before them (Jdg 6:2), some of the Israelites hid in whatever out-of-the-way places they could find (v.6; 14:11, 22). Others fled eastward across the Jordan River (v.7), where they sought safety in Gad and Gilead. (Both Transjordanian regions were between the Sea of Galilee and the Dead Sea, Gad being smaller than and south of Gilead during this period [cf. Barry J. Beitzel, *The Moody Atlas of Bible Lands* [Chicago: Moody, 1985], 120; also 2Sa 24:5–6].) David would later discover that caves (23:23; 24:3, 7–8, 10)—and one in particular (22:1; 2Sa 23:13)—would afford especially safe protection from Saul and other enemies.

The greatly reduced number of men who remained with Saul at Gilgal were understandably frightened (v.7). Saul, remembering Samuel's earlier command (10:8), waited seven days for his arrival (v.8). When the prophet failed to appear at the appointed time, even more of Saul's troops began to defect. Desperate, Saul decided to seek the Lord's favor (v.12) by sacrificing the offerings (v.9) that Samuel had told him he himself would make. It may be overly analytical to point out that Samuel prescribed "burnt offerings" (plural, 10:8) while Saul mentions "burnt offering" (singular, 13:9; cf. also vv.10, 12), since Samuel could have been speaking in general terms or the singular form could be understood as a collective.

Nevertheless, it is perhaps significant that the text indicates Samuel arrived on the scene just after Saul had offered up the burnt offering but before he had had time to sacrifice the fellowship offerings (v.10). "The narrator wants the reader to infer that Samuel was in fact close by, waiting to catch Saul and then to reprove him, as Samuel immediately does" (Preston, 34). The fact that upon Samuel's arrival Saul goes out to "greet" (lit., "bless"; cf. Ge 47:7 and NIV note there; also 2Ki 4:29; 10:15) him does not mollify him in this situation any more than his similar statement in similar circumstances would do later (15:13).

Saul's sin was not that as king he was forbidden by God's law to sacrifice burnt offerings and fellowship offerings under any and all circumstances. Later David (2Sa 24:25) and Solomon (1Ki 3:15) made the same kinds of offerings, and there is no hint of divine rebuke in either case. Saul sinned because he disobeyed God's word through the prophet Samuel (v.13)—a sin that he would commit again (15:26).

11–15 Saul's motivation to offer the sacrifice, however ill-advised (cf. 2Ch 26:16–21), seems genuine and appropriate. The Philistines were gathering for battle against Israel, his men were deserting him, and Samuel had not arrived on the scene when he had said he would (v.11). Saul therefore felt the urgent need to seek God's favor—or at least that was his excuse (v.12). What he apparently failed to realize, however, is that animal sacrifice is not a prerequisite for entreating God. In the OT there is no clear case of *ḥillâ ʾet-pᵉnê* ("sought the favor of [God/the LORD]") in a context where sacrifice was a necessary accompaniment (cf. Ex 32:11; 1Ki 13:6; 2Ki 13:4; 2Ch 33:12; Ps 119:58; Jer 26:19; Da 9:13; Zec 7:2; 8:21–22; Mal 1:9—notwithstanding K. Seybold to the contrary [*TDOT*, 4:408–9]). The fact is that Saul had not heeded the divine word through the prophet, and obedience is always better than sacrifice (15:22).

But there is more. It would seem that in ancient Israel rituals associated with holy war were not to be performed by the king unless a prophet was present. Both in ch. 13 and in ch. 15 Saul acted without the presence of Samuel, and in both cases his transgression was related to holy war ritual (vv.11–12; 15:3 [see also NIV note there], 7–11, 17–19). For these offenses Saul was rebuked by Samuel and rejected by God (cf. further Gerbrandt, 156–57).

Wolfgang M. W. Roth, "A Study of *skl*," 74, has perceptively observed that the four Niphal occurrences of *skl* ("act foolishly," v.13; 2Sa 24:10 = 1Ch 21:8; 2Ch 16:9) belong together:

> They refer to the action of an "anointed one of the LORD" (Saul, David, Asa) in conflict situations, when military or political considerations stand against certain prophetical concepts connected with Holy War, they occur either in the first or second person singular as accusations or confessions, and they mark the breaking point in the conflict between prophet and king.

The basic thrust of this verb is that of intellectual inability or incapability, and the Niphal brings out the reflexive-tolerative aspect and leads to the meaning "act foolishly in self-reliance" (ibid., 76–78). In Saul's case acting foolishly meant to disobey the divine command mediated through a prophet (v.13; cf. also 15:19, 23, 26; contrast Hezekiah's obedience in 2Ch 29:25).

Had Saul obeyed, his "kingdom" (*mamlākâ*) over Israel would have been divinely established *ʿad-ʿôlām* ("in perpetuity, for all time," v.13). Such a promise presents a difficulty in light of the Davidic covenant since the Lord affirms that David's throne will be established "forever" (2Sa 7:13, 16; cf. also Ge 49:10). It is possible, of course, that God's original choice of Saul (9:15–17; 10:1, 24), which appears in any case to have been intended as a foil to David, carried with it a genuine (though hypothetical) promise of a continuing dynasty that was never in danger of being fulfilled, given Saul's character.

A more helpful solution, however, is to compare the case of Saul with that of Jeroboam I, who in 1 Kings 11:38 is promised an "enduring dynasty" (*bayit-neʾᵉmān*) like that already promised to David ("lasting dynasty," 25:28; cf. also 2Sa 7:16: "Your house and your kingdom will endure forever"). It is clear that Jeroboam's dynasty would not replace David's but would exist alongside it. Similarly, Saul's kingdom/dynasty could theoretically have been established alongside that of David without endangering or contradicting the enduring character of the latter (cf. Howard, "The Case for Kingship," 23 n. 14).

But Saul, reminded twice that he had not obeyed the Lord's command (vv.13–14), is told in no uncertain terms that he will be replaced by a man "after his [God's] own heart" (lit., "according to his [God's] heart/will/desire," v.14; cf. 2Sa 7:21, where the same Heb. expression is used), a man who has been chosen by God (cf. GNB, The Message, NIrV), and therefore a man who has God's interests at heart (see Ac 13:22; for full discussion see Kevin C. Peacock, "A Man after God's Heart: Re-examining a Popular Yet Problematic Interpretation" [unpublished paper, 2006]). Saul will be replaced by a neighbor of his, a neighbor better than him (15:28).

Saul will later become so distraught over this prospect that he will beg David not to cut off his descendants or wipe out his name from his father's family (24:21). David Lys ("Who Is Our President? From Text to Sermon on 1 Samuel 12:12," *Int* 21/4 [1967]: 409) observes that Saul's "kingdom" will soon be ruled over by a "leader" (*nāgîd*, the transitional title used at the onset of monarchy in Israel; cf. also 25:30) appointed by God. "The Israelite king was rightly king only as far as he was the representative of *the* King; otherwise the Lord would reject him" (ibid., 417).

In verse 15 the MT has Samuel leaving Gilgal and going to Gibeah while Saul apparently stays in Gilgal. The LXX, however, has Samuel leaving Gilgal and going on his way while Saul and his troops go to Gibeah (see NIV note). Since Saul has already arrived at Gibeah in v.16, the LXX text perhaps preserves a genuine tradition about the sequence of events (for details see V. Philips Long, *The Reign and Rejection of King Saul*, 94–95). In any case, Saul takes a census of his fighting men to assess their numerical strength (cf. 11:8; 14:17). In spite of the original two thousand men (or three thousand, if he was already in Gibeah and the count would therefore include Jonathan's troops) mentioned earlier (v.2) and the general call to arms to supplement them (vv.3–4), wholesale defections had reduced his troops to "about six hundred" (cf. 14:2).

The books of Judges and Samuel often specify units of six hundred men (Jdg 3:31; 18:11, 16–17; 1 Sam 23:13; 27:2; 30:9; 2Sa 15:18), which J. B. Segal, 13, describes as a "modest military force." Fokkelman ("Saul and David," 27) observes: "The reduction of Saul's troops to 600 men is a literary way of telling us that he has an opportunity to become another Gideon, to achieve victory with only a small contingent of courageous followers."

NOTE

8 A few Hebrew manuscripts insert אמר (*ʾmr*) before שמואל (*šmwʾl*, "Samuel") in the difficult phrase למועד אשר שמואל (*lmwʿd ʾšr šmwʾl*), yielding the meaning "until the time that Samuel set" (cf. NIV). Thus the MT's reading might have resulted either from haplography of *ʾmr* after *ʾšr* or of *šm* before *šmwʾl*.

2. The Struggle against the Philistines (13:16–14:23)

[16]Saul and his son Jonathan and the men with them were staying in Gibeah in
Benjamin, while the Philistines camped at Micmash. [17]Raiding parties went out from the
Philistine camp in three detachments. One turned toward Ophrah in the vicinity of Shual,
[18]another toward Beth Horon, and the third toward the borderland overlooking the Valley
of Zeboim facing the desert.

[19]Not a blacksmith could be found in the whole land of Israel, because the Philistines
had said, "Otherwise the Hebrews will make swords or spears!" [20]So all Israel went down to
the Philistines to have their plowshares, mattocks, axes and sickles sharpened. [21]The price
was two thirds of a shekel for sharpening plowshares and mattocks, and a third of a shekel
for sharpening forks and axes and for repointing goads.

[22]So on the day of the battle not a soldier with Saul and Jonathan had a sword or spear
in his hand; only Saul and his son Jonathan had them.

[23]Now a detachment of Philistines had gone out to the pass at Micmash. [14:1]One day
Jonathan son of Saul said to the young man bearing his armor, "Come, let's go over to the
Philistine outpost on the other side." But he did not tell his father.

[2]Saul was staying on the outskirts of Gibeah under a pomegranate tree in Migron. With
him were about six hundred men, [3]among whom was Ahijah, who was wearing an ephod.
He was a son of Ichabod's brother Ahitub son of Phinehas, the son of Eli, the LORD's priest
in Shiloh. No one was aware that Jonathan had left.

[4]On each side of the pass that Jonathan intended to cross to reach the Philistine outpost was a cliff; one was called Bozez, and the other Seneh. [5]One cliff stood to the north
toward Micmash, the other to the south toward Geba.

[6]Jonathan said to his young armor-bearer, "Come, let's go over to the outpost of those
uncircumcised fellows. Perhaps the LORD will act in our behalf. Nothing can hinder the LORD
from saving, whether by many or by few."

[7]"Do all that you have in mind," his armor-bearer said. "Go ahead; I am with you heart
and soul."

[8]Jonathan said, "Come, then; we will cross over toward the men and let them see us. [9]If
they say to us, 'Wait there until we come to you,' we will stay where we are and not go up
to them. [10]But if they say, 'Come up to us,' we will climb up, because that will be our sign
that the LORD has given them into our hands."

[11]So both of them showed themselves to the Philistine outpost. "Look!" said the Philistines.
"The Hebrews are crawling out of the holes they were hiding in." [12]The men of the outpost
shouted to Jonathan and his armor-bearer, "Come up to us and we'll teach you a lesson."

So Jonathan said to his armor-bearer, "Climb up after me; the LORD has given them into
the hand of Israel."

[13]Jonathan climbed up, using his hands and feet, with his armor-bearer right behind
him. The Philistines fell before Jonathan, and his armor-bearer followed and killed behind
him. [14]In that first attack Jonathan and his armor-bearer killed some twenty men in an area
of about half an acre.
[15]Then panic struck the whole army—those in the camp and field, and those in the outposts and raiding parties—and the ground shook. It was a panic sent by God.
[16]Saul's lookouts at Gibeah in Benjamin saw the army melting away in all directions.
[17]Then Saul said to the men who were with him, "Muster the forces and see who has left
us." When they did, it was Jonathan and his armor-bearer who were not there.
[18]Saul said to Ahijah, "Bring the ark of God." (At that time it was with the Israelites.)
[19]While Saul was talking to the priest, the tumult in the Philistine camp increased more
and more. So Saul said to the priest, "Withdraw your hand."
[20]Then Saul and all his men assembled and went to the battle. They found the
Philistines in total confusion, striking each other with their swords. [21]Those Hebrews who
had previously been with the Philistines and had gone up with them to their camp went
over to the Israelites who were with Saul and Jonathan. [22]When all the Israelites who had
hidden in the hill country of Ephraim heard that the Philistines were on the run, they
joined the battle in hot pursuit. [23]So the LORD rescued Israel that day, and the battle moved
on beyond Beth Aven.

COMMENTARY

16–22 The combined forces of Saul and Jonathan at Gibeah (v.16) numbered only in the hundreds (14:2), while those of the Philistines at Micmash, scarcely four miles to the northeast, numbered in the thousands (v.5). Philistine "raiding parties" (lit., "the destroyer," thus bent on destruction and pillage; v.17; 14:15) left camp in three detachments, a common military strategy in those days (11:11; Jdg 7:16; 9:43; 2Sa 18:2) since it provided more options and greater mobility. The final destruction of each detachment is left deliberately vague, the word "toward" having the general meaning "in the direction of" (as in Jdg 20:42). They headed off in three different directions: One group went toward Ophrah in Benjamin (cf. Jos 18:23; modern et-Taiyibeh, six miles north of Micmash) in the region of Shual (otherwise unknown, unless related to Shaalim in 9:4; see comment there), a second (v.18) went toward (Upper) Beth Horon in Ephraim (cf. Jos 16:5; modern Beit Ur el-Foqa, ten miles west of Micmash) on the border of Benjamin, and the third went an undetermined distance eastward toward the Valley of Zeboim (location unknown).

Peter R. Ackroyd ("Note to **parzon* 'Iron' in the Song of Deborah," *JSS* 24/1 [1979]: 19–20) is correct in his contention that vv.19–22 provide an introduction to "a heroic tale of the exploits of Jonathan" and that their purpose is to describe the humiliation of Israel "with a corresponding exaltation of the power of Israel's God." But Ackroyd's further assumption that the passage has nothing to do with ironworking as an index of Philistine military superiority is surely wide of the mark. For decades archaeologists working at many different sites have unearthed iron artifacts in bewildering number and variety dating from the period of greatest Philistine power and leading to the general consensus that the metal was introduced into Canaan—at least for weapons, agricultural tools, and jewelry—by the Philistines (cf. G. Ernest Wright, "Iron in Israel," *BA* 1/2 [1938]: 5–8; James D. Muhly, "How Iron Technology Changed the Ancient World—And Gave the Philistines a Military Edge," *BAR* 8/6 [1982]: 40–54). Megiddo, Beth Shemesh, Gezer, Tell Qasileh, and other sites have yielded iron tools of various kinds (cf. Yigael Yadin, "Megiddo of the Kings of Israel," *BA* 33/3 [1970]: 78–79, 95). Perhaps most intriguing of all is the iron plow point from the time of Saul found at his citadel in Gibeah (cf. Lawrence A. Sinclair, "An Archaeological Study of Gibeah [Tell el-Ful]," *BA* 27/2 [1964]: 55–57).

As an effective method of denying weapons to the beleaguered Israelites, the Philistines had apparently deported all the Israelite blacksmiths (v.19; cf. similarly 2Ki 24:14, 16; Jer 24:1; 29:2). Hebrew fighting men were not to have swords or spears. (Saul and Jonathan, either with Philistine permission or by subterfuge, were the sole exceptions [v.22].)

Although the precise nature of some of the agricultural tools named in vv.20–21 remains uncertain (for a typical attempt to identify them from an archaeological standpoint, cf. G. Ernest Wright, "I Samuel 13:19–21," *BA* 6/2 [1943]: 33–36), the intention of the passage became clear when Samuel Raffaeli discovered that *pîm* ("two thirds of a shekel" [NIV], v.21) refers to a unit of weight (cf. O. R. Sellers and W. F. Albright, "The First Campaign of Excavation at Beth-zur," *BASOR* 43 [1931]: 9). Made of stone and other materials, weights marked *pym* have turned up in various excavations (cf. George L. Kelm and Amihai Mazar, "Excavating in Samson Country: Philistines and Israelites at Tel Batash," *BAR* 15/1 [1989]: 49). The *pym* has proven to be two-thirds of a shekel in weight. If silver was the medium of exchange in v.21, the Philistines charged the Israelites an exorbitant price for sharpening and repointing their tools.

Since Philistia was located on the coastal plains west of the foothills of Judah, Israelites who visited the Philistines for any purpose "went down" to them (v.20; see Jdg 14:19; 16:31; Am 6:2). The word for "plowshares," occurring again in the messianic oracle found in Isaiah 2:2–4 (= Mic 4:1–3; see also Joel 3:10), probably means more precisely "plow points," since plowshares themselves were made of wood in ancient times. The word "axes" is used elsewhere in contexts of cutting down trees and chopping wood (Jdg 9:48; Ps 74:5; Jer 46:22). A cognate form of the word for "goads," which is found only here and in Ecclesiastes 12:11 in the OT, is apparently now attested in Ugaritic (see Mitchell Dahood, "Hebrew-Ugaritic Lexicography II," *Bib* 45 [1964]: 404).

As in the days of Deborah (Jdg 5:8), the Israelites were woefully outgunned as the battle against the enemy loomed before them (v.22). Despite their lack of weapons, however, with God's help (14:6) they would rout the mighty Philistines just as David would later defeat the giant Goliath (17:45, 47).

13:23–14:14 The stage having been set in 13:16–22, the drama of Israel's victory over Philistia begins with a remarkably courageous attack by two men, who win a skirmish with a heavily armed enemy against overwhelming odds.

A "detachment" (the Heb. word is different from that in 13:17 and is translated "outpost" in 14:1, 4, 6, 11, 15) of Philistines had left their main camp at Micmash (13:16) and had gone out (v.23) to defend a pass leading to it. As in 13:3, so also in 14:1 it is Saul's son Jonathan, rather than Saul himself, who takes the initiative against the enemy. He suggests to his armor-bearer that they attack the recently established Philistine outpost. Armor-bearers in ancient times had to be unusually brave and loyal, since the lives of their masters often depended on them. David later served Saul in that capacity (16:21); and Saul's final valiant stand against the Philistines at Mount Gilboa took place alongside his faithful armor-bearer, who would die with him (31:4–6). In the present situation the function of Jonathan's armor-bearer is especially important because of the scarcity of weapons in Israel (13:22). Jonathan decides not to tell his father about his plans, perhaps not to worry him needlessly or because he feels that Saul would forbid him to go.

Meanwhile, Saul's modest army of six hundred men (14:2; 13:15) was with him near Gibeah, his hometown. Although the statement that Saul himself was sitting "under a pomegranate tree" contrasts his timidity and relative ease/luxury (the pomegranate being a highly prized fruit; cf. Nu 20:5; Dt 8:8; SS 4:13; 6:11; 7:12; Joel 1:12; Hag 2:19) with Jonathan's willingness to sacrifice his very life for Israel, it may simply be intended as an allusion to his role as leader (cf. Jdg 4:5). The specific location of Migron (v.2) and its relationship to the Migron of Isaiah 10:28 remain unclear.

Among the men with Saul was the priest Ahijah ("brother of the LORD"), son of Ahitub ("covenant brother"; for the root *ṭwb* used as a legal term in covenantal contexts, cf. Michael V. Fox, 41–42), grandson of Phinehas and great-grandson of Eli (v.3). Reference to Ahijah's ancestors recalls the divine curse on the house of Eli (2:30–33) and the deaths of Eli (4:18)—who had been "the LORD's priest in Shiloh," a city so recently destroyed by the Philistines (cf. Ps 78:60; Jer 7:12, 14; 26:6, 9)—and Phinehas (4:11). Later the text describes the deaths of Ahitub and his fellow priests (22:11–18)—including perhaps Ahijah, if Ahimelech is another name for Ahijah (22:9–11)—at the command of Saul himself. Especially poignant is the reference to Ahijah's "wearing an ephod" (v.3), a priestly description (cf. 2:28) stressed by the narrator as he reports the massacre of eighty-five descendants of Eli (22:18).

The apparently needless reference to Ichabod ("no glory"; cf. NIV note to 4:21) recalls yet another tragedy in Eli's family. Thus the rebuked king Saul is in the company of the priest Ahijah of the rejected house of Eli, and neither is "aware" that the courageous Jonathan son of Saul is on his way to fight the Philistines. David Jobling, 368, summarizes: "His own royal glory gone, where else would we expect Saul to be than with a relative of 'Glory gone'?"

The names of the cliffs flanking the Micmash pass (v.4; cf. Isa 10:28–29) were doubtless intended to pinpoint the site of the Philistine outpost, but their own locations are no longer known. "Cliff" (v.5) translates a Hebrew phrase that means literally "tooth of a cliff" (cf. Job 39:28, "rocky crag"), perhaps emphasizing the sharp and jagged nature of the rock formation. If the two cliffs are mentioned in the same order in vv.4 and 5, Bozez was on the north and Seneh was on the south. Bozez ("shining"?) would then perhaps be so named because its face, being on the south, would catch the rays of the sun. As for Seneh ("thornbush"[?]; cf. a similar Hebrew word in Ex 3:2–4; Dt 33:16), it may have been so-called because of thornbushes growing on or near its face (cf. Josephus' reference to "the Valley of Thorns, close to a village named Gibeah of Saul," *J. W.* 5.51 [2.1]). The suggestion of J. Maxwell Miller, 163, n. 17 (among others), that the "modern name, Wadi es-Suweinit [*sic*], is probably based on the same root" fails to account for the different sibilants in the two words or for the *t* in the modern name. In any case, the Wadi es-Suweinit (seven miles northeast of Jerusalem) is indeed the deep gorge near which the Philistine outpost was located (for general orientation cf. Yohanan Aharoni and

Michael Avi-Yonah, *The Macmillan Bible Atlas* [New York: Macmillan, 1968], 60).

When Jonathan repeats his suggestion of v.1 to his armor-bearer, he makes a significant change by calling the Philistines "those uncircumcised fellows" (v.6), a term of reproach used elsewhere of Goliath (17:26, 36) and other Philistines (31:4 = 1Ch 10:4; 2Sa 1:20) and serving to designate them as nonparticipants in the Abrahamic covenant (Ge 17:9–11).

Jonathan is confident that the Lord will fight for Israel and that nothing can keep God from saving them (cf. David's taunt to Goliath in 17:47). He knows that with God on his side even an insignificant number of men can achieve victory (v.6; cf. Jdg 7:4, 7). Other parallels with the story of Gideon commend themselves as well: the hero accompanied by only one servant (v.7; cf. Jdg 7:10–11); the sign (vv.9–10; cf. Jdg 7:13–15); the panic (v.15; cf. Jdg 7:21); the confusion, causing the enemy soldiers to turn on "each other with their swords" (v.20; cf. Jdg 7:22); reinforcements from the "hill country of Ephraim" (v.22; cf. Jdg 7:24); and the pursuit (v.22; cf. Jdg 7:23; similarly, Jobling, 369 n. 7; further, Garsiel, 87–93).

The armor-bearer's response to Jonathan (v.7) shows the extent of his loyalty: "Do all that you have in mind" (*bilᵉbābekā*, lit., "in your heart") finds its counterpoint in "I am with you heart and soul" (*kilᵉbābekā*, lit., "according to your heart," translated as hendiadys by the NIV). Their two hearts beating as one, the men will march into battle together. The verse is later echoed (almost verbatim in the Heb.) in a striking parallel (2Sa 7:3) when the prophet Nathan says to David, "Whatever you have in mind ... do it"—but this time the counterpoint (though not as verbally pleasing) is much superior: "The LORD is with you."

A brief comment by Jonathan (v.8) introduces the sign (vv.9–10) and its sequel (vv.11–14). As the dew on the fleece gave Gideon the faith to believe that God would save Israel by Gideon's hand (Jdg 6:36–37), so the appropriate Philistine response to the approach of Jonathan and his armor-bearer gave Jonathan the faith to believe that the Lord would give the enemy into their hands (vv.9–10).

When the Philistines caught sight of the two men (v.11), they assumed them to be Israelite deserters who had earlier hidden in caves and holes (13:6). Confident that they had nothing to fear, the Philistines shouted the fateful words: "Come up to us" (v.12). Goliath would learn the folly of saying "Come here" (17:44) to a mere boy who seemed to pose no threat. Like the Philistine outpost at the Micmash pass, he would feel the fatal sting of the God who had the power to give Israel's enemies into her hands (v.12; cf. 17:47).

Wasting no time, Jonathan and his companion climbed up to the outpost and began the slaughter. The use of the rare Polel of *mût* ("killed," v.13) invites further comparison to the account of David's victory over Goliath, where the same stem of the verb is used (17:51). Although outnumbered about ten to one, Jonathan and his armor-bearer dispatched "some twenty men" (v.14) in a "[furrowed] area" (*maᶜᵃnâ*; cf. Ps 129:3) of a field small enough to be plowed by a yoke of oxen in half a day (cf. NIV note here and at Isa 5:10)—that is, the Philistines were killed in a brief time and a short distance.

15–23 Confusion struck the Philistine troops (v.15; cf. vv.20, 22) whatever their location: in the camp at Micmash (13:16), out in the field, at the various outposts, with one or another of the three raiding parties (13:17–18). The panic, sent by God (cf. also 2Ki 7:6–7), was of the kind promised to Israel against her enemies when the people trusted him (Dt 7:23) but also part of the covenantal curse against Israel herself when she was apostate (Dt 28:20). During such times of terror, the ground may shake, as when the Lord led his people through the Sea of Reeds while at the same time overthrowing the Egyptians (Ps 77:18), or as an accompaniment to a theophany (2Sa 22:8 = Ps 18:7; cf. further Steven A. Austin and Mark L. Strauss, "Are Earthquakes Signs of the End Times?" *Christian Research Journal* 21/4 [1999]: 36), or—again—as a manifestation of God's displeasure against apostate Israel (Am 8:8).

So total was the Philistine panic and so noisy their flight (*hāmôn*, "army," in v.16 is translated "tumult" in v.19) that Saul's watchmen on the walls at Gibeah could see—and perhaps hear—many of the enemy soldiers as they scattered in all directions. The "melting [away]" of an enemy force is a vivid metaphor describing full retreat (cf. Isa 14:31; also Ex 15:15; Jos 2:9, 24). Curious about what was causing the Philistine flight, and perhaps considering the possibility of helping to turn it into a total rout, Saul decided once again to take a census of his troops (v.17; see 13:15)—but this time to see whether any of them had left the camp and were perhaps responsible for the Philistine panic. Amazingly enough, it was not until the census was complete that Saul became aware of the absence of Jonathan, his own son.

Still not quite ready to go to Jonathan's aid, however, Saul told the priest Ahijah to bring the ark of God before him (v.18). The LXX has "ephod" (doubtless reading *ʾpwd* instead of *ʾrwn*; cf. v.3 and NIV note on 14:18) instead of "ark of God"; the verb "bring" (*higgîš*) is used of the ephod (23:9; 30:7) but not of the ark, and lots are cast later in the chapter (vv.41–42). But the MT of v.18 uses the phrase "ark of God" twice (translated "it" by the NIV the second time; cf. also 3:3; 4:11, 13); a special point is made of the fact that it was "with the Israelites" at that time (presumably having been brought to Gibeah—temporarily, at least—from Kiriath Jearim; cf. 7:2), and Saul may well have wanted to carry it into battle against the Philistines in a superstitious attempt to guarantee victory (cf. 4:3–7). In any event, "the near-unanimous preference of older critics for 'ephod' of the LXX over 'ark' has now been reversed, and most recent authorities retain 'ark' as *lectio difficilior*" (Jobling, 369 n. 6; cf. Miscall, 92; Garsiel, 87).

Hearing the increasing tumult in the Philistine camp, Saul apparently changed his mind about the need to make use of the ark and told Ahijah to stop the ritual proceedings (v.19). Together with his men he then marched into battle (v.20), presumably without benefit of priestly blessing of any kind. The Philistines, meanwhile, had become filled with total "confusion" (*meḥûmâ*, a word assonant with *hāmôn*, "tumult," in the previous verse). Brother was wielding sword against brother, a scene to be repeated in the eschaton (Eze 38:21).

Saul, Jonathan, and the Israelite army were soon joined by two groups of reinforcements, distinguished from each other by the occurrence of *gam-hēmmâ* (lit., "also they") in vv.21 and 22. Some were Hebrews who had previously gone to the Philistine camp (v.21), perhaps either to have their agricultural tools sharpened (cf. 13:20) or, disgruntled with Israelite rule, to hire themselves out as mercenaries (cf. David among the Philistines in 29:6). In any event, it is not necessary to insist that "Hebrews" here should be differentiated from "Israelites" (see comment on 13:3) or that it stands for *ʿapirū*, a nonethnic designation for members of disparate groups of uprooted persons who exchanged their services for supplies and shelter (cf. Barry J. Beitzel, "Hebrew [People]," in *ISBE* rev., 2:657).

The second group of reinforcements (v.22) consisted of Israelite deserters who had been hiding (cf. 13:6) in the hill country of Ephraim, a large, partially forested plateau (Jos 17:15–18) north and west of Micmash. Saul himself would have known the area well (9:3–4). The "hot pursuit" of the combined Israelite forces under Saul and Jonathan would be tragically reversed in the final relentless attack of the Philistines against the king and his son (31:2 = 1Ch 10:2).

The Hebrew expression translated "So the LORD rescued Israel that day" (v.23) is a verbatim quotation of Exodus 14:30 ("That day the LORD saved Israel," NIV) in the narrative of the Sea of Reeds. Its deliberate use stresses the importance of Saul's victory while also giving all the glory to God (as Saul apparently also did; cf. v.39). The Israelite forces, however, were not satisfied with the results of their own efforts until they had driven the Philistines some distance west of Beth Aven (v.23) toward their own homeland beyond Aijalon (v.31).

NOTE

16 J. Maxwell Miller ("Geba/Gibeah of Benjamin," *VT* 25/2 [1975]: 165) has attempted to prove that "Geba, Geba of Benjamin, Gibeah, Gibeah of Saul, and, probably, Gibeath-elohim [Gibeah of God] were essentially identical and are to be associated with the site of present-day Jeba^{c}." But by the simple expedient of assuming גבע (*gb^{c}*, "Geba") to be an orthographic variant of גבעה (*gb^{c}h*, "Gibeah") in a few passages, the NIV successfully maintains the traditional distinction between Geba (in Benjamin)/Gibeah of God, on the one hand, and Gibeah (in Benjamin/of Saul), on the other (cf. NIV note to v.16; Jdg 20:10, 33).

3. The Cursing of Jonathan (14:24–46)

OVERVIEW

In this central section of chs. 13–15, the already developed contrast between Saul and Jonathan reaches its zenith. In vv.1–46 "Saul ... is not so much wicked as foolish and frustrated. His intentions are good, indeed thoroughly pious, but he pursues them in self-defeating ways, and events thwart them" (Jobling, 368).

24Now the men of Israel were in distress that day, because Saul had bound the people under an oath, saying, "Cursed be any man who eats food before evening comes, before I have avenged myself on my enemies!" So none of the troops tasted food.
25The entire army entered the woods, and there was honey on the ground. 26When they went into the woods, they saw the honey oozing out, yet no one put his hand to his mouth, because they feared the oath. 27But Jonathan had not heard that his father had bound the people with the oath, so he reached out the end of the staff that was in

his hand and dipped it into the honeycomb. He raised his hand to his mouth, and his
eyes brightened. 28 Then one of the soldiers told him, "Your father bound the army under
a strict oath, saying, 'Cursed be any man who eats food today!' That is why the men are
faint."

29 Jonathan said, "My father has made trouble for the country. See how my eyes brightened when I tasted a little of this honey. 30 How much better it would have been if the men
had eaten today some of the plunder they took from their enemies. Would not the slaughter of the Philistines have been even greater?"

31 That day, after the Israelites had struck down the Philistines from Micmash to Aijalon,
they were exhausted. 32 They pounced on the plunder and, taking sheep, cattle and calves,
they butchered them on the ground and ate them, together with the blood. 33 Then
someone said to Saul, "Look, the men are sinning against the LORD by eating meat that has
blood in it."

"You have broken faith," he said. "Roll a large stone over here at once." 34 Then he said,
"Go out among the men and tell them, 'Each of you bring me your cattle and sheep, and
slaughter them here and eat them. Do not sin against the LORD by eating meat with blood
still in it.'"

So everyone brought his ox that night and slaughtered it there. 35 Then Saul built an
altar to the LORD; it was the first time he had done this.

36 Saul said, "Let us go down after the Philistines by night and plunder them till dawn,
and let us not leave one of them alive."

"Do whatever seems best to you," they replied.

But the priest said, "Let us inquire of God here."

37 So Saul asked God, "Shall I go down after the Philistines? Will you give them into
Israel's hand?" But God did not answer him that day.

38 Saul therefore said, "Come here, all you who are leaders of the army, and let us find out
what sin has been committed today. 39 As surely as the LORD who rescues Israel lives, even if
it lies with my son Jonathan, he must die." But not one of the men said a word.

40 Saul then said to all the Israelites, "You stand over there; I and Jonathan my son will
stand over here."

"Do what seems best to you," the men replied.

41 Then Saul prayed to the LORD, the God of Israel, "Give me the right answer." And
Jonathan and Saul were taken by lot, and the men were cleared. 42 Saul said, "Cast the lot
between me and Jonathan my son." And Jonathan was taken.

43 Then Saul said to Jonathan, "Tell me what you have done."

So Jonathan told him, "I merely tasted a little honey with the end of my staff. And now
must I die?"

44Saul said, "May God deal with me, be it ever so severely, if you do not die, Jonathan."
45But the men said to Saul, "Should Jonathan die—he who has brought about this
great deliverance in Israel? Never! As surely as the LORD lives, not a hair of his head will fall
to the ground, for he did this today with God's help." So the men rescued Jonathan, and he
was not put to death.
46Then Saul stopped pursuing the Philistines, and they withdrew to their own land.

COMMENTARY

24–30 The scenes recorded here constitute a flashback to events simultaneous with the battle description in vv.20–23. Saul (v.24) had bound the "people" (*ʿam*, "troops," in this context, as often in Samuel; cf. the same word translated as "troops" later in the verse) under an oath of abstaining from food for the entire day of the battle. The result was that they were "in distress" (the same Heb. verb translated "hard pressed" in 13:6) from hunger. Thus Saul's motivation, however praiseworthy, resulted in his men's becoming "faint" (v.28) and "exhausted" (v.31).

Perhaps this result is why the narrator uses the Hiphil verbal form *wayyōʾel* ("had bound ... under an oath," from *ʾālâ*), since the form itself conjures up the root *yʾl*, which means "acted foolishly" in the Niphal stem, or for that matter the root *ʾwl*, a noun form of which means "fool" (*ʾewîl*) and is found often in Proverbs. Jobling (374 and n.32) sees here a deliberate pun that highlights Saul's "foolish oath" and that may be reflected in the double translation of the LXX: "Saul acted very foolishly ... and laid a curse on the people." Accompanying the fulfillment of the oath, intended to implement a religiously motivated fast that would energize the men and fill them with a fighting zeal, would be the opportunity for Saul to take vengeance on his enemies (cf. similarly Samson's prayer in Jdg 16:28). It was not uncommon for Israel's leaders to pronounce curses formally on friend and foe alike (cf. 26:19; Jos 6:26).

Just as a riddle about eating honey in a Philistine context got Samson into trouble (Jdg 14:8–20), so also tasting honey in a Philistine context almost cost Jonathan his life. Upon entering a forest (perhaps in the hill country of Ephraim [v.25; cf. comment on v.22]), Saul's troops noticed a honeycomb (cf. v.27) on the ground. Although it was filled with honey, no one so much as tasted any of it because they "feared" the oath (v.26)—that is, they took it seriously; they respected it (cf. Pr 13:13; further, Fox, 41). But Jonathan, unaware of the oath (v.27), used the end of his staff (perhaps to avoid being stung by bees) to dip some honey from the comb. (Compared with date honey, bees' honey was especially sweet and was virtually a luxury food [cf. SS 4:11; 5:1].)

When Jonathan ate it, his eyes "brightened" ("shone, lit up"), implying renewal of strength (cf. NIV note; Ezr 9:8; Ps 13:3). Especially instructive in this regard are the metaphors in Psalm 19:8–10: "The commands of the LORD are radiant, giving light to the eyes.... The ordinances of the LORD ... are sweeter than honey, than honey from the comb." On "his eyes brightened/lit up" see Robert Alter (*The David Story*, 81), who observes that "the idiom used for the refreshing effect of a taste of food is a pointed one because ... the verb 'to light up' (the Hebrew verb *ʾwr*) plays antithetically on Saul's 'cursed (*ʾārûr*) be the man.'"

One of Jonathan's fellow soldiers warned him about his father's oath (v.28), adding the observation that obeying it had caused the troops to become "faint" (the same verbal form is translated "exhausted" in v.31; cf. also Jdg 4:21; 2Sa 21:15). Jonathan's rebuttal, based on his refreshment after eating food, is that Saul "has made trouble [*ʿākar*; GK 6579] for the country" (v.29). The verb "*ʿkr* specifically means 'to bring into cultic jeopardy'" (Jobling, 370, though "cultic" may be an overtranslation), here in the context of holy war (cf. Jos 6:18; 1Ki 18:17–18; similarly, 1 Macc 3:5; 7:22). Of particular interest is the story of Achan, whose name (in the form Achar) became a wordplay on the root *ʿkr* (Jos 7:25; 1Ch 2:7; and NIV note) and after whom the Valley of Achor was named (Jos 7:26 and NIV note; Isa 65:10; Hos 2:15 and NIV note). Concerning Jonathan, Jobling, 370, summarizes: "He, not his father, has correctly interpreted Yhwh's will." Jonathan concludes (v.30) by arguing that even more Philistines would have been killed if Saul's men had eaten some of the food they "took" as plunder from the enemy. The verb *māṣāʾ* in this context means "found [with the intention of taking]" (cf. also Jdg 5:30; 21:12; 2Ch 20:25; Ps 119:162).

31–35 "That day" (v.31) is doubtless the same as "that day" in v.24, but Saul's men were no longer under his oath of abstinence (v.32) because it was after evening and the Philistines were totally routed. The Israelites had devastated them and driven them westward all the way to Aijalon (modern Yalo, about sixteen miles west of Micmash and seven miles southwest of [Upper] Beth Horon [cf. 13:18]), which had originally been assigned to the tribal territory of Dan (Jos 19:40–42) but which, after the Canaanites had prevented the Danites from coming into their full inheritance (Jdg 1:34; 18:1), was now in the hill country of Ephraim (1Ch 6:67–69).

Echoes of vv.32–35 reverberate throughout ch. 15: "pounce[d] on the plunder" (v.32; 15:19—the only two occurrences of the denominative verbal root *ʿyṭ* in the OT), sheep and cattle (v.32; 15:9, 14–15, 21), cattle and sheep (v.34; 15:3, translating a different pair of Hebrew words from that in the preceding set), sin(ning)/sinned (vv.33–34; 15:24, 30), "bring me" (v.34; 15:32—identical Hebrew in the two verses). Saul's commendable attempt to engage in proper ceremonial practice in vv.32–35 contrasts with his total failure in the same arena in ch. 15.

Famished, the Israelite troops seized sheep, cattle, and calves from the Philistine plunder, butchered them, and ate the meat without waiting for the blood to drain from it (v.32). Since eating meat with the blood still in it was forbidden to God's people throughout their history (cf. Lev 17:10–14; 19:26; Dt 12:16, 23–24; Eze 33:25; Ac 15:20), it is not surprising that Saul, on hearing of his men's sinful deed, immediately acted to absolve them of guilt. He first accused them of having betrayed their promise to God, of having "broken faith" (v.33; the root *bgd* is strikingly used five times in succession in Isa 24:16: "The treacherous betray! With treachery the treacherous betray!"). He then demanded that a large stone be rolled over to him so that animals could be properly slaughtered on it, not on the ground as before (v.32)—perhaps because the ground was reserved for receiving the drained blood (cf. Dt 12:16, 24).

Although Klein, 139, claims that the "large stone" in v.33 should be compared to that in 6:14, "which served as an altar for sacrifice at Beth-shemesh when the ark was returned from the Philistines," we observe that nothing is said in either chapter about a rock on which sacrifice was offered. In fact, 6:15, 18 state specifically that the "large rock" (the Heb. phrase thus translated in ch. 6 being the same as that for "large stone" in v.33) was used as a temporary pedestal for the ark. In any case, the issue in vv.32–34 is slaughtering animals for food, not sacrificing animals for atonement. We cannot even be sure that the large stone was incorporated into the altar that Saul built later (v.35), as asserted by some (e.g., Kirkpatrick, *1 Samuel*, 136).

Saul demanded that each of his men "bring" (v.34) their animals to him for slaughter. The same Hebrew phrase so translated appears on Saul's lips also in the account of his rebuke by Samuel (13:9) and on Samuel's lips in the account of Saul's rejection by God (15:32). Here in v.34 it poignantly underscores Saul's commendable attempt to right a sinful wrong perpetrated by his understandably hungry troops—a hunger originally caused by a well-intended but ill-advised oath that Saul had imposed on them. Spiritually sensitive Israelite leaders built altars as a matter of routine (cf. Samuel [7:17]; Gideon [Jdg 6:24]; David [2Sa 24:25; 1Ch 21:18]). In Saul's case a special point is made of the fact that this was the "first time" he had done so (v.35), probably a negative comment directed at Saul's lack of piety.

36–46 The literary integrity of this unit is highlighted by the inclusio that frames it: "Go down after the Philistines" (v.36) is mirrored by "stopped pursuing the Philistines" (lit., "went up from after the Philistines," v.46). Initially Saul determined to plunder and slaughter them until nothing and no one remained. The decision to attack at night and plunder till dawn (v.36) reflects the common practice of conducting military operations in the dead of night, when the number of attackers was small and therefore the element of surprise was important (cf. Jdg 16:3). Saul's men, apparently satisfied that he had their best interests at heart, were ready to follow him (vv.36, 40).

The priest Ahijah, however, sensed the need to "inquire of" God (lit., "draw near to," v.36; cf. Zep 3:2), perhaps by making use of the sacred lots stored in the ephod (v.3; cf. further vv.41–42). Agreeing, Saul "asked" (v.37; yet another Hebrew pun on the name "Saul") the Lord whether the defeat of the enemy was imminent (cf. similarly 7:8–9; Jdg 20:23). When he received no answer, he sensed that something was amiss in the army (v.38). Much later, after his rejection by God, Saul would understand that no approach or technique, however authorized in other contexts, would bring a divine response, however desperate his need (28:6, 15).

Saul called for the army "leaders" (lit., "corner[stone]s," v.38 [cf. Jdg 20:2; Isa 19:13; Zec 10:4]) to come before him to ascertain what sin had been committed (v.38) and who had committed it (v.39). Pronouncing the solemn asseverative oath "as surely as the Lord lives," which is used often (though not always) in contexts where life and death hang in the balance (cf. v.45; 19:6; 20:3, 21; 25:34; 26:10, 16; 28:10; 2Sa 4:9–10; 12:5; 14:11; 15:21), Saul affirmed that whoever had sinned "must die" (v.39; the Heb. construction underlying this phrase is translated "will surely die" in Ge 2:17 and is echoed verbatim in v.44). If necessary, he was even prepared to give up the life of his son Jonathan (vv.39, 44; cf. similarly Abraham and Isaac [Ge 22:10, 12, 16; Heb 11:17]; Reuben and his two sons [Ge 42:37]; Jephthah and his daughter [Jdg 11:31, 39]).

Respectful even in the face of Saul's shocking announcement, knowing that Jonathan had (however innocently) violated his father's imposed oath, aware that the brave Jonathan would likely die through no fault of his own, doubtless sympathizing with Jonathan's position as over against Saul's folly—none of his men "said a word" (lit., "was answering him") during those dramatic moments. Anticipating the casting of lots to determine by the process of elimination (cf. 10:19–21 and comments there; Jos 7:11–12, 14–18) who had committed the sin that imperiled further war against

Philistia (v.41), Saul made the "first binary division" (Klein, 140) by lining up his troops on one side and himself and Jonathan on the other (v.40). Again the text stresses the tenseness of the scene by noting the acquiescence of Saul's men.

At best, "Give me the right answer" in the MT of v.41 is difficult. A. Toeg ("A Textual Note on 1 Samuel XIV 41," *VT* 19/4 [1969]: 493–98), after surveying several attempts to maintain its authenticity—including reference to supposed Mesopotamian analogies such as *kettam šuknā* ("Put right," that is, "Grant me a clear and true response")—concludes that the longer LXX version (see NIV note) is the more original text (cf. also F. F. Bruce, "The Old Testament in Greek," *BT* 4/4 [1953]: 159). In any event, mention of the priestly ephod in v.3 and of the casting of lots in vv.41–42 provides a strong presumption for the accuracy of the tradition underlying the LXX text at this point, if not of its precise wording. (No Heb. equivalent for "lot" is found in the text in either verse, but in both cases the NIV correctly supplies the word based on the context, as it does also in Job 6:27.) The MT's *tāmîm* (rendered "right answer" in v.41) should surely be vocalized *tummîm* ("Thummim"), with the LXX.

The casting of lots proceeds swiftly, and the rest of the men are eliminated as "Jonathan and Saul" are taken (v.41; that Jonathan's name appears first is an ominous sign). As the final lot is cast, Saul is cleared and Jonathan taken (v.42). Saul's statement to Jonathan echoes Joshua's to Achan centuries earlier: "Tell me what you have done" (v.43; Jos 7:19). The NIV's translation of Jonathan's response makes him sound more indignant than the Hebrew text warrants: "I merely tasted a little honey with the end of my staff. And now must I die?" A more literal rendering reveals his willingness to accept the consequences of his action: "I indeed tasted a little honey with the end of my staff. I am ready to die" (cf. also Jobling, 370; Klein, 131). Even more solemn than the oath Saul had taken earlier (v.39) is the one he now takes (v.44; cf. also 25:22; Ru 1:17; 1Ki 2:23), and it seems that Jonathan's doom is sealed.

Unable to contain themselves any longer in the face of gross injustice, Saul's men remind him of how cruel it would be to execute Israel's deliverer (v.45). Jonathan would remember their cry of "Never!" as he later encouraged David (20:2). Because he was able to achieve victory with God's help (cf. Ge 4:1), not a single hair of his head would fall to the ground (so also of the son of the wise woman from Tekoa [2Sa 14:11]; of Adonijah [1Ki 1:52]; and of the men with Paul in the boat about to be shipwrecked [Ac 27:34]). Finally persuaded, Saul rescinds his order, and thus Jonathan is "rescued" (lit., "ransomed"; cf. Job 6:23) by the fervent pleas of the troops. Distracted by his determination to execute his own son, Saul loses his best opportunity to deal the Philistines a lethal blow (v.46).

NOTES

25 One Hebrew manuscript has הָעָם (*hāʿām*, "the people"; "army," NIV) instead of the MT's הָאָרֶץ (*hāʾāreṣ*, "the land"; cf. NIV note).

27 In 2007, remains of the first beehive colony dating from the biblical period were found in excavations at Tel Rehob four miles south of Beth Shan in the Jordan Valley. The apiary consisted of more than thirty hives and dates from the mid-tenth to early-ninth century BC (*Artifax* 22/4 [2007]: 6).

30 We would expect הַמַּכָּה (*hammakkâ*, "the slaughter"; thus the NIV) instead of the MT's מַכָּה (*makkâ*, without the definite article). Perhaps the MT's reading illustrates the phenomenon of shared consonants, the ־ה (*h*-) of the definite article being shared with the same letter that ends the preceding word (so Watson, 531).

32 The correctness of the *Qere* reading וַיַּעַט (*wayyaᶜaṭ*, "[and] pounced on") is confirmed by the occurrence of the same rare verb in the same phrase in 15:19. There is thus no need to connect the *Kethiv* reading וַיַּעַשׂ (*wayyaᶜaś*, lit., "and he did/made") with a presumed Arabic cognate meaning "turn," as does D. Winton Thomas, who does not mention the *Qere* ("Translating Hebrew ᶜāśâ," *BT* 17/4 [1966]: 192).

4. Further Wars of Saul (14:47–52)

OVERVIEW

Just before the account of the divine rejection of Saul in ch. 15, the end of his reign is marked by an editorial summary of his career (Jobling, 371 n. 15). Like other similar royal summaries (cf. that concerning Jeroboam II [2Ki 14:28]), it includes a brief statement about his military victories over his enemies (vv.47–48, 52). The names and relationships of important members of his family (vv.49–51) are also given.

[47]After Saul had assumed rule over Israel, he fought against their enemies on every side: Moab, the Ammonites, Edom, the kings of Zobah, and the Philistines. Wherever he turned, he inflicted punishment on them. [48]He fought valiantly and defeated the Amalekites, delivering Israel from the hands of those who had plundered them.

[49]Saul's sons were Jonathan, Ishvi and Malki-Shua. The name of his older daughter was Merab, and that of the younger was Michal. [50]His wife's name was Ahinoam daughter of Ahimaaz. The name of the commander of Saul's army was Abner son of Ner, and Ner was Saul's uncle. [51]Saul's father Kish and Abner's father Ner were sons of Abiel.

[52]All the days of Saul there was bitter war with the Philistines, and whenever Saul saw a mighty or brave man, he took him into his service.

COMMENTARY

47–48 The ambiguity (perhaps intentional) of the statement that Saul "assumed rule over" Israel (v.47) may be illustrated by the assertion in BDB, 540, that it refers to "Saul's seizing the kingdom, that is, acquiring it actually by force of arms," as opposed to BDB, 574, where we read that the phrase here simply means to "assume sovereignty over" the land. The verb *lākad* ("seize, take"; GK 4334) is used in vv.41–42 in the sense of being "taken" by lot. Although for the most part we do not know the times or extent of Saul's wars against his enemies, we read that he was successful wherever he turned: against the Transjordanian triad of Ammon (cf. 11:1–11), Moab, and Edom (northeast, east, and southeast of the Dead Sea respectively); against the Aramean kingdom of Zobah (north of Damascus), where David was similarly successful (2Sa 8:3–12; 10:6–19); and—last but not least—against the Philistines. In anticipation of Saul's fiasco in ch. 15, the narrator reserves the Amalekites (who inhabited large tracts of land southwest of the Dead Sea) for special attention (v.48).

On one or more occasions (otherwise unrecorded) during his reign, Saul "fought valiantly" against Amalek (v.48; other occurrences of the idiom associate it with God's help; "gain the victory," Ps 60:12 = 108:13; "has done mighty things," 118:15–16) and defeated them. Saul also saved Israel from the hands of "those who had plundered" them (the phraseology echoes the grand tradition of the judges; cf. Jdg 2:16, where the same Heb. participle is translated "raiders"). But Saul's incomplete victory in ch. 15, caused by his disobedience, led to divine rejection and the loss of his kingdom (15:28; 28:17–18).

49 The names of Saul's children are recorded in v.49 and those of other family members appear in vv.50–51. In addition to his firstborn, Jonathan, Saul had at least two other sons: Ishvi (meaning unknown), who is probably to be identified with Ish-Bosheth, since the latter was not killed (31:2) in Saul's last battle (2Sa 2–4; = Esh-Baal [1Ch 8:33 = 9:39]), and Malki-Shua ("My king is noble" [31:2 = 1Ch 10:2; 1Ch 8:33 = 9:39]). Each of the four references listed for Malki-Shua also includes the name of a fourth son, Abinadab ("My father is noble"); why he is not mentioned here in v.49 is unknown. Saul's two daughters, Merab (2Sa 21:8; better Merob, which perhaps means "Substitute, Compensation" [see comment on Jerub-Baal in 12:11]; cf. the Qumran and LXX vocalization of the name; and esp. Robert B. Lawton, 423–25) and Michal (perhaps contracted from Michael, "Who is like God?"; cf. 19:11–17; 2Sa 6:16–23), are listed in their proper genealogical order (cf. similarly Ge 29:16). Both were later offered in marriage to David (18:17–27).

50–51 Saul's wife (v.50) was Ahinoam ("My brother is pleasant") daughter of Ahimaaz (meaning unknown); nothing further is known of Ahimaaz (for Ahinoam see comment on 25:43). Saul also had a concubine named Rizpah (2Sa 3:7). The commander of Saul's army was his cousin Abner (spelled Abiner in the Hebrew only here), which means either "My father is Ner" (he is called "son of Ner") or "My father is the lamp" (a metaphor for God himself; cf. 2Sa 22:29; further, Robert Houston Smith, "The Household Lamps of Palestine in Old Testament Times," *BA* 27/1 [1964]: 21–22). Saul's father, Kish (v.51), and his uncle Ner were both sons of Abiel ("My father is God"; cf. 9:1).

52 Chapter 14 concludes with reminders of the never-ending and all-pervasive Philistine threat and of the king's continuing need for fresh troops (the latter of which Samuel had warned the people about when they had originally demanded a king; 8:11). This final verse also sends forth literary rays into the future. One of the "brave" men Saul will conscript is David (18:17); and David himself, after committing adultery with the wife of Uriah, would doom him by having him sent to the battlefront "where the fighting is fiercest" (2Sa 11:15; the Hebrew phrase is translated "bitter war" here in v.52). Once the husband of Bathsheba was dead, David "had her brought to" his house to become his wife (2Sa 11:27; the Hebrew phrase is translated "took him into his service" here in v.52).

NOTE

47 Excavations in 2002 at Khirbet en-Nahas ("ruins of copper" in Arabic), a copper-smelting site thirty miles south of the Dead Sea in Jordan, uncovered an Edomite monumental fortress and industrial-scale, metal-production facilities dating to the tenth century BC. Radiocarbon dating of the site itself establishes that occupation began there as early as the late twelfth century, a fact confirmed by the presence of Egyptian scarabs that date to the thirteenth and eleventh centuries—all of which demonstrates archaeologically that Edomites had in fact settled in the area long before Saul's reign began (see esp. Thomas E. Levy and Mohammad Najjar, "Edom and Copper: The Emergence of Israel's Ancient Rival," *BAR* 32/4 [2006]: 24–35); Najjar Levy et al., "High-Precision Radiocarbon Dating and Historical Biblical Arcaheology in Southern Jordan," *Proceedings of the National Academy of Sciences* 105 [2008]: 16460–65).

5. The Rejection of Saul (15:1–35)

OVERVIEW

Chapter 15, which concludes the account of Saul's decline (chs. 13–15), is the classic exposition of the theme of "prophetic opposition to reliance on anybody or anything but the LORD who alone leads Israel's Holy War" (Roth, "A Study of *skl*," 74–75). As in ch. 13 Saul's offering of an unauthorized sacrifice in the context of holy war led to Samuel's initial rebuke, so in ch. 15 Saul's intention to offer an unauthorized sacrifice in the context of holy war leads to God's final rejection. If at that earlier time Saul was denied a dynasty, now he is denied his kingship. Thus ch. 15 is climactic. "Saul's loss of kingship and kingdom are irrevocable; the rest of 1 Samuel details how in fact he does lose it all" (Miscall, 98).

[1]Samuel said to Saul, "I am the one the LORD sent to anoint you king over his people
Israel; so listen now to the message from the LORD. [2]This is what the LORD Almighty says:
'I will punish the Amalekites for what they did to Israel when they waylaid them as they
came up from Egypt. [3]Now go, attack the Amalekites and totally destroy everything that
belongs to them. Do not spare them; put to death men and women, children and infants,
cattle and sheep, camels and donkeys.'"
[4]So Saul summoned the men and mustered them at Telaim—two hundred thousand
foot soldiers and ten thousand men from Judah. [5]Saul went to the city of Amalek and set
an ambush in the ravine. [6]Then he said to the Kenites, "Go away, leave the Amalekites so
that I do not destroy you along with them; for you showed kindness to all the Israelites
when they came up out of Egypt." So the Kenites moved away from the Amalekites.

[7]Then Saul attacked the Amalekites all the way from Havilah to Shur, to the east of
Egypt. [8]He took Agag king of the Amalekites alive, and all his people he totally destroyed
with the sword. [9]But Saul and the army spared Agag and the best of the sheep and cattle,
the fat calves and lambs—everything that was good. These they were unwilling to
destroy completely, but everything that was despised and weak they totally destroyed.
[10]Then the word of the LORD came to Samuel: [11]"I am grieved that I have made Saul king,
because he has turned away from me and has not carried out my instructions." Samuel
was troubled, and he cried out to the LORD all that night.
[12]Early in the morning Samuel got up and went to meet Saul, but he was told, "Saul has
gone to Carmel. There he has set up a monument in his own honor and has turned and
gone on down to Gilgal."
[13]When Samuel reached him, Saul said, "The LORD bless you! I have carried out the LORD's
instructions."
[14]But Samuel said, "What then is this bleating of sheep in my ears? What is this lowing
of cattle that I hear?"
[15]Saul answered, "The soldiers brought them from the Amalekites; they spared the best
of the sheep and cattle to sacrifice to the LORD your God, but we totally destroyed the
rest."
[16]"Stop!" Samuel said to Saul. "Let me tell you what the LORD said to me last night."
"Tell me," Saul replied.
[17]Samuel said, "Although you were once small in your own eyes, did you not become
the head of the tribes of Israel? The LORD anointed you king over Israel. [18]And he sent you
on a mission, saying, 'Go and completely destroy those wicked people, the Amalekites;
make war on them until you have wiped them out.' [19]Why did you not obey the LORD? Why
did you pounce on the plunder and do evil in the eyes of the LORD?"
[20]"But I did obey the LORD," Saul said. "I went on the mission the LORD assigned me. I
completely destroyed the Amalekites and brought back Agag their king. [21]The soldiers
took sheep and cattle from the plunder, the best of what was devoted to God, in order to
sacrifice them to the LORD your God at Gilgal."
[22]But Samuel replied:

"Does the LORD delight in burnt offerings and sacrifices
as much as in obeying the voice of the LORD?
To obey is better than sacrifice,
and to heed is better than the fat of rams.
[23]For rebellion is like the sin of divination,
and arrogance like the evil of idolatry.
Because you have rejected the word of the LORD,
he has rejected you as king."

[24]Then Saul said to Samuel, "I have sinned. I violated the LORD's command and your
instructions. I was afraid of the people and so I gave in to them. [25]Now I beg you, forgive
my sin and come back with me, so that I may worship the LORD."
[26]But Samuel said to him, "I will not go back with you. You have rejected the word of
the LORD, and the LORD has rejected you as king over Israel!"
[27]As Samuel turned to leave, Saul caught hold of the hem of his robe, and it tore.
[28]Samuel said to him, "The LORD has torn the kingdom of Israel from you today and has
given it to one of your neighbors — to one better than you. [29]He who is the Glory of
Israel does not lie or change his mind; for he is not a man, that he should change his
mind."
[30]Saul replied, "I have sinned. But please honor me before the elders of my people and
before Israel; come back with me, so that I may worship the LORD your God." [31]So Samuel
went back with Saul, and Saul worshiped the LORD.
[32]Then Samuel said, "Bring me Agag king of the Amalekites."
Agag came to him confidently, thinking, "Surely the bitterness of death is past."
[33]But Samuel said,

"As your sword has made women childless,
so will your mother be childless among women."

And Samuel put Agag to death before the LORD at Gilgal.
[34]Then Samuel left for Ramah, but Saul went up to his home in Gibeah of Saul. [35]Until
the day Samuel died, he did not go to see Saul again, though Samuel mourned for him.
And the LORD was grieved that he had made Saul king over Israel.

COMMENTARY

1–3 The emphatic position of the independent pronoun—"I am the one"—stresses Samuel's role as the representative through whom God anointed Saul and through whom he now proclaims a further message to him (v.1). As Miscall, 98–99, correctly observes, Saul is here described for the first time as having been anointed *melek* ("king"; see also v.17); previously the transitional term *nāgîd* ("leader") is used at his anointing (9:16; 10:1). His fall from grace thus becomes all the more stark—and that of David in a similarly tragic situation (2Sa 12:7–10) mirrors the scene that unfolds in this chapter.

Soon to wrest the kingship from Saul's grasp, the Lord—the only true King in Israel's theocratic monarchy—is described as "the LORD Almighty" (v.2), a specifically royal name (see comment on 1:3). His message to Saul is that the time has come for the final destruction of the Amalekites, predicted and reiterated long ago (Ex 17:8–16; Nu 24:20; Dt 25:17–19). The summary of Saul's wars at the end of ch. 14 includes his defeat of Amalek on one or more otherwise unrecorded occasions (14:48), casting the failure of ch. 15 in even sharper relief. The geographical clues scattered throughout the chapter make it clear that the Amalekites referred to here are the traditional southern marauders rather than a smaller Amalekite enclave occupying an area in the hills of western Samaria. The only way that the northern Amalekite theory can be maintained is by the unacceptable means of assuming that all the clues are secondary insertions (cf. Edelman, "Saul's Battle," 71–84).

The significance and uniqueness of the divine command to annihilate the Amalekites is underscored by *ḥrm* (GK 3049), "the irrevocable giving over of things or persons to the LORD, often by totally destroying them" (NIV note, v.3). Although the root appears often enough elsewhere in the OT in contexts of holy war, it occurs in the books of Samuel only here in ch. 15. The verb ("completely/totally destroyed") is found, however, a total of seven times in this one chapter (vv.3, 8–9 [2x], 15, 18, 20), while its cognate noun ("what was devoted to God") appears once (v.21). The precise meaning of the verb in this context is secured by the verbs associated with it at its first occurrence in verse 3: "attack," "do not spare," "put to death." Although all the verbs except one in v.3 are in the singular, Saul is not expected to accomplish the grisly task himself. The key verb "totally destroy" is plural and thus implicates the Israelite troops as well.

It is furthermore clear that "everything that belongs to them" (v.3) here means "everything among them that breathes" (cf. strikingly Dt 20:16–17). Representative pairings of animate creatures doomed to destruction conclude the verse. This list is ominously echoed—almost verbatim—in 22:19, where Saul exterminates all the inhabitants of the town of Nob. Fokkelman ("Saul and David," 28) observes that "in killing everyone in Nob, including Yahweh's priests, Saul takes his revenge against God. Saul does to a town of Yahweh's priests what God through Samuel had ordered Saul to do to the Amalekites." The command in v.3 is specific: "Do not spare them"; Saul, however, rationalized the disobedience of that command (vv.9, 15).

We should not be surprised that Saul did not flinch at the prospect of killing ostensibly innocent women and children. Although outside of Israel the root *ḥrm* in the sense here outlined occurs only in line 17 of the Mesha inscription (Rudolf Smend and Albert Socin, *Die Inschrift des Königs Mesa von Moab* [Freiburg: Mohr, 1886], 12, 23), wars in the ancient Near East always had a religious dimension, and the battlefield was an arena of divine retribution. The Amalekites, in their persistent refusal to fear God (Dt 25:18), sowed the seeds of their own destruction. God is patient and slow to anger, "abounding in love and faithfulness" (Ex 34:6); he nevertheless "does not leave the guilty unpunished" (34:7).

The agent of divine judgment can be impersonal (e.g., the flood or the destruction of Sodom and Gomorrah) or personal (as here), and in his sovereign purpose God often permits entire families or nations to be destroyed if their corporate representatives are willfully and incorrigibly wicked (cf. Jos 7:1, 10–13, 24–26). For further discussion of this sensitive issue, see the nuanced treatments of Peter C. Craigie, *The Problem of War in the Old Testament* (Grand Rapids: Eerdmans, 1978); John W. Wenham, *The Enigma of Evil: Can We Believe in the Goodness of God?* (Grand Rapids: Zondervan, 1985), 99–101, 119–25, 165–68.

4–9 Saul's preparations for battle against the Amalekites are outlined in vv.4–6. He "summoned" (lit., "caused to hear"; cf. "called up" in 23:8) from Judah "ten thousand" men (v.4). The number probably denotes "the least number for a complete fighting force" (J. B. Segal, 5–6); thus there were only "ten thousand foot soldiers" left in the decimated army of Jehoahaz (2Ki 13:7). In addition Saul mustered "two hundred thousand foot soldiers," probably from Israel (on the analogy of 11:8; cf. comment there). Saul's troop strength had declined considerably since the battles against Nahash and the Ammonites (11:8), but it was more than adequate for the present task. Although the precise location of the mustering site (Telaim, probably = Telem in the Negev [Jos 15:21, 24]) is unknown, it has been suggested that the "city of Amalek" (v.5) is modern Tel Masos (about seven miles east-southeast of Beersheba) and that a destruction layer there attests to the successful ambush of Saul's troops (cf. Ze'ev Herzog, "Enclosed Settlements in the Negeb and the Wilderness of Beer-Sheba," *BASOR* 250 [Spring 1983]: 43, 47).

Before Saul's main attack against the Amalekites (vv.7–9), he urged the Kenites living in or near Amalekite territory (cf. 27:10; 30:29) to move out (at least temporarily) to avoid getting killed in the ensuing battle. Saul's regard for the welfare of the Kenites is in recognition of the fact that they "showed kindness" to the Israelite spies centuries earlier and had thus been spared in return (Jos 2:12–14; so Miscall, 100–101).

The Israelites attacked the Amalekites throughout their homeland—from Havilah (location unknown, but perhaps in northern Arabia) to Shur (on the eastern border of the Nile delta [v.7]; cf. also 27:8; Ex 15:22)—an extensive area that had formerly been settled by descendants of Ishmael (Ge 25:17–18). The powerful assonance evident in "totally destroyed [*ḥrm*] with the sword [*ḥrb*]" is not unique to v.8 (cf. Dt 13:15; Jos 6:21; Isa 34:5). The description of the total destruction of "all" the people (v.8) is hyperbolic, since the Amalekites as a whole survived to fight again (cf. 30:1). In any event, Saul spared Agag—but perhaps with the intent of later putting him to death, since the idiom "take alive" often describes an action preparatory to subsequent execution (cf. 2Ki 10:14; 2Ch 25:12; and esp. Jos 8:23, 29). It is noteworthy that Samuel nowhere berates Saul for having (temporarily?) preserved Agag's life.

Although Numbers 24:7 with its reference to "Agag" may be a specific prediction of the events in ch. 15, it is equally possible that Agag was a dynastic royal name among the Amalekites and that Numbers 24:7 merely speaks in general terms of the historical domination of Amalek by Israel. That Haman the "Agagite" (Est 3:1, 10; 8:3, 5; 9:24) was an Amalekite is taken for granted by Josephus, who states that Haman's determination to destroy all the Jews in Persia was in retaliation for Israel's previous destruction of all his ancestors (*Ant.* 11.211 [6.5]).

Besides sparing Agag, Saul and his troops also set aside the best of the enemy's animals while destroying those that were worthless and weak (v.9). When reproved by Samuel for not slaughtering even the best animals (vv.14, 19), Saul gave the excuse that his "soldiers" (vv.15, 21) intended to sacrifice them to the Lord. If Saul is sincere at this point, his reluctance to accept responsibility and his haste to shift the blame to his men is disquietingly reminiscent of similar situations in the past (Ge 3:12–13; Ex 32:21–24). The text, however, states that Saul and his men were "unwilling" to destroy—a verb specifically linked elsewhere with the sin of rebellion (Dt 1:26).

10–21 In truth, "the word of the LORD was rare" in those days (3:1). The phrase "the word of the LORD came to" is used of God's revelation to a prophet only three times in the books of Samuel—once in blessing (through Nathan to David [2Sa 7:4]) and twice in judgment (through Samuel to Saul [v.10]; through Gad to David [2Sa 24:11]). In each of two stages in this section (vv.10–15, 16–21), Samuel brings the condemning word of God to Saul for having disobeyed the divine command.

The use of the Niphal of the verb *nāḥam* ("repent"; GK 5714) in ch. 15 presents something of a problem because it appears to involve God in contradictory actions. In v.11 the Lord says, "I have repented" ("I am grieved," NIV; "I regret," TNIV); in v.29 Samuel says twice of him that he does not "repent" ("change his mind," NIV); and in v.35 the narrator says of him that he "repented" ("was grieved," NIV; "regretted," TNIV). Terence E. Fretheim, in an otherwise excellent article ("Divine Foreknowledge," 595, 602), speaks of "limited divine knowledge of the future," of "what God has learned, and how God adjusts in view of such learning." Much better is the analysis of John Goldingay (*Theological Diversity and the Authority of the Old Testament* (Grand Rapids.: Eerdmans, 1987), 16–17):

> To speak of God changing his mind about an act or regretting it suggests the reality of his interacting with people in the world.... His reactions to the deeds of others reflect a coherent pattern rather than randomness. Further, whereas human beings make their decisions unaware of all their consequences, so that those consequences can catch them out, God (so the OT assumes) can foresee not only the consequences of his own actions but also the nature of the responses they will meet with and the nature of other human acts, so that he can in turn formulate his response to these in advance. So the interaction between divine and human decision-making is real (there are genuine human acts to foresee), yet God is not caught out by the latter, and in this sense he does not have to change his mind.

Walter C. Kaiser Jr. (*Toward Old Testament Ethics* [Grand Rapids: Zondervan, 1991], 250) remarks, "God can and does change in his actions and emotions towards men so as not to be fickle, mutable, and variable in his nature or purpose" (see further Page H. Kelley, "The Repentance of God," *BI* 9/1 [1982]: 12–13). The NIV's "am/was grieved" in vv.11, 35 (references, we observe, that bookend a major section of ch. 15) is, of course, justifiable (cf. H. Van Dyke Parunak's contention ["A Semantic Survey of *NḤM*" *Bib* 56 (1975): 519] that *nḥm* means "suffer emotional pain" not only here but also in Ge 6:6–7; Jdg 21:6, 15; Jer 31:19 ["repented," NIV]). In such contexts the connection between "regret, suffer remorse, be grieved" and "repent, relent, reconsider" (cf. Ex 32:11–14; Jer 18:8, 10) is not far to seek. For a fine summary of the various issues involved in God's reconsidering/regretting/relenting/repenting see John Peckham, "The Passible Potter and the Contingent Clay: A Theological Study of Jeremiah 18:1–10," *Journal of the Adventist Theological Society* 18/1 (2007): 129–49.

Whether Samuel had by this time become reconciled—however reluctantly—to Saul's kingship is difficult to say. After all, God's role in making Saul king is stressed over and over in these chapters (9:17; 10:1, 24; 12:13; 13:13; 15:1). Although Samuel did not yet know it, Saul had "turned away" (v.11) from the Lord, an action fraught with the most serious of consequences (cf. Nu 14:43; 32:15; Jos 22:16, 18, 23, 29; 1Ki 9:6–7); to fail to carry out God's "instructions" (lit., "words") is to become his enemy (cf. Pss 50:16–17; 119:139). The Lord's "word" to Samuel in v.11 was clearly disturbing to him. It caused him to be "troubled" (lit., "angry"; cf. 18:8; 2Sa 3:8; and esp. 2Sa 6:8, where the divine execution of Uzzah makes David "angry") and to cry out (for help, often for someone else; cf. 7:8–9; 12:8, 10) to the Lord all night long.

Was Samuel, sympathetic to Saul's plight, trying to persuade God to forgive Saul and retain him as king? Or was Samuel, antagonistic toward Saul, pleading with God to maintain somehow Samuel's credibility (since it was Samuel who had anointed Saul as king)? Although the text is noncommittal on this point, attempts to explain Samuel's sense of urgency along these and similar lines are legion (cf. Fretheim, "Divine Foreknowledge," 601; Miscall, 103). Whatever the reason(s) for Samuel's distress/anger, and whatever the content of his cries for help, it was during his nightlong wrestling with God in prayer that he received the divine message of irreversible doom for Saul's kingdom (cf. v.16). God has now spoken; throughout the rest of the chapter Samuel mediates the divine word to the rejected Saul.

Wherever it was that Samuel expected to find Saul when he went out to meet him (v.12) and declare to him the message of doom, he was told that Saul had gone to Carmel (modern Khirbet el-Kirmil in the hill country of Judah [cf. 25:2, 5, 7, 40; Jos 15:48, 55], eight miles south-southeast of Hebron, not the northern Carmel on the Mediterranean coast). There Saul set up a monument (probably an inscribed victory stele) "in his own honor" (apparently not giving credit to the Lord). The word for "monument" is *yad* ("hand"), used in the same sense concerning the equally egotistical Absalom (2Sa 18:18). Having built the monument, Saul then "turned" (preparatory to leaving; cf. v.27) and went to Gilgal—the very place where Samuel had earlier rebuked him but that at the same time had in Saul's mind become associated with sacrifice (13:7–14; cf. v.21).

When Samuel arrived at Gilgal, Saul—either genuinely or pretending innocence—greeted him in the traditional way (v.13; cf. 23:21; 2Sa 2:5; Ru 2:19–20; 3:10) and told him he had carried out the Lord's "instructions" (lit., "word"—does he avoid saying "words" [cf. comment on v.10] because of having spared Agag and the best animals?). But Samuel, not to be denied, wanted to know why he heard the "bleating" of sheep and the "lowing" (lit., in both cases, "voice") of cattle in the background (v.14). The terms used in Samuel's question soon return to haunt Saul when Samuel says to him that "obeying" (lit., "hearing") the "voice" of the Lord pleases him more than bringing sacrifices to him (v.22; cf. also v.19; v.24 and comment).

Thus, Saul's meek retort in v.15 fails on two counts: (1) However commendable his declared motive, Saul was told to destroy every living thing and therefore should not have spared even the best of the animals; (2) even if his soldiers were primarily responsible for saving the animals, Saul was their leader and therefore should not have tried to shift the blame to them. Especially stark is the contrast between "they spared" and "we totally destroyed." Notice that in speaking to Samuel, Saul referred to "the LORD your God" (rather than "the LORD our God"; cf. vv.21, 30)—even though he had just invoked the name of the Lord in a personal way and had claimed to have obeyed him (v.13).

Samuel refused Saul's self-righteous protestations. With all the force of divine authority, he told Saul to "stop" (v.16; the same Hebrew verb translated "be still" in Ps 46:10)—a command analogous to "you acted foolishly" in 13:13 (so Miscall, 105)—and to listen to what God had revealed to him the previous night. He reminded Saul (v.17) that despite the fact that Saul had once considered himself too insignificant to be Israel's ruler (cf. 9:21; 10:22), the Lord had nevertheless anointed him as king. He then summarized (v.18) the divine commission of vv.2–3, emphasizing the intractable sinfulness of the Amalekites by calling them "wicked people" (lit., "[habitual] sinners," the same Heb. word used in Ps 1:1, 5) and reiterating the irrevocable, divine intention to destroy them completely (cf. similarly 2Sa 22:38 = Ps 18:37; 1Ki 22:11 = 2Ch 18:10; Jer 9:16). Quick to condemn his troops for having "pounced on the plunder"—including especially "sheep and cattle"—after defeating the Philistines (14:32–33), Saul discovered that "to pounce on the plunder" (v.19)—including especially "sheep and cattle" (v.21)—is to "do evil in the eyes of the LORD" (an echo of Israel's sinful demand for a king in the first place; cf. 12:17).

Saul has no better defense against Samuel's onslaught than to repeat in detail (vv.20–21) what he had already said in summary (v.13). Although he stresses his own obedience by speaking in the first person several times in v.20, he also tries to justify the actions of his troops (v.21) by attributing to them the worthy intention to sacrifice to the Lord the animals they had spared. Saul's terminology in v.21 and Samuel's in v.22 link the disobedience of Saul and his men to the earlier wickedness of Eli and his reprobate sons. As the latter had sinfully fattened themselves on the "choice parts" of Israel's offerings (2:29), so Saul's troops had stubbornly kept the "best" of the plundered animals in order to sacrifice them (v.21; the Heb. word in the two passages is identical and is not the same as the word for "best" in vv.9, 15). As the doom of Hophni and Phinehas was sealed because it was the Lord's "will" to put them to death (2:25), so the rejection of Saul is irreversible because the Lord does not "delight" in willful disobedience (v.22; the same Heb. root in both verses).

22–31 The poetic format of Samuel's well-known condemnation of Saul's objection (vv.22–23) in no way blunts its severity (cf. similarly v.33). As at the time of the fall (Ge 2–3), the matter at stake is one of obedience, and Saul failed as miserably as did Adam and Eve.

Verse 22, a classic text on the importance of obedience, moral conduct, and proper motivation vis-à-vis animal sacrifice, has a striking parallel in the Egyptian Instruction for Meri-ka-Re, written a millennium earlier: "More acceptable is the character of one upright of heart than the ox of the evildoer" (*ANET*, 417). If nothing else, the Egyptian parallel eviscerates the shopworn argument that v.22 and other biblical texts that have the same emphasis (e.g., Pss 40:6–8; 51:16–17; Isa 1:11–15; Jer 7:21–23; Hos 6:6; Mic 6:6–8; Mk 12:32–33) pit the prophetic stress on obeying the divine word against the priestly commitment to sacrificial ritual. Samuel, himself both prophet (3:20) and priest (cf. 2:35 and comment; also 3:1), not only received and proclaimed the word of God (vv.10–11, 16–17) but also brought sacrifices to the Lord (7:9; 9:12–13; 10:8). The issue here is not a question of either/or but of both/and. So practically speaking, sacrifice must be offered to the Lord on his terms, not ours. Saul's postponement of the commanded destruction, however well meaning, constituted flagrant violation of God's will.

Verse 22a asks a rhetorical question that is then answered in v.22b. The seriousness of disobedience is underscored in v.23a, and devastating application is made to Saul's situation in v.23b. The vocabulary of v.22 reverberates throughout Isaiah 1:11: "The LORD" takes no "pleasure" (the same Heb. root as "delight" in v.22) in "sacrifices" or "burnt offerings," in "rams" or the "fat" of other animals. Nevertheless, mutual "delight" between God and his children can be expected when the righteous among them meditate on his law (Ps 1:2) and heed his words as mediated through his prophets.

For the sake of clarity in English, the NIV has transformed the metaphors of v.23a into similes. In neither line is "like" represented in the Hebrew text, which is thus all the more blunt. The lexicon of disobedience is repulsive indeed. The open insurrection known as "rebellion" and the pushy presumption called "arrogance" (cf. Ge 19:9, where the same Heb. root has the wicked men of Sodom "bringing pressure" on the hapless Lot) are the equivalents of the sins of "divination" (found in association not only with other forms of spiritism but also with human sacrifice in Dt 18:10) and "idolatry" (the superstitious worship of household gods, *t^erāpîm*; contrast the godly purge initiated by Josiah in 2Ki 23:24). The alternative to obedience is costly: Selfish refusal to submit to the commands of the sovereign Lord results in slavery to malign forces in the demonic realm.

Just as Saul's earlier impetuous disobedience had brought the full force of Samuel's rebuke (13:14), so now Saul's halfhearted fulfillment of the divine command removes him from royal office. Rejection begets rejection (v.23b), and the doleful refrain echoes throughout the rest of the chapter and beyond (v.26; 16:1).

The note of finality in Samuel's voice finally brings Saul to his senses. To read his plea of remorse in vv.24–25 in connection with Exodus 10:16–17 is to recognize that Saul, perhaps unwittingly, is echoing the sentiments of an earlier beleaguered ruler, the pharaoh of the exodus (cf. also Ex 9:27). Like Balaam before him (Nu 22:34) and like David after him (2Sa 12:13; 24:10, 17 [cf. 1Ch 21:8, 17]; Ps 51:4), Saul says—twice—"I have sinned" (vv.24, 30). He confesses to having "violated the LORD's command" (v.24), apparently not having learned the lesson of his earlier failure (13:13). Such action has no hope of success (Nu 14:41; 22:18; 24:13). Fearing the people more than God (always a dubious enterprise; cf. Pr 29:25; Isa 51:12–13), Saul "gave in to them" (lit., "obeyed them") when all along he should have been obeying the voice of God through the prophet (vv.19, 22).

At first Saul's plea to Samuel for forgiveness (v.25) falls on deaf ears (v.26). As far as Samuel is concerned, the conversation is over, so he turns to leave the scene (v.27). At this point "Saul" (not in the MT but supplied by 4QSamuel[a], the LXX, and the NIV in the interests of clarity) in desperation seizes the hem of Samuel's robe. Saul may not have been aware of the full implications of his act, which seems to have been spontaneous and unpremeditated. But since a man's robe may symbolize his power and authority (cf. 2:19 and comment; also 18:4 and esp. 24:11), perhaps the narrator is telling us that the tearing of Samuel's robe implies an irreparable breach between Saul and Samuel as well as the more obvious sundering of the kingdom from Saul's personal rule and that of his descendants (v.28; cf. similarly 1Ki 11:11–13, 29–31), thus dashing whatever ambitions his sons Jonathan (18:1–5; 23:16–18) and Ish-Bosheth (2Sa 2:8–9) and his grandson Mephibosheth (2Sa 16:3) might eventually have had.

The "neighbor" destined to receive Saul's kingdom (v.28; cf. also 13:14) is David, whose identity is clearly revealed to Saul once and for all by the robed apparition of Samuel (28:14, 17–18). As obedience is "better than" sacrifice (v.22), so David is "better than" Saul. It goes without saying that the new ruler should be "better than" his or her predecessor (cf. Est 1:19), and it is ironic that Saul himself had originally been considered "better than" ("without equal among," NIV; 9:2) his peers.

The general statement in Numbers 23:19 concerning the immutability of God's basic nature and purpose (cf. the helpful summary article by Billy Graham, "God Has Not Changed," *Decision* 30/10 [1989]: 1–3) is now applied in v.29. Fretheim ("Divine Foreknowledge," 597–98) makes a strong case for referring this verse to God's irrevocable decision to give the kingdom to David rather than to God's irreversible determination to reject Saul by pointing out that the verb "lie" was used in Davidic covenantal contexts (cf. "betray" in Ps 89:33; Fretheim's reference to "lie" in 89:35 [cf. his n. 9] is to a different, though semantically equivalent, Heb. verb). In any event, Samuel gives to the unchangeable God a unique name by calling him the "Glory" (*nēṣaḥ*; GK 5905) of Israel (also used as an attribute of God; cf. the NIV's "majesty" in 1Ch 29:11).

Although some may attempt to assert that God is beyond gender since he is "not a man" (v.29; cf. also Nu 23:19; Hos 11:9), John W. Miller ("Depatriarchalizing God in Biblical Interpretation: A Critique," *CBQ* 48/4 [1986]: 612–13) correctly insists that the contrast in all three texts is not between a God beyond gender and man as male but between a God who is truthful and compassionate and man who is deceitful and merciless. He summarizes by stating that it cannot be argued "on the basis of these texts that a 'masculine label' for deity was thought to be dangerous or that a depatriarchalizing principle was at work in biblical religion."

Perhaps by now reconciled to the irreversible divine determination (for another example, cf. Eze 24:14) to reject him finally as king of Israel, Saul poignantly repeats (in summary fashion; v.30) his earlier statements of confession and of his desire for Samuel to "come back" with him (vv.24–25), whether back to Gilgal (v.33) or simply because Samuel is again about to leave (cf. v.27). Saul wants to save face before the elders and people of Israel by publicly worshiping the Lord and so demonstrating his allegiance to him. Samuel—a man, not God—this time relents (v.31).

32–35 There was one piece of business still to take care of, however. Using the language common to the ritual procedure of sacrifice (v.32), Samuel said, "Bring me [a verbatim echo of the same Heb. phrase in 13:9] Agag"—whom he then further describes as "king of the Amalekites," thus again underscoring Saul's failure to destroy them completely. In Samuel's mind Agag is an offering to be sacrificed to the Lord. Whatever Agag's physical condition or state of mind (he is brought before Samuel *maʿᵃdannōt*, which probably means "in chains" [see Notes]; the NIV renders "confidently"; the NIV note, "trembling"), he apparently feels that his life will be spared—although "surely the bitterness of death is past" could perhaps be understood as a statement of resignation to his fate.

Quickly dispelling whatever optimism Agag may have felt, Samuel's couplet (which rhymes in Heb.) applies the *lex talionis* to the Amalekite king (cf. similarly Jdg 1:7 and the statement of Jesus in Mt 7:2) and reminds him that bloodshed begets bloodshed (Ge 9:6; for a contrasting application of "like for like," cf. David's statement to Saul in 26:24). Without further ado Samuel then executes Agag, probably by hacking him in pieces (see Notes; for the treaty violation implications of such an act, cf. 11:12 and comment).

Following the death of Agag, Samuel and Saul go their separate ways—Samuel to his hometown of Ramah (v.34), just as he does after anointing David (16:13), and Saul to his hometown of Gibeah. "Until the day of [one's] death" or its equivalent often has negative connotations in the OT, as here in the case of Saul (v.35) and in 2 Samuel 6:23 in the case of Saul's daughter Michal. Although after this time Saul would go to see Samuel again on more than one occasion (19:23–24; 28:10–11), never again would Samuel initiate such a meeting. Samuel nonetheless "mourned" for Saul (cf. also 16:1), the narrator using the verb that is normally used of lamenting for the dead (*ʾbl*). Gunn (*The Fate of King Saul*, 147) observes, "As far as Samuel is concerned, Saul is a dead man."

The chapter ends with a doleful echo of v.11: "The LORD was grieved that he had made Saul king." Saul's rejection of God's word through his prophet had led to God's rejection of Saul's rule over his people. To end this part of our discussion on a relatively positive note, however, we do well to remember, with Fretheim ("Divine Foreknowledge," 597), that the divine rejection of the kingship of Saul does not imply a rejection of the person of Saul.

NOTES

9 The NIV translates the MT's משׁנים (*mšnym*, "second things") as "fat calves," presumably reading שׁמנים (*šmnym*) with one Hebrew manuscript (cf. the root *šmn* used similarly in Ne 8:10 ["choice food"]; Eze 34:16 ["sleek (sheep)"]; also the LXX's ἐδεσμάτων (*edesmatōn*, "foods, meats"). The alternate reading "grown bulls" may be an attempt to render the MT; cf. Barthélemy, 2:181, who states that "seconds" refers to "those animals which were kept and fattened after the first-born had been given to God."

12 יָד (*yād*, "hand") in the sense of "monument" is found also in Isaiah 56:5 ("memorial") and Ezekiel 21:19 ("signpost"). The Isaiah 56:5 reference in full, יָד וָשֵׁם (*yād wāšēm*, "a memorial and a name") has given the name Yad Vashem to the main Holocaust monument in modern Jerusalem, which contains records of systematic extermination of millions of Jews in concentration camps throughout eastern Europe during World War II. The use of the term "hand" to designate an inscribed stele occurs not only in v.12 (and perhaps also in 1Ch 18:3; cf. comment on 2Sa 8:3) but also a century earlier in an apology of Hattusilis III (cf. Edelman, "Saul's Battle," 76, 82 n. 17). Various theories proposed for calling such a monument a "hand" include (1) its roughly handlike shape (an upright shaft with a rounded top); (2) the fact that some stelae have one or more hands engraved on their sides; and (3) the use of *yd* in the sense of "phallus" at Qumran and in Ugaritic (De Moor, 144 n. 33; cf. also at least once in the OT; cf. Isa 57:8; "nakedness," NIV); esp. M. Delcor, "Two Special Meanings of the Word יד in Biblical Hebrew," *JSS* 12/2 (1967): 230–40.

18 "Wicked people" is in apposition to "Amalekites," making the two terms virtually synonymous. Later Judaism equated "sinner" with "Gentile" (= "pagan"; cf. Karl Heinrich Rengstorf, "ἁμαρτωλός [*hamartōlos*]," *TDNT*, 1:324–26), a fact reflected in the NT (cf. Mt 5:47 with Lk 6:32; Mt 26:45 with Lk 18:32; and esp. Gal 2:15). The connection is already implied, however, in such OT texts as Psalm 9:17, where "the wicked" and "the nations" are found in synonymous parallelism.

32 מַעֲדַנֹּת (*maʿadannōt*) has been derived from three different roots: (1) עדן (*ʿdn*, "luxuriate"; cf. "reveled," Ne 9:25), thus the NIV's "confidently" here; (2) מעד (*mʿd*, "totter"; cf. "wavering," Ps 26:1), thus the NIV margin's "trembling" (LXX, *tremōn*) here; (3) by metathesis ענד (*ʿnd*, "bind"; cf. Pr 6:21). Since *maʿadannōt* occurs elsewhere in the OT only in Job 38:31, where it parallels מֹשְׁכוֹת (*mōšekôt*, "cords"), it most likely means "chains, fetters" here as well as there (cf. second NIV note at Job 38:31) (so McCarter, *I Samuel*, 264 n. 32). For a full discussion of the options, see Robert G. Bratcher, "How Did Agag Meet Samuel? (1 Sam 15:32)," *BT* 22/4 (1971): 167–68 (but notice the caveat of Barthélemy, 2:182).

33 The targumic rendering of שׁסף (*šsp*), a *hapax legomenon* in the OT, is פשח (*pšḥ*, "tear in pieces"; cf. the Hebrew cognate in La 3:11, "mangled"). The NIV's "put ... to death" is more cautious, and not without reason; *šsp* has been analyzed as a Shaphel (causative) of סוף (*swp*, "come to an end"), thus meaning "put an end to" (cf. Dahood, "Hebrew-Ugaritic Lexicography XI," *Bib* 54/3 [1973]: 362).

III. ESTABLISHMENT OF MONARCHY IN ISRAEL (16:1–31:13)

OVERVIEW

Although monarchy in the person of Saul had long since arrived in Israel by the time of the events recorded in ch. 16, only with the anointing and rapid rise of David can it be said to have been truly established. Unlike Saul's abortive rule, a complex admixture resulting from popular demand and divine choice, David's reign was sovereignly instituted by God alone. Already in ch. 14 it is clear that Saul would not father a royal dynasty, for that chapter gives the distinct impression that the rift begun there between the king and his firstborn son, Jonathan, would only widen with the passing of the years. In fact, chs. 16–31 are as much the story of the decline and ultimate fall of Saul and Jonathan as they are the rise of David, although the beginnings of that decline and fall were already evident in chs. 13–15.

Looking at the Deuteronomic history as a whole, Gerbrandt, 158, observes that "a total of 40 [*sic*] chapters (1 Samuel 16–1 Kings 1) have [*sic*] David as the center of attention whereas the whole history from David to the end of the two kingdoms is dealt with in only 46 chapters.... Literally the David stories are right at the center of the history." Although this latter statement is somewhat imprecise, the basic centrality and dominance of David in the Deuteronomic history is beyond reasonable question. Despite his obvious faults, he is the man after God's own heart (see comment on 13:14), the key figure in the story, the ideal king against whom the characters and careers of his royal descendants on the throne are constantly measured.

P. Kyle McCarter Jr. sees in 1 Samuel 16:14–2 Samuel 5:10 "an old, more or less unified composition describing David's rise to power" ("Apology of David," 493), which "in its original formulation was of Davidic date" (502). Together with Herbert M. Wolf ("The Apology of Hattushilish Compared with Other Ancient Near Eastern Political Self-Justifications" [Ph.D. diss., Brandeis University, 1967]: 99–117) and Harry A. Hoffner Jr. ("Propaganda and Political Justification in Hittite Historiography," in *Unity and Diversity: Essays in the History, Literature, and Religion of the Ancient Near East*, ed. H. Goedicke and J. J. M. Roberts [Baltimore: Johns Hopkins Univ. Press, 1975], 49–62), McCarter ("The Apology of David," 495–99) sees the so-called apology of the Hittite king Hattusilis III (thirteenth century BC), which tells of his rise to power, his rebellion against his nephew and predecessor, and his ascription of success to his patron deity, as a useful model for determining the literary genre of the biblical account of David's rise. But while there may be some justification for McCarter's assertion that the "Apology of David" ends at 2 Samuel 5:10 (which concludes with the expression, "the LORD God Almighty was with him"; cf. v.18), there is little reason for his assumption that it does not begin until 1 Samuel 16:14, since the two halves of ch. 16 are clearly of a piece (cf. S. D. Walters, 567–89).

A. The Rise of David (16:1–28:2)

OVERVIEW

Just as the story of the advent of Israelite monarchy (chs. 8–15) begins with an account of the rise of Saul (chs. 8–12), so also the story of the establishment of that monarchy begins with an account of the rise of David. In this case, however, the rise of the latter is so intimately connected with the decline of the former that it occupies much more space in the telling. If at times the stories of Saul and David intersect, at other times they go their own way—only to interlace again and again in what Fokkelman refers to as "crossing fates." The result makes for one of the most fascinating and engrossing sections of the entire Samuel corpus.

1. The Anointing of David (16:1–13)

OVERVIEW

One of the many indications that the two halves (vv.1–13, 14–23) of ch. 16 are closely related is that each section is framed by an inclusio: "Horn with/of oil" is found in vv.1 and 13, and the phrase "Spirit ... departed from" constitutes the first words of v.14 and the last words of v.23 (see the MT; cf. Walters, 569–73, for this and other similarities between the two halves).

In addition to being the middle ch. of 1 Samuel, ch. 16 is pivotal in another way as well: Its first half (vv.1–13), ending with a statement concerning David's reception of the Spirit of God, describes David's anointing as ruler of Israel to replace Saul; its second half (vv.14–23), beginning with a statement concerning Saul's loss of the Spirit and its replacement with an "evil spirit" sent by God, describes David's arrival in the court of Saul. Thus the juxtaposition of vv.13 and 14 delineates not only the transfer of the divine blessing and empowerment from Saul to David, but also the beginning of the effective displacement of Saul by David as king of Israel. The transition at vv.13–14 can thus be arguably defined as the literary, historical, and theological crux of 1 Samuel as a whole.

[1]The LORD said to Samuel, "How long will you mourn for Saul, since I have rejected him
as king over Israel? Fill your horn with oil and be on your way; I am sending you to Jesse of
Bethlehem. I have chosen one of his sons to be king."
[2]But Samuel said, "How can I go? Saul will hear about it and kill me."
The LORD said, "Take a heifer with you and say, 'I have come to sacrifice to the LORD.'
[3]Invite Jesse to the sacrifice, and I will show you what to do. You are to anoint for me the
one I indicate."
[4]Samuel did what the LORD said. When he arrived at Bethlehem, the elders of the town
trembled when they met him. They asked, "Do you come in peace?"
[5]Samuel replied, "Yes, in peace; I have come to sacrifice to the LORD. Consecrate yourselves and come to the sacrifice with me." Then he consecrated Jesse and his sons and
invited them to the sacrifice.
[6]When they arrived, Samuel saw Eliab and thought, "Surely the LORD's anointed stands
here before the LORD."
[7]But the LORD said to Samuel, "Do not consider his appearance or his height, for I have
rejected him. The LORD does not look at the things man looks at. Man looks at the outward
appearance, but the LORD looks at the heart."
[8]Then Jesse called Abinadab and had him pass in front of Samuel. But Samuel said, "The
LORD has not chosen this one either." [9]Jesse then had Shammah pass by, but Samuel said,
"Nor has the LORD chosen this one." [10]Jesse had seven of his sons pass before Samuel, but

Samuel said to him, "The LORD has not chosen these." 11So he asked Jesse, "Are these all the sons you have?"

"There is still the youngest," Jesse answered, "but he is tending the sheep."

Samuel said, "Send for him; we will not sit down until he arrives."

12So he sent and had him brought in. He was ruddy, with a fine appearance and handsome features.

Then the LORD said, "Rise and anoint him; he is the one."

13So Samuel took the horn of oil and anointed him in the presence of his brothers, and from that day on the Spirit of the LORD came upon David in power. Samuel then went to Ramah.

COMMENTARY

1–5 After an indeterminate period of time, ch. 16 begins where ch. 15 ends: Samuel is still mourning for Saul (v.1)—perhaps over his loss of kingdom and dynasty, perhaps because of his disobedience, or perhaps for him personally. Ironically, the divine "how long" serves as a prophetic rebuke to the prophet Samuel (so Martin Kessler, "Narrative Technique in 1 Sam 16:1–13," *CBQ* 32/4 [1970]: 547 and n. 21). God has rejected Saul as king over Israel (13:13–14; 15:23, 26); thus a change of leadership is in order.

The Lord tells Samuel to go to "Jesse of Bethlehem" (v.1), a phrase that appears again in 17:58 and is thus used as an inclusio to frame and tie together chs. 16 and 17. (The only other occurrence of the expression is in 16:18, where Saul's servant gives a summary description of the young David.) At Bethlehem one of Jesse's sons will become the next ruler of Israel by being anointed with oil (as Saul had been anointed earlier [9:16; 10:1; cf. also 2Ki 9:1, 3, 6]). Jesse of the tribe of Judah (cf. Ru 4:12, 18–22) and his hometown, Bethlehem in Judah, will forever become associated with the Messiah (Isa 11:1–3, 10; Mic 5:2; Mt 1:1, 5–6, 16–17; 2:4–6).

The Lord also tells Samuel that he has "chosen" (lit., "seen," v.1) a son of Jesse. (For another case of "see" in the sense of "choose" in connection with the divine election of a king, see 2Ki 10:3.) Miscall, 115, 118 (cf. similarly Kessler, "Narrative Technique," 549) points out that various forms of the root *rʾh* ("see") occur throughout the chapter: v.1 ("chosen"), v.6 ("saw"), v.12 ("features"), v.17 ("find"), v.18 ("seen"), and, remarkably, a total of four times in v.7 ("appearance, look[s] at" [3x]). The contrasting expressions in 8:22 (lit., "make for them a king") and 16:1 (lit., "I have seen ... for myself a king") stress that while Saul was in reality the people's king, David will become the Lord's king (so Gunn, *The Fate of King Saul*, 125; Baldwin, 121; cf. similarly "for me" in v.3).

Samuel was understandably afraid that the rejected Saul would kill him if he learned that Samuel was on the way to Bethlehem to anoint Saul's successor (v.2; for an excellent treatment, see John Murray, *Principles of Conduct: Aspects of Biblical Ethics* [Grand Rapids: Eerdmans, 1957], 139–41). The Lord therefore reminded Samuel of an accompanying (if secondary) reason for making the journey: to sacrifice a heifer (presumably as a fellowship offering; cf. Lev 3:1) in conjunction with the ritual of anointing (cf. similarly

9:11–10:1; 11:15). It is unnecessary to refer to God's advice as a "pretext" (or other word with negative connotations), as Calvin (cited in K&D, 168), Gordon (*I and II Samuel*, 150), Richard D. Patterson ("The Old Testament Use of an Archetype: The Trickster," *JETS* 42/3 [1999]: 393–94), and others do.

The sacrificial ceremony was for a select few (including Jesse, his sons, and the elders of Bethlehem [vv.4–5]) and was therefore by invitation only (v.3; cf. similarly 9:24). God's promise to Samuel—"I [emphatic] will show you what to do"—echoes an early classic passage about prophetic enabling: "I [emphatic] ... will teach you what to do" (Ex 4:15; cf. also Jesus' assurance to Paul in Ac 9:6). Samuel is left with no doubt concerning God's sovereign role in the choice of Saul's successor: Samuel must anoint for the Lord the one whom the Lord indicates (v.3; cf. Dt 17:15).

Obedient to the Lord's command (v.4), Samuel went to Bethlehem (four miles south-southwest of Jerusalem). Perhaps awed by his formidable reputation (had they heard of the recent execution of Agag [15:33]?), the town elders "trembled when they met him" (as the priest Ahimelech would tremble later when meeting David [21:1]; the same Heb. verb is translated "quaking with fear" in 13:7). They asked Samuel the customary question in such circumstances: "Do you come in peace?" (cf. similarly 1Ki 2:13; 2Ki 9:22). Samuel's cordial response allayed their fears as he told them (part of) the reason he had come (v.5). In preparation for entering into God's presence, he had the elders consecrate themselves; then he personally consecrated the specially designated celebrants (Jesse and his sons). Such ceremonial cleansing, whether or not self-administered, was often accompanied by putting on fresh garments to heighten the symbolism (Ge 35:2–3; Ex 19:10–14).

6–10 Samuel, apparently eager to get on with the anointing of Israel's next king (v.6), "saw" Eliab (meaning "My God is father"), "David's oldest brother" (17:28), and felt sure that he was the Lord's chosen one, his "anointed" (*māšîaḥ*; see Notes on 2:10). As though in a courtroom, Samuel sees Eliab as standing "before" the Lord, the Judge (cf. 12:3, where the same Heb. word is translated "in the presence of"). Later hindsight, however, makes it clear that David, not Eliab or any other of Jesse's sons, will occupy a throne that will endure "before" the Lord forever (Ps 89:35–37).

Indeed, the divine response to Samuel's musings (v.7) immediately eliminates Eliab as Israel's future king. God rejects him (as he had rejected Saul [v.1]), knowing that Samuel is impressed by Eliab's physique (including especially his "height"; cf. the reference to Saul's height in 9:2 and Samuel's assumption that visible attributes of that kind are important in a king [10:23–24]). What Samuel "saw" externally (v.6) was Eliab's "appearance" (v.7; the same Heb. word underlies both words), but what a human being "looks at" is not what God "looks at." (Again the Heb. root is the same as that in "saw"; "looks at" is used three times in v.7.)

That God is not a human being is emphasized here, as it was in 15:29. "Man looks at the outward appearance"—an insight appreciated even by the notorious Machiavelli ("Men in general judge more from appearances than from reality"). Representing a different Hebrew root from that used earlier in the verse, the second occurrence of the word "appearance" means literally "eyes" (so also v.12; Lev 13:55). Human beings are impressed—and therefore often deceived—by what their eyes tell them, while God looks at the "heart" (cf. also 1Ki 8:39; 1Ch 28:9; Isa 11:3; 55:8–9), a contrast highlighted also by Jesus (Lk 16:15).

Abinadab and Shammah, the second and third sons of Jesse (17:13), fared no better than Eliab had. When Abinadab ("My [divine] father is noble") passed by, Samuel said, "The LORD has not chosen this one either" (v.8), a statement repeated verbatim in the MT with respect to Shammah in v.9 (modified slightly by the NIV, apparently for stylistic variation). The name Shammah is probably an abbreviation of its alternative forms, Shimea and Shimeah (2Sa 13:3, 32; 21:21 = 1Ch 20:7; 2:13), and thus means something like "Heard [by God]."

Verse 10 summarizes the rest of the proceedings with respect to the divine rejection of David's brothers. None of the seven is acceptable. It is clear not only from this context but also from 17:12–14 that David is the eighth. First Chronicles 2:13–15, however, lists and numbers Jesse's sons and calls David the "seventh"—an assessment that Josephus apparently agrees with in his account of David's anointing (*Ant.* 6.161 [8.1]). Walters, 585, thus suggests that the reference to David as the eighth son in connection with his anointing is "a witness to an eschatological reading. Since the world was created in seven days, eight is a suitable number to symbolize the beginning of a new order."

The Syriac version of 1 Chronicles 2:15, attempting to harmonize the text with 1 Samuel, lists Elihu as Jesse's seventh son and David as the eighth. Although an Elihu is named as a "brother of David" in 1 Chronicles 27:18, "Elihu" there may be a variant of "Eliab," or "brother" may be used in its broader sense of "relative." All things considered, it may be best to assume that one of David's seven older brothers died without offspring and is therefore omitted from the genealogy in 1 Chronicles 2:13–15.

11–13 Samuel, knowing God's determination that one of Jesse's sons will be king (v.1), but also knowing that God has not chosen any of the first seven (v.10), asks Jesse whether he has any other sons (v.11). Jesse informs him that there is one more, the "youngest" (cf. also 17:14), the Hebrew for which can also be translated "smallest." Perhaps the ambiguity is deliberate here, and a contrast is being drawn not only with Eliab (vv.6–7) but also with Saul (9:2; 10:23; so Kessler, "Narrative Technique," 550). In 11QPsa 151, a Hebrew pseudo-Davidic psalm that differs in important essentials from its LXX equivalent, David says:

> Smaller was I than my brothers, the youngest of my father's sons. So he made me shepherd of his flock.... He sent his prophet to anoint me, Samuel to make me great. My brothers went out to meet him, handsome of figure and of appearance. Though they were tall of stature, handsome because of their hair, the LORD God chose them not.

Although the NIV translates *w^ehinnēh* as "but" (v.11), it can just as easily (and thus less negatively and perhaps more appropriately) be rendered "and (in fact)." When we first meet Saul, he is looking for his father's donkeys (9:2–3); when we first meet David, he is tending his father's sheep. Since the metaphors of shepherd and flock for king and people respectively were widespread in the ancient world (cf. references to the king of Babylon as shepherd in the prologue to the Code of Hammurapi, eighteenth century BC), Jesse is speaking better than he knows as he unwittingly introduces his youngest son as Israel's next king. In the words of Walters, 574 n. 17: "The shepherd/flock image is a kind of *Leitmotif* for David from this point on.... The book's last story shows David deeply concerned for the flock [2Sa 24:17]" (cf. further 17:15, 20, 28, 34, 40; 2Sa 5:2; 7:8; also Eze 34:23).

At Samuel's request, Jesse sends someone to bring David in from the fields (v.12). Ironically, David, while presumably not a tall man, immediately presents a striking appearance. Although physical attractiveness is by no means a necessary attribute for a king, it is here elevated to the status of an important characteristic, if not a prerequisite. David is "ruddy" (cf. also 17:42; elsewhere the Heb. word *ʾadmōnî* appears only in Ge 25:25 ["red"], where it describes Esau [= Edom, "Red"] at his birth; cf. also the cognate form *ʾādôm*, used by the woman in Song 5:10 to describe her lover as "ruddy"), not the "pink-cheeked babyface" of Robert North's bizarre translation, which, according to North, makes David suitable as a "therapist for Saul in his advancing insanity" (North, 543).

David has "a fine appearance" (lit., "beautiful eyes," v.12; cf. v.7 and comment) and "handsome features." Since the phrases are virtually synonymous, their elements are therefore interchangeable (e.g., "fine" plus another word for "appearance" is translated "handsome" in describing David in 17:42). Good looks, while often desirable, contain their obvious pitfalls (cf. Absalom's "handsome appearance" [2Sa 14:25], or the "very beautiful" Bathsheba [2Sa 11:2]). Indeed, the most instructive example is the narrator's comparison between Saul and David in his use of *ṭôb* ("good") in the sense of "handsome" (David [v.12]) and of "impressive" and, negatively, "without equal" (Saul [9:2]). By using the same adjective, "the narrator carefully associates David with Saul and suggests that the 'rise-fall' pattern will be repeated in David" (Preston, 38).

No sooner was David brought into Samuel's presence than the Lord commanded Samuel to anoint him as Israel's next ruler (v.12), the first act in a series that would result eventually in a triple anointing (cf. 2 Sa 2:4; 5:3; for details cf. Brettler, 83–84). "He is the one" is literally "He is this one," reminiscent not only of "not ... this one, not ... these" of vv.8–10 with respect to David's older brothers, but also of "This is the man [who] ... will govern" (9:17) with respect to Saul. If Saul at one time had been God's choice, David is now surely the chosen one. Benjamin Harris stated it well under the alphabet letter "S" in *The New-England Primer* more than three centuries ago: "Samuel anoints whom God appoints."

In v.13 David is mentioned for the first time by name in the books of Samuel. His name was once thought to be related to a supposed *dawidum* ("chief [tain]") found in the Mari letters and elsewhere. It is now known, however, that the reading *da-Wi-du-um* is a syllabic writing for Akkadian *dabdûm* ("defeat, massacre"; cf. *CAD*, 3:14) and therefore has nothing to do with David's name. It is perhaps best to understand *dawid* to be a defectively written Qal passive participle of *dwd*, thus meaning "Beloved [of the LORD]" (cf. the similar name Jedidiah [*y*ᵉ*dîd*ᵉ*yāh*], the other name of David's son Solomon [2Sa 12:25], formed from the Qal passive participle of the byform *ydd* and thus likewise meaning "Beloved of the LORD").

Dwdh in line 12 of the Mesha inscription might then be not only a longer (Moabite) form of David's name but also an extrabiblical reference to King David himself (cf. John C. L. Gibson, *Hebrew and Moabite Inscriptions*, vol. 1, in *Textbook of Syrian Semitic Inscriptions* [Oxford: Clarendon, 1971], 80). For the possibility that David's name (written as *dwt*) has been found even earlier, in a late-tenth-century BC Egyptian inscription, cf. Kitchen, *Reliability*, 93; on the antiquity of the phrase "house of David" see note on 2Sa 3:1).

The narrator links Samuel's anointing of David ("in the presence of his brothers," so that there may be witnesses and also to make it clear that David, although the youngest of Jesse's sons, is truly God's choice) with David's accession of the Spirit of the Lord (v.13). Anointing with oil thus symbolized anointing with the Holy Spirit (cf. Isa 61:1). In David's case the divine accession was permanent ("from that day on"; cf. the similar expression in 30:25, "from that day to this"), while elsewhere the same Hebrew verb allows for the Spirit to come and go (twice for Saul [10:6, 10; 11:6]; three times for Samson [Jdg 14:6, 19; 15:14]).

Although the work of the Holy Spirit in David's life appears to be qualitatively different from that in the lives of other OT saints, it is often claimed that the normal experience of the Spirit in the OT was external and temporary as compared to the permanent indwelling of the Spirit beginning on the day of

Pentecost (Ac 2:1–4). As Daniel I. Block points out, however ("The Prophet of the Spirit: The Use of *rwḥ* in the Book of Ezekiel," *JETS* 32/1 [1989]: 40–41), such a view overlooks the indispensable animating role of the Spirit in effecting spiritual renewal in the OT (cf. Dt 30:6) and disregards the witness of Psalm 51:10–12 (where David's continued acceptance in the divine presence and the salvific work of the Spirit within him represent his only hope). This view also ignores Jesus' rebuke of Nicodemus for being ignorant of the regenerating power of the Spirit (Jn 3:8–10) and misses the point of Ezekiel 36:25–29, which anticipates the day when the transforming work of the Spirit in the lives of people will be the rule rather than the exception (cf. also Walter C. Kaiser Jr., *Toward Rediscovering the Old Testament* [Grand Rapids: Zondervan, 1987], 135–41, who emphasizes further the connection of the Holy Spirit with Christ as a distinguishing feature of the NT experience when compared with the OT).

Verse 13 concludes with Samuel's prophetic departure for his home in Ramah. Although he makes additional appearances later on, he no longer plays an active role in the books that bear his name. The anointing of David was the capstone to Samuel's career.

NOTES

1 Anointing oil is specially stated to have been poured from an animal "horn" (קֶרֶן, *qeren*) only in the case of David (vv.1, 13) and Solomon (1Ki 1:39), kings of the united monarchy during Israel's golden age (cf. also the intricate metaphor, lit., "horn, son of oil," in Isa 5:1 ["fertile hillside," NIV]). Horns served as convenient receptacles for other precious substances as well (cf. Job 42:14 for the name of Job's third daughter, Keren-Happuch, which means "Horn of antimony").

7 לֹא אֲשֶׁר יִרְאֶה הָאָדָם (*lōʾ ʾašer yirʾeh hāʾādām*, lit., "not what man looks at") is translated by the NIV as "[the LORD] does not look at the things man looks at," which correctly assumes an ellipsis (cf. KJV, RSV, and K&D, 169). Barthélemy, 2:183, suggests an even briefer ellipsis: "[It is] not [a matter of] what man sees." In any case, it is not necessary to assert, with Cross (on the basis of his restoration in 4QSamuel[b]), that "the phrase יראה האלהים appears to have fallen out by haplography due to *homoioarkton*" (Cross, "The Oldest Manuscripts," 166).

11 Since the Hebrew text of Sirach 32:1 uses the verb סבב (*sbb*, "surround, gather around") in the same sense of "sit down," it is not necessary for the NIV's footnote to cite "some LXX manuscripts" as justification for such a rendering.

2. The Arrival of David in the Court of Saul (16:14–23)

OVERVIEW

As noted above, the two halves of ch. 16 (vv.1–13, 14–23) are linked together in various ways and therefore constitute a literary unit. One link is the position of David's name. "In each of its first appearances it is the object of a verb: in verse 13 the spirit of YHWH 'seizes' (*ṣālaḥ*) David, and in verse 19 Saul asks Jesse to 'send' (*šālaḥ*) David to him.... The two verbs are very similar in sound, being distinguished only as the two sibilants *ṣ* and *š* are distinguished" (Walters, 572–73).

In addition, however, the hinge of the chapter underscores, as described in the title of an excellent article by David M. Howard Jr., "The Transfer of Power from Saul to David in 1 Samuel 16:13–14," 477:"The movements of the figures here—YHWH's Spirit, Samuel, the evil spirit—in relationship to each other effectively tell the story of the transfer of political power and spiritual power from Saul to David."

14Now the Spirit of the LORD had departed from Saul, and an evil spirit from the LORD
tormented him.
15Saul's attendants said to him, "See, an evil spirit from God is tormenting you. 16Let our
lord command his servants here to search for someone who can play the harp. He will play
when the evil spirit from God comes upon you, and you will feel better."
17So Saul said to his attendants, "Find someone who plays well and bring him to me."
18One of the servants answered, "I have seen a son of Jesse of Bethlehem who knows
how to play the harp. He is a brave man and a warrior. He speaks well and is a fine-looking
man. And the LORD is with him."
19Then Saul sent messengers to Jesse and said, "Send me your son David, who is with
the sheep." 20So Jesse took a donkey loaded with bread, a skin of wine and a young goat
and sent them with his son David to Saul.
21David came to Saul and entered his service. Saul liked him very much, and David
became one of his armor-bearers. 22Then Saul sent word to Jesse, saying, "Allow David to
remain in my service, for I am pleased with him."
23Whenever the spirit from God came upon Saul, David would take his harp and play.
Then relief would come to Saul; he would feel better, and the evil spirit would leave him.

COMMENTARY

14–18 The relationships of four movements in vv.13–14 are clarified in the following chart, which exhibits a chiastic pattern:

(1) The Spirit of Yahweh	comes upon	David (v.13c)
(2) Samuel	leaves	David (v.13d)
(3) The Spirit of Yahweh	leaves	Saul (v.14a)
(4) An evil spirit	comes upon	Saul (v.14b)

Howard summarizes: "When YHWH's Spirit came upon David his anointer left, leaving him in good hands. When YHWH's Spirit left Saul an evil spirit came upon him, leaving him in dire straits" (Howard, "The Transfer of Power," 481).

The Spirit's coming on David and the Spirit's leaving Saul are two climactic events that occur in close sequence to each other (cf. esp. 18:12: "The LORD was with David but had left Saul"). Just as the accession of the Spirit by David was an expected accompaniment of his anointing as

Israel's next ruler (v.13), so the departure of the Spirit from Saul (v.14) should be understood as the negation of effective rule on his part from that time on. No longer having access to Samuel's counsel, Saul eventually was forced to resort to the desperate expedient of consulting a medium because God had "turned away" from him (28:15; the Heb. verb is the same as the one rendered "departed" in v.14).

The "evil spirit" (v.14), the divinely sent scourge that "tormented" (lit., "terrified, terrorized") Saul, returned again and again (18:10; 19:9). Just as God had sent an evil spirit to perform his will during the days of Abimelech (Jdg 9:23), so also he sent an evil spirit on Saul—"both of whom proved to be unworthy candidates for the office" of king in Israel (Howard, "The Transfer of Power," 482). In both instances it was sent in response to their sin, which in Saul's case was particularly flagrant (13:13–14; 15:22–24). Although the "evil" spirit may have been a demon that embodied both moral and spiritual wickedness, it may rather have been an "injurious" (so NIV note) spirit that "boded ill for Saul, one that produced harmful results for him" (Howard, ibid., 482 n. 36). It was thus doubtless responsible for the mental and psychological problems that plagued Saul for the rest of his life.

That God uses alien spirits to serve him is taken for granted in the OT (cf. esp. 2Sa 24:1 with 1Ch 21:1). On occasion God's people "were not very concerned with determining secondary causes and properly attributing them to the exact cause. Under the divine providence everything ultimately was attributed to him; why not say he did it in the first place?" (Walter C. Kaiser Jr., *Hard Sayings*, 131; cf. also Archer, 180: "Saul's evil bent was by the permission and plan of God. We must realize that in the last analysis all penal consequences come from God, as the Author of the moral law and the one who always does what is right [Ge. 18:25]"; cf. Fredrik Lindstrom, *God and the Origin of Evil* [Lund: Gleerup, 1983]).

As French *maréchal* ("blacksmith") developed into marshal, and as *chambellan* ("bedchamber attendant") developed into chamberlain, so also *ᶜebed* ("servant") came to mean "attendant, official" in royal circles in Israel, beginning during the days of Saul. The title was conferred on high officials and is found inscribed on their seals. It was also employed side by side with the use of the term as a conventional way of referring to oneself while addressing a superior (cf. conveniently Talmon, 64 and nn. 34–36). Thus Saul's "attendants," aware that their king was being tormented by an evil spirit (v.15), referred to themselves as his "servants" (same Heb. word) who were ready and eager to help (v.16; cf. v.17; 17:32, 34, 36; 18:5 ["officers"], 22, 24; 19:1; 28:7).

Perhaps sensing that "music hath charms to soothe the savage breast," Saul's attendants offered to look for someone to play the "harp" (*kinnôr*; cf. comment on 10:5) to make their master "feel better" (v.16). Pictorial representations of the asymmetrical harp or lyre ranging from the twelfth to seventh centuries BC can help us visualize what David's harp looked like (cf. Bathja Bayer, "The Finds That Could Not Be," *BAR* 8/1 [1982]: 22, 30; [no author], "What Did David's Lyre Look Like," BAR, 8/1 [1982]: 34). Walters, 582, points out that of the fifteen OT occurrences of *niggēn* ("play [an instrument]"), seven appear in this section of 1 Samuel (vv.16 [2x], 17, 18, 23; 18:10; 19:9) and thus serve at the outset to highlight the reputation of David as "Israel's singer of songs" (2Sa 23:1).

Saul agreed with his attendants' counsel (v.17), and one of his "servants" (lit., "young men," a different Hebrew word from that rendered "attendants" in v.15 and "servants" in v.16) suggested that a certain son of Jesse would meet Saul's needs admirably (v.18). In the course of doing so, the servant gave—in a series of two-worded Hebrew phrases—as fine a portrayal of David as one could wish. Understandably, he began with a characterization of him as a musician and then continued by describing him as a "brave man" (the same Heb. phrase used of Saul's father, Kish, and translated "man of standing" in 9:1), a "warrior" (translated "fighting man" [of Goliath] in 17:33 and "experienced fighter" [of David] in 2Sa 17:8), a discerning and articulate speaker, and a handsome man as well.

The servant's final descriptive phrase—set off from what precedes by a major disjunctive accent in the MT—reminds us that just as the Lord was with Samuel (3:19), so also he was with David. This latter attribute becomes yet another *Leitmotif* for David (17:37; 18:12, 14, 28; 2Sa 5:10; so Walters, 570–71; McCarter, "The Apology of David," 499, 503–4). That God was "with" him, however, refers primarily to David's success rather than to his moral character (cf. Marti J. Steussy, *David: Biblical Portraits of Power* [Columbia, S.C.: Univ. of South Carolina Press, 1999]). In any event, Saul's servant has just introduced us to Israel's next king, although unwittingly.

A modern assessment of David's character and career sees him as "giant-slayer, shepherd, musician, manipulator of men, outlaw, disguised madman, loyal friend and subject, lover, warrior, dancer and merrymaker, father, brother, son, master, servant, religious enthusiast, and king" and then asks, "What are we to make of this enormous portrait? Where do we begin?" (Kenneth R. R. Gros Louis, "King David of Israel," in *Literary Interpretations of Biblical Narratives*, ed. Kenneth R. R. Gros Louis and James S. Ackerman [Nashville: Abingdon, 1982], 2:205). What, and where, indeed?

> Biblical scholars in the twentieth century have characterized David in one of two seemingly contradictory ways. The traditional version characterizes David as a pious shepherd who rises to become the king of Israel. The critical version presents David as a cunning usurper who murders and schemes his way to a throne not rightfully his. The first characterization arises from a "naïve" or "straightforward" reading of the biblical text. The second arises from a "hermeneutic of suspicion" reading "against the grain of the text." In fact, the biblical text allows both readings, and they are not as contradictory as may first appear. (Bosworth, 191–92)

In the rest of his fine and balanced treatment, which is well worth a careful reading in its entirety, Bosworth adduces and comments on representatives of both positions. Those who minimize David's flaws and magnify his virtues include David M. Howard (*ABD*, 2:41–49) and D. F. Payne (*ISBE*, 1:870–76); those who do the reverse include Baruch Halpern (*David's Secret Demons*); Steven L. McKenzie (*King David: A Biography* [New York: Oxford Univ. Press, 2000]); and Gary Greenberg (*The Sins of King David: A New History* [Naperville, Ill.: Sourcebooks, 2002], which includes a chapter titled "The Biblical David Versus the Historical David" [239–60]). Early on, Bosworth, 195, summarizes: "Although the pious tradition of David the upright hero is a simplistic idea in need of revision, the claim that David was a terrorist or a tyrant after the pattern of Joseph Stalin seems to be another simplistic idea."

When all is said and done, even a cursory reading of the OT reveals several Davids: the David of the books of Kings, which portray him as the ideal king against whose virtues all the rest of the kings of Judah are measured; the books of Chronicles, which emphasize his positive qualities and ignore his negative ones; the book of Psalms, which celebrates his gifts of poetry and music; the books comprising the Latter Prophets, which speak of a Messiah who will spring from David's royal line; and of course the books of Samuel, in which David appears in all of his delightful and deplorable complexity. The rest of our commentary can only tentatively analyze the multiform aspects of the personality and deeds of this admittedly most complex of all Israelite rulers. For now, a gentle irony: Although Saul's servant agreed with the positive contemporary consensus that kings and courtiers should be "fine-looking" (v.18), the same Hebrew word is preceded by a negative particle in its description of great David's greater Son as one who had "no beauty" (Isa 53:2).

19–23 Again Saul, influenced by a servant's suggestion, sent for the man described: Jesse's son—here, for only the second time so far, identified by the name David (v.19). Saul's reference to David as being "with the sheep" thus identifies him as a shepherd and uses "language which refers allusively to him as a kingly figure" (Walters, 575). Like Jesse earlier (cf. v.11 and comment) and then Saul's servant (cf. v.18 and comment), Saul unwittingly characterizes David as Israel's next king.

It is often stated that numerous inconsistencies, especially in matters of detail, exist in the early stories of David and Saul (for a typical list, see Emanuel Tov, "The Composition of 1 Samuel 16–18 in the Light of the Septuagint Version," in *Empirical Models for Biblical Criticism*, ed. Jeffrey H. Tigay [Philadelphia: Univ. of Pennsylvania Press, 1985], 121–22). The appropriate response to such alleged discrepancies is not, however, to seek refuge in the fact that in chs. 16–18 "the Masoretic Text has 80 percent more verses than does the LXX" (ibid., 99) and thus to attribute the differences to an attempt by the standardizers of the present Hebrew text to include variant readings whether or not they could be harmonized. Nor should one assume the prior existence of two or more different narratives of how David rose to power, along the lines of the now-discredited documentary hypothesis (for a lively survey of this approach, see North, 524–44; see comment on vv.11–13). Much to be preferred is the method of examining each so-called discrepancy on its own merits in an attempt to determine whether it is more apparent than real.

A case in point: If Saul recognizes David as Jesse's son in v.19, why does he later ask him whose son he is (17:58)? In the light of the differing contexts in the two chapters, a possible solution comes to mind. In ch. 16 Saul's initial interest in David was as a harpist, while in ch. 17 he is interested in him primarily as a warrior (according to his customary policy [14:52]). Saul's question in 17:58, in any event, is only a leadoff question; his conversation with David continued far beyond the mere request for his father's name (18:1). He probably wanted to know, among other things, "whether there were any more at home like him" (Archer, 175). It is of course not beyond the realm of possibility that Saul simply forgot the name of David's father during the indeterminate period between chs. 16 and 17.

A firm believer in the truth later expressed in Proverbs 18:16 ("a gift opens the way for the giver and ushers him into the presence of the great"), Jesse sends David to take bread, wine, and a young goat (staple items; cf. 10:3) to Saul (v.20). Obviously impressing Saul (v.21), David "entered his service" (*wayyaᶜᵃmōd lᵉpānāyw*, lit., "stood before him," a common idiom in the ancient Near East [cf. v.22, "remain in my service"]; the Akkadian semantic equivalent is *uzuzzu panī*) as an armor-bearer. Although skilled men can expect to be pressed into service by kings (Pr 22:29), Saul also "liked" David personally. (The same Heb. verb describes Jonathan's relationship to David and is translated "loved" [cf. 18:1, 3; 20:17].) At the same time the narrator may well be playing on the ambiguity of the verb *ʾāhēb* ("love"; GK 170) in these accounts, since it can also have political overtones in covenant/treaty relationships (so Thompson, 335).

Obviously delighted with David, Saul engages him as one of his servants (v.22). Sandwiched between the two occurrences of the noun *rûaḥ* ("spirit"; GK 8120) in v.23 is the verb *rāwaḥ* ("relief would come"). The noun and the verb both come from the same root (*rwḥ*) and thus constitute an elegant wordplay, stressing that David's skill as a harpist brings soothing "relief" that drives the evil "spirit" from the disturbed king (cf. similarly Walters, 578).

The chapter ends with a gifted young man, Israel's future king, coming to serve a rejected and dejected ruler who is totally unaware of the implications of his welcoming David into his court. Not just "a handsome yokel with a rustic lyre," Jesse's son is the anointed king (Walters, 581).

NOTE

16 יֹדֵעַ מְנַגֵּן (*yōdēaʿ mᵉnaggēn*, lit., "knows how, plays"; "can play," NIV) is a difficult grammatical construction. Since one manuscript reads נַגֵּן (*naggēn*) here, and since v.18 reads יֹדֵעַ נַגֵּן (*yōdēaʿ naggēn*, lit., "knows how to play"; so NIV), it is better to understand the *m* on *mngn* in v.16 to be a misplaced enclitic from the end of the preceding word than to assume that *ydʿmngn* is a conflation of *ydʿ(l)ngn* and *mngn* (cf. GKC, sec. 120*b* n. 1).

3. The Death of Goliath (17:1–58)

OVERVIEW

Just as Samuel's anointing of Saul (10:1) was followed by Saul's defeat of Nahash and the Ammonites (11:1–11), so also Samuel's anointing of David (16:13) was followed by David's defeat of Goliath and the Philistines (ch. 17). Although lacking time frames, the impression in both instances is that the Israelite victory occurred fairly soon after the anointing and thus demonstrated the courage, determination, and military expertise of the newly anointed leader.

The exciting story of David and Goliath is an excellent example of an attempt at representative warfare effected by means of a contest of champions. The purpose of such contests was "to obviate the necessity of a general engagement of troops which would spill more blood than necessary to resolve the dispute" (Hoffner, 220). Whether this kind of radical limitation on warfare is ever sincerely accepted by either side remains in itself a matter of dispute (for a nuanced treatment of the issue, cf. George I. Mavrodes, "David, Goliath, and Limited War," *RefJ* 33/8 [1983]: 6–8). It is clear, however, that contests of champions (to be carefully distinguished from duels, which are individual combats not representing larger groups) such as that between David and Goliath or between Menelaus and Paris (Homer, *Iliad*, bk. 3) were not uncommon in ancient times (for additional examples, see Hoffner, 220–25).

Partly because the LXX's text of ch. 17 is considerably shorter than the MT's (the LXX containing only thirty-two of the MT's fifty-eight verses), some assert that the David–Goliath story weaves together two or more separate accounts without regard to possible discrepancies (cf. Emanuel Tov, "The David and Goliath Saga: How a Biblical Editor Combined Two Versions," *BRev* 11/4 [1986]: 35–41). But David W. Gooding ("An Approach to the Literary and Textual Problems in the David–Goliath Story: 1 Sam 16–18," in *The Story of David and Goliath: Textual and Literary Criticism*, ed. Dominique Barthélemy et al. [Göttingen: Vandenhoeck & Ruprecht, 1986], 55–86, 99–106, 114–20, 145–54), among others, argues for the unity and integrity of the chapter in spite of the alleged differences between the LXX and the MT.

Indeed, close readings of the text in recent years have tended to regard the finished canonical narrative as an exquisitely structured whole. For example, T. A. Boogaart, 205, perceptively observes that vv.1–54 constitute a cycle of confrontation–challenge–consternation repeated three times.

I. Goliath's Challenge (vv.1–11)
   A. Confrontation: Philistines and Israelites Face Each Other; Goliath Appears (vv.1–7)
   B. Challenge: Goliath Defies the Ranks of Israel (vv.8–10)
   C. Consternation: Saul and Israel Are Dismayed and Terrified (v.11)

II. David Witnesses Goliath's Challenge (vv.12–39)
   A. Confrontation: David Appears in the Israelite Camp; Philistines and Israelites Face Each Other (vv.12–22)
   B. Challenge: David Hears Goliath Defying the Ranks of Israel (v.23)
   C. Consternation: David Converses with the Fearful Israelites, His Angry Brother, and an Indecisive Saul (vv.24–39)

III. David Meets Goliath's Challenge (vv.40–54)
   A. Confrontation: David and Goliath Face Each Other (vv.40–41)
   B. Challenge: David and Goliath Summon Each Other; David Kills Goliath (vv.42–51a)
   C. Consternation: Philistines Flee from Israelites (vv.51b–54)

This commentary will assume the validity of Boogaart's basic structure without following it slavishly.

1Now the Philistines gathered their forces for war and assembled at Socoh in Judah.
They pitched camp at Ephes Dammim, between Socoh and Azekah. 2Saul and the
Israelites assembled and camped in the Valley of Elah and drew up their battle line to
meet the Philistines. 3The Philistines occupied one hill and the Israelites another, with the
valley between them.

4A champion named Goliath, who was from Gath, came out of the Philistine camp.
He was over nine feet tall. 5He had a bronze helmet on his head and wore a coat of scale
armor of bronze weighing five thousand shekels; 6on his legs he wore bronze greaves, and
a bronze javelin was slung on his back. 7His spear shaft was like a weaver's rod, and its iron
point weighed six hundred shekels. His shield bearer went ahead of him.

8Goliath stood and shouted to the ranks of Israel, "Why do you come out and line
up for battle? Am I not a Philistine, and are you not the servants of Saul? Choose a man
and have him come down to me. 9If he is able to fight and kill me, we will become your
subjects; but if I overcome him and kill him, you will become our subjects and serve us."
10Then the Philistine said, "This day I defy the ranks of Israel! Give me a man and let us

fight each other." 11On hearing the Philistine's words, Saul and all the Israelites were dismayed and terrified.

12Now David was the son of an Ephrathite named Jesse, who was from Bethlehem in
Judah. Jesse had eight sons, and in Saul's time he was old and well advanced in years.
13Jesse's three oldest sons had followed Saul to the war: The firstborn was Eliab; the second,
Abinadab; and the third, Shammah. 14David was the youngest. The three oldest followed
Saul, 15but David went back and forth from Saul to tend his father's sheep at Bethlehem.

16For forty days the Philistine came forward every morning and evening and took his
stand.

17Now Jesse said to his son David, "Take this ephah of roasted grain and these ten
loaves of bread for your brothers and hurry to their camp. 18Take along these ten cheeses
to the commander of their unit. See how your brothers are and bring back some assurance from them. 19They are with Saul and all the men of Israel in the Valley of Elah, fighting
against the Philistines."

20Early in the morning David left the flock with a shepherd, loaded up and set out, as
Jesse had directed. He reached the camp as the army was going out to its battle positions,
shouting the war cry. 21Israel and the Philistines were drawing up their lines facing each
other. 22David left his things with the keeper of supplies, ran to the battle lines and greeted
his brothers. 23As he was talking with them, Goliath, the Philistine champion from Gath,
stepped out from his lines and shouted his usual defiance, and David heard it. 24When the
Israelites saw the man, they all ran from him in great fear.

25Now the Israelites had been saying, "Do you see how this man keeps coming out? He
comes out to defy Israel. The king will give great wealth to the man who kills him. He will also
give him his daughter in marriage and will exempt his father's family from taxes in Israel."

26David asked the men standing near him, "What will be done for the man who kills this
Philistine and removes this disgrace from Israel? Who is this uncircumcised Philistine that
he should defy the armies of the living God?"

27They repeated to him what they had been saying and told him, "This is what will be
done for the man who kills him."

28When Eliab, David's oldest brother, heard him speaking with the men, he burned with
anger at him and asked, "Why have you come down here? And with whom did you leave
those few sheep in the desert? I know how conceited you are and how wicked your heart
is; you came down only to watch the battle."

29"Now what have I done?" said David. "Can't I even speak?" 30He then turned away to
someone else and brought up the same matter, and the men answered him as before.
31What David said was overheard and reported to Saul, and Saul sent for him.

32David said to Saul, "Let no one lose heart on account of this Philistine; your servant
will go and fight him."

33 Saul replied, "You are not able to go out against this Philistine and fight him; you are
only a boy, and he has been a fighting man from his youth."

34 But David said to Saul, "Your servant has been keeping his father's sheep. When a lion or
a bear came and carried off a sheep from the flock, 35 I went after it, struck it and rescued the
sheep from its mouth. When it turned on me, I seized it by its hair, struck it and killed it. 36 Your
servant has killed both the lion and the bear; this uncircumcised Philistine will be like one of
them, because he has defied the armies of the living God. 37 The LORD who delivered me from
the paw of the lion and the paw of the bear will deliver me from the hand of this Philistine."

Saul said to David, "Go, and the LORD be with you."

38 Then Saul dressed David in his own tunic. He put a coat of armor on him and a bronze
helmet on his head. 39 David fastened on his sword over the tunic and tried walking
around, because he was not used to them.

"I cannot go in these," he said to Saul, "because I am not used to them." So he took
them off. 40 Then he took his staff in his hand, chose five smooth stones from the stream,
put them in the pouch of his shepherd's bag and, with his sling in his hand, approached
the Philistine.

41 Meanwhile, the Philistine, with his shield bearer in front of him, kept coming closer to
David. 42 He looked David over and saw that he was only a boy, ruddy and handsome, and
he despised him. 43 He said to David, "Am I a dog, that you come at me with sticks?" And
the Philistine cursed David by his gods. 44 "Come here," he said, "and I'll give your flesh to
the birds of the air and the beasts of the field!"

45 David said to the Philistine, "You come against me with sword and spear and javelin,
but I come against you in the name of the LORD Almighty, the God of the armies of Israel,
whom you have defied. 46 This day the LORD will hand you over to me, and I'll strike you
down and cut off your head. Today I will give the carcasses of the Philistine army to the
birds of the air and the beasts of the earth, and the whole world will know that there is a
God in Israel. 47 All those gathered here will know that it is not by sword or spear that the
LORD saves; for the battle is the LORD's, and he will give all of you into our hands."

48 As the Philistine moved closer to attack him, David ran quickly toward the battle line to
meet him. 49 Reaching into his bag and taking out a stone, he slung it and struck the Philistine on the forehead. The stone sank into his forehead, and he fell facedown on the ground.

50 So David triumphed over the Philistine with a sling and a stone; without a sword in his
hand he struck down the Philistine and killed him.

51 David ran and stood over him. He took hold of the Philistine's sword and drew it from
the scabbard. After he killed him, he cut off his head with the sword.

When the Philistines saw that their hero was dead, they turned and ran. 52 Then the
men of Israel and Judah surged forward with a shout and pursued the Philistines to the
entrance of Gath and to the gates of Ekron. Their dead were strewn along the Shaaraim

road to Gath and Ekron. [53]When the Israelites returned from chasing the Philistines, they plundered their camp. [54]David took the Philistine's head and brought it to Jerusalem, and he put the Philistine's weapons in his own tent.

[55]As Saul watched David going out to meet the Philistine, he said to Abner, commander of the army, "Abner, whose son is that young man?"

Abner replied, "As surely as you live, O king, I don't know."

[56]The king said, "Find out whose son this young man is."

[57]As soon as David returned from killing the Philistine, Abner took him and brought him before Saul, with David still holding the Philistine's head.

[58]"Whose son are you, young man?" Saul asked him.

David said, "I am the son of your servant Jesse of Bethlehem."

COMMENTARY

1–3 The imminent battle against the Philistines described in this chapter is only one of many that involved Saul's troops (cf. 13:12–14:46 and the summary statement in 14:47) since the Philistines were his inveterate enemies throughout his reign (14:52). On this occasion (v.1) the Philistines gathered "their forces" (lit., "their camps"; v.53 ends with the same Hebrew phrase ["their camp," NIV], thus forming an inclusio around the narrative) between Socoh and Azekah, two towns in the western foothills of Judah (Jos 15:20, 33, 35).

Modern Khirbet Abbad (seventeen miles west-southwest of Jerusalem) is the location of ancient Socoh, which was two and one-half miles southeast of Azekah (modern Khirbet Tell Zakariyeh). The latter town later became famous as one of the last two (the other being Lachish) to fall to Nebuchadnezzar II before the destruction of Jerusalem by the Babylonians in 586 BC (Jer 34:7; Lachish letter 4:10–13). The precise location of Ephes Dammim (called Pas Dammim in 1Ch 11:13; cf. also 2Sa 23:9 and comment), the Philistine campsite, is unknown but was probably on the southern slopes of the Valley of Elah (the modern Wadi es-Sant; v.2) and about one mile south of Azekah. The Israelite camp, on the northern slopes of the valley and perhaps less than a mile northeast of Socoh, was thus fewer than three miles east of Ephes Dammim.

The contest between David and Goliath took place on the floor of the valley itself, about halfway between (v.3) the two opposing campsites. (For a map of the area showing the major routes and locations, see Rasmussen, 113.)

4–7 The portrayal of Goliath may well be "the most detailed physical description of any found in scripture" (Boogaart, 207). In agreement with the non-Semitic background of the Philistines, the name "Goliath" (*golyāt*) has been connected with such Indo-European names as the Lydian *Aluattēs* (cf. William F. Albright, *CAH*, 2.2.33, p. 513 n. 8; Kitchen, "The Philistines" [in Wiseman, *Peoples of OT Times*], 67). In 2005 a pottery sherd containing the oldest Philistine inscription ever found (tenth to mid-ninth century BC) was unearthed in Gath (modern Tell es-Safi), Goliath's hometown, located five miles due west of Azekah. The first of two names on the sherd is *ʾlwt*, which excavator Aren Maeir notes is similar to, and indeed may be the equivalent of, the name Goliath ("Gath Inscription Evidences Philistine Assimilation," *BAR* 32/2 [2006]: 16; *Artifax* 21/1 [2006]: 24). Although Frank Moore Cross disputes the reading ("Cypro-Minoan Inscriptions Found in Ashkelon," *IEJ* 56/2 [2006]: 151–52), Maeir strongly disagrees (see note in *BAR* 33/1 [2007]: 12). Stay tuned.

In vv.4 and 23 Goliath is called a "champion" (*ʾîš-habbēnayim*). The Hebrew phrase, found nowhere else in the OT, means literally "the man between two [armies]" (BDB, 108) and is attested at Qumran in the sense of "infantryman." In Ugaritic a similar expression, *bnš bnny*, means "middleman, intermediary, representative" (William F. Albright, "Specimens of Late Ugaritic Prose," *BASOR* 150 [1958]: 38 n. 12).

By any standard of measure, the Philistine champion was a giant of a man (v.4). Some LXX manuscripts give his height as "four cubits and a span" (so also 1QSam[a]; Josephus, *Ant.* 6.171 [9.1]; for a robust defense of this reading, see J. Daniel Hays, "Reconsidering the Height of Goliath," *JETS* 48/4 [2005]: 701–14; critiqued by Clyde E. Billington, "Goliath and the Exodus Giants: How Tall Were They?" *JETS* 50/3 [2007]: 489–508; responded to by Hays, "The Height of Goliath: A Response to Clyde Billington," *JETS* 50/3 [2007]: 509–16). Other LXX manuscripts have "five cubits and a span." The MT reads "six cubits and a span" (thus the NIV note), making him "over nine feet tall." Other comparable heights in the OT are those of "an Egyptian who was seven and a half feet tall" (1Ch 11:23) and Og king of Bashan, whose size is not specified but whose bed/sarcophagus was "more than thirteen feet long" (Dt 3:11).

The MT's account of Goliath's height is paralleled in modern times by reports concerning Robert Pershing Wadlow, who was eight feet eleven inches tall at the time of his death on July 15, 1940, at the age of twenty-two (see www.guinnessworldrecords.com/records/human_body/extreme_bodies/tallest_man.aspx, accessed Oct. 23, 2008). According to *Guinness Book of World Records 2008*, in 2006 the world's tallest living human being was thirty-five-year-old Leonid Stadnyk, at eight feet five-and-a-half inches.

Goliath's armor and weapons are described at length (vv.5–7; for a useful summary together with photographs and drawings of Philistine and similar weaponry, see esp. Yadin, 265–66, 336–41, 344, 354–55). The Hebrew term for "helmet" in vv.5 and 38 (*k/qôbaʿ*) is doubtless a loanword from Hittite *kupaḫ(ḫ)i* (T. C. Mitchell, "Philistia," in *Archaeology and Old Testament Study*, ed. D. Winton Thomas [Oxford: Clarendon, 1967], 415).

A coat of mail such as Goliath wore was fashioned from several hundred small bronze plates (cf. Yadin, 196–97) that resembled fish scales and had to meet the needs of protection, lightness, and freedom of movement (ibid., 354). (The Hebrew masculine plural word for "scale" in v.5 is used of fish scales in its feminine singular form in Lev 11:9–10, 12; Dt 14:9–10.) The weight of Goliath's armor is thus all the more impressive ("about 125 pounds," NIV note). David, however, scorned both helmet and armor, finding his ultimate protection in God himself (vv.38–39, 45).

Like his helmet and coat of mail, the rest of Goliath's defensive armor was also made of bronze (v.6). Greaves protected the legs below the knee, and javelins were probably used to fend off attackers as often as they were used in offensive maneuvers. Goliath's most formidable offensive weapon seems to have been his spear (v.7), whose heavy "point" (lit., "flame," referring to its shape) was made of iron (a metal monopolized by the Philistines and denied to the Israelite troops; cf. comment on 13:19–22). Its shaft was "like a weaver's rod" (cf. also 2Sa 21:19 = 1Ch 20:5; 11:23), the leash rod of a loom (a block of wood separating the threads of the warp to offer passage for the threads of the woof), in that it had a loop and a cord wound around it so that the spear "could be hurled a greater distance with greater stability by virtue of the resultant spin" (Yadin, 354–55). Goliath's sword, mentioned later in vv.45, 51, doubtless had an iron blade. Receiving added protection from the large shield (*ṣinnâ*; cf. 1Ki 10:16 = 2Ch 9:15) carried by his aide, the Philistine giant must have felt—and appeared—invincible (cf. esp. A. Millard, "The Armor of Goliath").

8–11 Goliath hurls the challenge of representative combat into the teeth of the Israelite army (vv.8–10). Priding himself on his Philistine heritage, he addresses the Israelites as Saul's "servants" (v.8), an ambiguous term that can mean either "officials" or "slaves" (cf. comment on 16:15–16). What Goliath intends by it becomes readily apparent, however, in v.9, when he uses the same Hebrew word in the clear sense of "subjects" and then follows it with the verb "serve" (again from the same Heb. root). The Philistines (so Goliath thinks) will win a quick and easy victory over Israel, who will then be enslaved by them. But although Goliath means to "defy the ranks of Israel" (v.10; cf. v.25), David sees him as defying "the armies of the living God" (vv.26, 36)—yea, even God himself (v.45, although the relative *ʾᵃšer* ["whom"] could also be translated "which" and thus refer again to the armies).

Having thrown down the gauntlet, the Philistine challenger at first has no takers. In fact, Saul and his troops (v.11) are "dismayed and terrified" (a common Heb. verbal pairing, elsewhere always reversed; cf. "be afraid ... be discouraged" in Dt 1:21; 31:8; Jos 8:1; 10:25; 1Ch 22:13; 28:20; 2Ch 20:15, 17; 32:7; "be afraid or terrified" in Jer 23:4; Eze 2:6; 3:9; "fear ... be dismayed" in Jer 30:10; 46:27). Barring the response of an Israelite hero, Goliath will win by default, and the Philistines will continue to be Israel's masters.

12–16 Again we are introduced to David, Jesse's son (v.12; see comment on 16:19). Jesse, like Elimelech during the days of the judges (Ru 1:1–2), was an Ephrathite from Judahite Bethlehem. It is clear from Genesis 35:19; 48:7; Joshua 15:59a LXX; Ruth 4:11; and Micah 5:2 that Ephrath(ah) was another name for Bethlehem in Judah (as opposed to Bethlehem in Zebulun [Jos 19:10, 15]). Jesse, already an "old" man (perhaps an "elder"; see Notes) during Saul's reign, had eight sons, the first three of whom are again named here (v.13; cf. 16:6–11 and comment).

Jesse's three oldest sons, loyal warriors all, "followed" Saul into battle (vv.13–14). The MT emphasizes this fact by repeating the verb (lit., "walked [after]") three times in the two verses. (The NIV omits it once in v.13 for stylistic reasons.) By contrast David—"the youngest" (v.14)—"went back and forth [lit., 'was walking and returning'] from Saul" (v.15). Although having entered Saul's service earlier (16:21), David was currently engaged in his main task, tending his father's sheep—in preparation for a more important shepherding task later (cf. comments on 16:11, 19; further the similar description of Moses in Ex 3:1). Scornful of all such activity, Goliath came forward twice a day (v.16) for forty days (a month and then some; cf. J. B. Segal, 10–11) in continuing, taunting defiance. He "took his stand," like the kings of the earth in Psalm 2:2 (same Heb. verb), "against the LORD and against his anointed one" (Ps 2:2 NIV note).

17–22 Boogaart, 204, notes that Jesse's command to David was threefold: (1) to take provisions to David's brothers and their unit commander, (2) to find out how his brothers were getting along, and (3) to bring back a token (cf. NIV note on v.18) of their welfare (vv.17–18). He further observes that David fulfilled the first two parts of the command upon arriving at the camp (v.22; cf. also v.23), but the third part not until the end of the account, when he took Goliath's head and armor as trophies of war (v.54).

The urgency of Jesse's command ("hurry," v.17; cf. 20:6; lit., "run," as in vv.22, 48, 51—in each case stressing the youthful eagerness and energy that characterizes David in this chapter) underscores his concern for his sons' well-being and safety (cf. similarly Jacob in Ge 37:13–14). Jesse sent along the staple items of roasted grain (cf. Ru 2:14) and bread for David's brothers, while for the commander of their unit he provided a gift of "ten cheeses" (v.18; cf. J. B. Segal, 5). Jesse's observation that David's brothers and their comrades-in-arms were "fighting against the Philistines" (v.19) was doubtless spoken with pride and intended as a gentle rebuke to David.

The rest of ch. 17 describes David's transformation from being a shepherd of flocks to becoming a leader of people. He "left" his father's flock with a "shepherd" (lit., "keeper," v.20), and he "left" his "things" with the "keeper" of the "supplies" (v.22; the term is used in the sense of "military supplies" in 25:13; 30:24; cf. the comment on "baggage" in 10:22). In v.20 the rare word translated "camp" (*maʿgāl*; elsewhere in this sense only in 26:5, 7) means literally "wagon-wheel track" and probably refers to the "tracks" made by supply wagons that outlined the perimeter of the camp. David used the word metaphorically in the "shepherd psalm" ("paths of righteousness" [Ps 23:3]).

When he reached the battle lines, David "greeted" (v.22) his brothers (lit. Heb., "asked concerning [their] welfare/well-being [*šālôm*]," the same word used by Jesse in v.18: "how [they] are"; cf. the comment at 10:4; also the English greeting "How are you?").

23–30 Even from a distance Goliath's defiant challenge appears to have been loud enough to interrupt David's conversation with his brothers (v.23). The mere sight of the giant was enough to cause the men of Israel to flee in disorder and panic. ("Ran" in v.24 [lit., "fled"] does not translate the same verb as in v.22; unlike his fellow Israelites, who "ran from" Goliath, David "ran ... to meet him" [v.48] and "ran and stood over him" [v.51].) The narrator reminds us that nothing has changed in more than a month (v.16); the same Hebrew phrase translated "terrified" in v.11 is translated "in great fear" in v.24.

Boogaart, 208–9, points out the strong contrast between "the soldiers' words of resignation" (v.25) and "David's words of indignation" (v.26): The men of Israel call Goliath "this man," David calls him "this uncircumcised Philistine"; they say that Goliath has come out to "defy Israel," David says that he has come out to "defy the armies of the living God"; they refer to Goliath's potential victor as "the man who kills him," David refers to him as "the man who kills this Philistine and removes this disgrace from Israel." In short, the men of Israel "see an insuperable, fearsome giant who is reproaching Israel; David sees merely an uncircumcised Philistine who has the audacity to reproach the armies of the living God."

Giving one's daughter in marriage as a reward for faithful service (v.25) was not unprecedented in Israel (cf. Jos 15:13–17, where, again, the foe consisted of men of unusually tall stature, in this case the Anakites; cf. Nu 13:32–33; Dt 1:28; 2:10, 21; 9:2). In addition, Saul promised great wealth to Goliath's victor as well as making his father's family *ḥopšî* ("exempt") in Israel. Although N. P. Lemche ("חפשי [*ḥpšy*] in 1 Sam. xvii 25," *VT* 24/3 [1974]: 374) has suggested that here this term refers to receiving "supplies from the royal household," such an offer would be anticlimactic in light of the "great wealth" mentioned earlier in the verse.

Considering all the evidence from within the OT itself (the use of "free[d]" in Ex 21:2, 5, 26–27; Dt 15:12, 18; Job 3:19; Isa 58:6; Jer 34:9–11, 14,

16) as well as from elsewhere in the ancient Near East (the *ḫupšū*, mentioned in the Nuzi documents, Ugaritic literature, Amarna tablets, Assyrian laws, and Late Assyrian texts, being "free-born people" who "engaged primarily in agricultural pursuits as small land-holders and tenant-farmers" [I. Mendelsohn, "New Light on the *ḫupšū*," *BASOR* 139 (1955): 11]), the NIV's "exempt his father's family from taxes" remains the best understanding of the passage in this context (cf. *AIs*, 88; McCarter, *I Samuel*, 304; Talmon, 65–66).

In righteous indignation David implicitly offers himself to fight Goliath (v.26), an offer that becomes explicit in v.32. Nahash the Ammonite had intended to "bring disgrace on all Israel" (11:2), and in David's eyes the presence of Goliath, the "uncircumcised Philistine" (cf. comment on 14:6), has already brought on Israel a disgrace that must be removed (cf. further Isa 25:8). The Hebrew root for "disgrace" in v.26 is the same for "defy" later in the verse: Goliath is disgracing/defying Israel, and David—with God's help—intends to remove that disgrace/defiance. Since "defy" in v.26 answers to "defy" in v.25 (Boogaart, 208), the last sentence in v.26—especially in the light of *kî*'s introducing a clause after an interrogative clause—should doubtless be translated as follows: "Who is this uncircumcised Philistine? Why should he defy the armies of the living God?" (cf. comment on 11:5). Despite what the Philistines may think or believe, their god Dagon is a destroyed, dead idol (5:3–4). By contrast, "the LORD is the true God; he is the living God, the eternal King" (Jer 10:10; cf. also Dt 5:26; 2Sa 22:47; Isa 37:17; Jer 23:36).

Verses 27–30 constitute a literary unit framed by *wayyōʾmer ... kaddābār hazzeh* (lit., "And said ... according to this word"), translated "repeated ... what they had been saying" in v.27 and "brought up the same matter" in v.30. Both framing verses respond to David's desire to know what would be done for the man who killed Goliath (v.26), the details of which had been given in v.25.

Just as Joseph's older brothers reacted with jealous hatred to his dreams of sovereignty over them (Ge 37:4–36), so also David's oldest brother, Eliab, misunderstood and angrily questioned David's motives for coming down to the battlefield. Eliab, angered at David's seeming irresponsibility, unknowingly underscored David's transition from shepherd to ruler when he referred to the fact that David would "leave" a few sheep (v.28; see comment on "left" in v.20). David's response to Eliab was respectful but firm (v.29).

31 David's expressions of bravado were reported to Saul, who then decided that he wanted to talk to the young shepherd. "Sent for" and "took" (v.40) translate the same Hebrew verb and are probably intended to form an inclusio circumscribing this pericope (for other unifying features of the passage, cf. Ceresko, 61–62).

32–33 Knowing that the Lord is on his side, David offers to fight Goliath (v.32) in spite of the overwhelming odds against him (cf. Dt 20:1–4). His confident statement, "Let no one lose heart," is made all the more specific by the overly eager LXX (and some Old Latin manuscripts): "Let not the king lose heart." But Saul, unimpressed, insists that a fight between David and Goliath will be a mismatch (v.33): "You" (emphatic pronoun) are "only a boy," while "he" (emphatic pronoun) has been a "fighting man" ever since his boyhood days. Goliath, of course, agrees with Saul's assessment and despises David because he is "only a boy" (v.42).

David also agrees with Saul's "You are not able to go out" against the Philistines—but not in the sense that Saul intended. "I," says David, "cannot go" (v.39; the Heb. echoes Saul's warning) wearing this heavy armor because he is not used to it. As for Goliath's reputation as a "fighting man," David has already been referred to as a "warrior" (same

Heb. phrase) earlier in the text (16:18). The odds are therefore much more even than either Saul or Goliath might imagine, especially when the divine element is added to the equation.

34–35 In vv.34–37 David demonstrates beyond cavil that he "speaks well" (16:18). Though others may flee from lions and bears (Am 5:19), David does not. It would not be at all inappropriate to compare Goliath with "a roaring lion or a charging bear" (Pr 28:15). As a shepherd "keeping his father's sheep" (v.34; cf. 16:11), David often rescued them from the mouths of dangerous animals (v.35; cf. also Am 3:12). When they turned to attack him, he "struck ... and killed" (v.35) them. As a newly established leader of his Father's people, David soon "struck ... and killed" the dangerous Goliath (v.50).

36–37 The comparison between David as a herder of sheep and David as a leader of people ("The armies [flock] of the living God [father] were being threatened by a predator [Goliath]" [Boogaart, 209]) is made even more explicit in these verses. Goliath will be "like" (v.36) the lion or the bear, both of whom David had killed. As God had delivered David from the "paw" (lit., "hand") of the lion and of the bear, so he (*hûʾ*, an emphatic pronoun in v.37, untranslated in the NIV but answering to the "he" of v.33 [used there of Goliath], is the subject of the verb) will also deliver him from the "hand" of the Philistine (cf. further Ex 18:9–10).

Another more subtle comparison is also evident: As David routinely "rescued" sheep from wild animals (v.35), so also God had "delivered" David from them, and he will thus "deliver" him from Goliath (v.37; same Heb. verb). Indeed, deliverance from enemies depicted as predatory animals is a not uncommon motif in Scripture (Ps 22:21; cf. also 2Ti 4:17).

Saul, again impressed by David's bravado (cf. v.31), now tells him to "Go" (v.37b)—a command he was not initially willing to give him (v.33). Saul's added expression of encouragement ("the LORD be with you") echoes the original description of David given by Saul's servant (16:18) and unwittingly calls attention to the tragically disparate spiritual conditions of Saul and David (16:13–14).

38–40 Saul, desirous of giving David every advantage, clothes him in the same kind of armor and crowns him with the same kind of helmet that Goliath is wearing (v.38; cf. v.5). He also gives him his own "tunic" (v.38) and "sword" (v.39). Since it was believed that to wear the clothing of another was to be imbued with his essence and to share his very being (cf. Johannes Pedersen, *Israel: Its Life and Culture. I–II* [London: Oxford, 1926], 302–3), these latter acts are probably calculated so to bind Saul to David that Saul will be able to take credit for, or at least to share in, David's victory over the Philistine giant. In a similar way Jonathan will soon give to David his own "tunic" and "sword" (18:4), among other things, as visible tokens of his covenantal love for him (18:3).

David, however, denies Saul his potential moment of glory. Saul had said "Go" (v.37); but David, after "walking around," insists that he cannot "go" while wearing Saul's armor (v.39; the same Heb. verb in all three cases) because, not being used to it, he will be weighed down and therefore slowed down by it. After taking the armor off, he selects five sling stones (v.40) from the stream bed in the Valley of Elah. Such stones were part of the normal repertoire of weapons in the ancient world (cf. 2Ch 26:14), usually balls two or three inches in diameter and manufactured from flint (Ovid R. Sellers, "Sling Stones in Biblical Times," *BA* 2/4 [1939]: 41–42, 45). David, however, had a ready supply of naturally spherical stones of the right size at hand.

The sling itself "consisted of two long cords with a pocket in the center. The slinger placed a stone in the pocket, grasped the ends of the cords, whirled the stone, and shot by releasing one of the cords" (Sellers, "Sling Stones," 42; cf. Jdg 20:16; 1Ch 12:2; further Yadin, 9–10, 364). Thus propelled, a sling stone could easily reach a speed upwards of seventy miles per hour. And so, armed only with his shepherd's staff and the five stones "in the pouch of his shepherd's bag" (v.40), David the Israelite shepherd strides forth to do battle with Goliath the Philistine champion.

41–42 Together with his aide carrying a large shield (v.41; cf. v.7 and comment there), the huge Goliath must have considered himself invincible. He fails to understand, however, that he and his shield bearer are no match for David and his God. Goliath's observation merely echoes Saul's opinion that David, far from being a worthy opponent, is "only a boy" (v.42; cf. v.33). The Philistine, who "despised" David, is not impressed that he is "ruddy and handsome" (cf. 16:12). Goliath, unfortunately for him, does not reckon with the truth that such egotistical pride "goes before destruction, a haughty spirit before a fall" (Pr 16:18).

43–44 Apparently not noticing David's sling, or at least discounting its potentially lethal effectiveness against his full suit of armor, Goliath perceives that David is coming to fight against him with "sticks" (v.43; the singular form of the same Heb. word translated "staff" in v.40). Such weapons, he implies, are appropriate for beating a "dog" (*keleb*), the lowliest of animals (cf. similarly 24:14; 2Sa 3:8; 9:8; 16:9; Dt 23:18, where the word is an epithet applied to a male prostitute; Akkad. *kalbu* and Ugar. *klb*, used in similarly pejorative senses), but will be of no use whatever in trying to defeat a champion such as he. Goliath therefore curses David "by" (i.e., "by invoking, in the name of"; cf. 2Ki 2:24) his "gods" (or "god," as the Heb. word may also be translated, with the reference perhaps being to Dagon, the main Philistine deity during this period; cf. comment and Notes on 5:2). His curse indicates that he intends to give David's flesh to the "birds of the air and the beasts of the field" (v.44)—a curse that, in typical Near Eastern fashion, David promptly hurls back in his teeth (v.46; cf. also Jer 34:20).

45–47 David's taunting response begins and ends by declaring the ineffectiveness and irrelevance of "sword and spear" (vv.45, 47; in short supply in Israel in any case; cf. 13:19, 22) when the God of Israel is involved in the battle (for other rhetorical features binding these three verses together, cf. Ceresko, 73–74 n. 56). "You" (Goliath; v.45, emphatic pronoun) and "I" (David; emphatic pronoun) possess weapons that belong to totally different realms (cf. 2Ch 32:7–8; 2Co 10:3–4). David fights Goliath "in the name of" the Lord—that is, "as his representative" (BDB, 102; cf. 25:5, 9; 2Sa 6:18; Ex 5:23; Dt 10:8; 2Ch 14:11).

One of the names of the "God of the armies of Israel" is the regal name "LORD Almighty" (lit., "LORD of hosts/armies"—though the Heb. word for "armies" is different in the two expressions, and therefore "armies of Israel" cannot be used, without further ado, to define "hosts" in the name "LORD Almighty"; cf. comment on 1:3 for details). Goliath is on perilous ground: To defy "the armies of Israel" (v.45) is to defy "the armies of the living God" (v.36; cf. comment on v.10) and is tantamount to defying God himself. (The relative pronoun "whom," which the NIV takes as referring to God in v.45, could also be translated "which," in reference to "armies.")

Anxious to get on with the contest (v.48), David asserts (v.46) that Goliath will be killed "this day ... today" (same Heb. expression). The Lord, says David to Goliath, will "hand you over to me" (lit., "deliver you into my hand"; cf. 24:18; 26:8, the only other occurrences of the Heb. idiom using the Piel). David threatens to "cut off" the giant's head (lit., "remove" it, translating a different Heb. verb from that used in v.51). David's next words may reflect that section of the Ugaritic Baal epic

> in which Anath threshes the death-god, Mot. We are there told *(a)* that Mot's body will be food for the birds of the air, and, subsequently, *(b)* that El receives a sign that Baal "lives" and "exists." Thus the narrative of the combat between David and Goliath may be a polemical allusion to these features: David's victory will leave the foe slain on the battlefield as food for the birds, and thus "all the earth may know that God exists [*yēš*] for Israel," which is how the final words in the quotation may also be translated. (Mettinger, 87)

The contrast would then be between dead idols—such as the Philistine god Dagon—and the living God (cf. also Isa 37:4, 17, 19; Jer 10:1–16). Even though *kol-hāʾāreṣ* ("the whole world," v.46) should perhaps be here translated "the whole land" (i.e., the land of Israel, as often; cf. "all those gathered here," v.47), the point remains the same: All who hear will know that the God of Israel is the only true God. In addition, they will know that the Lord, not weapons of war (cf. also Ps 44:3, 6–7) or a human instrument, is the true deliverer (v.47), a fact understood by Jonathan as well (14:6). "The battle" belongs to the Lord alone (2Ch 20:15).

David begins his taunt of Goliath by referring to "you" and "I" (v.45), emphatic singular pronouns that echo Goliath's challenge in v.44. He concludes by warning that God will give "you" (plural) into "our" (plural) hands (v.47), thus reminding Goliath of his own earlier intention that their battle is indeed representative warfare, the results of which will have profound implications for the Philistines and Israelites as a whole (vv.8–9).

48–49 Undeterred, Goliath moves closer to "attack" (v.48) David, who in turn wastes no time in running (cf. also vv.22, 51) forward to "meet" him (same Heb. verb). One sling stone suffices; it fells the Philistine, who—like the idol of his god Dagon in an earlier episode—topples to the ground face-down (v.49; cf. 5:4). As inevitably as a prisoner sinks into the mud at the bottom of a cistern (Jer 38:6), so David's stone sank into Goliath's forehead.

50–51a With only a sling and a stone, not with a sword, David has vanquished Goliath. As David had earlier "struck ... and killed" wild animals threatening his father's sheep (v.35), so now he "struck down the Philistine and killed him" (v.50). The Hebrew of vv.50–51 is ambiguous (probably unintentionally) concerning whether David killed Goliath with a sling stone or with Goliath's own sword. Boogaart's analysis, 214 n. 8, seems best: Verse 50 is the narrator's personal comment, stating that David "killed" Goliath (eventually) and anticipating "the death of Goliath which is not recorded until verse 51." That is, David did not kill Goliath with an Israelite sword (v.50); irony of ironies, he did it with Goliath's own sword (v.51; cf. similarly Benaiah's exploit in 2Sa 23:21). Baldwin, 128, summarizes: "The stone had stunned the giant, and now the sword must kill him" (cf. Ariella Deem, "'And the Stone Sank into His Forehead': A Note on 1 Samuel xvii 49," *VT* 28/3 [1978]: 350).

The fact that David "ran" (v.51a) to the Philistine after felling him indicates that he wanted to kill Goliath before he regained consciousness. Whether David first despatched him by plunging the sword into his heart and then decapitating him or whether beheading him was the manner of his execution is impossible to say. In either case, as he had promised (v.46), he cut off the Philistine's head (v.51), reminiscent of the earlier decapitation of the statue of the Philistine god Dagon (5:4). Goliath's head was later displayed as a trophy of war (v.54); his sword as well became a battlefield trophy (owned by David; cf. 21:9).

Marking the beginning of the end for the Philistines, David's victory over Goliath has frequently been celebrated in art and literature. Michelangelo's magnificent statue of the encounter, made from a block of marble discarded by another sculptor, stands on a hilltop overlooking Florence in Italy. The LXX's Psalm 151 well summarizes David's daring feat: "I went out to meet the Philistine, and he cursed me by his idols. But I drew his own sword; I beheaded him, and I removed reproach from the people of Israel" (vv.6–7). The theological recapitulation of Ceresko, 72, is very much to the point: "David's defeat of the Philistine champion affirms the superiority of trust in Yahweh over any purported marvels of human technology or skill."

51b–54 Goliath's death produces panic in the Philistine ranks, and "they" (doubtless including Goliath's shield bearer) flee in disorder (v.51b). Goliath's original, defiant challenge—that the winner of the battle between himself and his Israelite counterpart would thus decide the future ruler-subject relationship between the two nations (v.9)—is now forgotten or ignored or both. The men of "Israel" and "Judah" (by now a traditional distinction made by the narrator; cf. comment on 11:8), with a shout of triumph (v.52; cf. God's exultation in Ps 60:8 = 108:9), set out in hot pursuit, chasing the Philistines all the way to Gath (Goliath's hometown; v.4) and Ekron (modern Khirbet el-Muqanna, about six miles north of Gath). Shaaraim (Jos 15:36), which means "Two Gates," was probably modern Khirbet Qeiyafa on the northern side of the Valley of Elah and less than seven miles east of Gath. Excavator Yosef Garfinkel dates the one-period site to about 1000–970 BC, thus contemporary with the time of David. It is the only Israelite city of the period with more than one gate (for further details, see Hershel Shanks, "New Discovered: A Fortified City from King David's Time," *BAR* 35/1 [2009]: 38–43). Qeiyafa was "built with megalithic stones, some weighing four to five tons" (*Artifax* 24/1 [Winter 2009]:3).

On returning from the slaughter of the Philistines, the Israelite army plunders the enemy camp (v.53) at Ephes Dammim (v.1). This common ancient practice is illustrated not only elsewhere in the OT (e.g., 2Ki 7:16) but also in other Near Eastern literature (e.g., the Egyptian Sinuhe, after defeating a "mighty man of Retenu," says: "What he had planned to do to me I did to him. I took what was in his tent and stripped his encampment" [*ANET*, 20]).

David's role in the plundering operation is perhaps summarized in v.54b, which informs us that he put Goliath's weapons in "his" own tent. The NIV assumes that David's tent is intended here ("his own tent"), but it is unlikely that David, a visitor to the battlefield, would have had his own tent. James K. Hoffmeier ("The Aftermath of David's Triumph over Goliath: 1 Samuel 17:54 in Light of Near Eastern Parallels," *ABW* 1/1 [1991]: 18–19) makes a strong case for the possibility that Goliath's tent is meant and that Goliath's weapons and tent alike were David's share of the plunder.

Humiliating one's enemies by cutting off and displaying the heads of their vanquished heroes was commonly practiced in the ancient Near East (cf. 31:9; 2Sa 4:7; 20:22; 1Ch 10:10; for a pictorial representation, cf. *ANEP*, no. 236). Thus David proceeded to put Goliath's head on public display. Some consider the fact that he took it to Jerusalem (v.54), a city not yet under Israelite control (cf. 2Sa 5:6–10), to be a "hopeless anachronism" (cf. Simon J. DeVries, "David's Victory over the Philistine as Saga and as Legend," *JBL* 92/1 [1973]: 24 n. 3). Hoffmeier ("The Aftermath of David's Triumph," 22) suggests that David was probably "putting the Jebusites on notice that just as the Philistine had fallen victim to David, Jerusalem's demise was only a matter of time." Perhaps under cover of night to avoid detection, David may have affixed Goliath's head to Jerusalem's wall (cf. 31:10

for the similar treatment of Saul's body by the Philistines).

55–58 The events recorded in v.54 postdate vv.55–58, as v.57 makes clear. Indeed, vv.55–56 synchronize with v.40, while vv.57–58 follow immediately on v.51a. For the difficulty posed by Saul's ignorance of the name of David's father in v.58, see the comment on 16:19. Psychologically, Saul's reaction to David in vv.55–58 as a whole may also be explained as "haughtiness fed by envy" (Herman M. van Praag, "The Downfall of King Saul: The Neurobiological Consequences of Losing Hope," *Judaism* 35/4 [1986]: 421).

Three times (vv.55–56, 58) Saul expresses a desire to know who this "young man" is, using the ordinary word *naʿar* in vv.55 and 58 but the extremely rare word *ʿelem* (found elsewhere only in 20:22 and perhaps emphasizing the strength and vigor of youth) in v.56 (cf. KB, 709; also the frequently attested Ugaritic cognate *ǵlm* ["young man"], for which see Aistleitner, *Wörterbuch der Ugaritischen Sprache*, no. 2150). Abner, Saul's cousin and the commander of his army (14:50–51), cannot of course be expected to know all of Saul's court favorites (v.55). Abner therefore uses the common oath formula—"As surely as you live" (see comment on 1:26)—to underscore his inability to answer the king's question.

Determined to know who the boy is, however, Saul says to Abner, "Find out" (lit., "You [emphatic pronoun] ask" [*š^{e}ʾal*, yet another wordplay on Saul's name], v.56). Immediately after David "returned" from his triumph over Goliath, therefore, Abner brings him to Saul (v.57), and David identifies himself as the son of "Jesse of Bethlehem" (v.58; for the significance of this phrase as terminating a literary unit, cf. comment on 16:1). David's fellow warriors (including Saul) will soon be "returning" home from the battlefield itself (18:6)—and Saul's misunderstanding of the welcome they receive from the women of Israel will trigger a long-standing and ultimately self-defeating jealousy toward David (18:7–9).

NOTES

4 If Goliath was indeed "over nine feet tall," he may well have suffered from a rare disease known as acromegaly, the advanced form of which sometimes includes visual field restriction (cf. vv.41–42, 44, 48). This condition, in turn, would have enabled David to maneuver quickly into position and sling a stone into the giant's forehead (V. M. Berginer, "Giant Problem," *BRev* 17/2 [2001]: 52).

8 It is not necessary to assume (with BDB, 136; Driver, 140) that the MT's בְּרוּ (*b^{e}rû*, "Eat," root *brh*) is a scribal error for בחרו (*bḥrw*). The NIV's "Choose" can just as well be a translation of a revocalized בֹּרוּ (*bōrû*, root *brr*; cf. the participial forms rendered "choice, chosen" in 1Ch 7:40; 9:22; 16:41; Ne 5:18).

12 "Old and well advanced in years" usually translates זָקֵן בָּא בַיָּמִים (*zāqēn bāʾ bayyāmîm*, lit., "old, coming [along] in[to] the days"; cf. Ge 24:1; Jos 13:1; 23:1). Here, however, the Hebrew reads זָקֵן בָּא בַאֲנָשִׁים (*zāqēn bāʾ ba^{a}nāšîm*, lit., "old, coming among men"). Barthélemy, 2:184, suggests "an elder, notable/distinguished among men," a proposal made all the more attractive when one compares 1 Chronicles 4:38, הַבָּאִים בְּשֵׁמוֹת (*habbāʾîm b^{e}šēmôt*, lit., "the ones coming with names"; "the men listed ... by name," NIV), perhaps to be understood as "the men distinguished by name." (Later in the same verse they are called "leaders of their clans.") One would have expected Jesse to be a "man of standing" (cf. Saul's father, Kish, in 9:1), especially since his grandfather Boaz is described in those terms (Ru 2:1).

18 חֲרִצֵי הֶחָלָב (*ḥ^a^riṣê heḥālāb*, "cheeses") means literally "cut(ting)s of milk." For the possible role that *ḥārîṣ* (found only here in the OT in the sense of "cheese") played in the popular (mis)understanding of the name of Jerusalem's Tyropoeon Valley ("Valley of the Cheesemakers"), see A. van Selms, "The Origin of the Name Tyropoeon in Jerusalem," *ZAW* 91/2 (1979): 170–76 (according to van Selms, *tyropoion* means "cutting[s], moat[s]").

עֲרֻבָּה (*ʿ^a^rubbâ*, "assurance"; GK 6859; "*some token;* or *some pledge of spoils,*" NIV note), although found elsewhere in the OT only in Proverbs 17:18 ("security"), is one of a number of cognate nouns derived from the relatively common verb עָרַב (*ʿārab*, "pledge, exchange"). Long a crux in this passage, the word is probably best understood in the sense of "token" (so NIV note) and refers in anticipation to Goliath's armor (v.54). (The Targum on the Prophets understands the phrase "bring back some assurance" to mean "bring back the divorce certificates of their wives," implying that before they went to war Saul's soldiers granted conditional divorces to their wives and thus made it possible for them to remarry if the men died in battle and no proof of their death was forthcoming.)

34 The NIV translates the difficult וּבָא הָאֲרִי וְאֶת־הַדּוֹב (*ûbāʾ hāʾ^a^rî w^e^ʾet-haddôb*) as "When a lion or a bear came," which in any event is clearly the basic intended sense of the clause. One Hebrew manuscript omits the *nota accusativi* אֵת (*ʾet*) in an attempt to resolve the grammatical difficulty it poses. Ceresko perhaps has outlined a better solution (based on an earlier proposal by Felix Perles). He revocalizes the consonantal text as אָתָ (*ʾātā*), defective writing for אָתָה (*ʾātâ*), and translates the resulting clause as "Whenever a lion came or a bear attacked" (see Ceresko, 60, 63–64, for details).

43 Aspects of Goliath's sarcastic question—"Am I a dog, that you come at me with sticks?"—are paralleled in Akkadian omen literature (e.g., Maqlu 5:43: "[May they chase the sorceress away] *kīma kalbi ina ḫaṭṭi* [like a dog with a stick]"), in the Amarna letters (e.g., EA 71:16–19, *Mīnu ʿAbdi-ʾAširta ardu kalbu u yilqu māt šarri ana šâšu*, "Who is Abdi-Ashirta, the slave, the dog, that he takes the land of the king for himself?"), and in the Lachish ostraca (e.g., 2:3–4, *ʿbdk klb*, "your slave, the dog"); for additional details see Youngblood, *The Amarna Correspondence*, 92–93.

49 Medieval Jewish commentators wondered (1) how David's stone could have sunk into Goliath's "forehead," which was presumably covered by his helmet, and (2) why, if struck on the forehead, Goliath would have fallen "facedown" instead of on his back. Deem ("'And the Stone Sank into His Forehead,'" 349–51) suggests that מֵצַח (*mēṣaḥ*), the ordinary Hebrew word for "forehead," should here be translated "greave" (cf. מִצְחַת נְחֹשֶׁת, *miṣḥat n^e^ḥōšet*, "greaves made of bronze," in v.6). David's sling stone would thus have struck Goliath on or near his knee, just above one of his two greaves, causing him to fall facedown and enabling David to rush forward and behead him with his own sword. Deem points out that such a reading has an interesting parallel in *Testament of Judah* 3:1: "I ran out alone against one of the kings, struck him on his leg armor, knocked him down, and killed him" (translation of H. C. Kee in *The Old Testament Pseudepigrapha: Apocalyptic Literature and Testaments*, ed. James H. Charlesworth [Garden City, N.Y.: Doubleday, 1983], 1:796). But Deem admits (1) there existed the occasional possibility of the forehead's exposure in helmets similar to that worn by Goliath; (2) the weight of Goliath's frontal armor and the momentum of his forward movement would surely have been enough to cause him to fall facedown rather than backward; and (3) a sling stone sinking "into his greave" seems much less threatening than one sinking "into his forehead."

52 The first occurrence of "Gath" here assumes the correctness of some LXX manuscript readings; instead of גַּת (*gat*), the MT has גַּיְא (*gay*ʾ, "valley"; cf. NIV note). Nor is the referent of "Gath" in this verse certain; it is possible that Gittaim (modern Ras Abu Humeid, four miles northwest of Gezer) is intended (cf. G. Ernest Wright, "Fresh Evidence for the Philistine Story," *BA* 29/3 [1966]: 80; Aharoni, 271).

4. The Jealousy of Saul (18:1–30)

OVERVIEW

A slight disruption in chronological order, a feature of ch. 17 (see comment on 17:55), characterizes ch. 18 as well. For example, Saul's promotion of David to a high rank in Israel's army, since it is introduced by "whatever Saul sent him to do" (v.5), postdates the army's return from the battlefield after David had killed Goliath (v.6). At the same time v.5 illustrates Saul's increasingly schizophrenic behavior, since his jealous fear of David (v.9) obviously, on occasion, abates long enough for him to appreciate David's service and reward him accordingly.

Up to the events recorded in ch. 18, Saul had apparently been favorably disposed toward David. The scene that unfolds in verses 6–9, however, changes all that. Concerning Saul's progressive disintegration, Gunn (*The Fate of King Saul*, 80) observes that "from this point on the negative side of his character comes increasingly to the surface."

[1]After David had finished talking with Saul, Jonathan became one in spirit with David,
and he loved him as himself. [2]From that day Saul kept David with him and did not let him
return to his father's house. [3]And Jonathan made a covenant with David because he loved
him as himself. [4]Jonathan took off the robe he was wearing and gave it to David, along
with his tunic, and even his sword, his bow and his belt.

[5]Whatever Saul sent him to do, David did it so successfully that Saul gave him a high
rank in the army. This pleased all the people, and Saul's officers as well.

[6]When the men were returning home after David had killed the Philistine, the women
came out from all the towns of Israel to meet King Saul with singing and dancing, with
joyful songs and with tambourines and lutes. [7]As they danced, they sang:

"Saul has slain his thousands,
  and David his tens of thousands."

[8]Saul was very angry; this refrain galled him. "They have credited David with tens of
thousands," he thought, "but me with only thousands. What more can he get but the kingdom?" [9]And from that time on Saul kept a jealous eye on David.

10The next day an evil spirit from God came forcefully upon Saul. He was prophesying
in his house, while David was playing the harp, as he usually did. Saul had a spear in his
hand 11and he hurled it, saying to himself, "I'll pin David to the wall." But David eluded
him twice.
12Saul was afraid of David, because the LORD was with David but had left Saul. 13So he
sent David away from him and gave him command over a thousand men, and David led
the troops in their campaigns. 14In everything he did he had great success, because the
LORD was with him. 15When Saul saw how successful he was, he was afraid of him. 16But all
Israel and Judah loved David, because he led them in their campaigns.
17Saul said to David, "Here is my older daughter Merab. I will give her to you in marriage;
only serve me bravely and fight the battles of the LORD." For Saul said to himself, "I will not
raise a hand against him. Let the Philistines do that!"
18But David said to Saul, "Who am I, and what is my family or my father's clan in Israel,
that I should become the king's son-in-law?" 19So when the time came for Merab, Saul's
daughter, to be given to David, she was given in marriage to Adriel of Meholah.
20Now Saul's daughter Michal was in love with David, and when they told Saul about it,
he was pleased. 21"I will give her to him," he thought, "so that she may be a snare to him
and so that the hand of the Philistines may be against him." So Saul said to David, "Now
you have a second opportunity to become my son-in-law."
22Then Saul ordered his attendants: "Speak to David privately and say, 'Look, the king is
pleased with you, and his attendants all like you; now become his son-in-law.'"
23They repeated these words to David. But David said, "Do you think it is a small matter
to become the king's son-in-law? I'm only a poor man and little known."
24When Saul's servants told him what David had said, 25Saul replied, "Say to David,
'The king wants no other price for the bride than a hundred Philistine foreskins, to
take revenge on his enemies.'" Saul's plan was to have David fall by the hands of the
Philistines.
26When the attendants told David these things, he was pleased to become the king's
son-in-law. So before the allotted time elapsed, 27David and his men went out and killed
two hundred Philistines. He brought their foreskins and presented the full number to the
king so that he might become the king's son-in-law. Then Saul gave him his daughter
Michal in marriage.
28When Saul realized that the LORD was with David and that his daughter Michal loved
David, 29Saul became still more afraid of him, and he remained his enemy the rest of his
days.
30The Philistine commanders continued to go out to battle, and as often as they did,
David met with more success than the rest of Saul's officers, and his name became well
known.

COMMENTARY

1–4 Some time after the conversation between David and Saul that concludes ch. 17, Saul's son Jonathan entered into a covenant with David (v.3). The ambiguous verb "loved" describes the relationship (vv.1, 3). Tom Horner (*Jonathan Loved David: Homosexuality in Biblical Times* [Philadelphia: Westminster, 1978]) asserts that the relationship between David and Jonathan was homosexual (see esp. pp.20, 26–28, 31–39). But the verb *ʾāhēb* ("love"; GK 170) is not used elsewhere to express homosexual desire or activity, for which the OT employs *yādaʿ* ("know"; GK 3359), in the sense of "have sex with" (Ge 19:5; Jdg 19:22). The latter verb is never used of David's relationship with Jonathan.

Rather, as conveniently summarized by Thompson, 334–38, "love" has political overtones in diplomatic and commercial contexts. Indeed, "we may suspect that already in 1 Samuel xvi 21 ['Saul liked (David),' NIV] the narrator is preparing us for the later political use of the term" (335). A clear example of the treaty/covenant use of "love" appears in 1 Kings 5:1, which says that Hiram king of Tyre "had always 'loved' David" (appropriately rendered in the NIV as "had always been on friendly terms with David"). To summarize: In vv.1, 3 the narrator probably uses "the ambiguous word *love ʾāhēb* because it denoted more than natural affection however deep and genuine this may have been" (Thompson, 336; cf. also vv.16, 20, 22 ["like," NIV], 28; 20:17; 2Sa 1:26).

The intimate friendship enjoyed by David and Jonathan—the only friendship between two men that appears in the entire OT and that has thus become proverbial—is further characterized by the phrase *nepeš ... niqšᵉrâ bᵉnepeš* ("became one in spirit with" [v.1], lit., "spirit bound with spirit"). The closest parallel is Genesis 44:30: *nepeš qᵉšûrâ bᵉnepeš* ("life ... closely bound up with ... life"), describing Jacob's profound love for his youngest son, Benjamin (cf. Ge 44:20). Peter R. Ackroyd ("The Verb Love," 213) makes the important observation that just as *ʾāhēb* in ch. 18 is intentionally ambiguous, so also "there is another verbal subtlety in 1 Sam. xviii 1 in the use of the root *qšr*." In its various conjugations the root can mean either "bind," "tie," or "conspire" (whether positively or negatively), depending on the context. Ackroyd, 213–14, summarizes: "The use here of another term which has both a nonpolitical and a political meaning is a further indication of the way in which an overtone is being imparted to what might at first sight appear to be a straightforward piece of narrative." Indeed, the word *nepeš* ("life, soul, spirit, self"; GK 5883) occurs twice in "became one in spirit with" and once in "he loved him as himself" (v.1; so also in v.3; 20:17), thus linking the two phrases together.

David's close relationship with Jonathan made Saul all the more determined to make David a permanent member of the royal household (v.2). The covenant between Jonathan and David (v.3; 20:8) was only one of many such agreements "made" (lit., "cut"; cf. comment on 11:1) over a long period of time, until David's kingship was firmly established (20:16–17; 23:18; 2Sa 3:13, 21; 5:3; cf. Thompson, 334). And when Jonathan took off his robe (a symbol of the Israelite kingdom; cf. 15:27–28 and comment) and gave it to David (v.4), he was in effect transferring to him his own status as heir apparent (cf. Gunn, *The Fate of King Saul*, 80). Saul had earlier tried to put his tunic and armor on David, but to no avail (17:38–39). Jonathan now gives his own tunic and armor (including a type of belt that was often used to hold a sheathed dagger; cf. 2Sa 20:8) to David, who apparently accepts it without further ado. "David can receive from Jonathan what he cannot receive from Saul" (ibid.).

5 This verse anticipates and summarizes David's continued successes as a warrior after his victory over Goliath (cf. the similarity with v.30). The root *śkl*, used to describe David's triumphs, combines the virtues of success and wisdom (cf. vv.14–15, 30 and NIV notes). Having experienced repeated military success himself (14:47), Saul appreciated its importance and honored David accordingly by giving him command over one or more army units (cf. also v.13; similarly, Joseph's elevation to the position of vizier over the land of Egypt in Ge 41:33, 40–43). David's skill as a warrior "pleased" (lit., "was good in the eyes of," in contrast to the song of the Israelite women, which "galled"—lit., "was bad in the eyes of"—Saul; v.8) all the *ʿam* ("people"; here more precisely "troops," as in v.13). After David became Israel's king, his ability to please his subjects would continue (2Sa 3:36).

6–8 When David the conquering hero returned to the Israelite camp (17:57) after killing Goliath, here (v.6) called simply "the Philistine" (par excellence; so also frequently in ch. 17; cf. further 19:5), and after the Israelite army had defeated their Philistine counterparts (17:52–53), all the troops (including Saul) returned home to be greeted by their fellow countrymen. Such victory celebrations were normally led by women, who came to meet the triumphant warriors with "dancing" accompanied by "tambourines" (cf. Ex 15:20; Jdg 11:34; Ps 68:24–25; 149:3; Jer 31:4) as well as with "singing" (cf. similarly Ex 15:21; Jdg 5:1).

The term *šālišîm*, derived from the Hebrew word "three" and found here uniquely in a context of celebration (elsewhere it means something like "third man in a chariot," hence "chariot officers," e.g., in Eze 23:15, 23), is translated "lutes" by the NIV (whether because of the supposed triangular shape of lutes or perhaps because they had three strings). Another possibility, however, is that the word designates a song pattern, since there are three beats in each line of the Hebrew original of the song quoted in v.7 (cf. Sellers, 45): "Saul has slain his thousands, and David his tens of thousands." It was sung by the women as they "danced" (different Hebrew root from v.6; "celebrated" would be preferable, as in 2Sa 6:5, 21).

Saul's reaction to the contents of the refrain is not surprising: He becomes angry (cf. 20:7) from assuming that David is receiving ten times more praise than he (v.8). But entirely apart from the fact that the refrain gives him pride of place (his name being mentioned before David's), "thousand ... ten thousand" is a stock parallel pair in the OT (cf. Ps 91:7; Mic 6:7) as well as in Ugaritic (cf. "a thousand fields, ten thousand acres" [V AB D 82; *ANET*, 137]). Each element in the pair is hyperbolic for a large number (cf. G. B. Caird, *The Language and Imagery of the Bible* [Philadelphia: Westminster, 1980], 133), and there is therefore no inherent necessity to interpret the second as greater than the first. It may well be that the song lavishes equal praise on both Saul and David (so also Stanley Gevirtz, *Patterns in the Early Poetry of Israel* [Chicago: Oriental Institute, 1963], 24; for the possibility that the refrain is intentionally ambiguous, see Gunn, *The Fate of King Saul*, 149 n. 8).

In any case, Saul now fears for his kingdom, as well he might—but not because of his misunderstanding of an innocently sung victory hymn. After Absalom's death David's men would later affirm that David was worth "ten thousand" of them (2Sa 18:3)—perhaps an intentional echo of a refrain that by their time had become proverbial (21:11; 29:5).

9–16 Just as "from that day on" signals a major literary break in 16:13, so also does the similar expression "from that time on" in v.9. David's military prowess made him Saul's equal, at the very least, in the perception of their fellow Israelites, and Saul's formerly positive attitude toward his young armor-bearer now became decidedly negative: He "eyed" him (a unique expression; the NIV rendering "kept a jealous eye on" should perhaps be modified to "kept a fearful eye on" in the light of vv.12, 15, 29).

Saul's paranoia concerning David was exacerbated by the frequent arrival of "an evil spirit from God" (v.10; see comment on 16:14). On more than one occasion in the past, Saul had received an accession of the Spirit of God, which "came upon him in power" (10:10; 11:6), but now the evil spirit "came forcefully upon" him (the same Heb. verb in all cases). Whether good or evil, such accessions sometimes induced "prophesying," often resulting in an altered state of consciousness (see comment on 10:5–6), accompanied at times by bizarre behavior (19:23–24). To bring relief to Saul when an evil spirit was tormenting him, David would play the harp (16:15–16, 23; cf. 19:9). The MT of v.10 states that David was playing the harp "with his hand" and then notes that there was a spear "in Saul's hand," thus underscoring the contrast between David's helpful service and Saul's murderous designs.

There would be at least one other time (cf. "twice," v.11) when Saul would try to pin David to the wall with a spear (19:10). Although Jonathan at first could not believe that Saul was determined to kill David (20:9), Saul's attempt to impale even his own son finally convinced him (20:32–33). Later given a similar opportunity to pin Saul to the ground with a spear, David declared that he would never "lay a hand on the LORD's anointed" (26:8–11).

Saul was apparently fearful (*yr*ʾ, vv.12, 28–29; different Heb. verb from that in v.15) because God was with David (Jonathan had no such fears; cf. 20:13) but had "left" him (cf. esp. 16:13–14 and comment); so he "sent away" David (v.13; "left" and "sent away" come from the same Heb. root). Saul made him commander of a "thousand" (probably a round number signifying a military unit; cf. 17:18 and NIV note there), something he was sure David would never do for the men of Benjamin (22:7). Saul's purpose, however, was sinister: He intended to place David at the head of the front rank of troops, where he would be sure to be killed by the Philistines (v.17; cf. David's similar treatment of Uriah in 2Sa 11:14–15).

For his part David "led the troops in their campaigns" (lit., "went forth and came back at the head of the troops," v.13; cf. also v.16). "To go forth and come back" is frequently used with military connotations (cf. Nu 27:16–17; also 1Sa 29:6 ["to have you serve (with me in the army)," NIV]; Jos 14:11 ["to go out (to battle)"]; further Thompson, 337 n. 1). David's military exploits, possible only because the Lord was "with him" (v.14), bound him all the more closely to "Israel and Judah" (v.16; for this phrase see comment on 11:8) in covenantal relationship ("loved"; see v.1 and comment). By contrast Saul "was afraid of" David (v.15; the Heb. verb *gwr* often means "be terrified," as in Nu 22:3) because of his success on the battlefield.

17–19 As a further means of assuring David's death at the hands of the Philistines, Saul offered him the distraction of his "older daughter Merab" (better "Merob"; see comment on 14:49) in marriage (v.17). But just as David's ancestor Jacob preferred Laban's younger daughter Rachel to her older sister Leah (Ge 29:16–18), so also David declined to marry Merob (v.18) and later became the husband of her younger sister, Michal (vv.26–28). Jacob's love for Rachel (Ge 29:11, 18, 20, 30), however, is not paralleled in David, who is never described as loving Michal. In fact, Michal loved David (vv.20, 28), a circumstance so unusual that Alter affirms it to be "the only instance in all biblical narrative in which we are explicitly told that a woman loves a man" (Alter, *Art of Biblical Narrative*, 118; cf.

similarly Berlin, "David's Wives," 70). Although Alter's statement is not quite accurate (cf. SS 1:7; 3:1–4), the mention of Merob in v.17 reminds us of Leah and Rachel and "sets up a parallel which underscores what David lacks in his relationship with Michal: love" (Lawton, esp. 425).

Saul's mandate to David in v.17—essentially "be brave and fight"—echoes the common battle cries of those days (cf. 4:9). David had already proven himself to be just the sort of man that Saul was eager to press into service in his army (14:52). Saul apparently understood that to fight Israel's battles (8:20) was in reality to fight the Lord's battles (cf. also 25:28; 2Ch 32:8). His duplicity, however, is evident in his intention not to raise his own hand against David but to place him in situations that would guarantee his death at "the hand of the Philistines" (v.17 MT; also in vv.21, 25).

David's self-effacing statement of reluctance to marry Merob (v.18) reprises Saul's earlier modest questioning of his own background and abilities (9:21). In spite of everything—whether intentionally or unintentionally, whether innocently or through carefully planned strategy—David would indeed soon become "the king's son-in-law" (22:14), but because Michal, not Merob, would be his wife (v.27). Saul gave Merob to another man (v.19), to whom she eventually bore five sons (2Sa 21:8).

20–26a The literary structure of vv.20–26a is chiastic (cf. similarly Gunn, *The Fate of King Saul*, 149–50 n. 10):

- A Michal's love for David pleases Saul (v.20)
  - B Saul wants David to fall at the Philistines' hands (v.21)
    - C Saul sends a message to David (vv.22–23a)
    - C' David sends a message to Saul (vv.23b–24)
  - B' Saul wants David to fall at the Philistines' hands (v.25)
- A' Becoming the king's son-in-law pleases David (v.26a)

The middle verses (vv.22–24) continue the tug-of-war concerning whether or not David will become Saul's son-in-law, with Saul playing the role of the suitor and David the role of the one being courted.

Every time either Merob or Michal appears in this chapter, she is referred to as the "daughter" of Saul (vv.17, 19–20, 27–28). David's marriage to one or both women could not escape the political implications of their being the daughters of the reigning king: If Saul (and Jonathan) should die, David's claim on the throne of Israel would be all the stronger if he were married to one of its princesses. In addition, the symbolism of David's marrying Saul's daughter should not be missed: When political marriages were arranged, it was usually the daughter of the ostensibly weaker ruler who married the stronger (cf. Ge 34:9; 1Ki 3:1; 2Ch 18:1). David's relentless climb to Israel's throne proceeds apace.

Michal's "love" for David (vv.20, 28) parallels that of Jonathan (vv.1, 3) and, while doubtless genuine, perhaps carries the same covenantal nuances. What is certain is that these two siblings "show more love and loyalty to their father's competitor than to their father. The biblical author further invites the comparison by juxtaposing their stories in 1 Sam. 18–20" (Berlin, "David's Wives," 70).

Saul and David were both "pleased" (vv.20, 26) at the prospect of Michal's marriage to David, but for different reasons. As Moses had been a "snare" to the Egyptian pharaoh (Ex 10:7) in the sense of tripping him up at every turn and keeping him off guard, so also Saul intended that Michal would be a "snare" to David (v.21) in the sense that Saul's demanded bride-price of a hundred Philistine foreskins would prove to be his undoing (v.25). David, however, brought back "two" hundred foreskins (v.27) and thus—ironically—capitalized on the "second opportunity" (v.21) that Saul gave him.

Saul, to confirm to David his desires concerning Michal, sent further word through his "attendants" (lit., "servants," v.22; see comment on 16:15–16). They were to approach David "privately" to make it appear as though they were speaking to him on their own rather than at Saul's command. They stressed their own loyalty to him (on "like" in v.22, cf. comment on 16:21), which matched that of the people as a whole (v.16).

David's response to them (v.23), however, once more emphasizes his humble origins (cf. v.18). He again demonstrates that he "speaks well" (16:18), this time by using a Hebrew wordplay captured by the NIV in "small matter" (from *qll*; cf. Isa 49:6) and "little known" (from *qlh*; cf. Pr 12:9, "a nobody"), each of which translates the same underlying consonantal text (*nqlh*). In addition David refers to himself as a "poor man," a description that will come back to haunt him in Nathan's parable (2Sa 12:1–4).

Saul, however, would not allow David to plead poverty as an excuse to get out of marrying Michal. A mere "hundred Philistine foreskins" would suffice as compensation for her (v.25). The Hebrew term *mōhar* ("bride-price"; elsewhere only in Ge 34:12; Ex 22:16[15]) refers to payment made by the groom to the bride's father (cf. similarly Dt 22:29) and is paralleled in other Semitic cultures from the earliest times (cf. W. Robertson Smith, *Kinship and Marriage in Early Arabia* [Cambridge: Cambridge Univ. Press, 1885], 78–80; *The Prophets of Israel and Their Place in History to the Close of the Eighth Century B.C.* [2nd ed.; London: A.&C. Black, 1919], 171, 410 n. 13). But "the *mohar* seems to be not so much the price paid for the woman as a compensation given to the family, and, in spite of the apparent resemblance, in law this is a different consideration. The future husband thereby acquires a right over the woman, but the woman herself is not bought and sold" (*AIs*, 27). Under certain circumstances, as here (cf. also Jos 15:16), "heroic deeds could be substituted for the *mōhar*" (I. Mendelsohn, "The Family in the Ancient Near East," *BA* 11/2 [1948]: 27).

In asking David to kill one hundred Philistines, Saul of course is hoping that David himself will be killed. Saul gives another reason, however, for his demand: that he might "take revenge" on his enemies (v.25) by decimating them (cf. 14:24; Jdg 15:7; and 16:28 for other examples of avenging oneself on the Philistine foe). Ironically, as Gunn (*The Fate of King Saul*, 150 n. 10) observes, David himself has become one of Saul's "enemies" (v.29; cf. also 19:17; 20:13; 24:4, 19; 25:26, 29).

26b–29 The word *hayyāmîm* (lit., "the days") occurs at the end of v.26b ("allotted time") and of v.29, thus forming a frame around this section. "Presented the full number" (v.27) echoes "elapsed" in v.26b (the same Heb. root underlies both expressions), thus further linking v.26b with what follows rather than with what precedes.

David's "men," later to become his loyal companions during the days of their mutual flight from Saul (cf. 23:3, 5; 24:3; 25:12–13), are first mentioned in v.27. The verbs "went out," "killed," and "brought" are singular in number, stressing David's leadership in fulfilling Saul's demand. "Presented," however, has a plural subject and involves David's men, without whose help he surely would have failed, in the overall success of his venture. For the MT's "two hundred" the LXX has "one hundred," which is sometimes assumed to be the correct reading on the basis of 2 Samuel 3:14. The latter verse, however, simply quotes Saul's original figure (v.25) as the price of Michal's hand. Saul, true to his word, gives his daughter to his enemy (v.27). "He is thus even more enmeshed with David: indebted to him for his harp-playing/healing and his military service, and tied to him through Jonathan's love and his daughter's marriage" (Gunn, *The Fate of King Saul*, 81).

The combination of the evidence of God's help for and presence with David (v.28; cf. vv.12, 14 and comment on 16:18) and of Michal's love for David (vv.20, 28) increased Saul's fear of David (v.29; cf. v.12), with the result that "he" (Saul) remained "his" (David's) enemy for the rest of his "days" (cf. 23:14).

30 The final verse of ch. 18 repeats the theme of David's success (cf. vv.5, 14–15). He soon proved that he was more than a match for the Philistine commanders; and even when they later joined in common cause against Saul, they justifiably remained wary of David (29:3–4, 9). In contrast to David's own earlier protestations concerning his unworthiness and obscurity (v.23), the text observes that his name was now "well known" (lit., "precious," as in Ps 139:17; Isa 43:4). The superlatives heaped on him are reminiscent of the earlier description of Saul (9:2), as though to remind us that David had become what Saul could no longer be.

NOTES

7 In an Egyptian victory hymn of the fifteenth century BC, Thutmose III says, "I bind the barbarians of Nubia by ten-thousands and thousands, the northerners by hundred-thousands as living captives" (*ANET*, 374). The Egyptian word for "hundred thousand" (*ḥfnw*) "also has the abstract meaning 'great quantity'" (James K. Hoffmeier, "Egypt As an Arm of Flesh: A Prophetic Response," in Gileadi, 86). Hoffmeier (95 n. 67) suggests that the Egyptian couplet may be a parallel to "thousands ... tens of thousands" in v.7.

18 חַיַּי (*ḥayyay*, "my life") should probably be repointed here as חַיִּי (*ḥayyî*) in the unique sense of "my family" (thus the NIV). Driver, 153, is perhaps correct in assuming that the following "my father's clan" is a scribal explanation of this rare term. Perhaps כִּי (*kî*) should here be translated by the interrogative "why" instead of the NIV's "that" (see comment on 11:5).

21 Saul's statement to David at the end of v.21, "Now you have a second opportunity to become my son-in-law," is probably to be understood as "a formal declaration over David which secures his betrothal to Michal, 'Today you shall be my son-in-law.' ... We find the head of his house acting unilaterally without recourse to the courts to bring about a change in legal status which as in divorce and adoption is effected by a specific spoken formula" (Anthony Phillips, "Another Example of Family Law," *VT* 30/2 [1980]: 241). The initial בִּשְׁתַּיִם (*bištayim*, "with a second [opportunity]" [hence the NIV]) could also be rendered (with approximately the same meaning) "in a second way" (cf. Job 33:14; so K&D, 192).

27 On an interior wall of his mortuary temple at Medinet Habu, Rameses III (ca. 1198–1166 BC) commissioned scenes depicting the counting of hands severed from his enemies in battle as a means of establishing a body count (cf. *ANEP*, no. 348). Elsewhere on the same temple walls is a panel that has been interpreted as picturing a pile of foreskins collected for the same purpose, perhaps from Philistines (whose armies were driven out of Egypt by Rameses III).

5. David the Refugee (19:1–24)

OVERVIEW

Although Saul is earlier described as desiring David's permanent residence at the palace (18:2), ch. 19 records the final break—however ambiguous from Saul's point of view (vv.6–7)—between the two men. Now determined once and for all to kill David, Saul forces David's flight, and the vocabulary of the refugee suffuses the chapter ("go into hiding," v.2; "eluded," v.10; "made good his escape," v.10; "run for your life," v.11; "fled and escaped," v.12; "escaped," v.17; "get away," v.17; "fled and made his escape," v.18).

[1]Saul told his son Jonathan and all the attendants to kill David. But Jonathan was very fond of David [2]and warned him, "My father Saul is looking for a chance to kill you. Be on your guard tomorrow morning; go into hiding and stay there. [3]I will go out and stand with my father in the field where you are. I'll speak to him about you and will tell you what I find out."

[4]Jonathan spoke well of David to Saul his father and said to him, "Let not the king do wrong to his servant David; he has not wronged you, and what he has done has benefited you greatly. [5]He took his life in his hands when he killed the Philistine. The LORD won a great victory for all Israel, and you saw it and were glad. Why then would you do wrong to an innocent man like David by killing him for no reason?"

[6]Saul listened to Jonathan and took this oath: "As surely as the LORD lives, David will not be put to death."

[7]So Jonathan called David and told him the whole conversation. He brought him to Saul, and David was with Saul as before.

[8]Once more war broke out, and David went out and fought the Philistines. He struck them with such force that they fled before him.

[9]But an evil spirit from the LORD came upon Saul as he was sitting in his house with his spear in his hand. While David was playing the harp, [10]Saul tried to pin him to the wall with his spear, but David eluded him as Saul drove the spear into the wall. That night David made good his escape.

[11]Saul sent men to David's house to watch it and to kill him in the morning. But Michal, David's wife, warned him, "If you don't run for your life tonight, tomorrow you'll be killed." [12]So Michal let David down through a window, and he fled and escaped. [13]Then Michal took an idol and laid it on the bed, covering it with a garment and putting some goats' hair at the head.

14When Saul sent the men to capture David, Michal said, "He is ill."
15Then Saul sent the men back to see David and told them, "Bring him up to me in his
bed so that I may kill him." 16But when the men entered, there was the idol in the bed, and
at the head was some goats' hair.
17Saul said to Michal, "Why did you deceive me like this and send my enemy away so
that he escaped?"
Michal told him, "He said to me, 'Let me get away. Why should I kill you?'"
18When David had fled and made his escape, he went to Samuel at Ramah and told
him all that Saul had done to him. Then he and Samuel went to Naioth and stayed there.
19Word came to Saul: "David is in Naioth at Ramah"; 20so he sent men to capture him. But
when they saw a group of prophets prophesying, with Samuel standing there as their
leader, the Spirit of God came upon Saul's men and they also prophesied. 21Saul was told
about it, and he sent more men, and they prophesied too. Saul sent men a third time, and
they also prophesied. 22Finally, he himself left for Ramah and went to the great cistern at
Secu. And he asked, "Where are Samuel and David?"
"Over in Naioth at Ramah," they said.
23So Saul went to Naioth at Ramah. But the Spirit of God came even upon him, and
he walked along prophesying until he came to Naioth. 24He stripped off his robes and
also prophesied in Samuel's presence. He lay that way all that day and night. This is why
people say, "Is Saul also among the prophets?"

COMMENTARY

1–7 "A king delights in a wise servant, but a shameful servant incurs his wrath" (Pr 14:35). The Hebrew root translated "wise" in this proverb is used to describe David's "success" in 18:5, 14–15, 30 (see comment on 18:5), a success that brought varied and inconsistent responses from Saul.

Although Saul's wise and successful "servant" (v.4), David is the object, not of the king's delight, but of his murderous intent. He commands his "attendants" (lit., "servants," v.1; see comment on 16:15–16), as well as his son Jonathan, to kill David. Saul's tortured duplicity becomes more and more evident as we recall that he had earlier ordered his attendants to tell David privately that the king was "pleased with" him (18:22). The narrator now states that Jonathan is "fond of" David (identical Heb. expression) and that Jonathan will therefore do everything in his power to save the life of his covenanted friend (cf. 18:1–3 and comment).

The NIV's "warned" (lit., "told," vv.2, 11) appropriately links the concern of Jonathan with that of his sister Michal, both of whom want no harm to come to David. Saul's determination, by contrast, is relentless. He "is looking" for an opportunity to kill David, he "tried" again to pin him to the wall with his spear (v.10), and he "plans" to destroy the town of Keilah because of David (23:10; the same

Heb. verb in all three passages). So Jonathan warns his friend, "Be on your guard" (v.2; cf. 2Sa 20:10 for the danger of ignoring such advice), using the same Heb. verb as in v.11, where Saul's men are told to "watch" David's house one night to prevent him from escaping so that they can kill him in the morning. God's servant must always be alert, because his enemy will surely be (1Pe 5:8).

Jonathan also tells David to "go into hiding and stay there" (lit., "stay in a secret place and hide," v.2). From this time on and for a long period of time, the man after God's own heart would be a hunted fugitive. He would hide from his best friend's father at the beginning of his career and from his own son near its end (2Sa 17:9). Miscall, 126, observes that David's hiding from Saul in a secret place "foreshadows his sin with Bathsheba 'in a secret place' (2 Sam 12:12)."

Jonathan's personal interest in helping David is underscored by use of the emphatic pronoun in the phrases "I will go out" and "I'll speak" (v.3). Jonathan promises to stand "with" (lit., "at the hand of") his father, Saul, as David's advocate (cf. v.4). By doing so, Jonathan is sure that he will be acting in the king's best interests (cf. 1Ch 18:17, "at the king's side" [lit., "hand"]; Ne 11:24, "the king's agent" [lit., "at the king's hand"]). The venue is the "field" where David is hiding (cf. also 20:5, 11, 24, 35), perhaps not far from Saul's fortress in Gibeah. Jonathan further promises to keep David fully informed (cf. David's fears expressed in 20:10).

The plea of Jonathan in vv.4–5 begins and ends with his hope that Saul will not "do wrong to" David, especially since the latter has not "wronged" the king (cf. also 24:11; in all cases the Heb. verb is *ḥāṭāʾ*, lit., "sinned [against]"; GK 2627). Jonathan further reminds his father that David's deeds have helped Saul, that David "took his life in his hands" (v.5; for the idiom cf. further 28:21; Jdg 12:3; Job 13:14; Ps 119:109) when he escaped Goliath's challenge, and that Saul himself had been pleased with the outcome (17:55–58). There is therefore no reason to kill "an innocent man"; such a crime could only bring bloodguilt on Saul (Dt 21:8–9). "Why" would his father want to do David harm, Jonathan asks—a question that he later has to repeat (20:32). The works of David should bring him praise, not death (cf. Pr 31:31).

Through David's initial success on the battlefield the Lord had "won a great victory" for all Israel (v.5), just as through Saul's earlier similar success the Lord had "rescued" Israel (see 11:13 and comment; same Heb. idiom). But whereas in ch. 11 Saul refused to allow his detractors to be put to death, in ch. 19 he orders the execution of one of his courtiers. Fortunately, Jonathan's rebuke of his father brought him to his senses, at least temporarily. He "listened to" (lit., "obeyed," v.6) Jonathan and took the most solemn of all oaths (cf. 14:39 and comment; also Jer 4:2; Hos 4:15), promising that David would not be put to death—a promise that he quickly and conveniently forgot (v.11). In the meantime, however, David was once again made a member of Saul's court in good standing (v.7; cf. 16:21; 18:2).

8–10 David's continued military success against the Philistines (v.8) evoked the repetition of a familiar scene (vv.9–10; see comment on 16:14, 16; 18:10–11).

11–17 Verse 10 ends by stating that "David made good his escape," and v.18 begins with "When David had fled and made his escape," the two expressions thus framing the account (vv.11–17) of Michal's helping David to escape (cf. Gunn, *The Fate of King Saul*, 83) from Saul's "men" (lit., "messengers," vv.11, 14–16). The account itself, structurally held together also by the repeated use of *šlḥ* ("send," vv.11, 14–15, 17), is one of a series of deception stories "in which the response to the opening situation is a deception. These stories have the following common structure or pattern: (1) a difficult situation provides the necessity for a party to act; (2) that party performs a deception to escape the situation; (3) the immediate threat of the opening situation is removed" (Robert C. Culley, "Themes and Variations in Three Groups of OT Narratives," *Semeia* 3 [1975]: 5). Other examples given by Culley are Abram's deceiving the Egyptian pharaoh (Ge 12:10–20); Lot's daughters' conceiving sons through their father (Ge 19:30–38); Tamar's conceiving a son through Judah (Ge 38); the midwives' deceiving the Egyptian pharaoh (Ex 1:15–21); the Gibeonites' deceiving the Israelites (Jos 9:3–15); and Ehud's killing the king of Moab (Jdg 3:12–30).

Tradition ascribes vv.11–17 as the original setting of Psalm 59, which includes in its title "When Saul had sent men to watch David's house in order to kill him," using the language and vocabulary of v.11. Although the mission of Saul's men was to kill David "in the morning," God's strength and love preserved him "in the morning" (Ps 59:16).

The human agent assuring David's rescue was Michal, his loving wife (18:20, 28). After warning him to flee the home they shared (v.11), she helped him escape by lowering him "through a window" (v.12; for other examples cf. Jos 2:15; 2Co 11:33). To give David time to put sufficient distance between himself and his pursuers, Michal fashioned a crude dummy to take his place in his bed (v.13). She further stalled for time by telling Saul's men that her husband was ill (v.14), thus implying that they should not disturb him.

Michal's dummy is described in connection with *t^erāpîm* (GK 9572; cf. NIV note on v.13), usually translated "idols, household gods" (thus the NIV's "idol" in vv.13, 16 and "idolatry" in 15:23). Since *t^erāpîm* is always plural and since the idols they denote are presumably always small (Ge 31:19, 34–35; Jdg 17:5; 18:14, 17–18, 20; 2Ki 23:24; Eze 21:21; Hos 3:4; Zec 10:2), the dummy was almost certainly not a single, man-sized idol. Michal's ruse was probably effected by piling clothing, carpets, or the like on David's bed and covering it with a garment, allowing only the goats' hair at the head to show. She did not place the household idols "on" or "in" (NIV, vv.13, 16) the bed but "at" or "beside" it (*ʾel* often has this meaning; cf. BDB, 40 sec. 8) to enhance the impression of David's illness (cf. similarly Ackroyd, "The Verb Love," 157–58). The Hebrew root of *t^erāpîm*, although unknown, may have been *rph* ("sink, drop, be weak") or *rpʾ* ("heal"; for an excellent summary, cf. Aubrey R. Johnson, *The Cultic Prophet in Ancient Israel* [Cardiff: Univ. of Wales Press, 1944], 31 n. 3).

Michal's use of household idols doubtless reflects pagan inclination or ignorance on her part. But the narrator also employs her actions to make yet another connection between David's wife Michal and Jacob's wife Rachel (see comment on 18:17). Each woman deceived her father by using teraphim (cf. Ge 31:33–35) and thus demonstrated that she was "more devoted to her husband than to her father" (Lawton, 425). Another final (though more remote) link between the two accounts is the use of the rare word *m^eraʾ^ašôt* (lit., "place[s] at the head") in vv.13, 16 and Genesis 28:11, 18 (the term occurs elsewhere only in 1Sa 26:7, 11–12, 16; 1Ki 19:6).

Michal's ruse worked to perfection; Saul's men were deceived (v.14). Saul, however, not satisfied with their report, sent his men back for another look, this time with orders to "bring [David] up" to Gibeah, bed and all, so that he might be killed there (v.15). By the time they arrived (v.16), of course, David was long gone. Near the end of his reign over Israel, Saul would command the medium at Endor to "bring up" Samuel (28:8, 11), with equally distressing results.

In v.5 Saul's son asked his father "why" he would want to kill David, and in v.17 Saul asks his daughter "why" she would "deceive" (lit., "betray"; cf. 1Ch 12:17; La 1:19) him and keep David from being killed. Michal's response repeats a key verb in Saul's question: Her "get away" and his "send ... away" both translate *šlḥ* (cf. further the comment on v.11). In addition, she brings the entire matter full circle by echoing her earlier words to David in v.11, where she warned him that if he did not flee he would "be killed." Alter observes: "Michal coolly turns around her own words to David and her actions of the previous night and pretends that David threatened her, saying, 'Help me get away or I'll kill you'" (Alter, *Art of Biblical Narrative*, 120).

Saul's own words identify David as his mortal "enemy" (v.17; cf. 18:29), thus barring forever his return to Saul's court at Gibeah. David's days as an outlaw, now begun in earnest, will continue until Saul's death.

18–24 Verse 18 reverts to the time when David had escaped after Michal's warning (v.12). He went to Ramah, Samuel's hometown (far to the northwest of Gibeah; see comment on 1:1), to inform the prophet about what Saul had done. Perhaps to escape detection, he and Samuel then went to Naioth (v.18) at Ramah (v.19). Naioth, possibly a common noun ("habitations") rather than a place name, may refer to the compound of dwellings in Ramah where Samuel's "group of prophets" (v.20) lived (cf. 2Ki 6:1–2).

In relentless pursuit of David, Saul sends men to Naioth to capture him. The Spirit of God, however, protects David by causing first three successive contingents of Saul's messengers (vv.20–21) and finally Saul himself to prophesy (vv.22–23). Saul's men "saw" (not "heard") Samuel's disciples "prophesying" (v.20), which—as in a similar situation earlier (10:5–6, 9–11)—probably means that the prophesying was in the form of succumbing to a divinely induced possession trance rather than of speaking a divinely given word (see comment on 10:5 for details). Each such group of prophets had a "leader" (as here, v.20) or "father" (10:12; 2Ki 2:12), in this case Samuel.

Finally realizing that his men were not going to apprehend David, Saul takes matters into his own hands by going to Ramah himself (v.22). Stopping at Secu (mentioned only here; meaning and location unknown), he "asked" (*šāʾal*—yet another pun on his name) for the exact whereabouts of Samuel and David. Told they had gone to Naioth, Saul continued on his way and began "prophesying" after receiving an accession of the Spirit of God (v.23).

An accompaniment of Saul's prophesying was that he, like those who had arrived before him (implied by "also," omitted by the NIV at the beginning of v.24), "stripped off" his garments. Since *ʿārōm* in context with *pāšaṭ* ("strip off") is elsewhere rendered "naked" (cf. Job 22:6; Hos 2:3), the NIV's discreet translation "that way" is unnecessary. In fact, the implication is that Saul, minus the robes symbolic of his rule (cf. comment on 2:19; 15:27)—yea, naked—demonstrates once again his forfeiture of any claim to be Israel's king. In addition, the rhetorical question demanding a negative answer—"Is Saul also among the prophets?"—underscores that forfeiture and thus takes an ironic twist: To question the genuineness of Saul's prophetic behavior was to question his legitimacy as king of Israel (see comment on 10:11).

The use of this proverb first in 10:11–12 and now here brackets the narrative descriptions of Saul's first and last encounters with Samuel as well as with the Spirit of God. Neither legitimate king nor genuine prophet, Saul continues to stumble toward his doom at the hands of the Philistines, when he will be "stripped" of his garments for the last time (31:8–9).

NOTES

10 According to *IBHS*, 313 n. 22, "the anarthrous phrase *blylh hwʾ* 'in that night' (Ge 19:33; 30:16; 32:23) is both anomalous and textually suspect" and should probably be amended to *blylh hhwʾ* on the basis of the Samaritan Pentateuch. But the same anarthrous phrase occurs here, and similar phenomena are attested elsewhere in the OT and in Moabite (cf. GKC, sec. 126*y*). Emendation of the MT therefore seems unnecessary.

13 William F. Albright, 207 n. 63, proposed "old rags" as a translation of תְּרָפִים (*tᵉrāpîm*; GK 9572) in vv.13, 16, especially since no man-sized idols have turned up in archaeological excavations in Palestine (114; so also Ronald F. Youngblood, "Teraphim," in *WBE*, 1685). But since *tᵉrāpîm* always means "(household) idols" elsewhere in the OT, it seems best to keep that sense here as well. For a possible alternative—namely, that *tᵉrāpîm* means "ancestor figurines/statuettes" throughout the OT—see H. Rouillard and J. Tropper, "*trpym*, rituals de guérison et culte des ancêtres d'après 1 Samuel xix 11–17 et les textes parallèles d'Assur et de Nuzi," *VT* 37/3 (1987): 351–61; Karel van der Toorn, "The Nature of the Biblical Teraphim in the Light of the Cuneiform Evidence," *CBQ* 52 (1990): 203–22.

20 "Group," "company," and the like are merely contextual guesses for MT *lhqt*, a word that occurs only here (unless it is a metathesis for *qhlt*, which seems unlikely). A more attractive proposal connects it with Ethiopic *lhq*, "old man, elder, dignitary," resulting in the translation "venerable group/company" in verse 20; cf. G. R. Driver, "Some Hebrew Words," *JTS* 29 (1928): 394; D. Winton Thomas, "A Note on לִיקְּהַת in Proverbs xxx.17," *JTS* 42 (1941): 154; E. Ullendorff, "The Contribution of South Semitics to Hebrew Lexicography," *VT* 6 (1956): 194; *HALOT*, 521 and references there.

6. Jonathan's Friendship (20:1–42)

OVERVIEW

The chronological continuation of ch. 20 from the preceding chapter is secured by the reference to "Naioth at Ramah" in v.1 (found elsewhere only in 19:18–23). The frequent repetition of key terms and motifs throughout ch. 20, which will be pointed out in the comments below, also guarantees its integrity as a cohesive literary unit. Especially noteworthy is the expression "The LORD is witness between you and me forever" (vv.23, 42), which concludes each of the chapter's roughly equal halves (cf. Polzin, *Samuel and the Deuteronomist*, 191–93; M. H. Segal, 183).

[1]Then David fled from Naioth at Ramah and went to Jonathan and asked, "What have I done? What is my crime? How have I wronged your father, that he is trying to take my life?"

2"Never!" Jonathan replied. "You are not going to die! Look, my father doesn't do
anything, great or small, without confiding in me. Why would he hide this from me? It's
not so!"
3But David took an oath and said, "Your father knows very well that I have found
favor in your eyes, and he has said to himself, 'Jonathan must not know this or he will be
grieved.' Yet as surely as the LORD lives and as you live, there is only a step between me and
death."
4Jonathan said to David, "Whatever you want me to do, I'll do for you."
5So David said, "Look, tomorrow is the New Moon festival, and I am supposed to dine
with the king; but let me go and hide in the field until the evening of the day after tomorrow. 6If your father misses me at all, tell him, 'David earnestly asked my permission to hurry
to Bethlehem, his hometown, because an annual sacrifice is being made there for his
whole clan.' 7If he says, 'Very well,' then your servant is safe. But if he loses his temper, you
can be sure that he is determined to harm me. 8As for you, show kindness to your servant,
for you have brought him into a covenant with you before the LORD. If I am guilty, then kill
me yourself! Why hand me over to your father?"
9"Never!" Jonathan said. "If I had the least inkling that my father was determined to
harm you, wouldn't I tell you?"
10David asked, "Who will tell me if your father answers you harshly?"
11"Come," Jonathan said, "let's go out into the field." So they went there together.
12Then Jonathan said to David: "By the LORD, the God of Israel, I will surely sound out my
father by this time the day after tomorrow! If he is favorably disposed toward you, will I
not send you word and let you know? 13But if my father is inclined to harm you, may the
LORD deal with me, be it ever so severely, if I do not let you know and send you away safely.
May the LORD be with you as he has been with my father. 14But show me unfailing kindness
like that of the LORD as long as I live, so that I may not be killed, 15and do not ever cut off
your kindness from my family—not even when the LORD has cut off every one of David's
enemies from the face of the earth."
16So Jonathan made a covenant with the house of David, saying, "May the LORD call
David's enemies to account." 17And Jonathan had David reaffirm his oath out of love for
him, because he loved him as he loved himself.
18Then Jonathan said to David: "Tomorrow is the New Moon festival. You will be missed,
because your seat will be empty. 19The day after tomorrow, toward evening, go to the
place where you hid when this trouble began, and wait by the stone Ezel. 20I will shoot
three arrows to the side of it, as though I were shooting at a target. 21Then I will send a boy
and say, 'Go, find the arrows.' If I say to him, 'Look, the arrows are on this side of you; bring
them here,' then come, because, as surely as the LORD lives, you are safe; there is no danger.
22But if I say to the boy, 'Look, the arrows are beyond you,' then you must go, because the

LORD has sent you away. [23]And about the matter you and I discussed—remember, the LORD
is witness between you and me forever."

[24]So David hid in the field, and when the New Moon festival came, the king sat down
to eat. [25]He sat in his customary place by the wall, opposite Jonathan, and Abner sat next
to Saul, but David's place was empty. [26]Saul said nothing that day, for he thought, "Something must have happened to David to make him ceremonially unclean—surely he is
unclean." [27]But the next day, the second day of the month, David's place was empty again.
Then Saul said to his son Jonathan, "Why hasn't the son of Jesse come to the meal, either
yesterday or today?"

[28]Jonathan answered, "David earnestly asked me for permission to go to Bethlehem.
[29]He said, 'Let me go, because our family is observing a sacrifice in the town and my
brother has ordered me to be there. If I have found favor in your eyes, let me get away to
see my brothers.' That is why he has not come to the king's table."

[30]Saul's anger flared up at Jonathan and he said to him, "You son of a perverse and
rebellious woman! Don't I know that you have sided with the son of Jesse to your own
shame and to the shame of the mother who bore you? [31]As long as the son of Jesse lives
on this earth, neither you nor your kingdom will be established. Now send and bring him
to me, for he must die!"

[32]"Why should he be put to death? What has he done?" Jonathan asked his father. [33]But
Saul hurled his spear at him to kill him. Then Jonathan knew that his father intended to
kill David.

[34]Jonathan got up from the table in fierce anger; on that second day of the month he
did not eat, because he was grieved at his father's shameful treatment of David.

[35]In the morning Jonathan went out to the field for his meeting with David. He had a
small boy with him, [36]and he said to the boy, "Run and find the arrows I shoot." As the
boy ran, he shot an arrow beyond him. [37]When the boy came to the place where Jonathan's arrow had fallen, Jonathan called out after him, "Isn't the arrow beyond you?"
[38]Then he shouted, "Hurry! Go quickly! Don't stop!" The boy picked up the arrow and
returned to his master. [39](The boy knew nothing of all this; only Jonathan and David
knew.) [40]Then Jonathan gave his weapons to the boy and said, "Go, carry them back to
town."

[41]After the boy had gone, David got up from the south side of the stone and bowed
down before Jonathan three times, with his face to the ground. Then they kissed each
other and wept together—but David wept the most.

[42]Jonathan said to David, "Go in peace, for we have sworn friendship with each other in
the name of the LORD, saying, 'The LORD is witness between you and me, and between your
descendants and my descendants forever.'" Then David left, and Jonathan went back to
the town.

COMMENTARY

1–4 Polzin (*Samuel and the Deuteronomist*, 191, 264 nn. 10–13) observes that the first half of ch. 20 contains a

> preponderance of definite, forceful, strident, and emotionally charged language.... The finite verb is strengthened or emphasized by a preceding infinitive absolute of the same stem no fewer than seven times in verses 1–21; both David and Jonathan frequently invoke the LORD's name in solemn oath, self-imprecation or blessing; the partners repeatedly protest, implore, and react in the strongest of terms; and they frequently punctuate their statements with the deictic *hinnēh* "behold."

The brief interchange between David and Jonathan recorded in vv.1–4 is bracketed by David's question, "What have I done ... that he is trying to take my life [lit., 'soul']?" (v.1), and Jonathan's words of assurance, "Whatever you [lit., 'your soul'] want me to do, I'll do for you" (v.4). David's flight from Saul at Naioth takes him back to the Gibeah fortress and to his friend (v.1), the only one he can trust. Like his ancestor Jacob before him (Ge 31:36; cf. similarly Abimelech's plea in Ge 20:9 and Obadiah's question in 1Ki 18:9), David wants to know the nature of the terrible sin he has supposedly committed that would bring on such frantic pursuit of him. The naked truth that Saul is "trying to take" (lit., "seeking") his life would be repeated over and over by Saul and others (22:23; 23:15; 25:29; 2Sa 4:8).

But to Jonathan, trusting son as well as loyal friend, it is incredible to think that Saul really intends to harm David (vv.2, 9; cf. also Saul's oath in 19:6)—until it became painfully obvious to him (v.33). Jonathan, reminded of how his comrades-in-arms had come to his defense with their "Never!" in the face of Saul's murderous intentions toward his own son (14:45), encourages David with the same interjection (vv.2, 9). He assures him that Saul does nothing without "confiding in me" (lit., "uncovering/opening my ear," an idiom used by Jonathan again in vv.12–13 ["let you know," NIV]).

David, however—more sensitive to Saul's unpredictability and changes of mood—responds to Jonathan's "Look.... Why would he hide this from me?" (v.2) with his own "Look ... let me go and hide in the field" (v.5). He swears (v.3; cf. also vv.17, 42) with the most solemn of oaths (cf. also v.21; 19:6; see comment on 14:39) that there is "only a step" between him and death at the hands of Saul.

As Abigail does later in a similar situation (25:26), David strengthens the assertion even further by adding "and as you live" (cf. also 17:55; for its significance see comment on 1:26). He thus affirms (v.3) that Saul, who "knows" of the high regard in which Jonathan holds David (cf. v.29), does not want his son to "know" of his evil designs on David's life or he would be "grieved" (cf. v.34). One major emphasis of the chapter concerns who knows (or does not know) this or that matter—and therefore, as Polzin observes, in ch. 20 "words using the root *YDʿ*, 'to know,' occur more often (twelve times) than in any other chapter in the book" (Polzin, *Samuel and the Deuteronomist*, 194).

5–7 Verses 5–23 constitute a three-act drama structured around ten "if-then" statements (vv.6, 7a, 7b, 8, 9, 10, 12, 13, 21, 22; cf. Polzin, *Samuel and the Deuteronomist*, 192, 264 n. 16], who discerns an eleventh [v.14]). The acts are arranged in chiastic order:

A David's plan to help Jonathan know (vv.5–7)
  B David and Jonathan's mutual covenant (vv.8–17)
A' Jonathan's plan to tell David that he now knows (vv.18–23)

The vocabulary of v.5 (which begins the drama) is echoed in that of v.24 (which begins the second half of the chapter). David's plan (vv.5–7) is simple: If Saul accepts Jonathan's explanation for David's absence from the forthcoming New Moon festival celebration, then David is safe; but if Saul becomes angry, then Jonathan will know that Saul is bent on harming David.

The monthly burnt offerings at the appearance of the new moon (Nu 28:14) were accompanied by celebration and rejoicing (Nu 10:10). David's emphatic "I" (v.5) probably contains an element of surprise that he should be invited and also of trepidation in the knowledge of what would happen to him if he attended. He therefore plans to hide in a "field" (near Saul's fortress in Gibeah; see 19:3 and comment) until the evening of the third day, by which time he would presumably expect to receive word from Jonathan concerning Saul's reaction toward his absence from the festival.

David's excuse for not attending (v.6) is relayed by Jonathan to Saul in vv.28–29 (with some additional details). The verb "asked permission" (vv.6, 28, the rare Niphal of *šāʾal*, attested elsewhere only in Ne 13:6) provides yet another opportunity to pun on the name "Saul." David's desire to participate in an "annual sacrifice" with his family would not have been considered unusual (1:21; 2:19). During Samuel's boyhood days the normal venue was Shiloh (1:3), the site of the tabernacle. By David's time, however, Shiloh had been destroyed (see comment on 4:11), and the tabernacle had no fixed location. Thus it was only to be expected that annual sacrifices would be offered in the celebrants' hometowns.

Understandably, David was risking Saul's wrath by pretending to substitute a competing festival for the one the king had invited him to. Perhaps Bethlehem, his hometown, had the additional stigma of being outside Saul's domain (as argued by G. W. Ahlström, "Was David a Jebusite Subject?" *ZAW* 92/2 [1980]: 285–87). In any case, David surely was not serious in asserting that Saul's ready agreement to allow him to go to Bethlehem would mean that he would then be back in the king's good graces (v.7)—"unless, of course, his entire strategy in having Jonathan lie about his absence is to provoke Saul to an angry outburst that would remove Jonathan's misconceptions, not his own" (Polzin, *Samuel and the Deuteronomist*, 189). David knew that Saul was determined to kill him (v.7); and although Jonathan had not yet brought himself to admit that cold fact (vv.9, 13), he soon would (v.33).

8–17 Covenantal terminology ("show kindness," vv.8, 14; "brought him into a covenant," v.8; "do not ever cut off your kindness," v.15; "made a covenant," v.16; "reaffirm his oath," v.17; "love[d]," v.17), used by both David and Jonathan, links together vv.8–17. Reminding Jonathan of the covenant they had made (18:3), David asks him to demonstrate covenantal loyalty, *ḥesed* ("kindness" [GK 2876], v.8)—conduct required in "the mutual relationship of rights and duties between allies" (Nelson Glueck, *Ḥesed in the Bible* [Cincinnati: Hebrew Union College, 1967], 46–47; contra K. Sakenfeld, *The Meaning of Hesed in the Hebrew Bible: A New Inquiry* [Decatur, Ga.: Scholars, 1978]).

David's willingness to die "if I am guilty" would later be echoed by his son Absalom (2Sa 14:32), though neither man believed himself deserving of death. David voiced his preference for dying at the hand of his covenanted friend Jonathan ("yourself" is emphatic) instead of his sworn enemy Saul. But Jonathan avowed that if he "had the least inkling" (lit., "knew at all," v.9) that his father intended to harm David, he would surely "tell" his friend. David, still wary, wants to know whether Jonathan would really "tell" (v.10) him if Saul answered "harshly" (a not uncommon quality in royal speech; cf. Ge 42:7, 30; 1Ki 12:13 = 2Ch 10:13) when he learned the reason for David's absence.

Cain had said to his brother Abel, "Let's go out to the field" (Ge 4:8), and used the privacy it afforded to kill him. By contrast Jonathan said the same thing to his covenanted brother David (v.11), but used the privacy of the field to assure him of his undying loyalty. The fact that David and Jonathan went to the field "together" (lit., "the two of them") underscores their close relationship and is reminiscent of the description of Abraham and Isaac at Moriah (Ge 22:6, 8).

The New Moon festival would be celebrated "tomorrow" (v.5), at which time Saul would react in one way or another to David's absence (v.7). In accord with David's wishes to learn of Saul's response by "the evening of the day after tomorrow" (v.5), Jonathan promises on oath to send David word no later than that time—whether the news is favorable (v.12) or unfavorable (v.13). In either case, Jonathan says, "I ... [will] send you away safely" (lit., "I will send you away, and you will go in peace"; cf. v.42 for the fulfillment of Jonathan's promise). "May the LORD deal with me, be it ever so severely" (lit., "May the LORD do thus to me, and thus may he add"; cf. also 3:17; 14:44) was perhaps "accompanied by a gesture, such as feigning to cut one's own throat" (William S. LaSor, David A. Hubbard, and Frederic W. Bush, *Old Testament Survey: The Message, Form, and Background of the Old Testament* [2nd ed.; Grand Rapids: Eerdmans, 1996], 177).

To the assessment of others concerning the Lord's presence "with" David (see 16:18 and comment; 17:37; 18:12, 14, 28), Jonathan now adds his own prayer to the same end (v.13). In so doing he parallels David's divine calling with that of Saul and thus recognizes—again (see comment on 18:4)—that David, and not he himself (Saul's disobedience had long since forfeited an enduring kingdom for himself and his descendants, 13:13–14), will be the next king of Israel.

In vv.14–15 covenantal friendship is the basis of Jonathan's plea that neither he nor his descendants be executed by David after he becomes king. The link between these two verses and 2 Samuel 9 is established by comparing *ḥesed yhwh* ("the kindness of the LORD"; appropriately in the NIV, "unfailing kindness like that of the LORD," v.14) with *ḥesed ʾelōhîm* ("the kindness of God"; that is, "kindness like that of God," preferable to the NIV's "God's kindness," 2Sa 9:3; cf. 2Sa 9:1, 7). Norman H. Snaith ("The Meanings of a Word," *BT* 16 [1965]: 47) suggests that since the divine name is sometimes used to denote the superlative, *ḥesed yhwh* in v.14 perhaps means "the greatest possible loyalty." In any case, "the word *chesed* plus the Sacred Name is used in 1 Sam 20:14 to express the close bond between David and Jonathan, the Hebrew equivalent of Roland and Oliver, Aeneas and Achates, Orestes and Pylades, the 'faithful friends' of history and romance and legend."

Jonathan's plea to David not to "cut off" (v.15) his kindness from Jonathan's "family" (lit., "house," paralleling "house" in v.16) forms a Hebrew wordplay not only with "cut off ... from the face of the earth" (v.15; for the idiom see Zep 1:3) but also with "made [lit., 'cut'; see comment on 11:1] a covenant" in v.16. By now Jonathan surely perceives that among David's "enemies" (v.15; cf. also v.16), whom he predicts will be cut off, is his own father, Saul (cf. 18:29; 19:17).

Thus Jonathan, on behalf of his family/house/descendants, extends in perpetuity ("ever," v.15; cf. vv.23, 42) his previous covenant with David (see 18:3 and comment; cf. also 22:8) to the house/family/descendants of the latter (v.16). In so doing he prays that the Lord may "call David's enemies to account" (lit., "demand an accounting [for the shedding of innocent blood] from the hand of David's enemies"; cf. 2Sa 4:11; for a parallel idiom, cf. Ge 9:5). Since covenants by nature and definition involve reciprocal obligations (v.42), Jonathan also has David reaffirm his side of the agreement (v.17), in context with the covenantal language of 18:1, 3: "He loved him as [he loved] himself."

18–23 Jonathan's suggested ruse (vv.18–22) begins by echoing the time and place of the venue David had originally proposed (v.5). He agrees that David will be "missed" because his seat will be "empty" (v.18; the same Heb. word in both cases). On the third day (v.19) David is to go to the field where he hid (David's suggestion as well; v.5) "when this trouble began" (probably referring to Saul's plans to kill him; 19:2). There he is to "wait" (lit., "sit"; instead of occupying a "seat" at Saul's religious festival [v.18], David will "sit" by himself in a nearby field) by a stone called Ezel (mentioned only here; location unknown).

Jonathan himself (the "I" at the beginning of v.20 being emphatic) will then aim three arrows at the stone, "shooting" (lit., "sending," a key verb in this section; cf. vv.21–22) as though at a target. The boy dispatched to find the arrows will be told either that the arrows are "on this side of" him (v.21) or "beyond" him (v.22). If the former is the case, David is "safe" (v.21), which, of course, is Jonathan's intention (v.13) and in which case David may return to the fortress at Gibeah. But if the arrows are beyond where the boy is at the time of Jonathan's shout, then David's life is in danger, and he must flee in response to the will of "the LORD" (v.22).

The first literary half of the chapter closes with Jonathan's reminder to David of the eternal nature of the covenant of friendship that binds them (v.23; cf. also v.42). Jonathan is especially concerned that David (the first "you" is emphatic) and his dynasty keep his promise, made on oath, not to break covenant with Jonathan (emphatic "I") and his descendants (vv.15–17). He therefore invokes the Lord as witness "between" the two men in a manner reminiscent of the ancient agreement between Jacob and Laban (Ge 31:48–53).

24–34 Playing out the charade to humor his friend, David hid in the field (v.24 echoes v.5). When the celebrants gathered for the New Moon festival, Saul took his customary seat "by the wall" (v.25), where he could feel relatively safe from surprise attack. Jonathan and Abner, Saul's army commander (and cousin; see 14:50; 17:55), occupied places of honor at the table, but David's place was "empty" (as Jonathan and David had planned; v.18).

Saul's ignorance of what was really taking place (he "said nothing," v.26) matched that of the boy sent by Jonathan to retrieve the arrows (he "knew nothing," v.39). When David did not appear on the first day of the New Moon festival, Saul assumed that something had happened to make him "ceremonially unclean" (v.26; cf. Lev 15:16, 18) and therefore disqualified from participating in a religious feast (cf. Nu 9:6). But Saul naturally wanted to know why David's seat was also empty on the second day of the *ḥōdeš* ("New Moon festival," v.27, as in vv.5, 18, 24; the NIV's "month," vv.27, 34, while possible, causes unnecessary confusion; for the likelihood that the New Moon was celebrated for at least two days, cf. *AIs*, 470). In referring to David as the "son of Jesse" (vv.27, 30–31; cf. also 22:7–9, 13, and esp. 25:10), Saul probably intended at least a mild insult (see comment on 10:11).

Jonathan's response to Saul's question (vv.28–29) reflects the language of David's original plan (v.6) but with the addition of a few details. Polzin (*Samuel and the Deuteronomist*, 264 n. 14), among others, calls attention to a wordplay in vv.27–28: David would rather celebrate with his humble family in "Bethlehem" (*bêt lāḥem*, v.28) than risk coming to a king's "meal" (*lāḥem*, v.27). Because of wariness of Saul's paranoia, David's excuse is also a lie. He knows, however, that he can trust Jonathan: "I have found favor in your eyes" (v.3, quoted by Jonathan in v.29). A subtle irony in David's desire to "get away" (*mālaṭ*) to see his brothers is evident in the frequent use of the verb in its more common sense of "flee, escape" with respect to his flight from Saul (e.g., 19:10, 12, 17–18), thus signaling yet another aspect of his fugitive status. Though Saul's grandson will always be welcome at King David's "table" (2Sa 9:7–13), David feels unwelcome at the "table" of King Saul (v.29).

As David had feared (v.7), Saul became violently angry (v.30) when Jonathan told him the reason for David's absence. For all intents and purposes, Jonathan and David are indistinguishable to Saul as he explodes in "foul-mouthed anger" (Hertzberg, 175). The vile epithet Saul hurls at his son Jonathan, which the NIV translates euphemistically as "You son of a perverse and rebellious woman," is difficult to render without being equally vulgar—although TEV's "You bastard!" and NJB's "You son of a rebellious slut!" come close. Saul, of course, is cursing Jonathan, not Jonathan's mother, as the rest of the verse makes clear. He accuses Jonathan of having "sided with" (lit., "chosen") David, and that not only to his own shame but also the shame of the "mother who bore you" (lit., "nakedness of your mother," a phrase that elsewhere has sexual connotations; cf. the MT of Lev 18:7).

Saul further reminds Jonathan that so long as David remains alive, neither Jonathan (emphatic "you," v.31) nor Jonathan's kingdom can survive. History will prove Saul's fears to be prophetic beyond his worst nightmares: Although the kingdom of Saul and his son will not be established (13:13–14), the kingdom of David and his son will be (2Sa 7:16, 26; 1Ki 2:12, 46). The word *bēn* ("son"), used twice by Saul in v.30, occurs twice again on Saul's lips in v.31. Its second occurrence is hidden in the NIV's "must die": *ben-māwet* (lit., "son of death" = a person characterized by or deserving of death). The idiom appears elsewhere only twice, both times in the books of Samuel (26:16; 2Sa 12:5), and its last occurrence—on the lips of David himself—will recoil to haunt him for the rest of his life as the prophet Nathan identifies David as the one worthy of death: "You are the man!" (2Sa 12:7).

Saul's demand for David's death (v.31) brings a predictable response from Jonathan: "Why?" (v.32; cf. 19:5). Jonathan's further question, "What has he done?" reflects his earlier reminder to Saul that David's actions had benefited the king (19:4). But Saul, though placated before (19:6), will not be denied this time. Saul, not having David as his target as on two previous occasions (18:10–11; 19:9–10), tries to pin David's surrogate, Jonathan, to the wall with his spear (v.33). Jonathan needs no further convincing that Saul indeed intends to kill David (something David obviously knew much earlier; cf. v.7) and that the spear was really meant for his covenanted friend. In Saul's eyes, Jonathan and David have momentarily become one.

It is Jonathan's turn to fly into a rage. (The Heb. phrase translated "fierce anger" in v.34 elsewhere describes the highest levels of disappointed human fury [cf. Ex 11:8; 2Ch 25:10; Isa 7:4].) Knowing of his father's murderous designs on and mistreatment of David causes Jonathan to be "grieved" (v.34), a response that his friend had foreseen (v.3). On the second day of the New Moon festival, neither David (v.27) nor Jonathan (v.34) ate at the king's table (vv.29, 34).

35–40 The final section of ch. 20 (vv.35–42) is divided into two unequal parts, each of which ends with "back to [the] town" (vv.40, 42).

Verses 35–40 describe the fulfillment of the ruse proposed earlier (vv.18–22). Jonathan had told David to wait by the stone Ezel on the second day of the New Moon festival "toward evening" (v.19). Jonathan had left unspecified the time of the shooting of the three arrows (v.20), which he now begins on the following morning (v.35), presumably because the flight of an arrow is more easily seen in daylight. The boy Jonathan takes with him (vv.21–22) is here described as being "small" (v.35) and thus less likely to ask embarrassing questions about the orders he is given.

Although the MT reads "arrows" (plural) the first time the word appears in vv.36–38 and "arrow" (singular) the other four times (so also NIV), the number of arrows that Jonathan actually shot remains uncertain. Except for the last of the four occurrences of the singular (where, in any event, many manuscripts join the *Qere* in reading the plural), the word for "arrow" is rare (found elsewhere only in 2Ki 9:24) and in each case is read as a plural in two or more Hebrew manuscripts. The four plural readings, however, may be a misguided scribal attempt to harmonize vv.36–38 with the "[three] arrows" of vv.20–22. Jonathan tells the boy to find the "arrows" he has shot (v.36a); but, since his aim is true, he discovers that he needs to shoot only one "arrow" (v.36b).

The arrow's landing beyond the running lad, loudly confirmed by Jonathan (v.37) so that David will be sure to hear it, is a signal to David that it is God's will for him to remain a fugitive from Saul (v.22). Jonathan's urgent commands to the boy (v.38) are obviously intended for David instead, but the boy of course does not know the reason behind the shooting of the arrow(s) in the first place (v.39). He therefore interprets his master's words as a command to retrieve the arrow(s) and return to him. Jonathan then sends him back to town with all the weapons (v.40), assuming (and doubtless hoping) that David might want a private moment to bid his friend farewell.

41–42 Getting up from his hiding place near "the stone" (v.41, implied from v.19), David bows down more than once (a not uncommon practice in ancient times; cf. Ge 33:3; often in the Amarna letters [Youngblood, *The Amarna Correspondence*, 15–19]) to acknowledge Jonathan's (covenantal) superiority ("with his face to the ground"; cf. further 24:8; 25:23, 41; 28:14). Their mutual kissing and weeping (v.41), in expectation of their coming farewell (v.42), is reminiscent of the poignantly emotional scene involving Joseph and his brothers (Ge 45:14–15).

Jonathan's "Go in peace" (*lēk lᵉšālôm*, v.42) reflects the "safe(ly)" of vv.7, 13, 21 (see comment on vv.13, 21) and is generally spoken by a superior to an inferior (cf. 1:17; 25:35). At the same time Jonathan magnanimously uses the emphatic "we" as he reminds David of their mutual—and everlasting—oath of friendship (cf. vv.17, 23). They had sworn to each other "in the name of the LORD" (cf. Dt 6:13; 10:20), thus employing an oath that the Decalogue solemnly warned the ancient Israelites not to "misuse" (Ex 20:7 = Dt 5:11; cf. also Lev 19:12). The covenant between Jonathan and David included their "descendants forever" (cf. v.15 and comment; cf. also 24:21).

The two friends part after Jonathan's farewell speech. Apart from one other brief meeting (23:16–18), this is the last time they see each other.

NOTES

1 Perhaps כִּי (*kî*) should here be translated by the interrogative "why" instead of the NIV's "that" (see comment on 11:5).

3 The opening words, וַיִּשָּׁבַע עוֹד דָּוִד (*wayyiššabaʿ ʿôd dāwid*, lit., "But David took an oath again"), present a difficulty since no previous oath is mentioned. The LXX and Syriac omit *ʿôd* (so also the NIV), as does Driver (assuming dittography at both ends of the word). Others preserve *ʿôd* but revocalize *wyšbʿ* as

וַיֵּשֶׁב (*wayyāšeb*, "But he replied"), assuming the MT's final ע (ʿ) to be dittography (so Gordon, *I and II Samuel*, 150; cf. similarly Hertzberg, Klein, McCarter, H. P. Smith). Barthélemy, however, prefers the MT, apparently either from willingness to allow the difficulty to remain or from understanding "again" as a way of expressing the addition of David's oath to his strong assertion of v.1.

10 The difficult phrase אוֹ מַה־יַּעַנְךָ אָבִיךָ קָשָׁה (*ʾô mah-yyaʿankā ʾābîkā qāšâ*) has provoked numerous suggestions for emendation (see the commentaries). But since *ʾô* ("or") occasionally means "if, when" (as in Lev 26:41), and since *mah* sometimes functions as a relative pronoun meaning "what(ever)" (as in 19:3), "if what your father answers you is harsh" (cf. similarly NIV) solves the problem nicely.

14 The best way to make sense out of the first two occurrences of וְלֹא (*wᵉlōʾ*, "and not") in v.14 is to repoint the consonantal text as וְלֻא (*wᵉluʾ*, "and if only"; cf. לוּא [*lûʾ*, "if (only)"] in 14:30). Verse 14 would then read (lit.): "And if only you, as long as I am alive—indeed, if only you would show me the kindness of the LORD—that I may not die!" (cf. NIV; also K&D, 210).

19 Although difficult, תֵּרֵד מְאֹד (*tērēd mᵉʾōd*, lit., "you/she will go down exceedingly") can hardly be separated from וְהַיּוֹם רַד מְאֹד (*wᵉhayyôm rad mᵉʾōd*, lit., "and the day went down exceedingly"; cf. Jdg 19:11, "and the day was almost gone," NIV). McCarter (*I Samuel*, 337 n. 19), who correctly links the two passages, nevertheless reads in v.19, "you will wander [from the verb רוּד, *rûd*] exceedingly" = "you will be long gone." But comparison with Isaiah 38:8, הַשֶּׁמֶשׁ ... יָרָדָה (*haššemeš ... yārādâ*, lit., "the sunlight ... had gone down") makes resort to the rare verb *rûd* unnecessary. In the phrase in v.19 *tērēd* is correctly vocalized from the root *yrd* and has as its subject the unexpressed feminine noun *šemeš*: "[the sun] goes down exceedingly" = "[the sun] has almost set." The NIV's "toward evening" expresses the same idea idiomatically.

25 The MT's וַיָּקָם יְהוֹנָתָן (*wayyāqom yᵉhônātān*, "and Jonathan got up"; cf. NIV note) is doubtless due to contamination from v.34. The NIV's text of v.25 follows the LXX, which reads "and he was in front of Jonathan," implying וַיְקַדֵּם (*wayyᵉqaddēm*; cf. Driver, 169, for details; also Barthélemy, 2:192).

30 "All English translations have treated ... *mardut* as 'rebellion,' deriving it from the root *m-r-d*, 'to rebel.' But this form ... would be anomalous in the Hebrew, whereas the vocalization of the received text yields a Hebrew word well known in rabbinic Hebrew and meaning 'discipline.' (The verbal root is *r-d-h*, 'to rule sternly.') She is 'perverse against discipline'" (Alter, *The David Story*, 128). Thus Alter's translation calls Jonathan a "son of a perverse wayward woman." See further *HALOT*, 632.

7. David and the Priest of Nob (21:1–9)

OVERVIEW

The last sentence in the NIV's rendering of 20:42 is 21:1 in the MT, accommodating the traditional one-verse numbering difference between the Hebrew and the English texts throughout ch. 21. The commentary follows the English numbering system.

Chapters 21–22 apparently record events later than those in the preceding chapters, since by this time David has gathered around him a sizable body of "men" (21:2, 4–5; 22:6) and has become their "leader" (22:2). The two chapters comprise a literary unit of three sections arranged in chiastic order.

Chapters 21:1–9 and 22:6–23 are concerned with the priestly compound at Nob in Benjamin, while the central section (21:10–22:5) summarizes David's flight to Gath in Philistia, Adullam in Judah, and Mizpah in Moab. The present section describes how David receives food (vv.1–6) and weapons (vv.8–9) from Ahimelech the priest, two sections that frame a brief notice regarding the presence in Nob of Doeg, one of Saul's servants (v.7).

1David went to Nob, to Ahimelech the priest. Ahimelech trembled when he met him, and asked, "Why are you alone? Why is no one with you?"

2David answered Ahimelech the priest, "The king charged me with a certain matter and said to me, 'No one is to know anything about your mission and your instructions.' As for my men, I have told them to meet me at a certain place. 3Now then, what do you have on hand? Give me five loaves of bread, or whatever you can find."

4But the priest answered David, "I don't have any ordinary bread on hand; however, there is some consecrated bread here—provided the men have kept themselves from women."

5David replied, "Indeed women have been kept from us, as usual whenever I set out. The men's things are holy even on missions that are not holy. How much more so today!" 6So the priest gave him the consecrated bread, since there was no bread there except the bread of the Presence that had been removed from before the LORD and replaced by hot bread on the day it was taken away.

7Now one of Saul's servants was there that day, detained before the LORD; he was Doeg the Edomite, Saul's head shepherd.

8David asked Ahimelech, "Don't you have a spear or a sword here? I haven't brought my sword or any other weapon, because the king's business was urgent."

9The priest replied, "The sword of Goliath the Philistine, whom you killed in the Valley of Elah, is here; it is wrapped in a cloth behind the ephod. If you want it, take it; there is no sword here but that one."

David said, "There is none like it; give it to me."

COMMENTARY

1–6 David, needing help in his continued flight from Saul, went to Nob (perhaps modern el-Isawiyeh, one and one-half miles northeast of Jerusalem [cf. Isa 10:32] and two and one-half miles southeast of Gibeah of Saul). As the site of a large contingent of priests (22:11, 18–19), Nob may for a time have been the location of the tabernacle (though not the ark of the covenant; see comment on 7:2). Ahimelech, one of the more prominent of Nob's priests and mentioned several times in these chapters, "trembled" when he "met" David (v.1), thus displaying fear for David's reputation and perhaps also recognizing his authority (cf. 16:4 for the similar reaction of Bethlehem's elders when confronted by Samuel).

Ahimelech's two questions—"Why are you alone?" and "Why is no one with you?"—may seem to be saying much the same thing, but David answers them separately. He is alone because there is a secret matter that he wishes to discuss with the priest (v.2a), and his men are not with him because he will meet them later (v.2b). Polzin (*Samuel and the Deuteronomist*, 195) suggests that the unnamed "king" in David's first answer is—in the narrator's mind, at least—not Saul but the Lord, who "charged" David with a certain matter and gave him "instructions" (v.2), just as he had earlier "appointed" him leader of his people to replace the discredited Saul (13:14; the same Heb. root in all three cases). Polzin's proposal is attractive in that the name Ahimelech means "The King [i.e., God] is my brother" and that the narrator is thus perhaps engaging in wordplay in v.2.

In addition Jonathan had been convinced that the Lord had "sent" David away (20:22), just as the divine King has now asserted to David that no one is to know about "your mission" (lit., "the mission that I am sending you on," v.2). David's statement concerning his meeting his men at a "certain" place employs a rare Hebrew idiom that is used when one either does not know the name of a person or place or when he is deliberately trying to conceal it from his audience (Ru 4:1, "my friend" ["such a one," KJV]; 2Ki 6:8, "such and such").

David next asks Ahimelech two questions (vv.3, 8), each of which is followed by the priest's answer (vv.4, 9a) and then David's response (vv.5, 9b). The questions are parallel in that both use the same rare idiom: "What do you have on hand?" (lit., "What is that under your hand/control?" v.3) and "Don't you have a spear or a sword here?" (lit., "Isn't there here a spear or sword under your hand/control?" v.8). David follows up his first question with a request: "Give me [lit., 'Give into my hand'] five loaves of bread"—a modest amount at best (cf. 17:17).

Echoing David's request, Ahimelech tells him what he has and does not have "on hand" (v.4): No "ordinary" (lit., "common") bread is available, but "there is" (for other examples of the rare emphatic position of *yēš* see the MT of Jdg 19:19; Isa 43:8) some "consecrated" (lit., "holy") bread that David and his men may eat. There was a condition, however: The men must not recently have had sexual relations with women, which would have rendered them ceremonially unclean (Ex 19:14–15; Lev 15:18) and therefore temporarily unfit to partake of the holy food.

David assured Ahimelech that women had indeed been "kept" (v.5; different Heb. verb from that in v.4) from himself and his men—his customary practice whenever he "set out" to do battle (for *yāṣāʾ* in this specialized sense, cf. 8:20; 17:20). Uriah the Hittite would later refuse to sleep with his wife, Bathsheba, while on military duty (2Sa 11:11). The sharp distinction between the "holy" (*qōdeš*; GK 7731) and the "common" (*ḥōl*; GK 2687; cf. Lev 10:10; Eze 22:26; 42:20; 44:23; 48:14–15) observed in v.4 is maintained in v.5. Even on "missions" (different Heb. word from the one in v.2) that are "not holy" (*ḥōl*), the "bodies" (see NIV note) of David's men are "holy" (*qōdeš*). How much more so, then, during this particular venture—though we are not told what David's mission is. (He may well have made up the story out of whole cloth, either to deceive Ahimelech into supplying his needs or to protect the priest from any accusation of complicity in his flight from Saul.)

Satisfied with David's rationale, Ahimelech gives him the consecrated/holy bread, now identified specifically as the bread of the (divine) "Presence" (*pānîm*, v.6; cf. the mandate of placing the bread regularly "before" [*lipnê*, lit., "in the presence of"] the Lord [Lev 24:8]). Such bread (Ex 25:30; 35:13; 39:36; 40:23; Lev 24:5–8; 1Ki 7:48 = 2Ch 4:19), after it had performed its symbolic function, became "a most holy part" of the customary share given to the priests, who were to eat it in a "holy" place (Lev 24:9).

Since priestly perquisites were for priests and their families only (cf. Ex 29:32–33; Lev 22:10–16), how could Ahimelech in good conscience give the consecrated bread to David and his men, who were not priests? The answer provided by Jesus (Mt 12:1–8; Mk 2:23–28; Lk 6:1–5), the authoritative "Lord of the Sabbath," seems to be that "human need takes priority over ceremonial law" (F. F. Bruce, *The Hard Sayings of Jesus* [Downers Grove, Ill.: InterVarsity Press, 1983], 33) and that it is always "lawful" on the Sabbath "to do good" (Mk 3:4). Possibly the incident recorded in vv.1–6 took place on a Sabbath day, since v.6 could imply that the consecrated bread being given to David had been replaced with a fresh supply ("hot bread") not long before (cf. Lev 24:8).

The reference to Abiathar (rather than to his father, Ahimelech) in Mark 2:26 is also puzzling (K&D, 218 n. 1, calls it "an error of memory" on Mark's part). Perhaps John W. Wenham has the best solution. He observes that the use of *epi* in *epi tou batou* ("in the account of the bush," Mk 12:26) may be paralleled to its use in *epi Abiathar archiereōs* in Mark 2:26, which should then be translated "in the account of Abiathar the high priest" (John W. Wenham, "Mark 2:26," *JTS* 1 [1950]: 156), especially since Abiathar was the only survivor of the slaughter of the priests of Nob (22:20) and in fact became much more noteworthy than his father (cf. chs. 22–30; 2Sa 15–20; 1Ki 1–4 [passim]; for a different [though related] solution, cf. Archer, 362).

7 Doeg the Edomite, perhaps a mercenary pressed into service as a result of Saul's war(s) against Edom (14:47), is introduced parenthetically in anticipation of his sinister role later (22:18–19). He had been detained "before the LORD" (i.e., at the tabernacle), probably for an undisclosed ceremonial reason (K&D, 219, suggests he may have been a proselyte "who wished to be received into the religious communion of Israel"). The verb "detained" echoes "kept" in v.5, both coming from the same Heb. root. Doeg's official role in Saul's employ was as his "head shepherd" (cf. Joseph's brothers in Ge 47:6: "Put them in charge of my own livestock," lit., "Make them chiefs [i.e., 'chief herdsmen,' thus the NEB] of my own livestock").

8–9 David's request for bread (v.3) is followed by one for weapons (v.8). His question to Ahimelech, "Don't you have?" (lit., "Isn't there under your hand?"), is mirrored in his further statement, "I haven't brought" (lit., "I haven't taken in my hand"). What David does not have in his hand he hopes is in Ahimelech's. The urgency of the "king's business" (v.8; cf. v.2, where the Heb. word for "business" is translated "a certain matter") is David's excuse for his lack of weapons. As in v.2 (see comment), the identity of the king remains shrouded in ambiguity.

The only weapon Ahimelech has to offer to David is the sword of Goliath, whom—as was apparently widely known—David had killed in the "Valley of Elah" (v.9; cf. 17:2, 19, 48–51). Although David first took the giant's sword as part of his share of the Philistine plunder (17:54), he must have eventually brought it to the sanctuary of the Lord (for a Hittite parallel, cf. Hoffner, 225). So Ahimelech tells David that it is in a storage place behind the "ephod" (the priestly garment that held the breastpiece containing the sacred lots; cf. Ex 28:28, 30), where David can find it protected in a "cloth" (lit., "garment" [v.9], often used as wrapping material in ancient times; cf. Ex 12:34; Jdg 8:25).

Although David had not "brought" (lit., "taken," v.8) his own sword, Ahimelech was able to supply one: If you "want" (lit., "will take for yourself," v.9) Goliath's sword, then "take" it. As David had earlier said concerning the bread, "Give me five loaves" (v.3), he now says concerning the sword, "Give it to me" (v.9).

Ahimelech says of Goliath's mighty weapon, "There is no sword ... but that one"; and David responds, "There is none like it" (v.9). David thus echoes Samuel's earlier description of Saul, the newly chosen king: "There is no one like him" (10:24). Polzin (*Samuel and the Deuteronomist*, 197) makes the important observation that

> the priestly transfer to David of the sword ... speaks of the holy and mysterious transfer of royal power from Saul to David.... Once David is installed as king in Jerusalem and the matter of his "everlasting" kingship revealed in the vision of Nathan, it is no accident that David prays to the LORD in words that recall the very sword of Goliath, even as they tie together the unique choice of David with the unique LORD [2Sa 7:22].

Polzin (ibid., 265 n. 23) also calls attention to the prayer of David's son Solomon in 1 Kings 8:23.

NOTES

2 David's response to Ahimelech's first question is chiastically arranged, the first half of the chiasm occurring in his opening statement and the second half in his quotation of the Lord's words. A literal translation is "The King *charged* me with a *mission* and said to me, 'No one is to know anything about the *mission* that I am sending you on and that I have *charged* you with.'"

6 The MT's plural form הַמּוּסָרִים (*hammûsārîm*, "that had been removed") is probably a mistake for singular הַמּוּסָר (*hammûsār*; thus 4QSam[b]) and arose by attraction to the preceding הַפָּנִים (*happānîm*; cf. Cross, "The Oldest Manuscripts," 168).

8. David the Fugitive: Gath, Adullam, Mizpah (21:10–22:5)

OVERVIEW

Gath in Philistia (21:10–15), Adullam in Judah (22:1–2), and Mizpah in Moab (22:3–5) are presented in sequence as three of the places of refuge to which David resorts in his continuing flight from Saul.

[10]That day David fled from Saul and went to Achish king of Gath. [11]But the servants of Achish said to him, "Isn't this David, the king of the land? Isn't he the one they sing about in their dances:

"'Saul has slain his thousands,
and David his tens of thousands'?"

[12]David took these words to heart and was very much afraid of Achish king of Gath. [13]So he pretended to be insane in their presence; and while he was in their hands he acted like a madman, making marks on the doors of the gate and letting saliva run down his beard.

14 Achish said to his servants, "Look at the man! He is insane! Why bring him to me? 15 Am
I so short of madmen that you have to bring this fellow here to carry on like this in front of
me? Must this man come into my house?"
22:1 David left Gath and escaped to the cave of Adullam. When his brothers and his
father's household heard about it, they went down to him there. 2 All those who were in
distress or in debt or discontented gathered around him, and he became their leader.
About four hundred men were with him.
3 From there David went to Mizpah in Moab and said to the king of Moab, "Would you
let my father and mother come and stay with you until I learn what God will do for me?"
4 So he left them with the king of Moab, and they stayed with him as long as David was in
the stronghold.
5 But the prophet Gad said to David, "Do not stay in the stronghold. Go into the land of
Judah." So David left and went to the forest of Hereth.

COMMENTARY

10–15 Immediately after departing from Nob ("that day," v.10) with the sword of Goliath, David went to Gath (ironically, Goliath's hometown [17:4]), possibly to seek employment as a mercenary soldier. The king of Gath was Achish son of "Maoch" (*māʿôk*, 27:2), perhaps an alternative form of "Maacah" (*maʿᵃkâ*, 1Ki 2:39), in which case Achish would have been the ruler of Gath for over forty years. In the title of Psalm 34, he is called Abimelech, possibly a Philistine royal or dynastic title (cf. Ge 20:2; 21:32; 26:1). The Philistine name Achish has been known for well over a century in the form "Ikausu," the seventh-century BC king of Ekron during the reigns of the Assyrian rulers Esarhaddon and Ashurbanipal (see Note on v.10).

Whatever David's intentions in going to Gath, the "servants" (perhaps in the sense of "officers" or "attendants"; cf. comment on 16:15) of Achish (v.11) were sufficiently impressed by David's reputation—as reflected in the ditty composed after he and Saul had defeated the Philistines (18:7; cf. esp. 29:4–5)—to be wary of him. Calling him "king of the land," however, may have been belittling his importance by considering him only one among many such local rulers (cf. Jos 12:7, 9–24).

David took the servants' words seriously (v.12; cf. the same Heb. idiom in Job 22:22). Having fled "from" (*mippᵉnê*) Saul (v.10[11]), David was now very much afraid "of" (*mippᵉnê*) Achish (v.12[13]). "Sensing danger [David] extracts himself from the situation by feigning madness. It creates a nice contrast. David controls madness. Madness controls Saul" (Gunn, *The Fate of King Saul*, 86).

In v.13 the verb translated "he acted like a madman" is used elsewhere to describe behavior resulting from drunkenness (Jer 25:16; 51:7) or terror (Jer 50:38) or to drive a chariot furiously or recklessly (Jer 46:9; Na 2:4). The manifestations of David's pretended insanity were "making marks" (Heb. verb used elsewhere only in Eze 9:4) on the doors of the (city) gate and letting saliva run down his beard—hardly the picture of a recently anointed king (contrast the positive image of oil running down the beard of Aaron in Ps 133:2).

Achish has seen enough. Sarcastically declaring that he already has sufficient madmen of his own, he makes it clear that he wants nothing more to do with this Israelite refugee (vv.14–15). David's deception of Achish has worked—as it would again (ch. 27) and again (ch. 29).

22:1–2 Leaving Gath (v.1) David "escaped" (probably a reference to his continuing flight from Saul; cf. 27:1) to a cave near Adullam (in the western foothills of Judah [Jos 15:35], perhaps modern Khirbet esh-Sheikh Madhkur, about ten miles east-southeast of Gath). His brothers and other family members went "down" (presumably from the higher ground at Bethlehem, their hometown; cf. also Ge 38:1; 2Sa 23:13 = 1Ch 11:15) to join him there. They may have feared royal reprisal if they remained in Bethlehem, where Saul would be sure to come looking for the fugitive David.

It is possible, though by no means certain, that David's relatives joined "those" (lit., "a man" [v.2], repeated three times in the verse; cf. also "men" near the end of the verse) who "gathered" around him (perhaps in anticipation of military action, as in 7:7 ["assembled"]). Numbering about "four hundred" (in itself a formidable force; cf. 25:13; 30:10, 17; Ge 33:1) even in the beginning, the ranks of David's men eventually swelled to as many as six hundred (23:13; 27:2; 30:9; cf. also 13:15 and comment; 14:2; 2Sa 15:18; Jdg 3:31; 18:11, 16–17). United by adverse circumstances of all sorts (e.g., the Hebrew phrase translated "discontented" means lit. "bitter of soul"; cf. 1:10), they were attracted to the charismatic David as their "leader" (v.2, a word with military connotations, often in contexts of raiding/looting; cf. 2Sa 4:2; 1Ki 11:24). Such bands of malcontents and other social misfits were not uncommon in the ancient Near East (cf. Jdg 9:4; 11:3) and were often elsewhere known as *ʿapirū* (cf. Edward F. Campbell Jr., "The Amarna Letters and the Amarna Period," *BA* 23/1 [1960]: 14; similarly, David O'Brien, "David the Hebrew," *JETS* 23/3 [1980]: 204).

3–5 The section begins and ends with reference to place names not found elsewhere in the OT. The location of the "forest of Hereth" (v.5) is unknown (except that it was somewhere in Judah), while this particular "Mizpah" (*miṣpēh*, "Watchtower," v.3; cf. 2Ch 20:24, "place that overlooks"; Isa 21:8) was located on one of the heights of the tableland east of the Dead Sea. It was understandable that David should seek refuge for his "father and mother" in Moab (which he would later conquer [2Sa 8:2]), since Moabite blood flowed through the veins of his ancestors on his great-grandmother's side (Ru 1:4; 4:13, 16–17).

In being solicitous of the needs of his parents, David was following common ancient practice (Jos 2:13, 18; 6:23; 1Ki 19:20) as well as obeying the fifth commandment (Ex 20:12; Dt 5:16). In addition, his desire to conform to God's will (v.3) not only finds precedent in his previous conduct (cf. 17:35–37, 45–47) but also will become increasingly evident throughout his days as a fugitive from Saul (cf. 23:1–2, 4, 10–11; 25:32; 26:11, 23). David's "stronghold" (vv.4–5; cf. 24:22; 2Sa 5:17; 23:14 = 1Ch 11:16), whose location is unknown, could not have been the cave of Adullam (contra Ackroyd, Hertzberg, Driver, McCarter, et al.) since the "stronghold" was not in Judah (v.5). David's true stronghold, of course, was ultimately God himself (2Sa 22:2–3 = Ps 18:2).

As the prophet Samuel had helped and advised Saul, so from now on "the prophet Gad" (v.5), among others, would perform the same functions for David (cf. 2Sa 24:11, where Gad is called "David's seer"). It was through such prophets that the word of God was mediated to Israel's leaders during the days of the monarchy, and it was often by such prophets that records of the royal reigns were written down (1Ch 29:29).

NOTES

10 That אָכִישׁ (ʾākîš, Achish) was in fact the West Semitic spelling of Ikausu is now certain. A royal dedicatory inscription discovered at Tel Miqne (ancient Ekron) in 1996 (see Note on 5:10) refers to אכיש בן פדי ("ʾkyš son of Padi"). Padi was the king of Ekron during the reign of the Assyrian ruler Sennacherib (*ANET*, 287–88), and Padi's son Ikausu was Ekron's king during the reigns of Sennacherib's immediate successors, Esarhaddon and Ashurbanipal (*ANET*, 291, 294).

> ʾkyš and Ikausu must have been derived from **Ik(h)ayus/š*, which eventually leads to Akhayus, that is, ʾAxaios or "Achaean," meaning "Greek." ... The assumption that Padi called his son "Achaean," or—more plausibly—that Akhayus himself adopted this appellation, may be of great importance to the discussion of the origin of the Philistines.... It seems likely that the name of the king of Ekron in the seventh century BC reflected on the name of the Philistine king(s) of Gath in the narrations of the time of Saul and Solomon. (Joseph Naveh, "Achish-Ikausu in the Light of the Ekron Dedication," *BASOR* 310 [1998]: 35–36)

13 The traditional title of Psalm 34, which includes the phrase "he pretended to be insane" (lit., "he changed/disguised his judgment/sense/taste"), places the psalm in the context of David's experience recorded in vv.10–15 (cf. esp. v.13). Although some have felt that the occurrence of the word "taste" in Psalm 34:8 attracted later traditionalists to make a literary link with the wording of v.13, several verses in the psalm itself make a historical connection between the two texts plausible if not certain (cf. "fear[s]" in 34:4, 7, and deliverance from "troubles" in 34:6, 17, 19). Indeed, the psalm as a whole is appropriately tied to the episode in David's life described in vv.10–15.

Somewhat less close is the relationship between David's experience and Psalm 56. Verse 13 in our text states that David was "in their hands"—at best a tenuous parallel to "the Philistines had seized him" in the title of the psalm. At the same time its general tenor lends itself to connection with the event in Gath (cf. "many are attacking me," Ps 56:2; "I will not be afraid," 56:4; "you have delivered me from death," 56:13); and it is therefore understandable that traditionalists might have linked the two passages.

22:4 The MT's וַיַּנְחֵם (*wayyanḥēm*, "and he led them"; root נחה, *nḥh*) has been vocalized as וַיַּנִּחֵם (*wayyanniḥēm*; root נוח, *nwḥ*) by the NIV to yield the more likely meaning "he left them" (cf. the same problem and solution in 2Ki 18:11, "settled them").

9. The Slaughter of the Priests of Nob (22:6–23)

OVERVIEW

Verses 6–23 serve the dual function of (1) describing the penultimate fulfillment of the Lord's promised judgment against the priestly house of Eli (see comment on 2:31–33; for the ultimate fulfillment see 1Ki 2:26–27), and (2) demonstrating the complete contrast between the contempt of the rejected king, Saul, for a priesthood he considered to be treacherous, and the respect and gratitude of the elected king, David, for a priesthood he considered to be an important mediator of God's will to his anointed.

The section begins with Saul the king "seated" (*yôšēb*, v.6) under a tree—a scene with possible pagan connotations—and concludes with Abiathar the priest of the Lord being advised by David: "Stay [*šᵉbâ*] with me" (v.23). The pericope as a whole has a chiastic arrangement:

A Saul berates his officials (vv.6–8);
  B Doeg informs on Ahimelech (vv.9–10);
    C Saul condemns Ahimelech and his fellow priests (vv.11–17);
  B' Doeg kills Ahimelech and his fellow priests (vv.18–19);
A' David protects Ahimelech's son (vv.20–23).

[6]Now Saul heard that David and his men had been discovered. And Saul, spear in hand,
was seated under the tamarisk tree on the hill at Gibeah, with all his officials standing
around him. [7]Saul said to them, "Listen, men of Benjamin! Will the son of Jesse give
all of you fields and vineyards? Will he make all of you commanders of thousands and
commanders of hundreds? [8]Is that why you have all conspired against me? No one tells
me when my son makes a covenant with the son of Jesse. None of you is concerned
about me or tells me that my son has incited my servant to lie in wait for me, as he does
today."

[9]But Doeg the Edomite, who was standing with Saul's officials, said, "I saw the son of
Jesse come to Ahimelech son of Ahitub at Nob. [10]Ahimelech inquired of the LORD for him;
he also gave him provisions and the sword of Goliath the Philistine."

[11]Then the king sent for the priest Ahimelech son of Ahitub and his father's whole family, who were the priests at Nob, and they all came to the king. [12]Saul said, "Listen now, son
of Ahitub."

"Yes, my lord," he answered.

[13]Saul said to him, "Why have you conspired against me, you and the son of Jesse, giving him bread and a sword and inquiring of God for him, so that he has rebelled against
me and lies in wait for me, as he does today?"

[14]Ahimelech answered the king, "Who of all your servants is as loyal as David, the king's
son-in-law, captain of your bodyguard and highly respected in your household? [15]Was that
day the first time I inquired of God for him? Of course not! Let not the king accuse your
servant or any of his father's family, for your servant knows nothing at all about this whole
affair."

[16]But the king said, "You will surely die, Ahimelech, you and your father's whole family."

[17]Then the king ordered the guards at his side: "Turn and kill the priests of the LORD,
because they too have sided with David. They knew he was fleeing, yet they did not
tell me."

But the king's officials were not willing to raise a hand to strike the priests of the LORD.

[18]The king then ordered Doeg, "You turn and strike down the priests." So Doeg the
Edomite turned and struck them down. That day he killed eighty-five men who wore the

linen ephod. [19]He also put to the sword Nob, the town of the priests, with its men and
women, its children and infants, and its cattle, donkeys and sheep.
[20]But Abiathar, a son of Ahimelech son of Ahitub, escaped and fled to join David. [21]He
told David that Saul had killed the priests of the LORD. [22]Then David said to Abiathar:
"That day, when Doeg the Edomite was there, I knew he would be sure to tell Saul. I am
responsible for the death of your father's whole family. [23]Stay with me; don't be afraid; the
man who is seeking your life is seeking mine also. You will be safe with me."

COMMENTARY

6–8 Christian E. Hauer Jr., 96, perceptively observes that whereas the information gatherers of King David's administration were adroit on the foreign field but inept at home, Saul seems to have been poor at gathering information from abroad but was adept at coping with matters of internal security (cf. 23:7, 19, 25, 27; 24:1; 26:1). In the present context (v.6) Saul "knew both David's whereabouts and the identity of the men with him." David and his men "had been discovered" (lit., "were known"; cf. Pr 10:9, "will be found out").

The description of Saul with "spear in hand" reminds us of what a constant threat he was to friend and foe alike (cf. 18:10–11; 19:9–10; 20:33). Although the location of a "tamarisk tree" could have neutral (31:13) or even positive (Ge 21:33) connotations, the "hill" outside Gibeah may well have been a place given over to pagan worship (cf. Eze 16:24–25, 31, 39, where the same Heb. word is translated "lofty shrine[s]" in a chapter devoted to apostasy of the most detestable kind). Saul's officials were dutifully "standing around him" (cf. v.9), ostensibly at his beck and call (cf. 4:20, "attending her").

Saul demands of his fellow Benjamites an answer to the question of whether the "son of Jesse" (a pejorative way of referring to David [v.7]; cf. vv.8, 13; and comment on 20:27) can provide for them more possessions and privileges than they already have as associates of Saul himself. Does David have the power of a Samuel or a Saul to appoint them to high positions (cf. 8:1; 18:13)? Would David be able to make them "commanders of thousands and commanders of hundreds" (which, if true, would mean that David had become king [v.7]; cf. 8:12 and comment; also 17:18 NIV note)? After all, David himself was merely a "leader" (v.2, translating the same Heb. word here rendered "commander") of a few hundred men.

In his paranoia Saul assumes that all his men (v.8)—indeed, the priest Ahimelech as well (v.13)—are co-conspirators with David against him. By using the verb *qāšar* ("conspired"), the narrator may be subtly implying that soldiers and priests alike had become "one in spirit with" David (see 18:1 and comment). Saul complains that no one "tells" (lit., "opens the ear of"; see comment on "confiding in me," 20:2) him about his son Jonathan's perceived acts of treachery: making a covenant with David (cf. 18:3; 20:16) and inciting David to ambush Saul. All this, Saul insists, demonstrates his servants' lack of concern for their master.

9–10 Like Saul's officials (v.6), Doeg the Edomite was "standing" (v.9) near him. Imitating Saul's reference (v.7) to David as the (despised) "son of Jesse," Doeg informs Saul that he witnessed David's meeting with Ahimelech at Nob (see 21:7). In this chapter Ahimelech is referred to several times as "son of Ahitub" (vv.9, 11–12, 20) to highlight his membership in the condemned family of the high priest Eli (see 14:3 and comment, where it is suggested that "Ahimelech" might be another name for "Ahijah").

Doeg reports to Saul that Ahimelech had "inquired" (root *šʾl* [v.10]—yet another wordplay on the name Saul; cf. vv.13, 15; 23:2, 4) of the Lord for David, a fact not mentioned in 21:1–9 but readily admitted to by the priest (v.15). In addition, Doeg continues, Ahimelech gave David "provisions" and "the sword of Goliath the Philistine" (cf. 21:6, 9). That both expressions are in emphatic position in their respective clauses stresses Doeg's opinion that Ahimelech was committing treasonable acts by assisting Saul's enemy.

According to its traditional title, Psalm 52 contains David's tirade against Doeg on this occasion. In the first stanza (52:1–4) David appears to accuse Doeg of falsehood, while in the second (vv.5–7) he foretells divine judgment on him. After David proclaims his confidence in God's unfailing love in his behalf (v.8), the psalm concludes with praise to the Lord for his deeds and presence ("name," v.9).

11–17 Doeg's report to Saul resulted in the king's sending for Ahitub's "whole" priestly family (v.11), who "all" responded by coming from Nob to Gibeah, scarcely two miles to the northwest. ("Whole" and "all" emphasize the almost total annihilation about to take place.) On their arrival Saul addressed Ahimelech in words that echo his statements to his officials in vv.7–8: "Listen ... son of Ahitub" (v.12). The epithet "son of Ahitub" is not only the pejorative equivalent of "son of Jesse" (vv.7–9, 13), demonstrating Saul's anger over what Ahimelech has done, but also forms a suitable literary parallel to his earlier reference to his officials as "men [lit., 'sons'] of Benjamin" (v.7). In response, Ahimelech's "Yes, my lord" is appropriately servile and obedient.

Saul's retort in v.13 combines the elements of Doeg's report in v.10 ("inquiring of God" for David as well as providing him with "bread and a sword") and the substance of his own accusations against his officials in v.8 ("conspired against me," "lies in wait for me," "as he does today"; cf. also "incited" [v.8] and "rebelled" [v.13], both of which are translations of forms of *qûm*, "rise up"). But whereas Saul is of the opinion that his men have conspired among themselves, he insists that Ahimelech is overtly in league with his enemy David ("you and the son of Jesse," v.13).

Ahimelech's response to Saul (vv.14–15) is polite but firm. He defends David's character by suggesting that none of the king's servants is as "loyal" (v.14) as David (cf. comment on "faithful," describing Samuel, in 2:35). After all, David is Saul's "son-in-law" (cf. 18:18). In addition, he is the "captain" of Saul's "bodyguard" (the word is later used of David's own bodyguard in 2Sa 23:23 = 1Ch 11:25) and "highly respected" (cf. comment on 9:6, again describing Samuel; cf. further the characterization of Benaiah, a valiant fighter in charge of David's bodyguard, in 2Sa 23:22–23, "held ... in honor").

Having evaluated David's reputation positively to his own satisfaction, Ahimelech emphatically denies that this was the first time he had consulted God on David's behalf. (The essential element of the Heb. idiom rendered "Of course not!" in v.15 is translated "Never!" in 14:45; 20:2, 9.) Saul should therefore not "accuse" (a strong verb in such contexts, elsewhere rendered "slander" [Dt 22:14, 17] and "charges" [Job 4:18]) Ahimelech or his father's family. In any case, Ahimelech claims to know nothing "at all" (lit., "small or great") of the crimes Saul attributes to David. Believing Ahimelech to be a liar, however, Saul tells him that he and his family "will surely die" (v.16; cf. Saul's intention concerning his own son Jonathan in 14:39, 44). Polzin (*Samuel and the Deuteronomist*, 199) observes:

> Ahimelech is playing here a kind of Jonathan role in the particular conjunction of death and ignorance that permeates their speech in chapters 20 and 22. In 20:2 Jonathan responded to David's worries, 'You shall not die. Behold, my father does nothing either great or small without disclosing it to me.' ... In Jonathan's formulation, knowledge of things great and small goes with life; in Ahimelech's case, ignorance of matters great or small will lead to death.

As good as his word, Saul issues orders for the execution of the priests of Nob. He first commands the "guards" (lit., "runners," v.17; cf. comment on 8:11) "at his side" (lit., "the ones standing around/with him," as in vv.6, 9) to "turn" (preparatory to acting; cf. v.18; also 15:12, 27) and kill them. The priests' crime is that although they knew David was fleeing, they did not "tell" Saul about it (cf. the similar reticence of his own men, v.8). More serious, however, is the fact that the priests "too" (along with David's followers [v.2]—and perhaps also [some of] Saul's men?)—are in league with David.

But Saul's orders fall on deaf ears, thwarted by the religious scruples of his officials. They refuse to raise "a hand" (lit., "their hand," echoing the terminology used earlier in the verse to describe the priests, who "have sided with" [lit., "their hand is with"] David) against the priests of the Lord. The fugitive David will later say, "I will not lift my hand against my master [Saul], because he is the LORD's anointed" (24:10), and after Saul's death he will rebuke an Amalekite for insensitivity in the same respect (2Sa 1:14).

Saul's officials are adamant: They are "not willing" to kill the Lord's priests (v.17). The same Hebrew verb is used later to describe David's unwillingness, as well as that of Saul's armor-bearer, to harm the Lord's anointed ("would not," 26:23; 31:4). Miscall, 136, appropriately compares what Doeg the Edomite was about to do to the priests with what Saul and his men had earlier refused to do to the Amalekites ("were unwilling," 15:9): "Through the hand of a foreigner, Saul perpetrates upon Israelites, priests of the Lord, what he himself did not perpetrate upon foreigners, the Amalekites."

18–19 When Saul, not to be denied, issues his ominous order to Doeg, the doom of the priests is sealed. As an Edomite, Doeg has no qualms about killing Israelite priests. The MT uses the emphatic pronoun "he" in connection with the verb "struck ... down" (v.18), paralleling the emphatic "you" earlier in the verse and stressing the willingness of a foreigner to do what Saul's Israelite officials refused to do. The number of priests murdered surely qualifies the deed as a massacre, and reference to them as wearing the "linen ephod" links this act to the prophecy against the house of Eli delivered by an unnamed man of God (2:28; cf. also 14:3 and the comment on "linen ephod" in 2:18).

Not satisfied with killing the eighty-five priests of Nob, Doeg extends the slaughter by putting the entire town "to the sword" (v.19; cf. the similar threat against Jerusalem recorded in 2Sa 15:14). The doleful list of victims at the end of the verse recalls once again the contrast to Saul's earlier reluctance to totally destroy the Amalekites (see comment on 15:3). "Put to the sword" is the usual NIV rendering of the MT's "strike with the edge [lit., 'mouth'] of the sword," perhaps a vivid description of the sickle-shaped blades of swords commonly used throughout much of the OT period (cf. Yadin, 204, 206–7).

20–23 Probably unknown to Saul at the time, "a" (lit., "one" [v.20], stressing the fact that he is the sole survivor) son of Ahimelech "escaped" (the same verb frequently used of David; cf. 19:10, 12, 17–18) and joined David's fugitive band. Abiathar ("The [divine] Father is excellent") by name (cf. Moses' father-in-law, the priest Jethro, whose name means

"His excellency"), he performed priestly functions for David for the rest of David's life (cf. 23:6, 9; 30:7; 2Sa 8:17); he was eventually replaced by Zadok under Solomon's reign (1Ki 2:27, 35; for the reference to Abiathar in Mk 2:26, see comment on 21:6).

When Abiathar informs David that Saul had issued orders resulting in the massacre of all the priests of Nob except himself (v.21), David tells him (v.22) that he had anticipated Doeg's act of betrayal ever since their earlier encounter at Nob (cf. 21:7). David then confesses that he himself, however unwittingly, is ultimately accountable for the massacre. In saying "I am responsible," David uses a form of the same Hebrew verb translated "turn, turned" in v.18. Although it was Doeg the Edomite who "turned" and killed the priests, it was David who, through his earlier presence at Nob, was "responsible" for causing their death. He therefore offers refuge to Abiathar, telling him not to "be afraid" (v.23; cf. Jonathan's similar reassurance to David in 23:17). Abiathar may count on David's protection: "You" (emphatic), David says, "will be safe with me." Saul now seeks the life (see comment on 20:1) of both of them; so they become partners in flight. King-elect and priest-elect have joined forces as fellow fugitives.

NOTES

6 Saul may have chosen a tamarisk tree—"found abundantly in deserts, dunes and salt marshes" (*Fauna and Flora of the Bible*, 182) but not native to the hill country of Gibeah—under which to officiate because its anomalous presence (like that of the palm tree under which Deborah sat [Jdg 4:5]) would have made it instantly recognizable from a distance. In addition, it provides delightful shade that is cooler than that of other trees (cf. Nogah Hareuveni, *Tree and Shrub in Our Biblical Heritage* [Kiryat Ono: Neot Kedumim, 1984], 24–26).

"Tamarisk" as the correct meaning of אֶשֶׁל (*ʾešel*) is defended by James Barr ("Seeing the Wood for the Trees? An Enigmatic Ancient Translation," *JSS* 13/1 [1968]: 11–20), who vigorously critiques other ancient and modern renderings such as "measure of length," "plot of land," "grove." Although the NEB gives "strip of ground" as the preferred rendering of *ʾešel* in Genesis 21:33, the 1989 REB prefers "tamarisk tree" in conformity with 1 Samuel 22:6; 31:13 (the only two other places in the OT where the Hebrew word appears).

14 "Captain" translates שַׂר (*śar*), probably the original reading (cf. the LXX's ἄρχων, *archōn*), for which the MT's סָר (*sār*, "turning [aside], departing") is doubtless an aural scribal error. Restoration of *śar* in this verse strengthens its function as a *Leitwort* throughout the chapter (cf. vv.2 ["leader"], 7 ["commanders"]).

10. The Rescue of Keilah (23:1–6)

OVERVIEW

Chapters 23 and 24 are linked together by the frequent occurrence of the word "hand," which appears twenty times in the two chapters. It is found nine times in ch. 23 (vv.4, 6 ["with him" = lit., "in his hand"], 7, 11 ["to him" = lit., "into his hand"], 12 ["to Saul" = lit., "into the hand of

Saul"], 14, 16 ["helped him find strength" = lit., "strengthened his hand"], 17, 20) and eleven times in ch. 24 (vv.4, 6, 10 [2x], 11 [2x, the second occurrence being "I am not guilty" = lit., "there is not in my hand"], 12, 13, 15, 18, 20). In ch. 23 the issue is usually that of the effective (or ineffective) use of "power" (a frequent metaphorical meaning of "hand"), while in ch. 24 the stress is more on the restraint of power than on its use (cf. Miscall, 139). The two unequal halves of ch. 23 (vv.1–6, 7–29) have in common David's use of the priestly ephod to inquire of the Lord (vv.6, 9), first to save the people of Keilah from the Philistines (vv.1–6) and then to save himself from Saul (vv.7–29).

[1]When David was told, "Look, the Philistines are fighting against Keilah and are
looting the threshing floors," [2]he inquired of the LORD, saying, "Shall I go and attack these
Philistines?"
The LORD answered him, "Go, attack the Philistines and save Keilah."
[3]But David's men said to him, "Here in Judah we are afraid. How much more, then, if we
go to Keilah against the Philistine forces!"
[4]Once again David inquired of the LORD, and the LORD answered him, "Go down to
Keilah, for I am going to give the Philistines into your hand." [5]So David and his men went
to Keilah, fought the Philistines and carried off their livestock. He inflicted heavy losses
on the Philistines and saved the people of Keilah. [6](Now Abiathar son of Ahimelech had
brought the ephod down with him when he fled to David at Keilah.)

COMMENTARY

1–6 The Philistine threat, relegated to the background for several chapters, returns to menace a town in Judah (v.1). Keilah, prominent in this chapter, is mentioned elsewhere in the OT only in Joshua 15:44 (which locates it in the western foothills of Judah; cf. Jos 15:21, 33) and Nehemiah 3:17–18 (where the name applies to an administrative district of Judah after the Babylonian exile; it had apparently also been an important town much earlier, as references to *Qīltu* in the fourteenth-century Amarna letters indicate; cf. *ANET*, 487, 489). Ancient Keilah is usually identified with the modern site of Khirbet Qila, located about eighteen miles southwest of Jerusalem and three miles southeast of Adullam.

Just as Saul had saved Israel from "those who had plundered" them (see 14:48 and comment), so also David saves the people of Keilah from the Philistines who were "looting" (v.1) their threshing floors (same Heb. verb). In ancient Near Eastern towns, threshing floors often served as storage areas (2Ki 6:27; Joel 2:24).

David's repeated inquiries to God concerning whether he should go to Keilah and attack the Philistines, together with their divine responses (vv.2, 4), are reminiscent of similar inquiries and responses during the period of the judges (Jdg 20:23, 28). Such inquiries usually made use of the sacred lots, the Urim and Thummim, stored in the priestly ephod (cf. v.6; see comment on 14:36, 40–42).

When "David's men" (v.3; see comment on 18:27) learned that the Lord had responded affirmatively to his first inquiry, they demurred. After all, they said, even in the relative security of certain parts of Judah—for example, the forest of Hereth (22:5–6)—"we" are afraid (v.3). (The emphatic "we" balances and contrasts with the emphatic "they," the subject of "are looting" in the MT of v.2.) But going to Keilah, closer to Philistines who were in battle array and armed to the teeth, would be even worse—in fact, it would be too frightening to contemplate.

David therefore inquired of the Lord again (v.4), and this time God told him that he himself (the "I" is emphatic) would guarantee David's victory over the Philistines. (The Lord's earlier response [v.2] had not spelled out the means by which David would "save Keilah.") The promise of divine help apparently reassured David's men, who then joined him in defeating the enemy. All the verbs in v.5, however, are singular in number (with David as subject), reflecting either (1) the lack of faith of David's men or (2) the common attribution of success to the leader, even though it was clearly understood that he could not have succeeded on his own. Thus David "saved" the people of Keilah (v.5), as God had commanded (v.2) and promised (v.4).

The account of the victory concludes with the parenthetical note that Abiathar had earlier brought the priestly ephod with him when he had fled from Nob and joined David (v.6; cf. 21:9; 22:20). As in ch. 17, so also here the Lord chooses not the rejected king but the fugitive king-elect to deliver his people from the Philistines.

11. The Pursuit of David (23:7–29)

OVERVIEW

In contrast to David's seeking and receiving divine guidance, which brings him victory (vv.1–6), Saul relies totally on human messages and reports (cf. vv.7, 13, 19, 25, 27), which bring him frustration and failure (vv.7–29). Ironically, the Hebrew verb translated "inquired" in vv.2 and 4 is *šāʾal*, a wordplay on Saul's name.

The section describes Saul's pursuit of David from Keilah (vv.7–13) to the Desert of Ziph (vv.14–24a) to the Desert of Maon (vv.24b–28) and concludes with David's flight to the strongholds of En Gedi (v.29).

[7]Saul was told that David had gone to Keilah, and he said, "God has handed him over to me, for David has imprisoned himself by entering a town with gates and bars." [8]And Saul called up all his forces for battle, to go down to Keilah to besiege David and his men.

[9]When David learned that Saul was plotting against him, he said to Abiathar the priest, "Bring the ephod." [10]David said, "O LORD, God of Israel, your servant has heard definitely

that Saul plans to come to Keilah and destroy the town on account of me. [11]Will the citizens of Keilah surrender me to him? Will Saul come down, as your servant has heard? O LORD, God of Israel, tell your servant."

And the LORD said, "He will."

[12]Again David asked, "Will the citizens of Keilah surrender me and my men to Saul?"

And the LORD said, "They will."

[13]So David and his men, about six hundred in number, left Keilah and kept moving from place to place. When Saul was told that David had escaped from Keilah, he did not go there.

[14]David stayed in the desert strongholds and in the hills of the Desert of Ziph. Day after day Saul searched for him, but God did not give David into his hands.

[15]While David was at Horesh in the Desert of Ziph, he learned that Saul had come out to take his life. [16]And Saul's son Jonathan went to David at Horesh and helped him find strength in God. [17]"Don't be afraid," he said. "My father Saul will not lay a hand on you. You will be king over Israel, and I will be second to you. Even my father Saul knows this." [18]The two of them made a covenant before the LORD. Then Jonathan went home, but David remained at Horesh.

[19]The Ziphites went up to Saul at Gibeah and said, "Is not David hiding among us in the strongholds at Horesh, on the hill of Hakilah, south of Jeshimon? [20]Now, O king, come down whenever it pleases you to do so, and we will be responsible for handing him over to the king."

[21]Saul replied, "The LORD bless you for your concern for me. [22]Go and make further preparation. Find out where David usually goes and who has seen him there. They tell me he is very crafty. [23]Find out about all the hiding places he uses and come back to me with definite information. Then I will go with you; if he is in the area, I will track him down among all the clans of Judah."

[24]So they set out and went to Ziph ahead of Saul. Now David and his men were in the Desert of Maon, in the Arabah south of Jeshimon. [25]Saul and his men began the search, and when David was told about it, he went down to the rock and stayed in the Desert of Maon. When Saul heard this, he went into the Desert of Maon in pursuit of David.

[26]Saul was going along one side of the mountain, and David and his men were on the other side, hurrying to get away from Saul. As Saul and his forces were closing in on David and his men to capture them, [27]a messenger came to Saul, saying, "Come quickly! The Philistines are raiding the land." [28]Then Saul broke off his pursuit of David and went to meet the Philistines. That is why they call this place Sela Hammahlekoth. [29]And David went up from there and lived in the strongholds of En Gedi.

COMMENTARY

7–13 The statements "Saul was told that David had gone to Keilah" (v.7) and "Saul was told that David had escaped from Keilah" (v.13) frame this literary unit. Whether sincerely or in a false display of piety, Saul affirms that God has "handed" David over to him (v.7; cf. v.20—where, however, the Heb. verb is different). Saul assumes that David is trapped, that he has "imprisoned himself" (cf. Eze 3:24, "shut yourself") in a walled town from which there may be only one exit. (The same Heb. verb underlies the renderings "surrender" in vv.11–12 and "handing ... over" in v.20.) "Gates and bars" is literally "two doors [cf. Isa 45:1 MT] and a bar."

Keilah perhaps had only one gateway in its wall, its two reinforced wooden doors hinged to posts at the sides of the entrance, meeting in the center and secured with a heavy metal bar spanning the entrance horizontally (for a possible parallel, cf. Jdg 16:3). Preparing to attack David at Keilah, Saul "called up" (v.8) his troops (the Heb. verb is the common *šāmaʿ* ["heard"] in its rare Piel form, the only other occurrence in the OT being in 15:4 [see comment]).

David soon found out (v.9) that Saul was "plotting" (lit., "thinking/planning evil"; cf. the same idiom in Pr 3:29, "plot harm") against him. He therefore told Abiathar to bring the ephod so that he might use the Urim and Thummim to inquire of the Lord (as he had in vv.1–6; cf. also 30:7–8). The verb "bring" is commonly used in cultic or ceremonial contexts (cf. 14:18; see 14:34 and comment).

David begins and concludes his plea (vv.10–11) with the words "O LORD, God of Israel," acknowledging the Lord as the true sovereign of his people. Just as Saul earlier was "looking for a chance" to kill him (19:2) and had "tried" to pin him to a wall (19:10), David now expresses his concern that Saul "plans" to destroy Keilah because of him (v.10; the same Heb. verb in all three cases).

Although David asks two questions (v.11), the Lord answers only the second one. David therefore repeats the first question (v.12), this time expressing his concern for the safety of his men also. The Lord now answers it as well. In each case the divine response consists of only one Hebrew word, which the NIV appropriately translates as tersely as possible. That the citizens of Keilah would even think of surrendering their deliverer and his men to Saul might seem like the height of ingratitude, but perhaps they feared royal retribution if they harbored fugitives.

In any case, because the Lord's answers to David's questions bode ill for David and his men, they leave Keilah and frequently change their location (v.13; for some of the places they eventually go to, see 30:27–31, where the verb "had roamed" renders the same Heb. verb as "kept moving" does here). Although since the last count (22:2) the number of David's men has increased to "about six hundred" (cf. also 25:13; 27:2; 30:9; see also comment on 13:15), David understandably feels that they are still no match for Saul and his army (cf. the reference to Saul's "three thousand chosen men" in 24:2). For his part, Saul changes his mind about going to Keilah when he learns that the fugitives have left.

14–24a Just as references to Keilah frame vv.7–13, so also references to Ziph frame vv.14–24a. Mentioned elsewhere only in v.15 and 26:2, the Desert of Ziph (v.14) was doubtless located east of Ziph (v.24), which had been allotted to Judah in the hill country west of the Dead Sea after Joshua's conquest of Canaan (Jos 15:48, 55). The modern site of the ancient town is Tell Zif, located twelve miles southeast of Keilah. Knowing that Saul is relentlessly continuing his search for him (vv.14, 25), David hides in various "strongholds" in the Desert of Ziph (vv.14, 19) and elsewhere (v.29).

Despite the careful description of the location of Horesh and its strongholds (vv.15, 19), the exact site is unknown (although Khirbet Khuresa, fewer than two miles from Tell Zif, may preserve the ancient name). Despite God's gracious and providential care (v.14), David was afraid, because Saul came out to take his life "while David was at Horesh in the Desert of Ziph" (v.15; see Notes). So Saul's son Jonathan went to Horesh to remind David of the Lord's concern for him and to encourage him (v.16). Jonathan said (v.17), "Don't be afraid, because" (*ʾal-tîrāʾ kî*, echoing *wayyirāʾ kî* in v.15; see Note for vowel pointing) Saul will not "lay a hand on you."

This occasion was not, of course, the first time Saul had "come out" against David to "take/seek his life" (v.15; cf. 20:1; 22:23)—nor would it be the last (25:29; 26:20). Miscall, 141, observes that Jonathan's helping David "find strength in God" (v.16) in this situation is paralleled by a similar crisis later: "David found strength in the LORD his God" when his own men were talking about stoning him (30:6). Jonathan's "Don't be afraid" (v.17) is mirrored—ironically—by David's earlier "don't be afraid" to the fugitive Abiathar in the face of the same threat (22:23). Miscall, 142, notes an earlier analogy for Jonathan's assurance to David that Saul's murderous intent would come to naught (see 20:2).

Jonathan vigorously continues to encourage David: "You [emphatic] will be king," while "I [emphatic] will be second to you"—an inevitable truth that Saul also knows (v.17). Although "second" in contexts of this kind means primarily "second-in-command, next in rank" (1Ch 16:5; 2Ch 28:7; 31:12; Est 10:3; Jer 52:24), Miscall, 142, makes the suggestive observation that it can also mean "double" or "copy" (Ge 43:12; Dt 17:18) and that therefore Jonathan is at the same time David's "copy, his equal." "The two of them" (v.18)—as equals—then make a covenant in the presence of the Lord, perhaps invoking his blessing and taking an oath in his name. While it is possible that this covenant constitutes a reaffirmation of the earlier one initiated by Jonathan between the two men (18:3; 20:8), it is better understood as a fresh, bilateral covenant defining their new relationship (see comment on 18:3). Having comforted his friend, Jonathan returns home to Gibeah—perhaps never to see David again. (No further meetings between the two men are recorded.)

Certain "Ziphites" go to Gibeah and reveal David's whereabouts, perhaps to ingratiate themselves to Saul. Their words to him—"Is not David hiding among us?"—are repeated verbatim in the title of Psalm 54, whose traditional setting is thus the narrative in vv.19–24a. In the psalm David prays for deliverance (Ps 54:1–2); complains that ruthless, ungodly men are seeking his life (v.3); pleads that their evil deeds will recoil on them (v.5); and promises a freewill offering to the Lord in gratitude for God's faithfulness in delivering him (vv.6–7). The psalm's center verse (v.4) focuses on David's assurance that the Lord is his help and sustainer.

The Samuel narrative locates David's hiding place on the hill of Hakilah (cf. 26:1, 3), an unknown location south of Jeshimon (cf. v.24; 26:1, 3), whose location is also unknown except generally as a "wasteland" (so the Heb. word; cf. Nu 21:20; 23:28) between Ziph and the Dead Sea. The Ziphites invite Saul to come to them "whenever it pleases you" (lit., "according to all the desire of your soul" [v.20], a rare idiom found also in Dt 12:15, 20–21 ["as much ... as you want"]; 18:6 ["in all earnestness"]; Jer 2:24 ["in her craving"]), at which time they promise to hand David over to him.

Saul's reply to the Ziphites, "The LORD bless you" (v.21), is a stereotyped expression (see comment on 15:13) that tells nothing about his piety (or lack of it; see v.7 and comment). His gratitude for their "concern" for him recalls the earlier episode where he "spared" Agag—like himself, a doomed king—and the best of the Amalekite livestock (15:9, 15) in direct violation of God's command through Samuel (15:3; same Heb. verb; cf. the similar observation in Polzin, *Samuel and the Deuteronomist*, 204). The NIV's "make further preparation" (v.22) is not on target in this context; "make sure once more" (NAB) is much better (cf. also NASB, NEB, RSV). Always the investigator relying on human ability, Saul tells the Ziphites to "find out" (lit., "know and see," vv.22–23; cf. 14:38) where David usually hides. David will later hurl Saul's phrase back at him ("understand and recognize," 24:11) in protestation of his own innocence (cf. further "See [how]" in 1Ki 20:7; 2Ki 5:7).

Saul is determined to track David down no matter where he goes or what it takes (vv.22–23; cf. Hushai's similar advice to Absalom against his father, David, in 2Sa 17:12–14). Under no circumstances will he permit the "crafty" David to outwit him (v.22; cf. Ge 3:1, where the same Heb. root describes the serpent). The Ziphites are to pinpoint every potential hiding place that David might use and then report back to Saul "with definite information" (v.23; the same Heb. root as that for "make ... preparation" in v.22; see Notes). Obedient to their presumed overlord, they return to Ziph and begin to comb the area in search of David and his men (v.24a).

24b–29 *Hālak* ("went"), the basic Hebrew verb of movement, gives unity to vv.25–28, for each verse contains the verb at least once ("began," v.25; "was going," "to get away," v.26; "come," v.27; "went," v.28). Verse 28 in the MT concludes ch. 23; v.29 of the English versions is 24:1 in the MT.

On the run as usual (v.13), David and his men go to "the Desert of Maon, in the Arabah south of Jeshimon" (v.24b; for Jeshimon see comment on v.19). Although "Arabah" is usually thought of as the name of the desert flatlands stretching for more than a hundred miles from the southern end of the Dead Sea to the northern end of the Gulf of Aqaba, in some contexts (as here) it clearly refers to northward extensions of those flatlands west and east of the Dead Sea and beyond, all the way to the southern end of the Sea of Galilee (for details see S. Cohen, *IDB*, 1:177–79; H. G. Andersen, *ZPEB*, 1:233–36). Like the Desert of Ziph (see comment on v.14), the Desert of Maon was named for a town that had been allotted to Judah in the hill country west of the Dead Sea after Joshua's conquest of Canaan (Jos 15:48, 55). Modern Khirbet Main, five miles south of Ziph, marks the location of the ancient site, and the Desert of Maon would thus most likely have been south of the Desert of Ziph (cf. the map in Rasmussen, 114).

Upon hearing that Saul had once again embarked on his relentless "search" for him (v.25; cf. v.14), David retreated with his men to "the rock" (soon to be given a name [v.28]) in the Desert of Maon. Informed of this (probably by the Ziphites), Saul pursued his quarry. He probably divided "his forces" (v.26) into two groups so that they could attack both flanks of David's men "on the other side" of the mountain, thus "closing in" on them. Although David had been able to "get away" from Saul on several occasions (cf. 18:11; 19:10), it appears that this time all was lost—at least from a human standpoint.

Providentially, however, a messenger arrived with the unsettling news that Philistines were raiding (v.27) part of Saul's sovereign territory. Sensing a greater threat from the Philistines, Saul had no choice but to postpone his pursuit of David (v.28). The "rock" (*sela*ᶜ, v.25) from which Saul and his men marched out to engage the Philistines in battle was called "Sela Hammahlekoth." The name originally may have meant "Smooth/Slippery Rock." (The same Hebrew root is used to describe David's five "smooth stones" in 17:40.) By popular etymology it came to mean "The Rock of Parting" (see NIV note; from the same Heb. root as the word translated "scatter[ed]" in Ge 49:7; La 4:16), apparently referring to the timely retreat of Saul's men from David's men on that occasion (for other examples of topographical features receiving memorable names, cf. 7:12; 2Sa 2:16; Jos 5:3; Jdg 15:17, 19).

God used the distraction of Philistines, rather than the aid of Ziphites or other Judahites, to rescue David from the tentacles of Saul (cf. similarly Miscall, 143). For his part David moved himself and his men to strongholds in the vicinity of the En Gedi oasis (v.29; modern Ain Jidi, near Tell ej-Jurn on the western shore of the Dead Sea fourteen miles east of Ziph). Known also as Hazazon Tamar (2Ch 20:2; cf. Ge 14:7), En Gedi's powerful, perennial spring provided abundant water for vineyards (SS 1:14) and played a prominent role in Ezekiel's vision of a restored Israel (Eze 47:10, 18–19; 48:28).

NOTES

7 The NIV's "God has handed him over to me" translates נִכַּר אֹתוֹ אֱלֹהִים בְּיָדִי (*nikkar ʾōtô ʾᵉlōhîm bᵉyādî*, "God has delivered him into my hand[s]"). For *nikkar* the LXX reads πέπρακεν (*pepraken*, "sold"), giving rise to the suggestion that *nikkar* is a scribal error for מָכַר (*mākar*; see Smith, 212; cf. Jdg 4:9 for the idiom). סִכַּר (*sikkar*, "hand over") has also been proposed on the basis of Isaiah 19:4 (see Driver, 184; Klein, 228; McCarter, *I Samuel*, 369–70). James Barr (*Comparative Philology and the Text of the Old Testament* [Oxford: Clarendon, 1968], 331) defends the existence of a rare verb *nkr* (which he defines as "acquire, sell"), points to the use of וָאֶכְּרֶהָ (*wāʾekkᵉrehā*) in Hosea 3:2 as a parallel example from the same root (although *wāʾekkᵉrehā* is usually derived from כָּרָה, *kārâ*; cf. BDB, 500), and adduces Ugaritic *nkr* (cf. also John Gray, *The Legacy of Canaan: The Ras Shamra Texts and Their Relevance to the Old Testament*, 2nd rev. ed. [Leiden: Brill, 1965], 141 n. 1, cf. 260; de Moor, 153 n. 24). Attention should also be called to Akkadian *nukkuru* ("to transfer/reassign/move someone to another location"), which has the added advantage of being in the same stem as *nikkar* (cf. *CAD*, 11:169 for examples).

9 4QSamuel[b] preserves a fragmentary text of vv.9–17 (see Cross, "The Oldest Manuscripts," 169–71). Although it presents a few modest deviations from the MT, one or two of which may be closer to the autographs of 1 Samuel, none is significant enough to require attention for the purposes of this commentary.

The so-called long forms of the Hebrew masculine singular imperative, which end in ָה (*â*), perhaps originally functioned as ventives, like Akkadian verbal forms ending in *-a(m)*. The ventive expresses action from the standpoint of its destination: "here," "to me," and so forth (Wolfram von Soden, *Grundriss der Akkadischen Grammatik* [Rome: Pontifical Biblical Institute, 1952], 1007–8; K. Riemschneider, *An Akkadian Grammar*, trans. Thomas A. Caldwell, John N. Oswalt, and John F. X. Sheehan [Milwaukee: Marquette Univ. Press, 1974], 51–52). Thus הַגִּישָׁה (*haggîšâ*) would have originally expressed fully the idea "bring to me" and only later—when the ventive nuance had been lost—would have required the kind of explicit expansion found in 30:7 (MT).

15 חֹרֶשׁ (*ḥōreš*) means "forest" (cf. 2Ch 27:4, "wooded areas"; Isa 17:9, "thickets"; Eze 31:3); so the trees of Horesh would have provided additional cover for David and his men.

In the light of the overall context, the MT's וַיַּרְא כִּי (*wayyarʾ kî*, "and he saw that"; "he learned that," NIV) is to be repointed as וַיִּרָא כִּי (*wayyirāʾ kî*, "and he was afraid, because"; so virtually all recent commentators—e.g., Baldwin, Driver, Gordon, Klein, McCarter). *Wayyarʾ* in 26:3 should not be used to justify the MT vocalization here because there the context demands "when he saw."

23 "At Nacon" (see NIV note) understands אֶל־נָכוֹן (*ʾel-nākôn*) as containing a proper name (cf. the similar situation in 26:4). But although Nacon is clearly a place name in 2 Samuel 6:6 (see comment there for the alternative form "Kidon" in the 1Ch 13:9 parallel), it seems best to understand it here as a common noun from the root כּוּן (*kûn*, "be firm, definite, prepared, sure") in light of the use of the same root in v.22 (see comment).

12. Sparing Saul's Life (24:1–22)

OVERVIEW

As noted earlier (see Overview to ch. 23), ch. 24 follows naturally ch. 23 from a literary standpoint in that the word "hand" appears frequently in both chapters. In addition, ch. 24 begins where ch. 23 ends: David is in the desert strongholds of En Gedi. Finally, Saul's relentless pursuit of David in ch. 23 continues in ch. 24. The link between the two chapters is thus secured.

At the same time, however, it is equally clear that chs. 24–26 form a discrete literary unit within 1 Samuel. Chapters 24 and 26 are virtually mirror images of each other, beginning with Saul's receiving a report about David's latest hiding place (24:1; 26:1), focusing on David's refusal to lift a hand against Saul, "the LORD's anointed" (24:6, 10; 26:11), and concluding with the words of a remorseful Saul and his returning home from pursuing David (24:17–22; 26:21, 25). The two chapters form a frame around the central ch. 25, where the churlish Nabal functions as an alter ego of the rejected Saul. In addition, divine protection that keeps David from shedding innocent blood runs as a unifying thread through all three chapters. In the words of Gordon ("David's Rise," 53): "From 24:1 to 26:25 we have a three-part plot in which there is incremental repetition of the motif of blood-guilt and its avoidance."

The last verse of ch. 23 in the NIV constitutes the first verse of ch. 24 in the MT, accommodating the traditional one-verse numbering difference between the Hebrew and the English texts throughout ch. 24 (for a similar phenomenon in ch. 21, see comment on Overview to ch. 21). Chapter 24 itself divides naturally into three roughly equal sections arranged in chiastic order:

A David spares Saul's life (vv.1–7)
  B David's *apologia* (vv.8–15)
A' David agrees to spare Saul's descendants (vv.16–22)

1After Saul returned from pursuing the Philistines, he was told, "David is in the Desert of
En Gedi." 2So Saul took three thousand chosen men from all Israel and set out to look for
David and his men near the Crags of the Wild Goats.
3He came to the sheep pens along the way; a cave was there, and Saul went in to relieve
himself. David and his men were far back in the cave. 4The men said, "This is the day the

LORD spoke of when he said to you, 'I will give your enemy into your hands for you to deal with as you wish.'" Then David crept up unnoticed and cut off a corner of Saul's robe.

[5]Afterward, David was conscience-stricken for having cut off a corner of his robe. [6]He said to his men, "The LORD forbid that I should do such a thing to my master, the LORD's anointed, or lift my hand against him; for he is the anointed of the LORD." [7]With these words David rebuked his men and did not allow them to attack Saul. And Saul left the cave and went his way.

[8]Then David went out of the cave and called out to Saul, "My lord the king!" When Saul looked behind him, David bowed down and prostrated himself with his face to the ground. [9]He said to Saul, "Why do you listen when men say, 'David is bent on harming you'? [10]This day you have seen with your own eyes how the LORD delivered you into my hands in the cave. Some urged me to kill you, but I spared you; I said, 'I will not lift my hand against my master, because he is the LORD's anointed.' [11]See, my father, look at this piece of your robe in my hand! I cut off the corner of your robe but did not kill you. Now understand and recognize that I am not guilty of wrongdoing or rebellion. I have not wronged you, but you are hunting me down to take my life. [12]May the LORD judge between you and me. And may the LORD avenge the wrongs you have done to me, but my hand will not touch you. [13]As the old saying goes, 'From evildoers come evil deeds,' so my hand will not touch you.

[14]"Against whom has the king of Israel come out? Whom are you pursuing? A dead dog? A flea? [15]May the LORD be our judge and decide between us. May he consider my cause and uphold it; may he vindicate me by delivering me from your hand."

[16]When David finished saying this, Saul asked, "Is that your voice, David my son?" And he wept aloud. [17]"You are more righteous than I," he said. "You have treated me well, but I have treated you badly. [18]You have just now told me of the good you did to me; the LORD delivered me into your hands, but you did not kill me. [19]When a man finds his enemy, does he let him get away unharmed? May the LORD reward you well for the way you treated me today. [20]I know that you will surely be king and that the kingdom of Israel will be established in your hands. [21]Now swear to me by the LORD that you will not cut off my descendants or wipe out my name from my father's family."

[22]So David gave his oath to Saul. Then Saul returned home, but David and his men went up to the stronghold.

COMMENTARY

1–7 On a previous occasion when the Israelites "returned from chasing the Philistines," they plundered their camp (17:53). This time, after Saul "returned from pursuing the Philistines" (v.1; cf. 23:28), he was told about David's general location (the desert west of En Gedi; see comment on 23:29) and set out with "three thousand chosen men" (v.2; see also 26:2), who outnumbered David's motley band (see 22:2 and comment) five to one (23:13; 25:13; 27:2; 30:9). The term "chosen men" refers to warriors who were especially skilled (Jdg 20:16) and courageous (Jdg 20:34, "finest men"). Saul narrowed his search to an area near the Crags of the Wild Goats (location unknown, although the reference to "wild goats" stresses the inaccessibility of the site—cf. Job 39:1, "mountain goats"; Ps 104:18—and thus sets up a contrast with En Gedi, which means "Spring of the [tame] young goat").

The "sheep pens" Saul "came to" (v.3) probably consisted of one or more enclosures made of low, stone walls flanking the entrance to a cave. Thus Saul would have entered the pens to gain access to the cave. ("Came" and "went in" translate the same Heb. verbal form.) His purpose in going into the cave was to "relieve himself" (lit., "cover his feet"; cf. other expressions such as "go outside" [Dt 23:12] and "sit down outside" [Dt 23:13], both translated "relieve yourself" by the NIV). The narrator may have chosen this particular euphemism for defecation because it occurs elsewhere only in Judges 3:24, where it is used of Eglon king of Moab, who "alone in the upper room of his summer palace" (Jdg 3:20) was killed by the judge Ehud. Saul king of Israel, going inside the cave in search of privacy, is similarly unaware that he is placing himself in mortal danger.

Unknown to Saul, David and his men are "far back in" that very cave (lit., "in the deepest recesses of"; cf. Jnh 1:5, where the same Heb. word is translated "below [deck]"). The traditional titles of Psalms 57 and 142 connect those psalms with this incident. In Psalm 57 David prays for divine help (Ps 57:1–5), crying out for deliverance from "those who hotly pursue" him (v.3) and whom he describes metaphorically as "lions" and "ravenous beasts" (v.4). In the latter half of the psalm (vv.6–11), he praises the Lord for his great "love" and "faithfulness" (v.10), which assure him of the deliverance he seeks. Psalm 142 similarly voices David's prayer for divine rescue from "those who pursue" him (v.6), as well as his plea for release from his "prison" (perhaps a reference to the cave). He is grateful for the anticipated deliverance that will take place because of the "goodness" of God (v.7). In both psalms David cries out for divine "mercy" (57:1; 142:1), and in both he affirms that the Lord, not the cave, is his true "refuge" (57:1; 142:5).

If the titles of Psalms 57 and 142 preserve an authentic tradition concerning their setting, David must have composed them long before Saul arrived on the scene, because David's men see in the presence of Saul inside the cave a golden opportunity to get rid of him once and for all (v.4). Whether we choose the NIV's text (which refers to a divine promise to David not mentioned previously) or footnote (which refers to God's providence working through present circumstances), the end result is the same: David now has a chance to eliminate his "enemy" (vv.4, 19; see also 18:29 and comment; the word is similarly used by Saul of David in 19:17).

Out of respect for Saul's divine anointing and therefore not willing to kill him, but at the same time wanting to let Saul know that he is not in control of his own destiny, David creeps up behind him "unnoticed" (cf. "quietly," which translates the same Heb. word in the sinister context of Jdg 4:21). In cutting off the corner of Saul's robe, David may have been symbolically depriving Saul of his royal authority and transferring it to himself (cf. v.11; see also comment on 15:27–28; 18:4). At the very least, parallels from cuneiform texts found at Mari and Alalakh "may imply that David's act in cutting off the 'wing' or hem of Saul's garment was an act of rebellion for which he was later repentant" (D. J. Wiseman, "Alalakh," in *Archaeology and Old Testament Study*, ed. D. Winton Thomas [Oxford: Clarendon, 1967], 128).

The fact that David was "conscience-stricken" (v.5) for what he had done is to be understood as recognition on his part that he has sinned (cf. 2Sa 24:10, the only other occurrence of the expression in the OT). A literary echo of this scene appears in 25:31, where Abigail's warning to David reminds him that vengeance belongs to God and that if he were to kill Nabal and his men, the guilt resulting from needless bloodshed would be on his "conscience."

Using a solemn oath (v.6, the essence of which is summarized in the parallel context in 26:11), David affirms to his men that he will never "do" (the same Heb. verb translated "deal [with]" in v.4) harm to his master Saul, who is "the LORD's anointed" (used seven times in chs. 24 and 26: 24:6 [2x], 10; 26:9, 11, 16, 23). Made the anointed of the Lord by divine appointment and human ministration (see 9:16 and comment; 10:1; cf. also 12:3, 5), Saul is king. David—himself also the Lord's anointed, and thus perhaps not wanting to do anything that could provide a precedent for his own murder later (Polzin, *Samuel and the Deuteronomist*, 210)—will not lay a hand on Saul (vv.6, 10; cf. also 26:9, 11, 23). Indeed, using metaphorically a strong verb that means "tear apart" (Lev 1:17; Jdg 14:6), David "rebukes" his men for even so much as thinking otherwise (v.7), and Saul leaves the cave none the wiser.

8–15 The brief *apologia* of David recorded here should be compared with that of Samuel (ch. 12)—not so much in terms of precise literary parallels as in terms of persuasive power. At the same time David's *apologia* is echoed at the end of ch. 26, where it functions in much the same way as that of Samuel, serving as a kind of farewell speech to Israel's king.

After Saul left the cave (v.7), David, after a short time, himself emerged and "called out" to Saul (v.8; the verb often implies physical distance between sender and receiver, as in 20:37). Addressing Saul as his acknowledged superior ("My lord the king!" echoed in 26:17, 19), David "bowed down and prostrated himself with his face to the ground"—the same expression used of Saul doing obeisance to an apparition of the deceased Samuel (28:14).

David begins his protestation and defense with a "Why?" (v.9), which echoes that of Saul, who had earlier accused Ahimelech of conspiracy with David against him (22:13). David assures Saul that he is not intent on "harming" him (v.9), nor is he guilty of "wrongdoing" (v.11; the same Heb. word in both cases). Unlike those who spread false rumors about his murderous plans, David refuses to listen to all who want to incite him to vengeance against Saul (v.10). Indeed, the king himself knows that David has just now had a unique opportunity to kill him, but David has refused to seize it.

Pressing his advantage, three times David says to Saul, *r*^{e}*ʾēh* : "See ... look ... recognize" (v.11). When he addresses Saul as "my father," he is probably not simply using a term of respect but is reminding the king that he is, after all, Saul's son-in-law (cf. 18:17–27; 22:14) and thus holds him in high regard. (Saul will later respond to David as "my son" [v.16].) Taking another tack, Gunn (*The Fate of King Saul*, 94–95) suggests that by calling Saul his father, "David has usurped Jonathan's sonship; symbolically he requires Saul as father in order for his future kingship to be (symbolically) legitimate," and "even the cutting of the robe ... confirms symbolically that Saul's status—as king *and* father (that is, dynast)—is in effect transferred to David."

The "piece/corner of [Saul's] robe," mentioned four times in this chapter (vv.4–5, 11 [2x]) and now in David's hand (v.11), is a "symbol of Samuel, of the kingdom, and of Saul's rejection." Moreover, it "points ahead to a future date when the Lord tears the kingdom from the hand of Solomon, David's son" (Miscall, 148; cf. comment on 15:27–28; 19:24; cf. also 28:14, 17; 1Ki 11:11–13, 29–31).

Continuing to protest his innocence, David wants Saul to "understand and recognize" (lit., "know and see," v.11; cf. comment on "find out" in 23:22–23) that he is not guilty of "wrongdoing," a plea he will repeat later. ("Wrong" in 26:18 translates the same Heb. word; see also comment on v.9 and note especially Abigail's warning to David in 25:28b.) Using the same verbal root as in 20:1, David reminds Saul that he has not "wronged" (lit., "sinned [against]") him (cf. also Jonathan's strong objections to his father in 19:4). There is therefore no reason, says David, for Saul to be "hunting" him down. (The verb, used elsewhere only in Ex 21:13, means "act with malicious intent"; compare the related noun in Nu 35:20, 22: "[un]intention[ally].")

Unwilling to submit their dispute to human arbitration, David prays that the only fair and impartial Judge (cf. Jdg 11:27), the Lord himself, might "judge between you and me" (v.12), a request repeated almost verbatim in the Hebrew of v.15 (there translated "decide between us"). But no matter what happens, David assures his king, "my hand will not touch you" (vv.12–13). After all, evil deeds are perpetrated only by evildoers, as an ancient proverb affirms (v.13). The proverb may in fact be double-edged, vindicating the refusal of the righteous David to harm Saul while at the same time condemning the wicked Saul for his malicious pursuit of David (cf. similarly A. S. Herbert, "The 'Parable' [*Māšāl*] in the Old Testament," *SJT* 7/2 [1954]: 183–84).

Earlier English versions (KJV, ASV, RSV, NEB) understood the two brief phrases at the end of v.14 as noninterrogative statements of fact or as exclamations. The meaning would then be that Saul should not waste his time chasing David, who is as insignificant as a "dead dog" (cf. also 2Sa 9:8; 16:9), a "single flea" (MT; echoed in 26:20). More recent versions (including the NIV), however, tend to treat the phrases as questions (NASB, REB) and thus as veiled threats to Saul: If he thinks that David will be easy to vanquish, he had better think again (cf. similarly Gunn, *The Fate of King Saul*, 154 n. 6).

David concludes his *apologia* by entreating the Lord to decide between himself and Saul (v.15). (The rare Heb. word translated "judge" is not the same as that in v.12 and occurs elsewhere only in Ps 68:5 ["defender"], where it again describes God.) Confident of the outcome, David affirms his belief that the Lord will "uphold" his "cause" against Saul, using a phrase that he will use again after the death of Nabal, Saul's alter ego (25:39; cf. Gordon, "David's Rise," 48). He prays to the Lord to "vindicate me [by delivering me] from" Saul. (The words in brackets are supplied by the NIV to fill what would otherwise be an English ellipsis. For another way of treating the same Heb. idiom, see 2Sa 18:19, 31, where David is informed that God has "delivered him from" his enemies—this time including Absalom, his son.)

16–22 Saul's remorseful response to David (vv.17–21) is framed by transitional v.16 and concluding v.22. It is no more necessary to deny Saul's sincerity here than it is in the parallel passage in 26:21,25. In each case Saul begins with the plaintive "Is that your voice, David my son?" (v.16; 26:17; cf. also 26:21, 25; for the significance of "my son" here, see the comment on "my father" in v.11). Speaking later to Nabal, David refers to himself as "your son David" (25:8), thus strengthening the suggestion that Nabal functions as Saul's alter ego (cf. Gordon, "David's Rise," 47–48). Miscall, 146, makes the important observation that Saul "will soon act to end David's status as royal son-in-law by giving Michal [Saul's daughter and David's wife, 18:27] to Palti (1 Sam 25:44)."

Meanwhile Saul, distressed and conscience-stricken, "wept aloud" when confronted with David's innocence. "Saul's weeping and his address to David as 'my son' will be echoed ... when David weeps over the death of ... Absalom, who has attempted to seize the throne from David, as Saul perceives David trying to do from him" (Preston, 35; cf. 2Sa 15:1–12; 18:33).

Mirroring Judah's words concerning his daughter-in-law Tamar (Ge 38:26), Saul says to his son-in-law David, "You are more righteous than I" (v.17). He then draws a contrast between David's exemplary conduct (emphatic "you") and his own deplorable actions (emphatic "I"). David has treated Saul "well" (v.17), Saul admits that what David has done to him is "good" (v.18), and Saul desires that the Lord will reward David "well" for what he has done (v.19), since a man never lets his enemy get away "unharmed" (lit., "in a good way"; the same Heb. word in all four cases). Saul admits to David, "I have treated you badly" (v.17, a Heb. idiom elsewhere only in Ge 50:17; Pr 3:30 ["done you ... harm"]; Isa 3:9 ["brought disaster upon"]). Gordon ("David's Rise," 48) notes the same contrast in David's words concerning Nabal: "He has paid me back evil for good" (25:21).

Saul's recognition that the Lord had "delivered" him into David's hands (v.18; different from the Heb. verb in v.10) is later echoed by Abishai (26:8; cf. also David's confident challenge to Goliath in 17:46: "The LORD will hand you over to me"). Understanding that David has every right not to let his "enemy" (v.19; cf. v.4) get away, Saul—with words reminiscent of what Boaz said to Ruth (Ru 2:12)—prays that God will reward David richly for what he has done.

Earlier Samuel had told Saul that because of his rebellion against God, his "kingdom" would not endure but would be given to a man after God's own heart (13:14)—"and now" (v.20; see Notes) Saul emphatically acknowledges that David will be ruler over the "kingdom of Israel" (cf. also 15:28; 18:8). Saul says "I know" that David will be king (v.20), an observation that Jonathan had earlier made about his father's knowledge (23:17).

Like Jonathan before him (see comments on 20:15, 42), Saul is concerned that David not "cut off [his] descendants" (v.21). And as David had sworn that he would show unfailing kindness to Jonathan and his family (20:14–17), so now he swears that he will not harm Saul's offspring or wipe out his name (vv.21–22). Because "name is inextricably bound up with existence" in the ancient world, "to cut off a name ... is to end the existence of its bearer" (R. Abba, *IDB*, 501).

Having secured David's oath, Saul returns to Gibeah. David, however, wisely continues to distrust Saul and therefore retreats to his "stronghold" (v.22; see 22:4–5 and comment).

NOTES

7[8] This verse ends with two common Hebrew words, וַיֵּלֶךְ בַּדָּרֶךְ (*wayyēlek baddārek*, "and went his way"), that appear elsewhere in this section only in v.2 ("and set out") and v.3 ("the way"). Two other verbs that help to tie the section together are עָשָׂה (*ʿāśâ*) in v.4[5] ("deal") and v.6[7] ("do") and קוּם (*qûm*) in v.4[5] ("crept up") and v.7[8] ("attack, left").

8[9] The word אַחֲרֵי (*ʾaḥᵃrê*, "after, behind") occurs seven times in vv.8–15 (three times in v.8[9] and four in v.14[15]), here usually left untranslated in the NIV to accommodate English idiom. It serves, however, not only to give cohesion to the literary unit but also to frame all but its last verse.

10[11] The NIV's "I spared" is elliptical for "my eye spared," a common OT idiom (cf. Dt 7:16; 13:8; 19:13 ["look on with pity, show pity"]). Although the Hebrew word for "eye" (feminine in gender) does not appear as the subject of the verb "spared" in v.10, the third person feminine singular verb (וַתָּחָס, *wattāḥos*) implies it, as the Vulgate recognizes (*pepercit ... oculus meus*) and as several translations (for example, ASV, KJV, NASB) and commentators agree (for example, Klein, K&D, McCarter). Although Saul has seen with his own "eyes" that the Lord has delivered him into David's hands, David's "eye" has spared Saul.

13[14] The NIV's "the old saying" renders מְשַׁל הַקַּדְמֹנִי (*mešal haqqadmōnî*, lit., "the proverb of the ancient one"). A DSS fragment (cf. *BHS*) reads the second word as a plural (cf. also Watson, 532), probably to smooth out the awkwardness of the phrase. The MT, however, is just as smooth if the singular *haqqadmōnî* is understood as a collective (observed already long ago by K&D, 236), a common phenomenon in nouns of the gentilic type (*IBHS*, 115).

14[15] The phrase *keleb mēt* ("dead dog") finds its Akkadian cognate parallel in the self-effacing description of one Urad-Gula, servant of chief exorcist Adad-shumu-usur: "Initially, in (the days of) the king's father, I was a poor man, son of a poor man, a dead dog (*kalbu mītu*), a vile and limited person" (State Archives of Assyria 10, 294.14).

The meaning "flea" for פַּרְעֹשׁ (*parʿōš*), a rare word at best, is secured by the various forms of its Akkadian cognate—*pu/iršaʾu, puruʾsu*—which also mean "flea" (Benno Landsberger, *Die Fauna des alten Mesopotamiens nach der 14. Tafel der Serie ḪAR.RA = ḫubullu* [Leipzig, 1934], 126).

20[21] The MT of v.21 begins with וְעַתָּה (*weʿattâ*, "And now"), which, as Polzin observes (*Samuel and the Deuteronomist*, 206, 268 n. 6), occurs twelve times in chs. 24–26 (24:20–21; 25:7, 17, 26 [2x], 27; 26:8, 11, 16, 19–20) and only twenty-one times in the rest of 1 Samuel. In these three chapters in particular the narrator records matters of emphasis, persuasion, and conviction that he tags by the use of *weʿattâ* not always expressed in translation by the NIV because of its stylistic redundancy in English.

13. David, Nabal, and Abigail (25:1–44)

OVERVIEW

Chapter 25 is the central panel in the triptych that comprises chs. 24–26. As such it not only anchors the literary unit but also facilitates the fact that chs. 24 and 26 mirror each other. Beginning with the death of David's friend Samuel, it ends with Saul's giving David's wife Michal to another man and thus considering David as good as dead. It is therefore possible to interpret ch. 25 as marking the low point in David's fortunes. At the same time, however, in the chapter David acquires a wise wife (Abigail), who had successfully persuaded him not to harm a quintessential fool (Nabal). Saul, who figures largely in chs. 24 and 26, appears only in the last verse of ch. 25. But it is hard to escape the implication that in ch. 25 Saul, though physically absent, is nonetheless figuratively present in Nabal, his alter ego (cf., for example, Gordon, "David's Rise," 43).

This chapter is structured chiastically as follows (cf. Stek, 65A):

A Samuel dies (v.1a)
  B David the fugitive is in the vicinity of the wealthy Nabal and his beautiful wife Abigail (vv.1b–3)
    C Hearing of Nabal's situation and later rebuffed by him, David prepares to avenge himself of the insult (vv.4–13)
      D Abigail prepares food to take to David (vv.14–19)
        E David meets Abigail (vv.20–35)
      D' Abigail returns home to find Nabal gorging himself on food (vv.36–38)
    C' Hearing of Nabal's death, David praises the Lord for having upheld his cause against Nabal (v.39a)
  B' David the fugitive takes the beautiful Abigail as his wife (vv.39b–43)
A' Saul treats David as though he were dead (v.44)

Detailed comparisons between the sets of parallel sections will be pointed out in the commentary.

1Now Samuel died, and all Israel assembled and mourned for him; and they buried him
at his home in Ramah.
Then David moved down into the Desert of Maon. 2A certain man in Maon, who had
property there at Carmel, was very wealthy. He had a thousand goats and three thousand
sheep, which he was shearing in Carmel. 3His name was Nabal and his wife's name was
Abigail. She was an intelligent and beautiful woman, but her husband, a Calebite, was
surly and mean in his dealings.
4While David was in the desert, he heard that Nabal was shearing sheep. 5So he sent ten
young men and said to them, "Go up to Nabal at Carmel and greet him in my name. 6Say
to him: 'Long life to you! Good health to you and your household! And good health to all
that is yours!
7"'Now I hear that it is sheep-shearing time. When your shepherds were with us, we did
not mistreat them, and the whole time they were at Carmel nothing of theirs was missing.
8Ask your own servants and they will tell you. Therefore be favorable toward my young
men, since we come at a festive time. Please give your servants and your son David whatever you can find for them.'"
9When David's men arrived, they gave Nabal this message in David's name. Then they
waited.
10Nabal answered David's servants, "Who is this David? Who is this son of Jesse? Many
servants are breaking away from their masters these days. 11Why should I take my bread
and water, and the meat I have slaughtered for my shearers, and give it to men coming
from who knows where?"
12David's men turned around and went back. When they arrived, they reported every
word. 13David said to his men, "Put on your swords!" So they put on their swords, and

David put on his. About four hundred men went up with David, while two hundred stayed with the supplies.

14One of the servants told Nabal's wife Abigail:"David sent messengers from the desert
to give our master his greetings, but he hurled insults at them. 15Yet these men were very
good to us. They did not mistreat us, and the whole time we were out in the fields near
them nothing was missing. 16Night and day they were a wall around us all the time we
were herding our sheep near them. 17Now think it over and see what you can do, because
disaster is hanging over our master and his whole household. He is such a wicked man
that no one can talk to him."

18Abigail lost no time. She took two hundred loaves of bread, two skins of wine, five
dressed sheep, five seahs of roasted grain, a hundred cakes of raisins and two hundred
cakes of pressed figs, and loaded them on donkeys. 19Then she told her servants, "Go on
ahead; I'll follow you." But she did not tell her husband Nabal.

20As she came riding her donkey into a mountain ravine, there were David and his men
descending toward her, and she met them. 21David had just said, "It's been useless—all
my watching over this fellow's property in the desert so that nothing of his was missing.
He has paid me back evil for good. 22May God deal with David, be it ever so severely, if by
morning I leave alive one male of all who belong to him!"

23When Abigail saw David, she quickly got off her donkey and bowed down before David
with her face to the ground. 24She fell at his feet and said:"My lord, let the blame be on me
alone. Please let your servant speak to you; hear what your servant has to say. 25May my lord
pay no attention to that wicked man Nabal. He is just like his name—his name is Fool, and
folly goes with him. But as for me, your servant, I did not see the men my master sent.

26"Now since the LORD has kept you, my master, from bloodshed and from avenging
yourself with your own hands, as surely as the LORD lives and as you live, may your enemies
and all who intend to harm my master be like Nabal. 27And let this gift, which your servant has brought to my master, be given to the men who follow you. 28Please forgive your
servant's offense, for the LORD will certainly make a lasting dynasty for my master, because
he fights the LORD's battles. Let no wrongdoing be found in you as long as you live. 29Even
though someone is pursuing you to take your life, the life of my master will be bound
securely in the bundle of the living by the LORD your God. But the lives of your enemies he
will hurl away as from the pocket of a sling. 30When the LORD has done for my master every
good thing he promised concerning him and has appointed him leader over Israel, 31my
master will not have on his conscience the staggering burden of needless bloodshed or
of having avenged himself. And when the LORD has brought my master success, remember
your servant."

32David said to Abigail, "Praise be to the LORD, the God of Israel, who has sent you today
to meet me. 33May you be blessed for your good judgment and for keeping me from

bloodshed this day and from avenging myself with my own hands. 34Otherwise, as surely
as the LORD, the God of Israel, lives, who has kept me from harming you, if you had not
come quickly to meet me, not one male belonging to Nabal would have been left alive by
daybreak."
35Then David accepted from her hand what she had brought him and said, "Go home in
peace. I have heard your words and granted your request."
36When Abigail went to Nabal, he was in the house holding a banquet like that of a king.
He was in high spirits and very drunk. So she told him nothing until daybreak. 37Then in
the morning, when Nabal was sober, his wife told him all these things, and his heart failed
him and he became like a stone. 38About ten days later, the LORD struck Nabal and he died.
39When David heard that Nabal was dead, he said, "Praise be to the LORD, who has
upheld my cause against Nabal for treating me with contempt. He has kept his servant
from doing wrong and has brought Nabal's wrongdoing down on his own head."
Then David sent word to Abigail, asking her to become his wife. 40His servants went to
Carmel and said to Abigail, "David has sent us to you to take you to become his wife."
41She bowed down with her face to the ground and said, "Here is your maidservant,
ready to serve you and wash the feet of my master's servants." 42Abigail quickly got on a
donkey and, attended by her five maids, went with David's messengers and became his
wife. 43David had also married Ahinoam of Jezreel, and they both were his wives. 44But Saul
had given his daughter Michal, David's wife, to Paltiel son of Laish, who was from Gallim.

COMMENTARY

1a "Saul's public recognition of David's coming kingship [24:20] is the cue for Samuel to leave the scene" (Gunn, *The Fate of King Saul*, 95). The notice of Samuel's death in v.1 apparently marks the point at which, according to Talmudic tradition, authorship of the books of Samuel passed from the prophet himself (who supposedly wrote chs. 1–24) to Nathan and Gad (who supposedly wrote chs. 25–31 and all of 2 Samuel; cf. *b. B. Bat. 14b–15a*). This tradition, however, is based on a misunderstanding of 1 Chronicles 29:29 and therefore has little to commend it (cf. McCarter, *I Samuel*, 3–4; S. Szikszai, *IDB*, 4:203; contrast H. Wolf, *ZPEB*, 5:260–61).

Loved and respected by his people, Samuel was mourned by them at his death. Elements of the laconic statement in v.1 are repeated in 28:3 ("all Israel,""mourned for him,""buried him,""Ramah"). "Assembled" is also echoed in 28:4, but with a sinister twist: In v.1 all Israel "assembled" to lament Samuel's death, while in 28:4 the Philistines "assembled" to fight all Israel. The Hebrew roots of "assembled" and "buried"—*qbṣ* and *qbr* respectively—provide a fine example of alliteration and assonance in v.1.

"Buried" appears in 1 Samuel only here, in its echo in 28:3, and in 31:13 (the last verse in 1 Samuel). Notices of the burials of Samuel and Saul in v.1 and 31:13 thus serve as a kind of inclusio framing the final seven chapters of the book. Although local tradition places Samuel's tomb in Nebi Samwil northwest of Jerusalem, such tradition depends on the unlikely identification of Nebi Samwil with Ramah (see comment on 1:1; for details, cf. S. R. Driver, in *Hastings' Dictionary of the Bible*, 4:198).

1b–3 The difference in social status between David and Nabal becomes immediately apparent (Stek, 65C): David "moved down" to the "Desert of Maon" (v.1; for the location of Maon and the desert named after it, see comment on 23:24), but he told his men to "go up" (v.5) to Nabal at "Carmel" (which means "Vineyard land, Garden spot"; for its location see comment on 15:12). Like David's later friend Barzillai (2Sa 19:32), Nabal was very "wealthy" (lit., "great" [v.2], as in 2Sa 3:38). The Hebrew word translated "property" here (so also REB, NAB) often means "occupation, work" (Ge 46:33; 47:3; Jdg 13:12; Isa 54:16) and is therefore rendered "business" in some modern translations (e.g., RSV, NASB, JB).

The observation that Nabal had "three thousand" sheep may be another attempt to present him as the alter ego of Saul, who had "three thousand chosen men" (24:2; 26:2; cf. Stek, 65G). Sheepshearing, a time for celebration (cf. 2Sa 13:23–24), took place "after the summer grazing when the profits were distributed" (Ralph Gower, *The New Manners and Customs of Bible Times* [Chicago: Moody Press, 1987], 143). Plucking by hand and/or with the help of bronze combs sufficed for shearing sheep until the Iron Age, when iron shears came into use (Nina Hyde, "Wool—Fabric of History," *National Geographic* 173/5 [1988]: 557).

Only four episodes of sheepshearing are recorded in the OT. In each of them, "sheepshearing provides the setting for avenging a wrong: (1) Jacob takes what rightfully belongs to him for tending Laban's flocks (Genesis 31); Tamar lures Judah into a sexual encounter to secure her rightful progeny (Genesis 38); (3) David seeks compensation for protecting Nabal's flocks (1 Samuel 25); and (4) Absalom kills Amnon for raping his sister, Tamar (2 Samuel 13)" (Jeffrey C. Geoghegan, "Israelite Sheepshearing and David's Rise to Power," *Bib* 87/1 [2006]: 55). Geoghegan, 63, concludes:

> An analysis of the relevant texts ... reveals that sheepshearing in ancient Israel was a significant celebration characterized by feasting, heavy dirinking [*sic*], and the settling of old scores. As a result of these associations, sheepshearing became an ideal backdrop for events in Israel's past involving the repayment of debts or the righting of wrongs. Because both David and Absalom took advantage of sheepshearing for this purpose—and in the process aided their own ascents to the throne—sheepshearing became intimately associated with the emergence of the royal clan (Genesis 38) and the establishment of the Davidic dynasty.

The contrast between Nabal and his wife Abigail (v.3) could scarcely be starker. Not only "beautiful" (lit., "lovely in form"—the same expression used to describe Rachel in Ge 29:17 and Esther in Est 2:7), Abigail was also "intelligent" (lit., "good in understanding"; cf. 2Ch 30:22; Ps 111:10; Pr 13:15). Nabal, however, was "mean" (lit., "evil")—and thus a polarity between "good" (*ṭôb*; GK 3202) and "evil" (*raʿ*; GK 8273) is set up at the beginning of ch. 25. As Gunn observes (*The Fate of King Saul*, 96, 154 n. 7), each of the two terms ("good" or "do good"; "evil" or "do evil") appears seven times in the chapter ("good," vv.3, 8 ["festive"], 15, 21, 30–31 ["brought ... success"], 36 ["high"]; "evil," vv.3, 17 ["disaster"], 21, 26 ["harm"], 34 ["harming"], 39 [2x: "wrong," "wrongdoing"]). Together they underscore one of the major themes of the story: Good brings its own reward, while evil recoils on the head of the wicked.

The names of Abigail ("My [divine] Father is joy") and Nabal ("Fool"; cf. v.25 and comment) well describe the characters of the couple. Nabal's parents, however, are not likely to have given their son the name "Fool." The Hebrew word *nābāl* (GK

5573) may therefore also have had one or more positive meanings (see, e.g., Levenson, 2:222); it is also possible that Nabal was a deliberately pejorative nickname applied to the man in later life rather than a praenomen given to him at birth.

According to the MT's vocalic text, Nabal was a "Calebite" (*kālibbî*), a word with the same root as *keleb* ("dog"), hence "doglike"—a description that is anything but complimentary (see comment on 17:43). According to the MT's consonantal text, however, Nabal was "like his heart" (*k^e libbô*), which is almost certainly "an allusion to Psalm 14:1 (53:2), 'the fool [*nābāl*] has said in his heart [*b^e libbô*], "There is no God."' If this is correct, then we have here an instance of scribal sarcasm. The consonantal text alludes to the prideful and ultimately stupid and arrogantly unperceptive character of this man, who seems to have recognized no authority other than his own (Levenson, 2:223)."

The beautiful and intelligent Abigail, though mismatched with Nabal, is a perfect match for David, whose commendable qualities complement hers (cf. 16:12, 18). In all respects she is David's equal (Levenson, 2:228; Stek, 65D). In fact, she should perhaps be identified with one of David's two sisters, the only other Abigail mentioned in the Bible (1Ch 2:15–16). According to 2 Samuel 17:25, David's sister Abigail was the daughter of Nahash, who was perhaps the Ammonite ruler of 11:1–2 and 12:12. This identification would help to explain the friendship between Nahash and David (2Sa 10:2). At the same time, since David was the son of Jesse, Abigail would then have been only his half sister (cf. similarly K&D, *The Book of Chronicles*, 62–63, although Keil apparently understands Nahash to have been a woman), so making it possible for him to marry her (v.42; cf. similarly Ge 20:12). If the two Abigails are thus identified (cf. G. R. H. Wright, "Dumuzi at the Court of David," *As on the First Day: Essays in Religious Constants* [Leiden: Brill, 1987], 52), her first husband would have been Jether (2Sa 17:25; 1Ch 2:17)—perhaps Nabal's real name (Levenson and Halpern, esp. 511–12).

4–13 After hearing that Nabal is shearing sheep (v.4), David sends ten young men (*n^e ͨārîm*) to him (v.5). Later Abigail, again proving herself to be a "fit partner" for David (Stek, 65E), goes to him attended by her "five" (a "modest" number [J. B. Segal, 9]) young women (*na ͨ^a rōteyhā*, v.42).

David's message to Nabal through his men (vv.5–8) begins by telling them to "greet him" (lit., "inquire of him concerning [his] well-being/welfare"; see comment on 10:4) in David's name (i.e., as his representative; cf. also v.9; see comment on 17:45). The boon of "well-being/welfare/peace/good health" is expressed in v.5 by the word *šālôm*, which reappears three times in v.6 ("Good health to you and [good health to] your household! And good health to all that is yours!").

Nabal's foolish rejection of David's friendly overtures (vv.10–11) evokes a threefold response from David in v.13, this time repeating the word *ḥereb* ("sword": "'Put on your swords!' So they put on their swords, and David put on his [sword]"). The opposition between *šālôm* and *ḥereb* found here is a striking prefiguration of Jesus' statement: "I did not come to bring peace, but a sword" (Mt 10:34).

"[And] now" (v.7)—David continues in his persuasive tone (see comment and Notes on 24:20) as he seeks a favor from Nabal. He senses that sheep-shearing time should put Nabal in a good mood, because it is a "festive" occasion (v.8). Utilizing the ancient equivalent of the protection racket (cf. Gunn, *The Fate of King Saul*, 96), David observes that his men did not mistreat Nabal's shepherds or steal anything from them (v.7; cf. Samuel's *apologia* in 12:4–5), perhaps implying that there were plenty of opportunities to do so. One of Nabal's servants later confirms to Abigail the claims of David (vv.14–15; cf. also v.8) and expresses his gratitude for the protection provided by David's men (v.16; cf. also David's complaint in v.21). David's concern for the welfare of Nabal's shepherds had in fact extended over a long period of time (vv.7, 15–16).

David's request that Nabal should "be favorable toward my young men" (lit., "the young men find favor in your eyes," v.8) is the epitome of courtesy (cf. 1:18; 20:29; 27:5). The season for sheepshearing provides opportunity for a "festive time" (lit., "good day"; cf. Est 8:17 ["celebrating"]; 9:19 ["joy and feasting"], 22 ["day of celebration"]; cf. also *T. Ash.* 4:4, where "good day" means "festival"). As Stek, 65G, observes, Nabal's negative response (vv.10–11) on a "good day" results in the likelihood of a time of "evil" ("disaster" [NIV], v.17) for him. David is simply requesting for himself and his men "whatever" supplies (primarily food; cf. v.11) Nabal might be willing to give them, since they depend on the generosity of others for the protection they provide (v.16). David's curious reference to himself as Nabal's "son" (v.8) makes sense if Nabal is functioning as Saul's literary surrogate in this chapter (cf. 24:16).

Arriving in Carmel, David's men act as faithful messengers by reporting to Nabal "this message" (lit., "according to all these words," v.9; the same Heb. expression translated "every word" in v.12) in the name of their leader. The verb rendered "waited" (lit., "rested") can also be translated "stopped" (cf. Nu 10:36, "came to rest"), here in the sense of "stopped speaking," implying that they did not add anything to David's words.

Possibly these "ten young men" (v.5) sent to Nabal by David were officers in his small army, since they are called his "servants" at the beginning of v.10 (for "servant" in the sense of "officer," see comment on 16:15–16; cf. also 18:5; 29:3). Nabal clearly uses the same word in the same verse with its most basic meaning. His repeated "Who?" is uttered with scorn, like that of David with respect to Goliath (17:26). Nabal also uses "son of Jesse" in an insulting and belittling way, as did Saul before him (see 20:27 and comment; 22:7). In so doing Nabal rejects David's courteous reference to himself as Nabal's "son" (v.8). The rebel Sheba would later dismiss the "son of Jesse" with similar contempt (2Sa 20:1; cf. Levenson, 2:237).

Nabal's contention that "many servants are breaking away from their masters these days" (v.10) is at least double-edged and perhaps even triple-edged: (1) He may be referring to David, who is fleeing from his master Saul; (2) he may be subtly suggesting to David's servants that they would be well advised to break away from their master, possibly even to join Nabal's household; and (3), ironically, he speaks better than he knows, since "he is about to find *himself* in the role of a master whose slaves break away, telling their mistress of her husband's stupidity and ethical vacuity" (Levenson, 2:225 [emphasis his]; cf. vv.14–17). Gunn (*The Fate of King Saul*, 97) makes an additional observation about v.10: "This scathing dismissal is strongly reminiscent of Saul's sarcastic outburst against David in chapter 22" (cf. 22:7–8).

Nabal is even unwilling to give to David and his men "bread and water" (v.11), the most basic food and drink (Nu 21:5; Dt 9:9, 18; 1Ki 13:8–9, 16–17; cf. the similar refusal of the officials of Succoth to the request of Gideon for his men in Jdg 8:4–6, 15)—much less the meat he had slaughtered for his workers. Nabal telegraphs his egotism in the MT of v.11, which uses "I" and "my" a total of eight times (four times apiece): "I take," "I slaughtered," "I give," "I know"; "my bread," "my water," "my meat," "my shearers."

Upon receiving Nabal's response, David's men "turned" (the verb often being used of an [abrupt] about-face, especially in military contexts; cf. Jdg 20:39, 41; Ps 78:9) and reported back to David (v.12). His immediate reaction is to retaliate by arming himself and his men with swords (v.13; for the literary function of the triple mention of "sword" in the MT here, see comment on v.6; cf. similarly Miscall, 151)—a poignant contrast to his earlier repudiation of the sword before his contest with Goliath (17:39, 45, 47). Splitting his six hundred men into two groups of unequal size, David sets out for Carmel with four hundred (a number often "associated with flight and with battles" [J. B. Segal, 12]) and leaves the rest behind with the "supplies" (a term with military connotations; see comment on "baggage" in 10:22 and on "supplies" in 17:22). The two hundred who "stayed with the supplies" are not to be considered in any way inferior and can expect to share in whatever plunder will be seized (cf. 30:24; for an identical deployment of David's men on a later occasion—though for a different reason—cf. 30:9–10).

14–19 This section begins with "told" (v.14) and ends with "did not tell" (v.19). In the MT in each case the clause starts with its object ("Abigail" in v.14, "her husband Nabal" in v.19), making the inclusio around the whole appear all the more striking and deliberate. The parallel section (vv.36–38) uses the same verb twice as well, this time beginning with a negative construction ("told ... nothing," v.36) and ending with a positive construction ("told," v.37; cf. similarly Stek, 65B).

Nabal's servant describes to Abigail (v.14) the shoddy treatment David's men have received at Nabal's hands. David had sent messengers to "give" Nabal "his greetings" (the verb "greet" here [cf. 2Sa 8:10 = 1Ch 18:10] literally meaning "bless, praise," as in vv.32–33, 39) but had been crudely rebuffed by him. Abigail's response to her meeting with David, by contrast, is a "gift" (lit., "blessing," v.27) of substantial proportions (v.18). Nabal, as we might suspect, hurls "insults" at David's men.

Nabal's servant continues to apprise Abigail of his favorable impression of David and his men (v.15), even repeating some of their terminology (cf. v.7). He especially stresses the physical proximity of Nabal's shepherds to David's men ("near them," vv.15–16) during "the whole time" (v.15; "all the time," v.16) they were in the fields. Like the fortress "wall" enclosing a city (v.16; the same metaphor used of God in Zec 2:5), the protection provided by David and his men continued around the clock ("night and day"). Afraid that the "good" deeds (v.15) of David's men will be repaid by "disaster" (v.17) against Nabal and his household because of his moral obtuseness, his servant appeals to Abigail for help.

"Think it over and see," the servant says to Abigail (lit., "know and see," a common phrase in 1 Samuel; see comment on "realize" in 12:17 and on "find out" in 23:22–23), pleading with her to make up for her husband's dereliction. "Disaster is determined/inevitable" (*kālᵉtâ hārāᶜâ*; "disaster is hanging [over]," NIV; cf. 20:7, 9 ["determined to harm"]; Est 7:7 ["decided (his) fate"]), because Nabal is a "wicked man" (*ben-bᵉlîyaᶜal*; cf. 2:12 of Eli's sons; also 10:27 ["troublemakers"]; see comment and Notes on "wicked woman" in 1:16; further, *ʾîš bᵉlîyaᶜal* in v.25). The servant concludes his appeal by observing that no one can talk to Nabal, thus implying that perhaps his wife Abigail may be able to persuade him of the folly of his ways.

Nabal's sloth is more than compensated for by Abigail's speed in meeting David's needs. She "lost no time" (v.18), she acted "quickly" (vv.23, 34, 42; the same Heb. verb in all four cases). Nabal's stinginess is counterbalanced by his wife's generosity; her itemized tally of foodstuffs for David and his men surpasses the size of a later, similar list drawn up for the same purpose (2Sa 16:1). "Cakes of raisins" and "cakes of pressed figs" (v.18) were especially prized, not only for their sweetness and nutritive value, but also because they could be kept for some time without spoiling (cf. 30:1, 11–12).

David had earlier asked Ahimelech the priest for "five loaves of bread," or "whatever you can find"

(21:3), and Ahimelech had responded—however reluctantly—by giving him consecrated bread, the only food available (21:6). When David's servants asked Nabal for "whatever you can find" (v.8; similar though not identical Heb. in 21:3), he refused to give them any "bread" at all (v.11). Now, in response to David's need, Abigail supplies him with "two hundred loaves of bread" in addition to large amounts of other provisions (v.18). Levenson, 2:227, observes that when Abigail finally tells Nabal about her gift to David (v.37; cf. v.19), his heart fails him "over a negligible loss"—the loss of "various perishables and exactly five sheep [v.18] out of his three thousand [v.2]." Perhaps a further irony is that among Abigail's provisions for David are two "skins" (*niblê*) of wine—a possible wordplay on *nābāl* ("Nabal").

20–35 Possessing its own literary unity, this central section of ch. 25 begins and ends with three-verse paragraphs (vv.20–22, 32–34) that reflect each other and frame the speech of Abigail, which constitutes the heart of the chapter (vv.24–31). Except for the suffix, the Hebrew rendered "toward her" (v.20) is the same as that translated "to meet me" (vv.32, 34). In addition vv.22 and 34 each begin with an oath and end with the Hebrew phrase translated "one male." Verse 23 (which introduces Abigail's speech) and v.35 (which concludes the whole) in the MT also share certain words: "See" (untranslated in the NIV but appearing before "I have heard" in the Heb. of v.35) answers to "saw" (v.23), and "your request" (lit., "your face," v.35) echoes "her face" (v.23).

Having sent her servants ahead with the provisions for David and his men, Abigail follows on a donkey (v.20; cf. also vv.23, 42), a common means of transportation in ancient times (Ex 4:20; Jos 15:18 = Jdg 1:14; 2Ch 28:15). She intercepts David near a mountain "ravine," an out-of-the-way place reminding us that he is still a hunted fugitive (the same Heb. word translated "hiding" in 19:2). He and his men are on their way to punish Nabal for his incivility. The MT is ambiguous concerning whether Abigail has heard David's words recorded in vv.21–22. (The NIV's "had just said" implies that she has not.) In any case, David feels cheated ("It's been useless," lit., "for deception/disappointment") by Nabal's action (or inaction).

Although guaranteeing that none of the property of "this fellow" (spoken in a scornful tone of voice; cf. 21:15) was "missing" (cf. also vv.7, 15), David has been "paid ... back evil for good" (an expression implying betrayal or cruelty; cf. Ge 44:4; Pr 17:13; Jer 18:20; also especially the Davidic Pss 35:12; 38:20; 109:5). David, intending to retaliate in the heat of his anger, will later praise the Lord for having "brought Nabal's wrongdoing [= evil] down on his own head" (v.39; the Heb. verb rendered "brought ... down" is translated "paid ... back" in v.21). With a strong oath of self-imprecation (v.22; see comment on 20:13), David swears that he will kill every male in Nabal's household by daybreak—although he later expresses his gratitude that the Lord (and Abigail) kept him from doing so (vv.33–34).

In preparation for responding at some length to David's threat against her husband (vv.24–31) and in contrast to Nabal's treatment of David and his men (vv.10–11), Abigail bows down respectfully before him (v.23). As D. M. Gunn ("Traditional Composition," 221–22) has pointed out, details of both form and content relating to Abigail's speech are paralleled in the account of the interview between David and the wise woman of Tekoa in 2 Samuel 14:1–20. With respect to content, both scenes involve a woman interceding with David for herself and her family, and both are concerned with themes of bloodguilt and revenge. With respect to form, the following details stand out (translating the Heb. literally and disregarding the order of the elements):

1 Samuel 25	2 Samuel 14
And she fell before David with her face to the ground, and she bowed down ... and she said (vv.23–24)	And she fell with her face to the ground, and she bowed down, and she said (v.4)
"On me, my lord, is the blame" (v.24)	"On me, my lord the king, is the blame" (v.9)
"Please let your servant speak in your ears, and hear the words of your servant" (v.24)	"Please let your servant speak a word to my lord the king" (v.12)
And he said to her, "Go up in peace to your home; see, I have heard your voice and granted your request" (v.35)	And the king said to the woman, "Go to your home, and I will issue an order in your behalf" (v.8)

Abigail's speech is a masterpiece of rhetoric, appealing not only to reason and the emotions, but also to her own credibility (Kenneth W. Shoemaker, "The Rhetoric of Abigail's Speech [1 Sam 25:24–31]" [paper presented at the annual meeting of the SBL, Boston, Mass., 1987], 6). Beginning with a formal exordium (v.24) and ending with a formal conclusion (v.31b), the main body of the speech treats matters of the past (v.25), present (vv.26–28a; vv.26a, 26b, and 27 all begin with "And now" in the MT), and future (vv.28b–31a; v.30 begins with "And it will be" in the MT; cf. Shoemaker, "Abigail's Speech," 20–21).

Riding alone "into a troop of four hundred armed men bent on violence [vv.20–22]" (Shoemaker, "Abigail's Speech," 4), the defenseless Abigail knows that she has very little time to change their minds. She immediately demonstrates an attitude of submission to David, referring to him as "my lord/master" in every verse of her speech and to herself as "your servant" in all but vv.26, 29, and 30 (cf. Hannah to Eli in 1:15–16; Ruth to Boaz in Ru 2:13). The contrast between her attitude toward David and that of Nabal could hardly be more striking. Gunn (*The Fate of King Saul*, 99) observes: "For Nabal, David is 'servant' [v.10]; for Abigail, he is 'master.'" In addition, although Nabal is "such a wicked man that no one can talk to him" (v.17), Abigail pleads for an opportunity to "speak to" David.

Abigail, the consummate diplomat, knows that she has to be careful

> neither to exculpate Nabal nor to appear disloyal to him.... In short, she must win David without betraying Nabal. Abigail devises the perfect solution to the dilemma: she intercedes on behalf of Nabal (v.24), although conceding that he has no case and no hope of survival (vv.25–26). In other words, while overtly defending him, she covertly dissociates herself from him. (Levenson, 2:230)

To save Nabal's life, she assumes his guilt (v.24). Her admission is "unacceptably lame, but it has succeeded in buying further time" (Shoemaker, "Abigail's Speech," 10). The urgency and insistence clearly detectable throughout her speech is modulated by a tone of courtesy and politeness, evidenced in her frequent use of the particle *nāʾ* ("please," vv.24–25 [omitted by NIV], 28).

Abigail's characterization of Nabal as a "wicked man" and a "fool" (v.25) has often been misunderstood as a heartless and self-serving denunciation of her husband. The contrary is the case, however: Her action is one of

> wit and tactical maneuvering.... It is very unlikely that David would have been eager to marry [vv.39–40, 42] any woman known for disloyalty, even though wealthy and beautiful, since such a treacherous woman in the royal chambers would

> be a constant threat. A wife's self-sacrificial loyalty to her spouse, on the other hand, would be a virtue prized by any husband. (Shoemaker, "Abigail's Speech," 13–14)

At the same time her integrity prevents her from pulling any punches. Since Nabal is a "wicked man" (see comment on v.17; cf. also 2Sa 20:1, where the same Heb. expression ["troublemaker"] is used of Sheba—who referred disparagingly to David as "son of Jesse," as Nabal had done earlier [v.10; cf. Levenson, 2:237]), one should "pay no attention" (cf. also 4:20) to him (Shoemaker ["Abigail's Speech," 7] suggests "not ... take ... seriously"; the same Heb. phrase is translated "do not worry" in 9:20 and "won't care" in 2Sa 18:3).

Abigail's statement that Nabal (*nābāl*, "Fool"; GK 5573) "is just like his name" is perhaps the best biblical illustration of the ancient perception that a name was not simply a label for distinguishing one thing from another but that "a more profound connection between the name and its bearer" should be sought (Mettinger, 7). In other words, "name" equals "person" (cf. Isa 30:27), and "Nabal"—whether name or epithet (cf. similarly Pr 21:24; see also commentary on v.3)—equals "Fool" with all the nuances implied in that term (cf. Isa 32:6, which says of the fool that, among other things, "the hungry he leaves empty and from the thirsty he withholds water"—a description that characterizes Nabal precisely [v.11], as observed by Levenson, 2:221–22). Thus "his name is Fool, and folly [*n*[e]*bālâ*] goes with him."

That the root *nbl* basically means "be foolish, fool, folly," is secured not only by numerous references in the OT (for a complete list, see BDB, 614–15) but also by versional renderings (LXX, Vul.) as well as Hebrew-Greek equivalences in Sirach (cf. 4:27; 21:22). At the same time the various Hebrew roots (including *nbl*) thus translated in the OT have not so much to do with people who are stupid, ignorant, or even naïve as they do with those who are "morally deficient" (NIV note at Pr 1:7). Tellingly and ironically, David's wife Ahinoam (v.43) bore his first son, Amnon, who proved to be "one of the wicked fools" (*n*[e]*bālîm*; 2Sa 13:13) capable of doing a "wicked thing" (*n*[e]*bālâ*; 2Sa 13:12; cf. Stek, 65E; also Jos 7:15, "disgraceful thing"). Although the Hebrew root is different, 26:21 records Saul's admission that he "acted like a fool," thus strengthening the observation that in ch. 25 Nabal functions as Saul's alter ego.

Although assuming her husband's blame (v.24), Abigail disavows having seen the "men" (v.25) David had sent to him (v.5, where the same Heb. word is translated "young men"). She senses that God has "kept" (v.26) David from harming Nabal and his men, a truth that David acknowledges (v.34—though placing the emphasis on not harming Abigail). At the same time David asserts the important role of Abigail herself in keeping him from "bloodshed" (v.33), recognizing in her the mediator of the Lord's intentions. Since vengeance belongs to God alone (Dt 32:35), David must not avenge himself (vv.26, 31, 33). To do so would be to usurp God's prerogatives, "act the fool and violate the wisdom" of Proverbs 20:22: "Do not say, 'I'll pay you back for this wrong!' Wait for the LORD, and he will deliver you" (thus Stek, 65E, who observes that the Heb. for "deliver" in Pr 20:22 is the same as that for "avenging/avenged" here in vv.26, 31, 33).

With the same double asseveration used earlier by David (see 20:3 and comment), Abigail expresses her desire that David's "enemies" (among whom Saul counts himself, 18:29; cf. also 26:8) and all who "intend to harm" him (the same Heb. phrase is translated "bent on harming" in 24:9) might "be like Nabal" (v.26). This apparently anticipates the death of her husband and also, by implication, foreshadows the death of Saul (cf. Gordon, "David's Rise," 49), Nabal's alter ego.

Though Nabal may be stingy, not so Abigail. She describes the generous supply of food that she brings to David and his men as a "gift" (v.27; lit., a "blessing"; cf. 2Ki 5:15; the same Heb. word is translated "present" in 30:26; Ge 33:11 and "special favor" in Jos 15:19 = Jdg 1:15). The narrator will later (v.42) demonstrate Abigail to be a fit partner for David by portraying her as "attended by her five maids" (*nʿrwt*, lit., "her five maids walking at her feet"), an echo of her description of David's contingent as "the men [*nʿrym*] who follow you" (lit., "the men who walk at the feet of my master"; cf. Stek, 65E).

Continuing to accept the blame for Nabal's folly, Abigail begs David's forgiveness for her own "offense" (v.28; the same Heb. root is translated "rebellion" in David's disclaimer in 24:11). In fact, Abigail's burden in v.28 is to plead with David not to do anything rash—anything that might endanger or even destroy the "lasting dynasty" (*bayit neʾemān*; cf. 1Ki 11:38, where the same Heb. expression is translated "dynasty as enduring") that God will give him. So clearly is Abigail's statement in this regard an adumbration of Nathan's prophecy in 2 Samuel 7:16 ("Your house ... will endure" [*neʾman bêtkā*]; cf. also 1Ch 17:23) that the rabbis of Talmudic times counted Abigail "among seven women who they believed had been graced by the holy spirit, the source of prophecy" (Levenson, 2:231; cf. also Brettler, 84). Unlike the king desired by the people of Samuel's day, a king who would "fight our battles" (8:20), David is to be a man who "fights the LORD's battles" (v.28)—as Saul had insincerely and hypocritically asked David to do (18:17).

Abigail warns David not to let "wrongdoing be found" in him (v.28)—a flaw that David's son Solomon would later use ("evil is found" [1Ki 1:52] translates the same Heb. phrase) as a reason/excuse to execute his half-brother Adonijah, a rival claimant to David's throne (1Ki 2:24–25). Shoemaker ("Abigail's Speech," 7) understands "as long as you live" (lit., "from your days") in the sense of "any of your days" ("from" with partitive force), arguing that the possibility of evil conduct on David's part "subtly includes the present day's affairs."

Although the "good/evil" terminology (see comment on v.3) is not used in v.29, the contrast is nonetheless evident: Abigail assures David that his life is safe but that the lives of his enemies are doomed. The "someone" intending to "take [David's] life" is, of course, Saul (see 20:1 and comment; see also 22:23 ["seeking your life ... seeking mine"]; 23:15). But neither Saul nor anyone else will be able to wrest David from the protection of the Lord his God, who secures him in the "bundle" of the living (the word translated "bundle" is found elsewhere in the sense of a "pouch/purse" containing money [Ge 42:35; Pr 7:20] or a "sachet" containing myrrh [SS 1:13]).

Conversely, the same Lord will "hurl away" into oblivion the enemies of David as though from the pocket of a "sling"—a clear echo of David's divinely empowered victory over Goliath. (In its only other occurrence in the Piel, the Heb. verb for "hurl away" is rendered "slung" in 17:49, while the noun "sling" appears in 17:40, 50.) G. M. Mackie suggests the possibility that Abigail's imagery serves the additional function of contrasting the two pouches used by the shepherd, the "bundle of the living" referring to the pouch that held food (symbolizing life) and the "pocket of a sling" the pouch that held the stone (symbolizing death; G. M. Mackie, *Bible Manners and Customs* [New York: Revell, 1898], 33).

Continuing to look into the future, Abigail again alludes to the Davidic covenant of 2 Samuel 7 (see comment on v.28). On the basis of Akkadian *ṭābūta dabābu* ("to discuss good/friendly relations, to establish a [favorable] treaty"; cf. *CAD*, 3:8), the idiom *dibbēr ṭôbâ* ("speak/promise good thing[s]") is often best translated the same way (cf. 1Ki 12:7, where "establish a covenant with them" is preferable to the NIV's "give them a favorable answer"; thus perhaps also similarly in 2Ki 25:28 = Jer 52:32). In the context of 2 Samuel 7, "established this covenant with" is better than "promised these good things to" in 2Sa 7:28 (= 1Ch 17:26). Likewise, Abigail refers to the time when the Lord will have done for David "according to every good thing that he spoke/promised" (*k^e^kōl ^ʾa^šer-dibber ʾet-haṭṭôbâ*, v.30; cf. NIV), that is, "according to everything in the covenant that he (will have) established" with David (cf. Fox, 41–42, esp. 42).

Although God has already "appointed him leader" (v.30), a fact earlier announced to Saul by Samuel (see 13:14 and comment), David will not exercise effective rule over Israel until after Saul's death. In the meantime, however, Abigail does not want David to do anything to jeopardize his future or endanger his throne. In a literary echo of 24:5 (see comment), she warns him not to burden his "conscience" (lit., "heart," v.31; cf. Ecc 7:22) with "needless bloodshed" against Nabal (cf. Jonathan's admonition to Saul in 19:5; cf. 1Ki 2:31). Such a burden would be "staggering" indeed, bringing David distress like that of the kind of chronic drunkenness that causes leaders to "stumble when rendering decisions" (Isa 28:7).

As Joseph had concluded his conversation with the Pharaoh's cupbearer by requesting that he "remember" Joseph when all "goes well" with him (Ge 40:14), so also Abigail ends her plea by asking that David "remember" her when the Lord "has brought ... success" to him (v.31; the same Heb. verbs in both verses). Levenson, 2:230, observing that Abigail is alone with David throughout her address, interprets the phrase "remember your servant" in a highly personal sense: "She offers victuals to David's men; to David, she offers herself" (cf. v.42).

David's three-verse response (vv.32–34) to the rhetorical brilliance of Abigail mirrors the three-verse paragraph (vv.20–22) with which this literary unit begins (see comment on vv.20–22). In addition, the response has its own literary symmetry: The phrases "the LORD, the God of Israel" and "to meet me" both occur in vv.32 and 34.

Although David was on his way to destroy Nabal's household, Abigail's sevenfold use of the divine name Yahweh (vv.26 [2x], 28 [2x], 29, 30, 31) has perhaps reminded him of the spiritual dimensions of his calling—or, as Shoemaker ("Abigail's Speech," 16) puts it, "David's Yahwistic perspective has been refocused." David sees in Abigail the Lord's envoy: "Praise be to the LORD [v.32; cf. v.39] ... who has sent you." "Praise be to" (v.32) and "May ... be blessed" (v.33) translate the same Hebrew root (*brk*; GK 1385; the NIV almost always avoids "bless" where God is the object).

David recognizes that "good judgment" is an admirable quality in a woman (cf. Pr 11:22 ["discretion"]). He also understands that God has used Abigail to keep him from bloodshed and from attempting to avenge himself (v.33; the Heb. verb rendered "keeping" [cf. Ps 119:101], however, is different from that in vv.26, 34). The oath "As surely as the LORD ... lives" (v.34) is frequently used where life and death hang in the balance (see comment on 14:39). Mass killings of the kind that David contemplated often occurred at night, giving point to his statement that not a male in Nabal's household would have survived till "daybreak" (v.34; cf. v.22; 14:36).

This lengthiest of pericopes in the chapter (vv.20–35) concludes with David's grateful acceptance of Abigail's gift of food for himself and his men (v.35). He makes it clear that she has succeeded in assuaging his wrath: "Go [lit., 'Go up,' usually to higher ground; cf. Ge 44:17, 'go back'] ... in peace." That he has been impressed and influenced by her impassioned arguments is clear from his acknowledgment: "I have heard your words" (lit., "I have listened to your voice"), an idiom that often implies obedience. In any event, his final words must have been like music to her ears: "I have ... granted your request" (lit., "lifted up your face"; cf. Job 42:8–9, "accept[ed] his [Job's] prayer"), guaranteeing that he will not be the instrument of Nabal's death. The basic elements of the idioms David uses here remind us of the Aaronic benediction: "The LORD turn [lit., 'lift up'] his face toward you" in blessing and peace (Nu 6:24–26).

36–38 The repetition of three crucial words gives unity to this brief paragraph: "heart" (vv.36 ["spirits"], 37), "died" (vv.37 ["failed"], 38), and "told" (vv.36–37; for the literary significance of this verb in the section, see the comment on its structural parallel in vv.14–19).

Abigail went to Nabal's "house" (v.36), doubtless in Carmel (cf. v.40), where his sheepshearing celebration was taking place (see v.2 and comment on vv.7–8). He was presiding at a banquet fit for a "king"—a cruel irony when it is remembered that his wife has just declared her allegiance to Israel's king-elect. At his feast Nabal proved to be "a fool [*nābāl*] who is full of food" (Pr 30:22), something the very earth cannot tolerate (Pr 30:21). Through overindulgence in wine he was "in high spirits" (lit., "his heart is good/merry"; cf. Jdg 16:25; Est 1:10; also David's firstborn son, Amnon, in 2Sa 13:28). Realizing that Nabal was in no condition to understand what she might say to him, Abigail decided to tell him "nothing" (lit., "nothing small or great"; see 22:15 ["nothing at all"] and comment) until "daybreak"—the time by which, ominously, David had originally sworn to kill every male in Nabal's household (v.34; cf. also v.22).

As it turns out, of course, Nabal's folly is his own worst enemy. By the next morning "Nabal was sober" (lit., "the wine had gone out of Nabal," v.37). Levenson, 2:227, observes that the consonants of Nabal's name can be vocalized as *nēbel* ("wineskin"; cf. v.18), and the narrator may well be using a wordplay: "In short, the man is equated with his bladder" (cf. also Levenson and Halpern, "The Political Import of David's Marriages," 514 n. 18; Gordon, "David's Rise," 51).

Pursuing Levenson's observations, Peter J. Leithart ("Critical Note: Nabal and His Wine," *JBL* 120/3 [2001]: 526) translates the construction as "while the wine was going out of Nabal" and suggests that "Abigail tells Nabal about the encounter with David while he is emptying his bladder, that is, while he is urinating after a night of heavy drinking." In the rest of Leithart's article (526–27) he teases out the implications of this understanding. Cf. second Note on v.22.

Feeling that the time is now ripe, Abigail tells her husband "all [so a few Heb. MSS] these things." When David's men had earlier given Nabal "this message" (lit., "all these things," v.9), he insulted them and David. When they returned to David and reported to him "every word" (lit., "all these things," v.12), he and his men prepared to march into battle against Nabal. Now, when Nabal hears from his wife "all these things" (v.37)—perhaps the entire story of her meeting with David, but doubtless including the list of provisions that she had so generously given to him and that Nabal would surely begrudge (see v.18 and comment)—the shock is too much for him in his materialistic greed. Nabal the "fool," Nabal the "wineskin," who was very drunk and "was in high spirits" (lit., whose "heart was good") just a day earlier (v.36), now suffers from a heart that goes bad: "His heart failed him" (lit., "died in him," v.37). Since the heart is the seat of courage (cf. David's statement to Saul: "Let no one lose heart on account of this Philistine," 17:32), Nabal is depicted as a coward as well.

The description of Nabal's becoming "like a stone" ("petrified" [BDB, 7]) should not be diagnosed as a specific illness (heart attack, stroke, etc.) but understood figuratively (cf. Ex 15:16, where Moses affirms that God's enemies will be "as still as a stone"). Indeed, reference to a "stone" may be yet another allusion to the Goliath narrative (cf. 17:50; see comment on v.29; cf. similarly Miscall,

154; Polzin, *Samuel and the Deuteronomist*, 211–12). At the same time, it is equally possible that the narrator looks at Nabal as receiving a "heart of stone" in exchange for his heart of flesh—the reverse of the promise in Ezekiel 36:26 (Levenson, 2:227; see also Marjorie O'Rourke Boyle, "The Law of the Heart: The Death of a Fool [1 Samuel 25]," *JBL* 120/3 [2001]: 401–27 [esp. 410, 412–26]).

Though not immediate, Nabal's death is not long in coming. After about ten days "the LORD struck" him (v.38). The same Hebrew phrase is used in 26:10 of the ultimate fate of Saul, Nabal's alter ego (cf. similarly Gordon, "David's Rise," 49). Thus Nabal "died" at God's hand. As Stek, 65F, observes, *wayyāmōt* ("and [it/he] died," vv.37 ["failed"], 38) forms an "inclusio that frames the account of Nabal's end."

39a David greets the news of Nabal's death with an outburst of praise, echoing that in v.32. As he had earlier entreated the Lord to "uphold" his "cause" against Saul (24:15), so now he expresses his gratitude to the Lord for having "upheld his cause" against Saul's alter ego (cf. similarly Gordon, "David's Rise," 48, who notes that these "are the only occurrences of the root ריב [*ryb*; GK 8189], in its forensic sense, in 1 Samuel"). Nabal's having treated David with "contempt" also makes him like Goliath, who brought "disgrace" on Israel (17:26; the same Heb. word in both cases).

The Lord's dealings with David and Nabal could hardly be more different: As for David, God has "kept his servant from doing wrong" (cf. the almost identical language in the Davidic Ps 19:13), while in Nabal's case he has "brought [his] wrongdoing down on his own head" (for the same idiom, see Jdg 9:57, "made (them) pay for all their wickedness"; 1Ki 2:44, "repay you for your wrongdoing"; cf. also Joel 3:4, 7, "return on your own heads what you have done").

39b–43 There are striking similarities between the occurrence, sequence, and subject(s) of verbs in this passage and in its parallel earlier in the chapter (see Notes on vv.4–13). The most important feature giving internal literary unity to the section is the phrase *lô lᵉʾiššâ* (lit., "to him as a wife") at the end of vv.39b, 40, and 42. It serves also to highlight David's marriage to Abigail as the theme of the pericope.

Nabal now dead, David "sent" his servants to Abigail to "take" her to become his wife (vv.39b–40). Miscall, 156, notes that David here "sends and takes, as he does with another woman at a future time (2 Sam 11:4)." Abigail, by no means unwilling, nevertheless continues to characterize herself as David's "maidservant" (v.41, using the same Heb. word translated "servant" in vv.24–25, 28, 31)—one of the many persons/things Samuel had warned Israel that their king would "take" (8:16; see comment on 8:11). Adopting the same posture of servile obedience with which she first met David (v.23), Abigail then expresses her readiness to go so far as to "wash the feet of my master's servants" (v.41). Since foot-washing normally was a self-administered act (Ge 18:4; 19:2; 24:32; 43:24; Jdg 19:21; 2Sa 11:8; SS 5:3), Abigail demonstrates her joyful willingness to be "slave of all" (Mk 10:44; cf. Jn 13:5–17). As Rebekah, accompanied by her maids, had returned with Abraham's servant to become Isaac's wife (Ge 24:61–67), so also Abigail, "attended by her five maids" (v.42), hurries back with David's messengers to become his wife (though she is probably his half sister; see comment on v.3).

Like its literary parallel (vv.1b–3), v.43 calls attention to a geographical site ("Jezreel," a southern town of unknown location in the hill country of Judah near Maon and Carmel, v.2; cf. Jos 15:21, 48, 55–56). The NIV's translation "David had also married [pluperfect] Ahinoam," which implies that his marriage to Ahinoam occurred before he took Abigail as his wife, is doubtless correct, since Ahinoam is always mentioned before Abigail when the two names occur together (27:3; 30:5; 2Sa 2:2;

3:2–3 = 1Ch 3:1–4). The only other Ahinoam mentioned in the Bible is the wife of Saul (14:50), and it has therefore been plausibly suggested that, before David took Abigail to become his wife, he had already asserted his right to the throne of Israel by marrying Queen Ahinoam—a tactic perhaps hinted at in Nathan's speech to David (2Sa 12:8; cf. Levenson, 2:241–42; also, however, the caution of Gordon, "David's Rise," 44).

David's polygamy, at first blush inconsistent with the description of him as a man after God's own heart (13:14), finds a typical ancient rationalization in the Qumran Damascus Document: "David had not read the sealed book of the Law which was in the ark.... And the deeds of David rose up ... and God left them to him" (CD 5:3–6, as translated by G. Vermes, *The Complete Dead Sea Scrolls in English* [rev. ed.; Baltimore: Penguin, 2004], 132). Thus the Qumran Covenanters might argue that David cannot be blamed for his polygamy because he was ignorant of God's intentions (cf. similarly Lucetta Mowry, "The Dead Sea Scrolls and the Background for the Gospel of John," *BA* 17/4 [1954]: 97). The truth, of course, lies elsewhere (see comments on 1:2 and 2Sa 12:8).

44 Whether or not Ahinoam of Jezreel is to be identified with the wife of Saul, he "had given" (pluperfect, v.44; thus also Alter, *The Art of Biblical Narrative*, 121) his daughter Michal, David's wife, to another man. From a literary standpoint the narrator may be describing Saul's intention to treat David as being as good as dead, thus balancing the account of Samuel's death at the beginning of the chapter (v.1a; cf. Stek, 65B). Conversely, Alter, 121, may be correct in assuming that since Michal is after all "David's wife" (v.44; cf. 18:27), Saul's motive may be "to demonstrate, however clumsily, that David has no bond of kinship with the royal family and hence no claim to the throne." The name of Michal's second husband was Paltiel, from Gallim. Although its location is unknown, it may be the same Gallim of Isaiah 10:30 (near Gibeah and Anathoth, and thus a few miles north of Jerusalem), which appears in association with Laishah, an expanded form of the name of Paltiel's father, Laish.

Thus ch. 25, whose main burden is a move by David to kill a man (Nabal) and later to marry his wife (Abigail), comes to a close. 2 Samuel 11, the story of David, Uriah, and Bathsheba, is the only other chapter in the books of Samuel with the same theme. First Samuel 25 is thus "a proleptic glimpse, within the context of David's ascent, of his fall from grace" (Levenson, 2:237).

NOTES

1 The NIV's "Maon" is based on the LXX (cf. NIV note). The MT reads פָּארָן (*pāʾrān*, "Paran"), as do a few LXX manuscripts, but the Desert of Paran is much too far south to figure in this context (cf. also "Maon" in v.2).

4–13 Several key verbs in this section are echoed in the same order in its parallel passage (vv.39–42), usually with the same subject: וַיִּשְׁמַע (*wayyišmaʿ*, "[David] heard," vv.4, 39); וַיִּשְׁלַח (*wayyišlaḥ*, "[David] sent," vv.5, 39); וַיָּבֹאוּ (*wayyābōʾû* "[David's men/servants] arrived/went," vv.9, 40); וַיְדַבְּרוּ (*way^{e}dabb^{e}rû*, "[David's men/servants] spoke/said," vv.9, 40); and וַיֹּאמֶר/וַתֹּאמֶר (*wayyōʾmer/wattōʾmer*, "[Nabal/Abigail] answered/said," vv.10, 41) (cf. similarly Stek, 65B).

6 The NIV's "Say to him: 'Long life to you!'" renders וַאֲמַרְתֶּם כֹּה לֶחָי (*wa^{ʾa}martem kōh leḥāy*, lit., "And you shall say thus: 'To the life!'"). It is perhaps preferable to read לְאָחִי (*l^{e}ʾāḥî*) instead of *leḥāy*, assuming elision of **א** (ʾ; cf. בָּנוּ, *bānû*, for בָּאנוּ, *bāʾnû*, "we come," in v.8). The entire expression would then be translated (lit.): "And you shall say thus to my brother" (cf. Vul., *et dicetis sic fratribus meis*).

14 The verb עִיט, *ʿyṭ*, "hurl insults, scream, shriek"), although unique to this verse, is cognate with the more common עַיִט (*ʿayiṭ*, "bird of prey"). Its homonym, also found only in 1 Samuel, means "pounce" (14:32; 15:19).

22 Instead of the MT's "David's enemies," the NIV here reads "David" (with the LXX; cf. NIV note), doubtless correctly (cf. also Barthélemy, 2:199), since the common formula of self-imprecation is used and since "David's enemies" scarcely makes sense here (cf., however, K&D, 242). McCarter (*I Samuel*, 394 n. 22) suggests that since David's threat is in fact never carried out, "a scribe has changed David's words [in the MT] to protect him (or his descendants!) from the consequences of the oath."

The NIV's euphemistic "one male" translates מַשְׁתִּין בְּקִיר (*maštîn bᵉqîr*, "one who urinates against a wall"). Outside this chapter the expression is used only in 1 Kings 14:10; 16:11; 21:21; 2 Kings 9:8, each time (as here) in a context where the extermination of an entire family or household is in view.

33 The Hebrew translated "May you be blessed for your good judgment" reads literally, "May your good judgment be blessed and may you be blessed." For other examples of blessing invoked on inanimate objects, cf. Deuteronomy 28:5 ("basket, kneading trough"); Proverbs 5:18 ("fountain").

44 פַּלְטִי (*palṭî*, "Palti"; see NIV nnote), which means "My deliverance," is the hypocoristicon (shortened form) of the theophoric name פַּלְטִיאֵל (*palṭîʾēl*, lit., "God is my deliverance/deliverer," 2Sa 3:15).

14. Sparing Saul's Life Again (26:1–25)

OVERVIEW

The striking similarities between chs. 24 and 26, already noted briefly (see Overview to 24:1–22) and expanded below, have led some scholars to assume that the same incident is in view. But the differences are equally striking. Therefore it is best to conclude with Mauchline, 173, that "there is no difficulty in supposing that there may have been two occasions, in different circumstances, when David spared Saul's life" (cf. K&D, 247–49). The most fundamental difference between the two chapters is expressed by Miscall, 158: "Chapter 24 was a study in David's restraint when given an opportunity to harm or kill Saul. Chapter 26 is a demonstration of David's ability to put himself in the position to kill Saul" (cf. Miscall, 162).

The chapter narrates the final confrontation between Saul and David, and its speeches are animated by the mutual irreconcilability of the two men (cf. Gordon, "David's Rise," 59). Its literary structure is arranged chiastically:

- A Saul searches for David, who then responds (vv.1–5)
  - B David keeps his man Abishai from killing Saul (vv.6–12)
  - B' David rebukes Saul's man Abner for not protecting Saul (vv.13–16)
- A' Saul talks to David, who then responds (vv.17–25)

1The Ziphites went to Saul at Gibeah and said, "Is not David hiding on the hill of Hakilah, which faces Jeshimon?"

2So Saul went down to the Desert of Ziph, with his three thousand chosen men of Israel, to search there for David. 3Saul made his camp beside the road on the hill of Hakilah facing Jeshimon, but David stayed in the desert. When he saw that Saul had followed him there, 4he sent out scouts and learned that Saul had definitely arrived.

5Then David set out and went to the place where Saul had camped. He saw where Saul and Abner son of Ner, the commander of the army, had lain down. Saul was lying inside the camp, with the army encamped around him.

6David then asked Ahimelech the Hittite and Abishai son of Zeruiah, Joab's brother, "Who will go down into the camp with me to Saul?"

"I'll go with you," said Abishai.

7So David and Abishai went to the army by night, and there was Saul, lying asleep inside the camp with his spear stuck in the ground near his head. Abner and the soldiers were lying around him.

8Abishai said to David, "Today God has delivered your enemy into your hands. Now let me pin him to the ground with one thrust of my spear; I won't strike him twice."

9But David said to Abishai, "Don't destroy him! Who can lay a hand on the LORD's anointed and be guiltless? 10As surely as the LORD lives," he said, "the LORD himself will strike him; either his time will come and he will die, or he will go into battle and perish. 11But the LORD forbid that I should lay a hand on the LORD's anointed. Now get the spear and water jug that are near his head, and let's go."

12So David took the spear and water jug near Saul's head, and they left. No one saw or knew about it, nor did anyone wake up. They were all sleeping, because the LORD had put them into a deep sleep.

13Then David crossed over to the other side and stood on top of the hill some distance away; there was a wide space between them. 14He called out to the army and to Abner son of Ner, "Aren't you going to answer me, Abner?"

Abner replied, "Who are you who calls to the king?"

15David said, "You're a man, aren't you? And who is like you in Israel? Why didn't you guard your lord the king? Someone came to destroy your lord the king. 16What you have done is not good. As surely as the LORD lives, you and your men deserve to die, because you did not guard your master, the LORD's anointed. Look around you. Where are the king's spear and water jug that were near his head?"

17Saul recognized David's voice and said, "Is that your voice, David my son?"

David replied, "Yes it is, my lord the king." 18And he added, "Why is my lord pursuing his servant? What have I done, and what wrong am I guilty of? 19Now let my lord the king listen to his servant's words. If the LORD has incited you against me, then may he accept an

offering. If, however, men have done it, may they be cursed before the LORD! They have now
driven me from my share in the LORD's inheritance and have said, 'Go, serve other gods.'
[20]Now do not let my blood fall to the ground far from the presence of the LORD. The king of
Israel has come out to look for a flea—as one hunts a partridge in the mountains."
[21]Then Saul said, "I have sinned. Come back, David my son. Because you considered my
life precious today, I will not try to harm you again. Surely I have acted like a fool and have
erred greatly."
[22]"Here is the king's spear," David answered. "Let one of your young men come over and
get it. [23]The LORD rewards every man for his righteousness and faithfulness. The LORD delivered you into my hands today, but I would not lay a hand on the LORD's anointed. [24]As surely
as I valued your life today, so may the LORD value my life and deliver me from all trouble."
[25]Then Saul said to David, "May you be blessed, my son David; you will do great things
and surely triumph."

So David went on his way, and Saul returned home.

COMMENTARY

1–5 The common verb *bôʾ* ("come, enter"), a unifying feature of this section, appears in all but one of its verses ("went," v.1 [a different word is used for "went" in v.2]; "followed," v.3; "arrived," v.4; "went," v.5). It occurs elsewhere in the chapter only in vv.7, 10, and 15.

Verse 1 is an abbreviated and slightly modified echo of 23:19 (see comment there concerning Hakilah and Jeshimon; for the location of Ziph, see comment on 23:14). Since there were "strongholds" (23:19) at Hakilah, it was an especially secure place for a fugitive to hide and was therefore doubtless used often by David and his men. Substituting for the specific "south of" in 23:19, the more flexible Hebrew idiom *ʿal pᵉnê* (lit., "near the face of"; cf. "near," 24:2) describes the general location of Hakilah in v.1 ("which faces"; "facing," v.3).

Having heard the report of the Ziphites, Saul goes "down" (v.2) from the high ground at Gibeah (v.1) with his "three thousand chosen men" (see 24:2 and comments) to the "Desert of Ziph." There he continues to "search ... for" David, as he had done earlier (23:14, 25; cf. 24:2, "look for"). David, sensing that Saul has followed him to the desert (v.3), sends scouts to confirm that fact (v.4; for the NIV note "had come to Nacon," see comment and Notes on 23:23).

After his scouts have pinpointed the exact location of Saul's camp, David waits until Saul and his men have retired for the night ("had lain down ... was lying," v.5) and then goes to look over the situation for himself. Saul's apparent invulnerability is detailed: (1) Abner, his cousin (see comment on 14:50–51) and the commander of "his" (MT) army, is lying beside him; (2) he is safely inside the "camp" (lit., "wagon-wheel track," vv.5, 7; see comment on 17:20); and (3) the rest of his army is encamped "around him" (v.5; cf. v.7). Nevertheless Gunn (*The Fate of King Saul*, 102) observes that "despite these impossible odds," David goes down to the camp.

6–12 Not to be confused with Ahimelech the priest (cf. ch. 21), "Ahimelech the Hittite" (v.6), mentioned only here, was one among many mercenaries who formed a part of David's burgeoning army (for a later example, cf. Uriah the Hittite [2Sa 11:3]). Together with Joab's brother, Abishai son of Zeruiah, Ahimelech is asked whether he is willing to join David in going down to Saul's camp. Zeruiah, David's sister, was the mother of Abishai and Joab (1Ch 2:15–16), who both figure prominently in 2 Samuel, especially after David becomes king following Saul's death.

Portending his later importance, Abishai (rather than Ahimelech the Hittite) volunteers to go down with David into the camp of Saul. The two men arrive after dark ("by night," v.7), when everyone is asleep, and leave before anyone wakes up (v.12). Since Saul and his men are in a "deep sleep" brought on by the Lord (v.12; cf. Ge 2:21; 15:12), David and Abishai can move about undetected and speak to one another without being heard. Like a scepter symbolizing the royal presence, a "spear" (v.7)—"that spear which is a hall-mark of Saul" (Gunn, *The Fate of King Saul*, 102; cf. 18:10; 19:9–10; 20:33; 22:6)—is stuck in the ground near his head. Abishai, anxious to be rid of Saul once and for all, wants to kill him with "the spear" (v.8 MT; "my spear" in NIV is unwarranted and detracts from the ironic potential of Saul's being assassinated with his own spear, an understanding preferred by many commentators [e.g., Baldwin, Driver, Hertzberg, Klein, Smith]).

Abishai's sense of urgency (a characteristic of the chapter as a whole) is conveyed by his "today" and his "now" (lit., "And now" [v.8], for which cf. David's words in vv.11, 16 ["And now look around you," MT], 19–20; see comment and Notes on 24:20). His words to David are strikingly reminiscent of David's to Goliath in 17:46: "This day [= 'Today' in v.8] the LORD will hand you over to me" (lit., "will deliver you into my hand"; see comment at 17:46; cf. 24:18). In addition, Gunn (*The Fate of King Saul*, 102) points out the similarity between the beginning of Abishai's speech and that of David's men in 24:4—although a different Hebrew verb (lit., "give") is used there (as also here in v.23 ["delivered," NIV]). All these cases, however, attest to a common theme: It is the sovereign Lord who brings deliverance, whether potential or actual, to his king-elect.

Abishai, however, envisions himself as the instrument of divine deliverance: "Let me pin him to the ground" (v.8). In so speaking he echoes—probably unwittingly—the narrator's description of Saul's murderous intentions against David (see 18:10–11 and comment; 19:10; cf. 20:33). Not characterized by restraint, Abishai is always quick to act (cf. his later proposals to kill Shimei on the spot [2Sa 16:9–10; 19:21–23]; and further Miscall, 159). He is also confident about his strength, claiming that he will be able to execute Saul without having to "strike him twice" (v.8; cf. the similar description of the brute strength of Abishai's brother Joab against the hapless Amasa in 2Sa 20:10).

As in ch. 24, David does not allow any of his men to press their advantage against the unsuspecting Saul. Because he is the "LORD's anointed" (v.9; see 24:6 and comment), no one—including David himself—is to "lay a hand on" him (vv.9, 11, 23; cf. "lift my hand against" in 24:6, 10). Jonathan's earlier question—"Why then would you do wrong to an innocent [*nāqî*] man like David by killing him?" (19:5)—receives a faint echo in that of David: "Who can [kill Saul] ... and be guiltless [*weniqqâ*]?" David's command to Abishai—"Don't destroy him!" (v.9)—may be the origin of the familiar *ʾal-tašḥēt* ("Do Not Destroy") in the titles of the Davidic Psalms 57–59, two of which have David's fugitive days as their traditional background (Pss 57; 59; cf. the title of the Asaphite Ps 75).

In v.10 David intones the solemn oath—"As surely as the LORD lives"—that is often used where matters of life and death are at stake (cf. v.16; see comment on 14:39). Then, in a series of three clauses separated by *ʾô ... ʾô* (which the NIV translates as "either ... or," assuming that the first clause governs the next two in the sense that the second and third clauses describe ways in which the Lord might put Saul to death; so also Gordon, "David's Rise," 49; Klein; McCarter), David describes potential ways that Saul might die.

It is equally possible, however, that the phrase here means "or ... or" and that v.10 outlines three options rather than two (thus Driver, Keil, Mauchline, Smith; cf. also Gunn, *The Fate of King Saul*, 103; Miscall, 159; Polzin, *Samuel and the Deuteronomist*, 212): (1) The Lord will "strike" him (fatally, as he did his alter ego Nabal [25:38]), "or" (2) when his "time" comes (lit., "day"; for the expression cf. Jer 50:27, 31; Eze 21:25, 29; and esp. Davidic Ps 37:13) he will die (i.e., a natural death), "or" (3) he will "perish" (lit., "be swept away," as in 12:25; for the same verb cf. 27:1, "be destroyed") in battle. Under any one of these three understandings, of course, the Lord is the ultimate cause of Saul's death, not only because of his sovereign will, but also because vengeance belongs to him, as Abigail reminded David (25:26, 31) and as he himself acknowledged (25:32, 39). The last of David's suggestions turned out to be a presentiment of Saul's fate (cf. 31:1–6).

Reflecting the language of 24:6, David uses another oath (v.11) to underscore his refusal to kill Saul. In 24:4 (see comment) he had taken "a corner of Saul's robe," a symbol of royal authority. Here he orders Abishai to take Saul's spear (a symbol of his authority but also of death) and water jug (a symbol of life; cf. 1Ki 19:4–6). As Saul was unprotected and unsuspecting in 24:3, so also here—indeed, he and his men are unable to awaken because of divinely induced slumber. Thus David and Abishai, unseen and unheard, steal away into the night (v.12).

Although Abishai doubtless obeyed David's command to take the spear and the water jug (v.11), he did so on David's behalf—and so the text attributes the act to David (v.12). Polzin (*Samuel and the Deuteronomist*, 212) contrasts the scene in this chapter to a similar episode in 22:6–23: "Whereas David's taking of bread and the sword of Goliath caused Saul to murder the priests of Nob, here his taking of water and the spear of Saul embodies a refusal to murder."

13–16 In addition to the single-minded theme of this section (David's rebuke of Abner), another unifying feature is the subtle inclusio formed by the occurrence of the root *rʾš* in vv.13 ("top") and 16 ("head").

After leaving Saul's camp, David places a safe distance between himself and his enemy. The idiom *ʿāmad mērāḥōq* ("stand/stay at a distance"; "stood ... some distance away" [NIV], v.13) means to distance oneself for reasons of fear, awe, respect, caution, etc. (cf. Ex 20:18, 21; 2Ki 2:7; Isa 59:14; and the Davidic Ps 38:11, "stay far away"). On a later occasion Shimei would similarly leave a valley between himself and David in order to curse him and throw stones at him with impunity (2Sa 16:13).

David calls out to Saul's army in general and to its commander, Abner, in particular (and thus by association to "the king" himself; v.14). David's question implies that he had to call several times, perhaps because the men were sleeping (v.12). Abner finally replies, "Who are you who calls [*qārāʾtā*] to the king?" (v.14). McCarter (*I Samuel*, 408) contends that David's reply to Saul in v.20 echoes Abner's question in v.14: David stands on a "mountain" ("hill" [NIV], v.13) calling (v.14), and he later complains to Saul that he is comparing David to a "partridge" (*qōrēʾ*, lit., "caller") being hunted in "mountains" (v.20; cf. a similar wordplay in Jdg 15:18–19, where En Hakkore probably meant "Spring of the Partridge").

David's first two questions in v.15 seem to be scornful, although it is also possible that they were uttered with incredulous pity. His third question rebukes Abner for dereliction of duty, a failing in which he also implicates Abner's men (v.16): Not to protect the king, "the LORD's anointed," is inexcusable—indeed, is worthy of death (for the phrase "deserve to die" [lit., "are sons of death"], see comment on "must die" in 20:31; cf. similarly "those condemned to die/death" in Pss 79:11; 102:20; for the circumstances leading to Abner's death, see 2Sa 3:22–27). The "someone" (lit., "one of [David's] soldiers") who came to "destroy" (v.15) the king was of course Abishai (v.9), whom David had already kept from doing so.

Whereas Jethro's stern rebuke of his son-in-law, Moses, had been nonetheless helpful (Ex 18:17), David's echo of it is a condemnation of Abner ("What you [singular] have done is not good," v.16). Gunn (*The Fate of King Saul*, 156 n. 14) calls attention to the irony that follows: "As Yahweh *lives* you deserve to *die*."

17–25 The final section of ch. 26 consists of a conversation between Saul and David, with Saul beginning and ending the interchange but with David doing most of the talking: Saul (v.17a), David (vv.17b–20), Saul (v.21), David (vv.22–24), Saul (v.25). The king addresses the fugitive as *b^enî dāwid* ("my son David") in the first, middle, and last verses (vv.17, 21, 25), thus giving literary unity to the section. Saul's initial question—"Is that your voice, David my son?" (v.17)—is a verbatim echo of 24:16. But whereas there David had addressed Saul not only as "my lord the king" (24:8) but also as "my father" (see 24:11 and comment), here Saul is simply "my lord the king" (v.17; cf. v.19). Saul has already acknowledged/designated David as his legitimate successor (24:20), and therefore David no longer needs the rejected "king" as his "father" (Gunn, *The Fate of King Saul*, 104).

David, recognizing his continuing fugitive status, begins and ends his first response to Saul with the verb *rādap* ("pursuing," v.18; "hunts," v.20). His "what have I done?" (v.18) is later mirrored by Saul's "you will do" (v.25). As before, so also now he is firm in his conviction that he is innocent of any "wrong[doing]" (v.18; cf. 24:11). Just as "I am not guilty of wrongdoing" (24:11) is more literally translated as "there is no wrongdoing in my hand," so also here its echo—"what wrong am I guilty of?"—is more literally "what wrong is in my hand?" The latter expression, in turn, is mirrored in v.23, where David tells Saul that the Lord delivered him "into my hands" (cf. "in my hand" in v.18). By deciding again not to "lay a hand" on the Lord's anointed (v.23), David refuses to make his guiltless hands guilty of wrongdoing.

In vv.19–20a David sets forth two possible sources of Saul's dogged pursuit of him. First, God may have "incited" Saul (as he later "incited" David to take a census [2Sa 24:1]) against him (v.19). In that case David hopes to appease God by bringing him an offering that he may "accept" (lit., "smell"; cf. Ge 8:20–21). Gunn (*The Fate of King Saul*, 156 n. 15) points out Saul's earlier perception that his son Jonathan had "incited" David (22:8, using a different Heb. verb) to lie in wait for Saul. Thus David and Saul interpret their mutually hostile relationship quite differently.

Second, men may be at fault. In that case David pronounces a solemn oath against them: "May they be cursed before the LORD!" (cf. Jos 6:26). David's sense of urgency in v.19 is underscored by his use of "now" (lit., "today," as in vv.21, 23–24): He is concerned that his fugitive status will prevent his participation in "the LORD's inheritance" (i.e., the land of Israel; cf. 2Sa 14:16; 20:19; 21:3). In ancient times it was commonly believed that to be driven from one's homeland was tantamount to leaving one's god(s) and being forced to "serve other gods," the gods of the alien territory of exile (cf. Youngblood, *The Book of Genesis*, 220; for a more general treatment, see Daniel I. Block, *The Gods of the Nations: Studies in Ancient Near Eastern National Theology* [Jackson, Miss.: Evangelical Theological Society, 1988]). David thus prays that Saul will not cause him to die "far from the presence of the LORD" (v.20)—in this case, in Philistia (see ch. 27). Gunn (*The Fate of King Saul*, 104) observes that Saul's pursuit of David is forcing him "to break the first and greatest commandment."

In a reprise of 24:14, David concludes his statement to Saul by stressing the incongruity of Saul's enterprise (v.20b): The most powerful man in the land ("the king of Israel") has taken it upon himself to "come out" (cf. also 23:15) to look for something trivial, something unworthy of his time and energy—a single "flea." In 24:14 the "flea" reference is in the form of a question and thus serves as a veiled threat. Here, however, the context is quite different: Looking for a single flea is compared to hunting a single "partridge" (lit., "caller"; see comment on v.14) in the mountains, something no one in his right mind would take the time or make the effort to do. Since the sand partridge (*Ammoperdix heyi*) is the only partridge found in the desert areas west of the Dead Sea, David's comparison of it to himself is particularly apt: "This partridge is a great runner and speeds along the ground when it is chased, until it becomes exhausted and can be knocked down by the hunter's stick" (*Fauna and Flora of the Bible*, 64).

Saul responds to David (v.21) with words that he has felt a need to utter before: "I have sinned" (cf. 15:24; contrast David's description of his own conduct in 24:11). Recognizing that David has "considered" Saul's "life precious" (for the idiom cf. 2Ki 1:13–14, "have respect for ... life"; also Ps 72:14, "precious is their blood in his sight"), Saul promises not to harm him. Apparently Saul's repentance is sincere this time. He admits that he has erred "greatly" (*harbēh mᵉʾōd*, "very greatly") and that—like his alter ego Nabal (see comment on 25:25)—he has "acted like a fool" (cf. Samuel's rebuke of Saul in 13:13). David's later confession to the Lord in 2 Samuel 24:10 (= 1Ch 21:8) is ironically and sadly reminiscent of Saul's words in v.21.

David's retort to Saul offers to return his spear (v.22), the symbol of death, but not the water jug, the symbol of life. Miscall, 161, suggests that keeping the jug "could be a sign of David's control" over the situation. The argument of David to the effect that God "rewards" (v.23; cf. similarly 2Sa 16:12) all who are characterized by "righteousness and faithfulness" (for the pairing of *ṣᵉdāqâ* and *ʾᵉmûnâ*, cf. Pr 12:17 ["truthful ... honest"]; Isa 59:4 ["justice ... integrity"]; Hab 2:4) is perhaps as much a condemnation of Saul's conduct as it is a commendation of David's own. As before (24:10; see comment on 22:17; cf. further 31:4 = 1Ch 10:4), so also now David refuses to lay a hand on Saul, the Lord's anointed. It is the Lord who has "delivered" Saul into David's hands (v.23), and as recompense for his respect for Saul's life he prays that the Lord will "deliver" him (v.24; different Heb. verbs) from "all trouble."

Although David has valued Saul's life, he does not ask Saul to reciprocate. Instead, he places in God's hand whatever worth his life might have (cf. similarly Gunn, *The Fate of King Saul*, 105). Likewise, deliverance from "all trouble" (cf. 2Sa 4:9 for David's confident assertion about God's past deliverance in every negative circumstance) will come from God, not from Saul—who in fact has been the major cause of "trouble" for David in any case.

Strangely enough, Saul's final words to David (v.25) are good wishes for his greatness and triumph. Three times Saul has called David his "son" (vv.17, 21, 25), and Saul now apparently knows that David will be his successor on Israel's throne as well (cf. similarly 24:19–20). His blessing on David virtually assures as much. David had prayed that any potential enemies of his might be "cursed" (v.19); Saul now leaves David after praying that he might be "blessed" (v.25; cf. David's words to Abigail in 25:33). Since there is now nothing more to be said, David and Saul part (cf. 24:22), never to see each other again.

NOTES

6 Two Hebrew bullae (clay seal impressions) from the late seventh or early sixth century BC display the name יהואב (*yhwʾb*, "Jehoab"), which is "the first known instance of the full form of the biblical name Joab" (Avigad, 43).

That Abishai, Joab, and Asahel (2Sa 2:18) are consistently referred to as sons of their mother Zeruiah rather than as sons of their father is unusual. It is perhaps best explained in the light of the reference to the tomb of Asahel's father in 2 Samuel 2:32, which suggests that he had already died "while his sons were children" (F. H. Cryer, "David's Rise to Power and the Death of Abner: An Analysis of 1 Samuel xxvi 14–16 and Its Redactional-Critical Implications," *VT* 35/4 [1985]: 388 n. 9).

8 The MT's בחנית ובארץ (*bḥnyt wbʾrṣ*, lit., "with the spear and into the ground") is difficult at best. Perhaps the words should be divided differently: *bḥnytw bʾrṣ* ("with his spear into the ground"; see comment on v.8).

12 Two MT manuscripts insert אֲשֶׁר (*ʾašer*, "that [are/were]") before מראשתי (*mrʾšty*, "near [Saul's] head"), in conformity with the same phrase in vv.11, 16. The *Qere* in v.12, however, vocalizes *mē-* ("from"; cf. LXX, ἀπό, *apo*), instead of as the nominal prefix *mᵉ-* (as in vv.11, 16). Keil is therefore probably correct in asserting that the *m-* does double duty in v.12 (*mē-* standing for *mim[ᵉ]-* [K&D, 250]; cf. similarly Watson, 532).

15 The idiom שָׁמַר אֶל־ (*šāmar ʾel-*, "watch over"; "guard," NIV; cf. 2Sa 11:16, "had ... under siege") has been thus interpreted in the Lachish ostraca and used to argue in favor of the view that the Lachish ostraca were draft letters written from, rather than to, Lachish (for details cf. Oded Borowski, "Yadin Presents New Interpretation of the Famous Lachish Letters," *BAR* 10/2 [1984]: 77).

19 David's way of addressing Saul—"Now let my lord the king listen to his servant's words"—finds an exact parallel in a seventh-century BC ostracon found at Mesad Hashavyahu, a fortress near Yavneh Yam ten miles south of Tel Aviv. Like David, the supplicant begins his plea to redress a wrong as follows: "Let my lord the governor listen to his servant's word" (cf. Alan R. Millard, "The Question of Israelite Literacy," *BRev* 3/3 [1987]: 27).

15. Achish the Philistine (27:1–28:2)

OVERVIEW

Technically speaking, the story of the rise of David continues beyond Saul's death (ch. 31) and through the accounts of David's elimination of other rivals to his divinely granted rule over Israel (2Sa 1–5). At the same time, however, there is a distinct literary break at 28:3, which begins the narrative that describes Saul's final hours. The vignette depicting David's settling in Philistia (27:1–28:2), therefore, is a convenient point to bring to an end—in a more restricted sense and in conformity with our overall outline—the story of David's rise (16:1–28:2), which, as we have seen, interlaces and oscillates with the story of Saul's decline.

God's name is not mentioned either in ch. 31 or 27:1–28:2, perhaps suggesting that Saul entered his final battle against the Philistines without God's help (cf., ominously, 28:6) and that David did not consult God (maybe believing that he could not do so because he was no longer in Israel, his homeland; see comment on 26:19–20) when he decided to escape to Philistine territory.

1But David thought to himself, "One of these days I will be destroyed by the hand of Saul. The best thing I can do is to escape to the land of the Philistines. Then Saul will give up searching for me anywhere in Israel, and I will slip out of his hand."

2So David and the six hundred men with him left and went over to Achish son of Maoch king of Gath. 3David and his men settled in Gath with Achish. Each man had his family with him, and David had his two wives: Ahinoam of Jezreel and Abigail of Carmel, the widow of Nabal. 4When Saul was told that David had fled to Gath, he no longer searched for him.

5Then David said to Achish, "If I have found favor in your eyes, let a place be assigned to me in one of the country towns, that I may live there. Why should your servant live in the royal city with you?"

6So on that day Achish gave him Ziklag, and it has belonged to the kings of Judah ever since. 7David lived in Philistine territory a year and four months.

8Now David and his men went up and raided the Geshurites, the Girzites and the Amalekites. (From ancient times these peoples had lived in the land extending to Shur and Egypt.) 9Whenever David attacked an area, he did not leave a man or woman alive, but took sheep and cattle, donkeys and camels, and clothes. Then he returned to Achish.

10When Achish asked, "Where did you go raiding today?" David would say, "Against the Negev of Judah" or "Against the Negev of Jerahmeel" or "Against the Negev of the Kenites." 11He did not leave a man or woman alive to be brought to Gath, for he thought, "They might inform on us and say, 'This is what David did.'" And such was his practice as long as he lived in Philistine territory. 12Achish trusted David and said to himself, "He has become so odious to his people, the Israelites, that he will be my servant forever."

28:1In those days the Philistines gathered their forces to fight against Israel. Achish said to David, "You must understand that you and your men will accompany me in the army."

2David said, "Then you will see for yourself what your servant can do."

Achish replied, "Very well, I will make you my bodyguard for life."

COMMENTARY

27:1–12 Chapter 27 occupies the lion's share of the account of David's relationship to Achish of Gath (27:1–28:2). Long a fugitive, David decides to flee to Philistia where he will be free of Saul's relentless pursuit once and for all. The chapter thus exudes permanence and stability and is characterized by such words as *yāšab* ("live," vv.3 ["settled"], 5 [2x], 7, 8, 11), *yôm* ("day," vv.1, 6, 6 ["since"], 7 [untrans. in NIV], 7 ["year"], 10 ["today"], 11 ["as long as"]), and *ʿôlām* ("ancient times," v.8; "forever," v.12). As Polzin (*Samuel and the Deuteronomist*, 216) observes, the chapter "ends with the narrator revealing the inner thoughts of Achish (as the inner thoughts of David were divulged at the beginning)": David "thought to himself" (lit., "said to/in his heart," v.1; cf. Ge 8:21), Achish "said to himself" (lit., "saying," the context implying "to himself," v.12).

David knows that it is only a matter of time before he will be "destroyed" (lit., "swept away"; cf. 12:25; 26:10 ["perish"]) by Saul (v.1). Polzin (*Samuel and the Deuteronomist*, 269 n. 1) notes correctly that "the use of *sapah* ['sweep away'] in 1 Samuel indicates a close connection between the fates of king and people." In v.1 David, in whom—by Saul's own testimony—the fate of the people of Israel resides (24:20), is in danger of being swept away by the king himself. David thus comes to the conclusion that "the best thing I can do is" (lit., "there is nothing better for me than"; for the idiom, cf. Ecc 3:12; 8:15) to "escape" (emphatic; the same verb, echoed later in the verse, is there translated "slip out") to Philistia. He feels that if he does so, Saul will "give up" his pursuit (lit., "despair in, find hopeless"; cf. Job 6:26; Isa 57:10; Jer 2:25 ["It's no use"]; 18:12).

David's confidence that he will then be able to "slip out of/escape from his hand" (cf. 2Ch 16:7; Jer 32:4; 34:3; 38:18, 23; Da 11:41, in each of which passages the idiom connotes deliverance from mortal danger) is confirmed when Saul stops "searching" for him (vv.1, 4), as he had relentlessly done while David was still in Israelite territory (23:14, 25; 24:2; 26:2, 20). "Thus a cycle is complete: David had come into Saul's life in large part through the Philistines (chapter 17), and now he moves out of Saul's life through the agency of the Philistines. The difference is that in the first place he had defeated them whereas now he joins them" (Gunn, *The Fate of King Saul*, 106).

So David and his "six hundred men" (v.2; for the significance of the number, see comment on 13:15; 23:13) seek refuge in Philistia with Achish son of Maoch king of Gath, to whom David had earlier fled for help (see 21:10 and comment for details concerning the names of Achish and his father). Since Gath is some thirty rugged miles northwest of the Desert of Ziph, where David had been hiding earlier (26:1–2), the task of moving himself, his two wives Ahinoam and Abigail (see comment on 25:3, 43), and his men and their families (v.3) must have involved considerable hardship.

David's settlement in Gath will doubtless be temporary, however, since David questions the advisability of living with a man who had earlier given him reason to fear (21:11–12). David therefore hopes that if he has "found favor" in the "eyes" of Achish (v.5)—implying that Achish can now trust him (see comment on 20:29)—the Philistine ruler will not insist that he live in the "royal city" (v.5), a term stressing the size, importance, and dominance of the city so described (cf. similarly 2Sa 12:26 ["royal citadel"]; Jos 10:2; *āl šarrūti* is the Akkadian equivalent [*CAD*, 1.1.382], *āl šarri* in Amarna Akkadian [*CAD*, 1.1.386; J. A. Knudtzon, *Die el-Amarna-Tafeln* (Leipzig: Hinrichs, 1915), 2:1368]). David is content to be assigned a country town;

so Achish gives him Ziklag (v.6), which originally had been part of the tribal patrimony of Simeon "within the territory of Judah" (cf. Jos 19:1, 5; cf. Jos 15:21, 31).

The modern site of ancient Ziklag is probably Tell esh-Shariah, about twenty miles east-southeast of Gaza (cf. esp. Anson F. Rainey, *ISBE*, 4:1196), although Tell Halif (in Judah, ten miles east of Tell esh-Shariah) has also been suggested (J. Simons, *The Geographical and Topographical Texts of the Old Testament* [Leiden: Brill, 1959], 145; [no author], "Digging in '89," *BAR* 15/1 [1989]: 28). Volkmar Fritz's proposal to identify Ziklag with Tell es-Seba^{c}, four miles east of the modern city of Beersheba ("Where Is David's Ziklag?" *BAR* 19/3 [1993]: 58–61), has been hotly disputed by Anson Rainey ("Disputes Ziklag Identification," *BAR* 19/6 [1993]: 80). In any event, Achish doubtless places David in Ziklag to protect Philistia against marauders from the south. David's settlement there anticipates the subsequent ownership of Ziklag by the "kings of Judah" (v.6), of whom he would become the ideal dynastic ancestor (2Sa 2:4). Altogether David lives in Philistine-controlled territory (vv.6, 11) for "a year" (lit., "days," translated "annual" in 1:21; 2:19; 20:6) "and four months" (v.7).

While vv.1–7 describe David's settlement in Philistia, vv.8–12 outline his raiding operations, in connection with which—for the second time—he succeeds in deceiving Achish (cf. 21:12–15). Since the Philistines themselves were often raiders (23:27), it is not surprising that a Philistine vassal or ally like David would also engage in raiding campaigns (vv.8, 10; the Heb. verb here and in 23:27 means "to strip off"). Among those whom David and his men raided were the Geshurites (a southern people mentioned elsewhere only in Jos 13:2 and not to be confused with the northern Geshurites, for which see comment on 2Sa 3:3), the Girzites (Kethiv, mentioned only here and otherwise unknown; the Qere's "Gizrites" would be the inhabitants of Gezer, which is, however, too far north to fit the present context), and the Amalekites (themselves characterized as raiders in 30:1, 14 [cf. 14:48]; see also comment on 15:7 for their connection with Shur).

All these peoples had lived in southern Canaan and northern Sinai "from ancient times" (v.8, perhaps a reference to the early confrontation between Amalek and Israel reported in Ex 17:8–16; for a close parallel to this nuance of *mē^{c}ôlām* see Jer 28:8 ["from early times"], making it unnecessary to read a posited *mṭlm*, "from Tela[i]m" [cf. 15:4], with the LXX, Garsiel, Driver, Gordon, McCarter, Klein, et al. [contrast K&D, RSV]). Saul had conducted a fateful campaign against the Amalekites (ch. 15), and David would soon fight them again (ch. 30).

David's "practice" (v.11) whenever he attacked an area was not to "leave a man or woman alive" (vv.9, 11). Unlike the situation in 15:3, however (see comment there), where total annihilation of the population was for religious purposes, David here kills everyone so that no survivors are left to report to Achish what has really happened (v.11). In addition to garments, he "took" as plunder (v.9; cf. the use of the verb in that sense also in 30:16, 18–20; Ge 14:11 ["seized"]; 1Ki 14:26) only animals, a procedure to be expected as a matter of course from kings (8:16), but not from prophets (see comment on 12:3).

Although David was raiding Geshurites, Girzites, and Amalekites (v.8), he told Achish that he was raiding various subdistricts of the Negev (v.10) that belonged to or were controlled by Judah (30:26–29): the "Negev of Judah" (in southern Judah near Beersheba; Joab would later complete David's census there [cf. 2Sa 24:7]), the "Negev of Jerahmeel" (probably in southern Judah in the eastern Negev basin), the "Negev of the Kenites" (see comment on 15:6; probably in the northeastern Negev basin near Arad; cf. Rasmussen, 246, and the map on 114). Far enough away from Gath so that Achish would be ignorant of his movements, David can lie to him with impunity—especially by leaving no survivors who might be able to contradict him. David thus has the best of both worlds. He implies to Achish that Judahite hostility toward David is increasing, and at the same time he gains the appreciation and loyalty of Judah toward himself by raiding their desert neighbors.

To his detriment, Achish trusts David (v.12) and is therefore deceived by his report. He is confident that David the Israelite has become "odious" to his own people (see comment on "stench" in 13:4; cf. 2Sa 10:6; 16:21) and will thus be forced to be a "servant" of Achish the Philistine. But "like Nabal, Achish seriously underestimates David by regarding him as a servant or slave" (Miscall, 165; cf. Gunn, *The Fate of King Saul*, 107). Another Philistine from Gath had likewise prematurely predicted much the same fate for David's fellow Israelites (17:9). The term *ʿôlām* ("forever"; GK 6409) means "for life" in this context (as in Ex 21:6; Lev 25:46; Dt 15:17) and is thus a virtual synonym of *kol-hayyāmîm* (lit., "all the days") in 28:2.

28:1–2 The brief paragraph that concludes this account of David's relationship with Achish is framed by "in those days" (v.1) and "all the days" (v.2; "for life," NIV).

Still laboring under the assumption that David is his faithful vassal, Achish forcefully reminds him ("must" is emphatic) that he and his men are expected to "accompany" (lit., "go/march out with," v.1) the Philistines to fight against Israel. David appears to acquiesce by responding that Achish will then "see" (echoing Achish's "understand," v.1; identical Heb. verb) for himself what David is capable of doing (v.2). In referring to himself as Achish's "servant," David reflects the thoughts of Achish concerning him (27:12)—although David intends nothing more than a polite expression equivalent to the personal pronoun "I" (cf. BDB, 714).

Continuing to misjudge David, Achish announces his desire to make him "my bodyguard" (lit., "guard/watcher for my head"). As Miscall, 167, observes, this is the same David who had "once cut off the head of another Philistine from Gath and whom the Philistine generals fear will reconcile himself to Saul 'with the heads of the men here' (1 Sam 29:4)." Achish, however, fails to "see" (v.2) that David and his men constitute a dangerous fifth column inside Philistine territory.

NOTES

8 "These peoples had lived" translates הֵנָּה יֹשְׁבוֹת (*hēnnâ yōšᵉbôt*). Although the feminine plural appears to be unprecedented, feminine singular forms are not unusual with reference to countries or populations of a country (cf. Driver's comment, 143, on ותערך, *wtʿrk*, "were drawing up," in 17:21).

10 Although K&D attempts to make sense of the MT's אַל (*ʾal*, "not") by construing it like the Greek μή (*mē*) in an interrogative sense ("You have not gone raiding today, have you?"), it is perhaps better to read אָן (*ʾān*, "Where?"; cf., however, Note on 10:14), with one or two manuscripts and the NIV (cf. BDB, 39). 4QSamuel[a] at this point unfortunately breaks off immediately after its reading על (*ʿl*, "Against" [?]) and therefore cannot be used to support the LXX's ἐπὶ τίνα (*epi tina*, "Against whom?").

B. The End of the Reign of Saul (28:3–31:13)

OVERVIEW

First Samuel concludes decisively with an account of the end of King Saul's reign, contrasting Saul with David for the last time. The four-chapter narrative is arranged chiastically:

A Saul's final night (28:3–25)
  B David's dismissal by the Philistines (29:1–11)
  B' David's destruction of the Amalekites (30:1–31)
A' Saul's final day (31:1–13)

The section as a whole is framed by notices of the burials of Samuel (28:3) and Saul (31:13; see also comment on 25:1a).

1. Saul and the Medium at Endor (28:3–25)

OVERVIEW

The strange story of the meeting of Saul with Endor's "witch" (so-called traditionally; better "necromancer" or "medium" [NIV]), resulting in the announcement that Saul would die at the hands of the Philistines (v.19), is preceded (27:1–28:2) and followed (29:1–11) by accounts of David's friendly relationships with the Philistines through Achish king of Gath. After an introductory verse that sets the stage for what follows (v.3), the chapter continues with a brief description of the problem Saul faces (vv.4–6), narrations of his conversations with the medium (vv.7–14) and with Samuel (vv.15–19), and the story of his final meal (vv.20–25).

3Now Samuel was dead, and all Israel had mourned for him and buried him in his own town of Ramah. Saul had expelled the mediums and spiritists from the land.

4The Philistines assembled and came and set up camp at Shunem, while Saul gathered all the Israelites and set up camp at Gilboa.
5When Saul saw the Philistine army, he was afraid; terror filled his heart.
6He inquired of the LORD, but the LORD did not answer him by dreams or Urim or prophets.
7Saul then said to his attendants, "Find me a woman who is a medium, so I may go and inquire of her."

"There is one in Endor," they said.

8So Saul disguised himself, putting on other clothes, and at night he and two men went to the woman. "Consult a spirit for me," he said, "and bring up for me the one I name."

9But the woman said to him, "Surely you know what Saul has done. He has cut off the mediums and spiritists from the land. Why have you set a trap for my life to bring about my death?"

10Saul swore to her by the LORD, "As surely as the LORD lives, you will not be punished for this."

11Then the woman asked, "Whom shall I bring up for you?"

"Bring up Samuel," he said.

12When the woman saw Samuel, she cried out at the top of her voice and said to Saul, "Why have you deceived me? You are Saul!"

13The king said to her, "Don't be afraid. What do you see?"

The woman said, "I see a spirit coming up out of the ground."

14"What does he look like?" he asked.

"An old man wearing a robe is coming up," she said.

Then Saul knew it was Samuel, and he bowed down and prostrated himself with his face to the ground.

15Samuel said to Saul, "Why have you disturbed me by bringing me up?"

"I am in great distress," Saul said. "The Philistines are fighting against me, and God has turned away from me. He no longer answers me, either by prophets or by dreams. So I have called on you to tell me what to do."

16Samuel said, "Why do you consult me, now that the LORD has turned away from you and become your enemy? 17The LORD has done what he predicted through me. The LORD has torn the kingdom out of your hands and given it to one of your neighbors — to David. 18Because you did not obey the LORD or carry out his fierce wrath against the Amalekites, the LORD has done this to you today. 19The LORD will hand over both Israel and you to the Philistines, and tomorrow you and your sons will be with me. The LORD will also hand over the army of Israel to the Philistines."

20Immediately Saul fell full length on the ground, filled with fear because of Samuel's words. His strength was gone, for he had eaten nothing all that day and night.

21When the woman came to Saul and saw that he was greatly shaken, she said, "Look, your maidservant has obeyed you. I took my life in my hands and did what you told me to do. 22Now please listen to your servant and let me give you some food so you may eat and have the strength to go on your way."

23He refused and said, "I will not eat."

But his men joined the woman in urging him, and he listened to them. He got up from the ground and sat on the couch.

24The woman had a fattened calf at the house, which she butchered at once. She took some flour, kneaded it and baked bread without yeast. 25Then she set it before Saul and his men, and they ate. That same night they got up and left.

COMMENTARY

3 Since v.3a reprises 25:1a (see comment there), the pluperfect "had mourned" is appropriate. The reminder that Samuel had died is coupled with the observation that Saul (perhaps in obedience to the law of Moses, such as Lev 19:31; 20:6–7; Dt 18:11) had expelled the mediums and spiritists from Israel; both events figure prominently in the rest of the chapter. Although the basic meaning of *ʾôb* was probably "spirit" (v.8; cf. the rendering "ghost" in Isa 29:4), by metonymy it came to mean "medium" (2Ki 21:6 [= 2Ch 33:6]; 23:24; 1Ch 10:13; Isa 19:3) in the technical sense of one who consulted "the dead on behalf of the living" (Isa 8:19). Harry A. Hoffner makes the intriguing suggestion that *ʾôb* originally meant "sacrificial pit," which was personified as *^{D}A-a-bi*, the god of the netherworld (*TDOT*, 1:131–32; cf. Clyde E. Billlington, "The Ghost Pits of Saul and Odysseus," *Artifax* 23/3 [2008]: 17–18). The term *yiddeʿōnî* ("spiritist", lit., "one who has [occult?] knowledge") is always found in association with *ʾôb(ôt)* ("medium[s]").

4–6 "The wording of this introduction (28:4f.) is notable, for it is strongly reminiscent of two other fateful confrontations between Saul and the Philistines, the first at Michmash/Gilgal (13:5f.), the second at Socoh/Elah (17:1f., 11)" (Gunn, *The Fate of King Saul*, 108). In addition, the first two words of the Hebrew consonantal text of v.4—*wyqbṣw plštym* ("the Philistines assembled/gathered")—echo v.1 and remind us yet again of the ever-present Philistine threat throughout Saul's reign.

Skillfully and tersely, v.4 describes the opposing forces: The Philistines "assembled" (*wyqbṣw*) and "set up camp" at Shunem, while Saul "gathered" (*wyqbṣ*) his forces and "set up camp" (the same Heb. root translated "army" in v.5) at Gilboa. Located in the northern tribal territory of Issachar (Jos 19:17–18), Shunem (modern Solem, at the southern foot of Mount Moreh, nine miles east-northeast of Megiddo) is mentioned in the fifteenth-century BC roster of Canaanite towns drawn up by Thutmose III, in the fourteenth-century Amarna letters, and in the tenth-century topographical list of Sheshonk. It was the hometown of Abishag, a young virgin who attended King David (1Ki 1:3), and of a well-to-do woman who assisted the prophet Elisha (2Ki 4:8, 12). Gilboa, a mountain (modern Jebel Fuquah) ten miles south-southeast of Shunem, is referred to elsewhere in the OT only as the site of Saul's death (31:1, 8 = 1Ch 10:1, 8; 2Sa 1:6, 21; 21:12).

When Saul "saw" the Philistines, he became "afraid" (v.5; both verbs translate the Hebrew consonants *wyrʾ* and thus constitute a wordplay)—not the first time that the appearance or approach of the Philistines had struck fear in Israelite hearts (17:11, 24; 23:3). Given the situation, it is understandable that Saul "inquired of" the Lord (v.6; *wayyišʾal šāʾûl*, lit., "and Saul asked," yet another pun on Saul's name). Although 1 Chronicles 10:14 states that Saul "did not inquire" of the Lord, a different verb (*drš*) is used. In addition, "it may be correctly remarked that Saul's attempts at inquiry were of so unworthy a nature that it would be an abuse of language to speak of him as really 'inquiring of Jehovah'" (Haley, 359–60; cf. further K&D, 173).

For all Saul's efforts—whether desperate, sincere, or otherwise—to receive an "answer" (v.6; cf. v.15) from the Lord, none came (a disquieting echo of 14:37; see comment). The normal modes of divine communication were silent: "dreams" (cf. v.15), "Urim" (the sacred lots stored in the priestly ephod; cf. comment on 23:6, 9; cf. also NIV note on 14:41 and comment on that verse), and "prophets" (cf. v.15).

7–14 Under such circumstances it is not surprising that Saul, even if out of sheer desperation, would resort to a forbidden source of information—indeed, to a "medium" (v.7), a necromancer of the sort that he himself had earlier expelled from the land (v.3). Fearful of Philistine strength, he wanted to know how to proceed (v.15) and thus was willing to go to any lengths to find out what to do.

The fascinating story of the medium at Endor was long remembered in ancient Israel (cf. its brief summary in 1Ch 10:13–14) and has been the subject of intense debate since the earliest times: "Was the woman actually able to raise up the righteous dead (that is, Satan having power over the saints) or was her craft one of mere delusion? Was Samuel resuscitated or was this a demon? Did Samuel appear due to the necromancer's craft or did God intervene and raise Samuel himself?" (Lewis, 115 n. 39). Individual proponents of one or more of these views, as well as of others of a similar nature, are not far to seek (e.g., Hoffner, *TDOT*, 1:133–34; Haley, 194–95; Archer, 180–81; *Seventh-day Adventists Believe* ... [Washington, D.C.: General Conference of Seventh-day Adventists, 1988], 355).

Early church fathers, fearful of affirming that the prophet Samuel was a shade in Sheol, that a medium was an appropriate intermediary between the divine and human worlds, and that necromancy is efficacious, "proceeded to undermine the literal text with one of two arguments: either sorcery is just demonic deceit, and what appeared was not really Samuel, but a demon in his guise; or, Samuel was not really in Hades but had been sent by God to announce Saul's fate" (Patricia Cox, "Origen and the Witch of Endor: Toward an Iconoclastic Typology," *AThR* 61/2 [1984]: 139).

As for Origen, in his typical fashion he was not bothered by what appears to be the plain, literal meaning of the text (that Samuel was really in the netherworld and that the medium really had the power to bring him up). Without denying that literal meaning, by tortuous allegorizing Origen's fertile mind came to the conclusion that the story is also typological of the mediating work of Christ, who voluntarily descended into hell, prophesied to souls in the depths, is a mediatorial figure who breaks the barrier between the netherworld and this world, and has the power to bring back the inhabitants of Hades and usher them through the flaming sword that guards the way to the tree of life (Cox, "Origen and the Witch of Endor," 140–44).

My own sympathies lie with the judgment of Gregory of Nazianzus, who was content to leave the text in its ambiguity: "Samuel was raised, *or so it seems* by the woman having a familiar spirit" (*Invective against Julian* 1.54; emphasis mine). An element of mystery suffuses this chapter, and it would be presumptuous to claim to have successfully plumbed its depths.

Having received no answer from the Lord (v.6), Saul sent his "attendants" (lit., "servants," v.7; see comment on 16:15–16) for help from another quarter. "Find" a medium (lit., "seek"; the verb has been used frequently of Saul's search for David, and now Saul uses it for the last time [cf. Gunn, *The Fate of King Saul*, 108]), the king says, thus violating his own earlier intention (v.3). Endor is probably not related to Dor on the Mediterranean coast but is rather to be sought inland from Taanach and Megiddo (Jos 17:11; Ps 83:9–10). It is almost certainly to be identified with modern Khirbet Safsafeh, located four miles northeast of Shunem and thus dangerously close to where the Philistines were encamped (v.4).

On the basis of Ugaritic parallels, Othniel Margalith ("Dor and En-Dor," *ZAW* 97/1 [1985]: 111) suggests that Endor means "Spring of the oracular sanctuary," a fitting name in light of the medium's reference to Samuel's apparition as a "god" (see comment on v.13). That Saul should prefer a "woman" as a medium (v.7) is not surprising (cf. Na 3:4, where the pagan city of Nineveh is compared to a "mistress of sorceries" enslaving nations "by her witchcraft"; cf. also Akkad. *šāʾiltu*, "she who asks questions [of the gods]"; see esp. A. Leo Oppenheim, "The Interpretation of Dreams in the Ancient Near East," *Transactions of the American Philosophical Society* 46/3 [1956]: 221). The narrator, perhaps deliberately, uses a different Hebrew word for "inquire of" in v.7 from the one he uses in v.6, where the Lord is the object.

Although Saul was obviously convinced that if he "disguised himself" (v.8) he would be able to conceal his identity, he was wrong (v.12)—and in any event the information he received through (or in spite of) the medium's efforts was hardly what he wanted to hear (vv.17–20). Centuries later King Ahab of Israel and King Josiah of Judah would reap similarly negative benefits from disguising themselves in order to gain the anonymity they hoped would protect them (1Ki 22:30, 34–35 = 2Ch 18:29, 33–34; 2Ch 35:22–24).

Since the netherworld is a place of darkness (Job 10:21–22; 17:13; Pss 88:12; 143:3; for details cf. Ronald F. Youngblood, "Qoheleth's 'Dark House' [Eccl 12:5]," *JETS* 29/4 [1986]: 397–410), "night" (v.8) provided the proper setting for communicating with one of its denizens (cf. Lewis, 114). In addition, necromancers may well have preferred to do their work at night (cf. Hoffner, *TDOT*, 1:133), and Saul would have found it easier to conceal his identity under cover of darkness.

Taking two men with him, the king went to the woman and asked her to "consult" a "spirit" (*ʾôb*, v.8; see comment on v.3) on his behalf. The root of the Hebrew word for "consult" is *qsm* (GK 7876), other forms of which are elsewhere translated "diviners, divination," a practice universally condemned as a pagan abomination (6:2) to be scrupulously avoided by Israel (Dt 18:10, 14; 2Ki 17:17). Saul's earlier rebellion against the Lord had been so heinous that Samuel had compared it to the "sin of divination" (15:23). Nevertheless, Saul is now commanding a diviner, a necromancer, to "bring up" for him (v.8; cf. vv.11, 13, 15) one who dwells in the "realm of death below" (Dt 32:22; for Hittite parallels of diviners who "pull up" a deity "from the pit" see *COS*, 1:164, 174). As the Geneva Bible puts it in its note on v.8, Saul "seeketh not to God in his misery, but is led by Satan to unlawful meanes."

Not yet recognizing Saul, the woman reminds him that Israel's king has "cut off" (v.9) all the land's mediums and spiritists. Her words to Saul drip with irony: "You know" (*yādaʿtā*) that "spiritists" (*yiddᵉʿōnî*) are no longer allowed here. Saul will later compound the irony by asking the wraith he believes to be Samuel "to tell me" (*lᵉhôdîʿēnî*) what to do (v.15). Meanwhile the woman wonders why her nocturnal visitor would want to put her life in jeopardy by begging her to do what royal decree has forbidden. Although "cut off" may not necessarily have implied death (cf. "expelled" in v.3), the execution of diviners was not without precedent in Israel (Jos 13:22).

In promising the woman that she would not be punished, Saul uses the most solemn of oaths by swearing to her in the Lord's name (v.10; see comment on 14:39). "The irony of Saul's doing this in a negotiation with a conjurer of spirits is vividly caught by the Midrash: 'Whom did Saul resemble at that moment? A woman who is with her lover and swears by the life of her husband' (Yalkut Shimoni 2:247:139)" (Alter, *The David Story*, 173). As Miscall, 168, observes, "This is the last time that Saul will speak the name of the Lord."

Saul's response to the medium's question (v.11) is specific: He wants her to bring up "Samuel" (the word is in emphatic position). Although Saul and Samuel had worked at cross-purposes throughout much of their time together, the king now desires a final word from his prophet. How—and whether—the woman engaged the dead we are not told. "Even the Rabbis did not speculate as to her technique in conjuring up Samuel, but simply stated 'she did what she did, and she said what she said, and raised him'" (Lewis, 115). The Geneva Bible note on v.11 is instructive: "He [Saul] speaketh according to his grosse ignorance, not considering the state of the saints after this life, and how Satan hath no power over them."

Whether she saw Samuel in the flesh or an apparition or simply an internal vision, the medium's reaction when Samuel appeared was one of shock and surprise: She "cried out" (v.12), an emotional outburst often linked with feelings of fear and dismay (cf. 4:13; 5:10). "The incident does not tell us anything about the veracity of claims to consult the dead on the part of mediums, because the indications are that this was an extraordinary event for her, and a frightening one because she was not in control" (Baldwin, 159). At the very least the woman must have been clairvoyant, because while in her trancelike state she was able to penetrate Saul's disguise and recognize him (cf. K&D, 262).

The irony continues: Saul, previously afraid because of the Philistine threat (v.5) and soon to be afraid "because of Samuel's words" (v.20), tells the necromancer not to be afraid (v.13). He then asks her what she sees, thus indicating that he is not privy to the apparition itself. She responds that she sees "a spirit"—literally "[a] god[s]" (*ʾelōhîm*, a different Hebrew word from that used in v.8). A living prophet could be compared to God in the sense that he was God's mouthpiece and therefore spoke with God's authority (cf. Ex 7:1–2; Dt 18:17–18). Here the situation is quite different, however. It seems that in ancient times the deceased could be referred to as "gods" in that they lived in the realm of the preternatural (cf. A. H. Sayce, *The Religions of Ancient Egypt and Babylonia* [Edinburgh: T&T Clark, 1903], 286; Lewis, 115–16; Tromp, 176–78; cf. Ps 106:28 with Nu 25:1–3; also Isa 8:19–22).

Indeed, the apparition of Samuel is seen coming up out of "the ground"—*hāʾāreṣ* (GK 824)—a word often used in the OT (cf., e.g., Job 10:21–22; Ps 71:20; Jnh 2:6) and elsewhere in the ancient Near East to refer to the netherworld, the realm of the dead (cf. Lewis, 114; Tromp, 23–46; for the Akkadian cognate *erṣetu* in the same sense, see *CAD*, 4:310–11). Ironically, although Saul had attempted to drive all the mediums and spiritists "from the land" (vv.3, 9), a medium now sees an apparition coming up "out of the ground/netherworld" (v.13; the same Heb. phrase in all three verses). This understanding of v.13 lends credence to the interpretation of Endor as "Spring of the assembly of the gods, Spring of the oracular sanctuary" (see comment on v.7).

Saul, unable himself to see the "spirit," wants to know what he looks like (v.14). When the medium describes him as "an old man wearing a robe," Saul is convinced that the apparition is Samuel, who in Saul's mind has always worn the robe of the prophet (15:27; cf. 2:18–19). "Samuel is clothed in a dead man's robe as he foretells the imminent death of Saul and his sons. The robe as shroud enfolds Saul's death as well as Samuel's" (Polzin, *Samuel and the Deuteronomist*, 219). That Saul now "knew" it was Samuel (v.14) plays on the medium's earlier statement to him: "Surely you know" (see comment on v.9). In a verbatim reprise of 24:8, in the context of which David had Saul's robe—and destiny—in his grasp (24:4), Saul "bowed down and prostrated himself with his face to the ground" (v.14). The intimate connection between the two passages has not been lost on Polzin (ibid., 271 n. 7): "It would appear that as David bowed down before Saul, the one who by now ought to be dead, so Saul now bows down before Samuel, the one who is really dead." Continuing in its conviction that Satan is behind the apparition (see vv.8, 11 and comments), the Geneva Bible note on v.14 concludes that the "spirit" (v.13) "was Satan, who to blinde his [Saul's] eyes tooke upon him the forme of Samuel, as he can doe of an Angel of light" [alluding to 2Co 11:14]).

15–19 Having concluded his conversation with the medium (vv.7–14), Saul now speaks (probably via the medium) to what he believes to be Samuel (or the "spirit" of Samuel). The apparition begins the interchange by complaining that Saul has "disturbed" him (v.15; the same Heb. verb translated "is astir" in Isa 14:9, where the spirits of the departed in Sheol are pictured as being roused at the arrival of another denizen; for other examples of death being compared to sleep see Job 3:13; 14:12; Ps 13:3; 90:5; Jer 51:39, 57). Saul's response—that he is in "distress" because of the Philistines—uses the same Hebrew phrase earlier translated "their situation was critical," describing Israel's plight when facing a similar Philistine threat (13:6).

Saul's claim to be in "great" distress reflects his desperate emotional state. Though speaking to a "spirit" (*ʾᵉlōhîm*, v.13), he knows full well that "God" (*ʾᵉlōhîm*, v.15) has abandoned him. Saul has felt it necessary to consult "[a] god[s]" because of the silence of the one true "God" (cf. similarly Lewis, 116), who "has turned away from" him (vv.15–16)—a fate that the Lord had consigned to Saul years before at the time of David's anointing (see comment on 16:14; cf. also 18:12).

The "not yet" of the Lord's revelation to Samuel (3:7) finds its bitter echo in the "no longer" of the Lord's response to Saul (v.15; thus approximately Polzin, *Samuel and the Deuteronomist*, 220). In v.6 the narrator observes that the Lord did not answer Saul "by dreams or Urim or prophets." In v.15 Saul tells "Samuel" that God does not answer him "either by prophets or by dreams," perhaps omitting "Urim" to hide from Samuel his slaughter of the priests of Nob (22:11–19; cf. similarly Polzin, ibid., 270 n. 4) and perhaps listing "prophets" first in his hope that the prophet Samuel will now fill that vacuum. In a sense Samuel obliges: Saul has complained that God no longer speaks "by" (lit., "by the hand of") prophets, and Samuel says that the Lord has done what he predicted "through" (lit., "by the hand of") Samuel himself (v.17). Meanwhile Saul wants Samuel to "tell" him (lit., "cause to know"; for the irony of his request, see the comment on v.9; for the function of pagan diviners in this regard, cf. 6:2) what to do—though he had paid little attention to Samuel's counsel up to this point (cf. 10:8 with 13:8–14).

Whether the "Samuel" of this chapter is the prophet himself or an apparition, his statements to Saul in vv.16–19 are in full agreement with what we know of Samuel in other contexts. As he had punned on Saul's name before (cf. 12:17, "asked"), so he does now (v.16, "consult"; for another example see the comment on "inquired of" in v.6). Although Saul uses the general word "God" in v.15, Samuel characteristically refers to "the LORD" in vv.16–19—seven times in all (the number of completion/perfection [see comment on 2:5]; cf. also independently Miscall, 169; Brueggemann, *First and Second Samuel*, 195).

The prediction in v.17 refers back to 15:28 and echoes much of the terminology found there. The imagery of tearing a kingdom away from one Israelite ruler and giving it to another is repeated with respect to the division of the monarchy in connection with Solomon's death (1Ki 11:11–13, 31; 14:8; 2Ki 17:21). Samuel had told Saul that the Lord had given the kingdom of Israel to "one of your neighbors—to one better than you" (see 15:28 and comment). The prophet now repeats that language verbatim (v.17) but specifies precisely the referent of the final phrase: "to David" (a fact that Saul himself had already admitted earlier, however; cf. 24:20, where Saul says that the kingdom would be established "in your [David's] hands," reflected here in v.17, which affirms that the kingdom would be torn "out of your [Saul's] hands"). Ironically, the prophet Nathan would later tell King David that, because of his sins against Bathsheba and Uriah, the Lord would take David's wives and give them to "one who is close to you" (i.e., Absalom; 2Sa 12:11; cf. 2Sa 16:20–22), the Hebrew for which is translated "one of your neighbors" in 15:28 and 28:17.

Verse 18 summarizes the two fateful decisions made by Saul that prompted the Lord to wrench the kingdom from his grasp: (1) He disobeyed the Lord's command through his prophet (see ch. 13), and (2) he refused to "carry out" (lit., "do"; cf. similarly Isa 48:14) fully the divine wrath against the Amalekites (see ch. 15). Saul had not been willing to "do" God's wrath against Amalek; therefore God has "done" (v.18) his will against Saul. Obeying God had never been easy for Saul (cf. 15:19, 22), and his impatient insistence on his own way cost him the kingdom.

Although throughout Samuel's lifetime the Israelites had been delivered "out of the hand/power of the Philistines" (cf. 7:3, 14), the Lord would now "hand over" Israel to them (v.19). On the last night of Saul's life, Samuel euphemistically predicts the slaughter on Mount Gilboa: "Tomorrow you and your sons will be with me" (in the netherworld, the realm of death; cf. David's plaintive words in 2Sa 12:23). Samuel's last-recorded words, describing the fate of "both Israel and you [Saul]" (v.19), reprise the final words of his *apologia*: "Both you [Israel] and your king [Saul] will be swept away" (12:25). Thus did Samuel, in the words of George Gordon, Lord Byron, rise "from the grave, to freeze once more / The blood of monarchs with his prophecies" (*Don Juan*, lines 82–83).

Apart from v.20, Samuel does not appear again in the two OT books named after him. His importance and influence, however, continue to leave their mark throughout the rest of the Bible. His family tree appears twice in the Chronicler's genealogies (1Ch 6:25–28, 33–38). If Moses is rightly celebrated as Israel's lawgiver par excellence, so also Samuel is justly heralded as the prototypical prophet (1Ch 11:3; 2Ch 35:18; Ps 99:6; Jer 15:1), standing at the head of the prophetic line (Ac 3:24; 13:20; Heb 11:32). Bearing the titles of both "prophet" and "seer" (1Ch 9:22; 26:28; cf. 1Sa 9:9, 19), he shared in recording the events of King David's life (1Ch 29:29). As priest, judge, prophet, counselor, and anointer of Israel's first two rulers, Samuel takes his place as one of ancient Israel's greatest and most godly leaders (cf. the encomium in honor of Samuel in Sir 46:13–20).

20–25 The chapter races to its conclusion: "Immediately" (v.20) and "at once" (v.24) are both forms of the verb *mhr* ("hasten"). His strength gone (vv.20, 22), King Saul falls on the ground "full length" (v.20), the narrator ironically using a word ("length/height") that qualifies a man for kingship in the eyes of his fellows but not in the eyes of God (16:7; cf. 10:23–24). Fearful earlier because of the Philistine threat (v.5), Saul is now "filled with fear" because of Samuel's words of doom. In addition he lacks physical strength because he has eaten no food "all that day and night," an expression used elsewhere in a ritualistic setting (19:24). Since eating nothing is also often a religious act (a "fast" [BDB, 37]; cf. Ezr 10:6), Lewis, 114, may be correct in his inference that "Saul's going without food 'all that day and night' in verse 20 is due to the requirements of the ritual" of necromancy (cf. further David T. Tsumura, *The First Book of Samuel* [NICOT; Grand Rapids: Eerdmans, 2007], 629).

The medium, politely referring to herself as Saul's "(maid)servant" (for the idiom see 1:11 and comment; 25:27), reminds him that she risked her own safety when she "took [her] life in [her] hands" (v.21; see comment on 19:5). The verb *šmʿ* ("hear, obey, listen to"; GK 9048) plays a prominent role in this section: The medium "obeyed" Saul (v.21) when she "did" (lit., "listened to") what he told her to do; she now wants him to "listen to" her (v.22) and eat some food; although he at first refused, he finally "listened to" her (v.23) when his men joined her in urging him.

To meet Saul's acknowledged need for food, the woman deftly uses the tactic of demanding reciprocity: "I took" (v.21) and "let me give" (v.22) both translate forms of *śîm* ("put, set"; cf. "set" in its first occurrence in 9:24), and after the phrase "please listen" in v.22 the MT includes the words "also you" (emphatic pronoun). The medium is thus determined that Saul respond to her on a quid-pro-quo basis. Her offer to give him "some food" (lit., "a piece of bread," v.22; see 1Ki 17:11 for the same Heb. expression) belies her intention to serve him a more sumptuous meal (vv.24–25).

In the light of Samuel's fateful words, Saul's response is understandably negative: He refuses to eat (v.23). Polzin (*Samuel and the Deuteronomist*, 271 n. 10) calls attention to the contrast in the way food functions at the beginning and at the end of 1 Samuel: When Hannah could not have a child, she "would not eat" (1:7); when Saul learns that he and his sons will soon die, he "will not eat." (The account of David's reaction to the news of his son's fatal illness comes to mind as well [2Sa 12:15–23].) It is only when Saul's men join their voices of encouragement to that of the woman that he gets up from the ground and agrees to have a meal.

The activity described in v.24 is similar, even in the choice of vocabulary, to the scenes of hospitality depicted in Genesis 18:6–7 and 19:3 (for a concise description of ancient Near Eastern hospitality, cf. Youngblood, *The Book of Genesis*, 174). "Fattened calf" was a delicacy (cf. Jer 46:21; Mal 4:2 ["calves released from the stall"]) available only to the wealthy (Am 6:4; cf. also Lk 15:22–30). That the woman had a calf "at/in the house" is not surprising in the light of archaeological evidence that domestic stables were probably located inside residences and not separate from them (for details see Philip J. King, *Amos, Hosea, Micah—An Archaeological Commentary* [Philadelphia: Westminster, 1988], 149–51; cf. also the wording of Jephthah's vow in Jdg 11:30–31).

Brueggemann (*First and Second Samuel*, 196) summarizes: "Read at its best, this meal is a kind of last supper, one final meal for a king (cf. 25:36) who will not be a king much longer. It is as though the woman wants one last regal gesture for Saul when no one else will give it (cf. Mk 14:3–9)." Having eaten, Saul and his men go out into the night—"that same night" (v.25) in which Samuel's words have sealed the fate of a doomed king. The last stanza of Rudyard Kipling's "En-Dor" provides a fitting conclusion to this tragic chapter:

> Oh the road to En-dor is the oldest road
> And the craziest road of all!
> Straight it runs to the Witch's abode,
> As it did in the days of Saul,
> And nothing has changed of the sorrow in store
> For such as go down the road to En-dor!

NOTES

8 With minor exceptions, the practice of "putting on other clothes" was virtually unknown among the ordinary population in ancient Israel, being restricted to royalty (2Sa 12:20; 2Ki 22:14 = 2Ch 34:22), the priesthood (Lev 6:11; Eze 42:14; 44:19), and probably the very rich (cf. Neufeld, 53 n. 31).

10 "You will not be punished" translates אִם־יִקְּרֵךְ עָוֺן (*ʾim-yiqqᵉrēk ʿāwōn*, lit., "punishment will not befall [קרה, *qrh*] you." The *dagesh* in *yiqqᵉrēk* is *dagesh forte dirimens* and serves to make the *shewa* more audible (cf. GKC, sec. 20*h*). For another example in 1 Samuel, see 1:6 (הַרְּעִמָהּ, *harrᵉʿimāh*).

13 The NIV note on אֱלֹהִים (*ʾᵉlōhîm*, "spirits/gods") recognizes not only the fact that *ʾᵉlōhîm* itself is a plural noun but also that its accompanying verb עֹלִים (*ʿōlîm*, "coming up") is plural. Since *ʾᵉlōhîm* in the sense of "God" normally takes singular verbs (cf. Ge 1:1), the construction in v.13 leads to the conclusion that "god(s)" rather than "God" is meant.

16 The rare עָר (*ʿār*, "enemy" [GK 6839], found elsewhere in the OT only in Psalm 139:20 ["adversaries"]) may be a dialectal variant of צַר (*ṣar*). Perhaps the narrator chose it as an anticipatory pun on רֵעַ (*rēaʿ*, "neighbor") in v.17.

17 The MT reads literally: "The LORD has done for him(self) what he predicted," the phrase "for himself" (לוֹ, *lô*) to be understood as a dative of advantage (cf. the *dativus ethicus* of GKC, sec. 119*s*; *IBHS*, 208). It is therefore unnecessary to read לְךָ (*lk*, "to you") with a few manuscripts and versions (for details cf. *BHS*).

19 Many modern commentators (e.g., Driver, Mauchline, McCarter) assert that the last sentence of this verse is a variant of its first clause and that therefore one or the other should be omitted as repetitive (for details see Lewis, 110). But in stating that the "army/camp" of Israel would "also" be handed over to the Philistines, the last sentence adds information not present earlier. Baldwin, 160, summarizes: "The people and their army are bound up with their king, and they too will suffer defeat as the result of Saul's disobedience." K&D, 264, takes a slightly different tack but with the same basic result: The "camp" of Israel was plundered (apparently in contrast to earlier references in the verse, which refer to the death of Saul, his people, and his sons).

23 "Urging" renders the root פרץ (*prṣ*), which many commentators assume is a mistaken metathesis of פצר (*pṣr*; cf. Lewis, 111). But although *pṣr* is indeed attested in the sense of "urge" (cf. 2Ki 5:16), it is no more common than *prṣ* with the same meaning (2Sa 13:25, 27; 2Ki 5:23). In fact, metatheses of consonants in roots with liquids and/or sibilants are relatively frequent in the Semitic languages, including Hebrew (for other examples see *IBHS*, 94, 424–25). In any event, Hebrew *prṣ* ("urge") is probably cognate to Akkadian *parāṣu* ("penetrate, pierce, bring pressure on"; for the root *pṣr* in the latter sense, cf. Ge 19:9) and perhaps also to Arabic *faraḍa* ("establish, stipulate, resolve, decide, impose"; cf. peculiarly BDB, 823, which asserts that Hebrew *pṣr* is "perh[aps] related" to the above Akkadian and Arabic roots "by transp[osition]" and then goes on to suggest that *prṣ* here and in 2Sa 13:25, 27; 2Ki 5:23 should "prob[ably]" be read as though from *pṣr*; cf. BDB, 829)—a tortuous argument at best.

24 The elision of א (ʾ) in ותפהו (*wtphw*), from אפה (*ʾph*, "bake"), also occurs elsewhere in first-radical-ʾ verbs in the books of Samuel (cf. J. Stek, "What Happened to the Chariot Wheels of Exodus 14:25?" *JBL* 105/2 [1986]: 293–302, esp. 293).

2. The Dismissal of David (29:1–11)

OVERVIEW

Although ch. 29 plays an important literary role in the story of the end of Saul's reign (see Overview to 28:3–31:13), it is also reminiscent of the events recorded in 27:1–28:2, as the following commentary will demonstrate. Thus 27:1–28:2 and ch. 29 frame the account of Saul and the medium at Endor (28:3–25), isolating it as a separate literary unit. In addition ch. 29, the narrative of David's third deception of Achish king of Gath (cf. 21:12–15; 27:8–12), introduces the report of David's defeat of the Amalekites (ch. 30), a stark contrast to Saul's earlier fateful failure (ch. 15) and his forthcoming death during a final battle against his nemesis, the Philistines (ch. 31).

Brief as it is, the chapter itself is nonetheless exquisitely crafted. It begins and ends at "Jezreel" (vv.1, 11), hard by the site of Saul's suicide. Its repeated use of other key words and phrases, which will be noted as they appear, is impressive. Finally, Achish's triple vindication of David's honor and dependability is spaced evenly throughout (vv.3, 6, 9).

1The Philistines gathered all their forces at Aphek, and Israel camped by the spring
in Jezreel. 2As the Philistine rulers marched with their units of hundreds and thousands,
David and his men were marching at the rear with Achish. 3The commanders of the
Philistines asked, "What about these Hebrews?"

Achish replied, "Is this not David, who was an officer of Saul king of Israel? He has already been with me for over a year, and from the day he left Saul until now, I have found no fault in him."

4But the Philistine commanders were angry with him and said, "Send the man back, that
he may return to the place you assigned him. He must not go with us into battle, or he will
turn against us during the fighting. How better could he regain his master's favor than by
taking the heads of our own men? 5Isn't this the David they sang about in their dances:

"'Saul has slain his thousands,
and David his tens of thousands'?"

6So Achish called David and said to him, "As surely as the LORD lives, you have been
reliable, and I would be pleased to have you serve with me in the army. From the day you
came to me until now, I have found no fault in you, but the rulers don't approve of you.
7Turn back and go in peace; do nothing to displease the Philistine rulers."

8"But what have I done?" asked David. "What have you found against your servant from
the day I came to you until now? Why can't I go and fight against the enemies of my lord
the king?"

[9]Achish answered, "I know that you have been as pleasing in my eyes as an angel of God; nevertheless, the Philistine commanders have said, 'He must not go up with us into battle.' [10]Now get up early, along with your master's servants who have come with you, and leave in the morning as soon as it is light."

[11]So David and his men got up early in the morning to go back to the land of the Philistines, and the Philistines went up to Jezreel.

COMMENTARY

1–11 The chapter begins by recalling the muster of Philistine and Israelite armies described in 28:4 (cf. 28:1). In reconciling the differences between the place names in v.1 and in 28:4, the summary of Aharoni, 290–91, is helpful:

> The Philistine rulers assembled their forces at Aphek at the sources of the Yarkon (1Sam 29.1) preparatory to marching on Jezreel (vs. 11). Saul's troops "were encamped by the fountain which is in Jezreel" (vs. 1); on the eve of the battle they ranged themselves on Mount Gilboa. The Philistines made camp across from them at Shunem (1Sam 28.4).

Verse 1, like its counterpart (28:4), describes the opposing forces in a terse and balanced way: The Philistines gathered their "forces" (lit., "camps") at Aphek, and Israel "camped" near Jezreel. Aphek, modern Ras el-Ain at the point where the Philistine plain meets the plain of Sharon, is mentioned in the books of Samuel only here and in 4:1. It was thus the staging area for Philistine troop deployment in the first and last battles between Israel and Philistia recorded in 1 Samuel. Jezreel (not to be confused with the southern site of the same name; see 25:43 and comment), located in the tribal territory of Issachar (Jos 19:17–18), is modern Zerin, on a spur of Mount Gilboa three miles south of Shunem. News about the death of Saul and Jonathan would soon be relayed from Jezreel (2Sa 4:4), which was to play a key (if ambiguous) role in the unfolding history of the northern kingdom (cf. 1Ki 21:1; Hos 1:4–5; 2:22–23).

The personal involvement of the Philistine "rulers" (vv.2, 6–7; see comment and Notes on 5:8) demonstrates their perception that the present battle was crucial. Most commentators distinguish between "rulers" and "commanders" (vv.3–4, 9) in this chapter (cf. Baldwin, Gordon, Klein, McCarter, Smith), although a few hesitate to commit themselves on the matter (cf. Ackroyd, Hertzberg). Others, however (e.g., K&D, Mauchline), equate the two terms—and, indeed, comparing vv.3–4 with v.6 provides little justification for making the distinction.

The resolute Philistines march out in traditional military units of "hundreds" and "thousands" (cf. 2Sa 18:4)—numbers that in such cases should probably be understood figuratively rather than literally (see comments on 4:2; 11:8). David and his men, mercenaries in the Philistine army (cf. 28:1), fall in behind at the behest of Achish king of Gath (see comment on 21:10).

The Philistine commanders, understandably wary of David (cf. 18:30), question the wisdom of including "Hebrews" (v.3) in the army ("Hebrew" was commonly used by non-Israelites as a synonym for "Israelite"; cf. 4:5–10; 13:19; 14:11; see also comments on 13:3; 14:21–22). But Achish, who had earlier made David his "bodyguard for life" (28:2), rises to his defense:

(1) Although David had at one time been an "officer" of Saul (lit., "servant"; for the nuance "officer, official," cf. 1Ki 11:26; 2Ki 25:8; Isa 36:9), he "left" Saul (lit., "fell away from"; cf. Jer 39:9, where "those who had gone over to" [lit., "the falling ones who had fallen to"] expresses the idea of transfer of allegiance).

(2) Having fled from Saul, David has now been with Achish for "over a year" (lit., "these days or these years," an idiom meaning something like "a year or two"; cf. 27:7, which notes that David lived in Philistine-controlled territory "a year and four months") and has therefore had sufficient time to demonstrate his loyalty.

(3) During this entire period ("until now," vv.3, 6, 8) Achish has found "no fault" in David (v.3, a sentiment repeated by Achish in v.6 and shared [cynically?] by David himself in v.8). The words "no fault" (lit., "nothing, not ... anything"), reflecting David's presumed innocence of wrongdoing, echo not only his earlier protestations in the story of Nabal and Abigail (25:7, 21) but also Samuel's self-justification in his *apologia* (12:5).

Unconvinced, the Philistine commanders demand that Achish "send" David "back" (v.4), a verb (*šwb*) repeated in various forms and to the same end throughout the rest of the chapter (vv.4 ["return"], 7 ["turn back"], 11 ["go back"]). They insist that he return to "the place (Achish) assigned him"—that is, Ziklag (see 27:6 and comment), to which David indeed eventually goes (vv.11; 30:1). They do not want David to go with them "into battle" (vv.4, 9) for fear that he will turn against them "during the fighting" (the same Heb. for both expressions). The verb "turn against" is literally "become an adversary against"; the word for "adversary" [*śāṭān*; GK 8477] was later specialized to refer to "the Adversary [par excellence]"—namely, "Satan" [cf. Job 1–2; 1Ch 21:1]; for the idiom used here, cf. Nu 22:22 ["oppose"]; 2Sa 19:22). As a potential fifth column in the Philistine ranks, David might kill some of them and take their "heads" as trophies of war (cf., ironically, 31:9; see also comment on 28:2). In so doing he would regain "his master's" (i.e., Saul's; cf. v.3) favor.

The Philistine commanders conclude their critique by reminding Achish of the victory refrain (v.5)—by now well known (see 18:7–8 and comment; 21:11)—sung by the women of Israel in honor of (Saul and) David. As the commanders do so, they sarcastically hurl Achish's own words back at him: "Isn't this the David" (identical Heb. to "Is not this David," v.3; cf. 21:11). In addition, the Philistines "take the song as a celebration of solidarity between David and Saul. Saul and David are linked in the Philistine perception in common military exploits. Obviously such a man cannot fight with the Philistines against Saul" (Brueggemann, *First and Second Samuel*, 198).

Achish, not willing to buck his peers on this point, tells David about the commanders' concern but without sharing any details with him (vv.6–7, 9). To assure David of the truth of what he is about to say, he takes a solemn oath in the name of David's God (v.6; see comment on 14:39). As far as Achish is aware (but cf. 27:8–11), David has been "reliable" (lit., "upright," as in Job 1:1). Thus, says Achish, "I would be pleased" (lit., "it would be pleasing in my eyes," as in v.9) to have you (David) "serve" (lit., "go forth and come back"; see comment on 18:16) in the army. The contrast between the attitude of Achish toward David and that of the other Philistine rulers toward him could not be more stark: "The rulers don't approve of" him (lit., he is "not pleasing in the eyes of the rulers," v.6)—indeed, David is in danger of doing something that will "displease" them (lit., be "displeasing in the eyes of" them, v.7). "Pleasing" (*ṭôb*, "good") and "displeasing" (*rā*ᶜ, "evil") set up the classic confrontation that began in the Garden of Eden (Ge 2:9, 17: 3:4, 22).

The narrator describes the perceptions of Achish and his fellow Philistine rulers in clearly contrasting terms: In the mind of Achish, David is good ("I have found no fault [*rāʿâ*, a different word from that used in v.3] in you"), while the other commanders consider him to be evil. Seeing no hope of reconciling the two opposing viewpoints, Achish advises David to "go in peace" (v.7), a cordial expression of farewell (2Sa 15:9; cf. 15:27). Furthermore, Achish is doubtless concerned about "the lucrative booty he is receiving from David [cf. 1Sa 27:9]. He readily accepts the generals' demand, because he does not want to jeopardize the relationship he has with David" (Miscall, 174).

David's response (v.8) echoes in part some of Achish's own words (cf. v.6). In addition, David wants to know "what [he has] done" to deserve such suspicion, again playing the role of the innocent victim, as he earlier had before his brother Eliab (17:29), his friend Jonathan (20:1), and his master Saul (26:18). He wants to fight (or pretends that he does) against the enemies of his "lord the king" (v.8)—Achish, at least in this context. But, as Miscall, 175, asks, is David's true lord and king Achish or Saul, or both or neither? "Is David being ironic?"

For the third time (v.9; cf. vv.3, 6) Achish vindicates David's honor and dependability. Brueggemann (*First and Second Samuel*, 200) sees in this a possible parallel to Pilate's threefold declaration concerning Jesus: "I find no basis for a charge against him" (Jn 18:38; 19:4, 6; cf. Lk 23:22). In Achish's eyes David is like "an angel of God," an epithet used elsewhere (cf. 2Sa 14:17, 20; 19:27; Zec 12:8) in "metaphorical reference to the king in court-etiquette fashion" (Talmon, 30 n. 67). The name of God is used only twice in this chapter (vv.6, 9), both times by Achish rather than David, perhaps implying that while David was in Philistine territory he did not consult the Lord (for a similar phenomenon see the comment on 27:1–28:2).

"Now" (v.10) echoes the beginning of v.7 (which also starts with "now" in the MT). This opening word underscores the urgency of Achish's request to David to return to Ziklag before he needlessly angers the Philistine rulers even further. David is to take with him his "master's" (Saul's; see comment on "my lord the king" in v.8) servants and "get up early/leave in the morning" (same Heb. expression). To go "as soon as it is light" would be to take advantage of the cool morning hours (cf. similarly Ge 44:3), especially if the journey was long (Ziklag was fifty miles from Aphek). That David and his men go back to the "land of the Philistines" (v.11) reflects the narrator's judgment that Aphek, strictly speaking, is not in Philistine territory.

Thus David, doubtless relieved, avoids fighting against his own countrymen—and does so with Philistine blessing. Brueggemann (*First and Second Samuel*, 199) observes a further irony: "The very same Philistines who will finally dispose of Saul (ch. 31) are the ones who unwittingly rescue David."

NOTES

1 עַל (*ʿal*) is the most common way of expressing "by" in association with bodies of water (cf. Ps 1:3). As here, however, in a few cases בְּ־ (*b-*) is used (cf. Eze 10:15, 20).

2 Usually "march" (in a military sense) is rendered in Hebrew by יָצָא (*yāṣāʾ*, "go [out]"; cf. 2Sa 18:6 and esp. 18:4). Here, however, the narrator twice chose עֹבְרִים (*ʿōbᵉrîm*, "passing[over/by/through]"; "marched, were marching," NIV), perhaps as an anticipatory pun on עִבְרִים (*ʿibrîm*, "Hebrews") in v.3.

4 "Go into battle" (as also in 26:10) is literally "go down into battle" (cf. 30:24). But when Achish later repeats the Philistine commanders' statement, he quotes them as saying "go up ... into battle" (v.9; cf. v.11; 7:7). Driver's resolution (219–20) of the apparent discrepancy is probably correct:

> The narrator must here allow the Philistines to speak from the *Israelite* point of view (cf. v.6, where Achish is represented as swearing by *Yahweh*), who would "go down" from the mountainous country of Judah to fight against the Philistines in their plains.... Here [in v.9] the Philistines speak from the point of view which would be natural to them, when they were invading the high central ground of Canaan.

10 After "come with you" the LXX inserts several clauses, which the NRSV takes to be original and therefore includes in its text, translating as follows: "and go to the place that I appointed for you. As for the evil report, do not take it to heart, for you have done well before me" (cf. similarly JB, NJB, NAB, NEB, REB). But together with v.9, v.10 just as it stands adequately answers David's questions (v.8). In addition, apart from "do not take it to heart," the insertion adds no new information and looks more like a characteristic LXX expansion than a mistaken MT omission.

3. The Defeat of the Amalekites (30:1–31)

OVERVIEW

Even when all seems lost, David continues to prosper. Although he arrives in Ziklag and finds it destroyed, through God's help he tracks the Amalekites down and recovers all the people and plunder they had taken. He then ingratiates himself to his troops and his neighbors by sharing his good fortune with them. Chapter 30 is a case study of the qualities that make for strong and compassionate leadership: persistence, empathy, faith in God, commitment to a cause, integrity, decisiveness, and generosity. Saul, disobeying God's prophet, defeated the Amalekites but lost his kingdom (ch. 15); David, seeking God's will, defeats the Amalekites and embarks on his reign (ch. 30).

The chapter displays a chiastic arrangement:

A David reaches destroyed Ziklag and finds it plundered (30:1–3)
  B David and his men are promised the Lord's help (30:4–8)
    C David defeats the Amalekites (30:9–20)
  B' David shares the Lord's plunder with his men (30:21–25)
A' David returns to Ziklag and distributes the remaining plunder (30:26–31)

[1]David and his men reached Ziklag on the third day. Now the Amalekites had raided the Negev and Ziklag. They had attacked Ziklag and burned it, [2]and had taken captive the women and all who were in it, both young and old. They killed none of them, but carried them off as they went on their way.

3When David and his men came to Ziklag, they found it destroyed by fire and their
wives and sons and daughters taken captive. 4So David and his men wept aloud until they
had no strength left to weep. 5David's two wives had been captured — Ahinoam of Jezreel
and Abigail, the widow of Nabal of Carmel. 6David was greatly distressed because the men
were talking of stoning him; each one was bitter in spirit because of his sons and daughters. But David found strength in the LORD his God.

7Then David said to Abiathar the priest, the son of Ahimelech, "Bring me the ephod."
Abiathar brought it to him, 8and David inquired of the LORD, "Shall I pursue this raiding
party? Will I overtake them?"

"Pursue them," he answered. "You will certainly overtake them and succeed in the
rescue."

9David and the six hundred men with him came to the Besor Ravine, where some
stayed behind, 10for two hundred men were too exhausted to cross the ravine. But David
and four hundred men continued the pursuit.

11They found an Egyptian in a field and brought him to David. They gave him water to
drink and food to eat — 12part of a cake of pressed figs and two cakes of raisins. He ate and
was revived, for he had not eaten any food or drunk any water for three days and three
nights.

13David asked him, "To whom do you belong, and where do you come from?"

He said, "I am an Egyptian, the slave of an Amalekite. My master abandoned me when
I became ill three days ago. 14We raided the Negev of the Kerethites and the territory
belonging to Judah and the Negev of Caleb. And we burned Ziklag."

15David asked him, "Can you lead me down to this raiding party?"

He answered, "Swear to me before God that you will not kill me or hand me over to my
master, and I will take you down to them."

16He led David down, and there they were, scattered over the countryside, eating, drinking and reveling because of the great amount of plunder they had taken from the land
of the Philistines and from Judah. 17David fought them from dusk until the evening of the
next day, and none of them got away, except four hundred young men who rode off on
camels and fled. 18David recovered everything the Amalekites had taken, including his
two wives. 19Nothing was missing: young or old, boy or girl, plunder or anything else they
had taken. David brought everything back. 20He took all the flocks and herds, and his men
drove them ahead of the other livestock, saying, "This is David's plunder."

21Then David came to the two hundred men who had been too exhausted to follow
him and who were left behind at the Besor Ravine. They came out to meet David and the
people with him. As David and his men approached, he greeted them. 22But all the evil
men and troublemakers among David's followers said, "Because they did not go out with
us, we will not share with them the plunder we recovered. However, each man may take
his wife and children and go."

23David replied, "No, my brothers, you must not do that with what the LORD has given
us. He has protected us and handed over to us the forces that came against us. 24Who will
listen to what you say? The share of the man who stayed with the supplies is to be the
same as that of him who went down to the battle. All will share alike." 25David made this a
statute and ordinance for Israel from that day to this.
26When David arrived in Ziklag, he sent some of the plunder to the elders of Judah, who
were his friends, saying, "Here is a present for you from the plunder of the LORD's enemies."
27He sent it to those who were in Bethel, Ramoth Negev and Jattir; 28to those in Aroer,
Siphmoth, Eshtemoa 29and Racal; to those in the towns of the Jerahmeelites and the
Kenites; 30to those in Hormah, Bor Ashan, Athach 31and Hebron; and to those in all the
other places where David and his men had roamed.

COMMENTARY

1–3 The section is framed by the notice that "David and his men reached/came to" (the same Heb. verb in both cases) Ziklag (vv.1, 3). Having been dismissed by Achish, David and his men begin the long trek from Aphek (29:1) to Ziklag (see comment on 27:6) in "the land of the Philistines" (29:11) and arrive there on the "third day" (v.1). The narrator observes that in the meantime the Amalekites (Israel's agelong enemies [cf. Ex 17:8–16], who inhabited large tracts of land southwest of the Dead Sea) had "raided the Negev and Ziklag," a summary statement that is given more detailed definition in v.14. "Raided" here and in v.14 means literally "stripped," the verb used in 31:9 of the Philistines' ignominious treatment of the vanquished Saul.

The Amalekites took advantage of David's absence from Ziklag, raiding the town in retaliation for when David had earlier "raided" them (27:8). They "attacked" Ziklag (v.1), and so—again quid pro quo—David later "fought" them (v.17; same Heb. verb). Their burning of Ziklag (vv.1, 3, 14) would be tragically echoed in the Philistines' burning of the bodies of Saul and his sons (31:12).

The Amalekites had also "taken captive" (vv.2–3) everyone who lived in the town, from the youngest to the oldest (vv.2, 19). The captured "women" receive pride of place in v.2, probably because David's two wives were included among them (v.5). Killing no one, the Amalekites "carried them off" (lit., "drove them," as in v.20, where the same Heb. verb is used in reference to livestock; cf. also 23:5). The allusion to "sons and daughters" in v.3 receives added emphasis in v.6, where they are the objects of special concern on the part of David's men (cf. v.19, where the same Hebrew phrase is translated "boy or girl").

4–8 Weeping aloud is an understandable reaction when the situation seems hopeless (see comment on 11:4). But the abject sorrow of David and his men (v.4) would soon be replaced by confident expectation as a result of the Lord's assurance of victory (v.8). David mourns the (apparent) loss of his two wives (v.5), Ahinoam of Jezreel and Abigail of Carmel (see comment on 15:12; 25:3, 43), whom he had moved to Ziklag after Achish had assigned the town to him (cf. 27:3–6).

Added to David's grief is the fact that he is "greatly distressed" (v.6) because his men blame him for their plight. Pointing to an earlier parallel where Saul is pictured as being "in great distress" (see 28:15 and comment), Brueggemann (*First and Second Samuel*, 201) comments: "Both David and Saul are portrayed as persons in deep crises of leadership, and both are deeply at risk. What interests us is the difference of response.... Saul seeks refuge in a medium," while David inquires of the Lord.

In the meantime, however, David's men consider "stoning him"—a much more serious threat than the later frivolous action of Shimei (even though the same Heb. verb is used; cf. 2Sa 16:6, 13). Convinced that they will never see their children again, the men are "bitter in spirit" (v.6; cf. 1:10, "in bitterness of soul"; 2Ki 4:27, "in bitter distress"). While in 22:2 people who were "discontented" (the same Heb. in all these cases) flocked to David's leadership, here his men are so distraught that they cannot think clearly and are prepared to do him harm.

David's spiritual discernment now comes to the fore: He "found strength" (v.6) in the right Person (cf. similarly Ezr 7:28, "took courage"; Da 10:19). Concerning the last sentence in v.6, Brueggemann (*First and Second Samuel*, 202) observes that it "anticipates Paul's wondrous two-sided statement of Philippians 2:12–13: 'Work out your own salvation ... for God is at work.' David counts heavily on God's being at work. At the same moment David is boldly at work on the rescue mission." Although the Hebrew phrase translated "had no strength" in v.4 is not from the same root, the contrast is nonetheless striking. By using the expression "the LORD his God," the narrator emphasizes David's intimate relationship with the One who from the beginning has always been "with him" (see 16:18 and comment).

As at Keilah, so also at Ziklag David says to Abiathar the priest (v.7), "Bring me the ephod" (see comments on 23:6, 9; also 22:20), which David then uses to inquire of the Lord (v.8; see comments on 23:2, 4; also comments on 14:36, 41–42). When the rejected Saul inquired of the Lord, no answer came (28:6); when the "man after [God's] own heart" (13:14) does the same, the Lord answers specifically and with precision (as here; cf. also 23:2, 4). "The contrast between Saul going to the necromancer in 1 Samuel 28 and David easily consulting YHWH in 1 Samuel 30 is heightened through the narrative proximity of these two events" (Brettler, 83).

In this case David asks whether he should "pursue" the Amalekite raiders and, if so, whether he would be able to "overtake" them. The Lord's response is immediate, clear, and full of encouragement: David is commanded to "pursue," he will "certainly overtake" (infinitive absolute plus finite verb), and in addition—the divine bonus—he will "succeed in the rescue" (again, infinitive absolute plus finite verb). True to his promise, the Lord makes sure that David "has recovered" everything, including the captives and plunder (vv.18, 22; "recovered" is from the same Heb. verb as "rescue" in v.8).

9–20 The staging area for the campaign against the Amalekites is the Besor Ravine, mentioned only in this chapter. Today called the Wadi Ghazzeh, it empties into the Mediterranean Sea about four miles south of Gaza. (Since the Wadi Ghazzeh in this area is not very deep, to call it a "ravine" is somewhat misleading; cf. Rasmussen, 212 n. 18.) Of David's "six hundred men" (v.9; for the significance of the number, see comment on 13:15; cf. 27:2), two hundred are too "exhausted" (vv.10, 21; "dead tired," Alter [*The David Story*, 185] suggestively proposes, relating the verb *pgr* to the noun *peger*, "corpse") to continue the rigorous march. David and the four hundred others, however, press on (for an identical deployment of David's men on an earlier occasion—though for a different reason—see 25:13 and comment).

Finding a starving Egyptian in a field (v.11), they give him water and food, including cakes of raisins and of pressed figs (v.12), items especially suitable for men on the march (see 25:18 and comment). His enforced three-day fast has apparently weakened him, because after eating he is "revived" (lit., "his spirit/strength returned to him" [v.12], as with Samson in a similar situation [Jdg 15:19; "revived" there renders a different Heb. verb]).

David's questions to the Egyptian (v.13) are reminiscent of Nabal's to David's servants in 25:10–11 (cf. Jnh 1:8)—although the selfish stinginess of Nabal, who had no intention of sharing his food and water with strangers, is no match for the generosity of David. While Nabal gave nothing to the "servants" of a fellow Israelite (for possible referents of "servants," see comment on 25:10), David supplies the needs of a hated Amalekite's Egyptian "slave" (v.13; the same Heb. word in both passages), whose cruel master had left him for dead simply because he had become ill.

The emphatic "we" at the beginning of v.14 suggests that the slave participated personally in the Amalekites' raids. The summary statement in v.1—"the Negev and Ziklag"—is now given definition: Among the pillaged regions were the Negev of the Kerethites ("probably S Philistine Plain area and W Negev region E and NE of Gaza" [Rasmussen, 246 and map on 114]), an undefined portion of Judahite territory (the MT does not justify the NIV's use of "the" before the "territory" in v.14), and the Negev of Caleb (named after the clan that occupied it and of which Nabal was a member [25:3], it was doubtless located in the "Hill Country of Judah, S of Hebron but NE of Beersheba" [Rasmussen, 246]; for other subdistricts of the Negev, see the comment on 27:10). Last of all, says the Egyptian, "Ziklag we burned" (the word order in the MT—which, when combined with Ziklag's placement at the end of the list, makes the town doubly emphatic as the focus of the Amalekite attack).

The Egyptian agrees to show David where the Amalekite raiding party has gone if David will swear not to kill him or "hand [him] over to" his master (lit., "deliver [him] up to the hands of"; cf. 23:11–12 ["surrender ... to"], 20; see comment on "imprisoned himself" in 23:7). Miscall, 180, observes, "There is poignancy to his speech, since it intones both Saul's earlier request for an oath from David not to kill him (1Sa 24:22 [EV v.21]) and Saul's death on Mt. Gilboa."

Although in the earlier episode David "gave his oath" (24:22), the present text is silent concerning whether he does the same here. In any event, the Egyptian leads David down to the Amalekite bivouac (v.16). The raiders are not only "eating" and "drinking"—in contrast to the former plight of the Egyptian slave (vv.11–12), who had considered himself one of their number (vv.13–14)—but also "reveling" (the Heb. verb usually means "go on pilgrimage, celebrate a [religious] festival"; cf. "festive" in Ps 42:4). After all, they had recently "taken" great quantities of plunder (cf. vv.18–20; see also comment on 27:9). Brueggemann (*First and Second Samuel*, 202–3) characterizes the scene: "The Amalekites are presented ... with an extra rhetorical flourish designed to make them as unattractive as possible. They are 'eating and drinking and dancing,' surely the marks of a degenerate people who practice excessive self-indulgence (cf. Ex. 32:6)."

David and his men are more than a match for the Amalekites, who must have far outnumbered the Israelites. Even after a full night and day of fighting (v.17), during which large numbers of Amalekites have fallen (cf. the hyperbolic "none of them got away"), "four hundred" of them—the same figure used to describe David's original army (v.10)—are still able to get away. Like an earlier horde of Midianite raiders (Jdg 6:3–5), the Amalekites rode on camels (the mount of choice of many Eastern peoples; cf. Isa 21:7), this time to make good their escape.

Emphasizing the completeness of the rout and the scope of David's victory, the narrator reports that everything the Amalekites had "taken" (vv.16, 18–19) David "took" back (v.20), including (most important of all) "his two wives" (v.18). Indeed, "nothing was missing" (v.19). As in 23:5 (during the rescue of Keilah, the account of which has much in common with that of the rescue of Ziklag), so also here the Hebrew verbs are in the singular ("fought," v.17; "recovered," v.18; "brought ... back," v.19; "took," v.20), rightly attributing success to David as the leader of his men (see comment on 23:5).

Note too that the retrieved spoil is referred to as "David's plunder" (v.20). Gunn (*The Fate of King Saul*, 110–11), noting that the rest of ch. 30 "is devoted to one theme—the spoil taken from the Amalekites," makes the further observation that "Samuel's words of rejection still ring in our ears (15:19) ... : 'Why did you not obey the voice of Yahweh?'" Brueggemann (*First and Second Samuel*, 203) summarizes: "The Amalekites are resented for taking spoil; Saul is rejected for taking spoil; David is saluted and championed for doing the same."

21–25 David, of course, understands that the plunder is ultimately not his but the Lord's (vv.23, 26), and he must therefore exercise the utmost care in its disposition. Returning to the Besor Ravine, he and his troops are met by the two hundred men who had remained behind (v.21; cf. vv.9–10). As was his custom on such occasions (17:22; 25:5–6), David "greeted" them (lit., "asked about" their "well-being/welfare"; see comment on 10:4).

As Saul had his "troublemakers" (10:27; see comment on 25:17) at the beginning of his reign, so also David has his (v.22). They declare their unwillingness to share the plunder with men who had not participated in the campaign against the Amalekites, and even their concession to allow the two hundred to receive their families back is marred by the verb they use ("take" is lit., "drive, lead," ordinarily used to express forced movement, as with livestock [v.20]; see comment on v.2).

David, generously calling the troublemakers "my brothers" (v.23; cf. Jesus' polite use of "friend" in Mt 20:13), reminds them that the booty is not, as they think, "the plunder we recovered" (v.22) but rather "what the LORD has given us" (v.23). God has enabled them to defeat the "forces" (the same Heb. word translated "raiding party" in vv.8, 15) that came against them. However exhausted the men who remained behind might have been, they deserve a reward for staying with and guarding the "supplies" (v.24; see comment on "baggage" in 10:22). They are thus not to be considered inferior and are to share equally in the plunder (cf. similarly 25:13) with those who "went down to the battle" (see Notes on 29:4). Like his ancestor Abraham (Ge 14:24), the magnanimous David—who knows full well that he has been divinely deputized to distribute the Lord's plunder as he wishes (cf. similarly Mt 20:14–15)—makes sure that loyal service is suitably compensated (cf. further 1Co 3:8). "The basis of distribution is not risk or victory or machismo but simply membership in the community" (Brueggemann, *First and Second Samuel*, 205).

The last word of the sentence "All will share alike" (v.24c) reappears as a grisly echo in 31:6, which reports that Saul and all his comrades died "together" (same Heb. word). David (v.25) makes the principle of equal sharing of plunder a "statute and ordinance" (a technical term for divinely established laws, as in Ex 15:25, "a decree and a law"; Jos 24:25, "decrees and laws"; cf. also Ps 81:4, "decree ... ordinance") for Israel in perpetuity ("from that day to this"; cf. the action of Joseph, with similar long-term effects, in Ge 47:26).

26–31 The final section of ch. 30 begins as does the first: "David arrived in/reached Ziklag" (vv.1, 26; the same Heb. verb in both verses). The fact that David sends some of the plunder to Judah (v.26) leads Brueggemann (*First and Second Samuel*, 206) to characterize him as a "giver, not a taker [see comment on 8:11, 13–17]. It is his propensity to give that makes his new kingdom possible." Representing Judah, the elders (cf. 2Sa 19:11) receive a "present" (lit., "blessing") from David, who thus reciprocates the earlier generosity of Abigail, who gave a "gift" (lit., "blessing") to David and his men (see 25:27 and comment). The Judahite elders, who are David's "friends" (v.26), stand in contrast to the Amalekite raiders, who are "the LORD's"—and therefore David's—"enemies."

Concluding the chapter, vv.27–31 list the specific places where David's "present" was distributed and give additional information concerning the areas raided by the Amalekites. Bethel (v.27, not the famous site in Benjamin at modern Beitin twelve miles north of Jerusalem, for which see 7:16; 10:3; 13:2) is probably the Judahite Kesil (Jos 15:30; LXX^B, *Baithēl*), alternatively called Bethul (Jos 19:4) or Bethuel (1Ch 4:30), "House of God," doubtless because a temple had been built there.

Ramoth Negev ("Heights of the Negev"), probably the same as Ramah in the Negev (Jos 19:8), is mentioned in one of the Arad ostraca and is perhaps to be located at modern Khirbet Ghazzeh (cf. Yohanan Aharoni, "Arad: Its Inscriptions and Temple," *BA* 31/1 [1968]: 17–18) twenty miles south-southeast of Hebron.

Jattir, a town for the Levites (Jos 21:14; 1Ch 6:57) in the hill country of Judah (Jos 15:48), is modern Khirbet Attir thirteen miles south-southwest of Hebron.

Aroer (not the same as the Reubenite Aroer; Jos 13:16; 1Ch 5:8) is perhaps modern Khirbet Ararah (probably = *ʿadʿādâ* in Jos 15:22 [cf. LXX^B, *Arouēl*], with Hebrew *d* mistakenly written for *r*; cf. Aharoni, 117), about fifteen miles south of Jattir. Because of the absence of any signs of habitation at Khirbet Ararah during David's time, however, Avraham Biran prefers the site of Tel Esdar, about a mile to the north (Steven Feldman, "Return to Aroer," *BAR* 28/1 [2002]: 54).

The location of Siphmoth, mentioned only here, is unknown.

Eshtemoa/Eshtemoh, modern es-Semu nine miles south-southwest of Hebron, was (like Jattir) a town for the Levites in the hill country of Judah (Jos 15:50; 21:14; 1Ch 6:57).

The word "Racal" (v.29), otherwise unknown, may be a scribal error for "Carmel" (*ZPEB*, 5:17; cf. LXX^B, *Karmēlō*), the modern Khirbet el-Kirmil four miles northeast of Eshtemoa. Various "towns of the Jerahmeelites and the Kenites" (v.29; see comment on 27:10) are also objects of David's generosity.

Although the location of Hormah (v.30) is uncertain (for details cf. Aharoni, 215–16), it is probably modern Khirbet el-Meshash four miles north of Aroer and is mentioned in connection with Kesil/Bethul/Bethuel in Joshua 15:30; 19:4 and 1 Chronicles 4:30 (see comment on Bethel in v.27). Hormah had been the site of an early Amalekite victory over Israel (Nu 14:45), who later attacked and destroyed it (Nu 21:3; Jos 12:14; Jdg 1:17).

Bor Ashan, mentioned only here, is probably the same as Ashan, like Jattir and Eshtemoa, a Judahite town (Jos 15:42; 19:7) for the Levites (1Ch 6:59), perhaps to be identified with modern Tell Beit Mirsim about twelve miles southwest of Hebron (cf. Aharoni, 261–62, 354).

"Athach," otherwise unknown, may be a scribal error for "Ether" (Jos 19:7; cf. already K&D; cf. Jos 15:42, where LXX^B reads *Ithak*), probably modern Khirbet el-Ater fifteen miles northwest of Hebron.

Although v.31 concludes with a general statement concerning "other places where David and his men had roamed" (see 23:13 and comment), the list of specific sites that began in v.27 ends here with Hebron, the most important city where plunder was sent (cf. also Jos 10:3; for the significance of the similar position of Ziklag in an earlier list, see v.14 and comment). While this is the only mention of Hebron in 1 Samuel, it plays a key role in 2 Samuel, where it appears about twenty-five times (most of the occurrences being clustered in chs. 2–5). Located in the hill country of Judah (Jos 15:54), twenty-seven miles northeast of Ziklag, Hebron was the seat of David's rule for seven years and six months (2Sa 5:5) before he made Jerusalem, eighteen miles to the north-northeast, his political and religious capital.

David thus ingratiates himself to the elders and other inhabitants of Judah by sharing with them the plunder recovered from the Amalekites. And even before David the king-elect has finished currying favor with Israelites living in the south, King Saul has died while fighting the Philistines in the north, a story vividly and tersely related in the last chapter of 1 Samuel.

NOTES

2 The MT does not read "and all," but the NIV is justified in filling the ellipsis because the context demands some such phrase (cf. vv.3, 6, 19). Indeed, the LXX *ad sensum* reads καὶ πάντα (*kai panta*), and the NASB inserts "and all" in italics.

5 "Widow" here and in 27:3 renders אִשָּׁה (*ʾiššâ*) contextually in the sense of "[former] wife [of a deceased man]." The common Hebrew word for "widow" is אַלְמָנָה (*ʾalmānâ*).

14 Elsewhere in the books of Samuel the Kerethites always appear alongside the Pelethites, both groups together constituting a corps of foreign mercenaries used as David's bodyguard (2Sa 8:18; 20:7, 23; cf. *AIs*, 123). "Kerethites" later served as a synonym of "Philistines" (Eze 25:16; Zep 2:5). Although "Kerethite" almost surely means "Cretan" (cf. K. A. Kitchen, in Wiseman, *Peoples of OT Times*, 56), it is remotely possible that it is a common noun meaning "executioner" or the like from כרת (*krt*, "cut"; for details see M. Delcor, "Les Kéréthim et les Crétois," *VT* 28/4 [1978]: 420).

15 An episode in the story of Esther provides an eerie if unintentional parallel to the present account. Like the Egyptian slave, Esther is an unwilling foreigner in unfamiliar surroundings. Like him, she does not "eat or drink for three days, night or day" (Est 4:16). Like him, she then goes to a king (or king-elect). And like him, in so doing she places her life at risk.

21 The NIV's "people" presumably intends to include the Israelite captives mentioned in vv.18–19. Elsewhere in the chapter, however, עַם (*ʿam*; GK 6639) is always used in the technical sense of "troops" (as commonly in the books of Samuel) and is therefore translated "men" (vv.4, 6). In fact, the phrase translated by the NIV as "the people with him"—הָעָם אֲשֶׁר־אִתּוֹ (*hāʿām ʾašer-ʾittô*)—is rendered in v.4 "his [that is, David's] men." Indeed, *hāʿām* near the end of v.21 itself is translated "his men." Thus "men" would be better than "people" in this context.

22 The NIV translates *ad sensum* "with us" (cf. a few Heb. manuscripts), as do the LXX and Vulgate. The MT reads "with me," explained (however improbably) by K&D as referring to "the person speaking."

25 שִׂים מִשְׁפָּט (*śîm mišpāṭ*, "make/establish an ordinance, lay down a ruling") corresponds to the Mari expression *šipṭam nadānum/šakānum* (cf. Abraham Malamat, "Mari," *BA* 34/1 [1971]: 19).

27 In Joshua 19:8 the NIV implies that Ramah in the Negev is the same as Baalath Beer (cf. Marten H. Woudstra, *The Book of Joshua* [NICOT; Grand Rapids: Eerdmans, 1981], 281). The identification is not certain, however; compare Rasmussen, 228, where the two sites are equated, with 128, where a map locates them more than twenty miles apart.

28 A silver hoard discovered recently in the ruins of Eshtemoa was at first thought to be part of the booty that David sent to the town. The clay jugs in which the silver was found, however, were made at least a century after the event took place (cf. Zeʾev Yeivin, "The Mysterious Silver Hoard From Eshtemoa," *BAR* 13/6 [1987]: 41–43).

4. The Death of Saul and Jonathan (31:1–13)

OVERVIEW

> Chapters 30 and 31 gain in poignancy and power if we regard their events as simultaneous. In the far south, David is anxious about his own and about spoil, while in the far north Saul and the Israelite army perish [cf. also 2 Sam 1:1–4]....While David smites (*hikkah*) ["fought," 30:17] the Amalekites, and they flee (*nus*) [30:17], the Philistines smite (*hikkah*) ["killed," v.2] Saul and his sons, and Israel flees (*nus*) [vv.1, 7]. (Miscall, 181–82).

Consonant with a narrative suffused with violence and death, most of the verbs in ch. 31 reflect the carnage at Mount Gilboa. Having consigned Saul to his inexorable fate, God is not mentioned in the chapter (cf. 27:1–28:2 and Overview).

In slightly abbreviated form, ch. 31 is repeated in 1 Chronicles 10:1–12, where it serves as an introduction to the Chronicler's story of David, which comprises the rest of 1 Chronicles. The commentary below will note only those places where the differences between the two texts are significant or where the Chronicler makes his own unique contribution.

Focusing on Saul's death, the narrator of ch. 1 works quickly and sparsely. The chapter divides most naturally into two parts: vv.1–7 describe the battle itself, while vv.8–13 relate its aftermath. Verses 1 and 8 (the initial verses in each section) contain the only references in the chapter to the "slain" ("dead," NIV [v.8]) who fell "on Mount Gilboa."

1 Now the Philistines fought against Israel; the Israelites fled before them, and many fell
slain on Mount Gilboa. 2 The Philistines pressed hard after Saul and his sons, and they killed
his sons Jonathan, Abinadab and Malki-Shua. 3 The fighting grew fierce around Saul, and
when the archers overtook him, they wounded him critically.

[4]Saul said to his armor-bearer, "Draw your sword and run me through, or these uncircumcised fellows will come and run me through and abuse me."
But his armor-bearer was terrified and would not do it; so Saul took his own sword
and fell on it. [5]When the armor-bearer saw that Saul was dead, he too fell on his sword
and died with him. [6]So Saul and his three sons and his armor-bearer and all his men died
together that same day.
[7]When the Israelites along the valley and those across the Jordan saw that the Israelite
army had fled and that Saul and his sons had died, they abandoned their towns and fled.
And the Philistines came and occupied them.
[8]The next day, when the Philistines came to strip the dead, they found Saul and his
three sons fallen on Mount Gilboa. [9]They cut off his head and stripped off his armor, and
they sent messengers throughout the land of the Philistines to proclaim the news in the
temple of their idols and among their people. [10]They put his armor in the temple of the
Ashtoreths and fastened his body to the wall of Beth Shan.
[11]When the people of Jabesh Gilead heard of what the Philistines had done to Saul, [12]all
their valiant men journeyed through the night to Beth Shan. They took down the bodies
of Saul and his sons from the wall of Beth Shan and went to Jabesh, where they burned
them. [13]Then they took their bones and buried them under a tamarisk tree at Jabesh, and
they fasted seven days.

COMMENTARY

1–7 The Philistine threat has hung like a pall over Israel throughout 1 Samuel almost from the beginning (cf. 4:1–2), and the end is not yet. Even now, "as Samuel promised, the Philistines fight Israel (cf. 28:19)" (Brueggemann, *First and Second Samuel*, 207)—and, as all too often under Saul's erratic leadership, "many" Israelites "fell slain" (v.1). The present scene stands in marked contrast to David's killing of Goliath, which galvanized the Israelite army with the result that the Philistine "dead were strewn" along the roadside (17:52; the Heb. phrase is the same as that for "fell slain" in v.1). Symbolizing defeat for Israel, the verb "fell" appears three times in this section (vv.1, 4–5; cf. also "fallen" in v.8). Mount Gilboa would always be remembered as the place where Saul and his sons died (see comment on 28:4).

Although Saul and Jonathan had earlier engaged "in hot pursuit" of the Philistines (14:22), now the tables are tragically turned: The Philistines "pressed hard" after Saul and his sons (v.2; same Heb. phrase; cf. also 2Sa 1:6, "almost upon him"; Jdg 20:45). Of the four sons of Saul (for details see comment on 14:49), three (including Jonathan, who should have been the heir apparent) are killed (vv.2, 6, 8) before Saul himself commits suicide. The other son, Esh-

Baal/Ish-Bosheth, may not have been present on the battlefield. (He makes his first appearance in the narrative in 2Sa 2:8.)

With Saul helpless and virtually alone, the Philistines moved in for the kill. As the fighting grew "fierce" around him (lit., "heavy," v.3; cf. Jdg 20:34), the archers "overtook him" (lit., "found him" in the sense of finding their mark, as an axehead might "hit" [lit., "find"; Dt 19:5] and kill a man), and he was badly wounded.

Saul does not want the Philistines, "these uncircumcised fellows" (v.4; see comment on 14:6), to finish him off and "abuse" him (cf. Jdg 19:25; "Saul is afraid of being tortured before he dies" [McCarter, *I Samuel*, 443]). Relying on his armor-bearer to do as he is told (for the importance of an armor-bearer to his master, see comment on 14:1), Saul tells him, "Draw your sword and run me through" (v.4). David had earlier drawn Goliath's sword from its scabbard and used it to kill the Philistine giant (17:51), but Saul's armor-bearer—like David before him (26:23)—"would not" kill the Lord's anointed (see comment on "not willing" in 22:17). Miscall, 182, observes: "Saul, in his last moment, is not supported by his armor-bearer—this one or his earlier armor-bearer. 'David came to Saul ... and became his armor-bearer' (1 Sam 16:21–22). Again we are subtly reminded that David is not there at Mt. Gilboa."

Since Saul is determined to die on his own terms, he has no alternative but to take his own sword and fall on it. Just as Eli, a failed priest for forty years, died by falling off "his" (lit., "the") chair (4:18), so also Saul, a hapless king for forty years (Ac 13:21), dies by falling on "his" (lit., "the") sword. Polzin (*Samuel and the Deuteronomist*, 224) suggests yet another comparison:

> Wounded in battle, both Abimelech and Saul ask their armor bearers to kill them lest they bear the ignominy of being killed by one who is uncircumcised (in Abimelech's case by a woman, in Saul's by the Philistines). The differing responses of their armor bearers is significant: Abimelech's young man thrusts him through (Jdg. 9:54), but Saul's is unwilling to kill his master, forcing the king to commit suicide.

Although one could conceivably read into Saul's suicide the decision of a desperate man who was as good as dead, the narrative itself provides its own rationale. "There is a reasoned and controlled quality in this final act—'lest these uncircumcised come and slay me and make mockery of me' (31:4)—that stands in marked contrast to his earlier rashness (14:18, 24)" (Humphreys, 98).

> Saul thus kills himself for a noble reason, the same reason in essence that David had given earlier for refusing to kill Saul.... Saul dies on the battlefield, doing the job he had been anointed and elected to do—leading the army of Israel against her enemies. Through all the reluctance, failure, and madness, he kept his bargain to the end, dying as the military king. (Preston, 37)

But in another sense the Philistines do in fact kill Saul, since their archers wound him beyond hope of recovery. Thus the man who had originally been introduced as the one who would "deliver [God's] people from the hand of the Philistines" (9:16) meets his end by dying at their hands.

Seeing that his king is dead, the armor-bearer follows his example and falls on his own sword (v.5). Perhaps in order to stress the camaraderie and mutual loyalty within the Israelite army, the narrator states that all the warriors—Saul, his sons, his armor-bearer, his men—die "together" (v.6; see comment on "alike" in 30:24). Miscall, 170, observes that "Saul and his sons, like Eli and his sons, die on the same day, a day on which the Philistines defeat Israel" (cf. 2:34; 4:10–12, 17–18). Although many Israelites not directly involved in the fighting manage to escape the Philistine onslaught, the extent of the enemy victory is impressive: They occupy deserted Israelite towns in "the valley" (v.7; doubtless the Valley of Jezreel, as in Jdg 7:1, 8, 12 [cf. 6:33]) and in Transjordan.

The three stanzas of "Song of Saul before His Last Battle" by George Gordon (Lord Byron) imaginatively reconstruct Saul's last words to his men, his armor-bearer, and his son Jonathan:

Warriors and chiefs! should the shaft or the sword
Pierce me in leading the host of the Lord,
Heed not the corse, though a king's in your path:
Bury your steel in the bosoms of Gath!

Thou who art bearing my buckler and bow,
Should the soldiers of Saul look away from the foe,
Stretch me that moment in blood at thy feet!
Mine be the doom which they dared not to meet.

Farewell to others, but never we part,
Heir to my royalty, son of my heart!
Bright is the diadem, boundless the sway,
Or kingly the death, which awaits us to-day!

8–13 The following day (v.8) the Philistines come back to the battlefield to "strip the dead"; on a later occasion David's men would return the favor (2Sa 23:9–10). Brueggemann (*First and Second Samuel*, 208) suggests that the Philistines may have been able to identify Saul's body "not only by his height but by his special armor (17:38)." As David had earlier cut off the head of the Philistines' champion (see 17:51 and comment), they now cut off the head of Israel's king (v.9), soon to put it on display in the temple of Dagon as a trophy of war (1Ch 10:10; see comment on 5:4).

They also strip Saul of his armor, soon to display it in the temple of their goddesses (v.10; for "Ashtoreths" meaning "goddesses" see comment on 7:3–4; cf. also "gods" in the parallel passage in 1Ch 10:10, in this case probably meaning "goddesses," for which Heb. had no specific word). Messengers are sent to "proclaim the news" of the resounding victory and its aftermath—good news, but only from the Philistine standpoint (see 4:17 and comment; cf. 2Sa 1:20; 4:10).

The report is to be broadcast throughout Philistia but especially "in the temple of their idols" (v.9). Whether the various temples mentioned in vv.9–10 and in the parallel texts in 1 Chronicles are different designations for the same building or refer to more than one building is impossible to say (although at least two buildings seem intended). It is indeed ironic, however, that a book that begins at the "house/temple of the LORD at Shiloh" (1:24; cf. 1:9; see also comment on 1:7) ends at the "house/temple" of one or more pagan deities.

With respect to archaeological excavations at Beth Shan, T. C. Mitchell ("Bethshean, Bethshan," *NBD*, 136) comments: "In level V (*c.* 11th century) two temples were uncovered, one (the S) dedicated to the god Resheph and the other to the goddess Antit, and [A.] Rowe [field director of the excavations from 1925–28] has suggested that these are the temples of Dagon and Ashteroth in which Saul's head and armour were displayed by the Philistines" (for a brief description of the excavation results, see G. M. FitzGerald, "Beth-shean," *Archaeology and Old Testament Study* [ed. D. Winton Thomas; Oxford: Clarendon, 1967], 193–96).

As for the mutilated bodies of Saul and his sons (Saul's suicide did not in fact prevent his body from being abused; v.4), the Philistines fasten them to Beth Shan's wall (vv.10, 12, probably to the face of it; for a parallel, cf. the following from a stela of Amenhotep II in the temple of Amada in Nubia: "Six men of these enemies were hanged on the face of the wall of Thebes.... Then the other foe was ... hanged to the wall of Napata, to show his majesty's victories" [John A. Wilson, *ANET*, 248]). Beth Shan is modern Tell el-Husn, an impressive and picturesque mound of ruins fifteen miles south-southwest of the Sea of Galilee at the junction of the Jezreel and Jordan valleys. The name of the ancient city is preserved in that of the nearby town of Beisan.

At the beginning of his reign, Saul's first military action had been to rescue the people of Jabesh Gilead (see comment on 11:1) from the Ammonites (11:1–11). At the end of his reign, after his final military action (which cost him his life), the grateful people of Jabesh (v.11) pay tribute to Saul and his sons by retrieving their bodies from Beth Shan and giving them an honorable burial (vv.12–13; 2Sa 2:4–5). The "valiant men" of Jabesh (v.12; the Heb. idiom implies unusual courage; cf. 2Sa 11:16, "strongest defenders"; 23:20 Qere, "valiant fighter"), doubtless at great personal risk (cf. Brueggemann, *First and Second Samuel*, 209), travel by night (probably to increase their chances of avoiding detection [cf. 2Sa 2:29, 32; 4:7], esp. since they have to cross the Jordan) to Beth Shan, about twelve miles to the northwest. There they lovingly remove the bodies of Saul and his sons and take them to Jabesh, where they burn them (perhaps to avoid "risk of infection from the quickly decomposing bodies" [Baldwin, 171]; cf. Am 6:10).

"In the end, Saul is humiliated and then honored" (Brueggemann, *First and Second Samuel*, 208; cf. also Hertzberg, 234). The last verse of 1 Samuel describes the Jabeshites' two final acts of respect: They "buried" (see comment on 25:1a; 28:3–31:13) Saul and his sons, and they "fasted." The bones were interred "under a ['the,' MT] tamarisk tree" (called "the great tree" in 1Ch 10:12)—an ironic twist on Saul's position of haughty authority "under the tamarisk tree" at Gibeah, his hometown (22:6). The fasting of the men of Jabesh for Saul and his sons would be repeated by David and his men, though for a shorter period of time (2Sa 1:12). "Seven days" is frequently associated with "ceremonies involving ritual uncleanness" (J. B. Segal, 15–16; cf. Lev 13:4–6, 21, 26–27, 31–34, 50–51, 54; 14:8–9, 38–39; 15:13, 19; Nu 6:9; 12:14–15; 19:11–12). In this case it may have been a period of mourning as well as fasting (cf. Lewis, 44–45; cf. Ge 50:10; Sir 22:12).

In its final chapter 1 Samuel thus ends on a high note "by putting aside allusion to Saul's dark and clouded days. It closes ... with pathos, with a memory of Saul's finest hour" (Miscall, 182). Though Saul "was predestined to fail and he did, as a commander, a father, a friend, the founder of a monarchy," he nevertheless "perseveres in the mission for which he was chosen, the protection of Israel from annihilation by the surrounding enemies. Therein lies his greatness. Though he lost favor in the eyes of the Lord of Israel, yet Saul continued to feel compassion for the Children of Israel" (Herman M. van Praag, "The Downfall of King Saul: The Neurobiological Consequences of Losing Hope," *Judaism* 35/4 [1986]: 424).

At best, however, Saul remains a complex and enigmatic figure, at once hero and villain. "What [R. B.] Sewall [*The Vision of Tragedy* (New Haven, Conn.: Yale Univ. Press, 1962), 32] says of *Oedipus the King* can be said of the tragedy of King Saul as well: 'At the end ... much remains to praise, much to blame, and much to wonder at'" (Humphreys, 102). Perhaps the fittest conclusion to the story of

Saul, as well as the most appropriate transition from 1 Samuel to 2 Samuel, is the Chronicler's inspired coda: "Saul died because he was unfaithful to the LORD; he did not keep the word of the LORD and even consulted a medium for guidance, and did not inquire of the LORD. So the LORD put him to death and turned the kingdom over to David son of Jesse" (1Ch 10:13–14).

The king is dead.

Long live the king!

NOTES

3 "They wounded him critically" renders וַיָּחֶל מְאֹד מֵהַמּוֹרִים (*wayyāḥel m^e^ʾōd mēhammôrîm*, lit., "he was wounded exceedingly by the archers"). Unpointed, ויחל (*wyḥl*) may be parsed as a Qal imperfect from חול (*ḥwl*) or חלל (*ḥll*), one of which in this case is probably a byform of the other; see especially רַב מְחוֹלֵל (*rab m^e^ḥôlēl*, "an archer who wounds"; Pr 26:10), in which *m^e^ḥôlvēl* is either a Poel participle from *ḥll* or a Polel participle from *ḥwl* (cf. מְחוֹלֶלֶת, *m^e^ḥôlelet*, "who pierced"], a similarly ambiguous form in Isa 51:9). Given the root *ḥll* in v.1 ("slain") and v.8 ("dead"), it would seem best to assume that root here as well.

The MT apparently understands *wayyāḥel* from *ḥwl*/*ḥyl* in the sense of "he was in anguish, he was afraid"; cf. the possible semantic parallels in v. 4: יָרֵא מְאֹד (*yārēʾ m^e^ʾōd*, "was terrified") and 28:5: וַיֶּחֱרַד לִבּוֹ מְאֹד (*wayyeḥ^e^rad libbô m^e^ʾōd*, "terror filled his heart," lit., "his heart was afraid exceedingly"). Very few commentators (e.g., K&D, Klein) and versions (e.g., ASV) translate the passage in that way, however, and the NIV's rendering is contextually preferable (cf. KJV, NKJV, NASB, RSV, NEB/REB, TEV).

4 הָעֲרֵלִים ... וְהִתְעַלְּלוּ (*hāʿ^a^rēlîm* ... *w^e^hitʿall^e^lû*, "uncircumcised fellows will ... abuse") is a fine example of assonance.

6 By substituting "all his house died together" for "his armor-bearer and all his men died together," 1 Chronicles 10:6 perhaps stresses the faithfulness of the warriors who stood with Saul to the end. In either case "all" is hyperbolic, since many Israelites were not involved in the battle (v.7) and since Saul's son Ish-Bosheth, a member of Saul's "house," did not die until later (2Sa 4:7–8).

10 Beth Shan is spelled בֵּית שַׁן (*bêt šan*) here and in 2 Samuel 21:12, בֵּית שְׁאָן (*bêt š^e^ʾān*) elsewhere (Jos 17:11, 16; Jdg 1:27; 1Ki 4:12; 1Ch 7:29). Although the name would appear to mean "Temple of [the God] Shan," a divine name Shan/Shaʾan is thus far unattested. Beth Shan should perhaps therefore be analyzed as Akkadian *bītu ša Ani* ("Temple of Anu"; cf. the writing of Beth Shan as *bīt[u] ša-a-ni* in Tell el-Amarna letter 289:20). For Anu, the Sumero-Babylonian god of the heavens, compare Herman Wohlstein, *The Sky-God An-Anu: Head of the Mesopotamian Pantheon in Sumerian-Akkadian Literature* (Jericho, N.Y.: Paul Stroock, 1976).

12 Since the bones of Saul and his sons remained after the Jabeshites burned their bodies, cremation (which reduces a corpse to ashes) is not in view. Nor should "burned them" be understood as meaning "burned spices for them" or "anointed them with spices" (cf. NEB) on the basis of 2 Chronicles 16:14; 21:19; Jeremiah 34:5 ("make a fire in [one's] honor," NIV), where the Hebrew idiom is quite different (as pointed out long ago by K&D).

2 SAMUEL

I. CONSOLIDATION OF MONARCHY IN ISRAEL (1:1–20:26)

OVERVIEW

The overriding theme of the books of Samuel is the beginning of Israel's monarchy in the eleventh century BC. Having discussed the prelude (1Sa 1:1–7:17), advent (1Sa 8:1–15:35), and establishment (1Sa 16:1–31:13) of the monarchy, the author next turns to its consolidation under David, Israel's greatest king.

Many scholars assume that the story of David's rise, which begins in 1 Samuel 16:1, does not end until 2 Samuel 5:10 (cf. McCarter, "The Apology of David," 489–504; *II Samuel*, 142–43; Brueggemann, *First and Second Samuel*, 236, 244) or perhaps until the early chapters of 2 Samuel (for a summary listing see Mabee, 89 n. 1). The Deuteronomic historian himself, however, has provided an important clue that contravenes all such assessments. If—as seems likely—the books of Joshua, Judges, Samuel, and Kings were written/compiled/edited by the same individual(s), it is surely to the point to observe that just as Joshua begins with "After the death of Moses" and Judges begins with "After the death of Joshua," so also 2 Samuel begins with "After the death of Saul." (Although 2 Kings begins similarly, the corresponding phrase sits differently in the verse and is therefore appropriately rendered in a slightly different way by the NIV: "After Ahab's death.") In other words, the narrator telegraphs to his readers as sharp a break at 2 Samuel 1:1 as he had at Joshua 1:1 and Judges 1:1 (a break later confirmed by whomever it was who divided the scroll of Samuel into two books).

In addition, as my overall outline of 2 Samuel indicates (see the Introduction: Outline), the first twenty chapters constitute a carefully crafted literary masterpiece that divides into four sections of varying lengths, each of which ends with a four-verse list of names. The first two sections (1:1–3:5; 3:6–5:16) conclude respectively with a list of sons born to David in Hebron (3:2–5) and children born to David in Jerusalem (5:13–16), while each of the last two sections (5:17–8:18; 9:1–20:26) concludes with a list of David's officials (8:15–18; 20:23–26). Such a structure bears every indication of being deliberate rather than accidental. (For a similar—though not identical—analysis arrived at independently, see Martin, 37–39. For 2 Samuel 1:1 as the start of "the narration of events centered solely around David," compare Mabee, 90 and n. 3. For chs. 1–20 as a single literary unit, compare Baldwin, 176.)

Beginning with the list of sons born to David in Hebron (3:2–5), much of 2 Samuel is paralleled in 1 Chronicles (a process already begun in 1Sa 31; see comment on 1Sa 31:1–13):

2 Samuel	1 Chronicles
3:2–5	3:1–4a
5:1–3	11:1–3
5:4–5	3:4b; 29:26–27 (cf. 1Ki 2:11)
5:6–10	11:4–9
5:11–12	14:1–2
5:13–16	3:5–8; 14:3–7
5:17–25	14:8–16
6:1–11	13:5–14

(Continued on the next page)

(Continued)

2 Samuel	1 Chronicles
6:12b–19a	15:25–16:3
6:19b–20a	16:43
7:1–17	17:1–15
7:18–29	17:16–27
8:1–14	18:1–13 (cf. 1Ki 11:23b–24a)
8:15–18	18:14–17
10:1–19	19:1–19
11:1	20:1a
12:29–31	20:1b–3
21:18–22	20:4–8
23:8–23	11:11–25
23:24–39	11:26–41a
24:1–9	21:1–6
24:10–17	21:7–17
24:18–25	21:18–27

In addition, ch. 22 is paralleled in Psalm 18. For detailed comparisons between the MT of 2 Samuel and its parallels in 1 Chronicles and Psalm 18 (as well as elsewhere in the OT), see especially Abba Bendavid, *Parallels in the Bible* [Jerusalem: Carta, 1972], 31–70); for detailed comparisons in English, see William Day Crockett, *A Harmony of the Books of Samuel, Kings, and Chronicles* (London: Revell, 1897), 106–41, and esp. James D. Newsome Jr., ed., *A Synoptic Harmony of Samuel, Kings, and Chronicles with Related Passages from Psalms, Isaiah, Jeremiah, and Ezra* (Grand Rapids: Baker, 1986), 23–79. The commentary below will note only those places where the differences between 2 Samuel and parallel texts are significant or where the parallel text makes its own contribution. Given the fact that the Chronicler, in order to highlight the enduring values of David's reign, tends to omit those episodes in 2 Samuel that are unflattering to David, comparisons between 2 Samuel and 1 Chronicles have continued to hold a special fascination for generations of readers of the OT.

A. David's Accession to Kingship over Judah (1:1–3:5)

OVERVIEW

The story of David's rise to the kingship of Judah begins with an account of the decimation of Saul's line (1:1–16) and ends with a summary of David's fecundity (3:2–5). Nestled in the center of the literary unit is the narrative of David's anointing as king over Judah (2:1–7), signaling the replacement of Saul and his house in southern Canaan.

1. The Death of Saul and Jonathan (1:1–16)

OVERVIEW

Second Samuel begins as 1 Samuel ends—with an account of the death of King Saul and his son Jonathan, the heir apparent. But while 1 Samuel 31 describes the events as they actually occurred, 2 Samuel 1:1–16 consists of a report of the events filtered through the not disinterested words of an

Amalekite alien. The section displays a chiastic arrangement:

- A David strikes down the Amalekites (1:1)
  - B David questions an Amalekite (1:2–5)
    - C The Amalekite tells David his story (1:6–10)
    - C' David and his men react to the Amalekite's story (1:11–12)
  - B' David questions the Amalekite again (1:13–14)
- A' David strikes down the Amalekite (1:15–16)

[1]After the death of Saul, David returned from defeating the Amalekites and stayed in
Ziklag two days. [2]On the third day a man arrived from Saul's camp, with his clothes torn
and with dust on his head. When he came to David, he fell to the ground to pay him
honor.

[3]"Where have you come from?" David asked him.

He answered, "I have escaped from the Israelite camp."

[4]"What happened?" David asked. "Tell me."

He said, "The men fled from the battle. Many of them fell and died. And Saul and his son Jonathan are dead."

[5]Then David said to the young man who brought him the report, "How do you know that Saul and his son Jonathan are dead?"

[6]"I happened to be on Mount Gilboa," the young man said, "and there was Saul, leaning
on his spear, with the chariots and riders almost upon him. [7]When he turned around and
saw me, he called out to me, and I said, 'What can I do?'

[8]"He asked me, 'Who are you?'

"'An Amalekite,' I answered.

[9]"Then he said to me, 'Stand over me and kill me! I am in the throes of death, but I'm still alive.'

[10]"So I stood over him and killed him, because I knew that after he had fallen he could not survive. And I took the crown that was on his head and the band on his arm and have brought them here to my lord."

[11]Then David and all the men with him took hold of their clothes and tore them. [12]They
mourned and wept and fasted till evening for Saul and his son Jonathan, and for the army
of the LORD and the house of Israel, because they had fallen by the sword.

[13]David said to the young man who brought him the report, "Where are you from?"

"I am the son of an alien, an Amalekite," he answered.

[14]David asked him, "Why were you not afraid to lift your hand to destroy the LORD's anointed?"

[15]Then David called one of his men and said, "Go, strike him down!" So he struck him
down, and he died. [16]For David had said to him, "Your blood be on your own head. Your
own mouth testified against you when you said, 'I killed the LORD's anointed.'"

COMMENTARY

1 Verses 1 and 15–16 frame the literary unit by referring to David's "striking down" (Hiphil of *nākâ*) the Amalekite(s) ("defeating," v.1; "struck him down," v.15 ["strike him down" earlier in v.15 derives from the Hebrew root *pgʿ*]). Verse 1 and 8:13 also form an inclusio surrounding a larger section (chs. 1–8) that immediately precedes the court history (chs. 9–20): David "returned from defeating" the Amalekites (v.1); David "returned from striking down" the Edomites (8:13). David's earlier successful returning home from battle (1Sa 17:57) had aroused Saul's jealousy (1Sa 18:6–9)—and the resulting paranoia had contributed to his decline and ultimate demise.

2–5 Saul's defeat and death at the hands of the Philistines and David's victory over the Amalekites (for the full account see 1Sa 30–31) occurred at approximately the same time (as the syntax of vv.1–2 indicates; cf. K&D). The distance from Mount Gilboa (v.6; see comment on 1Sa 28:4) to Ziklag (v.1; see comment on 1Sa 27:6) is more than eighty miles, a three-day trip for the Amalekite fugitive (v.2). His arrival in Ziklag is underscored by the use of three different forms of the same Hebrew verb (translated "arrived," v.2; "came," v.2; "come," v.3), and the place from which he fled is called "Saul's camp" by the narrator (v.2) and "the Israelite camp" by the Amalekite himself (v.3).

The story in vv.2–5 echoes the similar account of the Benjamite fugitive's report in 1 Samuel 4:12–17 (cf. "his clothes torn and [with] dust on his head," v.2; 1Sa 4:12; "What happened?" v.4; 1Sa 4:16) and should be compared with it (see comment on 1Sa 4:12; cf. also independently Garsiel, 102–6). Garsiel, 106, summarizes:

> The author of Samuel established a deliberate connection between the two stories in order to set up an analogy between the fates of Saul's house and of Eli's.... The comparison indicates that there is a clear rule of law which connects a leader's conduct with his fate and the fate of his house. A degenerate leader, whether it is himself who has sinned or his sons, will ultimately be deposed ... or come to a tragic end, just as Eli and his sons die on the same day, and so do Saul and his.

Torn clothes (v.2; cf. v.11) and dust on one's head are signs of anguish and distress (cf. 15:32; Jos 7:6; Ne 9:1), appropriate and understandable behavior in a man who has so recently witnessed a battlefield scene of suffering and death. Like Abigail before him (1Sa 25:23), the man demonstrates his submission to David by prostrating himself in his presence.

David's desire to know where the man has come from (v.3) is doubtless prompted by the man's forlorn and unkempt appearance (cf. similarly 1Sa 30:13). His response—that he has escaped from the Israelite camp—makes David all the more curious; so he demands that the man "tell" him what has happened (v.4). Continuing to characterize the man, the participial form of the verb *ngd* ("tell"; cf. 18:11) is rendered "who brought ... the report" in vv.5, 13 (cf. similarly 4:10; the NIV leaves the word untranslated in v.6 in deference to English style). Rendered elsewhere as "messenger" (cf. 15:13; Jer 51:31), the term in this context thus reduces the function of the Amalekite to that of a bearer of news.

The Amalekite's report reveals that the Israelites "fled" from the battle against the Philistines and that many of them "fell and died" (v.4; cf. 1Sa 31:1). What is more, continues the man—who obviously thinks that he is bringing David good news (4:10)—"Saul and his son Jonathan are dead." As noted by Terence Kleven ("Rhetoric and Narrative Depiction in 2 Samuel 1:1–16," *Proceedings of the Eastern Great Lakes and Midwest Biblical Societies*

9 [1989]: 62), the fugitive is referred to in v.2 by the most general term, a "man," but in v.5, as the conversation progresses, he is called a "lad" ("young man," NIV). This is "one of the first indications of the naivety [*sic*] of the man's actions." David, of course, wants to know how the messenger can be so sure that Saul and Jonathan are indeed dead (v.5), so the man tells his story (vv.6–10).

6–10 The Amalekite's account of Saul's death deviates in several important respects from that given in 1 Samuel 31. Arnold gives a concise summary of the most obvious differences: "In 1 Samuel 31 ... the king committed suicide, here the Amalekite killed him; there he was wounded by archers, here his enemies were charioteers; there the Philistines took his armor, here the Amalekite brought his crown and armlet to David" (Bill T. Arnold, "The Amalekite's Report of Saul's Death: Political Intrigue or Incompatible Sources?" *JETS* 32/3 [1989]: 290).

Most of the proposed solutions to the problem—for example, that the narrator has transmitted two mutually contradictory accounts, or that the Amalekite's story is true (which would mean that the report in 1 Samuel 31 is false), or that the so-called contradictions can be dissolved by postulating separate literary sources in vv.1–16 (a theory effectively answered by Arnold in "The Amalekite's Report," 290–94)—only serve to complicate it further. Commentators have therefore tried to harmonize the two accounts.

Typical is the early reconstruction by Josephus. He claimed that when Saul's armor-bearer refused to kill him, the king tried to fall on his own sword but was too weak to do so. Saul then turned and saw the Amalekite, who, upon the king's request, complied by killing him. After the Amalekite had taken the king's crown and armband and fled, Saul's armor-bearer killed himself (Josephus, *Ant.* 6.370–72 [14.7]). Josephus's attempt at conflation, while commendable and in some respects helpful, errs in his basic assumption that the Amalekite was telling the truth.

The messenger begins his report to David (v.6) by stating that he "happened" (better something like "just happened," to bring out the force of the Hebrew infinitive-absolute-plus-finite-verb construction) to be on Mount Gilboa (the scene of Saul's last battle [1Sa 31:1]; see comment on 28:4). There he encountered the wounded Saul, who was supporting himself by "leaning on his spear"—a parable of his tendency to rely on human effort rather than on divine resources (cf. Isa 10:20; 31:1, where "rely" translates the same Heb. verb as "leaning" does here). Philistine "chariots and riders," feared far and wide (see comment on 1Sa 13:5), were "almost upon him" (see comment on 1Sa 31:2, where "pressed hard" renders the same Heb. verb).

Seeing the Amalekite nearby, Saul called out to him (v.7). The man replied with the response commonly used by servants: "What can I do?" (*hinnēnî*, lit., "Behold me," "Here I am" [see comment on 1Sa 3:4–10; see also Ge 22:1, 11; Isa 6:8], in this case "How can I [possibly] help you?"). Perhaps to be sure that the man was not a Philistine, who might abuse the Israelite king if he had the chance (cf. 1Sa 31:4), Saul asked the man to identify himself (v.8). His answer—that he was an "Amalekite"—gives to the account an ironic touch, since David had recently returned to Ziklag after defeating an Amalekite raiding party (v.1; cf. 1Sa 30). Indeed, "David's vivid memories of the battle with the Amalekites makes [*sic*] it improbable that David (would have) much sympathy for an Amalekite who brings him the news of Saul's death" (Kleven, "Rhetoric and Narrative Depiction," 61).

Satisfied as to the general identity of the young man, Saul uttered words reminiscent of the earlier description of David's dispatching of Goliath: "Stand over me and kill me" (v.9; cf. 1Sa 17:51).

Although in mortal agony and wanting to die, Saul was unable—or (at least temporarily) unwilling (cf. 1Sa 31:4)—to take his own life.

Apparently happy to oblige, the Amalekite claims to have fulfilled Saul's wish to the letter (v.10). He "knew" that the fallen king could not survive, and—since he himself had killed him—he could also "know" for certain (v.5) that Saul was dead. After killing the king, the Amalekite took Saul's "crown" (*nēzer*), the primary symbol of his royal authority (cf. 2Ki 11:12 = 2Ch 23:11), as well as a band (lacking the definite article in the MT) that he was wearing on his arm. The armlet (*ʾeṣʿādâ*) may have been made of gold (cf. the same Heb. word in Nu 31:50) and was perhaps another symbol of royalty. Arnold ("The Amalekite's Report," 296) surmises:

> In the Joash enthronement passage (2 Kings 11:12) we read that "then they brought out the king's son, and put the crown (*nēzer*) upon him, and gave him the testimony (*hāʿēdût*)." *BHK* and many commentators read *haṣʿādôt* ("the armlets") for "the testimony," thus providing a perfect illustration of the crown and armlet as the primary royal insignia.

But although the proposed emendation is both attractive and modest (requiring the addition of only one Hebrew consonant), and although the form *haṣṣᵉʿādôt* does in fact occur in Isaiah 3:20 ("ankle chains," NIV; perhaps better "armlets"), the NIV's "copy of the covenant" in 2 Kings 11:12 (= 2Ch 23:11) faithfully translates *hāʿēdût* there and makes equally good sense in the context. In any case, Arnold's plausible reconstruction ("The Amalekite's Report," 296–97) of the sequence of events is not dependent on the Joash enthronement passage:

> After Saul's serious wound, and in light of the imminent arrival of the Philistines and his armor-bearer's reluctance to mercifully kill him, he committed suicide. In the ensuing chaos the Amalekite, whose connections with the Israelite camp are unknown, took the royal insignia from the king's corpse. The next morning the Philistines found Saul's body and stripped him of his armor. But the most substantial spoils of war, the royal crown and armlet, were already being carried to Ziklag with the message that Saul was dead.

11–12 Having once been a valued member of Saul's court, David undoubtedly recognizes the crown and armlet in the hands of the Amalekite. But the messenger could scarcely have been prepared for the response of David and his men, who tear their clothes (v.11) for much the same reason that the Amalekite had earlier torn his (see comment on v.2). With genuine and heartfelt expressions of grief over Saul and Jonathan (cf. also vv.17–27) and the other fallen Israelite warriors, David and his men mourn (v.12; cf. 11:26; 1Sa 25:1; 28:3) and weep (cf. also v.24). They also fast, but only "till evening," which was apparently David's usual practice in such situations (cf. 3:35; contrast the weeklong fast of the Jabeshites for Saul and his sons [see comment on 1Sa 31:13]). Their sorrow extends to the "house of Israel" (v.12), a reference to the people as a whole ("house" in the sense of "family, community"; see comment on 1Sa 7:2), since all Israel has suffered tragic and irreparable loss in the death of their king.

13–14 Apparently after the period of mourning (vv.11–12) is over, David questions the messenger again (cf. vv.2–5). David's "Where are you from?" (v.13) does not repeat his earlier "Where have you come from?" (v.3), which is concerned with the man's most recent location (cf. "Where do you come from?" in 1Sa 30:13). Here David wants to know something of the man's background, probing even more deeply than Saul's "Who are you?" in v.8. Thus, in addition to repeating the information that he is an Amalekite (v.13; cf. v.8), the man affirms that he is the son of an "alien."

It would seem that David has now learned all he needs to know concerning the Amalekite. Since his father is a resident alien, living in Saul's realm, the young man can be expected to have at least minimal knowledge about Israel's basic traditions, including the inviolability of "the LORD's anointed" (vv.14, 16). David's question to him (v.14) is therefore entirely in order. By the Amalekite's own testimony (cf. v.16), he had lifted his hand (see comment on 1Sa 22:17) to "destroy" (see comment on 1Sa 26:9; for another example of "destroy" with a human object, cf. 2Sa 14:11) the Lord's anointed king—something David had never done, though he had had more than one opportunity to do so (see 1Sa 24:6 and comment; 24:10; 26:9 and comment; 26:11).

15–16 Far from receiving the reward that he thinks David will surely give him because of the "good news" he thought he was bringing (4:10), the Amalekite's callous bravado (v.14) has sealed his own doom. As David would later order his men to execute the murderers of Ish-Bosheth son of Saul (4:12), so now he calls one of his "men" (lit., "young men," v.15) to strike down the "young man" (v.13) who claims to have killed Saul. The command of execution—"Strike him down!" (v.15)—was all too common in the early days of Israel's monarchy (cf. 1Sa 22:18; 1Ki 2:29). In this case the subsequent statement, "So he struck him down," uses a different verb from that used earlier in the verse, probably to form an inclusio with v.1 (see comment there; the latter verb is the same as that used of David's striking down Goliath in 1Sa 17:50).

The Amalekite's own words—that he had "killed" (v.16; cf. v.10) Saul—proved to be his undoing. Before the Amalekite's summary execution David told him, "Your blood be on your own head," a stock phrase pronounced to protect the one who authorizes an execution by clearing him of bloodguilt against the murdered man (cf. 1Ki 2:31–33)—in this case Saul, of whose death David (soon to become the de facto king of Israel) thus declares himself innocent. A gentle irony: Early on, a disobedient Saul had been "too weak to kill the Amelekite [*sic*] Agag [1Sa 15], while David appropriately inflicts capital punishment upon the Amelekite [*sic*] who inappropriately [claimed to have] killed Saul" (Brettler, 82). That Amalekite, hoping for a reward by bringing to David the crown that had been on Saul's "head" (v.10), discovers—too late—that his claim to have killed Saul has brought on his own "head" bloodguilt against the Lord's anointed (v.16).

The story ends as it began: David "strikes down" one or more hated "Amalekites" (see comment on v.1). Although he acts in accord with the messenger's own words, we have no way of knowing whether David in fact believes them. In the light of 1 Samuel 31, it is clear that the young man's claim to have killed Saul is false, however much the rest of his story may appear to have the ring of truth. Arnold's summary statement is apropos: "The events described in 1 Samuel 31 and 2 Samuel 1 are historically consistent if it is assumed that the Amalekite messenger was attempting to deceive David" (Arnold, "The Amalekite's Report," 298).

NOTES

1 The MT's הָעֲמָלֵק (*hā*^{ca}*mālēq*, "the Amalek") is unique in the OT and should doubtless be vocalized to be read as the gentilic הָעֲמָלֵקִי (*hā*^{ca}*mālēqî*, "the Amalekite[s]") with several Hebrew MSS (cf. BDB, 766).

9 "I am in the throes of death" is literally "the שָׁבָץ [*šābāṣ* being a *hapax legomenon* of unknown meaning] has seized me." If the word is related to the root *šbṣ*, used in various forms elsewhere of the fabrication of priestly garments in the sense of "[intricately] weave [cloth]," "mount/set [gems]" (Ex 28:4, 11, 13–14, 20, 25, 39; 39:6, 13, 16, 18), the rendering "throes [of death]," with its implications of (intricate?) convulsion, may be close to what the narrator intended.

The sentence כִּי־כָל־עוֹד נַפְשִׁי בִּי (*kî-kol-ʿôd napšî bî*, "But I'm still alive," lit., "But my life is still in me") finds a striking parallel in Job 27:3: כִּי־כָל־עוֹד נִשְׁמָתִי בִי (*kî-kol-ʿôd nišmātî bî*, "As long as I have life within me").

12 The LXX reads Ἰούδα (*Iouda*, "Judah," apparently from a Hebrew text that had יהודה [*yhwdh*] instead of the MT's יהוה [*yhwh*, "the LORD"]), thus paralleling "army [lit., 'people'] of Judah" and "house of Israel" (for the significance of similar pairings in the books of Samuel, see comment on 1Sa 11:8). Siegfried Herrmann ("King David's State" [in Barrick and Spencer], 269; for full argumentation see 268–72) observes, however, that "עם יהוה [*ʿm yhwh*] refers to the tribal levies, but בית ישראל [*byt yśrʾl*] refers to the totality represented by the 'people of the Lord,' or, in other words, to the 'state' of Israel."

2. David's Lament for Saul and Jonathan (1:17–27)

OVERVIEW

"David's lament over Saul and Jonathan is powerful, passionate poetry commonly regarded as being directly from David's hand" (Brueggemann, *First and Second Samuel*, 213). That David was the author of this remarkable poem and that its date of composition was therefore about 1000 BC or slightly earlier is widely recognized (cf. Freedman, "Divine Names and Titles," 55, 57, 72, 96; Gevirtz, 72; Holladay, 154).

The poem is strikingly secular, never once mentioning God's name or elements of Israel's faith (see comment on v.21). Although OT laments over individuals are not uncommon (cf. 1Ki 13:30; Jer 22:18; 34:5; Eze 28:12–19; 32:2–15), the only other such recorded lament by David is that over Abner in 3:33–34 (again making "no reference to God" [David Noel Freedman, "The Age of David and Solomon," in Freedman, *History and Religion*, 286–87]).

It is generally agreed that vv.19–27 constitute the limits of the poem, secured by the inclusio formed by "How the mighty have fallen!" in vv.19 and 27. Although a few scholars would begin the poem with v.18, it is possible to do so only by resorting to radical and extensive emendation (cf. Gevirtz, 73–76; Holladay, 162–68). My treatment of David's lament itself will thus begin with v.19 and will assume that vv.17–18 establish its historical and literary context.

The most satisfying structural outline of vv.19–27 is William H. Shea's "Chiasmus and the Structure of David's Lament." He understands the body of the poem to consist of five stanzas (vv.20, 21, 22–23, 24–25, 26) framed by vv.19 and 27. In addition "the lament was composed in an overall chiasm by form in which the poetic units of the piece lengthen progressively toward its center and then decrease progressively after having reached that point" (14). Although I agree with much of Shea's analysis, it breaks down in his poetic scansion of the central section as well as in his combining vv.24 and 25 into one stanza. I also disagree, however, with the NIV's scansion, which incorrectly combines v.22 with v.21. In my judgment Shea has proven that vv.22 and 23 belong together.

My seven-stanza outline, which focuses on the reference in each verse to Saul and/or Jonathan (named or unnamed), exhibits a basically chiastic arrangement (though less pristine than that of Shea):

A_1 1:19: Jonathan (unnamed)
A_2 1:20: both men (unnamed)
  B 1:21: Saul (named)
    C 1:22–23: Jonathan and Saul (both named)
  B' 1:24: Saul (named)
A_1' 1:25–26: Jonathan (named)
A_2' 1:27 both men (unnamed)

17 David took up this lament concerning Saul and his son Jonathan, 18 and ordered that the men of Judah be taught this lament of the bow (it is written in the Book of Jashar):

19 "Your glory, O Israel, lies slain on your heights.
  How the mighty have fallen!

20 "Tell it not in Gath,
  proclaim it not in the streets of Ashkelon,
lest the daughters of the Philistines be glad,
  lest the daughters of the uncircumcised rejoice.

21 "O mountains of Gilboa,
  may you have neither dew nor rain,
  nor fields that yield offerings of grain.
For there the shield of the mighty was defiled,
  the shield of Saul—no longer rubbed with oil.
22 From the blood of the slain,
  from the flesh of the mighty,
the bow of Jonathan did not turn back,
  the sword of Saul did not return unsatisfied.

23 "Saul and Jonathan—
  in life they were loved and gracious,
  and in death they were not parted.
They were swifter than eagles,
  they were stronger than lions.

24 "O daughters of Israel,
  weep for Saul,
who clothed you in scarlet and finery,
  who adorned your garments with ornaments of gold.

25"How the mighty have fallen in battle!
  Jonathan lies slain on your heights.
26I grieve for you, Jonathan my brother;
  you were very dear to me.
 Your love for me was wonderful,
  more wonderful than that of women.

27"How the mighty have fallen!
  The weapons of war have perished!"

COMMENTARY

17–18 "Took up ... lament" (v.17) renders the cognate accusative construction *qyn ... qînâ* (GK 7801, 7806; cf. also Eze 32:16 ["chant," NIV]; 2Sa 3:33 omits the noun, while Jer 9:10; Eze 28:12; 32:2; Am 5:1 use the verb *nś᾽* for "take up"). The term *qînâ* in the OT "is used of a formal utterance which expresses grief or distress. It ... could be learned [cf. v.18] and practiced" (David L. Zapf, "How Are the Mighty Fallen! A Study of 2 Samuel 1:17–27," *Grace Theological Journal* 5/1 [1984]: 116). The Irish word "keen," which is a funeral song accompanied by wailing, may derive ultimately from the Hebrew root *qyn*. Since 3:2 meter is commonly (though not exclusively) employed in OT poems of the lament genre (cf. often in the book of Lamentations), the 3:2 pattern is sometimes called *qinah* meter. All attempts to find *qinah* rhythm in vv.19–27, however, have thus far proven unsuccessful.

The NIV adds "this lament of the" (v.18) in deference to the needs of English translation. Zapf ("How Are the Mighty Fallen!" 116) points out that *qšt* (["The] Bow") is probably the title of the lament (cf. also K&D). The word appears in v.22 as a weapon used by Jonathan, who was probably a skilled bowman (cf. 1Sa 20:18–22, 35–40), and Saul had been mortally wounded by archers (1Sa 31:3).

Like Joshua's poetic address to the sun and moon (Jos 10:12–13), David's lament was eventually written down in "the Book of Jashar" (v.18; cf. also 1Ki 8:13 [LXX 8:53, which adds: "It is written in the book of the song (*tēs ōdēs*)," the last two words of which are generally believed to be based on a Hebrew text that read *hšyr*, a transcriptional error for *hyšr* ["Jashar"]). Hebrew *hayyāšār* means literally "the upright," perhaps an overall descriptive term for the contents of the poetic collection. Freedman ("Divine Names and Titles," 99 n. 18) suggests that the earliest editions of the "Book of the Wars of the LORD" (Nu 21:14) and the Book of Jashar "may well go back to the time of the judges, but the final published form must be dated in the monarchic period."

19 Shea, "Chiasmus," 20, observes that the inclusio formed by vv.19 and 27 displays "How the mighty have fallen!" in the second colon of v.19 and in the second-to-last colon of v.27, thus providing an additional element of symmetry to the poem. "How" followed immediately by a verb in the perfect tense often signals the beginning of a lament (the best-known example is La 1:1). Holladay, 166–67, expects *gibbôrîm* ("[the] mighty") to be paralleled by *ḥayil* ("power[ful]"), as often elsewhere in the OT (see, e.g., Gevirtz, 89), and therefore sees irony in the fact that *ḥālāl* ("slain") appears instead of *ḥayil.* In v.22, however, "blood of the slain" is parallel to "flesh of the mighty," and in that verse there can be no question of emending "slain" to "power(ful)" since the phrase "blood of the slain" is secured by its occurrence in Numbers 23:24 ("blood of his victims").

In any event "mighty" in v.19 is probably best understood as being parallel to "glory," and thus "slain" is parallel to "fallen" (cf. similarly in v.25; note especially the phrase "fell slain" in 1Sa 31:1 [see comment]). The word *gibbôrîm* ("mighty") appears in another ancient poem, the Song of Deborah (Jdg 5:13, 23), and the root *gbr* is thematic of David's lament, occurring no fewer than six times in its nine verses: vv.19, 21, 22, 23 ("stronger"), 25, 27.

Bāmôt (GK 1195) usually means "high places" in the sense of open-air worship sites (authorized or not; see comment on 1Sa 9:12), but "heights" in the more general sense of topographical elevations is also common for *bāmôt* especially in poetry (cf. Dt 32:13; Hab 3:19). "Heights" here refers to Gilboa (v.21), located in "Israel," which was Saul's main realm and to whose people David's lament is addressed. Not yet king over all Israel, David orders that the lament be taught only to the men of "Judah" (v.18), where he has already gained considerable influence (see 1Sa 30:26–31 and comment).

According to David Noel Freedman ("The Refrain in David's Lament," 120), *haṣṣ^ebî* ("Your glory," v.19 [NIV]) should be translated "the gazelle" as a nickname or sobriquet for Jonathan. He summarizes: "In our opinion, 'Jonathan' in vs. 25 explicates 'the gazelle' in vs. 19." Freedman is surely correct in his analysis: "Gazelle" is used as a simile for a fleet-footed warrior in the immediate context (2:18; cf. also 1Ch 12:8), Saul and Jonathan are compared to "eagles" and "lions" in v.23, and the simile of a deer is employed in connection with "heights" in 22:34 (cf. Hab 3:19). That Jonathan should be compared to a gazelle is entirely appropriate (cf. 1Sa 14:4–5, 10, 12–13).

Although Saul and Jonathan are each named four times in David's lament (Saul, vv.21, 22, 23, 24; Jonathan, vv.22, 23, 25, 26), Jonathan is given pride of place when the two are first mentioned together (v.22) and is featured in the false coda (v.25). It is therefore not surprising that he is alluded to, even if not by name, at the beginning of the poem. Zapf's translation of *haṣṣ^ebî* ("the gazelle/glory") ("How Are the Mighty Fallen!" 117) arises from his conclusion that it "is probably purposely ambiguous both in reference and meaning." If Zapf's reasoning that led him to his decision is somewhat convoluted (see 106–7), his summary is nonetheless helpful: "Saul is not slighted, but Jonathan is given a certain preference" (107). In the first stanza of his lament, therefore, David serves notice to the reader that he intends to highlight his relationship to "the gazelle," his "dear" friend (v.26), Jonathan.

20 The Hebrew verbs rendered "tell" (cf. Mic 1:10 and NIV note) and "proclaim" occur together again in 4:10 ("told," "bring good news"; for other examples see Gevirtz, 83), recalling the frequent use of *ngd* ("tell") in the story concerning the Amalekite earlier in the chapter (see comment on v.4). The verb translated "proclaim" almost always implies good news—in this case, of course, only from the standpoint of the Philistines (see comment on 1Sa 31:9), who can be expected to spread the report of Saul's death like wildfire. "Streets" in this context is better rendered "bazaars"or the like (Lawrence E. Stager, "The Fury of Babylon: Ashkelon and the Archaeology of Destruction," *BAR* 22/1 [1996]: 63, 68; cf. 1Ki 20:34, "market areas," for the same Heb. word). "Gath, standing at the eastern edge of Philistine territory near the hill country of Israel, and Ashkelon by the sea represent all of Philistine territory" (Zapf, "How Are the Mighty Fallen!" 113). The words of an Akkadian proverb are apt in this context: "Secret knowledge is not safeguarded by an enemy" (*ANET*, 425 [1.14–15]).

The "daughters of the Philistines/uncircumcised" (cf. 1Sa 31:1, 4; see also comment on 1Sa 14:6), from whom the news of the Israelite defeat is to be kept if at all possible, will "be glad" and "rejoice" if they hear of it (the Heb. verbs are paralleled also in Pr 23:15–16; Jer 50:11; Zep 3:14; cf. Gevirtz, 84). In David's lament they appear in poetic opposition to the "daughters of Israel," who are commanded to "weep for Saul" (v.24).

21 The alleged difficulties in the third stanza have attracted more attention from commentators than the rest of the verses in the poem combined, especially the phrase the NIV renders "nor fields that yield offerings of grain." Despite references in ancient Egyptian literature to the "Field of Offerings," a kind of paradise, the goal of the deceased (cf. Leonard H. Lesko, "Some Observations on the Composition of the *Book of Two Ways*," *JAOS* 91/1 [1971]: 30–43), perhaps similar to the "Elysian field(s)" of Greek mythology, the heavenly destination of Saul and Jonathan is not in view here. The verse consists of something more mundane: a curse on the "mountains of Gilboa," the site of the Israelite defeat (cf. comment on v.6), which is described topographically by William H. Shea, "David's Lament," *BASOR* 221 (1976): 141–42:

> Gilboa is not a solitary mountain peak, nor a series of peaks, but a ridge some eight miles long and three to five miles wide running southeast and south from Jezreel. It forms the watershed between the plain of Esdraelon and the plain around Beth-shean, dropping away sharply to the north and east. It slopes gradually to the west, however, and on this gentle fertile terrain, barley, wheat, figs and olives are grown.... [It was] this western slope to which rain and dew were denied by the curse of this poem.

Other texts demonstrating that the land is affected adversely by murderous acts include Psalm 106:38 and Hosea 4:2–3. For a defense of "O field of heights," the most likely rendering of the disputed phrase, see the Notes.

The parallelism between "dew" and "rain" occurs also in 1 Kings 17:1—again in a context in which their absence signifies a curse against the land. (The two words are paralleled also, but in reverse order, in Dt 32:2; Job 38:28.) In Hebrew thought, dew was often a symbol of resurrection or the renewing of life (cf. Ps 110:3; Isa 26:19; also the name Abital [2Sa 3:4], "My [divine] father is dew" or "[Divine] father of dew"; for parallels elsewhere in the ancient Near East, cf. Magnus Ottosson, "The Prophet Elijah's Visit to Zarephath," in Barrick and Spencer, 190–91).

The Hebrew root *mgn* (usually "shield"; GK 4482) on occasion seems to mean "king, sovereign, donor," or the like (cf. Ge 15:1; Pss 47:9; 84:9; 89:18 and NIV notes; for details see esp. M. O'Connor, "Yahweh the Donor," *AuOr* 6 [1988]: 47–60). Although "there are cases in which it is impossible to decide clearly between *māgēn*, 'shield', and *mgn*, 'donor'" (52), the context in v.21 tips the scales in favor of "shield." Whether *nigʿal* means "defiled" (NIV) in the sense that, in the words of Shea, "David's Lament," 142, "the Philistines treated [Saul's shield as they wished] like the Israelites did Goliath's armor and sword" (cf. 1Sa 17:54; 21:9), or whether it means "rejected (with loathing)" in the sense that, in the words of Driver, 237, the shield is pictured "as lying upon the mountains, no longer polished and ready to be worn in action, but cast aside as worthless, and neglected," the verb is more suited to shields than to sovereigns.

The rendering "sovereign" in v.21 is not without its proponents (cf. Mitchell Dahood, "Northwest Semitic Notes on Genesis," *Bib* 55/1 [1974]: 78), but it can only be justified by assuming that "rubbed [lit., 'anointed'] with oil" refers to Saul and thus by translating *b^{e}lî* ("no longer") asseveratively in the sense of "surely, firmly, duly" (cf. O'Connor, "Yahweh the Donor," 57–58; Freedman, "The Refrain of David's Lament," 122–23; Terence Kleven, "Reading Hebrew Poetry: David's Lament Over Saul and Jonathan [2Sa 1:17–27]," *Proceedings of the Eastern Great Lakes and Midwest Biblical Societies* 11 [1991]: 59–60)—a questionable procedure at best. In favor of "shield" is the appearance of "bow" and "sword" in v.22 (cf. the sequence "bow" ["arrows," NIV], "shield," "sword" in Ps 76:3 [observed also by Shea, "David's Lament," 142 n. 5]). In addition to Isaiah 21:5, which urges the Babylonians to "anoint/oil the shields" (to keep them in good condition), an Old Babylonian text from Tell Asmar lists "one sila of oil to rub shield(s)" (cf. Alan R. Millard, "Saul's Shield Not Anointed With Oil," *BASOR* 230 [1978]: 70).

22–23 Shea, "Chiasmus," 17, has demonstrated conclusively that vv.22 and 23 together constitute a stanza that resides at the center of the poem (cf. also Fokkelman, "Saul and David," 30; Holladay, 179). Each of the two verses refers to both Saul and Jonathan by name—the only verses in the lament to do so. Verse 22 mentions Jonathan before Saul (thereby giving Jonathan pride of place), while v.23 reverses the names. In addition, the MT of the first two lines of v.22 parallels that of the last two lines of v.23 in striking ways: Both units employ pairs of the preposition *min* ("from ... from" in v.22, "than ... than" in v.23); the last noun of the first unit ("the mighty") and the last verb of the second unit ("they were stronger") come from the same root (*gbr*); and *ḥ^{a}lālîm* ("the slain," v.22) and *qallû* ("they were swifter," v.23) convey somewhat similar sounds. Holladay, 179 n. 5, makes the further observation that the ubiquitous word *lō*ʾ ("not") occurs three times in vv.22–23 and nowhere else in the lament.

In no uncertain terms vv.22–23 summarize the bravery, determination, comradeship, and ability of King Saul and his son Jonathan. Verse 22 reflects the language of Deuteronomy 32:42, a verse that concludes the words of the Lord in another ancient Israelite poem, the Song of Moses. There "the blood of the slain" (a singular collective; for the exact phrase found here, cf. Nu 23:24 ["the blood of his victims"], which concludes Balaam's second oracle) is mentioned, and we are told that "arrows" drink "blood" and that the "sword" devours "flesh" (cf. Isa 34:5–6). Likewise here Jonathan's "bow" did not turn back from "blood" and Saul's "sword" did not return (to its sheath; cf. Eze 21:5) "unsatisfied" (lit., "empty[-handed]"; cf. Isa 55:11; Jer 14:3 ["unfilled"]; 50:9) from "flesh" (lit., "fat," translating a different Hebrew word from that in Dt 32:42). (For the parallelism between "blood" and "fat," compare again Isa 34:6–7, where a battle is compared to a sacrifice; cf. also Jer 46:10; Eze 39:17–19; Gevirtz, 88; Holladay, 177.)

The MT of v.23 juxtaposes "in life" (lit., "during their lifetime[s]; cf. 18:18) with "and in death," placing the two phrases between "they were loved and gracious" and "they were not parted." The effect is to suggest that both verbal clauses pertain to both temporal expressions. The king and his son, inseparable in life as in death, will continue to be honored in death as in life. The Hebrew roots underlying "loved" and "gracious," applied here to Saul and Jonathan, are in v.26 applied to Jonathan alone, though in reverse order ("dear" and "love"; cf. independently Gevirtz, 91).

"Swifter than eagles" recurs in Jeremiah 4:13 and Lamentations 4:19 (for other examples of the eagle simile/metaphor, cf. Dt 28:49; Jer 48:40; 49:22; Hos 8:1), and "stronger than lions" reprises Judges 14:18 (but with a different Hebrew verb for "stronger"; cf. also Nu 23:24; 24:9; Isa 38:13; Jer 51:38; La 3:10; Eze 22:25). Ironically, the other two places in the OT where "swift" and "strong" are parallel (Am 2:14 uses a different Heb. word for "strong"—though the sentiment is much the same) may be applied to the tragic end of Saul and Jonathan: "The race is not to the swift or the battle to the strong" (Ecc 9:11); "The swift cannot flee nor the strong escape" (Jer 46:6).

24 The central stanza of David's lament (vv.22–23) is flanked by the only two stanzas that mention Saul alone and by name (vv.21, 24). Verse 24 mirrors v.20, where David deplores the likelihood that the news of the Israelite defeat at Gilboa will spread throughout Philistia, causing the "daughters of the Philistines/uncircumcised" to "be glad/rejoice"; here David calls on the "daughters of Israel" to "weep" for Saul, as he and all his men have done (v.12). Weeping for/over a person (or a personified place) was a universal custom in ancient Israel (3:34; Job 30:25; Jer 22:10; 48:32; Eze 27:31).

Although it is possible that the "daughters of Israel" in this case were professional mourners (compare the "daughters of the nations" who chant a lament in Eze 32:16 and the professional "wailing women" of Jer 9:17 in the context of the command, "Teach your daughters how to wail," in Jer 9:20), the reference is probably rather to the wealthy women of the land, since Saul is described as having lavished fine clothes and expensive jewelry on them. The rare word *ᶜᵃdānîm*, here translated "finery," occurs elsewhere in the OT only twice, in both cases with reference to food or drink ("delights," Ps 36:8; "delicacies," Jer 51:34). The term was perhaps used in this verse because of its assonance with *ᶜᵃdî* ("ornament[s]").

Gevirtz, 93, observes that "scarlet" and "ornaments of gold" are paralleled again in Jeremiah 4:30 ("jewels of gold"; cf. also Jer 2:32 for "jewelry" as a rendering of *ᶜᵃdî*). The Hebrew words for "scarlet" and "garments/clothes" are found in close association also in the poem concerning the wife of noble character that concludes the book of Proverbs (cf. Pr 31:21–22). Shea, "Chiasmus," 18, comments on the literary artistry in the MT of the last two lines of v.24, pointing out that "the verb for 'clothe' occurs at the beginning of the first colon, and the noun for 'clothes' appears at the end of the second."

25–26 Verses 25–26—the only two verses in which Jonathan appears alone by name—combine to form a stanza. Verse 25 reflects v.19 (where Jonathan is called "the gazelle"; see comment). "How the mighty have fallen" echoes v.19 verbatim and at first gives the impression that the lament concludes at this point. The addition of "in battle," however, signals the possibility that v.25 is a false ending—a possibility that is confirmed as the poem continues.

Verse 25 is best described as a false/fake coda used by David to heap further praise on his friend Jonathan. Indeed, "the separate treatment of Jonathan in a fake coda subtly shows David's preference for him [over Saul]" (Zapf, "How Are the Mighty Fallen!" 121). The two lines of v.25 reverse the elements of v.19, its mirror image. As in v.19, so also in v.25, "your heights" refers to Israel's heights on the slopes of Mount Gilboa.

The relatively common idiom *ṣar lᵉ-* ("to be in distress," lit., "it is distressing to/for"; cf. 1Sa 13:6) occurs only twice in 2 Samuel, both times on the lips of David (1:26 ["I grieve"]; 24:14). Its placement in the first and last chapters serves as a kind of inclusio that highlights the lament theme with which the book begins and ends. With respect to the structure of v.26 itself, Shea, "Chiasmus," 20, observes that in the MT "the suffixed preposition *lî* ... occurs in first position ['I'] in the first colon, in second position ['to me'] in the second colon, in third position ['for me'] in the third colon, and it does not appear at all in the fourth colon. This distribution appears to be more by design than by accident."

David's grief in v.26 is for Jonathan, his "brother"—not in the sense of "brother-in-law" (a true enough description; cf. 1Sa 18:27 and comment) but of "treaty/covenant brother" (as in Nu 20:14; 1Ki 9:12–13; 20:32–33; for Akkadian examples, see

CAD, 1.1.200–201). David's further statement that Jonathan's "love" for him was "more wonderful than that of women," although occasionally (and perversely) understood in a homosexual sense, should rather be understood to have covenantal connotations, "love" in such contexts meaning "covenantal/political loyalty" (see comment on 1Sa 18:1–4; cf. also Robert North, "Social Dynamics from Saul to Jehu," *BTB* 12/4 [1982]: 112). Indeed, the Hebrew word for "love" is translated "friendship" in a similar context (Ps 109:4–5).

The Hebrew roots underlying the words "dear" and "love" in v.26 are repeated from v.23 but in reverse order ("loved and gracious"). "The first word bespeaks physical attraction, a trait [Jonathan] shared with David himself (cf. 1 Sam 16:12). The second word expresses an elemental devotion, a devotion he shared distinctively with David. Taken together the two words articulate a peculiar and precious bonding with David" (Brueggemann, *First and Second Samuel*, 216–17). Since *nʿm* ("gracious, dear, pleasant, beloved") does not occur in 1 Samuel 16:12, Brueggemann might better have called attention to 2 Samuel 23:1, where David is described as Israel's "beloved" (*neʿîm*) singer (see NIV note there).

Mary Joan Winn Leith ("Biblical Views," *BAR* 34/1 [2008]: 24, 81) sees an admittedly remarkable parallel to vv.25–26 in Achilles' outpouring of grief over his slain friend Patroklos: "... my dear companion has perished, Patroklos, whom I loved beyond all other companions, as well as my own life. I have lost him" (Homer, *Iliad* 18.80–82).

27 Just as Jonathan is hidden in a metaphor ("the gazelle") in the first line of David's lament (see v.19 and comment), so also Saul and Jonathan are hidden in a metaphor ("the weapons of war"; see comment on 1Sa 8:12; cf. also Gevirtz, 95) in its last line (v.27). The first and last lines (highlighting respectively the slaying of Jonathan and the perishing of Saul and Jonathan) not only support but also frame the inclusio—"How the mighty have fallen!"—which is the theme of the entire poem (cf. also v.25).

"The artful execution of this work serves as a fitting tribute both to its esteemed author and to those whom he commemorated by composing it" (Shea, "Chiasmus," 25). In addition, the lament of David for Saul and Jonathan is characterized by both passion and restraint. While giving full vent to his feelings upon hearing the report of their death, David displays no bitterness toward his mortal enemy Saul. As Holladay, 189, remarks: "The judgment of T. H. Robinson is certainly justified: 'We know nothing of David which presents him in a better light.'"

Carlson, 48, rightly calls attention to the similarity between v.18, where David orders that the men of Judah be "taught" his lament for Saul and Jonathan, and Deuteronomy 31:19 (cf. also 31:22), where the Lord commands Moses to write down a song (Dt 32:1–43) and "teach" it to the Israelites. Apparently the epic hymns of Israel's history were intended to be taught and applied from generation to generation. David's lament may well have been a favorite, if 1 Maccabees 9:21 is a reliable indication. There we read that the lamentation for the slain Judas Maccabeus, leader of the Jewish rebellion against their Seleucid overlords, began with these words: "How the mighty has fallen!"

NOTES

18 Among the best known English "translations" of an allegedly genuine Hebrew book of Jashar is *The Book of Jasher* (the KJV's spelling of the word) by Jacob Ilive (Bristol: Philip Rose, 1829), originally published in London in 1751. Ilive claimed that Alcuin, abbot of Canterbury, had found the Hebrew text in Gazna, Persia, and had then translated it into English. That Ilive—a known plagiarist and opportunist—himself wrote the book out of whole cloth, however, is clear from the patent absurdity of its contents. The text of the Hebrew "Book of Jashar" has apparently been irretrievably lost.

21 For the interruption caused by ־בְּ (*b-*) in the construct phrase הָרֵי בַגִּלְבֹּעַ (*hārê baggilbōaᶜ*, "the mountains of Gilboa"), a not uncommon phenomenon in the OT, see also the Ketiv of 10:9: בְּחוּרֵי בְיִשְׂרָאֵל (*bᵉḥûrê byiśrāʾēl*, "the best troops of/in Israel").

Dahood ("Hebrew-Ugaritic Lexicography X," *Bib* 53/3 [1972]: 398) translates the first three lines of v.21 as follows:

O mountains of Gilboa,
  no dew and no rain upon you,
O upland fields!

(cf. also Freedman, "The Refrain in David's Lament," 121–22; Jan P. Fokkelman, " שדי תרומת in 2 Samuel 1:21a—A Non-Existent Crux," *ZAW* 91/2 [1979]: 290–93; Zapf, "How Are the Mighty Fallen!" 108, 118; Shea, "Chiasmus," 15).

תְּרוּמָה (*tᵉrûmâ*, "offering, contribution") is almost always found elsewhere in sacral contexts (see BDB, 929, for a complete list of passages), the only apparent exception being Proverbs 29:4 ("[greedy for] bribes"). In this otherwise thoroughly secular lament, therefore, it seems best to assume that *tᵉrûmâ* (from רום, *rûm*, "to be high"]) at one time had a wider semantic range and to understand וּשְׂדֵי תְרוּמֹת (*ûśᵉdê tᵉrûmōt*) as "O [vocative use of the conjunction; for details see Dahood, 'Hebrew-Ugaritic Lexicography X,' 398] fields of heights!" (cf. the cognate expression מְרוֹמֵי שָׂדֶה, *mᵉrômê śādeh*, "the heights of the field," in the similar battle context of Jdg 5:18), parallel to "O mountains of Gilboa." Fokkelman defends the parallelism on the basis of the overall chiastic structure of v.21:

O mountains of Gilboa,
  no dew
  and no rain on you,
O high fields!
For there was defiled [כִּי שָׁם נִגְעַל, *kî šām nigᶜal*]
  the shield of the mighty,
  the shield of Saul—
no longer rubbed with oil [בְּלִי מָשִׁיחַ בַּשָּׁמֶן, *bᵉlî māšîaḥ baššāmen*].

Fokkelman, 291, observes: "In verse 21b the alliteration *sham ni- … shamen* contributes to the chiasmus" ("שדי תרומת in II Sam 1:21a," 291).

Despite the valiant efforts of T. L. Fenton to salvage it ("Comparative Evidence in Textual Study: *M. Dahood on 2 Sam. i 21 and CTA 19 [1 Aqht], I, 44–45*," *VT* 29/2 [1979]: 162–70), H. L. Ginsberg's celebrated emendation of וּשְׂדֵי תְרוּמֹת (*ûśᵉdê tᵉrûmōt*) on the basis of its supposed Ugaritic exemplar must be given up. Rendering Ugaritic *bl ṭl bl rbb bl šrᶜ thmtm* as "No dew, no rain; no welling-up of the deep," he proposed reading the MT's *ʾl-ṭl wʾl-mṭr wśdy trwmt* similarly, assuming transcriptional error in the last two words (H. L. Ginsberg, "A Ugaritic Parallel to 2 Samuel 1:21," *JBL* 57 [1938]: 209–13; "Ugaritic Studies and the Bible," *BA* 8/2 [1945]: 56–57; *ANET*, 153 n. 34).

The emendation was summarily adopted by, among others, the RSV and numerous commentators (cf. Holladay, 170–72; Gevirtz, 85–86). Since שׂרע (*śrʿ*) is not sufficiently similar graphically to שׂדי (*śdy*), however, Robert Gordis invented a new Hebrew word (שְׂדִי, *śᵉdî*), claimed it to have cognates in Arabic, Syriac, and Aramaic, and gave it the meaning "outpouring" (Robert Gordis, "The Biblical Root *ŠDY-ŠD*: Notes on 2 Sam. i. 21; Jer. xviii. 14; Ps. xci. 6; Job v. 21," *JTS* 41/1 [1940]: 36). But the supposed parallel between the Ugaritic and OT texts breaks down syntactically as well: Ugaritic *bl* ... *bl* ... *bl* is quite different from the MT's *ʾl* ... *wʾl* ... *w-* in which the last *w-* would surely be followed by *ʾl* if "nor" were intended. In any event, few translations and commentators agree with Ginsberg today; the NRSV, for example, renders "bounteous fields" (cf. also Walter Harrelson, "Recent Discoveries and Bible Translation," *Religious Education* 85/2 [Spring 1990]: 192–93; cf. similarly Gonzalo Baez-Camargo, "Biblical Archaeology Helps the Translator," *BT* 31/3 [1980]: 319—although he vacillates between other options as well).

Uncertainty as to whether to read מָשִׁיחַ (*māšîaḥ*) with most MT MSS or מָשׁוּחַ (*māšûaḥ*) with about twenty MSS should probably be decided in favor of the latter. Although both words are passive participles of the verb meaning "anoint," the first is used again and again in the books of Samuel to refer to the "anointed" leader of the Lord's people (cf. 1Sa 2:10, 35; 12:3, 5; 24:6, 10; 26:9, 11, 16, 23; 2Sa 1:14, 16; 19:21; 22:51; 23:1). The latter form, differing slightly from the former, would thus heighten the grisly wordplay in the verse: Saul, anointed with oil at the beginning of his reign (cf. 1Sa 10:1), has now at the end of his reign lost his shield, "no longer rubbed with oil." In addition, as Holladay, 175, observes, שָׁאוּל (*šāʾûl*, "Saul") and *māšûaḥ* share the same vowel pattern and thus display assonance.

22 Holladay, 178, calls attention to "the most remarkable assonantal symmetry of the whole verse": *ḥl* in the last word of line one (חללים, *ḥllym*, "slain"), *ḥlb* in the first word of line two ("flesh"), *ḥr* in the last word of line three (אחור, *ʾḥwr*, "back"), and *ḥrb* in the first word of line four ("sword").

24 Although referring to the same object ("daughters of Israel"), הַמַּלְבִּשְׁכֶם (*hammalbiškem*, "who clothed you") and לְבוּשְׁכֶן (*lᵉbûšken*, "your garments") display different pronominal suffixes (second person masculine plural and feminine plural respectively). Some Hebrew MSS level the two words out in one direction, others in another (cf. *BHS*). But the masculine suffixed pronoun is often used for a feminine antecedent, and in fact the same alternation between masculine and feminine suffixes in v.24 is attested in Isaiah 3:16–17 (with "daughters" as the antecedent): "The women [lit., 'daughters'] of Zion are haughty ... with ornaments jingling on their [masculine plural] ankles. Therefore the LORD will bring sores on the heads of the women [lit., 'daughters'] of Zion; the LORD will make their [feminine plural] scalps bald."

26 The anomalous form נִפְלְאַתָה (*niplᵉʾatâ*, "was wonderful"; GK 7098) has occasioned considerable discussion. If it was intended as a feminine singular participle, we would have expected נִפְלֵאת (*niplēʾt*), as in Deuteronomy 30:11. If, however, it was intended as a third-person feminine perfect (as seems more likely), we would have expected נִפְלְאָה (*niplᵉʾâ*) or, as in Psalm 118:23, נִפְלָאת (*niplāʾt*). But, as Holladay, 183, observes, "We may have here an archaic form because of the assonance with *ʾahᵃbātᵉkā* which follows; so it is best to leave the vocalization as the MT gives it."

3. David Anointed King over Judah (2:1–7)

OVERVIEW

In many respects chs. 2–8 form

> the crux of the book. Here the fertility motif reaches a peak. The thesis of the author—that Israel is blessed with fertility when the nation (and the epitome of the nation, the king) is following the covenant—is demonstrated in these chapters. The king, the ark (representing the presence of God and the Word of God, the covenant), and fertility are all intertwined in a beautifully artistic way. (Martin, 37)

Nestled in the heart of the literary unit that describes David's triumph over the remnant of Saul's house (1:1–3:5), 2:1–7 divides most naturally into two roughly equal sections (vv.1–4a, 4b–7), each of which ends with a statement declaring that the house of Judah has anointed David to be king over them (vv.4a, 7b; cf. similarly Carlson, 49).

[1]In the course of time, David inquired of the LORD. "Shall I go up to one of the towns of Judah?" he asked.
The LORD said, "Go up."
David asked, "Where shall I go?"
"To Hebron," the LORD answered.
[2]So David went up there with his two wives, Ahinoam of Jezreel and Abigail, the widow
of Nabal of Carmel. [3]David also took the men who were with him, each with his family, and
they settled in Hebron and its towns. [4]Then the men of Judah came to Hebron and there
they anointed David king over the house of Judah.
When David was told that it was the men of Jabesh Gilead who had buried Saul, [5]he
sent messengers to the men of Jabesh Gilead to say to them, "The LORD bless you for
showing this kindness to Saul your master by burying him. [6]May the LORD now show you
kindness and faithfulness, and I too will show you the same favor because you have done
this. [7]Now then, be strong and brave, for Saul your master is dead, and the house of Judah
has anointed me king over them."

COMMENTARY

1–4a With King Saul now dead and buried, the time has come for the private anointing of David (1Sa 16:13) to be reprised in public (see Notes on v.1). Saul's death made it possible for David and his men to move about more freely, so he decides to leave Ziklag (1:1)—but not without seeking divine guidance. Unlike Saul (cf. 1Ch 10:14; see comment on 1Sa 28:6), David "inquired of the LORD" (v.1), doubtless by asking his friend Abiathar the priest to consult the Urim and Thummim stored in the ephod that he had brought with him from Nob (1Sa 22:20; 23:6; see comment on 1Sa 14:36, 40–42; 23:2). This is not the first time David inquired of God in so formal a way (cf. 1Sa 23:1–4, 9–12; 30:7–8), nor would it be his last (cf. 5:19, 23–24).

David wants to know whether he should "go up" (v.1) to one of the towns in the hill country of Judah (the Heb. verb, thematic of the section, appears a total of five times in vv.1–3: "go up" [2x], "go," v.1; "went up," v.2; "took" [lit., "caused to go up"], v.3). By means of the sacred lots, the Lord responds affirmatively. When David then asks for a more precise destination, the lots (through the process of elimination; see comment on 1Sa 10:20–21) pinpoint Hebron as the place. Located twenty-seven miles northeast of Ziklag, Hebron was the most important city David sent plunder to after defeating the Amalekites (see 1Sa 30:31 and comment) and looms large in chs. 2–5.

Obedient to the divine command, David severs his ties with Philistine Ziklag (see comment on 1Sa 27:6) and, with his two wives Ahinoam and Abigail (27:3; 30:5; see comment on 1Sa 25:3, 43), moves to Judahite Hebron (v.2). He also takes with him the army of men who have rallied to his leadership (see 1Sa 22:2 and comment), and they together with their families settle in Hebron and its nearby villages (v.3). With the nucleus of his future government now his loyal neighbors, David is publicly anointed by the "men of Judah" (perhaps the elders; cf. 5:3; also 1Sa 30:26) as king over the "house of Judah" (v.4; cf. also vv.7, 10–11), that is, the people of Judah as a whole ("house" in the sense of "family, community"; see comment on 1:12). David's elevation to kingship, however, though administered by men, is fundamentally due to divine anointing (5:3, 12; 12:7; 1Sa 15:17; see comment on 1Sa 15:1; 16:13).

4b–7 Word eventually reaches David that the men of Jabesh Gilead (see comment on 1Sa 11:1) had given Saul a decent burial (v.4; 1Sa 31:11–13). Since Jabesh is an Israelite (not Judahite) town and therefore presumably still loyal to Saul's house (in speaking to the Jabeshites, David twice refers to "Saul your master" [vv.5, 7]), David realizes that he must try to win them over to his side. He therefore sends messengers to them with overtures of peace and friendship, an approach that stands in sharp contrast to the tactics used by David's men in the rest of the chapter. Brueggemann's summary is apropos (*First and Second Samuel*, 220): "The much later crisis of 1 Kings 12 suggests that the Davidic hold on the north is never deeply established. In our chapter we are given two episodes of David's attentiveness to the north. One (vv.4b–7) is a peaceable act of friendship. The other (vv.8–32) is an act of confrontation and hostility."

Although "The LORD bless you" was a traditional form of greeting (see comment on 1Sa 15:13), it here further "expresses appreciation and praise for the outstanding loyalty of the Jabesh-Gileadites to their dead king" (Anderson, 29). The Jabeshites are commended for "showing ... kindness" (in the sense of demonstrating loyalty; cf. 3:8, where "I am loyal" translates the same Heb. idiom) to Saul (v.5). "Kindness" (*ḥesed*; GK 2876; see comment on 1Sa 20:8, 14–15) of this sort ultimately derives from God, as David himself recognizes (cf. 9:1, 3, 7; also 1Ki 3:6). Indeed, he invokes the Lord's "kindness and faithfulness" on the Jabeshites (v.6; cf. 15:20; Ge 32:10; cf. esp. Ex 34:6, where "love and faithfulness" [the same Heb. phrase] are part of the very nature of God himself).

"Love/kindness and faithfulness" are part and parcel of all genuine covenantal relationships, and David stresses his eagerness (emphatic "I" in v.6) to transfer the Jabeshites' covenantal loyalty from Saul to himself. He offers to "show you the same favor" (*ʾeʿeśeh ʾittᵉkem haṭṭôbâ hazzōʾt*, lit., "do with you this good [thing]") that Saul had shown them. The "favor/good thing" in this case is a "treaty of friendship" (cf. Delbert R.

Hillers, "A Note on Some Treaty Terminology in the Old Testament," *BASOR* 176 [1964]: 47; cf. Dt 23:6; see also comment on 1Sa 25:30), since *ʿāśâ ṭôbā* ("do [a] good [thing]") here corresponds to Akkadian *ṭābūta epēšu* and Sefire *ʿbd ṭbtʾ* with the same meaning (for which cf. W. L. Moran, "A Note on the Treaty Terminology of the Sefire Stelas," *JNES* 22 [1963]: 173–76; for additional bibliography, cf. esp. Edelman, "Saul's Rescue," 202 n. 30). This understanding obviously has implications for the proper exegesis of the phrase rendered "promised these good things" in 7:28 (see comment).

Just as in v.6 David had said that "I" (emphatic) would make the same treaty of friendship with the Jabeshites that Saul had made with them, so also in v.7 he reminds them that Saul their master is now dead and that the house of Judah has anointed "me" (emphatic) king. "David wishes to take Saul's place as suzerain of Jabesh-Gilead. Since treaties did not automatically continue in force when a new king took the throne, it was necessary for David actively to seek a renewal of the pact" (Hillers, "Treaty Terminology," 47). David's enthusiasm is also demonstrated in his repeated use of "now [then]" in vv.6–7. (In the MT the word occurs at the beginning of both verses.)

David concludes his offer to enter into a covenantal relationship with the Jabeshites by encouraging them to "be strong and brave" (v.7). The Hebrew phrase rendered "be strong" means literally "let your hands be strong" (as in Zec 8:9, 13; cf. also 2Sa 16:21), an idiom that often means "be encouraged" (cf. Jdg 7:11). "Be brave" is literally "become sons of power/might" (cf. also 13:28; in 1Sa 18:17 the same Heb. phrase is translated "serve ... bravely"), the term "son of might" implying "one characterized by might"—that is, a "brave man/soldier" (17:10; 1Sa 14:52). With Saul dead and David anointed king over Judah, David invites the Jabeshites to enter into a mutual defense treaty with him. But there is more than one fly in the ointment, as the rest of the chapter clearly suggests.

NOTE

1 וַיְהִי אַחֲרֵי־כֵן (*way*[e]*hî ʾaḥ*[a]*rê-kēn*, lit., "And it was after this"; cf. 2Ch 20:1), rendered by the NIV as "In the course of time," recurs in 8:1; 10:1; 13:1; and, somewhat unexpectedly, 21:18. With the exception of 1 Samuel 24:5 ("Afterward"), all other instances of the formula *wyhy ʾḥry-kn* in the OT, including those in 2 Samuel, "appear at the beginning of episodes in the accounts of the reign of a particular individual.... The formula's function is controlled, not by the genre of the material it introduces, but rather by the redactor's intention, positing a sequence of events internal to a reign" (Bailey, 56–57).

4. War between Saul's House and David's House (2:8–3:1)

OVERVIEW

Saul may be dead, but Saulide interests are very much alive. With the future of "all Israel" (v.9) at stake, it is understandable that there should be rival claimants for the tribal territories. Although the story of the struggle between Saul's house and David's house begins in 2:8 and does not end until

5:3, the main outlines are established in 2:8–32 and the inevitable outcome is summarized in 3:1. The literary structure of 2:8–32 is chiastic:

A Ish-Bosheth is king in Mahanaim; David is king in Hebron (vv.8–11)
  B Abner suggests that hostilities begin (vv.12–17)
    C Abner kills Asahel (vv.18–23)
  B' Abner suggests that hostilities cease (vv.24–28)
A' Ish-Bosheth's men return to Mahanaim; David's men return to Hebron (vv.29–32)

8Meanwhile, Abner son of Ner, the commander of Saul's army, had taken Ish-Bosheth son of Saul and brought him over to Mahanaim. 9He made him king over Gilead, Ashuri and Jezreel, and also over Ephraim, Benjamin and all Israel.

10Ish-Bosheth son of Saul was forty years old when he became king over Israel, and he reigned two years. The house of Judah, however, followed David. 11The length of time David was king in Hebron over the house of Judah was seven years and six months.

12Abner son of Ner, together with the men of Ish-Bosheth son of Saul, left Mahanaim and went to Gibeon. 13Joab son of Zeruiah and David's men went out and met them at the pool of Gibeon. One group sat down on one side of the pool and one group on the other side.

14Then Abner said to Joab, "Let's have some of the young men get up and fight hand to hand in front of us."

"All right, let them do it," Joab said.

15So they stood up and were counted off—twelve men for Benjamin and Ish-Bosheth son of Saul, and twelve for David. 16Then each man grabbed his opponent by the head and thrust his dagger into his opponent's side, and they fell down together. So that place in Gibeon was called Helkath Hazzurim.

17The battle that day was very fierce, and Abner and the men of Israel were defeated by David's men.

18The three sons of Zeruiah were there: Joab, Abishai and Asahel. Now Asahel was as fleet-footed as a wild gazelle. 19He chased Abner, turning neither to the right nor to the left as he pursued him. 20Abner looked behind him and asked, "Is that you, Asahel?"

"It is," he answered.

21Then Abner said to him, "Turn aside to the right or to the left; take on one of the young men and strip him of his weapons." But Asahel would not stop chasing him.

22Again Abner warned Asahel, "Stop chasing me! Why should I strike you down? How could I look your brother Joab in the face?"

23But Asahel refused to give up the pursuit; so Abner thrust the butt of his spear into Asahel's stomach, and the spear came out through his back. He fell there and died on the spot. And every man stopped when he came to the place where Asahel had fallen and died.

24 But Joab and Abishai pursued Abner, and as the sun was setting, they came to the hill of
Ammah, near Giah on the way to the wasteland of Gibeon. 25 Then the men of Benjamin rallied behind Abner. They formed themselves into a group and took their stand on top of a hill.
26 Abner called out to Joab, "Must the sword devour forever? Don't you realize that this will
end in bitterness? How long before you order your men to stop pursuing their brothers?"
27 Joab answered, "As surely as God lives, if you had not spoken, the men would have
continued the pursuit of their brothers until morning.'"
28 So Joab blew the trumpet, and all the men came to a halt; they no longer pursued
Israel, nor did they fight anymore.
29 All that night Abner and his men marched through the Arabah. They crossed the Jordan, continued through the whole Bithron and came to Mahanaim.
30 Then Joab returned from pursuing Abner and assembled all his men. Besides Asahel,
nineteen of David's men were found missing. 31 But David's men had killed three hundred and
sixty Benjamites who were with Abner. 32 They took Asahel and buried him in his father's tomb
at Bethlehem. Then Joab and his men marched all night and arrived at Hebron by daybreak.
3:1 The war between the house of Saul and the house of David lasted a long time. David
grew stronger and stronger, while the house of Saul grew weaker and weaker.

COMMENTARY

2:8–11 "Abner son of Ner, the commander of Saul's army" (v.8; cf. also 1Sa 17:55; 26:5) and Saul's cousin (see comment on 1Sa 14:50), had either avoided or escaped from the battle on Mount Gilboa that had resulted in the death of "Saul and his three sons" (1Sa 31:8). Still ostensibly loyal to the dead king, Abner had taken a fourth son, Ish-Bosheth, and "brought him over" (eastward across the Jordan; cf. v.29, where the same Heb. verb is translated "crossed") to Mahanaim ("Two Camps"; see Ge 32:2 and NIV note), far away from the continuing Philistine threat. Located just north of the Jabbok River in the tribal territory of Gad (Jos 13:26, 30; 21:38), ancient Mahanaim is probably the modern Tell edh-Dhahab el-Gharbi, about seven miles east of the Jordan. Later in David's reign, Mahanaim would serve as a place of refuge for him during the rebellion of his son Absalom (17:24, 27; 19:32; 1Ki 2:8).

Ish-Bosheth ("Man of Shame"), mentioned only in chs. 2–4, is perhaps to be identified with Ishvi in 1 Samuel 14:49 (see comment). Not killed in Saul's last battle (cf. 1Sa 31:2), he may have been something of a coward. In any event, "it is Abner, not Ishbosheth, who holds the real power" (Brueggemann, *First and Second Samuel*, 221). Scribal tradition often substituted the word *bōšet* ("shame"; see Note on 1Sa 7:4) for the hated name of the Canaanite god Baal (cf. Jer 3:24; 11:13 ["shameful god(s)"]; Hos 9:10 ["shameful idol"]). Thus Ish-Bosheth's real name was E/Ish-Baal, "Man of Baal" (cf. 1Ch 8:33; 9:39 and NIV note), Mephibosheth's (2Sa 4:4) was Merib-Baal (1Ch 8:34; 9:40 and NIV note), and Jerub-Besheth's was Jerub-Baal (2Sa 11:21 and NIV note; cf. also Jdg 6:32 and NIV note).

Since *baʿal* is also a common noun meaning "lord, owner, master" and could therefore be used occasionally in reference to the one true God (cf. Hos 2:16 and NIV note), it is possible that Saul did not intend to honor the Canaanite god Baal when he named his son Ish-Baal (which would mean "The man of the Lord")—especially since the name of his firstborn son, Jonathan, means "The LORD has given." The scribes who transmitted the Hebrew Scriptures, however, alert to the dangers of ambiguity in such names, provided a *caveat lector* in the instances noted above.

Although David became king over "the house of Judah" by popular anointing (v.4), Abner single-handedly makes Ish-Bosheth king over "all Israel" (v.9), thus demonstrating that he is the real power behind the throne of Israel now that Saul is dead. The first three names in v.9 are of regions, each introduced by the preposition *ʾel* ("to, over"), and the last three are of tribal territories, each introduced by the preposition *ʿal* ("upon, over"). Gilead, the area east of the Jordan between the southern end of the Sea of Galilee and the northern end of the Dead Sea, included the town of Jabesh Gilead (v.4), which was located thirteen miles north of Mahanaim (v.8)—indicating something of the difficulty David faced in attempting to win the Jabeshites over to his side. The location of Ashuri (mentioned only here) remains unknown and is hardly the tribal territory of Asher (cf. NIV note), since tribal names are restricted to the last triad in the verse. (K&D, 295, declares that the reading "Ashuri[tes]" is "decidedly faulty" and is content to affirm that "the true name cannot be discovered"; cf. similarly Driver, 241.) Jezreel is the extensive valley that separates the hill country of Manasseh from that of Galilee and is the region in which the town of Jezreel was located (cf. 4:4; see also comment on 1Sa 29:1).

The territories of Ephraim and Benjamin are probably selected to represent those areas within Israel that could be reasonably considered to have been under Saul's control ("all [emphatic] Israel" [v.9] is an obvious hyperbole for the northern tribes; cf. similarly 4:1). Ephraim was the largest tribal territory in the north, and Benjamin (cf. also vv.15, 25, 31) was the homeland of Saul (1Sa 9:1–2). A. D. H. Mayes (*Judges* [OTG; Sheffield: JSOT, 1985], 87) makes this useful observation:

> The Song of Deborah [Judges 5] and the event it commemorates presuppose a national consciousness, and self-identification as the people of Yahweh, which could have appeared surely not long before the Israelite monarchy under Saul. The area over which Saul reigned, described in 2 Sam 2:9, is almost exactly that from which contingents came, or were expected to come, to the help of Deborah and Barak against Sisera.

It is this realm that Ish-Bosheth son of Saul now inherits—with the ambitious Abner son of Ner pulling the strings behind the scenes.

The formal notice summarizing the reign of Ish-Bosheth (v.10) follows the typical pattern of the regnal formula (cf. 1Ki 14:21; see also comment on 1Sa 13:1) by recording (1) his age when he became king and (2) the length of his reign. After the murder of Ish-Bosheth (ch. 4), the regnal formula is reserved exclusively for southern kings (beginning with David [5:4])—and, indeed, even v.10, written ostensibly to honor Ish-Bosheth, ends as follows: "The house of Judah, however, followed David." Since David is the man after God's own heart (see comment on 1Sa 13:14), following David implies following the Lord (see esp. comment on 1Sa 12:14). "Followed" (v.10) renders *hāyû ʾaḥªrê* (lit., "were/went after"). It is therefore sadly ironic that when the united kingdom was torn in two after the death of David's son Solomon and when Jeroboam was made king over "all Israel" (the northern tribes), only the tribe of Judah "remained loyal to" (*hāyâ ʾaḥªrê*) the house of David (1Ki 12:20).

It is conceivable that "the distinctive concepts of 'Judah and Israel' evolved during David's kingdom in Hebron, and after a period of reunification these entities were allowed to live on in the United Monarchy, though without an official division" (Zechariah Kallai, "Judah and Israel—A Study in Israelite Historiography," *IEJ* 28/4 [1978]: 257). In any event, during the coexistence of Ish-Bosheth's and David's reigns "Israel" is referred to several times in contrast/opposition to "Judah" (2:10–11, 17, 28; 3:10, 12, 17–19, 21, 37–38; 4:1). Since David became king of Israel shortly after Ish-Bosheth's death (4:12–5:3), and since David's reign in Hebron was more than five years longer than Ish-Bosheth's in Mahanaim (2:10–11; cf. also 5:5), it must have been several years after Saul's death before Ish-Bosheth had gained enough support to become king over the northern tribes. Thus Ish-Bosheth's two-year reign would have coincided with the last two years of David's seven-and-one-half-year reign over Judah.

12–17 It is only to be expected that David and Ish-Bosheth would each attempt to seize the other's kingdom. Full-scale warfare was not the only way to accomplish such a goal, however. "A general engagement of troops could ... be avoided by the substitution of a contest of teams of champions. It appears that such was the case with the two teams of twelve men each who fought for David and Ish-baal at the pool of Gibeon" (Hoffner, 221; cf. also F. Charles Fensham, "The Battle between the Men of Joab and Abner as a Possible Ordeal by Battle?" *VT* 20/3 [1970]: 356–57).

During the days of Joshua, Gibeon (v.12) "was an important city, like one of the royal cities" (Jos 10:2). Allotted to the tribe of Benjamin (Jos 18:21, 25), the ancient site is today known as el-Jib (an abbreviation that reflects the original name), six miles northwest of Jerusalem. Although Gibeon was located in Saulide territory, the fact that the combat between the Israelites and the Judahites took place there "might not be accidental, because from another part of the book of Samuel it is clear that Saul during his life acted treacherously to the Gibeonites by breaking the treaty in Jos. ix (cf. 2 Sam. xxi). It is thus to be expected that the Gibeonites should side with David and not with the Saulites" (Fensham, "The Battle between the Men of Joab and Abner," 357). Once again the hand of God can be seen working in David's behalf.

So Saul's cousin Abner, together with Ish-Bosheth's men (v.12), meet David's nephew Joab (see comment on 1Sa 26:6), together with David's men, at the "pool of Gibeon" (v.13), apparently a well-known site (perhaps the same as the "great pool in Gibeon" of Jer 41:12). It is often identified with the round, rock-cut pool excavated on the northeastern side of el-Jib in 1956 by an archaeological expedition directed by James B. Pritchard. The pool is a cylindrical shaft thirty-seven feet in diameter and thirty-five feet deep. Its five-foot-wide spiral stairway, which winds downward around the inside wall of the pool in a clockwise direction, continues below the floor level to an additional depth of forty-five feet. "From the fill of the pool came two jar handles bearing the name 'Gibeon' inscribed in good Hebrew script.... This discovery would seem to make the identification of the site of el-Jib with the biblical Gibeon certain" (James B. Pritchard, "The Water System at Gibeon," *BA* 19/4 [1956]: 70; for additional details, cf. idem, "Industry and Trade at Biblical Gibeon," *BA* 23/1 [1960]: 23–24; and *Gibeon, Where the Sun Stood Still: The Discovery of the Biblical City* [Princeton, N.J.: Princeton Univ. Press, 1962], 64–74).

Ish-Bosheth's men and David's men sit down on opposite sides of the pool of Gibeon, probably facing each other (v.13). Abner makes a proposal, which Joab accepts, that some of the young men in one group "fight hand to hand" with some in the other (the verb *śiḥaq* in v.14, "play, make sport of," is in this case a euphemistic technical term for hand-to-hand combat; cf. Y. Sukenik, "Let the Young

Men, I Pray Thee, Arise and Play before Us," *JPOS* 21 [1948]: 110–16; cf. also Brueggemann, *First and Second Samuel*, 222). Twelve from each group are "counted off" (*yaᶜabrû bᵉmispār*, lit., "they pass/cross over by number" [v.15], an idiom drawn from the practice of making animals pass under a shepherd's rod or hand as they are being counted; cf. Lev 27:32; Jer 33:13; Eze 20:37; similarly Ex 30:13–14; 38:26). The number twelve here doubtless stands for the twelve tribes of "all Israel" (v.9), whose fate hangs in the balance: "12 of the men of Ishbosheth fought 12 of the men of David to decide the succession to the throne" (J. B. Segal, 7).

The initial skirmish ends quickly (v.16). Each man "grabbed" (forcibly; cf. 13:11; 1Sa 17:35 ["seized"]) his opponent by the head and thrust a dagger into his side. Just as all the men had met at the pool "together" (v.12 [untrans. in NIV]), so also all the men now fall down "together" (v.16). From that day forward the site of the mutual massacre was called Helkath Hazzurim, which means either "Field of daggers" (from *ṣûr/ṣōr* "rock, flint"; cf. Ex 4:25; Jos 5:2–3; Ps 89:43 ["edge (of his sword)"]; Eze 3:9; the word for "dagger" in v. 16 is *ḥereb*, usually translated "sword" as in Ps 89:43; its plural is rendered "knives" in Jos 5:2–3) or "Field of hostilities" (from *ṣrr*, "be hostile toward"; cf. NIV note).

In this case "the contest ended in a draw with each man slaying his opponent [v.16], so that a general engagement ensued [v.17]" (Hoffner, 221). Thus v.17, the middle verse in the chapter, not only looks backward to the standoff in vv.12–16 but also—and supremely—looks forward to the resounding defeat of the "men of Israel" (summarized in vv.30–31). "The battle ... was very fierce" (v.17) is eerily reminiscent of "the fighting grew fierce" (1Sa 31:3)—fighting that led to the defeat and death of Saul king of Israel.

In an ancient Hittite account of representative combat, the gods are described as having given "the verdict by an ordeal on the guilty party.... Although nowhere in the narrative of 2 Sam. ii 12ff." is the Lord "*expressis verbis* called in as Judge to decide the ordeal by battle, the role of the Lord who has chosen David and rejected Saul is clearly discernable [*sic*] in the background" (Fensham, "The Battle between the Men of Joab and Abner," 357).

18–23 The word *ʾaḥᵃrê* ("after, behind, rear part") occurs a total of fifteen times in ch. 2 and is usually left untranslated by the NIV in the interests of English idiom. In addition to its appearance in 2:1 (see Note) and v.10 (see comment), it is found—remarkably—at least once in ten consecutive verses (vv.19–28) as well as in v.30. A particle implying pursuit, it thus gives unity and texture to the theme of chase that dominates vv.19–28: "chased [after], pursued [after]," v.19; "behind," v.20; "chasing [after]," v.22; "butt, back," v.23; "pursued [after]," v.24; "behind," v.25; "pursuing [after]," v.26; "pursuit of [/after]," v.27; "pursued [after]," v.28 (cf. also "pursuing [after]" in v.30).

The "sons of Zeruiah" (v.18) are "the ruthless devotees of David who always smell blood (cf. I Sam. 26:6–9; II Sam. 3:39; 16:9)" (Brueggemann, *First and Second Samuel*, 222; cf. also 18:14; for additional details see Rosenberg, 164–71). Of the three sons mentioned here, only Asahel ("God has made/done") appears for the first time (see Notes on 1Sa 26:6). Like Jonathan (see comment on 1:19), Asahel is compared to a gazelle (whether *gazella dorcas* with yellowish-brown fur, or *gazella arabica* with grey fur, is impossible to say), whose "only means of defence are its colour and the speed with which it can escape" (*Fauna and Flora of the Bible*, 34; cf. 1Ch 12:8; Pr 6:5). The "fleet-footed" (v.18; cf. Am 2:15) Asahel would eventually find himself undone by his very speed as a runner (cf. v.23).

The initial combat between Ish-Bosheth's men and David's men, which had ended in a draw (vv.12–16), now broadens and becomes more dangerous. Abner, not spoiling for a fight and eager to get out of harm's way, flees the scene of the massacre. Undeterred Asahel ("turning neither to the right nor to the left," v.19), however, is determined to overtake and kill Abner. After identifying his pursuer to his own satisfaction (v.20), Abner tells Asahel to "turn aside to the right or to the left" (i.e., give up the chase; v.21). He advises him to appease his desire for vengeance in another—perhaps less deadly—way: "Take on" (lit., "seize, grab," as in v.16) one of the young men fleeing from Gibeon and "strip him" (cf. similarly Jdg 14:19) of his weapons. The single-minded Asahel, however, is adamant (v.21).

Abner then issues a final warning: Unless he stops chasing Abner, Asahel will be the one who dies (v.22). Why would he want Abner to strike him "down" (lit., "to the ground"; cf. 18:11)? And if Abner kills Asahel, how can he "look" Asahel's brother Joab "in the face"? The Hebrew idiom means literally "lift up one's face," sometimes "without shame" (Job 11:15), in this case probably without fear—and Abner's fear of Joab proves to be not unfounded (cf. 3:27, 30).

Asahel, however, refuses to listen. Continuing to run full speed ahead, he closes the gap between himself and Abner, and the latter suddenly turns to face his pursuer. Asahel's momentum hurls him onto the butt of the spear of Abner, who thrusts it through Asahel's "stomach" (v.23; cf. the similar fate of Abner himself [3:27], of Ish-Bosheth [4:6], and of Absalom's army commander Amasa ["belly," 20:10]), thus killing him on the spot. "Every man" who "stopped when he came" to the place where Asahel had died (v.23) does not refer to travelers or others who stop to pay their respects, as some commentators hold, but to David's men, who stand transfixed in horror at the death of a fallen comrade (cf. the similar situation in 20:12, where "everyone who came ... stopped" renders the same Heb. phrase). If some "stop" (v.23; 20:12) because of fear or revulsion, others continue to "pursue" (v.24; 20:13) in order to right a wrong. The same Hebrew verb translated "stopped" in v.23 is rendered "came to a halt" in v.28, where it again refers to Joab's men.

Asahel, though dead because of his headlong pursuit of Abner, would be long remembered in Israel. He is listed first among the "Thirty," David's military elite (23:24 = 1Ch 11:26). The untimely death of Asahel, commander of the fourth of David's army divisions, early in David's reign made it necessary for his son to succeed him in that post (1Ch 27:7). It would only be a matter of time, however, before Asahel's brother Joab would avenge his great loss (3:30).

24–28 Although others may come to a halt—even if only momentarily—at the sight of their dead comrade, Joab and Abishai continue their pursuit of Abner (v.24). At sunset they (and presumably a contingent of troops with them; v.27) arrive at the hill of Ammah near Giah (both of which are otherwise unmentioned and whose locations are unknown), somewhere in the wasteland east of Gibeon. Confronting them, the Israelites (here called "men of Benjamin" [v.25; cf. also vv.9, 15, 31], probably because they were the largest contingent as well as because Benjamin was Saul's [and thus Ish-Bosheth's] tribal homeland) take their stand "on top of a [nearby] hill"—an ideal vantage point from which to direct or engage in battle if necessary (cf. Ex 17:9–10).

Just as Abner had earlier proposed that hostilities begin (v.14), so also—doubtless sensing the hopelessness of his situation—he now proposes that they cease (v.26). Across the valley between the two hills on which their respective troop contingents are deployed, Abner calls out to Joab: "Must the sword devour forever?" Brueggemann (*First and Second Samuel*, 224) makes a helpful observation at this point:

It is striking that the phrase, "sword devouring," is twice addressed to Joab. In the first usage, by Abner, the warning causes Joab to stop the killing. In the second usage (11:25), by David, the words are flippant and dismissive. The two uses of the phrase are realistic about the bloody dimensions of royal power. They mock Joab as the man at the center of the killing.

The phrase itself may derive from the shape of the blades of swords used throughout much of the OT period (see comment on 1Sa 22:19).

"How long" (v.26) commonly introduces questions implying a rebuke (see comment on 1Sa 16:1; cf. also 1Sa 1:14; Hos 8:5; Zec 1:12), and Abner uses it to good effect. He cleverly baits Joab by referring to the two groups of antagonists as "brothers"—and Joab bites by accepting the identification (v.27). He suggests that Joab's men "stop pursuing" Abner's—and the end result was that Joab "returned from pursuing" Abner (v.30; same Heb. expression). When brothers fight brothers, the result can only be "bitterness" (v.26) and shame (Ob 10).

Commentators differ on their understanding of Joab's response in v.27 (after the introductory oath formula, for which see comment on 1Sa 14:39). Some connect Joab's reply to v.14 (cf. K&D, 298: "'*If thou hadst not spoken* [*i.e.* challenged to single combat, ver. 14], *the people would have gone away in the morning, every one from his brother,*' *i.e.* there would have been no such fratricidal conflict at all"; cf. similarly first NIV footnote on v.27). But the NIV's text (and that of the second footnote), in assuming that Joab is responding to Abner's words in the nearer context (v.26), gives the more natural reading of the Hebrew original. The verb *na*^{ca}*lâ*, translated "gone away" by K&D, is elsewhere rendered "took oneself away" in the sense of lifting a siege (Jer 37:5, 11 ["withdraw"]). Joab calls off the chase (v.28), and Abner's timely plea thus leads to results remarkably similar to those described in 1 Samuel 25:34. Three times in 2 Samuel Joab blows the ram's-horn trumpet (v.28; 18:16; 20:22), and on each occasion his act signals the cessation of hostilities.

29–32 Paralleling vv.8–11, which begin by bringing Ish-Bosheth to Mahanaim and end with David in Hebron, vv.29–32 begin by returning Abner's (= Ish-Bosheth's) men to Mahanaim and end by returning Joab's (= David's) men to Hebron. In each case the men march all night to reach their respective home bases (vv.29, 32). It was customary for armies to travel at night, probably to be as inconspicuous as possible (see comment on 1Sa 31:12).

The Arabah (v.29; cf. also 4:7) refers here to the Jordan Valley between the Dead Sea and the Sea of Galilee. Marching eastward across the Jordan, Abner and his men continue through the Bithron (not mentioned elsewhere; location unknown) and arrive at Mahanaim, more than thirty miles from the wasteland east of Gibeon.

Including Asahel, a total of twenty of David's men are "missing" in action (v.30), presumably all dead. The body count of Ish-Bosheth's men, however, is "three hundred and sixty" (v.31). The eighteen-to-one ratio in favor of David demonstrates how terrible was the cost of Abner's arrogance (v.14) and how thoroughly "Abner and the men of Israel were defeated by David's men" (v.17).

Joab's men "took" (lit., "lifted up," v.32; the same Heb. verb is used in 4:4 with the crippled Mephibosheth as its object) Asahel's body to Bethlehem, the hometown of David and his clan (1Sa 20:6), where Asahel—Joab's brother and David's nephew (see comment on v.13)—would soon be given a proper burial in "his father's tomb." During much of ancient Israelite history, multiple burials in family tombs cut into the underlying rock of the slopes of hills were commonplace (cf. Robert

E. Cooley, "Gathered to His People: A Study of a Dothan Family Tomb," in *The Living and Active Word of God: Studies in Honor of Samuel J. Schultz*, ed. Morris Inch and Ronald Youngblood [Winona Lake, Ind.: Eisenbrauns, 1983], 49–58). Having left the body of their fallen comrade in Bethlehem, Joab and his men continue on their way to Hebron, more than twenty miles southwest of the wasteland east of Gibeon.

3:1 The first verse of ch. 3 serves as a summary of 2:8–32. Together with v.6 it also brackets the list of sons born to David while he was king in Hebron (vv.2–5). Though virtually unmentioned up to this point, at least in the sense of ruling dynasties, the "house of Saul" and the "house of David" (cf., however, comment on 1Sa 20:16) figure prominently in the next several chapters (cf. esp. ch. 7 for David's "house"). War—almost inevitable when rivals aspire to the same throne—continues between them "a long time" (at least for the two years of Ish-Bosheth's reign over Israel [v.10] and perhaps longer).

But Ish-Bosheth's weakness is no match for David's strength, and the outcome is a foregone conclusion. Indeed, as though to emphasize David's invincible, divinely given power (cf. 5:10), the narrator pits David alone, who "grew stronger and stronger" (singular Heb. verbs), against the entire "house of Saul," who "grew weaker and weaker" (plural Heb. verbs). As Gideon had learned in an earlier era, weakness is an asset only when God's presence accompanies it (Jdg 6:15–16). Long ago the Spirit of the Lord had come upon David and departed from Saul (see comment on 1Sa 16:14).

NOTES

8 Another way of handling the problem of the name "Baal" occurring in proper names was to substitute the generic word אֵל (*ʾēl*, "God"; cf. "Eliada" [5:16] for "Beeliada" [1Ch 14:7 and NIV note]).

12 Apart from the two occurrences of "young men" (נְעָרִים, *neʿārîm*) in vv.14 and 21, various terms for "men" (in the sense of able-bodied men who can fight in a battle) occur more than a dozen times in vv.12–32, always in carefully articulated patterns. The "men" of Ish-Bosheth (v.12) or of David (vv.13, 15 [untrans. in NIV], 17, 30–31) are called עֲבָדִים (*ʿabādîm*, lit., "servants"), reflecting their submissive obedience to the kings of their respective realms (see comment on 1Sa 17:8). The "men" of Israel (v.17) or of Abner (vv.29, 31 [untrans. in NIV]) are אֲנָשִׁים (*ʾanāšîm*), the ordinary word for "men," while the "men" of Joab (vv.26–28, 30) are called עַם (*ʿam*, "people"), commonly used in the books of Samuel in the sense of "soldiers" or "troops"; here the difference in terminology may be intended to highlight—subtly, to be sure—the fact that Joab's mighty "soldiers" are sure to defeat Abner's mere "men." Not until the battle is over and Israel has been overwhelmingly defeated (v.31) are the victors, Joab's "men" (v.32), called *ʾanāšîm*. The only other place in the chapter where the word "men" is reflected in a Hebrew equivalent is in reference to the "men" of Benjamin in v.25, where בָּנִים (*bānîm*, "sons") is used (probably to exploit its euphony with "Benjamin").

23 The Hebrew for "died on the spot" means literally "died under him" (i.e., "died [on the place that was] under him"). The closest parallel elsewhere in the OT is Jeremiah 38:9, "where he will starve to death" (lit., "and he will die [on the place that is] under him because of starvation").

24 According to *HALOT*, 1.62, the proper name אַמָּה (*ʾammâ*, "Ammah") means "canal"; the proper name גִּיחַ (*gîaḥ*, "Giah") is probably related to a water source of some kind (Aharoni, 109). The Hebrew root of the latter is used of movement of or in water (cf. "surge," Job 40:23; "thrashing about," Eze 32:2). Gihon, an expanded form of the same word, is the name of one of the four rivers of Eden (Ge 2:13) as well as of a major spring located outside the eastern wall of Jerusalem (1Ki 1:33) that even today provides water to its citizens. As Alter (*The David Story*, 206) suggestively observes, both names "may be related to an aquaduct [*sic*] system linked to the pool at Gibeon."

29 בִּתְרוֹן (*bitrôn*), perhaps not a place name, may have meant "ravine" or "morning" or the like (see NIV note). For the latter see W. R. Arnold, who translates "forenoon" on the basis of what he perceives as parallelism with "night" earlier in the verse ("The Meaning of בתרון," *AJSL* 28 [1911–12]: 274–83; cf. also NAB, NASB, NJB, REB, RSV, TEV).

31 The NIV's "Benjamites who were with Abner" understands מבנימן ובאנשי אבנר (*mbnymn wbʾnšy ʾbnr*, lit., "from Benjamin and among/from the men of Abner") in the sense of "from Benjamin—namely, from Abner's men." The NIV's rendering is supported by 4QSamuel[a], which reads מאנשי (*mʾnšy*, "from the men of") instead of the MT's *wbʾnšy*, thus clarifying the sense of the preposition and eliminating the ambiguous copula entirely (cf. also NAB, McCarter). In any case, the interchangeability of the two prepositions is clear from other passages in 2 Samuel (see Notes on 5:13; 13:30; 17:12; 22:9; cf. esp. Sarna, 310–13).

3:1 The phrase "house/dynasty of David," which first appears in 1 Samuel 20:16, occurs more than twenty times in the OT overall (cf. BDB, 109–10, for details). It was found inscribed in the form ביתדוד (*bytdwd*) on an Aramaic stela in an undisturbed ninth-century BC stratum at Tel Dan in northern Israel in 1993 (see A. Biran and J. Naveh, "An Aramaic Stele Fragment from Tel Dan," *IEJ* 43 [1993]: 81–98; "The Tel Dan Inscription: A New Fragment," *IEJ* 45 [1995]: 1–18; Anonymous, "'David' Found at Dan," *BAR* 20/2 [1994]: 26–39). Typical of the attempts of minimalist/nihilist/reductionist scholars (who doubt the existence of David as an historical figure) to read *byt dwd* as "house/temple of uncle" or "temple of (the god) Dod" or "house of beloved" or "house of kettle" or the like is that of Philip R. Davies, "'House of David' Built on Sand: The Sins of the Biblical Maximizers," *BAR* 20/4 (1994): 54–55. Davies was answered briefly by Anson Rainey, "The 'House of David' and the House of the Deconstructionists," *BAR* 20/6 (1994): 47.

The Dan discovery inspired Lemaire to reread the ninth-century Mesha inscription, where he noted the same phrase (see A. Lemaire, *Studi Epigrafici e Linguistici sul Vicino Oriente Antico* 11 (1994): 17–19). Another possible early mention of David has been noted by K. Kitchen in "A Possible Mention of David in the Late Tenth Century BCE and Deity *Dod as Dead as the Dodo?" (*JSOT* 76 [1997]: 29–44, esp. 29). It is written in Egyptian as *dwt* in the place-name *h(y)dbt dwt* ("Heights of David"), one of the toponyms in Pharaoh Shishak's list on the exterior south wall of the temple of Amun-Re at Karnak in southern Egypt. For a convenient summary of the importance of these three inscriptions—one Aramaic, one Moabite, and one Egyptian—see especially H. Shanks, "Has David Been Found in Egypt?" (*BAR* 25/1 [January–February 1999]: 34–35; Kitchen, *On the Reliability of the Old Testament*, 92–93; V. Philips Long, in I. Provan, V. P. Long, and T. Longman III, *A Biblical History of Israel* [Louisville: Westminster John Knox, 2003], 216–17). See further the comment on 1 Samuel 16:13 concerning the possibility that the name "David" also occurs in line 12 of the Mesha inscription.

5. Sons Born to David in Hebron (3:2–5)

OVERVIEW

The fact that vv.2–5 are flanked by references to "the war between the house of Saul and the house of David" (vv.1, 6) not only confirms the literary unity of the section but also highlights its function: to portray the growing strength of David's house in contradistinction to that of Saul (for other examples of this technique in the books of Samuel and the various purposes it serves, cf. Burke O. Long, 385–99). The verses have their own inclusio as well ("were born to David in Hebron," vv.2, 5; given the clear Pual in v.5, the debate between Niphal [*Qere*] and syncopated Pual [*Kethiv*] in v.2 as the original Hebrew verbal stem underlying "were born" should perhaps be settled in favor of the latter, the *Qere* Niphal then being viewed as a scribal harmonization with 5:13). Verses 2–5 are paralleled in 1 Chronicles 3:1–4a.

[2]Sons were born to David in Hebron:
His firstborn was Amnon the son of Ahinoam of Jezreel;
[3]his second, Kileab the son of Abigail the widow of Nabal of Carmel;
the third, Absalom the son of Maacah daughter of Talmai king of Geshur;
[4]the fourth, Adonijah the son of Haggith;
the fifth, Shephatiah the son of Abital;
[5]and the sixth, Ithream the son of David's wife Eglah.
These were born to David in Hebron.

COMMENTARY

2–5 Anointed king over Judah in Hebron, David settled down with his two wives, Ahinoam and Abigail, and began to build a substantial family during his seven-and-a-half-year rule from there (vv.2–3; cf. 2:1–2, 4, 11). His firstborn son, Am(i)non ("Faithful"; for the alternative spelling, cf. the MT of 13:20), the son of Ahinoam, would ultimately be killed by the men of Absalom (13:28–29), David's third son (v.3). His second son, Kileab, whose mother was Abigail (v.3), is mentioned only here and apparently died before he was able to enter the fray to determine who would be David's successor as king of Israel.

Ab(i)s(h)alom ("My [divine] father is peace" or "[Divine] father of peace"; for the alternative spelling [although a different Absalom is in view], cf. 1Ki 15:2, 10 and NIV note) was the son of Maacah (v.3), a Geshurite princess, whom David may have married as part of a diplomatic agreement with Talmai, the Geshurite king. Fearing royal reprisal over the murder of Amnon, Absalom would eventually flee to the protection of his grandfather and stay in

Geshur for three years (13:37–38). Although it is tempting to equate Maacah's homeland with the southern Geshur mentioned in 1 Samuel 27:8 (see comment), Talmai's Geshur was a small Aramean kingdom (cf. 15:8) northeast of the Sea of Galilee and often associated with the neighboring kingdom of Maacah (Dt 3:14; Jos 12:5; 13:11, 13), the namesake of Talmai's daughter. Another Absalom would later name his own daughter "Maacah," and she would become the wife of Rehoboam son of Solomon (1Ki 15:2, 10; 2Ch 11:20–22).

Adonijah ("My Lord is the LORD," v.4) the son of Haggith ("Festal one"; cf. "Haggai," a masculine form of the same name) would figure prominently in the struggle for David's throne (cf. 1Ki 1–2), eventually to be assassinated in favor of Solomon. Of Shephatiah ("The Lord judges") the son of Abital ("My [divine] father is dew" or [Divine] father of dew"; see comment on 1:21) and of Ithream (perhaps "[My divine] kinsman is abundance") the son of Eglah ("Heifer") nothing further is known. That Eglah alone is called "David's wife" (v.5) may be due to the fact that she is the last on the list and that her relationship to David therefore summarizes that of the other women. David's polygamy, begun with Ahinoam and Abigail (see comment on 1Sa 25:43), continues unabated—indeed, it increases—in Hebron.

In addition to summarizing David's fecundity in Hebron (one or more of David's wives bore him other children as well; cf. Absalom's sister Tamar [13:1]), vv.2–5 also have their political ramifications. Brueggemann observes that the important names in the section are "Amnon (v. 2; cf. chs. 13–14), Absalom (v. 3; cf. chs. 15–19), and Adonijah (v. 4; cf. 1 Kings 1–2). The sequence of Amnon, Absalom, and Adonijah provides an outline for the coming drama" (Brueggemann, *First and Second Samuel*, 255).

NOTE

3 Commentators often assume a relationship between כִּלְאָב (*kilʾāb*, "Kileab") and כָּלֵב (*kālēb*, "Caleb") in light of the Calebite ancestry of Nabal (1Sa 25:3), the deceased husband of Abigail. But apart from the fact that the intrusive א (ʾ) is then difficult to explain, the last three letters of *klʾb* ("Kileab") coincide with the first three letters of *lʾbygl* ("[the son] of Abigail"), which immediately follows *klʾb* in the MT. The suspicion of dittographic corruption in the MT at this point is therefore strong (cf. Driver, Kirkpatrick). In addition, the parallel text in 1 Chronicles 3:1 reads "Daniel" instead of "Kileab," and both 4QSamuel[a] and the LXX display *d* rather than *k* as the first consonant in the name of David's second son. Another possibility is that Kileab and Daniel were alternative names for the same man (thus K&D). Patrick, 345, provides a typical explanation:

> And the Hebrew Doctors give this Reason for both Names. He called him, say they, when he was born *Daniel* (which was his *Fundamental* that is, his primary Name) because, said he, *God hath judged* or *vindicated* me from *Nabal*. And afterwards he called him *Chileab* as much as to say, *like to his Father*. Because in his Countenance he resembled *David*. And this he did, for this reason, to silence the Mockers of that Age: Who said *Abigail* had conceived by *Nabal* whose Son this was. For the confuting of which Calumny, God was pleased to order that the Fashion of his Face should be perfectly like to *David's*.

Archaeologists working at Tell Hadar, an important city in the land of Geshur northeast of the Sea of Galilee, have unearthed an eleventh-century beer strainer in the burnt debris of a building tentatively identified as a palace. They interpret their discovery as confirming "the Biblical narrative that the land of Geshur existed during the period between the careers of Joshua and King David" (Timothy Renner and Ira Spar, "The Land of Geshur Project," *New Jersey Archaeological Consortium Newsletter* 3 [1988]). The palace may have been that of King Talmai himself ("Any Time, Any Place: A Dig for Every Interest," *BAR* 23/1 [1997]: 31). See especially Moshe Kochavi, Timothy Renner, Ira Spar and Esther Yadin, "Rediscovered! The Land of Geshur," *BAR* 18/4 (1992): 30–44. Geshur is almost certainly mentioned in the Amarna letters as "the land of Ga<su>ru" (EA 256), a league of seven cities (EA 256:19–28) in the fourteenth century BC (for details see Zvi U. Maᶜoz, "Gesher," *ABD*, 2:996).

B. David's Accession to Kingship over Israel (3:6–5:16)

OVERVIEW

The story of how David became king of all Israel follows, in most essentials, the same outline already established in the account of his accession to kingship over Judah (1:1–3:5). Both begin with a warrior trying to curry David's favor (an unnamed Amalekite in 1:1–13; Saul's army commander Abner in 3:6–21) and continue with the execution or murder of the warrior (1:14–16; 3:22–32), followed by a lament uttered by David (over Saul and Jonathan in 1:17–27; over Abner in 3:33–34). Near the center of each literary unit is a brief report of the anointing of David as king (over Judah in 2:1–7; over Israel in 5:1–5). David and his men are then successful in defeating their enemies (2:8–3:1; 5:6–12), and each unit concludes with a list of sons/children born to David (in Hebron in 3:2–5; in Jerusalem in 5:13–16). The similarities between the two sections point to the careful craftsmanship of a single author, who now sets about to tell his readers that just as the house of David has replaced Saul and his house in southern Canaan (1:1–3:5), so too is David's house about to replace that of Saul in the rest of the land (3:6–5:16).

1. Abner's Defection to David (3:6–21)

OVERVIEW

The devastating defeat of Ish-Bosheth's men by David's men (2:30–31) has made its impact on Saul's cousin Abner. Ruthless and ambitious, Abner is a canny politician who sees the handwriting on the wall. He therefore sets about to transfer Ish-Bosheth's kingdom over to David—and Ish-Bosheth can only sit by, helplessly watching the inevitable unfold (vv.9–11).

A key word in the narrative, used only and always by Abner, is *yād* ("hand"). Although Abner has not yet "handed" Ish-Bosheth "over to" (lit., "caused [him] to be found in the hand of") David (v.8), he will soon "help" (lit., "[his] hand will be with"; see comment on 1Sa 22:17) David to bring all Israel over to him (v.12). The Lord had earlier promised that "by" (lit., "by the hand of") David he would rescue Israel from the "hand" of the Philistines—indeed, from the "hand" of all her enemies (v.18). Doubtless hoping for a prominent place in David's kingdom, Abner wants to be the divinely chosen agent in delivering Israel to David's rule.

[6]During the war between the house of Saul and the house of David, Abner had been
strengthening his own position in the house of Saul. [7]Now Saul had had a concubine
named Rizpah daughter of Aiah. And Ish-Bosheth said to Abner, "Why did you sleep with
my father's concubine?"
[8]Abner was very angry because of what Ish-Bosheth said and he answered, "Am I a
dog's head—on Judah's side? This very day I am loyal to the house of your father Saul and
to his family and friends. I haven't handed you over to David. Yet now you accuse me of an
offense involving this woman! [9]May God deal with Abner, be it ever so severely, if I do not
do for David what the LORD promised him on oath [10]and transfer the kingdom from the
house of Saul and establish David's throne over Israel and Judah from Dan to Beersheba."
[11]Ish-Bosheth did not dare to say another word to Abner, because he was afraid of him.
[12]Then Abner sent messengers on his behalf to say to David, "Whose land is it? Make an
agreement with me, and I will help you bring all Israel over to you."
[13]"Good," said David. "I will make an agreement with you. But I demand one thing of
you: Do not come into my presence unless you bring Michal daughter of Saul when you
come to see me." [14]Then David sent messengers to Ish-Bosheth son of Saul, demanding,
"Give me my wife Michal, whom I betrothed to myself for the price of a hundred Philistine
foreskins."
[15]So Ish-Bosheth gave orders and had her taken away from her husband Paltiel son of
Laish. [16]Her husband, however, went with her, weeping behind her all the way to Bahurim.
Then Abner said to him, "Go back home!" So he went back.
[17]Abner conferred with the elders of Israel and said, "For some time you have wanted
to make David your king. [18]Now do it! For the LORD promised David, 'By my servant David I
will rescue my people Israel from the hand of the Philistines and from the hand of all their
enemies.'"
[19]Abner also spoke to the Benjamites in person. Then he went to Hebron to tell David
everything that Israel and the whole house of Benjamin wanted to do. [20]When Abner, who
had twenty men with him, came to David at Hebron, David prepared a feast for him and
his men. [21]Then Abner said to David, "Let me go at once and assemble all Israel for my lord
the king, so that they may make a compact with you, and that you may rule over all that
your heart desires." So David sent Abner away, and he went in peace.

COMMENTARY

6 Echoing v.1a, v.6a is thematic of the rest of ch. 3 and all of ch. 4 in its reminder of the continuing struggle between the Saulides and the Davidides. Echoing v.1b, v.6b parallels Abner's "strengthening" position in Saul's house with David's "stronger and stronger" control of his own fortunes, both of which contrast sharply with Ish-Bosheth's "weaker and weaker" hold on Israel's throne. Verse 6 also implies that Abner is not only well positioned to wrest Israel's kingdom from the hapless Ish-Bosheth but also to do with it whatever he pleases—including deliver it to David. It may therefore not be inappropriate to observe yet another contrast in the wider context: While Abner was "strengthening his own position" (*mtḥzq*) in the house of Saul, it was characteristic of David that he "found strength" (*wytḥzq*) in the Lord his God (1Sa 30:6).

7–11 Ish-Bosheth's surprise question to Abner—"Why did you sleep with my father's concubine?" (v.7)—arrives like a bolt out of the blue. "It springs on us a situation where one agent reproaches another for a full-blown and explosive affair of which we have had no inkling, let alone any queries" (Sternberg, 241).

Saul's concubine, Rizpah daughter of Aiah, is mentioned elsewhere only in 21:8–11 (where she protects the exposed corpses of seven of Saul's male descendants [including two of her own sons] from the ravages of wild animals). "Sleep with" is literally "come to," a common Hebrew euphemism for sexual intercourse. Ish-Bosheth accuses Abner of "coming to" King Saul's concubine (and now presumably Ish-Bosheth's, since Saul is dead)—an act by Abner that would probably be intended to assert his claim to Saul's throne (cf. vv.8–10; 16:20–22; 1Ki 1:1–4; 2:13–22; cf. Levenson and Halpern, 508; Brueggemann, *First and Second Samuel*, 225–26). Later Abner "came to" David at Hebron (v.20), offering to deliver to him the kingdom that apparently he considered his to dispose of as he wished (v.21). But for now Abner responds indignantly to Ish-Bosheth: "Am I a dog's head?" (v.8).

William A. C. Propp ("Acting Like Apes: The Bible's Alpha Males" [*BRev* 20/3 (2004): 36]) suggests that this derogatory epithet "conceivably refers to the cynocephalous, or dog-headed, baboon." Although unique, the expression is clearly to be taken as self-depreciating and uncomplimentary (see comment on 1Sa 17:43). How can Ish-Bosheth possibly think that Abner would defect to Judah? Abner protests that although "this very day" he has been loyal to Saul's house, Ish-Bosheth is accusing him "now" (same Heb. word in both cases). "I am loyal" translates the same Hebrew-covenant idiom rendered "showing kindness" in 2:5 (see comment) and makes all the more reasonable Abner's forthcoming request of David to "make an agreement" with him (v.12; cf. vv.13, 21).

Abner compounds his arrogance by claiming allegiance not only to Saul but also to his "family" (lit., "brothers/relatives") and "friends" (for the same two terms in parallelism, cf. Pr 19:7). After all, he continues, he has not "handed" Ish-Bosheth "over to" (lit., "caused [him] to be found in the hand of"; cf. Zec 11:6) David. He therefore pretends not to be able to understand how Ish-Bosheth can "accuse" him "of an offense" involving Rizpah—a bold protestation indeed, since the Heb. phrase rendered "accuse of offense" is elsewhere rendered "punish for sin/guilt/wickedness" in a number of key theological texts (Ex 20:5 = Dt 5:9; Ex 34:7; Lev 18:25; Nu 14:18; Isa 13:11; 26:21; Jer 25:12; 36:31; Am 3:2).

Far from denying Ish-Bosheth's accusation, however, Abner takes a strong oath of self-imprecation (v.9; cf. v.35; see comment on 1Sa 20:13), vowing that he will become God's instrument in bringing about what the Lord had promised to David (the reference being perhaps to 1Sa 15:28 and/or 16:1)—namely, transferring Saul's kingdom to him. "David's throne" (v.10), already established over Judah (2:4) and soon to be established over Israel, would someday soon be occupied by David's son Solomon (1Ki 2:12, 24, 45), later be discredited by Solomon's reprobate descendants, who would be destroyed by the Lord himself (Jer 13:13–14; 29:16–17), and eventually be inherited by the Lord's Messiah, who will reign forever in peace and with justice and righteousness (Isa 9:6–7). For now, however, during his lifetime David will rule over "Israel and Judah" (cf. 5:5; 12:8; 24:1; see also comment on 2:10) all the way "from Dan to Beersheba" (cf. 17:11; 24:2, 15; see comment on 1Sa 3:20). Cowardly (see comment on 2:8) and powerless, Ish-Bosheth for his part can do nothing to stem the tide of Abner's ambitions (v.11).

12–16 Divided into two parts by the expression "sent messengers" (vv.12, 14; cf. MT paragraph indicators), vv.12–16 constitute the central section of the present literary unit (vv.6–21) and focus on David's recovery of and reunion with his wife Michal.

The preliminary meeting between Abner and David takes place through messengers rather than face to face. Abner's rhetorical question, "Whose land is it?" (v.12), is perhaps intentionally ambiguous. It could mean, "The land of Israel is mine to give" (and therefore David should make an agreement "with me"), or it could mean, "The land of Israel is yours because of God's promise" (and therefore Abner will act as God's agent and "help you bring all Israel over to you"). Abner's ambition tips the scales in favor of the former interpretation. Indeed,

> it may be that Abner, as *de facto* ruler of all Israel, offered David his allegiance in exchange for the position of *śar ṣābāʾ* [commander of the army], the equivalent of his office in Eshbaal's army and the post currently held by Joab. V. 12 suggests something of the sort when it speaks of a *personal* deal between these two men. (Vanderkam, 531–32)

In either case it is clear that the Lord is working behind the scenes to deliver the northern tribes into David's hands. (The Heb. expression rendered "bring ... over to" is translated "turn[ed] ... over to" in 1Ch 10:14; 12:23, the process in both cases occurring because of divine initiative.) "Make an agreement" is literally "cut your covenant" (for the idiom "cut a covenant/treaty," see comments on 1Sa 11:1; 18:3) and emphasizes the personal nature of the deal that Abner wants to strike with David.

For his part, David is willing to accept Abner's proposal only on one condition: that he bring Michal, Saul's younger daughter (see comment on 1Sa 14:49), with him when he comes to Hebron (v.13). David is adamant, warning Abner not to "come into my presence" (lit., "see my face") without bringing Michal when he comes to "see me" (lit., "see my face," repeating the same Heb. phrase for emphasis).

Clines, 271, points out that David chooses his words carefully in vv.13–14. When speaking to Abner he refers to Michal as "daughter of Saul" (v.13), thus reminding Abner that if he agrees to bring her with him, he has turned his back on Ish-Bosheth for good and has assented to David's succession to Saul's throne. When speaking through messengers to Ish-Bosheth, however, David calls Michal "my wife" (v.14), thus reminding Ish-Bosheth that she is David's wife, not Paltiel's, and that the responsibility for her being now with Paltiel is Ish-Bosheth's, since he is the son and heir of Saul (Ish-Bosheth is mentioned several times in ch. 3, but only in v.14 is he called "son of Saul"), who wrongfully gave her to Paltiel in the first place (1Sa 25:44).

Alter (*The Art of Biblical Narrative*, 122) makes the further observation that Paltiel

> is called twice in close sequence [vv.15, 16] Michal's man or husband (*ᵓish*), a title to which at least his feelings give him legitimate claim, and which echoes ironically against David's use in the preceding verse [v.14] of *ᵓishti* my wife or woman, to describe a relationship with Michal that is legal and political but perhaps not at all emotional on his side.

Now that Saul's death has given him a free hand, David wants to strengthen his claim to Saul's throne by retrieving the woman for whom, after all, he had earlier paid the demanded bride-price of "a hundred Philistine foreskins" (v.14)—indeed, he had paid double what had been required of him (see comments on 1Sa 18:25–27).

Michal's guardian and brother Ish-Bosheth, powerless as ever, readily consents to David's demand and takes Michal away from her husband "Paltiel son of Laish" (v.15; see comment and note on 1Sa 25:44). When Abner and Michal depart for Hebron, the heartsick and weeping Paltiel tags along as far as Bahurim (v.16, mentioned elsewhere only in Davidic contexts [16:5; 17:18; 19:16; 1Ki 2:8]), where Abner orders him to go back home (probably to Mahanaim). Although the precise location of Bahurim is uncertain (somewhere near the Mount of Olives, however; cf. 15:30, 32; 16:1, 5), it is perhaps the modern site of Ras et-Tumeim, about one and a half miles northeast of Jerusalem and thus almost twenty miles southwest of Mahanaim.

And so it is that Michal is added to David's roster of wives. His repossession of her does not violate the terms of Deuteronomy 24:1–4, "since his separation from his wife was involuntary. The right of a husband to reclaim his wife ... is well entrenched in Mesopotamian law, and may be assumed to have operated in Israel" (Gordon, *I and II Samuel*, 219).

17–21 Like the previous section (vv.12–16), so also vv.17–21 divide into two roughly equal halves. In vv.17–19 Abner tries to convince the elders of Israel and the Benjamites that the time is ripe for them to make David their king. In vv.20–21 Abner arrives in Hebron, offers to facilitate a compact between all Israel on the one hand and David on the other, and then departs. The theme of the opening and closing verses of the section—that Israel would soon make David their king—is echoed and summarized in the terminology of 5:3: "the elders of Israel" (v.17; 5:3) "make/made a compact" (v.21; 5:3).

The time when Abner "conferred" (to gain support for his cause [v.17]; cf. 1Ki 1:7) with Israel's elders was probably antecedent to the events of vv.15–16 (thus Kirkpatrick), since the elders were doubtless headquartered for the most part in Mahanaim and served as Ish-Bosheth's advisors there, while it is equally clear that Abner escorted Michal to Hebron (cf. vv.13, 16). Abner's counsel to the elders is straightforward: There is no reason to delay any longer in making David king over all Israel (vv.17–18). God had promised David that he would be divinely endowed to "rescue/deliver my people Israel from the hand of the Philistines" (v.18), a word originally spoken concerning Saul—who, however, failed miserably in that endeavor (see 1Sa 9:16 and comment). In any event, God himself is the true deliverer of his people (cf. esp. 1Sa 7:8) and thus sovereignly chooses whom and when he will. David is called the Lord's "servant" (v.18) more than thirty times in the OT, usually in reference to the historical David (cf. 7:5, 8, 26; the titles of Pss 18; 36) but also to the eschatological, messianic David (cf. Eze 34:23–24; 37:24–25).

On his way to Hebron, Abner pays special attention to the Benjamites, who are Saul's (and Ish-Bosheth's) kinsmen. He "spoke" to them "in person" (v.19) and then continued on to "tell"

David (the Heb. idiom underlying both expressions means literally "speak into the ears of") what Israel and Benjamin wanted to do. Though counted among the northern tribes and an indispensable part of the kingdom of Israel, the "house of Benjamin" (v.19) would eventually become inextricably linked to the house of Judah (cf. 1Ki 12:21–23).

Arriving in Hebron with Michal, Abner and his twenty men sit down to a feast prepared for them by David (v.20). Whether the feast is in celebration of David's (re)marriage to Michal (cf. Vanderkam, 532; further Ge 29:21–22; Jdg 14:10; Mt 22:2) or is part of the protocol of covenants recently made (vv.12–13; cf. Abraham Malamat, "Organs of Statecraft in the Israelite Monarchy," *BA* 28/2 [1965]: 35; further Ge 26:28–30; 31:44, 53–54) is difficult to say, although the latter is perhaps more likely (cf. vv.20–21 with Ge 26:28–31).

With his offer to bring "all Israel" into a covenantal relationship with David (v.21), Abner's defection to the house of Judah is complete. The earlier "agreement" between the two men (vv.12–13) was personal and is not to be confused with the national "compact" (v.21; cf. also 5:3) now to be made between north and south, even though *b*ᵉ*rît*, usually translated "covenant," underlies both words. Abner assures David that the end result of the compact will be that "you may/will rule over all that your heart desires," a phrase ironically echoed in the Lord's words to Jeroboam in prediction of the rupture of the united kingdom after the death of Solomon (1Ki 11:37). To David's kingdom the ten northern tribes will soon be added; from his son Solomon's kingdom the ten northern tribes will eventually be taken away.

Abner's mission now complete, David sends him away and he goes "in peace" (v.21). The phrase is repeated in vv.22–23, perhaps to emphasize the fact that David had promised Abner safe conduct (cf. REB; also 15:27; Ge 26:29, 31). The promise, if such it was, would prove to be tragically meaningless, as the next section demonstrates.

NOTES

7 Although the name Ish-Bosheth does not appear in the MT of v.7, the NIV correctly supplies it in the context (cf. v.8). It in fact occurs in a few Hebrew MSS, and 4QSamuel[a], the LXX, and the Syriac seem to reflect a Hebrew text that read "Ish-Bosheth son of Saul" (cf. *BHS*).

8 Early Jewish commentators (e.g., Rashi, Kimchi) frequently understood the phrase "dog's head" to mean "head/commander over dogs." Abner thus accuses Ish-Bosheth of treating him, "the commander of Saul's army" (2:8), as though he were merely the captain of a pack of dogs (cf. Patrick, 347).

16 בָּכֹה אַחֲרֶיהָ עַד־בַּחֻרִים (*bākōh ʾaḥ*ᵃ*reyhā ʿad-baḥurîm*, "weeping behind her ... to Bahurim") is a fine example of assonance in the MT.

18 The NIV's "I will rescue" renders the MT's הוֹשִׁיעַ (*hôšîaʿ*, "to rescue" [Hiphil infinitive construct] or "he rescued" [Hiphil third person masculine singular perfect]). Although many Hebrew MSS here read אוֹשִׁיעַ (*ʾôšîaʿ*, "I will rescue" [Hiphil first person singular imperfect]; cf. also the ancient versions), Barthélemy, 2:214, remarks, "the infinitive here may be interpreted as a decision to save, 'I will save.'" It is also possible that the MT's form is a mispointed Hiphil infinitive absolute (for examples cf. GKC, sec. 53*k*) used as a finite verb.

2. The Murder of Abner (3:22–39)

OVERVIEW

Chapter 3 concludes with a detailed account of the events preceding, including, and following the death of Abner. It centers on v.30, a parenthetical statement that explains why Joab found it necessary to kill his northern counterpart. Various elements in the two halves of the section parallel one another, producing a symmetrical outline:

A Joab kills Abner (3:22–27)
  B David protests his innocence of Abner's death (3:28)
    C David curses Joab (3:29)
[The narrator summarizes (3:30)]
A' David mourns Abner's death (3:31–35)
  B' Everyone acknowledges David's innocence (3:36–37)
    C' David praises Abner and curses Joab (3:38–39)

[22]Just then David's men and Joab returned from a raid and brought with them a great
deal of plunder. But Abner was no longer with David in Hebron, because David had sent
him away, and he had gone in peace. [23]When Joab and all the soldiers with him arrived, he
was told that Abner son of Ner had come to the king and that the king had sent him away
and that he had gone in peace.
[24]So Joab went to the king and said, "What have you done? Look, Abner came to
you. Why did you let him go? Now he is gone! [25]You know Abner son of Ner; he came to
deceive you and observe your movements and find out everything you are doing."
[26]Joab then left David and sent messengers after Abner, and they brought him back
from the well of Sirah. But David did not know it. [27]Now when Abner returned to Hebron,
Joab took him aside into the gateway, as though to speak with him privately. And there, to
avenge the blood of his brother Asahel, Joab stabbed him in the stomach, and he died.
[28]Later, when David heard about this, he said, "I and my kingdom are forever innocent
before the LORD concerning the blood of Abner son of Ner. [29]May his blood fall upon the
head of Joab and upon all his father's house! May Joab's house never be without someone who has a running sore or leprosy or who leans on a crutch or who falls by the sword
or who lacks food."
[30](Joab and his brother Abishai murdered Abner because he had killed their brother
Asahel in the battle at Gibeon.)
[31]Then David said to Joab and all the people with him, "Tear your clothes and put on
sackcloth and walk in mourning in front of Abner." King David himself walked behind

the bier. 32They buried Abner in Hebron, and the king wept aloud at Abner's tomb. All the people wept also.
33The king sang this lament for Abner:

"Should Abner have died as the lawless die?
34 Your hands were not bound,
your feet were not fettered.
You fell as one falls before wicked men."

And all the people wept over him again.
35Then they all came and urged David to eat something while it was still day; but David
took an oath, saying, "May God deal with me, be it ever so severely, if I taste bread or anything else before the sun sets!"
36All the people took note and were pleased; indeed, everything the king did pleased
them. 37So on that day all the people and all Israel knew that the king had no part in the
murder of Abner son of Ner.
38Then the king said to his men, "Do you not realize that a prince and a great man has
fallen in Israel this day? 39And today, though I am the anointed king, I am weak, and these sons
of Zeruiah are too strong for me. May the LORD repay the evildoer according to his evil deeds!"

COMMENTARY

22–27 Key verbs in vv.22–27 are *bôʾ* ("come" [GK 995]; v.22 ["returned," "brought"], v.23 ["arrived," "had come"], v.24 ["went," "came"], v.25 ["came," "movements"]) and *yādaʿ* ("know" [GK 3359]; v.25 ["know," "observe," "find out"], v.26). Three verses in succession conclude with the report that David sent Abner away, and Abner went "in peace" (vv.21–23). In the middle of this otherwise tranquil scene (v.22) the narrator states that David's men and Joab "returned" from a raid (the verb is singular, stressing Joab's leadership), the theme in this case being not "peace" but "plunder" (the word being in emphatic position in its clause).

Arriving in Hebron and learning that Abner has already come and gone (v.23), Joab goes to David and demands to know why he released Abner—the only genuine obstacle to David's sitting on Israel's throne—when he had him firmly in his grasp (v.24). After all, the man whom David has allowed to leave is not just any "Abner" (v.24); he is "Abner son of Ner" (v.25), a cousin of Saul, who must therefore be an opponent of David (cf. Clines, 274–75). Indeed, Abner has doubtless come to Hebron for the sole purpose of learning everything that might well prove useful in the future (cf. similarly the mission of the envoys of Merodach-Baladan king of Babylon in the days of Hezekiah, 2Ki 20:12–18 = Isa 39).

"Movements" (v.25) is the NIV's rendering of the merism "going(s) out and coming(s) in," a common OT expression capable of a wide range of applications (cf. Dt 28:6, 19) that probably originated in such mundane activities as going out to the fields in the morning and returning at night and that was eventually pressed into service as a *terminus technicus* for the "exits and entrances" of buildings (cf. Eze 43:11; 44:5). Joab's accusation that David allowed Abner to "deceive" him (v.25) is ironic in the light of his own subsequent treachery (v.27). The principle elucidated in Proverbs 24:28–29 is surely apropos: "Do not ... use your lips to deceive. Do not say, 'I'll do to him as he has done to me; I'll pay that man back for what he did.'"

"A striking feature of the scene in which Joab excoriates his royal master (2 Sam 3:24–25) is the complete silence of David" (Vanderkam, 533 n. 39)—who, however, is realistic enough to recognize that he is still too weak to risk a showdown with the sons of Zeruiah (v.39). The brash Joab thus feels free to leave David without so much as waiting for a response to his rebuke (v.26); nor is David told that Joab's men pursue Abner and bring him back from the "well" (better "cistern"; cf. NAB, RSV; similarly NJB) of Sirah (mentioned only here, perhaps to be identified with modern Sirat el-Ballai about two and a half miles north of Hebron; for details see Simons, *The Geographical and Topographical Texts of the Old Testament* [Leiden: Brill, 1959], 330).

Joab's deception of Abner is chillingly similar to Cain's treachery toward his brother Abel (Ge 4:8). Pretending that he wants to discuss a private matter with him, Joab takes Abner "into" (lit., "to the midst of," v.27) the gateway, doubtless to a relatively secluded area within what was often a beehive of activity. Then, "to avenge" (*b*ᵉ-, lit., "[in exchange] for"; cf. v.14, where the same Heb. preposition is translated "for the price of") the blood of his brother Asahel, Joab kills Abner. The method used—he "stabbed him in the stomach" (v.27)—is the same used in Abner's killing of Asahel (see comment on 2:23) and thus illustrates the lex talionis ("principle of retaliation in kind"; cf. Ex 21:23–25).

28 The expansive phrase *mē*ʾ*aḥ*ᵃ*rê kēn* ("later," lit., "from after this") lends a touch of formality to David's protestation of innocence. (The idiom occurs only twice elsewhere: 15:1 ["in the course of time"]; 2Ch 32:23 ["from then on"].) In addition, Clines, 275, observes that from here to the end of the chapter Abner is given his legal/formal title "Abner son of Ner" only in vv.28 and 37. Furthermore, David's use of "forever" adds to the solemnity of his statement (cf. 1Ki 2:33).

Upon hearing of Abner's murder, David declares himself—and his kingdom, doubtless including his future royal heirs—innocent of all personal responsibility for Abner's death. The motif of David as "innocent" is first recorded in the assessment of his friend Jonathan (1Sa 19:5) and recurs in the Davidic psalms (cf. Pss 19:13; 26:6; 64:4). Needless to say, that opinion is not shared by disaffected Israelites, who hold David accountable for the massacre of the Saulides and continue to think of him as a "man of blood" (Shimei's description of David in 16:7–8, an evaluation shared by not a few modern scholars [cf. Vanderkam, passim]).

29 For his part, however, David disavows all such responsibility. He places the blame squarely where it belongs by cursing the "head of Joab" (cf. the words of Solomon in 1Ki 2:33) and devoutly hoping that Abner's blood will "fall" (lit., "swirl"; cf. Jer 23:19; 30:23) upon it—that is, that Joab's bloodguilt will eventually bring about his own destruction (see comment on 1:16 for the similar expression, "Your blood be on your own head") through the medium of divine vengeance (cf. v.39). Just as David had absolved himself and his "kingdom" of all guilt in the matter (v.28), so also now he includes Joab's "father's house" in Joab's condemnation.

That the land of Israel could be adversely affected by murderous acts is clear from 1:21 (see comment). "Apart from the land, blood pollution also affects persons directly (Gen 42:22; Judg 9:24; 2 Sam 3:28–29; 16:7–8; 1 Kings 2:33; Jer 26:15; 51:35; Ezek 16:38; 22:4; 23:45; 35:6; Joel 3:19, 21 [4:19, 21 MT]; Lam 4:13)" (David Wright, "Deuteronomy 21:1–9 as a Rite of Elimination," *CBQ* 49/3 [1987]: 395 n. 24).

As he weaves the tapestry of his curse against Joab, David's penchant for colorful language is given full rein. He pleads that Joab's house "may never be without" (lit., "may there never be cut off from Joab's house," v.29; cf. the similar curse context of Jos 9:23, where Joshua uses the same Heb. idiom in telling the Gibeonites that they "will never cease" to be servants of the Israelites) people who will suffer in five categories: (1) "running sore[s]" (the Heb. word is often translated "bodily discharge" [cf. Lev 15:2; 22:4] and refers to such infectious conditions as diarrhea and urethral emissions); (2) "leprosy" (the Heb. term is elsewhere sometimes translated "infectious skin disease" and does not always necessarily denote Hansen's disease; see NIV note; cf. also Lev 14:3 and NIV note); (3) the need to "lean on a crutch" (*pelek*, here translated "crutch," occurs elsewhere only once [Pr 31:19], where it means "spindle" [cf. Akkad. *pilakku*]); (4) falling by the sword (the fate of Israel's army at Mount Gilboa [1:12]); and (5) lack of food (cf. 1Sa 2:36; Pr 12:9; Am 4:6). The first three curses relate to physical ailments, the fourth to war, and the fifth to famine—a deadly triad in the ancient world (cf. "sword, famine and plague," which occurs fifteen times in Jeremiah alone: Jer 14:12; 21:7, 9; 24:10; 27:8, 13; 29:17, 18; 32:24, 36; 34:17; 38:2; 42:17, 22; 44:13).

30 The central verse in this literary unit implicates Abishai in Joab's murder of Abner, as does the final verse ("sons of Zeruiah," v.39). Since "the blood of a kinsman must be avenged by the death of the one who shed it" (*AIs*, 11), Joab and Abishai invoked the hoary custom of the blood feud as a rationale for murdering Abner (who, after all, had killed "their brother Asahel"). Abner, however, had killed Asahel "in the battle," and it is therefore questionable whether the blood vengeance of Joab and Abishai was justified in this case. Indeed, David later excoriates Joab for having shed the blood of Abner "in peacetime as if in battle" (1Ki 2:5). Joab, of course, may have had an ulterior motive in wanting Abner out of the way: the fear that Abner, the "commander of Saul's army" (2:8), might supersede him as commander of David's army (8:16; 20:23; 1Ki 1:19; 11:15, 21).

31–35 David issues commands concerning Abner's funeral (v.31). As Brueggemann (*First and Second Samuel*, 230) notes:

> We need not doubt David's genuine respect for Abner, but the funeral is also a media event. It is like a U.S. president with the returned body of a soldier from an unauthorized war. The president must lead national mourning, which is genuine, but at the same time must stage a media event designed to legitimate policy.

The murderer Joab is required to attend, as are all his men, referred to seven times in vv.31–37 as "all the people" (vv.31, 32, 34, 35 ["they all"], 36 ["all the people,""them"], 37). That the phrase means Joab's men is clear from their description as being "with him" at their first appearance (v.31) and as being distinguished from "all Israel" at their last (v.37; cf. also 2:26–28, 30 and Notes on 2:12).

David's weeping and mourning over a slain family member, comrade, or friend is not only a concession to custom but also—and far more significantly—an indication of his tender heart (cf. 1:12; 13:36–37; 18:33; 19:1–4). Joab and his men are ordered to walk in front of the funeral procession, with David bringing up the rear as he walks behind the "bier" (translating the most common Heb. word for "bed/couch," as in 1Sa 19:13, 15–16).

> David is in charge and Joab is humiliated.... The narrator seems to grasp the dramatic power of this moment, for he refers to David as "King David" (v.31). While David had previously been identified as "king" (2:4, 7, 11; 3:17, 21–24), this is the first formal use linking personal name and royal office. It is when the threat of the north has been decisively

> eliminated in the death of Abner that the throne is secure enough to warrant this powerful phrase. (Brueggemann, *First and Second Samuel*, 230)

Although Abner was a Benjamite (1Sa 9:1; 14:50–51) and under ordinary circumstances would have been taken to his hometown for burial, David honors him by burying him in the royal city of Hebron (v.32; 4:12). Expressing his grief, the king "wept aloud" (lit., "raised his voice and wept"; see comment on 1Sa 11:4) at Abner's tomb.

The weeping of Joab's men ("all the people," vv.32, 34; see comment on v.31) frames David's brief lament for Abner (vv.33b–34) together with its introduction (v.33a). As did his only other recorded lament (1:19–27), David's lament (see comment on 1:17) for Abner again demonstrates the emotive powers of his literary genius. An exquisitely crafted quatrain, it is arranged chiastically: The two outer lines bemoan Abner's unjust death, while the two inner lines celebrate his unfettered life. Lines 1 and 4 begin with an infinitive construct preceded by the preposition *k-* ("as"); lines 2 and 3 begin with words that sound alike (*yādekā*, "your hands"; *ragleykā*, "your feet"), followed immediately by *lō*ʾ ("not"). In addition, as Holladay, 156, observes, v.33 "plays on *ʾabnēr* and *nābāl*"; cf. also Holladay, *Jeremiah: A Fresh Reading* [New York: Pilgrim, 1990], 21–22).

The rhetorical question that begins the lament requires a negative answer. Hands not bound and feet not fettered, Abner was surely not "lawless" (*nābāl* recalling Nabal, whose name Abigail said means "Fool, and folly goes with him" [1Sa 25:25; see comment], and whose alter ego was Saul [see Overview to 1Sa 25], not Abner). The parallel to "lawless" (v.33) in v.34 is "wicked men" (*b*ᵉ*nê-*ᶜ*awlâ*; cf. also 7:10 ["wicked people"]), lit., "sons of wickedness"—again reminiscent of Nabal, whom Abigail called a "wicked man" (*ben-b*ᵉ*lîya*ᶜ*al*, lit., "son of wickedness" [see 1Sa 25:17 and comment]).

As in the case of Saul and Jonathan and their comrades in arms, so also for Abner, David fasts till evening (v.35; see 1:12 and comment). Try as they might, Joab's men are unable to induce David (who takes a strong oath of self-imprecation; cf. v.9; see comment on 1Sa 20:13) to eat the customary funeral meal (cf. Jer 16:5, 7; Eze 24:17) "before the sun sets." Although David could not have been completely unhappy about the death of his most powerful rival for control, his grief is genuine. If he mourned at length for Saul and Jonathan, he mourns no less for Abner.

36–37 David's magnanimity impresses Joab's men and is sure to draw them ever closer to his inner circle of advisors. Indeed, in their eyes he can do no wrong (v.36). Even more important in the immediate circumstance, however, is the clear understanding not only of Joab's men but also of "all Israel" that David was not an accessory to Abner's death (v.37). His protestation of innocence (v.28), believable then to his own cohorts, is ratified now by the northern tribes. Appropriately regal, David stands above the fray. In any event, needless to say, "the fact that the biblical text absolves David of responsibility for a murder does not mean that David was guilty of that murder" (Bosworth, 199).

38–39 The chapter concludes with David's final brief encomium for Abner (v.38) and final imprecation against Joab and Abishai (v.39), both of which are directed to his own men. Just as it was important that all Israel "knew" that David was innocent of the death of Abner (v.37), so also David wants his men to "realize" that in Abner a great man has been lost to Israel (v.38; same Heb. verb). The NIV's translation of the Hebrew phrase (*śar w*ᵉ*gādôl*) that David uses to describe Abner—"a prince and a great man"—is as old as the KJV and has been used as a eulogy in countless funerals for generations. Its closest OT parallel (although in a negative context) is Micah 7:3, where "judge" (*šōpēṭ*) is flanked by *śar* ("ruler") and *gādôl* ("powerful"). But since *śar* is frequently used elsewhere of Abner in the sense of "commander" (see 2:8 and comment), it is surely better to understand *śar w^e gādôl* in the present context as a hendiadys and to render it "a great commander"—a title whose significance could not have been lost on Joab (who, however, may not have been within earshot on this occasion).

"This day" (v.38) and "today" (v.39) connect the two verses and lend a note of immediacy to them. David harbors no illusions about the fact that although he is "the anointed king" (lit., "anointed [as] king"; cf. 2:4; for the unusual form *māšûaḥ* see comment and Notes on 1:21), he is nevertheless "weak" (cf. 1Ch 22:5; 29:1, where he uses the same Heb. word to describe his son Solomon as "inexperienced").

By contrast Joab and Abishai (the "sons of Zeruiah" [cf. 2:18], constant thorns in David's side; cf. 16:10; 19:22) are "strong"; and David, exercising commendable caution, realizes that he is not presently able to rebuke them with any semblance of authority. In the hearing of his own men (v.38), however, he repeats the curse against Joab (cf. v.29, where no hearers are mentioned), perhaps this time including Abishai—although the language of the imprecation is nonspecific: "May the LORD repay the evildoer according to his evil deeds!" (v.39; cf. Solomon's prayer in 1Ki 8:32; also Pss 18:20, 24; 28:4 [both Davidic psalms]; in the NT, cf. 2Ti 4:14; Rev 20:12–13).

NOTE

29 For בית אביו (*byt ʾbyw*, "his father's house"), 4QSamuel[a] reads בית יואב (*byt ywʾb*, "Joab's house"). Although this reading makes equally good sense, the Qumran reading is doubtless an anticipation of the same phrase a few words later in the verse. The MT is thus *lectio difficilior* and should therefore be retained (so also LXX, McCarter).

Although McCarter (*II Samuel*, 118) claims that *plkm* in the Phoenician Karatepe inscription means "crutches," the context there (lines 26–27) also allows "spindles" as a possible translation (thus, e.g., Franz Rosenthal in *ANETSup*, 654 n. 4). In any event, although translations and commentators are divided here between "staff/crutch" (ASV, KJV; Hertzberg, K&D, Kirkpatrick, McCarter, Smith) and "spindle/distaff" (which would imply effeminacy, or at least doing the work of women; NAB, NASB, NJB, REB, RSV, TEV; Anderson, Baldwin, Driver, Gordon, Mauchline; cf. also Lemos, 235 and nn. 34–36), the context favors "staff/crutch" (see comment above).

3. The Murder of Ish-Bosheth (4:1–12)

OVERVIEW

Saul the king is dead, Jonathan the heir apparent is dead, Abinadab and Malki-Shua (two of Jonathan's brothers) are dead (1Sa 31:2), Abner the commander of the army is dead—and no other viable claimants or pretenders continue to block David's accession to the throne except Saul's son Ish-Bosheth and Jonathan's son Mephibosheth. Chapter 4 removes them from the scene, one explicitly and the other implicitly. The chapter is a masterpiece of literary artistry, as the following outline demonstrates.

A. The *dramatis personae* (4:1–4)
  1. Ish-Bosheth, Baanah, Recab (4:1–3)
  2. Mephibosheth, lame in both feet (4:4)
B. The deed (4:5–8)
  1. The murder of Ish-Bosheth (4:5–7)
  2. His head brought to David (4:8)
C. The consequences (4:9–12)
  1. The verdict of David (4:9–11)
  2. The execution of Recab and Baanah, whose hands and feet are cut off (4:12)

Each of the three main sections contains four verses, further divided into a three-verse unit followed by a one-verse conclusion (each of which features one or more parts of the body). Verses 1 and 12 form an inclusio the common elements of which are "Ish-Bosheth" (see Notes on v.1), "Abner" (mentioned only in vv.1, 12 in this chapter), "Hebron," and "hands" (used in the plural only in vv.1, 12 in this chapter; see comment on v.1).

[1]When Ish-Bosheth son of Saul heard that Abner had died in Hebron, he lost courage,
and all Israel became alarmed. [2]Now Saul's son had two men who were leaders of raiding
bands. One was named Baanah and the other Recab; they were sons of Rimmon the
Beerothite from the tribe of Benjamin — Beeroth is considered part of Benjamin, [3]because
the people of Beeroth fled to Gittaim and have lived there as aliens to this day.
[4](Jonathan son of Saul had a son who was lame in both feet. He was five years old
when the news about Saul and Jonathan came from Jezreel. His nurse picked him
up and fled, but as she hurried to leave, he fell and became crippled. His name was
Mephibosheth.)
[5]Now Recab and Baanah, the sons of Rimmon the Beerothite, set out for the house of
Ish-Bosheth, and they arrived there in the heat of the day while he was taking his noonday
rest. [6]They went into the inner part of the house as if to get some wheat, and they stabbed
him in the stomach. Then Recab and his brother Baanah slipped away.
[7]They had gone into the house while he was lying on the bed in his bedroom. After
they stabbed and killed him, they cut off his head. Taking it with them, they traveled all
night by way of the Arabah. [8]They brought the head of Ish-Bosheth to David at Hebron
and said to the king, "Here is the head of Ish-Bosheth son of Saul, your enemy, who tried
to take your life. This day the LORD has avenged my lord the king against Saul and his
offspring."
[9]David answered Recab and his brother Baanah, the sons of Rimmon the Beerothite, "As surely as the LORD lives, who has delivered me out of all trouble, [10]when a
man told me, 'Saul is dead,' and thought he was bringing good news, I seized him and
put him to death in Ziklag. That was the reward I gave him for his news! [11]How much
more — when wicked men have killed an innocent man in his own house and on his

own bed—should I not now demand his blood from your hand and rid the earth of you!"

12So David gave an order to his men, and they killed them. They cut off their hands and feet and hung the bodies by the pool in Hebron. But they took the head of Ish-Bosheth and buried it in Abner's tomb at Hebron.

COMMENTARY

1–3 When David "heard" that Abner had died, he declared his own innocence and cursed Abner's murderer (3:28–29). When Ish-Bosheth "heard" that Abner had died, "he lost courage" (lit., "his hands became weak/limp" [v.1], a common and picturesque idiom; cf. 17:2; 2Ch 15:7 ["give up"]; Ne 6:9; Isa 13:7; Jer 6:24; 50:43; Eze 7:17; 21:7; Zep 3:16)—a typical and expected reaction (cf. 3:11). Abner's death left a power vacuum in the north, and it is therefore not surprising that all Israel became "alarmed" (the Heb. verb is translated "shaken" in 1Sa 28:21).

Among the opportunists eager to take charge are two of Ish-Bosheth's men who are "leaders of raiding bands" (v.2; in the singular the phrase is translated "leader of a band of rebels" in 1Ki 11:24). Such groups functioned under David's authorization as well (3:22; 1Ch 12:18) and were not uncommon elsewhere during the early days of Israel's monarchy (cf. 1Sa 30:1, 8, 15). Ish-Bosheth's men, Baanah and Recab, were Beerothites (for another prominent Beerothite, who became Joab's armor-bearer, see 23:37 = 1Ch 11:39) from Beeroth in Benjamin, Ish-Bosheth's tribal homeland.

A town of the Gibeonite tetrapolis (Jos 9:17) assigned to Benjamin (Jos 18:21, 25), ancient Beeroth is probably modern Khirbet el-Burj, located four and one-half miles northwest of Jerusalem. Its indigenous population had become "aliens" (v.3; cf. 1:13) in Gittaim (modern Ras Abu Humeid, seventeen miles northwest of Beeroth) at the edge of Philistine territory, doubtless because they were driven out by invading Benjamites. Beeroth is thus considered "part of" Benjamin (v.2)—unlike Gibeonites proper, who, though Saul had tried to annihilate them, were not a "part of" Israel (21:2) because Joshua had earlier "made a treaty of peace with them to let them live" (Jos 9:15).

Though from Beeroth, Baanah and Recab were members of the tribe of Benjamin and thus ostensibly loyal to Saul (and Ish-Bosheth). It is therefore incorrect to state that their plot against Ish-Bosheth is "an effort at revenge for the violence with which Saul had apparently treated the Gibeonites, Israel's treaty partners" (Vanderkam, 534 n. 40). McCarter (*II Samuel*, 128) notes that the treachery of Baanah and Recab "is born not of revenge but of crass opportunism and the hope of a reward from David."

4 Jonathan's son Mephibosheth is introduced parenthetically to demonstrate that his youth and physical handicap disqualify him for rule in the north. Patrick, 364, provides another possible reason: "to show, what it was that emboldened these Captains [Banaah and Recab] to do what follows: Because he, who was the next Avenger of Blood, was very young; and besides was lame and unable to pursue them."

In brief compass the verse provides information concerning why the Mephibosheth is "lame in both feet" (the same Heb. phrase is echoed in 9:3 ["crippled in both feet"]). Soon after the death of Saul and Jonathan (1Sa 31:2–6), news concerning the tragedy was relayed from Jezreel (see comment on 1Sa 29:1) to the remaining members of the Saulide clan, probably by Israelites fleeing the battlefield (1Sa 31:7). When the nurse of Jonathan's son learned that the boy's father had been killed, she too decided to flee with the boy to a safer location. In her headlong flight (cf. the similar incident in 2Ki 7:15) Mephibosheth fell from her grasp and became permanently crippled (for Mephibosheth's subsequent history, see ch. 9; 16:1–4; 19:24–30; 21:7). Five years old when his father died, Mephibosheth would still have been only twelve (cf. 2:11) at the time of the assassination of his uncle Ish-Bosheth.

5–7 The story of that assassination is the focus of the chapter. Mabee, 100, helpfully titles vv.5–8 "The Deed" and vv.9–12 "Consequence" (cf. similarly my outline in comment on 4:1–12), though his insistence on a judicatory backdrop in the account is overdone. Baanah's name appears before that of Recab in v.2, perhaps because he was the older of the two men. In the rest of the chapter, however, Recab's name always occurs first (vv.5–6, 9), probably indicating that he is the prime instigator of the murder of Ish-Bosheth.

The two brothers go to the "house of Ish-Bosheth" (doubtless in Mahanaim; v.5; cf. 2:8, 12, 29) and arrive there at siesta time, in "the heat of the day" (i.e., high noon; cf. Ge 18:1; see esp. 1Sa 11:9, 11 and comment), knowing full well that Ish-Bosheth would be sleeping. As Abner had been murdered in the "midst/inner part" of the gateway at Hebron (see comment on "into" in 3:27), so also Ish-Bosheth will be murdered in the "inner part" (same Heb. word) of his house (v.6). As Joab had lured Abner to his death ("as though to speak with him privately"; 3:27), so Recab and Baanah will gain access to Ish-Bosheth's sanctum through subterfuge ("as if to get some wheat"). And Ish-Bosheth will die as Abner had died. In each case the assailant(s) "stabbed him in the stomach" (v.6; 3:27)—a technique rapidly becoming the preferred method of killing during David's reign (see comment on 2:23).

Ish-Bosheth is assassinated while lying on "the bed in his bedroom" (v.7), luxuries available only to the wealthy or to royalty in those days (Ex 8:3; 2Ki 6:12; Ecc 10:20). "The narrative uses three verbs to characterize [the murderers'] action (v. 7). They strike, they kill, they decapitate (cf. 1 Sam 17:46 [also 17:50]). Ish-Bosheth, pitiful creature bereft of Abner, is three times dead" (Brueggemann, *First and Second Samuel*, 234; cf. also 2Sa 20:22, "where the head of the rebel leader Sheba is used to evidence his death" [Lemos, 236]). The verb "cut off" (cf. also 16:9; 2Ki 6:32) is literally "remove" and evokes a crude and grisly image. Recab and Baanah had entered Ish-Bosheth's house as though to "get" (lit., "take," v.6) wheat; they are now "taking" (v.7; cf. also v.12) Ish-Bosheth's head to David as a trophy of their vile deed. To avoid easy detection they travel through the night by way of the Arabah (see comment on 2:29) from Mahanaim to Hebron, a distance of almost thirty miles.

8 Presenting the head of Ish-Bosheth to David, Recab and Baanah remind him that Ish-Bosheth's father, Saul, had been David's "enemy" (see comments on 1Sa 18:29; 19:17; 24:4). Indeed, Saul had "tried to take" (lit., "sought") David's "life" on many occasions (see comment on 1Sa 20:1). But now, say the assassins, the Lord himself—to whom belongs all vengeance (cf. David's words to Saul in 1Sa 24:12; also Dt 32:35; Ro 12:19; Heb 10:30)—has "avenged" (cf. 22:48–49a = Ps 18:47–48a) David not only against Saul but also against Saul's "offspring" (including Ish-Bosheth, the last viable scion of the Saulide line). And now that none of Saul's descendants remains an obstacle to Davidic pretensions or ambitions, "the gift of Ish-Bosheth's head [to David] is at the same time the gift of the kingdom" (Gunn, "David and the Gift of the Kingdom," 17).

9–11 The assassins' offer (v.8) and the king's response (vv.9–11) are the only direct quotations in the chapter. Agreeing that it is the Lord who avenges and rescues, David takes an oath in his name (v.9; see esp. 1Sa 14:39 and comment). The MT of David's entire statement in v.9 is echoed verbatim in 1 Kings 1:29 (where the NIV renders "every trouble" instead of "all trouble," as here). The two asseverations form an inclusio surrounding the time span of David's reign as king in Jerusalem, the first being spoken just after his rival Ish-Bosheth is killed and the last just before his own son Solomon becomes king. "Delivered me" is literally "redeemed/ ransomed my life," a phrase commonly used by Israel's psalmists (e.g., Pss 34:22; 49:8, 15; 55:18; 71:23). To the assassins' reminder that Saul had tried to take David's "life" (v.8) the king responds that the Lord delivers his "life" (v.9) out of "all trouble" (including the difficulties he had faced when he was a fugitive from Saul's wrath; see comment on 1Sa 26:24).

Like the Amalekite who claimed to have killed Saul (1:10), Recab and Baanah can hardly have expected David's blistering response to their murder of Saul's son Ish-Bosheth (vv.10–11; see 1:14, 16). The man who had "told" David that Saul was dead (v.10) was, of course, the Amalekite (see comment on 1:4). Although he thought he was bringing "good news" (see comments on 1:20; 1Sa 31:9), he brought about only his own death at David's headquarters in Ziklag (cf. 1:1). Expecting a "reward" for his news (cf. 18:22), he received death instead. "While Paul's discussion of the rights of the Christian preacher is based on different premises in 1 Corinthians 9:1–18, his references to his personal 'reward' for his preaching of the 'good news' (vv.16–18) could hint at the custom reflected here" (Gordon, *I and II Samuel*, 223).

If David condemned the Amalekite for delivering the coup de grâce to the mortally wounded Saul on the battlefield, the a fortiori—"how much more" (v.11; cf. 1Sa 14:30; 21:5; 23:3)—is self-evident in this context: (1) Recab and Baanah, "wicked men," have killed Ish-Bosheth, an "innocent" (lit., "righteous") man (cf. similarly Solomon's condemnation of Joab for killing Abner and Amasa, both of whom were more "upright" [1Ki 2:32; same Heb. word] than he). Mabee, 104 and n. 48, further observes:

> The criminality of the defendants is clearly shown in their designation as רשעים [*rš*ʿ*ym*], while the deceased is termed צדיק [*ṣdyq*].... Therefore the crime is not regicide—even though it is a king who is murdered.... Although Ish-Bosheth was crowned king, he was not anointed (2 Sam 2:9). Thus, there is an implicit denial of Ish-Bosheth's kingship at the point where David refers to him as a "righteous man." Of course, the case is quite different at 2 Sam 1:14.

(2) Although Saul was killed in a context of danger and violence in battle, Ish-Bosheth was murdered in what should have been the secure and peaceful serenity of "his own house and on his own bed" (v.11; since David is aware of this detail, the assassins must have told him more than the summary statement of v.8 implies). David's outrage (whether real or pretended) over the circumstances of Recab and Baanah's assassination of Ish-Bosheth causes him to "demand his blood from your hand"—that is, hold them accountable for his death (see comment on 1Sa 20:16; cf. similarly Ge 9:5; Eze 3:18, 20; 33:6, 8). Again and again Saul had "tried to take" (lit., "sought," v.8) David's life; now David is in a position to "demand" (lit., "seek") the blood of Saul's son Ish-Bosheth from the hands of his assassins.

12 "All who draw the sword will die by the sword," said Jesus (Mt 26:52). Death begets death. The Amalekite claimed to have killed Saul, and in retaliation David "put him to death" (v.10); Recab and Baanah have "killed" Ish-Bosheth (v.11), so David gives the order that they in turn be "killed" (v.12; same Heb. verb in all three cases).

As Adoni-Bezek had been mutilated by having "his thumbs and big toes" (lit., "the thumbs of his hands and of his feet") "cut off" (Jdg 1:6), so David's men mutilate the dead bodies of Recab and Baanah by "cut[ting] off" (same Heb. verb) their "hands" (see comment on the Overview to vv.1–12; cf. v.1 and comment) and "feet" (cf. v.4). Patrick, 366, makes the quaint observation that this was done "by *David*'s Order no doubt: They having slain their Master with their *hands* made their escape from Justice with their *feet*."

Since the object of "hung" is left unexpressed in the MT, commentators are divided concerning whether it is "hands and feet" (e.g., Kirkpatrick, Mauchline, H. P. Smith) or "bodies" (supplied by the NIV; cf. also Anderson, Gordon, K&D). The latter is preferable, however, since it was the ancient custom to expose to public view the entire corpse of the victim (whether mutilated or not) whenever possible (cf. 21:9–10; 1Sa 31:9–10; Dt 21:22–23; Jos 10:26–27; Est 2:23). It is ironic indeed that the prolonged struggle between Ish-Bosheth's men and David's men begins and ends by the placid waters of a pool. Although the location of the "pool of Gibeon" is almost certainly known (see comment on 2:13), that of the "pool of Hebron" remains obscure (for discussion see Anderson, 72).

The contrast between the treatment of the remains of the assassins and of Ish-Bosheth could hardly be more striking. That the Hebrew word for "head" is in emphatic position in v.12b justifies the NIV's "But" at the beginning of the sentence. While the dead bodies of Recab and Baanah are impaled in a public setting to disgrace them and deter others, Ish-Bosheth's head is given an honorable burial in Abner's tomb at "Hebron"—the headquarters of David, their political rival. "Just as Abner takes (לקח) Ish-Bosheth and makes him king (2:8–9), now David and his men take (לקחו) the head of Ish-Bosheth and bury it" (Mabee, 105; Ish-Bosheth's head is also the object of the verb "taking" in v.7). Erstwhile comrades in life, Abner and Ish-Bosheth sleep in the same tomb in death. If at Abner's funeral David walked behind the dead man's "bier" (*miṭṭâ*, 3:31), David now oversees the funeral of Ish-Bosheth, ruthlessly killed while lying peacefully in "bed" (*miṭṭâ*, v.7).

With the death of Ish-Bosheth, no other viable candidate for king remains for the elders of the northern tribes. Meanwhile David sits in regal isolation, above the fray as always, innocent of the deaths of Saul, Jonathan, Abner, and now Ish-Bosheth. The way is open for his march to the throne of Israel.

NOTES

1 As in 3:7 (see Notes), so also here (and in v.2) the name "Ish-Bosheth" is not present in the MT. Although it is possible that "a deliberate excision of the offensive name is to be presumed" in vv.1–2 (Clines, 286), a more satisfactory solution has been given by F. M. Cross (*The Ancient Library of Qumran and Modern Biblical Studies* [Garden City, N.Y.: Doubleday Anchor, 1961], 191 n. 45):

> In II Sam. 4:1, 2 the *MT* reads *wyšmʿ bn šʾwl … hyw bn šʾwl*.… The latter phrase makes no sense whatever; the former is not happy. In both the *LXX* and 4QSam[a] the reading is *wyšmʿ mpybšt bn šʾwl* [v.1], which grammatically makes perfect sense. However, Mephibosheth is an obvious blunder. Ishbosheth is meant in both instances.

The reviser of the text did not replace the erroneous reading with the correct one; rather he excised the mistake and left the text standing. In the case of *hyw lmpybšt bn šʾwl* [v.2], he cut out not only *mpybšt* but also *l* and forgot to replace it before *bn šwl* [*sic*], leaving nonsense.

3 Gittaim ("Two Gaths"), mentioned by its full name elsewhere only in Nehemiah 11:33, may be the same as the Gath of 1 Chronicles 7:21 and 8:13.

4 Since children in ancient Israel were normally weaned by the age of three (see comment on 1Sa 1:22), Mephibosheth's "nurse" was not a wet nurse but a hired attendant who "cared for" him (as the same Heb. verb is translated of Naomi's relationship to Obed in Ru 4:16).

As scribal tradition often substituted "Ish-Bosheth" (which means "Man of shame"; see Note on 1Sa 7:4) for "E/Ish-Baal" (which means "Man of Baal"; see comment on 2:8), so also Mephibosheth's real name was Merib-Baal (cf. 1Ch 8:34; 9:40; and NIV note). Although מְרִיב בָּעַל (*mᵉrîb bāʿal*) is usually translated "Baal defends [my] case" (see Albright, 113) or the like, it should probably rather be considered an *Ersatzname* and rendered "Baal Substitutes" (for details see Notes on Jerub-Baal in 1Sa 12:11).

The second occurrence (untrans. in NIV) of Merib-Baal's name in 1 Chronicles 9:40 is spelled מְרִי־בַעַל (*mᵉrî-baʿal*; all LXX recensions also exhibit only one *b* in Meri[b]-Baal in 1 Chronicles), which perhaps means "Rebel[lion] of Baal" (cf. מְרִי, *mᵉrî*, ["rebellion"] in 1Sa 15:23). As for מְפִיבֹשֶׁת (*mᵉpîbōšet*), "One who scatters shame" is the probable meaning (for details see Werner Weinberg, "Language Consciousness in the OT," *ZAW* 92/2 [1980]: 201 n. 40)—although revocalizing the MT to read מִפִּיבֹשֶׁת (*mippîbōšet*) would produce the translation "From the mouth of shame."

6 The MT's הֵנָּה (*hēnnâ*, "they"; or revocalized as הִנֵּה, *hinnēh*, "behold"]) at the beginning of the verse is superfluous in English and is therefore justifiably omitted by the NIV. Considering v.7 a doublet of v.6, many translations (e.g., NAB, NJB, REB, RSV, TEV) and commentators (e.g., Driver, Gordon, Hertzberg, Kirkpatrick, Mauchline, McCarter, Smith; cf. also *BHK*) have been attracted to the LXX's version of v.6: "And behold, the woman guarding the house had been cleaning wheat, and she had nodded off and fallen asleep. So Recab and his brother Baanah slipped in." The MT, however, yields good sense as it stands (esp. if v.7 is rendered in the pluperfect) and has therefore been retained by many translations (e.g., KJV, ASV, NASB, NIV) and commentators (e.g., K&D, Anderson, Baldwin [although hesitantly]; cf. *BHS*, Barthélemy). In any event, repetition of information in successive verses (as in vv.6–7) is a common feature of Hebrew narrative and is attested here in the immediate context (3:22–23—which, interestingly, also begins with "Behold" ["Just then," NIV]).

7 *BHS*'s אֶל (*ʾal*) is a typographical error for עַל (*ʿal*, "on"; cf. *BHK*). The custom of possessing a severed head as a victory trophy was common in ancient times and was practiced by Sumerians, Egyptians, Assyrians, and Romans (among others). An excellent example of such a trophy is the head of the Elamite king Teumman. Reliefs from the reign of Ashurbanipal (669–626 BC) picture Teumman being decapitated, his head being transported in a captured Elamite mule-drawn wagon, and his preserved (perhaps embalmed) head attached to a large ring suspended from the upper branches of a pine tree (for details, including photographs of the reliefs, see Pauline Albenda, "Landscape Bas-Reliefs in the *Bīt-Ḫilāni* of Ashurbanipal," *BASOR* 225 [1977]: 29–33).

9 The idiom "redeem/ransom [one's] life" (see comment) is almost always translated "redeem [one's] soul" in the KJV. Although in the present context the phrase does not have salvific significance, Kidner is surely on target in his comment on Psalm 34:22: "At whatever level David himself understood his affirmation of 22a, *the Lord redeems the life* ..., the whole verse is pregnant with a meaning which comes to birth in the gospel, and which is hardly viable in any form that falls short of this" (Derek Kidner, *Psalms 1–72: An Introduction and Commentary on Books I and II of the Psalms* [TOTC; Downers Grove, Ill.: InterVarsity Press, 1973], 141–42).

4. David Anointed King over Israel (5:1–5)

OVERVIEW

Just as the account of the anointing of David as king over Judah (2:1–7) nestles near the center of the first major literary unit of 2 Samuel (1:1–3:5), so also the report of his anointing as king over all Israel (5:1–5) is located near the center of the second major unit (3:6–5:16). And just as 2:1–7 divides naturally into two roughly equal sections (vv.1–4a, 4b–7), so also does 5:1–5 (vv.1–3, 4–5). "All the tribes of Israel came to David at Hebron" (v.1) forms an inclusio with "When all the elders of Israel had come to King David at Hebron" (v.3), and vv.3 and 5 end by referring to David as *mlk* ("king," v.3; "reigned," v.5) "over (all) Israel" (cf. similarly Carlson, 52).

The rationale for the division is further strengthened by the fact that vv.1–3 are paralleled in 1 Chronicles 11:1–3, while vv.4–5 are paralleled in 1 Chronicles 3:4b; 29:26–27 (cf. also 1Ki 2:11).

[1]All the tribes of Israel came to David at Hebron and said, "We are your own flesh and
blood. [2]In the past, while Saul was king over us, you were the one who led Israel on their
military campaigns. And the LORD said to you, 'You will shepherd my people Israel, and you
will become their ruler.'"

[3]When all the elders of Israel had come to King David at Hebron, the king made a compact with them at Hebron before the LORD, and they anointed David king over Israel.

[4]David was thirty years old when he became king, and he reigned forty years. [5]In
Hebron he reigned over Judah seven years and six months, and in Jerusalem he reigned
over all Israel and Judah thirty-three years.

COMMENTARY

1–3 That the kingdom about to be established under King David is intended as a truly united monarchy is underscored by the use of the word "all" three times (vv.1, 3, 5). The "elders" of Israel (v.3; cf. 17:4, 15; 1Sa 4:3; 8:4; 15:30), representing the "tribes" (v.1), come to David at Hebron with the express purpose of submitting to his rule. Preliminary consultations with the elders had already been initiated by Abner (3:17), but his death had postponed further discussion. In any event, David may have preferred not to pursue the matter until after Ish-Bosheth's abortive reign was no longer a factor. The eagerness of the elders to make David the king over all Israel without further delay is reflected in the consistent double expression of personal subject (explicit in the MT) throughout their brief plea to David: "We [ourselves] are" (v.1), "you [yourself] were" (v.2a), "you [yourself] will" (v.2b), "you [yourself] will" (v.2c).

At the very least, the elders' reference to themselves as "your own flesh and blood" (lit., "your bone and your flesh," v.1) signifies their sense of kinship with him (cf. Wilfred G. E. Watson, "Some Additional Word Pairs" [in Eslinger and Taylor], 186; cf. also 19:12–13; Ge 2:23; 29:14; Jdg 9:2). Thus the elders declare their first reason for desiring David as their king: He is a "brother Israelite" (Dt 17:15; so already Patrick, 367). In addition, however, Brueggemann ("Of the Same Flesh and Bone," 536, 538; cf. 532–42 for full discussion; cf. also idem, *First and Second Samuel*, 237) has argued that "[We are your] bone and flesh" is "a statement of loyalty in initiating and affirming a treaty relationship ... a covenant formula which describes the commitments of partners to each other who have obligations to each other in all kinds of circumstances, thick and thin (*ʿṣm* and *bśr*)." The elders' affirmation to David, then, anticipates the covenant-making scene of v.3.

The elders' second reason is that during Saul's reign David was Israel's best army officer—a fact recognized even by the Philistines (1Sa 29:3, 5; cf. Brueggemann, *First and Second Samuel*, 237). Indeed, David was "the one who led Israel in their military campaigns" (v.2), the rendering of a Hebrew phrase that means literally "the one who led out and the one who brought back Israel" (cf. Nu 27:17, 21; see also comment on 1Sa 18:13, 16). In the days of the prophet Samuel, the elders of Israel (1Sa 8:4) had demanded "a king to lead us and to go out before us and fight our battles" (1Sa 8:20). Saul was to some extent such a king, but David would be supremely so—as events will soon demonstrate (vv.6–12, 17–25).

Their understanding that the Lord has chosen David (a perception shared by Abner; cf. 3:18) is the elders' third reason for wanting him to ascend to Israel's throne. They sense that the Lord has invested David with the titles of "shepherd" and "ruler" (v.2) as well as "king" (v.3). With respect to the term "shepherd," Patrick, 368, is technically correct in his observation that this is "the first time we find a Governour described by this Name in Scripture." Apart from God himself (Ge 48:15; 49:24), David is the first example of a specific person being called a "shepherd," although the idea in principle antedates him by several centuries (cf. Nu 27:17). Moreover, the motif of David as shepherd was prefigured at his earliest anointing (see comment on 1Sa 16:11; for details cf. the fine summary by Walters in Eslinger and Taylor, 574–75).

Understanding that the figure of the shepherd would be immediately familiar to their subjects and that they would readily associate it with gentleness, watchfulness, and concern, ancient Near Eastern rulers commonly referred to themselves as "the shepherd" (see Notes). Since it is the shepherd's task to lead, feed, and heed his flock, the shepherd metaphor was a happy choice for benevolent rulers and grateful people alike (cf. Jer 3:15; 23:4). David thus becomes the paradigm of the shepherd-king (cf. Ps 78:70–72; Eze 34:23; 37:24), and it is not surprising that "great David's greater son," Jesus Christ, should be introduced frequently and glowingly in the NT as the "good shepherd" (Jn 10:11, 14), the "great Shepherd" (Heb 13:20), and the "Chief Shepherd" (1Pe 5:4), the one who provides for his sheep all things needful for the abundant life.

Needless to say, a benevolent shepherd can change into a tyrannical despot. Forgetting that he is supposed to lead his sheep to verdant pastures, he can drive them mercilessly and trample them underfoot (Jer 23:1–2; Eze 34:1–10; Zec 11:4–17). "It is not accidental that Nathan's parable utilizes the shepherd-sheep metaphor to indict David (12:1–4). In the episode of Bathsheba and Uriah, David misuses his role as shepherd and at enormous cost works only to enhance his own situation" (Brueggemann, *First and Second Samuel*, 238). In the beginning David could do no wrong (3:36), but with the passing of time his power will become increasingly seductive and intoxicating—to the detriment of himself, his family, and his people.

In addition to being called "shepherd," David is also called *nāgîd* ("ruler"; GK 5592). Carlson, 53, notes that "the 'shepherd' motif is also connected with the term *nāgîd* in 7:8" (more precisely, 7:7–8), thus linking the two passages together. The title "ruler, leader" provided a convenient transition between judgeship on the one hand and kingship on the other. Although more than a judge, the *nāgîd* was not yet a king in the full sense of that term (see comment on 1Sa 9:16).

Dale Patrick ("The Covenant Code Source," *VT* 27/2 [1977]: 152) suggests that "there is only one account in Biblical literature of a covenant being made between a human king and his subjects where sovereignty itself was at issue: 2 Sam 5:1–3" (cf. also in the same article, 152–53, Patrick's helpful comparisons between covenant-making elements in the narrative framework [Ex 19:3–8; 24:3–8] and similar elements in vv.1–3). David's sovereignty is underscored by the threefold reference to him as "king" in v.3. He does not go to Israel's elders in Mahanaim—they come to him in Hebron. Their need for him is greater than his for them, though the stakes are enormous on both sides.

Abner had suggested earlier that Israel "make a compact" (lit., "cut a covenant/treaty," for which see comments on 1Sa 11:1; 18:3) with David (see 3:21 and comment). But now that the moment for such an agreement has arrived, it is the king who initiates the compact with his (future) subjects, not the other way around (v.3; cf. similarly Jer 34:8). At the same time, however, the covenant should not be understood as bestowing on David the role of all-powerful suzerain and dooming the Israelites to become his craven vassals. "The evident meaning is that David bound himself formally to certain contractual obligations toward the Israelites" (McCarter, *II Samuel*, 132; cf. similarly Brueggemann, *First and Second Samuel*, 239). The covenant-making formalities take place "before the LORD" (v.3), acknowledging that the proceedings are under his guidance and enjoy his blessing (v.12; see 1Sa 11:15 and comment).

As David had earlier been anointed king over Judah (see 2:4 and comment), so now he is anointed king over Israel, "as the LORD had promised through Samuel" (1Ch 11:3; cf. 1Sa 15:28; 16:13). "There is, thus, a duality in the kingship of David, a duality which reasserted itself in the breaking free of Israel from Judah and the Davidic dynasty after the death of Solomon" (Cross, *Canaanite Myth and Hebrew Epic*, 230; cf. "all Israel and Judah," v.5). The news of the anointing will soon become well enough known to cause concern in the hearts of the Philistines (v.17). Although for a while David will bask in the afterglow of his divine unction, his failure to live up to God's expectations for it and demands connected with it will evoke prophetic wrath (12:7)—as in the case of his predecessor, Saul (1Sa 15:17–19).

4–5 Before its use to characterize David's reign, the regnal formula—"So-and-so was *x* years old when he became king, and he reigned *y* years" (v.4)—was used of Saul (1Sa 13:1) and of Ish-Bosheth son of Saul (2Sa 2:10); from here on it is reserved exclusively for kings headquartered in Judah (for details see comments on 1Sa 13:1).

As Jacob's son Joseph had become vizier of Egypt at the age of thirty (Ge 41:46), so Jacob's descendant David became king in Hebron when he was thirty years old (v.4)—the approximate age of Jesus "when he began his ministry" (Lk 3:23). David's overall reign of forty years matches that of his predecessor Saul (cf. Ac 13:21; see also comment on 1Sa 13:1) as well as that of his son and successor Solomon (1Ki 11:42). If thirty years represents the age when a man reached his maturity and could thus (if from the tribe of Levi) enter service at the Israelite tabernacle (Nu 4:47), forty years "represents the period of a complete generation" (J. B. Segal, 11; cf. Ps 95:10). David's total life span matches the psalmist's ideal: "The length of our days is seventy years" (Ps 90:10).

The forty-year reign of David consisted of seven and a half years in Hebron over Judah alone (v.5; 2:11; 1Ch 3:4; the seven years of 1Ki 2:11 and 1Ch 29:27 is intended only as a round number) and thirty-three years in Jerusalem over all Israel and Judah (the Lucianic text of Samuel "has adjusted the text in verse 5 to read 'thirty-two years and six months'" [Stephen Pisano, "2 Samuel 5–8 and the Deuteronomist: Textual Criticism or Literary Criticism?" in *Israel Constructs Its History*, ed. Albert de Pury, Thomas Römer, and Jean-Daniel Macchi (Sheffield: Sheffield Academic Press, 2000), 263]). Although Jerusalem had not been unknown to David before the elders of Israel anointed him (see 1Sa 17:54 and comment), he is now determined to make it his capital.

NOTE

2 מוֹצִיא וְהַמֵּבִי (*môṣîʾ wᵉhammēbî*) should be corrected to הַמּוֹצִיא וְהַמֵּבִיא (*hammôṣîʾ wᵉhammēbîʾ*, "the one who led out and the one who brought back") on the basis of the *Qere* and 1 Chronicles 11:2. In the MT the loss of the ה (*h*) at the beginning of the first word and of the א (ʾ) at the end of the second was due either to haplography or to the phenomenon of shared consonants (for the latter see Watson, 531).

In the prologue to his celebrated code of laws, Hammurapi of Babylon (ca. 1792–1750 BC) refers to himself as "the shepherd, called by Enlil," and as "the shepherd of the people"; in the epilogue he speaks of the people "whose shepherding Marduk had committed to me," calls himself "the beneficent shepherd," and pronounces a blessing upon his successor if the latter heeds the words of Hammurapi's statutes: "May he shepherd his people in justice!" (cf. *ANET*, 164–65, 177–78).

The etymological origins of עַם (*ʿam*, "people"; GK 6639) remain obscure despite an attempt of Robert McClive Good (*The Sheep of His Pasture: A Study of the Hebrew Noun* ʿAm(m) *and Its Semitic Cognates* [HSM 29; Chico, Calif.: Scholars, 1983], 2): "The noun *ʿam(m)* represents the sound made by caprine beasts and originally signified 'flock.'" Good's theory is especially tantalizing in the light of OT references to shepherding of people, but his philological arguments are based primarily on hypothetical evidence derived from a supposed Arabic cognate—and Hebrew-Arabic isoglosses are distressingly few in number at best. Reviewers of Good's book with its thesis have been understandably skeptical (cf. Carol Meyers in *CBQ* 48/1 [1986]: 106–8; J. J. M. Roberts in *JBL* 105/2 [1986]: 325–26).

Although it is well known that Matthew 2:6 quotes Micah 5:2, it is not commonly recognized that the latter half of Matthew 2:6 also cites the present passage, "doubtless due to the suggestion in Micah 5:4" (Robert L. Reymond, *Jesus, Divine Messiah: The Old Testament Witness* [Ross-shire, Scotland: Christian Focus, 1990], 56; cf. also Homer Heater Jr., "Matthew 2:6 and Its Old Testament Sources," *JETS* 26/4 [1983]: 395–97; A. J. Petrotta, "A Closer Look at Matthew 2:6 and Its Old Testament Sources," *JETS* 28/1 [1985]: 47–52).

5. David's Conquest of Jerusalem (5:6–12)

OVERVIEW

In the MT *wayyēlek* ("he went") stands at the beginning of v.6 ("marched") and verse 10 ("became"), thus forming an inclusio around vv.6–10. Other verbs that tie the section together are *yšb* ("live, take up residence"; vv.6, 9) and *bw*ʾ ("get in, enter"; vv.6 [2x], 8). The terms "fortress" (vv.7, 9) and "the city of David" (vv.7, 9) are repeated as well. That vv.6–10 constitute a literary unit separate from vv.11–12 emerges also from the fact that vv.6–10 are paralleled in 1 Chronicles 11:4–9 while vv.11–12 are paralleled in 1 Chronicles 14:1–2. The larger section is further divisible into the account of how David conquered Jerusalem (vv.6–8) and how he then settled in the city and built it up (vv.9–10).

The separation between 1 Chronicles 11:4–9 and 14:1–2 opens up the possibility that the order of events from 2 Samuel 5:6 onward may be thematic rather than chronological. Eugene H. Merrill ("The 'Accession Year' and Davidic Chronology," *JANESCU* 19 [1989]: 108) argues that such is in fact the case. Concerning ch. 5 he observes:

> 2 Sam. 5:1–9a can ... be confidently assigned to [David's accession] year. The commencement of building activities (9b) must also have taken place then, but it is inconceivable that they were completed within the year (5:11–12) and that David's becoming "more and more powerful" (5:10) and his accumulation of a large family all transpired in that brief time (5:13–16). The Philistine wars (5:17–25), on the other hand, almost certainly preceded the conquest of the city and yet, as the historian emphasizes, followed David's accession to the Saulide throne (5:17). The reason for the inclusion of the Philistine campaigns here no doubt lies in the fact that the ark—the subject of chapter 6—was in Philistine territory at Kiriath-jearim and the defeat of the Philistines would explain how the ark could be safely removed from there to Jerusalem.

Thus David's palace (v.11) may not have been built until as long as twenty-five years after the wars against the Philistines (vv.17–25) and the conquest of Jerusalem (vv.5–8; cf. Merrill, *Kingdom of Priests*, 244). Although one might quibble with one or more details of Merrill's analysis, he demonstrates conclusively that the author/compiler of 2 Samuel did not intend to provide a strictly chronological narrative. Indeed, vv.6–16 highlight key events of David's entire reign and are followed by summaries of his experiences in the military (vv.17–25), cultic (ch. 6), and theological (ch. 7) arenas.

[6]The king and his men marched to Jerusalem to attack the Jebusites, who lived there. The Jebusites said to David, "You will not get in here; even the blind and the lame can ward you off." They thought, "David cannot get in here." [7]Nevertheless, David captured the fortress of Zion, the City of David.

8On that day, David said, "Anyone who conquers the Jebusites will have to use the water shaft to reach those 'lame and blind' who are David's enemies." That is why they say, "The 'blind and lame' will not enter the palace."

9David then took up residence in the fortress and called it the City of David. He built up the area around it, from the supporting terraces inward. 10And he became more and more powerful, because the LORD God Almighty was with him.

11Now Hiram king of Tyre sent messengers to David, along with cedar logs and carpenters and stonemasons, and they built a palace for David. 12And David knew that the LORD had established him as king over Israel and had exalted his kingdom for the sake of his people Israel.

COMMENTARY

6–8 "These verses are among the most difficult in the books of Samuel" (Brueggemann, *First and Second Samuel*, 239). Jones, 119–41, however, has greatly advanced their understanding and, by building on the suggestions of earlier interpreters, has cleared up many problems.

The catchword "Jerusalem" (v.6) links vv.6–8 to the previous section (Carlson, 55; cf. v.5). Jerusalem, although usually thought to mean "Foundation of [the God] Shalem" (cf. *IDB*, 2:843), probably means "City of [the God] Shalem" (cf. Ronald F. Youngblood, "Ariel, 'City of God,'" in *Essays on the Occasion of the Seventieth Anniversary of the Dropsie University [1909–1979]*, ed. Abraham I. Katsh and Leon Nemoy [Philadelphia: Dropsie, 1979], 460; cf. independently Mauchline, 216). Far and away the most important city in the Bible, Jerusalem is mentioned there more often than any other. Geographically and theologically it is located "in the center of the nations" (Eze 5:5). Known also by its abbreviated name "Salem" (Ps 76:2), it makes only one appearance in the OT before the time of Joshua (Ge 14:18; cf. also Heb 7:1–2, where *šālēm* is defined as "peace" [*šālôm*] through wordplay).

The gloss in 1 Chronicles 11:4 (cf. also Jos 15:8; 18:28; Jdg 19:10) explains that Jerusalem was also known as Jebus (meaning unknown), whose pre-Israelite, pagan inhabitants were thus called Jebusites, probably of Hurrian/Hittite origin (Eze 16:3, 45; for details cf. Harry A. Hoffner Jr., "The Hittites and Hurrians" [in Wiseman, *People of Old Testament Times*], 225). Since the earlier inhabitants of Jerusalem were Amorites (Jos 10:5; cf. also Eze 16:3, 45), "it appears that Jerusalem was not Jebusite till the time of the Israelite Conquest" under Joshua (Benjamin Mazar, "Jerusalem in the Biblical Period," in *Jerusalem Revealed: Archaeology in the Holy City 1968–1974*, ed. Y. Yadin [Jerusalem: Israel Exploration Society, 1975], 4).

Edward Lipinski (in *Itineraria Phoenicia* [OLA 127; Leuven: Peeters, 2004], 502), however, suggests that an Amorite ethnic group known as the *Yabusiʾum*, referred to in an eighteenth-century BC Mari letter, "implies the existence of a tribe or clan of *Yabusi*, or Jebusites"—which, however, "may not be the same as the clan of Jebusites living in pre-Davidic Jerusalem" (Edward Lipinski, "Who Were the Jebusites," *BAR* 32/2 [2006]: 17). In any event, "the Jebusite settlement in Jerusalem ... was so firmly established in the city that it could not be dislodged by the Israelites, but remained as a foreign enclave in their midst when they settled in the land and persisted in this way until David conquered Jerusalem" (Jones, 122).

Soon after being anointed king over all Israel and Judah (v.5), David deploys his men for a march on Jerusalem "to attack the Jebusites, who lived in the land" ("lived there," v.6 [NIV]). The phrase "in the land" is problematic since the Jebusites seem to have been confined to Jerusalem (and only part of the city at that). Watson has thus suggested that *hayᵉbusî yôšēb hāʾāreṣ* ("the Jebusites, who lived in the land") be translated "the Jebusite ruler of the city" (Wilfred G. E. Watson, "David Ousts the City Ruler of Jebus," *VT* 20/4 [1970]: 501–2). But (1) 1 Chronicles 11:4 clearly understands the singular form "Jebusite" in v.6 as a collective by following it with the plural form *yōšᵉbê*, and (2) that *ʾereṣ* never means "city" in the OT remains to be proven and should therefore not be used to promote a rendering that is suspect on other grounds.

The solution proposed by Jones, 125–26, is much to be preferred: Jerusalem was the name for the Jebusite settlement on two hills, one of which was heavily defended (the "fortress of Zion," v.7) and was located in the southeastern sector of the present city while the other consisted of unprotected open country located in the southwest. In addition, the "threshing floor of Araunah the Jebusite" (24:16), where the temple of Solomon would eventually be built (2Ch 3:1), was north of the fortress in an open area. It is clear, therefore, that many Jebusites lived outside the fortress and could be referred to as being "in the land"—either in the sense of living in the open country, or by synecdoche: "Because they inhabited the region around the south-eastern hill, the text is correct; but it lacks precision in that it uses the name of the whole for the part, and does not specify that, when David went up to Jerusalem, he was going to attack the fortress on the south-eastern hill" (Jones, 126).

The two-site location of Jebusite Jerusalem also explains the apparent contradiction between Joshua 15:63 and Judges 1:8. The former text states that at the time of the conquest Israel "could not dislodge the Jebusites, who were living in Jerusalem" (cf. also Jdg 1:21)—a reference to the fortress on the southeastern hill. The latter text asserts that the men of Judah "attacked Jerusalem ... and took it. They put the city to the sword and set it on fire"—a reference to the open settlement on the southwestern hill. It may even be the case that the OT name of Jerusalem, *yᵉrûšāla[y]im* (lit., "Two Jerusalems"), referred to the two distinct sites of the Jebusite city.

The interchange about the "blind" and the "lame" in vv.6 and 8, although interpreted in numerous ways (for a convenient summary, see Gilbert Brunet, "Les aveugles et boiteux Jebusites," in *Studies in the Historical Books of the Old Testament* [VTSup 30; ed. J. A. Emerton; Leiden: Brill, 1979], 72), is best understood as "an example of pre-battle verbal taunting, somewhat similar to the exchanges between the Rabshakeh and the Jerusalemites in 2 Kings 18:19–27" (Jones, 125). Thus in v.6 the Jebusites smugly claim that even disabled people can withstand any attack on their fortress, while in v.8 David retaliates in kind by characterizing all Jebusites—"David's enemies"—as "lame and blind" (whether the defenders of the fortress could hear all or part of David's rejoinder is impossible to say).

The overconfident Jebusites, however, do not reckon with the skill and determination of David, who captures the fortress of Zion and renames it the "City of David" (vv.7, 9; cf. Jones, 123). Its conqueror, he also becomes its owner and gives it his name. But David's defeat of the Jebusites does not mean that he wipes them out.

> On the evidence of the friendly negotiations between David and Araunah in 2 Sam 24:18–25, and David's insistence on paying a fair price for the Jebusite's threshing-floor rather than taking possession of it as conqueror, it can be suggested that there was no outright slaughter of the Jebusites or an attempt to oust them from their stronghold.... Jerusalem is usually described as a city-state, and the position envisaged after its storming by David and his troops is that it remained a city-state; the coming of David meant only a change of city ruler.... The inhabitants remained, but their fortress had now become the personal possession of David and was under his control. (Jones, 135)

According to 4Q522, one of the Joshua apocrypha found among the Dead Sea scrolls, the Lord tells Joshua that he is not to take Jerusalem but that "a son ... born to Perez, son of Ju[dah,... is to take] the Rock of Zion and from there he is to possess the Amorites" (Geza Vermes, trans., *The Complete Dead Sea Scrolls in English* [rev. ed.; London: Penguin, 2004], 582). And so it was that David attacked and "captured the fortress of Zion" (v.7).

Although occurring more than 150 times in the OT, the name "Zion" (meaning unknown) appears only six times in the historical books (beginning here [= 1Ch 11:5]; cf. also 1Ki 8:1 = 2Ch 5:2; 2Ki 19:21, 31). Referring in v.7 to the Jebusite citadel on the southeastern hill, the name is later used elsewhere of the temple mount (e.g., Isa 10:12) or of the entire city of Jerusalem (e.g., Isa 28:16).

Up to this time Jerusalem had been on the border between Judah in the south (Jos 15:1, 5, 8) and Benjamin in the north (Jos 18:11, 16). Tied to no tribe, the "City of David" (a name the southeastern hill continued to bear long after David's time [Isa 22:9; cf. also 29:1]) could champion its neutrality, central location, and virtual impregnability as qualities that made it and its environs the ideal capital for David's newly established, united kingdom.

> David's renaming of Jerusalem as "City of David" has distinct parallels in the ancient Near East. It was a common practice to name cities after their founders. For example, Kar Tukulti-Ninurta is named after the Assyrian king Tukulti-Ninurta I; Dur Sharru-ken is named after the Assyrian king Sargon II; and Azitiwadiya is named after its founder, the king of Adana. (Nadav Na'aman, "Cow Town or Royal Capital? Evidence for Iron Age Jerusalem," *BAR* 23/4 [1997]: 46)

What was David's Jerusalem like? Does 2 Samuel 5 provide an accurate and reliable historical account, or is the information it gives based on retrojection from a much later age in order to glorify David and enhance his reputation? The area of the Jebusite settlement and its environs has undergone repeated (though intermittent) excavation for decades by eminent archaeologists, including R. A. S. Macalister and J. Garrow Duncan (1923–25), Kathleen Kenyon (1961–67) and Yigal Shiloh (1978–85). "Virtually every archaeologist to have excavated in the City of David has found architecture and artifacts dating to the period of the United Monarchy" (Jane Cahill, "Jerusalem in David and Solomon's Time," *BAR* 30/6 [2004]: 27), so the historicity debate centers around the fact that the excavated remains seem relatively meager, especially when compared to those of the later divided monarchy.

For example, Margreet Steiner (a fine archaeologist in her own right), after an exhaustive review of those remains, expresses grave doubts about their significance for, or even their relationship to, the biblical account of David's reign in Jerusalem ("It's Not There: Archaeology Proves a Negative," *BAR* 24/4 [1998]: 26–33, 62–63). Archaeologist Cahill, by contrast, accuses Steiner of ignoring "most of the published evidence" ("It Is There: The Archaeological Evidence Proves It," *BAR* 24/4 [1998]: 34) and mounts a strong critique of the ways in which Steiner interprets the evidence she does discuss

(34–41, 63). Cahill, 36, also notes, among other things, that archaeological excavation in the City of David is impeded by the local topography, by the reuse of earlier building stone by later builders, by Roman quarrying and Byzantine construction, and by the fact that the summit is now covered by modern buildings.

Cahill is joined in her critique of Steiner by Nadav Naʾaman, who focuses most of his attention on the six 14th-century BC Amarna letters sent by ʿAbdi-Heba, king of Jerusalem, to the Egyptian pharaoh (for translation see William L. Moran, *The Amarna Letters* [Baltimore: Johns Hopkins Univ. Press, 1992], 325–44) and observes a number of useful comparisons between the Late Bronze Age ruler and his Jerusalem, on the one hand, and David, the Iron Age ruler of his Jerusalem, on the other (Nadav Naʾaman, "It Is There: Ancient Texts Prove It," *BAR* 24/4 [1998]: 42–44). Concerning Steiner's survey, Naʾaman, 44, warns that we should be "cautious about drawing conclusions from supposedly negative archaeological evidence" (see further V. Philips Long, "The Early Monarchy," 228–30).

Since v.7 describes the fortress of Zion (see comment on v.9) as already captured and v.8 records David's instructions to its potential captor, "said" (v.8) is better rendered as a pluperfect ("had said," as in 1Ch 11:6). The "one who conquers the Jebusites" (v.8) would turn out to be Joab, who as a result would be rewarded with the position of commander-in-chief of the armies of united Israel (1Ch 11:6). Exactly how the fortress was captured remains unclear because the meaning of *ṣinnôr* is somewhat uncertain. Here translated "water shaft," it is rendered "waterfalls" in its only other occurrence in the OT (Ps 42:7; cf. perhaps also *ṣantᵉrôt* ["pipes (for pouring out oil)," in Zec 4:12]). Assuming that "water shaft" or the like is correct, Joab (perhaps assisted and accompanied by his men) would then have either (1) climbed up through a tunnel that led from a water source outside the city to a location somewhere within the city, or (2) cut off the citadel's water supply and thus forced the "lame and blind"—the Jebusite defenders—to surrender.

Despite its attractiveness, the earlier theory that the Jebusite *ṣinnôr* is to be identified with the water shaft that leads from the Gihon Spring to the southeastern hill and that was discovered by Charles Warren in 1867 remains unproven (cf. Anderson, 84; Kathleen M. Kenyon, *The Bible and Recent Archaeology*, rev. ed. [Atlanta: John Knox, 1987], 92; Philip J. King's review of Harry Thomas Frank, *Discovering the Biblical World*, ed. James F. Strange; rev. ed. [Maplewood, N.J.: Hammond, 1988], in *BAR* 15/1 [1989]: 13). Indeed, whether Warren's Shaft itself was ever used to draw water into the city has been debated (cf. Hershel Shanks, "Did Ancient Jerusalem Draw Water through Warren's Shaft?" *BAR* 33/2 [2007]: 64–69, 77), although that it was part of a complex earlier water system is beyond dispute. According to geologist Dan Gill ("Subterranean Waterworks of Biblical Jerusalem: Adaptation of a Karst System," *Science* 254 [December 1991]: 1467–70):

> ... ancient Jerusalem has long been known to possess a system of subterranean waterworks by which the spring of Gihon, which issues outside the walls, could be approached from within the city, and its waters diverted to an intramural pool.... Geological investigation has revealed the waterworks to be part of a well-developed karst system, a network of natural dissolution channels and shafts, in the limestone and dolomite underlying the city. Thus, it was not through primary planning but by means of skillful adaptation of these pre-existing natural features that the city was ensured of a dependable water supply during both war and peace [1467]....
>
> The apparent "mistakes" in the waterworks are so fundamental and numerous that it is unlikely that they were deliberately planned. Previous authors tried to rationalize each anomaly indi-

> vidually instead of looking for a common reason. A reexamination of the waterworks suggests that it was fashioned essentially by skillful enlargement of natural (karstic) dissolution channels and shafts and their integration into a functional water supply system [1469]....
>
> [Therefore] ancient (Jebusite) Jerusalem could be entered from at least two extramural points on the eastern hillside: the cave of Gihon, and the upper tunnel of W[arren's] S[haft] I[nstallation], which both connected to pre-existing natural passages, but whose whereabouts was most likely known only to insiders. Thus, if anything, the present findings provide support for Joab's exploit (the capturing of Jerusalem by using a hidden passage), based on geologic fact rather than on linguistic assumptions [1470].

In the late 1990s Ronny Reich and Eli Shikron participated in renewed excavations in the area of the City of David ("Light at the End of the Tunnel," *BAR* 25/1 [1999]: 22–33, 72). South and west of an existing springhouse over the Gihon Spring they discovered the remains of a tower built around the spring to protect it. The Spring Tower (as they called it) is huge (forty-five feet by fifty-five feet on the outside) and was "part of a large, complex water system that promised the residents of Jerusalem a secure supply of water" (ibid., 30). A second gigantic tower (the Pool Tower) was discovered a short distance west of the Spring Tower. Potsherds found associated with the two towers were all from a single period: Middle Bronze II (eighteenth to seventeenth centuries BC). After a thorough review and evaluation of all the available research reports, Terence J. Kleven ("The Water System of Jerusalem and Its Implications for the Historicity of Joab's Conquest," *Near East Archaeological Society Bulletin* 47 [2002]: 35–48) concludes (46): "As recent geological, philological and archaeological evidence converges in affirming the existence of some type of substantial water system in Jebusite Jerusalem, it appears that a reasonable case can be made for the plausibility of the depiction in 2 Samuel 5." Indeed, archaeologist Eilat Mazar, who believes that she has located the ruins of David's palace (cf. comment on v.11), claims also to have discovered the water tunnel that provided Joab and his men with their means of access into the Jebusite city (Etgar Lefkovits, "First-Temple era water tunnel uncovered in the City of David dig," *Jerusalem Post* [10/30/2008], 5).

David's declaration that the Jebusites, the "lame and the blind," are his enemies eventually gave rise to an epigram: "The 'blind and lame' will not enter the palace" (v.8b)—a palace that would be built at an indeterminate time in the future (v.11). The revulsion of David for the Jebusites barred them from associating with him from that day onward. The observation of Carlson, 57, that in its context the saying expresses "the idea that Mephibosheth is disqualified by his lameness from filling the functions of the sacral king in the palace and the temple" forges a useful link between v.8 and related texts (cf. Lev 21:18; Dt 15:21; Mal 1:8, 13).

Saul M. Olyan ("'Anyone Blind or Lame Shall Not Enter the House': On the Interpretation of Second Samuel 5:8b," *CBQ* 60/1 [1998]: 218–27), building on that and related links, asserts that "there is a consensus among scholars that the aphorism was originally independent from its present context" (218), argues that *hbyt* ("the house"; "the palace," NIV) in v.8b is "a sanctuary, probably the temple of Jerusalem" (220), and affirms that the blind and the lame "and their counterparts in Deut 23:2 [MT; NIV 23:1]" are to be viewed "as synecdoches, representative of all blemished worshipers disqualified for cultic participation according to the circles responsible for these texts" (225). His conclusion: "At all events, 2 Samuel 5:8b suggests that a ban on worshipers with at least some physical defects was in force in Jerusalem at some point in time" (227).

Anthony R. Ceresko ("The Identity of 'the Blind and the Lame' [ʿiwwēr ûpissēaḥ] in 2 Samuel 5:8b," *CBQ* 63/1 [2001]: 23–30), however, uses a "quite different" approach, following "in general" my "reading of verses 6–10" as the background for his proposal (23 n. 1). For Ceresko, "the primary meaning of *habbayit* in verse 8b is 'palace.' But allusions to 'temple' and 'kingship' are not, therefore, excluded" (25). He agrees with Carlson's proposal (see above) that "the lame" referred to in v.8b is "the lame Mephibosheth [cf. 4:4; 9:13], the son of Jonathan and heir to Saul's kingship" (Carlson, 24). And the reference to "the blind" is echoed in 2 Kings 25:7, which "describes the fate of the last Davidic king to rule in Jerusalem, Zedekiah" (Carlson, 24). Ceresko also notes "the irony of 2 Kings 25:29. David had invited the lame Mephibosheth, the heir of Saul, to dine 'at the king's table' [2Sa 9:13].... It is now the turn of a descendant of David (and nephew of the blinded Zedekiah), Jehoiachin, to 'dine regularly in the presence of the king (of Babylon)'" (29). Ceresko's summary: "The mention of 'the blind and the lame' in the epigram does not refer solely to David's exclusion of the Jebusites from his palace. At another level it affirms the supplanting of Saul's house ('the lame') by David and foreshadows the eventual exclusion of the Davidic dynasty ('the blind') from kingship as well" (30).

Well stated—but perhaps it would not be amiss to trace the trajectory of progressive revelation a bit further: Just as David would eventually welcome the lame Mephibosheth (9:13) into the royal palace, so also in the messianic age the blind and the lame will be special recipients of divine favor (cf. Isa 35:5–6; Jer 31:8; Mt 12:22; 21:14; Ac 3:7–8). "In the old Jerusalem of this text, the blind and lame are excluded and despised. In the new Jerusalem envisioned by the gospel, all are welcomed.... David, the provoked warrior, might exclude. David, the embodiment of Israel's best hope, will eventually include" (Brueggemann, *First and Second Samuel*, 241–42; cf. also esp. M. Dennis Hamm, *The Beatitudes in Context: What Luke and Matthew Meant* [Wilmington, Del.: Michael Glazier, 1990], 90–91, 105).

9–10 David thus "took up residence" (v.9) in Jerusalem, where the Jebusites "lived" (v.6; same Heb. verb). Expropriating the "fortress" (of Zion, v.7; see comment) as his private property, he renamed it "the City of David" (v.9; see comment on v.7) and lived there until his own palace was built (v.11; see comment). He then set about to repair the surrounding areas "from the supporting terraces inward." The term rendered "supporting terraces" is "Millo" (see NIV note), which means "fill(ing)." For several decades archaeologists have been excavating intermittently a massive structure (known as the Stepped-Stone Structure) consisting of a huge fill constructed by Canaanites/Jebusites in the fourteenth and thirteenth centuries BC. It was built at the highest point of the extreme northern end of the City of David and served as the foundation of a two-thousand-square-foot level platform. The "fortress of Zion" was probably constructed on it.

In the 1960s Kathleen Kenyon suggested, probably correctly, that the Stepped-Stone Structure is the Millo of v.9. Depending on the topography, fill on which other structures could be erected (in Jdg 9:6 and 2Ki 12:20, the proper name Beth Millo means "House of [i.e., built on] Fill") might consist of rock, tamped earth, or a combination of them. As the city expanded, the terraces would expand accordingly (1Ki 9:15, 24; 11:27); in any event, it would be in constant need of repair and reinforcement (2Ch 32:5). First Chronicles 11:8 observes that, in addition to David's building activities, Joab (David's commander-in-chief and the point man in Jerusalem's conquest) "restored the rest of the city" (parts of which were doubtless damaged or destroyed as a result of Joab's attack to capture it).

The assertion that David "became more and more powerful" (v.10) is reminiscent of 3:1 (see comment). Now as earlier, however, David himself is not the source of his strength. The narrator is quick to remind his readers that "the LORD God Almighty" (a title for God that is more royal than military; see comment on 1Sa 1:3), the true king of Israel, grants his power and, as always, is "with him" (see 1Sa 16:18 and comment; cf. also 1Sa 17:37; 18:12, 14, 28).

11–12 The fact that vv.6–10 are paralleled in 1 Chronicles 11:4–9 while vv.11–12 are not paralleled until 1 Chronicles 14:1–2 hints at the possibility that the events described in vv.11–12 occurred a long time after those recorded in vv.6–10. That possibility becomes a certainty when it is noted that Hiram (v.11) did not become king of Tyre (a part of Phoenicia) until about 980 BC (and thus more than twenty years after David was anointed king over Israel and conquered Jerusalem). Hiram continued his friendly relations with Israel's royal house well into the reign of David's son Solomon (1Ki 5:1–12; 9:10–14).

Hiram's name, an abbreviation of Ahiram, means "Brother of the exalted (God)," as does the variant spelling Huram, which occurs often in Chronicles (see NIV note on 2Ch 2:3). Located just beyond the border of the tribal territory of Asher (Jos 19:24, 29) more than fifty miles north of Jerusalem, Tyre ("Rock") was a well-fortified island in the Mediterranean Sea with a supply depot (called Ushu by the Assyrians) on the coast nearby. The former island is now joined to its mainland sister, and the two sites exist as es-Sur today.

During the latter part of David's reign and much of Solomon's, Hiram traded building materials (which Israel lacked) for agricultural products (which Phoenicia lacked). Thus Hiram sends to David logs of "cedar" (v.11; *cedrus libani*, whose "fragrant wood is much sought after for building purposes, as it does not easily rot" [*Fauna and Flora of the Bible*, 108]; cf. 1Ki 5:6–10; 6:9–10; 9:11; 1Ch 22:4; 2Ch 2:3, 8), doubtless lashed into rafts and floated down the Mediterranean coast to Joppa, from which they would be transported overland to Jerusalem (cf. 1Ki 5:8–9; Ezr 3:7). He also sends David carpenters and stonemasons (cf. also 2Ki 12:11–12; 1Ch 22:15), both of which are in short supply in Israel (cf. 1Ki 5:6, 18).

All this activity will eventuate in a "palace for David" (v.11). Archaeologist Eilat Mazar believes that she located the ruins of David's palace in 2005 ("Did I Find King David's Palace?" *BAR* 32/1 [2006]: 16–27, 70). They constitute what remains of an impressive Iron Age public building (which she calls the "Large-Stone Structure") that had been erected on top of the Stepped-Stone Structure outside the northern fortifications of the City of David. The earliest construction phase of the Large-Stone Structure dates to the tenth century BC.

David's palace will eventually fill him with a certain unease (7:1–2). Brueggemann (*First and Second Samuel*, 246) puts his finger on at least part of the problem that David faces:

> David has joined the nations. David is a practitioner of alliances and accommodations.... Jeremiah later sees that cedar and its accompanying opulence will talk Judean kings out of justice (Jer. 22:13–18). Verse 11 sounds like a historical report, but it is in fact an ominous act of warning.

For now, however, David—witnessing God's evident blessing on his life—once again acknowledges the Lord's role in establishing "him as king over Israel" (v.12). Indeed, David's throne and dynasty will be established forever (7:11b–16; 22:51; 1Sa 25:28), culminating in the eternal reign of "great David's greater son" (cf. Lk 1:30–33). As Israel's ideal ruler, David has the privilege of seeing his kingdom "exalted" (v.12; "highly exalted," 1Ch 14:2) by the Lord himself. All this is not for his own sake alone but also—and primarily—for the sake of "his" (i.e., God's) people.

NOTES

6 Patrick, 371, calls attention to the following commonly held theory (among others):

> A great many by *the blind and the lame* understand the Images of their Gods.... As if they had said, our Gods, whom ye call blind and lame, that have Eyes and see not, Feet and walk not (as it is CXV. *Psal.*) they shall defend us: And you must overcome them, before you overcome us. *Luther* himself thus explains the Sense; *These blind and lame* saith he, *were the Idols of the Jebusites; which to irritate David, they set upon their Walls, as their Patrons and Defenders: And they did as good as say, thou dost not fight with us, but with our Gods; who will easily repel thee.*

Similar to this is a Hittite soldiers' oath (see *ANET*, 354) calculated to strike terror into the hearts of all who would presume to oppose the Hittite rulers:

> They parade in front of them a (blind woman) and a deaf man and [you speak] as follows: "See! here is a blind woman and a deaf man. Whoever does evil to the king (and) the queen, let the oaths seize him! Let them make him blind! Let them [ma]ke him [deaf]! ... Let them [annihilate him], the man (himself) together with his wife, [his children] (and) his kin!"

8 The fact that צִנּוֹר (*ṣinnôr*) means "water duct/pipe/spout" in Mishnaic and modern Hebrew supports the interpretation given in the comment on v.8. The NIV note ("scaling hooks") is based primarily on an Aramaic cognate, as are similar renderings offered by a few versions (e.g., the REB) and commentators (e.g., William F. Albright, "The Old Testament and Archaeology," in *Old Testament Commentary*, ed. Herbert C. Alleman and Elmer E. Flack [Philadelphia: Muhlenberg, 1948], 149; Unger, 13–14; Yadin, 268). Other translations have also been proposed (for a typical list see Gilbert Brunet, "David et le *Sinnor*," in *Studies in the Historical Books of the Old Testament* [VTSup 30; ed. J. A. Emerton; Leiden: Brill, 1979], 74 n. 9; for a convenient, brief summary of the philological arguments favoring "water shaft" or the like as well as a comprehensive list of other proposed translations of the Heb. word, see Terence Kleven, "Up the Water-spout," *BAR* 20/4 [1994]: 34–35).

"David's enemies" renders either the *Kethiv* שָׂנְאוּ נֶפֶשׁ דָּוִד (*śān^{e}ʾû nepeš dāwid*, "they hate David's soul") or the *Qere* revocalized שֹׂנְאֵי נֶפֶשׁ דָּוִד (*śōn^{e}ʾê nepeš dāwid*, "haters of David's soul"). The NIV note ("hated by David") translates the *Qere*'s שְׂנֻאֵי נֶפֶשׁ דָּוִד (*ś^{e}nuʾê nepeš dāwid*, "hated of/by David's soul"). 1QSamuel^{a} reads the verb as שׂנאה (*śnʾh*), resulting in the translation "David's soul hates" and making active the passive *Qere* reading. Although any one of the readings makes good sense, the epigram in v.8b gives a slight edge either to the rendering in the NIV margin or to the Qumran reading (for a defense of the latter see Olyan, "'Anyone Blind or Lame Shall Not Enter the House,'" *CBQ* 60/1 [1998]: 219 n. 3).

9 בָּיְתָה (*bāy^{e}tâ*), here translated "inward" (cf. Ex 28:26 = 39:19 ["inside"]; 1Ki 7:25 = 2Ch 4:4 ["toward the center"]), could also be translated "to the palace," especially since בַּיִת (*bayit*) means "palace" in vv.8 and 11. Fortunately both renderings lead to the same result.

11 Although Alberto R. Green ("David's Relations with Hiram: Biblical and Josephan Evidence for Tyrian Chronology," in Meyers and O'Connor, 373–97) places Hiram's accession to the throne of Tyre too early (ca. 1000 BC), his detailed treatment of all the data available for determining the date is invaluable. Whereas Green (389–91) gives Hiram a reign of half a century, other representative scholars whose calculations Green records (392) assign the Tyrian king a total of thirty-four regnal years, ranging from as early as 980–947 BC to as late as 962–929 BC.

The phrase translated "stonemasons," חָרָשֵׁי אֶבֶן קִיר (*ḥārāšê ᵓeben qîr*), means literally "craftsmen of stone of wall," in which the word for wall refers to the wall of a building (as opposed to a city wall). The parallel in 1 Chronicles 14:1 omits *ᵓeben* ("stone").

6. Children Born to David in Jerusalem (5:13–16)

OVERVIEW

As the list of sons born to David in Hebron (3:2–5) concludes the account of his accession to kingship over Judah (1:1–3:5), so the roster of children born to David in Jerusalem concludes the narrative of his accession to kingship over Israel (3:6–5:16). The two lists may originally have been parts of one (as in 1Ch 3:1–8) and only later separated, as the phrase "after he left Hebron" (v.13) suggests (cf. 3:5b: "These were born to David in Hebron"). In any case and at the very least, "after he left Hebron" indicates that the lists are chronologically sequential.

[13]After he left Hebron, David took more concubines and wives in Jerusalem, and more sons and daughters were born to him. [14]These are the names of the children born to him there: Shammua, Shobab, Nathan, Solomon, [15]Ibhar, Elishua, Nepheg, Japhia, [16]Elishama, Eliada and Eliphelet.

COMMENTARY

13–16 In violation of the divine decree that Israel's kings not "take many wives" (Dt 17:17), David takes "more" concubines and wives (v.13)—that is, in addition to his wives Ahinoam and Abigail (see comment on 1Sa 25:43) and to the wives he had already taken in Hebron (see comment on 3:5). Here is the first mention of concubines in connection with David (cf. also 1Ch 3:9)—and also the only occurrence of the phrase "concubines and wives" in the Bible (the usual order is "wives and concubines"; cf. 19:5; 1Ki 11:3; 2Ch 11:21; Da 5:2–3, 23). By placing the word "concubines" in emphatic position, the narrator is perhaps deploring David's proclivity for the trappings of a typical ancient Near Eastern monarch, including a harem.

David fathered many "sons and daughters" (v.13) in Jerusalem. Although vv.14–16 list only sons born to him by his wives (as 1Ch 3:9 states), the name of at least one of David's daughters has survived—that of Tamar, the sister of Absalom (cf. 13:1; 1Ch 3:9).

Verses 13–16 are paralleled in 1 Chronicles 3:5–8 and 14:3–7. The following chart prepared by James W. Flanagan (*David's Social Drama: A Hologram of Israel's Early Iron Age* [JSOTSup 73; Sheffield,

Almond, 1988], 348) is useful for comparing the three passages:

2 Samuel 5:14–16	1 Chronicles 3:5–8	1 Chronicles 14:4–7
Shammua	Shimea	Shammua
Shobab	Shobab	Shobab
Nathan	Nathan	Nathan
Solomon	Solomon	Solomon
Ibhar	Ibhar	Ibhar
Elishua	Elishama	Elishua
	Eliphelet	Elpelet
	Nogah	Nogah
Nepheg	Nepheg	Nepheg
Japhia	Japhia	Japhia
Elishama	Elishama	Elishama
Eliada	Eliada	Beelida [*sic*]
Eliphelet	Eliphelet	Eliphelet

The most obvious difference among the three lists is the omission of two names (El[i]p[h]elet, Nogah) in 2 Samuel 5. Scribal error is the probable cause, since the names from Ibhar to the end are correctly added up as nine in 1 Chronicles 3:8. The first of the two names may have been omitted either because of its similarity to Elishua, which immediately precedes it, or its identicalness to Eliphelet (the last name in the list). As for Nogah, it may have dropped out by haplography because of its similarity to Nepheg, which immediately follows it.

Apart from the two omissions, the list in 2 Samuel 5 is almost identical to that in 1 Chronicles 14. The only exception is Eliada ("God knows," v.16) in place of Beeliada ("Baal knows," 1Ch 14:7), which—although doubtless the original name—was considered shameful by one or more of the scribes who transmitted 2 Samuel and was therefore altered. (For a similar phenomenon see comment on Ish-Bosheth in 2:8.) It is likely, therefore, that 1 Chronicles 14 is the most accurate of the three lists, faithfully preserving the correct forms of the names of all thirteen of David's sons who were born in Jerusalem.

The list in 1 Chronicles 3 is the most poorly transmitted of the three, although with only modest variations from the other two. Shimea (1Ch 3:5) is an alternative form of Shammua, both names meaning "Heard (by God)." While 2 Samuel 5:15 and 1 Chronicles 14:5 have Elishua ("My God is salvation"), 1 Chronicles 3:6 reads Elishama ("My God hears"), a duplicate of the antepenultimate name in all three lists. And while 1 Chronicles 14:5 has Elpelet ("God is deliverance"), 1 Chronicles 3:6 contains the variant Eliphelet ("My God is deliverance"), a duplicate of the last name in all three lists. In addition, 1 Chronicles 3:5 also misspells Bathsheba as "Bathshua" (see NIV note on 1Ch 3:5–6 for details on this and other related matters).

The first four names in the list (v.14) are of sons born to David by Bathsheba (1Ch 3:5); two of the names appear elsewhere in the biblical narratives (the only two among the thirteen sons in the lists to do so; cf. Baldwin, 199). Nathan ("[God] gives"; not to be confused with the famous prophet of the same name) is mentioned in Luke 3:31 in the genealogy of Jesus. Solomon ("[God is] his peace"), appearing here for the first time in the Bible and David's tenth son overall (David himself was an eighth son), would eventually outlast his rivals for the throne and rule over the united kingdom (cf. 1Ki 1:28–39).

It is worth noting that at least four of David's sons born in Jerusalem (five, if Beeliada/Eliada is included) had names containing the element El ("God")—Elishua, Elpelet (1Ch 14:5), Elishama, Eliphelet—while none of the names contained the element Yah ("LORD"). Of the sons born to David in Hebron, however, none bore El names while two—Adonijah, Shephatiah (3:4)—had names containing Yah. The relatively high proportion (a third of the total at each site) seems to be deliberate and may reflect the often claimed preference of Judahites for the name Yah(weh) and of Israelites (members of the northern tribes) for the name El(ohim) respectively. If so, David may have had political considerations in mind by catering to northern predilections in naming his Jerusalemite sons.

A final observation: The two main claimants to David's throne in his later years were Absalom (his third-born, 3:3) and Solomon (his tenth-born). Although the first means "(Divine) father of peace" and the second "(God is) his peace," it is hardly accidental that each of the two men was anxious to rule over Jerusalem—a city whose name, dominated by the same basic root (*šlm*), probably means "City of (the God) Shalem" (see comment on v.6; cf. similarly Jones, 127; Talmon, 152 n. 19).

NOTES

13 "In Jerusalem" translates מִירוּשָׁלַם (*mîrûšālaim*, lit., "from Jerusalem"). That מִן (*min*, "from") means "in" here would seem to be clear from the parallel in 1 Chronicles 14:3, which reads בִּירוּשָׁלָם (*bîrûšālāim*; for other examples see Sarna, 312–13). If, however, *min* is taken in the partitive sense, some of the women added to David's harem may have been local Jebusites, and the marriages may have been politically motivated (Andrew E. Hill, "On David's 'Taking' and 'Leaving' Concubines [2 Samuel 5:13; 15:16]," *JBL* 125/1 [2006]: 129–39).

16 The alternation between Eliada (v.16) and Beeliada (1Ch 14:7) is strikingly paralleled in the book of Judges. A god named Baal-Berith appears in Judges 8:33, and the "temple of Baal-Berith" is mentioned in Judges 9:4. But the same building is later called the "temple of El-Berith" (Jdg 9:46). In this case, however, the variation in name was an intra-Canaanite issue: "El was the nominal head of the Canaanite pantheon, but his position was virtually taken over by Baal, the great, active god, in a process taking many generations" (Arthur E. Cundall, *Judges: An Introduction and Commentary* [Chicago: InterVarsity Press, 1968], 135).

C. David's Powerful Reign (5:17–8:18)

OVERVIEW

As the story of David's accession to kingship over Judah (1:1–3:5) parallels that of his accession to the throne of Israel (3:6–5:16), each concluding with a list of his sons (3:2–5; 5:13–16), so the account of his powerful reign (5:17–8:18) parallels that of his court history (chs. 9–20), each concluding with a roster of his officials (8:15–18; 20:23–26).

The narrative before us is especially representative of those early chapters of 2 Samuel that Carlson, 39, describes as "David under the blessing." A key verse in this respect, highlighting as it does the manifest blessing of the Lord on David and his activities, is 7:29, containing the final, emphatic words of David's prayer: "Now be pleased to bless the house of your servant, that it may continue forever in your sight; for you, O Sovereign LORD, have spoken, and with your blessing the house of your servant will be blessed forever."

Excluding the appendix (8:15–18), 5:17–8:18 may be outlined as follows.

A. The Philistines Defeated (5:17–25)
B. The Ark Brought to Jerusalem (6:1–23)
C. The Lord's Covenant with David (7:1–17)
D. David's Prayer (7:18–29)
E. David's Enemies Defeated (8:1–14)

The section detailing the provisions of the Davidic covenant is of supreme importance and therefore occupies pride of place at the center of the literary unit.

1. The Philistines Defeated (5:17–25)

OVERVIEW

Paralleled in 1 Chronicles 14:8–16 (which contains a few significant and helpful differences), 5:17–25 describes two Israelite victories over the Philistines, their agelong enemies. The two confrontations (vv.17–21, 22–25) are similar in several ways: (1) The Philistines are the aggressors (they "went up/came up [same Heb. verb] ... and spread out," vv.17–18, 22); (2) the locale is the same ("the Valley of Rephaim," vv.18, 22); (3) David's response to the challenge is the same (he "inquired of the LORD," vv.19, 23); (4) David obeys God's command ("So David went/did," vv.20, 25); (5) the battles end in the same way (David "defeated/struck down" [the same Heb. verb] the enemy, vv.20, 25); and (6) "YHWH—not David—is prominent as Israel's ultimate warrior" (Howard, "The Case for Kingship," 113; cf. vv.19, 24). Although by no means the only battles King David fought against the Philistines (cf. 8:1), these serve as a paradigm to summarize the continuing conflict.

17When the Philistines heard that David had been anointed king over Israel, they
went up in full force to search for him, but David heard about it and went down to the
stronghold. 18Now the Philistines had come and spread out in the Valley of Rephaim; 19so
David inquired of the LORD, "Shall I go and attack the Philistines? Will you hand them over
to me?"

The LORD answered him, "Go, for I will surely hand the Philistines over to you."

20So David went to Baal Perazim, and there he defeated them. He said, "As waters break
out, the LORD has broken out against my enemies before me." So that place was called
Baal Perazim. 21The Philistines abandoned their idols there, and David and his men carried
them off.

22Once more the Philistines came up and spread out in the Valley of Rephaim; 23so
David inquired of the LORD, and he answered, "Do not go straight up, but circle around
behind them and attack them in front of the balsam trees. 24As soon as you hear the

sound of marching in the tops of the balsam trees, move quickly, because that will mean the LORD has gone out in front of you to strike the Philistine army." 25So David did as the LORD commanded him, and he struck down the Philistines all the way from Gibeon to Gezer.

COMMENTARY

17–21 "David's capture of Jerusalem ... has been placed [by commentators] before, after, and between the two Philistine incursions on the valley of Rephaim" (Christian E. Hauer Jr., "Jerusalem, the Stronghold, and Rephaim," *CBQ* 32/4 [1970]: 571; cf. similarly Jones, 121). Although Hauer (ibid., 572–75) himself argues that the events in ch. 5 are roughly chronological and that David seized Jerusalem "immediately after his anointment as king over all Israel," K&D, 323, is surely correct in its observation that both of David's victories over the Philistines "belong in all probability to the interval between the anointing of David ... and the conquest of the citadel of Zion." It is as soon as the Philistines learn "that David had been anointed" that they become concerned (v.17), not at a later time. Furthermore, they go to "search" for him, an unnecessary task if David had already occupied the formidable fortress of Zion.

Both armies rely on military intelligence reports as they deploy their forces: The Philistines "heard" and "went up," and then David "heard" and "went down" (v.17). The tentacles of David's intelligence system were evidently widespread and effective (10:7, 17; cf. Hauer, "Foreign Intelligence," 97).

The "stronghold" (*meṣûdâ*, v.17) to which David retreats is not the "fortress" of Zion (*meṣudâ*, vv.7, 9), in spite of the fact that the two Hebrew words are morphologically identical. That the first is here written *plene* and the second defectively suggests that the author intends to make a distinction between them. Also David "went down" to the stronghold, an act that cannot describe the ascent necessary to reach the hill on which Zion rests. Although the cave of Adullam is a possible candidate for the "stronghold" (thus Hauer, "Jerusalem, the Stronghold, and Rephaim," 575–78; Carlson, 56 n. 2), the latter, while sometimes mentioned in association with Adullam (23:13–14; 1Sa 22:1–5), is never equated with the cave itself and in at least one case cannot be so equated (see comment on 1Sa 22:4–5). The precise identification and location of David's stronghold must therefore remain uncertain.

The NIV pluperfect "had come" (v.18) is correct, both grammatically (cf. Tidwell, 206) and contextually (the Philistine action in v.18 is antecedent to that of David in v.17). In 1 Chronicles 14:9, 13, the verb "raided," which is substituted for "spread out" in the present section (vv.18, 22), merely indicates that the Philistines have more than one purpose in mind and should not be used to argue that vv.18–21 were originally written to describe a less momentous occasion and only later became displaced into the present context (as asserted by Tidwell, 195–98, 205, 211–12). If "spread out" is often used in scenes suggestive of plunder (cf. Jdg 15:9), it is also used in a more general sense (cf. Isa 16:8).

The locale of the two battles is the "Valley of Rephaim" (vv.18, 22; cf. also 23:13 and comment), west-southwest of Jerusalem on the border between the tribal territories of Judah and Benjamin (Jos 15:1, 8; 18:11, 16). A relatively flat area, its fertile land produced grain that not only provided food for Jerusalem (Isa 17:5) but also attracted raiding parties. It is known today as el-Baqʿa, "through which the modern railway achieves its Jerusalem terminus" (Hauer, "Jerusalem, the Stronghold, and Rephaim," 573 n. 10).

Bruce K. Waltke (*ZPEB*, 5:64–66) asserts that *r*^{e}*pāʾîm* (GK 8329), from *rpʾ* ("heal") and/or *rph* ("sink, relax," thus "sunken/powerless ones"), is used in the OT in three distinct senses, the relationship between which is obscure.

1. Inhabitants of the netherworld ("dead," "departed spirits," "spirits of the dead/departed": Job 26:5; Ps 88:10; Pr 2:18; 9:18; Isa 14:9; 26:14, 19). "The most that can be said with certainty about this use of *rephaim* is that the Israelites applied the term to people who were dead and gone" (Waltke, *ZPEB* 5:64).
2. Pre-Israelite inhabitants of Transjordan ("Rephaites": Ge 14:5; 15:20; Dt 2:11, 20; 3:11, 13; Jos 12:4; 13:12; 17:15), noted for their great height (Dt 2:10–11; 3:11).
3. Giants who were descendants of Rapha, the eponymous ancestor of one distinct group of Rephaim (21:16, 18, 20, 22; 1Ch 20:4 ["Rephaites"], 6, 8). Goliath, the Philistine giant (1Sa 17:4), may have been such a "Rephaite" (21:19; 1Ch 20:5).

It is impossible to know whether the Valley of Rephaim was named after one of these three groups (see, however, Tidwell, 203–4).

To meet the Philistine threat David, as always, "inquired of the LORD" (v.19) by consulting the Urim and Thummim through a priest (see comments on 2:1; 1Sa 14:36, 40–42; 23:2; for structural similarities between several of these passages, see Tidwell, 208). Having gone "down" to the stronghold (v.17), David now asks the Lord (1) whether he should "go" (lit., "go up") and attack the Philistines and (2) whether the Lord will hand them over to him (v.19). The divine answer is emphatically affirmative to both questions ("go" is again lit. "go up").

In obedience to God's command, David "went" (v.20; the verb is singular; the parallel in 1Ch 14:11 uses a plural verb, which the NIV translates by adding "and his men" after "David" [see also comment on v.25]) to engage the Philistines in battle at Baal Perazim (location unknown, although modern ez-Zuhur, four miles southwest of Jerusalem, has been suggested). Meaning "The Lord [in this case Yahweh, not Baal] who breaks out" (see NIV note), Baal Perazim was so named because of David's affirmation following the Philistine defeat: "As waters break out, the LORD has broken out against my enemies before me" (v.20). The phrase "before me" underscores the divine initiative in the Lord's fighting on David's behalf, as does "in front of you" in v.24 (the same Heb. in both instances).

Purposeful divine wrath may "burst/break out" at any time, not only against God's enemies, but also against his own people (Ex 19:22, 24; 1Ch 15:13; Job 16:14; Ps 60:1; 106:29). A string of names involving the element "Perez" began early in Israel's history when Judah's son was named Perez ("Breaking out"; see NIV note on Ge 38:29) because he had "broken out" of his mother's womb. In addition to Baal Perazim, another place name—Perez Uzzah ("The outbreak against Uzzah"; see NIV note at 6:8)—would soon arise, this time from the Lord's anger breaking out against a disobedient Israelite (6:8 = 1Ch 13:11).

In full retreat from the forces of Israel, the Philistines abandon "their idols" (v.21), which they probably brought onto the battlefield as protective talismans (see comment on 1Sa 4:3 concerning a similar use of the ark by the Israelites). Although other renderings have been suggested for *ʿăṣabbêhem* in this case (e.g., vessels or containers for carrying plunder [Tidwell, 211]; scimitars as religious images [F. Willesen, "The Philistine Corps of the Scimitar from Gath," *JSS* 3/4 (1958): 333–34]), the traditional translation is preferable in the light of 1 Chronicles 14:12, where the parallel has "their gods" (cf. also LXX). The purpose of carrying the Philistine idols away from the battlefield (v.21; cf. similarly 2Ch 25:14) was so that, at David's command and in accordance with Mosaic prescription (Dt 7:5, 25), they could be burned up (1Ch 14:12).

22–25 On an indeterminate subsequent occasion ("once more," v.22), the Philistines again "came up" (cf. "went up," v.17). The narrator echoes the first battle account by stating that they "spread out in the Valley of Rephaim" (see v.18 and comment). As before (v.19), David inquires of the Lord (v.23). Unlike earlier, however, this time David is told not to "go [straight] up" (v.23; see comment on v.19, where "go" renders the same Heb. verb). Apparently the first confrontation was with a smaller contingent of Philistines, whereas now a flanking movement ("circle around behind them") is strategically preferable. The Israelite attack is apparently to take place in front of a grove of "balsam" trees, although the identification of the kind of tree/shrub (*bᵉkāʾîm*) remains uncertain (the KJV, e.g. renders "mulberry"; the REB, "aspen"; the NAB, "mastic"; cf. Hertzberg, "mastic terebinth"). It may well be that the Valley of Baca (*bākāʾ*), in the vicinity of Jerusalem (Ps 84:5–6), received its name from the event recorded here.

The Lord instructs David to "move quickly" (v.24) as soon as he hears the sound of "marching" in the treetops. Related to a Hebrew root meaning "step, pace, march," the noun translated "marching" nevertheless occurs only here. Chaim Herzog and Mordechai Gichon, 80, make the intriguing suggestion that David, "aware of the fact that the daily breeze from the sea reaches the Jerusalem area at about noon,... timed his attack for this hour, so that the rustle of the trees would cover the steps of the stealthily approaching Israelites." However that may be, the significance of the sound in the treetops again stresses the divine initiative: "The LORD has gone out in front of you" (v.24), an almost verbatim echo of Judges 4:14, "Has not the LORD gone ahead of you?" (Carlson, 56–57; cf. also Gerbrandt, 148). Indeed, Howard ("The Case for Kingship," 113) calls attention to the contrast between the present text "and 1 Samuel 8:20, where Israel had asked for a king who would 'go out before us and fight our battles.'"

David, acting at God's command (a common OT response; cf. Ge 50:12; Ex 7:10, 20; Nu 8:3; Jos 4:8; Eze 12:7), "struck down" (the parallel in 1Ch 14:16 includes David's men by reading "they struck down") the Philistines (v.25, echoing "strike" in v.24; see comment on "defeated" in v.20). In describing the complete rout of the enemy, the narrator uses a common idiom of retreat in stating that they were pursued "all the way from" (cf. 1Sa 15:7) Gibeon (six miles northwest of Jerusalem; see comment on 2:12) to Gezer. A city in the northern foothills in the tribal territory of Ephraim just east of the Philistine plain, Gezer remained a Canaanite enclave because of the ultimate failure of the Israelites to drive out its inhabitants (Jos 16:3, 10; Jdg 1:29). Today called both Tell Jezer and Tell Abu Shusheh, Gezer is located fifteen miles due west of Gibeon and is one of the most important archaeological sites in the entire region. Philistine as well as Israelite remains have been unearthed there (cf. the early summary articles by H. Darrell Lance, "Gezer in the Land and in History," and William G. Dever, "Excavations at Gezer," *BA* 30/2 [1967]: 34–62).

"The biblical record does not claim that David actually conquered Philistia. He merely pushed the Philistines out of his territory as far as Gezer.... Without conquering, David was still able to maintain nominal control over Philistia" (Hoffmeier,

"Egypt as an Arm of Flesh: A Prophetic Response" [in Gileadi], 82). It is to David's credit that, under the Lord's direction, he knew when and how much to conquer. He has thus taken his place in history among those warriors who were at one and the same time courageous, clever, and compassionate. "Medieval chivalry chose David as one of its main paragons from among *les neuf-preux*.... The nine exemplary knights of Christendom, consisting of Joshua, David, Judas Maccabeus, Hector, Alexander, Caesar, Arthur, Charlemagne and Godefroi of Bouillon" (Herzog and Gichon, 75, 230–31 n.1).

NOTES

18 Ancient mythological texts from Ugarit refer to *rpum*, "a (semi-)divine guild of chariot-riding warriors" (B. Margulis, "A Ugaritic Psalm [RS 24.252]," *JBL* 89/3 [1970]: 301; Tidwell, 204; contra Marvin Pope, "The Cult of the Dead at Ugarit," in *Ugarit in Retrospect: Fifty Years of Ugarit and Ugaritic*, ed. Gordon Douglas Young [Winona Lake, Ind.: Eisenbrauns, 1981], 174). A striking parallel between the Ugaritic *rpum* and the biblical Rephaites is that both are stated to have been headquartered at Ashtaroth and Edrei in Transjordan (Jos 12:4; 13:12; cf. Margulis, "A Ugaritic Psalm," 293–94; Pope, "The Cult of the Dead at Ugarit," 172 n. 40).

21 עזב (*ʿzb*, "abandon") and עצב (*ʿṣb*, "idol") provide an excellent example of alliteration and assonance in the Hebrew text.

24 Patrick, 377–78, makes the quaint suggestion that בְּרָאשֵׁי (*bᵉrāʾšê*) "should not be rendered *in the tops* (for Men do not walk on the Trees) but *in the beginnings*; in the very entrance of the place, where the Mulberry Trees were planted: Where God intended to make a sound, as if a vast number of Men were marching to fall upon the *Philistines*." But ראשׁ (*rōʾš*) does in fact refer to the top(s) of trees elsewhere (Isa 17:6; Eze 17:4, 22), and when it is used in the sense of "beginning," it is almost always temporal rather than spatial. In any event, it is never a synonym for "entrance."

25 The MT's גֶּבַע (*gebaʿ*, "Geba") is a scribal error for גִּבְעוֹן (*gibʿôn*, "Gibeon"; cf. LXX; cf. also 1Ch 14:16), as virtually all commentators agree (cf. NIV note; in any case, Geba's location about five miles north-northeast of Jerusalem effectively removes it from the present context). Many assume further that Isaiah 28:21 refers to the event(s) here recorded (cf. Carlson, 56 n. 3; Blenkinsopp, 151 n. 30), although the episode related in Joshua 10:10–14 is another possible referent for the Isaiah passage.

2. The Ark Brought to Jerusalem (6:1–23)

OVERVIEW

Apart from its appearance in 1 Samuel 14:18 (see comment), the ark of the covenant has not been mentioned in the books of Samuel since 1 Samuel 7:2, where the narrator comments that it remained at Kiriath Jearim for twenty years. Although it is impossible to say whether 6:1–23 was originally a part of a longer narrative that began in 1 Samuel 4 (see comment on 1Sa 4:1b–7:17), the two accounts (compare esp. 1Sa 6 with 2Sa 6) are

> similar enough to suggest the lineaments of a type-scene: in both, there is a triumphal procession; in both, there is great rejoicing and the offering of thanksgiving sacrifices; in both, there is a wagon and oxen; in both, there is retribution for unwarranted proximity to the Ark; and in both, the itinerant Ark proves its sufficiency against its enemies and against the hazards of travel. (Rosenberg, 116)

Thus the story of the ark is now resumed in 2 Samuel 6. Since the "twenty years" of 1 Samuel 7:2 perhaps "refers to the period between the ark's return from Philistia [1Sa 6:21–7:1] until the battle reported in" 1 Samuel 7:7–13 (Klein, 65)—or alternatively until the end of Samuel's judgeship (1Sa 7:15)—to the twenty years must be added at least the forty years of Saul's reign (see comment on 1Sa 13:1) plus a few years into the reign of David, leading to a grand total of more than sixty years that the ark languished in exile (for a similar estimate based on "the well-established view that Shiloh was destroyed about 1050 BC and that David began to reign around the turn of the millennium," see Blenkinsopp, 145).

The account of the ark's arrival in Jerusalem is entirely consonant with similar ceremonies elsewhere in the ancient Near East.

> In light of ... Akkadian and Phoenician parallels ... we are in a position to understand 2 Samuel 6 as the record of a historically unique cultic event, viz., the ritual dedication of the City of David as the new religious and political capital of the Israelites, the people of Yahweh. The purpose of the ceremony was the sanctification of the City of David for the installation of the ark in the hope that Yahweh's presence would assure the success of David's government and the welfare of the people. (P. Kyle McCarter Jr., "The Ritual Dedication of the City of David in 2 Samuel 6," in Meyers and O'Connor, 276; cf. similarly Brueggemann, *First and Second Samuel*, 249)

So David adds to political centralization in Jerusalem a distinctly religious focus by bringing to the city the most venerable and venerated object of his people's past: the Lord's ark—repository of the covenant, locus of atonement, throne of the invisible Yahweh. It is no wonder that the story of the ark's solemn procession is told not only in 2 Samuel 6 but also in 1 Chronicles 13, 15–16, where the Chronicler, true to his affection for matters liturgical and Levitical, preserves numerous details not found in the more concise and matter-of-fact Samuel account. Close parallels between the two narratives, however, are nonetheless frequent: 1 Chronicles 13:5–14 echoes vv.1–11; 1 Chronicles 15:25–16:3 reprises vv.12b–19a, and 1 Chronicles 16:43 is the equivalent of vv.19b–20a. The Chronicler omitted the confrontation between David and Michal in vv.20b–23, perhaps because he construed it as presenting David in a somewhat unfavorable light.

Furthermore, direct quotations as well as reminiscences of 2 Samuel 6 and 1 Chronicles 13, 15–16 are scattered throughout several psalms. The Davidic Psalms 24 and 68 reflect on the ceremonial procession of the ark, probably for a later festival commemorating the event (cf. Ps 24:7–10, the last verse of which uses the name "LORD Almighty" [cf. 2Sa 6:2]; Ps 68:16–17, 24–27, 29, 35). Psalm 132, a song of ascents perhaps used at royal coronation ceremonies (cf. 132:18), appears to summarize events beginning with David's reign (including the arrival of the ark in Jerusalem: cf. 132:6–9 and especially the reference to Kiriath Jearim in 132:6 ["Jaar"]) and continuing through the early decades of Israel's monarchy (cf. the quotation of 132:8–10 in 2Ch 6:41–42). The ark narrative of 2 Samuel 6 (and its parallels in 1 Chronicles) may also have influenced the Korahite Psalm 47 (see esp. 47:5, 8) and the anonymous Psalm 99 (see esp. 99:1–2, 9).

Particularly impressive is David's psalm of thanks in 1 Chronicles 16:8–36, which has almost verbatim parallels in three additional anonymous psalms (1Ch 16:8–22 = Ps 105:1–15; 1Ch 16:23–33 = Ps 96; 1Ch 16:34–36 = Ps 106:1, 47–48). It has been suggested that the difficult Song of Songs 6:12 be translated "I knew not my heart; it made of me the chariots of Ammi-nadab" (cf. NIV note) in metaphorical reference to the "new cart(s)" that the "sons of Abinadab" (2Sa 6:3) used to transport the ark (for details see Raymond Jacques Tournay, *Word of God, Song of Love: A Commentary on the Song of Songs* [Mahwah, N.J.: Paulist, 1988], 98–106). All things considered, then, David's bringing the ark of the covenant of the Lord to the City of David in Jerusalem made a notable impact on Israel's history as reflected in substantial portions of several sections of the OT.

In addition to 2 Samuel 6 and 1 Chronicles 13:5–14; 15:25–16:3, 43, a third Hebrew text (4QSamuel[a]) witnesses to the events recorded here. Ulrich, 197 (cf. also 220–21), ranks the three texts as follows: 4QSamuel[a] is "the best," 1 Chronicles is "a close second," and the MT of Samuel, in this chapter as elsewhere, "retains its reputation as a poorly preserved text." The NIV notes on vv.3–5 confirm the overall accuracy of Ulrich's analysis, and the commentary below will make use of the readings from 4QSamuel[a] and 1 Chronicles.

In the overall structure of the larger narrative describing David's powerful reign (5:17–8:18), the story of the ark's journey to Jerusalem parallels the moving prayer of David as recorded in 7:18–29 (see Overview on 5:17–8:18). My analysis of 2 Samuel 6 is based on the following symmetrical outline, which attempts to divide the chapter into its natural components:

A David's unsuccessful attempt to transport the ark (6:1–5)
    B Judgment against Uzzah (6:6–11)
A' David's successful attempt to transport the ark (6:12–19)
    B' Judgment against Michal (6:20–23)

1David again brought together out of Israel chosen men, thirty thousand in all. 2He and
all his men set out from Baalah of Judah to bring up from there the ark of God, which
is called by the Name, the name of the LORD Almighty, who is enthroned between the
cherubim that are on the ark. 3They set the ark of God on a new cart and brought it from
the house of Abinadab, which was on the hill. Uzzah and Ahio, sons of Abinadab, were
guiding the new cart 4with the ark of God on it, and Ahio was walking in front of it. 5David
and the whole house of Israel were celebrating with all their might before the LORD, with
songs and with harps, lyres, tambourines, sistrums and cymbals.
6When they came to the threshing floor of Nacon, Uzzah reached out and took hold of
the ark of God, because the oxen stumbled. 7The LORD's anger burned against Uzzah because
of his irreverent act; therefore God struck him down and he died there beside the ark of God.
8Then David was angry because the LORD's wrath had broken out against Uzzah, and to
this day that place is called Perez Uzzah.

9 David was afraid of the LORD that day and said, "How can the ark of the LORD ever come
to me?" 10 He was not willing to take the ark of the LORD to be with him in the City of David.
Instead, he took it aside to the house of Obed-Edom the Gittite. 11 The ark of the LORD
remained in the house of Obed-Edom the Gittite for three months, and the LORD blessed
him and his entire household.

12 Now King David was told, "The LORD has blessed the household of Obed-Edom and
everything he has, because of the ark of God." So David went down and brought up the
ark of God from the house of Obed-Edom to the City of David with rejoicing. 13 When
those who were carrying the ark of the LORD had taken six steps, he sacrificed a bull and
a fattened calf. 14 David, wearing a linen ephod, danced before the LORD with all his might,
15 while he and the entire house of Israel brought up the ark of the LORD with shouts and
the sound of trumpets.

16 As the ark of the LORD was entering the City of David, Michal daughter of Saul watched
from a window. And when she saw King David leaping and dancing before the LORD, she
despised him in her heart.

17 They brought the ark of the LORD and set it in its place inside the tent that David had
pitched for it, and David sacrificed burnt offerings and fellowship offerings before the
LORD. 18 After he had finished sacrificing the burnt offerings and fellowship offerings, he
blessed the people in the name of the LORD Almighty. 19 Then he gave a loaf of bread, a
cake of dates and a cake of raisins to each person in the whole crowd of Israelites, both
men and women. And all the people went to their homes.

20 When David returned home to bless his household, Michal daughter of Saul came out
to meet him and said, "How the king of Israel has distinguished himself today, disrobing in
the sight of the slave girls of his servants as any vulgar fellow would!"

21 David said to Michal, "It was before the LORD, who chose me rather than your father
or anyone from his house when he appointed me ruler over the LORD's people Israel—I
will celebrate before the LORD. 22 I will become even more undignified than this, and I
will be humiliated in my own eyes. But by these slave girls you spoke of, I will be held in
honor."

23 And Michal daughter of Saul had no children to the day of her death.

COMMENTARY

1–5 The parallel passage in 1 Chronicles 13:5–8 is preceded by a paragraph (1Ch 13:1–4) in which David confers with his army officers (v.1) before announcing to the "whole assembly of Israel" (vv.2, 4) his plans to bring the "ark of our God" (v.3) to Jerusalem in accordance with the "will of the LORD our God" (v.2). The "territories of Israel" (v.2) to which the joyful news was sent included the area "from the Shihor River" (1Ch 13:5; probably either the northeastern section of the Pelusiac branch of the Nile in the eastern part of Egypt's delta or a frontier canal at the delta's edge) "to Lebo Hamath" (modern Lebweh, forty-five miles north of Damascus in the Beqa[c] of Lebanon).

Kiriath Jearim (see comment on 1Sa 6:21) is located about halfway "between Jerusalem and Gezer, which David had reached when pursuing his enemies (5:25). Here we have the associative point of departure for the incorporation of the account of the transfer of the Ark to Jerusalem, 6:1–23" (Carlson, 58). Thus the rout of the Philistines "all the way ... to Gezer" (5:25) enables David to consider the possibility of bringing Israel's most sacred object to the political nerve center of his realm.

For the third time ("again," v.1; cf. 5:17–21, 22–25) David assembles his troops (cf. similarly Blenkinsopp, 151), here to serve as a military escort for the ark of the covenant. David's "chosen men" (cf. 10:9 = 1Ch 19:10) are reminiscent of Saul's elite corps of soldiers (see comment on 1Sa 24:2)—although David's troops outnumber Saul's by a factor of ten, perhaps to underscore the significance and solemnity of David's mission (cf. Carlson, 64–65). While "thirty thousand" (cf. also 1Sa 4:10) perhaps means rather "thirty units of soldiers" here (see comment on 1Sa 4:2), it is also possible that the number is to be taken literally in this context.

Just as Kiriath Arba was an earlier name of Hebron (Jos 14:15; 15:13) and Kiriath Sepher of Debir (Jos 15:15), so also Kiriath Jearim ("City of forests") was doubtless the original name of "Baalah of Judah" (v.2 and first note in the NIV; cf. 1Ch 13:6; cf. similarly Blenkinsopp, 146–47). In summary, Kiriath Jearim (Jos 9:17; 15:9; 1Ch 13:5–6) = Kiriath Baal (Jos 15:60; 18:14) = Baal(ah) (Jos 15:9–10) = Baal(ah) of Judah (v.2; 1Ch 13:6). Furthermore, Jaar (Ps 132:6) is an abbreviated form of Kiriath Jearim (see NIV note on Ps 132:6; cf. also 132:8). Blenkinsopp, 147–48, observes (1) that Kiriath Jearim occupied the nodal point on the boundaries of Judah, Benjamin, and Dan, and (2) that expressions such as "Mount Jearim" (Jos 15:10), "Mount Baalah" (Jos 15:11), and "fields of Jaar" (Ps 132:6) suggest that the name Kiriath Jearim "may have covered a fairly large area" (ibid., 147, n. 16).

In any event, for half a century or more the ark of the covenant had been sequestered in "the house of Abinadab, which was on the hill" (v.3; see comments on 1Sa 7:1), either inaccessible to the Israelites because of Philistine control of the region or languishing in neglect (perhaps partially because King Saul had shown no interest in it; cf. 1Ch 13:3).

The solemnity of the scene that unfolds in ch. 6 is enhanced by the grandiose description of the ark and the repeated references to it. As in 1 Samuel 4:4 (see comment), the ark is depicted in v.2 as the seat of authority of "the LORD Almighty" (see comment on 1Sa 1:3), "who is enthroned between the cherubim" (cf. 2Ki 19:15 = Isa 37:16; Pss 80:1; 99:1).

It is also referred to as the "ark of God" (vv.2–4, 6–7, 12 [2x]) and the "ark of the LORD" (vv.9–11, 13, 15–17). Although there is no discernible reason for the alternation in the divine names in these expressions, it is noteworthy that in the chapter each of the names occurs seven times (the number of completion/perfection) in connection with the ark. Indeed, the ark "is called by the name/Name" (v.2), an idiom denoting ownership (BDB, 896; cf. 12:28 ["will be named after"]; 1Ki 8:43 ["bears your Name"]; 2Ch 7:14; Jer 25:29 ["bears my Name"]) and thus here emphasizing that the ark is the Lord's property.

The term "Name" (unmodified grammatically with a divine title following it), appearing in the books of Samuel only here and in 7:13, not only refers to the Lord's name but also stands for his presence (cf., e.g., Ex 23:21; Lev 24:11, 16; see also comment on 1Sa 25:25) and is especially common in Deuteronomy in connection with the centralized place of worship that the Lord would choose for his people in the Promised Land (Dt 12:5, 11, 21; 14:23–24; 16:2, 6, 11; 26:2). "From this deeper meaning of 'the name of God' we may probably explain the repetition of the word שֵׁם [*šēm*, 'name'], which is first of all written absolutely (as at the close of Lev. xxiv. 16), and then more fully defined as 'the name of the Lord of hosts'" (K&D, 330). הַשֵּׁם (*haššēm*, "The Name" [par excellence]), has often been used by Jews through the centuries as a reverent substitute for YHWH, the OT name above all names.

David's intention to "bring up" (v.2; cf. v.15) the ark to the City of David (cf. v.12) is of course not only commendable but also entirely appropriate (cf. 1Ki 8:1, which records Solomon's desire to "bring up" the ark from the City of David to the temple). At the same time, however, his first attempt to do so follows Philistine rather than Levitical procedure. David and his men "brought" (lit., "carried," v.3; cf. v.13) the ark from Abinadab's house by transporting it on a "new cart," the method earlier used by the Philistines (see 1Sa 6:7–8 and comments). If Abinadab had not already died, he was surely an elderly man by this time. It is therefore possible that Uzzah and Ahio were Abinadab's grandsons rather than his "sons" (v.3; the Heb. word for "son" often means "grandson," as in 9:9–10; 19:24). Their task was to guide the cart, Ahio walking in front (v.4) and Uzzah presumably bringing up the rear.

With David taking the lead, the whole "house of Israel" (v.5, with "house" being used here in the sense of "family, community"; see comment on 1Sa 7:2) begins "celebrating" (though sometimes associated with dancing [cf. 1Ch 15:29], celebrating is not identical to it; see comment on "danced" in 1Sa 18:7). In this context "before the LORD" (v.5; cf. v.14) is virtually tantamount to "before the ark" (a literal translation of "in front of it," v.4). "With all (their) might" is echoed verbatim in v.14 ("with all [his] might"; cf. Gunn, *The Story of King David*, 73–74) and contributes to the enthusiastic abandon that characterizes the chapter as a whole.

"Songs" (perhaps of victory; see comment on 1Sa 18:6), the singular of the Hebrew for which is sometimes equivalent to "music" (cf. 1Ch 25:6–7), introduce the list of accompanying musical instruments that follows. "Harps, lyres, tambourines" were staple elements on such joyful occasions (see comments on 1Sa 10:5; 16:16; 18:6). The "sistrum," mentioned only here in the OT, was used widely throughout the ancient Near East, especially in Egypt. It consisted of a handle fitted to "a metal loop with holes through which pieces of wire were inserted and bent at the ends. Since the holes were larger than the wire, the instrument produced a jingling sound when shaken. The Hebrew word comes from a verb which means 'shake;' so it is reasonable to suppose that the *menaᶜanᶜim* were sistra" (Sellers, 44–45).

"Cymbals" were of two kinds, one set of which were struck vertically (harsh/noisy cymbals) and the other horizontally (clear cymbals). The former may be reflected in the "clash of cymbals" and the latter in the "resounding cymbals" of Psalm 150:5. The cymbals here were probably clear cymbals (similar to but smaller than their modern descendants), bronze examples of which (cf. 1Ch 15:19) archaeologists have found at several sites in Israel (e.g., Beth Shemesh [cf. Sellers, 46, fig. 12:c]; Hazor [cf. Bathja Bayer, "The Finds That Could Not Be," *BAR* 8/1 [1982]: 24]). While not mentioning sistrums, the parallel passage in 1 Chronicles 13:8 concludes the list with "trumpets," resulting in a total of six different musical instruments used to accompany the first attempt to bring the ark from Kiriath Jearim to Jerusalem.

6–11 Just as "David and the whole house of Israel" (*dāwid wᵉkol-bêt yiśrāʾēl*) begins the last verse of the previous section (vv.1–5), so also "Obed-Edom and his entire household" (*ᶜōbēd ʾᵉdōm* *w*[e]*ʾet-kol-bêtô*) ends the last verse of the present section (vv.6–11). The contrast is stark: David and Israel's house celebrate while the ark is being mishandled, whereas Obed-Edom and his house are blessed because the ark is under his protection.

Since threshing floors were often places of sanctity (cf. 24:16, 18, 21, 24–25; Ge 50:10; 1Ki 22:10; Hos 9:1), the "threshing floor of Nacon" (v.6) may also have been a holy site (cf. Porter, 171). Unfortunately, it is mentioned only here ("Nacon" as a proper noun is a secondary reading in 1Sa 23:23; 26:4; see NIV notes there; see Notes on 1Sa 23:23), its location is unknown, and even the spelling of its name is uncertain (e.g., 1Ch 13:9 reads "Kidon" instead of "Nacon"). "Two verbs with which *nacon* could be connected are *kûn*, 'to be fixed or prepared', or *nākâ*, 'to smite'; indeed the latter occurs in verse 7 ['struck him down']. The name may have been coined to encapsulate memories of the disaster, witnessed by the great company of worshippers" (Baldwin, 207–8; cf. similarly Carlson, 78).

In any event, the threshing floor is fraught with peril for Uzzah (whose name, ironically, means "Strength," from the same Heb. root translated "might" in v.5). Sensing that the oxen pulling the cart were stumbling (v.6) and might therefore cause the ark to fall to the ground, Uzzah "reached out" (elliptical for "reached out his hand," as in 1Ch 13:9, 4QSam[a], and several ancient versions; cf. Ulrich, 195, and *BHS*) to steady the ark. In so doing he "took hold of" it, and thus his doom was sealed despite whatever good intentions he may have had.

The wrath of divine judgment fell on Uzzah "because of his irreverent act" (v.7), a phrase that is unique in the OT (for discussion see Carlson, 79) and that is understood in 1 Chronicles 13:10 to mean in this context, "because he had put his hand on the ark" (cf. also probably 4QSam[a]; Ulrich, 195). Although this act in itself would have been enough to condemn him, (1) Uzzah was transporting the ark in a cart rather than carrying it on his shoulders, and (2) there is no evidence that he was a Kohathite Levite in any event (see Nu 4:15; cf. similarly Terence Kleven ["Hebrew Style in II Samuel vi" (paper presented at the annual meeting of the ETS, New Orleans, La., November 1990), 6], who calls attention as well to such related texts as Ex 25:12–15; Nu 3:29–31; 7:9; Dt 10:8). Just as God had "struck down" and put to death some of the men of Beth Shemesh for looking into the ark (1Sa 6:19; cf. Nu 4:20), so also God "struck [Uzzah] down" (v.7) for touching the ark (cf. also 1Sa 5:6–12).

It is sometimes claimed that the ark, a wooden chest overlaid inside and out with gold (Ex 25:10–11), functioned as a huge Leyden jar that produced enough static electricity while bumping along the rocky road to electrocute Uzzah when he touched it. But it is also conceivable that a member of the ark's military escort used his spear (one Heb. word for which is *kîdōn* [cf. Jer 50:42], the name of the threshing floor according to 1Ch 13:9) to dispatch Uzzah. In any event, the Lord was the ultimate cause of Uzzah's death, whether or not he used secondary means to accomplish the act of judgment.

As though to emphasize the threshing floor as the locale of Uzzah's death, the narrator states not only that Uzzah died "there" but also that God struck him down "there" (omitted from the NIV in the interests of English style). An additional irony is that he died "beside" (*ʿim*, usually "with," but cf. similarly "near" in 1Sa 10:2) the ark, which he had been attempting to rescue from real or imagined harm. ("Beside the ark of God" [v.7] and "with the ark of God" [v.4] translate the same Heb. phrase.) John Stek, 69, observes that the fate of Uzzah brings to mind "the deaths of Nadab and Abihu, Lev. 10:1, 2; Achan, Josh. 7; and Ananias and Sapphira, Acts 5:1–11; all of whom failed to take Yahweh's rule seriously—at the dawn of new eras in the history of the kingdom of God."

The Lord's anger (v.7) causes David to react first with anger of his own (v.8) and then with fear (v.9). David is understandably indignant that the divine "wrath" (lit., "breaking out," v.8) has broken out against Uzzah and resulted in his death, a seemingly harsh penalty for so small an infraction. Indeed, it may have been David himself who named the place of Uzzah's death Perez Uzzah (v.8), "The outbreak against Uzzah" (see NIV note; see also comment on Baal Perazim in 5:20).

It is not surprising that David's anger against God should be mingled with fear of him (v.9). His fear was experienced "that day" (i.e., the day of Uzzah's death, as opposed to "this day" [v.8], the time of the narrator of 2 Samuel; see comment on 1Sa 6:18), in the light of which he questions whether the ark can "ever" (implied in the context, though not explicitly represented in the MT) come to him. Although written from a different perspective, Blenkinsopp's observation (151 n. 33) is surely correct: "The question of David ... is answered in the liturgy of Ps 24 (vss. 4f.)."

David decides that a cooling-off period is in order before he is willing to give further consideration, if any at all, to taking the ark to be "with him" (remembering what happened when it was with Uzzah) in the "City of David" (v.10, the new name so recently given to the fortress of Zion; see comment on 5:7). Instead, he gives the ark a temporary home in the house of "Obed-Edom" ("Servant of Edom," in which "Edom" is probably the name of either a god or a tribe; see Driver, 241) the Gittite.

While it is true that "Gittite" can refer to someone whose hometown was the Philistine city of Gath (cf. Goliath in 1Sa 17:4, 23; 2Sa 21:19), it is unlikely that David would entrust the ark to the care of a Philistine. Since *gat* is the ordinary word for "(wine)press," the epithet "Gittite" can be used with respect to any activity (cf. the enigmatic feminine form *gittît* in the titles of Pss 8; 81; 84) or place name (cf. Gath Hepher [Jos 19:13; 2Ki 14:25]; Gath Rimmon [Jos 19:45; 21:24–25; 1Ch 6:69]) related to winepresses. Indeed, it is even possible that Obed-Edom was originally from Gittaim ("Two [Wine]presses"; see Notes on 4:3).

In any case, despite the skepticism of some commentators (e.g., McCarter, Smith), Obed-Edom was a Levite (1Ch 15:17–18, 21, 24–25; 16:4–5, 38; Josephus, *Ant.* 7.83 [4.2])—in fact, he was a Kohathite Levite if Gath Rimmon in Dan or Manasseh was his hometown (Jos 21:20, 24–26; 1Ch 6:66, 69; cf. Kirkpatrick). The house of Obed-Edom was probably located "somewhere on the southwestern hill of Jerusalem" (Carlson, 79; on the two-site location of Jebusite Jerusalem see comment on 5:6). There the ark remained for three months (v.11), during which time the Lord blessed the house of Obed-Edom, as soon to be reflected in the confidence of David that the Lord would bless the house of David forever (7:29). In the case of Obed-Edom, the divine blessing (as often in the OT) would ultimately come in the form of numerous descendants: "62 in all" (1Ch 26:8; cf. "For God had blessed Obed-Edom," 1Ch 26:5).

12–19 That vv.12–19 constitute a literary unit is strengthened by the fact that vv.12b–19a are paralleled in 1 Chronicles 15:25–16:3. In addition v.12 begins with a reference to the Lord's blessing the household of Obed-Edom, while v.20, which starts the next unit, begins with a reference to David's blessing his own household. Finally, *wayyēlek* ("went") in vv.12 and 19 serves to frame the whole. (The NIV's unjustifiable translation "went down" in v.12 needlessly muffles the echo in v.19.)

True to form, the Chronicler precedes his parallel narrative with a lengthy account that details the functions of the Levites with respect to the triumphal procession of the ark (1Ch 15:1–24). In the center of his addendum, the Chronicler summarizes the reasons for the failure of the initial attempt to bring the ark to the City of David: "It was because you, the Levites, did not bring it up the first time that the LORD our God broke out in anger against us. We did not inquire of him about how to do it in the prescribed way" (1Ch 15:13).

Eventually David is told of the Lord's blessing on the house of Obed-Edom "because of the ark of God" (v.12). Sensing that it is therefore now safe to bring the ark up to the fortress, David proceeds to do so. In this endeavor he is accompanied by "the elders of Israel and the commanders of units of a thousand" (1Ch 15:25). Although David's leadership role is emphasized by the use of verbs in the singular number ("he sacrificed," v.13; "David sacrificed," v.17), the Chronicler is at pains to point out that David had help ("they sacrificed," 1Ch 15:26 [obscured by the NIV's rendering in the passive]; 16:1). If in the case of the first attempt there was celebration and singing (v.5), now there is "rejoicing" (v.12).

> Vss 13–14 are the central verses in the chapter which mark the changes David makes in the transportation of the ark.... First, individuals are now carrying the ark.... Second,... after the procession has marched six steps, David sacrifices.... Third,... David wears a linen ephod.... Each of the changes are [*sic*] a clue that laws for the transport of the ark are now being obeyed. The ark was not to be moved in the manner of the Philistines, but as enjoined by Israelite law. (Kleven, "Hebrew Style in II Samuel vi," 8–9)

"Those who were carrying the ark" (v.13) were, of course, (Kohathite) Levites (1Ch 15:26; cf. also 2Sa 15:24). Although v.13 may intend to state that when the Levites had taken six steps a bull and a fattened calf were sacrificed, after which the procession continued uninterrupted on its way to the City of David, Assyrian parallels make it more likely that sacrifices were offered every six steps (cf. McCarter, "Ritual Dedication" [in Meyers and O'Connor], 273–74, 277 n. 1; also Carlson, 80, 86). Given the proximity of the house of Obed-Edom to the City of David (see comment on v.10), such a procedure would not have been needlessly cumbersome or time-consuming. The six-step ritual may have been memorialized in the six steps of David's son Solomon's throne, where a total of twelve lions standing on the steps (1Ki 10:19–20) probably symbolized Israel's twelve tribes.

Oxen/bulls (v.13) were commonly sacrificed as "burnt offerings and fellowship offerings" (vv.17–18; cf. Lev 1:4–6; 4:10; 9:4, 18), and the "fattened calf" (v.13) would be sacrificed with increased frequency during Solomon's reign (1Ki 1:9, 19, 25; cf. also Lk 15:23–30). The "seven bulls and seven rams" of 1 Chronicles 15:26 (cf. also 4QSam[a]) are perhaps also to be understood as part of the overall picture of burnt offerings and fellowship offerings here described (for the use of rams as sacrifices, cf. Lev 9:2, 4).

Prefiguring the priestly functions of King David (v.14), the prophet Samuel had earlier worn a "linen ephod" (see 1Sa 2:18 and comment; cf. also 1Sa 22:18). First Chronicles 15:27 states that, in addition to the ephod, David was "clothed in a robe of fine linen," doubtless the "robe of the ephod" that was worn under the ephod itself (cf. Ex 28:31). During the time of the Israelite monarchy, kings occasionally officiated as priests (cf. 24:25; 1Ki 8:64; 9:25). At the same time, however,

> we must note that the instances where the king's personal action is beyond question are all very special or exceptional: the transference of the Ark, the dedication of the altar or sanctuary, the great annual festivals. Ordinarily, the conduct of worship was left to the priest (2 Kings 16:15). Anointing did not confer on the king a priestly character ... he was not a priest in the strict sense. [*AIs*, 114]

"With all his might" (v.14; cf. also v.5) David "danced" (or "[was] dancing," as in v.16; in both cases the verb is a participle) "before the LORD"—in this case before the ark, the symbol of the divine presence (see comment on v.5). The Hebrew verb translated "danced/dancing" is unique to this chapter, although it occurs in Ugaritic with the same meaning (cf. G. W. Ahlström, "KRKR and TPD," *VT* 28/1 [1978]: 100–101, responding to Y. Avishur, "KRKR in Biblical Hebrew and Ugaritic," *VT* 26/3 [1976]: 257–61, who argues that the verb means "play").

As "David and the whole house of Israel" (v.5) had celebrated during the earlier procession of the ark, so "he and the entire house of Israel" (v.15; the MT is the same in both cases) now "brought up" (or "were bringing up," a participial form; cf. "was entering," "leaping," "dancing" in v.16) the ark from the house of Obed-Edom. The scene is punctuated with "shouts" of excitement and triumph, as on a similar earlier occasion (see 1Sa 4:5–6 and comment; cf. also 2Ch 15:14: Ezr 3:11–13) and with the sound of ram's-horn "trumpets" (or perhaps "a trumpet," since the form is singular; cf. also Ps 47:5, which may be a reference to this event). First Chronicles 15:28 has "rams' horns and trumpets" (cf. the similar distinction between rams' horns and trumpets in Ps 98:6) as well as cymbals, lyres, and harps (instruments used also during the first procession of the ark; cf. v.5).

Halfway through the literary unit (vv.12–19) the narrator pauses to inject a discordant note (v.16). "Michal daughter of Saul" (so described because here and in v.20 she is depicted as being critical of David and is therefore "acting like a true daughter of Saul"; Clines, 272) "watched" the proceedings "from a window" (cf. Sisera's mother [Jdg 5:28]; Jezebel [2Ki 9:30]; the Heb. phrase is the same in all three cases). The "Frau im Fenster" ("woman at the window") may be

> the best-known motif in the Phoenician tradition of art, certainly the most common of the Phoenician ivory motifs.... There is only one example at Samaria, but it appears frequently at Nimrud and Khorsabad in Assyria, at Arslan Tash in Syria, and in Cyprus. Adorned with an Egyptian wig or headdress, the woman peers through a window within recessed frames overlooking a balcony balustrade (a low railing) supported by voluted (scroll-shaped) columns. (Philip J. King, *Amos, Hosea, Micah—An Archaeological Commentary* [Philadelphia: Westminster, 1988], 146)

(See also A. S. Murray, "Excavations at Enkomi," in *Excavations in Cyprus*, ed. A. S. Murray, A. H. Smith, and H. B. Walters [London: British Museum, 1900], 10, cited by Gloria A. London, "Canaan's Relations with Cyprus," in *100 Years of American Archaeology in the Middle East* [Boston: American Schools of Oriental Research, 2003], 157; Porter, 166; *ANEP*, figs. 131, 799.)

Perhaps still smarting from her earlier separation from her former husband Paltiel (cf. 3:13–16), Michal looks at her present husband, David, with something less than the love she at one time had for him (see 1Sa 18:20 and comment). Seeing him "leaping and dancing" (the same Heb. verbs in the Piel stem are not found in the OT outside the present context [for "dancing" see comment on v.14]; 1Ch 15:29 ["dancing and celebrating"] substitutes two Heb. verbs more commonly attested)—even though "before the LORD"—she reacts with disgust. Once Michal, Saul's daughter, had helped David escape through a window (1Sa 19:12); now, peering at him through a window, she despises him "in her heart" (v.16). And in striking contrast to the theme of "the lameness of Saul's heir (2 Sam 4:4) and to the exclusion of 'the lame' declared in 2 Sam 5:8b ... the agile David, 'leaping and dancing ... before the LORD' (v.16), *enters* the gates of his new capital and takes up residence in the royal 'house' (cf. 7:1)" (Anthony R. Ceresko, "The Identity of 'the Blind and the Lame' in 2 Samuel 5:8b," *CBQ* 63/1 [2001]: 28).

Although later returning to the encounter between David and Michal (vv.20–23), the narrator first concludes the story of the ark's procession into the City of David. The ark is brought in and "set" (the same Heb. verb is used similarly in 1Sa 5:2) in its predetermined place "inside the tent David had pitched for it" (v.17; cf. 2Ch 1:4). David had apparently pitched the tent at some time prior to his appointment of and conference with the personnel who accompanied the procession (cf. 1Ch 15:1, 3 with 16:1). "This construction of a new tabernacle to house the ark ... was necessitated by the destruction of the original Mosaic tent, evidently when the Philistines overran Shiloh about 1050 BC and carried away the ark" (Unger, 20; see also comment on 1Sa 4:11).

Apparently at a somewhat later date, another tabernacle was constructed and installed at the high place in Gibeon (1Ki 3:4; 1Ch 16:39; 21:29; 2Ch 1:3, 5, 13), about six miles northwest of Jerusalem (see comment on 2:12). Thus there were in effect two tabernacles: the one in Jerusalem serving as the repository for the ark (1Ch 16:37), and the one in Gibeon housing the other tabernacle furnishings (1Ch 16:39–40; cf. 1Ki 1:39; 2:28–30; 3:4). Nowhere in the books of Samuel, Kings, or Chronicles is the ark associated with Gibeon or with a sanctuary there. Just before Solomon's prayer at the dedication of the temple, the priests "brought up the ark of the LORD ['from Zion, the City of David,' 1Ki 8:1] and the Tent of Meeting and all the sacred furnishings in it [from Gibeon]" (1Ki 8:4). Although reference to the Gibeon tabernacle as the one that "Moses the LORD's servant had made in the desert" (2Ch 1:3; cf. 1Ch 21:29) may mean the original Mosaic tabernacle had survived for over four hundred years, the phrase can also be taken in a metaphorical sense (i.e., the Gibeon tabernacle was made in strict accordance with the Mosaic pattern).

During the time the Mosaic tabernacle was not in use (for whatever reason), various offerings continued to be sacrificed without necessary benefit of the bronze altar of burnt offering. Thus David sacrifices "burnt offerings and fellowship offerings" (v.17; cf. also 24:25; 1Sa 13:9) as an act of gratitude (cf. 1Sa 6:14–15) and consecration (cf. 1Ki 8:63–64) "before the LORD" (i.e., honoring the divine presence symbolized by the ark). In particular, the fellowship offering (traditionally, "peace offering"; see NIV note) signified the desire of the worshipers to rededicate themselves to God in covenantal allegiance and to reaffirm their king as God's covenanted temporal ruler (see comment on 1Sa 11:15). It is therefore possible that the present ritual procedures also imply David's formal (re)investiture as king over Israel in Jerusalem, especially in the light of Mesopotamian *šulmānu* ("present, gift," thus "peace offering") parallels (cf. James W. Flanagan, "Social Transformation and Ritual in 2 Samuel 6," in Meyers and O'Connor, 368–69).

After bringing an unspecified number of offerings (vv.17–18), David blesses the *ʿam* ("people" [v.18] in this case rather than "troops," since "both men and women" are included [v.19]). Because the act of blessing was a function of spiritual leadership (cf. 1Sa 2:20; also Ge 14:18–19), David once again performs the role of a priest (see comment on v.14). As he had challenged Goliath "in the name of the LORD Almighty" (see comment on 1Sa 1:3)—that is, as the Lord's representative (see comment on 1Sa 17:45)—so he blesses Israel in the same powerful name (v.18). Carlson, 89, observes: "Just as the removal of the Ark from Kiriath-jearim was begun with the calling out of the divine name over the Ark [v.2], so the enterprise was concluded with a blessing pronounced in the same divine name." Thus "the name of the LORD Almighty" (vv.2, 18) forms a literary and theological inclusio that frames the account of the procession of the ark of the covenant of the Lord.

David adds to his blessing the distribution of food (v.19), an association also found in Psalm 132:15 (an ark-procession psalm [see Overview to 6:1–23]; cf. Porter, 168). The universal nature of the royal largesse could hardly be stated more explicitly in the MT: (lit.) "to all the people, to the whole crowd of Israelites, both men and women, to each person." Although staple foods, at least one of the three items given by David to the people ("cake of raisins") is found once in a ritual context (Hos 3:1). "Cake of dates" as the meaning of *ʾešpār*, which is attested only here (and in the parallel in 1Ch 16:3), is secured by an Arabic cognate (cf. Koehler, 15; KB, 95). The italics in the KJV rendering ("good piece *of flesh*") in this case demonstrate uncertainty (for a defense of the KJV, as well as for a critique of an even more fanciful interpretation ["sixth part of a bullock"], see Patrick, 388). To summarize (Martin, 38):

> The blessing of the people and the giving out of cakes made with fruit (an Oriental fertility motif) was [*sic*] a sign to the people that now that God was in their midst and now that they were dedicated to living according to the covenant there would be fertility in the land. Such was the significance of David's sending each one to his own house (6:19).

20–23 Just as the preceding section (vv.12–19) began with a blessing on a household (v.12), so also does the present section. Having blessed the Israelites who witnessed the procession of the ark (v.18), David returns home to "bless" his own household (v.20). Although the Hebrew verb sometimes means "greet" (preferred here by Alter, *The Art of Biblical Narrative*, 124), Carlson, 92 n. 3, is surely correct in stating that such a connotation in this context "is far too weak," especially in the light of the frequent use of the verb earlier in the chapter (vv.11–12, 18). Indeed, the contrast between the inevitable success of the Lord's blessing on the household of Obed-Edom (see v.11 and comment) and the failure of David's aborted blessing on his own household (see comment on v.23) is striking.

When a warrior returned victorious from battle, the women of his hometown would come out to meet him and would celebrate with music and dancing (see comment on 1Sa 18:6). David might have expected his wife, "Michal daughter of Saul" (see comment on v.16), to celebrate his similar triumph in much the same way. If so, he is quickly disappointed: "Until the final meeting between Michal and David, at no point is there any dialogue between them—an avoidance of verbal exchange particularly noticeable in the Bible, where such a large part of the burden of narration is taken up by dialogue. When that exchange finally comes, it is an explosion" (Alter, *The Art of Biblical Narrative*, 123).

Although only one sentence long (v.20), Michal's words drip with the "How" of sarcasm (cf. Job 26:2–3; Jer 2:23): David, the "king of Israel" (an office once occupied by her father, Saul), has "distinguished himself" (lit., "honored himself," as in v.22 ["be held in honor"]; see comment on "highly respected" in 1Sa 9:6). Michal punctuates her disdain by doubly emphasizing the time of the event (in the MT "today" appears again after "disrobing") as well as by underscoring the act itself three times (in addition to the NIV's "disrobing," the final clause of the verse reads lit.: "as any vulgar fellow, disrobing, would disrobe"; for the uniqueness of the infinitive construct followed by the infinitive absolute, see Driver, 272). It may be that the "repeated expression indicates continual action: 'uncovered himself like [vulgar fellows] go and uncover themselves'" (Carlson, 91).

To what extent David's state of undress was scandalous (cf. Alter, *The David Story*, 229: "The verb 'to expose' is clearly used in the sexual sense") is impossible to say (earlier he had been wearing at least a "linen ephod" [v.14] and a "robe of fine linen" [1Ch 15:27])—although Josephus claims that, at least by the time of Michal's outburst, he was "naked" (*gymnoumenos*; Josephus, *Ant.* 7.87 [4.3]). Hints of this sort (including also mention of "slave girls" in vv.20, 22) have led some commentators to detect orgiastic overtones in David's dancing and/or to assume that "it was a prelude to the sacred marriage" rite (Porter, 166). Such extreme interpretations, however, do not tally well with David's own explanation of his actions in vv.21–22. Far from the kind of "vulgar fellow" (lit., "empty, worthless person," v.20; cf. Jdg 9:4 ["adventurers"]; 11:3; 2Ch 13:7) who would be an exhibitionist in the sight of the slave girls of his "servants" (or "officers," another possible rendering of *ᶜᵃbādîm*; see comment on 1Sa 16:15–16), David makes it clear that he is very much concerned about how the Lord evaluates his actions.

The centerpiece in the literary unit in which it appears, David's response (vv.21–22) to Michal (not called "daughter of Saul" in v.21, perhaps because "attention now focuses on David, who is the subject of the sentence" [Clines, 272]) is honest and direct. He begins and ends his first sentence by insisting that he is celebrating "before the LORD" (noted also by Brueggemann, *First and Second Samuel*, 252; cf. vv.14, 16), not before the slave girls. In his rebuke of Michal, David takes pains to dissociate himself from Saul ("your father") and the Saulides by asserting that God had chosen him rather than them, a sentiment shared by the representatives of Israel's tribes (5:2).

David, of course, knows that the Lord had in fact chosen Saul (see 1Sa 10:24 and comment), but he also knows that Saul's abortive kingship has been replaced by his own anointed reign (cf. 1Sa 16:8–13; 1Ki 8:16 = 2Ch 6:5–6; 1Ch 28:4; Ps 78:70). David is "ruler" (*nāgîd*) over Israel by divine appointment (see 1Sa 13:14 ["leader"] and comment; cf. also 1Sa 25:30), as his son Solomon would be after him (cf. 1Ki 1:35). The phrase "ruler over the LORD's people Israel" (v.21) contains distinct echoes of "my people Israel, and you will become their ruler" in 5:2 (Gunn, *The Story of King David*, 74). Thus David, in a spirit of gratitude and dedication, is quick to "celebrate before the LORD" (v.21), as he had been during the first (unsuccessful) attempt to bring the ark to Zion (see v.5 and comment; cf. further Dt 12:7; 16:1).

David now preempts the verb *kābēd* (lit., "be heavy"; GK 3877) used by Michal in v.20 ("distinguished himself") and opposes it to the verb *qālal* (lit., "be light"; GK 7837). He revels in the fact that he will become even more "undignified" (*qll*, v.22) than he now appears, to the extent that he will be "humiliated" (lit., "low"; cf. similarly Mal 2:9) in his own "eyes" (as opposed to the "sight" of the slave girls [v.20]—the same Heb. noun in both cases). But by those same slave girls (v.22), whom Michal herself has already mentioned (v.20)—"by them" (emphatic; *ᶜimmām* left untrans. in NIV)—David will be "held in honor" (*kbd*; cf. the description of David's mighty men in 23:19, 23).

The counterpoise between *kbd* and *qll* also appears elsewhere in the books of Samuel. In 1 Samuel 2:30 the Lord says, "Those who honor [*kbd*] me I will honor [*kbd*], but those who despise me will be disdained [*qll*]." And in the earlier ark narrative in 1 Samuel 6, the Philistine priests and diviners suggest to their questioners that they should "pay honor [*kbd*] to Israel's god. Perhaps he will lift [*qll*] his hand from you.... Why do you harden [*kbd*] your hearts as the Egyptians and Pharaoh did?" (1Sa 6:5–6). In such passages there is something of "the exalted being humbled and the humbled being exalted (Matt. 23:12; Luke 14:11; 18:14). David is indeed the one who humbles himself and who, by the power of God, is exalted" (Brueggemann, *First and Second Samuel*, 253).

The chapter ends on a somber note: "Michal daughter of Saul" remains childless to her dying day (v.23). The use of the patronymic in this case "presumably means: 'Here is the punishment for an opponent of David the divinely chosen king', and perhaps also: 'So David fails to legitimise his succession to Saul's throne through Michal'" (Clines, 272). In ancient times childlessness, whether natural or enforced, was the ultimate tragedy for a woman (see comment on 1Sa 1:2). Negative connotations are also implied in the expression "to the day of (one's) death" (cf. 1Ki 15:5; see also 1Sa 15:35 and comment). "The whole story of David and Michal concludes on a poised ambiguity through the suppression of casual explanation: Is this a punishment from God, or simply a refusal by David to share her bed, or is the latter to be understood as the agency for the former?" (Alter, *The David Story*, 230).

While the Lord's blessing on Obed-Edom resulted in a large number of descendants for him (see comment on v.11), David's intended blessing on his own household (v.20) was effectively nullified by Michal's tragic criticism of her husband. Her resulting childlessness "gave David the opportunity to pass the leadership on to his sons by other wives.... The return of Michal and her barrenness serve as the pivot upon which the transition of ruling houses turned" (Flanagan, "Social Transformation and Ritual in 2 Samuel 6," 367).

At the same time, David's treatment of Michal is less than exemplary. In this respect Alter's summary (*The Art of Biblical Narrative*, 124–25; cf. 1Sa 18:20, 28; 19:11–17) is worth pondering:

> The writer ... does not question the historically crucial fact of David's divine election, so prominently stressed by the king himself at the beginning of his speech; but theological rights do not necessarily justify domestic wrongs, and the anointed monarch of Israel may still be a harsh and unfeeling husband to the woman who has loved him and saved his life.

NOTES

1 The two Hebrew words that begin the narrative of David's first attempt to transport the ark (vv.1–5) echo those that begin the narrative of his second battle against the Philistines (5:22–25): Compare וַיֹּסִפוּ עוֹד (*wayyōsipû ʿôd*, "Once more" [lit., "they added again"], 5:22; root *ysp*) with וַיֹּסֶף עוֹד (*wayyōsep ʿôd*, "again brought together," 6:1; root *ʾsp*). That the MT's וַיֹּסֶף (*wayyōsep*, "added," an auxiliary verb) stands for וַיֶּאֱסֹף (*wayyeʾesōp*, "brought together") is clear from the parallel in 1 Chronicles 13:5, where the text reads וַיַּקְהֵל (*wayyaqhēl*, "assembled"). The elision of א (ʾ) also occurs elsewhere in first-radical-ʾ verbs in the books of Samuel (e.g., 20:9; 1Sa 28:24; cf. J. Stek, "What Happened to the Chariot Wheels of Exod 14:25?" *JBL* 105/2 [1986]: 293–302, esp. 293).

כָּל־בָּחוּר בְּיִשְׂרָאֵל (*kol-bāḥûr beyiśrāʾēl*, "every chosen man in Israel"; "out of Israel chosen men" [NIV], v.1) and כָּל־בֵּית יִשְׂרָאֵל (*kol-bêt yiśrāʾēl*, "the whole house of Israel," v.5) form an inclusio that gives literary unity to vv.1–5.

2 Although the first NIV note states that בַּעֲלֵי יְהוּדָה (*baʿalê yehûdâ*) is "a variant of *Baalah of Judah*" (cf. 1Ch 13:6), it is surely better to assume, with M. H. Segal, 199 n. 24, that the "final *yod* [on בעלי, *bʿly*] was dittographed from the initial *yod* in the next word [יהודה, *yhwdh*]." The resulting "Baal of Judah" would then be another way of expressing "Kiriath Baal (that is, Kiriath Jearim), a town of the people of Judah" (Jos 18:14; cf. also Ulrich, 204; Driver, 265–66).

As the second NIV note indicates, the MT's שֵׁם (*šēm*, "[the] name") appears only once in the LXX and Vulgate (and probably also in 4QSam[a]; cf. Ulrich, 194). Instead of the first occurrence, many MSS have שָׁם (*šām*, "there"), which, however, makes less sense and in any case is probably influenced by מִשָּׁם (*miššām*, "from there") earlier in the verse.

3 Although the name Ahio could be revocalized to mean "his brother/brothers," Ahio ("Brother/kinsman of the LORD") is attested as a proper name elsewhere in the OT (1Ch 8:31; 9:37).

4 At the beginning of the verse, the MT repeats "and brought it from the house of Abinadab, which was on the hill" from v.3. The dittography in the MT—doubtless caused by the fact that "new cart," which appears before the two clauses in v.3, recurs at the end of that verse—is not found in 4QSamuel[a] (cf. Ulrich, 195) or in some MSS of the LXX (see NIV note on vv.3–4).

5 The MT's בְּכֹל עֲצֵי בְרוֹשִׁים (*bᵉkōl ʿᵃṣê bᵉrôšîm*, "with all [kinds] of wood[en instruments made] of pine") is doubtless a scribal error for בְּכָל־עֹז וּבְשִׁירִים (*bᵉkol-ʿōz ûbᵉšîrîm*, "with all [their] might, with songs"; cf. NIV note; also Ulrich, 195), especially since "with all [his] might" (v.14) echoes v.5.

צֶלְצְלִים (*ṣelṣelîm*, "cymbals") appears elsewhere in the OT only in Psalm 150:5 (2x). The parallel text in 1 Chronicles 13:8 substitutes מְצִלְתַּיִם (*mᵉṣiltayim*), a dual form found frequently in Chronicles and once each in Ezra and Nehemiah. Although the latter has understandably been considered an apparently later equivalent of *ṣelṣelîm* (BDB, 853), its attestation in Ugaritic (*mṣltm*) opens up the possibility of early origin and a northern provenance (cf. Stanley Gevirtz, "Of Syntax and Style in the 'Late Biblical Hebrew'–'Old Canaanite' Connection," *JANESCU* 18 [1986]: 25–26 and n. 7).

6 For the MT's נכון (*nkwn*), the parallel in 1 Chronicles 13:9 reads כידן (*kydn*) and 4QSamuel[a] reads either נודן (*nwdn*) or נידן (*nydn*; cf. Ulrich, 195). The letters ד (*d*), כ (*k*), and נ (*n*) are similar enough to one another not only to account for all the readings but also to make it difficult if not impossible to choose between them (Ulrich, 213).

7 שַׁל (*šal*), the key word in עַל־הַשַּׁל (*ʿal-haššal*, "because of his irreverent act"), may be cognate to the Aramaic שָׁלוּ (*šālû*, "neglect"; Ezr 4:22; 6:9 ["fail"]; Da 6:4 ["negligent"]; cf. Carlson, 79). If so, של (*šl*) should perhaps be read as שלו (*šlw*), the ו (*w*) on the following word (וימת, *wymt*) doing double duty (cf. Watson, 531).

16 At the beginning of the verse, the MT reads והיה (*whyh*), which usually means "and it will be." 4QSamuel[a] and 1 Chronicles 15:29, however, read correctly ויהי (*wyhy*, "and it was"; cf. LXX's καὶ ἐγένετο, *kai egeneto*).

3. The Lord's Covenant with David (7:1–17)

OVERVIEW

Although it is helpful to consider ch. 7 as an integral whole in the sense that 7:18–29 is David's prayerful response to Nathan's oracle (7:4–17), which in turn is introduced by a temporal and spatial backdrop (7:1–3), there is virtually unanimous agreement among scholars that 7:1–17 constitutes a discrete literary unit within the Deuteronomic history. As such it is the center and focus of (1) the narrative of David's powerful reign over Israel (see Overview to 5:17–8:18), (2) the story of David's life as a whole (cf. similarly Gerbrandt, 160), and indeed (3) the Deuteronomic history itself (cf. similarly Carlson, 127; McCarthy, "II Samuel 7," 131, 134, 137; see comment on 1Sa 12:1–5).

In fact, from a theological standpoint 7:1–17 (or 7:1–29) is the "highlight of the Books of Samuel ... if not of the Deuteronomistic History as a whole" (Anderson, 112; cf. also Brueggemann, *First and Second Samuel*, 253). Cross (*Canaanite Myth and Hebrew Epic*, 252) "finds it surprising that more attention has not been given to the Deuteronomistic idiom of the chapter. It fairly swarms with expressions found elsewhere in works of the Deuteronomistic school," many of which will be noted below. "[Second] Samuel 7 is rightly regarded as an 'ideological summit,' not only in the 'Deuteronomistic History' but also in the Old Testament as a whole" (Gordon, *I and II Samuel*, 235).

Heinz Kruse, 139–41, enumerates more than forty separate texts that may have been influenced by Nathan's prophecy, ranging widely through the Pentateuch, the Former and Latter Prophets, and the Writings—and including a few references in the books of the Apocrypha as well. Other passages could easily be added to the list (cf. Ronald E. Clements, "The Deuteronomistic Interpretation of the Founding of the Monarchy in I Sam. VIII," *VT* 24/4 (1974): 399 n. 3). Given such statistics, it would be difficult to dispute the contention of Jon D. Levenson ("The Davidic Covenant and Its Modern Interpreters," *CBQ* 41/2 [1979]: 205–6) that the Lord's covenant with David "receives more attention in the Hebrew Bible than any covenant except the Sinaitic."

"This chapter was to become the source of the messianic hope as it developed in the message of prophets and psalmists" (Baldwin, 213; cf. also Gordon, *I and II Samuel*, 236; Brueggemann, *First and Second Samuel*, 257; Carlson, 127). Judging from 4QFlorilegium, a midrash on 7:10b–14a (cf. Geza Vermes, trans., *The Complete Dead Sea Scrolls in English* [rev. ed.; London: Penguin, 2004], 525–26), the Qumran sectarians also detected clear messianic overtones in Nathan's oracle (see commentary below). It remained for the NT, however, to exploit fully the messianic implications inherent in 7:4–17. While it is true that direct citations of ch. 7 are few and far between (vv.8, 14 in 2Co 6:18; v.14 in Heb 1:5), various elements of the Davidic covenant are alluded to in the NT again and again, as the commentary will demonstrate. Indeed, Stephen concludes his summary of Israel's history with transparent references to the divine promise to David, "who enjoyed God's favor and asked that he might provide a dwelling place for the God of Jacob. But it was Solomon who built the house for him.... 'What kind of house will you build for me? says the Lord. Or where will my resting place be?'" (Ac 7:46–47, 49).

Although ch. 7 nowhere contains the word "covenant," it is universally recognized that it describes the Lord's covenant with David (cf. its inclusion among the covenants listed under *b^erît* ["covenant"] in BDB, 136). Several OT texts do in fact refer to Nathan's oracle as the exposition of a "covenant" established by the Lord with his servant (cf. 23:5; 1Ki 8:23; 2Ch 13:5; Pss 89:3, 28, 34, 39; 132:12; Isa 55:3; Jer 33:21; also Sir 45:25), and covenantal terminology appears at various points in the chapter as well (see, e.g., comments on "love" in v.15 and "good things" in v.28).

The precise nature of the Davidic covenant, long a matter of dispute (usually cast in terms of whether it is "conditional," "unconditional," or a combination of the two), has been illuminated by Weinfeld's important distinction (184–85, italics his):

> Two types of official judicial documents had been diffused in the Mesopotamian cultural sphere from the middle of the second millennium onwards: the political treaty which is well known to us from

> the Hittite empire and the royal grant, the classical form of which is found in the Babylonian *kudurru* documents (boundary stones).... The structure of both types of these documents is similar. Both preserve the same elements: historical introduction, border delineations, stipulations, witnesses, blessings and curses. Functionally, however, there is a vast difference between these two types of documents. While the "treaty" constitutes an obligation of the vassal to his master, the suzerain, the "grant" constitutes an obligation of the master to his servant. In the "grant" the curse is directed towards the one who will violate the rights of the king's vassal, while in the treaty the curse is directed towards the vassal who will violate the rights of his king. In other words, the "grant" serves mainly to protect the rights of the *servant* while the treaty comes to protect the rights of the *master*. What is more, while the grant is a reward for loyalty and good deeds already performed, the treaty is an inducement for future loyalty.

Weinfeld, 185, goes on to assert that the Davidic covenant is of the grant type, not the vassal type. As the promissory covenant included gifts bestowed on the vassal for loyally serving his master, so "David was given the grace of dynasty because he served God with truth, righteousness and loyalty (I Kings III, 6; cf. IX, 4, XI, 4, 6, XIV, 8, XV, 3)."

Although it would be tempting to characterize the treaty/obligatory/law type of covenant as "conditional" and the grant/promissory/oath type as "unconditional" without further ado, the truth of the matter is far more complex (cf. Ronald F. Youngblood, "The Abrahamic Covenant: Conditional or Unconditional?" in *The Living and Active Word of God: Essays in Honor of Samuel J. Schultz*, ed. Morris Inch and Ronald Youngblood [Winona Lake, Ind.: Eisenbrauns, 1983], 31–46). Weinfeld, 195–96, himself admits to a conditional element within the Davidic covenant, although he attributes it (needlessly, in my judgment) to "the Deuteronomist, the redactor of the Book of Kings." That the grant type of covenant, by its very nature, tends toward unconditionality by no means eliminates the possibility of its having conditions or obligations, which in any case comprise the essence of the covenantal concept itself (cf. Youngblood, "The Abrahamic Covenant," 33, 35, 37–38, 45).

It is not surprising, therefore, that many commentators find one or more conditional elements in Nathan's oracle (Kruse, 159; Gerbrandt, 166–69; Carlson, 126 and n. 5; Mettinger, 143–45; E. Theodore Mullen, Jr., "The Sins of Jeroboam: A Redactional Assessment," *CBQ* 49/2 [1987]: 216 n. 12; *The Scofield Reference Bible*, ed. C. I. Scofield (New York: Oxford Univ. Press, 1909], 362 n. 2; Ronald W. Pierce, "Spiritual Failure, Postponement, and Daniel 9," *TJ* 10/2 [Fall 1989]: 219 n. 34; William J. Dumbrell, "The Prospect of Unconditionality in the Sinaitic Covenant" [in Gileadi], 154 n. 1; Avraham Gileadi, "The Davidic Covenant: A Theological Basis for Corporate Protection" [in Gileadi], 159).

Waltke notes, on the one hand, that "YHWH's grant to David places no obligations on David for its enactment or perpetuation. It is unilateral, and in that sense unconditional" (Bruce K. Waltke, "The Phenomenon of Conditionality within Unconditional Covenants" [in Gileadi], 130). On the other hand, however, "the explicit condition put upon the Davidic covenant, extending the irrevocable grant only to a faithful son who keeps the obligations of the treaty, is found not only in putative D[euteronomist] (compare 1 Kings 2:4; 6:12–13; 8:25; 9:4 ff.) but also in the apparently ancient Psalm 132 [vv.11–12]" (ibid., 132; cf. also 23:5–7; 1Ki 3:14; 2Ch 6:16; 7:17–22; Jer 22:1–9). To summarize:

> In reiterating the terms of the Davidic covenant to Solomon (1 Kings 9:4–9), eminently clear conditions are laid down by God. The tension between divine commitment to an unalterable promise

> on the one hand and the inexorable human bent toward sin on the other is explored in Psalm 89 and in 132:11–12.... The fact that a covenant that is everlasting from the divine standpoint may in the course of time be broken by sinful human beings need not give us pause (cf. Isa 24:5). (Youngblood, "The Abrahamic Covenant," 41)

Outside the OT, the closest ancient Near Eastern parallels to the Davidic covenant of grant are Hittite and Assyrian documents (Weinfeld, 189; cf. also Weinfeld, "Addenda to *JAOS* 90 [1970], 184ff.," *JAOS* 92/3 [1972]: 468–69) rather than the Egyptian *Königsnovelle* ("King's Letter"; contrast Martin Noth, *The Laws in the Pentateuch and Other Studies* [Philadelphia: Fortress, 1967], 257 and n. 23). "The Akkadian royal inscriptions provide close analogies to 2 Samuel 7.... Since the Assyrian texts range in date from the third and second millennia to 859 BC, they provide us with a good opportunity to trace the development of literary patterns through the centuries until the time of David and Solomon" (Laato, 248).

Within the OT itself, the grant type of covenant includes the Noahic (Ge 9:8–17) and Abrahamic (Ge 12:1–3; 15:1–21; 17:1–27) as well as the covenant with Phinehas (Nu 25:10–13). Relationships between the Abrahamic and Davidic covenants are especially close (cf. Clements, 47–60; James Freeman Rand, "Old Testament Fellowship with God," *BSac* 109/433 [1952]: 52).

The most important OT covenant of the treaty type is the Mosaic/Sinaitic (Ex 19–24). Of course, differences between the two types of covenant should not be allowed to obscure their similarities or to set them in opposition to each other. Waltke ("The Phenomenon of Conditionality" [in Gileadi], 125, 135) argues: "YHWH's grants and treaty do not rival or exclude, but complement one another.... YHWH irrecoverably committed himself to the house of David, but rewarded or disciplined individual kings by extending or withholding the benefits of the grant according to their loyalty or disloyalty to His treaty" (cf. also Clements, 53; McCarthy, "II Samuel 7," 136; Youngblood, "The Abrahamic Covenant," 42; Levenson, citing Ps 78:68–72 ["The Davidic Covenant," 218]). The period of the judges, with its recurring cycle of rebellion/retribution/repentance/restoration (cf. Jdg 2:11–19; Ne 9:26–29), made it clear that Israel's corporate vassalage to Yahweh as divine suzerain was virtually impossible to realize. Thus,

> the Davidic covenant did away with the necessity that all Israel—to a man—maintain loyalty to YHWH in order to merit his protection. In the analogy of suzerain-vassal relationships, David's designation as YHWH's "son" and "firstborn" (2 Sam 7:14; Pss 2:6–7; 89:27) legitimized him as Israel's representative—as the embodiment of YHWH's covenant people, also called his "son" and "firstborn" (Exod 4:22).... Henceforth, the king stood as proxy between YHWH and his people. (Gileadi, "The Davidic Covenant" [in Gileadi], 160)

Indeed, Frederick C. Prussner finds ("The Covenant of David and the Problem of Unity in Old Testament Theology," in *Transitions in Biblical Scholarship* [Essays in Divinity 6; ed. J. Coert Rylaarsdam; Chicago: Univ. of Chicago Press, 1968], 29–41) in the conjunction of the Sinaitic and Davidic covenants the theological center of OT faith.

The location of ch. 7 in its present position is doubtless thematic rather than chronological. Nathan's oracle came to David after "the LORD had given him rest from all his enemies around him" (v.1)—but the account of David's defeat of his enemies is related in 8:1–14 (cf. also 23:9–17). As Merrill, 243, observes: "It was not until these kingdoms [Philistia, Moab, Zobah, Damascus, Ammon, Amalek, Edom] were actually subdued that David turned wholeheartedly to religious pursuits." Along similar lines, David's "palace" (v.1) was probably not constructed until relatively late in his reign (see comment on 5:11).

Pursuing his proposal that the Davidic covenant describes a grant recognizing prior loyal vassalage, Weinfeld, 187 n. 28, suggests that ch. 7 follows ch. 6 because "the promise of dynasty to David is to be seen as a reward for his devotion," while Porter, 169, sees the link between the two chapters as springing from the posited mutual relationship to Psalm 132. And whereas Kruse, 150, asserts that if the Davidic covenant was a reward, "we may suppose that it was given before David proved himself unworthy of it by his sin against Uriah (2 Sam. xi)," Waltke ("The Phenomenon of Conditionality" [in Gileadi], 131) proposes more plausibly that by placing ch. 11 after ch. 7 the narrator "subtly instructs us that the beneficiaries' darkest crimes do not annul the covenants of divine commitment."

The literary structure of 7:1–17 may be outlined as follows.

A. Setting (7:1–3)
B. Nathan's oracle (7:4–17)
  1. Introduction (7:4)
  2. Body (7:5–16)
    a. God's questions (7:5–7)
    b. God's promises (7:8–16)
      (1) to be realized during David's lifetime (7:8–11a)
      (2) to be fulfilled after David's death (7:11b–16)
  3. Conclusion (7:17)

Second Samuel 7:1–17 is paralleled in 1 Chronicles 17:1–15.

[1]After the king was settled in his palace and the LORD had given him rest from all his
enemies around him, [2]he said to Nathan the prophet, "Here I am, living in a palace of
cedar, while the ark of God remains in a tent."
[3]Nathan replied to the king, "Whatever you have in mind, go ahead and do it, for the
LORD is with you."
[4]That night the word of the LORD came to Nathan, saying:
[5]"Go and tell my servant David, 'This is what the LORD says: Are you the one to build me
a house to dwell in? [6]I have not dwelt in a house from the day I brought the Israelites up
out of Egypt to this day. I have been moving from place to place with a tent as my dwelling.
[7]Wherever I have moved with all the Israelites, did I ever say to any of their rulers
whom I commanded to shepherd my people Israel, "Why have you not built me a house
of cedar?"'
[8]"Now then, tell my servant David, 'This is what the LORD Almighty says: I took you from
the pasture and from following the flock to be ruler over my people Israel. [9]I have been
with you wherever you have gone, and I have cut off all your enemies from before you.
Now I will make your name great, like the names of the greatest men of the earth. [10]And I
will provide a place for my people Israel and will plant them so that they can have a home
of their own and no longer be disturbed. Wicked people will not oppress them anymore,

as they did at the beginning [11]and have done ever since the time I appointed leaders over
my people Israel. I will also give you rest from all your enemies.
"'The LORD declares to you that the LORD himself will establish a house for you: [12]When
your days are over and you rest with your fathers, I will raise up your offspring to succeed you, who will come from your own body, and I will establish his kingdom. [13]He is the
one who will build a house for my Name, and I will establish the throne of his kingdom
forever. [14]I will be his father, and he will be my son. When he does wrong, I will punish him
with the rod of men, with floggings inflicted by men. [15]But my love will never be taken
away from him, as I took it away from Saul, whom I removed from before you. [16]Your
house and your kingdom will endure forever before me; your throne will be established
forever.'"
[17]Nathan reported to David all the words of this entire revelation.

COMMENTARY

1–3 David, victorious over his enemies, is settled in his royal house (v.1), and his regal status is now beyond question. "The shepherd boy in his tent has become a king, enthroned in his palace" (Carlson, 97). David is thus referred to as "the king" three times in three successive verses in the MT (vv.1–3; the NIV uses "he" in v.2 in deference to English style) and is not called by his personal name until v.5 (the Chronicler, however, in 1Ch 17:1–2, substitutes "David"—to the Chronicler, the human name above all others—for "the king" in all three places).

David decides that the time has finally come for him to do what any self-respecting king worthy of the name should do: build a house for his God. The contrast between his own house and that of the Lord is stark: The human king ("I," v.2; emphatic) is "living" (*yšb*, translated "was settled" in v.1) in a sumptuous "palace" (lit., "house"; vv.1–2), while the "ark of God" (v.2, emphatic)—the symbolic throne of the divine King (see 1Sa 4:4 and comment)—"remains" (*yšb*) in a mere tent. Constructed of the finest materials and with the best available workmanship (see 5:11 and comment), David's palace overwhelms in size and splendor the relatively simple "tent" (see Notes on v.2). To David's credit he recognizes that the imbalance needs to be rectified.

Safe within his well-fortified palace and behind secure frontiers, the king would doubtless have plenty of time for a major construction project. The Lord has "given him rest from all his enemies around him" (v.1; cf. v.11; similarly 1Ki 5:4; 1Ch 22:9, 18; 23:25; 2Ch 14:7; 15:15; 20:30), thus fulfilling during David's reign a promise he had made to Israel centuries earlier (cf. Dt 3:20; 12:10; 25:19; Jos 1:13, 15) and had already fulfilled during the lifetime of Joshua (Jos 21:44; 22:4; 23:1). "David completed what Joshua had begun: the taking possession of Canaan. It is this completion of Joshua's work which is reflected in 2 Sam 7:1, 11. Now David plans to build a temple as the sequel of the LORD's having granted him rest from his enemies" (Roth, "The Deuteronomic Rest Theology," 8).

Verse 1 may also be characterized "as a fulfillment of the prayer with which [the royal psalm in 1 Sam 2:1–10] concludes: 'May he (Yahweh) give strength to his king, and exalt the power of his anointed,' verse 10b" (Carlson, 99–100; see comment on 1Sa 2:10). The expansionist LXX text of 1 Samuel 10:1 suggests that the task of saving the people "from the power of their enemies round about" (see NIV note on 1Sa 10:1) "was first of all given to Saul and later transferred to David" (Carlson, 90; see comment below on v.15).

That David had determined to build a "palace of cedar" (*byt ʾrzym*, v.2; see 5:11 and comment) for himself is not unexpected (cf. Jer 22:14–15). But "the plushness of the proposed temple [v.7, 'house of cedar' (*byt ʾrzym*)] contradicts Yahweh's self-understanding. Yahweh will not be bought off, controlled, or domesticated by such luxury" (Brueggemann, *First and Second Samuel*, 254). For the Ugaritic Baal, building a "house of cedar" (*bt arzm*) for himself might serve the function of "guaranteeing the future existence of the cosmos" (Carlson, 98; cf. de Moor, 55). The Lord, however, requires no such assurances. If a house is to be built for him—not that he needs it to dwell in, of course (cf. 1Ki 8:27; Isa 66:1–2; Ac 7:48; 17:24–25; Heb 8:1–2; 9:24; *Sibylline Oracles* 4:8–11), but as a symbol of his presence among his people—he himself will name the time, the place, and the builder (vv.5–7).

Just as Saul had been advised by Samuel, who had been "attested as a prophet" (1Sa 3:20; for the etymology and meaning of the Hebrew word for "prophet," see comment on 1Sa 9:9), so also David would be helped and counseled by various prophets (see comment on 1Sa 22:5). The most important and famous of these was "Nathan the prophet" (v.2), who appears here for the first time in the text. In addition to being the recipient of the divine oracle outlining the Davidic covenant (vv.4–17), Nathan ("[God] gives") confronts David after his sin with Bathsheba (ch. 12) and plays a prominent role in the anointing of Solomon (rather than Adonijah) as David's successor (1Ki 1). He was also responsible for recording many of the events of the reigns of David (1Ch 29:29) and Solomon (2Ch 9:29).

With respect to David's implied desire to build a temple to house the ark of God (v.2), Nathan agrees that the king should do whatever he has "in mind" (v.3). The statement is that of a loyal subject following customary protocol (see 1Sa 14:7 and comment) and, in the case of Nathan, has "no bearing whatever on (his) later judgment or oracle as Yahweh's prophet" (Cross, *Canaanite Myth and Hebrew Epic*, 242; cf. also Noth, *The Laws in the Pentateuch*, 257–58; Kruse, 147; Baldwin, 217; Brueggemann, *First and Second Samuel*, 254). In any event, "for all his prompt complaisance, Nathan is not to be compared with the kind of fawning time-servers who surrounded Ahab and told him what he wanted to hear (1 Kings 22:6); his subsequent behaviour here, as also in ch. 12, puts him in a different class" (Gordon, *I and II Samuel*, 237). Indeed, Nathan understands that David will ultimately follow the path of obedient servanthood (v.5) because "the LORD is with" him (v.3; cf. v.9; see also 5:10; 1Sa 16:18 and comments; further Cross, *Canaanite Myth and Hebrew Epic*, 250 n. 130; 252).

4 Nathan's oracle proper (vv.5–16) is framed by an introduction (v.4) and a summary statement (v.17). Of the three times the phrase "the word of the LORD came to" is used of God's revelation to a prophet in the books of Samuel (see comment on 1Sa 15:10), only here does it appear in an oracle of blessing. In all three cases, however, the oracle came during the night, as Carlson, 108, observes (cf. 24:11; 1Sa 15:10, 16). Here it is referred to as a *ḥizzāyôn* ("revelation/vision," v.17; GK 2612), which was often received at night (cf. Job 4:13 ["dreams"]; 7:13–14; 20:8; 33:15). Nathan's oracle thus serves as a counterpoise to Samuel's dream theophany (see comment at Overview to 1Sa 3:1–4:1a).

5–7 The messenger formula ("This is what the LORD says," v.5) pinpoints Nathan as the mediator of the divine oracle to David. "This is not a unique circumstance, since other examples of royal legitimation through prophetic oracles in the ancient Near East are known: the so-called Eshnunna prophecy, a prophecy from Mari, and Neo-Assyrian royal prophecies" (Laato, 257).

In contrast to his title as "the king" in the opening verses of the chapter (see comment on vv.1–3), David is now referred to by the Lord as "my servant David" (vv.5, 8; see comment on 3:18; cf. also 1Ki 11:13, 32, 34, 36, 38, 14:8; 2Ki 19:34; 20:6; Jer 33:21–22, 26; Eze 34:23–24), a description that he willingly and humbly accepts (v.26).

> The only other occurence [*sic*] of this precise phrase, "my servant N.," in the whole of the Deuteronomic work is "my servant Moses" in the words of Yahweh to Joshua when he takes over the leadership of Israel [Josh 1:2, 7]. Not even Joshua himself merits the title.... This calls attention to David's importance—he merits comparison with Moses—and the important new thing, the institution of the Davidic monarchy, which begins with him. [McCarthy, "II Samuel 7," 132; cf. Gerbrandt, 170]

The substantive contents of the present literary unit (vv.5–7) are framed by two questions asked by the Lord, both of which pertain to building a temple for him (vv.5, 7). The first—"Are you the one to build me a house to dwell in?"—has been interpreted in a variety of ways (for a typical list see Gerbrandt, 162). After examining a number of ancient Near Eastern texts that deal with the building/rebuilding/repairing of temples, Michiko Ita ("A Note on 2 Sam 7," in *A Light unto My Path: Old Testament Studies in Honor of Jacob M. Myers* [Gettysburg Theological Studies 4; ed. Howard N. Bream, Ralph D. Heim, and Carey A. Moore; Philadelphia: Temple Univ. Press, 1974], 406; cf. Carlson, 109) concludes:

> The real issue is that both the initiative to build a temple and the choice of the person for the task must come from God and not from an individual king.... First, God has not commanded the building of a temple either to any of the past leaders or to David himself (vss 6–7). Second, the choice of the person is God's affair. God's denial—put in the interrogative form (vs 5)—concerns the person of David and not the temple itself. The emphatic position of the pronoun (*hʾth*) makes this point more than clear. Moreover, this denial of David results in the positive choice of his successor in vs 13, where the emphatic *hwʾ ybnh* ["He is the one who will build"] is to be noted as a counterpart of the emphatic denial in vs 5.

That the question in v.5 expects a negative answer is clear not only from the succeeding context but also from the LXX's *ou sy* ("Not you") and from the Chronicler's parallel: "You are not the one" (1Ch 17:4).

Needless to say, the prohibition of v.5 is merely temporary. "This is confirmed by the later verses in the chapter, by verses such as 1 Kings 5:3–5, as well as by the positive emphasis on the temple throughout the remainder of the history" (Gerbrandt, 162). David's son Solomon (see comments on vv.12–13) would eventually build the Lord's house (cf. 1Ki 5:3–5; 6:1). In the broader context, at least two reasons are given for the fact that David himself did not build the temple: (1) He is too busy waging war with his enemies (1Ki 5:3); (2) he is a warrior who has shed much blood (1Ch 22:8; 28:3). The reasons are complementary rather than contradictory, the first being practical and the second theological (cf. similarly Walter C. Kaiser, "The Blessing of David,"

304 n. 21). Neither reason dims David's vision, however (cf. similarly Ps 132:1–5), and before his death he makes extensive preparations for the temple that would eventually be built by Solomon (cf. 1Ch 22:2–5; 28:2).

But the time for construction has not yet arrived. The tabernacle still suffices as the Lord's dwelling (v.6). Although David is "living" (*yšb*; GK 3782) in a palace (v.1), the Lord has never "dwelt" (*yšb*; also "dwell" in v.5) in a permanent house, not "from the day" (cf. Jdg 19:30) he "brought the Israelites up out of Egypt" (v.6)—a common phrase recalling the miracles of the Exodus redemption (cf. 1Sa 8:8; 10:18; Dt 20:1; Jos 24:17; for additional examples cf. Cross, *Canaanite Myth and Hebrew Epic*, 253; see comment on 1Sa 12:6). The Lord has been content with "moving from place to place" (*mthlk*; cf. v.7, "moved"; also Dt 23:14, "moves about"), demonstrating his continuing desire to "walk" (*hthlk*) among his people (Lev 26:12; cf. Ge 3:8; further Gregory K. Beale, "Eden, the Temple, and the Church's Mission in the New Creation," *JETS* 48/1 [2005]: 7).

Referred to as "tent(-curtain[s])" in v.2 (see Notes), the tabernacle is called both a "tent" (*ʾōhel*; GK 185) and a "dwelling" (*miškān*; GK 5438) in v.6. The latter term is commonly translated "tabernacle" in the OT (cf. Ex 25:9) and occurs elsewhere in association with the former (cf. Ex 26:12–13), especially in the phrase "tent over the tabernacle" (Ex 26:7; 36:14; 40:19). The irony in v.6 must not be missed: Although God condescends to accompany his people on their journey with a tent as his dwelling (v.6b), a tent carried by them, all along they have in fact been carried by him (v.6a).

Like the first, the second question in the present literary unit (vv.5–7) expects a negative answer (see comment on v.5). Beginning with the word "did," it implies that the Lord never required the Israelites to build for him a "house of cedar" (v.7; see comment on v.2). "Any of their rulers" translates *ʾaḥad šibṭê yiśrāʾēl* (lit., "one of the tribes of Israel"). Since the same Hebrew phrase occurs in 15:2 in its literal sense, Philippe de Robert wants to translate it the same way here ("Judges ou tribus en 2 Samuel VII 7?" *VT* 21/1 [1971]: 116–18; cf. also the LXX's *phylēn* ["tribe"]). As Driver, 274, had already pointed out long ago, however, there is no example of any tribe's having been divinely commissioned to "shepherd" (see 5:2 and comment; cf. also 24:17) Israel. (But compare Kirkpatrick [*Second Book of Samuel*, 98], who suggests that "tribes" may be understood "of the different tribes which through the Judges and leaders chosen from them successively attained the supremacy, as Ephraim in the time of Joshua, Dan in the days of Samson, Benjamin in the reign of Saul" [cf. 1Ch 28:4; Ps 78:67–68].) Many commentators therefore substitute *šōpṭê* ("judges, leaders") for *šibṭê* on the basis of 1 Chronicles 17:6 (where the LXX, however, has *phylēn*) and the subsequent context (vv.10–11; cf. McCarthy, "II Samuel 7," 133 and n. 7; Driver, 274).

The best solution to the problem would seem to be that of Patrick Reid, who suggests revocalizing the MT's *šibṭê* as *šōbṭê*, "a denominative qal participle ... of *šēbeṭ* meaning 'the one who wields a staff,'" thus "staff bearers," which "fits the imagery of the passage much better than 'judges.' One would expect that the persons bearing the shepherd's staff would be commissioned 'to shepherd'" (Patrick V. Reid, "*šbṭy* in 2 Samuel 7:7," *CBQ* 37/1 [1975]: 18; cf. 17–20 for full argumentation; similarly McCarter, *II Samuel*; also the use of *šēbeṭ* ["scepter"] as a metaphor for authoritative rule in the messianic texts Ge 49:10; Nu 24:17). The NIV's "rulers" (v.7; "ruler" in v.8 renders a different Heb. word) is a term general enough to capture the basic idea.

"People" used with reference to Israel is an important *Leitmotif* in the chapter (cf. independently Carlson, 118), employed four times in each half (vv.7, 8, 10, 11; vv.23 [3x], 24; see also comment on 6:21). "The people of God is one of the most prominent themes in the Bible" (John Goldingay, *Theological Diversity and the Authority of the Old Testament* [Grand Rapids: Eerdmans, 1987], 59; for full discussion see 59–96). "I will be your God, and you will be my people" or the equivalent is doubtless the most characteristic covenantal expression in the entire OT (cf. v.24; Ex 6:7; Lev 26:12; Dt 26:17–18; Jer 7:23; 30:22; 31:1, 33; 32:38; Eze 34:30; 36:28; 37:23; Hos 1:9–10; 2:23; also Heb 8:10).

8–11a The repetition of the messenger formula (see comment on v.5) marks v.8 as the start of a new section of Nathan's oracle. Here, however, the word "LORD" (v.5) has been augmented by "Almighty," a regal title (see comment on 1Sa 1:3) that stresses the Lord's function as covenantal suzerain of David, his "servant" vassal (see comment on v.5). Characteristically, David in his response to God willingly acknowledges both roles (vv.26–27). In Paul's citation of v.14a in 2 Corinthians 6:18, the apostle similarly acknowledges the solemnity and importance of "Almighty" in describing the Lord in this context.

The divine grant to David is divided into two parts: "promises to be realized during David's lifetime (2 Sam 7:8–11a) and promises to be fulfilled after his death (7:11b–16)" (Waltke, "The Phenomenon of Conditionality" [in Gileadi], 130). Verses 7b–8a constitute a brief historical prologue in which the Lord reviews his earlier blessings on his servant David. He begins by reminding David of where he found him: "I [emphatic] took you ... from following the flock" (v.8). At the time of David's earlier private anointing, Samuel had said, "Send for him" (lit., "Send and take him"; 1Sa 16:11); the Lord now observes that it was he himself who "took" David. As in the case of Amos, the Lord took him "from following the flock" (in Am 7:15, "from tending the flock"—the same Heb. expression in both passages). Once a mere shepherd boy (see comments on 5:2; 1Sa 16:11), David has been given a much weightier responsibility: to be "ruler" over the Lord's people Israel (see comments on 5:2; 6:21; 1Sa 9:16; 10:1; cf. also Hezekiah in 2Ki 20:5 ["leader"]). "Yahweh could use David, not because he was a great military leader, but because he was faithful. In this way a good king can be an agent by which the people are blessed" (Gerbrandt, 171).

Verse 9 is linked to v.6 through the use of the durative form *wā'ehyeh* ("I have been"): As the Lord had been "moving from place to place" with his people (v.6; cf. also v.7), so he has been "with" (v.9; see v.3 and comment; cf. also Carlson, 114; cf. esp. Ex 3:12) David "wherever" he has gone (cf. v.7; 8:6, 14; Jos 1:7, 9; also Ge 28:15). The Lord had promised to "cut off" David's enemies from before him (cf. also 1Sa 20:15).

Verses 9b–11a contain three elements: The Lord will (1) make David's "name great" (v.9b), (2) "provide a place" for Israel (v.10), and (3) give David "rest" from all his enemies (v.11a; Carlson, 114–15). The divine promise to make the name of David great is a clear echo of the Abrahamic covenant (cf. Ge 12:2), which in turn stands in sharp contrast to the self-aggrandizing boasts of the builders of the tower of Babel: "so that we may make a name for ourselves" (Ge 11:4). An example of David's name becoming great is 8:13, where the narrator reports that David "became famous" (lit., "made a name"; cf. 1Ki 1:47) after defeating the Edomites (cf. similarly 1Sa 18:30). But again David testifies to his reliance on God's power as he affirms that redemption takes place in the context of God's determination to "make a name for himself" (vv.23, 26; cf. Jer 13:11; 32:20; see 1Sa 12:22 and comment).

That God will provide a "place" for his people (v.10) had been predicted long ago: "Every place where you set your foot will be yours: Your territory will extend from the desert to Lebanon, and from the Euphrates River to the western sea" (Dt 11:24; cf. Jos 1:3–4). "Since this promise is identical with that given to Abraham in Gen 15:18 ... the introduction of the *māqōm* ['place'] idea in [2Sa] 7:10 [cf. also 1Sa 12:8] implies that the Covenant made with Abraham is fulfilled through David" (Carlson, 116; cf. 8:1–4). And far from being temporary, the "place" that God will provide will be the land where he "will plant them" (v.10; cf. Ex 15:17; Pss 44:2; 80:8; Isa 5:2; Jer 2:21; Am 9:15). Plant imagery is frequently applied to David's dynasty in the OT (e.g., Ps 80:15; Isa 11:1, 10; Jer 23:5; 24:5–6; 33:15; Eze 19:10–14; Zec 3:8; 6:12; cf. Talmon, 218 n. 26).

Having a home of their own, David and his countrymen will no longer "be disturbed" (v.10; i.e., "tremble" in fear [Dt 2:25; same Heb. verb in both cases]) by "wicked people" (lit., "sons of wickedness" [see comment on "wicked men" in 3:34], which contrasts with "Israelites" [lit., "sons of Israel"] in vv.6–7). Indeed, "wicked people will not oppress them anymore" (a phrase echoed in Ps 89:22), as had been their fate earlier in their history ("at the beginning"; cf. Ge 15:13, where the Lord predicted that Abraham's descendants would be "mistreated" [thus also Dt 26:6; same Heb. verb as that rendered "oppress" here] four hundred years—yet another link between the Abrahamic and Davidic covenants [cf. Carlson, 118]). Although oppression had been virtually endemic in Israel during the entire period of the "judges" (v.11; NIV note), such will no longer be the case.

"David and his line are presented as the true successors of the judges who will bring on the lasting rest from Israel's enemies which the earlier leaders were unable to achieve" (McCarthy, "II Samuel 7," 133; cf. Gerbrandt, 171 n. 186; Roth, "The Deuteronomic Rest Theology," 8; Howard, "The Case for Kingship," 113 n. 36). As always, of course, the ultimate giver of the rest is God himself (v.11a; see v.1 and comment). The Chronicler's parallel notes that the method the Lord will use to "give [David] rest from" all his enemies will be to "subdue" them (1Ch 17:10).

11b–16 Just as the divine pronouncements in vv.5–7 and 8–11a are introduced with the messenger formula "This is what the LORD [Almighty] says," so also vv.11b–16 begin with the oracular preface "The LORD declares to you" as a means of introducing God's promises to David's descendants: a "house" (= dynasty, vv.11b, 16; cf. "offspring," v.12); a throne (vv.13, 16), and kingdom (vv.12–13, 16) that will last forever (vv.13, 16); a "house" (= temple, v.13); and a Father-son relationship (v.14) including a covenantal love that will never be taken away (v.15). The importance of "house" in the sense of "dynasty" in Nathan's oracle is underscored by its appearance at the beginning (v.11b) and end (v.16) of the literary unit, thus serving to frame the whole.

That "house" is used with two different meanings in these verses is clear from the verbs used with it: In v.11b the verb is *ʿśh* ("establish," lit., "make"; cf. 1Ki 2:24, where "made a house" is translated "founded a dynasty"), while in verse 13 the verb is *bnh* ("build," as in v.5; see comment). Although David is not to build a "house" (temple) for the Lord (v.5), the Lord will establish a "house" (dynasty) for David (v.11; cf. similarly Brueggemann, *First and Second Samuel*, 255). It is David's "offspring" (v.12) who will build the Lord's temple (v.13).

All the promises in this section will be fulfilled after David's death, after his being laid to "rest" (lit., "lie down," v.12; a different Heb. verb is used for "rest" in vv.1, 11) with his "fathers" (cf. 1Ki 1:21; 2:10)—an expression used of Moses (Dt 31:16) and others (cf. Ge 47:30). It reflects the ancient Israelite practice of having multiple burials in family tombs (see comment on 2:32).

"Like Abraham, David is receiving promises concerning a son yet unborn" (Gordon, *I and II Samuel*, 239). Saul's earlier plea to David not to cut off "my descendants" (lit., "my seed after me," 1Sa 24:21; cf. Ru 4:12 for "seed/offspring" applied to David's ancestor[s]) is reprised in the Lord's determination with respect to David to "raise up your offspring to succeed you" (lit., "your seed after you"; cf. similarly 1Ki 15:4; similar language is also used in Esarhaddon's royal inscriptions ["royal seed, offspring of an eternal dynasty"], in which the Akkadian cognate of the Hebrew word for "seed/ offspring" appears [Laato, 254]). The emphasis that David's offspring will "come from your own body" (lit., "loins" as the locus of procreation, v.12) forges yet another striking link to the Abrahamic covenant (cf. Ge 15:4), as does the repeated reference to Abraham's "seed/descendants after you/him" in Genesis 17:7–10, 19.

Although Carlson, 122, assumes that the offspring of v.12 is Absalom because of the occurrence of "is of my own flesh" (lit., "has come from my own loins") in 16:11, Patrick, 395, long ago understood that the future tense in v.12 "shows that he speaks of one, who was not yet born, *viz. Solomon:* And that *Absalom, Adonijah* and the rest who pretended to the Kingdom, were not designed for it: Being already proceeded from him" (cf. 3:2–5, which lists the sons born to David in Hebron). Furthermore, the Lord promises to "establish" (vv.12–13, 16; see 5:12 and comment; the verb is *kwn*, different from that used in v.11 [see comment]) the "kingdom" and throne of Solomon, not Absalom. Although Saul's kingdom could earlier have been theoretically "established" alongside that of David (see 1Sa 13:13 and comment), such was not to be (cf. v.15).

The possibility of understanding "seed" ("offspring," NIV) as either singular or plural (cf. Ps 89:4, 29, 36, where the Heb. word for "seed" is translated "line" in connection with the Davidic covenant) is exploited by Paul in Galatians 3:16: "The promises were spoken to Abraham and to his seed. The Scripture [Ge 12:7; 13:15; 24:7] does not say 'and to seeds,' meaning many people, but 'and to your seed,' meaning one person, who is Christ" (cf. also "the Seed" [= Christ] in Gal 3:19 and "Abraham's seed" [= Christians] in Gal 3:29). The trajectory from the Abrahamic covenant through the Davidic covenant to the new covenant in Christ is strengthened by the repetition of words such as "seed" used in a messianic sense (cf. similarly John M. G. Barclay, *Obeying the Truth: A Study of Paul's Ethics in Galatians* [Edinburgh: T&T Clark, 1988], 89; cf. also Jn 7:42 and NIV note there; Ac 13:23 ["descendants"]; cf. further Dale Goldsmith, "Acts 13:33–37: A *Pesher* on 2 Samuel 7," *JBL* 87/3 [1968]: 321–24).

Unlike vv.11 and 16, v.13 uses "house" in the sense of a building (cf. also vv.1–2 ["palace"], 5–7), in this case a house of worship, a temple. David's offspring (v.12)—"he" (emphatic, v.13), answering to the emphatic "you" (David) of v.5 (see comment)—has been designated to build a temple for the Lord's "Name" (i.e., his presence, v.13 [for "name" = "presence" cf. Jn 1:12]; see comment on 6:2; cf. also 1Ki 3:2; 5:3, 5; 8:16, 18–19, 44, 48; 9:7). "Within the [Deuteronomic] History this ['he'] is an obvious reference to Solomon. This verse could be interpreted both as a justification for Solomon's building the temple, and as a sign legitimating his rise to the throne (the one who builds the temple is the God-chosen successor to David)" (Gerbrandt, 163; cf. Brueggemann, *David's Truth*, 75–76). Indeed, "1 Kings 6–8 is the fulfilment of the oracular promise in 7:13a, cf. 1 Kings 8:14–21, 24" (Carlson, 120; Gerbrandt, 165). As for v.13b, it promises that the Davidic dynasty, throne, and kingdom will endure "forever" (a fact mentioned seven times in ch. 7: vv.13b, 16a, 16b, 24, 25, 29a, 29b; cf. also 22:51; 1Ki 2:33, 45; 1Ch 22:10; Ps 89:4).

Not the least because they are cited twice in the NT (2Co 6:18; Heb 1:5), the Lord's words in v.14a are doubtless the best known as well as the most solemn in the entire chapter: "I [emphatic] will be his father, and he [emphatic] will be my son." In its original setting the son is Solomon, as the subsequent context makes clear (cf. also 1Ch 22:9–10). The statement in the first instance was not a formula of begetting but of adoption (Edmond Jacob, *Theology of the Old Testament* [New York: Harper, 1958], 236; cf. also Pss 2:7; 89:26; Shalom M. Paul, "Adoption Formulae: A Study in Cuneiform and Biblical Legal Clauses," *Maarav* 2/2 [1980]: 173–85; Anthony Phillips, "Another Example of Family Law," *VT* 30/2 [1980]: 240–41). The formula "provides both the judicial basis for the gift of the eternal dynasty (compare Pss 2:7–8; 89) and the qualification that disloyal sons will lose YHWH's protection (compare 1 Kings 6:12–13; 9:4, 6–7)" (Waltke, "The Phenomenon of Conditionality" [in Gileadi], 131; cf. Weinfeld, 190).

Because of its typological use in 2 Corinthians 6:18 and Hebrews 1:5, v.14a has long been considered messianic in a Christological sense. 4Q174 (Florilegium), an eschatological midrash primarily on vv.10b–14a (although other OT passages, including Ps 1:1; 2:1, are also treated in it), demonstrates that the Dead Sea sectarians also understood v.14a to be messianic (for text cf. J. M. Allegro, "Fragments of a Qumran Scroll of Eschatological *Midrāšîm*," *JBL* 77/4 [1958]: 350–54; Yigael Yadin, "A Midrash on 2 Sam. vii and Ps. i–ii [4QFlorilegium]," *IEJ* 9 [1959]: 95–98; for a literate and readily accessible translation, see Geza Vermes, trans., *The Complete Dead Sea Scrolls in English* [rev. ed.; London: Penguin, 2004], 525–26). William R. Lane ("A New Commentary Structure in 4QFlorilegium," *JBL* 78/4 [1959]: 344) observes that 4QFlorilegium divides naturally into two parts, the first of which concentrates mainly on vv.10b–14a and deals with "the establishment of the true house of Israel under the Davidic Messiah and the subsequent era of peace" and the second with "the wicked and their affliction of the elect during the final struggle."

Needless to say, the Qumran sectarians interpreted the OT "prooftexts" according to their own agenda. The fact that they understood v.14a messianically, however, is surely significant for the NT passages that do the same. No longer is it possible to insist that the NT writers overstepped their bounds in claiming that the divine sonship of the Messiah (in their case, Jesus) is adumbrated in 2 Samuel 7, Psalm 2, and elsewhere. They were making use of well-established, exegetical methodologies that had long been recognized in Jewish scholarly circles. Indeed, 4QFlorilegium "suggests that the Qumran community ... inherited a messianic reading of [Nathan's] oracle from earlier times.... Christian and Qumran interpreters shared a basic approach to the verses, but their exegesis led in rather different directions" (Donald Juel, *Messianic Exegesis: Christological Interpretation of the Old Testament in Early Christianity* [Philadelphia: Fortress, 1988], 61–62; cf. also 87–88). At the same time, what is particularly striking about the 4QFlorilegium commentary is that it

> betrays no embarrassment regarding the use of father-son imagery in verse 14. That is notable only in light of later targumic and rabbinic tradition that took great pains to ensure that the

> imagery from this text be understood as figurative. Later tradition was hesitant to use "son" to speak of the Messiah; the Qumran interpreter shows no such reservations. (Ibid., 68; cf. also 78)

Like 4QFlorilegium, Hebrews 1:5 also quotes v.14a and Psalm 2 (this time, however, Ps 2:7: "You are my Son; today I have become your Father"). The author of Hebrews uses the two texts to demonstrate that Jesus, the Son of God, "became as much superior to the angels as the name he has inherited is superior to theirs" (Heb 1:4) when he "sat down at the right hand of the Majesty in heaven" (Heb 1:3). Furthermore, "the 'Son of God' is a title applied to Jesus by the gospel writers to highlight his messianic and divine origin as the fulfilment of such Old Testament prophecies as Psalm 2:7 and 2 Samuel 7:14" (Craig L. Blomberg, *The Historical Reliability of the Gospels* [Downers Grove, Ill.: InterVarsity Press, 1987], 251). And such passages as Luke 1:32–33 reverberate with echoes of Nathan's oracle: "[Jesus] will be great and will be called the Son of the Most High. The Lord God will give him the throne of his father David, and he will reign over the house of Jacob forever; his kingdom will never end."

At the same time, "son" in v.14a could be understood by NT writers in a collective sense, as 2 Corinthians 6:18 demonstrates: "I will be a Father to you, and you will be my sons and daughters, says the Lord Almighty" (see NIV note). Murray J. Harris notes: "The unique divine-human relationship, first promised to David's offspring and later extended to include the whole nation ('I am Israel's father, and Ephraim is my firstborn son,' Jer 31:9), now finds its fulfillment, Paul is saying, in the filial relationship of believers to God as Father (cf. Gal 3:26; 4:6)" (*Revised EBC*, 11:489). Father-son imagery representing God's relationship to the people of Israel is common in the OT. Besides Jeremiah 31:9, it is found in such texts as Exodus 4:22–23; Deuteronomy 14:1; 32:6, 19; Isaiah 1:2; 30:1; 43:6; 45:10; 63:16; 64:8; Jeremiah 3:19; Hosea 1:10; 11:1; and Malachi 1:6; 2:10.

A further aspect of the father-son metaphor is its covenantal setting. In Mesopotamia, for example, "employment of familial metaphors to express political ties was ... a well-known phenomenon in the diplomatic lexicon of the second millennium. Thus *abbūtu* 'fathership' signifies suzerainty, *mārūtu* 'sonship'—vassalship" (Paul, "Adoption Formulae," 177). The use of "father" for God and "son" for Solomon in v.14a is thus entirely appropriate in what has justifiably come to be known as the Davidic covenant. At the same time the most characteristic of all covenantal formulas—"I will be your God, and you will be my people"—is taken from "the sphere of marriage/adoption legal terminology like its Davidic counterpart in II Sam. VII, 14" (Weinfeld, 200).

Although the Davidic king is to enjoy the unique relationship of being the Lord's "son," he will thereby be brought "all the more firmly within the constraints of Yahweh's fatherly discipline" (Gordon, *I and II Samuel*, 239), as v.14b indicates. The Lord will use men as agents of divine judgment on Solomon (and his dynastic successors) "when he does wrong" (cf. Solomon's words in 1Ki 8:47 in their context). It is not an idle promise: "The rod" (v.14b; cf. also Ps 89:32) of divine wrath will fall on Jerusalem and her citizens because of the sins of David's descendants (cf. La 3:1). The Chronicler's parallel leaves out v.14b entirely because of his characteristic desire to display the Davidic dynasty in the best possible light. His omission of the negative threat makes it tempting to assume that Hebrews 1:5, referring to the sinless Christ, cites 1 Chronicles 17:13 rather than 2 Samuel 7:14 (cf. Robert L. Reymond, *Jesus, Divine Messiah: The Old Testament*

Witness [Ross-shire, Scotland: Christian Focus, 1990], 11 n. 6). Patrick, 395, however, prefers to call v.14 "a mixt [*sic*] Prophecy, some part of which belongs to Christ, and the other part to *Solomon* and his Successors in the Kingdom of *Israel*."

But neither expedient seems necessary. Although the NT leaves no doubt that v.14a is fulfilled typologically in Jesus, it is also clear that in its original setting the entire verse refers to the Lord's adoption of Solomon (and his royal descendants) as his son/vassal: "The son given into adoption has the duties of a son (= respecting his parents) but also has the privileges of a son: he has to be treated like the son of a free citizen and not like a slave.... What is then meant in II Sam. VII, 14 is that when David's descendants sin they will be disciplined like rebellious sons by their father but they will not be alienated" (Weinfeld, 192–93). Such an understanding in no way denies the interpretation that Solomon, the type, prefigures Jesus, the antitype.

Taken together, vv.14b–15 have often been understood to mean that the Davidic covenant is unconditional: No matter what David's descendants do (v.14b), the Lord's love will "never be taken away" from them (v.15). But although the verses "may point in that direction, it is striking that a passage so clearly grounded in the royal cults of that time would emphasize that Yahweh will punish the king for disobeying the law. This must be seen as at least qualifying the promise if not making it conditional. These verses point out that kings are not to use the Davidic promise as a justification for any style of behavior" (Gerbrandt, 164).

At the same time, however, the "when" of v.14b gives way to the "but" of v.15. Brueggemann (*First and Second Samuel*, 259) remarks:

> Sound interpretation requires us to recognize that while the covenantal "if" is silenced in this theology, it has not been nullified. Therefore, interpretation must struggle with the tension of "if" and "nevertheless" that is present in the Bible, in our own lives, and in the very heart of God.... The historical process teaches us about the reality of judgment and condition, so that we know about the "if" of reality from our own experience. The other side of the tension, God's unconditional commitment, will be operative in biblical faith only if Nathan's bold oracle of "nevertheless" is sounded as the gospel.

All three verbs in v.15 ("be taken away," "took ... away," "removed") are forms of the verb *swr* ("turn aside"; GK 6073), the second and third occurrences of which are identical (*hᵃsirōtî*). The Lord promises that although he "turned aside" his love from Saul (whom the Chronicler in his parallel, reluctant to mention Saul by name, simply calls David's "predecessor" [1Ch 17:13]), David's mortal enemy whom the Lord "turned aside" from before him, the divine love will never "turn aside" from David's seed ("offspring," v.12), David's son Solomon (and his descendants)—and ultimately great David's greater Son, Jesus Christ. Carlson, 122, notes that "the emphasized *hēsīr* element in v.15 derives from the previous description of Saul and David, cf. 1 Sam 16:14, 18:12, 28:15 f." (see comments on 1Sa 16:14; 28:15–16). In addition *lōʾ-yāsûr* ("will never be taken away") echoes the same phrase in Genesis 49:10 ("will not depart"; cf. Carlson, 108).

God's covenant with David assures him that his covenantal "love" (*ḥesed*, v.15; GK 2876; see comments on 2:6; 1Sa 20:8, 14–15; cf. Roger T. Beckwith, "The Unity and Diversity of God's Covenants," *TynBul* 33 [1987]: 102 n. 26) will never leave David's son as it had left Saul. An important emphasis in v.15 is the fact that it constitutes "an endorsement of the Davidic claim to the throne over against the Saulide and any others that may emerge" (Levenson, "The Davidic Covenant and Its Modern Interpreters," *CBQ* 41/2 [1979]: 217). The word *ḥesed* becomes a virtual synonym for *b^e^rît* ("covenant") in later allusions to the Davidic covenant (cf. 22:51 ["unfailing kindness"]; 1Ki 3:6 ["kindness"]; 2Ch 6:42 ["great love"]; Ps 89:28, 33, 49; Isa 55:3; 1 Macc 2:57 [for the last reference, cf. Kruse, 148, who observes that *eleos* ("mercy") = *ḥesed* in this context; cf. further Pierre Bordreuil, "Les 'Graces de David' et 1 Maccabees ii 57," *VT* 31/1 (1981): 73–76]).

With respect to Isaiah 55:3 (cited in Ac 13:34 to demonstrate that Jesus' resurrection was further proof of God's covenantal love to David), Kaiser ("The Unfailing Kindnesses Promised to David," 92) makes the helpful observation that "the phrase *ḥasdê dāwid hanneʾemānîm* ['faithful love promised to David'] ... echoes 2 Sam 7:15–16: 'My *ḥesed* I will not remove from him.... Sure [*neʾman*] are your house and your kingdom before me forever." Verse 16 itself reprises earlier promises in the near context in summary fashion (for "house/dynasty" see comment on v.11b; for "kingdom" and "throne"—which are linked contextually to "house/dynasty"—and "forever" see comment on v.13b; for "established" see comment on v.12).

That David's "house" will "endure" (v.16) echoes Abigail's insight in 1 Samuel 25:28 (see comment on "lasting dynasty" there; see also comment on "firmly [established his] house" in 1Sa 2:35; cf. 1Ki 11:38 ["dynasty as enduring"]—the Hebrew expression is virtually the same in all four passages). *Nʾmn* ("enduring, true, established, confirmed" is applied also to the divine promises made to David (1Ki 8:26; 1Ch 17:23; 2Ch 1:9; cf. further Mettinger, 144–45, who calls attention to the fact that "Isaiah's address to the Davidide Ahaz [Isa 7:9] ... contains a play on the Nathan prophecy"; cf. similarly Gordon, *I and II Samuel*, 240), which comprise the covenant itself (which "will never fail," Ps 89:28).

Through Solomon (cf. 1Ch 22:6–11; 28:5–7) and his descendants, David's throne will "be established" (*kwn*, v.16; GK 3922; cf. 1Ki 2:45 ["remain secure"]; Ps 89:37). It should also be noted that "data from the ancient Near East ... indicate that there is no *prima facie* reason to regard the central idea in 2 Samuel 7—the promise of an eternal dynasty to David—as an anachronistic element in the account of the reigns of David and Solomon" (Laato, 263).

When A. G. Hebert wrote a book that he subtitled *A Study of the Fulfilment of the Old Testament in Jesus Christ and His Church*, he could think of no better main title than *The Throne of David* (London: Faber and Faber, 1941). More than any other, Christ fulfills the promises of the Davidic covenant. "The failure of the kings generally leads not to disillusion with kingship but to the hope of a future king who will fulfill the kingship ideal—a hope which provides the most familiar way of understanding the significance of Jesus of Nazareth, the *Christ* coming in his *kingdom*" (Goldingay, *Theological Diversity and the Authority of the Old Testament*, 70). That the throne of David will remain "forever" (v.16) refers ultimately to "none but Christ, for *David*'s Kingdom had an end, but Christ's hath none" (Patrick, 396; cf. Lk 1:31–33). In the words of Martin Luther, "his kingdom is forever."

17 Nathan's oracle (vv.5–16) having come to an end, a summary statement functions, together with the introduction (v.4), to frame the oracle itself. It was incumbent on a prophet to report "all the words" the Lord commissioned him to proclaim (cf. Jer 42:4 ["everything"]), and Nathan keeps nothing back. "The task of the prophet, to convey the message of the Lord faithfully and accurately, is carried out by Nathan, though it involved contradicting what he had already said to David by way of personal opinion" (Baldwin, 217; see v.3 and comment).

The Lord's "revelation/vision" (*ḥizzāyôn*; see v.4 and comment) to Nathan concerning David and his dynasty is perhaps referred to in Psalm 89:19 ("vision," *ḥāzôn*), which may allude also to the divine communication to Samuel in 1 Samuel 16:12.

NOTES

2 "In a tent" is literally "inside the curtain(s)" and refers to "the" tent earlier pitched by David and "inside" which he had set the ark in its place (6:17). As in Exodus 26:1–13, the noun translated "curtain(s)" almost always refers to the curtains of the tabernacle (see comment on 6:17).

6 The NIV's "with a tent as my dwelling" (lit., "in a tent and in a dwelling") is rendered as a hendiadys also by Carlson ("in a tent-dwelling," 106). The Chronicler captures the durative aspect of the entire sentence ("I have been moving from place to place with a tent as my dwelling") with a creative rendering of the hendiadys: "I have moved from one tent site to another, from one dwelling place to another" (1Ch 17:5). Cross (*Canaanite Myth and Hebrew Epic*, 242–43) observes that the pair of words surfaces in Psalm 78:60 ("tabernacle, tent") in reference to its abandonment by the Lord at Shiloh (see comment on 1Sa 4:11).

7 The NIV's "did I ever say" apparently vocalizes the first word in דבר דברתי (*dbr dbrty*) as the infinitive absolute דַּבֵּר (*dabbēr*) rather than following the MT's cognate accusative דָּבָר (*dābār*). Although Cross (*Canaanite Myth and Hebrew Epic*, 253) affirms the MT's vocalization and lists many other examples of *dbr* in cognate accusative constructions from elsewhere in the Deuteronomic corpus, all of them interpose one or more graphemes (for example, *ʾšr*) between the verbal form and its object and are thus not true parallels to *dbr dbrty*. The juxtaposition of the two forms in the present verse, as well as the LXX's εἰ λαλῶν ἐλάλησα (*ei lalōn elalēsa*, "speaking have I ever spoken") both here and in the parallel in 1 Chronicles 17:6, make the infinitive absolute construction the better choice.

8 The legitimation of King Zimrilim in a prophecy from Mari "contains many motifs similar to those found in connection with the legitimation of David.... [For example] the installation of the king is expressed in first singular form both in the Mari prophecy ('I restored him to the throne,' MP, lines 16–17; cf. 19) and in 2 Sam 7:8 ('I took you from the pasture ... that you should be prince over my people')" (Laato, 261; for additional similarities cf. 262–63).

9 A few commentators have attempted to equate David's promised "great name" (שֵׁם גָּדוֹל, *šēm gādôl*) with its literal Egyptian equivalent, *ren wer*. But since the Egyptian phrase is a technical term referring to a fivefold royal titulary and is never used in the sense of "fame" or "renown," it is entirely different from its Hebrew counterpart (cf. Kitchen, *Ancient Orient*, 110–11).

10 A lively debate concerning the best translation of *mqwm* (GK 5226) emerged in the 1990s. It was touched off by A. Gelston ("A Note on II Samuel 7 10," *ZAW* 84 [1972]: 92–94), who proposed that the word in question sometimes means "cultic centre" or "temple" in the OT and that here it should be understood "as referring to the projected temple" that Solomon would build. D. F. Murray ("*MQWM* and the Future of Israel in 2 Samuel VII 10," *VT* 40/3 [1990]; 298–320) responded belatedly and at length to Gelston by affirming the traditional rendering ("place") followed by most translators and commentators. He in turn elicited a detailed response from David Vanderhooft ("Dwelling beneath the Sacred Place: A Proposal for Reading 2 Samuel 7:10," *JBL* 118/4 [1999]: 625–33), who translates 2 Samuel 7:10a literally as follows: "I will establish a place [= temple] for my people Israel, and I will plant him, then he will dwell beneath it and will not tremble any more" (625), comparing this nuance of "place" with numerous passages in Deuteronomy 12, 14, etc., where, he says, "the reference is to the place of worship" (629)—that is, the future temple.

All three articles present strong arguments favoring their positions. But since *mqwm* can in any event refer to a sacred site on occasion (cf., e.g., *HALOT*, 1.627—although not citing 2Sa 7:10), it would seem that the default rendering "place" is preferable here. Vanderhooft's "beneath it" for the Hebrew *tḥtyw*, which leads to his understanding of the verse as referring to the idea that Israel will "dwell beneath God's sacred precinct, in its protective shade" (631), is clever but both tendentious and unnecessary since the preposition *tḥt* is often used as a substantive (NIV here, "a home of their own"). Indeed, the substantives *mqwm* and *tḥtyw* are both found (coincidentally, to be sure, as well as in reverse order) in 2:23 ("on the spot ... place"). When all is said and done, then, it would seem safest to render *mqwm* neutrally as "place" and to agree with Eslinger, 33, that here the Lord "combines the language of the book of Deuteronomy about the place that Yhwh would place his name and the language of verse 6 about his own itinerant past.... The party to be anchored to a 'place' is Israel; the place to be 'established' (*śm*) is that for Israel, not a temple for God (as per Deuteronomy)" (cf. also 33 n. 4: "Yahweh's point here is to rebut absolutely any notion of staking him down to a sacred locale. The hyperbolic reversal of the deuteronomic 'place ideology' is aimed only as far as saying that it is God who will situate Israel, not an Israelite [David] who will situate God. The language of Deuteronomy is a convenient tool [since it treats of the temple] for restating the central point of covenantal ideology from God's point of view: divine control over his people").

12 One of the two pillars standing in front of Solomon's temple was named "Jakin" (1Ki 7:21; 2Ch 3:17). R. B. Y. Scott ("The Pillars Jachin and Boaz," *JBL* 58/2 [1939]: 143–49) has plausibly suggested on the basis of ancient Near Eastern parallels that יָכִין (*yākîn*, "he establishes, he will establish") may well be the first word of a royal dynastic oracle on the basis of such texts as vv.12–13, 16, thus explaining why it was customary for kings of Judah to stand "by the pillar" on ceremonial occasions (2Ki 11:14; 23:3). The entire sentence may have been "The Lord will establish your throne forever" or the like (cf. Albright, 139; D. J. Wiseman and C. J. Davey, *NBD*, rev. ed., 545).

16 The reading "before me" (i.e., the Lord) with a few Hebrew MSS and the LXX is clearly preferable to the MT's "before you" (i.e., David; see NIV note), which "may have been subject to secondary influence from the expressions in verses 26 and 29 ['in your sight'], with which it stands in a factual connexion" (Carlson, 108). On the other hand, the MT's reading לפניך (*lpnyk*) might have arisen from dittography, since the following word begins with כ (*k*).

4. David's Prayer to the Lord (7:18–29)

OVERVIEW

The heartfelt response of King David to the oracle of the prophet Nathan is one of the most moving prayers in Scripture. (Other nonpsalmic prayers of a similar genre include 1Ki 3:6–9; 8:22–53; 1Ch 29:10–19; Ezr 9:6–15; Ne 1:4–11; 9:5–38; Job 42:2–6; Jer 32:16–25; Da 9:4–19; Jnh 2:2–9; Mt 6:9–13; and Lk 2:29–32; 10:21–22.) In it he humbly expresses his gratitude to the Lord for revealing his will to him through Nathan and declares his own desire that the divine promises might indeed be fulfilled to the greater glory of God.

In the overall chiastic arrangement of the narrative of David's powerful reign over Israel (see comment on 5:17–8:18), David's prayer parallels the story of the procession of the ark into the city of Jerusalem (ch. 6). The literary structure of vv. 18–29 may be outlined as follows (cf. similarly C. F. D. Erdmann, "The Books of Samuel," in *Commentary on the Holy Scriptures: Critical, Doctrinal, and Practical*, ed. John Peter Lange [Grand Rapids: Zondervan, n.d.], 5:433, 435, 437).

A. The present: gratitude for God's favor (7:18–21)
B. The past: praise for what God has already done (7:22–24)
C. The future: prayer for God's fulfillment of covenantal promises (7:25–29)

Second Samuel 7:18–29 is paralleled in 1 Chronicles 17:16–27.

18Then King David went in and sat before the LORD, and he said:
"Who am I, O Sovereign LORD, and what is my family, that you have brought me this
far? 19And as if this were not enough in your sight, O Sovereign LORD, you have also spoken
about the future of the house of your servant. Is this your usual way of dealing with man,
O Sovereign LORD?
20"What more can David say to you? For you know your servant, O Sovereign LORD. 21For
the sake of your word and according to your will, you have done this great thing and
made it known to your servant.
22"How great you are, O Sovereign LORD! There is no one like you, and there is no God
but you, as we have heard with our own ears. 23And who is like your people Israel—the
one nation on earth that God went out to redeem as a people for himself, and to make a
name for himself, and to perform great and awesome wonders by driving out nations and
their gods from before your people, whom you redeemed from Egypt? 24You have established your people Israel as your very own forever, and you, O LORD, have become their
God.
25"And now, LORD God, keep forever the promise you have made concerning your servant and his house. Do as you promised, 26so that your name will be great forever. Then
men will say, 'The LORD Almighty is God over Israel!' And the house of your servant David
will be established before you.
27"O LORD Almighty, God of Israel, you have revealed this to your servant, saying, 'I will
build a house for you.' So your servant has found courage to offer you this prayer. 28O
Sovereign LORD, you are God! Your words are trustworthy, and you have promised these
good things to your servant. 29Now be pleased to bless the house of your servant, that it
may continue forever in your sight; for you, O Sovereign LORD, have spoken, and with your
blessing the house of your servant will be blessed forever."

COMMENTARY

18–21 In response to the Lord's promises as mediated through Nathan, David "went in" (probably into the tent he had pitched for the ark; v.18) and sat "before the LORD" (i.e., before the ark; see 6:17 and comment). Since the customary posture of prayer was standing or kneeling, the fact that David "sat" before the Lord was perhaps "in accordance with the prerogative of the Davidic kings (*cf.* Ps 110:1)" (Gordon, *I and II Samuel*, 241). "The verb 'sat,' *yašav*, is identical with the verb at the beginning of the chapter that also means 'dwell,' and thus establishes a structural parallel between the passage on the postponed building of the temple and David's prayer" (Alter, *The David Story*, 234).

Beginning his prayer with appropriate humility and deference ("Who am I ... that you have brought me this far?" [cf. the similar plea of Moses in Ex 3:11]), David addresses God as "Sovereign LORD," which he employs seven times (vv.18, 19 [2x], 20, 22, 28, 29) and which occurs only here in the books of Samuel. Michael A. Grisanti ("The Davidic Covenant," *MSJ* 10/2 [1999]: 246) calls attention to the fact that the parallel passage in 1 Chronicles 17, by contrast, uses "LORD God" (1Ch 17:16–17), "God" (17:17) and "LORD" (17:19–20, 26–27) "instead of the title originally used by David." (As Carlson, 127, notes, the name "Sovereign LORD" is "used by Abraham when addressing his God in Gen 15:2, 8.")

A further link between the Davidic and Abrahamic covenants is thus established. Kaiser ("The Unfailing Kindnesses Promised to David," 310 n. 43) calls attention to five additional earlier attestations of the name, each "in a prayer to God as in this passage: Moses' prayers in Deuteronomy 3:24; 9:26; Joshua's prayer in Joshua 7:7; Gideon's prayer in Judges 6:22; and Samson's prayer in Judges 16:28." And if God is sovereign to David, he recognizes his own status as vassal by referring to himself ten times as the Lord's "servant" (vv.19, 20, 21, 25, 26, 27 [2x], 28, 29 [2x]; see comments on v.5; 3:18; 1Sa 1:11; 25:24).

The central theme of the prayer is David's *bayit* ("house/dynasty"). Like the special name David uses to address the Lord, it too appears in the first and last verses of the prayer and occurs seven times (vv.18 ["family"], 19, 25, 26, 27, 29 [2x]; cf. Cross, *Canaanite Myth and Hebrew Epic*, 247). Though his household is insignificant at present (v.18), David is confident that it will become great in the future because of the proven reliability of God and his promises.

That the Lord has brought him to this point in his experience (v.18) will be sufficient for David, but he gratefully recognizes that in God's eyes it is "not enough" (*qṭn*, lit., "small," v.19). The Lord has even better things in store for him in the future. The NIV's rendering, "Is this your usual way of dealing with man?" although barely possible, remains problematic (see Notes).

"Confessing that to say more would be as inadequate as it would be unnecessary (vs. 20; cf. Ps 139:4; Isa 65:24), David yet continues with gratitude for the divine message" (Matitiahu Tsevat, "The House of David in Nathan's Prophecy," *Bib* 46 [1965]: 354). The Lord has honored his servant (cf. 1Ch 17:18) beyond measure, and David asserts that there is scarcely anything more that he can say (cf. his descendant Hezekiah's similar concern in Isa 38:15). David affirms that the Lord "know[s]" his servant (v.20), perhaps including the fact that he has "chosen" him (cf. Ge 18:19, where the Heb. verb is the same; similarly Am 3:2). David had earlier reminded Michal that the Lord "chose" him (6:21, though a different Heb. verb is used there) rather than anyone from Saul's household (cf. also 1Sa 16:1).

Recognizing the unconditional aspect of the Lord's covenant with him (v.21), David "accepts the promises as certain, with no obligations imposed on him" (Waltke, "The Phenomenon of Conditionality" [in Gileadi], 131). If David earlier knew that the Lord had blessed him "for the sake of" his people Israel (5:12), he now confesses that the Lord has done a great thing simply "for the sake of" his "word" (v.21). The Lord has also acted according to his "will" (lit., "heart")—a blessing that David later echoes in claiming that he himself has found "courage" (lit., "his heart") to offer his prayer to God (v.27).

The greatness of God and his deeds overwhelm David, who refers to the "great thing" the Lord has done (v.21; cf. "great deeds" in the Davidic Ps 145:6; also Ps 92:5), to how "great" the Sovereign Lord is (v.22; cf. Ps 104:1), to the "great" wonders the Lord has performed in the past (v.23), and to how "great" the Lord's name is (v.26). (The parallel in 1Ch 17:19 adds to the list by substituting "made known all these great promises" for "made it known to your servant" in v.21.) And the God who "know[s]" his servant (v.20) is also the God who makes his great deeds "known" to his servant (v.21).

22–24 Verse 22 is only one among many OT texts describing God as unique, as sui generis (for details cf. esp. Labuschagne, 8–30, 64–123). That there is "no one like" the Lord is a major theme in the Song of Hannah (1Sa 2:2) as well as a point of comparison used by the prophet Samuel as he presents Saul to the people as their first king (see 1Sa 10:24 and comment). That there is "no God but/except/besides/apart from" the Lord rings like a refrain throughout the words of psalmist (cf. 22:32 = Ps 18:31) and prophet alike (cf. Isa 45:5, 21; 64:4; Hos 13:4; for the importance of the prophetic proclamations of the unity and uniqueness of the God of Israel in Isa 40–48, cf. Menahem Haran, "The Literary Structure and Chronological Framework of the Prophecies in Is. XL–XLVIII," VTSup 9 [Leiden: Brill, 1963], 134).

> From Deut. 33:29, II Sam. 7:23 and Deut. 4:7 [cf. also Dt 4:8, 33–34] it appears that there is a close connection between Yahweh's incomparability and that of his people. Because Yahweh is incomparable, it follows that the people He elected as His own and with whom He entered into communion, who of themselves had no qualities worthy of this attribute, may also be considered incomparable. The application of a divine attribute to the nation does not denote their deification, and there is no evidence whatsoever that Israel regarded herself deified as a result of the application to herself of an attribute of Yahweh. (Labuschagne, 149–50)

Three times in v.23 Israel is referred to as God's "people" (*ʿam*), the one elect "nation" (*gôy*) out of all the "nations" (*gôyim*). Israel's powerful "God" is contrasted with the nations' impotent and ineffective "gods" (same Heb. word in both cases).

Israel's matchless Lord, who brooks no rivals, has gone out to do three things for his grateful people: "redeem" them (cf. Dt 7:8; 9:26; 13:5; 15:15; 21:8; 24:18; Ne 1:10; Jer 31:11), "make a name" for himself (see comment on v.9; cf. also v.26), and "perform great and awesome wonders" (cf. Dt 10:21; also Dt 7:21; 10:17; Ne 9:32; Pss 99:3; 106:22; 145:6; Isa 64:3; Da 9:4; Joel 2:31 ["great and dreadful"]; Mal 4:5 ["great and dreadful"]) by driving out the enemy.

In connection with "perform great and awesome wonders," the MT includes the phrase "for you, on your behalf" (plural; omitted from the NIV, apparently in the interests of economy of style in English), indicating that divine victories for Israel's ancestors continue to bless the people of David's time. Indeed, in vv.23–24 the Sinaitic covenant is cited in support of the Davidic (for details see Gileadi, "The Davidic Covenant" [in Gileadi], 160). The ancient establishment of Israel as God's own people "forever" (v.24) is now to be channeled through David and his dynasty, which will continue "forever" (vv.25, 29 [2x]; see also v.13 and comment). The old Abrahamic and Sinaitic covenantal formula—"I will be your God, and you will be my people"—undergoes yet another variant (see comment on "I will be his father, and he will be my son" in v.14) as David emphasizes that the Lord has "become their [Israel's] God" (v.24; cf. Ge 17:7–8; 28:21; Ex 6:7; 29:45; Lev 11:45; 22:33; 25:38; 26:12, 45; Nu 15:41; Dt 26:17; 29:13). Thus the OT manifestation of the kingdom of God is now to be mediated through the Davidic monarchy (vv.24–25).

25–29 That the concluding verses of David's prayer constitute a literary unit in their own right is clear not only from the multiple use of the word "forever" (vv.25–26, 29 [2x]) but also from the fact that *wᶜth* ("And now") begins vv.25, 28 (untrans. in NIV), and 29. David is very much concerned about the permanence of the "promise" (v.25) the Lord has "made" (lit., "promised," as at the end of the verse; cf. also 1Ki 6:12; 8:24–26) concerning the Davidic dynasty. *Dibbēr* ("speak") in the special sense of "promise" is common in the Deuteronomic corpus (Cross, *Canaanite Myth and Hebrew Epic*, 254; cf. Dt 1:11; 6:3; 9:3, 28; 10:9 ["told"]; 11:25; 12:20; 15:6; 18:2; 26:18; 27:3; 29:13; Jos 13:14, 33; 22:4; 23:5, 10).

The covenanted establishment of David's house (v.26; cf. v.16) will be a visible sign of the greatness of God's name. Indeed, "LORD Almighty" (vv.26–27) will become widely known as the appropriate royal title of the Great King, the God of Israel (see comments on v.8; 1Sa 1:3). In the light of God's sovereignty, David willingly and humbly refers to himself seven times as the Lord's "servant" (vv.25, 26, 27 [2x], 28, 29 [2x]; see comment on v.5).

David is grateful that God has "revealed ... to" him (lit., "uncovered the ear of," v.27; see 1Sa 9:15 and comment; cf. also 1Sa 20:2 ["confiding in"], 12–13 ["let ... know"]; 22:8 ["tells" (2x)], 17 ["tell"]) his plans and purposes: "I will build a house for you" (see comment on a similar expression in 1Sa 2:35), which declaration reprises v.11 (though the verb is different; see comment). He acknowledges that the sovereign Lord alone is God (v.28; "you" is emphatic), as the prayers of Elijah and Hezekiah will also confess (1Ki 18:37; 2Ki 19:15, 19; cf. also Ne 9:6–7). Just as the widow at Zarephath will affirm that the "word" of the Lord from Elijah's mouth is the "truth" (1Ki 17:24), so also David now states that the "words" of the Lord are "trustworthy" (v.28; same Heb. terms in both cases; see also Ps 119:142, 151, 160).

Although 2 Samuel 7 never uses the term "covenant" (*bᵉrît*) of God's promises to David, "good things" (*ṭôbâ*, v.28; GK 3208) is a technical term synonymous with "covenant" in contexts such as this (cf. Michael V. Fox, "*Ṭôb* as Covenant Terminology," *BASOR* 209 [1973]: 41–42; Abraham Malamat, "Organs of Statecraft in the Israelite Monarchy," *BA* 28/2 [1965]: 64; see 2:6 and comment; 1Sa 25:30 and comment). It is possible (if not probable) that *wayᵉdabbēr ʾittô ṭōbôt* ("He spoke kindly to him"; 2Ki 25:28 = Jer 52:32) should rather be rendered "He established a covenant with him."

David concludes his prayer with a request (expressed in the form of a command) to the Lord to "be pleased" (v.29, softened in the 1Ch 17:27 parallel: "you have been pleased"; cf. 1Sa 12:22; Job 6:28 ["be so kind as"]) to bless the Davidic dynasty. The root *brk* ("bless"), which occurs three times as a summarizing *Leitmotif* in v.29, often relates to the propagation of numerous descendants (e.g., Ps 115:14–15; see 6:11 and comment; cf. also 6:12). "Through the descendants of Abraham the nations of the earth would acquire blessing for themselves.... It is not unimportant, therefore, that one of Israel's royal psalms [Ps 72:17] gives voice to the hope that the Davidic king will become a symbol of blessing to the nations" (Clements, 58–59).

Since it is the sovereign Lord himself who has promised ("you" is emphatic), David speaks with the calm assurance of a man who knows that his house will continue forever "in your sight" (v.29, using the same Heb. expression translated "before you" in v.26). The prayer of David thus ends on a note of confident contentment.

NOTES

19 וְזֹאת תּוֹרַת הָאָדָם (*wᵉzōʾt tôrat hāʾādām*) is literally "And this is the law of man" (NIV's "Is this your usual way of dealing with man?"). Not only is the customary Hebrew sign of the interrogative ה (*h*) lacking, but also the translation of *tôrat* as "usual way of dealing with," however "frequent in rabbinic Hebrew" (Tsevat, "The House of David in Nathan's Prophecy," 354 n. 1), would be unique to this passage as far as the OT is concerned (cf. BDB, 436; the expected word is מִשְׁפָּט, *mišpāṭ*, as in 1Sa 2:13 ["practice"]; 27:11 ["practice"]). While it is not quite true that the phrase as a whole has "defied the wits of the exegetes" (Kruse, 157 n. 44), all proposed emendations of the MT here, whether or not based on the parallel in 1 Chronicles 17:17 ("You have looked on me as though I were the most exalted of men"), are unsatisfactory, as recognized long ago by Driver, 277.

The best suggestion to date is that of Kaiser ("The Blessing of David," 311–15). He chooses the nuance "charter" because the continuance of David's house into the future is "the plan and prescription for God's kingdom whereby the whole world shall be blessed with the total content of the promise doctrine. It [the Davidic covenant] is a grant conferring powers, rights, and privileges to David and his seed for the benefit of all mankind" (ibid., 314). Indeed, the phrase *tôrat hāʾādām* may find its cognate reflex in Akkadian *têrēt nišī*, "oracular decisions given to man" (cf. *CAD*, 11/2:284; cf. Henri Cazelles, "Shiloh, the Customary Laws and the Return of the Ancient Kings," in *Proclamation and Presence: Old Testament Essays in Honour of Gwynne Henton Davies*, ed. John I. Durham and J. R. Porter [repr., Macon, Ga.: Mercer, 1983], who renders the Hebrew and Akkadian phrases "the decree concerning humanity in general" [250]; cf. also Carlson, 125 and n. 4; Anderson, 126–27; TNIV footnote on 7:19: "[this decree is] *for the human race*"; "may this be the law/torah of man" [Eslinger, 71]). The promises of the Abrahamic covenant, already universal in scope (cf. Ge 12:3), are thus confirmed in the Davidic as well.

21 The parallel in 2 Chronicles 17:19 reads עבד (*ʿbd*, "servant") instead of the MT's דבר (*dbr*, "word"; cf. also δοῦλον, *doulon*, "servant," in some MSS of the LXX). The MT, however, should be retained as the *lectio difficilior*. In addition, the variant "servant" can be explained as *lapsus calami* under the influence of the same word at the end of the verse as well as near the end of the previous verse. Moreover, David's use of "servant" ten times in his prayer (see comment on v.19) may be intentional and would thus allow no further occurrences.

23 When used of the God of Israel, אֱלֹהִים (*ʾᵉlōhîm*) usually takes singular agreement; when used of pagan gods, it takes plural agreement. There are a few exceptions to this general rule, however, and הָלְכוּ (*hālᵉkû*, "went out" [pl.]) is a case in point. (The parallel in 1Ch 17:21 uses the singular.) For discussion of honorific plural nouns, see *IBHS*, 122–24.

The difference between the textual and marginal readings in the NIV focuses on one Hebrew word. The MT's לארצך (*lʾrṣk*, "for your land") is surely to be read לגרש (*lgrš*, "by driving out"), with the parallel in 1 Chronicles 17:21 (cf. also LXX).

25 Though not uncommon elsewhere in the OT, the compound divine title "LORD God" occurs only here in the books of Samuel, and for unknown reasons. In any case, the MT's vocalization indicates that the Hebrew name is to be pronounced in the same way as the compound Hebrew title translated seven times as "Sovereign LORD" (see comment on v.18)—in other words, *ʾădōnāy ʾĕlōhîm*.

27 In the MT "offer ... prayer" is a cognate accusative construction (lit., "pray ... prayer"; cf. 1Ki 8:28–29).

5. David's Enemies Defeated (8:1–14)

OVERVIEW

Recapitulating David's military victories during his years as king over Israel and Judah in Jerusalem, vv.1–14 parallel the account of the defeat of the Philistines (5:17–25) in the overall structure of the narrative of David's powerful reign (5:17–8:18; see Overview). The summary may not be intended as all-inclusive, since other wars and skirmishes are mentioned later in the book (cf. ch. 10; 21:15–22; 23:8–23).

The section leaves no doubt about the fact that David's armies were invincible and that no nation, however numerous or powerful its fighting men, could hope to withstand the Israelite hosts. The account teems with verbs denoting military action: *nkh* ("defeat/fight/strike down," vv.1–3, 5, 9–10 ["(gain) victory"], 13); *knʿ* ("subdue," v.1); *lqḥ* ("take," vv.1, 7–8); *hyh lʿbdym* ("become subject," vv.2, 6, 14); *lkd* ("capture," v.4); *lḥm* ("[do] battle," v.9); and *kbš* ("subdue," v.11).

At the same time, however, a striking summary statement appears twice in the section as though to emphasize that the reader—and David himself—must never forget the identity of the real conqueror: "The LORD gave David victory wherever he went" (vv.6, 14).

Geographical arrangement of the conquered foes seems intentional and produces the following outline.

A. Enemies defeated in the west (v.1)
B. Enemies defeated in the east (v.2)
C. Enemies defeated in the north (vv.3–12)
D. Enemies defeated in the south (vv.13–14)

Second Samuel 8:1–14 is paralleled in 1 Chronicles 18:1–13 (cf. also 1Ki 11:23b–24a).

1 In the course of time, David defeated the Philistines and subdued them, and he took Metheg Ammah from the control of the Philistines.

2 David also defeated the Moabites. He made them lie down on the ground and measured them off with a length of cord. Every two lengths of them were put to death, and

the third length was allowed to live. So the Moabites became subject to David and
brought tribute.
[3]Moreover, David fought Hadadezer son of Rehob, king of Zobah, when he went to
restore his control along the Euphrates River. [4]David captured a thousand of his chariots,
seven thousand charioteers and twenty thousand foot soldiers. He hamstrung all but a
hundred of the chariot horses.
[5]When the Arameans of Damascus came to help Hadadezer king of Zobah, David
struck down twenty-two thousand of them. [6]He put garrisons in the Aramean kingdom of
Damascus, and the Arameans became subject to him and brought tribute. The LORD gave
David victory wherever he went.
[7]David took the gold shields that belonged to the officers of Hadadezer and brought
them to Jerusalem. [8]From Tebah and Berothai, towns that belonged to Hadadezer, King
David took a great quantity of bronze.
[9]When Tou king of Hamath heard that David had defeated the entire army of Hadadezer, [10]he sent his son Joram to King David to greet him and congratulate him on his
victory in battle over Hadadezer, who had been at war with Tou. Joram brought with him
articles of silver and gold and bronze.
[11]King David dedicated these articles to the LORD, as he had done with the silver and
gold from all the nations he had subdued: [12]Edom and Moab, the Ammonites and the Philistines, and Amalek. He also dedicated the plunder taken from Hadadezer son of Rehob,
king of Zobah.
[13]And David became famous after he returned from striking down eighteen thousand
Edomites in the Valley of Salt.
[14]He put garrisons throughout Edom, and all the Edomites became subject to David.
The LORD gave David victory wherever he went.

COMMENTARY

1 The formula "in the course of time" is used often in 2 Samuel to denote narrative sequence, whether chronological or thematic (see 2:1 and Notes). It is impossible to know for certain whether the divine promises of ch. 7 preceded or followed the divine victories of ch. 8 (cf. 7:1, "After ... the LORD had given him rest from all his enemies around him"; 7:11, "I will also give you rest from all your enemies"). At the same time, however, Merrill, 247, plausibly argues that "David was occupied by military affairs throughout his early years; not until after the subjugation of Rabbah [in Ammon; cf. v.12; ch. 10; 11:1; 12:26–27, 29] did he move the ark and make any plans for a temple" (and thus, presumably, receive and respond to Nathan's oracle [ch. 7]). Carlson, 115–16, however, argues that the Lord's promise to "provide a place" for his people (7:10) is fulfilled by David's conquests described in ch. 8.

Although in my judgment Merrill's overall treatment of the chronological problems (243–48) is more persuasive, final resolution must await further evidence (if any).

In any event, it would seem that the narrator intends the account of the Philistine defeat (v.1) to resume the story told in 5:17–25 (cf. Baldwin, 219; Gordon, *I and II Samuel*, 242). The verb *nkh* ("strike," 5:24; "struck down," 5:25) is echoed in v.1 ("defeated"). As for the verb *knʿ* ("subdued," v.1), Carlson, 57, is of the opinion that the expression alludes "to the greatest triumph in the period of the Judges, 4:23" (cf. also Dt 9:3; 1Ch 17:10; Ne 9:24; Ps 81:14). It is better, however, to relate it to 1 Samuel 7:13, which reports that during Samuel's judgeship "the Philistines were subdued and did not invade Israelite territory again"—especially since additional terms in v.1 reprise the same context in 1 Samuel: *lqḥ* ("took," v.1) is rendered "had captured" in 1 Samuel 7:14, and "from the control [*yad*] of the Philistines" (v.1) is translated as "from the power [*yad*] of the Philistines" in 1 Samuel 7:14.

Exactly what it was that David "took" from the Philistines cannot be determined with certainty. If *meteg hāʾammâ* is a place name ("Metheg Ammah," NIV), it occurs nowhere else, and attempts to relate it to "the hill of Ammah" (2:24) simply compare one obscure/unknown site to another. The word *meteg* elsewhere means "bit, halter" (2Ki 19:28 = Isa 37:29; Ps 32:9; Pr 26:3), and *ʾammâ* may here be cognate to *ʾēm* ("mother"). The phrase *meteg hāʾammâ* would then mean "the authority of the mother-city/metropolis" (BDB, 52; ASV; Driver, 277; cf. 20:19, which refers to a "city that is a mother [*ʾēm*] in Israel"). Most commentators agree that this meaning conveys the general sense of the phrase and note that the parallel in 1 Chronicles 18:1 interprets it to refer to "Gath and its surrounding villages" (lit., "its daughters"). The summary of Kirkpatrick (*Second Book of Samuel*, 105) is typical:

> The most probable explanation of this obscure expression is *took the bridle of the metropolis out of the hand of the Philistines*, i.e. wrested from them the control of their chief city. This is equivalent to the statement in I Chr. xviii.I that "David took Gath and her towns out of the hand of the Philistines"; and it may be noticed that the metaphor of the "mother-city" is employed there, for the word translated "towns" literally means *daughters*.

A less acceptable solution is that of Hertzberg, 288 n. b, who prefers to understand *ʾammâ* in its more common sense of "forearm, cubit" and to render the phrase "the reins of the forearm, the leading reins." Thus "up to this point, the Philistines were in the saddle in Palestine; from now on it is Israel, i.e. David" (290).

The importance of the conquest of Philistia by David can scarcely be overestimated: "The Philistines considered themselves the legitimate heirs of the Egyptian rule in Palestine and their defeat by David implied the passage of the Egyptian province of Canaan into the hands of the Israelites" (Malamat, 100).

2 As David "defeated" the Philistines (v.1), so also he "defeated" the Moabites (v.2). Why he fought against Moab is unknown, especially since the Moabite Ruth was his ancestor (cf. Ru 4:10, 13, 16–17) and Moab had at one time sheltered his parents (see comment on 1Sa 22:3–4). "A Jewish tradition relates that the king of Moab betrayed his trust and murdered David's parents" (Kirkpatrick, *Second Book of Samuel*, 105). If it be true that David is presaged in the messianic promise of Numbers 24:17 (see comment on 7:7), Patrick, 402, may be correct in asserting that the Moabite defeat fulfills that prophecy (cf. Kirkpatrick, *Second Book of Samuel*, 105).

David's method of executing a specified number of prisoners of war is not attested elsewhere. Making them lie down on the ground and then measuring them off with a length of cord, he puts two-thirds of them to death. Since the terminology in this description is often used of the measuring and allocation of land (cf. Jos 19:51; Pss 16:6; 60:6 = 108:7; 78:55; Am 7:17; Mic 2:5), a few earlier commentators assumed that "made them lie down" is to be understood metaphorically as "laying level their strong Holds and fortified Places" (Patrick, 402) and that, after the country was carefully surveyed ("measured ... off"), two-thirds of it was depopulated. Although the end result would be the same under either interpretation, the consensus among recent commentators strongly favors the rendering adopted by the NIV. David's destruction of Moab means that only one third of its inhabitants are "allowed to live"—ironically, a more humane treatment than his earlier attacks on other areas, during which he did not "leave" anyone "alive" (see 1Sa 27:9, 11 and comment; same Heb. verb in both passages). Characteristically, the parallel in 1 Chronicles 18:2 omits the account of David's atrocity in v.2.

Like the Arameans (v.6) and Edomites (v.14), the Moabites "became subject to" David (v.2). In the case of Moab and Aram, vassalage to David explicitly included bringing tribute to him (vv.2, 6; cf. Wiseman, "'Is It Peace?'" 313). Although not stated in the text, bringing of tribute may be implied in the Edomite subjugation as well. The Hebrew word for "tribute" often means "gift(s)/offering(s)" presented as sacrifices (cf. 1Ch 16:29; Ps 96:8), which are thus understood as tribute brought into the throne room of the Great King. After David's death, nations conquered by him would continue to bring tribute to his son Solomon (1Ki 4:21) and his successors. The Moabite contribution to King Ahab would be substantial: "a hundred thousand lambs and ... the wool of a hundred thousand rams" (2Ki 3:4).

3–12 Despite the limited information available about Aram during David's reign, the space given to its conquest in this chapter testifies to its overall significance in the scheme of things.

> The kingdom of Aram Zobah ... whose strength is difficult to estimate from the fragmentary evidence found in the Bible, expanded during the reign of its king Hadadezer ... over vast territories. In the south it apparently reached the frontier of Ammon, as can be deduced from the intervention of Aramaean troops on the side of the Ammonites in their war with David (II Samuel 10:6 ff.). In the northeast the kingdom of Zobah extended to the river Euphrates and even to territories beyond it (II Samuel 8:3; 10:16). In the east it touched the Syrian desert and in the west it included Coele-syria. (Malamat, 100)

(See also Mazar, "The Aramean Empire," esp. 102, which locates the focal point of the Zobah kingdom "probably in the northern part of the Lebanon valley.")

The events in this section are sometimes interrelated with those of 10:1–11:1 and 12:26–31 by seeing them as describing the same situation or by viewing them as sequential. It is probably best, however, to understand 8:3–12 as a record of battles that occurred after the campaigns reported in chs. 10–12 (cf. John Bright, *A History of Israel*, 4th ed. [Louisville: Westminster John Knox, 2000], 202 n. 38; Leon J. Wood, *A Survey of Israel's History* [rev. ed.; Grand Rapids: Zondervan, 1986], 226).

As David had "defeated" the Philistines (v.1) and Moabites (v.2), so he also "fought" (v.3) and "defeated" (v.9) the Arameans (same Heb. verb in each case). His main adversary is "Hadadezer [vv.3, 5, 7–10, 12; 10:16, 19; 1Ki 11:23] son of Rehob." (The mention of Rehob only in vv.3 and 12 serves to form an inclusio that demarcates the literary unit.) "Hadadezer" ("[The God] Hadad is [my] help") is the Hebrew form of an Aramean dynastic royal title that appears in transcription in Assyrian annals as *(H)adad-(ʿ)idri* (cf. *ANET*, 279) (cf. the name of Saul's son-in-law Adriel ["My help is God"; 21:8; 1Sa 18:19], which corresponds to the name "Azriel" in Hebrew [1Ch 5:24; 27:19; Jer 36:26]).

This particular Hadadezer was king of Zobah (vv.3, 5, 12; 10:6, 8; 23:36; title of Ps 60), an Aramean nation Saul had earlier fought against with success (see 1Sa 14:47 and comment). "Hadad" was the most common personal name of the Canaanite storm god, better known by the appellative title *baʿal*, meaning "lord." During the Hyksos period (seventeenth–sixteenth centuries BC) he was identified with the Egyptian storm god Seth, and it was probably at that time that "Baal" came into use as a personal name for Hadad (cf. William F. Albright, *Yahweh and the Gods of Canaan: A Historical Analysis of Two Contrasting Faiths* [Garden City, N.Y.: Doubleday, 1968], 124).

The ambiguous pronoun "he" (v.3), whose antecedent could be either "David" or "Hadadezer," has puzzled scholars for centuries (cf. Patrick, 404). Most recent commentators, however, prefer Hadadezer (cf. K&D, 358: "The subject ... must be Hadadezer and not David; for David could not have extended his power to the Euphrates before the defeat of Hadadezer"). The phrase "restore [cf. 9:7; 16:3 ('give ... back')] his control" translates *lᵉhāšîb yādô*, for which the parallel in 1 Chronicles has *lᵉhaṣṣîb yādô* (rendered "establish his control" in the NIV). But the latter expression surely means "set up his monument" (cf. CEV; NRSV; REB; Tanakh), referring to "the erection of a victory stele" (Gordon, *I and II Samuel*, 243; cf. Driver, 281; see comments on 18:18; 1Sa 15:12; cf. esp. Hoffner, 222 n. 6).

Such monuments were located in prominent places (cf. 18:18), such as near the "Euphrates River" (v.3), the greatest river in western Asia (and therefore sometimes called simply "the River" [par excellence]). Marking the eastern reaches of David's realm, the Euphrates was also one of the fixed boundaries of the land promised to Abraham (Ge 15:18). Reference to it here thus forges yet another link between the Abrahamic and Davidic covenants (cf. also Dt 1:7; 11:24; Jos 1:4; 1Ki 4:21, 24).

The general tenor of the account implies that David drove back the forces of Hadadezer all the way to the Euphrates. In so doing he captured substantial numbers of chariots, charioteers, and foot soldiers (v.4). Philistine chariots and riders/charioteers were feared far and wide (see comments on 1:6; 1Sa 13:5), and there is no reason to assume that Aramean chariots and riders were feared any less. The number of Aramean foot soldiers was about twenty thousand (cf. also 10:6), which, although a standard figure for a large army (cf. J. B. Segal, 6–7), is nevertheless smaller than the number that Saul was able to muster against the Amalekites (1Sa 15:4). In any event, since *ʾelep* ("thousand") sometimes means "(military) unit" in battle contexts (see comment on 1Sa 4:2), a measure of uncertainty obtains for at least some of the occurrences of *ʾelep* in ch. 8.

David's seizure of a thousand Aramean chariots included the capture of the chariot horses that pulled them. He "hamstrung" most of the horses (that is, severed the large tendon above and behind their hocks to disable them; cf. also Jos 11:6, 9). The mutilated horses "were likely put to some other, peaceable, use, probably in agriculture and haulage, but especially breeding" (Halpern, 139). Although it is often assumed that David hamstrung them because he did not understand the value of chariots in warfare and that not until the days of Solomon did chariot squadrons become an integral part of Israel's armed forces, Yadin, 285, makes a good case for David's use of chariots despite the present hamstringing incident. David's own chariot units may have already been up to full strength; he could not have successfully fought a formidable Aramean chariot force far from home without comparable vehicles of his own, and "the Biblical references to the chariots of Absalom [15:1] and Adonijah [1 Kings 1:5] show that they must have [also] been a common sight in the army of David."

Damascus (v.5), a key player in the Aramean league of nations (cf. Merrill F. Unger, *Israel and the Arameans of Damascus* [London: James Clarke, 1957], 38–51) that included Zobah (v.3) and (Beth) Rehob (10:6, 8), sends a huge contingent of troops to "help" (*ʿzr*) Hadadezer. The obvious wordplay on Hadadezer's name (see comment on v.3) is especially poignant, since his god Hadad is clearly of no help to him. Indeed, David strikes down "twenty-two thousand" of the Damascus reinforcements, a number used in the OT to represent a "large national force" (cf. J. B. Segal, 7, for details).

David then puts "garrisons" (v.6; cf. also v.14) throughout the Aramean kingdom of Damascus, with the result that the Arameans become tributary to him. Since *nᵉṣîb* ("garrison"; cf. also 1Sa 10:5; 13:3 ["outpost"]) can also mean "monument/pillar" (Ge 19:26) or "governor" (1Ki 4:19), it is possible that "governors" is intended here (and in v.14; cf. Mazar, "The Aramean Empire," 104). Larry E. McKinney, however ("David's Garrisons in Edom," *BI* 10/1 [Fall 1983]: 62), observes that the various nuances are not necessarily mutually exclusive and cogently argues that the word "likely encompasses something of each of these possible meanings." The "garrison," then, would have served as a "monument" to David's control over Aram and would have been commanded by a "governor."

A characteristic formula stressing divine enablement recurs (with variations) throughout the book of Judges: "Then the LORD raised up judges, who saved [*yšʿ*] them out of the hands of these raiders" (Jdg 2:16; cf. Jdg 2:18; 3:9, 31; 6:14; 10:1). Talmon, 51 n. 36, plausibly suggests that "the author of the Book of Samuel employed this formula in reference to David, but with an interesting change: 'And the Lord gave victory [*yšʿ*] to David wherever he went'" (vv.6, 14; see also comments on "rescue[d]" [*yšʿ*] in 3:18; 1Sa 14:23). In the present section this sentence serves to frame the rest of the story of David's conquests (cf. Burke O. Long, 387, 398) and in so doing stresses that God, not David, is the true Savior of his people. Indeed, the Lord not only grants victory to David but is also with him "wherever" he goes (see 7:9 and comment).

Part of the tribute that David "took" (vv.7–8) from Hadadezer was his officers' "gold shields" (v.7). Though they "belonged to" (or were "carried by," as the parallel in 1Ch 18:7 states) the officers, they were obviously ceremonial or decorative shields and were not used in battle (cf. SS 4:4; Eze 27:11). Whether they were made of solid gold or simply bossed with gold or supplied with golden fittings is impossible to say (contrast the shields mentioned in 1Ki 10:16–17; 14:26). Brought to Jerusalem and eventually placed in Solomon's temple where they remained for well over a century, the shields now "belonged to" David (2Ki 11:10). Brueggemann (*David's Truth*, 81) notes that David's rapacious ways, as evidenced by the verb "took" (vv.7–8), were not limited to shields and similar items of booty. Later he sent messengers to Bathsheba "to get her" (lit., "and he took her," 11:4).

Three towns that belonged to Hadadezer (Tebah, Berothai [v.8], and Cun [cf. the 1Ch 18:8 parallel]) yielded a "great quantity of bronze" to King David. *Harbēh mᵉʾōd* ("great quantity," v.8) is echoed in 12:2, where the prophet Nathan intimates that David is a rich man who has a "very large number" of sheep and cattle. From this later perspective the Chronicler adds to v.8 the note that Solomon used the bronze "to make the bronze Sea, the pillars and various bronze articles" for his temple (1Ch 18:8; cf. 1Ki 7:13–47). It is therefore ironic that the identical bronze items became booty in the hands of the

Babylonians when Solomon's temple was destroyed in 586 BC (cf. 2Ki 25:13–14).

The MT's "Betah" (v.8) is doubtless a metathesized form of Tebah (cf. Tibhath, another form of the same name in the parallel in 1Ch 18:8 [see NIV note there]; cf. also some MSS of the LXX [see NIV note here]), the Tubikhi of Egyptian inscriptions (cf. *ANET*, 477 and n. 31; exact location unknown). Tebah appears in a list of Abraham's descendants (Ge 22:24) in association with Aram (Ge 22:21). The ancient site of Berothai (probably the same as Berothah in Eze 47:16) is doubtless modern Bereitan, thirty miles north-northwest of Damascus. Ancient Cun is perhaps modern Ras Baalbek, thirty miles north-northeast of Berothai. All three towns were therefore located in the northern part of the Lebanese Beqaᶜ. References to Berothai and Cun have apparently been found in close association with each other in an Eblaite gazetteer (cf. Mitchell Dahood, "Philological Observations on Five Biblical Texts," *Bib* 63/3 [1982]: 390–91; for additional details on all three sites, see McCarter, *II Samuel*, 250).

The news of David's defeat of the entire army of Hadadezer eventually reaches the ears of Tou, king of Hamath (v.9). The capital city of a nation with the same name, ancient Hamath is modern Hama (on the middle Orontes River about 120 miles north of Damascus). Added to the fact that David had already pursued Hadadezer "as far as Hamath" (1Ch 18:3), it is understandable that Tou would want to make peace with the conquering Israelite king. He therefore sends his son to "greet" David (lit., "ask about the well-being/welfare of," v.10; cf. 1Sa 10:4; 30:21; see comments on 1Sa 17:22; 25:5) and to "congratulate" him (lit., "bless"; cf. 1Ki 1:47; see comment on "give ... greetings" in 1Sa 25:14) on his "victory" (from *nkh*, "strike down," a different root from the one used in vv.6, 14; see comment on v.6) over Hadadezer.

Indeed, the Aramean king has been "at war with" Tou (lit., "a man of battles of/against"; cf. Driver, 282, who interprets the idiom to mean "a man engaged often in conflict with"; cf. also "those who wage war against," Isa 41:12 [same Heb. phrase as here]). The word *ṣbh* ("Zobah") in Aramean script has been found on bricks excavated at Hamath and dating from as early as the tenth century BC, a discovery that probably testifies to "an ancient connection between Zobah and Hamath" (Malamat, 101 n. 22).

Joram, the name of Tou's son, means "The Lord is exalted." His original Aramean name, Hadoram (that is, *Haddu-rām*, "Hadad is exalted"; cf. NIV note, LXX, and the parallel in 1Ch 18:10), may have been modified by David. If so, it is not implausible "to see a certain Israelite influence on internal affairs in Hamath" (cf. Yutaka Ikeda, "Solomon's Trade in Horses and Chariots in Its International Setting" [in Ishida], 237 and n. 126).

Although Joram brings "articles of silver and gold and bronze" to David (v.10), this does not necessarily mean that Hamath was now tributary to Israel in a formal sense but should probably be understood as a voluntary gift to gain David's good will (cf. similarly 1Ki 15:18–19; contrast Wiseman, "'Is It Peace?'" 319; Mazar, "The Aramean Empire," 103; Malamat, 101 and n. 23, who, however, admits that "the country of Hamath, of course, was not really annexed to Israel, and therefore it is often mentioned in the Biblical literature in connection with the northern frontier of the Israelite kingdom"). Since silver was often rarer (and therefore more valuable) than gold in the ancient Near East (cf. R. J. Forbes, *Studies in Ancient Technology* [Leiden: Brill, 1964], 8:209–26 passim), the mention of silver before gold in vv.10–11 (cf. also 21:4) may indicate their relative value during David's time (cf., however, the parallel in 1Ch 18:10, where the order is reversed).

In grateful acknowledgment of divine blessing, David dedicates all the articles—whether received as gift, tribute, or plunder—to the Lord (vv.11–12). Although v.12 concludes the relatively lengthy account of his campaigns against the north (Aram), the narrator also includes in it a summary of David's conquest of neighboring nations in every direction: south (Edom; cf. also vv.13–14), east (Moab [cf. v.2] and Ammon [cf. also chs. 10–12, esp. 12:29–31 (cf. Bailey, 78); see also 1Sa 11:1 and comment]), west (Philistia; cf. v.1), and southwest (Amalek; cf. also 1:1; 1Sa 30; see also comments on 1Sa 14:48; 15:2; 28:18).

13–14 The statement in v.13 that David "returned from striking down" the Edomites echoes the assertion in 1:1 that David "returned from striking down" the Amalekites and with it forms an inclusio that surrounds a large literary section of 2 Samuel (see comment on 1:1; cf. also 1Sa 17:57; 18:6). At the same time *nkh* ("striking down") not only serves to introduce the present literary unit (as it does the other three in this section: v.1 ["defeated"], v.2 ["defeated"], v.3 ["fought"]) but also forms an inclusio with the same verb in v.1, thus helping to demarcate the narrative of the defeat of David's enemies in vv.1–14. Although Abishai son of Zeruiah (see 1Sa 26:6 and comment) did the actual "striking down" (see the parallel in 1Ch 18:12), David is the supreme commander and thus gets the credit ("became famous" [v.13] = lit., "made a name"; cf. 1Ki 1:47; see comment on 7:9).

Abishai strikes down eighteen thousand Edomites (v.13), while his brother Joab, commander of Israel's army (v.16), strikes down twelve thousand (see the title of Ps 60), apparently in the same battle. Whether the twelve thousand should be added to the eighteen thousand or are part of them is impossible to say. The proposal of Patrick, 408, is as typical as it is attractive: "*Abishai* who began the Fight, perhaps slew six Thousand, and then *Joab* coming in with his Reserve slew twelve Thousand more; which in all make eighteen Thousand." The "Valley of Salt" (cf. also 2Ki 14:7; 2Ch 25:11) was perhaps either the Wadi el-Milh (Arabic for "valley of salt") east of Beersheba or was located in the es-Sebkha region south of the Dead (Salt) Sea.

Having conquered the Edomites, David (through Abishai; cf. 1Ch 18:12–13) "put garrisons throughout Edom" (literally and emphatically "put in Edom garrisons, in all Edom he put garrisons," v.14) as he did similarly in the Aramean kingdom of Damascus (see comment on "garrisons" in v.6). McKinney ("David's Garrisons in Edom," 64–65) points to Umm el-Bayyara (near Petra) and Ezion Geber (at the northern end of the Gulf of Aqaba) as the most likely locations for Israelite garrisons and suggests the possibility that "David's desire to exploit Edom's abundant copper mines was a chief cause of his war with the Edomites." The narrator's summary, which replicates v.6b (see comment), concludes the section on a note of triumph—"The LORD gave David victory wherever he went"—and serves again to remind the reader that it is because God is with him that David succeeds.

Malamat, 100, observes that the "unprecedented territorial expansion" of David's realm "may be explained by assuming that David's kingdom based itself on comprehensive political organizations which had existed before and which, through David's victories over their rulers, passed into his hands with their complex systems intact." It was also made possible by the power vacuum left by the decline and/or fall of the great empires (Hittite, Egyptian, Babylonian, Assyrian) in the twelfth and eleventh centuries BC (cf. Mazar, "The Aramean Empire," 102). By any method of calculation, the regions added to David's realm through the defeat of the nations surrounding him more than doubled the territory of Israel. The successful military campaigns described in ch. 8 initiated the golden age of Israelite history.

David's new boundaries, resulting from his conquest of Philistia (v.1), Moab (v.2), Cis-Euphrates (vv.3–4), Aram of Damascus (vv.5–12), Ammon, Amalek (v.12), and Edom (vv.13–14), correspond to those outlined in the divine promise to Abraham: "To your descendants I give this land, from the river of Egypt to the great river, the Euphrates" (Ge 15:18; cf. also Dt 11:24; Jos 1:4). Yet another link is thus forged between the covenants of Abraham and David. Indeed, as Carlson, 116, expresses it, "the Covenant made with Abraham is fulfilled through David" (cf. also 1Ki 4:21, where David's realm as bequeathed to Solomon is described in similar terms).

How large, however, was David's realm? Do the maps at the backs of many of our Bibles give a true historical picture of the size and impact of David's empire? That depends. If we define "empire" in terms of the Hittite or Assyrian or Babylonian or Persian empires, the "empire" of David pales by comparison. According to Kitchen, *Reliability*, 97–102, for example, David's realm was the latest in a series of four "mini-empires" that existed "ca. 1200–900—neither earlier nor later." In chronological and geographical (north-to-south) succession they may be listed as follows:

1. Tarhuntassa/Tabal in eastern Turkey, whose "great kings" were successors of the last kings of the Hittite empire that had broken up under the impact of external attack at the end of the thirteenth century
2. Carchemish southeast of Tabal and centering on a relatively small heartland surrounding the storied city of Carchemish, with subject allies under the authority of its "great kings" for a hundred miles or so in all directions, including Hamath and environs to the south, until about 1000 BC
3. Aram Zobah under its "king" Hadadezer, with its heartland southeast of Phoenicia, its conquests southeast of Hamath, and its subject allies in the areas around Damascus
4. Israel and Judah as the heartland with Jerusalem as its capital, under its "king" David, whose major conquests included Aram, Ammon, Moab, and Edom and whose subject allies inhabited Maacah, Geshur and Hamath

> Thus David's mini-empire ... included three levels of rule: home core, subjugated territories (under governors and subject kings), and subject allies, less closely tied to Israel's regime. Similar profiles appear in the cases of the other mini-empires also.... All four of our mini-empires took over defeated opponents and their territories as they stood, without much territorial change; thus such units could readily break away as natural political entities when the central power weakened. It is a considerable contrast with the vast Neo-Assyrian, Neo-Babylonian, and Persian empires, where (increasingly) new large-scale provinces became the norm. (Kitchen, *Reliability*, 102–3)

David Noel Freedman also notes: "In an era of profound Egyptian weakness and slow Assyrian rise David was himself king of Israel, king of Judah, owner of Jerusalem, chief of Moab and Ammon, and overlord of Aram Zobah, Aram Beth-rehob, Edom, and the Canaanite city-states of Palestine" (Freedman, "The Age of David and Solomon," in Freedman, *History and Religion*, 1:305).

While applauding Baruch Halpern for providing "a mass of informative detail with regard to the issues of 2 Sam 8 (*Secret Demons*, 133–226)," Campbell (*2 Samuel*, 82) rebukes him for asserting that "the authors of 2 Samuel ... *suggested, implied, insinuated* that David's achievements were a great deal more extensive than in reality they were. But they did not openly prevaricate, on this subject at least" (ibid., 206–7; emphasis added). Apart from the issue of authorial intention (and that in itself is a grave issue), it is unwise to speak of the "author of 2 Sam 8 ... [as] a highly skilled propagandist" (Halpern, *Secret Demons*,

158), without discussion of the complex and differing traditions incorporated into this compilation.

In summary, "we may conclude that the notion of a Davidic empire, as biblically defined, is entirely plausible, and the notion of it being an anachronistic retrojection from the postexilic period can be safely laid to rest" (V. Philips Long, "The Early Monarchy," 232; cf. his full treatment on 230–32).

NOTES

1 According to Carlson, 116 n. 1, אַמָּה (*ʾammâ*) "should probably be interpreted as an Akkadianism, *ammatu* 'land.'" Akkadian *ammatu* in this sense, however, is rare (cf. *ammatu B* in *CAD*, 1/2:75). Indeed, *ammatu* in Akkadian can just as readily be a synonym for *ummu*, "mother" (cf. *ammatu C* in *CAD*, 1/2:75; see comment on v.1).

3 The famed tenth-century AD Aleppo Codex, one of the oldest and best MSS of the MT in existence, is referred to in Hebrew as *Keter Aram Zova* ("The Crown of Aram Zobah") and represents the Ben Asher text of the Hebrew Bible. Held up as a model by Moses Maimonides, the great twelfth-century philosopher and Bible scholar, it experienced a harrowing pilgrimage. "Several times it was stolen by kings and conquerors and held for ransom. Maimonides saw it in Cairo after the Jews there ransomed it from the Seljuk Turks, who had looted it from Jerusalem. It arrived in the thriving metropolis of Aleppo ... sometime around 1478, after Jewish Aleppines paid off the Ottoman sultan" (Harvey Minkoff, "The Aleppo Codex: Ancient Bible from the Ashes," *BRev* 7/4 [1991]: 27). In 1947 a quarter of it was consumed by fire in a synagogue in Syria, but the remainder was rescued from the ashes and eventually found its way to Israel in 1958, where it is now in the custody of the Hebrew University in Jerusalem.

The NIV's "Euphrates" reads with the *Qere* (cf. the parallel text of 1Ch 18:3) rather than with the *Kethiv*, which omits the consonants of פְּרָת (*pᵉrāt*). The other places in the MT where vowels appear without the appropriate consonants written above them are 16:23 (see Note); 18:20; Jdg 20:13; 2Ki 19:31, 37; Jer 31:38; 50:29. The Hebrew form *Perath* derives from Akkadian *Purattu*, ultimately from Sumerian B/PURANUN. English "Euphrates" transliterates Greek Εὐφράτης (*Euphratēs*), which in turn also comes from Akkadian *Purattu* via Old Persian *Ufratu*.

4 The NIV's "captured a thousand of his chariots, seven thousand charioteers" reflects the wording of the parallel in 1 Chronicles 18:4 as well as the LXX and the probable reading in 4QSamuel[a] (for additional reasons justifying the NIV note and departure from the MT, see Ulrich, 56–57).

7 The Hebrew word rendered "shields" here and elsewhere in the OT more likely means "quivers" (for full discussion see *HALOT*, 2.1522–23; see also Alter, *The David Story*, 237; NEB; CEV; Tanakh fn.). At the end of the verse, 4QSamuel[a] adds the following parenthetical note: "(which, [later on, were] also [taken by Shoshak king of Egypt, when] he [w]ent up to Je[rusalem] in the days of Rehoboam son of Sol[omon])." Although the Qumran lacunae can be filled in by the LXX, which exhibits a similar plus, the addition is suspect because of the unexpected, premature mention of Shishak and Rehoboam (for which cf. 1Ki 14:25–26).

9 The MT's תֹּעִי (*tōʿî*, "Toi"; cf. NIV note) is a variant spelling of Tou, as the ancient versions make clear (cf. McCarter, *II Samuel*, 245; also 1Ch 18:9–10).

12–13 The NIV's "Edom(ites)" instead of "Aram(eans)" is not only based on the parallels in 1 Chronicles 18:11–12 but also has the support of the LXX and Syriac as well as of some Hebrew MSS (see NIV note). Because of the similarity between ד (*d*) and ר (*r*), אדם (*ʾdm*) and ארם (*ʾrm*) were often confused in scribal transmission.

13 It is also possible that "made a name" ("became famous," NIV) should rather be read "built a monument" (CEV; "victory monument," The Message). If so, then "twin references to monuments [vv.3, 13] frame the Aramean war report" (Halpern, 195–96). The "Valley of Salt" may have been known earlier as the Valley of Siddim (Ge 14:3, 8, 10; cf. Rasmussen, 44). It has been suggested that שִׂדִּים (*śiddîm*) is derived from the Hittite *siyantas*, "salt" (*ZPEB*, 5:426).

6. David's Officials (8:15–18)

OVERVIEW

The first twenty chapters of 2 Samuel divide rather naturally into four sections of varying length, each of which ends with a four-verse list of names (see Introduction: Outline). Each of the last two sections (5:17–8:18; chs. 9–20) concludes with a list of David's officials (8:15–18; 20:23–26). After a brief but majestic introduction (v.15), the present list proper (vv.16–18) includes the names, patronymics, and offices of the men in David's cabinet. Second Samuel 8:15–18 is paralleled in 1 Chronicles 18:14–17.

15David reigned over all Israel, doing what was just and right for all his people. 16Joab
son of Zeruiah was over the army; Jehoshaphat son of Ahilud was recorder; 17Zadok son
of Ahitub and Ahimelech son of Abiathar were priests; Seraiah was secretary; 18Benaiah
son of Jehoiada was over the Kerethites and Pelethites; and David's sons were royal
advisers.

COMMENTARY

15 A mighty warrior (vv.1–14), King David now reigns over "all" Israel (the description perhaps includes many if not most of the conquered territories) and administers justice and equity to "all" his people. Just as the statement that David "reigned over all Israel" is followed by a list of his officials, so also is the statement that his son Solomon "ruled over all Israel" (1Ki 4:1) followed by a similar list (1Ki 4:2–6).

"Doing what was just and right" was the hallmark of a strong king in the ancient Near East and included such reforms as the elimination of oppression and exploitation (cf. esp. Ps 72). Finding a precise parallel in Akkadian *kittum u mīšarum* (cf. *CAD*, 10/2:117–18), *mišpāṭ ûṣ^e dāqâ* ("just[ice] and right[eousness]") are qualities that the Great King himself exemplifies (cf. Ps 103:6) and that he expects in his people as well as in his rulers (cf. Isa 5:7; Am 5:7, 24; 6:12). In the eschaton the Messiah will demonstrate and implement them in their fullness (Isa 9:7).

16–18 "David's officialdom ... has been shown to have been organized in part at least on Egyptian models ... doubtless ... through Phoenician or other intermediaries," especially in differentiating between the recorder (v.16) and secretary (v.17; Unger, 17; cf. also McCarter, *II Samuel*, 255). As expected, the commander of David's army (v.16; cf 20:23; 1Ki 1:19) is Joab son of Zeruiah (see 1Sa 26:6 and comment; cf. also 2:13). Jehoshaphat ("The Lord judges") son of Ahilud (cf. 20:24) is recorder and remains so into the reign of Solomon (1Ki 4:3). The function of the recorder (cf. also 2Ki 18:18, 37; 2Ch 34:8) was apparently either to have oversight of state records and documents or to serve as a royal herald, equivalent to the Egyptian *whm.w* ("speaker"), whose role was to make reports to the king and transmit royal decrees (cf. Anderson, 136; McCarter, *II Samuel*, 255).

The identity and function of each of the three officials mentioned in v.17 swarm with problems, as commentaries, special studies, and monographs amply attest. Though appearing here by name for the first time, Zadok ("Righteous") was probably one of the preliminary fulfillments of the oracle of the man of God in 1 Samuel 2:35 (see comment; cf. also Jones, 133; Olyan, 183 n. 34). It is striking, and perhaps intentional, that Jehoshaphat (*yhwšpṭ*, v.16) and Zadok (*ṣdwq*, v.17) should be listed in sequence so soon after David is described as doing what is "just [*mšpṭ*] and right [*ṣdqh*]" (v.15).

The root *ṣdq* (GK 7405) is found in the names of priests and kings of Jerusalem from the earliest times (cf. Melchizedek [Ge 14:18]; Adoni-Zedek [Jos 10:1]), and Zedekiah was the last king of Judah before Jerusalem was destroyed by Nebuchadrezzar II in 586 BC. One of the postexilic priests in Jerusalem bore the name J(eh)ozadak (1Ch 6:14–15; Ezr 3:2, 8; 5:2; 10:18; Ne 12:26; Hag 1:1, 12, 14; Zec 6:11). In Ezekiel's theocracy, centering around Jerusalem, the "sons of Zadok" are "the only Levites who may draw near to the LORD to minister before him" (Eze 40:46; cf. also 43:19; 44:15; 48:11), while the Sadducees, the aristocratic priestly party headquartered at the Jerusalem temple beginning as early as the second century BC, almost certainly derive their name from Zadok. Partly because of the frequent use of *ṣdq* in names of priests/kings associated with Jerusalem, Zadok's origins are often linked to the so-called Jebusite hypothesis, which seeks to demonstrate that Zadok was the Jebusite priest of God Most High (like Melchizedek [Ge 14:18]) in Jerusalem before the conquest of the city of David (cf. H. H. Rowley, "Zadok and Nehushtan," *JBL* 68/2 [1939]: 113–41; Christian E. Hauer Jr., "Who Was Zadok?" *JBL* 82/1 [1963]: 89–94).

It is clear, however, that "Zadok son of Ahitub" (v.17) is not a Jebusite but a Levite (cf. 1Ch 6:1, 8, 52–53), not to be confused with the later Zadok son of Ahitub (1Ch 6:12; Zadok and Ahitub were both common priestly names [for Ahitub cf. 1Sa 14:3; 22:9, 11–12, 20; for Zadok cf. 1Ch 9:11; Ne 11:11]). Indeed, he should perhaps be identified with the Levite Zadok mentioned in 1 Chronicles 12:28 as a contemporary of David (cf. J. Barton Payne, *EBC*, 4:378). Cross (*Canaanite Myth and Hebrew Epic*, 214 n. 72) translates *naᶜar* as "aide" in the phrase *naᶜar gibbôr ḥāyil* (1Ch 12:28), which the NIV renders "brave young warrior." Cross thus understands the entire phrase to imply that Zadok was a "noteworthy/powerful aide" (or the like) in the service of the Levite Jehoiada (1Ch 12:27; cf. Olyan, 188–89 and n. 50; for *naᶜar* in the sense of "aide," cf. Ne 6:5). Benaiah (v.18), another of

David's officials, was probably the son of this same Jehoiada (for details cf. Olyan, 185).

In any event, Zadok was not from the line of Eli (see comment on 1Sa 2:35), whose only remaining descendant was apparently Abiathar (see 1Sa 22:20 and comment). Since Abiathar was the son of an Ahimelech who did not survive Doeg's slaughter of the priests of Nob (1Sa 22:16, 20), many commentators follow the Syriac version and read "Abiathar son of Ahimelech" (cf. also 1Sa 23:6; 30:7) instead of "Ahimelech son of Abiathar" in v.17. But there is no reason why the principle of papponymy (naming a male child after his grandfather), a widespread practice in ancient times (cf. 1Ch 6:9b–10a; 7:20), should not apply here. In addition, "Ahimelech son of Abiathar" as the name of one of David's priests is firmly attested elsewhere (cf. 1Ch 18:16 [where the reading "Abimelech" is clearly secondary; see NIV note]; 24:6). The young Ahimelech may have sometimes substituted for his father, Abiathar (cf. 15:24; 20:25), when the latter was unable to serve because of illness or the like (for discussion of various possibilities, see K&D, 365–67).

"Zadok a descendant of Eleazar [cf. 1Ch 6:4–8] and Ahimelech a descendant of Ithamar" (1Ch 24:3) shared priestly duties during at least part of the reign of David. Whether Zadok at first represented the southern half of the kingdom (originally headquartered in Hebron) and Ahimelech (or, alternatively, Abiathar) the northern (centered in Jerusalem after its capture by David), as some assert (cf. Cross, *Canaanite Myth and Hebrew Epic*, 214–15; Olyan, 183), is impossible to say. During the early years of David's reign, Zadok may have been appointed to offer sacrifices at the tabernacle in Gibeon (cf. 1Ch 16:39–40) and Abiathar/Ahimelech to minister before the ark of the covenant in Jerusalem (so also independently K&D, 365; see comment on 6:17 for the likelihood that there were two tabernacles during the reign of David).

The function of Seraiah ("The Lord prevails") as "secretary" (v.17) was as much that of a secretary of state as it was that of a royal scribe (cf. *AIs*, 131). In the parallel in 1 Chronicles 18:16, David's secretary is called Shavsha, while other secretaries bear the names of "Sheva" (20:25) and "Shisha" (1Ki 4:3) respectively. The similarity of the latter three names (which indeed may be alternative spellings of the same name and therefore refer to the same person) and their dissimilarity to that of Seraiah (which, unlike the others, contains a ר [*r*]) have led Aelred Cody ("Le titre égyptien et le nom propre du scribe de David," *RB* 72 [1965]: 387) to make the tantalizing suggestion that they reflect eighteenth/nineteenth dynasty Egyptian *sš-sʿt* or *sḥ-šʿt*, a compound expression that combines words meaning "scribe" and "official message," hence a term for a government scribe.

Cody goes on to note that this term translated into cuneiform appears in an Amarna letter addressed to the Egyptian court and concludes that in its OT occurrences it is simply the Egyptian equivalent of the Hebrew word for "secretary"—a proposal that makes sense in light of the fact that David's cabinet may have been patterned after Egyptian models (see comment on v.16). Attractive though the suggestion is, however, it would then leave the secretary unnamed/unidentified (and thus unique) in each list in which the term appears. Although Shavsha (1Ch 18:16) may be an alternative name for Seraiah in v.17, it is equally possible that he served as secretary in Seraiah's absence (for whatever reason).

Benaiah ("The Lord builds") is the son of Jehoiada (v.18), perhaps the same Jehoiada who was an older colleague of Zadok (v.17; cf. again 1Ch 12:27–28 and esp. 27:5, where Jehoiada is called a "priest"). Benaiah, in charge of David's bodyguard (23:22–23), eventually became a royal executioner (cf. 1Ki 2:25, 34, 46; also 2Sa 23:20–21) and rose to the position of commander-in-chief of Israel's army (1Ki 4:4). In the present context he is in charge of the "Kerethites and Pelethites" (v.18). The Kerethites are "'Cretans' without qualms" (K. A. Kitchen, "The Philistines," in Wiseman, *Peoples of the OT World* [Grand Rapids: Baker, 1998], 56), while the Pelethites are doubtless Philistines, the word *p^e lēṯî* being formed on the analogy of *k^e rēṯî*. (Pelethites are never mentioned apart from Kerethites [v.18; 15:18; 20:7, 23; 1Ki 1:38, 44; 1Ch 18:17].) Some of the Kerethites had apparently settled in or near Philistine territory (see comment on 1Sa 30:14).

Together with the Pelethites, the Kerethites constituted a corps of foreign mercenaries employed as David's bodyguard (for details see Notes on 1Sa 30:14; cf. also D. Huttar in *ZPEB*, 1:787; for full discussion, see M. Delcor, "Les Kéréthim et les Crétois," *VT* 28/4 [1978]: 409–22). "It seems likely that David sought to protect his kingship by having a bodyguard of foreign mercenaries who were independent of inner tensions in the court. They were professional soldiers, who are called 'David's mighty men' [*gibbôrîm*; 'special guard,' NIV] in 1 Kings 1:8" (Jones, 43; cf. also Brueggemann, *David's Truth*, 83).

The list of David's officials concludes by reporting that his sons (how many and who they were is not stated) were *kōh^a nîm* (the word is in emphatic position), which the NIV translates as "royal advisers." In v.17, however, with reference to Zadok and Ahimelech, the same word is rendered "priests" in the NIV (cf. also NIV note on v.18). Indeed, in another list of David's officials, Zadok and Ahimelech are called "priests" (20:25), after which the text continues by stating that Ira the Jairite was David's "priest" (20:26). These and similar considerations have led Carl E. Armerding ("Were David's Sons Really Priests?" in *Current Issues in Biblical and Patristic Interpretation: Studies in Honor of Merrill C. Tenney Presented by His Former Students*, ed. Gerald F. Hawthorne [Grand Rapids: Eerdmans, 1975], 76), among others, to assert that there were "priests in early Israel who were (1) connected with the royal house, (2) not of the Levitical order, and (3) serving a function that is still largely unknown to us."

Although the validity of Armerding's three points would seem beyond dispute, two interrelated questions remain: (1) Does the performance of priestly functions on occasion (cf. 24:25; 1Ki 8:64) automatically make the performer a "priest" in the strict sense of that word? I have argued earlier that it does not (see comment on 6:14; cf. similarly Rowley, "Zadok and Nehushtan," 129 n. 44).

(2) Does *kōhēn* (GK 3913) in contexts such as the present always mean "priest"? Not necessarily. Although in v.17 the LXX rightly refers to Zadok and Ahimelech as *hiereis* ("priests"), in v.18 it calls David's sons *aularchai* ("princes of the court"; cf. KJV's "chief rulers"). The parallel to v.18 in 1 Chronicles 18:17 understands *kōh^a nîm* to mean "chief officials at the king's side." After listing Zadok and Abiathar as "priests" in the Solomonic court (1Ki 4:4), the narrator describes Zabud son of Nathan as "a priest and personal adviser to the king" (1Ki 4:5), a phrase that would perhaps be better translated as "a priest—that is, a personal adviser to the king" (there is no "and" in the text), the latter phrase thus explaining what "priest" (*kōhēn*) means in this case. Similarly, Ira was probably David's "royal adviser" (*kōhēn*) rather than his "priest" (20:26). In a note on 1 Chronicles 18:17, J. Barton Payne defines *kōh^a nîm* as "a term that by Ezra's time was restricted to 'priests' but that in Samuel preserves an older, broader meaning of 'official ministers'" (*EBC*, 4:399; cf. BDB, 434, which defines *kōhēn* in certain situations as a chieftain/prince exercising priestly functions). In short, then, *kōhēn* does not always mean "priest" *sensu stricto*.

The relationship between vv.15–18 and 20:23–26 is discussed in the comment on the latter passage.

NOTE

18 The NIV's "over" translates על (*ʿl*), which appears in only one Hebrew MS but occurs in several ancient versions (cf. *BHS*) as well as in the parallel in 1 Chronicles 18:17. Its absence in the MT may be partially explained on the basis of haplography, since the previous word ends in ע (ʿ).

Although it does not deal adequately with the appearance of כהן (*khn*; GK 3913) in 20:26 and 1 Kings 4:5, the suggestion that כהנים (*khnym*, "priests") may be a transcriptional error for סכנים (*sknym*, "stewards") in 2Sa 8:18 is otherwise attractive. The parallel in 1 Chronicles 18:17 might then be attempting to explain the rare word סֹכֵן (*sōkēn*, GK 6125), which is found elsewhere in the OT only in Isaiah 22:15, where it is defined as one who is "in charge of the palace." The latter expression is used of Ahishar in the list of Solomon's cabinet officers (1Ki 4:6; for additional details see G. J. Wenham, "Were David's Sons Priests?" *ZAW* 87/1 [1975]: 79–82).

D. David's Court History (9:1–20:26)

OVERVIEW

The lengthy account of the court history of David that begins in ch. 9 is "the earliest and greatest example of Hebrew historiography" (Jackson, 195). Robert H. Pfeiffer's justifiably glowing description of these chapters is often quoted [*Introduction to the Old Testament*, rev. ed. [New York: Harper, 1948], 357):

> Ahimaaz, or whoever wrote the early source in Samuel, is the "father of history" in a much truer sense than Herodotus half a millennium later. As far as we know, he created history as an art, as a recital of past events dominated by a great idea.... David's biographer was a man of genius. Without any previous models as guide, he wrote a masterpiece, unsurpassed in historicity, psychological insight, literary style, and dramatic power.

(See also Jackson, 183 n. 4; Wharton, 341; Whybray, 10.) Indeed, David's court history has been claimed to be "the most brilliant historical narrative of antiquity" (Halpern, 133) and to function as the worthy conclusion to one of the greatest epics of all time (cf. Robert H. Pfeiffer and William G. Pollard, *The Hebrew Iliad: The History of the Rise of Israel under Saul and David* [New York: Harper, 1957], 86–120).

Ever since Rost's isolation of 2 Samuel 9–20 and 1 Kings 1–2 as a discrete literary unit (Rost, 65–114, esp. 84–87), it has been customary to refer to the account as the Succession Narrative (cf. Jackson, 183; Walter Brueggemann, "On Trust and Freedom," 3–4). But while there can be no doubt that the succession to David's throne is a prominent theme in these chapters, "the title *Court History* is preferable to *Succession History* (or the like) because the latter term focuses attention too narrowly upon one of its concerns, which, while it is extremely important, is hardly the only one. Thus a neutral title such as *Court History* more adequately reflects the contents" (Vanderkam, 522 n. 2). In a closely reasoned treatment James W. Flanagan ("Court History or Succession Document? A Study of 2 Samuel 9–20; 1 Kings 1–2," *JBL* 91/2 [1972]: 172–81) suggests that the bulk of chs. 9–20 constitutes a court history of David to which certain Solomonic sections, including 1 Kings 1–2, were later added, the end result comprising a succession narrative.

Flanagan's study raises the issue of the beginning and the ending of the narrative, including—but not restricted to—the question of whether 1 Kings 1–2 is part of it. Although most commentators would contend that 2 Samuel 9–20; 1 Kings 1–2 constitute a continuous literary unit (cf. Jackson, 195; Ackerman, 57; Perdue, 79), many would begin the story earlier than 2 Samuel 9, and/or conclude it later than 1 Kings 2, and/or remove from the chapters certain sections under the assumption that they are not part of the original account.

In any event, it is becoming increasingly clear that "it is difficult to think of I Kings 1–2, in which the urgency of the succession question is obvious, as deriving from the same hand as II Samuel 9–20, where it is not" (McCarter, "'Plots, True or False,'" 361). Flanagan ("Court History or Succession Document?" 173) points out that while there are literary similarities between 2 Samuel 9–20 and 1 Kings 1–2, there are differences as well. Although his attempt is not entirely successful, it demonstrates the unity of theme and purpose in the section as a whole. He concludes (ibid., 181) that 1 Kings 1–2 (plus the Bathsheba episode in 2Sa 11–12) were added to the court history by a later hand (cf. similarly McCarter, "'Plots, True or False,'" 361–62, 365–66).

Detailed characterizations of *dramatis personae*, intimate descriptions of human flaws and foibles, lengthy episodes instead of summary vignettes—these and other features lend to chs. 9–20 an impression of verisimilitude and unmistakably eyewitness quality (cf. Stuart Lasine, "Fiction, Falsehood, and Reality in Hebrew Scripture," *HS* 25 [1984]: 28). The entire account must have been written late in the reign of David or early in the reign of Solomon (cf. Jackson, 183–84; Whybray, 54–55), and the author, whether Ahimaaz or Abiathar or someone else (cf. Jackson, 190 and n. 27; Rost, 106), must himself have been a major player in the events he recorded.

If we allow for understandable hyperbole, the opinion of Jackson, 185, concerning the purpose of David's court history is helpful: "to display, in all their richness and depth, the varied relations of men who no longer walk by faith in the cultic religious symbols of the past but contend for temporal power and freedom of self-expression in the mundane world of daily, i.e. secular life." According to Whybray and others, wisdom influence is prominent throughout the narrative. Since most of chs. 9–20 can be justifiably characterized as "David under the Curse" (Carlson, 25) because of the section's uncomplimentary portrayal of David, it is not surprising that the Chronicler's parallels to these chapters include only the account of David's victory over the Ammonites (10:1–11:1; 12:29–31 = 1Ch 19:1–20:3; cf. similarly Perdue, 82 n. 15). Conspicuous by their absence in 1 Chronicles are the Bathsheba/Uriah episodes (11:2–12:25).

Despite Flanagan's valiant attempt ("Court History or Succession Document?" 177–81), no persuasive or convincing overall literary structure for chs. 9–20 has yet emerged. The most that can be suggested is a series of interlocking themes that weave their way throughout the tapestry of the text: rebukes delivered to David (Jackson, 187), sexual escapades (ibid., 189, 193 n. 31; Martin, 39), news reports (Jackson, 193 n. 33), the difficulty of distinguishing between good and evil (Ackerman, 42, 53), deception/treachery (Harry Hagan, "Deception as Motif and Theme in 2 Sam 9–20; 1 Kings 1–2," *Bib* 60/3 [1979]: 301–26). The narrator calls attention to divine purpose and activity only rarely, as, for example, in 11:27; 12:24; 17:14 (cf. Rost, 106; Jackson, 184–85; Brueggemann, "On Trust and Freedom," 9; Gerhard von Rad, "The Beginnings of Historical Writing in Ancient Israel," in *The Problem of the Hexateuch and Other Essays* [repr., London: SCM, 1984], 198–201; Whybray, 64). In numerous other instances the characters themselves express their belief that God is—or is not—at work.

As the previous literary unit (5:17–8:18) ends with a list of David's officials (8:15–18), so do chs. 9–20 (20:23–26). And as the succeeding literary unit (chs. 21–24) begins with a narrative concerning the survivors in Saul's family (21:1–14), so do chs. 9–20 (ch. 9; cf. esp. the reference to the "house" of "Saul" in the first verse of each unit [9:1; 21:1] and the foregrounding of Mephibosheth as the key survivor in each [9:6; 21:7]).

This latter fact weakens the thesis of Keys that David's court history begins in ch. 10 rather than ch. 9 (Gillian Keys, *The Wages of Sin: A Reappraisal of the 'Succession Narrative'* [JSOTSup 221; Sheffield: Sheffield Academic, 1996], 71–99). At the same time, however, her proposal (95–99) that the "succession narrative" was composed by a single "author/compiler" who then brought together various materials (chs. 1–9; 21–24) to serve as a framework for chs. 10–20, thus unifying the whole of 2 Samuel, is laudable. In addition, she is to be praised for her classification of the "succession narrative" as a theological biography whose main didactic purpose is "to present the lessons that may be learned from the experiences of David regarding Sin and Punishment" (214–15; capitals hers).

1. Kindness to Mephibosheth (9:1–13)

OVERVIEW

Two themes dominate the section: showing kindness (vv.1, 3, 7) and eating at the king's table (vv.7, 10–11, 13). Meeting in the middle verse of the chapter (v.7), they lead to the following chiastic outline (cf. similarly Sacon, 48–49):

A David intends to favor the survivors in Saul's family (9:1);
  B David speaks to Saul's servant Ziba (9:2–5);
    C David expresses favor to Mephibosheth (9:6–8);
  B' David speaks to Saul's servant Ziba (9:9–11a);
A' David implements favor to survivors in Saul's family (9:11b–13).

[1]David asked, "Is there anyone still left of the house of Saul to whom I can show kindness for Jonathan's sake?"

[2]Now there was a servant of Saul's household named Ziba. They called him to appear before David, and the king said to him, "Are you Ziba?"

"Your servant," he replied.
3 The king asked, "Is there no one still left of the house of Saul to whom I can show God's
kindness?"
Ziba answered the king, "There is still a son of Jonathan; he is crippled in both feet."
4 "Where is he?" the king asked.
Ziba answered, "He is at the house of Makir son of Ammiel in Lo Debar."
5 So King David had him brought from Lo Debar, from the house of Makir son of Ammiel.
6 When Mephibosheth son of Jonathan, the son of Saul, came to David, he bowed down
to pay him honor.
David said, "Mephibosheth!"
"Your servant," he replied.
7 "Don't be afraid," David said to him, "for I will surely show you kindness for the sake of
your father Jonathan. I will restore to you all the land that belonged to your grandfather
Saul, and you will always eat at my table."
8 Mephibosheth bowed down and said, "What is your servant, that you should notice a
dead dog like me?"
9 Then the king summoned Ziba, Saul's servant, and said to him, "I have given your
master's grandson everything that belonged to Saul and his family. 10 You and your sons
and your servants are to farm the land for him and bring in the crops, so that your master's
grandson may be provided for. And Mephibosheth, grandson of your master, will always
eat at my table." (Now Ziba had fifteen sons and twenty servants.)
11 Then Ziba said to the king, "Your servant will do whatever my lord the king commands his servant to do." So Mephibosheth ate at David's table like one of the king's sons.
12 Mephibosheth had a young son named Mica, and all the members of Ziba's
household were servants of Mephibosheth. 13 And Mephibosheth lived in Jerusalem,
because he always ate at the king's table, and he was crippled in both feet.

COMMENTARY

1 Now that he is the undisputed king, a fact emphasized again and again in this chapter (vv.2, 3, 4, 5, 9, 11), David can afford to be magnanimous. Although during his days as a fugitive from Saul, David would have had no compunctions about killing all who were still "left" of his foes, whether real or imagined (cf. 1Sa 25:34), and although during his early and somewhat tenuous years as king in Hebron he considered all members of the "house of Saul" his mortal enemies (cf. 3:1, 6, 8, 10), he now actively seeks out anyone "still left of the house of Saul" (vv.1, 3) so that he might bestow the royal largesse on him.

To any remaining members of Saul's family David desires to show kindness "for Jonathan's sake" (vv.1, 7). The "kindness" (*ḥesed*; GK 2876) he speaks of (vv.1, 3, 7) derives from his long-standing covenantal relationship with the deceased Jonathan. David had asked Jonathan to show him kindness (see 1Sa 20:8 and comment), and for his part Jonathan had echoed the same request (see 1Sa 20:14 and comment). Just as the Jabeshites had shown kindness to Saul by burying him (see 2:5 and comment), so also now David wishes to show kindness to Saul's house.

2–5 Contact between David and the house(hold) of Saul is made through one of its servants, a man named Ziba (v.2; cf. 19:17). Called to appear before the king, he answers David's question concerning his identity with the customary submissive response of an inferior to his superior: "Your servant" (see comment on 1Sa 25:24).

In a virtual echo of his question in v.1, David asks Ziba (v.3) whether Saul's house "still" has a survivor to whom David would be able to "show kindness like that of God" (a translation preferable to the NIV's "God's kindness"; see 1Sa 20:14 and comment). Ziba responds that there "still" remains one of Jonathan's sons, a man who is "crippled in both feet" (v.3; for possible implications of this description, see comment on 4:4, where the NIV renders the same Hebrew phrase as "lame in both feet").

David's question concerning the whereabouts of Jonathan's son brings a response that is both immediate and precise: A specific town and a specific house in that town are named. The house belongs to Makir son of Ammiel (vv.4–5; cf. also 17:27). Although Ammiel ("My [divine] kinsman is God") was also the name of Bathsheba's father (1Ch 3:5; in 2Sa 11:3 he is given the variant name Eliam ["The (divine) kinsman is my God"]), there is no reason to equate the two men.

As for Makir, every reference to his earlier namesake calls him either the (firstborn) son of Manasseh (Ge 50:23; Nu 26:29; 27:1; 32:39–40; 36:1; Jos 13:31; 17:1, 3; 1Ch 7:14; in Jdg 5:14 Makir is doubtless a synonym for Manasseh) or the father of Gilead (Nu 26:29; 1Ch 2:21, 23; 7:14–17; cf. Dt 3:15), thus establishing his Transjordanian provenance. The town of Lo Debar (vv.4–5) was also located east of the Jordan River, as indicated by its association with Mahanaim (formerly the headquarters of Saul's now-deceased son Ish-Bosheth; see 2:8 and comment), Rabbah, Rogelim (cf. 17:27), and Karnaim (cf. Am 6:13). The various spellings of Lo Debar in the MT—*lô d^e^bār* (vv.4–5), *lōʾ d^e^bār* (17:27), *lōʾ dābār* (Am 6:13)—make its meaning ambiguous and prompt Ackerman, 42–43, to refer to the name as "an interesting designation, which can imply 'no thing' (*lōʾ dābār*), or 'he has a word/thing,' that is, up his sleeve (*lô dābār*)." Although the exact location of Lo Debar is uncertain, a likely identification is with modern Umm ed-Dabar, ten miles south-southeast of the Sea of Galilee.

6–8 In this central and pivotal section of the chapter, David meets "Mephibosheth son of Jonathan, the son of Saul" (v.6; for the meaning of Mephibosheth see Note on 4:4). The double patronymic is used here because "the ancestry of Mephibosheth is fundamental to the narrative" (Clines, 275). In the rest of the chapter the unadorned name is employed.

As in v.2, so also in v.6 David's pronouncing of the name of his visitor evokes the response "Your servant." Here, however, the visitor bows down to pay honor to David, and here in addition Mephibosheth prefaces "your servant" with the word "Behold" (untrans. in NIV).

Doubtless knowing what had happened to his uncle Ish-Bosheth (cf. 4:5–8), Mephibosheth is understandably apprehensive. To put him at ease David tells Mephibosheth not to be afraid (v.7; cf. the identical reassurances uttered by David [1Sa 22:23] and Jonathan [1Sa 23:17]). True to his earlier promise (vv.1, 3), David declares emphatically that he will show Mephibosheth kindness for Jonathan's sake (see comment on v.1). David's specific expressions of covenantal loyalty to Saul's grandson will consist of (1) restoring to him all the land that had belonged to Saul and (2) welcoming him as a perennial guest at the royal table.

As for the first demonstration of the king's generosity, Ziba's later statement that Mephibosheth hopes that "the house of Israel will give me back my grandfather's kingdom" (16:3) may reflect wishful thinking on Mephibosheth's part right from the start ("restore" in v.7 and "give ... back" in 16:3 both render the same Hebrew verb)—or at least a misunderstanding of David's intentions. It is clear that by "land" (lit., "field," v.7; cf. 19:29) David means "(farm)land" (lit., "ground," v.9), not "land" over which one rules (i.e., "kingdom," as in 16:3).

As for the second demonstration—that Mephibosheth would always "eat at my table" (vv.7, 10; the MT reads "eat food at my table" in both verses)—a similar ambiguity exists.

> Given David's loathing for "the lame and the blind" since the war against the Jebusites (2 Sam 5:6–8), one is brought up short by his decision to give Jonathan's son Mephibosheth, "lame in both feet" (9:3, 13), a permanent seat at the royal table.... Is David willing to undergo such a daily ordeal just in memory of his friendship with Jonathan, as he himself declares, or as the price for keeping an eye on the last of Saul's line? Considering David's genius for aligning the proper with the expedient, he may be acting from both motives. (Sternberg, 255; cf. also Ackerman, 43; Perdue, 75; Curtis, "East Is East ...," 357)

What is beyond dispute is that "eating (food) at the (king's) table" (cf. also vv.11, 13; 19:28) can be understood as a metaphor referring to house arrest (cf. 2Ki 25:29 = Jer 52:33). Indeed, David himself had experienced what it was like to feel somewhat unwelcome at the table of a king (see comment on 1Sa 20:29).

The central section of the chapter ends as it began: Mephibosheth "bowed down" (vv.6, 8) and, speaking to the king, referred to himself as "your servant" (vv.6, 8). He was grateful that David should "notice" him (*pānâ ʾel-* ["pay/give attention to"]; cf. 1Ki 8:28 = 2Ch 6:19). Becoming more craven still in his submission to David, Mephibosheth refers to himself as a "dead dog" (v.8; cf. 3:8; see also the comment and Notes on 1Sa 17:43)—an epithet earlier applied by David to himself (1Sa 24:14) and later hurled by Abishai at Shimei, "a man from the same clan as Saul's family" (16:5, 9).

9–11a Like its parallel section (vv.2–5), the present literary unit states that Ziba is "summoned" into David's presence (v.9; "called" in v.2 translates the same Heb. verb). Ziba is here referred to as the *naʿar* ("steward") of Saul (cf. 16:1; 19:17; the NIV's "servant" in v.9 obscures the fact that everywhere else in the chapter "servant" renders *ʿebed*).

David announces to Ziba that he has turned over to Mephibosheth the property belonging to Saul and his "family" (lit., "house," v.9; the announcement thus echoes "house of Saul," "Saul's household" in vv.1–3). As though to stress the extent of the royal bounty, David uses the word *kōl* ("all") twice in v.9: "everything," "entire family/house" ("entire" untrans. in NIV).

David then gives Ziba the responsibility to "farm" (*ʿābad*, lit., "serve, work"; cf. Ge 2:5; 3:23; 4:2, 12) the land on Mephibosheth's behalf (v.10). Ziba is also to "bring in the crops" (the object, contextually implicit in the Heb. verb, being made explicit by the NIV; cf. Ne 13:15; Hag 1:6 ["harvested"]) so that Saul's grandson may "be provided for" (lit., "have food and eat it"—a phrase that seems to cast a cloud over David's generous pledge that Mephibosheth would always "eat [food] at [the king's] table" [vv.7, 10–11, 13], since it appears that Mephibosheth will be supplying some if not most of his own provisions). In any event, Ziba's "fifteen sons and twenty servants" (v.10; 19:17), all of whom are in turn servants of Mephibosheth (v.12), will comprise a sufficient work force to help Ziba carry out the king's commands (v.11a).

11b–13 David's intention to show kindness to Saul's survivors (v.1) is now implemented. The literary section begins and ends with the reminder that Mephibosheth always "ate" (lit., "was eating," emphasizing the habitual and continuing nature of the activity) at the king's table (vv.11b, 13).

Some time has passed since the earlier mention of Mephibosheth in 4:4, when he was no more than twelve years of age (see comment on 4:4). He is now old enough to have a "young son" named Mica(h) (v.12), whose descendants are listed in 1 Chronicles 8:35–38; 9:41–44. The meaning of Micah's name, which is the same as that of the famous prophet, is "Who is like (Yahweh)?"—quite a contrast to the meaning of the name of Mephibosheth himself (see Notes on 4:4).

So Mephibosheth was moved from Lo Debar (vv.4–5) to Jerusalem (v.13), where from that day on he "lived" continually (lit., "was living"; see comment on v.11b). The chapter concludes with a final—and perhaps ominous—reminder that he was "crippled in both feet" (cf. 19:26; see comments on v.3; 4:4).

NOTES

4 The MT's לִדְבִר (*lidbir*) in Joshua 13:26 ("Debir," NIV) should probably be revocalized as לֹדְבָר (*lōdᵉbār*; cf. *BHS*) and equated with the Transjordanian Lo Debar (cf. Driver, 286). As in 2 Samuel 17:27, so also in Joshua 13:25–26, it shares proximity with Rabbah and Mahanaim.

7 Thérèse Glardon ("Handicap et royauté: le fabuleux destin de Mefibosheth," *Hok* 90 [2006]: 26–49) has provided her own suggestive application of a method "dear to rabbinic exegesis." (All translations of her French original are mine.) She notes that the consonants of בֹּשֶׁת ("shame") constitute not only part of the name *mpybšt* ("Mephibosheth") but also, when rearranged, part of the verb *hšbty* ("I will restore"). She then observes that "this play on words between *mpybšt* and *hšbty* permits us to glimpse a radical change in this man's life, a decisive passage from shame to dignity." And she concludes by proposing that "at the two ends of the word *hšbty*, framing the miracle of transformation and the appearance of this entirely new gift, there appear—as in letters of gold—the consonants of the divine name *YH*, the distinctive signature of the true Author of this wonderful act!" (Glardon, "Handicap et royauté," 38).

11 The NIV correctly reads "David's table" (with the LXX; see NIV note) for the MT's "my table" (which K&D, 371, labels a "mistake"). To read "As for Mephibosheth, *said the king*, he shall eat at my table" (KJV) is contextually awkward. The reading "my table" in v.11 probably arose by contamination from the same phrase in vv.7 and 10.

2. The Ammonites Defeated (10:1–19)

Chapters 10–12 constitute a distinct literary unit within the Court of History of David (chs. 9–20), as demonstrated by several factors:

- 10:1 and 13:1 both begin with "in the course of time," a phrase that always inaugurates a new section (cf. Roth, "You Are the Man!" 4; Lawlor, 193).
- 10:1–11:1; 12:26–31 describe Israel's military victories over the Ammonites, thus forming a frame around the central narrative of

David-Bathsheba-Uriah-Nathan-Solomon (11:12–12:25; cf. Bailey's summary description of these chapters in the title of his book *David in Love and War: The Pursuit of Power in 2 Samuel 10–12*).

- The parallel in Chronicles (1Ch 19:1–20:3) is the equivalent of 10:1–11:1 plus 12:29–31, thus spanning chs. 10–12 while at the same time omitting the unsavory picture of David that forms the heart of the section.
- The *Leitwort šālaḥ* ("to send"; GK 8938) appears twenty-three times in chs. 10–12. (It is found only twenty-one times in the rest of the court history and only thirteen times in chs. 1–8, 21–24.) Its concentration in these chapters probably represents "a conscious development of a power motif" (Lawlor, 196; cf. Bailey's similar insight in the subtitle of his book *David in Love and War: The Pursuit of Power in 2 Samuel 10–12*).

The story of the Ammonite wars is the only extensive narrative in the court history that casts David in a favorable light. To be sure, elsewhere the narrator of the history sometimes views David positively—or at least sympathetically—in briefer sections (cf. 12:13, 22–23; 18:32–33; 19:38–39). On the whole, however, chs. 9–20 deserve the label given by Carlson to the last two-thirds of 2 Samuel: "David under the Curse" (Carlson, 7, 25, 140).

It may well be that various episodes in chs. 10–12 are not set forth in chronological order. The events cover a period of at least two years, which raises the legitimate question as to whether Joab's military campaigns against the Ammonites would have lasted all that time. As Lawlor, 204 n. 33, states, the reports in 10:1–11:1; 12:26–31 might be "an example of deliberate narrative framing without concern for linear chronology/sequence." With respect to their chronological relationship to events narrated elsewhere in 2 Samuel, it is probably best to see the episodes of chs. 10–12 as having occurred earlier than those recorded in 8:3–12 (see comment; cf. also Carlson, 146 n. 4).

Attempts to discern a comprehensive literary structure (often chiastic) for chs. 10–12 fail to convince, nor does the rather straightforward narrative of ch. 10 itself yield readily to literary analysis. At the same time, internal considerations (discussed below) lead to a tripartite division of the chapter:

A. The Ammonites humiliate David's delegation (10:1–5).
B. The Ammonites and their Aramean allies flee from Joab (10:6–14).
C. David defeats the Arameans (10:15–19).

Second Samuel 10:1–19 is paralleled in 1 Chronicles 19:1–19.

1In the course of time, the king of the Ammonites died, and his son Hanun succeeded
him as king. 2David thought, "I will show kindness to Hanun son of Nahash, just as his
father showed kindness to me." So David sent a delegation to express his sympathy to
Hanun concerning his father.
When David's men came to the land of the Ammonites, 3the Ammonite nobles said to
Hanun their lord, "Do you think David is honoring your father by sending men to you to

express sympathy? Hasn't David sent them to you to explore the city and spy it out and
overthrow it?" [4]So Hanun seized David's men, shaved off half of each man's beard, cut off
their garments in the middle at the buttocks, and sent them away.

[5]When David was told about this, he sent messengers to meet the men, for they were
greatly humiliated. The king said, "Stay at Jericho till your beards have grown, and then
come back."

[6]When the Ammonites realized that they had become a stench in David's nostrils,
they hired twenty thousand Aramean foot soldiers from Beth Rehob and Zobah, as
well as the king of Maacah with a thousand men, and also twelve thousand men from
Tob.

[7]On hearing this, David sent Joab out with the entire army of fighting men. [8]The Ammonites came out and drew up in battle formation at the entrance to their city gate, while
the Arameans of Zobah and Rehob and the men of Tob and Maacah were by themselves
in the open country.

[9]Joab saw that there were battle lines in front of him and behind him; so he selected
some of the best troops in Israel and deployed them against the Arameans. [10]He put the
rest of the men under the command of Abishai his brother and deployed them against
the Ammonites. [11]Joab said, "If the Arameans are too strong for me, then you are to come
to my rescue; but if the Ammonites are too strong for you, then I will come to rescue you.
[12]Be strong and let us fight bravely for our people and the cities of our God. The LORD will
do what is good in his sight."

[13]Then Joab and the troops with him advanced to fight the Arameans, and they fled
before him. [14]When the Ammonites saw that the Arameans were fleeing, they fled before
Abishai and went inside the city. So Joab returned from fighting the Ammonites and
came to Jerusalem.

[15]After the Arameans saw that they had been routed by Israel, they regrouped. [16]Hada-
dezer had Arameans brought from beyond the River; they went to Helam, with Shobach
the commander of Hadadezer's army leading them.

[17]When David was told of this, he gathered all Israel, crossed the Jordan and went to
Helam. The Arameans formed their battle lines to meet David and fought against him.
[18]But they fled before Israel, and David killed seven hundred of their charioteers and forty
thousand of their foot soldiers. He also struck down Shobach the commander of their
army, and he died there. [19]When all the kings who were vassals of Hadadezer saw that they
had been defeated by Israel, they made peace with the Israelites and became subject to
them.

So the Arameans were afraid to help the Ammonites anymore.

COMMENTARY

1–5 The opening formula "in the course of time" (v.1) is often used in 2 Samuel to introduce narrative sequence, whether chronological or thematic. It does not necessarily imply that what follows it is chronologically later than what precedes it (see Notes on 2:1; comment on 8:1). Indeed, the relationship between ch. 10 and ch. 9 is literarily associative in that ch. 10 echoes key words from ch. 9: "Cf. the expression 'show kindness' in 10:2 (*bis*) and 9:1, 3, 7. Among other *verba associandi* in this connexion may be named 'servant', 10:2–4 [NIV's 'men'] to 9:10–12, and Zobah, 10:6, 8, *ṣābā* ('host'), 10:7, 16, 18 [NIV's 'army'], to Ziba in 9:2–3, 9–12" (Carlson, 145 n. 3).

The deceased "king of the Ammonites" (v.1) was Nahash (v.2; cf. 1Sa 12:12). If his name means "Snake" (see comment on 1Sa 11:1), then that of his son Hanun—although generally understood to mean "Favored (by God)" or the like (cf. BDB, 337)—might, in the eyes of the OT narrator and his readers, mean "Loathsome" (cf. Bailey, 163 n. 99), as the same Hebrew root is translated in Job 19:17. When political power is based on dynastic rule, a king about to die can reasonably expect his son to succeed him as king (cf. 2Ki 13:24). Thus Hanun becomes king of Ammon as a result of his father's death.

Assuming that the Nahash of v.2 is the same Ammonite king defeated by Saul (1Sa 11:1–11), the kindness Nahash showed to David may have been expressed during David's days as a fugitive from the Israelite royal court. David now wants to reciprocate by showing kindness to Nahash's son, thereby cementing the alliance already existing between Israel and Ammon. As David showed "kindness" (*ḥesed*; GK 2876) to Mephibosheth for the sake of his father Jonathan (9:7), with whom he had established a covenantal relationship many years earlier (see comments on 1Sa 20:8, 14), so he also shows "kindness" to Hanun for the sake of his father Nahash, with whom he had probably already concluded a prior treaty arrangement (cf. Lawlor, 194 n. 3). The former act promoted domestic harmony and solidified David's own position inside Israel, and the latter is calculated to maintain the viability of one of David's international agreements and strengthen his position outside Israel (cf. similarly Pinhas Artzi, "Mourning in International Relations," in *Death in Mesopotamia: Papers Read at the XXVI*[e] *Rencontre Assyriologique Internationale* [Copenhagen Studies in Assyriology 8; ed. Bendt Alster; Copenhagen: Akademisk, 1980], 169 n. 18).

The means chosen by David to show kindness to his deceased ally's son is sending a delegation to "express his sympathy" (*nḥm*, vv.2–3; GK 5714). Fokkelman (*Narrative Art*, 1:43) observes that this "'comforting' alliterates with *Nāḥāš* as well as *Ḥānūn* and connects them both." Artzi provides extrabiblical examples of acts of official mourning over the demise of a foreign king and notes that, although they are insufficient as a means of solving crises, they express solidarity in common human fate and may thus contribute to peaceful coexistence (Artzi, "Mourning in International Relations," 161–70). He suggests further that such mourning belongs to the same level of graciousness as that expressed in the sending of a delegation to convey wishes of good health "on the eve of recovery from a dangerous illness" (ibid., 167; cf. 170 n. 24, where Merodach-Baladan's apparent concern for Hezekiah [2Ki 20:12] is cited as an example). The verb "sent" (v.2), used frequently throughout this chapter (vv.3 [2x], 4, 5, 6 [the NIV's "hired" is literally "sent and hired"], 7, 16 [the NIV's "had ... brought" is literally "sent and caused ... to go out"]), reflects in most cases the deliberate maneuvering for power that is taking place during these days (see comment on 10:1–19).

Upon the arrival of David's delegation to the land of the Ammonites, the Ammonite "nobles" (*śārîm*, v.3; perhaps here "[army] commanders," as in 1Sa 29:3 [cf. Gordon, *I and II Samuel*, 250]) share their suspicions with Hanun. "They mistrust David's motives and urge a harsh response (cf. a parallel of advisers in 1 Kings 12:6–11)" (Brueggemann, *First and Second Samuel*, 270). Citing yet another parallel—the reaction of Joab to Abner's visit in 3:24–25—Gunn (*The Story of King David*, 97) observes that "in the political world of Joab and the courtiers suspicion is the order of the day. An unsolicited offer of friendship belongs to unreality."

Hanun's men are sure that David's delegation, like the Danite warriors of Judges 18:2, have been sent into alien territory to "explore" and "spy out" the region. In this case the focus of their interest is said to be "the city" (v.3; probably Rabbah [cf. 11:1], the capital city, today known as Amman [capital of the Hashemite Kingdom of Jordan] and located about forty miles east-northeast of Jerusalem)—although the parallel in Chronicles hints at the possibility that the Ammonites are accusing David's men of having designs on "the country" (*hāʾāreṣ*) as a whole (1Ch 19:3). In either case the Israelites have come to "overthrow" the Ammonite birthright. The same Hebrew verb elsewhere almost always has the Lord as its subject (cf. Ge 19:21, 25, 29; Dt 29:23; Job 9:5 ["overturns"]; 12:15 ["devastate"]; 34:25; Jer 20:16; La 4:6; Am 4:11; Hag 2:22 [2x: "overturn," "overthrow"]).

Accepting the assessment of his men, Hanun decides to refuse David's cordial overtures and to humiliate David's messengers. He (probably through his henchmen rather than personally) begins shaving off "half of each man's beard" (v.4; 1Ch 19:4 summarizes by stating simply that he shaved "them"), no doubt vertically rather than horizontally to make them look as foolish as possible. Although voluntarily shaving off one's beard was a traditional sign of mourning (Isa 15:2; Jer 41:5; 48:37), forcible shaving was considered an insult and a sign of submission (cf. Isa 7:20; for a modern example of insulting a man by cutting off half his beard see Boyd Seevers, "Select Biblical Customs in Light of the Cultural Practices of the Rwala Bedouin Tribe," *Near East Archaeological Society Bulletin* 52 [2007]: 18–19). Hanun then cuts off their garments "in the middle at the buttocks" (whether vertically or horizontally in this case is difficult to say) and then sends them on their way. Forced exposure of the buttocks was a shameful practice inflicted on prisoners of war (cf. Isa 20:4).

Hanun's treatment of David's men was clearly a violation of "the courtesies normally extended to the envoys of other states" in ancient times (Wiseman, "'Is It Peace?'" 315). Indeed, the indignities heaped on them are a grotesque parody of the normal symbolic actions that accompanied mourning (cf. similarly Artzi, "Mourning in International Relations," 170 n. 22; cf. also Lemos, 233–34). "In all this, we observe an extravagant reflection of the symbolic violation of Saul by David when he cut off a corner of the king's robe" (Alter, *The David Story*, 245; cf. 1Sa 24:4, 11).

Introductory formulas located at strategic points throughout ch. 10 almost certainly refer to intelligence data gathered by David's scouts to keep him informed of significant developments on the international scene: "When David was told about/of this" (vv.5, 17), "On hearing this" (v.7; cf. Hauer, 97–98). Knowing that the maltreatment of his men by Hanun is causing them to be "greatly humiliated" (v.5; cf. Nu 12:14 ["have been in disgrace"]; Ps 74:21 ["in disgrace"]), David sends messengers to tell them to stay at Jericho (modern Tell es-Sultan, six miles west of the Jordan River and just north of a major ancient highway leading from Rabbah to Jerusalem) until their beards have grown back. Only after remaining there (presumably out of public view) for a suitable length of time do they have to return to Jerusalem.

As the hair on Samson's shorn head ultimately grew back (Jdg 16:22) and proved to be a bad omen for the Philistines, so also the regrowth of the beards of David's men would portend disaster for the Ammonites. Hanun's foolish miscalculation will bring about his own defeat. "The misfortune of the comforting delegation of David is the actual cause of the (already looming) war against the Ammonite-Aramean coalition" (Artzi, "Mourning in International Relations," 166).

6–14 Verses 6 and 14 begin with the same statement—"When the Ammonites saw [NIV's 'realized' in v.6] that"—thus forming an inclusio that frames the literary unit (cf. Fokkelman, *Narrative Art*, 1:46; the major variation in the two verses is that they use two different Qal forms of the same Hebrew verb). The Ammonites' perception of themselves is accurate: They have become a "stench" in David's nostrils (v.6)—not necessarily a situation to be deplored (cf. 16:21), although in the present case it is tantamount to affirming that David will almost surely be expected to declare war against Ammon (see 1Sa 13:4 and comment).

In anticipation of that likelihood the Ammonites, at enormous cost, hire a large army of Arameans to supplement their own troops. Although *ʾelep* sometimes means "(military) unit" (see comments on 8:4; 1Sa 4:2), the huge amount of silver (see 1Ch 19:6 and footnote) expended in the Ammonites' enlistment and supply of the Arameans makes it virtually certain that the word is intended in its ordinary sense of "thousand" throughout this chapter.

The hiring of mercenaries, who thus owed their livelihood and security to their master, was not uncommon in ancient times (cf. 2Ki 7:6; 2Ch 25:6). In the present situation Arameans are hired from Beth Rehob (v.6, called simply Rehob in v.8), an Aramean district north of Laish/Dan (Jdg 18:28; cf. also Nu 13:21), probably located in the Beqaʿ region of Lebanon; Zobah (cf. the title of Ps 60; for the location see comment on 8:3); Maacah (assigned to the tribal territory of East Manasseh [Jos 13:8, 11] but not conquered by Israel [Jos 13:13]), comprising the northeastern portion of the Huleh Valley and the northwestern Golan Heights region; and Tob, a town and district where the judge Jephthah found protection (Jdg 11:3, 5; cf. perhaps also 1 Macc 5:13; 2 Macc 12:17) and today identified as modern et-Taiyibeh, located forty-five miles northeast of Rabbah (for a map showing the relative locations of these four regions, see Rasmussen, 117). From the fact that the Ammonites choose to hire Arameans, it is possible to infer the earlier expansion of Aram to the borders of Ammon itself (cf. Malamat, 100).

The parallel account of the Aramean muster recorded in 1 Chronicles 19:6–7 (cf. similarly 4QSam[a]; LXX) differs in several particulars from the narrative in v.6. Assuming that the numbers have been transcribed accurately in both accounts, we can nevertheless harmonize the two passages as follows: "Aram Naharaim" (i.e., northwestern Mesopotamia; cf. 1Ch 19:6 and note) includes Beth Rehob and Tob in v.6; "the king of Maacah with his troops" (1Ch 19:7) are "the king of Maacah with a thousand men" of v.6; and "thirty-two thousand chariots and charioteers/horsemen" (1Ch 19:7; cf. also 1Ch 19:6) represent the numerical strength of the chariot force hired by Hanun and equal the "twenty thousand foot soldiers" plus the "twelve thousand men" of v.6. Apparently "charioteer/horseman," used here in the sense of "rider" (an infantryman conveyed from place to place in a chariot), could be interchanged with "foot soldier" in both 2 Samuel and 1 Chronicles (cf. Zane C. Hodges, "Conflicts in the Biblical Account of the Ammonite-Syrian War," *BSac* 119/475 [1962]: 241–42; see also comment on v.18).

Upon learning that the Ammonite-Aramean coalition has been formed, David takes no chances. He sends out the entire army, under the leadership of his commander Joab, to engage them (v.7). While the Ammonites prepare to defend their city (probably Rabbah, the capital) by amassing at its most vulnerable point, the "entrance to their city gate" (v.8; cf. similarly Jdg 9:40), the troops from the various Aramean districts (each army apparently led by its own king; cf. 1Ch 19:9) are deployed in "the open country" (lit., "the field[s]"; cf. 11:23 ["the open"]; 18:6). The scene is described in solemn, formal terms: The Ammonites "came out and drew up in battle formation," an expression that echoes Goliath's taunt in 1 Samuel 17:8 by using the same Hebrew phrase ("Why do you come out and line up for battle?").

Before the battle is joined, Joab decides on strategy (vv.9–10) and encourages his brother Abishai (vv.11–12; see 1Sa 26:6 and comment). Just as the double assertion that the Ammonites "saw" (vv.6, 14) frames the longest literary unit in the chapter (see comment on v.6), so also the statement that Joab "saw" (v.9) begins the crucial central paragraph (vv.9–12) of that unit. Joab perceives enemy "battle lines" (*p^e^nê hammilḥāmâ*, lit., "the face[s] of the battle") "in front of him" (*mippānîm*, lit., "from face[s]") and behind him (cf. similarly 2Ch 13:14), thus recognizing that he must divide his army if he is to prevail.

Sensing that the Arameans are the stronger of the two forces in the enemy coalition, he "selected" some of the "best troops" (the root is *bḥr* in both cases; see Notes on "chosen men" in 6:1 and comment on 1Sa 24:2) and decided to lead them personally to fight against the Arameans (cf. Herzog and Gichon, 83). The rest of the "men" (lit., "people," often used in the sense of "troops" in military contexts in the books of Samuel [cf. v.13]; v.10) he puts under the command of Abishai, who leads them against the Ammonites. "Deployed" (vv.9–10; cf. also 1Sa 4:2) is the same verb of action (*ʿrk*) rendered "drew up" in v.8 and "formed" in v.17.

Joab's heartening speech to his brother (vv.11–12) uses the verb *ḥzq* ("be strong") twice in each verse (the second occurrence in v.12 is rendered "let us fight bravely"). Failing to size up one's opponent adequately, for whatever reason, can prove disastrous (cf. 1Ki 20:23). Joab therefore stresses vital communication between the two commanders so that either can come to the other's "rescue" if necessary (v.11)—an outcome that the Ammonites and Arameans will be unable to accomplish with respect to each other (cf. v.19, where "to help" renders the same Hebrew verb translated "to rescue" in v.11b).

Shouts and cheers calculated to raise the spirits of one's comrades and to urge them on to success and victory have resounded from the earliest times. Joab's "be strong" (v.12) is clearly reminiscent not only of the ringing words of encouragement of Moses and the Lord to Joshua and to all Israel (Dt 31:6–7, 23; Jos 1:6–7, 9) but also of those of the Transjordanian tribal leaders to Joshua (Jos 1:18). Joab's "let us fight bravely" echoes the Philistines' "be strong" in 1 Samuel 4:9 (same Heb. verbal form in both texts). Joab senses that he is responsible not only for the people of Israel but also for "the cities of our God" (for an attempt at identification with sites in southern Transjordan, see Raphael Giveon, "'The Cities of Our God' [II Sam 10:12]," *JBL* 83/4 [1964]: 415–16). Like Eli before him (see 1Sa 3:18 and comment), Joab resigns himself to divine sovereignty: "The LORD will do what is good in his sight" (v.12).

Leading Israel's finest troops and convinced of the Lord's guidance, Joab marches into battle against the Arameans, who turn tail and flee (v.13). As soon as the Ammonites learn of Aram's headlong retreat, they flee to the protection of the walls of Rabbah (v.14). Apparently unable to pursue his advantage against the Ammonites by besieging the city—for now, at least—Joab returns to Jerusalem.

15–19 That the Arameans are "routed by/before Israel" (v.15) is reminiscent of an earlier episode in which the Philistines were "routed before the Israelites" (1Sa 7:10), especially since in both cases the Lord played the key role in the enemy retreat. Undeterred by what they consider a minor setback, however, the Arameans regroup their forces. Hadadezer (v.16; see 8:3 and comment) sends for Aramean reinforcements from beyond the eastern side of the Euphrates River (cf. Malamat, 102), and his army commander Shobach (later killed in battle; v.18) leads them to Helam (possibly modern Alma, about seven miles north of Tob; cf. perhaps also Alema in 1 Macc 5:26, 35 [cf. Gordon, *I and II Samuel*, 251–52]).

When David's intelligence network informs him of the exact location of the Aramean forces (v.17), he musters his entire army and crosses the Jordan River eastward to engage the Arameans in battle. Although the Arameans "regrouped" (v.15), the Israelites David "gathered" (v.17) proved to be more than a match for them (same Heb. verb). The contrast between David's leading his own army (cf. also 12:29) in this situation and his remaining behind in Jerusalem in the next episode (11:1) is noteworthy (cf. Lawlor, 195).

No braver than the Aramean mercenaries hired by the Ammonites, Hadadezer's reinforcements also flee from the Israelites (v.18; cf. v.13). This time, however, David and his men press their advantage and inflict huge numbers of casualties on the enemy. Unless an error in transcription has occurred, the discrepancy between "seven hundred of their charioteers" here (v.18) and "seven thousand of their charioteers" in the parallel passage (1Ch 19:18) is perhaps best resolved by understanding *rekeb* in v.18 to mean "(men of) chariots" or "(men of) chariot divisions" and in 1 Chronicles 19:18 to mean "charioteers" (cf. Hodges, "Conflicts in the Biblical Account," 242 n. 6; Patrick, 425).

As to the "foot soldiers" in 1 Chronicles 19:18, where v.18 here has the Hebrew word for "horsemen" (see NIV note), the two texts can be reconciled by assuming either that the terms were interchangeable (see comment on v.6) or that foot soldiers and horsemen "were mixed together.... And that in all there were slain forty thousand of them, part Horsemen, and part Footmen" (Patrick, 425). In any event, these texts clearly distinguish not only between "charioteers" and "foot soldiers" (cf. also 8:4) but also between "charioteers" and "horsemen" (cf. the MT of v.18).

The forty thousand horsemen/foot soldiers (cf. also Jdg 5:8) probably represent four armies of troops (cf. J. B. Segal, 12). Carlson, 146, makes the intriguing observation that the numbers four and seven, here boding ill for Aram, are reprised in the passing of judgment on David in ch. 12 (cf. 12:6, 18).

Noting that the MT of v.19 features verbs with the same consonants (*wyrʾw*)—though with different meanings ("saw," "were afraid")—at the beginning and near the end, Fokkelman *Narrative Art*, 1:50) suggests the following (slightly modified) outline for the verse:

A When saw the kings—
  B the vassals (*ʿbd*) of Hadadezer—
    C their defeat by Israel,
    C' they made peace with Israel
  B' and became subject (*ʿbd*) to them.
A' Therefore were afraid the Arameans.

The "kings" refers back to v.8 (cf. 1Ch 19:9, which makes the reference explicit). The defeat of the Arameans at the hands of Israel leaves them no option: They sue for peace (cf. Wiseman, "'Is It Peace?'" 313; similarly Jos 10:1, 4; also Dt 20:12; Jos 11:19) and become subject to the Israelites (cf. 8:6; for implications see comment on 8:2). By substituting "David" for "the Israelites" and "him" for "them," 1 Chronicles 19:19 highlights the personal role of the king in the proceedings (cf. also 22:44).

Aram's fear of going to the aid of the Ammonites after the present debacle may have sprung at least partly from the first-rate intelligence system that David enjoyed (cf. Hauer, 98). In any case, the Ammonites, to their detriment, are now on their own (cf. 11:1; 12:26–31).

NOTES

9 Because בישׂראל (*byśrʾl*, "in Israel") follows immediately after a construct noun, many Hebrew MSS exhibit a *Qere* reading that omits the preposition (cf. *BHS*). It is not unusual, however, for a prepositional phrase to stand after a construct participle, as here (cf. *IBHS*, 165).

15–19 The MT of the final section of ch. 10 begins and ends similarly: וַיַּרְא אֲרָם (*wayyarʾ ʾărām*, "After the Arameans saw," v.15); וַיִּרְאוּ אֲרָם (*wayyirᵉʾû ʾărām*, "So the Arameans were afraid," v.19b). In addition v.19a echoes v.15a: "After/When ... saw that they had been routed/defeated by Israel" (the same Heb. verb is rendered "routed" in v.15 and "defeated" in v.19). The total effect is to form an inclusio that frames the literary unit. At the same time, v.15 ("After ... saw") echoes the beginning of the previous section: "When ... realized/saw" (see v.6 and comment; cf. Fokkelman, *Narrative Art*, 1:48–49).

15 Instead of the MT's ויאספו יחד (*wyʾspw yḥd*, "they gathered themselves together"; "they regrouped," NIV), two MSS read the final word in the verse as יחדו (*yḥdw*; cf. *BHS*). Although the translation remains the same in either case, it may well be that the MT intends the reading *yḥdw* by sharing the ו (*w*) with which the next verse begins (cf. Watson, 531).

16 הדדעזר (*hddʿzr*, "Hadadezer") is erroneously spelled הדרעזר (*hdrʿzr*, "Hadarezer") in 1 Chronicles 18:3, 5, 7–10; 19:16, 19, doubtless due to similarity between the consonants ד (*d*) and ר (*r*). שׁוֹבַךְ (*šôbak*, "Shobach") is spelled alternatively שׁוֹפַךְ (*šôpak*, "Shophach") in 1 Chronicles 19:16, 18. The interchange between *b* and *p* is fairly widespread in all the Semitic languages (cf. Anton C. M. Blommerde, *Northwest Semitic Grammar and Job* [BibOr 22; Rome: Pontifical Biblical Institute, 1969], 5–6); cf. דְּבַשׁ (*dᵉbaš*, "honey") with Akkadian *dišpu* ("honey"); נֹפֶת (*nōpet*, "honey [from the comb]") with Akkadian *nūbtu* ("honeybee") and Ugaritic *nbt* ("honey"; cf. KB, 203, 628).

3. David's Sin against Bathsheba (11:1–5)

OVERVIEW

Although ch. 11 is a discrete unit in a larger complex consisting of chs. 10–12 (see comment on 10:1–19), references to David, Joab, the Ammonites, Rabbah, and Jerusalem in 11:1 and in 12:26–31 make it likely that chs. 11–12 constitute an integral section within that complex. A close reading of the section produces the following chiastic outline (cf. similarly Samuel A. Meier, "The Historiography of Samuel" [master's thesis, Dallas Theological Seminary, 1978], 8–9; for a comparable though slightly divergent analysis, cf. Sacon, 42–44):

A David sends Joab to besiege Rabbah (11:1)
B David sleeps with Bathsheba, who becomes pregnant (11:2–5)
C David has Uriah killed (11:6–17)
D Joab sends David a message (11:18–27a)
E The Lord is displeased with David (11:27b)
D' The Lord sends David a messenger (12:1–14)
C' The Lord strikes David's infant son, who dies (12:15–23)
B' David sleeps with Bathsheba, who becomes pregnant (12:24–25)
A' Joab sends for David to besiege and capture Rabbah (12:26–31)

The contrast between the folly of David (as played out in chs. 11–12) and the "wisdom of Solomon" (1Ki 10:4; cf. 4:29–34) is masterfully explicated by Carole Fontaine, 61–77. In the course of his downward slide from temptation into sin, David manages to disobey three of the Ten Commandments: "You shall not covet your neighbor's wife"; "you shall not commit adultery"; "you shall not murder" (Ex 20:17, 14, 13). His execrable conduct in ch. 11 is a parade example of the truths expressed in James 1:14–15: "Each one is tempted when, by his own evil desire, he is dragged away and enticed. Then, after desire has conceived, it gives birth to sin; and sin, when it is full-grown, gives birth to death."

1In the spring, at the time when kings go off to war, David sent Joab out with the king's
men and the whole Israelite army. They destroyed the Ammonites and besieged Rabbah.
But David remained in Jerusalem.
2One evening David got up from his bed and walked around on the roof of the palace.
From the roof he saw a woman bathing. The woman was very beautiful, 3and David sent
someone to find out about her. The man said, "Isn't this Bathsheba, the daughter of Eliam
and the wife of Uriah the Hittite?" 4Then David sent messengers to get her. She came to
him, and he slept with her. (She had purified herself from her uncleanness.) Then she went
back home. 5The woman conceived and sent word to David, saying, "I am pregnant."

COMMENTARY

1 "The story of David and Bathsheba has long aroused both dismay and astonishment; dismay that King David, with his manifest piety, could stoop to such an act, and astonishment that the Bible narrates it with such unrelenting openness, although the person involved is David, the great and celebrated king, the type of the Messiah" (Hertzberg, 309). David's sin against Bathsheba, while described in the most laconic fashion imaginable, is nonetheless significant for all that. Indeed, "the David-Bathsheba episode ... is pivotal to our understanding of his reign" (Rosenberg, 125).

The story, continuing the account begun in ch. 10, is set "in the spring, at the time when kings go off to war" (v.1; cf. 1Ki 20:22, 26). "The month of March, named after Mars the Roman god of war, affords a parallel" (Gordon, *I and II Samuel*, 252). Springtime, which marks the end of the rainy season in the Middle East, assures that roads will be in good condition (or at least passable), that there will be plenty of fodder for war horses and pack animals, and that an army on the march will be able to raid the fields for food (cf. *AIs*, 190, 251). Less likely is the theory that "the spring" (lit., "the [re] turn of the year") in this case refers to "a particular historical date (one year after the kings of Aram went forth to join the Ammonites against Israel)" (an option proposed by Sternberg, 194; cf. 10:6; 1Ch 19:9).

David "sent" (v.1; for the importance of *šlḥ* in chs. 10–12 see comment on 10:2; for its importance in ch. 11 in particular cf. Simon, 209) his army commander Joab, his "men" (lit., "servants," doubtless the mercenary troops), and the "whole Israelite army" (the tribal muster) to continue the battle against Ammon. The result is the mass slaughter of the Ammonites and the siege of Rabbah, their capital city (see comment on 10:3), the reduction and capture of which is yet to come (cf. 12:26–29).

The narrator thus leaves the impression that every able-bodied man in Israel goes to war—everyone, that is, except the king himself: "But David remained in Jerusalem." The contrast between David and his men can hardly be expressed in starker terms. Staying home in such situations was not David's usual practice, of course (cf. 5:2; 8:1–14; 10:17). Indeed, leading his troops into battle was expected to be the major external activity of an ancient Near Eastern ruler (see 1Sa 8:5–6, 20 and comments). Although therefore reprehensible in itself, David's conduct on this occasion opens the way for royal behavior that is more despicable still.

2–5 Another contrast now surfaces. Although King David's army marches off to war "at the time when kings" do so (v.1), King David himself gets out of bed "one evening" (lit., "at the time of evening," v.2). Perhaps because of the oppressive heat of a spring sirocco, he has apparently lengthened his afternoon siesta into the cooler part of the day (cf. Ge 24:11). Getting up "from" (lit., "from upon") his bed and taking a stroll, "from" (lit., "from upon") the roof of his palace (probably the highest point in the city, he sees a woman bathing. As Bailey, 86, notes, the other occurrences of *hthlk* ("walked around") used of David occur in contexts with a negative flavor, and we are therefore probably justified in assuming that here as well "some questionable conduct is about to occur" (cf. 1Sa 23:13 ["moving from place to place"]; 25:15 ["were"]; 30:31 ["roamed"]). The roof of the royal palace in Jerusalem will later become the focus of yet another sinful act (cf. 16:22; similarly Da 4:29–30; see also 1Sa 9:25–26 and comment).

"Remember all the commands of the LORD, that you may obey them and not prostitute yourselves by going after the lusts of your own hearts and eyes" (Nu 15:39). Failing to heed the warning expressed in that and/or similar texts, David "saw" a woman (v.2) and wanted her. Concerning Matthew 5:29, F. F. Bruce (*The Hard Sayings of Jesus* [Downers Grove, Ill.: InterVarsity, 1983], 54) observes, "Matthew places this saying immediately after Jesus's words about adultery in the heart, and that is probably the original context, for it provides a ready example of how a man's eye could lead him into sin"—a sin that Job was determined to avoid at all costs (Job 31:1).

The woman David sees is "very beautiful," which translates a Hebrew phrase reserved for people of striking physical appearance (e.g., Rebekah [Ge 24:16; 26:7], Vashti [Est 1:11], Esther [Est 2:7], and—not to discriminate against men—David himself [see comment on 1Sa 16:12, where a cognate Heb. expression is used]). The woman David sees is bathing, and the sight of her naked body arouses him. His virgin-conceived descendant would one day condemn such voyeurism for the sin that it is: "Anyone who looks at a woman lustfully has already committed adultery with her in his heart" (Mt 5:28).

For now, however, the heat of an unusually warm spring day has not only extended David's normal siesta period and then brought him outdoors for a refreshing walk on the palace roof; it has also forced the woman to bathe outside to escape the suffocatingly hot atmosphere of her house. Such heat makes people more susceptible to sexual encounters (cf. H. Hirsch Cohen, "David and Bathsheba," *JBR* 33/2 [1965]: 144), and in his vulnerability David succumbs. Continuing the use of a key verb as established earlier in the chapter, the narrator states that David "sent" (v.3; see comment on v.1) someone to find out about the woman and then, having learned her identity, "sent" (v.4) messengers to get her.

In addition to simply stating her given name—Bathsheba ("Daughter of an oath" or "Daughter of seven" [i.e., perhaps "Seventh daughter/child"])—the man sent to identify the woman tells David that she is the daughter of Eliam (given the variant name Ammiel in 1Ch 3:5; for the meaning of the names, see comment on 9:4) and the wife of Uriah the Hittite (v.3). The rhetorical "Isn't this Bathsheba?" perhaps intentionally echoes the earlier "Isn't this David?" (cf. 1Sa 21:11; 29:3, 5). The reference to Eliam probably reflects Bathsheba's upper-class pedigree, because Eliam was the son of Ahithophel (23:34), who was in turn David's counselor (see 15:12 and comment; cf. Hayim Tadmor, "Traditional Institutions and the Monarchy: Social and Political Tensions in the Time of David and Solomon" [in Ishida, 247]). Since Eliam was one of David's warriors and thus perhaps a foreign mercenary, and since Bathsheba is listed along with the pagan ancestresses of Jesus (Mt 1:3–6), we "have to reckon with the possibility that [she] was of non-Israelite origin" (Jones, 43–44; cf. Fontaine, 66; Gene R. Smillie, "'Even the Dogs': Gentiles in the Gospel of Matthew," *JETS* 45/1 [2002]: 75 and n. 5).

As for Uriah the Hittite (v. 3), in spite of his mercenary status as another of David's warriors (cf. 23:39), he was apparently a worshiper of the Lord (his name probably means "Yahweh is my light"; for the less likely possibility that it is of Hurrian derivation and is related to that of Araunah the Jebusite, see C. J. Mullo Weir, "Nuzi," in *Archaeology and Old Testament Study*, ed. D. Winton Thomas [Oxford: Clarendon, 1967], 82). Like Ahimelech the Hittite before him (see 1Sa 26:6 and comment), Uriah depends on his master David for sustenance and support. In return he gives total loyalty to "king, nation, and fellow warriors.... This loyalty of a foreigner is emphasized twice more in the behavior of Ittai and Hushai" (Perdue, 76; cf. chs. 15–18). An attempt to define Uriah's Hittite origins is made, among others, by Richard H. Beal ("The Hittites after the Empire's Fall," *BI* 10/1 [1983]: 81): "Although Uriah may have been a free-lance soldier from one of the numerous north-Syrian Syro-Hittite states, he more likely was a descendant of those Hittite refugees who more than a century earlier had settled in the land of Palestine, in flight from the collapsing Hittite Empire."

It is the wife of this trusted servant whom David is about to violate, and v.4 mercifully tells the story in the briefest possible compass. Master of all he surveys, David has everything—and yet does not have enough (for a useful comparison with Adam's/Everyman's sin in the Garden of Eden, see Vogels, 245). David sends messengers to "get" (lit., "take") her (see 5:13; 12:4; 1Sa 8:11–17 and comment on 8:11; see further Linafelt, 109). "The ironic contrast with 2 Sam 2–4 is marked: the king who was content to be given his kingdom must seize by force (against Uriah if not Bathsheba) a wife" (Gunn, "David and the Gift of the Kingdom," 19; cf. also 35).

Upon being summoned, Bathsheba "came to him, and he slept with her" (v.4; cf. the same Heb.

idiom in Ge 19:34 ["go in and lie with him"]). (The verb *bô*ʾ ["enter, come in"] is often used by itself, governing various prepositions, with the nuance "have sexual intercourse," although a man is almost always the subject [cf. BDB, 98].) The parallel section near the end of the narrative repeats the scene, but this time David is the subject of both verbs: "He went [lit., "came'] to her and lay with her" (12:24). If in the latter case Bathsheba is already David's wife, in the former the relationship is blatantly adulterous.

> Gratifying the desire conceived as he walked about on his palace roof (*wayyithallēk*, 11:2), David lies with the wife of a trusted and trusting servant (*wayyiškab* ʿ*immāh*, 2 Sam 11:4), thereby rejecting the teachings of wisdom on adultery in Proverbs 6:22, teachings which "will lead you when you walk (*b*ᵉ*hithallekkā*)" and "watch over you when you lie down (*b*ᵉ*šokb*ᵉ*kā*)." (Fontaine, 65)

The parenthetic sentence—"She had purified herself from her uncleanness"—is a circumstantial clause (Driver, 289) that describes "Bathsheba's condition at the time of the action, and is thus to be rendered in English by a perfect tense (i.e. it is something that happened before but about which the reader only learns now)" (Berlin, "David's Wives," 80). Its purpose is

> to inform the reader that Bathsheba was clearly not pregnant when she came to David, since she had just been "purified from her uncleanness." Shortly thereafter she found that she was, and that leaves no doubt that the child is David's, since her husband had been out of town during the interlude between the bath and her visit to the palace. Moreover, the phrase may also alert the reader to the fact that Bathsheba was, at this time in her cycle, most likely to become pregnant. (ibid.)

(See also Simon, 213; Fokkelman, *Narrative Art*, 1:52; cf. already W. Robertson Smith, *Kinship and Marriage in Early Arabia* [Cambridge: Cambridge Univ. Press, 1885], 275–76.) Referring to her menstrual period (cf. Lev 15:25–26, 30; 18:19; Eze 36:17), Bathsheba's "uncleanness" is ceremonial rather than hygienic—although the two are not necessarily unrelated (cf. the English proverb "Cleanliness is next to godliness"; also the Mishnaic saying, "Heedfulness leads to physical cleanliness, and physical cleanliness leads to ritual purity" [*m. Soṭah* 9.15], quoted by Neufeld, 64).

Verse 5 begins and ends with the same verb, thus emphatically implicating David: "The woman conceived [lit., 'became pregnant'] ... 'I am pregnant.'" Of all the fateful conceptions recorded in the OT (cf. Hagar [Ge 16:4–5]; Lot's daughters [19:36]; Rebekah [25:21]; Tamar [38:18]; Jochebed [Ex 2:2]), Bathsheba's ranks near the top of the list in terms of future repercussions. As Lawlor, 197, notes, the message she sends to David—"I am pregnant"—are her "only words in the entire narrative.... The only recorded speech of Bathsheba, brief though it is, sets in motion a course of action which ultimately results in her husband's death."

NOTES

1 "Kings" renders the *Qere*, which assumes a reading מלכים (*mlkym*) along with many Hebrew MSS and several versions (cf. *BHS*). The MT's מלאכים (*mlʾkym*, "messengers") is clearly inferior (though not without its supporters; cf. Fokkelman, *Narrative Art*, 1:50–51), especially in light of the unequivocal testimony of the parallel text (1Ch 20:1) and of the fact that "it applies the time-indicator to the season of the year appropriate for campaigning and not to the sending of messengers, an operation in which the seasonal time factor is of no significance" (Simon, 209 n. 1). Rosenberg, 126, suggests—more cleverly than convincingly, however—that the two readings may be due to studied and deliberate ambiguity, in which "we find ourselves with an oddly convoluted inversion of kingly function in the king's preference of agents to represent him. In this transition of a sedentary monarchy, the agent within the king and the king within the agent seem at war with each other."

2 A pottery figurine of a woman bathing in an oval bathtub, found at Aczib in 1942 and dating from the eighth or seventh century BC, illustrates the domestic bathtub of the kind that Bathsheba might have used. Royal families and the wealthy also had luxurious bathrooms in their elaborate houses (cf. Neufeld, 41, 51–52).

3 4QSamuel^{a} and Josephus' *Antiquities* (7.131 [7.1]) preserve a tradition that Uriah was "Joab's armor-bearer," thus enhancing his importance in the upper echelons of David's mercenary corps.

4 The NIV's note is contextually invalid (see comment above). The proposal of Martin Krause ("II Sam 11 4 und das Konzeptionsoptimum," *ZAW* 95 [1983]: 434–37) that Leviticus 15:19–28 helps us to pinpoint David's sexual liaison with Bathsheba to a time subsequent to the fourteenth day after she began menstruating, is somewhat too precise.

4. The Murder of Uriah (11:6–27)

OVERVIEW

As in the earlier verses of ch. 11 (vv.1, 3–5), so also in vv.6–27 the verb *šlḥ* ("to send"; GK 8938) continues to be prominent (vv.6 [3x], 12, 14, 18, 22, 27 ["had her brought"]) as an index of royal power (see comments on v.1 and introduction to 10:1–19). But another verb now rears its ugly head: *mwt* ("to die," vv.15, 17, 21 [2x], 24 [2x], 26; GK 4637)—the ever-present potential fate of the powerless victims of royal sending run amok. Uriah the Hittite, loyal subject and servant of King David, is soon to die by regnal fiat, his only crime being that he gets in the way of royal lust and power through no fault of his own. Although Bailey, 86–88, and others have suggested that Bathsheba was a complicit partner in a prearranged tryst with David, Richard M. Davidson ("Did King David Rape Bathsheba? A Case Study in Narrative Theology," *Journal of the Adventist Theological Society* 17/2 [2006]: 82) argues convincingly and at length that David alone is entirely at fault and that Bathsheba is "a victim of a 'power rape' on the part of David" (for details see 81–93).

6So David sent this word to Joab:"Send me Uriah the Hittite." And Joab sent him to
David. 7When Uriah came to him, David asked him how Joab was, how the soldiers were
and how the war was going. 8Then David said to Uriah, "Go down to your house and wash

your feet." So Uriah left the palace, and a gift from the king was sent after him. 9But Uriah
slept at the entrance to the palace with all his master's servants and did not go down to
his house.

10When David was told, "Uriah did not go home," he asked him, "Haven't you just come
from a distance? Why didn't you go home?"

11Uriah said to David, "The ark and Israel and Judah are staying in tents, and my
master Joab and my lord's men are camped in the open fields. How could I go to my
house to eat and drink and lie with my wife? As surely as you live, I will not do such a
thing!"

12Then David said to him, "Stay here one more day, and tomorrow I will send you back."
So Uriah remained in Jerusalem that day and the next. 13At David's invitation, he ate and
drank with him, and David made him drunk. But in the evening Uriah went out to sleep on
his mat among his master's servants; he did not go home.

14In the morning David wrote a letter to Joab and sent it with Uriah. 15In it he wrote, "Put
Uriah in the front line where the fighting is fiercest. Then withdraw from him so he will be
struck down and die."

16So while Joab had the city under siege, he put Uriah at a place where he knew the
strongest defenders were. 17When the men of the city came out and fought against Joab,
some of the men in David's army fell; moreover, Uriah the Hittite died.

18Joab sent David a full account of the battle. 19He instructed the messenger: "When you
have finished giving the king this account of the battle, 20the king's anger may flare up,
and he may ask you, 'Why did you get so close to the city to fight? Didn't you know they
would shoot arrows from the wall? 21Who killed Abimelech son of Jerub-Besheth? Didn't
a woman throw an upper millstone on him from the wall, so that he died in Thebez? Why
did you get so close to the wall?' If he asks you this, then say to him, 'Also, your servant
Uriah the Hittite is dead.'"

22The messenger set out, and when he arrived he told David everything Joab had
sent him to say. 23The messenger said to David, "The men overpowered us and came out
against us in the open, but we drove them back to the entrance to the city gate. 24Then
the archers shot arrows at your servants from the wall, and some of the king's men died.
Moreover, your servant Uriah the Hittite is dead."

25David told the messenger, "Say this to Joab: 'Don't let this upset you; the sword
devours one as well as another. Press the attack against the city and destroy it.' Say this to
encourage Joab."

26When Uriah's wife heard that her husband was dead, she mourned for him. 27After the
time of mourning was over, David had her brought to his house, and she became his wife
and bore him a son. But the thing David had done displeased the LORD.

COMMENTARY

6–17 Early in Israel's history an Egyptian pharaoh had concocted a three-phase plan to solve what he considered a serious problem: the strength and large numbers of Israelites in his kingdom. Each phase was more ruthless than the preceding: (1) The Egyptian slave masters oppressed the Israelites with forced labor (Ex 1:11–14). When that did not work, (2) the Hebrew midwives were commanded to kill every newborn Hebrew male infant (Ex 1:15–21). When the midwives disobeyed the pharaoh's edict, (3) all the Egyptians were ordered to throw every newborn male into the Nile (Ex 1:22).

In a similar way, David hatches a three-phase scheme to solve the serious problem of Bathsheba's pregnancy, each phase more ruthless than the preceding. Whereas the pharaoh's best efforts had failed, David succeeds—temporarily at least—in concealing his sin. Vogels, 246, refers to David's effort as a series of three "cover-ups": a "clean" one (vv.6–11), a "dirty" one (vv.12–13), and a "criminal" one (vv.14–17).

As Bathsheba had sent word to David informing him of the problem (v.5), David now sends word to Joab to begin the process of seeking a solution (v.6). At David's command Joab sends him "Uriah the Hittite," the full description once again underscoring Uriah's mercenary status and therefore presumably also his loyalty to David (see comment on v.3). Having been "sent" for by David, Uriah "came to him" (v.7), just as Bathsheba had come under similar circumstances (v.4).

David begins his conversation with Uriah in an apparently solicitous and cordial way by asking about the welfare/progress (*šālôm*; GK 8934; see 1Sa 10:4; 17:22 and comments) of Joab, the soldiers, and the war (v.7). Such queries by the king would later return to haunt him (cf. 18:29, 32, where "safe" renders the same Hebrew idiom containing the word *šālôm*).

Ostensibly satisfied concerning how things are going on the battlefield, David tells Uriah to go down to his house and "wash" his "feet" (v.8). Although usually an expression describing an act affording refreshment and relaxation in a land where dusty roads are the rule (see 1Sa 25:41 and comment; cf. also Lk 7:44; 1Ti 5:10), the phrase may well be intended here as a double entendre, given the euphemistic use of "feet" in the sense of "genitals" (cf. Ex 4:25; Dt 28:57 ["womb," NIV]; Isa 7:20 ["legs," NIV]). David would thus be suggesting to Uriah that he "enjoy his wife sexually" (Gale A. Yee, "'Fraught With Background': Literary Ambiguity in II Samuel 11," *Int* 42/3 [1988]: 245; cf. Simon, 214). Thus Bathsheba's washing ("bathing," v.2; same Heb. verb) and Uriah's washing would both involve or eventuate in sexual cohabitation.

In any event, Uriah "left" (*yṣʾ*, lit., "went out," v.8) the palace, and a royal gift "was sent" (lit., "went out," not *šlḥ*, the usual verb translated "send"; see v.1 and comment) after him. *Masʾēt* (lit., "that which rises/is lifted"; cf. BDB, 673, for its various nuances) means "gift" in other contexts as well, especially where granted by a superior to an inferior (cf. Ge 43:34 ["portion(s)"]; Est 2:18; Jer 40:5 ["present"]).

"And Uriah slept" (possible translation of v.9). "For a moment it looks as though the king's plan is going to work, but the text immediately veers around" (Sternberg, 200). The ambiguous conjunction that begins the verse must therefore be rendered adversatively: "But Uriah slept" (thus correctly NIV)—not with Bathsheba, as David had hoped, but "at the entrance to the palace with all his master's [doubtless David's] servants." Foiling David's plan (cf. v.8), Uriah steadfastly refuses to "go down to his house" (v.9; cf. also vv.10 ["go home" (2x)], 13 ["go home"]; same Heb. expression).

The next day, when David learns that Uriah did not in fact go down to his house (and therefore did not sleep with his wife), he obviously wants to know why (v.10). He reminds Uriah that he has just come from a "distance" (lit., "way"), a term that sometimes means "military campaign" (cf. Jdg 4:9 ["expedition," NIV note]; 1Sa 21:5 ["missions"]; 1Ki 8:44 ["wherever," lit., "on the way/campaign where"]). Thus "David's importunings to Uriah ... can also be taken to reflect the celibacy devolving on those going into battle" (Simon, 214). Uriah's retort in v.11, then, becomes "doubly trenchant, if we take it not as an open defiance but as an indirect, unconscious rebuke. The sting of the words is accordingly palpable only to David. Uriah is not ready to do legitimately what [David] has done criminally" (ibid., 214; on the question of whether Uriah might be expected to have known about David's liaison with Bathsheba, see esp. Sternberg, 201–9).

Just as David and his men had always "kept themselves from women" whenever they set out to do battle (1Sa 21:4–5; see comment there), so now Uriah refuses to sleep with his wife, even while on a brief furlough from military duty (v.11). Unlike David, who "remained" (*yšb*) in Jerusalem (see v.1 and comment), the ark (for the practice of carrying the ark of the covenant out to the battlefield, see comment on 1Sa 4:3) and the tribal musters from Israel and Judah (equivalent to the "whole Israelite army" in v.1; see comment there) are "staying" (*yšb*) at military campsites. The NIV's "in tents" (*bassukkôt*) should doubtless be rendered "in Succoth" (see the NIV's note at 1Ki 20:12, 16). Succoth (modern Tell Deir Alla, a Transjordanian site almost forty miles northeast of Jerusalem) was evidently the forward base that served as a suitable staging area for Israel's battles against the Ammonites (and against the Arameans as well; cf. Yadin, 274–75, who gives additional reasons—not the least of which is the fact that the ark was ensconced in an *ʾōhel* ["tent"; see 6:17 and comment] rather than in a *sukkâ* ["hut"]—for rejecting the translation "tents" in this context; cf. also McCarter, *II Samuel*, 287).

Although "master" and "lord(s)" (v.11) render the same Hebrew noun, the NIV is probably correct in distinguishing the first (Joab) from the second (David) since "my lord's men" (lit., "the servants of my lord") are in all likelihood the same as "the king's men" (lit., "his servants," the mercenary corps) in v.1 (see comment). Thus each unit in v.11 (with the exception of the ark) has its correspondent in v.1 (as might be expected). It is understandable that Uriah would speak of Joab as "my master Joab" (v.11), which "is indeed how one makes a deferential reference to one's [immediate] commanding officer" (Sternberg, 204).

In light of the fact that David's entire army is on the battlefield, how could Uriah in good conscience "eat" and "drink" and "lie" with his wife (v.11; all three verbs will be used again with telling effect in Nathan's rebuke [see comment on 12:3])? David had already "slept/lain" with Uriah's wife (v.4; same Heb. verb as in v.11)—a matter about which Uriah probably has no knowledge—while Uriah himself has "slept" and would "sleep" only among David's servants (vv.9, 13). Indeed, both David and Bathsheba had sinned when she "came [*bwʾ*] to him, and he slept [*škb*] with her" (v.4), while Uriah refuses to "go" (*bwʾ*) to his house and "lie" (*škb*) with his wife (v.11; cf. similarly Fokkelman, *Narrative Art*, 1:55). That he calls Bathsheba "my wife" could hardly have failed to rebuke David, who had callously violated the relationship between Uriah and the person most precious to him.

Uriah concludes his statement to David by emphatically rejecting the king's offer. Taking a solemn oath, which translates literally as "by your life, and by the life of your soul" (the NIV condenses the two expressions into one: "as surely as you live"; cf. similarly 14:19; 15:21; see also comments on 1Sa 1:26; 20:3), Uriah swears that he will not so much as think of doing the unthinkable—he will not do "such a thing" (lit., "this thing," a phrase that occurs again in v.25 ["this" (first occurrence), NIV; cf. comment on 12:6]). "Uriah's name turns out to be Yahwist, after all. In the heart of the imperial phalanges we find an orthodox Israelite, quietly observing the wartime soldier's ban against conjugal relations (cf. I Sam. 21:4–7)" (Rosenberg, 132).

Failing in his first attempt to cover up his sin, David tries again: "'Stay [*yšb*] here one more day'.... So Uriah remained [*yšb*]" (v.12)—indeed, against his better judgment Uriah "remained in Jerusalem" at the behest of the king, who had earlier (perhaps selfishly) done the same thing (v.1), and with disastrous results.

Although Uriah will not go to his own house to eat and drink (v.11), he has no such scruples in the king's house (v.13). When David gets him drunk, he assumes that Uriah's inhibitions will be overcome (cf. Hab 2:15) and that he will automatically go home, sleep with Bathsheba, and thus absolve David of any charge of her child's paternity. At first it appears that David's plan will succeed: "Indeed, 'in the evening he went out to lie on his bed' [v.13]—on his bed at home? With his wife? No, on his bed of the past two nights, 'with the servants of his lord, and did not go down to his house'" (Sternberg, 201).

His second attempt at covering up his affair with Bathsheba having failed, David senses that he has exhausted his options and so decides to have Uriah killed. The narrative is ambiguous concerning what David thinks Uriah knows (for a penetrating discussion of possible hypotheses, see Sternberg, 209–13). In any event, David takes no chances: In the morning he "wrote a letter to Joab and sent it with [*wayyišlaḥ bᵉyad*, lit., 'sent by the hand of'; see comment on 12:25] Uriah" (v.14). Probably unwittingly, Uriah carries his own death warrant to Joab.

Comparison of the contents of David's letter to those of the infamous Jezebel's letters concerning Naboth (cf. 1Ki 21:9–11) is not out of place, since in both cases an innocent man is executed at an Israelite monarch's whim. David orders Joab to put Uriah in the front line of battle against the Ammonites where "the fighting is fiercest" (v.15)—a phrase that echoes the "bitter war" against the Philistines in the days of Saul (see 1Sa 14:52 and comment; same Heb. expression). Uriah is then to be abandoned to his fate: He will be "struck down [*nkh*] and die."

"Cursed is the man who kills [*nkh*] his neighbor secretly [*bassāter*]," intones Deuteronomy 27:24. David "struck down [*nkh*]" Uriah and took his wife (12:9), and these things were done "in secret [*bassāter*]" (12:12). The implication is obvious: David's heinous actions are punishable under the divine curse (cf. Carlson, 141).

At this point in the account, however, Uriah is still alive. When Joab receives David's letter, he recognizes the fact that to isolate Uriah as the only fatality in the attack would cast suspicion on David's motives. He therefore "makes improvements on the plan, implementing it in spirit rather than to the letter.... He realized that the saving in casualties, however desirable in itself, is also the weak spot in the king's plan. It is better for many to fall, he decides, than for the conspiracy to stand revealed" (Sternberg, 214). Joab thus besieges "the city" (v.16)—that is, Rabbah, the Ammonite capital (cf. v.1)—and puts Uriah at a "place" where its best troops are defending it (for "place" as a technical term in battle narratives, cf. Jos 8:19 ["position"]; Jdg 20:33). But he also sends other "men" (*ʿām*, lit., "people," a term often used in the sense of "soldiers" in military contexts; see comment on 1Sa 11:11) in David's "army" (lit., "servants" and thus mercenaries, like Uriah himself; see comment on v.1) to accompany Uriah into the heat of battle (v.17).

And so it is that "some" (vv.17, 24) of the mercenaries are sacrificed so that one, relatively unnoticed, might die. "In this fashion, the circle of lethal consequences of David's initial act spreads wider and wider" (Alter, *The David Story*, 254). The literary unit closes with David's criminal purpose finally accomplished—"Uriah the Hittite was dead"—a doleful refrain repeated in the rest of ch. 11, each time emphasizing not only a brave warrior's mercenary status but also his unswerving loyalty to his liege lord: "Your servant Uriah the Hittite is dead" (v.21), "Your servant Uriah the Hittite is dead" (v.24; cf. also v.26). The poignancy and pathos of his death are not dimmed by the matter-of-fact way in which the reports of it—whether by the narrator, by Joab, or by Joab's messenger—are treated as an addendum: "moreover" (v.17), "also" (v.21), "moreover" (v.24; in each case *gam*). More than three centuries ago, Benjamin Harris summarized the sordid story of David's adultery and Uriah's death under the letter "U" in *The New-England Primer*: "Uriah's beautious Wife, Made David seek his Life."

18–27a "Joab has performed his task so well that he got Uriah killed without giving the show away. Now he must effectively disguise his report to the king, concealing from the messenger the true purpose of his mission. While the messenger believes that he is carrying news about the abortive battle, Joab smuggles into the message the crucial item about Uriah's death" (Sternberg, 215). Sending a complete "account of the battle" (vv.18–19) to David through a messenger, Joab warns the latter that the king's anger may "flare up" (v.20; same Heb. verb used of the Lord's anger in 2Ch 36:16 ["was aroused"])—presumably when he learns of the high casualty count. Indeed, says Joab, David may ask a series of questions designed to reveal the stupidity (in his opinion) of Joab's battle plans against Rabbah.

Sternberg, 219, may well be correct in his evaluation of Joab's hypothetical reconstruction of David's words as suggesting "a picture of a general who not only gives his messenger the contents of the king's anticipated response but also acts the part of the king, expressively mimicking the intonations and speech patterns of royalty in rage." At the same time, however, the potential response as recorded is a literary masterpiece in miniature, chiastically arranged:

A Why did you get so close (*ngš*) to the city (v.20b)?
  B Didn't you know they would shoot from (*mʿl*) the wall (v.20c)?
    C Who killed Abimelech (v.21a)?
  B' Didn't a woman throw something from (*mʿl*) the wall (v.21b)?
A' Why did you get so close (*ngš*) to the wall (v.21c)?

David's supposed questions thus focus attention on the central issue in the parallel: "Who (really) killed Abimelech" (= Uriah)?

To get too near a city wall in ancient times was to flirt with mortal danger, since arrows and other missiles rained down from protected positions. Joab thus senses that when David hears about the casualties he will want to know why his men needlessly risked their lives. In fact, Joab surmises, David—an acknowledged expert in military lore—will probably also remind Joab's messenger of the story of the death of Abimelech son of Gideon, who lost his life because of his foolhardiness (v.21; cf. Jdg 9:50–54). In the days of the judges, during the siege of Thebez (exact location unknown, although probably a few miles northeast of Shechem; for possible identifications, see Aharoni, 265) "a woman dropped [*hšlyk*; cf. v.21 ("throw")] an upper millstone on

[Abimelech's] head and cracked his skull" (Jdg 9:53).

As Sternberg, 219–22, notes, the parallels between Abimelech on the one hand and Uriah and David on the other are multifaceted. Abimelech and Uriah are "struck down/killed" (*nkh*, vv.15, 21) because of a woman—and David falls because of a woman as well. The story of Abimelech conjures up the image of disgrace brought on royalty because of a woman's hand and an attempt to cover up the disgrace for fear that rumors would spread among the people (cf. Jdg 9:53–54). Of course

> David, God's anointed and a great king, is otherwise poles apart from a petty thug like Abimelech.... [But] that David is likened to Abimelech has—because of the very distance between them—the effect of diminishing his image. The more so since Abimelech fell at a woman's hands while at the head of his army: David falls at a woman's hands precisely because he plays truant from war. (Sternberg, 221–22)

Arriving in Jerusalem, Joab's messenger tells David "everything" his master has sent him to communicate (v.22). Apparently he somewhat elaborates the words of Joab, however, by giving (or concocting) a few additional details. The powerful Ammonites, says the messenger, "came out" from Rabbah (v.23; cf. v.17) to engage the Israelites in "the open," but David's men were able to drive them back to "the entrance to the city gate" (for the tactical significance of these locations, see 10:8 and comment). If the influence of wisdom has made an impact on chs. 11–12, the observation of Fontaine, 65, is apropos: "Unlike Wisdom at the gate, bringing life through her teachings (Prov 1:20 ff.; 8:1 ff.), the woman at the wall of Thebez brings death, and the allusion to the incident conjures up a feminine shadow of death hovering over Uriah at the gate of Rabbah (2 Sam 11:23b), all because of his failure to stand father to David's child."

As the messenger completes the fulfillment of his mission to David, his words remind us that the tragedy has come full circle: The archers' death volley was fired "from" (*mēᶜal*, lit., "from upon") the wall (v.24; cf. also vv.20–21), echoing the same prepositional phrase used earlier in the chapter (see comment on v.2). And it is not the guilty king, safe in his fortress palace in Jerusalem, who suffers; the enemy's arrows find their mark in his innocent "servants" (v.24), in his innocent "men" (lit., "servants"), who are sacrificed so that David can inconspicuously dispose of his ultimate target, his "servant" Uriah the Hittite.

The verbal element of the initial clause of David's response to Joab through the messenger—"May this thing/matter not be evil [*rᶜᶜ*] in your eyes" ("Don't let this upset you," NIV; v.25)—reverberates suggestively throughout the various ambivalent attitudes toward monarchy in the books of Samuel. The Israelite elders' original request for a king had "displeased" Samuel (see 1Sa 8:6 and comment), and David's popularity had "galled" Saul (1Sa 18:8). In the present context, although David tries to placate Joab with the assurance that the casualties among the mercenaries should not be allowed to "upset" him (v.25), "the thing David had done displeased the LORD" (v.27; cf. also 12:9; for additional examples, cf. Carlson, 151 and n. 3).

Temporarily oblivious to the divine displeasure, David resorts to a platitude: "The sword devours one as well as another" (v.25; see 2:26 and comment; see also comment on 18:8 [lit., "the forest devoured more lives ... than the sword devoured"]). From his own selfish perspective the king is basically saying that what is done is done, that it cannot be helped, and that innocent people will often get caught in the crossfire when vital goals are pursued. What is more, David further masks his true concerns by telling the messenger to authorize Joab to "press" the attack against Rabbah (cf. in addition

12:26–31) as part of the royal message that will "encourage" him (v.25; same Heb. verb).

When the news of Uriah's death reaches Bathsheba, she mourns for him—probably with more feeling than formality (cf. v.26, which reads lit., "When Uriah's wife heard that her husband Uriah was dead, she mourned for her husband," a sentence that also implicitly condemns David's adultery by stressing three times the husband-wife relationship between Uriah and Bathsheba). Although David had "mourned and wept and fasted" for the fallen Saul and Jonathan and their troops, as well as for Israel as a whole (see 1:12 and comment), unlike Bathsheba he apparently sheds no tears for Uriah (not to mention the other mercenaries).

The husband of Bathsheba now dead and the period of her mourning now over, the way is open for David to bring her to his house. The Hebrew phrase translated "had her brought" (v.27) is literally "sent and collected her" and emphasizes the abuse of royal power that David is increasingly willing to exercise (see comments on v.1; 10:1–19; the same Heb. verb is rendered "took ... into his service" in 1Sa 14:52 [see comment there]).

Bathsheba becomes David's wife, and in due course a son is born of their earlier adulterous act. That the child is not named is perhaps because "his life was so short and he died within seven days after birth [see 12:18 and comment], which was before the time for giving him a name (cf. Lk. 1:59)" (Jones, 112). Although short-lived and unnamed, however, he will not be unloved during the days of his fatal illness (cf. 12:16–24).

27b Serving as the hinge of chs. 11–12 (see comment on 11:1–5), v.27b looks backward to v.25 (see comment) and forward to 12:6, 9. It thus functions not as a later "redactional link" (as suggested by Jones, 96) but takes its rightful place as an integral part of the original narrative.

David's third cover-up, the death of Uriah, "is not the end: the last word belongs to Someone else: 'But what ["the thing," NIV] David had done displeased Yahweh'" (Vogels, 247). This is the only reference to "the LORD" in the entire chapter, but it is ironic indeed that the Hittite Uriah's name, which contains Yahweh's name in abbreviated form (see comment on v.3), appears an astounding seventeen times in the same chapter. And it is furthermore ironic that "Yahweh does not act. Rather, 'the deed' ... is subject of the verb. The deed did evil 'in the eyes of Yahweh.' Yahweh does not act or move or intervene or assert himself. *He is simply there*" (Brueggemann, "On Trust and Freedom," 10; italics his). The Lord's people are confident that he himself will "do what is good in his sight" (10:12), even though all too often they do the reverse (cf. Ge 38:10; Isa 59:15 ["was displeased"]). David will later confess that his sin with Bathsheba is known to God and is therefore deserving of divine judgment: "Against you, you only, have I sinned and done what is evil in your sight" (Ps 51:4).

NOTES

20 W. F. Albright reads *it-ta[g](!)-šu* in a damaged line on a cuneiform letter found at Taanach by Ernst Sellin in 1903–1904 ("A Prince of Taanach in the Fifteenth Century BC," *BA* 94 [1944]: 22 n. 63). If his reading is correct (which seems likely in context), the resulting phrase—*ittagšu ana ālāni*—means literally "gets close to the cities" and reflects the same idiom as נִגַּשְׁתֶּם אֶל־הָעִיר (*niggaštem ʾel-hāʿîr*, "you get close to the city"). Thus the Taanach phrase, though ostensibly written in Akkadian, exhibits a strong Canaanite overlay and provides another example of *ngš* in the sense of "approach, go near," as opposed to standard Akkadian *nagāšu*, which means "leave, wander" (cf. *CAD*, 11:108).

21 Abimelech was the son of Gideon, whose other name was Jerub-Baal (cf. NIV note; also 1Sa 12:11 and comment). For the rationale behind the pejorative Jerub-Besheth, see comments on 2:8 and 1 Samuel 12:11 (see also Note on 1Sa 7:4). "Upper millstone" (cf. also Dt 24:6; Jdg 9:53) is literally "millstone of riding," because it rides back and forth on top of its lower (and larger) counterpart (for details cf. *IDB*, 3:380–81; *ZPEB*, 4:227). For "lower millstone" as a simile of hardness, cf. Job 41:24.

23 "But we drove them back" reads literally "But we were against them," the preposition in this case being of the kind that can exist "dependent on a verb (generally a verb of motion), which, for the sake of brevity, is not expressed, but in sense is contained in what is apparently the governing verb" (GKC, sec. 119*ee*).

24 The *Kethiv* of the words rendered "archers" and "shot arrows" assumes the Aramaic form of the verb ירא (*yrʾ*), as in 2 Chronicles 26:15, whereas the *Qere* recognizes the א (ʾ) as superfluous and vocalizes on the basis of the more common Hebrew form ירה (*yrh*), as in v.20; 1 Samuel 20:20, 36, 37 ("had fallen"); 31:3. For examples of the same phenomenon in other verbs with ה (*h*) as the third radical, see GKC, sec. 75*rr*.

25 The troublesome accusative particle אֶת־ (ʾ*et-*) before הַדָּבָר הַזֶּה (*haddābār hazzeh*, "this thing/matter") is omitted from a few Hebrew MSS (cf. *BHS*), in effect making the phrase the subject of the sentence. Driver, 291, however, understands it to be construed as an accusative *ad sensum* and gives additional examples.

Although זֹה (*zōh*, "this") is often considered to be late biblical Hebrew (cf. by implication BDB, 262), the phrase כָּזֹה וְכָזֶה (*kāzōh wᵉkāzeh*, "one as well as another," lit., "like this and like this") demonstrates that "the corpus of what have been perceived to be uniquely LBH [Late Biblical Hebrew] traits is dwindling" (Stanley Gevirtz, "Of Syntax and Style in the 'Late Biblical Hebrew'–'Old Canaanite' Connection," *JANESCU* 18 [1986]: 26; cf. 25 n. 3; also Jdg 18:4 ["what"]; 1Ki 14:5 ["such and such an answer"]).

5. Nathan's Rebuke (12:1–25)

OVERVIEW

With respect to literary structure and context, ch. 12 combines with ch. 11 to form an integral section (see comment on 11:1–5) within the larger complex consisting of chs. 10–12 (see comment on 10:1–19). As such it follows naturally and relentlessly upon the sins of David described so laconically in ch. 11 and provides the divine response to his adultery with Bathsheba and his murder of her husband, Uriah (together with the other mercenaries who were also innocent victims of David's desperate maneuvering). Each of the segments of the chapter is chiastically parallel to its corresponding segment in ch. 11 (cf. 12:1–14 with 11:18–27a; 12:15–23 with 11:6–17; 12:24–25 with 11:2–5; and 12:26–31 with 11:1 [see comment on 11:1–5]).

1The Lord sent Nathan to David. When he came to him, he said, "There were two men
in a certain town, one rich and the other poor. 2The rich man had a very large number
of sheep and cattle, 3but the poor man had nothing except one little ewe lamb he had
bought. He raised it, and it grew up with him and his children. It shared his food, drank
from his cup and even slept in his arms. It was like a daughter to him.

4"Now a traveler came to the rich man, but the rich man refrained from taking one of
his own sheep or cattle to prepare a meal for the traveler who had come to him. Instead,
he took the ewe lamb that belonged to the poor man and prepared it for the one who
had come to him."

5David burned with anger against the man and said to Nathan, "As surely as the Lord
lives, the man who did this deserves to die! 6He must pay for that lamb four times over,
because he did such a thing and had no pity."

7Then Nathan said to David, "You are the man! This is what the Lord, the God of
Israel, says: 'I anointed you king over Israel, and I delivered you from the hand of Saul.
8I gave your master's house to you, and your master's wives into your arms. I gave you
the house of Israel and Judah. And if all this had been too little, I would have given you
even more. 9Why did you despise the word of the Lord by doing what is evil in his eyes?
You struck down Uriah the Hittite with the sword and took his wife to be your own.
You killed him with the sword of the Ammonites. 10Now, therefore, the sword will never
depart from your house, because you despised me and took the wife of Uriah the Hittite
to be your own.'

11"This is what the Lord says: 'Out of your own household I am going to bring calamity
upon you. Before your very eyes I will take your wives and give them to one who is close
to you, and he will lie with your wives in broad daylight. 12You did it in secret, but I will do
this thing in broad daylight before all Israel.'"

13Then David said to Nathan, "I have sinned against the Lord."

Nathan replied, "The Lord has taken away your sin. You are not going to die. 14But
because by doing this you have made the enemies of the Lord show utter contempt, the
son born to you will die."

15After Nathan had gone home, the Lord struck the child that Uriah's wife had borne to
David, and he became ill. 16David pleaded with God for the child. He fasted and went into
his house and spent the nights lying on the ground. 17The elders of his household stood
beside him to get him up from the ground, but he refused, and he would not eat any food
with them.

18On the seventh day the child died. David's servants were afraid to tell him that the
child was dead, for they thought, "While the child was still living, we spoke to David but
he would not listen to us. How can we tell him the child is dead? He may do something
desperate."

[19]David noticed that his servants were whispering among themselves and he realized
the child was dead. "Is the child dead?" he asked.
"Yes," they replied, "he is dead."
[20]Then David got up from the ground. After he had washed, put on lotions and changed
his clothes, he went into the house of the LORD and worshiped. Then he went to his own
house, and at his request they served him food, and he ate.
[21]His servants asked him, "Why are you acting this way? While the child was alive, you
fasted and wept, but now that the child is dead, you get up and eat!"
[22]He answered, "While the child was still alive, I fasted and wept. I thought, 'Who knows?
The LORD may be gracious to me and let the child live.' [23]But now that he is dead, why
should I fast? Can I bring him back again? I will go to him, but he will not return to me."
[24]Then David comforted his wife Bathsheba, and he went to her and lay with her. She
gave birth to a son, and they named him Solomon. The LORD loved him; [25]and because the
LORD loved him, he sent word through Nathan the prophet to name him Jedidiah.

COMMENTARY

1–14 The account of the Lord's sending the prophet Nathan to David to announce God's judgment on him includes Nathan's parable (vv.1–4), David's indignant reaction (vv.5–6), Nathan's two-word condemnation (v.7a [MT]), two divine oracles (vv.7b–12), David's confession (v.13a), and Nathan's announcement of judgment tempered by grace (vv.13b–14).

Although vv.1–4 exhibit characteristics of fable (George W. Coats, "Parable, Fable, and Anecdote: Storytelling in the Succession Narrative," *Int* 35/4 [1981]: 368–82) and melodrama (Lasine, 101–24), the overall category of "parable" best defines the literary genre of Nathan's tale (cf. Graffy, 404–6; Brad H. Young, *Jesus and His Jewish Parables: Rediscovering the Roots of Jesus' Teaching* [Mahwah, N.J.: Paulist, 1989], 5, 13 n. 11, 108–9, 241; Simon, 220–42). In a later article Coats himself observes that "Nathan's response to the king's judgment makes the function of the fable as a parable explicit" (George W. Coats, "2 Samuel 12:1–7a," *Int* 50/1 [1986]: 170).

At the same time, however, it would seem best not to attempt a more restrictive definition, such as "juridical parable" (Simon, 220–25) or "self-condemnation parable" (Graffy, 408) or "disguised parable" (Lawrence M. Wills, "Observations on 'Wisdom Narratives' in Early Biblical Literature," in *Of Scribes and Scrolls: Studies on the Hebrew Bible, Intertestamental Judaism, and Christian Origins. Presented to John Strugnell on the Occasion of His Sixtieth Birthday*, ed. Harold W. Attridge, John J. Collins, and Thomas H. Tobin [Lanham, Md.: Univ. Press of America, 1990], 60). In any event, Simon, 221, and Graffy, 404–8, agree that 14:1–20; 1 Kings 20:35–42/43; Isaiah 5:1–7; and Jeremiah 3:1–5 are four parables that resemble Nathan's parable in one or more ways (cf. similarly Wills, "Observations on 'Wisdom Narratives,'" 59). Graffy has identified four structural elements that appear in each of the five parables, and it is useful to set them forth as they occur in Nathan's parable and in the parable of the wise woman of Tekoa (14:1–20):

	12:1–7a	14:1–20
Introductory formula	v.1a	vv.1–5a
Presentation of the case	v.1b–4	vv.5b–7, 15–17
Judgment of the case	vv.5–6	vv.8–11
True meaning revealed	v.7a	vv.12–14, 18–20

If ch. 11 is liberally flecked with the verb *šlḥ* ("send") as an index of human power (see comments on 10:1–19; 11:1), ch. 12 begins by using it with God as the subject: "The LORD sent Nathan to David" (v.1a). A few Hebrew MSS add "the prophet" to "Nathan" here, as does the LXX. In any case, it is clearly in his prophetic role that Nathan is sent by the Lord to proclaim his convicting word to the king (see comments on 7:2; 1Sa 22:5).

Initially, the divine word takes the form of a parable. Briskly told, its vocabulary would later be used by the prophet Zechariah to describe the injustice of the "rich" (*ʿšr*) against the "flock" (*ṣʾn*) whose "buyers" (*qnh*) slaughter them and whose own shepherds do not "spare" (*ḥml*) them, with the result that the Lord would no longer "pity" (*ḥml*) the people of the land (Zec 11:4–6; cf. here: *ʿšr* [vv.1–2, 4]; *ṣʾn* ["sheep," vv.2, 4]; *qnh* ["bought," v.3]; *ḥml* ["refrained," v.4]; *ḥml* [in David's angry response, v.6]; cf. similarly Lasine, 104 and n.6). That Nathan's rebuke begins with a parable makes it no less effective, since its verisimilitude is reflected in the modern Bedouin custom of *Adayieh* ("attack"), which clarifies "two motives in the parable: the urgency and supremacy of the duty of hospitality, on the one hand, and the reality of the emotional attachment of man to his beast—the ewe that was like a daughter" (Simon, 229; for additional details, see 227–30).

The immediate use of the word "men" (*ʾănāšîm*) in v.1b and the triple occurrence of "man" (*ʾîš*) in the concluding verse of the parable (v.4: "rich man" [first occurrence], "poor man," "one"), combined with David's double use of the word "man" in v.5, prepare the reader for Nathan's powerful accusation in v.7a. Now a rich man, David should have remembered what it was like to be "poor" (v.1b) because by his own admission he himself had once been a "poor man" (see 1Sa 18:23 and comment). The "very large number" of sheep and cattle owned by the rich man (= David; v.2) echoes the "great quantity" of bronze taken by David from the Arameans (see 8:8 and comment; same Heb. phrase). The "sheep and cattle" in the parable symbolize David's many wives, a fact clarified in the succeeding verses.

By contrast the "poor man" (= Uriah) has "nothing except" (*ʾên-kōl kî ʾim*) one little "ewe lamb" (= Bathsheba; v.3). The description is reprised in a similar tale of poverty, in which a poor widow announces that she has "nothing ... except" a little oil (2Ki 4:2; same Heb. expression). The verbs used of the ewe lamb in the rest of v.3 indicate that it is prized as a genuine member of the poor man's family: He "raised it" (lit., "caused it to live"; cf. Eze 16:6), it "grew up" with the other family members (cf. 1Sa 2:21; 3:19; Eze 16:7), it "shared" (lit., "ate") his food and "drank" from his cup and "slept/lay" in his arms (the latter three verbs echo Uriah's refusal to "eat" and "drink" and "lie" with his wife in 11:11; cf. Lawlor, 198, 201). "Food" (v.3) is literally "piece (of bread)," meager fare at best (cf. 1Sa 2:36; see also 1Sa 28:22 and comment).

The expression "slept in his arms" (cf. "he gathers the lambs in his arms," Isa 40:11) is frequently used of a woman lying in a man's embrace or near him (cf. ironically 1Ki 1:2 ["lie beside him"]; also Mic 7:5). That the ewe lamb stands for Uriah's wife becomes clear at the end of v.3, where the narrator states that it "was like a daughter/*bat* (as in *bat-šeba*ᶜ) to him" (Ackerman, 44; for additional helpful details concerning the description of the lamb in human terms, see Coats, "Parable, Fable, and Anecdote," 371).

By no means the ordinary word for "traveler" (v.4, first occurrence), *hēlek* (lit., "walking, walker") appears elsewhere only once in the OT (1Sa 14:26 ["oozing out"]; for a more common word for "traveler" [v.4, second occurrence], cf. Jdg 19:17; Jer 9:2; 14:8). It is perhaps used here to remind the reader that David's trouble began in the first place because he had earlier "walked around" (*wayyithallēk*) on the roof of his palace (see 11:2 and comment). Bound by culture and tradition to provide hospitality for his guest (see comment on 1Sa 28:24), the rich man sets about to prepare a meal for him. Instead of slaughtering one of his own animals, however, he "took" (v.4) the poor man's one ewe lamb instead—just as David had sent messengers to "get" (lit., "take," 11:4; see comment there) Bathsheba.

That the rich man "refrained" (*wayyaḥmōl*) from taking one of his own animals (v.4) is the key element in understanding the main point of Nathan's parable. David would soon condemn the man because "he had no pity" (*lōʾ-ḥāmāl*, v.6). The observations of Lasine, 112–13, are perceptive:

> The prophet only says that the rich man spared ("had pity on") his own animals. He leaves it to the hearer to notice a connection between the villain's "pitying" of his own flocks and his lack of pity for the poor man's ewe. David not only notices this connection but focuses on it.... He shows that the rich man's "pity" for his own property equals "no-pity" for the poor man and his little lamb. But by correcting these perversions of justice and sensibility, David creates a *new* opposition between himself and the story, one involving *his* relationship to pity. His pity for the victims in the story is in stark contrast to his lack of pity for Uriah, his victim in real life. (italics his; cf. similarly Lawlor, 201–2)

Understandably, David's moral indignation against the rich man in Nathan's parable takes the form of burning anger (v.5) that will not be assuaged until justice is done (unlike the lack of resolution of David's anger following the incident of Amnon's rape of Tamar; see 13:21 and comment). As in 1 Samuel 26:16, David uses the Lord's name in a solemn oath (cf. 14:11; see 1Sa 14:39 and comment), and as in 1 Samuel 26:16, David declares that someone "deserves to die" (lit., "is a son of death"; see comments at 1Sa 20:31; 26:16), in this case "the man who did this"; David is, of course, oblivious to the fact that he himself is "the man" (v.7a). Thus "David has been trapped by his own sentence" (Ackerman, 44).

Since theft of a lamb was not a capital crime, David's outburst is an exaggeration "designed to express the gravity of the sin involved in the callous ignoring of the poor man's attachment to his ewe" (Simon, 230). It "reflects the inadequacy of the civil law in this particular case.... The rich man deserved death for his callous act, but was protected by the law itself" (Anthony Phillips, "The Interpretation of 2 Samuel xii 5–6," *VT* 16/2 [1966]: 243). Thus the man's penalty is that he must pay for the confiscated lamb "four times over" (v.6) as mandated by Exodus 22:1 (cf. also the promise made by Zacchaeus in Lk 19:8). His guilt is clear: He must make restitution "because [*ᶜēqeb ʾašer*] he did such a thing" (i.e., took the poor man's only ewe lamb)—just as David will soon be told that he is guilty "because [*ᶜēqeb kî*] you ... took the wife of Uriah the Hittite" (v.10). Unlike the pharaoh's daughter, whose heart was so touched at the sight of the crying Hebrew baby that she "felt sorry" for him (Ex 2:6), the rich man (= David) had no "pity" (v.6; same Heb. verb; see also v.4 and comment). "The Egyptian princess, a person who held Moses in her power, a foreigner, not a member of the covenant community, has what David did not have. She has compassion for the baby" (Coats, "II Samuel 12:1–7a," 171).

Many have seen (correctly, in my opinion) in the fourfold restitution as applied to David "an allusion to the death of four of David's sons, namely Bathsheba's first child [v.18], Amnon [13:28–29], Absalom [18:14–15] and Adonijah [1 Kings 2:25]" (Jones, 103). Indeed, Ackerman, 50, observes, "the narrator has unobtrusively introduced a lamb motif as he describes [the last three] sons and their fate." Less likely is the suggestion of the rabbinic tractate *Yoma* 22B (cited by Alter, *The David Story*, 258) that the four victims are Bathsheba's first child, Tamar, Amnon, and Absalom, since (1) the introduction of a female child in the series would be unexpected and (2) Tamar's fate was rape, not death.

Up to this point in the MT, the narrator has used "man" and "men" six times—four times from the lips of Nathan (vv.1, 4 ["rich man," first occurrence; "poor man"; "one"]) and twice from the lips of David (v.5). Now the identity of the culprit in the parable becomes explicit in the seventh appearance of the incriminating word as Nathan delivers his terse rebuke to David: "You are the man" (v.7a), a statement that McDonald calls "the most dramatic sentence in the Old Testament" (J. Ian H. McDonald, "The Bible and Christian Practice," in *Theology and Practice* [ed. Duncan B. Forrester; London: Epworth, 1990], 24; cf. further Linafelt, 104: "The Hebrew phrase ... wonderfully emphasizes that, in the final analysis, David is simply a man. David is not addressed as 'king,' or 'lord,' or even 'prince,' but simply as *haʾish*, the man").

On the broader horizon it can be affirmed that "David, royal judge, is shown to be a rich oppressor," whose dynasty has "sprung from an adulterously begun union" (Roth, "You Are the Man!" 10). In the shorter term, however, Nathan's abrupt application "draws a parallel between the rich man's exploitation of the poor on account of his superior status and the king's misuses of his own position of authority. Attention is thus focused not on the simple case of theft, but on the exploitation of the weak by one enjoying a superior position" (Jones, 100). Thus identification with the rich man implies that David is not merely "a man who deserves to die, but who can only be sued in tort: he is, by his murder of Uriah, an actual murderer who should suffer execution under Israel's criminal law. It is only due to Yahweh's direct pardon that David is to be spared (2 Sam. xii 13)" (Phillips, "The Interpretation of 2 Samuel xii 5–6," 244).

Appropriately, a few Hebrew manuscripts insert a closed paragraph marker after "You are the man" to separate v.7a from v.7b. Verses 7b–12, the divine oracles that continue Nathan's rebuke, divide naturally into two unequal sections separated by a closed paragraph marker (vv.7b–10 and vv.11–12), each section beginning with the prophetic messenger formula "This is what the LORD says" (cf. vv.7b, 11). In addition, "the two sections concentrate on different aspects of David's sin, the first being more concerned with the murder of Uriah and the second relating exclusively to David's adultery with Bathsheba" (Jones, 101–2). Perhaps most significantly vv.9–10, the middle two verses of the six that make up the oracles, can be arguably defined as the literary, historical, and theological crux and center of 2 Samuel as a whole (see comment below).

After Nathan strengthens the basic messenger formula by referring to the Lord as "the God of [the entire nation of] Israel" (v.7b), the first section of the divine oracle begins with the two occurrences of the emphatic pronoun: "*I* anointed" and "*I* delivered." The Lord reminds David that it was he who anointed him king (more than once; see 1Sa 16:13; 2Sa 2:4a; 5:3 and comments) and that it was he who delivered him from Saul's clutches (more than once; see 1Sa 24:15; 26:24; 27:1; 2Sa 4:9 and comments). Just as Saul, the Lord's anointed, had fallen from grace, so also would David—though not in the same way or to the same degree (see comment on 1Sa 15:1; cf. also 15:17–23).

In addition, the Lord who "gave" Saul's "house" (= family and property; see comments on 9:9–11a) and wives to David and who "gave" the "house" (= kingdom) of "Israel and Judah" (see comment on 5:3) to David (v.8) would soon "give" the wives to someone else (v.11). In light of the monogamous ideal outlined in Genesis 2:22–24, the gift of "wives" in vv.8 and 11 would seem to be a divine concession to the polygamy that was relatively common (at least among the upper classes) in ancient Near Eastern culture (see comments on 1Sa 1:2; 25:43). Saul's "wives" presumably included at least Ahinoam (see comment on 1Sa 25:43; cf. also Levenson and Halpern, 507, 513) and perhaps also his concubine Rizpah (cf. 3:7). The fact that they are given into David's "arms" (v.8) is an ironic allusion to Nathan's parable (cf. v.3; also Mic 7:5 ["embrace"]). And the God whose generosity knows no bounds (cf. Ex 34:6) would have "given" (lit., "added") even more to David if he had considered it appropriate to do so.

But David's unbridled desire and willful murder have foreclosed any such options. The first section of the divine oracle (vv.7b–10) concludes with vv.9–10, which are closely tied to each other by their use of the terms "despise(d)," "Uriah the Hittite," "sword," and "took ... wife ... to be your own." The verses perform the same function for 2 Samuel as 1 Samuel 16:13–14 perform for 1 Samuel (see comment on 1Sa 16:1–13): By leaving no doubt concerning the Lord's displeasure with the king's sins and his determination to punish him, verses 9–10 constitute the literary, historical, and theological center not only of the oracle itself but also of the entire book. To use Carlson's helpful rubric, David is now truly and undeniably "under the Curse" (Carlson, 7, 25, 140).

If Saul lost the kingdom through having "rejected the word of the LORD" (1Sa 15:23), David is judged because he has decided to "despise the word of the LORD" (v.9). "Here, we have for the first time a pronouncement of evil upon David" (Linafelt, 104). To despise the Lord's word is to break his commands and thus to incur guilt and punishment (cf. Nu 15:31), and that without remedy (cf. 2Ch 36:16). Proverbs 13:13 is apropos: "He who scorns/despises [though not having the same three consonants, the Heb. verbs translated 'despise' here (*bwz*) and in v.9 (*bzh*) spring from the same biconsonantal root] instruction [*dbr*] will pay for it, but he who respects a command is rewarded." To despise the Lord's "word" (*dbr*) is to do "what is evil in his eyes" (v.9; see comment on 11:27b), a link David later acknowledges when he confesses to God that he has done "what is evil in your sight, so that you are proved right when you speak [*dbr*]" (Ps 51:4). Taking 11:27b, 12:9, and Proverbs 13:13 together, Brueggemann ("On Trust and Freedom," 11) argues that "'in the eyes of Yahweh' can most plausibly be understood as that benevolent life-giving ordering upon which the wise reflected and which David in his foolishness violated."

In v.9 the emphatic position of "Uriah the Hittite," "his wife," and "him"—objects that in each case precede their governing verbs—underscores the callous and heinous nature of David's sins against them. People who above all others he should have cherished and cared for became instead the degraded and destroyed targets of royal lust and caprice. The trusted mercenary Uriah is "struck down" (see 11:15 and comment) and "killed" by the sword of the enemy. Although the Lord "gave" and would have given "even more" (v.8), David "took" (see comment on v.4; see also 5:13 and comment) someone else's wife to be his own (vv.9–10). Unfeeling acquisitiveness is of the very nature of royalty (see 1Sa 8:11, 13–17, and comment).

Despising the word of the Lord (v.9) is tantamount to despising the Lord himself (v.10; cf. Note on v.14). In doing both, David finds himself in unsavory company (cf. 1Sa 2:29–30). With respect to the statement that "the sword will never depart from [David's] house," Carlson, 158, observes: "David's ominous words in ... 11:25 ['the sword devours one as well as another'] recoil upon his own house in 12:10" (cf. also Alter, *The David Story*, 259). David's "never" in his colorful curse against Joab's "house" in 3:29 also returns to haunt him in the inexorable language of divine judgment (v.10).

The second section of the Lord's oracle (vv.11–12) is relentless in the immediacy with which it threatens retaliation against the king. "Out of your own household" (v.11) renders the same Hebrew expression translated "from your house" in v.10. As David has done what is "evil" (v.9), so the Lord will bring "calamity" upon him (v.11; same Heb. word); and as David has done evil "in [the Lord's] eyes" (v.9), so the Lord will bring calamity upon the king "before [his] very eyes" (v.11). Indeed, the Hebrew grammatical construction translated "I am going to bring calamity" is perhaps better rendered "I am about to bring calamity" (as in, e.g., 1Sa 3:11), emphasizing the imminence of the events described (cf. GKC, sec. 116*p*)—events such as Amnon's rape of Tamar (13:1–14), Absalom's murder of Amnon (13:28–29), Absalom's rebellion against David (15:1–12), and more. David's punishment for his crimes against Bathsheba and Uriah is a clear example of a conditional element in the Davidic covenant (see comment on 7:1–17; cf. Waltke, "The Phenomenon of Conditionality" [in Gileadi], 132).

As David "took" Uriah's wife (vv.9–10), so the Lord will "take" David's wives (v.11). As the Lord "gave" Saul's property and Israel's kingdom to David (v.8), so he says that he will now "give" David's wives to someone else, to "one who is close to you" (v.11)—ironically, an expression earlier used of David himself in similar circumstances (see 1Sa 15:28; 28:17 ["one of your neighbors"] and comments). The "one who is close" to David turns out to be his own son Absalom: "David's voyeurism in 2 Sam 11:2 and Nathan's curse in 12:11 foreshadow Absalom's rooftop orgy (16:20–22)" (Levenson and Halpern, 514). Although Uriah had refused to "lie" with his own wife (11:11), David had "slept" with her (11:4)—and soon Absalom will "lie" with David's wives (v.11; same Heb. verb). As the Lord will take David's wives "before [his] very eyes," so Absalom will lie with them "in broad daylight" (lit., "before the eyes of this sun," v.11).

David's despising of God (v.10) and his commands (v.9) resulted in his "doing" evil in the Lord's eyes (v.9). But although David "did" evil "in secret" (see comment on 11:15), the Lord will "do" his will against David "in broad daylight" (v.12; not the same expression as in v.11, it reads literally "before [*neged*] the sun"; cf. Nu 25:4) and thus "before [*neged*] all Israel" (cf. the fulfillment "in the sight of all Israel" in 16:22). As it turns out, three of David's sons will prove themselves "unfit to rule by recapitulating, each in his turn, their father's sin.... Just as David willfully takes Bathsheba for himself (II Sam. 11:2–4), so Amnon forces Tamar (II Sam. 13:8–14), Absalom enters the royal harem (II Sam. 16:22), and Adonijah tries to claim his deceased father's concubine (I Kings 2:13–17)" (McCarter, "'Plots, True or False,'" 359).

To his credit, David confesses to the prophet Nathan that he has broken God's law: "I have sinned against the LORD" (v.13a; cf. David's words in 24:10, 17 and especially in Ps 51:4: "Against you, you only, have I sinned"; for Saul's earlier agonized admission to the prophet Samuel in similar circumstances, see 1Sa 15:24, 30 and comment). Though he could have vacillated or indignantly denied Nathan's accusation or ridded himself of Nathan in one way or another, David accepts full responsibility for his actions. "In his total and immediate response of repentance ... there is no hint in the narrative that this is anything less than an authentic, rightly intentioned confession. It is presented without irony or suspicion" (Brueggemann, "On Trust and Freedom," 8).

And, as might be expected, the prophet does not leave the king comfortless. Nathan comes to David with words of divine grace. "Only the man who accepts that he was wrong can be forgiven. 'Yahweh, for his part, forgives your sin [v.13b]'" (Vogels, 251). In judging the rich man for his cruelty (v.5), David had unwittingly chosen his own death penalty (cf. Lev 20:10; Dt 22:22). But the Lord, through his prophet, announces the forgiveness of David's "sin" (against Bathsheba) and preserves David's life: "You are not going to die." The fact that God does not hesitate to strike people down for what might be considered lesser infractions (see 6:7 and comment) makes his forbearance in David's case all the more noteworthy.

At the same time, however, the Lord is not yet through with David: "By doing this you have shown utter contempt for the LORD" (NIV note on v.14, which is doubtless the intention of the narrator and is preferable to the NIV's textual reading; see Notes below). In this respect David finds himself in the company of Eli's reprobate sons, who had been in the habit of "treating the LORD's offering with contempt" and whose sin was therefore "very great in the LORD's sight" (1Sa 2:17; cf. "evil in his eyes," v.9). David will not "die" (v.13), but the son born to him will (v.14). Tit for tat: Having "show[n] utter contempt" (infinitive absolute plus finite verb) for the Lord, David's son will "die" (infinitive absolute plus finite verb; better, "surely die" [cf. Ge 2:17, where the same grammatical construction appears]). "When David slept with the woman and created new life, the woman did not belong to him but to Uriah. The child cannot belong to David. He cannot enrich himself through his sin, and in a sense, justice is done to Uriah" (Vogels, 251).

15–23 The account of the death of David's infant son, a result of David's sin (vv.15–23), is paralleled by the story of Uriah's death, a crime of which David was guilty (11:6–17; see comment on 11:1–5). And just as in 11:15–26 the verb *mwt* ("to die") occurs numerous times (see comment on 11:6–27), so also it appears numbingly often in vv.15–23 (vv.18 [3x], 19 [3x], 21, 23).

Having fulfilled his prophetic mission, Nathan leaves the palace and goes home. The Lord then strikes Bathsheba's newborn son (v.15) with what proves to be a fatal illness (cf. 1Sa 25:38; see also comment on 1Sa 26:10). The phrase "the child that Uriah's wife had borne to David" underscores the fact that David's adultery and murder will claim yet another innocent victim.

Despite the prophet's pronouncement that the child's fate is sealed (v.14), David is not yet willing to resign himself to the death of his son. He therefore intercedes for the child's life (v.16). "Supplication is more humbling than resignation" (Simon, 239). Ostensibly as a symbol of mourning (see also v.20 and comment), he "fasted" (see comments on 1:12; 3:32–35; 1Sa 31:13). Although the series of consecutive perfects beginning with "went" is correctly rendered as repeated action in the NIV (cf. also Driver, 291), commentators in general seem not to have noticed that going "into (one's) house" and spending one's nights "lying on the ground" are incompatible activities, unless the house has a dirt floor—which was surely not the case in David's palace.

In any event, the MT does not have "into his house" in v.16 (contrast "went to his [own] house" in v.20), and thus "went" (*bā*ʾ) should probably be understood here as an auxiliary verb used to initiate action (cf. the analogous use of imperative *bô*ʾ with auxiliary function in cohortative constructions as noted in *IBHS*, 574). Outside the royal palace, David "spent the nights lying on the ground"—ironically, just as Uriah and his fellow soldiers had done (cf. 11:9, 11; cf. Vogels, 261).

If Genesis 24:2 is any indication ("the chief/oldest servant in his household" is literally "his servant, the elder in his household"), "the elders of [David's] household" (v.17) must have been loyal servants to whom David had delegated important tasks. Concerned for his welfare, they stand "beside" (or "over," as in 1:9) him, urging him to get up and take care of his personal needs. He refuses, however, and will not so much as "eat" any food with them. Koehler, 6, argues cogently that the root *brh* (here written *br*ʾ) "means 'eat invalid food, or the food of mourners'" (see also 3:35 and comment; cf. 13:6, 10).

The death of the child—son of Bathsheba, "Daughter of seven" (see comment on 11:3); son of David, chosen above his seven brothers (see 1Sa 16:10 and comment; cf. Vogels, 252)—takes place on "the seventh day" (v.18). Although it is impossible to know whether the day the child died was "the seventh Day after its Birth before it was circumcised; or the seventh after it fell sick" (Patrick, 446), on balance the former is the more attractive (see comment on 11:27a). David's "servants" (vv.18–19, 21), doubtless to be identified with the "elders of his household" (v.17), are reluctant to tell him of the child's death for fear that their master may do something "desperate" (lit., "evil, disastrous"; for the same idiom, cf. Jer 26:19; 41:11 ["crimes ... had committed"]).

Aware of the whispering of his servants and thus realizing that the child is dead, David gives verbal expression to his own worst nightmare (v.19). Whether or not he voices it in the form of a question (two Hebrew manuscripts do not exhibit the *he-* interrogative particle; cf. *BHS*), the servants finally affirm to him that the child is indeed dead.

Having admitted to himself the inevitable, David gets up from the ground (v.20). After he had "washed" (cf., ironically, 11:2 and 8, where the Heb. verb is the same) and put on lotions (a procedure sometimes associated with the absence or cessation of mourning; cf. 14:2), he "changed his clothes." Although some have understood the latter act simply as a privilege of David's royal status (as opposed to that of commoners; cf. Neufeld, 53 n. 31), it is surely better to see it as the shedding of mourning garb and the reverting back to normal clothing, especially since "lying in sackcloth (on the ground)" is the attested reading in v.16 in 4QSamuel[a], most manuscripts of the LXX (including the Lucianic recension), one Old Latin manuscript, and Josephus (*Ant.* 7.154 [7.4]; for details see Ulrich, 100; also Simon, 240 n. 1).

After entering the "house of the LORD" (the tabernacle; see 1Sa 1:7 and comment) to worship him, apparently resigned to divine judgment against himself and his child, David then goes to "his own house" (v.20). There he breaks his fast (cf. v.16) and eats ordinary food (as opposed to the food of mourners that he had earlier rejected [see comment on v.17; the verb "ate" is here *ʾkl*, not *br*ʾ]).

Understandably, David's servants are confused. While the child was alive, David—acting like a mourner—had "fasted and wept" (v.21; for the association of fasting and weeping with mourning, see 1:12; 3:31–35 and comments; cf. also Jdg 20:26; Est 4:3; Ps 69:10–11; Joel 2:12). Now that his son is dead, however, the king puts on garments befitting royalty and enjoys a good meal.

Concerning David's response to his perplexed servants (vv.22–23), Perdue, 77, asks: "Are these the words of a grief-stricken father, or of a callous ruler realizing he had failed to negate Nathan's prophecy predicting trouble from the king's own house, a prediction whose initial sign was the death of the child?" Walter Brueggemann (*In Man We Trust*, 36) had already answered Perdue's question:

> David's reaction to the death of his child ... is an act of profound faith in the face of the most precious tabus of his people.... David had discerned, for whatever reasons, that the issues of his life are not to be found in cringing fear before the powers of death, but in his ability to embrace and abandon, to love and to leave; to take life as it comes, not with indifference but with freedom, not with callousness but with buoyancy.

David readily admits that his conduct might have appeared peculiar, that his mourning might have seemed premature (v.22). But he was counting on the open door of the divine "perhaps": "Who knows?" (cf. similarly Joel 2:13–14; Jnh 3:9). "To be sure, David's hope in this instance was ill-founded, but his use of *mî yôdēaᶜ* functions in the same way the prophetic *ʾûlay* ('perhaps') does in Amos v 15 and comparable passages. The emphasis falls on the sovereignty of God, but human beings still dare to hope that compassion will gain the upper hand" (James L. Crenshaw, "The Expression *Mî Yôdēaᶜ* in the Hebrew Bible," *VT* 36/3 [1986]: 275; cf. also Simon, 239 n. 1).

Resigned to the death of his child, David asks his servants why he should "fast" (the participle is better rendered "continue fasting"). Since the netherworld is the "Land of No Return" (Akkad. *erṣet lā târi*, the name by which it was often described in ancient Mesopotamia; for OT observations of a similar nature, cf. Job 7:9 ["he who goes down to the grave (= Sheol) does not return"]; 10:21 ["place of no return"]; 16:22 ["journey of no return"]; Pr 2:18–19; Eze 26:20; for discussion see Tromp, 189–90), the child "will not return" to David, and nothing that David can do will "bring him back again" (v.23). Indeed, David's only option for a reunion with his son is to "go to him" (cf. similarly George W. Coats, "II Samuel 12:1–7a," *Int* 40/2 [1986]: 173). But however far this may fall short of Christian confidence in the eventual resurrection of the body and the life everlasting (cf. Kirkpatrick, *Second Book of Samuel*, 131), not all is lost: "David comes to terms with his own mortality, and even in that finds hope, because he looks forward to being reunited with his child. The Lord who had sent Nathan to David had had the last word and, though David was bereft, he was content" (Baldwin, 241).

A final word: "By way of personal conclusion, one could read and meditate on Psalm 51. The biblical tradition has understood this psalm as reflecting the feelings and prayer 'of David, when the prophet Nathan came to him because he had been with Bathsheba'" (Vogels, 254).

24–25 As noted above (see comment on 11:1–5), vv.24–25 mirror 11:2–5. At the beginning of the narrative, Bathsheba had been "the wife of Uriah the Hittite" (see 11:3 and comment), but as an outcome of the sin of King David she has become "his wife" (v.24). "David is able, but with apparent impunity now, to do precisely what he had done to set the story in motion: he can have sexual intercourse with Bathsheba, the woman of his desire (11:4; 12:24)" (Gunn, "David and the Gift of the Kingdom," 20).

If Isaac's marriage to Rebekah helped him find comfort after his mother's death (Ge 24:67), David "comforted" Bathsheba (who doubtless mourned her son's death) when he "went to her and lay with her" (v.24; see 11:4 and comment). In due course she gives birth to yet another son, later to be recognized as a "wise son" given to David by the Lord (1Ki 5:7). The boy is named Solomon, which apparently means "(God is) his peace" (see comment on 5:14; for another possibility, cf. Jones, 113 ["His replacement/substitution"]). That his name contains the same Hebrew root (*šlm*) as does Jerusalem (see comment on 5:6) is probably not coincidental (cf. similarly Talmon, 152 n. 19).

The statement that the Lord "loved" Solomon (v.24; cf. Ne 13:26; similarly Dt 4:37; 7:8; Ps 146:8;

Pr 3:12; 15:9) perhaps has covenantal overtones and should therefore include the technical nuance that the Lord "honors his treaty commitments to the dynasty" (Brueggemann, "On Trust and Freedom," 13 and n. 32; for "love" in the sense of "covenantal/political loyalty," see comments on 1:26; 1Sa 18:1–4). If so, the suggestion that the name Solomon means something like "His submission (is to the Lord)" becomes more attractive (for discussion, see Z. W. Falk, "Hebrew Legal Terms: II," *JSS* 12/2 [1967]: 244).

On the basis of his love for Solomon, the Lord "sent word through" (lit., "sent by the hand of," v.25—an ironic touch; see 11:14 and comment) the prophet Nathan, who is thereby instructed to call David's newborn son Jedidiah ("Loved by the LORD" [see NIV note]; cf. *y^edîd yhwh*, "the beloved of the LORD" [Dt 33:12], a phrase used to describe Benjamin), a name similar to that of David himself (for details see comment on 1Sa 16:13).

Why the boy was given two names is a question that has been much discussed. Since Jedidiah is an unambiguously orthodox name, Jones suggests that it was calculated to "satisfy the Israelite [as opposed to the Jebusite] element in Jerusalem" (Jones, 114). It seems more likely, however, that "Solomon" should be understood "as a throne name which David ... conferred upon his son Jedidiah ... so as to suggest his (future) appointment as king in (Jeru)salem" (Talmon, 152). The dual naming thus anticipates "the change of name which Solomon himself assumed when he succeeded to the throne" (Talmon, 152).

If at the beginning of ch. 12 Nathan rebuked the king (vv.7–14), at its end he comforts him (v.25). But Nathan's ministry with respect to David and Solomon/Jedidiah is not yet finished. During David's last days Nathan would play a key role in making sure that Solomon succeeds his father as king of Israel (cf. 1Ki 1:11–14, 24–27). In fact, Nathan would share in Solomon's anointing (1Ki 1:34, 45), the most solemn act of all.

NOTES

5 When Lasine states that "Nathan's tale evokes a vehement emotional response from David, who ... does not view it as a melodrama" (Lasine, 103), he seriously undercuts his own analysis of the literary genre of Nathan's rebuke by claiming to understand the prophet's words better than David did. The Egyptian Tale of the Eloquent Peasant, which predates David by more than half a millennium, also excoriates anyone who plunders the property of the poor: "Do not despoil a poor man of his possessions, a feeble man whom you know, for his possessions are (the very) breath to a poor man, and to take them away is to stop up his nose" (translation by R. O. Faulkner in *The Literature of Ancient Egypt: An Anthology of Stories, Instructions, and Poetry* [new ed.; ed. William Kelly Simpson; New Haven, Conn.: Yale Univ. Press, 1973], 43).

6 Although Josephus (*Ant.* 7.150 [7.3]), the Lucianic recension of the LXX, and some Targum MSS join the MT in reading "four times," the LXX prefers "seven times"; cf. also Peter W. Coxon, "A Note on 'Bathsheba' in 2 Samuel 12,1–6," *Bib* 62/2 (1981):

> To retain the "sevenfold" is to recognise that with two deft strokes the snare is laid which will bring the king down. I would like to suggest here that, Jacob-like, David the deceiver is cajoled by Nathan's smooth narration to the extent that he fails to recognise the subtle intrusion of Bathsheba's name. Could one doubt for one instance [*sic*] that the wider circle of Nathan's audience remained oblivious to the suggestive combination of *bt*

> [v.3] and the stem of *šbʿtym* [v.6]? Nathan confronted David with the name of his mistress and David's partisan judgement only served to heap coals of wrath upon his head. (Coxon, ibid., 250)

But

> while it is possible that the punitive damages were later increased, it is more likely that sevenfold is a later proverbial expression indicating that perfect restitution must be made. A later scribe might have altered the MT to conform to the law, but it would seem more probable that the LXX rendering is due to a recollection of the proverbial saying preserved in Prov. vi 31, which also reads sevenfold. As the amount of compensation was fixed by law, it is unlikely that David would need to resort to a proverbial saying. (Anthony Phillips, "The Interpretation of 2 Samuel xii 5–6," *VT* 16/2 [1966]: 243)

It is therefore unnecessary to insist that "the reading 'fourfold' must be taken (as most exegetes do) to be secondary—and, we may add, post-Deuteronomic" (Carlson, 156).

14 Since נִאֵץ (*niʾēṣ*) is never causative elsewhere in the OT (cf. BDB, 611), the NIV's "you have made the enemies of the LORD show utter contempt" is suspect from the outset. The reading in the NIV note, "you have shown utter contempt for the LORD," is clearly the author's intent—but it is not necessary to omit "the enemies of." Kitchen provides the solution: "The literal reading is no fault of the text, it is simply a euphemism to avoid saying 'having slighted the Lord ...' by transferring the insult verbally to God's enemies. Remarkably enough, *exactly* the same euphemism has been noticed in an Egyptian decree of the seventeenth century BC" (Kitchen, *Ancient Orient*, 166; italics his). For the same conclusion, cf. the detailed discussion of M. J. Mulder ("Un euphémisme dans 2 Sam. xii 14?" *VT* 18/1 [1968]: 108–14), who also calls attention (113) to the possibility that "David's enemies" in 1 Samuel 20:16; 25:22 is likewise a euphemism for David himself (cf. NIV note on 1Sa 25:22; further McCarter, *II Samuel*, 296). An alternative possibility is to adopt the reading of 4QSamuel[a]: "[because] by [doing this you have] despised the word of the LORD" (cf. v.9).

16 That consultation of the dead was commonly practiced in the ancient world is beyond cavil (cf. the warnings in Dt 18:10–11; Isa 8:19; 57:9; 65:2, 4; see also 1Sa 28:7–14 and comment), but the theory that אַרְצָה (*ʾārṣâ*, "on the ground") here means "to/into the netherworld" and that David is therefore "ritually acting out a descent into the netherworld to try to bring his son back from the clutches of death" (Lewis, 43) can only be described as eccentric.

6. The Ammonites Defeated (12:26–31)

OVERVIEW

In the overall scheme of chs. 10–12, 10:1–11:1 and 12:26–31 describe Israel's military victories over Ammon and thus bracket the central narrative of David-Bathsheba-Uriah-Nathan-Solomon (11:2–12:25; see comment on 10:1–19). At the same time, however, in the light of the fact that chs. 11–12 constitute an integral section within the larger complex, 12:26–31 mirror 11:1 (see comment on 11:1–5) and bring to a successful conclusion the siege of Rabbah that was mounted at the beginning of ch. 11. Since it is unlikely that the siege itself lasted for the minimum of two years implied in the events of chs. 11–12, chronological considerations appear to have yielded to literary and thematic concerns in the narrator's presentation. The NIV's "meanwhile" in v.26 is therefore entirely in order.

The present literary unit (vv.26–31) divides naturally into two sections, the first (vv.26–28) with Joab as the major actor and the second (vv.29–31) featuring David. That only vv.29–31 are paralleled by the Chronicler (cf. 1Ch 20:1b–3) is fully compatible with his interest in highlighting the positive aspects of David's reign.

26Meanwhile Joab fought against Rabbah of the Ammonites and captured the royal
citadel. 27Joab then sent messengers to David, saying, "I have fought against Rabbah
and taken its water supply. 28Now muster the rest of the troops and besiege the city and
capture it. Otherwise I will take the city, and it will be named after me."
29So David mustered the entire army and went to Rabbah, and attacked and captured
it. 30He took the crown from the head of their king — its weight was a talent of gold,
and it was set with precious stones — and it was placed on David's head. He took a
great quantity of plunder from the city 31and brought out the people who were there,
consigning them to labor with saws and with iron picks and axes, and he made them work
at brickmaking. He did this to all the Ammonite towns. Then David and his entire army
returned to Jerusalem.

COMMENTARY

26–28 Tying three verses together is the verb *lkd* ("take, capture," vv.26, 27, 28 [2x]). Intensifying the siege of Rabbah (the Ammonite capital city; see comment on 10:3), the onset of which is recorded in 11:1 (see comment), Joab captures its "royal citadel" (*ʿîr hammᵉlûkâ*, "city of royalty," v.26), probably the major fortification either within the city or guarding the approaches to it (for a similar expression, see comment on 1Sa 27:5). The city now rendered defenseless, Joab sends word to David that he has fought against Rabbah and taken its "water supply" (*ʿîr hammāyim*, "city of water[s]," v.27).

Although the latter expression is clearly to be linked in some way to the former (indeed, two Heb. manuscripts read *hammᵉlûkâ* instead of *hammāyim* in v.27; cf. *BHS*), the "city of water[s]" is patently not the "beautiful harbor" of the Living Bible. (Rabbah is seventy miles inland from the Mediterranean Sea.) The phrase is doubtless elliptical for "citadel protecting the water supply" or the like (cf. Anderson, 136). Josephus (*Ant.* 7.159 [7.5]) understood "took the city of waters" to refer to cutting off the main Ammonite water supply (noted by Patrick, 451). In 1969, salvage archaeological excavations on the citadel

> uncovered structures dating to the tenth or ninth century B.C.E.... The excavators were able to delineate the outline of a city wall.... Within the area enclosed by the wall, a 6-foot tunnel had been cut down through the bedrock to a stairway,

> which in turn descended into a large underground chamber 20 feet wide, 55 feet long and 23 feet high—parts of which were located outside (though below) the city wall. This ... chamber resembles hidden underground water systems at Megiddo and other Iron Age sites in Israel, so it is possible that it is indeed the "King's Pool" captured by Joab, a reservoir that kept Rabbath Ammon's citizens supplied with drinking water. This reservoir extending outside the walls of the northern part of the city ... was the weakest part of the town's natural defenses. (Timothy Harrison, "'Rabbath of the Ammonites,'" *Archaeology Odyssey* 5/2 (2002): 16–17)

McCarter (*II Samuel*, 310) summarizes: "Perhaps 'the Royal Citadel' (v.26) was the official name used by the narrator and 'the citadel of the water supply' (v.27) was not a name ['the Citadel of Waters'] but rather Joab's descriptive way of identifying its strategic importance to David."

With Rabbah now in dire straits, Joab advises David to muster the "rest of the troops" (lit., "people," v.28; see 10:10 and comment) and lead them in the final attack against the city. Joab warns that if the king refuses to become personally involved, he himself will capture Rabbah, in which case it will be named after Joab rather than after David. Although the victor may not always have sole control of distributing the spoils, Joab apparently reserves for himself the privilege of renaming the conquered site (see comments on 5:7, 9; see also 6:2 and comment; cf. Robin Gallaher Branch, "David and Joab: United by Ambition," *BAR* 19/4 [2003]: 22–23).

One of the most strategically significant cities in the Transjordanian region, Rabbah was now to become part of David's domain. It was therefore vital that David, not Joab, be credited with seizing it. "Joab clearly discerned that it was important for David to preserve his mastery and domination in the east and that all possible ties be made with the king" himself (Curtis, "'East Is East ...,'" 357; cf. Simon, 209).

29–31 In vv.29 and 31, references to "David" and "the entire army" (lit., "all the people" [= troops; see comment on v.28]) form an inclusio that serves to frame the literary unit. (The NIV's "his" in v.31 is not represented in the MT and muffles its echo of v.29.) The unit is paralleled by 1 Chronicles 20:1b–3.

Although 1 Chronicles 20:1b ("Joab attacked Rabbah and left it in ruins") seems intended as a summary of vv.26–28, it can also be viewed as functioning in much the same way as v.29—namely, to introduce the account of David's plunder of Rabbah and his forced levy of its people (vv.30–31). In any case, David finishes what Joab has begun: Having "mustered" the necessary troops (the same Heb. verb is rendered "gathered" in 10:17; see comment), he captures the city (v.29).

Of the many trophies seized by David, one of the most spectacular was a gold crown that had rested on the Ammonite king's head and was now transferred to David's (v.30; cf. S. H. Horn, "The Crown of the King of the Ammonites," *AUSS* 11 [1973]: 170–80). Set with "precious stones" (for possible examples cf. Eze 28:13), the crown was of such enormous weight and value (see second NIV note) that it was probably used only on ceremonial occasions. The Ammonite king's crown was by no means unique. The crown of Sassanian ruler Shapur II (AD 310–379), for example, weighed so much that it was literally "unwearable: A sixth-century visitor to the Sassanian palace wrote that the king's crown was so heavily encrusted with emeralds, rubies and pearls that the crown had to be suspended above the ruler's head by a thin gold chain" ("Worldwide," *BAR* 25/2 [1999]: 70).

"Plunder from the city" (v.30) and "the people [probably = troops, as throughout these verses] who were there" (v.31) are in emphatic position in their respective sentences, and both phrases are objects of the verb *hôṣîʾ* ("brought out"; rendered "took" in v.30). The "plunder" was in "great quantity" (*harbēh m*[e]*ʾōd*), the first word of which may be a subtle pun on *rabbâ* ("Rabbah").

As for the "people," earlier interpreters explained that David "put them under saws, and under harrows of iron, and under axes of iron, and made them pass through the brick-kiln" (v.31 [KJV]; cf. also Patrick, 452–53). That David was capable of such atrocities is not disputed (see 8:2 and comment). But "consigning them to labor with ... and with ..." is more likely to represent a correct rendering of the key preposition *b*- than "put them under ... and under...." Apparently David forced the defeated Ammonites to work on various building projects. The "saws," for example, were of the kind used to trim the faces of blocks of stone (cf. 1Ki 7:9).

Only after David had extended the forced labor requirement to the other defeated Ammonite towns did he and his troops return to Jerusalem (v.31). The Israelite victory was thus both thoroughgoing and complete. David's accomplishment was all the more impressive when it is remembered that

> the number and strength of [the Ammonite] fortress dwellings ... point to a dynamic civilization with a well-organized center of political authority. And the effectiveness of their defensive set-up is attested by the fact that, as far as we know, only once in some six centuries of Ammonite history was the ring of defenses around their capital at Rabbah-ammon ever breached, and the capital itself besieged and taken: in the 10th century BC, when Israelite military power was at its height, under the leadership of David and his commander Joab. (George M. Landes, "The Material Civilization of the Ammonites," *BA* 24/3 (1961): 74)

NOTES

30 The MT's מלכם (*mlkm*) can be vocalized either as מַלְכָּם (*malkām*, "their king" [NIV text]) or as מִלְכֹּם (*milkōm*, "Milcom," a variant of the name of the chief Ammonite god Molech [NIV note]; cf. 1Ki 11:5, 33). The same ambiguity obtains in the case of Jeremiah 49:1, 3; Amos 1:15; and Zephaniah 1:5, as attested by the NIV notes on those verses. Needless to say, the correct reading in each context must be judged on its own merits. Here "their king" is probably to be preferred, not only because it is unlikely that David would have worn the crown of a pagan idol, but also because the transfer of the crown from one head to another was doubtless emblematic of the transfer of sovereign authority over the Ammonites from the head of their king to that of David (cf. Baldwin, 245–46 n. 1; for fallen crowns as symbols of the loss of royal authority, cf. Jer 13:18). An ornate limestone bust of an Ammonite king wearing a crown, dating from the ninth century BC and said to have been unearthed in the vicinity of Rabbah, is pictured on the cover of *Biblical Archaeology Review* 8/5 (1982). In Egyptian style, the crown bears an ostrich feather on each side with flowered reliefs carved in front.

31 "He made them work at brickmaking" is an attempt to render הֶעֱבִיר אוֹתָם בַּמַּלְבֵּן (*he*[ʿe]*bîr ʾôtām bammalbēn*, reading the final word with the *Qere* rather than with the anomalous *Kethiv* במלכן, *bmlkn*), a clause of uncertain meaning (see NIV note). That *malbēn* means something like "brickmaking" is secured by Jeremiah 43:9 ("brick pavement") and Nahum 3:14 ("brickwork"). The NIV's text apparently assumes a scribal error and reads העביד (*hʿbyd*, "caused to work") instead of העביר (*hʿbyr*, "caused to pass (through)" (ד [*d*] and ר [*r*] being similar in appearance). Precedent for such a variant is attested in Genesis 47:21, where the Samaritan Pentateuch reads *hʿbyd ʾtw lʿbdym* ("reduced the people to servitude," NIV) for the

MT's *hʿbyr ʾtw lʿrym* ("moved the people into the cities," NIV note). Forcing captive people to work hard in brickmaking was not uncommon in ancient times (cf. Ex 1:13–14).

7. Amnon's Sin against Tamar (13:1–22)

OVERVIEW

Within the court history of David (chs. 9–20), the longest definable literary section is the story of Absalom in chs. 13–20 (more precisely, 13:1–20:22; cf. Conroy, v, 6 n. 31). Absalom's name appears in the OT approximately one hundred times, more than 90 percent of which occur in chs. 13–20. Although Absalom dies in ch. 18 (cf. 18:14–15), his memory and influence continue down to the end of the court history (cf. 20:6).

If the integrity of chs. 13–20 as a literary unit of the highest order is beyond question (cf. Conroy, 1), it is equally clear that the section contains two readily distinguishable subsections: chs. 13–14, which may be characterized as exhibiting for the most part a "desire/fulfillment of desire" pattern, and chs. 15–20, which prefer a "departure/return" pattern (for details see Conroy, 89–93; for the same basic division, cf. Eskhult, 58–59; Carlson, 42).

Although my parameters for the four segments within chs. 13–14 (i.e., 13:1–22, 23–39; 14:1–20, 21–33) are more traditional than those of Conroy (i.e., 13:1–22, 23–38, 39–14:27 [14:25–27 he calls a "descriptive parenthesis" (Conroy, 92)], 28–33) and thus differ slightly from them, his insight into the basic theme of the chapters is helpful and suggestive. Literary clues leading to the isolation of chs. 13–14 as a separate unit include (1) "in the course of time" at 13:1 (*wayᵉhî ʾaḥᵃrê-kēn*) and 15:1 (*wayᵉhî mēʾaḥᵃrê kēn*), signaling the start of a new section; (2) *lᵉʾabšālôm* (lit., "to Absalom") at the beginning of 13:1 and the end of 14:33, forming an inclusio to frame the whole; and (3) the "two years" of 13:23, "three years" of 13:38, and "two years" of 14:28, specific time spans arranged in chiastic order and adding up to seven years, the number seven symbolizing completion (cf. similarly Carlson, 164).

The furies unleashed by David in ch. 11, having already taken their toll in the death of the unnamed infant son of David and Bathsheba (12:19), continue unimpeded in the rape and desolation of David's daughter Tamar (13:14, 20), the murder of David's son Amnon (13:28–29), and the enforced exile and quarantine of David's son Absalom (13:34, 37–38; 14:28). Chapters 13–14 are thus aptly characterized as "family tragedies" (Eskhult, 58–59).

> Clearly we are expected to see in chapter 13 a recapitulation of what had gone before in chapter 11. David had seen a beautiful woman, had taken her and lain with her; then, in order to prevent discovery through the birth of an obviously illegitimate child, he had attempted to trick the husband into a false paternity and, failing this, had finally engaged in an intrigue which led to Uriah's death. Amnon, David's son, desires a beautiful girl, he conspires to trick her into a position where he can seize and lie with her, but is in turn conspired against and murdered. David finds, coming to expression within his own family, the elements of his own earlier experience.... His sin has come home to roost. (Gunn, *The Story of King David*, 98–99; cf. also Ackerman, 49; Preston, 41]

George P. Ridout, 50–56, has provided a detailed chiastic outline of 13:1–22, reproduced here with slight modifications:

A Amnon in love with Tamar (13:1–2)
B Intervention of Jonadab (13:3–5)
C Tamar's arrival (13:6–9a)
D Amnon's servants ordered to leave (13:9b)
E Amnon's command to Tamar to come to bed with him; her unavailing plea (13:10–14a)
F Amnon's rape of Tamar; the turning of love to hatred (13:14b–15a)
E' Amnon's command to Tamar to depart; her unavailing plea (13:15b–16)
D' Amnon's servant recalled (13:17)
C' Tamar's departure (13:18–19)
B' Intervention of Absalom (13:20)
A' Absalom's hatred for Amnon (13:21–22)

Although it is relatively easy to indulge in minor quibbles with Ridout's attempt (cf. Conroy, 20; Fokkelman, *Narrative Art*, 1:100–101), his analysis has the advantage of showing how a narrative that begins with love (vv.1–2) and ends with hatred (vv.21–22) centers on an act of violence that turns love into hatred (vv.14b–15a). His outline will therefore be followed here. Fokkelman's modest rearrangement of and additions to the chain-structure outline by Shimon Bar-Efrat ("Some Observations on the Analysis of Structure in Biblical Narrative," *VT* 30/2 [1980]: 162–63]) leads to the same broadly chiastic conclusion (Fokkelman, *Narrative Art*, 1:101–2).

love/hatred (vv.14b–15a)
Tamar–Amnon (vv.8–16)
(v.7) David–Tamar   Amnon–servant (v.17)
(v.6) Amnon–David   servant–Tamar (v.18)
(vv.3–5) Jonadab–Amnon   Tamar–Absalom (vv.19–20)
(vv.1–2) *love*   *hatred* (vv.21–22)

In a number of respects the account of Amnon's sin against Tamar echoes that of Shechem's against Dinah in Genesis 34, both verbally (cf. v.12 with Ge 34:7; v.14 with Ge 34:2) and thematically:

> Taking the two stories together, the message is clear: Whoever violates a virgin daughter of Israel will suffer for it—whether it is achieved by seduction or force, whether the guilty man is a Jew or a Gentile (Amnon or Shechem), whether he loves her or hates her, whether he offers to marry her or drives her out of his house, death will be the verdict and the outcome. The punishment will be inflicted by her near kinsmen, full brothers as it happens. (David Noel Freedman, "Dinah and Shechem, Tamar and Amnon," in Freedman, *History and Religion*, 1:494–95)

For a helpful overview of the horrific implications of sexual transgression in every area of life, see Andrew J. Schmutzer, "A Theology of Sexual Abuse: A Reflection on Creation and Devastation," *JETS* 51/4 (2008): 786–812 (esp. 811 n. 146).

1In the course of time, Amnon son of David fell in love with Tamar, the beautiful sister of Absalom son of David.

2Amnon became frustrated to the point of illness on account of his sister Tamar, for she was a virgin, and it seemed impossible for him to do anything to her.

3Now Amnon had a friend named Jonadab son of Shimeah, David's brother. Jonadab was a very shrewd man. 4He asked Amnon, "Why do you, the king's son, look so haggard morning after morning? Won't you tell me?"

Amnon said to him, "I'm in love with Tamar, my brother Absalom's sister."

5"Go to bed and pretend to be ill," Jonadab said. "When your father comes to see you, say to him, 'I would like my sister Tamar to come and give me something to eat. Let her prepare the food in my sight so I may watch her and then eat it from her hand.'"

6So Amnon lay down and pretended to be ill. When the king came to see him, Amnon said to him, "I would like my sister Tamar to come and make some special bread in my sight, so I may eat from her hand."

7David sent word to Tamar at the palace: "Go to the house of your brother Amnon and prepare some food for him." 8So Tamar went to the house of her brother Amnon, who was lying down. She took some dough, kneaded it, made the bread in his sight and baked it. 9Then she took the pan and served him the bread, but he refused to eat.

"Send everyone out of here," Amnon said. So everyone left him. 10Then Amnon said to Tamar, "Bring the food here into my bedroom so I may eat from your hand." And Tamar took the bread she had prepared and brought it to her brother Amnon in his bedroom. 11But when she took it to him to eat, he grabbed her and said, "Come to bed with me, my sister."

12"Don't, my brother!" she said to him. "Don't force me. Such a thing should not be done in Israel! Don't do this wicked thing. 13What about me? Where could I get rid of my disgrace? And what about you? You would be like one of the wicked fools in Israel. Please speak to the king; he will not keep me from being married to you." 14But he refused to listen to her, and since he was stronger than she, he raped her.

15Then Amnon hated her with intense hatred. In fact, he hated her more than he had loved her. Amnon said to her, "Get up and get out!"

16"No!" she said to him. "Sending me away would be a greater wrong than what you have already done to me."

But he refused to listen to her. 17He called his personal servant and said, "Get this woman out of here and bolt the door after her." 18So his servant put her out and bolted the door after her. She was wearing a richly ornamented robe, for this was the kind of garment the virgin daughters of the king wore. 19Tamar put ashes on her head and tore the ornamented robe she was wearing. She put her hand on her head and went away, weeping aloud as she went.

[20]Her brother Absalom said to her, "Has that Amnon, your brother, been with you? Be quiet now, my sister; he is your brother. Don't take this thing to heart." And Tamar lived in her brother Absalom's house, a desolate woman.

[21]When King David heard all this, he was furious. [22]Absalom never said a word to Amnon, either good or bad; he hated Amnon because he had disgraced his sister Tamar.

COMMENTARY

1–2 That vv.1–22 constitute a pericope with literary integrity is clear: "The three personal names (Absalom, Tamar, and Amnon) form an *inclusion* between v.1 and v.22b. The beginning and end ... are also linked by way of a reversal: Amnon loves ... at v.1, he is hated ... at v.22" (Conroy, 17). The transitional formula "in the course of time" does not "mark a completely new beginning but rather a new episode which shares something with the foregoing" (ibid., 41). Although not necessarily signifying chronological sequence (see Notes on 2:1 and comments on 8:1; 10:1), the phrase in this context appears in any case to introduce an account of events occurring later than those in chs. 10–12.

As an indication of the fact that the story of Amnon's sin against Tamar is part of the larger narrative of Absalom's relentless march to usurp the throne of Israel now occupied by his father David, Absalom's name appears first in the Hebrew text of v.1. The half brothers "Absalom son of David" (David's third son) and "Amnon son of David" (David's firstborn; see 3:2–3 and comments) contextually surround Tamar (v.1), "sister to Absalom and object of desire to Amnon.... They move between protecting and polluting, supporting and seducing, comforting and capturing her" (Trible, 38). Tamar's name means "Palm Tree" (as in SS 7:7–8, where a palm tree's height is compared to a woman's stature and its clusters of fruit to her breasts).

Sister of Absalom and half sister of Amnon, Tamar is "beautiful" indeed (v.1). Good looks were not at a premium in David's family: The "handsome" Absalom (14:25) would father a "beautiful" daughter also named Tamar (14:27)—probably in memory of his sister—and David himself was "handsome" (1Sa 16:12; 17:42). In addition, David was attracted to "beautiful" women such as Abigail (1Sa 25:3) and, of course, Bathsheba (11:2; the same Heb. word in all verses except the last). Thus it is not surprising that David's son Amnon "fell in love with" Tamar (cf. also v.4; for the ingressive mode of the verb, cf. Eskhult, 59).

As a "virgin" (v.2), however, strictly speaking "Tamar is protected property, inaccessible to males, including her brother" (Trible, 38). Amnon is therefore "frustrated" (or "distressed/in distress," as the same Hebrew expression is translated in 24:14; 1Sa 28:15; 30:6) to the extent that he becomes lovesick (cf. "faint with love" in SS 2:5; 5:8; the Heb. root rendered "faint" is the same as that for "illness" in v.2). The statement that "it seemed impossible for him to do anything to her" is perhaps deliberately ambiguous since "the key verb's literal sense and its supporting syntax permit a double entendre: 'And it was awesome in the eyes of Amnon to do something to her'" (Rosenberg, 140).

In general, *l^ehippālēʾ min* normally means "to be beyond the powers of, to be too hard/difficult for" someone (to do/contemplate; cf. Ge 18:14; Dt 30:11; Jer 32:17, 27), whereas *l^ehippālē^ʾ b^{eʿ}ênê* means "to be wonderful/marvelous in the eyes of" someone (cf. Ps 118:23; Zec 8:6 ["seem marvelous to"]; for additional details see Rosenberg, 244 n. 51). Since the latter form of the Hebrew expression is used here, it may not at all seem "impossible" for Amnon to violate his half sister Tamar. Indeed, given her unusual beauty, it may in fact seem quite possible—perhaps even "awesome"—for him to do so.

3–5 Jonadab's intervention on Amnon's behalf (vv.3–5) and Absalom's intervention on Tamar's behalf (v.20) are similar in that both begin with one or more questions (vv.4, 20a) and then continue with words of advice (vv.5, 20b). More immediately important from a structural standpoint, however, is a comparison between a literal rendering of the Hebrew texts of vv.1 and 3: "And to Absalom ... a sister ... and her name Tamar" (v.1); "And to Amnon a friend, and his name Jonadab" (v.3; cf. similarly Trible, 39). Tamar may be "beautiful" (v.1), but Jonadab is "very shrewd/wise" (v.3). At first blush it would seem that Tamar is no match for Jonadab and that his counsel to Amnon will surely contribute to her undoing.

As the son of David's brother Shimeah (called "Shammah" in 1Sa 16:9; 17:13 and "Shimea" in 1Ch 2:13), Jonadab (a name that means "The LORD is noble" and that was perhaps deliberately chosen to reflect the name of Shimeah's older brother Abinadab, which means "My [divine] father is noble"; see 1Sa 16:8 and comment) is Amnon's cousin, and thus all the people mentioned by name in vv.1–22 are members of the same family circle. Jonadab is also Amnon's "friend" (*rēaʿ*), perhaps in this case connoting

> a special office or association with the royal family (especially in light of his role as a counselor in David's cabinet; cf. 13:32–35). During Solomon's reign, Zabud son of Nathan has the title of priest and "king's friend" (*rēʿeh hammelek*, 1 Kgs 4:5 ["personal adviser to the king," NIV]). It may well be that with Jonadab (and others?) this cabinet post has its rudimentary beginnings in the Davidic monarchy. (Hill, 387; cf. perhaps also 16:16–17)

Since counsel was often sought from wise men and women during David's reign (cf. 14:2; 20:16), it is doubtless better to translate *ḥākām* (GK 2682) by the more neutral "wise" than the more nuanced (and possibly incorrect) "shrewd" (v.3). Jonadab is then a wise man, and the ploy suggested by him "to Amnon for the seduction of Tamar was known to him by virtue of his standing in the royal court as a sage" (Hill, 388), as we will see.

Jonadab begins by asking Amnon why he—who is, after all, the "king's son" (v.4)—looks so "haggard" all the time (the Heb. word has various shades of meaning, including "weak" [3:1; Ps 41:1] and "scrawny" [Ge 41:19]). Jonadab's urbane "Won't you tell me?" is much more polite than David's terse "Tell me" (1:4), a difference readily explained by observing who is speaking to whom. Amnon's response (v.4b), as reported by the narrator, is a masterpiece of alliteration in the MT, with all six words beginning with the same letter: *ʾet-tāmār ʾ^aḥôt ʾabšālōm ʾāḥî ʾ^anî ʾōhēb* (lit., "Tamar, the sister of Absalom my brother, I love"). The alliteration in *ʾ* (*āleph*) "gives the impression of a succession of faltering sighs" (Conroy, 29 n. 38). The word "Tamar" is in emphatic position and is thus highlighted as referring to the object of Amnon's desire.

If Egyptian contacts with and influence on the Israelite united monarchy (attested for Solomon's reign; cf. 1Ki 3:1; 4:30) began during the days of David, Jonadab's familiarity with Egyptian wisdom literature may have led him to reflect on the practical application of words such as these (from an Egyptian love poem of the Nineteenth Dynasty [ca. 1303–1200 BC]; translation by Michael V.

Fox, *The Song of Songs and the Ancient Egyptian Love Songs* [Madison, Wis.: Univ. of Wisconsin Press, 1985], 13):

I will lie down inside,
and then I will feign illness.
Then my neighbors will enter to see,
and then (my) sister will come with them.
She'll put the doctors to shame
(for she) will understand my illness.

So strikingly similar to the above excerpt are certain elements of Jonadab's advice to Amnon in v.5—"Go to bed" (lit., "Lie down [cf. v.8] on your bed"), "pretend to be ill," "come to see," "my sister ... to come"—that the relationship between the two texts can hardly be coincidental. Without comparing the boy in the Egyptian poem to Amnon (and therefore without referring to the fact that "illness" [lit., "making himself ill," v.2] and "pretend[ed] to be ill" [vv.5–6] are the only occurrences of Hithpael *ḥlh* in the OT), Fox says of the boy that "perhaps the illness he feigns is more real than he realizes, for the last line speaks of his illness as a real one that cannot be diagnosed by the physicians, but only by his beloved" (Fox, ibid., 13).

The similarities between such Egyptian love songs and the story of Amnon and Tamar should not be allowed to obscure the differences, however: "There is a strong and effective contrast between the scenes of idyllic charm which are associated with the motif of love-sickness in Egyptian poetry and the act of brutal selfishness which will be the outcome of Amnon's love-sickness" (Conroy, 27; cf. Hill, 388–89).

Jonadab knows that when David hears of his son Amnon's "illness," he will come "to see" him (v.5; for another example of sickbed visitation, cf. Ps 41:6). At that point Amnon should tell his father that he wants Tamar to come and "give" him something "to eat" (for the rare verb *brh*, "[give to] eat" [in the sense of "eat food intended for mourners/sick people"; vv.5–6, 10] and its cognate noun *biryâ*, "food intended for mourners/sick people" [vv.5, 7, 10], cf. Koehler, 6; see also 12:17 and comment). Tamar would also "prepare" (lit., "do") the food in Amnon's "sight" (v.5), a procedure that recalls the impossibility/awesomeness in Amnon's "eyes/sight" to "do" something to Tamar (see v.2 and comment; cf. Trible, 41). There is perhaps here also an echo of Nathan's parable, which included a privileged rich man who "prepared" a poor man's ewe lamb for a visiting traveler (12:4).

When Tamar arrives in his "sickroom," Amnon will surely want to "watch [her]" (v.5; an ambiguous phrase, since there is no object in the MT)—but in what sense? Trible, 41, suggests: "Though David must be made to think that Amnon wants to see the food being prepared, the reader knows that he wants to see Tamar." If so, Amnon's desire to "watch" reprises his father's earlier voyeurism ("he saw" [see 11:2 and comment]; same Heb. verb).

Does Jonadab act alone in the advice he gives to Amnon? Perhaps not. Since Absalom is David's third son while Amnon is his firstborn, Absalom may be willing to sacrifice his sister in a power play for the throne. At the same time Jonadab may be attempting to secure his own political future by casting his lot with the ambitions of the aggressive Absalom, whom he sees as eventually winning out over the dissolute Amnon in any case. Jonadab would thus be a "co-conspirator with Absalom in the whole affair, since both men have much to gain" (Hill, 389).

6–9a Tamar's arrival into Amnon's presence (vv.6–9a) is shaped by the verbs *bwʾ* ("come [in]," v.6) and *hlk* ("go/went," vv.7–8), while her departure from Amnon (vv.18–19) is described by the verbs *yṣʾ* ("go out," v.18 ["put ... out"]) and *hlk* ("went," v.19 [2x]). In addition Tamar's "hand" is to serve food to Amnon in v.6 (cf. also v.5) but symbolizes mourning and desolation in v.19.

Amnon readily accepts the advice of Jonadab, whom he perceives as acting in his best interests (v.6). But although on David's arrival Amnon at first quotes Jonadab's words verbatim ("I would like my sister Tamar to come," v.6; cf. also v.5), he inserts his own vocabulary in describing what he wants her to do after she actually comes.

(1) The phrase "make some special bread" is an attempt to render the rare noun *l*ᵉ*bibôt* and its equally rare denominative verb *libbēb* (the words being found only here and in vv.8, 10). The fact that elsewhere the root *lbb* always means "heart" has led commentators to translate the noun in ch. 13 as "heart-shaped cakes" (*IBHS*, 412) or "heart-cakes ... a heart-strengthening kind of pastry" (K&D, 398) or—an especially felicitous rendering—"hearty dumplings" (McCarter, *II Samuel*, 322). Since the cognate verb is translated "you have stolen my heart" in Song of Songs 4:9 (for the connection between "heart" and "love" in ancient Israel, cf. also SS 5:2; 8:6), it is possible that Amnon is being deliberately ambiguous: The cakes/dumplings will strengthen his heart (the nuance he hopes David will choose), but they will also reflect his amorous intentions (the true meaning under his hidden agenda). Indeed, the ambiguity is perhaps furthered by the explicit mention of "two" cakes/dumplings in the MT of v.6 (for details cf. Fokkelman, *Narrative Art*, 1:105–6; Ackerman, 45).

(2) Amnon plays on David's sympathies by using the verb *brh* ("eat [invalid food]") in the phrase "eat from her hand" (v.6) instead of *ʾkl*, the ordinary verb "eat," suggested by Jonadab in "eat ... from her hand" (v.5).

Without hesitation Tamar obeys David's command to go to the house of her "brother Amnon" (vv.7–8; the constant repetition of "sister" [vv.2, 5–6, 11, 20, 22] and "brother" [vv.7–8, 10, 12, 20] describing their relationship throughout ch. 13 heightens the tragedy about to ensue). As might be expected, Amnon is "lying down" (v.8), a "posture of power devastating for Tamar" (Trible, 43). Eskhult, 59, observes that "in verses 8b–9a the rapid succession of *wayyiqṭol*-clauses creates the impression of bustling activity," a series of six verbs divided into two sets of three that, as Trible, 43, perceptively notes, not only "detail (Tamar's) activities" but also "focus on Amnon's eyes": "And she took some dough, and she kneaded it, and she made the bread *in his sight*; and she baked it, and she took the pan, and she served him the bread" (NIV slightly modified; italics mine). The verb "knead" and its object "dough" are sometimes used, whether literally or figuratively, in contexts where spiritual adultery is deplored (Jer 7:18; Hos 7:4).

Amnon's response to Tamar's six acts of solicitude on his behalf is a climactic seventh act of the capricious sort so characteristic of spoiled and pampered royalty: He "refused" to eat (v.9a; cf. vv.14, 16, where the Heb. verb, however, is different).

9b In vv.9b and 17, Amnon's initial commands in both cases are plural in number in the MT ("Send [everyone] out," v.9b; "Get [this woman] out," v.17) and include the expression *mēʿālay* ("out of here," lit., "from upon me"). Although addressing an individual in v.17 (and perhaps also in v.9b), Amnon uses the indefinite/impersonal plural imperative (for similar phenomena cf. *IBHS*, 71). In v.9b "Send everyone out [*hôṣîʾû*] of here" is perfectly matched by its response: "So everyone left [*wayyēṣ*ᵉ*ʾû*, lit., 'went out'] him" (lit., "from upon him").

The peremptory command of Amnon in v.9b echoes verbatim that of Joseph centuries earlier: "Have everyone leave my presence!" (Ge 45:1; identical Heb. sentence). But while Joseph desired privacy so that he could be alone when he made himself known to his brothers, Amnon wants to be alone so that, unseen and unhindered, he can ravish his sister.

10–14a The structure of vv.10–14a and vv.15b–16 is similar in that each contains (1) a terse command addressed by Amnon to Tamar (vv.11, 15b), (2) a strong negative plea by Tamar (vv.12–13, 16a), and (3) the same concluding response by Amnon: "But he refused to listen to her" (vv.14a, 16b).

Once they are alone, Amnon tells Tamar to bring the "[invalid] food" to him so that he might "eat [the invalid food]" from her hand (v.10). The language Amnon uses is designed to perpetuate the charade of his pretended illness (cf. vv.5–6). Unsuspecting, Tamar brings the "bread" (see comment on v.6) to Amnon, her "brother" (see comment on v.7), in the "bedroom"—a locale usually reserved for rest and bliss but where betrayal and violence all too often hold sway (cf. 4:7).

As soon as the gullible Tamar was within arm's reach, Amnon "grabbed" her (v.11; forcibly, expressed by the Hiphil of *ḥzq*; see 2:16 and comment; the Qal of *ḥzq* is used in v.14, where Amnon is described as being "stronger" than Tamar). His lustful demand, however elegant from a literary standpoint, is both ominous and insensitive: "Come to bed with me, my sister" (*bôʾî šikᵉbî ʿimmî ʾᵃḥôtî*). "In v.11 the change to shorter sentences conveys the violence of Amnon's desire which is reflected too by the assonance in *-î* (four times) and by the staccato rhythm of his words" (Conroy, 30; cf. Trible, 59 n. 31).

> The dialogue in the story of Amnon and Tamar ... looks like a conscious allusion to the technique used in the episode of Joseph and Potiphar's wife. Amnon addresses to his half-sister exactly the same words with which Potiphar's wife accosts Joseph—["Come to bed with me!" (Gen 39:7)]—adding to them only one word, the thematically loaded "sister" (2 Sam 13:11). She responds with an elaborate protestation, like Joseph before her. [Alter, *The Art of Biblical Narrative*, 73]

"Come to bed" (v.11) is literally "Come, lie down," the latter verb (*škb*) being used in an entirely different way from that in vv.5–6, 8 (see also 11:4 and comment; 12:24). The ambiguity of "my sister" is also notable, since Amnon may be simultaneously referring to Tamar not only as his half sister but also as his potential sexual companion (for the latter, cf. SS 4:9–10, 12; 5:1–2; for "sister" in the same sense in Egyptian love poems, cf. Fox, *The Song of Songs*, xii–xiii, 8, 136).

Tamar's immediate response to Amnon is indignant as well as frantic: "Don't" (v.12)—or, more simply, "No" (as in v.16; cf. 1Sa 2:24; Jdg 19:23). She matches his "my sister" with "my brother," but in the sibling rather than in the amorous sense. One by one, her short sentences bespeak her terror: "Don't force me" (v.12; cf. vv.14 ["raped"], 22 ["disgraced"], 32 ["raped"]; same Heb. verb). The Piel of *ʿānâ* in the sense of "force a woman to have sexual intercourse" is attested both in legal contexts (Dt 21:14; 22:24, 29) and in narrative passages (Ge 34:2; Jdg 19:24; 20:5; La 5:11; Eze 22:10–11; for details see Beth Glazier-McDonald, "Malachi 2:12: *ʿēr wᵉʿōneh*—Another Look," *JBL* 105/2 [1986]: 296).

The list of things that, in the minds of those who decide to make pronouncements on the subject, "should not be done" (v.12) is long enough (cf. Ge 20:9; 29:26; Lev 4:2, 13, 22, 27; 5:17), and sexual sins in particular are among those that should not be committed "in Israel" (vv.12–13; Ge 34:7; Dt 22:21; Jdg 20:6, 10; Jer 29:23; cf. also Jos 7:15). Indeed, Tamar calls Amnon's intended act of rape a *nᵉbālâ* ("wicked thing," v.12), the kind of activity engaged in only by "wicked fools" (*nᵉbālîm*, v.13).

Anthony Phillips, among others, observes that *nᵉbālâ* ("folly, disgraceful/outrageous thing, vileness";

GK 5576) appears in "connection with outrageous sexual offences" and adds to the above list Judges 19:23–24 ("*NEBALAH*—A Term for Serious Disorderly and Unruly Conduct," *VT* 25/2 [1975]: 237). Pointing out that "*nebalah* is reserved for extreme acts of disorder or unruliness which themselves result in a dangerous breakdown in order, and the end of an existing relationship," he defines it as "'an act of crass disorder or unruliness' or 'acting in an utterly disorderly or unruly fashion'" (ibid., 238). It is, in fact, "action which is to be utterly deplored" (ibid., 237), as its application to "that wicked man Nabal" indicates (see comment on "folly" in 1Sa 25:25). Thus,

> Amnon's rape of his half-sister Tamar [violates] the ancient prohibition on casual sexual relations outside marriage with women whom one could expect to find living under the same family roof.... While Amnon could certainly have married Tamar with his father's consent ... to force her was indeed an act of crass disorder, extreme unruliness (*nebalah*), which inevitably led to bloodshed within the royal family. (ibid., 239)

The *casus pendens* constructions in v.13 ("What about me? ... And what about you?") contribute to the staccato effect of Tamar's series of objections. As far as she herself is concerned, she wants to know "where" (cf. the plaintive cry of the similarly distraught Reuben [Ge 37:30]) she could possibly get rid of her "disgrace" (*ḥerpâ*; cf. 1Sa 25:39 ["contempt"]; Pr 6:32–33; Isa 47:3 ["shame"]; Eze 16:57 ["scorned"]). And as far as Amnon is concerned, Tamar warns him that if he gives vent to his lustful desires, he will be like one of Israel's "wicked fools" (see comment on "lawless" in 3:33).

Having asked and answered her own rhetorical questions, Tamar voices her final plea (v.13): "Now then [omitted from the NIV; see, however, comment on v.20]," she implores Amnon, "please speak to the king" (referring to him not as their father but by his title, since she anticipates his acting in an official capacity rather than as a family member). She is sure that David will not keep her from "being married to" Amnon. (Although the MT does not include the phrase in quotation marks, the NIV correctly supplies it.) After all, had not her ancestor Abraham married his half sister Sarah (cf. Ge 20:12)?

Although we are not told whether Tamar would object to becoming Amnon's wife, she does not appear to be inherently opposed to such a prospect. As Propp notes, marrying Amnon "would solve her problem: instead of a [*sic*] unmarriageable nonvirgin princess, she might (even) become queen" (William H. C. Propp, "Acting like Apes: The Bible's Alpha Males," *BRev* 20/3 [2004]: 40). What Tamar is adamantly against, however, is sexual intercourse with Amnon outside the marriage relationship. "Marriage between a half-brother and half-sister is forbidden in Pentateuchal law (Lev 18:9, 11; 20:17; Dt 27:22), though whether such a law operated in this period is open to question" (Gordon, *I and II Samuel*, 263). It would therefore seem likely that Amnon was about to become "guilty of rape, not of incest" (Conroy, 18 n. 4; cf. also Trible, 60 n. 37)—although if in her desperation Tamar is clutching at straws, incest is indeed a possible concomitant of Amnon's crimes (cf. K&D, 398–99; Baldwin, 248; Alter, *The David Story*, 268).

Tamar's most eloquent pleadings, however, are to no avail. Her three "Don't"s in v.12 and her three "And"s in v.13 (lit., "And as for me," "And as for you," "And now") meet with the same climactic seventh act—this time a paradigm of ominous insensitivity—as before: Amnon "refused to listen to her" (v.14a; see comment on v.9a).

14b–15a The center of the chiasm that structures this section (see comment on 13:1–22) focuses on Amnon's unspeakable violence against his half sister. He had "grabbed" her earlier (v.11), and he has apparently not released her throughout the entire dreary episode. He is, after all, "stronger" than she (v.14b; same Heb. verb in both cases). A painful irony is evident in comparing the story of David and Goliath with that of Amnon and Tamar: The young underdog David "triumphed over" the hitherto invincible Philistine (1Sa 17:50), while David's firstborn son "was stronger than" his weak and innocent half sister (v.14b; identical Heb. verbal construction in both texts).

So Amnon "raped her"—literally, "forced her [see v.12 and comment] and laid her." The latter verb echoes v.11, where Amnon commands Tamar: "Come to bed with me"—literally, "Come, lie down [*škb*] with me." Here, however, the verb *škb* does not govern the particle of accompaniment *ʿim* ("with") but the accusative particle *ʾēt*, hence "laid her" (cf. Trible, 46; similarly Sternberg, 536–37 n. 4). Whereas David had "slept/lain with [*škb ʿm*]" Bathsheba (11:4), implying at least the possibility of consent on her part, Amnon "laid" (*škb ʾt*) Tamar, thus forcing her against her will. (The same comparison between father and son, although highlighting other verbs in the two passages, is made by Gunn [*The Story of King David*, 100].)

The immediate denouement of the rape (v.15a) is poignantly anticlimactic. A rapist's emotional response following the crime is unpredictable: If Shechem "loved" Dinah after he "violated" (*ʿnh*) her (Ge 34:2–3), Amnon "hated" Tamar after he "forced" (*ʿnh*) her (vv.14b–15a). Needless to say, hatred subsequent to the act of sexual intercourse is not confined to situations of rape; it can arise in the marriage bed as well (cf. Dt 22:13, 16; 24:3, where in each case "dislikes" is literally "hates").

Verse 15a (through "In fact, he hated her") includes a chiasm that, when translated literally, underscores the intensity of Amnon's newly found hatred for Tamar (cf. Fokkelman, *Narrative Art*, 1:107; cf. similarly Trible, 47; Conroy, 32):

A Then Amnon hated her
  B with a hatred
    C great
      D exceedingly;
      D' indeed,
    C' great
  B' was the hatred
A' with which he hated her.

The latter sentence concludes with the phrase "more than the love with which he had loved her" (literal rendering). Thus the fourfold reference to "hate" that constitutes the subject matter of the chiasm is flanked (vv.1, 4; v.15a) by two sets of twofold references to "love." Although the fires of love may often burn away hatred (and perhaps even postpone death; cf. SS 8:6), hatred may often extinguish the fires of "love"—especially when it takes on the nuance of "lust" (cf. similarly Trible, 47). Love in any form will not appear again in vv.15b–22, but hatred will (v.22).

15b–16 Scarcely has Tamar had a chance to catch her breath after being ravished by Amnon before he delivers to her "a curt asyndetic pair of imperatives" (Conroy, 33): "Get up and get out!" (v.15b). The Hebrew expression (*qûmî lēkî*), though only half as long as its counterpart in v.11b, is characterized by the same staccato rhythm as well as the same assonance in *-î*. It thus conveys the intensity of Amnon's hatred as vividly as his earlier commands had imparted the passion of his desire (see comment on v.11b). Before, consumed by lust, he had begun by begging Tamar to "come [in]"; now, repulsed by disgust, he concludes by banishing her with the words "get/go out." And Amnon's final word to Tamar also resonates within a wider literary context: It is "the same as the first word [*lky*, 'go'] spoken to her by the king in v. 7" (Conroy, 33).

Although Tamar's response here (v.16) is much briefer than her earlier pleas (vv.12–13), she is no more ready to obey Amnon's commands now than she was before. And just as he dropped the seductive "my sister" (v.11) from his concluding terse statement (v.15b), so also she omits the plaintive "my brother" (v.12) from her final words to him. She begins in the same way as she had before, however: "No!" (v.16; see comment on v.12). As in the case of Samson's intention to do more "harm" to the Philistines than he had done before (Jdg 15:3), Amnon's sending Tamar away would only add insult to injury by involving him in a greater "wrong" than the rape itself (v.16; same Heb. word in both passages).

For the third time, however, Amnon "refused" (vv.9, 14, 16)—and this time his rejection of Tamar's plea echoes the previous one almost verbatim (v.14a reads lit., "But he refused to listen to her voice [i.e., refused to obey her]").

17 Although Amnon speaks to his personal servant, his first command to him is a plural imperative (as in the parallel in v.9b; see comment there). In v.9b he wanted everyone else out of his bedroom so that, without the presence of witnesses, he could have his own way with Tamar; here he wants Tamar out of his bedroom so that, in her absence, he will not be reminded unduly of the awful sin he has committed.

Brusque and impassive, Amnon wants to get rid of Tamar. "This woman" translates the unadorned feminine demonstrative *zōʾt*, the masculine equivalent of which (*zeh*) is often used in a derogatory sense (cf. 1Sa 10:27, "this fellow" [= Saul]; 21:15, "this fellow," "this man" [= David]; 25:21, "this fellow" [= Nabal]). Thus perhaps *zōʾt* here is best rendered simply "this thing," reflecting the contempt in which Amnon now holds Tamar: "One could hardly express more clearly Amnon's revulsion at his act, or the fact that he had treated his half-sister as a thing, not as a person" (Jackson, 190; cf. Trible, 48). Like Pharaoh to Moses ("Get out of my sight [*mēʿālāy*, lit., 'from upon me']," Ex 10:28), so Amnon to Tamar ("Get this woman out of here [*mēʿālay*]"): Both are nervous at the prospect of seeing the face of an unwanted or rejected person at an undetermined time in the future.

Amnon's second command to his servant is to "bolt the door after her." The purpose of securing doors is all too often to prevent or conceal a questionable or evil deed—for example, a homosexual act in the case of Lot (cf. Ge 19:6), a murder in the case of Ehud (cf. Jdg 3:21–24), a rape in the case of Amnon. Needless to say, a door keeps people not only out but also in, and thereon hangs an illustration: "On the surface, it is Tamar who is shut out, but upon Amnon too a door is closed. His fate is sealed from this moment" (Conroy, 33).

18–19 Although Tamar's arrival into Amnon's presence was carefully orchestrated (vv.6–9a), her forced departure is abrupt indeed. Obedient to a fault, the servant of Amnon wastes no time: He "put her out" (v.18; same Heb. verb as in v.9b ["Send ... out"; see also comment there]). Once the man (in this case Amnon) has satisfied his lustful desires, he discards the woman (cf. similarly Jdg 19:25) as though she were so much refuse.

But Tamar is one of "the virgin daughters [see comment on v.2] of the king" (v.18), a status that should have made her doubly untouchable. By no means trash, she wears a "richly ornamented robe" that befits her regal position. Now no longer a virgin, she tears her robe (v.19) as a symbol of her ravished state: "Worn (v. 18a), it signifies her status as an unmarried princess; torn (v.19a), it symbolizes the ruin of her life (v. 20b)" (Conroy, 34). The act of tearing her garment also gives expression to her mourning over her irreparable loss (cf. v.31; 15:32), as do her putting "ashes on her head" (cf. similarly 1:2 and comment; 1Sa 4:12 and comment; Est 4:1) and her "weeping/crying aloud" (cf. 19:4).

Tamar's putting her "hand" (see comment on v.6; perhaps better "hands" [cf. *BHS*]) on her head is probably emblematic not only of mourning (for details see *AIs*, 59) but also of exile or banishment (cf. Jer 2:37; for a relief at Medinet Habu depicting prisoners of Rameses III with their arms/hands on/over their heads, see *ANEP*, fig. 7). "In her plea to Amnon at v. 13 Tamar asked, 'where shall I carry (*HLK* hif ["get rid of"]) my shame'?; now in vv. 19f. she goes (*HLK* twice in v. 19 ['went']) to her brother Absalom" (Conroy, 34).

20 Absalom's advice to Tamar parallels Jonadab's counsel to Amnon (vv.3–5; see Overview to 13:1–22), thus strengthening the suggestion that Jonadab and Absalom are working in concert (see comment on v.5; cf. also Rosenberg, 156–59). In terms of literary structure, the verse is exquisitely ordered:

A "her brother" (Absalom)
  B "your brother" (Amnon)
    C "my sister" (Tamar)
  B' "your brother" (Amnon)
A' "her brother" (Absalom)

> Bar-Efrat, from whom this beautiful observation is derived, points out how not only the substantives are concentrically arranged ... but also in their possessive suffixes, indicating the 3rd, 2nd, 1st, 2nd, and 3rd person respectively.... Tamar stands in the centre and is, in the first place, surrounded and enclosed by her evil brother, but he is, in turn, surrounded and enclosed ... by the good brother whose loving "my sister" originates in the centre. [Fokkelmann, *Narrative Art*, 1:111–12]

At the same time, the narrator reminds his readers that the whole sordid episode is a family affair.

The advice of Absalom is both matter-of-fact and calculating. Choosing his words carefully, he asks Tamar whether Amnon (spelled "Aminon" in the MT only here; see comment on 3:2) has "been with" her—an expression that, though not sexually explicit, is at least suggestive of potential involvement (cf. Ge 39:10). He counsels her to be quiet about the matter "now" (cf. v.13 [MT])—that is, "for the time being" (cf. Trible, 51). Since Amnon is Tamar's "(half) brother," the problem will be solved within the parameters of the family. Therefore Tamar should not "take this thing to heart" (i.e., pay undue attention to it or worry about it; cf. 1Sa 4:20; 9:20, where the same Heb. idiom, or its equivalent, is used).

For the foreseeable future Tamar will live in her brother Absalom's "house" ("not ... a residence removed from the royal palace but merely an area within it" [M. O'Connor, "The Grammar of Finding Your Way in Palmyrene Aramaic and the Problem of Diction in Ancient West Semitic Inscriptions," in *Focus: A Semitic/Afrasian Gathering in Remembrance of Albert Ehrman* (Current Issues in Linguistic History 58; ed. Yoel L. Arbeitman; Philadelphia: John Benjamins, 1988), 356 n. 5]). There she will remain "desolate," which "includes the meanings 'unmarried' and 'childless': see Isa 54:1. For a Hebrew woman it was a living death (cf. 2 Sam 20:3)" (Conroy, 35 n. 70).

21–22 David and three of his children (Amnon, Absalom, Tamar) are linked together in the final segment (vv.21–22) of the literary unit under review (vv.1–22), just as they were in the beginning segment (vv.1–2). There the interrelationships were reasonably positive, and love was the keynote (v.1); here, however, all semblance of harmony has dissolved, and emotions such as anger (v.21) and hatred (v.22) dominate.

When David hears about Amnon's rape of Tamar and its sequel, he is understandably "furious" (v.21)—just as he had "burned with anger" after learning of the despicable conduct of the rich man in Nathan's parable (see 12:5 and comment; same Heb. expression in both cases). But even though he is "King David" (the title is an ironic touch), he perhaps feels that he is powerless to act because he himself is guilty of a similar sin: his adultery with Bathsheba. If Dinah's brothers, hearing about the rape of their sister and thus becoming angry (Ge 34:7), proceeded to take what they considered to be the necessary steps to avenge her (Ge 34:25–29), David's guilt in an analogous situation paralyzes him.

Indeed, David's responses throughout ch. 13 are reactive rather than proactive (cf. vv.37, 39).

> The results of David's sin with Bathsheba become evident in his relations with his sons, for how can a father discipline his children when he knows that he has done worse than they? When David's son Amnon rapes Tamar ... David is very angry (2 Sam 13:21), and yet David takes no action, for he, too, has committed his own sexual offense. The upshot is that Tamar's brother, Absalom, murders Amnon (2 Sam 13:29), but David again does nothing, for he, too, has a murder on his head. (Paul J. and Elizabeth Achtemeier, *The Old Testament Roots of Our Faith* [Philadelphia: Fortress, 1979], 94; see also Ackerman, 48; Lasine, 102)

David is as clearly unable to control his sons' passions as he is his own (cf. Jackson, 189).

Meanwhile Absalom bides his time (v.22), saying nothing "either good or bad" to Amnon (cf. Ge 31:24, 29)—that is, nothing "one way or the other" (Ge 24:50; same Heb. idiom in all four texts). Absalom's remarkable forbearance, which would last two years (v.23), provides further evidence in favor of the conspiracy theory (see comment on v.5). He "remained silent and inactive, although [*kî*, untrans. in NIV] he hated Amnon" (Conroy, 18 n. 6; cf. similarly W. Malcolm Clark, "A Legal Background to the Yahwist's Use of 'Good and Evil' in Genesis 2–3," *JBL* 88/3 [1969]: 269 n. 14).

Amnon's acquired hatred for his half sister Tamar (v.15) is reprised in Absalom's acquired hatred for his half brother Amnon (v.22). The phrase *ʿal-dᵉbar ʾᵃšer* ("because") followed by a verb occurs only here and in Deuteronomy 22:24 (2x); 23:4 ("for"). "In the legal texts of Dt the phrase introduces the reason for a condemnation or sentence, and a similar nuance may be had at 2 Sam 13,22: Absalom's silence and separation from Amnon means that the latter has already been sentenced" (Conroy, 35 n. 74).

NOTES

3 Instead of the MT's "Jonadab" (first occurrence), "Jonathan" is read in 4QSamuel[a] and the Lucianic recension of the LXX, probably by contamination from 21:21 (where Jonathan, another son of Shimeah, is mentioned).

16 Although Driver, 298, declares אַל־אוֹדֹת (*ʾal-ʾôdōt*) to be "untranslateable" (cf. Kirkpatrick, Smith), K&D suggests that "nothing more is needed than to supply תְּהִי [*tᵉhî*]" to arrive at the clear (literally rendered) translation: "Do not become the cause of this great evil, (which is) greater than another that thou hast done to me, to thrust me away." Another possibility is to translate, with Goldman, 260, "Not so, because this great wrong in putting me forth is worse than the other that thou didst unto me." Since many MSS read עַל (*ʿal*) instead of אַל (*ʾal*; cf. BHS), the MT may have originally read *ʾal ʿal-ʾôdōt* ("No, because"), with *ʾal* dropping out of some MSS because of haplography and *ʿal* out of others for the same reason (for *ʿal-ʾôdōt*, "because of," cf. Ge 21:11 ["because it concerned"], 25 ["about"]; Ex 18:8 ["for (the) sake (of)"]; Nu 12:1; 13:24; Jdg 6:7; Jer 3:8). In any case, emendations of the MT based on the LXX are uncalled for, since the LXX may have been translating *ad sensum* a Hebrew *Vorlage* identical to or close to the MT.

18 The meaning of פַּסִּים (*passîm*; GK 7168), which renders "(richly) ornamented" in vv.18–19 as well as in Genesis 37:3, 23, 32, remains uncertain (see NIV note here and at Ge 37:3; cf. also the extended discussion in McCarter, *II Samuel*, 325–26). The two most common translations are "long-sleeved" (based on the LXX's renderings here) and "embroidered" (perhaps "based on one meaning of *pas* in Rabbinic Hebrew, namely, 'strip, stripe'—thus *k^etōnet passîm* 'gown of strips' or 'striped gown'" [ibid., 325]; cf. Joseph's "coat of *many* colours" [KJV]). It is impossible to choose definitively between the two, nor do the "embroidered garments" worn by the royal bride in Psalm 45:14 constitute an unassailable parallel, since the phrase translates a different Hebrew word (cf. similarly Jdg 5:30).

21 At the end of the verse, the NRSV appends "but he would not punish his son Amnon, because he loved him, for he was his firstborn." The added words (cf. already Josephus, *Ant.* 7.173 [8.2]; JB; NAB; NEB; also Barthélemy, 2:234–35) "can be restored on the basis of the Greek and Old Latin texts and a fragment of the longer reading in a Hebrew manuscript from Qumran (4QSam[a])" (McCarter, "'Plots, True or False,'" 366 n. 20; cf. similarly Driver, 301, based on the LXX alone). Although the addition is attractive (cf. "His father had never interfered with [Adonijah]" in 1Ki 1:6, which looks like a literary reminiscence of the versional "he would not punish his son" [same Heb. idiom in both cases]), Conroy, 152–53, issues a helpful caveat.

8. The Murder of Amnon (13:23–39)

OVERVIEW

Bracketed by the "two years" of Absalom's silent waiting (v.23) and the "three years" of his voluntary exile (v.38), vv.23–39 constitute a distinct literary unit. Although it has been argued that v.39 is more closely linked to what follows it than to what precedes it (cf. Sacon, 42; Fokkelman, *Narrative Art*, 1:126), at the very least it is better to treat it as a transitional verse connecting ch. 13 to ch. 14.

The entire unit divides most naturally into two main sections that describe, respectively, Amnon's murder (vv.23–29) and its aftermath (vv.30–39; cf. similarly Fokkelman, ibid., 114). The former section refers to David exclusively as "the king" (vv.24–26; cf. also "the king's sons" [vv.23, 27, 29]), while the latter often uses the proper name (vv.30, 32, 37, 39 [MT; see NIV note]). Both sections appear to be arranged chiastically:

A Absalom invites the king and his officials to the sheepshearing (13:23–24)
  B Despite Absalom's urging, the king refuses (13:25)
    C Absalom requests that Amnon alone be allowed to come (13:26a)
  B' Due to Absalom's urging, the king agrees (13:26b–27)
A' Absalom orders his men to kill Amnon (13:28–29)

A David and his servants mourn (13:30–31)
  B Jonadab speaks to David (13:32–33)
    C Absalom alone flees (13:34)
  B' Jonadab speaks to David (13:35)
A' David and his servants mourn (13:36–39)

The latter chiasm is similar to certain elements of the analysis suggested by Sacon, 41–42, who, however, needlessly complicates the outline by attempting to draw vv.23–29 into one large overall chiasm. The result is a top-heavy structure that parallels vv.23–29b with vv.37–38b. My proposal has the advantage of isolating the two main *dramatis personae*: Amnon the victim as the center of attention in v.26a, and Absalom the murderer as the focal point in v.34.

23Two years later, when Absalom's sheepshearers were at Baal Hazor near the border of
Ephraim, he invited all the king's sons to come there. 24Absalom went to the king and said,
"Your servant has had shearers come. Will the king and his officials please join me?"
25"No, my son," the king replied. "All of us should not go; we would only be a burden to
you." Although Absalom urged him, he still refused to go, but gave him his blessing.
26Then Absalom said, "If not, please let my brother Amnon come with us."
The king asked him, "Why should he go with you?" 27But Absalom urged him, so he sent
with him Amnon and the rest of the king's sons.
28Absalom ordered his men, "Listen! When Amnon is in high spirits from drinking wine
and I say to you, 'Strike Amnon down,' then kill him. Don't be afraid. Have not I given you
this order? Be strong and brave." 29So Absalom's men did to Amnon what Absalom had
ordered. Then all the king's sons got up, mounted their mules and fled.
30While they were on their way, the report came to David: "Absalom has struck down all
the king's sons; not one of them is left." 31The king stood up, tore his clothes and lay down
on the ground; and all his servants stood by with their clothes torn.
32But Jonadab son of Shimeah, David's brother, said, "My lord should not think that they
killed all the princes; only Amnon is dead. This has been Absalom's expressed intention
ever since the day Amnon raped his sister Tamar. 33My lord the king should not be concerned about the report that all the king's sons are dead. Only Amnon is dead."
34Meanwhile, Absalom had fled.
Now the man standing watch looked up and saw many people on the road west of him, coming down the side of the hill. The watchman went and told the king, "I see men in the direction of Horonaim, on the side of the hill."
35Jonadab said to the king, "See, the king's sons are here; it has happened just as your servant said."
36As he finished speaking, the king's sons came in, wailing loudly. The king, too, and all his servants wept very bitterly.
37Absalom fled and went to Talmai son of Ammihud, the king of Geshur. But King David mourned for his son every day.
38After Absalom fled and went to Geshur, he stayed there three years. 39And the spirit of
the king longed to go to Absalom, for he was consoled concerning Amnon's death.

COMMENTARY

23–24 Two full years having passed (lit., "And it was for two years, [namely] days," v.23; for the same Heb. construction, cf. 14:28; see also comment on 13:1–22), Absalom determines that the time is ripe to avenge the rape of his sister Tamar. He chooses sheepshearing, a festive season (see comment on 1Sa 25:2), as a suitable if macabre backdrop for the murder of his brother Amnon. As the sheep of Absalom would lose their wool (vv.23–24), so David's firstborn, the potential shepherd of Israel, would lose his life (vv.28–29). Indeed, Amnon is to be the second "lamb" of the four that will die, by David's own reckoning, as payment for David's sins against Bathsheba and Uriah (see 12:6 and comment).

The locale is Baal Hazor, perhaps the same as the Benjamite village of Hazor (cf. Ne 11:33) and identified with modern Jebel/Tel Asur (about fifteen miles north-northeast of Jerusalem), the highest peak (3,333 feet above sea level) in the hill country of Ephraim (cf. Rasmussen, 40; also Aharoni, 29). A magnificent site, it is the place to which Absalom invites the king, together with all of his sons and officials, to join in celebrating their mutual prosperity. Absalom's words to his father David (v.24) are well chosen in terms of both politeness and protocol. Referring to himself as "your servant," he continues his request: "Will the king and his officials [lit., 'servants'] please join me [lit., 'your servant']?"

25 The king's two brief responses to Absalom, combined with the phrase "Absalom urged him," link v.25 to vv.26b–27 as parallel elements in the chiastic structure of vv.23–29. From a literary standpoint, David's "No, my son" reprises Tamar's "No, my brother" (see v.12 and comment; cf. further Rosenberg, 147). From an exegetical standpoint, however, it is a much gentler rebuff (cf. Naomi's "No, my daughters" in Ru 1:13) than Tamar's desperate cry for help. In any event, David knows that if his entire retinue would accompany Absalom, it would be "a burden to" him (lit., "heavy [up]on," as in Ne 5:18). Absalom's urging to the contrary notwithstanding, David refuses to go and gives him his "blessing" (or "farewell"; cf. NIV note on Ge 47:10).

26a After asking for the impossible (doubtless knowing that he would be refused), Absalom cannily requests that Amnon alone be allowed to come (for *wālō'* [lit., "and not"] in the sense of "if not," cf. 2Ki 5:17). He probably realizes that David, knowing that Absalom may intend to harm Amnon because of what he did to Tamar, will not accede to his latter request any more than he did to the former. Or perhaps Absalom hopes that the two years that have elapsed since the rape have dimmed the event in his father's mind. In addition, Absalom refers to Amnon as "my brother" (only here in the entire chapter), apparently to assuage whatever lingering fears David may have.

26b–27 To Absalom's chagrin, David does not agree immediately. His "Why ...?" (v.26b) smacks more of the suspicious than of the incredulous. This time, however, Absalom's urging (v.27; cf. the parallel in v.25) is successful—and perhaps beyond his wildest expectations: The indecisive king not only allows his son Amnon to go but also sends the rest of his sons along with him. "David puts himself at ease by giving Amnon the company of his brothers. For Absalom they are no hindrance, however, but a good cover needed to receive Amnon fittingly at his country-seat" (Fokkelman, *Narrative Art*, 1:116).

28–29 Emboldened by his increasing success (in vv.24–27 he alternates between requesting and urging), Absalom now commands (the verb "order" is used of/by him three times in vv.28–29). He gets the attention of his men by telling them to "listen" (lit., "see/look," as in Ex 25:40; 2Ki 6:32; cf. also Ps

45:10). To be "in high spirits from drinking wine" (v.28) is often to invite mischief at best (cf. Est 1:10–11) and disaster at worst (see 1Sa 25:36 and comment; cf. further Jeffrey C. Geoghegan ("Israelite Sheepshearing and David's Rise to Power," *Bib* 87/1 [2006]: 56–57)—in this case mayhem ("kill him"). Sandwiched between Absalom's words of encouragement and reassurance—"Don't be afraid" (see 9:7 and comment) and "Be strong and brave" (lit., "Be strong and become sons of power/might"; for the latter clause see 2:7 and comment)—is the "I" (emphatic) of potentially royal mandate.

As the daughter of Jephthah died because "he did to her as he had vowed" (Jdg 11:39), so the brother of Absalom dies because "Absalom's men did to Amnon what Absalom had ordered" (v.29; similar Heb. euphemistic form of expression in both cases). Panic-stricken, the rest of the king's sons decide against waiting to find out whether Absalom's execution order will extend to them. They get on their "mules" (the mount of choice for royalty during the early monarchy; cf. 18:9; 1Ki 10:25; 18:5) and flee for their lives.

Thus David's adultery with Bathsheba is mirrored in his son Amnon's rape of Tamar, and David's murder of Uriah is reprised in Absalom's execution of Amnon. "It will suffice here to conclude that Amnon and Absalom are chips off the old block" (Fokkelman, *Narrative Art*, 1:125). Applicable to the present situation, a principle enunciated by Paul is terser still: "A man reaps what he sows" (Gal 6:7).

30–31 Before the princes arrive in Jerusalem, a false "report" comes to David (v.30), claiming that Absalom has killed "all the king's sons." It would seem that David's usually reliable intelligence network (see 10:5 and comment) has failed him this time. Like far too many rumors, the one that reaches David is a gross exaggeration. As far as the king's sons are concerned, apart from Absalom "not one of them is left." (For the same Heb. expression, cf. Ps 106:11, where it is said of Israel's Egyptian pursuers in the days of the Exodus that "not one of them survived.")

David's immediate reaction to the news is both predictable and understandable. He "stood up" in alarm (v.31), bolt upright, just as his sons had done when their brother Amnon was killed ("got up," v.29; same Heb. verb in both cases). Echoing the behavior of his disgraced daughter Tamar, who tore her robe to bewail the loss of her virginity, David tears his clothes as a sign of mourning (see v.19 and comment), and his "servants" dutifully follow suit (v.31; cf. also v.36 [the same Heb. word is translated "officials" in v.24; see 1Sa 16:15–16 and comment]). As a further symbol of his grief, the king lies "on the ground" (v.31), just as he had done while pleading to God for the life of his illegitimate son (see comment on 12:16).

32–33 The false "report" (*šᵉmuʿâ*, v.30) is quickly challenged by a wise man who may have been a member of David's cabinet (see comment on v.3): Jonadab son of "Shimeah" (*šimʿâ*, v.32; for the observation that the consonantal structure of the two Heb. words is the same, see Fokkelman, *Narrative Art*, 1:118). Jonadab's prior knowledge that "only Amnon is dead" (vv.32–33) and that his murder has been Absalom's expressed "intention" (cf. similarly K&D, Anderson; *śûmâ* is attested only here) for the past two years lends further credence to the theory that Absalom and Jonadab had long ago hatched a plot to do away with Amnon, David's heir apparent and thus an obstacle to Absalom's pretensions. Although the erroneous report had stated that "Absalom" had struck down all the princes (v.30), Jonadab knows that "they [Absalom's men] killed" only Amnon (v.32 [cf. v.29]; cf. Hill, 390). Jonadab's confident assertion being the true state of affairs, David should not "be concerned about the [false] report" that has come to him (lit., "lay [*śym*, cognate to and punning on *śûmâ* in v.32] the word upon his heart," v.33; see comment on 1Sa 21:12 ["took these words to heart"]).

34 Whereas the king's sons had "fled" to avoid Amnon's fate (v.29), Absalom has meanwhile also "fled," in this case to escape royal retribution (v.34; different Heb. verbs). Although the other princes escape to the refuge of Jerusalem, Absalom flees across the Jordan, far from Jerusalem—a flight of such import that it is mentioned three times in the space of five verses (vv.34, 37, 38). Ironically, David himself will later "flee" to "escape from Absalom" (15:14; cf. also 1Sa 19:12, 18; 22:17).

One of the watchmen atop the walls of Jerusalem sees a number of men "on" (for *min* ["from"] in the sense of "in, on," see Notes on 5:13) the road leading to the city from the west. He reports to David that they are "in the direction of Horonaim" (or "on the road from Horonaim"; cf. similarly "on the road down from Beth Horon" in Jos 10:11). Meaning literally "Two Horons," Horonaim here is not the Moabite town mentioned in Isaiah 15:5 and Jeremiah 48:3, 5, 34 (= *ḥwrnn* in lines 31–32 of the Mesha stele) but refers to the Levitical city (cf. Jos 21:20, 22; 1Ch 6:66, 68) of Upper and Lower Beth Horon, modern Beit Ur el-Foqa and Beit Ur el-Tahta respectively, located in Ephraim two miles apart on a ridge ten to twelve miles northwest of Jerusalem. Fleeing from Baal Hazor (see comment on v.23), the royal party must have traveled "by way of Bethel and picked up the Horonaim road near Gibeon" (McCarter, *II Samuel*, 333).

35 As Jonadab had earlier assured the king that of all his sons only Amnon was dead (see vv.32–33 and comments), so he now advises David to see with his own eyes that "the king's sons are here." He then adds a statement that is doubtless intended to ingratiate himself to David: "It has happened just as your servant said."

36–39 The scene of mourning described in vv.36–39 balances that in vv.30–31. Appearing at the beginning of vv.36 ("finished") and 39 ("longed"), the verb *klh* frames this literary unit.

The Hebrew clause rendered "the king's sons came in" (v.36) echoes verbatim the one translated, "See, the king's sons are here" in v.35. David's servants and sons join him in weeping and wailing "loudly" and "bitterly" (v.36; for other examples of David's mourning over a slain family member, comrade, or friend, see comment on 3:32). "Wailing loudly" is an idiomatic rendering of the picturesque phrase "raised their voice(s) and wept" (see comment on 1Sa 11:4), while "wept ... bitterly" (cf. also Jdg 21:2) translates a cognate accusative construction that means literally "wept a great weeping." The effect of both expressions used together is to emphasize the pathos and sense of utter hopelessness that surrounds the tragic loss of a firstborn son.

For his part Absalom, David's third son, flees for his life to Geshur (v.37) in Aram (cf. 15:8) to find protection in the household of Talmai, his grandfather on his mother's side (see 3:3 and comments). "Like Jacob before him, Absalom fled to Aramaean kinsmen in the North-east" (Carlson, 164). "King David" (though the words are not in the MT, they appear in the LXX and are rightly supplied contextually by the NIV) continues to mourn for "his son"—doubtless Amnon, although the fact that the narrator does not name him leaves open the slight possibility that Absalom, "the favorite now in exile" (Sternberg, 231), is intended. (David's later grieving for his son Absalom is one of the most poignant scenes in all of Scripture [cf. 18:33–19:4].) The depth of David's grief over Amnon's death is underscored in the statement that he mourned for his son "every day" (lit., "all the days"), an emphatic expression elsewhere translated "always" (cf. 1Sa 2:35) and "for life" (cf. 1Sa 28:2).

Meanwhile, "only after a three-year self-imposed exile in Geshur [v.38] ... does [Absalom] return to Jerusalem [14:23] to make preparations for his own kingship by undermining popular allegiance to David.... Certainly this belies a carefully constructed strategy for seizing control of the monarchy and bespeaks a man of considerable foresight, determination and ability" (Hill, 389–90). "When revolt against David did finally come, it is not surprising that its roots were in the east.... One must wonder if Absalom did not expect to receive aid in his revolt from his eastern allies" (Curtis, "'East Is East ...,'" 357–58).

Absalom's rebellion, however, is still in the future. For now the narrator briefly explores David's attitude toward Absalom after the period of mourning for Amnon is over. The rendering represented by the NIV ("the spirit of the king longed to go to Absalom," v.39) "is opposed ... to the conduct of David towards Absalom as described in ch. xiv—namely, that after Joab had succeeded by craft in bringing him back to Jerusalem, David would not allow him to come into his presence for two whole years" (K&D, 405). Noting that *klh* is stronger than "long, yearn," meaning rather "fail, be finished, be spent" (cf. esp. Ps 84:2 ["faints"]; 143:7), McCarter (*II Samuel*, 344) translates: "The king's enthusiasm for marching out against [Absalom] was spent" (cf. the alternative rendering in Barthélemy, 2:238). The Hebrew idiom *yṣʾ ʾl* ("go [out] to") is used in the sense of "march out against" in Deuteronomy 28:7 ("come at," NIV). The first clause of v.39 thus asserts that "David is no longer openly hostile to [Absalom] and, therefore, ready to be prodded step by step towards a reconciliation" (McCarter, *II Samuel*, 344).

NOTES

23 Geoghegan ("Israelite Sheepshearing," 58) observes that there are several noteworthy connections

> between Judah's daughter-in-law, Tamar, and the Judahite king's (David's) daughter. First of all, recompense for the violations against both Tamars is obtained during the time of sheepshearing: Tamar deceitfully lures Judah into a sexual encounter in order to secure her rightful offspring, while Absalom deceitfully lures Amnon to his sheepshearing to avenge his sister's rape (Ge 38,12; 2 Sam 13,23). In addition, both Tamars are involved in incestuous relationships: the former with her father-in-law, the latter with her half-brother.

Driver's linguistic arguments (301–2; cf. also BDB, 68b sec. 6) for equating "Ephraim" here with the town of "Ephron" (*Qere*: "Ephrain") in 2 Chronicles 13:19 are effectively negated by his own note: "But it is odd that the site of a conspicuous hill ... should have to be defined by its nearness to a place ... nearly 500 ft. in the valley below it." As for McCarter's observation (*II Samuel*, 333) that "the preposition *ʿim* means 'near, in the vicinity of,' not 'within,'" the NIV's rendering "near the border of" satisfactorily resolves the alleged difficulty, both linguistically and geographically.

25 For פרץ (*prṣ*) in the sense of "urge" here and in v.27, see Notes on 1 Samuel 28:23. To see "error" in this root wherever it means "urge" (cf. Lewis, 111) is unwise as well as unnecessary.

27 Barthélemy, 2:235, recommends an addendum: "And Absalom prepared a feast like a king's feast" (cf. also JB, NAB, NEB, NRSV; for details regarding support from ancient versions and possibly also from 4QSam[a], see McCarter, *II Samuel*, 330). It would seem just as likely, however, that the putative Hebrew *Vorlage* of the versions has suffered from contamination from 1 Samuel 25:36 as that the MT has lost a sentence through scribal error. In any case, sheepshearing was known as a time for celebration (see comment on 1Sa 25:2), and therefore further elaboration is not called for every time it is mentioned.

30 נוֹתַר (*nôtar*, "be left, survive") is one among several verbs that may employ either בְּ- (*b*[e]-; cf. 17:12; Lev 8:32; 14:18) or מִן (*min*, as here; cf. also Lev 7:17; 14:29) as the subordinating preposition (for examples of other verbs, see Sarna, 312).

32 The fact that the Hebrew consonants of the words rendered "report" (v.30) and "Shimeah" (v.32) are identical in the MT (see comment on v.32) may have influenced the narrator's choice of "Shimeah" (rather than its variants "Shammah," "Shimea") here and in v.3 (see comment there).

34 The last sentence of the verse is based on the LXX and is not included in the MT (see NIV note). As reconstructed, the Hebrew *Vorlage* was probably something like: ויבא הצפה ויגד למלך ויאמר אנשים ראיתי מדרך חרנים מצד ההר (*wyb*ʾ *hṣph wygd lmlk wy*ʾ*mr* ʾ*nšym r*ʾ*yty mdrk ḥrnym mṣd hhr*, "The watchman went and told the king, 'I see men in the direction of Horonaim, on the side of the hill'"; cf. Driver, 301–2; McCarter, *II Samuel*, 333); this presumably dropped out of the MT when a scribe's eye skipped from the first occurrence of *mṣd hhr* ("from/on the side of the hill") to the second.

39 Since the verb rendered "longed" is feminine, the MT's "David" (דוד, *dwd*) cannot be its subject. "Spirit" (רוח, *rwḥ*), however, is almost always feminine and is therefore either the explicit (see NIV text) or implied subject of the verb (see NIV note; for details justifying the NIV's textual reading, see Ulrich, 106–7).

9. The Wise Woman of Tekoa (14:1–20)

OVERVIEW

The "desire/fulfillment-of-desire" motif exhibited in ch. 13 continues in ch. 14, which itself contains additional literary clues that lead to the isolation of chs. 13–14 as a separate unit (for details see Overview to 13:1–22) within the court history of David (chs. 9–20). As a whole, ch. 14 is concerned with Joab's successful attempt to bring Absalom back to Jerusalem from his self-imposed exile in Geshur. Apart from the incidental reference to Absalom's daughter Tamar in v.27, Joab and Absalom are the only two *dramatis personae* specifically named in the chapter. The other two players are "the king" (obviously David, though never referred to by name) and the wise woman from Tekoa. David at this point still commands the respect of his subjects (however grudgingly it may be in some cases) since each of the other three main characters in ch. 14 bows down, "face to the ground" (vv.4, 22, 33), before him.

Despite various suggestions concerning the division of ch. 14 into more than two subsections, the traditional bipartite analysis (vv.1–20, 21–33) remains the simplest and best. As a whole, the chapter is framed by an inclusio formed by the appearance of the name "Absalom" at the end of vv.1 and 33. The only other verse in ch. 14 ending with "Absalom" is v.21, which thus begins a subsection that mirrors the structure of the full chapter. As for the section constituted by vv.1–20, the verb that begins its first verse and concludes its last verse is *yd*ʿ ("know"), reflecting the fact that Joab understands David's intentions (v.1) and David understands Joab's (v.20; cf. Leonard, 143–44).

Helpful parallels between vv.1–20 and other episodes in the books of Samuel have often been observed. Echoes of David's meeting with Abigail in 1 Samuel 25:20–35 have been explored by David M. Gunn ("Traditional Composition," 221–22; for details see comment on 1Sa 25:23) as well as by R. Bickert ["Die List Joabs und der Sinneswandel Davids," VTSup 30 [1979]: 42–43). Structural elements common to the story of the Tekoite woman and Nathan's parable (12:1–7a) have been noted by Graffy, 406–7 (cf. also Fokkelman, *Narrative Art*, 1:141–42; for details see comment on 12:1–14), while similarities between the narrative of the "wise woman" of Tekoa and that of the "wise woman" of Abel Beth Maacah (20:14–22) have been pointed out by Claudia V. Camp, 14–29. My commentary will elaborate on the various comparisons as they occur and where considered necessary.

The question of whether the narrator pictures wisdom as residing in the Tekoite woman or in Joab has been hotly debated. Whybray, 59, states flatly that the story of "Joab's use of the woman of Tekoa is really a story of Joab's wisdom rather than of the woman: Joab applied his wisdom 'in order to change the course of affairs' (v. 20)" (for detailed argumentation, see George G. Nicol, "The Wisdom of Joab and the Wise Woman of Tekoa," *ST* 36/2 [1982]: 97–104). J. Hoftijzer, 419–44, argues differently: "The author of the story does not present Joab as wise, but the woman. Her wisdom is that she was able to handle a very tricky case, a case that remained a real test case for her even if she was fully instructed" (444 n. 1; cf. also Camp, 17–18 n. 8).

It seems best, however, to admit that the dispute between the two views is not a matter of either/or but of both/and: Joab is wise in knowing whom to delegate to approach David and in knowing what to tell her to say, and the Tekoite woman is wise in knowing how to implement Joab's instructions in the midst of a delicate situation. If the scales must be tipped in one direction or the other, the woman gets the nod. She, after all, is the one who is called "wise" (v.2).

The pericope as a whole appears to be structured chiastically:

A Joab "knew" (14:1)
  B Joab instructs the wise woman (14:2–3)
    C The woman makes a request of the king (14:4–5a)
      D She makes her first appeal (14:5b–10)
        E She successfully pleads for her son's life (14:11)
      D' She makes her second appeal (14:12–17)
    C' The king makes a request of the woman (14:18–19a)
  B' She admits that Joab has instructed her (14:19b)
A' The king "knows" (14:20)

[1]Joab son of Zeruiah knew that the king's heart longed for Absalom. [2]So Joab sent someone to Tekoa and had a wise woman brought from there. He said to her, "Pretend you are in mourning. Dress in mourning clothes, and don't use any cosmetic lotions. Act

like a woman who has spent many days grieving for the dead. 3Then go to the king and speak these words to him." And Joab put the words in her mouth.

4When the woman from Tekoa went to the king, she fell with her face to the ground to pay him honor, and she said, "Help me, O king!"

5The king asked her, "What is troubling you?"

She said, "I am indeed a widow; my husband is dead. 6I your servant had two sons. They got into a fight with each other in the field, and no one was there to separate them. One struck the other and killed him. 7Now the whole clan has risen up against your servant; they say, 'Hand over the one who struck his brother down, so that we may put him to death for the life of his brother whom he killed; then we will get rid of the heir as well.' They would put out the only burning coal I have left, leaving my husband neither name nor descendant on the face of the earth."

8The king said to the woman, "Go home, and I will issue an order in your behalf."

9But the woman from Tekoa said to him, "My lord the king, let the blame rest on me and on my father's family, and let the king and his throne be without guilt."

10The king replied, "If anyone says anything to you, bring him to me, and he will not bother you again."

11She said, "Then let the king invoke the LORD his God to prevent the avenger of blood from adding to the destruction, so that my son will not be destroyed."

"As surely as the LORD lives," he said, "not one hair of your son's head will fall to the ground."

12Then the woman said, "Let your servant speak a word to my lord the king."

"Speak," he replied.

13The woman said, "Why then have you devised a thing like this against the people of God? When the king says this, does he not convict himself, for the king has not brought back his banished son? 14Like water spilled on the ground, which cannot be recovered, so we must die. But God does not take away life; instead, he devises ways so that a banished person may not remain estranged from him.

15"And now I have come to say this to my lord the king because the people have made me afraid. Your servant thought, 'I will speak to the king; perhaps he will do what his servant asks. 16Perhaps the king will agree to deliver his servant from the hand of the man who is trying to cut off both me and my son from the inheritance God gave us.'

17"And now your servant says, 'May the word of my lord the king bring me rest, for my lord the king is like an angel of God in discerning good and evil. May the LORD your God be with you.'"

18Then the king said to the woman, "Do not keep from me the answer to what I am going to ask you."

"Let my lord the king speak," the woman said.

19The king asked, "Isn't the hand of Joab with you in all this?"

The woman answered, "As surely as you live, my lord the king, no one can turn to the right or to the left from anything my lord the king says. Yes, it was your servant Joab who instructed me to do this and who put all these words into the mouth of your servant.
20Your servant Joab did this to change the present situation. My lord has wisdom like that of an angel of God—he knows everything that happens in the land."

COMMENTARY

1 The full name "Joab son of Zeruiah" (see comment on 1Sa 26:6) signals a new beginning in the narrative (Joab has not been mentioned since 12:27). "Longed for," intended by the NIV to continue the thought of 13:39 (see comment), is represented in the MT only by the preposition *ʿal* ("on"). "The king's heart longed for Absalom" is therefore better rendered "The king's mind was on Absalom" (cf. Job 1:8, "Have you considered" [lit., "Have you set your heart/mind on"])—implying, in the context, that Joab chooses a time when he knows that David is thinking about Absalom, "trying (presumably) to decide how to handle the matter" of potential reconciliation between father and son (McCarter, *II Samuel*, 351).

2–3 Determined to enlist an expert to help his cause, Joab sends for a "wise woman" (cf. the wise woman from Abel Beth Maacah [20:15–16]) to be brought to Jerusalem. His choice of a woman rather than a man is perhaps related to the nature of his mission, and his decision to engage a stranger rather than an intimate (such as Jonadab; see comments on 13:3, where "wise" is preferable to "shrewd") may be calculated to catch David off guard and therefore help him ultimately to view his relationship to Absalom more objectively. Speaking with the voice of authority and uttering proverbs are two traits, often associated with wisdom, that are exhibited by the wise woman from Tekoa and her counterpart from Abel (cf. Camp, 17–18). In the present narrative, wisdom is mentioned again only in v.20 (see comment) and thus strengthens the inclusio formed by the occurrences of the verb "know" in vv.1 and 20.

The woman is from Tekoa, the birthplace of one of the earliest of the writing prophets (Am 1:1), a town located in the desert of Judah (cf. 2Ch 20:20) about ten miles south of Jerusalem at a site today called Khirbet Tequ. Upon her arrival in Jerusalem, Joab tells the woman (v.2) to pretend that she is in "mourning," to dress in "mourning" clothes, and to act as though she is "grieving" for the dead. (All three words are forms of the same Heb. root, *ʾbl*.) She is thus asked to play a fictitious role, to participate in a "dramatic fiction," as Luis Alonso Schökel labels the episode ("David y la mujer de Tecua: 2 Sam 14 como modelo hermenéutico," *Bib* 57/2 [1976]: 192).

By telling the woman to pretend that she has "spent many days grieving for the dead," Joab is—doubtless intentionally—comparing her with David, who "mourned for his son every day" (see 13:37 and comment; same Heb. verb). Indeed, the woman from Tekoa and the king of Israel are twice bereaved: She has lost her husband and a son, and he has lost an illegitimate son born through Bathsheba as well as Amnon, his firstborn. The link between the woman's situation and David's earlier loss is highlighted by Joab's command to her not to "use any cosmetic lotions" (v.2; see 12:20 and comment).

Joab next orders the woman to go to the king and "speak these words" to him (v.3), the narrator here using a Hebrew idiom that can mean "give this advice" (cf. 17:6). But the contents of the message Joab wants the Tekoite to deliver are specific, so he "put[s] the words in her mouth" (cf. the woman's admission to that effect in the parallel passage [v.19b]). In cases where the context is clear, this phrase is always used when a superior instructs a subordinate (cf. Hoftijzer, 419 n. 3; cf. Ex 4:15; Nu 22:38; 23:5, 12, 16; Ezr 8:17 ["told them what (to say)"]). At the same time, however, the authority that inheres in the words put in someone's mouth should not be confused with the personal authority that the chosen vessel might carry (for a carefully nuanced treatment, see Camp, 18 n. 8). Joab is to be commended for choosing a messenger who is perceptive (= "wise") enough to take the words he gives her and use them in the most persuasive way before the king.

4–5a Arriving at the royal court in Jerusalem, the woman of Tekoa gains an audience with David (v.4), as Joab had commissioned her to do (v.3). To pay the king due respect, she falls before him, "face to the ground," as Joab (v.22) and Absalom (v.33) will later do (cf. also 1:2; 18:28; 24:20; 1Ki 1:23; see esp. 1Sa 25:23 and comment). Her initial request—"Help me [*hôšiʿâ*], O king!"—will be echoed not only by another woman to another king of Israel (cf. 2Ki 6:26; also Mt 15:25) but also by the crowds on Palm Sunday: "Hosanna to the Son of David!" (Mt 21:9 [see NIV note, citing Ps 118:25–26]; for discussion see Leonard, 146–48).

In his role as judge and paramount (for the term, see Bellefontaine, 57–58), David asks the woman, "What is troubling you?" (v.5a). Although the Hebrew idiom (lit., "What to you?" [*mah-llāk*]) may seem harsh because of its terseness, it often carries with it elements of genuine concern: "What can I do for you?" (Caleb to his daughter Acsah [Jos 15:18]); "What is it you want?" (David to Bathsheba [1Ki 1:16]); "What's the matter?" (2Ki 6:28, in response to "Help me, my lord the king!" [2Ki 6:26; see comment on v.4 above]).

5b–10 The woman begins her first appeal to David by identifying herself as a widow and then adding: "My husband is dead" (v.5b). The latter clause, which belabors the point and is clearly successive in the mind of the speaker, justifies Eskhult's description of the Tekoite as a "pretended widow" (Eskhult, 60; cf. also Brueggemann, *First and Second Samuel*, 292). As the sequel indicates, she is a consummate actress and spins a tale that is eminently believable.

Using the submissive language of the ancient Near East in the presence of a superior, she refers to herself as David's "servant" (vv.6–7, 12, 15–17, 19; see 1Sa 1:11 and comment; 28:21–22; and esp. 25:24–25, 27–28, 31, 41; 2Sa 20:17). She states that her two sons "got into a fight," as brothers (or friends or kinsmen) often will (cf. Ex 2:13; 21:22; Lev 24:10; Dt 25:11). The goal of one of the sons was apparently mayhem, or perhaps even murder, and thus the battleground of choice was at some distance from their village—a field, where the presence of witnesses and/or rescuers would be unlikely (cf. Ge 4:8; Dt 21:1; 22:25–27). There, says the Tekoite, one of the brothers "struck the other and killed him" (v.6), a fate that would some day claim Absalom himself (18:15; cf. similarly 1:15; 4:7; 21:17).

The "widow" then states that, after the slaying of her son, clan loyalty took over and demanded retribution against the murderer (v.7). Whether members of the clan who wanted revenge appealed to regulations such as those recorded in Exodus 21:12 and Numbers 35:18–19 (cf. Leonard, 136) is not stated. The Hebrew word here translated "clan" may have represented an association of extended families coextensive (or nearly so) with the village or town in which they lived (as perhaps also in 16:5 and 1Sa 20:6; cf. Bellefontaine, 50). As such they would have been the local community that normally determined the penalty for such matters as homicide, perhaps on the basis of certain provisions of tribal law, elements of which would then have eventually been incorporated into covenantal law.

In any event, the Tekoite comes to David, not to dispute the general custom of blood vengeance (see comment on 3:30), but to question its strict application to her only surviving son. She wants the king to overrule the decision of the clan and to exhibit flexibility "on the basis of certain extenuating circumstances: there were no witnesses to the crime; it appeared to be unpremeditated; the mother's widowhood and dependence on the remaining son; and the role of her son as heir and preserver of the lineage" (Bellefontaine, 54–55).

To fortify her claim that the entire clan has "risen up" (i.e., "rebelled"; see 1Sa 22:13 and comment) against her (v.7), the woman of Tekoa makes up out of whole cloth the very words of their supposed demand. Her calculated deceit is similar to that reflected in Michal's statement to Saul: "(David) said to me, 'Let me get away. Why should I kill you?'" (1Sa 19:17; see comment there; for discussion of various types of nonverifiable quoted speech, see Berlin, *Poetics and Interpretation*, 96–97).

Fabrication though it is, the Tekoite's story is persuasive enough to convince David that she is telling the truth. She claims that she has been ordered to "hand over" her other son, the accused murderer (cf. 20:21). The clan will then execute him "for" (i.e., "in exchange for," *bêt pretii* as in 1Sa 3:13 ["because of"]; cf. GKC, sec. 119*p*) having "killed" his brother (similarly, Joab and Abishai murdered Abner because he had "killed" their brother Asahel [3:30; see comment]). The sad fact that David had earlier "killed" Uriah (12:9) is yet another example of unchecked power that uses murder to gain its own ends.

Concluding her supposed citation of the clan's demands, the woman hints at the likelihood that their ulterior motive in putting her only surviving son to death was to get rid of the "heir" (cf. Jer 49:1) and thereby gain possession of the family property (cf. also v.16). She thus raises the issue of a possible conflict of interest on their part (cf. Bellefontaine, 55).

In a final personal plea (v.7), the wise woman of Tekoa uses a vivid figure of speech to add a note of pathos to her request. She accuses the clan members of wanting to extinguish, to "put out" (cf. similarly 21:17; Isa 42:3 ["snuff out"]), the only "burning coal" remaining to her (for Akkadian parallels, see Hoftijzer, 422 n. 2). He is all she has "left," and when he is gone, her deceased husband will be without "descendant" (these two words derive from the same Heb. root; for the latter word, cf. Ge 45:7 ["remnant"]). In addition, her husband's "name" (cf. Dt 25:5–6; Isa 14:22)—and therefore his very existence (see 1Sa 24:21 and comment)—will be blotted out and thus forgotten. Every memory of him will be expunged from "the face of the earth" (cf. 1Sa 20:15; Zep 1:2–3).

The wise woman from Tekoa has spun an admirable tale. Plausible enough for David to believe it, the situation it describes differs enough from his own (cf. already Patrick, 470) to keep him from becoming suspicious of her true purposes. Her story prepares the groundwork for what Joab wants her to accomplish.

Although David surely has the power and authority to reverse the decision of the members of the woman's clan, he at first treads cautiously so as not to alienate a group that "forms part of his own power base" (Bellefontaine, 61). Unlike his earlier forceful and decisive response to Abigail ("Go home in peace. I have heard your words and granted your request," 1Sa 25:35), his statement to the Tekoite is uncharacteristically vague: "Go home, and I will issue an order in your behalf" (v.8).

Undeterred, the woman is not to be dismissed quite so easily. Like Abigail before her, she makes a confession of guilt ("let the blame rest on me," v.9; cf. 1Sa 25:24) in the hope that doing so will force David to take action. It seems probable, then, that in both situations the confession is meant to support the plea, so that "the central point of these texts is *not* who takes (or has to take) the responsibility in the case under consideration" (Hoftijzer, 427). The Tekoite's desire that the king and his throne "be without guilt" (v.9; cf. Ex 21:28 ["not be held responsible"]) is merely a polite addendum to her main assertion. Surely David's throne, having begun a long and distinguished history (see comment on 3:10; cf. also 7:13, 16), is not to be sidetracked by a local family squabble.

Impressed by the woman's persistence, the king commits himself personally to making sure that no one who chose to interfere with the royal decision concerning her would ever "bother" her again (v.10; cf. Ge 26:11 ["molest"]; 1Ch 16:22 ["touch"]).

11 The center of the chiasm (see Overview to 14:1–20) focuses on the successful plea of the "widow" for the life of her "son," which emboldens her to launch her second plea (vv.12–17). It also contains the first of the woman's seven references to God (vv.11, 13, 14, 16, 17 [2x], 20), as well as David's only use of the divine name in the chapter.

Pleading that the king will pray to the Lord in her behalf, the Tekoite asks for divine help in preventing the "avenger of blood" from killing her only surviving son (for the function of the avenger of blood, see Nu 35:6–28; Dt 19:1–13; Jos 20). She pretends that she wants to keep the avenger from "adding [*Qere*: *harbat*] to the destruction," from causing "a really 'big killing,' so then she will not only have lost one son, but also the second, her last one" (Hoftijzer, 429 n. 2). She wants to make sure, she says, "that my son will not be destroyed" (lit., "that they [i.e., the clan members] will not destroy my son"; cf. v.7, where "get rid of" translates the same Heb. verb rendered "destroyed" here; for another example of "destroy" with a human object, see comment on 1:14—where, however, a different Heb. verb is used [one translated "destruction" in 14:11]).

Just as in his response to Nathan's parable, so also in the case of the Tekoite woman David uses the Lord's name in a solemn oath (see 12:5 and comment; see also 1Sa 14:39 and comment). He promises her that not one hair of her "son" (the NIV's rendering, "son's head," clarifies the terse Heb. idiom) will "fall to the ground" (for other occurrences of this trope, see comment on 1Sa 14:45). David's reference to the "hair" of the woman's "son" is both ironic and poignant: The hair of his own son Absalom was not only an index of his handsome appearance (cf. vv.25–26) but would also contribute to his undoing (cf. 18:9–15).

Referring to the language of the Heidelberg Catechism Question 1 in describing the secure refuge afforded by the gospel ("Jesus Christ ... watches over me so well that without the will of my Father in heaven not a hair can fall from my head"; cf. also Lk 21:18), Brueggemann (*First and Second Samuel*, 293) goes on to make a striking comparison with our text: "Imagine, the protection of every hair on the head by a royal father who is utterly attentive and utterly powerful."

12–17 Having received the assurance she needs, the woman is now ready to make her second appeal. Her words echo those of Abigail: "Let your servant speak" (v.12; cf. 1Sa 25:24). When David gives the Tekoite permission to say whatever she wishes, she addresses him in an open and forthright way. In the light of his firm determination to intervene in behalf of the murderous sibling for whose life she has just pleaded, she asks why the king has "devised" (v.13—or, more strongly, "done"; cf. Hoftijzer, 434, who argues that when interpreting the verb *ḥšb*, "it is very difficult to make a clear cut division between devising and doing") a thing "like this" (a phrase that often has negative connotations; cf. 1Sa 4:7).

Unlike her own situation, which involves only a relatively small clan, by allowing (or forcing) Absalom to remain in exile David has jeopardized the future welfare of all the "people of God" (cf. Jdg 20:2; the term is equivalent to "people of the LORD" in the Deuteronomic corpus, as observed by R. Bickert, "Die List Joabs und der Sinneswandel Davids," in *Studies in the Historical Books of the Old Testament*, ed. J. A. Emerton [Leiden: Brill, 1979], 46 and nn. 55–56; cf. 6:21; 1Sa 2:24; for related expressions, see also 1:12 and comment).

To make sure that David understands the ramifications of what she is saying, the woman points out that his willingness to help her "son" convicts the king himself because he has not "brought back" (used of straying sheep in Eze 34:4, 16) Absalom, his own banished son. Just as her first appeal had asked "that a fratricide go unpunished and that the offender be restored to his family and to his status as a son and heir (v.7)," so also the

> second appeal (by Joab through the woman) requests that another fratricide go unpunished and the offender be restored to "the people of God" (v.13) and, by implication, to his status as son and heir. In neither case is the murderer declared innocent, granted pardon or excused for his deed. But their actions with their consequences are weighed in the balance of a broader context, namely, the suffering and disaster which would befall others if due sanctions were imposed. (Bellefontaine, 63)

Like the wise woman of Abel Beth Maacah (cf. 20:18), the woman of Tekoa demonstrates her expertise and authority in the arena of wisdom by making use of a proverb (v.14), the common identificational type (cf. Camp, 16, 20). Her selection in this case, referring as it does to water spilled on "the ground," may have been triggered at least partially by David's promise that not a hair of her son's head would fall to "the ground" (v.11). Although the exact application of the proverb is debatable (e.g., whether it means that life once lost cannot be recovered, or that death is inevitable, or that punishment for sin is irrevocable, or something else), the image of wasted water is suggestive ("an obvious and effective counterpoint to her previous image of the ember that should not be quenched" [v.7; Alter, *The David Story*, 278]) and therefore appropriate in any event (cf. similarly Job 11:16; Pss 22:14–15; 58:7; Pr 17:14).

Just as in 12:14 the expression "will surely die" (see comment there) refers to "untimely death as a punishment for sins of others" (Hoftijzer, 432 n. 2; 433 n. 1), so also "the people of God" (v.13)—"we" (v.14)—"must die" (or "will surely die"; same Heb. expression as in 12:14) an "untimely death, because they will be punished for the king's sin" (Hoftijzer, 433) in not bringing Absalom back from exile.

Despite the understanding of many commentators (cf. already Patrick, 473), the NIV's "take away life" (v.14) seems to be unprecedented for the relatively common expression *nś᾽ npš* (GK 5951, 5883). In the present context it apparently means something like "dedicate himself" (cf. Hoftijzer, 436–37; Camp, 16 n. 5; cf. Ps 24:4 ["lift up his soul" = "dedicate himself"]; Pr 19:18 ["be a willing party"]; Hos 4:8 ["relish" = "direct their activities toward"]). It is therefore best to translate v.14b (cf. also v.13b) as a rhetorical question: "But will not God dedicate himself, and will he not devise ways to make sure that a banished person does not remain banished/estranged from him?" It was commonly believed in ancient times that estrangement from God's presence was automatic—and potentially permanent—if a person was driven from his homeland (see 1Sa 26:19–20 and comment).

The Tekoite implies that God will effect Absalom's return from Aram to Israel. Although David has "devised" one thing (v.13), God "devises" another (v.14). The difference between the actions of the king and of the Lord is underscored as well by the two occurrences of *l^{e}biltî* ("in order that not": "the king has not brought back his banished son" [v.13]; "so that a banished person may not remain estranged from him" [v.14]; cf. Schökel, "David y la mujer de Tecua," 200–201).

Having made her point, the woman concludes her second appeal by intermingling elements of it with those of her first appeal. Since the "people" (the "whole clan" [v.7], the "people of God" [v.13]) had "made [her] afraid" (v.15; cf. 2Ch 32:18; Ne 6:9 ["frighten"]), she had nothing to lose by seeking an audience with the king. In her desire that "the king" would "do what his servant asks" (v.15), she unwittingly cements her relationship with her mentor Joab, who will later be grateful that "the king has granted his servant's request" (v.22; same Heb. in both cases). She hopes that the king will "deliver his servant [i.e., the woman herself] from the hand of" the avenger (v.16); in so doing she uses a common idiom employed elsewhere of what a king is expected to do on a national scale (cf. 19:9; similarly 1Sa 8:20) or of what the Lord does in behalf of his chosen ones (cf. 22:1; 1Sa 4:3; 2Ki 20:6; 2Ch 32:8, 11; Ezr 8:31).

The woman of Tekoa is afraid that her clan members will "cut off" (lit., "destroy"; see comment on v.11) her and her son from "God's inheritance" ("the inheritance God gave us" [NIV], v.16), a term that, although found nowhere else, is doubtless equivalent to "the LORD's inheritance" (20:19; 21:3; 1Sa 26:19) and may be interpreted as referring either to the land and people of Israel (see comment on 1Sa 10:1 and the expansionist LXX text translated in the NIV note there; cf. also Hoftijzer, 439 n. 3; Harold O. Forshey, "The Construct Chain *naḥ^{a}lat YHWH/ʾ^{e}lōhîm*," *BASOR* 220 [1975]: 51–53) or to an individual "family's landed property or its share in Yahweh's land" (Anderson, 189; cf. also Leonard, 137–38, and the expression "the inheritance of my fathers" applied to Naboth's vineyard in 1Ki 21:3–4). Bellefontaine, 55, observes that the avenger may have an ulterior motive in wanting to kill the woman's only surviving son: to "gain possession of the family property on the death of the heir."

The Tekoite introduces the final words of her second appeal by echoing verbatim what she had stated earlier: "Your servant thought/says" (vv.15, 17). She wants David's decision to bring her "rest"—that is, relief from a bad situation (cf. Hoftijzer, 440; cf. Ru 1:9; Isa 28:12; cf. esp. Jer 45:3). Like Achish before her (see 1Sa 29:9 and comment) and Mephibosheth after her (cf. 19:27), she compares David to an "angel of God"—not merely to flatter him (contra Hoftijzer, 441) but, more importantly, to recognize that in some respects at least the king is "the embodiment of the divine power.... Perhaps a bit of this is *Hofstil* (cf. 1Sa 29:9), but solid reality stands behind it. The king was expected to give judgments of more than human wisdom" (Dennis J. McCarthy, "Compact and Kingship: Stimuli for Hebrew Covenant Thinking" [in Ishida], 82).

Like an angel of God, David is capable of "discerning [lit., 'hearing'; same Heb. verb as 'agree' in v.16] good and evil" (v.17), a merism (cf. Hoftijzer, 441) that not only intends to encompass all moral knowledge (cf. 19:35 ["what is good and what is not"]; Ge 2:9, 17; 3:5, 22; Dt 1:39 ["good from bad"]; 30:15 ["prosperity ... and destruction"];

Pss 34:14; 37:27; Isa 7:15–16 ["wrong and ... right"]; Am 5:14–15; cf. esp. 1Ki 3:9) but also "presupposes God's moral inerrancy.... That the speaker means to praise David rather than God only underscores the powers of divinity, which so unthinkingly surface as an ideal norm and basis for comparison" (Sternberg, 90; see also comment on v.20). The woman's stated desire that the Lord might be "with" the king (v.17) not only expresses her hope that God will help him make the right decision(s) but also echoes a recurring *Leitmotif* for David in the books of Samuel (see comment on 1Sa 16:18).

18–19a Balancing the woman's request of the king (cf. vv.4–5a), David now makes a request of her. Using language reminiscent of Eli's demand to the young Samuel (cf. 1Sa 3:17), the king insists that the Tekoite not "keep" (lit., "hide," v.18) the truth from him. He senses that she is not acting entirely on her own initiative and wants to know whether Joab's "hand" is "with" her in what she is doing (v.19a)—that is, whether Joab is behind all this and is giving her support in what the king now recognizes is her (= Joab's) effort to return Absalom to Jerusalem (for the Heb. idiom "hand is with" in the sense of "support," cf. 2Ki 15:19; Jer 26:24).

19b To swear to the truth of what she is about to say, the woman takes a solemn oath that translates literally as "by the life of your soul" (cf. 15:21; 1Sa 17:55; 25:26; see also comments on 2Sa 11:11; 1Sa 1:26; 20:3). She is firmly convinced that no one can turn "to the right or to the left" (for the idiom, cf. Isa 30:21) of anything David says, implying that the "king's words hit the mark precisely; he discerns the exact state of the case" (Kirkpatrick, 146; cf. K&D, 410–11). Reprising v.3b, she readily admits that Joab engineered her deceptive gambit when he "put all these words in (her) mouth."

20 Ultimately, of course, David is not fooled by the woman's/Joab's fictitious story. Although Joab "knew" (v.1), the king "knows" even more. Like an angel of God, David discerns good and evil (see v.17 and comment); like an angel of God, David knows "everything that happens in the land," the simile in this case presupposing God's omniscience (Sternberg, 90). If Joab has been able to "change" (*sabbēb*, lit., "turn around") the present situation, his ploy is transparent to David. The woman may be "wise" (v.2), but the "wisdom" of the king is compared to that of a divine messenger and, by implication, to that of God himself.

At the same time, however, the Tekoite's compliment is not without its backlash. Her ingratiating simile is "exposed as an empty superlative by way of opposition to reality past (the 'David did not know' formulas that punctuate the story of Abner's murder, or his falling into the trap set by Nathan's parable) and to come" (Sternberg, 93). Rounded off within itself, the account of the wise woman of Tekoa serves as a socio-political example of "the process by which the judicial authority of the chief [David] was expanded and strengthened while that of the autonomous local groups [clan members] was gradually weakened" (Bellefontaine, 64). In its wider context, the narrative depicts the kind of royal power that Absalom—and others—will either try to undermine or seek to usurp.

NOTES

4 "Went," attested in many MSS of the MT as well as in the LXX, Vulgate, and Syriac (cf. *BHS*; see also NIV note), answers to "go" in v.3. Although most MT MSS have וַתֹּאמֶר (*wattōʾmer*, "said/spoke";

probably by contamination by the same word later in the verse), "went" would appear to be the superior reading (contra Barthélemy, 2:239).

5 The construction of the verse is strikingly similar to that of 2 Kings 4:14. In each case a speaker asks a solicitous question, which is then followed by a brief, two-part response beginning with אֲבָל (*ʾᵃbāl*). Although "indeed" (v.5) and "well" (2Ki 4:14) are possible translations of *ʾᵃbāl*, the latter seems more natural and would be equally appropriate here: "Well, I am a widow; my husband is dead."

13 Since all other occurrences of מִדַּבֵּר (*middabbēr*, "says") are clearly Hithpael forms (rendered "speaking" in Nu 7:89; Eze 2:2; 43:6), there is no compelling reason to take it as מִן (*min*, "from, because of") plus Piel here (as is done by Hoftijzer, 430 n. 1)—especially because the resulting translation would not improve on that of the NIV. Indeed, since in the other three cases the subject of the verb is the invisible God, the use of the Hithpael in v.13 adds to the solemnity and significance of the word of David, who is twice described by the Tekoite as being like "an angel of God" (vv.17, 20).

16 The NIV's "is trying" is supplied *ad sensum* as in the LXX and Vulgate (for details cf. *BHS*). It is not necessary to assume that a word has dropped out of the MT (contra Forshey, "The Construct Chain," 52 n. 14). נַחֲלַת אֱלֹהִים (*naḥᵃlat ʾᵉlōhîm*, "the inheritance of God") is rendered "the inheritance of (one's) ancestors" by Lewis, 178 n. 14. But although it is true that *ʾᵉlōhîm* occasionally refers to human beings (cf. BDB, 43, for examples), translations other than "God/god(s)" should be resorted to only when all else fails.

19 In context the NIV's "no one" is a possible translation of the MT's אִשׁ (*ʾš*), whether understood as defective writing of אִישׁ (*ʾyš*, "man"), with many MSS, or as a rare alternative spelling of יֵשׁ (*yš*, "there is"), with a few MSS (cf. *BHS* for details), as in Micah 6:10 (where, however, the NIV translates *ʾš* as a defectively written form of the verb נשׁה, *nšh*, "forget"). The latter is preferable syntactically and has the support of 4QSamuel[c], which reads *yš* (cf. Eugene C. Ulrich Jr., "4QSam[c]: A Fragmentary Manuscript of 2 Samuel 14–15 from the Scribe of the *Serek Hay-yaḥad* (1QS)," *BASOR* 235 [Summer 1979]: 1–25, esp. 6, 12). The spelling with ʾ is normal in Ugaritic and Aramaic (*ʾt*).

4QSamuel[a] and 4QSamuel[c] may now be added to the few MSS that insert א (ʾ) into its proper place (cf. *BHS*) in להשׂמא(י)ל (*lhśmʾ[y]l*, "turn ... to the left"; cf. Ulrich, "4QSam[c]: A Fragmentary Manuscript," 6, 9). The MT omits ʾ, as also in Ezekiel 21:21[16].

10. Absalom's Return to Jerusalem (14:21–33)

OVERVIEW

As a whole, ch. 14 is framed by an inclusio formed by the occurrence of "Absalom" at the end of vv.1 and 33, and the subsection consisting of vv.21–33 is bracketed by an inclusio formed in the same way. But although the name "Absalom" appears prominently in the section (being absent only from vv.22 and 26), the key player is clearly Joab, who mediates between the king and his son and is eventually the catalyst who brings about their reconciliation. Joab is the central figure in the two exchanges of direct discourse at the beginning and end of the pericope: (1) The king speaks (v.21), Joab speaks (v.22), the king speaks (v.24); (2) Absalom speaks (v.30), Joab speaks (v.31), Absalom speaks (v.32).

Like the first half of the chapter (see comment on vv.1–20), the second half appears to be structured chiastically:

A The king tells Joab to bring Absalom back (14:21)
  B The king refuses to grant Absalom a royal audience (14:22–24)
    C Absalom is described as being handsome (14:25)
      D Absalom periodically cuts his hair (14:26)
    C' Absalom's daughter is described as being beautiful (14:27)
  B' Absalom insists on a royal audience (14:28–32)
A' The king summons Absalom into his presence (14:33)

21The king said to Joab, "Very well, I will do it. Go, bring back the young man Absalom."
22Joab fell with his face to the ground to pay him honor, and he blessed the king. Joab
said, "Today your servant knows that he has found favor in your eyes, my lord the king,
because the king has granted his servant's request."
23Then Joab went to Geshur and brought Absalom back to Jerusalem. 24But the king
said, "He must go to his own house; he must not see my face." So Absalom went to his
own house and did not see the face of the king.
25In all Israel there was not a man so highly praised for his handsome appearance as
Absalom. From the top of his head to the sole of his foot there was no blemish in him.
26Whenever he cut the hair of his head—he used to cut his hair from time to time when it
became too heavy for him—he would weigh it, and its weight was two hundred shekels
by the royal standard.
27Three sons and a daughter were born to Absalom. The daughter's name was Tamar,
and she became a beautiful woman.
28Absalom lived two years in Jerusalem without seeing the king's face. 29Then Absalom sent
for Joab in order to send him to the king, but Joab refused to come to him. So he sent a second time, but he refused to come. 30Then he said to his servants, "Look, Joab's field is next to
mine, and he has barley there. Go and set it on fire." So Absalom's servants set the field on fire.
31Then Joab did go to Absalom's house and he said to him, "Why have your servants set
my field on fire?"
32Absalom said to Joab, "Look, I sent word to you and said, 'Come here so I can send you
to the king to ask, "Why have I come from Geshur? It would be better for me if I were still
there!"' Now then, I want to see the king's face, and if I am guilty of anything, let him put
me to death."
33So Joab went to the king and told him this. Then the king summoned Absalom, and
he came in and bowed down with his face to the ground before the king. And the king
kissed Absalom.

COMMENTARY

21 Although Joab may have been listening in as the woman of Tekoa wove the elaborate tapestry of her fictitious story, it is more likely that he was waiting in the wings to learn of its outcome (v.19 implies his absence from the audience room). In any case the king, impressed by the urgency and logic of the woman's arguments in her desire to save the life of her son, applies them to his own situation. David tells Joab that he will "do it" (lit., "do this thing")—that is, (give the order to) bring Absalom back from exile. Verse 21 thus serves an additional function as a transition between the two main sections of the chapter, since "do it" reprises "did this" (v.20) and anticipates "has granted [his servant's] request" (lit., "has done [his servant's] word/thing," v.22).

Since David will force Absalom to wait for a long time before allowing him to come into his presence (cf. vv.24, 28), his calling Absalom a "young man" (v.21) is doubtless more a reference to his immaturity and temperament than to his endearing qualities.

22–24 Like the Tekoite before him (cf. v.4) and Absalom after him (cf. v.33), Joab falls, "face to the ground" (v.22), before the king (see Overview to vv.1–20; v.4). The statement that Joab "blessed" David surely implies a prayer directed to God, a prayer that David would receive a divine blessing (as in Ps 72:15; for details and additional references, see *TDOT*, 2:291–92; also 1Sa 26:25 and comment). Continuing in an attitude of humility mingled with courtesy, Joab expresses his gratitude that he has "found favor in [the king's] eyes" (v.22; cf. 16:4; 1Sa 1:18; 16:22 ["pleased with"]; 20:3, 29; see also comments on 25:8 ["be favorable toward"]; 27:5), a perception suggested by the fact that David has "granted his servant's request" (see comment on "do what his servant asks" in v.15).

Through the good offices and personal mission of Joab, Absalom's three-year, self-imposed exile at Geshur in Aram (see 13:37–38 and comments) now comes to an end as he returns to Jerusalem (v.23). Not yet welcome in David's quarters or the royal court, however, Absalom must "go to his own house" within the palace precincts (v.24; see comment on 13:20). The verb "go" (*sbb*, lit., "go around") is a weak echo of "change" (*sabbēb*) in v.20 (see comment) and reflects the reality that Joab's ultimate goal remains unfulfilled. David is still not ready to allow Absalom to "see" his "face"—that is, have an audience with him (cf. Ex 10:28; the Heb. expression "and did not see the face of the king" at the end of this unit [v.24] is repeated verbatim at the beginning of the parallel unit ["without seeing the king's face," v.28]; see also the comment on 3:13 ["come into my presence," "see me"]).

25 Since he has a "handsome" father (1Sa 16:12; 17:42) and a "beautiful" sister (see comments on 13:1), it is not surprising that Absalom himself should be "handsome." Although the expression "from the top of (one's) head to the sole of (one's) foot" or its equivalent usually encompasses the range or scope of a disease or injury (cf. Lev 13:12; Dt 28:35; Job 2:7; Isa 1:6), in Absalom's case it describes his striking appearance. Like the most ideal of priests (cf. Lev 21:17–18, 21, 23 ["defect"]) or the most desirable of women (cf. SS 4:7 ["flaw"]), Absalom is totally without "blemish." Such uncommon good looks often attract fawning praise (cf. Ge 12:14–15; but contrast Pr 31:30); so handsome is Absalom that in Israel he is the most "highly praised" of all.

Adonijah, a younger son of David, will reprise various aspects of Absalom's life (cf. McCarter, "'Plots, True or False,'" 365), including the characteristic of being "handsome" (1Ki 1:6, although the Heb. term is different). A pleasing appearance, after all, was often considered to be "a prerequisite for royal leadership" (Burke O. Long, 396)—but only from a human standpoint (see 1Sa 16:7 and comment). If Absalom "is a type of David, it is a particularly hollow and romantic version, laden with posturing and public relations, and markedly heavy on the visual and superficial" (Rosenberg, 156).

26 As a child of the court, Absalom has learned to cultivate "a certain narcissism centered in the hair" (Rosenberg, 156). Refraining from cutting one's hair was an emblem of the Nazirites (cf. Nu 6:5) and, in the case of Samson, a badge of strength (cf. Jdg 16:17). For Absalom, however, it is a sign of vanity, and he therefore cuts it only when it becomes too heavy for him—probably once a year ("from time to time" is lit. "from end of days to the days"; for a similar expression rendered "year after year/each year," cf. 1Sa 1:3; 2:19; BDB, 399; see also comment on "years" in 13:23). Its weight (see NIV note), if too great to be believable, should doubtless be attributed to hyperbole rather than to scribal error (contra K&D, 412).

As the center of the chiasm in the first section of the chapter focuses on hair (see comment on v.11), so also here. What Absalom proudly considers his finest attribute will prove to be the vehicle of his ultimate downfall (cf. 18:9–15).

27 Perhaps to mock Absalom's forthcoming pretensions to royalty, the narrator notes that children "were born to" him (the phrase occurs elsewhere in the books of Samuel only in 3:2 and 5:13, where the lists of King David's children in Hebron and Jerusalem are given). Since 18:18 indicates that Absalom had no sons to carry on his name, his three unnamed sons mentioned here may have died in infancy (cf. K&D, 412; Lewis, 118). But the name of his daughter has been preserved, probably because it is the same as that of her aunt and namesake, the beautiful Tamar, Absalom's sister, whose beauty his daughter reflects (see 13:1 and comment).

It is also possible, however, that Absalom named his daughter "Tamar" for an entirely different reason: "'Tamar,' after all, is the name of the dynastic mother (Ge 38) of the Judahite line of Perez, from which both David and Absalom have sprung. In naming his daughter 'Tamar,' Absalom may be expressing his own ambition to be a dynastic founder" (Rosenberg, 159). Tamar should not be confused with Maacah, the daughter of another Absalom (cf. 1Ki 15:2, 10 and NIV note; see comment on 3:3). In terms of the literary structure of vv.21–33, the fact that Tamar is "beautiful" (v.27) matches the description of her father as "handsome" in the parallel passage (v.25; same Heb. in both verses).

28–32 Although Absalom's exile is over, he is forced to cool his heels in Jerusalem for "two years" (v.28; for the structural significance of the "two years" here and in 13:23 and the "three years" of 13:38, see Overview to 13:1–22) before being invited to see "the king's face" (for the meaning of this phrase and its importance with respect to its parallel unit, see comment on v.24). The literary subsection under consideration (vv.28–32) is delimited by the phrases "without seeing the king's face" in v.28 and "I want to see the king's face" in v.32.

No more persuasive with Joab (v.29) than he had earlier been with David (cf. 13:25), Absalom decides to take drastic measures. In an act reminiscent of that of Samson against the Philistines (cf. Jdg 15:3–6), he instructs his servants to torch a nearby field belonging to Joab (v.30) as a means of not only getting his attention but also of getting even for being slighted by him. "Perhaps the parallel with Samson [cf. also v.26 and comment] is meant to foreshadow Absalom's fate as a powerful leader whose imprudence brings him to an early death" (Alter, *The David Story*, 280). The loss of an entire crop of barley was a tragedy in ancient times (cf. Ex 9:28–31; Joel 1:11), even in the best of circumstances. On the basis of the Mosaic law (cf. Ex 22:6), Joab would have every right to demand adequate compensation, especially since the fire was set deliberately.

If Joab's indignant reaction (v.31) is understandable, Absalom has a ready answer. Joab has been unresponsive to Absalom's repeated pleas for his mediation, leaving Absalom with few alternatives. Unless the king grants him an audience soon, he might as well never have left Geshur (v.32; cf. v.23 in the parallel passage) in the first place (cf. similarly Ex 14:11–12; 16:3; 17:3; Nu 11:5, 18, 20; 14:2–4; 20:3–5; 21:4–5; Jdg 6:13). Echoing verbatim the earlier words of his father to his friend Jonathan ("if I am guilty"; see 1Sa 20:8 and comment), Absalom declares himself ready to be "put ... to death"—and thus he unwittingly reprises the penalty that the wise woman of Tekoa knew would be incurred by her only surviving "son" because of his alleged fratricide (cf. v.7).

33 The three chief players (the king, Joab, Absalom) in the beginning of the drama (v.21) come together again at its end (v.33). Joab, suitably chastened by Absalom's rebuke, submits to his request and relays his desires to David. Summoned to the court, Absalom prostrates himself with his "face to the ground" (see Overview to vv.1–20). He wanted to see "the king's face" (v.32), and now he gets his wish. He humbles himself "before the king" (lit., "to the king's face"). But perhaps Absalom also gets the last laugh, at least for a while; although he "bowed down" to King David and then was "kissed" by the king (who acts according to royal protocol and not as Absalom's father; cf. 19:39), David's subjects will soon "bow down" before Absalom himself, who will then "kiss" them (15:5). Absalom will thus steal the hearts of the men of Israel (cf. 15:6) as a first step on his march to his father's throne.

NOTES

26 "The royal standard" is literally "the stone of the king" (אֶבֶן הַמֶּלֶךְ, *ʾeben hammelek*), in which "stone" refers to a specific weight (cf. "stone" as a fourteen-pound weight in the modern British system). Stones of various sizes, carefully polished and often sculpted and/or inscribed, were used as sets of weights in ancient times and frequently turn up in archaeological excavations. The phrase אבני מלכא (*ʾbny mlkʾ*, lit., "the stones of the king") occurs frequently in *Aramaic Papyri Discovered at Assuan* (ed. A. H. Sayce; London: Alexander Moring, 1906; cf. A 7; B 14–15; C 15; D 14, 21; F 10; G 5, 6–7, 9, 10, 14–15, 34–35, 36; H 15; J 16).

30 4QSamuel[c] exhibits two divergences from the MT that are of interest. Instead of ולו (*wlw*, "and he has"), the Qumran text reads ולוא (*wlwʾ*, "but there was no"; cf. Ulrich, "4QSam[c]: A Fragmentary Manuscript," 7 [see Note on 14:19]; some MT MSS have ולא, *wlʾ*; cf. *BHS*), implying that Joab's barley field contained only stubble when it was set on fire. But torched barley stalks make Joab's reaction (v.31) much more understandable, and the MT's *wlw* gains credence in light of the second of the significant Qumran readings in v.30. 4QSamuel[c] appends to the verse an entire sentence (cf. also LXX), which translates literally as follows: "Joab's young men went to him with their garments torn and said, 'Absalom's servants set the field on fire.'" Since the young men's statement duplicates the last sentence of v.30 in the MT, some assume that the MT omitted the 4QSamuel[c] material by haplography (cf. Ulrich, "4QSam[c]: A Fragmentary Manuscript," 14). The characteristic terseness of Hebrew prose, however, advises caution in such matters. (The NAB is the only recent English version that includes the Qumran reading.)

11. Absalom's Conspiracy (15:1–12)

OVERVIEW

Chapters 15–20 constitute the major part of the longest definable literary section (chs. 13–20; more precisely, 13:1–20:22) of the court history of David (chs. 9–20; see Overview to 13:1–22). Unlike chs. 13–14, which exhibit for the most part a "desire/ fulfillment of desire" pattern, chs. 15–20 prefer a "departure/return" pattern. As such the section lends itself readily to chiastic analysis, variations on which are offered by most literary critics (cf. David M. Gunn, "From Jerusalem to the Jordan and Back: Symmetry in 2 Samuel xv–xx," *VT* 30/1 [1980]: 109–13). Perhaps the most satisfying attempt overall has been made by Conroy, 89:

A Rebellion breaks out (15:1–12)
  B The king's flight: meeting scenes (15:13–16:14)
    C Clash of counselors (16:15–17:23)
    C' Clash of armies (17:24–19:8)
  B' The king's return: meeting scenes (19:9–41)
A' The king returns to Jerusalem, and the final stirrings of rebellion are crushed (19:42–20:22)

My own analysis, which coincides with that reflected in the NIV's subheadings, differs from that of Conroy but nevertheless converges with his at several points:

A Absalom rebels against David (15:1–12)
  B David flees from Jerusalem (15:13–37)
    C David expresses kindness to Ziba (16:1–4)
      D Shimei curses David (16:5–14)
        E Ahithophel offers advice to Absalom (16:15–17:29)
      D' Joab's men kill Absalom (18:1–18)
    C' David mourns for Absalom (18:19–19:8)
  B' David returns to Jerusalem (19:9–43)
A' Sheba rebels against David (20:1–22)

The brief summary narrative of Absalom's rebellion against his father (15:1–12) is happily characterized as a "diptych" by Fokkelman (*Narrative Art*, 1:165). Each of its two panels (vv.1–6, 7–12) begins with a time-lapse phrase: "In the course of time" (v.1), "At the end of four years" (v.7).

[1]In the course of time, Absalom provided himself with a chariot and horses and with
fifty men to run ahead of him. [2]He would get up early and stand by the side of the road
leading to the city gate. Whenever anyone came with a complaint to be placed before the
king for a decision, Absalom would call out to him, "What town are you from?" He would
answer, "Your servant is from one of the tribes of Israel." [3]Then Absalom would say to him,
"Look, your claims are valid and proper, but there is no representative of the king to hear
you." [4]And Absalom would add, "If only I were appointed judge in the land! Then everyone
who has a complaint or case could come to me and I would see that he gets justice."

[5]Also, whenever anyone approached him to bow down before him, Absalom would
reach out his hand, take hold of him and kiss him. [6]Absalom behaved in this way toward
all the Israelites who came to the king asking for justice, and so he stole the hearts of the
men of Israel.
[7]At the end of four years, Absalom said to the king, "Let me go to Hebron and fulfill a
vow I made to the LORD. [8]While your servant was living at Geshur in Aram, I made this vow:
'If the LORD takes me back to Jerusalem, I will worship the LORD in Hebron.'"
[9]The king said to him, "Go in peace." So he went to Hebron.
[10]Then Absalom sent secret messengers throughout the tribes of Israel to say, "As
soon as you hear the sound of the trumpets, then say, 'Absalom is king in Hebron.'" [11]Two
hundred men from Jerusalem had accompanied Absalom. They had been invited as
guests and went quite innocently, knowing nothing about the matter. [12]While Absalom
was offering sacrifices, he also sent for Ahithophel the Gilonite, David's counselor, to
come from Giloh, his hometown. And so the conspiracy gained strength, and Absalom's
following kept on increasing.

COMMENTARY

1–6 In the light of 13:1 (see comment; see also Overview to 13:1–22), it might be expected that 15:1 should also begin with *way*^{e}*hî ʾaḥ*^{a}*rê-kēn* as 4QSamuel^{c} does (cf. Ulrich, "4QSam^{c}: A Fragmentary Manuscript," 7 [see Note on 14:19]) and as Ulrich insists it should (ibid., 14–15), rather than with *way*^{e}*hî mēʾaḥ*^{a}*rê kēn*. One could also argue, however, that the slight difference in the two phrases is intentionally designed not only to maintain continuity between chs. 13–14 and ch. 15 but also to signal the substantially new beginning that occurs in 15:1 (cf. Conroy, 41; see also Overview to vv.1–12). In any event, the expansive *mēʾaḥ*^{a}*rê kēn* phrase is relatively rare (see comment on 3:28) and serves in this case to carry the narrative forward chronologically.

Immediately after the introductory formula, the text reads *wayyaʿaś . . . ʾabšālôm* ("Absalom provided"), which combines with the same Hebrew phrase in v.6 (there rendered "Absalom behaved") to form an inclusio that brackets the intervening material. Absalom's providing himself with a "chariot and horses" and "men to run ahead of him" symbolizes his ambition to acquire the trappings of royalty (see 1Sa 8:11 and comment; cf. Ge 41:43; see also comment on "guards" in 1Sa 22:17) and will later (after Absalom's death) be imitated by another pretender to the throne, his younger brother Adonijah—even to the number of outrunners (cf. 1Ki 1:5).

Absalom's plan to ingratiate himself to the people of Israel is as simple as it is subtle. Early each morning he takes up a position alongside the main road leading to Jerusalem's city gate (v.2), the place where disaffected citizens expected to be able to bring their complaints for royal adjudication (cf. *AIs*, 152–53, 155; similarly Jos 20:4). He then asks such a person what town he is from, the sort of question a superior (especially a king) might be expected to ask an inferior (cf. 1:3, 13; see 1Sa 30:13 and comment).

If the plaintiff responds that he is from "one of the tribes of Israel" (v.2; see comment on "any of their rulers" in 7:7), Absalom then assures him—apparently without further ado or investigation—that his claims are valid and "proper" (v.3; cf. Pr 8:9 ["right"]). He proceeds to commiserate with the person by deploring the fact that the king has no representative on hand to "hear" the case (cf. Dt 1:16–17; Job 31:35; cf. esp. 1Ki 3:11 ["administering"])—although the wise woman of Tekoa had earlier observed that David is indeed capable of "discerning" good and evil (see comment on 14:17).

Needless to say, a solution for the plaintiff's dilemma is ready at hand: Absalom himself, he wistfully suggests ("If only," v.4; cf. 23:15 ["Oh, that someone would"]), should be appointed judge. Everyone could then come "to me" (emphatic), and he would personally see to it that justice was served. Continuing his royal posturing, Absalom proceeds to "take hold of" (probably forcibly [v.5]; see comments on "grabbed" in 2:16; 13:11) and "kiss" (cf. also 19:39) anyone who approaches him to "bow down" to him (see 14:33 and comment). In everything he does Absalom implies that he himself, and not King David, is best suited to provide the people with the "justice" (*mišpāṭ*, v.6; cf. 1Ki 3:11) they deserve (for other examples of the root *špṭ* in this section, cf. vv.2 ["decision"], 4 ["judge," "case"]; also La 3:59 ["cause"]; Nu 27:5).

By means of such behavior—now flattering, now forceful—Absalom "stole the hearts" of the men of Israel (v.6; cf. "deceived" in Ge 31:20, 26), all the while successfully concealing his subversive activity from his father (cf. v.13). Absalom's

> approaching the people prior to their reaching the court seems propagandistic, intended (1) to turn them away in their quest convinced that their suit would not be heard; (2) to raise doubts about David's competence to rule; and (3) to sow seeds of yearning for Absalom to be chief judge ... in Israel. Hence, 2 Sam 15:2–6 is not a trustworthy statement of David's fulfillment of his role as judge. It does, however, demonstrate that Absalom's desire to be "judge" in Israel was due, not to a concern about justice, but to his ambition to replace his father as chief in the land. (Bellefontaine, 59)

Nevertheless, something must have gone awry with David's rule that might serve to explain the readiness with which the people were willing to abandon him and follow his son. Noting that the title of Psalm 3 attributes its writing to David "when he fled from his son Absalom," Midrash Tanhuma calls attention to Psalm 3:2 ("Many are saying of me, 'God will not deliver him'") and then observes: "They were saying of David: '(How) can there be salvation for a man who had taken the lamb captive and slew the shepherd [referring to David's affair with Bathsheba and the murder of Uriah] and who caused Israel to fall by the sword [criticizing David's ruthless military campaigns, in which countless Israelite soldiers must have lost their lives]?'" "Taking the two reasons given ... they would account realistically for the rebellion against [David] and the recourse to the machinery prepared by Absalom and ready to hand for his forceable removal from the throne" (J. Weingreen, "The Rebellion of Absalom," *VT* 19/2 [1969]: 266; see 264 for the midrashic citation).

Absalom, of course, was by no means the only prince in ancient times to try to usurp power from his father. A striking Ugaritic parallel has been pointed out by Victor H. Matthews and Don C. Benjamin (*Old Testament Parallels: Laws and Stories from the Ancient Near East* [Mahwah, N.J.: Paulist, 1991], 205), describing Prince Yassib's challenge to King Keret:

"Listen to me carefully!" Yassib threatens:
"If enemies had invaded the land while you were ill,
They would have driven you out,
Forced you into the hills.
Your illness made you derelict:
You did not hear the case of the widow,
You did not hear the case of the poor,
You did not sentence the oppressor,
You did not feed the orphan in the city,
... nor the widow in the country....
Step down from the kingship,
Allow me to reign.
Relinquish your power,
Let me sit on your throne."

Substitute "Absalom" for "Yassib" in the first line, and the parallel becomes immediately transparent.

7–12 After he has lived in Jerusalem for four years, Absalom decides that the time has finally come for him to seize the kingdom. As a way of masking his true intentions, he asks David for permission to go to Hebron, where he intends to "fulfill a vow" (v.7; cf. Pss 50:14; 66:13; 116:14, 18) that he had made to the Lord. David Marcus (*Jephthah and His Vow* [Lubbock, Tex.: Texas Tech, 1986], 19–21) observes that Absalom's vow (vv.7–8) and the four other examples of vows recorded in the OT (Jacob's [Ge 28:20–22]; Israel's [Nu 21:2]; Jephthah's [Jdg 11:30–31]; Hannah's [1Sa 1:11]) share several characteristics:

1. Each is preceded by an introduction that contains the verb *ndr* ("to vow") and its cognate accusative (in this case "a vow I made," v.7; cf. also "I made this vow," v.8).
2. The deity to whom the vow is addressed is named (here "the LORD," v.7).
3. A form of the verb "to say" introduces the vow proper (here *lēʾmōr* [v.8], rendered in this case simply as a colon).
4. A protasis introduced by "if" (v.8) contains (except for Jacob's vow) an infinitive absolute plus the finite verb in the imperfect (here *yāšôb yᵉšîbēnî*, "[ever] takes me back," v.8).
5. An apodosis is expressed by the perfect consecutive (here *wᵉᶜābadtî*, "I will worship," v.8—that is, Absalom promises to offer sacrifices to the Lord in Hebron [cf. v.12]).

The statement that Absalom desires to go to "Hebron" (v.7), a city that figures largely in this passage (vv.8–10), reminds the reader that David had earlier been anointed king over Israel there (cf. 5:3). During the three years Absalom was "at Geshur in Aram" (v.8) he may have been attempting to drum up support among his eastern allies (see 13:38 and comment), looking forward to the time when he would rebel against his father. David, apparently unsuspecting (cf., however, Wiseman, "'Is It Peace?'" 324), tells his son to "go in peace" (v.9), a cordial expression of farewell (see comment on 1Sa 29:7) that perhaps in this case also includes a promise of safe conduct (cf. v.27; see comment on 3:21).

Meanwhile Absalom sends "secret messengers" (v.10; cf. Nu 21:32 ["spies"]; 1Sa 26:4 ["scouts"]) throughout Israel. Their mission is to alert the various tribal territories that a prearranged signal ("the sound of the trumpets") is their mandate to declare Absalom king of Israel. A large contingent of men from Jerusalem, unsuspecting of Absalom's true intentions, has accompanied him to Hebron (v.11).

If the Lord's earlier reminder to Samuel to sacrifice a heifer in conjunction with the anointing of David was not a pretext to distract the rejected Saul (see 1Sa 16:2 and comment), the same cannot be said for Absalom's offering of sacrifices (v.12) in connection with a supposed vow that he had previously made (see comments on vv.7–8). Realizing that if his designs on Israel's throne are to have any chance of success he will need all the expert advice he can get, he sends for David's own counselor, Ahithophel.

Ahithophel means "My brother is foolishness" (cf. v.31, where, however, a different Heb. root is used), the latter element of which is vocalized like *bōšet* ("shame"; see comment on the name Ish-Bosheth, "Man of Shame," in 2:8). The scribal treatment of Ahithophel's name alludes "to his 'shameful' role as a deserter to Absalom and his death in degradation, 17:23" (Carlson, 252). Ahithophel's son Eliam (cf. 23:34) is doubtless to be identified with Bathsheba's father (see 11:3 and comment), and it is therefore understandable that "as Bathsheba's grandfather he [Ahithophel] was an enemy of David" (Hugo Gressmann, "The Oldest History Writing in Israel," in *Narrative and Novella in Samuel: Studies by Hugo Gressman and Other Scholars 1906–23*, ed. David M. Gunn [JSOTSup 116; Sheffield: Almond Press, 1991], 39).

Years before, David had experienced the exhilaration of growing "stronger and stronger, while the house of Saul grew weaker and weaker" (3:1). Now, however, the shoe is on the other foot. To David's detriment, the evil alliance of Absalom's ambition and Ahithophel's advice makes it inevitable that Absalom's following will continue to increase (v.12).

NOTES

7 Since the MT's "forty" is contextually impossible, the reading "four," attested in several ancient witnesses (see NIV note), surely represents the original text (cf. K&D, 415–16).

8 Although the infinitive absolute יָשׁוֹב (*yāšôb*) and the following verb יְשִׁיבֵנִי (*yᵉšîbēnî*) are from two different roots (*yšb* and *šwb* respectively), the phenomenon is not unique to this text; compare אָסֹף אָסֵף (*ʾāsōp ʾāsēp*, "I will sweep away" [Zep 1:2]), in which the root of the first verb is *ʾsp* and the second *swp*. In Zephaniah 1:2 the infinitive absolute *ʾāsōp* was "chosen for assonance" (BDB, 692), and the same considerations were doubtless in view here as well.

Not in the MT, "in Hebron" is nevertheless at least implied in the context to avoid the impression that Absalom intends to worship the Lord in Jerusalem. The phrase in fact appears in some MSS of the LXX (see NIV note) in its Lucianic recension (cf. Driver, Mauchline, McCarter, Smith).

12 Since the idiom "sent for" requires the addition of a form of קרא (*qrʾ*, "called") to שלח (*šlḥ*, "sent"; cf. 1Sa 22:11), the apparent supralinear restoration of ויקרא (*wyqrʾ*) after וישלח (*wyšlḥ*) in 4QSamuel[c] (cf. Ulrich, "4QSam[c]: A Fragmentary Manuscript," 8, 16) probably reproduces the original text (cf. also LXX's καὶ ἐκάλεσεν, *kai ekalesen*; the MT lacks *wyqrʾ*).

The hometown of Ahithophel "the Gilonite" was Giloh, a town in the hill country of Judah (cf. Jos 15:48, 51). Although its exact location remains unknown, its association with Anab, Eshtemoh, and Anim (Jos 15:50), all of which were located south of Hebron, places it in that general vicinity, perhaps "at the southernmost end of the Judean mountains, close to the northern Negev" (Amihai Mazar, "Giloh: An Early Israelite Settlement Site Near Jerusalem," *IEJ* 31/1–2 [1981]: 2). In any event, Ahithophel's hometown is not the site of the same name near Jerusalem that has recently been undergoing excavation (for which cf. ibid., 1–36).

12. *David's Flight (15:13–37)*

OVERVIEW

A narrative whose main subject is fleeing is likely to contain a large number of verbs of motion, and these verses are no exception. The most important of them are *ʿbr* ("pass by, cross over, move on, march"), which occurs nine times (vv.18 [2x], 22 [2x], 23 [3x], 24 ["leaving"], 33 ["go"]); *šwb* ("return, go back") eight times (vv.19, 20, 20 ["take"], 25 ["take," "bring ... back"], 27, 29 ["took ... back"], 34); *bwʾ* ("come, enter, arrive") seven times (vv.13, 18 ["accompanied"], 20, 28, 32, 37 [2x]); and *hlk* ("go, walk, come") seven times (vv.14 ["leave"], 19, 20 [3x, two of which are rendered as portions of other idioms in the interests of English style], 22, 30 ["was barefoot," lit., "was walking barefoot"]).

In his discussion of the court history of David, Wharton, 353, makes an especially noteworthy observation concerning vv.13–37:

> All the utterly real issues between people and people and between God and people that swirl throughout 2 Samuel 9–20, 1 Kings 1–2 also swirl about Jesus as he moves toward the cross. One must think that the Gospel writers were acutely aware of this when they depicted Jesus' Maundy Thursday walk to the Mount of Olives in ways so graphically reminiscent of the "passion" of the first *Meshiach* in 2 Samuel 15:13–37. Even the detail of Judas' betrayal of Jesus, and his subsequent suicide, have no remote parallel anywhere in Scripture, with the remarkable exception of Ahithophel, who betrayed the Lord's anointed and thus opened the door to suicidal despair (2 Samuel 17:23).

The literary unit divides naturally into four roughly equal sections. A paragraph summarizing the preparations for and the beginning of the flight (vv.13–18) is followed by David's instructions to three of his supporters, one at the outset of the journey (Ittai [vv.19–23]) and the other two en route (Zadok [vv.24–31] and Hushai [vv.32–37]).

13A messenger came and told David, "The hearts of the men of Israel are with Absalom."
14Then David said to all his officials who were with him in Jerusalem, "Come! We must flee, or none of us will escape from Absalom. We must leave immediately, or he will move quickly to overtake us and bring ruin upon us and put the city to the sword."
15The king's officials answered him, "Your servants are ready to do whatever our lord the king chooses."
16The king set out, with his entire household following him; but he left ten concubines
to take care of the palace. 17So the king set out, with all the people following him, and they
halted at a place some distance away. 18All his men marched past him, along with all the Kerethites and Pelethites; and all the six hundred Gittites who had accompanied him from Gath marched before the king.

19The king said to Ittai the Gittite, "Why should you come along with us? Go back and
stay with King Absalom. You are a foreigner, an exile from your homeland. 20You came only
yesterday. And today shall I make you wander about with us, when I do not know where
I am going? Go back, and take your countrymen. May kindness and faithfulness be with
you."

21But Ittai replied to the king, "As surely as the LORD lives, and as my lord the king lives,
wherever my lord the king may be, whether it means life or death, there will your servant
be."

22David said to Ittai, "Go ahead, march on." So Ittai the Gittite marched on with all his
men and the families that were with him.

23The whole countryside wept aloud as all the people passed by. The king also crossed
the Kidron Valley, and all the people moved on toward the desert.

24Zadok was there, too, and all the Levites who were with him were carrying the ark of
the covenant of God. They set down the ark of God, and Abiathar offered sacrifices until all
the people had finished leaving the city.

25Then the king said to Zadok, "Take the ark of God back into the city. If I find favor in
the LORD's eyes, he will bring me back and let me see it and his dwelling place again. 26But
if he says, 'I am not pleased with you,' then I am ready; let him do to me whatever seems
good to him."

27The king also said to Zadok the priest, "Aren't you a seer? Go back to the city in
peace, with your son Ahimaaz and Jonathan son of Abiathar. You and Abiathar take your
two sons with you. 28I will wait at the fords in the desert until word comes from you to
inform me." 29So Zadok and Abiathar took the ark of God back to Jerusalem and stayed
there.

30But David continued up the Mount of Olives, weeping as he went; his head was
covered and he was barefoot. All the people with him covered their heads too and
were weeping as they went up. 31Now David had been told, "Ahithophel is among the
conspirators with Absalom." So David prayed, "O LORD, turn Ahithophel's counsel into
foolishness."

32When David arrived at the summit, where people used to worship God, Hushai the
Arkite was there to meet him, his robe torn and dust on his head. 33David said to him, "If
you go with me, you will be a burden to me. 34But if you return to the city and say to Absalom, 'I will be your servant, O king; I was your father's servant in the past, but now I will be
your servant,' then you can help me by frustrating Ahithophel's advice. 35Won't the priests
Zadok and Abiathar be there with you? Tell them anything you hear in the king's palace.
36Their two sons, Ahimaaz son of Zadok and Jonathan son of Abiathar, are there with
them. Send them to me with anything you hear."

37So David's friend Hushai arrived at Jerusalem as Absalom was entering the city.

COMMENTARY

13–18 *Wayyābō᾿* ("came, arrived") begins vv.13 and 37, thus becoming a part of an inclusio that brackets that literary unit. The word rendered "messenger" (v.13; cf. Jer 51:31) is a participial form of *ngd* ("tell"; cf. 18:11) and refers to one who brings a report, usually a bearer of bad news (see comment on 1:5), as in this case: The hearts of the men of Israel are now "with" Absalom; they are following him with total devotion (for the idiom, cf. 1Ki 11:4, where the heart of David's son Solomon is described as having been turned "after" other gods [same Heb. word in both cases]) because he "stole the[ir] hearts" (see v.6 and comment). Thus Israel's "gift of the kingdom to David is revoked.... The kingdom is now taken from him" (Gunn, "David and the Gift of the Kingdom," 22).

David sees no way out but to "flee" (v.14; cf. the title of Ps 3), an activity that is not new to him (cf. 1Sa 19:12, 18; 22:17)—and a cruelly ironic twist on Absalom's earlier flight from Jerusalem to escape his father (see 13:34, 37–38, and comment). To his officials David counsels the utmost speed (*mhr*, "immediately") since Absalom can be expected to "move quickly" (*mhr*). If Absalom succeeds in overtaking David and his men, they will be brought to ruin and Jerusalem will be "put ... to the sword," a terrifying fate at best (see 1Sa 22:19 and comment).

Loyal to a fault (v.15), the king's "officials" indicate that they, his "servants" (same Heb. word; see comments on 1Sa 1:11; 16:15–16), are ready to abide by whatever decision he "chooses" (*bḥr*, perhaps a deliberate wordplay on *brḥ* ["flee"] in v.14). And so it is (vv.16–17) that "the king set out, with" virtually everyone in the palace ("his entire household," v.16; "all the people," v.17) "following him." In addition to his numerous wives (see comments on 3:2; 12:8; 1Sa 25:43), David also had many concubines (see 5:13 and comment), ten of whom he leaves behind to take care of the palace (for their identification and significance see Note on 5:13; cf. also 12:11–12 and comment). Ahithophel will soon counsel the triumphant usurper, Absalom, to have sexual relations with David's concubines in full public view (cf. 16:21–22), as a result of which David will eventually put them under house arrest "till the day of their death" (20:3).

The first stop reached by the fleeing king and his retinue is a "place some distance away" (*bêt hammerḥāq*, v.17), perhaps the "last house" on the eastern edge of Jerusalem, whether inside or beyond the city walls (cf. Alter, *The David Story*, 286; further Anderson, Gordon, McCarter). David pauses temporarily as all his officials, together with his crack mercenary corps (the "Kerethites and Pelethites," v.18; see comment on 8:18), march on ahead. In addition, "six hundred" (cf. 1Sa 23:13; 27:2; 30:9; for the significance of the number, see comment on 1Sa 13:15) "Gittites" (originally citizens of the Philistine city of Gath [modern Tell es-Safi, about twenty-four miles west-southwest of Jerusalem]), doubtless also mercenaries, march before the king (cf. Herzog and Gichon, 87). By any reckoning David has a sizable and dependable military force to protect him from whatever contingency might arise from Absalom's delusions of grandeur.

19–23 The first high official in David's retinue to whom the king speaks is Ittai (v.19), the leader of the Gittite mercenaries, who is apparently considered trustworthy enough to share command of Israelite troops as well (see comment on 18:2). Apparently of Philistine origin, the name Ittai can hardly be separated from Itiya and Witiya, names of one or more governors of the Philistine city of Ashkelon who appear in several Amarna letters written almost four centuries before the time of

David (cf. M. Delcor, "Les Kerethim et les Cretois," *VT* 28/4 [1978]: 412–13). Since the name is non-Semitic, it does not mean "(God is) with me" or the like. Although *ʾittay* ("Ittai") is found in association with *ʾittānû* ("with us," v.19) and *ʾittô* ("with him," v.22), the appearance of the alternative forms *ʿimmānû* ("with us") and *ʿimmāk* ("with you," v.20) at a greater distance from "Ittai" perhaps make it more likely that the *ʾitt-* forms are wordplays than that they are attempts to define the name.

Polzin ("Curses and Kings," 204), however, argues rather forcefully that the "narrative role of Ittai,... whose very name suggests 'loyalty' or 'companion', *is to be with David wherever he goes*" (italics his). Polzin's subsequent attempts (ibid., 204–6) to make similar narrative capital out of the names of Zadok and Hushai, however, are less convincing.

Addressing Ittai, David wants to know why "you" (v.19), of all people (the pronoun being emphatic), would wish to accompany him in his flight. "The king" (David) recommends that Ittai return to Jerusalem and stay with "the king" (thus the MT; the NIV renders "King Absalom" to resolve the ambiguity [cf., however, Alter, *The David Story*, 287]). It would seem that David considers Absalom's coup d'état is a fait accompli (cf. v.34). Ittai has nothing to gain and everything to lose by remaining with David. After all, he is already a displaced person from his Philistine homeland. Because of Ittai's recent arrival on the scene, David is reluctant to make him "wander about" (v.20; cf. Ps 59:11), like the Israelites in the Sinai desert (cf. Nu 32:13), on a journey of uncertain destination. Commending him to the "kindness and faithfulness" of God (for the importance of this phrase to covenantal relationships, see 2:6 and comment), he therefore commands him to return to Jerusalem with his fellow Gittites.

Not to be dissuaded, however, Ittai takes the most solemn of oaths (v.21; see comments on 11:11; 1Sa 14:39; 20:3; 25:26) as he swears undying loyalty to David. Like Ruth before him in a similar situation (cf. Ru 1:16–17), Ittai pledges that he will never leave the king, whether in "life or death" (a Deuteronomic phrase [cf. Dt 30:15, 19]; here, however, lit., "whether for death or for life": "Given the grim circumstances, this loyal soldier unflinchingly puts death before life in the two alternatives he contemplates" [Alter, *The David Story*, 287]). And as in the case of Naomi (cf. Ru 1:18), David—however reluctantly—honors Ittai's determination and agrees to let him march on, together with all his men and "the families" that are with him (lit., "all the children" [v.22], the latter term serving here as synecdoche; for details and additional references see *TDOT*, 5:348–49).

Whatever problems certain citizens of Jerusalem and other towns may have with David (see comment on v.6), people living in the countryside see him in a different light. He is their king—and as he and his followers pass by, the people weep "aloud" (v.23; cf. 1Sa 28:12 ["at the top of her voice"]) as an expression of their fear for an uncertain future. Prefiguring the passion of another anointed King centuries later (cf. Jn 18:1), David crosses the Kidron Valley, a stream bed east of Jerusalem that is dry most of the year. Large numbers of his followers continue on toward the northern part of the desert of Judah, with David and his immediate retainers apparently moving along at a somewhat slower pace (cf. 16:1). Just as vv.30–31 serve as a transition between David's conversations with Zadok and Hushai, so also v.23 serves as a natural segue from David's discussion with Ittai to that with Zadok.

24–31 Sharing priestly duties during at least part of the reign of David, Zadok and Abiathar (v.24; 20:25; for details see comments on 8:17; 1Sa 22:20) decide to accompany him on his flight from Jerusalem. Not wanting to leave the ark of the covenant in the city and perhaps trusting in its supposed powers as a military palladium if war should break out (see 1Sa 4:3–4 and comment), Levites carry it (see comments on 6:13; 1Sa 6:15) across the Kidron. As during another procession of the ark (see 6:13 and comment), the Levites halt long enough for sacrifices to be offered. The ceremony continues until all the refugees have left Jerusalem (cf. similarly Jos 3:17; 4:11).

David's instructions to Zadok are divided into two parts, the first having to do with the return of the ark to Jerusalem (vv.25–26) and the second with the role of Zadok and Abiathar as listening posts there to keep David informed of important developments concerning Absalom's burgeoning rebellion (vv.27–29). Sensing no need for the ark to accompany him, David directs Zadok to take it back to the city (v.25). Like Gideon (cf. Jdg 6:17), he hopes to "find favor in the LORD's eyes" (cf. also Ge 6:8). Indeed, he is prepared to resign himself to the will of God, to whatever seems good "to him" (lit., "in his eyes," v.26).

David is confident that if the Lord so chooses, he will bring him back to Jerusalem to see again not only the ark in its proper setting but also the Lord's "dwelling place" (v.25), probably in this context a reference to the city itself (cf. Isa 33:20, where Jerusalem is called a peaceful "abode" [same Heb. word in both cases]). But if the Lord declares that he is not "pleased" with David (v.26)—unlike during his many experiences of fleeing from his enemies, when he reveled in the fact that the Lord "delighted" in him (22:20; same Heb. word)—he will accept that also with equanimity.

Like the Gibeonites in the presence of Joshua (cf. Jos 9:25, the wording of which is echoed here), David is "ready" to throw himself on the mercy of the court. (The equivalent of *hinenî* ["I am ready"], the characteristic response of the servant [often translated "Here I am"; cf. Ge 22:1, 11], is rendered simply "We are" in Jos 9:25.) As the people of Gibeon were prepared to accept "whatever seems good" to Joshua, so David is resigned to "whatever seems good" to the Lord.

In vv.27–28 (David's second statement to Zadok), he begins with a form of the verb *rʾh* ("see"; GK 8011; *reʾû* ["See"] at the beginning of v.28 is omitted from the NIV in the interests of style). Although "Aren't you a seer?" (v.27) is a possible translation of *hrwʾh ʾth* (for the role of a seer in ancient Israel, see 1Sa 9:9 and comment), the Hebrew phrase is not stated negatively. In addition, the presence of *rʾw* in v.28 (the same word as is translated "Listen!" in 13:28) makes it likely that the two expressions should be understood in the same way. "Do you see?" (in the sense of an imperative "see, look") would parallel nicely the "see" that begins v.28 (for a similar example compare *hrʾh ʾth* ["do you see," Eze 8:6] with *hrʾyt* ["do you see, have you seen"] in the same context [Eze 8:12, 15, 17]; cf. 1Sa 10:24; 17:25).

If it be argued that Zadok is here called a "seer" because his divinely imparted knowledge will enable him to "inform" David (v.28), it is necessary to point out that (1) ordinary human knowledge is sufficient to "inform" (the verb, a participial form of which occurs in v.13 ["messenger"; see comment], commonly means simply "tell"); (2) more than one person will "inform" David (the "you" before "to inform" is plural); (3) when "Zadok does inform David, it is because he in his turn is informed by Hushai (2 Sam. xvii 15), not because of Zadok's position as oracle priest" (J. Hoftijzer, "A Peculiar Question: A Note on 2 Sam. xv 27," *VT* 21/5 [1971]: 607; for additional details see 606–9).

Zadok will be of more help to David back in Jerusalem than if he flees with him, so David tells him to return to the city with his son Ahimaaz and Abiathar's son Jonathan (v.27). "Ahimaaz" and "Jonathan" have occurred already in the books of Samuel as the names of other men (1Sa 13:2; 14:50). (Zadok's son Ahimaaz as well as Abiathar have been suggested as possible authors of David's court history [see comments on 9:1–20:26].) The specificity (and perhaps also the urgency) of David's request is underscored by his addendum: "your [plural] two sons with you [plural]" (v.27; the NIV prefaces the phrase with "you and Abiathar take" to clarify in English the Heb. intention). David wants to make sure that Zadok understands that the two priests and their two sons—all four of them—are to return to Jerusalem.

As for David himself, he will continue on his way and wait at the "fords [reading *ᶜabrôt* with the *Kethiv*; cf. 17:16, where many MSS likewise read *ᶜabrôt* (cf. *BHS*) instead of *ᶜarbôt* (thus *Qere* in v.28), "steppes"] in the desert" (v.28) on the west bank of the Jordan (cf. 17:16; further 19:18). Although the exact site is unknown, "fords" is a more likely reading than "steppes" because "it gives a more specific location for the purpose of passing on the information" (Anderson, 201). David expects Zadok and Abiathar to be involved together in gathering data about Absalom's plans ("you" in v.28 is plural). Following David's instructions (v.29), the two men "took" (the verb is singular, stressing Zadok's primary responsibility) the ark back to Jerusalem (cf. vv.25–26) and "stayed" (plural) there (cf. vv.27–28).

After dismissing Zadok and Abiathar, David ascends the storied hill east of Jerusalem (cf. 1Ki 11:7; Eze 11:23), the Mount of Olives (v.30)—eventually linked to Jesus' triumphal entry (cf. Lk 19:29, 37), his teaching ministry (the so-called Olivet discourse; cf. Mk 13:3), his agony at Gethsemane (cf. Lk 22:39), his ascension (cf. Ac 1:11–12), and his second advent (cf. Zec 14:4). Facing the eminence on which Solomon's temple was later built, the Mount of Olives is about twenty-seven hundred feet high and rises about two hundred feet above the city itself. As David and the people with him climb the hill, they express their sorrow and sense of love by "weeping" (v.30) and their despair and sense of foreboding by covering their heads (cf. Est 6:12; 7:8; Jer 14:3–4). In addition, David walks barefoot to symbolize the shameful exile on which he is now embarking (cf. Isa 20:2–3; similarly Mic 1:8).

"Uneasy lies the head that wears a crown," wrote William Shakespeare (*King Henry IV*, part 2, 3.1.31). A harried king feels surrounded by conspirators (cf. v.12; see comment on 1Sa 22:8, 13), and David's intelligence network (see 10:5 and comment) informs David that Ahithophel (see v.12 and comment) is among them (cf. v.31). The news alarms David, and he turns to God for help with the prayer: "O LORD, turn Ahithophel's counsel into foolishness" (v.31; cf. Isa 44:25 ["nonsense"]).

> It was clear to David ... that Ahithophel as counsellor of the king not only held one of the highest court positions of confidence but also that whoever had the benefit of his advice in political or military matters would be successful.... This makes all the more understandable why David appealed as a last resort to the only power he thought able to intervene and to disqualify the counsel of a man considered practically infallible. (Roth, "A Study of *skl*," 71)

32–37 The summit of the Mount of Olives was a place "where people used to worship God" (v.32)—and where false gods would later be worshiped (cf. 1Ki 11:7). Upon arriving there David finds Hushai the Arkite waiting to "meet" him (*qrʾ*; cf. also 16:1), his robe "torn" (*qrᶜ*; the wordplay is perhaps intentional), and dust on his head (signs of anguish and distress; see comments on 1:2; 13:19; 1Sa 4:12). Hushai's clan, the Arkites (*ʾarkî*), lived near Ataroth (cf. Jos 16:2) "in NE Ephraim on the border with Manasseh" (Rasmussen, 227) and should not be confused with the Arkites (*ᶜarqî*), who were one of the ten traditional tribal groups in the Canaanite orbit (cf. Ge 10:17) and who lived in Arqat ("Irqata" in the Amarna letters; for details see Youngblood, *The Amarna Correspondence*, 104–5), modern Tell Arqa (about 120 miles north-northeast of the Sea of Galilee).

As in the case of Zadok and Abiathar (cf. vv.24–29), David is convinced that Hushai will be of more value to him back in Jerusalem than as a fellow refugee. Hushai will only be a "burden" to the king if he accompanies him (v.33; cf. 19:35 for Barzillai's perceptive self-evaluation in the parallel section; also Nu 11:11, 17; Job 7:20). David therefore tells Hushai to return to the city and promise Absalom the same kind of faithful service that he had already given to David himself (v.34). By becoming a member of Absalom's inner council, Hushai will be able to assist David by "frustrating" Ahithophel's advice (a not uncommon role of competent and clever counselors in ancient times; cf. Ezr 4:5).

David had already prayed that the Lord would turn Ahithophel's "counsel" into foolishness (v.31), and now he is convinced that Hushai can be a divinely empowered instrument to accomplish the goal of "frustrating" (and so it would be; cf. 17:14) Ahithophel's "advice" (v.34; same Heb. word as that for "counsel" in v.31). Hushai thus becomes a key link in David's resources of "statecraft and espionage in order to counter the sagacity of Ahithophel" (McKane, 57).

Zadok and Abiathar are to be David's eyes and ears in the palace while the king is fleeing (see v.28 and comment), and he wants Hushai to collaborate with them by telling them anything he hears there (v.35; "you hear" is singular). The three men will then send the priests' two sons to David with whatever helpful information they have been able to gather (v.36; "send" and "you hear" are plural). And so it is that Absalom, the king's treasonous son, and Hushai, the king's loyal "friend" (v.37; 16:16; see Notes below), arrive at Jerusalem simultaneously.

NOTES

19 לִמְקוֹמֶךָ (*limqômekā*, "from your homeland") provides an excellent example of לְ־ (*l-*) in the sense of "from," as the ancient versions understood it here (cf. *BHS*; for other examples, see Mitchell Dahood, "Hebrew-Ugaritic Lexicography IV," *Bib* 47/3 [1966]: 406).

23 "Toward the desert" translates עַל־פְּנֵי־דֶרֶךְ אֶת־הַמִּדְבָּר (*ʿal-pᵉnê-derek ʾet-hammidbār*, lit., "over the face of the road/direction of the desert"). The particle אֶת־ (*ʾet-*), whether it here means "with" or is understood as the sign of the definite accusative, is without analogy. Driver and others therefore assume it to be a scribal error for זַיִת (*zayit*, "olive"), on the basis of the Lucianic recension of the LXX, and *derek (haz)zayit* is then read "the Olive Way" (McCarter, *II Samuel*, 333). But the difficulty in the MT is relieved considerably if *ʾet-* is omitted (with many MSS) or if אֶל־ (*ʾel-*, "to, toward") is read in its place (with two MSS; cf. *BHS*). Emendation is thus unnecessary.

24 וַיַּעַל (*wayyaʿal*) in the Qal would mean "went up" (see NIV note), while in the Hiphil it can mean "offered (sacrifices)" even without an object (cf. 24:22; in 1Sa 2:28 "go up to my altar" can also be rendered alternatively "offer sacrifices on my altar"). The NIV's textual reading "offered sacrifices" is surely correct here, since "went up" would be contextually awkward (for details cf. Hertzberg, 343 n. a; Fokkelman, *Narrative Art*, 1:455).

34 For a detailed study of the differences in vv.34–35 between the MT, LXX, and Lucianic recension of the LXX, see Julio Trebolle, "Espías contra consejeros en la revuelta de Absalón (II Sam., xv, 34–36): Historia de la recensión como Método," *RB* 86/4 (1979): 524–43. Although McCarter (*II Samuel*, 367) accepts the lengthy LXX addition in v.34, Anderson (201) wisely advises caution.

37 "Friend" (*rēʿeh*) is used here and in 16:16, not in the sense of "acquaintance," but as a technical term for an important cabinet post (see comment on 13:3). The Hebrew word is rendered "personal adviser" in 1 Kings 4:5, and Hushai himself is called the king's "friend" in a list of David's officials (1Ch 27:33; cf. NIV note on 1Ki 1:8; for discussion, see McCarter, *II Samuel*, 372).

13. Kindness to Ziba (16:1–4)

OVERVIEW

David now encounters Ziba (vv.1–4), the first of two men with links to the house of Saul (the other being Shimei [vv.5–14]). Although Ziba attempts to ingratiate himself to David and Shimei curses him, David treats each with courtesy. The brief account of the king's kindness to Ziba has obvious connections with the narrative of his kindness to Mephibosheth (ch. 9), many of which will be noted below. Chapter 16 begins "a short distance beyond the summit" (v.1) and ends "on the roof" of the palace in Jerusalem (v.22)—two spatial high points whose significance is explored by Polzin ("Curses and Kings," 216–17). The first verse establishes the backdrop for the next three, each of which begins with *wayyōʾmer hammelek* ("And/Then the king said/asked").

1 When David had gone a short distance beyond the summit, there was Ziba, the steward of Mephibosheth, waiting to meet him. He had a string of donkeys saddled and loaded with two hundred loaves of bread, a hundred cakes of raisins, a hundred cakes of figs and a skin of wine.

2 The king asked Ziba, "Why have you brought these?"

Ziba answered, "The donkeys are for the king's household to ride on, the bread and fruit are for the men to eat, and the wine is to refresh those who become exhausted in the desert."

3 The king then asked, "Where is your master's grandson?"

Ziba said to him, "He is staying in Jerusalem, because he thinks, 'Today the house of Israel will give me back my grandfather's kingdom.'"

4 Then the king said to Ziba, "All that belonged to Mephibosheth is now yours."

"I humbly bow," Ziba said. "May I find favor in your eyes, my lord the king."

COMMENTARY

1 Proceeding beyond the summit of the Mount of Olives, David is met (see 15:32 and comment) by Ziba (see comment on 9:2), the steward of Saul's grandson Mephibosheth (cf. 9:6; see Notes on 4:4). Ziba's entourage includes donkeys loaded with all kinds of provisions, items especially suited for men on the march. Apparently Ziba wants to demonstrate his loyalty to David. Although *ṣemed* normally means "two" (cf. Jdg 19:3, 10), "pair of" (cf. 1Sa 11:7), the NIV's rendering "string of" is probably contextually preferable here (since v.2 seems to demand more than two donkeys) and receives support from the somewhat broad usage of Akkadian cognates *ṣimdu*, *ṣimittu* (cf. *CAD*, 16:197–99).

The foodstuffs for David and his men assembled years before by Abigail (see 1Sa 25:18 and comments) surpassed in amount and variety those described here, but Ziba's gift is nonetheless generous—even though it may have come from Mephibosheth's resources rather than his own (cf. Brueggemann, *First and Second Samuel*, 305–6). Indeed, Mephibosheth will later claim that he himself had "saddled" a donkey so that he might join David in his flight from Absalom—unlike the pretentious use made of "saddled" donkeys by the conniving Ziba, whom Mephibosheth will accuse of having "betrayed" him (19:26).

2–4 Suspicious either of Ziba's motives or of the origin of the supplies he has brought, David asks, "Why have you brought these?" (lit., "What are these to/for you?" v.2; cf. similarly Ge 33:5, 8; Eze 37:18). Ziba deftly dodges the question of whether he has a right to bring them and concentrates instead on their purposes, all of which are good and proper: The donkeys are for the king's household to ride on (and are therefore doubtless more than two in number; see comment on v.1; see also 1Sa 25:20 and comment), and the foodstuffs are for nourishment and refreshment. The Hebrew word for "fruit" in v.2 is the same as that for "figs" in v.1, the NIV probably understanding the word in v.2 as encompassing the raisins and figs in v.1. People on an arduous journey quickly become "exhausted" and need special attention (v.2; cf. Jdg 8:4, 15), particularly if they are fleeing for their lives. Ziba, whatever his ulterior motives may be, declares his willingness to help.

Still skeptical, David wants to know where Mephibosheth is (v.3), perhaps to speak directly to him to find out whether Ziba is telling the truth. Ziba's response—later indignantly denied by Mephibosheth (cf. 19:26–28)—is that the latter has decided to stay in Jerusalem in the belief that the house of Israel will return the kingdom (for a similar false hope, cf. 1Ki 12:21 = 2Ch 11:1) to the house of Saul and therefore to Mephibosheth himself. David had earlier agreed to "restore" to Mephibosheth all the land that belonged to Saul (see 9:7 and comment), but he had never agreed to "give ... back" Saul's kingdom to him (v.3; same Heb. verb). Apparently Ziba either did not know or did not care that the kingdom of Israel had long ago been torn from Saul by divine decree and given to David (see 1Sa 15:27–28 and comments). In any case, Ziba attributes to Mephibosheth words whose genuineness it is impossible to verify.

For the moment at least, David chooses to believe Ziba (v.4). Without hearing the other side of the story, David punishes Mephibosheth in absentia by giving Ziba everything that formerly belonged to his master. Not unexpectedly, Ziba's response is servile: "I humbly bow." Mephibosheth has taught him well (cf. 9:6, 8).

NOTE

3 Wordplay between ישׁב (*yšb*) and שׁוב (*šwb*), noted already in 15:8 (see Notes), occurs also in 16:3 ("is staying," "give ... back"; cf. Conroy, 121, who appropriately cites 15:19 ["go back," "stay"] and 15:29 ["took ... back," "stayed"] as well).

14. Shimei's Curse (16:5–14)

OVERVIEW

The second Saulide encountered by David in ch. 16 (see Overview to vv.1–4) is Shimei, whose reaction to the king is diametrically opposite to that of Ziba. While the latter is ingratiating and submissive, Shimei is insulting and defiant.

The chiastic structure of the literary unit is exquisite, as demonstrated by Ridout, 56–70, and amplified by Walter Brueggemann ("On Coping with Curse," 177) (the titles of the sections are my own):

A David approaches Bahurim (16:5a)
  B Shimei pelts David with stones (16:5b–6)
    C Shimei curses David (16:7–8)
      D Abishai wants to kill Shimei (16:9)
    C' David accepts Shimei's curses (16:10–12)
  B' Shimei pelts David with stones (16:13)
A' David arrives at his destination (16:14)

Although Brueggemann does not organize the speeches of Shimei, Abishai, and David (vv.7–12) chiastically, such an arrangement seems transparent. The focus of the unit is thus Abishai's desire for Shimei's execution.

[5]As King David approached Bahurim, a man from the same clan as Saul's family came
out from there. His name was Shimei son of Gera, and he cursed as he came out. [6]He
pelted David and all the king's officials with stones, though all the troops and the special
guard were on David's right and left. [7]As he cursed, Shimei said, "Get out, get out, you
man of blood, you scoundrel! [8]The LORD has repaid you for all the blood you shed in the
household of Saul, in whose place you have reigned. The LORD has handed the kingdom
over to your son Absalom. You have come to ruin because you are a man of blood!"
[9]Then Abishai son of Zeruiah said to the king, "Why should this dead dog curse my lord
the king? Let me go over and cut off his head."
[10]But the king said, "What do you and I have in common, you sons of Zeruiah? If he is
cursing because the LORD said to him, 'Curse David,' who can ask, 'Why do you do this?'"
[11]David then said to Abishai and all his officials, "My son, who is of my own flesh, is trying to take my life. How much more, then, this Benjamite! Leave him alone; let him curse,

for the Lord has told him to. 12It may be that the Lord will see my distress and repay me with good for the cursing I am receiving today."

13So David and his men continued along the road while Shimei was going along the hillside opposite him, cursing as he went and throwing stones at him and showering him with dirt. 14The king and all the people with him arrived at their destination exhausted. And there he refreshed himself.

COMMENTARY

5a On the line of march of David and his party is Bahurim (for possible location see comment on 3:16). "Approached" (*ûbāʾ*) and "arrived" (*wayyābōʾ*, v.14) form a suitable inclusio to frame the intervening verses.

5b–6 Bahurim is the hometown of Shimei son of Gera (the latter name being clearly Benjamite; cf. Ge 46:21; Jdg 3:15; 1Ch 8:3, 5, 7), a member of one of the Saulide clans (v.5b). Shimei is in an ugly mood. As he comes out of the town, he curses David (cf. the parallel in v.13), much as Goliath had done years earlier (cf. 1Sa 17:43). To curse a descendant of Abraham is to invite divine retribution (cf. Ge 12:3), and Shimei's headstrong actions will not ultimately go unpunished (1Ki 2:8–9) despite his repenting of them (cf. 19:18–20). Not content with hurling curses at the king (for a fine discussion of the Deuteronomic historians' penchant for pinpointing "kings or those individuals who support them" as "favorite objects of curses," see Polzin, "Curses and Kings," 219–22)—a particularly heinous act in itself, the equivalent of blasphemy (cf. Ex 22:28)—Shimei pelts David and his officials with stones (v.6) as a palpable means of expressing his great displeasure (cf. similarly Ex 21:18). Fortunately for David, his armed escort is protecting him on all sides ("right and left," v.6; cf. similarly Ps 16:8).

7–8 The three speeches that form the center of the literary unit (Shimei's [vv.7–8]; Abishai's [v.9]; David's [vv.10–12]) contain the phrase *hēšîb yhwh* ("the Lord has repaid/will repay") twice (vv.8, 12) within the larger unit (cf. Brueggemann, "On Coping with Curse," 177). Shimei continues his curse by demanding that David get out of Benjamite territory (v.7). He refers to David not only as a "man of blood" (vv.7–8; cf. the plural form "bloodthirsty men" in Pss 5:6; 26:9; 55:23; 59:2; 139:19—ironically, all of them psalms of David; cf. also Pr 29:10 [a proverb of David's son Solomon]) but also as a "man of Belial" ("scoundrel" [NIV], v.7; see Notes on 1Sa 1:16; also comments on 1Sa 25:17, 25).

In the tradition of Nathan (cf. 12:10–12), Shimei tells David that his sins will be punished (v.8; cf. Brueggemann, "On Coping with Curse," 179). Although the referents Shimei has in mind in speaking of the "blood" that David has shed "in the household of Saul" (v.8) remain uncertain—whether "Meribaal, Abner, Ish-baal, Saul, Uriah" (Brueggemann, "On Coping with Curse," 177), or, assuming a dischronologized narrative, the seven male descendants of Saul mentioned in 21:4–6, 8–9 (cf. Hertzberg, 299, 381; Vanderkam, 537–39)—Shimei insists that David's ruin is inevitable because of it. Of course, David had earlier disavowed any responsibility for the "blood" of Abner (3:28), as one might expect (but see comment there). In addition, Shimei's curses ring somewhat hollow in the light of the fact that Saul's house itself is "blood-stained" (21:1). In any event, Shimei (and doubtless many if not most of his compatriots) are apparently ready to acknowledge David's son Absalom as their new king (v.8).

9 The focus of the present literary unit centers on Abishai's rash suggestion that Shimei should be summarily put to death. Not characterized by cautious restraint, this "son of Zeruiah" (see comment on 1Sa 26:6) is always quick to act, especially when he thinks execution is the best way to solve a problem (see 1Sa 26:8 and comment). Indeed, the present situation is not the only time Abishai will recommend that Shimei should be killed for cursing the king (cf. 19:21).

Abishai cannot understand why a "dead dog" (a reference to the lowest of animals and therefore, with or without the qualifying adjective "dead," a term of reproach and insult; cf. 3:8; 1Sa 24:14; see comments on 9:8; 1Sa 17:43; see also Notes on 1Sa 17:43) should be allowed to curse David with impunity. To get rid of a minor annoyance like Shimei, Abishai wants to "cut off his head"—the earlier fate of the Philistine Goliath (cf. 1Sa 17:46) and the Saulide Ish-Bosheth (see 4:7 and comment; for full discussion of this macabre motif see Polzin, "Curses and Kings," 222–24).

10–12 The words of Shimei's curse (vv.7–8) include his belief that God is not displeased with it (cf. v.8), and each verse of the parallel passage (vv.10–12) underscores David's conviction either that the Lord has told Shimei to curse him (vv.10–11) or that Shimei's curse finds its origin in the Lord himself (see comment on v.12).

Knowing that the "sons of Zeruiah" (v.10; cf. also 19:22) usually work in concert, David's rebuke to Abishai apparently includes his brother Joab (cf. K&D, 425; already Patrick, 503). "Sons of Zeruiah" is probably used in a disparaging or contemptuous sense here (see comments on 2:18 and 3:39; see also comments on "son of Kish" in 1Sa 10:11 and "son of Jesse" in 1Sa 20:27). "What do you and I have in common?" echoed verbatim in an identical context in 19:22, is literally "What to me and to you?" (the pronoun is plural here and in 19:22), a phrase that is often used elsewhere when the speaker senses a threat (cf. Jdg 11:12 ["What do you have against us?"]; 1Ki 17:18; 2Ch 35:21 ["What quarrel is there between you and me?"]) or lack of common purpose (cf. 2Ki 3:13 ["What do we have to do with each other?"]; cf. the Semitism in Jn 2:4 ["Why do you involve me?"] pointed out by Snaith, 14). David's long experience with God's intimate presence has taught him that if the Lord has prompted Shimei's curse, no one should question Shimei's motivation (cf. similarly Job 9:12; Ecc 8:4; further Brueggemann, "On Coping with Curse," 184), however vindictive or unworthy it might be.

Widening his audience, David now addresses not only Abishai but also "his [David's] officials" (v.11; cf. v.6). The king knows that his throne is coveted by his son, a common threat in ancient times (cf. 2Ch 32:21). The Lord's covenant with David had promised him that he would be succeeded by a son who would "come from [his] own body" (7:12; cf. Ge 15:4)—but that son would be Solomon (see comment on 7:12), not Absalom ("is of my own flesh," v.11; same Heb. in both cases). Indeed, Absalom is "trying to take [David's] life," as Saul had attempted to do on more than one occasion (see comments on 4:8; 1Sa 20:1).

It is not surprising, then, that the Saulide Shimei—"this Benjamite" (cf. 1Sa 9:21; 1Ki 2:8)—should be bent on David's ruin. But although centuries later another counselor would warn another king that it would not be in the king's best interests to "tolerate" a certain community of Jews (Est 3:8), among whom were Benjamites (cf. Est 2:5), David's mandate concerning Shimei is clear and forthright: "Leave him alone" (v.11; same Heb. verb).

Like Hannah before him (see comment on "look upon [my] misery" in 1Sa 1:11), David hopes that the Lord will "see [his] distress" (v.12; same Heb. idiom) and "repay" him with good—the opposite of what Shimei's curse intends (cf. "has repaid" in v.8). The "good" that David yearns for (v.12) is perhaps a reflection on the contents of the Lord's covenant with him (see comment on "good things" in 7:28; cf. Brueggemann, "On Trust and Freedom," 15 n. 33).

In any event, David realizes that the curse of Shimei is not an "undeserved curse" (Pr 26:2). The phrase "the cursing I am receiving" (v.12) is literally "his curse"—that is, God's curse, as Vanderkam, 536, correctly observes. Thus in all three verses of the literary unit, David, while still pleading for divine mercy, reckons with the punishment that God is inflicting on him. As Vanderkam notes, David's statements constitute "a confession of guilt" with respect to his crimes against the Saulides, and—especially in v.12—he expresses his confidence in the fact that although the Lord's "response cannot be anticipated or predicted it can be trusted" (Brueggemann, "On Coping with Curse," 189).

13 Shimei's pelting David with stones and cursing him (cf. vv.5b–6) do not stop. Shimei's persistence in such potentially dangerous activity bears eloquent witness to the depth of his anger and frustration. As David and his party continue slowly on their way, Shimei keeps pace along a hillside that parallels the road. The phrase "cursing as he went" echoes "cursed as he came out" in v.5b. In addition to his stone-throwing, Shimei begins "showering [David] with dirt," a colorful cognate accusative construction (lit., "dirting him with dirt") that uses a denominative Hebrew verb found only here in the OT.

14 The king had "approached" Bahurim (v.5a), and now he has "arrived" at his destination. (The same Heb. verb begins each of the two verses [see comment on v.5a].) With him are "all the people" (*ʿam*; cf. 17:22), here doubtless including not only "all the troops" (*ʿam*) but also "all the king's officials" and the "special guard" (v.6) as well as others in his retinue. Although their destination is not named in the text, it is "clear from ch. xvii. 18, that the halting-place was not Bahurim, but some place beyond it" (Kirkpatrick, 161), possibly the Jordan River (for details see Alter, *The David Story*, 293–94).

The physical and psychological stresses of the journey leave David and his company "exhausted" (cf. 17:29 ["tired"]; 1Sa 14:28 ["faint"], 31), and he therefore takes the opportunity to "refresh" himself (the Heb. verb, a denominative from *nepeš*, "throat, being, breath, soul," includes the nuance of "catch one's breath, rest," and is found elsewhere only in the Sabbath contexts of Exodus 23:12 ["refreshed"] and 31:17 ["rested"]; GK 5882).

NOTES

5 The otherwise attractive proposal of Roger T. Beckwith ("The Early History of the Psalter," *TynBul* 46/1 [1995]: 19) that "'Cush, a Benjamite' in the title of Psalm 7 ... is probably a play on the name of Kish the father of Saul, and refers to Shimei ... (whose) relationship to Kish is inferred from the genealogy of Mordecai, another Benjamite, in Esther 2:5, where Mordecai is described as 'the son of Jair, the son of *Shimei*, the son of *Kish*,'" is rendered somewhat unlikely in that (1) the vowels in the two names are different and (2) "Cush" is spelled throughout with an initial כ (*k*) while "Kish" always begins with a ק (*q*).

10 In its rendering "If ... because," the NIV has chosen the *Kethiv* reading of the first particle and the *Qere* of the second. Although other options and permutations are possible (for example, *Qere*'s "in this way" instead of "if" yields equally good sense; for a full discussion, see Vanderkam, 536 and n. 44), *Qere's* "because" is surely preferable to *Kethiv's* "and if" in light of the repetition of "because the LORD said to him" in v.11 ("for the LORD has told him to").

12 The NIV's "my distress" renders עניי (*ʿnyy*) with a few MSS, a reading apparently presupposed also by the ancient versions (cf. *BHS*), as opposed to the MT *Kethiv's* עוני (*ʿwny*, "my iniquity/guilt"). The *Qere's* עיני (*ʿyny*, "my eyes") also has its adherents, who understand it in the sense of "my tears" (for discussion cf. Snaith, 16–17; Vanderkam, 536 n. 45).

15. The Advice of Hushai and Ahithophel (16:15–17:29)

OVERVIEW

The central unit of chs. 15–20 (more precisely, 15:1–20:22) deals with the conflicting advice of Ahithophel and Hushai (16:15–17:29; for the overall outline of chs. 15–20 see Overview to 15:1–12). It begins by reprising the end of ch. 15, which describes the coming of Absalom and Hushai to Jerusalem (cf. 15:37; 16:15–16), and it ends as the previous section (16:5–14) ended: The king and all the people with him arrive at their destination "exhausted/tired" (17:29; see comment on 16:14). Three key verses, interspersed throughout (16:23; 17:14, 23), provide the clue for analyzing the section as three chiasms arranged within a larger chiastic structure, the clash between Ahithophel's advice and Hushai's advice serving as the focus of the whole:

A Arriving in Jerusalem, Absalom is befriended (16:15–19)
  B_1 Ahithophel advises Absalom (16:20–22)
    B_2 Ahithophel is described in glowing terms (16:23)
  B_3 Ahithophel advises Absalom (17:1–4)
    C_1 Hushai advises Absalom (17:5–13)
      C_2 Hushai's advice is declared better than Ahithophel's (17:14)
    C_3 Hushai advises Zadok and Abiathar (17:15–16)
  B_1' David crosses the Jordan (17:17–22)
    B_2' Ahithophel commits suicide (17:23)
  B_3' Absalom crosses the Jordan (17:24–26)
A' Arriving in Mahanaim, David is befriended (17:27–29)

[15]Meanwhile, Absalom and all the men of Israel came to Jerusalem, and Ahithophel was
with him. [16]Then Hushai the Arkite, David's friend, went to Absalom and said to him, "Long
live the king! Long live the king!"

[17]Absalom asked Hushai, "Is this the love you show your friend? Why didn't you go with
your friend?"

[18]Hushai said to Absalom, "No, the one chosen by the LORD, by these people, and by all
the men of Israel — his I will be, and I will remain with him. [19]Furthermore, whom should I
serve? Should I not serve the son? Just as I served your father, so I will serve you."
[20]Absalom said to Ahithophel, "Give us your advice. What should we do?"
[21]Ahithophel answered, "Lie with your father's concubines whom he left to take care of
the palace. Then all Israel will hear that you have made yourself a stench in your father's
nostrils, and the hands of everyone with you will be strengthened." [22]So they pitched a tent
for Absalom on the roof, and he lay with his father's concubines in the sight of all Israel.
[23]Now in those days the advice Ahithophel gave was like that of one who inquires of
God. That was how both David and Absalom regarded all of Ahithophel's advice.
[17:1]Ahithophel said to Absalom, "I would choose twelve thousand men and set out
tonight in pursuit of David. [2]I would attack him while he is weary and weak. I would strike
him with terror, and then all the people with him will flee. I would strike down only the
king [3]and bring all the people back to you. The death of the man you seek will mean the
return of all; all the people will be unharmed." [4]This plan seemed good to Absalom and to
all the elders of Israel.
[5]But Absalom said, "Summon also Hushai the Arkite, so we can hear what he has to say."
[6]When Hushai came to him, Absalom said, "Ahithophel has given this advice. Should we
do what he says? If not, give us your opinion."
[7]Hushai replied to Absalom, "The advice Ahithophel has given is not good this time.
[8]You know your father and his men; they are fighters, and as fierce as a wild bear robbed
of her cubs. Besides, your father is an experienced fighter; he will not spend the night with
the troops. [9]Even now, he is hidden in a cave or some other place. If he should attack your
troops first, whoever hears about it will say, 'There has been a slaughter among the troops
who follow Absalom.' [10]Then even the bravest soldier, whose heart is like the heart of a
lion, will melt with fear, for all Israel knows that your father is a fighter and that those with
him are brave.
[11]"So I advise you: Let all Israel, from Dan to Beersheba — as numerous as the sand on
the seashore — be gathered to you, with you yourself leading them into battle. [12]Then we
will attack him wherever he may be found, and we will fall on him as dew settles on the
ground. Neither he nor any of his men will be left alive. [13]If he withdraws into a city, then
all Israel will bring ropes to that city, and we will drag it down to the valley until not even a
piece of it can be found."
[14]Absalom and all the men of Israel said, "The advice of Hushai the Arkite is better
than that of Ahithophel." For the LORD had determined to frustrate the good advice of
Ahithophel in order to bring disaster on Absalom.
[15]Hushai told Zadok and Abiathar, the priests, "Ahithophel has advised Absalom and the
elders of Israel to do such and such, but I have advised them to do so and so. [16]Now send

a message immediately and tell David, 'Do not spend the night at the fords in the desert;
cross over without fail, or the king and all the people with him will be swallowed up.'"
[17]Jonathan and Ahimaaz were staying at En Rogel. A servant girl was to go and inform
them, and they were to go and tell King David, for they could not risk being seen entering
the city. [18]But a young man saw them and told Absalom. So the two of them left quickly
and went to the house of a man in Bahurim. He had a well in his courtyard, and they
climbed down into it. [19]His wife took a covering and spread it out over the opening of the
well and scattered grain over it. No one knew anything about it.
[20]When Absalom's men came to the woman at the house, they asked, "Where are Ahimaaz and Jonathan?"
The woman answered them, "They crossed over the brook." The men searched but
found no one, so they returned to Jerusalem.
[21]After the men had gone, the two climbed out of the well and went to inform King
David. They said to him, "Set out and cross the river at once; Ahithophel has advised such
and such against you." [22]So David and all the people with him set out and crossed the
Jordan. By daybreak, no one was left who had not crossed the Jordan.
[23]When Ahithophel saw that his advice had not been followed, he saddled his donkey
and set out for his house in his hometown. He put his house in order and then hanged
himself. So he died and was buried in his father's tomb.
[24]David went to Mahanaim, and Absalom crossed the Jordan with all the men of Israel.
[25]Absalom had appointed Amasa over the army in place of Joab. Amasa was the son of a
man named Jether, an Israelite who had married Abigail, the daughter of Nahash and sister
of Zeruiah the mother of Joab. [26]The Israelites and Absalom camped in the land of Gilead.
[27]When David came to Mahanaim, Shobi son of Nahash from Rabbah of the Ammonites,
and Makir son of Ammiel from Lo Debar, and Barzillai the Gileadite from Rogelim
[28]brought bedding and bowls and articles of pottery. They also brought wheat and barley,
flour and roasted grain, beans and lentils, [29]honey and curds, sheep, and cheese from cows'
milk for David and his people to eat. For they said, "The people have become hungry and
tired and thirsty in the desert."

COMMENTARY

15–19 Resuming the narrative that ends in 15:37, v.15 describes Absalom's arrival in Jerusalem with "all the men of Israel" (lit., "all the people/troops, the men of Israel"), the main Israelite army, together with Ahithophel, who had formerly been "David's counselor" (see comment on 15:12) but has now defected to Absalom—doubtless because he believes the future lies with the son rather than with the father.

Enter Hushai (v.16; see 15:32 and comment), who will turn out to be the fly in Ahithophel's ointment, an integral member of David's fifth column in Absalom's fledgling court. He is again described as David's "friend" (*rēᶜeh*), his official cabinet title (see Notes on 15:37). A Davidic loyalist, Hushai speaks to Absalom in words that are an exercise in studied ambiguity. If Absalom understands Hushai's twice-spoken "Long live the king!" (v.16; see 1Sa 10:24 and comment) as a reference to himself, it is virtually certain that in his own mind Hushai is thinking of David.

Although the first part of Absalom's response to Hushai (v.17) may be intended as a question (the Hebrew interrogative particle, though common, is not mandatory; cf. *IBHS*, 316 n. 1), it is also possible to read it as a caustic comment: "So this is the love you show your friend!" (cf. Snaith, 21). Absalom is doubtless belittling Hushai's official title by sarcastically using the ordinary word for "friend, acquaintance" twice (*rēaᶜ*; cf. *AIs*, 123; McCarter, *II Samuel*, 372, 384). He questions Hushai's "love," his covenantal fidelity, to David (see 1Sa 20:15 and comment). He also wonders aloud why the supposedly faithful Hushai did not "go with" David. After all, two hundred men had "accompanied" Absalom (15:11; same Heb. idiom)—however unknowingly—from Jerusalem to Hebron, had they not?

Hushai counters by ostensibly declaring his loyalty to Absalom. Beginning with the emphatic "No" (v.18; for other examples, cf. 24:24; 1Sa 2:16; 10:19; 12:12), he affirms that he will remain with the one whom the Lord has "chosen." (The verb is singular, perhaps implying that the roles of the people and of the men of Israel in the choice of a king are being downplayed.) By appearing to refer to the pretender Absalom, Hushai is engaging in flattery, since nowhere is Absalom stated to be the Lord's choice. The OT, however, fairly teems with references to David as the one whom God has chosen (cf. 6:21; 1Sa 16:8–13; 1Ki 8:16; 11:34; 1Ch 28:4; 2Ch 6:5–6; Ps 78:70)—and thus Hushai once again probably has David in mind, although of course he wants Absalom to think otherwise.

As Hushai concludes his assurances to Absalom, he becomes less ambiguous (v.19), although even here he avoids mentioning Absalom's name directly. David had earlier asked Hushai to offer the same service to Absalom that he had formerly performed for David (cf. 15:34), and Hushai now fulfills that request. To his own rhetorical question concerning whom he should serve, Hushai says, "Should I not serve the son?" (lit., "Should it not be before his son?"), and following his assertion that just as he has served "your father" (David), Hushai says, "So I will serve you" (lit., "so I will be before you").

The peculiar phraseology and careful indirection of Hushai's language enable him to have it both ways. Commenting on the question "Should it not be (before) his son?" Baldwin, 264, writes: "Indeed it should, if [Hushai] were loyal to [Absalom's] father. As it is, Hushai will serve Absalom while at the same time being loyal to Absalom's father. Hushai has kept his integrity, Absalom has been blinded by his own egoism, and the reader is permitted to see one example of the outworking of God's providence."

20–22 The first of three chiasms in the present literary unit contains two pieces of advice given by Ahithophel to Absalom (16:20–22; 17:1–4), bracketing a highly complimentary description of Ahithophel himself (16:23). Having listened to Hushai's pledge of fealty (vv.16–19), Absalom turns his attention to a counselor he feels confident he can trust.

The idiom "Give ... your advice" (v.20) occurs in Judges 20:7 ("give your verdict") in a context of hearing the evidence and then making the wisest and best judgment on the basis of it. Although other advisers may have been present ("give" is plural), Absalom is primarily interested in Ahithophel's observations concerning the current situation.

Ahithophel first suggests that Absalom preempt his father's harem and that he have sexual relations with the ten concubines David had left behind in Jerusalem to take care of the palace (v.21; see 15:16 and comment). David had illicitly slept with a woman who was not his wife (cf. 11:4), and now his son is counseled to follow in his father's footsteps. Doing so, Absalom will make himself a "stench" in David's nostrils—a fact not necessarily to be deplored, although not without its inherent dangers (see comments on 10:6; 1Sa 13:4). In this case, however, Ahithophel clearly believes that the "hands" of Absalom's supporters will be "strengthened" (an idiom that often implies encouragement; see comment on 2:7) by such a bold move on his part.

Having the utmost confidence in Ahithophel's advice, Absalom agrees to it. A tent is pitched on the "roof" of the palace (v.22), doubtless the very roof on which his father had earlier committed an equally sinful act (see 11:2 and comment). The "tent" (*ʾōhel*) may have been intended to symbolize the *ḥuppâ* ("pavilion") occupied by the bridegroom and bride on their wedding night (as in Ps 19:4–5; cf. Joel 2:16 ["chamber"]; for similar customs among modern nomadic Arabs, see the observations of W. Robertson Smith, *Kinship and Marriage in Early Arabia* [Cambridge: Cambridge Univ. Press, 1885] 167–69).

Thus with the full knowledge of the people of Israel ("in the sight of all Israel," v.22; see comment on 12:11–12), Absalom sleeps with his father's concubines—little remembering that to do so may well jeopardize his inheritance rights (cf. Ge 35:22; 49:3–4) and compel him to forfeit them to another (cf. Youngblood, *The Book of Genesis*, 277). Nor will the concubines, however loudly they might protest their innocence, remain guiltless. Upon his return to Jerusalem, David will put them under house arrest, where they will remain "till the day of their death, living as widows" (20:3).

23 In theory, of course, Ahithophel's advice concerning David's concubines was entirely appropriate, since it was expected that a king's harem would pass to his successor (cf. 12:8). "Possession of the harem was a title to the throne" (*AIs*, 116). It is therefore understandable that both David and Absalom should respect the "advice" (*ʿēṣâ*) of Ahithophel (see comments on 15:31, 34) and regard it as equal to that of one who "inquires of God" (lit., "consults the word [*dābār*] of God"). The value of Ahithophel's advice was like that of a priestly oracle divinely sent.

> The *ʿēṣā* which brings success is that of the sagacious statesman, and failure to heed it brings such consequences as are comparable with those resulting from a failure to obey God. God is represented as controlling history through the mediation of human decisions: that is, to neglect *ʿēṣā* is to be exposed to the judgment of God. (McKane, 56)

At the same time, needless to say, it can be "dangerous or risky *for kings to seek counsel*" (Polzin, "Curses and Kings," 225), as 17:14 so clearly indicates (for full discussion see ibid., 224–26).

17:1–4 Sensing that he has successfully shored up Absalom's claims to kingship over Israel, at least in the eyes of the citizens of Jerusalem (cf. 16:20–22), Ahithophel now suggests to Absalom a bold military expedition that he is convinced will result in David's death (17:1–4). Whether literally or figuratively, Ahithophel puts himself in the position of an army commander whose job it is to "choose" (v.1; cf. Jos 8:3) the correct number of men to carry out the appropriate strategic goals. "I would choose ... and set out ... in pursuit of" renders a series of cohortative verbs that translate literally as, "Let me choose ... and let me set out ... and let me pursue" (see NIV note).

Ahithophel's militarily correct advice is thus both terse and urgent: "There is not a moment to lose, the only course is to hit David hard before he can regroup his forces, and the statement itself has no time for fancy rhetorical maneuvers" (Alter, *The Art of Biblical Narrative*, 74). "Twelve thousand" may be Ahithophel's way of asserting the need to muster at least one "thousand/unit" (see comment on 1Sa 4:2) from each of the twelve tribes in order to demonstrate the involvement of all Israel in Absalom's rebellion.

Although the first-person verbal forms in vv.2–3 are more varied than in v.1 (see NIV text and note on v.2), the sense of urgency does not diminish. Ahithophel advises an attack on David while he is "weary" (v.2; cf. Dt 25:18) and "weak." The latter term is literally "limp/feeble of hands" (cf. Job 4:3; Isa 35:3)—an expression often implying discouragement (see comment on 4:1)—and appears to be in deliberate contrast to the earlier description of Absalom's followers, whose "hands ... will be strengthened" and who would thus be encouraged (see 16:21 and comment).

The large number and mobility of the troops proposed by Ahithophel is calculated not only to "strike" David himself "with terror" (cf. similarly Eze 30:9) but also to frighten his men into running for their lives (cf. Zec 1:21). Ahithophel's strategy involves a lightninglike surgical strike that will hopefully result in the death of only "the king" (v.2)—a title that Ahithophel still uses for David (perhaps out of habit) but that surely does not please Absalom. All the other people will then be brought back to Jerusalem unharmed (v.3).

Absalom seems just as impressed by Ahithophel's advice on this occasion as he was earlier (cf. 16:20–22)—an opinion shared by the "elders of Israel" (v.4), upon whom, after all, the ultimate responsibility for entering into covenant with a new king devolves (see 3:17; 5:3 and comments). Nevertheless Absalom, realizing that whatever plan he adopts must be as nearly foolproof as possible, decides to get a second opinion.

5–13 Absalom therefore summons Hushai the Arkite (see comment on 15:32), whom he knows to be a trusted confidant of David (see 16:16–17 and comments) but who—like Ahithophel (cf. 15:12)—has offered his services (even though in Hushai's case the offer may be more apparent than real; see 16:18–19 and comments). Before taking any action Absalom wants to "hear" (v.5; cf. Nu 9:8 ["find out"]; Ps 85:8 ["listen to"]) "what [Hushai] has to say" (lit., "what is in his mouth"; cf. 1:16; similarly 14:3, 19b). The phrase *gam-hûʾ* ("also he"), although perhaps implied in the NIV's rendering, stresses Absalom's insistence on comparing Hushai's views with those of Ahithophel (a move that will "prove to be a fatal error" [Alter, *The David Story*, 297]) and should thus be represented in the translation (e.g., by adding "as well" to the end of v.5).

The root *dbr* (GK 1819) in its nominal ("word") and verbal ("speak") functions appears four times in v.6 (in chiastic order: verb, noun, noun, verb) in Absalom's statement to Hushai, a literal translation of which reads as follows: "Ahithophel has spoken according to this word [see comment on 14:3]. Shall we do this word? If not, you [emphatic] speak." The effect of such a rendering is to highlight Absalom's apparent understanding of Ahithophel's advice as having the potential of being the equivalent of a divine oracle (see comment on 16:23). At the same time, however, it would seem that Absalom is open to giving Hushai's counsel the same standing.

In his response to Absalom, Hushai first of all denigrates Ahithophel's second piece of advice (vv.1–3) by asserting that it is "not good" (v.7)—a judgment that, although totally at odds with the narrator's (cf. v.14), reflects the Lord's determination to frustrate Ahithophel's counsel (cf. v.14). For all intents and purposes, the phrase "the advice Ahithophel has given" (lit., "has advised," v.7) echoes "the advice Ahithophel gave" (lit., "advised," 16:23) and once again calls attention to the difference between the narrator's positive evaluation (of Ahithophel's first piece of advice, to be sure) in the latter text as compared to Hushai's here. "Devise your strategy" (lit., "Advise advice"), the prophet thunders (Isa 8:10), "but it will be thwarted" (see 15:34 ["frustrating"] and comment)—because "God is with us" (Isa 8:10; cf. 2Sa 17:14).

What follows (vv.8–13) is Hushai's "brilliant rhetorical contrivance," which counters Ahithophel's "militarily correct advice.... But rhetoric is not necessarily evil in the Bible, and the contrastive technique takes a dialectical turn here, for Absalom is, after all, a usurper, and Hushai, bravely loyal to David, is using his ability to deceive through words in order to restore the rightful king to his throne" (Alter, *The Art of Biblical Narrative*, 74). The two parts of Hushai's speech (vv.8–10, 11b–13)—separated by "So I advise you" (v.11a)—make use of the repetition of key words and/or ideas that have enabled Bar-Efrat ("Some Observations on the Analysis of Structure in Biblical Narrative," *VT* 30/2 [1980]: 170–71) to construct the following skeletal outline (with slight modifications):

A "know your father ... fighters" (v.8a)
  B "as a wild bear" (v.8b)
    C "the troops" (v.8c)
      X "some other place" (*bʾḥd/t hmqwmt*, v.9a)
    C' "the troops" (v.9b)
  B' "like ... a lion" (v.10a)
A' "knows ... your father ... a fighter" (v.10b)
D "all Israel ... be gathered" (*yēʾāsēp*, v.11b)
  E "as the sand on the seashore" (v.11c)
      X' "wherever" (*bʾḥt hmqwmt*, v.12a)
  E' "as dew settles on the ground" (v.12b)
D' "withdraws [*yēʾāsēp*) ... all Israel" (v.13)

The first part (A–A') reveals the weak points (from Hushai's perspective, of course) in Ahithophel's advice, while the second (D–D') offers Hushai's alternative plan, which is supposedly better. In the first section of the first part (A–C) Hushai shows why Ahithophel's plan will be unsuccessful, and in the second (C'–A') he states that in fact it will do more harm than good. The first section of the second part (D–E) describes the elaborate preparations necessary before attacking David, and the second section (E'–D') outlines the effects of the attack. The transitional clause (X) in the first part observes that "in one of the places" David remains "hidden," while the transitional clause (X') in the second expresses the confidence that "in one of the places" he will be "found." And so it is that Hushai the Arkite uses rhetorical artistry of the highest order in his attempt to convince Absalom that the counsel of Ahithophel the Gilonite will result in a course of action that cannot but fail, while his own advice, if followed, can only succeed.

Hushai makes capital of David's long-standing reputation as a "fighter" (*gibbôr* [vv.8, 10]; cf. the early description of him as *gibbôr ḥayil* ["a brave man," 1Sa 16:18]). Indeed, David and his men are as "fierce" (lit., "bitter of soul," v.8; see 1Sa 1:10 and comment; cf. Jdg 18:25 ["hot-tempered"]), and therefore as dangerous, as a "wild bear robbed of her cubs" (cf. Pr 17:12; Hos 13:8; also 2Ki 2:24). Due caution must be exercised in trying to outsmart or overpower David, whose fame as an "experienced fighter" (*ʾîš milḥāmâ*, lit., "man of war") is widely known (see comment on 1Sa 16:18 ["warrior"]).

Although *yālîn* (GK 4328) in v.8 could be understood as a Hiphil, with the resulting translation being something like "he will not let the troops rest overnight" (cf. Hertzberg, 347) in the sense that "none of them will be asleep and they will be ready, from an ambush, to cause some initial slaughter among Absalom's men" (Snaith, 29), this occurrence would be the only case of Hiphil *lw/yn* in the OT (cf. BDB, 533). In addition the traditional Qal parsing of the verb, adopted by the

NIV ("he [David] will not spend the night with the troops"), is better contextually in that it forges a more natural link with v.9: "Even now, he is hidden [see comment on 1Sa 19:2] in a cave or some other place." David is a past master at knowing how—and where—to hide from pursuers (see 1Sa 23:22–23 and comment). If indeed he is trying to escape from his son Absalom by cowering in a "cave" (cf. also Jer 48:28) that is hard to find, it is ironic that Absalom's final resting place will be a large "pit" in a forest (18:17; same Heb. noun).

Warning Absalom that David on the offensive would have the strategic advantage and would therefore draw first blood, Hushai points out that the exaggerated news of the initial defeat ("a slaughter," v.9; cf. 1Sa 4:17 ["(heavy) losses"]) would cause uncontrollable panic among Absalom's troops (v.10). Absalom's "bravest soldier" (*ben-ḥayil*, lit., "son of power/might"; see 2:7 and comment) is no match for David's "brave" men (*b*ᵉ*nê-ḥayil* [v.10]), who in this regard emulate their leader (see 1Sa 18:17 and comment). Though their hearts be like that of a lion, Absalom's troops will "melt" (cf. Ps 22:14; Eze 21:7; Na 2:10) with fear. David, after all, is a "fighter" (see comment on v.8) who has not flinched in the presence of lions (cf. v.10) or bears (cf. v.8), among the most dangerous of animals (see 1Sa 17:34–37 and comment; cf. Pr 28:15; Hos 13:8).

After eloquently belittling Ahithophel's counsel, Hushai gives some advice of his own. If followed, his plan is so elaborate that it will consume enough time for Hushai to send instructions to David concerning what to do in the light of Absalom's troop movements. Hushai suggests to Absalom that he needs a much larger force than the mere "twelve thousand" men (see v.1 and comment) proposed by Ahithophel. Absalom must enlist every able-bodied Israelite, "from Dan to Beersheba" (v.11; see comments on 3:10; 1Sa 3:20)—an enormous army, "as numerous as the sand on the seashore" (see 1Sa 13:5 and comment). The ultimate flattery: Absalom will personally (*pāneḵā*, "you yourself" [v.11]; for *pānîm* in the sense of "personally," cf. Dt 7:10 ["to their face," NIV (2x)]; Pr 7:15 ["(looked for) you" (NIV), lit., "your face" = "personally"]) lead them into battle.

Apparently swept along by his own glibness, Hushai rhetorically joins in the fray himself: "We will fall" on David (*naḥnû* from *nûaḥ* [cf. BDB, 59; K&D, 430–31; Driver, 323; Snaith, 32], not an alternative form of the independent personal pronoun *ʾ*ᵃ*naḥnû*, "we") as "dew" settles on the ground (v.12; cf. similarly Ps 110:3 [NIV note]), a comparison that emphasizes total coverage (McCarter, *II Samuel*, 384), and/or irresistibility (Leslie C. Allen, *Psalms 101–150* [WBC; Waco, Tex.: Word, 1983], 81), and/or silence/effortlessness (Alter, *The David Story*, 298). Neither David nor any of his men will be able to survive such an onslaught (cf. 1Sa 14:36).

Adopt whatever tactics he will, David cannot possibly escape—not even if he "withdraws" (lit., "gathers himself," v.13; same Heb. verb as translated "be gathered" in v.11) into the presumed safety of a city. Using a vivid hyperbole, Hushai envisions the entire Israelite army attaching ropes to that city in order to "drag" it down into the valley. The Hebrew verb *sāḥab* is used elsewhere only in Jeremiah, where it always suggests the humiliation of being "dragged away" to destruction as though by an animal (cf. Jer 15:3; 22:19; 49:20b = 50:45b). David's supposed haven will be so thoroughly demolished that not a "piece" (the Heb. word referring to a small "pebble"; cf. Am 9:9) of it will be found.

14 Second Samuel 16:15–17:29 constitutes the central section in the chiastic structure of chs. 15–20 (see Overview to 15:1–12), and 17:5–16 is the central chiasm in the carefully crafted arrangement of literary units in 16:15–17:29 (see Overview to this section). Since 17:14 is the focal point of vv.5–16, it serves also as the literary center of chs. 15–20.

The three key verses in 16:15–17:29 (16:23; 17:14, 23) are intimately linked to one another. The MT of all three verses makes use of the root *yʿṣ* ("advise, counsel") in its verbal and nominal forms (16:23 [3x]; 17:14 [3x]; 17:23 [1x]). But whereas 16:23 and 17:23 refer only to Ahithophel's counsel, 17:14 compares the advice of Ahithophel with the advice of Hushai—and records the judgment of "Absalom and all the men of Israel" that the latter is better than the former. If the fortunes of Ahithophel rose to their zenith in 16:23, they sink to their nadir in 17:23.

The critical turning point is 17:14. The delays inherent in Hushai's counsel give David and his troops time to escape across the Jordan and then regroup; thus Hushai's rhetoric wins the day. Absalom has made his fateful choice, and Hushai becomes the point man in the Lord's determination to "frustrate" (see 15:34 and comment) Ahithophel's counsel. The admittedly "good advice of Ahithophel," described so glowingly in 16:23, and the forthcoming "disaster on Absalom," implied in and hastened by Ahithophel's suicide (17:23), thus flank the erroneous judgment of Absalom and his men as reported in 17:14.

> It is intriguing to see Ahithophel's first counsel to Absalom accepted and executed, making the break between father and son final and public (2 Sam. xvi 20–22), but his second and more crucial advice (2 Sam. xvii 1–4) at once countered by Hushai's verbose arguments (xvii 5–13). If Absalom and his companions had followed Ahithophel's second advice as they had the first, the rebel would have defeated his father and won the kingdom, but, as the narrator affirms, "the Lord had ordained to defeat the good counsel of Ahithophel" (2 Sam. xvii 14 b). (Roth, "A Study of *skl*," 71)

And the litany of the divinely sent "disaster" against Israel's royal house has only just begun (cf. 1Ki 21:21, 29; 2Ki 21:12; 22:16–17; Jer 4:6; 6:19).

15–16 Having given Absalom advice that, if implemented, will turn out well for David (vv.5–13), Hushai now gives similar advice to the priests Zadok and Abiathar (vv.15–16; see 15:24 and comment), who are in a position to carry out Hushai's instructions through their sons Ahimaaz and Jonathan (see 15:35–36 and comment). In v.15 he quickly rehearses the substance of Ahithophel's advice to "Absalom and the elders of Israel" (see vv.1–4 and comments) and then contrasts it with his own obviously superior counsel (cf. vv.5–13; the "I" in v.15 is emphatic).

Since there is no time to lose, Hushai's advice (vv.15–16) and its execution (vv.17–22) are suffused with an atmosphere of urgency ("immediately" [v.16], "quickly" [v.18], and "at once" [v.21] all render *mᵉhērâ*). His message for David is that it would be too dangerous to spend even one more "night" (v.16; cf. v.1) at the "fords in the desert" (see 15:28 and comment). The king's only option is to "cross" the Jordan "without fail." (Augmenting the finite verb, the infinitive absolute underscores the need for swift and decisive action.) If he refuses to do so, he and his entire party will be "swallowed up" (cf. Job 37:20; Isa 9:16 ["led astray"]; for a discussion of the metaphor, cf. Conroy, 126 n. 51).

17–22 The final internal chiasm (vv.17–26) in the present literary unit (see Overview to 16:15–17:29) brackets the suicide of Ahithophel (v.23) with two accounts of royal figures crossing the Jordan (David the king [vv.17–22], and Absalom the crown prince [vv.24–26]). Gunn ("Traditional Composition," 224) observes that the narrative in vv.17–22 shares a number of features with the story of the spies at Jericho in Joshua 2:

> There are two spies in or at a city. The king of the city learns of their presence and sends men to find them. They are hidden in a house (under something) by a woman. The king's men come to the house and demand the spies be given up. But

the woman gives false directions, the pursuers go on their way, fail to find the spies, and return to the city. The spies escape.

But simply comparing shared features, however striking, between the two accounts in no way "argues strongly for their being derived from a common stereotype" (Gunn, ibid., 225). The most one can surmise in such cases is that the narrator of the books of Samuel chose to stress elements in his episode that recalled similar elements in the Jericho story, perhaps to remind his readers that God provides similarly in corresponding situations. In any event, the differences between the two accounts far outweigh their common characteristics.

The messengers designated to bring word to David (cf. v.16) are Jonathan and Ahimaaz (v.17), sons of Abiathar and Zadok respectively (see 15:27–28, 36 and comments). In order not to be accused of attempting to subvert Absalom's plans originating in Jerusalem while at the same time wanting to be near enough to keep in touch with developments there, Jonathan and Ahimaaz are staying at En Rogel (v.17), a spring (modern Bir Ayyub ["The Well of Job"]) in the Kidron Valley on the border between Benjamin and Judah (cf. Jos 15:1, 7; 18:11, 16) less than a mile south-southeast of the capital city. The locale of the later abortive coronation of David's son Adonijah (cf. 1Ki 1:9, 25), its name (lit., "Washerman's Spring") derives from a Hebrew root that elsewhere means "spy." It thus forms a wordplay on the mutual spying and intrigue that take place throughout these chapters between Absalom's men and David's men (see comments on "secret messengers" in 15:10 and on "Rogelim" in 17:27).

David's need for up-to-date news is reflected in the frequent use of the verb *ngd* ("tell," vv.16–17; "inform," vv.17, 21). A servant girl from Jerusalem relays the necessary information to Jonathan and Ahimaaz, who cannot risk "being seen" entering the city (v.17). But in spite of their caution a young man who "saw" them (v.18) reports their whereabouts to Absalom (ironically the verb *rʾh* ["see"] plays an important role in 15:27–28 as well; see comments). Knowing that they must act "quickly" (v.18; see comment on "immediately" in v.16), the two men leave En Rogel and go to Bahurim (about two miles to the northeast; see comment on 3:16; cf. also 16:5). There they climb down into a well in a residential courtyard (cf. Ne 8:16), and the wife of the house's owner keeps their presence secret by spreading a covering over (cf. similarly 2Ki 8:15; Ps 105:39) the mouth of the well (v.19). She then scatters "grain" over the covering, ostensibly to dry it out (for discussion cf. Snaith, 37; the Heb. word here rendered "grain" appears elsewhere only in Pr 27:22). The ruse works, and the men's hiding place is kept secret.

When Absalom's men arrive in Bahurim and ask the woman where Ahimaaz and Jonathan are, she says that they have already left. Apparently not believing her, they search the area, returning to Jerusalem only after failing to find the two fugitives (v.20). As soon as Absalom's men are gone, the two climb out of the well and go to deliver Hushai's instructions (cf. vv.15–16) to David (v.21), who is presumably still at the unspecified "destination" mentioned in 16:14 (see comment there). They advise him to cross the Jordan (cf. v.22) "river" (*mayim*, lit., "water") and to do so "at once" (see comment on "immediately" in v.16) in the light of Ahithophel's advice (v.21) to Absalom to strike quickly and decisively (see comments on vv.1–4). Sensing that there is no time to lose, David and his entire party cross over to the eastern side of the Jordan River under cover of darkness (v.22; see comment on 1Sa 14:36).

23 If in 16:23 Ahithophel is described in glowing terms as being at the height of his power and influence because of the extraordinary brilliance and dependability of his "advice," the parallel passage in 17:23 (see Overview to 16:15–17:29) depicts him as realizing that his "advice"—though not having lost any of its luster or suitability (see vv.1–4 and comments)—has not been followed this time. Knowing that the implementation of Hushai's advice will not result in the death of David, who will thus return to Jerusalem seeking revenge on his enemies, Ahithophel, "a deliberate, practical man to the very end" (Alter, *The David Story*, 301), therefore decides that the only course of action left open to him is suicide.

After he returns to Giloh, his hometown (see Notes on 15:12), and has "put his house in order" (cf. 2Ki 20:1 = Isa 38:1; the phrase *way*ᵉ*ṣaw* ʾ*el-bêtô* implies the giving of one's last will and testament in anticipation of imminent death; cf. late and modern Heb. *ṣawwā*ʾ*â* "[verbal] will"), he strangles himself (*ḥnq*; cf. Job 7:15; Na 2:12). Although the precise means that Ahithophel used to commit suicide by strangling is not specified (cf. Patrick, 517, who cites the bizarre interpretation of those who assert that "being full of Anguish, Anger and Vexation ... these Passions cast him into so violent a Distemper, that he was strangled by it"), it was probably by hanging from a rope. Accounts of suicide are infrequent in the OT (see 1Sa 31:4–5 and comments; cf. Jdg 9:54; 1Ki 16:18; also 2Mc 10:13; 14:41).

After his death Ahithophel is buried "in his father's tomb" (v.23), the normal place of interment in those days (see 2:32 and comment; cf. Jdg 8:32; 16:31). As K&D, 433, observes, David's prayer (see 15:31 and comment) is now answered. And just as Ahithophel had betrayed an anointed king of Israel (see 15:12 and comment) and finished his days as a suicide, so also would the betrayer of another Anointed King come to the same inglorious end (cf. Mt 27:4–5; Ac 1:18; cf. Wharton, 353).

24–26 The account of the crossing of the Jordan by Absalom parallels the similar narrative concerning David (vv.17–22; see Overview to 16:15–17:29), who stays one step ahead of his pursuers by continuing on to Mahanaim (vv.24, 27), the earlier headquarters of his rival Ish-Bosheth about seven miles east of the river in the tribal territory of Gad (see 2:8 and comment). Since Joab had apparently accompanied David on his flight from Jerusalem (see comment on 16:10), Absalom had appointed another leader "over the army" (v.25; see 8:16 and comment) to replace him. The new commander is Amasa, whose name in emphatic position as the first word in the MT of v.25 attests to his notoriety if not his importance (cf. 19:11–13).

Amasa's father was Ithra/Jether (see NIV note; cf. 1Ki 2:5, 32), perhaps Nabal's real name (see comment on 1Sa 25:3), and his mother was Nahash's daughter Abigal/Abigail (see NIV note; cf. 1Ch 2:17), David's half sister (and probably his wife; see comment on 1Sa 25:3) as well as the sister of Zeruiah—which makes Amasa a relative not only of David but also of Joab. Although the exact location of Absalom's camp is not specified, at this time the "land of Gilead" (v.26) presumably encompassed Gad and therefore Mahanaim—an ominous prospect for David and his men.

27–29 As Absalom had been befriended upon his arrival in Jerusalem (16:15–19), so in the parallel passage David is befriended upon his arrival in Mahanaim (vv.27–29; see Overview to 16:15–17:29). Three staunch allies come to his aid (v.27): the Ammonite Shobi (mentioned only here) son of Nahash (probably the Nahash of v.25, for which see comments on 1Sa 11:1; 12:12) from Rabbah (see comment on 10:3), Mephibosheth's patron Makir from Lo Debar (see 9:4–5 and comment), and the Gileadite Barzillai ("Iron Man") from Rogelim (mentioned elsewhere only in 19:31, its location [though uncertain] is perhaps modern Bersinya or nearby Dhaharat Soqa, about ten miles east-southeast of Lo Debar and forty miles northwest of Rabbah). The Hebrew form of the word "Rogelim," which means "Washermen," is the plural of "Rogel" in the place-name En Rogel (v.17; see comment).

In addition to various housekeeping items (v.28a), David's friends also bring essential foodstuffs to supply his needs and those of the people with him (vv.28b–29a; for similar lists see 16:1; 1Sa 17:17–18; 25:18 and comments): flour (see 1Sa 1:24 and comment; cf. 28:24) and roasted grain (see 1Sa 17:17 and comment; cf. 25:18), beans and lentils (cf. Eze 4:9; also Ge 25:34), "honey and curds" (often food of last resort, eaten in times of political turmoil; cf. Isa 7:15, 22; and Ronald F. Youngblood, *The Book of Isaiah* [Eugene, Ore.: Wipf and Stock, 2001], 49), sheep, and "cheese from cows' milk" (*š^e^pôt bāqār* [the first word is a *hapax legomenon*]). Knowing full well that the rigors of the desert flight have caused David and his party to become "tired" (see 16:14 ["exhausted"] and comment) and that they are "hungry and thirsty" (cf. Ps 107:4–5; also Ps 3, which may reflect this period in David's life), Shobi, Makir, and Barzillai want to give them the rest and provisions they need.

Refreshed, David and his troops will engage Absalom and his army. The battle will be joined in Transjordan, and the outcome there will determine which of the two men will rule over all Israel (cf. Curtis, "'East Is East ...'" 358).

NOTES

16:18 The NIV reads "his" (לוֹ, *lô*) with the *Qere* and the ancient versions. The *Kethiv*'s לֹא (*lō*ʾ, "no, not"), probably arose by contamination from "No" earlier in the verse.

19 Although שֵׁנִית (*šēnît*) means literally "(a) second (time)," the NIV's "furthermore" is clearly preferable here. For the same phenomenon with respect to the cognate Akkadian adverb *šanītam*, see the discussion in Youngblood, *The Amarna Correspondence*, 47–48.

23 "One who inquires" renders יִשְׁאַל (*yišʾal*, "he inquires"), with or without the *Qere*'s אִישׁ (*ʾîš*, "man, one") that follows the verb. As Driver, 320, observes, the *Qere* "is not needed."

17:3 "The death of the man you seek will mean the return of all" renders a Hebrew clause that translates literally as "like the return of all (is) the man whom you are seeking." The NIV thus includes "the death of" *ad sensum* in the light of v.2 (cf. similarly K&D, 429). Emendations on the basis of the LXX are therefore unnecessary, as are claims that the MT clause in question is "defective" (McCarter, *II Samuel*, 381) or "unintelligible" (Snaith, 26).

9 As the lack of discussion in the commentaries attests, כִּנְפֹל בָּהֶם בַּתְּחִלָּה (*kin^e^pōl bāhem batt^e^ḥillâ*, lit., "according to the fall of against/among them at the first") can be rendered with equal plausibility as "if he should attack your troops first" (NIV text; cf. Jdg 1:1; 20:18; Hertzberg; K&D) and as "when some of the men fall at the first attack" (NIV note; cf. Anderson, Driver, McCarter).

12 For the idiom נוֹתַר מִן/בְּ־ (*nôtar min/b^e^-*, "survive/be left among"), see Note on 13:30.

16 Comparing the cognate Arabic verb *balaġa*, A. Guillaume ("A Note on the Root בלע," *JTS* 13 [1962]: 320–22) makes a persuasive case for the meaning "suffer mishap, be afflicted, be distressed" for בלע (*blʿ*, "be swallowed up") here and in a number of other OT texts (cf. also McCarter, *II Samuel*, 388).

19 "The opening of the well," פני הבאר (*pny hb*ʾ*r*, lit., "the face/surface of the well"), is usually expressed by פי הבאר (*py hb*ʾ*r*, lit., "the mouth of the well"; cf. Ge 29:2–3, 8, 10), a reading that is found in some MT MSS and that is probably more original here also (but cf. Hertzberg, 348 n. b).

20 "They crossed over the brook" renders עָבְרוּ מִיכַל הַמָּיִם (*ʿābrû mîkal hammāyim*, lit., "They crossed over the brook of water," possibly a reference to the Jordan River; see comment on v.21), in which *mîkal* ("brook"?) is a *hapax legomenon* of uncertain meaning (cf. the NIV note "They passed by the sheep pen toward the water"; Alter (*The David Story*, 300) tentatively suggests "reservoir," perhaps "derived from a verbal root that means 'to contain.'" The narrator may have chosen the rare word *mîkal* to recall the stratagem of David's wife Michal on a previous occasion (cf. 1Sa 19:11–17).

25 Despite the support of some LXX MSS, the MT's "Israelite" can hardly be the correct reading here and may have been influenced by the appearance of "Israel" in vv.24 and 26. For the likelihood that "Jezreelite" (cf. some LXX MSS) was in the autograph because it best explains the readings "Israelite" and "Ishmaelite" (cf. 1Ch 2:17 and some LXX MSS; see NIV note), see the discussion of Levenson and Halpern, 511–12. In the light of 19:11–13 (see comment on 19:13), the Jezreel in question would be the southern town of unknown location in the hill country of Judah (see comment on 1Sa 25:43).

28 The Hebrew word translated "and roasted grain" appears twice in the MT of v.28. The second occurrence is probably due to dittography and is therefore omitted in most LXX MSS and in Syriac (see NIV note; cf. however K&D, 434–35).

16. Absalom's Death (18:1–18)

OVERVIEW

In the overall structure of 15:1–20:22, the story of Absalom's death (18:1–18) provides a counterpoise to that of Shimei's curse (16:5–14; see comment on 15:1–12). Just as in the earlier narrative an adversary of David (Shimei) curses him (16:5, 7–8, 13), so also here an adversary of David (Absalom) opposes him in battle (vv.6–8); just as in the earlier account David demands that Shimei be spared (16:11), so also here David demands that Absalom be spared (vv.5, 12); and just as in the earlier episode a son of Zeruiah (Abishai) is ready to kill Shimei (16:9), so also here a son of Zeruiah (Joab [v.2]) is ready to kill Absalom—and indeed wounds him, perhaps mortally (vv.14–15).

The literary unit is best divided into three sections of unequal length (cf. similarly Conroy, 55–66): (1) David's mustering of his troops (vv.1–5); (2) the battle between David's men and Absalom's men (vv.6–8); (3) Absalom's death (vv.9–18).

[1]David mustered the men who were with him and appointed over them commanders of thousands and commanders of hundreds. [2]David sent the troops out—a third

under the command of Joab, a third under Joab's brother Abishai son of Zeruiah, and a third under Ittai the Gittite. The king told the troops, "I myself will surely march out with you."

[3]But the men said, "You must not go out; if we are forced to flee, they won't care about us. Even if half of us die, they won't care; but you are worth ten thousand of us. It would be better now for you to give us support from the city."

[4]The king answered, "I will do whatever seems best to you."

So the king stood beside the gate while all the men marched out in units of hundreds and of thousands. [5]The king commanded Joab, Abishai and Ittai, "Be gentle with the young man Absalom for my sake." And all the troops heard the king giving orders concerning Absalom to each of the commanders.

[6]The army marched into the field to fight Israel, and the battle took place in the forest of Ephraim. [7]There the army of Israel was defeated by David's men, and the casualties that day were great — twenty thousand men. [8]The battle spread out over the whole countryside, and the forest claimed more lives that day than the sword.

[9]Now Absalom happened to meet David's men. He was riding his mule, and as the mule went under the thick branches of a large oak, Absalom's head got caught in the tree. He was left hanging in midair, while the mule he was riding kept on going.

[10]When one of the men saw this, he told Joab, "I just saw Absalom hanging in an oak tree."

[11]Joab said to the man who had told him this, "What! You saw him? Why didn't you strike him to the ground right there? Then I would have had to give you ten shekels of silver and a warrior's belt."

[12]But the man replied, "Even if a thousand shekels were weighed out into my hands, I would not lift my hand against the king's son. In our hearing the king commanded you and Abishai and Ittai, 'Protect the young man Absalom for my sake.' [13]And if I had put my life in jeopardy — and nothing is hidden from the king — you would have kept your distance from me."

[14]Joab said, "I'm not going to wait like this for you." So he took three javelins in his hand and plunged them into Absalom's heart while Absalom was still alive in the oak tree. [15]And ten of Joab's armor-bearers surrounded Absalom, struck him and killed him.

[16]Then Joab sounded the trumpet, and the troops stopped pursuing Israel, for Joab halted them. [17]They took Absalom, threw him into a big pit in the forest and piled up a large heap of rocks over him. Meanwhile, all the Israelites fled to their homes.

[18]During his lifetime Absalom had taken a pillar and erected it in the King's Valley as a monument to himself, for he thought, "I have no son to carry on the memory of my name." He named the pillar after himself, and it is called Absalom's Monument to this day.

COMMENTARY

1–5 "The inclusions between verses 1 ['commanders of thousands and commanders of hundreds'] and 4 ['units of hundreds and of thousands'] and between verses 2 and 5 (the names of the generals) ... interlock to give a firm unity to the passage" (Conroy, 55). The numbers in vv.1 and 4 are arranged chiastically as well. In addition *ʿam* ("men, troops") occurs at least once in each of these five verses.

Whether "thousands" and "hundreds" (vv.1, 4; cf. also v.3) are to be understood literally or figuratively (in the sense of "military units"; see comments on 1Sa 4:2; 18:13; see also 1Sa 17:18 and NIV note; cf. 1Sa 8:12; 22:7), it is clear that David has formidable military strength at his disposal. Having "mustered" or "counted" his troops (v.1; see 1Sa 11:8 and comment) and having separated them into three divisions (v.2, a common strategy in ancient times; see comment on 1Sa 11:11; cf. 13:17–18), he sends them out under the "command" (lit., "hand"; cf. similarly Nu 31:49) of Joab (the overall commander of David's army; see comments on 8:16; 1Sa 26:6), his brother Abishai (see comment on 1Sa 26:6), and Ittai.

Though a Philistine, Ittai the Gittite—who is leader of one of the most important of David's mercenary detachments (see 15:19 and comment)—is considered loyal enough also to share command of the Israelite regulars with Joab and Abishai. While David is mentioned by name in each of the first two verses, from v.2b to the end of the section (v.5) the narrator refers to him no fewer than five times as "the king," not only stressing the fact that he is the legitimate ruler of Israel, but also leaving no doubt concerning who is really in charge.

David announces to the assembled troops that he ("I myself," emphatic) intends to march out with them as well (v.2). Conroy observes in v.3 a reversal of 17:11: "Hushai who was not speaking for Absalom's good had urged him to lead his forces personally into battle, but David's men who are genuinely concerned for his welfare urge him to stay behind" (Conroy, 57). The men point out that if they are forced to flee, or even if half of them are killed in battle, Absalom's soldiers "won't care" (v.3; see comment on "pay no attention" in 1Sa 25:25) "about us" (the phrase, used twice in the MT of v.3, is omitted the second time from the NIV). But "you" (emphatic, referring to David), however, are "ten thousand" times as important as the troops.

Since "ten thousand" men was "the smallest number appropriate to an army" (J. B. Segal, 6), the statement of David's men is tantamount to saying that he is equal to all of them put together. They are convinced that he will be of more help to them—in terms not only of morale but also of giving them a cause to fight for—if he remains behind in "the city" (i.e., Mahanaim, 17:24, 27).

Acquiescing to their wishes, David stands "beside the gate" (v.4) of the city, a prominent and visible location (cf. 15:2; Pr 8:3) from which to review the troops as they march off to battle. Their "units of hundreds and of thousands" (numbers that should perhaps be understood figuratively; see comment on v.1) might have brought back to David memories of his days as a mercenary in a Philistine army (see 1Sa 29:2 and comment). His final order to his three commanders (v.5)—an order that all the troops hear as well—is that they be "gentle" (*ʾaṭ*; GK 351; cf. Job 15:11; Isa 8:6) with Absalom, that is, that they not deal too hastily (cf. Ge 33:14 ["slowly"]) with him. David's reference to his son as "the young man" (cf. also vv.12, 29, 32) indicates, together with his words "for my sake," his paternal affection in spite of Absalom's destructive ambition, arrogance, and treachery.

6–8 The brief account of the battle between the armies of David and Absalom is a tightly knit section, framed by an inclusio formed by the occurrence of "battle" and "forest" in vv.6 and 8. While the repetition of "that day" (vv.7–8) and of *ᶜam* ("people," vv.6–7 ["army"]; v.8 ["lives"]) serves to unify the section as well, the most striking feature is the use of *watt*ᵉ*hî* ("and it was") in all three verses ("took place," v.6; "were," v.7; part of the periphrastic expression "spread out," v.8). The resemblance in construction between vv.6b–7a ("and the battle took place in the forest of Ephraim. There the army of Israel was defeated by David's men") and 2:17 ("The battle that day was very fierce, and Abner and the men of Israel were defeated by David's men"), the middle verse in ch. 2 (see comment on 2:17), is also noteworthy (cf. Conroy, 59 n. 50).

The locale of the initial confrontation is "the field" (v.6), which provides ample room for large-scale troop movements (see comments on "the open [country]" in 10:8; 11:23). In spite of the fact that the "forested hill country" of Ephraim and Manasseh (cf. Jos 17:15, 17–18) was west of the Jordan River, the location of the armies of David and Absalom in Transjordan demands an eastern site for the specific "forest of Ephraim" mentioned here (v.6; cf. George Adam Smith, *The Historical Geography of the Holy Land* [22nd ed.; London: Hodder and Stoughton, n.d.], 335 n. 2, who observes that Ephraimites had settled "in Gilead in such large numbers that the western Ephraimites call the Gileadites fugitives from Ephraim [Judges xii. 4]"; for full discussion see LaMoine DeVries, "The Forest of Ephraim," *BI* 10/1 [1983]: 82–85). A "pit in the forest" would prove to be the ignominious burial place of Absalom following his summary execution (v.17).

If in v.6 "army" (*ᶜam*, lit., "people"; see comment on v.1) refers to David's troops, in v.7 it signifies Absalom's men. The "army of Israel" consists of "the levies from the northern tribes" (Siegfried Herrmann, "King David's State" [in Barrick and Spencer], 269) and is equivalent to the "army of the LORD" in 1:12 (see Notes there). The verb "defeated" (see comments on 10:15 ["routed"]; 1Sa 4:2; cf. 1Sa 7:10 ["routed"]) and the noun "casualties" (see comment on 17:9 ["slaughter"]; cf. 1Sa 4:17 ["losses"]) translate the same Hebrew root (*ngp*), which is used more often of plague or disease than in battle contexts (cf. Conroy, 59 n. 53); this term highlights not only the total devastation that has befallen Absalom's troops but also the key role played by the Lord in their overthrow. The "twenty thousand" men killed by David's troops represents a "large army" (J. B. Segal, 6; see comment on "ten thousand" in v.3).

That the battle is spread out "over the whole countryside" (v.8) echoes 1 Samuel 30:16, where the narrator states that the Amalekites were scattered "over the countryside" celebrating the great amount of plunder they had seized in a raid (identical Heb. expression). The Hebrew sentence rendered "the forest claimed more lives ... than the sword" may be literally translated as "the forest was greater to devour among the people than that which the sword devoured" (for the image of the devouring sword, see comments on 2:26; 11:25). Natural phenomena are often more deadly than human enemies (cf. Jos 10:11; cf. Conroy, 59 n. 54). Of the many suggestions concerning what it means that the forest "claimed/devoured" more than the sword, McCarter's (*II Samuel*, 405) seems best: The dense "forest of Ephraim" (v.6), characterized by uneven and dangerous terrain, was a battleground "where the numerically superior force of [Absalom's] conscript army would be at a disadvantage against David's more skilled private army, with its considerable experience of guerrilla warfare" (see also comment on v.17).

9–18 *Wayyiqqārēᵓ* ("happened"), which begins v.9, is echoed as a homonym in v.18, where it means "is called." The two occurrences of the word thus form an inclusio that brackets the literary unit.

Verses 9–18 provide a macabre example of how a forest can "devour." Riding his "mule," a suitably regal animal (v.9, see comment on 13:29), Absalom gets his "head" caught in a tangle of "thick branches" (rendering a word found only here, although a word derived from the same Heb. root is translated "mesh" in parallelism with "net" in Job 18:8; for further examples cf. Conroy, 61 n. 59) growing out from a large oak tree as the mule passes under them and leaves its owner behind. Conroy's comment is appropriate: "The mule was a royal mount; losing his mule Absalom has lost his kingdom" (Conroy, 60).

Although it is possible to understand Absalom's predicament as having gotten his neck caught in a fork formed by two of the branches, Conroy observes that "the reader who recalls 14,26 will almost certainly visualize Absalom's hair in connection with the entanglement ... and will easily draw a contrast between promise and pride on the one hand and humiliation and doom on the other" (Conroy, 44 n. 4). Indeed, the word "head" is used as synecdoche for "hair" in 14:26 ("hair of his head" is literally "his head"; see also comment there). "In midair" is the NIV's rendering of a colorful phrase that translates literally as "between heaven and earth" (cf. 1Ch 21:16; Eze 8:3; Zec 5:9).

Among David's "men" (lit., "servants/officers," v.9, as also in v.7) is "one of the men" (*ʾîš ʾeḥād*—that is, "a certain man," v.10 [see 1Sa 1:1 and comment; cf. Snaith, 45]) who is the first to see Absalom hanging in the tree. In reporting to Joab what he has seen (v.10), the man is characterized as a *maggîd* (v.11; "who had told," NIV), a messenger who ordinarily brings bad news (see comments on 1:5; 15:13). To Joab, however, the news is bad only in the sense that Absalom is still alive.

Whichever of the two main approaches one takes to translating the *hinnēh* in Joab's response, its call for violence and vengeance is totally in character. The NIV's "What! You saw him?" or the like is preferred by Conroy (61 n. 61) as being the "stronger sense" and therefore preferable. Snaith, 46, by contrast, reads "if you saw him ..."—a construction that has precedent in the books of Samuel (cf. "If we go,..." [1Sa 9:7]). In any event, Joab cannot understand why the man did not kill Absalom on the spot. Had he done so, Joab says, it would have been incumbent on Joab ("I would have had" [v.11] is emphatic) to give the man ten shekels of silver (about four ounces [see NIV note], a not inconsiderable sum; cf. Jdg 17:10, where it represents the annual stipend offered to a Levite in addition to his food and clothing) as well as a warrior's belt (cf. 1Ki 2:5).

Not nearly so insensitive and unscrupulous as Joab, the man affirms that even a hundred times as much silver could not induce him to "lift" his "hand against" Absalom (v.12; see comments on "raise a hand" in 1Sa 22:17 and on "lay a hand on" in 1Sa 26:9), who is after all the "king's son." He had been among the troops who had heard David order his three commanders to "be gentle with the young man Absalom" (v.5; see comment there), and he now reminds Joab of that fact (v.12). He knows that if he had killed Absalom, Joab would not have defended him (v.13; for "kept your distance," cf. Ex 2:4; Ob 11 ["stood aloof"]), since ultimately "nothing is hidden from" David (see comment on 14:18; cf. Pss 69:5; 139:15; Hos 5:3), who, like an angel of God—indeed, like God himself—"knows everything that happens in the land" (14:20; see comment). The king would therefore surely execute the murderer of his son.

Petulant and impatient, Joab declared his unwillingness to wait for his man to kill Absalom and decided to take matters into his own hands (v.14). Whether the weapons he used were "javelins" cannot be determined with certainty (the LXX reads *belē*, "darts"). In any case, Joab "plunged" (cf. Jdg 3:21; 4:21 ["drove"]) three sharp-pointed instruments of some kind into Absalom. They pierced his "heart" (i.e., "chest"; cf. Na 2:7 ["breasts"]; also Ps

37:15) while he was still alive in "the heart of" (the NIV omits the Heb. expression) the oak tree. Mortally wounded, Absalom was then "surrounded" (v.15; cf. Jdg 16:2; 2Ki 3:25; 6:15; Ecc 9:14) by ten of Joab's "young men" (Heb.), who finished the grisly task of striking and killing (see comment on 14:6) the "young man" Absalom (vv.5, 12).

In doing this, these young men perform one of the functions of "armor-bearers" (cf. 23:37), who were expected to be ready to fight and kill when the occasion arose (cf. Jdg 9:54; 1Sa 14:13–14; 31:4; see comment on 1Sa 14:1). If "ten" shekels were Joab's spurned offer to pay for Absalom's death (v.11), "ten" armor-bearers (v.15) are prepared to assassinate the king's son for nothing. The death of Absalom by hanging is a macabre reprise of the earlier death of his counselor Ahithophel (17:23). Absalom's death also brings to three the number of sons whom David has lost as a result of his sins against Bathsheba and her husband, Uriah the Hittite (see 12:6 and comment).

Israel's erstwhile leader now dead, Joab "sounded" the trumpet (v.16; the same Heb. verb is rendered "plunged" in v.14 and is a wordplay on it, as also in Jdg 3:21, 27; cf. Conroy, 63–64 n. 79) to recall his troops (see 2:28 and comment). Echoing Hushai's suggestion that perhaps David was hiding in a "cave" (see 17:9 and comment), the narrator states that after Absalom's death his corpse is thrown into a large "pit" (v.17; the Heb. noun is the same) in the "forest" (of Ephraim; see v.6 and comment). An enormous (*gādôl m*e*ʾōd*, "very large") heap of rocks is then piled up over him (a common practice to mark the graves of infamous people; cf. Jos 7:26; 8:29). The survivors among Absalom's troops have meanwhile fled to their "homes" (lit., "tents"; cf. 19:8; 20:1, 22; 1Sa 4:10; 13:2).

The account of Absalom's demise concludes with a brief flashback summary of his self-serving attempt to perpetuate his name (v.18). From a literary standpoint it is linked closely to what precedes it, not only in the echo of the homonym *wayyiqqārēʾ* ("is called," from v.9; see comment), but also in the use of "erected," which renders the Hiphil of *nṣb*, as does "piled up" in v.17. There are thus two monuments commemorating Absalom (the "heap of rocks" in v.17, the "pillar" in v.18), each in its own way as pitiable as the other.

If Saul and his son Jonathan were inseparable "in life" (1:23), Absalom's tragedy is compounded by the fact that "during his lifetime" (v.18; same Heb. expression) he had no son who was willing or able to memorialize him. Although the setting up of memorial pillars was not uncommon in ancient times (cf. Ge 28:18, 22, 31:13; 35:14), the only other example of a funereal pillar in the OT is the one that "marks Rachel's tomb" (Ge 35:20). The precise function of the pillar erected by Absalom has been long debated, since *hzkyr šmy*, here translated "carry on the memory of my name" (for the same expression and/or concept, cf. Ge 21:2; 48:16; Nu 27:4; Dt 25:6–7; Ru 4:5, 10; Ps 45:17; see also comments on 14:7; 1Sa 24:21), might also be rendered "invoke my name" on the basis of cognate phrases in Akkadian and Aramaic (for discussion cf. Lewis, 96, 119, 173).

An additional factor is the comparison often made between v.18 and the role of the devoted son described in Ugaritic text *2 Aqht* (*CTA*, 17) 1:27, 45: *nṣb skn ilibh bqdš* ("who erects the stele/monument of his *ilib* in the sanctuary"). If the comparison is justified and *ilib* means "ancestral spirit(s)" (cf. G. R. Driver, *Canaanite Myths and Legends* [OTS 3; Edinburgh: T&T Clark, 1956], 49), then ancestor worship may be in view (for discussion see Theodor H. Gaster, *Thespis: Ritual, Myth, and Drama in the Ancient Near East*, rev. ed. [New York: Harper, 1966], 333–35). If, however, *ilib* means "ancestral god(s)" (cf. de Moor, 228), then idolatry would be implied (cf. Anson F. Rainey, "Institutions: Family, Civil, and Military," in *Ras Shamra Parallels: The Texts from Ugarit and the Hebrew Bible* [AnOr 50; ed. Loren R. Fisher; Rome: Pontifical Biblical Institute, 1975], 2:78–79).

While there is nothing inherently inconceivable about the possibility of Absalom's having adopted one or more of the customs of his pagan neighbors/relatives (his mother, after all, was the daughter of an Aramean king; see 3:3 and comment), it is far from certain that the Ugaritic text in question is in fact an apt parallel of v.18 (for discussion see Conroy, 65 n. 88). Indeed, apart from the example of filial piety (or, perhaps, the lack of same; see comment below), the only clearly shared element is the verb *nṣb* ("to erect"). Since Absalom sets up the monument "to himself" (thus NIV; *lô* is probably not intended as a dative of advantage ["ethical dative"] here), and since he names the pillar "after himself" (*ʿal-šᵉmô*, lit., "according to his [own] name"; cf. Ge 48:6 ["under the names of"]; Ex 28:21 ["with the name of"]), it is best to understand *hazkîr šᵉmî* in its normal sense of "carry on the memory of my name" (cf. Carl F. Graesser, "Standing Stones in Ancient Palestine," *BA* 35/2 [1972]: 40).

Like the equally egotistical Saul before him (see 1Sa 15:12 and comment), Absalom decides to memorialize himself by erecting a monument (perhaps an inscribed stele of some sort) in his own honor. His plaint that he has "no son" to do it for him is usually understood to mean that all three of the unnamed sons mentioned in 14:27 (see comment) had already died. It is also possible, however, that one or more of his sons were unwilling (for whatever reason) to perpetuate their father's memory. If so, the monument stands as yet another poignant act of desperation by its builder (cf. similarly Stan Rummel, "Using Ancient Near Eastern Parallels in Old Testament Study," *BAR* 3/3 [1977]: 10).

"Absalom's Monument" (lit., "Absalom's hand"; see comments on 8:3; 1Sa 15:12; cf. also Isa 56:5 ["memorial"]; cf. M. Delcor, "Two Special Meanings of the Word יד in Biblical Hebrew," *JSS* 12/2 [1967]: 230; Hoffner, 222 n. 6), erected in the "King's Valley" (known also as the "Valley of Shaveh" [Ge 14:17], a place of uncertain location but probably near Jerusalem), could be seen "to this day" (v.18)—that is, the time of the narrator of 2 Samuel (cf. 4:3; 6:8; Ge 35:20; see also 1Sa 6:18 and comment).

The monument is not to be identified with the fifty-two-foot-tall, bottle-shaped "Tomb/Pillar of Absalom," a monolith cut out of a cliff in the Kidron Valley east of Jerusalem that probably received its name because of its resemblance to a pillar. Its burial chamber "is reminiscent of Hellenistic and Roman sepulchers and is to be dated to the first part of the first century AD" (W. Harold Mare, *The Archaeology of the Jerusalem Area* [Grand Rapids: Baker, 1987], 195). It thus predates the celebrated Copper Scroll (3Q15), found by archaeologists in Cave 3 of Qumran during the excavations of 1952 and listing sixty-four hiding places where various items of value are said to have been deposited. The directions to site number fifty read as follows: "Under the 'Hand' of Absalom on the western side dig twelve notches: 80 talents" (Geza Vermes, trans., *The Complete Dead Sea Scrolls in English*, rev. ed [London: Penguin, 2004], 630).

NOTES

2 "Will surely march out" renders a strengthening infinitive absolute construction. Although it is relatively infrequent with the verb יצא (*yṣʾ*), the parallel literary section (16:5–14) contains another example ("as he came out," 16:5).

3 The basic difference between the NIV's textual reading and marginal reading of the verse is that between "you" (אַתָּה, ʾattâ) and "now" (עַתָּה, ʿattâ). "You," the choice of virtually all commentators, is the contextually superior variant. Although deciding in favor of "now," the KJV rendered correctly *ad sensum*: "But now *thou art* worth ten thousand of us." The first "now" in the MT of v.3 probably arose from contamination by the second occurrence of "now" later in the verse (cf. independently K&D, 435).

"To give ... support" renders either the Hiphil *Kethiv* לעזיר (*lʿzyr*), for an original להעזיר (*lhʿzyr*, "to provide help"; cf. GKC, sec. 53*q*), or the Qal *Qere* לעזור (*lʿzwr*, "to help"). Since the existence of Hiphil *ʿzr* in the OT is suspect (the only other possible occurrence being the problematic מעזרים [*mʿzrym*] in 2 Chronicles 28:23—where, however, the initial *m* is probably due to dittography [cf. *BHS*]), the Qal form is preferable (for discussion cf. Driver, 328).

4 "General descriptions of city gates appear in several texts, such as 2 Sam. 18:4, 24, a passage that refers to a lower and an upper gate, an inner chamber, and two towers. This, of course, fits precisely the plan of the 10th-century city gates of Hazor, Megiddo, and Gezer" (William G. Dever, *What Did the Biblical Israelites Know and When Did They Know It?* [Grand Rapids: Eerdmans, 2001], 199).

9 "He was left hanging" translates וַיֻּתַּן (*wayyuttan*, lit., "and he was put/placed," from נתן, *ntn*). The same rendering results from what is doubtless the correct reading—ויתל (*wytl*, from תלה, *tlh*)—as demonstrated by 4QSamuel[a] and LXX (for details cf. McCarter, *II Samuel*, 401; also תָּלוּי [*tālûy*, "hanging"] in v.10).

12 Though attested in only two Hebrew MSS (cf. *BHS*), "for my sake" (לִי, *lî*) is also assumed in several ancient versions (see NIV note) and has the advantage of echoing the same phrase in v.5. The alternative noted in the NIV note attempts to make sense of MT מִי (*mî*, "who[ever]"; cf. further K&D, 438).

13 The textual reading is based on the *Qere*'s "my life," whereas the marginal rendering prefers the *Kethiv*'s "his life." (The Hebrew may be translated literally as "And/Or if I had dealt falsely/recklessly with my/his life" [for discussion cf. Kirkpatrick, 172; McCarter, *II Samuel*, 397, 401].)

16 חָשַׂךְ (*ḥāśak*, "halted, held back") could also be rendered "spared" here (cf. BDB, 362; for discussion cf. Conroy, 62 n. 73).

17. David's Mourning for Absalom (18:19–19:8a)

OVERVIEW

Although the similarities between 18:19–19:8 and its counterpart (16:1–4) in the architectonic structure of chs. 15–20 (more precisely, 15:1–20:22) are not as numerous or convincing as are other parallel sections in that structure (see Overview to 15:1–12), they are not totally absent. If in 16:2–4 David reveals his skepticism as he addresses a series of questions to Ziba concerning Mephibosheth, a pretender to the throne of Israel, in 18:28–32 he demonstrates equal skepticism as he questions Ahimaaz and a Cushite concerning Absalom, another pretender to Israel's throne.

Moreover, if in 16:2–4 David's statements are introduced three times by the formulaic *wayyōʾmer hammelek* ("And/Then the king said/asked"; see comment on 16:1–4), in the present section they are prefaced six times in the same way (cf. vv.25b, 26b, 27b, 29, 30, 32). Thus *wayyōʾmer hammelek* occurs nine times in 16:1–4; 18:19–19:8—an impressive figure in the light of the fact that it is found only nine times in the rest of the larger literary complex (15:19, 25, 27; 16:10; 18:2; 19:23, 33, 38; 20:4).

Two clearly distinguishable units comprise 18:19–19:8: (1) 18:19–33, which recounts in exquisite detail how two messengers relay the news of Absalom's death (indirectly, to be sure) to David; (2) 19:1–8, which records the words of Joab's rebuke to the mourning king. While the latter consists of a summary description of David's inconsolable grief (19:1–4) followed by Joab's rebuke and David's response to it (19:5–8), the former is divided into three sections arranged in chiastic order (as noted by Fokkelman, *Narrative Art*, 1:251 [the titles of the sections are mine]):

A The messengers are sent to bring news to David (18:19–23)
  B David anxiously waits for news concerning Absalom (18:24–27)
A' David receives the messengers and their news (18:28–33)

Two key verbal roots recurring frequently throughout 18:19–33 are *rwṣ* ("run," vv.19, 21, 22 [2x: "run," "go"], 23 [3x], 24, 26 [2x], 27 [2x; the NIV omits the second occurrence), and *bśr* ("[bring] news," vv.19, 20 [3x: "take the news," "take the news," "do so"], 22, 25, 26, 27, 31). At least one of the two roots occurs in each verse from v.19 through v.27, and their interplay has the effect of slowing down the action while at the same time heightening the suspense. As noted by Gunn ("Traditional Composition," 227–28), 18:19–33 bears a certain resemblance to the messenger scene in 2 Kings 9:17–20.

19Now Ahimaaz son of Zadok said, "Let me run and take the news to the king that the LORD has delivered him from the hand of his enemies."

20"You are not the one to take the news today," Joab told him. "You may take the news another time, but you must not do so today, because the king's son is dead."

21Then Joab said to a Cushite, "Go, tell the king what you have seen." The Cushite bowed down before Joab and ran off.

22Ahimaaz son of Zadok again said to Joab, "Come what may, please let me run behind the Cushite."

But Joab replied, "My son, why do you want to go? You don't have any news that will bring you a reward."

23He said, "Come what may, I want to run."

So Joab said, "Run!" Then Ahimaaz ran by way of the plain and outran the Cushite.

24While David was sitting between the inner and outer gates, the watchman went up to
the roof of the gateway by the wall. As he looked out, he saw a man running alone. 25The
watchman called out to the king and reported it.

The king said, "If he is alone, he must have good news." And the man came closer and closer.

26Then the watchman saw another man running, and he called down to the gatekeeper, "Look, another man running alone!"

The king said, "He must be bringing good news, too."
27The watchman said, "It seems to me that the first one runs like Ahimaaz son of Zadok."
"He's a good man," the king said. "He comes with good news."
28Then Ahimaaz called out to the king, "All is well!" He bowed down before the king
with his face to the ground and said, "Praise be to the LORD your God! He has delivered up
the men who lifted their hands against my lord the king."
29The king asked, "Is the young man Absalom safe?"
Ahimaaz answered, "I saw great confusion just as Joab was about to send the king's
servant and me, your servant, but I don't know what it was."
30The king said, "Stand aside and wait here." So he stepped aside and stood there.
31Then the Cushite arrived and said, "My lord the king, hear the good news! The LORD has
delivered you today from all who rose up against you."
32The king asked the Cushite, "Is the young man Absalom safe?"
The Cushite replied, "May the enemies of my lord the king and all who rise up to harm
you be like that young man."
33The king was shaken. He went up to the room over the gateway and wept. As he
went, he said: "O my son Absalom! My son, my son Absalom! If only I had died instead of
you — O Absalom, my son, my son!"
19:1Joab was told, "The king is weeping and mourning for Absalom." 2And for the whole
army the victory that day was turned into mourning, because on that day the troops
heard it said, "The king is grieving for his son." 3The men stole into the city that day as men
steal in who are ashamed when they flee from battle. 4The king covered his face and cried
aloud, "O my son Absalom! O Absalom, my son, my son!"
5Then Joab went into the house to the king and said, "Today you have humiliated all
your men, who have just saved your life and the lives of your sons and daughters and the
lives of your wives and concubines. 6You love those who hate you and hate those who
love you. You have made it clear today that the commanders and their men mean nothing to you. I see that you would be pleased if Absalom were alive today and all of us were
dead. 7Now go out and encourage your men. I swear by the LORD that if you don't go out,
not a man will be left with you by nightfall. This will be worse for you than all the calamities that have come upon you from your youth till now."
8So the king got up and took his seat in the gateway. When the men were told, "The
king is sitting in the gateway," they all came before him.

COMMENTARY

19–23 Jubilant over the fact that Absalom's army has been defeated by David's troops (cf. v.7), Ahimaaz (see comments on 15:27, 36) asks Joab for permission to report to the king: "[Please] let me run" (v.19; same Heb. expression as in v.22). His desire to "take the news" is doubtless prompted by his feeling that David will be as happy about the outcome of the battle as he himself is (the verb *bśr* and its cognate forms almost always connote news for David that is good; see comment on 1Sa 4:17). What could be better news for David than that the Lord has "delivered him" (lit., "vindicated him [by delivering him]," vv.19, 31; see 1Sa 24:15 and comment) from the rebellious Israelite troops, who have therefore become "his" enemies? (Whether the antecedent is David or the Lord, the end result is the same [see comment on "the LORD's enemies" in 1Sa 30:26].)

Joab, however, at first refuses to send Ahimaaz (v.20), perhaps because he does not want to endanger the life of a messenger who will in fact have brought bad news to the king. Three times he tells Ahimaaz that he is not to take the news "today" ("another time" is lit. "another day"), the third time underscoring his point by using "today" in emphatic position (lit., "but today you must not take the news"). Whether at this juncture Ahimaaz knows that Absalom is dead is a moot point since, as McCarter (*II Samuel*, 408) observes, the last clause in v.20 is probably the narrator's comment rather than a part of Joab's statement to Ahimaaz: "This was because the king's son was dead."

Another more likely messenger comes to Joab's attention: "a [lit., 'the'] Cushite" (v.21). To equate him with the Benjamite "Cush" in the title of Psalm 7, where the LXX reads *Chousi* ("Cushite"; cf. *BHS* there), is unproductive since the contents of the psalm imply that "Cush(i)" is David's enemy (as many if not most Benjamites were). As a gentilic the term "Cushite" can refer to a person born either in the upper Nile region (a Nubian [cf. Eli's son Phinehas; see comment on 1Sa 1:3]) or in central and southern Mesopotamia (cf. Youngblood, *The Book of Genesis*, 129–30). In their relationships with the people of Israel, Cushites in the OT are alternately friendly (cf. Jer 38:7–13; 39:15–18) or hostile (cf. 2Ch 14:9–15).

After surveying several proposed identifications and interpretations of the Cushite in v.21, Conroy appropriately summarizes: "Rather than speculate on the possibly baleful significance ... of the possibly black skin ... of the possibly Nubian messenger, it is preferable to think that Joab chose the Cushite simply because he was an alien and hence, if the worst came to the worst, more expendable" (Conroy, 69 n. 102). Nevertheless, it is also possible that "the Cushite served David as an official courier, a specially gifted and trained runner" (Larry Helyer, "'Come What May, I Want to Run': Observations on Running in the Hebrew Bible," *Near East Archaeological Society Bulletin* 48 [2003]: 8). In any event, "this casual reference to a Cushite in David's army seems to indicate that the presence of Cushite troops was not at all unusual" (J. Daniel Hays, "From the Land of the Bow: Black Soldiers in the Ancient Near East," *BRev* 14/4 [1998]: 31). Thus Joab sends him on his way and instructs him simply to tell David what he has seen.

Undeterred and unafraid, Ahimaaz again requests permission to take the news to David, "come what may" (vv.22–23). "Please let me run" (v.22; see v.19 and comment), he says, "also me" (an emphatic expression not reflected in the NIV). As before, however, Joab tries to deter him. Whether "my son" (v.22) was a conventional way of addressing a messenger (cf. 1Sa 4:16) is uncertain, although it is surely going too far to assert (with Conroy [70 n. 106] and McCarter [*II Samuel*, 408]) that here it is condescending, patronizing, or ironic. In any event, Joab attempts to convince Ahimaaz that none of the news he has can be expected to "bring ... a reward" (lit., "find [anything]," v.22; cf. Job 31:25 ["had gained"]; Hos 12:8 ["have become"]; for *bᵉśôrâ* ["news"] in a similar context implying reward, see 4:10 and comment).

Persistent to the end, Ahimaaz pleads a third time—and Joab finally relents (v.23). So intent is Ahimaaz on performing his mission well that, even though the Cushite has a head start, Ahimaaz outruns him. If the forest of Ephraim (see comment on v.6) was along the eastern border of the "plain" (cf. Ge 19:17, 25)—that is, the plain of the Jordan (see NIV note; cf. Ge 13:10–11; 1Ki 7:46 = 2Ch 4:17)—Ahimaaz's route, though less direct and therefore a mile or two longer than that of the Cushite, would be over smoother and more level ground than the Cushite's and would therefore enable him to arrive at Mahanaim in less time (for a plausible reconstruction of the two routes, see the map of Yohanan Aharoni and Michael Avi-Yonah, *The Macmillan Bible Atlas*, rev. ed. [New York: Macmillan, 1977], 71; for a detailed description of the terrain see Helyer, "'Come What May, I Want to Run,'" 8–10). In addition Ahimaaz from the outset may have been stronger and more athletic than the Cushite (cf. 17:17–21).

24–27 The scene shifts to Mahanaim, the temporary headquarters of David (v.24; see 17:24 and comment). There the king, waiting for news of the outcome of the battle, sits between "the inner and outer" (lit., "the two") gates of the city, perhaps in one of the guardrooms. A watchman, standing on the roof of the gateway complex that forms part of the city wall, looks out toward the horizon and catches sight of a lone runner approaching the city. When the watchman calls to the king below and reports what he has seen, the king assumes that if the runner is by himself "he must have good news" (lit., "good news must be in his mouth," v.25; see comment on 17:5).

But the narrator's observation that the man "came closer and closer," reprising as it does the earlier description of the Philistine Goliath who "kept coming closer" to David (1Sa 17:41), has an unsettling and ominous ring. The watchman then sees another man running, and this time he calls the information down to the city "gatekeeper" (v.26), whose duties included the dissemination of news to interested parties (cf. 2Ki 7:10–11). The king is thus duly notified, and his response is the same as before.

Ahimaaz's reputation as a superb athlete has preceded him, and the watchman recognizes his running style even before he has gotten close enough for his face to be visible (v.27). For the third time David responds favorably, characterizing Ahimaaz as a "good" man and the news he brings as "good." (The MT adds "good" [the explicit use of which with *bśr* is unnecessary; see comments on v.19; 1Sa 4:17] to "news" only here in the entire narrative.) If we agree for the sake of the argument that 1 Kings 1–2 is in fact a part of David's court history (chs. 9–20; for discussion see comments on 9:1–20:26), the observation of Gunn ("Traditional Composition," 228) is especially apt:

> Just as the watchman's identification of Ahimaaz draws the comment from the king that "He is a good man [*ʾyš ṭwb*] and comes with good news [*ʾl bśwrh ṭwbh ybwʾ*]," so in 1 Kings 1:42–43 the arrival of Jonathan the son of Abiathar with news for Adonijah prompts Adonijah to say, "Come in [*bʾ*] for you are a worthy man [*ʾyš ḥyl*] and bring good news [*ṭwb tbśr*]."

In the eyes of the recipients, however, in both cases the news turns out to be anything but good.

28–33 Whereas in vv.19–23 Joab sends two messengers to bring news to David, in the parallel section (vv.28–33) David receives Joab's messengers and their news. The chiastic effect (see Overview to 18:19–19:8) is enhanced by the fact that in the earlier passage the Cushite was sent before Ahimaaz while here Ahimaaz (who outran the Cushite) is received first. In addition the name "David" is used only once (v.24) in the entire literary unit (vv.19–33), and that in its central section (vv.24–27). The bracketing sections (vv.19–23, 28–33) refer to him as "the king" consistently throughout. Cohesion is given to the present section by the striking wordplay between the three occurrences of *šālôm* (vv.28 ["All is well!"], 29 ["safe"], 32 ["safe"]) and the five occurrences of *ʾabšālôm* (vv.29, 32, 33 [3x]).

Arriving in Mahanaim, Ahimaaz first reassures the king with the common *šālôm* greeting (v.28; see 1Sa 25:5–6 and comments). As the Cushite had bowed down before Joab (cf. v.21), Ahimaaz bows down before King David—but in the most respectful of ways, as Absalom himself had once done: "with his face to the ground" (v.28; cf. 14:33; see comment on 14:4). Beginning with an outburst of praise (see comment on 1Sa 25:32), Ahimaaz informs David that the Lord has "delivered up" the king's enemies. The idiom is the same as that in 1 Samuel 17:46; 24:18; and 26:8, but here it is used absolutely (without "into the hand of"; see comment on 1Sa 17:46). In every case it is the sovereign Lord (cf. independently Conroy, 72 n. 118), not mighty armies, who brings deliverance.

But, with respect to the reports not only of Ahimaaz (v.28) but also of the Cushite (v.31), Conroy, 74, observes: "It is as if [David] had not really heard their words at all. They were interested in the plural of the defeated forces; he is concerned only about the singular of his son." Again referring to Absalom as "the young man" (v.29; see comment on v.5), David insists on knowing whether he is "safe" (*šālôm*). Conroy's remark, 74, is to the point: "The insistence on *šlwm* here reminds the reader that the last word spoken to Absalom both by his father (15,9 ['peace']) and by Ahithophel (17,3 ['unharmed']) was *šlwm*."

For his part Ahimaaz, who perhaps does not know that Absalom is dead (see comment on v.20), responds simply that he saw great "confusion" (v.29), a not uncommon phenomenon in battle situations (see comments on 1Sa 14:19–20). Indeed, there was so much tumult that he does not "know what it was." (The NIV adds the last two words for clarity; Ahimaaz concludes his speech with *mâ* ["what"], as in Proverbs 9:13: "without knowledge" [lit., "does not know what"].) His question unanswered, due perhaps to Ahimaaz's nervous and somewhat incoherent statements (so Alter, *The David Story*, 309), David tells Ahimaaz to step aside and "wait here" (v.30), echoing verbatim the command of Balaam to Balak centuries earlier (in Nu 23:15).

After David dismisses Ahimaaz, the Cushite arrives with his report. He may have overheard the original request of Ahimaaz to Joab because he uses the same idiom to describe Israel's defeat: "The LORD has delivered you ... from the hand of [your enemies]" (v.31; see comment on v.19 [the NIV here omits "the hand of"]). When the king asks him the same question he had asked Ahimaaz (v.32), the Cushite responds—euphemistically, to be sure—that Absalom is dead: "May the enemies of my lord the king and all who rise up to harm you be like that young man." Garsiel, 106, perceptively observes:

> There is a clear rule of law which connects a leader's conduct with his fate and the fate of his house. A degenerate leader, whether it is himself who has sinned or his sons, will ultimately be deposed (see the story of Samuel and his sons) or come to a tragic end, just as Eli and his sons die on the same day, and so do Saul and his. This law holds true of David also ... just as in the stories of the death of Eli, Saul and their sons, in the story of Absalom there appears a runner who announces the evil tidings of his death in battle (2 Sam 18:19–32); and before that, in the story of Amnon's murder, a rumor comes to the king of the killing of all his sons, although it is found that only Amnon had been killed (2 Sam 13:30–36). With this, the criticism of all four leaders described in the book of Samuel, together with their sons, reaches its conclusion.

In the light of his obvious concern about his son, David's reaction to the news of Absalom's death is totally predictable: He is shaken (v.33), he mourns (19:1; for another example of parallelism between *rgz* ["shake, tremble"] and *ʾbl* ["mourn"], cf. Am 8:8; also Conroy, 75 n. 130). Seeking privacy to weep alone, he goes up to the room over the city gateway (see v.24 and comment) and laments as he goes: "O my son Absalom! My son, my son Absalom! If only I [emphatic] had died instead of you—O Absalom, my son, my son!" Totally unlike the otherwise similar complaint of certain grumbling Israelites on their trek through the desert following the Exodus ("If only we had died ... in Egypt!" [Ex 16:3]), David's mournful cry is filled with the pathos of a father's grieving heart: "If only I had died instead of you."

By no means is this the first time that David weeps over the death of someone—a compatriot (cf. 3:32), a close friend (cf. 1:11–12), even a son (cf. 13:33, 35–36)—but here his grief knows no bounds, and his language is therefore unique. The

> extreme possibility of repetition, where the device has a totally dramatic justification as the expression of a kind of mental stammer, is bound to be relatively rare, especially in nondramatic literature, but it does occur occasionally in the Bible, most memorably when David is informed of Absalom's death.... The poet-king, who elsewhere responds to the report of death with eloquent elegies, here simply sobs, "Absalom, Absalom, my son, my son," repeating "my son" eight times in two verses [18:33; 19:4]. (Alter, *The Art of Biblical Narrative*, 92)

Writers as different as George Gordon Lord Byron and William Faulkner have been moved by David's poignant words to incorporate them into their own writings in one form or another. Indeed, in weeping and in addressing Absalom as "my son," David himself echoes an earlier occasion in which Saul had done the same with respect to him, even while perceiving David as one who was attempting to seize the throne of Israel—just as Absalom has tried to do (see 1Sa 24:16 and comment).

But the narrative of the events immediately preceding and following Absalom's death as recorded in ch. 18 recalls another emotion-laden story as well (see Ackerman, 50):

> The description of Absalom's demise resonates with allusions to Abraham's binding of Isaac in Genesis 22.... Both Absalom and the ram are caught in a thicket (*śôbek/sĕbak*). Whereas Abraham is commanded not to send forth his hand (*ʾal tišlaḥ yadĕkā*) unto the lad (22:12), Joab's soldier refuses to send forth his hand (*lōʾ ʾešlaḥ yādî*) unto the son of the king (18:12). And finally, Abraham offers up the ram in place of his son (*taḥat bĕnô* [22:13]). It takes a while for David to help us perceive this analogy, but finally he makes it clear: "would that I had died in place of you (*taḥtekā*), O Absalom, my son, my son."

The last verse of ch. 18 in the NIV constitutes the first verse of ch. 19 in the MT, accommodating a traditional one-verse numbering difference between the Hebrew and English texts throughout ch. 19 (for the same phenomenon in 1Sa 24, see comment on 1Sa 24:1–22; for a similar phenomenon in 1Sa 21, see comment on 1Sa 21:1–9). The commentary below will follow the English numbering system.

19:1–8 Verses 1–8, which conclude the literary unit that begins at 18:19 (see Overview to 18:19–19:8), themselves comprise a discrete subunit that uses an inclusio to frame the whole: "Joab was told, 'Behold [MT *hinnēh*, omitted from the NIV], the king is weeping and mourning for Absalom'" (v.1); "The men were told, 'Behold [again omitted from the NIV], the king is sitting in the gateway'" (v.8; cf. Fokkelman, *Narrative Art*, 1:269). Avoiding the personal name "David," the account employs "the king" throughout (see comment on 18:28–33 for the same phenomenon in certain sections of ch. 18). In vv.1–8 the "exclusive use of *hmlk* ... (where David is most a father and least a king) is quite striking and could perhaps be taken as a deliberate contrast and an implied criticism on the part of the narrator" (Conroy, 81).

The subsection divides into two equal halves, vv.1–4 providing a summary description of David's grief and vv.5–8 recording Joab's lengthy rebuke and David's brief response. Verse 4 concludes by condensing the poignant lament with which ch. 18 ends, repeating verbatim only its first ("O my son Absalom!") and last ("O Absalom, my son, my son!") clauses.

In vv. 1–4 Joab, a beneficiary of David's intelligence network (see comment on 10:5), is eventually "told" (v.1) of David's "weeping" (see comment on 18:33) and "mourning" for his son Absalom (see 13:37 and comment for David's similar reaction to the death of his son Amnon; see also comment on 14:2). It is not long before Joab's entire army hears of it as well (v.2), with the result that what should have been for them a great "victory" (brought about by the Lord; cf. 23:10, 12; see 1Sa 19:5 and comment) has become a cause for "mourning" (a noun from the same Heb. root used in v.1).

Far from capitalizing on their triumph as an occasion for celebration, the men slink into Mahanaim like those who "steal in" (lit., "make themselves move around like thieves," v.3; cf. similarly Snaith, 54) because cowardice has forced them to flee the battlefield. Meanwhile David "covered his face" (v.4; "the verb used, *laʾat*, is the same one David chose when he said, 'Deal gently [*leʾat*] with the lad Absalom'" [18:5; Alter, *The David Story*, 312]) while continuing to cry aloud (cf. 13:19) as he mourns for his dead son.

In vv. 5–8 Rosenberg, 166, aptly characterizes this subsection: "Joab, asserting the reasons of state security that demanded Absalom's death, accuses David of grave discourtesy to his supporters and friends—the words [vv.5–7] are extraordinarily frank and represent Joab's only open rebuke of the king throughout the entire Davidic history." It is a rebuke that will cost him dearly (cf. v.13), at least temporarily.

Whereas the narrator employs *ʿam* ("people") to describe David's "army/troops/men" (vv.2–3, 8), Joab uses *ʿᵃbādîm* ("servants")—a term implying loyalty, obedience, dependence—for the same purpose (vv.5–7). Stressing not only the thoughtless immediacy of the king's insensitivity but also the urgent need for prompt action, Joab makes use of the word "today" no fewer than five times (2x in v.5 ["Today," "just"], 3x in v.6 [omitted once by the NIV]).

David's army commander goes "into the house" (v.5) to talk to the king. "The implication is that Joab speaks with David in private. The thematic opposition to this is 'in the gate' ['gateway,' NIV; v.8], where Joab will send David [v.7]" (Alter, *The David Story*, 312). Joab begins by upbraiding David for humiliating the very men ("your men," v.5) who are responsible for having saved the king's life as well as the lives of all who are near and dear to him (*nepeš* ["life"], which appears four times in the verse, is omitted from the NIV before "[your] concubines"), including those of his "wives and concubines" (for which see comments on 5:13; 12:8; 1Sa 25:43; see also 1Sa 1:2 and comment).

Joab is, of course, correct: "David's men" (18:7) have in fact won the battle. But the heart of Joab's complaint is that David loves those who hate him and hates those who love him (v.6). Although Joab's accusation has been called a "colossal hyperbole" (Fokkelman, *Narrative Art*, 1:272), "it accurately reflects the topsy-turvy nature of the king's extreme emotions. Its similarity to the description of Amnon's swing from love to hatred (13:15) reminds the reader that such emotions are common to father and son, both of whom commit grave acts of injustice" (Lasine, 117). Whatever else it may involve, at the very least "love" in this context surely implies covenantal loyalty (see comments on 1:26; 1Sa 16:21; 18:1–4; 20:17; cf. also Conroy, 79 and n. 151).

Joab has received the clear impression that the "commanders" (including himself, Abishai, and Ittai [cf. 18:5]; v.6) and their men mean nothing at all to the king. Indeed, in his present frame of mind David would trade Absalom's life for those of everyone else (ironically, "if [*lu*ʾ] Absalom were alive" echoes 18:12: "if [*lu*ʾ] a thousand shekels were weighed out into my hands, I would not lift my hand against the king's son"). Conroy, 79, observes on 18:33, "David wished that he had died himself instead of Absalom, but here Joab accuses him of wishing Absalom were alive even if that meant the loss of the whole army." The ambiguity of David's behavior when issues of life and death are at stake is explored also in 12:18–23 (see comments).

Joab's final statement in his rebuke begins and ends with "now" (v.7; see comment on "today" in vv.5–6). He swears on oath to David that if the king does not immediately go out and "encourage" (lit., "speak to the heart of," v.7; cf. 2Ch 32:6 ["encourage"]) his "men" (*ʿᵃbādîm*), by nightfall, not a "man" (*ʾîš*) will remain loyal to him. The troops of Judah thus having deserted David, no greater calamity for him throughout his entire life could possibly be imagined.

However reluctantly, the king is prodded into action by Joab's harsh words. If David formerly sat in the gateway of Mahanaim awaiting news of the battle's outcome (cf. 18:24), he now takes his seat there (v.8) in his official capacity of adjudicating the grievances (see 15:2 and comment; cf. also 1Ki 22:10) of any and "all" of the "men" (lit., "people"; see comment on v.5) of Judah. The literary unit ends by echoing the earlier report that the Israelites had "fled to their homes" (18:17; the NIV has wrongly placed v.8b, the contents of which constitute one of a series of concluding statements [cf. v.39; 18:17; 20:22; also 1Sa 2:11; 7:17; 10:25–26; 15:34; 24:22; 26:25], at the beginning of the next section).

NOTES

20 The *Qere*'s כִּי־עַל־כֵּן (*kî-ʿal-kēn*, lit., "because therefore") is the preferred reading. The omission of *kēn* in the *Kethiv* is doubtless due to haplography because of the following בֵּן (*ben*, "son of"; cf. K&D, 440; Driver, 331; McCarter, *II Samuel*, 402).

26 "Look, another man" is literally "Look, a man" (the NIV has inserted "another" *ad sensum*). The comment of Conroy, 71, is apropos:

> One would almost have expected the word "another" in the sentinel's words (*hnh ʾyš ʾḥr rṣ lbdw*), and indeed this is had by the ancient versions [cf. *BHS*], but the MT form without *ʾḥr* has its own effect. It expresses well the impersonal attitude of the sentinel who reports just what he sees at this moment and makes no connection with what he has seen previously, and this contrasts with the king's impatient eagerness and anxiety.

19:8[9] A gate complex and its pavement were built at Dan near the northern border of Israel at the end of the tenth century BC (cf. Avram Biran, "Tel Dan," *BA* 37/2 [1974]: 49). Near the entrance to the gate itself was found an unusual structure, built of ashlars and originally having at its four corners small columns with decorated capitals or bases. "The columns may have supported a canopy which covered the structure. The use of this structure could not be determined archaeologically, but it is possible that it served as a base for a throne.... The reference in 2 Samuel 19:8 surely must refer to some special structure [at Mahanaim] where David sat and where the people could see him" (Biran, "Tel Dan," 45, 47; cf. also 46 for photographs of the structure at Dan).

18. David's Return to Jerusalem (19:8b–43)

OVERVIEW

In the overall structure of chs. 15–20 (more precisely 15:1–20:22), the literary unit describing the return of "King David" (v.11) to Jerusalem (vv.9–43) parallels that depicting his flight (15:13–37) caused by Absalom's rebellion (see Overview to 15:1–12). If the earlier account included David's instructions to three of his supporters (Ittai, 15:19–23; Zadok, 15:24–31; Hushai, 15:32–37), the present narrative contains meetings with three representatives of "important constituencies with which David must come to terms" (Brueggemann, *First and Second Samuel*, 326): Shimei (vv.15b–23), Mephibosheth (vv.24–30), and Barzillai (vv.31–39).

These three sections are in turn bracketed by a prologue (vv.9–15a) and an epilogue (vv.40–43), each of which deals with the question of who—Israel or Judah—should escort the king on his triumphant return to his capital city (cf. the threefold repetition of *lhšyb ʾt-hmlk* ["to bring back the king"] in vv.10–12, echoed in v.43: *lhšyb ʾt-mlky* ["to bring back our (lit., 'my') king"]).

The resulting chiastic outline thus focuses on Mephibosheth (see comment on v.24):

A Israel or Judah? (19:9–15a)
  B Shimei the Benjamite (19:15b–23)
    C Mephibosheth the Saulide (19:24–30)
  B' Barzillai the Gileadite (19:31–39)
A' Judah or Israel? (19:40–43)

In addition to structural similarities, a number of shared lexical elements link the two parallel sections, among which are references to Zadok and Abiathar (v.11; 15:24, 27, 29, 35–36); the root *mhr* ("hurry," v.16; 15:14 ["immediately, move quickly"]); the word "ford" (v.18; 15:28); the unusual expression *hāyâ lᵉmaśśāʾ ʾel/ʿal* ("be a burden to," v.35; 15:33); and the idiom "do to/for" a person "whatever pleases/seems good to" him (vv.37–38; 15:26).

Meanwhile, the Israelites had fled to their homes. 9Throughout the tribes of Israel,
the people were all arguing with each other, saying, "The king delivered us from the
hand of our enemies; he is the one who rescued us from the hand of the Philistines. But
now he has fled the country because of Absalom; 10and Absalom, whom we anointed
to rule over us, has died in battle. So why do you say nothing about bringing the king
back?"

11King David sent this message to Zadok and Abiathar, the priests: "Ask the elders of
Judah, 'Why should you be the last to bring the king back to his palace, since what is being
said throughout Israel has reached the king at his quarters? 12You are my brothers, my

own flesh and blood. So why should you be the last to bring back the king?' 13And say to Amasa, 'Are you not my own flesh and blood? May God deal with me, be it ever so severely, if from now on you are not the commander of my army in place of Joab.'"

14He won over the hearts of all the men of Judah as though they were one man. They sent word to the king, "Return, you and all your men." 15Then the king returned and went as far as the Jordan.

Now the men of Judah had come to Gilgal to go out and meet the king and bring him across the Jordan. 16Shimei son of Gera, the Benjamite from Bahurim, hurried down with the men of Judah to meet King David. 17With him were a thousand Benjamites, along with Ziba, the steward of Saul's household, and his fifteen sons and twenty servants. They rushed to the Jordan, where the king was. 18They crossed at the ford to take the king's household over and to do whatever he wished.

When Shimei son of Gera crossed the Jordan, he fell prostrate before the king 19and said to him, "May my lord not hold me guilty. Do not remember how your servant did wrong on the day my lord the king left Jerusalem. May the king put it out of his mind. 20For I your servant know that I have sinned, but today I have come here as the first of the whole house of Joseph to come down and meet my lord the king."

21Then Abishai son of Zeruiah said, "Shouldn't Shimei be put to death for this? He cursed the LORD's anointed."

22David replied, "What do you and I have in common, you sons of Zeruiah? This day you have become my adversaries! Should anyone be put to death in Israel today? Do I not know that today I am king over Israel?" 23So the king said to Shimei, "You shall not die." And the king promised him on oath.

24Mephibosheth, Saul's grandson, also went down to meet the king. He had not taken care of his feet or trimmed his mustache or washed his clothes from the day the king left until the day he returned safely. 25When he came from Jerusalem to meet the king, the king asked him, "Why didn't you go with me, Mephibosheth?"

26He said, "My lord the king, since I your servant am lame, I said, 'I will have my donkey saddled and will ride on it, so I can go with the king.' But Ziba my servant betrayed me. 27And he has slandered your servant to my lord the king. My lord the king is like an angel of God; so do whatever pleases you. 28All my grandfather's descendants deserved nothing but death from my lord the king, but you gave your servant a place among those who eat at your table. So what right do I have to make any more appeals to the king?"

29The king said to him, "Why say more? I order you and Ziba to divide the fields."

30Mephibosheth said to the king, "Let him take everything, now that my lord the king has arrived home safely."

31Barzillai the Gileadite also came down from Rogelim to cross the Jordan with the king and to send him on his way from there. 32Now Barzillai was a very old man, eighty years of age. He had provided for the king during his stay in Mahanaim, for he was a very wealthy man. [33]The king said to Barzillai, "Cross over with me and stay with me in Jerusalem, and I will provide for you."

[34]But Barzillai answered the king, "How many more years will I live, that I should go up to Jerusalem with the king? [35]I am now eighty years old. Can I tell the difference between what is good and what is not? Can your servant taste what he eats and drinks? Can I still hear the voices of men and women singers? Why should your servant be an added burden to my lord the king? [36]Your servant will cross over the Jordan with the king for a short distance, but why should the king reward me in this way? [37]Let your servant return, that I may die in my own town near the tomb of my father and mother. But here is your servant Kimham. Let him cross over with my lord the king. Do for him whatever pleases you."

[38]The king said, "Kimham shall cross over with me, and I will do for him whatever pleases you. And anything you desire from me I will do for you."

[39]So all the people crossed the Jordan, and then the king crossed over. The king kissed Barzillai and gave him his blessing, and Barzillai returned to his home.

[40]When the king crossed over to Gilgal, Kimham crossed with him. All the troops of Judah and half the troops of Israel had taken the king over.

[41]Soon all the men of Israel were coming to the king and saying to him, "Why did our brothers, the men of Judah, steal the king away and bring him and his household across the Jordan, together with all his men?"

[42]All the men of Judah answered the men of Israel, "We did this because the king is closely related to us. Why are you angry about it? Have we eaten any of the king's provisions? Have we taken anything for ourselves?"

[43]Then the men of Israel answered the men of Judah, "We have ten shares in the king; and besides, we have a greater claim on David than you have. So why do you treat us with contempt? Were we not the first to speak of bringing back our king?"

But the men of Judah responded even more harshly than the men of Israel.

COMMENTARY

9–15a The use of "all" twice in v.9 (rendered once as "throughout") forges a transitional link with the final verse of the preceding section (see comment on v.8). Animated discussion ("arguing with each other," v.9) is the order of the day as some Israelites remind their countrymen that David, despite whatever flaws he may have, had in fact been their conquering hero in the past—indeed, "he is the one" (emphatic) who had long since rescued them from their perennial enemies, the Philistines (see 5:17–25; 8:1 and comments).

At the same time, however, he has now "fled" (*bāraḥ*) the country (an activity to which David was no stranger; cf. 1Sa 20:1) "because of" Absalom (*mēʿal*; better, "from"; cf. Ne 13:28, where *wʾbryḥhw mʿly* is rendered "And I drove him away [lit., 'caused him to flee'] from me"). David's partisans continue their apologia by pointing out that Absalom himself, whom Israel had "anointed" to rule over them (the only reference to Absalom's anointing; v.10), is now dead. They therefore insist "now" (omitted from the NIV) on knowing why their fellow Israelites ("you," emphatic plural) "say nothing" (lit., "remain quiet/silent"; cf. 13:20) about returning David to his rightful place on the throne in Jerusalem.

If there are any doubts at this point in the account concerning who is really king, the narrator erases them by using the title "King David" (v.11). Sending word to his friends Zadok and Abiathar, the priests (cf. 15:27–29, 35; 17:15–16; see also 15:24 and comment), David tells them to ask the elders of Judah (whom he had counted as his friends many years before; see 1Sa 30:26 and comment) why they should be the "last" to bring the king back to the city. The men of Israel would later chide the men of Judah by claiming that Israel, not Judah, was the "first" to speak of bringing the king back (v.43)—although, of course, the desire to do so was by no means unanimous throughout Israel (cf. v.10).

In the meantime David is privy to the substance of the ongoing discussions, the news of which has reached him at his "quarters" in Mahanaim (lit., "house," v.11; the same Heb. word refers to David's "palace" in Jerusalem earlier in the verse). At least partly because of his ancestry (cf. Ru 4:12, 18–22), David senses a special tie between himself and the Judahite elders; so he repeats his incredulous question: "Why should you be the last to bring back the king?" (v.12b). His close relationship to them as he describes it in v.12a reads literally as follows: "My brothers are you [emphatic], my bone and my flesh are you [emphatic]."

> It can of course be argued that this reference is to blood ties. But such can be the case only in a most general sense. More likely, "brother" and "bone and flesh" refer to the sharing of covenant oaths. [Johannes] Pedersen [*Israel: Its Life and Culture. I–II* (London: Oxford, 1926), 57–60] shows that "brother" refers to all those who have ties of community and commitments to solidarity. Thus David's reference here is not to blood ties, though they may be present, but rather that mutual covenant commitments must be honored because the vows assume fidelity through thick and thin. (Brueggemann, "Of the Same Flesh and Bone," 536)

"Bone and flesh," rendered by the NIV as "own flesh and blood" (v.12), describes a claim to relationship with David made earlier by the tribes of Israel as well (see 5:1 and comment). It is the men of Judah, however, who will try to convince the Israelites that David is more "closely related to us" (v.42) than he is to them.

Also to "Amasa" (emphatic, v.13)—clearly a blood relative of David (see 17:25 and comment)—Zadok and Abiathar are to say, "Are you [emphatic] not my own flesh and blood?" Although Joab was also related to David (see 1Sa 26:6 and comment), he was Absalom's chief executioner as well (cf. 18:14–15), and thus his position as David's army commander (cf. 18:2; see also comments on 8:16; 1Sa 26:6) is in jeopardy (cf. in addition his recent rebuke of the king, however well received [see 19:5–8 and comments]). Echoing verbatim the strong oath of self-imprecation that he took on an earlier occasion (cf. 3:35; see comment on 1Sa 20:13), David replaces Joab with Amasa as the commander of his army "from now on" (lit., "all the days," v.13), an emphatic expression the NIV translates "for life" in a similar context (1Sa 28:2). Ironically, some time earlier "Absalom had appointed Amasa over the army [of Israel] in place of Joab" (17:25), and now Joab is ousted as Judah's army commander as well.

> Still the practical politician, David sought by maintaining Amasa as commander-in-chief to placate

> the dissident elements in the east who had been allied with Absalom.... Thus David had met the challenge of Transjordanic Israel and had proved the master. (Curtis, "'East Is East ...'" 358)

Although it is impossible to know for certain whether it was David who "won over the hearts of all the men [ʾîš] of Judah" (v.14; the Lucianic recension of the LXX makes Amasa the subject), the end result is that they send word to the king to return to Jerusalem with all his "men" (*ʿᵃbādîm*, lit., "servants, officials"). Happy to comply with their request, David leaves Mahanaim and arrives at the Jordan River (v.15a). The question concerning whether Israel (vv.9–10) or Judah (vv.11–12) will "bring the king back" (vv.10–12) is resolved—at least temporarily—in favor of Judah.

15b–23 Various other significant constituencies, however, also vie for David's approval. Shimei the Benjamite (vv.15b–23), Mephibosheth the Saulide (vv.24–30), and Barzillai the Gileadite (vv.31–39) are the three key figures who represent them (see Overview to 19:9–43). Each section is characterized at the outset as a meeting scene: "Judah had come to Gilgal to go out and meet the king" (v.15b); "Mephibosheth, Saul's grandson, also went down to meet the king" (v.24); "Barzillai the Gileadite also came down from Rogelim to cross the Jordan with the king" (v.31). Eskhult, 67, correctly observes that the three episodes "are all commenced by a circumstantial clause of the type (*wə*)*subj–qṭl*": *wîhûdâ bāʾ* ("Now [the men of] Judah had come," v.15b); *ûmᵉpîbōšet ben-šāʾûl yārad* ("Mephibosheth, Saul's grandson, also went down," v.24); *ûbarzillay haggilʿādî yārad* ("Barzillai the Gileadite also came down," v.31).

That "Judah" in v.15b means "the men of Judah" (NIV) is clear in that it is flanked in vv.14 and 16 by the phrase *ʾîš yᵉhûdâ* in reference to the same entity. They intend to bring David "across the Jordan" (v.15b; cf. v.41) from the eastern side to Gilgal (the very "gathering place where Saul was consecrated as king [1 Sam 11:14–15] and later severed by Samuel from his role as God's anointed [1 Sam 15:12–29]" [Alter, *The David Story*, 319]; perhaps modern Khirbet el-Mefjer, about four miles west of the Jordan and sixteen miles northeast of Jerusalem), from which he—like Joshua before him (cf. Jos 10:7)—would lead his followers to ultimate triumph over the land.

Accompanying the men of Judah is "Shimei son of Gera, the Benjamite from Bahurim" (v.16; see 16:5, 11 and comments). He who had earlier been quick to curse David and pelt him with stones (see 16:5–14 and comments) now hastens ("hurried," v.16; "rushed," v.17) to beg for mercy (vv.18b–20). With him are not only a "thousand" (perhaps here "military unit"; see comments on 18:1, 4; 1Sa 4:2) of his countrymen but also "Ziba, the steward of Saul's household, and his fifteen sons and twenty servants" (v.17; see 9:1–2, 9–10 and comments). Shimei and his companions have come to take the king and his household westward across the "ford" of the Jordan (v.18; see 15:28 and comment). In addition, they are eager to "do whatever he wished" (lit., "do whatever is/was pleasing in his eyes")—just as Mephibosheth ("do whatever pleases you," v.27) and Barzillai ("do ... whatever pleases you," v.37) will later desire for David (same Heb. idiom in all three cases).

Because the reference to Ziba in v.17 has temporarily interrupted the story of Shimei, the latter is reintroduced in v.18b as "Shimei son of Gera" (cf. v.16). "The function of the full 'XbY' name form can be explained ... as indicating the refocussing of attention on Shimei" (Clines, 276). Arriving in David's presence on the eastern side of the Jordan, Shimei, while fully admitting that earlier he "did wrong," begs that the king not hold him "guilty" (v.19; the verb and substantive are both forms of the root *ʿwh*). On another occasion David declares that anyone "whose sin the LORD does not count against him" is blessed (Ps 32:2), a statement that employs the essentially same phrase here rendered "May my lord not hold me guilty."

Although punishment is only to be expected when one "does wrong" (7:14; cf. 24:17), Shimei hopes that David will not "remember" (v.19) what he had done to the king on the day he left Jerusalem (see 16:5–14 and comments)—a plea that contrasts sharply with Abigail's request that David "remember" her and her good deeds in his behalf when the Lord has brought him success (1Sa 25:31). Shimei earnestly desires that David "put ... out of his mind" (v.19) the spiteful and foolish behavior of his servant; he does not want the king to "take it to heart" (as the Heb. idiom is elsewhere translated; cf. 1Sa 21:12).

A short time ago Shimei had called David a "man of blood" (16:7–8), a "scoundrel" (16:7); now he addresses him respectfully—indeed, in an attitude of complete submission—as "my lord (the king)" and refers to himself as "your servant" (vv.19–20; see 1Sa 25:24 and comment). Recognizing how inappropriate his earlier conduct was, he readily confesses, "I [emphatic] have sinned" (v.20). In so doing he echoes the similarly contrite words of Saul, his deceased fellow Benjamite (see 1Sa 26:21 and comment).

In Shimei's mind, however, his misdeeds are part of a past that he would just as soon forget. It is now "today," and he wants to be the "first of the whole house of Joseph" (v.20)—the "first" among all the Israelites (cf. v.43; for "house of Joseph" [the largest and most prominent of the northern tribes; cf. Ge 49:22–26; Jos 17:17] as synecdoche for "Israel," cf. Jos 18:5; Jdg 1:22, 35; 1Ki 11:28; Am 5:6; Ob 18; Zec 10:6)—to "come down" (because "his hometown of Bahurim is in the high country near Jerusalem" [Alter, *The David Story*, 315]) and "meet my lord the king" (implying his desire that David return to his rightful place in Jerusalem).

But "Abishai son of Zeruiah" (v.21), one of David's army commanders (see 18:2 and comment), will hear none of it. Because David, "the LORD's anointed" (see comments on 5:3; 1Sa 16:13), had been "cursed" by Shimei (see 16:10–12 and comments), Abishai wants him "put to death," not only because such rashness is entirely in character for Abishai (see 16:9 and comment), but perhaps also because "to curse the king was considered a capital offense ... like cursing God (I Kings 21:10; cf. Ex 22:27 [EV v. 28])" (Talmon, 30).

David's reply to Abishai (v.22) echoes verbatim his earlier response to him in an identical context: "What do you and I have in common, you sons of Zeruiah?" (see 16:10 and comments). By using *hayyôm* ("today, this day") three times in rapid succession, David underscores the fact that he himself is in full control of the situation and that he alone will determine Shimei's fate. Although "you have become" is plural, thus making it virtually certain that David is speaking to Joab as well as to Abishai (cf. "sons [plural] of Zeruiah" earlier in the verse), it is equally clear that Abishai is the main addressee (*śāṭān* ["adversary"] is singular). The word for "adversary" was later specialized to refer to "the Adversary (par excellence)"—namely, Satan (see comment on 1Sa 29:4).

In the present context "my adversary" probably means "a legal accuser on my behalf" since the language of both Shimei (vv.19–20) and Abishai (v.21) is demonstrably forensic (for discussion cf. Peggy L. Day, "Abishai the *śāṭān* in 2 Samuel 19:17–24," *CBQ* 49/4 [1987]: 543–47). Wanting to know why Abishai thinks he has to stand up for the king's rights, David rhetorically asks whether anyone should be "put to death in Israel today"—that is, summarily executed. In reprising the similar statesmanlike declaration of his predecessor Saul (see 1Sa 11:13 and comment), David exhibits "a flash of that magnanimity which marked him at his best" (Gunn, "David and the Gift of the Kingdom," 32).

As in the case of Saul's words to Jonathan in 1 Samuel 20:30, David's "do I not know" (v.22) is intended as a rebuke to Abishai. "In his earlier rejection of Abishai's desire to kill, David gave a theological reason (16:11–12). Now David gives a more practical reason. David ['I' is emphatic] is 'king over Israel' (v.22)" (Brueggemann, *First and Second Samuel*, 327). Turning to Shimei, he promises him on oath that his life will be spared (v.23). Although at the end of his days David will change his mind and strongly urge Shimei's execution (cf. 1Ki 2:8–9), at least for now geopolitical considerations seem to demand his "affirmation of Shimei as a larger strategic gesture to reclaim the loyalty of the north" (Brueggemann, *First and Second Samuel*, 327).

24–30 The second—and central—of the three key men who come to meet David is "Mephibosheth, Saul's grandson" (v.24; see comments on 4:4; 9:6). The pericope that describes the meeting is delimited by the balanced statements "the king ... returned [*bāʾ*] safely" (v.24) and "the king has arrived [*bāʾ*] ... safely" (v.30).

David's exile from Jerusalem has encompassed many days if not weeks, and during that entire time ("from the day the king left until the day he returned," v.24) Mephibosheth has not cared for his feet, mustache, or clothes in a way befitting a guest of royalty (cf. 9:7, 10–12). That he has not "taken care of [*ʿāśâ*] his feet" probably means that he has not "trimmed his toenails" (cf. LXX; for discussion cf. McCarter, *II Samuel*, 417, 421), since the following clause ("trimmed his mustache") also uses the verb *ʿāśâ*. Indeed, the two clauses are identical except for the object of the verb (*wᵉlōʾ-ʿāśâ raglāyw wᵉlōʾ-ʿāśâ śᵉpāmô*, lit., "and he did not do his feet, and he did not do his mustache"). To "cover one's mustache" (NIV's "cover [the lower part of] one's face") was a sign of ceremonial uncleanness (cf. Lev 13:45), mourning (cf. Eze 24:17, 22), or shame (cf. Mic 3:7). Mephibosheth's refusal to wash his clothes is likewise more than a matter of careless hygiene; it demonstrates his desire to remain ceremonially unclean during the king's absence (cf. Ex 19:10, 14).

Employing the verb translated "left" (*hlk*) in v.24, David wants to know why Mephibosheth decided not to "go" with him (v.25) when he was forced to flee from Absalom (cf. 1Sa 30:22 for the potentially negative implications of not accompanying a king on risky ventures). Mephibosheth counters by stating that he had indeed wanted to "go" (*hlk*, v.26) with the king but that since he is "lame" (see comments on 5:8; 9:13; see also 4:4 and comment) he needed to have his donkey "saddled" so that he could "ride on" it. But his servant "Ziba" (not in the MT of v.26) had betrayed him. Mephibosheth may be implying that the string of donkeys Ziba had earlier "saddled" (see 16:1 and comment) and brought to David for his household to "ride on" (16:2) included Mephibosheth's own private mount, leaving him without means of transportation. He further accuses Ziba of having "slandered" (*rgl*) him in David's presence (v.27)—at the very time when Mephibosheth was experiencing discomfort and humiliation by not taking care of his "feet" (*rgl*, v.24).

Mephibosheth, however, consoles himself with "the confidence that David will not be fooled by the misrepresentation of Ziba, but will get to the bottom of the affair and separate truth from falsehood" (McKane, 59). After all, he asserts, King David is "like an angel of God" (v.27) and therefore not only "knows everything that happens in the land" (14:20) but also exercises divine wisdom "in discerning good and evil" (14:17; see comments on 14:17, 20; 1Sa 29:9). He readily admits that Saul's descendants—including, presumably, himself—"deserved" only "death" (lit., "were men of death," v.28; cf. 1Ki 2:26; see also comments on the Heb. expression "son[s] of death" in 12:5; 1Sa

20:31; 26:16) from David, whose life Saul had persistently and mercilessly tried to take from him (see comments on 4:8; 1Sa 20:1).

By contrast, Mephibosheth is grateful that David has given him the privilege—at least as he himself understands it—of being among those who "eat at" the king's "table" (v.28; see comment on 9:7). He does not use his own "right(s)" (lit., "righteousness") as a basis for claiming royal reward (see comment on 1Sa 26:23), nor does he sense that he deserves to make further "appeals" to the king (lit., "cries"; same Heb. root as in v.4).

David responds to Mephibosheth by ordering him and Ziba to divide "the fields" (v.29)—"the land" that he had originally restored to Mephibosheth (see 9:7 and comment; same Heb. word in both cases) but had later turned over to Ziba (cf. 16:4). Did David's decision to share the estate between the two men reflect "his conclusion that there was no possibility of ascertaining which of them was telling the truth" (McKane, 59)? Or was it "a compromise taking the place of a judgement based on fact-finding, which might have been too troublesome at that time" (Z. W. Falk, "Hebrew Legal Terms: III," *JSS* 14/1 [1969]: 41)?

Probably neither. As David's son Solomon would later threaten to divide a living baby in order to discern which of two mothers was telling the truth (cf. 1Ki 3:24–25), so David here demands the division of the fields in order to discern whether Mephibosheth or Ziba is the liar. Damrosch observes that just as the real mother of the living baby offered the child to the false claimant in order to preserve its life (cf. 1Ki 3:26), so also Mephibosheth offers the entire estate to Ziba (David Damrosch, *The Narrative Covenant: Transformations of Genre in the Growth of Biblical Literature* [San Francisco: Harper, 1987], 247; cf. v.30).

Indeed, the comparison between the episodes of Solomon and David may be even closer. The Talmudic tractate *Šabbat 56b* records a comment of R. Judah: "When David said to Mephibosheth, 'Thou and Ziba divide the land,' a Heavenly Voice said to him, 'Rehoboam and Jeroboam shall divide the kingdom.'" If the baby remained undivided because Solomon had "wisdom from God" (1Ki 3:28), and if the command of David (who was "like an angel of God," v.27) to "divide the fields" (v.29) became moot because of Mephibosheth's magnanimity (v.30), the death of Solomon would eventually bring about the division of the kingdom (cf. 1Ki 11:11–13) and the divine assignment of ten of the twelve tribes of Israel to Jeroboam I (cf. 1Ki 11:29–31; see also comment on v.43 below).

31–39 The third and last of the three representatives to meet David at the Jordan is "Barzillai the Gileadite" from "Rogelim" (v.31; see 17:27 and comments). "David's three encounters at the ford of the Jordan form a progressive series on the scale of loyalty: first Shimei, who has heaped insults on him and now pleads for forgiveness; then Mephibosheth, whose loyalty, though probably genuine, has been called into question by Ziba; and then the unswervingly devoted old man, Barzillai" (Alter, *The David Story*, 318). Verse 31, which speaks of Barzillai's leaving his hometown, and v.39, which records his return to his home, form an inclusio that frames the literary unit (these two verses also share the name "Barzillai," refer to "the king," and include the phrase "cross[ed] the Jordan"; in both cases the verbal form is *wayyaᶜᵃbōr*). A chiastic outline characterizes the section (cf. similarly Fokkelman, *Narrative Art*, 1:305):

A Introduction (19:31–32)
  B David speaks to Barzillai (19:33)
    C Barzillai speaks to David (19:34–37)
  B' David speaks to Barzillai (19:38)
A' Conclusion (19:39)

In some respects the presence of Barzillai at the Jordan is more significant than that of either Shimei or Mephibosheth. It is not only that he symbolizes the vast Transjordanian regions, the control of which were crucial to any Israelite king, but also that with respect to David he has the prestige ("eighty years of age," v.32; cf. Ps 90:10) and wherewithal ("very wealthy," v.32; cf. the description of Nabal in 1Sa 25:2) to "send him on his way" back to Jerusalem (v.31; cf. 1Sa 9:26). "He" (emphatic) it was, after all, who along with others "had provided for the king" (v.32) during the royal exile in Mahanaim (see 17:27–29 and comments).

David makes it clear, however, that he wants to repay Barzillai's kindness: "You [emphatic] cross over with me" (lit. trans., v.33). David's goal is to induce his friend to take up residence with him in Jerusalem so that the king can "provide" for him (v.33) as he had earlier "provided" for the king (v.32; for discussion of *kwl* with a more inclusive meaning than simply "to feed," see Alan J. Hauser, *From Carmel to Horeb: Elijah in Crisis* [JSOTSup 85; Sheffield: Almond, 1990], 14, 85 n. 9).

But Barzillai protests that the number of years left in his life is limited at best and that therefore it would make no sense for him to move to Jerusalem (v.34). He points out that he is "now" (lit., "today"—i.e., "at this very moment," v.35) eighty years old (see comment on v.32). In stating that he cannot tell the difference "between what is good and what is not" (lit., "between good and evil"), Barzillai may be implying that he is too old to appreciate the good life at David's court, since it is not necessarily only little children who are unable to distinguish good from bad (cf. Dt 1:39; Isa 7:15–16; Jnh 4:11).

At the same time, however, since Barzillai's words echo 14:17 (see comment), Ackerman, 42, may be correct in asserting that

> these three passages [14:17, 20; 19:35] combine to articulate a theme that runs throughout the Court History: the role of the king involves a keen discernment that helps him judge between good and evil. It is almost a superhuman knowledge that is required, like that of the angel of God [see comment on v.27]—bridging the epistemological gap among humans, as well as between the human and the divine. Thus, the phrase heaped on the king [in 14:17, 20] is also a challenge—both to the king and to the reader—to read situation and text closely, to perceive what is going on and why. Can anyone—characters or reader—discern good and evil?

In any event, the aged Barzillai, like other elderly sages of his time and all times, observes that his tastebuds have been dulled and his ability to "hear" singing (the Heb. verb intends, more precisely, "*listen to* ... with satisfaction or enjoyment" [Driver, 337]) has declined (v.35; cf. Ecc 12:4). Like Hushai in the parallel literary section (15:13–37; see comment on 15:1–12), Barzillai does not want to be a "burden" to David (v.35; see 15:33 and comment), perhaps in the sense that he would require constant care and attention (cf. Patrick, 548). He wants only to accompany the king across the Jordan "for a short distance" (v.36) and has no desire for further rewards. He will then return to Rogelim, where he will die and be interred in the family burial site (v.37; see 2:32 and comment).

If the king agrees, Kimham (probably one of Barzillai's sons, a tradition preserved in some LXX MSS [cf. *BHS*]; cf. 1Ki 2:7) will be Barzillai's surrogate at the royal court. To the final request of Barzillai to David—"Do for him [Kimham] whatever pleases you [David]" (v.37)—the king replies, "I [emphatic] will do for him whatever pleases you [Barzillai]" (v.38; for this idiom as a lexical link to the parallel literary section, see Overview to vv.9–43). David then adds that he is prepared to do for Barzillai anything his friend desires.

Formalities concluded, the crossing of the Jordan by the king and his party takes place (v.39) opposite Gilgal (v.40; see v.15b and comment). Before Barzillai returns to his home, David kisses him (for kissing as an act of royal protocol, see comment on 14:33) and gives him his "blessing" (or, perhaps better, "farewell"; see comment on 13:25; cf. NIV note on Ge 47:10; for *nšq* used alone in the sense of "kiss good-by," cf. Ge 31:28; Ru 1:14; 1Ki 19:20).

40–43 Like its counterpart (vv.9–15a; see Overview to vv.9–43), vv.40–43 address the question of whether it is Israel or Judah that will accomplish the vital mission of bringing David back to Jerusalem. Further tying together the two sections is the use of "brothers" in the general sense of allies or compatriots (vv.12, 41; see comment on v.12). After a brief introduction (v.40), the "men of Israel" and the "men of Judah" speak alternately (v.41; v.42; v.43a), with the men of Judah having the final say—although exactly what they say is left unrecorded (v.43b).

David's escort had consisted of "all the troops of Judah" and "half the troops of Israel" (v.40). Since Israel had a much larger army to begin with (see 17:11 and comment), that only half its troops had participated in the crossing might be understood merely in terms of logistics. But perhaps the narrator is subtly granting Judah pride of place. (In any case Judah, David's tribe, is mentioned first.) The acrimony between the two groups increases when the men of Israel complain to the king that the men of Judah—ostensibly their "brothers" (v.41; see comment above)—might as well have "kidnapped" David and his men (as the verb here rendered "steal ... away" is translated in Ex 21:16; Dt 24:7) to keep as many as possible of the men of Israel from sharing the privilege of accompanying the king westward to Gilgal.

The men of Judah have a ready answer, of course: As a member of their tribe, David is more "closely related" to Judah than he is to Israel (v.42). Thus there is no need for the men of Israel to be angry over what seems to the men of Judah to be perfectly natural. Nor have the latter taken advantage of their relationship to the king. Indeed, they strongly deny that they have either "eaten any" of his provisions or "taken anything" from his supplies. (The force of both finite verbs in the MT is strengthened by a preceding infinitive absolute form.)

But the men of Israel reject all such explanations. Judah is only one tribe, while Israel has ten "shares" (lit., "hands," v.43; cf. Ge 47:24 ["fifths"]; 2Ki 11:7 ["companies"]) in the king—that is, ten tribes in the overall kingdom (for Ugar. *yd* ["hand"] meaning "share" [plural *ydt*, as in the Heb. of v.43(44)], cf. *ydty*, "my portions" [Baal V.i.21]; for Akkad. *qātu* ["hand"] in the sense of "share [of an inheritance/estate]," cf. *CAD*, 13:196–97). The fact that the only other occurrence of *ʿeśer yādôt* ("ten shares") is in Daniel 1:20 ("ten times"), where the figure ten is doubtless metaphorical, leads Conroy to the conclusion that "*ʿśr ydwt* is more likely to be a round figure expressing superiority ... than a reference to the ten northern tribes" (Conroy, 123 n. 32).

Far more plausible, however, is comparison with "the tearing of Ahijah's mantle into twelve pieces giving Jeroboam ten (1 Kings 11:30–31, 35). In these last two texts [v.43; 1Ki 11:30–31, 35] there is clearly a stylized reference to the restricted Israel, to the 'Ten Tribes' of the divided kingdom" (Zechariah Kallai, "Judah and Israel—A Study in Israelite Historiography," *IEJ* 28/4 [1978]: 256). Such elements in the narrative "point forward to, and possibly reflect awareness of, the later division of the kingdom" (Gordon, *I and II Samuel*, 293) and have obvious implications for the date of the writing of the books of Samuel. (Indeed, K&D, 11, states categorically that "they were not written till after the division of the kingdom under Solomon's successor.")

Since the men of Israel "have ten shares in the king," they conclude that it logically follows ("besides," v.43) that they "have a greater claim on David" than Judah has. David's sizable land grant to Mephibosheth (cf. 9:7–13) and—even more impressive—the extensive tribal territories to which Ish-Bosheth fell heir (see 2:9–10 and comments) give substance to the assertion of Israel's men. They therefore want to know why the men of Judah "treat" them "with contempt" (lit., "humble" them, v.43; cf. Isa 9:1; 23:9), and they conclude their part of the debate by reminding the Judahites that they—the men of Israel—were the "first" to speak of returning David to his rightful place in Jerusalem (see v.20 and comment).

The words of the men of Israel, however, cause the men of Judah to respond more "harshly" still. By using the root *qšh*, the narrator not only echoes the earlier fears of David as he anticipated King Saul's wrath (cf. 1Sa 20:10) but also foreshadows the foolish attitude of Rehoboam as he—king of Judah and potentially king of all Israel—irrevocably alienates the northern tribes (cf. 1Ki 12:13 = 2Ch 10:13).

NOTES

9[10] "Arguing with each other" renders נָדוֹן (*nādôn*), a Niphal participle from דין (*dyn*, "judge, dispute"; cf. LXX κρινόμενος, *krinomenos*). But since this would be the only example of Niphal *dyn* in the OT, perhaps the original reading was נָלוֹן (*nālôn*), a Niphal participle from לין II (*lyn*, "grumble, murmur"; cf. the Lucianic recension of the LXX γογγύζοντες, *gongyzontes*), used with relative frequency of Israel's grumbling against the Lord's servants (cf. Nu 16:41[17:6]: וַיִּלֹּנוּ, *wayyillōnû*; LXX ἐγόγγυσαν, *egongysan*; cf. *BHS*) and employed once in the absolute sense (Ps 59:15[16]: וילינו, *wylynw*, "howl"; LXX γογγύσουσιν, *gongysousin* [58:16]).

13[14] The root of תֹּמְרוּ (*tōmᵉrû*, "[you] say") is אמר (*ʾmr*), the quiescent א (*ʾ*) of תֹּאמְרוּ (*tōʾmᵉrû*) having dropped out in the orthography.

18[19] "They crossed at the ford" (NIV) presumably assumes dittography of ה (*h*) in the MT's ועברה העברה (*wʿbrh hʿbrh*) and defective writing of the verb in וְעָבְרָ הָעֲבָרָה (*wᵉʿābᵉru hāʿᵃbārâ*, "They crossed back and forth"; frequentative use of the perfect with *waw* consecutive, for which cf. GKC, sec. 112*e*–*o*; cf. similarly Driver, 335, who states further that the words "will then describe the purpose with which Ziba and his attendants ... came down to the Jordan").

31[32] "From there" renders אֶת־בַּיַּרְדֵּן (*ʾet -bayyardēn*), a syntactically impossible construction in which the sign of the direct object (*ʾet-*) is followed by a phrase that means "in/from the Jordan." The best solution is perhaps to omit *ʾet-* (as a few Hebrew MSS do; cf. *BHS*) and to translate "from the Jordan" (= NIV "from there") with the Lucianic recension of the LXX.

32[33] שִׂיבָתוֹ (*śîbātô*), translated "his stay," is a difficult form at best if derived from the root ישב (*yšb*), which is called for here. It is thus better to read the infinite construct form שִׁבְתּוֹ (*šibtô*) with some Hebrew MSS (cf. *BHS*).

40[41] *Qere*'s העבירו (*hʿbyrw*, "had taken ... over") is much to be preferred to the syntactically inept *Kethiv* ויעברו (*wyʿbrw*), which probably arose by contamination from the same form ("bring ... across") in v.41[42] (where it is used correctly).

19. Sheba's Rebellion (20:1–22)

OVERVIEW

The account of Sheba's rebellion against David serves as a counterpoise to the story of Absalom's conspiracy (15:1–12) in chs. 15–20, which constitute the major part of the narrative in chs. 13–20 (more precisely, 13:1–20:22), the longest definable literary section of the court history of David (chs. 9–20; see Overviews to 13:1–22; 15:1–12). David's statement to Abishai in v.6 highlights the comparison between the two episodes and underscores the seriousness of Sheba's revolt: "Now Sheba son of Bicri will do us more harm than Absalom did."

Since vv.1 and 22b both contain the phrases *wayyitqaᶜ baššōpār* ("he sounded the trumpet") and *ʾîš leʾōhālāyw* ("every man to his tent/each returning to his home"), the two verses form an inclusio that brackets the literary unit, which may be outlined chiastically:

A Sheba deserts David (20:1–2)
  B David takes steps to foil Sheba (20:3–7)
    C Joab kills his rival Amasa (20:8–13)
  B' The wise woman of Abel defeats Sheba (20:14–22a)
A' Joab returns to David (20:22b)

1 Now a troublemaker named Sheba son of Bicri, a Benjamite, happened to be there. He
sounded the trumpet and shouted,

"We have no share in David,
  no part in Jesse's son!
Every man to his tent, O Israel!"

2 So all the men of Israel deserted David to follow Sheba son of Bicri. But the men of
Judah stayed by their king all the way from the Jordan to Jerusalem.
3 When David returned to his palace in Jerusalem, he took the ten concubines he had
left to take care of the palace and put them in a house under guard. He provided for them,
but did not lie with them. They were kept in confinement till the day of their death, living
as widows.
4 Then the king said to Amasa, "Summon the men of Judah to come to me within three
days, and be here yourself." 5 But when Amasa went to summon Judah, he took longer than
the time the king had set for him.
6 David said to Abishai, "Now Sheba son of Bicri will do us more harm than Absalom did.
Take your master's men and pursue him, or he will find fortified cities and escape from

us."[7]So Joab's men and the Kerethites and Pelethites and all the mighty warriors went out
under the command of Abishai. They marched out from Jerusalem to pursue Sheba son of
Bicri.

[8]While they were at the great rock in Gibeon, Amasa came to meet them. Joab was
wearing his military tunic, and strapped over it at his waist was a belt with a dagger in its
sheath. As he stepped forward, it dropped out of its sheath.

[9]Joab said to Amasa, "How are you, my brother?" Then Joab took Amasa by the beard
with his right hand to kiss him. [10]Amasa was not on his guard against the dagger in Joab's
hand, and Joab plunged it into his belly, and his intestines spilled out on the ground. Without being stabbed again, Amasa died. Then Joab and his brother Abishai pursued Sheba
son of Bicri.

[11]One of Joab's men stood beside Amasa and said, "Whoever favors Joab, and whoever is for David, let him follow Joab!" [12]Amasa lay wallowing in his blood in the middle of
the road, and the man saw that all the troops came to a halt there. When he realized that
everyone who came up to Amasa stopped, he dragged him from the road into a field and
threw a garment over him. [13]After Amasa had been removed from the road, all the men
went on with Joab to pursue Sheba son of Bicri.

[14]Sheba passed through all the tribes of Israel to Abel Beth Maacah and through the
entire region of the Berites, who gathered together and followed him. [15]All the troops
with Joab came and besieged Sheba in Abel Beth Maacah. They built a siege ramp up to
the city, and it stood against the outer fortifications. While they were battering the wall to
bring it down, [16]a wise woman called from the city, "Listen! Listen! Tell Joab to come here
so I can speak to him." [17]He went toward her, and she asked, "Are you Joab?"

"I am," he answered.

She said, "Listen to what your servant has to say."

"I'm listening," he said.

[18]She continued, "Long ago they used to say, 'Get your answer at Abel,' and that settled
it. [19]We are the peaceful and faithful in Israel. You are trying to destroy a city that is a
mother in Israel. Why do you want to swallow up the LORD's inheritance?"

[20]"Far be it from me!" Joab replied, "Far be it from me to swallow up or destroy! [21]That is
not the case. A man named Sheba son of Bicri, from the hill country of Ephraim, has lifted
up his hand against the king, against David. Hand over this one man, and I'll withdraw
from the city."

The woman said to Joab, "His head will be thrown to you from the wall."

[22]Then the woman went to all the people with her wise advice, and they cut off the
head of Sheba son of Bicri and threw it to Joab. So he sounded the trumpet, and his men
dispersed from the city, each returning to his home. And Joab went back to the king in
Jerusalem.

COMMENTARY

1–2 Mentioned eight times throughout the chapter, the rebel is always given his full name, "Sheba son of Bicri" (vv.1–2, 6–7, 10, 13, 21–22; the NIV has added "Sheba" in vv.14 and 15 for purposes of clarity), a highly unusual phenomenon that calls for explanation. In Jeremiah 2:23 the people of Judah are compared to "a swift she-camel [*bikrâ*], running here and there" (i.e., rebellious), and Isaiah 60:6 speaks of "young camels [*bikrê*] of Midian and Ephah," mentioning also the land of "Sheba" in that context. Clines, 277, observes that

> the implication could perhaps be that Sheba is a true son of בֶּכֶר [*beker*; GK 1146], stubborn, rebellious, and self-willed. It may be more than coincidental that in Isa. lx 6 Sheba is referred to as a region of camels (בכר [*bkr*]). Of course there is no real connection between the place name שְׁבָא [*š*[e]*bā*ʾ] and the personal name שֶׁבַע [*šeba*ʿ], but it is not impossible that a link between the refractory Sheba son of בֶּכֶר [*beker*] and a well-known home of the בֶּכֶר [*beker*] was intended by the story-teller, who referred invariably to "Sheba b. Bichri" in order to reinforce his view of Sheba's character, which he blackens at the very beginning with the epithet "son [*sic*] of Belial" (xx 1).

Sheba is introduced as a "troublemaker" (lit., "man of Belial," v.1 [cf. 1Sa 10:27; 30:22]; see comment on "scoundrel" in 16:7; see also Note on 1Sa 1:16 and comments on 1Sa 25:17, 25), a "'reckless' person, one who disregards the proprieties or disturbs the *status quo*" (Gunn, *The Story of King David*, 140 n. 20). Reference to him as a "Benjamite" marks him as a northerner and perhaps a Saulide partisan as well (cf. 1Sa 9:1). The narrator's statement that Sheba "happened" (v.1) to be at the scene of the debate that ends ch. 19 (i.e., Gilgal [19:40]) ties him contextually to Absalom, who "happened" to meet David's men (18:9) and thus lost his life (the Niphal of *qr*ʾ in the sense of "happen," rare at best, occurs in only these two places in the books of Samuel). It is as though the text is telling its readers that Sheba picks up the baton dropped by Absalom.

Sounding a ram's-horn trumpet, Sheba delivers (perhaps even composes) a brief but powerful statement (v.1) that would become a rallying cry for future secessionists (cf. 1Ki 12:16 = 2Ch 10:16). He declares that he and his compatriots have no "share" in David's realm (i.e., David's inheritance; cf. Ge 31:14) and no "part" in "Jesse's son." Notwithstanding Clines, 285–86, to the contrary, the phrase "Jesse's son" is doubtless used in a disparaging or contemptuous sense here (see comment on the parallelism between "David" and "son of Jesse" in 1Sa 25:10; see also comments on 1Sa 20:27; 22:7).

Sheba, having lost patience with David, orders "every man to his tent" (i.e., his home; cf. v.22; 1Ki 8:66; the phrase may derive "from a time when the nation dwelt actually in tents" [Driver, 148]—although, as David Noel Freedman [*History and Religion*, 1:291 n. 9] asserts, the reference to tents many not be "archaizing but military in connotation, suggesting that when troops were assembled for war their quarters were temporary [cf. 1 Sam. 17:54; Jer. 37:10]"). Despite the fact that David had been divinely anointed king over "Israel" (v.1; cf. 19:21; see comments on 5:3; 12:7; 1Sa 16:13), Sheba apparently suspects that David's loyalties basically lie in the south and therefore urges the representatives of the northern tribes to secede.

Although the men of Judah "stayed by" their king (lit., "clung to" him, v.2; cf. Ru 1:14; the verb is used figuratively "of loyalty, affection etc., [sometimes] with idea of physical proximity retained" [BDB, 179]), escorting him "all the way from the Jordan to

Jerusalem," the "men of Israel"—following Sheba's lead—deserted David.

Gunn (*The Story of King David*, 140 n. 20) makes the important observation that "nowhere is it said that Sheba actually engaged in armed rebellion, merely that he called for the men of Israel to disband and go home, though of course the implication is secession." The time to secede is not yet ripe, however. "It is no coincidence that independence is declared in practically identical terms in the cry of 2 Samuel 20:1b and 1 Kings 12:16. Sheba ben Bichri was before his time—so a 'worthless fellow.' After Ahijah's intervention, the time had come" (Antony F. Campbell, *Of Prophets and Kings: A Late Ninth-Century Document [1 Samuel–2 Kings 10]* [CBQMS 17; Washington, D.C.: Catholic Biblical Association, 1986], 83).

3–7 The steps David takes to foil Sheba's rebellion involve three (groups of) people: concubines (v.3), Amasa (vv.4–5), and Abishai (vv.6–7).

Before his flight from Jerusalem in the wake of Absalom's conspiracy, David had "left" ten concubines to "take care of" the palace (v.3; see comments on 15:16; 16:21). Returning now to his "palace," he takes the concubines who were supposed to care for the "palace" and puts them in a "house" under guard (same Heb. word in all three cases), virtually incarcerating them. (Indeed, the phrase *bêt-mišmeret*, here rendered "house under guard," is closely paralleled by *bêt mišmār*, "prison," in Ge 42:19.) Although he "returned" (*bw*ʾ) to the palace, David did not "lie" (*bw*ʾ) with the concubines—as his treasonous son Absalom had done (see 16:21–22 and comments). "There is a wry echo in all of this of that early moment of David's investment of Jerusalem when he was confronted by another wife he had left behind who had slept with another man—Michal. She had no child 'till her dying day'—an image of interrupted conjugality that is multiplied tenfold here with the concubines" (Alter, *The David Story*, 322).

To be sure, David makes certain that the concubines' needs are "provided" for (see comment on 19:33); but he also keeps them in confinement under house arrest, and they are forced to remain in that situation—as though "widows"—for the rest of their lives (v.3). Brueggemann observes (*First and Second Samuel*, 330):

> the presence of concubines [at the palace in Jerusalem] suggests how much the monarchy has embraced the royal ideology of the Near East, which is inimical to the old covenant tradition. David takes a drastic step of confining the concubines and presumably having no more to do with them. His action is most likely a concession and conciliatory gesture to the north.... In making this move, David not only distances himself from his own former practice but also offers a contrast to the conduct of Absalom (16:21–22).

The second step taken by David is to order Amasa (v.4), his new army commander (see 19:13 and comment), to "summon" the men of Judah (for military action; cf. Jdg 4:10) to come to Jerusalem within three days, and Amasa is to be there personally as well ("yourself" is emphatic). Amasa, however, takes longer than the time allotted to him (v.5).

Apparently losing patience with Amasa (and perhaps fearing that he may have defected), David takes the third step by giving a command to Abishai (v.6), another of his generals (see 18:2 and comment). After describing the danger if Sheba is left to do as he wishes (see Overview to vv.1–22), David speaks directly and forcefully to Abishai (the MT places an emphatic "you" before "take" in v.6). He is to muster his "master's men" (i.e., David's men [cf. Hertzberg, 372], described further in v.7) and "pursue" Sheba (cf. vv.7, 10, 13). David is afraid that Sheba will "find" refuge in a fortified city (cf. Ps 107:4) and so "escape from us" (thus the NIV, apparently following the Vulgate and the Lucianic recension of the LXX [for other options see Alter, *The David Story*, 323]; the

MT's *hiṣṣîl ʿênēnû* is best understood to mean "tear out our eye[s]," a metaphor meaning "do us serious injury" [cf. K&D, 453]; for gouging out eyes as a cruel expedient, see 1Sa 11:2 and comment; for full discussion of other options, cf. Driver, 342).

That David ignores Joab in his planning is noteworthy (see 19:13 and comment). "Joab's men" (v.7; see 18:2 and comment) now march out "under the command of Abishai" (as the NIV justifiably renders *ʾaḥ^a^rāyw*, lit., "after him"), who is also over the Kerethites and Pelethites (David's mercenary troops; see comments on 8:18; 15:18) as well as all the "mighty warriors" (*gibbōrîm*, perhaps also mercenaries), professional soldiers who are called David's "special guard" in 16:6 and 1 Kings 1:8 (same Heb. word; see comment on 8:18) and are perhaps here to be identified with the Gittites of 15:18 (for discussion see Kirkpatrick, 153). The immediate task of Abishai's substantial army is to "pursue [see comment on v.6] Sheba son of Bicri" (v.7), a phrase repeated as a refrain in the next section.

8–13 Focusing on the death of Amasa at the hands of Joab, his rival for power (see 19:13 and comment), the central section of the present literary unit (vv.1–22) divides naturally into two parts, each of which ends with the phrase "pursue[d] Sheba son of Bicri" (as does the preceding section; see v.7 and comment): Joab's murder of Amasa is reported in vv.8–10, and the removal of Amasa's body is described in vv.11–13.

The story of Amasa's death is eerily reminiscent of several other violent episodes recorded in chs. 2–4. In particular, 3:27 and 20:8–10 "describe respectively Joab's assassination of Abner and Amasa," assassinations that

> took place soon after each had decided to transfer his allegiance to David. This probably explains why in 1 Kgs ii 5 and ii 32, the two assassinations are mentioned together by David and Solomon. In fact, since it was on account of these two assassinations that David instructed Solomon to not let Joab die in peace (1 Kgs ii 5–6), and since Solomon did cite these two assassinations as justification for having Joab killed (1 Kgs ii 31–32), one can argue that the two assassinations, though briefly described, are indeed significant as defining events in Joab's life. But what is most interesting is that these two accounts ... seem to bear an uncanny resemblance to the account of Ehud's assassination of Eglon.... At the basic plot level, all three assassinations involve the use of deception as a key tactic in the elimination of unsuspecting victims. Furthermore, the weapon used in all three cases appears to be the sword, and in all three, the unsuspecting victims were killed by a single blow to the belly. (Gregory T. K. Wong, "Ehud and Joab: Separated at Birth?" *VT* 61/3 [2006]: 399–401)

As for Amasa, he belatedly joins Abishai's army at "the great rock [otherwise unknown; for tentative identifications, see McCarter, *II Samuel*, 429] in Gibeon" (modern el-Jib, six miles northwest of Jerusalem; v.8). Although located in the tribal territory of Benjamin, Gibeon was probably more likely to side with David than with the Saulides (see comment on 2:12). Joab is there, and he wears a "military tunic" that was doubtless much like that worn earlier by Jonathan, which included a type of belt often used to hold a sheathed dagger (see comment on 1Sa 18:4). Not concealed, the dagger was fastened on over the tunic (cf. 1Sa 17:39; 25:13) and was therefore in plain view. Wearing a sword or dagger at one's side did not hamper certain kinds of activity (cf. Ne 4:18).

And so it was that Joab "stepped forward" (v.8)—an ominous choice of terminology by the narrator, since the same Hebrew verb is translated "went out" and "marched out" in v.7 in a clearly military context. Joab contrives to allow his dagger to fall out of its sheath, and with "a natural motion, given such circumstances, he picks it up with his left hand and continues to greet Amasa" (Edward A. Neiderhiser, "2 Samuel 20:8–10: A Note for a Commentary," *JETS* 24/3 [1981]: 210), referring to him as his "brother" (v.9, probably in the general sense of "comrade in arms" [see comment on 19:12], even though the two men were indeed blood relatives [see comment on 17:25]). The fact that Joab wields his dagger with his left hand almost certainly echoes the similar ruse of Ehud (Jdg 3:15–22; for details of this and other comparisons see Wong, "Ehud and Joab," 401–10).

Joab "took" (lit., "seized") Amasa "by the beard" with his right hand, ostensibly to "kiss" him (v.9; for the kiss of greeting, cf. 14:33; 15:5; Ge 33:4) but in reality to kill him (cf. 1Sa 17:35, where David is reported to have "seized" a lion "by its hair" [lit., "beard"] in order to strike and kill it). The kiss of Joab thus turns out to be the kiss of a Judas (cf. Lk 22:47–48).

"The 'accidentally' dropped sword dangling idly in [Joab's] left hand is not a recognizable danger" (Neiderhiser, "2 Samuel 20:8–10," 210), and therefore Amasa is "not on his guard" against it (that is, he pays no attention to it; v.10; see comment on 1Sa 19:2 for the importance of being vigilant). Before Amasa realizes what is happening, Joab has "plunged" the dagger into his "belly" in a frightening reprise of earlier events (see 2:23; 3:27; 4:6 and comments; in all four cases the Hebrew verb is *nkh* ["thrust, stabbed, plunged"] and the noun is *ḥōmeš* ["stomach, belly"]). "Without being stabbed again" (v.10; the Heb. phrase echoes "won't strike him twice" in 1Sa 26:8 [see comment there]), Amasa dies. "There is something almost cruelly comic about the portrait: Amasa was the man whose loss of a battle [17:25; 18:7] gained him a command [19:13], who failed to keep an appointment [20:4–5], and who could not spot the sword in his rival's hand" (Gunn, *The Story of King David*, 140 n.21). After Amasa's murder, Joab and Abishai continue the pursuit of Sheba.

Even as one of Joab's men attempts to rally his comrades to the chase by linking loyalty to the discredited Joab (see comments on v.7; 19:13) with loyalty to David (v.11; cf. Ex 32:26; Jos 5:13; 2Ki 10:6), a dramatic pause in the action is effected by the threefold use of *ʿāmad* in vv.11 ("stood") and 12 ("came to a halt," "stopped"). The corpse of Amasa lies wallowing in its blood in the middle of the "road" (vv.12–13), right where Joab had killed him. Since the "road" (*mᵉsillâ*, "a prepared road leading across country" [*TDOT*, 3:278]) was doubtless a major highway used by David's troops, Amasa's body proves to be an unacceptable distraction that slows their progress as they stop to gawk. Seeing this, the man trying to rally the troops drags the body into a field and covers it with a "garment" (v.12). Only then is the pause in the action broken as all the men finally join Joab and continue the pursuit of Sheba (v.13).

14–22a The account of Sheba's defeat, which parallels the attempt of David to foil him (vv.3–7; see Overview to vv.1–22), is divided into two unequal sections. The first episode (vv.14–15), which exhibits numerous verbal connections to the previous pericope (vv.8–13; see comments below), describes the violent siege of Abel Beth Maacah by the ruthless Joab. The second episode (vv.16–22a) relates the story of the subtler and more nuanced approach of the wise woman of Abel and illustrates the truism that less is more.

Trying to drum up support for his secessionist cause, Sheba has stayed one step ahead of his pursuers as he "passed" (v.14; the same Heb. verb is rendered "went on" in v.13) throughout Israel, eventually arriving at Abel Beth Maacah, modern Abil el-Qamh, more than ninety miles north of the vicinity of Gilgal. Since Abel is four miles west of Dan (cf. 1Ki 15:20) at the northernmost end of the land (see comment on 1Sa 3:20), it was indeed necessary for Sheba to travel "through all the tribes of Israel" to reach it. Apparently, however, he was able to enlist only the "Berites" (v.14), who "gathered together" to follow his lead (for *qhl* [*Qere*] in the sense of assembling for mutual protection and/or [possible] warfare, cf. Jos 22:12; Jdg 20:1; Est 8:11; 9:2, 15 ["came together"], 16, 18; Eze 38:7). Mentioned only here, *bērîm* is probably a scribal error for *bikrîm* (LXX *en Charri*), "Bicrites" referring to Sheba ben Bicri's own clan (cf. Baldwin, 280; Gordon, *I and II Samuel*, 295, 362 n. 210; William White Jr., *ZPEB*, 1:610). Compared to those who were ready to "follow Joab" (v.11), the number of men who "followed" Sheba (v.14) is pitiable indeed.

Lacking neither confidence nor desire when it comes to besieging cities (cf. 11:1), Joab leads his troops against Sheba in Abel Beth Maacah (v.15). If Joab is responsible for the fact that Amasa's intestines "spilled out" (*špk*) on the ground (v.10), he also takes credit for the fact that his men "built" (*špk*) a "siege ramp" at Abel (*sōlᵉlâ* ["siege ramp"] shares with *mᵉsillâ* ["highway," vv.12–13] the root *sll* ["lift up, construct"]). The ramp (cf. 2Ki 19:32 = Isa 37:33; Jer 6:6; Eze 4:2; 26:8) stands against the "outer fortifications" or ramparts (cf. Isa 26:1; La 2:8) of the city and serves as a means of access for attackers to pull down the city wall itself.

At this point a "wise woman" (unnamed, like her counterpart from Tekoa; see comment on 14:20) makes her appearance. As in 14:1–20, so also in 20:16–22a, the term "wise woman" (14:2; 20:16) is echoed at the end of its respective episode by the word "wisdom" (14:20; 20:22a ["wise advice"]), the four elements thus forming a double inclusio that brackets the whole. Calling out from the city (perhaps from the top of the wall), the woman of Abel pleads for patience as she shouts "Listen!" (pl.) twice to the besiegers (v.16) and speaks the same word (sing.) once to Joab (v.17). Having confirmed his identity (his name and reputation have obviously preceded him) and gained his attention, she submissively refers to herself as his "servant" (as her predecessor had earlier done to David; see 14:6 and comment). He in turn responds politely to her "Listen!" by saying "I'm listening."

The wise woman now establishes the credentials of her city, her fellow citizens, and herself—not only as purveyors of wisdom but also as peacemakers. From antiquity Abel Beth Maacah has been justly famed as a place to which people resorted to find solutions for difficult problems (v.18). The woman therefore rebukes Joab for besieging the city as she speaks on behalf of its inhabitants: "We are [lit., 'I am'; emphatic] the peaceful [ones] and faithful [ones] in Israel" (v.19).

Describing the admirable qualities of Abel's people, she uses language that reflects several Davidic psalms (cf. 7:4; 12:1; 31:23). By way of contrast ("you" is emphatic), she accuses Joab of trying to "destroy" (lit., "put to death") a city that is a "mother [see comment and Notes on Metheg Ammah in 8:1] in Israel." The epithet "mother in Israel" is applied elsewhere only to the prophetess Deborah (cf. Jdg 5:7). As Camp, 28, notes:

> Abel is characterized in the proverb [v.18] as a city with a long reputation for wisdom and faithfulness to the tradition of Israel. It is, therefore, a mother in the same way Deborah was: a creator and hence a symbol of the unity that bound Israel together under one God Yahweh. And it is the wise woman's implicit appeal to this unity that stops Joab in his tracks.

The woman wishes to know why Joab wants to swallow up "the LORD's inheritance" (v.19; cf. 21:3; 1Sa 26:19), a phrase referring either to the land and people of Israel or to the share of Abel Beth Maacah in that land (see 14:16 and comment).

Impressed by the logic of the woman's arguments as well as by her sincerity, Joab relents. In the strongest possible terms ("Far be it from me!" v.20; cf. 1Sa 2:30; 12:23; also 1Sa 14:45; 20:2, 9 ["Never!"]; 22:15 ["Of course not!"]; 24:6; 26:11 ["The LORD forbid"]), he categorically denies that it is his intention either to "swallow up" (v.20; cf. v.19) or "destroy" (different Heb. verb from that used by the woman in v.19 but same as the one rendered "battering" in v.15). He assures her that he is interested only in apprehending Sheba, whom he characterizes as being from the "hill country of Ephraim" (v.21), a large, partially forested plateau that extended into the tribal territory of Benjamin (cf. v.1) from the north. He asserts that Sheba has "lifted up his hand" against David, implying that his treachery with respect to the king must be punished. Since the relatively common idiom *nś᾽ yd* is found only here and in 18:28 in the sense of "rise in rebellion" (cf. Conroy, 72 n. 119), Joab's use of it links the revolt of Sheba to that of Absalom and his fellow conspirators.

Joab tells the wise woman that if the citizens of Abel will release Sheba to him ("hand over" is plural; same Heb. verb as in 14:7, providing yet another parallel to the narrative of the wise woman of Tekoa), he and his men will pull back from the city. Promising Joab that Sheba's head will be thrown to him "from" the wall (*bᵉᶜad*, v.21; perhaps better "through [an opening in]" the wall; cf. 6:16 ["from" in the sense of "through"]; 1Sa 19:12; 2Ki 1:2), the woman relays her proposal to the people of the city. Impressed by her "wise advice" (lit., "wisdom." v.22; cf. 1Ki 4:34), they proceed to cut off Sheba's head (see comments on 1Sa 17:51; 31:9; cf. further Lemos, 236) and toss it out to Joab.

And so the rebellion of Sheba son of Bicri comes to an inglorious end, but with a surgical strike against one man rather than by destroying an entire city—and all because of the calming advice of the wise woman of Abel. "Sagacity, faithfulness, a commanding presence, and readily acknowledged influence with her peers—these are the attributes that clearly mark this woman" (Camp, 26). Brueggemann has observed: "Wise words override ruthless policy. At the end, not only the woman and the city are saved; something of David's dignity and self-respect are also rescued from Joab's mad, obedient intent" (Brueggemann, *First and Second Samuel*, 332).

22b By echoing the language of v.1 ("he sounded the trumpet," "each returning to his home"; see Overview to vv.1–22), the narrator brings the story of Sheba's revolt to a fitting conclusion. Whereas Sheba had sounded a trumpet to rally secessionists, Joab does so to call off the siege of Abel and send his men on their way. Although the verb *pûṣ* in battle contexts normally means "scattered" after defeat (cf. 1Sa 11:11; Nu 10:35; Ps 68:1), here it bears the unusual sense of "dispersed, demobilized" after victory (cf. Conroy, 59 n. 52).

With Joab's return to the king in Jerusalem, the grand symphony known as the court history of David reaches its conclusion for all practical purposes (at least as far as 1 and 2 Samuel are concerned; see Overview to 9:1–20:26). The last four verses of ch. 20 constitute a suitably formal coda, serving the same function for the court history that the last four verses of ch. 8 do for the narrative of David's powerful reign (see Overview to 5:17–8:18).

NOTES

1 In addition to its occurrence in ch. 20, the personal name Sheba (שֶׁבַע, *šbᶜ*) appears on a Hebrew seal and on Samaria ostracon 2:6 as well as on a fragment of a bulla (seal impression) recently discovered in Jerusalem (cf. Avigad, 111).

3 אַלְמְנוּת חַיּוּת (*ʾalmᵉnût ḥayyût*, lit., "widowhood of life") is translated "living as widows" by the NIV, which apparently repoints the MT as אַלְמָנוֹת חַיּוֹת (*ʾalmānôt ḥayyōt*, "living widows"; cf. LXX). Although the consonantal text, however vocalized, remains difficult (cf. Driver, 341, for discussion), the NIV's rendering is surely preferable to that of Allegro, who resorts to an Arabic cognate (often a dubious procedure at best) to arrive at his translation "widowhood of shame" (J. M. Allegro, "The Meaning of *Ḥayyût* in 2 Samuel 20:3," *JTS* 3 [1952]: 40–41).

5 The *Qere's* ויוחר (*wywḥr*, "he took longer"; preferable to the *Kethiv's* וייחר, *wyyḥr*) is from the root אחר (*ʾḥr*). For other examples of this phenomenon in the books of Samuel, cf. ותחז (*wtḥz*, "took," v.9), from אחז (*ʾḥz*), and see also Notes on 6:1; 19:13; 1 Samuel 28:24.

14 Abel Beth Maacah would later be conquered by the Aramean king Ben-Hadad I (cf. 1Ki 15:20 = 2Ch 16:4 [where it is called Abel Maim]) and still later by the Assyrian ruler Tiglath-Pileser III (cf. 2Ki 15:29), who referred to it in his annals as Abilakka (cf. *ANET*, 283) or, if a scribal lapse is assumed, Abil<ma>akka (cf. Aharoni, 372). The NIV margin's reading, "Abel, even Beth Maacah," analyzes the ו־ (*w-*) as *wāw explicativum* (for which cf. GKC, sec. 154*a* n. b), another example of which occurs in v. 19 ("that is"). The name of the site was sometimes abbreviated to Abel, as in v.18 (cf. also *ʾ-b-r* no. 92 in Thutmose III's roster of Canaanite towns [cf. Aharoni, 162]).

19 "A city that is a mother" (עִיר וְאֵם, *ʿîr wᵉʾēm*) brings to mind the term "metropolis," which appears as a loanword (*mṭrpwls*) in an Old Syriac sale deed found at Dura (cf. M. O'Connor, "The Arabic Loanwords in Nabatean Aramaic," *JNES* 45/3 [1986]: 228 n. 94).

20. David's Officials (20:23–26)

OVERVIEW

As the outline of 2 Samuel indicates (see Introduction), chs. 1–20 divide into four literary units of varying length, each of which ends with a four-verse list of names. Each of the last two units (5:17–8:18; chs. 9–20) concludes with a list of David's officials (8:15–18; 20:23–26) that provides the names, patronymics (for the most part), and offices of the men in David's cabinet. Despite the caveats of McCarter (*II Samuel*, 435), it seems best to understand the list in 8:15–18 as coming from the earlier years of David's reign and the present list as deriving from the later years.

[23]Joab was over Israel's entire army; Benaiah son of Jehoiada was over the Kerethites and Pelethites; [24]Adoniram was in charge of forced labor; Jehoshaphat son of Ahilud was recorder; [25]Sheva was secretary; Zadok and Abiathar were priests; [26]and Ira the Jairite was David's priest.

COMMENTARY

Although the roster of officials in 8:15–18 begins with the statement that David "reigned over all Israel" and the list in 1 Kings 4:2–6 begins by informing the reader that his son Solomon "ruled over all Israel" (1Ki 4:1), vv.23–26 do not begin with a reference to David's reign. While it may be overstating the case to "assume that by omitting David's name from it, the second list of David's high officials tells us, though implicitly, that the *de facto* ruler was then Joab, who ranked at the top of the list (2 Sam 20:23a)" (Tomoo Ishida, "Solomon's Accession to the Throne of David—A Political Analysis" [in Ishida], 185), at the very least the omission reflects David's weakened position in the wake of the rebellions of Absalom and Sheba.

All rivals for power (including Amasa; see v.10 and comment) now eliminated, Joab—as earlier (see 8:16 and comment)—is commander of "Israel's entire army" (v.23), while Benaiah (rather than Abishai; v.7) retains formal control over the Kerethite and Pelethite mercenaries (see comment on 8:18).

A new and ominous figure—Adoniram—makes his appearance in the royal cabinet (v.24). He is in charge of the corvée, the age-old institution (cf. *ANET*, 485 n.7) that involved impressing prisoners of war into "forced labor" (*mas*) on such projects as the building of highways, temples, and palaces. Foreseen as early as the time of Moses (cf. Dt 20:10–11), it was apparently inaugurated in Israel's monarchy by David at least partially in anticipation of the construction of a temple by his son Solomon (see 7:12–13 and comments). In choosing Adoniram, however, "David had appointed a man who was to play a prominent part in the apostasy of the Northern Kingdom, 1 Kings 12:18 f." (Carlson, 180).

Just as earlier in David's reign, so also now Jehoshaphat is recorder (see comments on 8:16). Apparently, however, Sheva has replaced Seraiah as secretary (v.25; for possible relationships between the names Sheva, Seraiah, Shisha [1Ki 4:3], and Shavsha [1Ch 18:16], see comment on 8:17). With respect to the substitution of "Zadok and Abiathar" (v.25) for "Zadok ... and Ahimelech son of Abiathar" in the earlier list, as well as for discussion concerning possible relationships between the three men, see comment on 8:17. Although it is possible that Ira the Jairite (presumably either a descendant of Jair or an inhabitant of one of the settlements known as Havvoth Jair; cf. Nu 32:41; 1Ki 4:13) shared the priesthood with Zadok and Abiathar, it is perhaps better to understand *kōhēn* (rendered "priest" in v.26) in the sense of "royal adviser" (as in 8:18 [see comment there]; cf. Goldman, 236, 319).

> The initial offer of Israel's throne was in the form of a covenant (5:1–3), but the presence of these officers tells against a covenantal version of royal power. The raw political strength that dominates this story of David's return to power presents the wise woman of 20:16–22 as an important contrast.... In the midst of Jerusalem's *Realpolitik* ... she can still imagine that careful speech, peaceable treasuring, and secure trust offer another way in public life. There is more to public life than David's sexual politics or Joab's killing fields. (Brueggemann, *First and Second Samuel*, 332–33)

NOTES

23 "Kerethites" (כרתי, *krty*) is the reading not only of the *Qere* but also of many Hebrew MSS and most versions (cf. *BHS*). "Carites" (כרי, *kry* [*Kethiv*]; cf. also 2Ki 11:4, 19) is doubtless incorrect since "Pelethites" is invariably preceded by "Kerethites" in the OT (cf. v.7; 8:18; 15:18; 1Ki 1:38, 44; 1Ch 18:17). The similarity between the two words, together with the fact that *krty* is found in parallelism with *kry* in Ugaritic (cf. M. Delcor, "Les Kerethim et les Cretois," *VT* 28/4 [1978]: 415), readily accounts for the reading of the *Kethiv*.

24 Second Samuel 20:24; 1 Kings 4:6; 5:14; 12:18 = 2 Chronicles 10:18 in the NIV all state that Adoniram ("My [divine] Lord is exalted") was in charge of forced labor under David/Solomon/Rehoboam. The MT of v.24, however, reads "Adoram" (although "Adoniram" is attested in some LXX MSS; cf. NIV note), as does the MT of 1 Kings 12:18 (although "Adoniram" appears in some LXX MSS as well as in the Syriac; cf. NIV note). In 2 Chronicles 10:18, on the other hand, the MT reads "Hadoram"—which the NIV's note there explains as "a variant of Adoniram." But while it is indeed possible to understand Hadoram in 2 Chronicles 10:18 as a spelling variant of Adoram (which in turn would probably be a contracted form of Adoniram), in the light of 2 Samuel 8:10 (see comment there) it is equally possible to explain it as a name in its own right with the meaning "Hadad is exalted."

The name Adoram can also be analyzed, however, as meaning "Adad is exalted" (for the alternative spellings of the divine name, see Albright, 157–58; for alternative spelling as a personal name, cf. the MT of 1 Kings 11:17, which translates literally as follows: "And Adad fled, he and some Edomite men who had been servants of his father with him, to go to Egypt; and Hadad was a small boy"). In that case "the Masoretes may thus have had good reason for using the more Canaanite-sounding form Adoram in 20:24 and 1 Kings 12:18, as against Adoniram in 1 Kings 4:6" and 5:14 (Carlson, 180).

26 Instead of היארי (*hyʾry*, "the Jairite"), the Lucianic recension of the LXX reads ὁ Ιεθερ (*ho Iether*, "the Ithrite"), which, if correct, would identify the Ira of v.26 with one of David's elite "Thirty" (cf. 23:38).

II. EPILOGUE (21:1–24:25)

OVERVIEW

If in fact the books of Samuel have as their basic theme the beginnings of Israel's monarchy in the eleventh century BC, and if chs. 1–7 of 1 Samuel describe the prelude to that monarchy, chs. 8–15 its advent, chs. 16–31 its establishment, and chs. 1–20 of 2 Samuel its consolidation under David, then the last four chapters of 2 Samuel—which for all intents and purposes conclude the magisterial history of the judgeship of Samuel, the reign of Saul, and the reign of David—function as an epilogue to the books of Samuel as a whole, "a coda to the [David story proper] rather than ... a series of appendices" (Alter, *The David Story*, 329).

Despite the miscellaneous character and dischronologized nature of chs. 21–24, many commentators have recognized the undoubted chiastic arrangement of their overall contents (cf. the discussion by Brueggemann, *First and Second Samuel*, 335). On this point Sternberg, 40, makes a useful observation: "It is suggestive that the most conspicuous and large-scale instance of chiasm in Samuel applies to a hodgepodge that has the least pretensions to literariness and, even with the artificial design thrown in, hardly coheres as more than an appendix." Indeed, it "deliberately subordinates expository to aesthetic coherence, business to pleasure" (ibid., 42).

At the same time, however, it would be a serious mistake to assume that the epilogue is disinterested in theological reflection or that it is otherwise inferior to the celebrated court history (chs. 9–20) that immediately precedes it. The narrator's masterful use of prose and poetry alike provide a fitting conclusion to the career of Israel's greatest king. "In sum, the final four chapters, far from being a clumsy appendix, offer a highly reflective, theological interpretation of David's whole career adumbrating the messianic hope" (Brevard S. Childs, *Introduction to the Old Testament as Scripture* [Philadelphia: Fortress, 1979], 275).

The following literary analysis was arrived at independently:

A The Lord's wrath against Israel (21:1–14)
  B David's heroes (21:15–22)
    C David's song of praise (22:1–51)
    C' David's last words (23:1–7)
  B' David's mighty men (23:8–39)
A' The Lord's wrath against Israel (24:1–25)

If it be claimed that an outline of this sort is more clever than credible, I would simply call attention to the double inclusio that links together the first and last sections—an inclusio that is all the more impressive since it interlocks the first verse of ch. 21 with the last verse of ch. 24: "a famine for three successive years" (21:1), "three years of famine" (24:13); "God/the LORD answered prayer in behalf of the land" (21:14; 24:25). The verb translated as "answered prayer" is "relatively rare; in Samuel–Kings, it occurs only in this collection's two 'atonement' passages, here [21:14] and in 2 Sam 24:25" (Campbell, *2 Samuel*, 191).

A. The Lord's Wrath against Israel (21:1–14)

OVERVIEW

The account of the Gibeonites' revenge (vv.1–14) begins with the Lord's wrath against Israel as expressed in a three-year famine (v.1) and ends with the Lord's answer to Israel's prayers by removing it (v.14). David's request (vv.1–4), Gibeon's demand (vv.5–6), David's acquiescence (vv.7–9), Rizpah's vigil (v.10), and David's final act of respect to the house of Saul (vv.11–14) constitute the various segments of the episode.

[1]During the reign of David, there was a famine for three successive years; so David sought the face of the LORD. The LORD said, "It is on account of Saul and his blood-stained house; it is because he put the Gibeonites to death."

[2]The king summoned the Gibeonites and spoke to them. (Now the Gibeonites were not a part of Israel but were survivors of the Amorites; the Israelites had sworn to spare them, but Saul in his zeal for Israel and Judah had tried to annihilate them.) [3]David asked the

Gibeonites, "What shall I do for you? How shall I make amends so that you will bless the LORD's inheritance?"

[4]The Gibeonites answered him, "We have no right to demand silver or gold from Saul or his family, nor do we have the right to put anyone in Israel to death."

"What do you want me to do for you?" David asked.

[5]They answered the king, "As for the man who destroyed us and plotted against us
so that we have been decimated and have no place anywhere in Israel, [6]let seven of his
male descendants be given to us to be killed and exposed before the LORD at Gibeah of Saul—the Lord's chosen one."

So the king said, "I will give them to you."

[7]The king spared Mephibosheth son of Jonathan, the son of Saul, because of the oath
before the LORD between David and Jonathan son of Saul. [8]But the king took Armoni and
Mephibosheth, the two sons of Aiah's daughter Rizpah, whom she had borne to Saul, together with the five sons of Saul's daughter Merab, whom she had borne to Adriel son
of Barzillai the Meholathite. [9]He handed them over to the Gibeonites, who killed and
exposed them on a hill before the LORD. All seven of them fell together; they were put to death during the first days of the harvest, just as the barley harvest was beginning.

[10]Rizpah daughter of Aiah took sackcloth and spread it out for herself on a rock. From the beginning of the harvest till the rain poured down from the heavens on the bodies, she did
not let the birds of the air touch them by day or the wild animals by night. [11]When David was
told what Aiah's daughter Rizpah, Saul's concubine, had done, [12]he went and took the bones
of Saul and his son Jonathan from the citizens of Jabesh Gilead. (They had taken them secretly from the public square at Beth Shan, where the Philistines had hung them after they
struck Saul down on Gilboa.) [13]David brought the bones of Saul and his son Jonathan from
there, and the bones of those who had been killed and exposed were gathered up.

[14]They buried the bones of Saul and his son Jonathan in the tomb of Saul's father Kish, at Zela in Benjamin, and did everything the king commanded. After that, God answered prayer in behalf of the land.

COMMENTARY

1–4 Lengthy famines were common in the ancient world (cf. Ge 12:10; 26:1; 41:54–57; Ru 1:1; 2Ki 4:38), and it is therefore not surprising that at least one famine of unusual severity should occur at some point during the forty-year "reign of David" (v.1). The MT's description is especially vivid, informing the reader that the famine continues for "three years, year after year" ("three successive years," NIV). Since it is often only "in their misery" that God's people pray to him (Hos 5:15), it may well be that David has not "sought the face of the LORD" (v.1) until Israel is *in extremis* (cf. 2Ch 7:14; cf. esp. the Davidic expressions of need recorded in 1Ch 16:11; Pss 24:6; 27:8). "In the secular realm, [the idiom 'seek the face of'] is used in referring to the king, 'seek the face of the king' (Prov. 29:26; cf. 1 K. 10:24; 2 Ch. 9:23), evidently meaning to 'obtain the favor of the king.'... [The act] assumes the personal movement of the one seeking toward the one being sought" (*TDOT*, 2:237), "to seek an audience (with a ruler)" (Alter, *The David Story*, 329). David thus makes his way to the divine throne room, perhaps entering the tabernacle itself, in order to receive mercy and help for his people.

The Lord's answer is not long in coming: "Saul and his blood-stained house" are to blame, since "bloodshed pollutes the land" (Nu 35:33; cf. Dt 19:10). Saul's crime is that he had "put the Gibeonites to death" (for the location of Gibeon, see comment on 20:8) and in so doing had violated the age-old "treaty with the Gibeonites" made with them by Joshua (Jos 9:16). One of its provisions was that the Israelites would "let them live" (Jos 9:15, 20–21). Despite the fact that Israel's people "did not kill them" (Jos 9:26), Israel's first king "put [some of them] to death" (v.1).

David, Israel's second king, is determined to right the wrong of Saul against the Gibeonites, so he summons them in order to discuss the matter with them. "Not a part of Israel" (v.2), the Gibeonites are characterized as "Hivites" (Jos 9:7; 11:19), as "survivors of the Amorites," a relatively nonbelligerent people during this period (see comment on 1Sa 7:14). The statement that the Israelites had "sworn to spare them" (lit., "sworn an oath to them," v.2) echoes the language of the narrative in Joshua many times over (cf. Jos 9:15, 18–19, and esp. 20: "We will let them live, so that wrath will not fall on us for breaking the oath we swore to them"). Although enthusiasm, when properly directed, is commendable (cf. Nu 11:29), Saul's misplaced zeal for "Israel and Judah" (v.2; see comments on 5:3; 1Sa 11:8; 15:4; 17:52) has now brought famine on the land. It is not the first time that Saul had "tried" to wipe out a real or supposed enemy (see comments on 1Sa 19:2, 10; 23:10).

Wanting to rectify the situation, David asks the Gibeonites whether there is anything he can do to "make amends" (lit., "make atonement," v.3; cf. Ex 32:30; Nu 16:46–47; 25:13).

> Since the verb *kipper* is used absolutely here, it is impossible to say from the construction alone whether it means to propitiate or to expiate. From the context, however, it is clear that it means both. David is seeking both to satisfy the Gibeonites and to "make up for" the wrong done to them. It is equally clear that he cannot achieve the latter without the former. There is no expiation without propitiation. (Paul Garnet, "Atonement Constructions in the Old Testament and the Qumran Scrolls," *EvQ* 46/3 [1974]: 134)

David pursues reconciliation with the Gibeonites "so that you will bless [an imperative used in a voluntative sense 'for the purpose of expressing with somewhat greater force the intention of the previous verb' (Driver, 350); cf. precisely the same construction—with the same verbal root—in Gen 12:2: 'and (= so that) you will be a blessing'] the LORD's inheritance" (i.e., the land and people of Israel; see comments on 14:16; 20:19; 1Sa 26:19). David apparently wants the Gibeonites, when their requirements have been met, to pray that God will bless David's people (cf. *TDOT*, 2:292; see also comment on 14:22).

The Gibeonites begin by indicating to David two things that they have no right to demand: (1) "silver or gold" from Saul's family (v.4; see comment on 8:11); (2) the death of "anyone [*ʾîš*, lit., 'a man'] in Israel" (for the custom of blood vengeance, see comments on 3:30; 14:7). They are asking neither for money from the extended clan of the man who murdered their fellow citizens nor for the execution of Israelites in general. It is only when David expands his initial question ("What shall I do for you?" v.3) to "What do you want me to do for you?" (lit., "What are you saying I should do for you?" v.4; cf. 1Sa 20:4) that the Gibeonites become more specific in their demand.

5–6 The Gibeonites' desire for vengeance concerns one "man" (*ʾîš*, v.5; see comment on v.4) and, since he is now dead, focuses on his descendants. Because of Saul, the Gibeonites have been "destroyed" (cf. 22:38; 1Sa 15:18 ["wiped ... out"]), plotted against, decimated, and deprived of a place in Israel. They therefore request that "seven" of Saul's male descendants be turned over to them (v.6), seven in this case not only being intended literally (cf. v.8) but also perhaps to be understood in the sense of full retribution (see 1Sa 2:5 and comment). Saul's "blood-stained house" (v.1) will now be completely avenged (cf. Nu 35:33; see comment on 16:7–8 for the possibility that Shimei's curse reflects the present situation).

While vv.1–9 surely constitute a parade example of the fact that "if the original offender was no longer alive vengeance could be exercised even upon his descendants" (Isaac Schapera, "The Sin of Cain," in *Anthropological Approaches to the Old Testament*, ed. Bernhard Lang [Philadelphia: Fortress, 1975], 28), it is also clear that much more than a simple blood feud is in view here. As stated earlier (see comment on v.1), David has discovered "that the famine was due to the breaking of the covenant between Gibeon and Israel, brought about by an act of Saul, years before. Propitiation could only be effected by the death of the sons of Saul at the hands of the Gibeonites" (F. Charles Fensham, "The Treaty between Israel and the Gibeonites," *BA* 27/1 [1964]: 99; for ancient Near Eastern parallels that report plague, drought, famine, and other disasters believed to result from breach of covenant, see 100).

Seven of Saul's descendants are therefore to be "killed and exposed" (v.6; cf. vv.9, 13; Nu 25:4). The Hebrew verb designates "a solemn ritual act of execution imposed for breach of covenant," probably involving the "cutting up or dismembering [of] a treaty violator as a punishment for treaty violation" (Polzin, "*HWQYʿ* and Covenantal Institutions," 229, 234; cf. Cross, *Canaanite Myth and Hebrew Epic*, 266). In addition to natural calamities such as those mentioned above (plague, drought, famine, etc.; cf. Fensham, "The Treaty between Israel and the Gibeonites," 100), Polzin singles out two other covenantal curses attested in extrabiblical sources from the ancient Near East: "The progeny of the transgressor shall be obliterated; and the corpse of the transgressor will be exposed. All three of these curses are involved in 2 Sam 21:1–14" (Polzin, "*HWQYʿ* and Covenantal Institutions," 228 n. 4).

As Agag was put to death "before the LORD" (1Sa 15:33), so also Saul's descendants are to be killed and "exposed before the LORD" (v.6; cf. v.9), perhaps so that his blessing might be sought (see comments on 5:3; 1Sa 11:15). Ironically, the act is to take place at "Gibeah of Saul" (modern Tell el-Ful, three miles north of Jerusalem), the hometown (see comment on 1Sa 10:10) of the one who had "put the Gibeonites to death" (v.1) in the first place. The citizens of Gibeon then compound the irony by sarcastically referring to Saul as the Lord's "chosen one" (v.6), a descriptive title used often of God's people in general but applied specifically elsewhere only to Moses (cf. Ps 106:23), David (cf. Ps 89:3), and the servant of the Lord (cf. Isa 42:1). Saul, however, is in fact referred to as "the man the LORD has chosen" in 1 Samuel 10:24 (see comment). With whatever ulterior motives (if any; cf. Anderson, 251–52; Mauchline, 303–4), David acquiesces in the Gibeonites' request.

7–9 Because of the "oath before the LORD" (v.7) sworn long ago between David and Saul's son Jonathan (see 1Sa 20:42 and comment; cf. also 1Sa 20:14–17), the king spares Jonathan's son Mephibosheth (see also 19:24–30 and comments), whose future is presumably now secure. Although he is never again mentioned in the OT, his namesake—a son of "Aiah's daughter Rizpah" (v.8), Saul's concubine (see 3:7 and comment)—has the misfortune of being one of the seven descendants of Saul to be handed over to the Gibeonites. The other six are Rizpah's son Armoni (brother of the hapless Mephibosheth) and the five sons of Saul's daughter Merab (better Merob, for which see comment on 1Sa 14:49), whom she had borne to Adriel the Meholathite (cf. 1Sa 18:19; Adriel's father Barzillai is not to be confused with David's friend Barzillai the Gileadite, for which see comment on 17:27).

After being delivered over to the Gibeonites by David, the seven are "killed and exposed ... before the LORD" (v.9; see comments on v.6) on a hill where they could be easily seen. All seven of them "fell down together," a phrase that reprises 2:16, the context of the start of the civil war at Gibeon (cf. Alter, *The David Story*, 331). The verb "fell" is used to portray their execution in a picturesque way (cf. 11:17; 1Sa 14:13) and is parallel to "were put to death" (v.9), an idiom that often implies summary execution (see comments on 19:22; 1Sa 11:13; cf. also 1Sa 19:6; 20:32).

The time of year is carefully specified as "during the first days of harvest, just as the barley harvest was beginning," the latter phrase adding a touch of precision to the former. In ancient Israel, reapers began harvesting the barley crop (cf. Ru 1:22) in late April (for discussion cf. Edward F. Campbell Jr., *Ruth* [AB 7; Garden City, N.Y.: Doubleday, 1975], 108). So important was the time of barley harvest in the agricultural year that it served as one of the reference points in the tenth-century Gezer calendar (cf. G. Ernest Wright, *Biblical Archaeology* [Philadelphia: Westminster, 1957], 180–84).

10 Rizpah, bereft of two sons (cf. v.8), spreads "sackcloth" (a sign of mourning; cf. 3:31) on a rock, where she will stay day and night (cf. 1Ki 21:27; Est 4:3; Isa 58:5; Joel 1:13) for the foreseeable future. She intends to remain there at least until the "rain" comes down (lit., "water," as in Jdg 5:4; Job 5:10)—probably an unseasonable late-spring or early-summer shower (cf. Gordon, McCarter) rather than the heavy rains of October (cf. Kirkpatrick). In either case she refuses to leave the exposed bodies of her sons and the other five victims until the drought ends as a sign that Saul's crime has been expiated. Furthermore, to allow the "birds of the air" and the "wild animals" to feast on the carcasses would be not only to subject them to the most ignominious treatment possible (cf. 1Sa 17:44, 46; Ps 79:2; Jer 16:4) but also to resign them to the curse reserved for covenantal violators (cf. Fensham, "The Treaty between Israel and the Gibeonites," 100; cf. Jer 34:20).

Roland De Vaux (*Studies in Old Testament Sacrifice* [Cardiff: University of Wales, 1964], 61) has proposed that several features mentioned in vv.1–10 and paralleled in a Ugaritic text mark the account as one reporting "a human sacrifice to assure fertility." "The Gibeonites are not Israelites, they are descendants of the old population of Canaan: with David's consent, they indulged in a Canaanite fertility rite" (ibid., 62). As McCarter (*II Samuel*, 44) correctly notes, however, such suggestions "disregard the reason for the execution offered by the text itself. The Saulides are crucified in propitiation of divine wrath arising from the violation of a treaty sanctioned by solemn oaths.... It is a matter of propitiatory justice, of restitution exacted upon those who bear the guilt for a gross breach of a divinely sanctioned oath."

11–14 Upon being told of Rizpah's vigil (v.11)—and perhaps also of her implied desire to make sure that the remains of Saul's seven descendants be given a proper burial—David is conscience-stricken to follow her example. He makes the long journey to Jabesh Gilead (v.12, probably modern Tell el Maqlub about fifty miles northeast of Jerusalem; see comment on 1Sa 11:1) to retrieve the bones of Saul and Jonathan from its citizens, who had buried them there (see 2:4b and comment) after having "taken them secretly" (lit., "stolen them") from Beth Shan's "public square" (apparently near the section of the city wall where the Philistines had hung the bodies of the two men after they had been struck down at Gilboa; see 1Sa 31:8–13 and comments).

Reinterment of bones was not uncommon in ancient times (for the odyssey of Joseph's bones, see Ge 50:25–26; Ex 13:19; Jos 24:32), and David now intends to give those of Saul and Jonathan an honorable—if secondary—burial (v.13; contrast the prediction of Jehoiakim's burial in Jer 22:19). The bones of the seven male descendants of Saul who were "killed and exposed" (v.13; see comment on v.6) are also gathered up, perhaps to be interred near (or even with, as the LXX of v.14 states; cf. also Baldwin, K&D, Mauchline, Smith) the bones of Saul and Jonathan.

And so Saul and his son Jonathan arrive at their final resting place, the tomb of "Saul's father Kish" (v.14; see comment on 1Sa 9:1). Attempts to equate "Zelzah on the border of Benjamin," the location of "Rachel's tomb" (1Sa 10:2), with "Zela in Benjamin" (v.14), where Kish was buried, are philologically unconvincing. Zela(h), mentioned elsewhere only in Joshua 18:28, is a site of unknown location.

As noted earlier (see comment on v.10), the three-year "famine" (v.1) caused by drought came to an end when God sent rain on the land. The execution of the seven had atoned for Saul's sin and propitiated the divine wrath. Thus the last sentence of v.14 not only reiterates the fact that the Lord has come to his people in grace but also serves to bring the section to a close: God has "answered prayer in behalf of the land" (for the significance of the echo of this phrase in the last verse of 2 Samuel, see Overview to 21:1–24:25).

NOTES

1 Although most commentators are content to state that Saul's crime against Gibeon is mentioned nowhere else in the OT (for discussion cf. McCarter, *II Samuel*, 441), Jorn Halbe, "Gibeon und Israel: Art, Veranlassung und Ort der Deutung ihres Verhältnisses in Jos. IX," *VT* 25/3 [1975]: 634), has suggested that the flight of the people of Beeroth to Gittaim (cf. 4:2–3) may have been a result of Saul's persecution of the Gibeonites. Joshua 9:17 locates Beeroth as within Gibeon's sphere of influence and therefore presumably under the protection of Israel's treaty with its citizens. For a defense of the years 996–993 BC as the most likely time for the three-year famine of vv.1–14, cf. Merrill, 253–54.

6 "Be given" renders either the *Qere*'s יֻתַּן (*yuttan*), a Qal passive form, or the *Kethiv*'s ינתן (*yntn*), universally vocalized as a Niphal (יִנָּתֵן, *yinnātēn*; cf. Driver, 351). Given the fact that the Gibeonites were "survivors of the Amorites" (v.2), however, it is perhaps better to vocalize the *Kethiv* as יֻנְתַּן (*yuntan*), an unassimilated Qal passive form that, like *antinnu* ("I will ... give/permit") in a Byblian Amarna letter of the fourteenth century BC, "illustrates the Amorite tendency to avoid the assimilation of the consonant *n* to a following dental or sibilant" (Ronald F. Youngblood, "Amorite Influence in a Canaanite Amarna Letter [EA 96]," *BASOR* 168 [1962]: 26).

Although the root of הוקיע (*hwqy*ʿ, "kill and expose") is clearly יקע (*yq*ʿ, "be dislocated"; GK 3697; cf. Ge 32:25 ["wrenched"]), the byform נקע (*nq*ʿ, "be severed/alienated"; GK 5936) also provides helpful semantic background. The two roots are used synonymously in Ezekiel 23:18: "I turned away from her in disgust [*yqʿ*], just as I had turned away [*nqʿ*] from her sister." In Arabic the root *nqʿ* is employed to denote a plundered animal that is sacrificed and eaten after a raid but before the division of the rest of the booty. The practice seems to have served a ritual purpose (W. Robertson Smith, *Lectures on the Religion of the Semites*, 2nd ed. [London: A. and C. Black, 1894], 491–92; cf. also Polzin, "*HWQYʿ* and Covenantal Institutions," 232).

7 "Oath" (שְׁבֻעַת, *šbʿt*) forms a wordplay with "seven" in v.6 (שִׁבְעָה, *šbʿh*) and "seven of them" in v.9 (שְׁבַעְת[ָי]ם, *šbʿt[y]m*).

8 In the light of 1 Samuel 18:19, "Merab/Merob" (cf. NIV) is surely to be preferred to "Michal" despite its weaker MS attestation (cf. NIV note for details). The KJV's "the five sons of Michal the daughter of Saul, whom she brought up for Adriel" is apparently based (at least partially) on a Targumic explanation and ignores the fact that יָלַד לְ־ (*yld l-*) means "bear to," not "bring up for." The tortuous attempt of ben-Barak to retain "Michal" in the text by stating (among other things) that "Adriel" is the Aramaic equivalent of the Hebrew name "Paltiel" (3:15) is unconvincing (Zafrira ben-Barak, "The Legal Background to the Restoration of Michal to David," *Studies in the Historical Books of the Old Testament*, ed. J. A. Emerton [VTSup 30; Leiden: Brill, 1979], 26–27).

9 "They were put to death" translates הֵם הֻמְתוּ (*hm hmtw* [*Kethiv*]), where הֵמָּה הֻמְתוּ (*hmh hmtw*) is expected (thus the *Qere*). Perhaps the הֻ־ (*h-*) at the beginning of the verb was intended to be shared with that at the end of the pronoun (cf. Watson, 531).

For בִּימֵי קָצִיר בָּרִאשֹׁנִים (*bymy qṣyr brʾšnym*, "during the first days of the harvest"), the Lucianic recension of the LXX reads ἐν ἡμέραις ζειῶν (*en hēmerais zeiōn*, "during the days of spelt"), a phrase that "at once arouses suspicion, for not only does it make little sense, but it also introduces a serious chronological difficulty, in that emmer, or spelt, was harvested *later* than barley" (S. P. Brock, "An Unrecognized Occurrence of the Month Name Ziw [2 Sam. xxi 9]," *VT* 23/1 [1973]: 101; cf. Ex 9:31–32). Thus it may well be that *zeiōn* in the Lucianic text is a scribal error for ζειου (*zeiou*, "Ziv"), the second month (mid-April to mid-May). Since the MT, however, reads smoothly as is, it is unnecessary to emend it to conform to the Lucianic reading (contra Brock, ibid., 103).

B. David's Heroes (21:15–22)

OVERVIEW

Parallel to the narrative of David's mighty men in 23:8–39 (see Overview to 21:1–24:25), the present account summarizes four noteworthy battles that David and his men fought against his nemesis, the Philistines. How the various skirmishes are related chronologically to those mentioned in 5:17–25; 8:1, 12; 23:9–17—or, for that matter, to each other—is impossible to ascertain.

The first and last verses (vv.15, 22) of the literary unit refer to David and "his men" (*ʿᵃbādāyw*, lit., "his servants/officers"; in v.17 "men" renders *ʾanšê*) and thus serve to frame the whole. Verse 22, the epilogue that concludes the section, observes that the four slain Philistine champions were descendants of "Rapha," the eponymous ancestor of one distinctive group of Rephaim (see comment and

Notes on 5:18). The rest of the unit, arranged chiastically, includes two shorter passages nestling at the center, each of which relates to a battle at "Gob" and begins with *wthy-ʿwd hmlḥmh* (lit., "And again there was the battle") while the two bracketing passages (vv.15–17, 20–21) each begin with *wthy-ʿwd mlḥmh* (lit., "And again there was a battle"):

A Abishai kills Ishbi-Benob at an unnamed site (21:15–17)
 B Sibbecai kills Saph at Gob (21:18)
 B' Elhanan kills "Goliath" at Gob (21:19)
A' Jonathan kills an unnamed opponent at Gath (21:20–21)

15 Once again there was a battle between the Philistines and Israel. David went down
with his men to fight against the Philistines, and he became exhausted. 16 And Ishbi-Benob,
one of the descendants of Rapha, whose bronze spearhead weighed three hundred
shekels and who was armed with a new sword, said he would kill David. 17 But Abishai
son of Zeruiah came to David's rescue; he struck the Philistine down and killed him. Then
David's men swore to him, saying, "Never again will you go out with us to battle, so that
the lamp of Israel will not be extinguished."
18 In the course of time, there was another battle with the Philistines, at Gob. At that time
Sibbecai the Hushathite killed Saph, one of the descendants of Rapha.
19 In another battle with the Philistines at Gob, Elhanan son of Jaare-Oregim the Bethlehemite killed Goliath the Gittite, who had a spear with a shaft like a weaver's rod.
20 In still another battle, which took place at Gath, there was a huge man with six fingers
on each hand and six toes on each foot — twenty-four in all. He also was descended from
Rapha. 21 When he taunted Israel, Jonathan son of Shimeah, David's brother, killed him.
22 These four were descendants of Rapha in Gath, and they fell at the hands of David and
his men.

COMMENTARY

15–17 Battles between Israel and the Philistines, Israel's age-long enemy, were not uncommon during the early years of the united monarchy (cf. 1Sa 4–7; 12–14; 17–19; 23; 28–31; see also Overview to 21:15–22). It was often necessary for David and his troops to go "down" (v.15) from the heights of his capital city to the Philistine foothills and plains (which were at a much lower elevation than Jerusalem). On this occasion the long march and the rigors of battle leave him "exhausted" (cf. also 1Sa 14:31).

Ishbi-Benob (known only from this text) decides to take advantage of David's situation and kill him (v.16). The weight of his bronze spearhead (see NIV note ["about 7½ pounds"]), although only half that of Goliath's (cf. 1Sa 17:7), nevertheless marks him as a man of unusual size and strength. *Qayin*, occurring as a noun only here and translated "spearhead," at the very least "signifies a sort of weapon, especially one used by a brute"—and it is therefore hardly coincidental that the name of the murderer Cain is spelled the same way in Hebrew (Yehuda T. Radday, "Humour in Names," in *On Humour and the Comic in the Hebrew Bible*, ed. Yehuda T. Radday and Athalya Brenner [JSOTSup 92; Sheffield: Almond, 1990], 75).

Ishbi-Benob is also "armed" with a "new" weapon of some sort, the nature of which is not specified in the text. The NIV supplies "sword," an excellent guess supported by the fact that (1) the Hebrew adjective rendered "new" is feminine and the Hebrew word for "sword" is likewise feminine, (2) several ancient versions add "sword" (cf. *BHS*), and (3) "armed" (lit., "girded") occurs in 20:8 ("was wearing") in relation to "sword" ("dagger"; compare also Jdg 18:11, 16–17 with Jdg 18:27).

Like the other combatants, Ishbi-Benob is one of the "descendants" of "Rapha" (v.16; cf. vv.18, 20 and the summary statement in v.22). Although the Hebrew word translated "descendants" is used elsewhere of the progeny of huge ancestors (cf. "descendants of Anak" in Nu 13:22, 28; Jos 15:14), and although "Rapha" (*rph*) seems clearly to be the forefather of at least one group of the "Rephaim" (*rpʾym*; cf. the spelling *rpʾ* for Rapha in 1Ch 20:6, 8; see also comment and Notes on 5:18), quite different understandings have been proposed for each of the two words.

Willesen argues that *yālîd* (GK 3535), conventionally translated as "son, descendant," never has that meaning "but always denotes a person of slave status.... So the *ylydy hrph* of II Sam. xxi were members of a corps called *hrph* [GK 8335]" (F. Willesen, "The Philistine Corps of the Scimitar from Gath," *JSS* 3/4 [1958]: 328). Following Willesen's lead, L'Heureux proposes that "the term *yālîd* does not designate a physical descendant, but one who is born into the group by adoption, initiation or consecration" and that in vv.15–22 the word should be rendered as "votaries"—although "with considerable reservation" (Conrad E. L'Heureux, "The *yᵉlîdê hārāpāʾ*—A Cultic Association of Warriors," *BASOR* 221 [1976]: 84 and n. 15; cf. also McCarter, *II Samuel*, 449–50).

As for "Rapha," Willesen asserts that the *h* on the front of the word is not the Hebrew definite article but is part of the root of the word itself. Because of the non-Semitic, Aegean origin of the Philistines, "it seems plausible to search Greek for an equivalent of *hrph* and here the word ἅρπη 'sickle, scimitar' recommends itself.... To sum up, the Philistine *ylydy hrph* was a body of warriors dedicated to a deity whose symbol was the royal Syro-Palestinian scimitar" (Willesen, "The Philistine Corps," 331, 335). L'Heureux, correctly observing that "few Semitists are likely to be comfortable with *harpē* as the source of *hārāpâ*," nevertheless agrees in principle that "the term *rpʾ* was a divine epithet" of some sort and thus translates the phrase in question "the votaries of Rapha," who "were fighting men initiated into an elite group whose patron was *(h)rp*ʾ" (L'Heureux, "The *yᵉlîdê hārāpāʾ*," 84–85).

Two decisive considerations, however, weigh heavily against all such interpretations: (1) The warriors in question are not simply referred to by the *terminus technicus yālîd* (vv.16, 18; 1Ch 20:4) but, even more frequently, are described through the use of other forms of the verbal root *yld*: *yullad* (v.20) and *yullᵉdû* (v.22), both of which are probably Qal passive perfect forms; *nôlad* (1Ch 20:6) and *nûllᵉdû* (1Ch 20:8), both of which are Niphal perfects (for the anomaly of the latter, cf. GKC, sec. 69*t*). Indeed, *yālîd* itself is a Qal passive participle of the same root.

(2) Although 2 Samuel consistently uses the root *rph* (cf. vv.16, 18, 20, 22), 1 Chronicles just as consistently uses *rpʾ* (cf. 1Ch 20:4, 6, 8)—a root that can hardly be separated from the *rpʾ(m)* of the Ugaritic texts (cf. similarly *ANET*, 149 n. 2). In fact, 1 Chronicles 20:4 calls the warriors in question *yᵉlîdê hārᵉpāʾîm* ("the descendants of the

Rephaites"). All things considered, therefore, it is difficult to escape what seems to be an inevitable conclusion: The *ylydy (h)rph/(h)rpʾ(ym)* are descendants of Rapha, the eponymous ancestor of at least one group of Rephaites (see comment and Notes on 5:18).

Despite his unusual size, Ishbi-Benob (v.16) faces a formidable opponent in "Abishai son of Zeruiah" (v.17), who, totally in character (see 16:9; 19:21; 1Sa 26:8 and comments), comes to David's "rescue" (lit., "help") by killing the Philistine. Sensing that the king has just experienced a close shave, his men swear to him that he will never again accompany them when they go out to battle (see comments on 11:1; 18:3). They want to make sure that David, the "lamp" of Israel—he who, with God's help, has brought the light of continued prosperity and well-being to the whole land (cf. 22:29; 1Ki 15:4; Ps 132:17; also Job 18:5–6; Pr 13:9)—will not be "extinguished" (see 14:7 and comment). The lamp imagery is probably derived from the seven-branched lampstand in the tabernacle (see 1Sa 3:3 and comment).

18 At this point the parallels between 2 Samuel and 1 Chronicles resume, to be continued sporadically throughout the rest of the book (for details see Overview to 1:1–20:26). The commentary below will note only those places where the differences between vv.18–22 and 1 Chronicles 20:4–8 are significant or where the parallel text makes its own contribution. Since "in the course of time" normally marks a substantially new departure in the narrative (though not necessarily with chronological overtones; see Notes on 2:1 and comments on 8:1; 10:1; 13:1), its occurrence here is surprising. Its presence at the beginning of the second segment of its overall literary section (see Overview to 21:15–22), however, may have played a part in the Chronicler's decision to omit the Ishbi-Benob pericope.

This time the location of the battle is "Gob" (*gôb*, vv.18–19), which it is tempting to read as "Nob" (*nôb*) in both verses, as many Hebrew MSS do (cf. *BHS*). Nob would echo nicely the name of Ishbi-Benob (v.16), which apparently means something like "Inhabitant of Nob," the "town of the priests" whose citizens Saul had massacred (see 1Sa 21:1; 22:18–19 and comments). First Chronicles 20:4, however, seems to indicate that Gob (mentioned nowhere else in the OT) was "another name for Gezer" (Rasmussen, 237), which is located just east of the Philistine plain twenty miles west-northwest of Jerusalem (see comment on 5:25).

The Rephaite Saph (given the alternative name Sippai in 1Ch 20:4) is killed by David's hero Sibbecai the Hushathite, known elsewhere as one of the Thirty (see comment and NIV note on 2Sa 23:27; cf. 1Ch 11:29) and also as a commander in charge of one of twelve army divisions, each of which consists of twenty-four thousand men (cf. 1Ch 27:11). At the end of the parallel verse in Chronicles, the narrator adds the comment that the Philistines "were subjugated" (1Ch 20:4), perhaps in part as a result of the death of Saph/Sippai.

19 A third battle against the Philistines also takes place at Gezer/Gob (see comment on v.18). This time the Israelite hero is "Elhanan son of Jair" (cf. 1Ch 20:5). Since it is universally recognized that the first occurrence of *ʾōrᵉgîm* is an erroneous scribal insertion caused by the appearance of the word at the end of the verse (where it forms part of the expression rendered "weaver's rod"), the name "Jaare-Oregim" (and the NIV's note, which suggests the translation "Jair the weaver") can be safely scuttled. In the light of the well-known fact that David son of "Jesse of Bethlehem" (1Sa 16:1, 18; 17:58) killed Goliath (cf. 1Sa 17:51, 57; 18:6; 19:5; 21:9), it is often suggested that "David" is Elhanan's throne name and that "Elhanan son of Jaare" (*yʿry*) is a scribal error for "Elhanan son of Jesse" (*yšy*;

cf. A. M. Honeyman, "The Evidence for Regnal Names among the Hebrews," *JBL* 67/1 [1948]: 23–24; Emanuel Tov in a letter to the editor, *BRev* 3/3 [1987]: 6).

To attempt to answer the question of who killed Goliath by equating David with Elhanan, however, fails to reckon with the references to "David"—not "Elhanan"—that flank v.19 (vv.15, 17, 21–22). Nor does it adequately address the parallel text: "Elhanan son of Jair killed Lahmi the brother of Goliath the Gittite" (1Ch 20:5; cf. also NIV note on v.19). Although the MT of 1 Chronicles 20:5 (*ʾt-lḥmy ʾḥy glyt*, "[killed] Lahmi the brother of Goliath") appears to be original and the text of v.19 (*byt hlḥmy ʾt glyt*, "The Bethlehemite [killed] Goliath") seems to be a corruption of it, it is also possible that the original text read "the Bethlehemite [killed] the brother of Goliath"—or, for that matter, "the Bethlehemite [killed] Lahmi the brother of Goliath."

Whatever option one chooses, however, "the fact of the matter then is that David slew Goliath, and that Elhanan slew the brother of Goliath" (Edward J. Young, *An Introduction to the Old Testament*, rev. ed. [Grand Rapids: Eerdmans, 1960], 198; cf. K&D, 465–66; Archer, 178–79). That there was more than one Goliath (cf. Haley, 336; Kirkpatrick, 197) or that "Goliath" was a common noun that "had come to designate a type" (Hertzberg, 387) seem less likely solutions.

In any event, "Elhanan son of Jair the Bethlehemite" (if that is the correct reading) is to be distinguished from "Elhanan son of Dodo from Bethlehem" (23:24)—although an attempt to equate them on the part of a copyist of 2 Samuel may have resulted in the (incorrect?) reading "the Bethlehemite" in v.19 (cf. J. Barton Payne in *EBC*, 4:404; for a judicious and helpful survey of possible resolutions of the differences between v.19 and 1Ch 20:5, cf. D. F. Payne in *New Bible Commentary*, rev. ed. [ed. D. Guthrie and J. A. Motyer; Grand Rapids: Eerdmans, 1970], 318–19).

The main weapon of Goliath's brother, "a spear with a shaft like a weaver's rod," matched that of Goliath himself (see comment on 1Sa 17:7). On another occasion one of David's men faced a similar spear, again wielded by a giant—this time an Egyptian (cf. 1Ch 11:23).

20–21 The last of the four battles against the Philistines takes place at "Gath" (v.20), the hometown of Goliath (cf. v.19; see 1Sa 17:4 and comment), modern Tell es-Safi (see comment on 1Sa 5:8), located about twelve miles south-southwest of Gezer. A nameless Rephaite, a "huge" man (cf. Nu 13:32 ["of great size"]; 1Ch 11:23 ["tall"]; Isa 45:14) with an extra digit on each hand and foot, makes his appearance. Barnett has observed that "in the Levant, polydactylism—an excess of fingers or toes—was considered to be ... a characteristic of giants, or of people with super powers or extra strength" (Richard D. Barnett, "Polydactylism in the Ancient World," *BAR* 16/3 [1990]: 46, 51).

This particular Rephaite taunts Israel (as Goliath had done many years earlier; v.21; see comment on 1Sa 17:10 ["defy"]). He is soon dispatched, however, by "Jonathan [not to be confused with David's friend of the same name] son of Shimeah, David's brother" (for various spellings of the name of Shammah, the third oldest brother of David, see comment on 1Sa 16:9). It is therefore somewhat ironic that a seventh-century Assyrian omen text affirms that "if a woman gives birth, and [the child] has six fingers [and toes] on each of its right and left hands and right and left feet—the land will live undisturbed" (cited by Barnett, "Polydactylism," 49).

22 Thus "four" (the number is omitted in 1Ch 20:8, since the death of Ishbi-Benob is not recorded in 1Ch 20:4–7) Rephaite giants are killed by David's men. If there is no indication in the text that David personally did battle with them, he nevertheless shares the credit for their death because he is king and his men act under his command. Relatively rare, the idiom "fall at/into the hands of" occurs again in 24:14 and therefore serves to enhance the inclusio effect discussed in the Overview to 21:1–24:25.

NOTE

21 Some LXX MSS read Ιωναδαβ (*Iōnadab*, "Jonadab") instead of "Jonathan" (cf. *BHS*), doubtless on the basis of 2 Samuel 13:3 (see comment). Since the LXX's reading is otherwise unfounded, it is better to assume that "Jonathan and Jonadab were brothers" (McCarter, *II Samuel*, 449).

C. David's Song of Praise (22:1–51)

OVERVIEW

It has long been recognized that 2 Samuel 22 is not only one of the oldest major poems in the OT but also that, because Psalm 18 parallels it almost verbatim, it is a key passage for the theory and practice of OT textual criticism. "The importance of this poem for the study of textual transmission can scarcely be overemphasized. No other ancient piece of comparable length appears in parallel texts in the OT" (Cross and Freedman, "A Royal Song," 15).

Although defective spelling and the presence of other orthographic archaisms are more common in 2 Samuel 22 than in Psalm 18 (cf. Cross and Freedman, "A Royal Song," 15–17), the relatively poor scribal transmission of the text of Samuel renders moot the question of whether 2 Samuel 22 contains a more original text overall than does Psalm 18. Whereas Robert Alter voices his opinion that 2 Samuel 22 is "the probably more authentic text" (Alter, *The Art of Biblical Poetry*, 29), the notes in the NIV footnotes declare four Psalm 18 readings superior to those of 2 Samuel 22 and only one Samuel reading superior to that of Psalm 18. Since the NIV chose not to footnote numerous other differences between the two texts, however, the four-to-one statistic is somewhat misleading. It is often difficult to decide between equally viable variant readings. In any event, it is likely that more than one version of David's poem was in circulation, and it is even possible (if not probable) that he himself produced more than one draft of the song. K&D, 469, gives a typical summary:

> Neither of the two texts that have come down to us contains the original text of the psalm of David unaltered; but the two recensions have been made quite independently of each other, one for the insertion of the psalm in the Psalter intended for liturgical use, and the other when it was incorporated into the history of David's reign, which formed the groundwork of our books of Samuel. The first revision may have been made by David himself when he arranged his Psalms for liturgical purposes; but the second was effected by the prophetic historian, whose object it was ... not so much to give it with diplomatic literality, as to introduce it in a form that should be easily intelligible and true to the sense.

The commentary below will note only the more significant differences between ch. 22 and Psalm 18 (note that all references to Ps 18 refer to English versification; for Heb. add one verse).

Attempts have been made to demonstrate that David's psalm is combined from two separate and readily discernible psalms, the one spoken by an individual who celebrates victory over the enemy (vv.2–31) and the other by the monarch who celebrates the dispersion of the enemy (vv.32–51). Among others, however, J. Kenneth Kuntz, 19–21, makes a good case for the literary integrity and theological unity of the psalm by (1) noting that the "old gnomic quatrain (vv.26–27)," which is "located at the psalm's midpoint, fulfills a crucial pivotal function in effectively uniting the poem in its several parts" as it looks backward as well as forward; (2) examining the way in which divine names and appellatives are employed throughout the psalm (cf. *ṣûrî*, "my rock," used of God in the introductory and concluding words of praise [vv.3, 47]); and (3) pointing out the repeated use of various nouns and verbs within both halves.

In addition, Alter (*The Art of Biblical Poetry*, 33) makes the observation that of the eight essentially synonymous lines in the psalm, "two occur at the very beginning [vv.2, 3a–b] and three at the very end [vv.49, 50, 51a–b] of the poem, leading one to suspect that the poet reserved this paradigmatic form of static parallelism for the purpose of framing, while parallelism in the body of the poem is preponderantly dynamic."

Virtually unanimous agreement on such matters as genre and data is not far to seek. Claus Westermann (*The Praise of God in the Psalms* [Richmond, Va.: John Knox, 1965], 103–4) identifies the framework of the psalm as a "declarative psalm of praise (psalm of thanks) of the individual" (for his penetrating discussion of the fact that the expression of thanks to God is a way of praising, see 25–30), a more precise description than the traditional "(royal) psalm/song of thanksgiving" (cf. Kuntz, 3; Peter R. Ackroyd, "The Succession Narrative [so-called]," *Int* 35/4 [1981]: 393; see also Kirkpatrick; Baldwin; Gordon; K&D; Hertzberg; Mauchline; Anderson; note the title of Cross and Freedman's article. "A Royal Song of Thanksgiving: II Samuel 22 = Psalm 18").

It is also generally held that the psalm dates from the tenth century BC (cf. Cross and Freedman, "A Royal Song," 20, 23 n. 13; William F. Albright, *Yahweh and the Gods of Canaan: A Historical Analysis of Two Contrasting Faiths* [Garden City, N.Y.: Doubleday, 1968], 25; Freedman, "Divine Names and Titles," 57, 96; Kuntz, 3) and that certain sections of it (esp. the theophany in vv.8–16) draw on still earlier sources (cf. Cross and Freedman, "A Royal Song," 21). In addition, internal attribution of authorship to David himself has held up well under scholarly scrutiny (cf. Freedman, "Divine Names and Titles," 76; K&D; Kirkpatrick; Gordon; Baldwin).

The position of ch. 22 within 2 Samuel is appropriate indeed: "With its title referring to the deliverance of David from the power of all his enemies, [it] comes fittingly after the near-escape of David from death described in the hero section of 21:15–22" (Ackroyd, "Succession Narrative," 393). Located near the end of the books of Samuel, it nicely balances the Song of Hannah near the beginning (1Sa 2:1–10) and shares several of its terms and themes (see comment on 1Sa 2:1–2; cf. also Freedman, "Divine Names and Titles," 75–76, 87, 89, 95).

With respect to the wider context of the entire OT, "the attribution to David of a thanksgiving poem (2 Sam 22) followed by his 'last words' in 23:1–7 provides a correspondence to the placing of the Song and Blessing of Moses in Deuteronomy 32 and 33" (Ackroyd, "Succession Narrative," 393). Finally, as Alter (*The David Story*, 336) has noted, "it was a common literary practice in ancient times to place a long poem or 'song' (*shirah*) at or near the end of a narrative book—compare Jacob's Testament, Genesis 49, and the Song of Moses, Deuteronomy 32."

Apart from its setting (v.1), ch. 22 may be analyzed as follows. (The minimal sections agree with the NIV's scansion.)

A. Introductory words of praise (22:2–4)
B. Reasons for praise (22:5–46)
   1. David's deliverance from his enemies (22:5–20)
      a. Though death threatened, the Lord heard me (22:5–7)
      b. Great is the Lord of heaven and earth (22:8–16)
      c. Though great in heaven, he saved me on earth (22:17–20)
   2. The basis of God's saving deliverance (22:21–30)
      a. The Lord saves those who are righteous (22:21–25)
      b. The Lord's justice is evident in his actions (22:26–30)
   3. The outworking of God's saving deliverance (22:31–46)
      a. The Lord, whose way is perfect, makes my way perfect (22:31–37)
      b. I gained the victory over my enemies (22:38–43)
      c. The Lord enabled me to gain the victory (22:44–46)
C. Concluding words of praise (22:47–51)

Leitwörter that characterize the psalm include *yšʿ* ("save, deliver"; cf. Alter, *The Art of Biblical Poetry*, 32) and *ṣûr* ("rock"; cf. Kuntz, 20–21).

[1] David sang to the LORD the words of this song when the LORD delivered him from the
hand of all his enemies and from the hand of Saul. [2] He said:

"The LORD is my rock, my fortress and my deliverer;
3 my God is my rock, in whom I take refuge,
my shield and the horn of my salvation.
He is my stronghold, my refuge and my savior—
from violent men you save me.
[4] I call to the LORD, who is worthy of praise,
and I am saved from my enemies.

[5] "The waves of death swirled about me;
the torrents of destruction overwhelmed me.
[6] The cords of the grave coiled around me;
the snares of death confronted me.
[7] In my distress I called to the LORD;
I called out to my God.
From his temple he heard my voice;
my cry came to his ears.

8 "The earth trembled and quaked,
the foundations of the heavens shook;
they trembled because he was angry.
9 Smoke rose from his nostrils;
consuming fire came from his mouth,
burning coals blazed out of it.
10 He parted the heavens and came down;
dark clouds were under his feet.
11 He mounted the cherubim and flew;
he soared on the wings of the wind.
12 He made darkness his canopy around him —
the dark rain clouds of the sky.
13 Out of the brightness of his presence
bolts of lightning blazed forth.
14 The LORD thundered from heaven;
the voice of the Most High resounded.
15 He shot arrows and scattered ⌞the enemies⌟,
bolts of lightning and routed them.
16 The valleys of the sea were exposed
and the foundations of the earth laid bare
at the rebuke of the LORD,
at the blast of breath from his nostrils.

17 "He reached down from on high and took hold of me;
he drew me out of deep waters.
18 He rescued me from my powerful enemy,
from my foes, who were too strong for me.
19 They confronted me in the day of my disaster,
but the LORD was my support.
20 He brought me out into a spacious place;
he rescued me because he delighted in me.

21 "The LORD has dealt with me according to my righteousness;
according to the cleanness of my hands he has rewarded me.
22 For I have kept the ways of the LORD;
I have not done evil by turning from my God.
23 All his laws are before me;
I have not turned away from his decrees.
24 I have been blameless before him
and have kept myself from sin.

25 The LORD has rewarded me according to my righteousness,
according to my cleanness in his sight.

26 "To the faithful you show yourself faithful,
to the blameless you show yourself blameless,
27 to the pure you show yourself pure,
but to the crooked you show yourself shrewd.
28 You save the humble,
but your eyes are on the haughty to bring them low.
29 You are my lamp, O LORD;
the LORD turns my darkness into light.
30 With your help I can advance against a troop;
with my God I can scale a wall.

31 "As for God, his way is perfect;
the word of the LORD is flawless.
He is a shield
for all who take refuge in him.
32 For who is God besides the LORD?
And who is the Rock except our God?
33 It is God who arms me with strength
and makes my way perfect.
34 He makes my feet like the feet of a deer;
he enables me to stand on the heights.
35 He trains my hands for battle;
my arms can bend a bow of bronze.
36 You give me your shield of victory;
you stoop down to make me great.
37 You broaden the path beneath me,
so that my ankles do not turn.

38 "I pursued my enemies and crushed them;
I did not turn back till they were destroyed.
39 I crushed them completely, and they could not rise;
they fell beneath my feet.
40 You armed me with strength for battle;
you made my adversaries bow at my feet.
41 You made my enemies turn their backs in flight,
and I destroyed my foes.
42 They cried for help, but there was no one to save them —
to the LORD, but he did not answer.

43 I beat them as fine as the dust of the earth;
I pounded and trampled them like mud in the streets.

44 "You have delivered me from the attacks of my people;
you have preserved me as the head of nations.
People I did not know are subject to me,
45 and foreigners come cringing to me;
as soon as they hear me, they obey me.
46 They all lose heart;
they come trembling from their strongholds.

47 "The LORD lives! Praise be to my Rock!
Exalted be God, the Rock, my Savior!
48 He is the God who avenges me,
who puts the nations under me,
49 who sets me free from my enemies.
You exalted me above my foes;
from violent men you rescued me.
50 Therefore I will praise you, O LORD, among the nations;
I will sing praises to your name.
51 He gives his king great victories;
he shows unfailing kindness to his anointed,
to David and his descendants forever."

COMMENTARY

1 Psalm 18 agrees with ch. 22 that the psalm recorded in both books originates with David, who in Psalm 18 is called "the servant of the LORD." Although "of David" in the title of the psalm doubtless implies authorship, the elasticity of the Hebrew preposition makes it hazardous to assume that proper names following it in other psalm titles are always the authors of their respective psalms (despite the fact that in many cases they surely are). The Lord is the eminently worthy recipient of David's song, but the narrator is probably not telling us that David "sang" it to him. In parallel contexts *dbr* is more properly rendered "recited" (Dt 31:30) or "spoke" (Dt 32:44). When "song" (*šîr*) is the object of "sing" in similar situations, the normal way of expressing the Hebrew verb is to use the cognate *šyr* (cf. Ex 15:1; Ps 137:3).

If God's people tend to believe that the ark of the covenant (cf. 1Sa 4:3 [see, however, Notes there]) or the king of Israel (see comments on 14:16; 19:9) saves them from the hand of their enemies, David knows full well that the Lord is the one who has "delivered him." Exactly "when" the psalm was first recited is uncertain, although it must have been after the prophet Nathan's announcement of God's covenant with him (see comments on v.51; 7:1–17; see also comment on "given him rest from all his enemies around him" in 7:1).

2–4 In his introductory words of praise, David affirms that the Lord is everything to him, that the Lord is all he needs. Nine epithets underlining God's protecting presence are divided into three sets of three: "my rock" (*salʿî*; GK 6152), "my fortress," "my deliverer" (v.2); "my rock" (*ṣûrî*; GK 7446), "my shield," "the horn of my salvation" (v.3a); "my stronghold," "my refuge," "my savior" (v.3b). The first two sets begin with synonyms for "rock"; the second two sets end with words derived from the root *yšʿ* ("save"; GK 3828), a *Leitwort* throughout the psalm (cf. also "you save me" [v.3b] and "I am saved" [v.4]); and the first and third sets end with the only two participles among the nine terms, both stressing the theme of rescue ("deliverer," "savior"). Each of the nine terms is personalized by adding the suffix *-î* ("my"), which also produces an impressive rhyming effect. A final participle, "worthy of praise" (*m*^{e}*hullāl*), begins v.4 in the MT and thus contributes a tenth and climactic epithet to the list.

Numerous words and phrases throughout David's poem are echoed again and again in the book of Psalms, and the divine titles in vv.2–4 are no exception. (The following examples are representative rather than exhaustive.) "My rock" (*salʿî*) and "my fortress" (v.2) appear together in Davidic Psalm 31:3 (= Ps 71:3), while "my rock" occurs alone in Psalm 42:9. Remarkably, Davidic Psalm 144 displays five of the epithets: "my Rock" (*ṣûrî*, v.1), "my fortress," "my stronghold," "my deliverer," "my shield" (v.2). "My fortress" is found also in Psalm 91:2 and "my deliverer" (*m*^{e}*palṭî*) in Davidic Psalm 40:17 (= 70:5). In addition the root *plṭ* (GK 7117) is echoed in v.44, where David gratefully asserts, "You have delivered me."

By virtue of their respective positions near the beginning of 1 Samuel and near the end of 2 Samuel, the Song of Hannah (1Sa 2:1–10) and the Song of David constitute a kind of overall inclusio framing the main contents of the books and underscoring the fact that the two books were originally one. Both hymns begin by using "horn" as a figure of speech for "strength" (see NIV note on v.3; also comment on 1Sa 2:1), by referring to God as the "rock," and by reflecting on divine "deliverance/salvation" (*yšʿ*; cf. 1Sa 2:1–2; 2Sa 22:3); and both hymns end by paralleling "his king" with "his anointed" (1Sa 2:10; 2Sa 22:51).

In terms of inner inclusios, however, the hymns go their separate ways: The Song of Hannah concentrates on "horn" (1Sa 2:1, 10), while the Song of David emphasizes "rock" (vv.3, 47 [2x]) and "salvation" (vv.3, 47 ["Savior"], 51 ["victories"]). God as David's "rock" (*ṣûr*) appears in Psalms 19:14; 28:1 as well (cf. also 92:15). Such a God, without peer as protector of his chosen servants, is one in whom David can confidently "take refuge" (v.3; cf. Davidic Pss 2:12; 11:1; 16:1; 31:1 [= 71:1]; also 118:8–9).

The Lord as "shield" not only protects David from his enemies (v.3) but also ensures the safety of all who are godly (cf. v.31). It is not always possible to tell whether *mgn*, used frequently of God (and sometimes of Israel's king) in the Psalms, should be translated "shield" or "sovereign" (cf. the NIV notes on Davidic Pss 7:10; 59:11 as well as on Pss 84:9; 89:18; also "kings" in Ps 47:9, where the NIV note's alternative is "shields"). When the former is intended, the root is *gnn* ("protect"); when the latter is in view, the root is apparently *mgn* ("give") as in Proverbs 4:9 ("present"; cf. also Ugar. *mgn*, "give, present"; Joseph Aistleitner, *Wörterbuch der Ugaritischen Sprache* (Berlin: Akademie, 1963), 178–79).

The rendering "sovereign" in such cases is surely preferable to "donor" or the like (contrast M. O'Connor, "Yahweh the Donor," *AuOr* 6 [1988]: 47–60; see also comment on 1:21). The association of "shield" with "salvation/victory" (*yšʿ*) is relatively common in the Psalms (cf. v.36; Pss 3:2

["deliver"], 3; 7:10; cf. John S. Kselman, "Psalm 3: A Structural and Literary Study," *CBQ* 49/4 [1987]: 576 n. 12).

"Stronghold/fortress" (*miśgāb*; GK 5369), a secure, lofty retreat that the enemy finds inaccessible, is a frequent metaphor for God in the Psalms (cf. Davidic Pss 9:9 ["refuge ... stronghold"]; 59:9, 16–17; 62:2, 6; 144:2 ["stronghold"]; also Pss 46:7, 11; 48:3; 94:22). As such the Lord is the "refuge" of his chosen one (cf. Davidic Ps 59:16; also Jer 16:19). That the Lord is therefore eminently able to save him from "violent men" (v.3) is a theme to which David returns at the end of the poem (v.49), and that God delights to "give victory to" his people, to "save/rescue" them from all their enemies and from every calamity is a prominent thread running throughout 1 and 2 Samuel (see comments on 3:18; 8:6; 1Sa 10:19; 14:23; for *yšʿ* as an important *Leitwort* in ch. 22, cf. vv.3–4, 28, 36, 42, 47, 51).

Having described at length the God who is strong to save, David states for the record what has become his habitual exercise: "I call to the LORD" (v.4; cf. v.7; Davidic Ps 86:3, 5, 7)—a practice he shares with saints of all times and places (cf. Job 27:10; Ps 50:15; Isa 55:6; La 3:57; Ro 10:12; 1Pe 1:17). Such a God, supremely "worthy of praise" (cf. Davidic Ps 145:3; also Pss 48:1; 96:4), specializes in assuring his people that they will ultimately be "saved/rescued" from their "enemies" (cf. Nu 10:9; similarly Jer 30:7).

5–7 Among the reasons David gives for praising the Lord (vv.5–46) is, indeed, the fact that God has already delivered him from his enemies (vv.5–20). Whether in images watery (v.5) or terrestrial (v.6), "death" formed an all-encompassing inclusio (vv.5a, 6b) that threatened to swallow David. As exemplified in the modern Grim Reaper, death in ancient times was personified and/or localized through the use of proper nouns: *m[w]t* ("Death"), the Canaanite deity known from the Ugaritic epics (cf. similarly Job 28:22); *bᵉlîyaʿal* ("Destruction"), rendering a Hebrew word that came into the NT as "Belial," a name virtually synonymous with Satan (cf. 2Co 6:15; see Notes on 1Sa 1:16); *šᵉʾôl* ("Sheol"; see NIV note) or "the grave," the realm of the afterlife, the place of departed spirits (see Notes on 1Sa 2:6 [the Song of Hannah], where "death" and "the grave" are parallel, as they are here in v.6; cf. also Ps 116:3).

The metaphor of "waves" (lit., "breakers," v.5) as an instrument of divine judgment occurs elsewhere in psalmic literature as well (cf. Pss 42:7; 88:7; Jnh 2:3). "Swirled about" (*ʾpp*, v.5) and "coiled around" (*sbb*, v.6), parallel verbs in Jonah 2:5 ("engulfing," "surrounded"), are equally at home in the sea (*ʾpp*, Jnh 2:5; *sbb*, Ps 88:17; Jnh 2:5) and on land (*ʾpp*, Davidic Ps 40:12; Ps 116:3 ["entangled"]; *sbb*, Davidic Ps 22:12, 16; Pss 49:5; 118:10–11, 12 ["swarmed around"]; Hos 7:2). "Overwhelmed" (lit., "terrified, terrorized, frightened," v.5; see comment on "tormented" in 1Sa 16:14) is used of divine visitants again and again in the book of Job (cf. Job 3:5; 9:34; 13:11, 21; 15:24 ["fill ... with terror"]; 18:11 ["startle"]; 33:7 ["alarm"]; also Isa 21:4 ["makes ... tremble"]); and just as the snares of death "confronted" David (v.6), so did days of suffering "confront" Job (cf. Job 30:27).

In v.6 death is pictured as a hunter setting traps for his victims. If the "cords of the grave" and the "snares of death" confronted David with mortal danger, the "cords of death" and the "anguish of the grave" did the same to an unnamed poet in Psalm 116:3. The book of Proverbs speaks of a "fountain of life"—the "teaching of the wise" (Pr 13:14), the "fear of the LORD" (Pr 14:27)—that neutralizes the "snares of death."

Just as calling to the Lord should be our lifelong response to an all-sufficient God (vv.2–3), who is worthy of praise (v.4), so also calling to the Lord should be our immediate reaction (v.7) when we are threatened by nameless dread or mortal danger (vv.5–6). When in "distress/trouble," David (v.7; cf. Ps 59:16)—and other afflicted saints (cf. Pss 66:14; 102:2)—knew whom to turn to. From his "temple," his heavenly dwelling (v.7; cf. Davidic Pss 11:4; 29:9; also Isa 6:1; Mic 1:2; Hab 2:20; cf. Cross and Freedman, "A Royal Song," 23 n. 11), God heard the plea of David, whose "cry" for help (cf. Davidic Pss 39:12; 40:1; also 1Sa 5:12; Ps 102:1; La 3:56) reached the ears of the Lord.

8–16 Situated at the center of David's paean of praise to God for having delivered him from his enemies (vv.5–20) is a magnificent theophany (vv.8–16) that shares motifs and vocabulary with other OT theophanic sections, both early (cf. Ex 19:16–20; Jdg 5:4–5; Davidic Ps 68:4–8, 32–35) and late (cf. Isa 6:1–8; Hab 3:3–15; Eze 1:4–28; 10:1–22). The "foundations of the earth" (v.16) answer to the "foundations of the heavens" (v.8), a merism that not only forms an inclusio delimiting the literary unit but also reminds us of God's greatness through the vast reaches of his creation. Another linkage that gives integrity to the section is the similarity between *geḥālîm bāʿᵃrû mimmennû* ("burning coals blazed out of it," v.9) and *bāʿᵃrû gaḥᵃlê-ʾēš* ("bolts of lightning blazed forth," v.13; cf. also the repeated references to "his nostrils" [vv.9, 16]). Beginning with two tristichs (vv.8–9), the unit continues to the end in a series of eight distichs (vv.10–16), the total of ten matching the number of divine epithets in the introductory words of praise (vv.2–4). If the opening section concentrates on God's majestic being, the theophany focuses on his mighty omnipotence.

The poetic description of the divine self-manifestation is cast in terms of natural phenomena related to earthquake and storm. An earth set to quaking and trembling by the power of God (v.8) is a common motif (cf. Jdg 5:4b = Davidic Ps 68:8a; Job 9:6; Pss 46:2; 77:18; Isa 13:13; Jer 51:29; see esp. 1Sa 14:15 and comment). Serving as an appropriate counterpoise to the quaking earth is the shaking of the "foundations of the heavens" (v.8), probably a reference to the "mountains on which the vault of heaven seems to rest" (Kirkpatrick, 201; cf. "vaulted heavens," Job 22:14; "pillars of the heavens," Job 26:11)—indeed, Psalm 18:7 reads "foundations of the mountains" (as do the Syriac and Vulgate; see NIV note on 2Sa 22:8).

Earth and heaven alike tremble when the Lord is "angry" (cf. Isa 13:13) at the enemies of his people (cf. 1Sa 14:15). The Hebrew idiom rendered "he was angry" (v.8) means literally "it burned for him," an expression that leads naturally into the terrifying portrait of God as a smoke-spewing, fire-breathing nemesis (v.9; the imagery is similar to that used of the leviathan in Job 41:18–21). Unlike the smoke and fire of the altar in the Isaianic theophany (cf. Isa 6:4, 6), the present context seems to define the "smoke" as storm clouds (compare Ex 19:16 with 20:18) and the "fire" and "burning coals" as flashes of lightning. (In v.13, "bolts of lightning" is lit. "coals of fire.") "Smoke" in the Lord's "nostrils" (v.9) depicts the judgment of divine wrath against his enemies (cf. Isa 65:5; also Eze 38:18 ["my hot anger," lit., "my anger in/from my nostrils"]), and "burning coals" can metaphorically represent instruments of divine punishment (cf. Eze 10:2).

In theophanic splendor the Lord "parted the heavens and came down" (v.10; Davidic Ps 144:5; cf. also Isa 64:1, where the more vigorous expression "rend the heavens" is used). "The sense of the root, *nṭy*, here must be, 'to spread out, to spread apart, to spread open (as curtains)'" (Cross and Freedman, "A Royal Song," 24 n. 23). When God "comes down/goes down/descends" from heaven, his appearance is awesome indeed (cf. Ex 19:11, 18, 20; Ne 9:13). Although on occasion he comes down to rescue (cf. Ex 3:8; Nu 11:17), more often than not his descent is for the purpose of judgment (cf. Ge 11:5; 18:21; Isa 31:4; 64:1, 3; Mic 1:3). At such times his "feet" (v.10; cf. Na 1:3; similarly Ex 24:10; Hab 3:5 ["steps"]; Zec 14:4) are planted on "dark clouds," which signal the ominous approach and destructive power of a violent thunderstorm (cf. Dt 4:11; 5:22; Ps 97:2–4).

One or more "cherubim" (v.11; the Heb. word is singular) are the metaphorical means of transportation that the Lord "mounted/rode" (*rkb*). If above the ark of the covenant the cherubim (winged sphinxes) support the throne from which God reigns over his people (see comments on 6:2; 1Sa 4:4), in storm theophanies the cherubim support (or pull) a chariot, pictured in the form of swift clouds that scud across the heavens (cf. Davidic Ps 68:4, 33; Dt 33:26; Isa 19:1). As the seraphs in Isaiah's inaugural vision "flew" (cf. Isa 6:2, 6), so the cherubim in David's poem—and, with them, their divine passenger—"flew," in this case driven along on the "wings of the wind" (for the imagery cf. esp. Ps 104:3; also Hos 4:19, where "whirlwind" is lit. "wind with its wings"). In the Ugaritic epic literature the Canaanite god Baal is described as the "rider of the clouds" (*rkb* ʿ*rpt*; cf. *ANET*, 130–31; for a sensitive treatment of such Ugaritic epithets and their parallels in the OT, see Peter C. Craigie, *Ugarit and the Old Testament* [Grand Rapids: Eerdmans, 1983], 77–79).

Darkness shrouds the middle verse (v.12) of the theophany. The God of wind and rain is pictured as though dwelling in storm clouds, which form his "canopy" and from which he thunders (cf. Job 36:29 ["pavilion"]; also Dt 5:23; Isa 40:22). Interfacing with the darkness is the "brightness" (*nōgah*, v.13; GK 5586) of the Lord's presence, a "brilliant light" (Eze 1:4, 27) or "radiance" (Eze 1:28; 10:4) that surrounds him, a brightness that in lesser measure he condescends to share with his chosen rulers (cf. 23:4).

Thunder (v.14), lightning (v.15), and their effects (v.16) round out the theophany, the final three verses of which provide its only explicit references to the name of "the LORD" (vv.14, 16). "The efficacy of Yahweh's self-manifestation ... is artfully imparted in verses 14–16 and a perceptible climax is reached" (Kuntz, 11). That God "thundered from heaven" against his enemies (v.14) is yet another example of a common OT motif (see comments on 1Sa 1:6; 2:10; 7:10; see also Notes on 1Sa 2:10). His "voice" is a vivid image of thunder, not only in the OT (for a representative listing see Moshe Held, "The *YQTL-QTL* [*QTL-YQTL*] Sequence of Identical Verbs in Biblical Hebrew and in Ugaritic," in *Studies and Essays in Honor of Abraham A. Neuman*, ed. Meir Ben-Horin, Bernard D. Weinryb, and Solomon Zeitlin [Leiden: Brill, 1962], 287 n. 4), but also elsewhere in the ancient Near East (see comments on 1Sa 7:10; 12:17; cf. also, in a Ugaritic poem with reference to Baal, "of the giving forth of his voice [*tn qlh*] in the clouds, of his letting loose the lightnings to the earth" [de Moor, 54]).

"The voice of the Most High resounded" (v.14) is literally "the Most High gave forth his voice" (*ytn qwlw*), the predicate of which is normally rendered by the verb "thunder" in the NIV (cf. Jer 25:30; Joel 2:11; 3:16; Am 1:2). Alter (*The Art of Biblical Poetry*, 34) suggests that the reason "thundered" occurs before "gave forth his voice" has to do with "the issue of consequentiality. I would assume that thunder precedes the voice of the Lord because that is the way it was experientially for the ancient Near Eastern imagination: first the awestruck observer heard the peal of thunder; then he realized that God must be speaking."

The word "arrows" as a figure of speech for "bolts of lightning" (v.15) appears also in Habakkuk 3:9 (cf. 3:11) and Zechariah 9:14. The context of Davidic Psalm 144:6, with which v.15 has much in common, indicates that the NIV is justified in understanding the masculine plural suffix on *wypyṣm* as referring to "enemies" in both verses (cf. similarly NAB; for discussion see K&D, 475). Together with thunder, lightning is a common accompaniment of theophanies (cf. Ex 19:16; Ps 77:18; Eze 1:13–14). And as thunder "routed" the Philistines in the days of Samuel (1Sa 7:10), so lightning has "routed" David's enemies.

With its emphasis on cosmic phenomena, the closing verse of the theophany (v.16) reprises its opening (v.8). If the heavens respond to the earth in v.8, the "earth" (lit., "world") answers the "sea" in v.16. The phrase *ʾpqy ym* ("valleys of the sea") is related semantically (though not theologically) to the Ugaritic expression *apq thmtm* ("sources/channels of the [two] seas"; cf. G. R. Driver, *Canaanite Myths and Legends* [OTS 3; Edinburgh: T&T Clark, 1956], 96–97, 108–9). In Psalm 18:15, therefore, *ʾpyqy mym* should probably be divided differently and read *ʾpyqy-m ym*, with the first *m* to be understood as an enclitic between the two elements of a construct phrase (cf. Cross and Freedman, "A Royal Song," 26 n. 41; Cross and Freedman, *Studies in Ancient Yahwistic Poetry*, 28; Mitchell Dahood, "Hebrew-Ugaritic Lexicography IV," *Bib* 47/3 [1966]: 418).

The reading *ʾpyqy mym* in Psalm 18 probably arose by being attracted to the same expression in Psalm 42:1; Song of Songs 5:12; and Joel 1:20, where it means "streams of water." That *mayim* ("water[s]") in Psalm 18:15 is intended in the sense of "sea" is a less plausible explanation for the variant. The word *ʾpyqy* with the meaning "valleys of" is attested in Joel 3:18, where it is translated "ravines of" and where "water" appears in the same clause.

However firm and stable the foundation of the "heavens" (v.8) and the "earth/world" (v.16) may be in the normal course of events (cf. Pss 93:1; 96:10; Pr 8:29; Isa 40:21; Jer 31:37; Mic 6:2), the Lord of the universe can shake them and lay them bare (v.16) in accordance with his sovereign will (cf. Ps 82:5; Isa 24:18–19; see also comment on 1Sa 2:8e). Dislocation and exposure of so severe a kind takes place "at the blast of breath" from his nostrils, a display of divine wrath (cf. Ex 15:7–8; Job 4:9; Isa 30:27–28; 59:18–19). The parallel word "rebuke" (*gʿr*; GK 1721) often takes on the nuance of "explosive blast" in contexts of "forceful and destructive movement of air accompanied by loud, frightening noise" (James M. Kennedy, "The Root *GʿR* in the Light of Semantic Analysis," *JBL* 106/1 [1987]: 59, 64; cf. Job 26:11; Pss 76:6; 80:16; 104:7; 106:9; Isa 50:2; 66:15; Na 1:4). The rebuke of the Lord (v.16) as an index of his anger (v.8) has thus brought the theophany full circle.

17–20 David concludes his overall description of deliverance from his enemies (vv.5–20) by asserting that the self-revealing, all-powerful Sovereign of the universe (vv.8–16) reached down from heaven and saved him on earth (vv.17–20). The Lord lives not only "on high" (v.17; cf. Mic 6:6 ["exalted"]) but also "with him who is contrite and lowly in spirit" (Isa 57:15), the better to rescue him from whatever danger befalls him. Just as the pharaoh's daughter "drew" David's great predecessor, Moses, from the waters of the Nile (Ex 2:10), so also the Lord "drew" David (v.17; the Heb. verb *māšâ* occurs three times in the OT [cf. Ps 18:16(17)]) out of "deep waters" (*mayim rabbîm*, lit., "many waters"), a cosmic metaphor that symbolizes the most threatening of perils (cf. Davidic Pss 32:6 ["mighty waters"]; 144:7).

Although "powerful" (v.18; cf. Davidic Ps 59:3 ["fierce men"]), David's enemies were no match for God, who "rescued" him (v.18; different Heb. verb in v.20). If the snares of death "confronted" David without lasting effect (v.6), his foes "confronted" him in vain (v.19). In speaking of the "day of my disaster" (v.19), David uses a common expression that elsewhere refers to an experience of divinely sent judgment, punishment, or vengeance (cf. Dt 32:35; Job 21:30 ["calamity"]; Pr 27:10 ["when disaster strikes"]; Jer 18:17; 46:21; Ob 13).

The linguistic and cultural background of *ʾêd* ("disaster"; GK 369) is perhaps to be sought in the widespread practice of the "river ordeal" (cf. *ʾēd* ["streams"] in Ge 2:6; Job 36:27), a form of legal trial in which a suspected criminal was thrown into a river and his success or failure in attempting to swim to shore was interpreted as a divinely sent index of his innocence or guilt. The semantic development of *ʾēd/ʾêd* would thus have been from "river, stream" to the specialized nuance "river ordeal" to the more general meaning "ordeal, calamity, distress" (cf. P. Kyle McCarter, "The River Ordeal in Israelite Literature," *HTR* 66/4 [1973]: 403–12).

In the present context the case for such a relationship is strengthened by the proximity of "day of my disaster" (v.19) to the "deep waters" that threatened David in v.17. Through every trial, the Lord himself was David's "support" (v.19), the Hebrew word for which (*mišʿān*) was recently found in Jerusalem as a personal name on a clay seal impression dating from the early sixth century BC. It is "probably a shortened form of an unknown theophoric name, such as Mishʿaniyahu ['The Lord is my support'], which expresses a desire for divine support of the new-born infant" and which is based on v.19 (Avigad, 78).

That the Lord safely "brought [David] out" (v.20) of the ordeals through which he had gone (cf. Ps 66:12) implies that he is the God who "sets [his chosen ones] free" from the worst their enemies can do to them (v.49; same Heb. verb). David was released into a "spacious place," a term that elsewhere suggests freedom from bondage and oppression (cf. Davidic Ps 31:8; Ps 118:5 ["setting ... free"]; Hos 4:16 ["meadow"]).

21–25 The fact that the Lord "delighted in" David (v.20; see 15:26 and comment) provides a convenient transition to the psalm's second main section, in which David describes the basis of God's saving deliverance (vv.21–30) as consisting of two main factors: the righteousness of those who are rescued by God (vv.21–25) and the justice of God himself (vv.26–30). The present unit clearly displays its own internal literary integrity by framing the whole with phrases repeated in vv.21, 25: "according to my righteousness," "has rewarded me," and—if the LXX, Vulgate, and Psalm 18:24 are followed (see NIV note on v.25)—"according to the cleanness of my hands" (cf. similarly the independent treatment of Kuntz, 12).

Is David saying that his "righteousness" (vv.21, 25) has earned God's favor? Hardly.

> The psalmist is not talking about justification by works, much less about sinless perfection, but about "a conscience void of offence toward God and men" (Ac 24:16). In the issue between himself and his opponents right was on his side, or Yahweh would not have savingly interposed. As verses 26–28 make clear, Yahweh may intervene for good or ill, and all depending upon the integrity or otherwise of the human element. [Gordon, *I and II Samuel*, 306]

Far from taking matters into his own hands, David had "kept the ways of the Lord" (v.22; cf. Ge 18:19; Jdg 2:22; also 1Ki 2:3) and had waited for divine vindication against his enemies. "Now that vindication had come, and therefore he could safely conclude that he was right with God (*cf.* Ps 66:18–19)" (Baldwin, 288). Not pretending to be perfectly righteous, David was simply laying claim "to sincerity and single-heartedness in his devotion to God. Compare his own testimony (I Sam xxvi. 23), God's testimony (I Kings xiv. 8), and the testimony of history (I Kings xi. 4, xv. 5), to his essential integrity" (Kirkpatrick, 204–5). It is in this context that David's self-evaluation in vv.21–25 must be understood.

"Cleanness" (*bōr*) of hands, while intended here (and in Job 22:30) in a moral and spiritual sense (cf. the similar expression in Davidic Ps 24:4), is an idiom that derives ultimately from the practice of washing one's hands with "soda" (*bōr*; cf. Job 9:30; Neufeld, 50). That the Lord was a God who "rewarded" people according to their righteousness (vv.21, 25) was a principle David had embraced long before he became king (cf. 1Sa 26:23).

Central in this section, as well as in David's concern, is his determination to keep God's laws before him so that he may not be tempted to turn away from the divine "decrees" (v.23; cf. Ps 89:31), as his son Solomon would later do (cf. 1Ki 11:11). David's testimony that he has been "blameless" before the Lord (v.24; cf. Dt 18:13) is echoed later not only in the statement that God shows himself "blameless" to those who are "blameless" (v.26) but also in David's realization that the God whose way is "perfect" (v.31) makes "perfect" the way of his chosen one (v.33; same Heb. root).

As noted above (see comment on v.21), vv.21 and 25 form an inclusio that brackets the literary section, a fact that argues against the omission of v.25 on the grounds that it "seems out of place in the present context" (Cross and Freedman, "A Royal Song," 28 n. 59). The literary and theological summary of Kuntz, 12, is apropos: "As a meaningful sense unit, this strophe [vv.21–25] is committed to the assumption that as Yahweh's servant, the king's righteousness is firmly anchored in his unwavering commitment to Yahweh and his covenant. Accordingly, royal self-exultation is in no wise permitted."

26–30 The second main factor in David's description of the basis of God's saving deliverance (vv.21–30; see comment on v.21) is the Lord's justice, which is evident in his actions (vv.26–30). At the precise center of the entire poem is "apparently an old gnomic quatrain" (vv.26–27; Cross and Freedman, "A Royal Song," 28 n. 60), the first three cola of which are introduced by *ᶜim* ("to") and exhibit God's positive, reciprocal response to those whose lives are holy, and the fourth colon of which is introduced by *wᵉᶜim* ("but to") and exhibits God's negative response to the ungodly.

To the "faithful" (*ḥāsîd*; GK 2883), the one who has appropriated the (covenantal) love (*ḥesed*; GK 2876) demonstrated to him by the Lord (see comments on 1Sa 2:9; 20:8), God shows himself faithful (v.26a). To the "blameless" (*tāmîm*; GK 9459), the one who has been made "perfect" in God's eyes (see comment on v.24), the Lord shows himself blameless (v.26b; cf. Ps 84:11). To the "pure" (*nābār*; GK 1405), the one whose hands are characterized by "cleanness" (see comment on v.21; same Heb. root), God shows himself "pure" (v.27a; cf. Isa 52:11, where the same verb is used to describe those "who carry the vessels of the Lord"). But to the "crooked" (*ᶜiqqēš*, v.27b; GK 6836), the one whose words are "perverse" (cf. Pr 8:8; also Davidic Ps 101:4; Pr 11:20; 17:20) and whose paths are littered with traps for the unwary (cf. Pr 22:5 ['wicked']), the Lord shows himself "shrewd."

Although Psalm 18:26 preserves the correct form of the verb (*titpattāl*, from the root *ptl*; cf. *ᶜiqqēš ûpᵉtaltōl*, "warped and crooked" [Dt 32:5]; *niptāl wᵉᶜiqqēš*, "crooked or perverse" [Pr 8:8]), the anomalous form *tittappāl* (from the root *tpl*) in v.27 may be a deliberate wordplay on the name of David's enemy Ahithophel, which means "My brother is foolishness" (see comment on 15:12). Thus for the Lord to show himself "shrewd" toward those who are "crooked" means—in the 2 Samuel 22 version of David's psalm—that he turns them into fools (cf. Carlson, 251–52). At the hinge of the poem, therefore, David acknowledges himself (and his God) to be "faithful," "blameless," and "pure," whereas his enemies are "crooked" and are made to be "fools" by the same Lord who is David's deliverer.

The contrast established between the godly and the godless in vv.26–27 is summarized in v.28. Continuing to address God in the second person (a notable characteristic of vv.26–30), David asserts that the Lord saves the "humble" (cf. Pr 3:34; 16:19 ["oppressed"]) but that his eyes bring low the "haughty" (for the Ps 18:27 variant—"those whose eyes are haughty"—cf. Davidic Ps 131:1; Pr 6:17; 21:4; 30:13). In a similar context (Ps 147:6), God's sustenance of the "humble" is set over against the fact that he "casts" the wicked to the ground (same Heb. verb translated "bring ... low" in v.28). More important still is the Song of Hannah's description of the Lord (see Overview to 22:1–51) as one who "humbles" and "exalts" (1Sa 2:7; same Heb. roots as those rendered "bring ... low" and "haughty" in v.28).

David as the "lamp" of Israel (see comment on 21:17) merely reflects the blinding light of the glory of God, who is the "lamp" of David himself (v.29). "If the king could be regarded as a lamp or luminary, then God certainly could be also, as celestial gods were in the Canaanite tradition" (Robert Houston Smith, "The Household Lamps of Palestine in Old Testament Times," *BA* 27/1 [1964]: 21). "You, O LORD, keep my lamp burning" (Ps 18:28) is probably an expansive variant of v.29a (for an explanation of how it might have entered the text, see Cross and Freedman, "A Royal Song," 29 n. 64).

With God on his side, David feels invincible (v.30). Since "scale a wall" is clearly the meaning of the second line of the verse (for *dillēg*, "scale, leap [over]," cf. SS 2:8; Isa 35:6), the alternative translation in the NIV's note ("run through a barricade") provides a more suitable parallel in the first line than "advance against a troop" (see Notes). Either reading, of course, reflects David's confidence that with the Lord's help he can accomplish anything, no matter how difficult.

31–37 The psalm's third major section (vv.31–46), which expounds the outworking of God's saving deliverance, begins by describing the Lord as the enabler of his servant David (vv.31–37). Several of the epithets used of God in the introductory words of praise (vv.2–4) recur here.

God's name (*hāʾēl*, lit., "the God") is placed front and center ("As for God," v.31) as a means of foregrounding his presence and power (cf. vv.33 ["It is God"], 48 ["He is the God"]). The Lord, whose works and ways are "perfect" (v.31; Dt 32:4; see comment on v.24), makes David's "way perfect" (v.33) by providing him with everything he needs to ensure victory over his enemies. The Lord, whose "word" (cf. Ps 119:140 ["promises"]) is "flawless" in the sense that like precious metals in a refiner's furnace it has been "tested" to the point of proving its purity (Ps 119:140), is a "shield" who protects all who "take refuge" in him (see v.3 and comments; cf. also Pr 30:5, where Agur appears to quote the last three lines of v.31).

The Lord's irresistible and omnipotent ability is linked to his absolute incomparability. David's two rhetorical questions in v.32 demand the uncompromisingly negative answer "no one." There is no god "besides the LORD" (cf. Isa 43:11; 44:6; 45:21); there is no "Rock" apart from our God (see comments on v.3; 1Sa 2:2; cf. also Dt 32:31 and esp. Isa 44:8). Uniquely beyond compare, the Lord brooks no rivals (cf. Labuschagne, 114–23; also 7:22 and comment).

In the remainder of the present literary unit, David glorifies the God who readies him for battle against the enemy (vv.33–37). The Lord "arms [him] with strength" (v.33, a reading superior to that of the MT [see NIV note for details; cf. also v.40]; see 1Sa 2:4 and comment), thus making him physically, mentally, and spiritually powerful. Kirkpatrick,

207, observes "the analogy between the perfection of God's way (v.31) and His servant's" and invites comparison with Matthew 5:48: "Be perfect, therefore, as your heavenly Father is perfect."

Habakkuk borrows freely from the language and phraseology of v.34 in the last verse of the psalm that concludes his prophecy (cf. Hab 3:19). David is grateful to the Lord for giving him the surefootedness of a deer, enabling him even to stand on the perilous "heights" (the final consonant of *bmwty*, otherwise difficult to explain, perhaps being a dittography of the first consonant of the following word) without fear of falling (cf. Dt 32:13; Isa 58:14). The Lord also "trains [David's] hands for battle" (v.35; cf. Davidic Ps 144:1) and strengthens his arms so that they are powerful enough to bend a bow of "bronze" (a hyperbole, since bows [whether simple or composite] were always made of wood; cf. Yadin, 6–8; for bronze as a symbol of strength, cf. Job 6:12; 40:18; Jer 1:18; 15:12, 20). The Hebrew phrase here translated "bow of bronze" is contextually rendered "bronze-tipped arrow" in Job 20:24.

The last two verses (vv.36–37) of David's description of God as enabler (vv.31–37) address the Lord directly. He gives David a "shield" that guarantees "victory" (v.36; for the association of "shield" with "salvation/victory" [*yšʿ*] in the Psalms, see v.3 and comment), and he condescends to "stoop down" (*ʿnh* III; cf. BDB, 776) in order to make David great. He also broadens the "path" beneath David's feet (lit., "step," v.37—here metonymy for "path"; cf. La 4:18, where "[our] step[s]" is parallel to "our streets"), so that his ankles do not "turn" (cf. Davidic Ps 37:31 ["slip"]; Job 12:5 ["slipping"]).

38–43 Adequately strengthened and properly equipped by the Lord (vv.31–37), David was able to gain victory over his enemies with God's help (vv.38–43). As he describes the thoroughness of his triumph, he virtually exhausts the lexicon of Hebrew verbs that have to do with annihilation, several of which appear earlier in the books of Samuel. He "crushed" (v.38; cf. 21:5 ["decimated"]; 1Sa 24:21 ["wipe out"]) his enemies "till they were destroyed" (see 21:5 and comment; *ʿad-kallôtām*, rendered "until you have wiped them out" in 1Sa 15:18 [see comment there]). "Crushed" in v.39 (cf. Davidic Ps 68:21; also Dt 32:39 ["wounded"]; 33:11 ["smite"]; Hab 3:13) translates a different Hebrew verb from that in v.38 and is augmented (not in Ps 18:38, however) by a form of the same Hebrew verb rendered "destroyed" in v.38, resulting in the phrase "crushed them completely." Thus David's enemies "fell" (cf. 1:12; see 1Sa 31:1 and comment), never to "rise" again (cf. Isa 43:17).

As in the last two verses (vv.36–37) of the previous section (vv.31–37), so also in the middle two verses (vv.40–41) of the present section (vv.38–43) David addresses the Lord directly. God has "armed" David "with strength" (v.40; see comment on v.33) and "made" his enemies "bow" before him in craven submission (cf. Davidic Ps 17:13 ["bring ... down"]; also Ps 78:31 ["cutting down"]). David's "adversaries" (lit., "those who rose" against him, v.40) will "rise" no more (v.39). If the Lord has broadened David's path "beneath" him (v.37), and if his enemies have fallen "beneath" his feet (v.39), David joyfully confesses that the Lord has caused them to bow "at my feet" (lit., "beneath me," v.40). The Lord has made David's enemies "turn their backs" (v.41; cf. Ex 23:27; Jos 7:8 ["has been routed"], 12; Jer 48:39) in flight, and David has thus "destroyed" (*ṣmt*, different from the Heb. verb in v.38; cf. Davidic Pss 54:5; 69:4; 101:5, 8 ["put to silence"]; 143:12 ["silence"]; also Pss 73:27; 94:23) his "foes" (lit., "those who hated" him; cf. Davidic Pss 68:1; 69:4; also Dt 33:11).

Although David's enemies tried to find relief from his onslaught, there was "no one to save them" (v.42; see comment on "no one comes to rescue us" in 1Sa 11:3; cf. also Dt 28:29, 31; Jdg

12:3 ["wouldn't help"]; Isa 47:15). "Cried for help" renders *yšwʿw* and is based on one Hebrew MS, ancient versions, and Psalm 18:41 (cf. BHS). But the MT *yšʿw* ("looked," from the root *šʿh*) may be an intentional wordplay on *yšʿ*, the most important *Leitwort* in David's psalm (cf. Alter, *The Art of Biblical Poetry*, 32), and may therefore be the more original reading.

Giving his enemies no quarter, David "beat" them (v.43; cf. Ex 32:36 ["grind"]; Job 14:19 ["wears away"]) as fine as the "dust" (cf. Dt 9:21; 2Ki 23:6, 15) of the "earth." ("Borne on the wind" in Psalm 18:42 translates *ʿl-pny-rwḥ* and may be a scribal error imported from *ʿl-knpy-rwḥ* ["on the wings of the wind"] in v.11 [cf. Cross and Freedman, "A Royal Song," 32 n. 94].)

He "trampled" them with his feet (cf. Eze 6:11; 25:6) as though they were "mud in the streets" (cf. Mic 7:10; Zec 10:5). Mud, mire, and refuse in streets and alleys reflect conditions that were "not accepted as a matter of fact, but rather were referred to with a sense of shame and disgrace" (Neufeld, 45). The similes in v.43 thus portray David's enemies as objects of humiliation and contempt.

44–46 Concluding the third main section (vv.31–46) of his reasons for praising the Lord (vv.5–46), David gives credit to God for enabling him to gain the victory over his enemies (vv.44–46). If earlier he had confessed that the Lord is his "deliverer," he now acknowledges the fact that God has "delivered" him (v.44) from "attacks" on all sides (cf. Davidic Ps 55:9 ["strife"]; also Jdg 12:2 ["struggle"]; Isa 41:11 ["(those who) oppose"]). Although it is possible to understand David as saying that he has been attacked by "my people" (*ʿammî*), all other references in the present literary unit are to his external enemies. It is therefore better to read the suffix as an archaic genitive indicator (for another example see Notes on v.24) and to translate "the people" (as in Ps 18:43, where the MT reads *ʿām*). A suitable parallel is thus supplied for the "nations" over whom David has been "preserved" (*šmr*) as head or been "made" (*śym*, the variant in Ps 18:43) the head.

David's conquests resulted in large numbers of people he "did not know" becoming "subject to" him (v.44; see 8:2; 10:19 and comments; cf. also 8:6). Since the enemies of God can be expected to "cringe" before him (Pss 66:3; 81:15), there is no reason why foreigners under David's control should not "come cringing" to the Lord's anointed (v.45). Indeed, "as soon as they hear" (lit., "at the hearing of an ear," *lišmôaʿ* / *lᵉšēmaʿ ʾōzen* [for *lᵉšēmaʿ*, cf. Ps 18:44]) they obey him. William Morrow ("Consolation, Rejection, and Repentance in Job 42:6," *JBL* 105/2 [1986]: 220) argues forcefully that *šēmaʿ ʾōzen*, traditionally translated "the hearing of the ear," is better understood as "rumor" or "mere report." Thus in v.45 "the nations proffer their obeisance to Israel's king at the *šmʿ ʾzn* concerning him. According to the psalmist, 'mere report' or 'rumor' of his might was enough to secure their fealty" (cf. also K&D, 483).

Bny nkr ("foreigners") begins vv.45 and 46, and the repetition would ordinarily not be infelicitous in English translation. But since the two lines of Psalm 18:44 are transposed (as compared to the parallel in 2Sa 22:45), Psalm 18:44b, 45a both begin with *bny nkr*, resulting in a harsh juxtaposition when both are translated the same way. The NIV thus renders "They all" at the beginning of Psalm 18:45 (and therefore also 2Sa 22:46) for stylistic reasons.

David's power and reputation strike terror in subject and foreigner alike, and they all "lose heart" (v.46; cf. Ex 18:18 ["wear ... out"]). Their only recourse is to "come trembling" (reading *wyḥrgw* with Ps 18:45 and certain ancient versions; see NIV note) from their "strongholds" (cf. Mic 7:17 ["dens"], where "come trembling" in a similar context renders the root *rgz* and secures the same meaning in David's psalm for the otherwise unattested root *ḥrg*). Utterly dejected, the peoples in and around David's realm cower before him and his God.

47–51 The impressive coda to this Song of David consists of a joyful paean of praise. Although *ḥay-yhwh* (v.47) could be read as a solemn oath introducing the rest of the section ("As surely as the LORD lives"; cf. 1Sa 14:39 and comment), it is probably better (with the NIV) to understand it as an exclamation—"The LORD lives!"—that echoes David's description of the Lord as "the living God" decades earlier (see 1Sa 17:26 and comment).

From the fact that God is indeed alive springs the rest of David's words of exultation. He begins with a common outburst of praise to which he is no stranger (see 1Sa 25:32 and comment; cf. also the words of Ahimaaz in 18:28), directing it to the omnipotent Lord who is his "Rock" (*ṣûr*; see comment on v.3). The God who is himself "exalted" (v.47; cf. Davidic Pss 21:13; 57:5, 11; also Ps 46:10) has "exalted" his servant David (v.49; cf. Davidic Pss 9:13 ["lift ... up"]; 27:5 ["set ... high"]; Hos 11:7).

If the second occurrence of "Rock" is retained (see, however, the Notes on v.47), then "the Rock, my Savior," is reprised in similar divine epithets elsewhere (cf. Dt 32:15; Pss 89:26; 95:1 ["Rock of our salvation"]). If, however, "Rock" is omitted (as in Ps 18:46), the title "Savior" alone is echoed not only in several Davidic psalms (cf. Pss 24:5; 25:5; 27:9; 51:14 ["who saves me"]; 65:5) but also in numerous other passages (cf. Pss 79:9; 85:4; 88:1 ["who saves me"]; 1Ch 16:35; Isa 17:10; Mic 7:7; Hab 3:18). In any event, the first occurrence of "Rock" and the reference to God as "Savior" remind his people that his mighty power works hand in hand with his redemptive grace.

When the Lord "avenges" his chosen king (v.48; see comment on 4:8), he "puts" the nations (Hiphil of *yrd*; cf. Davidic Ps 56:7 ["bring down"]; Ps 18:47 displays the Hiphil of *dbr*, "subdues," as a variant reading) "under" him (see comment on v.40) and "sets" him "free" from his enemies (lit., "brings" him "out," v.49; see comment on v.20). Indeed, David is exalted above his "foes" (lit., "those who rose" against him, v.49; see comment on "adversaries" in v.40) and is rescued from "violent men" (see comment on v.3; cf. Davidic Ps 140:1, 4, 11; Pr 3:31; 16:29).

Because of all that God has done for David, none of which he can possibly repay, he speaks to the Lord directly and announces his determination to "praise" him "among the nations" (v.50; cf. Davidic Ps 108:3), to "sing praises" to his "name" (cf. Pss 92:1 ["make music"]; 135:3), the name of him who alone is worthy of praise (cf. Davidic Ps 8:1, 9; also 1Ch 16:10; 29:13 [both in Davidic psalms]; Ps 45:17 ["memory"]; 1Ki 8:33, 35; Isa 26:13). That the nations of the world will share in David's praise to the Lord was a firm belief of the apostle Paul, who in Romans 15:9 quotes 2 Samuel 22:50: "Therefore I will praise you among the Gentiles, I will sing hymns to your name."

Like the Song of Hannah many years earlier, the magnificent Song of David ends with parallel references to the Lord's "king" and the Lord's "anointed" (v.51; 1Sa 2:10; see comment on 1Sa 2:1–2; cf. also Pss 2:2 [alternative reading in NIV note]; 89:38, 51; 132:10, 17). To his king the Lord gives great "victories" (see comments on 8:6; cf. 1Sa 14:45; 19:5; cf. Hab 3:8), and to his anointed—to David and his "descendants" (cf. Jer 33:21–22, 26)—he shows "kindness" (see comment on 2:6; cf. 1Ki 3:6).

God's covenant with David guarantees that the "kindness" (*ḥesed*) here affirmed, the unfailing "love" that is given freely and knows no bounds (cf. Ps 89:28, 33), will continue to bring untold blessing to the Davidic line for all future generations (see 7:15 and comment; cf. also 7:13, 16, 25; 23:5; Ps 89:4, 29, 36). The "messenger of the covenant" (Mal 3:1), the Lord's representative and Messiah, will confirm and establish the Davidic covenant; the Lord's messianic servant, himself a "covenant for the people" (Isa 42:6; 49:8), will fulfill the Davidic covenant as king through unending days (cf. Isa 9:7; Lk 1:31–33). It is thus both serendipitous and satisfying that the Song of David, a psalm of impressive scope and exquisite beauty, should begin with "The LORD" (v.2), the Eternal One, and end with "forever" (v.51).

NOTES

2 Psalm 18 begins David's praise hymn with "I love you, O LORD, my strength" (v.2 MT), a verse that does not appear in 2 Samuel in the MT but is included in the Syriac as well as in the Lucianic recension of the LXX. "My deliverer" is enhanced by לִי (*lî*, "of/belonging to me") in v.2 but not in Ps 18:2[3]. Since *lî* occurs in the same expression in Psalm 144:2, however, it is doubtless original in 2 Samuel as well (cf. also צרי ואיבי לי, *ṣry w*ʾ*yby ly*, "my enemies and my foes [belonging to me]" in another Davidic psalm, Ps 27:2).

3 The NIV vocalizes the MT's אֱלֹהֵי (ʾ*elōhê*) as אֱלֹהַי (ʾ*elōhay*, "my God"), doubtless correctly (cf. אֵלִי, ʾ*ēlî*, in Ps 18:2 [3]; also v.7). By the same token, therefore, the MT's ʾ*elōhê* in Psalm 43:2 should be revocalized as ʾ*elōhay*, with the resulting line reading either "You are my God, my stronghold," or "You, my God, are my stronghold" (cf. ʾ*elōhāy*, "my God," in 43:4–5).

After "my stronghold," Psalm 18:2[3] omits "my refuge and my savior—from violent men you save me," thus resulting in a different poetic scansion of its lines from that in 2 Samuel (cf. Ps 18:2 [NIV]).

5 Although אפפני (ʾ*ppny*) is in the perfect "tense" and יבעתני (*ybʿtny*) is in the imperfect, both are correctly translated as past-tense verbs ("swirled about," "overwhelmed"). The frequent alternation of perfect and imperfect verbs is "a technique of Hebrew poetic craft, without significance in meaning" (John S. Kselman, "Psalm 3: A Structural and Literary Study," *CBQ* 49/4 [1987] 577 n. 13; cf. similarly Cross and Freedman, *Studies in Ancient Yahwistic Poetry*, 28).

Instead of "waves of death," Psalm 18:4[5] reads "cords of death," doubtless a scribal error imported from "cords of the grave" in the next verse. "Waves" is a much better parallel for "torrents" than is "cords."

7 Whereas v.7 reads "I called ... I called ... my cry," Psalm 18:6[7] has "I called ... I cried [for help] ... my cry." A good case can be made for both variants, since in the original text the second element could have been intended as a reflection of either the first or the third.

The MT translates literally as "my cry ... to his ears," with the verb "came" being understood elliptically rather than expressed formally. תָּבוֹא (*tābôʾ*, "came") occurs in the text of Psalm 18:6[7]. For the possibility that it accidentally dropped out of the Samuel text and for a suggestion concerning how it might have happened, see Cross and Freedman ("A Royal Song," 23 n. 13).

9 The antiquity of the theophanic description (vv.8–16) is well illustrated in its frequent use of בְּ- (*b*-) in the sense of "from" (*b*- being the normal way of representing "from" in Ugaritic): "from his nostrils" (v.9), "from heaven" (Ps 18:13; 2Sa 22:14 employs מִן, *min*), "at/from the rebuke" (v.16; Ps 18:15 reads *min*; cf. Cross and Freedman, *Studies in Ancient Yahwistic Poetry*, 27–28; Sarna, 312–13).

11 "Soared" (וידא, *wydʾ*), parallel to "flew," is clearly better than וירא (*wyrʾ*), "appeared" (for details see NIV note). The scribal error in most MSS of the MT is due to the similarity between ד (*d*) and ר (*r*) as well as to the rarity of the verb דָּאָה (*dāʾâ*, "soar, swoop [down]"), which is found elsewhere only in Deuteronomy 28:49, Psalm 18:10[11], and Jeremiah 48:40; 49:22. It is also possible that וייראו (*wyr*ʾ*w*), which begins v.16 in the MT, had its baleful influence on the errant scribe.

12 The MT's סכות (*skwt*, "canopies") is probably a scribal error caused by metathesis of סכתו (*sktw*, "his canopy"; for *sktw* cf. Ps 18:11[12]; also similar readings in several Hebrew MSS and in some ancient versions of verse 12 as documented in *BHS*).

"Dark" (חשכת, *ḥškt*), as in Psalm 18:11[12], is surely the correct reading instead of the MT's "massed" (חשרת, *ḥšrt*; see NIV note), a word unattested elsewhere. For an attempt to connect *ḥšrt* with late Hebrew *ḥšrh* ("sieve") and therefore to understand the word as suggesting sieve-like clouds through which rainwater drops, see Cross and Freedman ("A Royal Psalm," 25 n. 33).

13 "Bolts of lightning [lit., 'coals of fire'] blazed forth" answers to "burning coals blazed out" in v.9. "Clouds advanced" (עָבָיו עָבְרוּ, *ʿābāyw ʿābᵉrû*), added in Psalm 18:12[13], was perhaps influenced by "clouds" in Psalm 18:11[12] and a metathesis of "blazed" (בָּעֲרוּ, *bāʿᵃrû*) in v.13. "With hailstones and" (בָּרָד וְ־, *bārād wᵉ-*), also added, possibly arose from a corruption of "blazed" as well, and the repetition of "with hailstones and bolts of lightning" in Psalm 18:13[14] compounded the problem (see NIV note there).

14 For the probable parallelism between "LORD" and "Most High" in the Song of Hannah, see Notes on 1 Samuel 2:10 (cf. also Freedman, "Divine Names and Titles," 67, 90–91).

15 The *Kethiv's* ויהמם (*wyhmm*, "and routed them") is to be preferred over the suffixless *Qere's* ויהם (*wyhm*), not only because of Psalm 18:14[15], but also because of the similar reading in Psalm 144:6.

16 The version of David's poem in Psalm 18 personalizes the final phrases of the theophany by reading "your rebuke, O LORD," and "your nostrils" (Ps 18:15[16]) instead of "the rebuke of the LORD" and "his nostrils" respectively.

17 "He reached down" is elliptical for "reached down his hand" (cf. Davidic Ps 144:7; similarly Cross and Freedman, "A Royal Song," 26 n. 44).

23 The MT of v.23b translates literally, "As for his decrees, I have not turned away [אָסוּר, *ʾāsûr*; Qal] from them" (מִמֶּנָּה, *mimmennâ*; to be analyzed either as the preposition plus third person feminine singular suffix, "her/it" [understood collectively], or as the preposition plus a remnant of the third person feminine plural suffix "from them" [for which cf. Cross and Freedman, "A Royal Song," 27 n. 55; also LXX's ἀπ' αὐτῶν, *ap' autōn*]). The MT of the parallel in Psalm 18:22[23] translates literally as follows: "His decrees I have not turned away [אָסִיר, *ʾāsîr*; Hiphil] from me" (מֶנִּי, *mennî*), an alternative way of expressing the same idea.

24 What appears to be a first person singular suffix (ִי־, *-î*) on "sin" is probably to be analyzed instead as "an old genitive case ending" (Cross and Freedman, "A Royal Song," 28 n. 58).

28 Since the sign of the definite accusative is extremely rare in poetry, it is better to vocalize את (*ʾt*) as אַתָּ (*ʾattā*, "you"; cf. אַתָּה, *ʾattâ*, in Ps 18:27[28]; also σύ, *sy*, in some MSS of the LXX) than as אֶת (*ʾet*) with the MT.

30 Although גְּדוּד (*gᵉdûd*, "troop, raiding band/party") is attested elsewhere in the books of Samuel (cf. 4:2; 1Sa 30:8, 15, 23 ["forces"]), the Lucianic recension of the LXX reads πεφραγμένος (*pephragmenos*, "fenced, fortified, walled"), suggesting גָּדוּר (*gādûr*, "wall[ed]") in its Hebrew exemplar. The final ד (*d*) in the MT's גדוד (*gdwd*) is thus perhaps a scribal error for ר (*r*).

33 Although the Hebrew MS evidence for וַיִּתֵּן (*wayyittēn*, "and makes") is extremely weak (cf. *BHS*), the NIV prefers it (perhaps because of Ps 18:32[33]) to the MT's וַיַּתֵּר (*wayyattēr*), a Hiphil form of נתר

(*ntr*), which means either "cause to tremble" (cf. Hab 3:6) or "let loose, release, set free, untie" (cf. Job 6:9; Pss 105:20; 146:7; Isa 58:6). Attempts to parse the form as though from יתר (*ytr*, "be affluent, rich"; cf. Mitchell Dahood, "Hebrew-Ugaritic Lexicography III," *Bib* 46 [1965]: 325–26), from תור (*twr*, "spy out, go around"; cf. K&D, 479), or from תאר (*tʾr*, "trace out, draw in outline"; cf. McCarter, *II Samuel*, 459) are unconvincing.

35 "Bend" translates נחת (*nḥt*, masculine singular) here and נחתה (*nḥth*, feminine singular) in Psalm 18:34[35]; neither form, however, exhibits concord with the Hebrew feminine plural word underlying "arms" (but cf. GKC, sec. 145*o* for the former, 145*k* for the latter). An alternative is to read with one Hebrew MS נחתת (*nḥtt*) from the root חתת (*ḥtt*), to understand "bow" as the subject, and to translate: "A bow of bronze is broken by my arms." Although the resulting text is somewhat more difficult grammatically, reading the root *ḥtt* has the advantage of forging yet another link between the Song of David and the Song of Hannah (see 1Sa 2:4 and comment).

36 Between "you give me your shield of victory" and "you stoop down to make me great," Psalm 18:35[36] inserts the line "and your right hand sustains me," for the secondary nature of which see the discussion in McCarter, *II Samuel*, 460.

38 "Crushed" (אשמידם, *ʾšmydm*) and "overtook" (אשיגם, *ʾśygm*; Ps 18:37[38]) are "old variants" (Cross and Freedman, "A Royal Song," 31 n. 86).

40 The form ותזרני (*wtzrny*, "You armed me") is contracted from ותאזרני (*wtʾzrny*; cf. Ps 18:39[40]). For other examples of the elision of first-radical א (ʾ) in Piel forms, see GKC, sec. 68*k* (see also Notes on 20:5).

41 "You made" renders נָתַתָּה (*nātattâ*) from נתן (*ntn*) in Psalm 18:40[41]. Here in v.41 the form is simply תַּתָּה (*tattâ*), probably a scribal error for יָתַתָּ(ה) (*yātattā[h]*), "a Canaanite dialectal form (root, *ytn*), as in Ugar. and Phoen." (Cross and Freedman, "A Royal Song," 32 n. 91). The loss of the -י (*y*-) may have resulted from haplography, since the previous word ends in *y* (cf. also Watson, 538).

43 "I pounded," parallel to "I beat," translates אדקם (*ʿdqm*) and is doubtless the correct reading. "I poured ... out" (אריקם, *ʾryqm*; Ps 18:42[43]) arose because of the common confusion between ד (*d*) and ר (*r*).

47 "Rock" appears in the second line of v.47 (but not in the second line of Ps 18:46[47]), perhaps repeated by mistake from the first line. In any case, if "Rock" is retained אֱלֹהֵי (*ʾelōhê*, "God") should be revocalized as אֱלֹהַי (*ʾelōhay*, "my God"), since the MT's construct form is ungrammatical as it stands. The NIV has in fact performed the same revocalization in v.3 (see Notes there), and doing it here would thus enhance the inclusio already demonstrable between the two verses (see comment on vv.2–4).

D. David's Last Words (23:1–7)

OVERVIEW

Sharing with the Song of David (ch. 22) the center of the extensive structural chiasm that makes up chs. 21–24 (see Overview to 21:1–24:25) is 23:1–7, characterized by the narrator as the "last words of David" (v.1). Like their counterpart in ch. 22, the present verses are generally acknowledged to have been written by David himself (cf. Hertzberg, 400; Kruse, 148; G. Del Olmo Lete, 430

n. 40) and are therefore given a date in the tenth century BC (cf. Cross, *Canaanite Myth and Hebrew Epic*, 234; H. Neil Richardson, "The Last Words of David: Some Notes on 2 Samuel 23:1–7," *JBL* 90/3 [1971]: 257; Freedman, "Divine Names and Titles," 73, 88, 96; for a concise summary of the extensive ancient Near Eastern context in which David's gifts as poet and musician find their natural home, see Kitchen, *Reliability*, 104–7).

In 11QPsalms[a], "which contains apocryphal compositions interspersed with canonical psalms in a radically different order" (Gerald H. Wilson, "The Qumran *Psalms Scroll* [11QPs[a]] and the Canonical Psalter: Comparison of Editorial Shaping," *CBQ* 59 [1997]: 448), 2 Samuel 23:7 is placed after Psalm 150 and between two "apocryphal" pieces known as "Hymn to the Creator" and "David's Compositions" (for a table listing the complete ordering of the fifty-one canonical and apocryphal compositions in 11QPsalms[a], see Wilson, ibid., 450–51; further Joseph A. Fitzmyer, *A Guide to the Dead Sea Scrolls and Related Literature*, rev. and exp. ed. [Grand Rapids: Eerdmans, 2008], 110–12).

Although it is common for students of David's elegant peroration to emphasize its undoubted wisdom motifs (cf. P. A. H. de Boer, "Texte et traduction des paroles attribuées à David en 2 Samuel xxiii 1–7," in *Volume du Congres: Strasbourg 1956* [VTSup 4; Leiden: Brill, 1957], 48), Del Olmo Lete, 434–47, has made a good case for prophetic and royal-dynastic elements in addition to sapiential features. Indeed, "the metaphors, 'morning of sunshine light' and 'fertilizing rain' [v.4], take in and synthesize the whole royal ideology of the Near East, adopted by Israel and reinterpreted conditionally according to the Yahwistic covenant system depending on behaviour" (Del Olmo Lete, 431; cf. Brueggemann, *Power, Providence, and Personality: Biblical Insight into Life and Ministry* (Louisville: Westminster John Knox, 1990), 97–99; Aubrey R. Johnson, *Sacral Kingship in Ancient Israel* [Cardiff: Univ. of Wales Press, 1967], 14–17; see also comments on 7:1–17).

After the narrator's superscript (v.1a), the poem itself begins. Two internal chiasms (vv.2a/3b, vv.5a/5de; cf. Richardson, "The Last Words of David," 259, 262, 264 [following unpublished observations made by David Noel Freedman]) supplement the overall chiastic structure of David's oracle (cf. similarly Del Olmo Lete, 424, 430):

A David speaks in the third person about himself (23:1b–e)
  B David speaks in the first person (23:2–3ab)
    C The Lord speaks (23:3cd–4)
  B' David speaks in the first person (23:5)
A' David speaks in the third person about evil men (23:6–7)

By nestling the divine description of the ideal king in the middle of the poem, David's "last words" give God the central—and therefore the final—word.

1These are the last words of David:

"The oracle of David son of Jesse,
  the oracle of the man exalted by the Most High,
the man anointed by the God of Jacob,
  Israel's singer of songs:

2"The Spirit of the LORD spoke through me;
his word was on my tongue.
3The God of Israel spoke,
the Rock of Israel said to me:
'When one rules over men in righteousness,
when he rules in the fear of God,
4he is like the light of morning at sunrise
on a cloudless morning,
like the brightness after rain
that brings the grass from the earth.'

5"Is not my house right with God?
Has he not made with me an everlasting covenant,
arranged and secured in every part?
Will he not bring to fruition my salvation
and grant me my every desire?
6But evil men are all to be cast aside like thorns,
which are not gathered with the hand.
7Whoever touches thorns
uses a tool of iron or the shaft of a spear;
they are burned up where they lie."

COMMENTARY

1a As de Boer ("Texte et traduction," 48) observes, "Words of (דִּבְרֵי, *dibrê*) David" recalls Proverbs 30:1 with respect to Agur and Proverbs 31:1 with respect to King Lemuel (*dibrê* is translated "sayings of" in both verses). Like Agur and King Lemuel, King David has gained the reputation of being a wise man—in his case, more than a wise man (see comments on 14:17, 19b, 20.)

Even allowing for dischronologization in the books of Samuel, the phrase "last words" need not be understood as the last words David spoke during his lifetime (cf., e.g., 1Ki 2:2–9) but is doubtless used in a way analogous to "last will and testament" or the like. Verses 1b–7 summarize his final literary legacy to Israel.

1b–e David begins by identifying his poem as an "oracle" and by providing his listeners/readers with a laudatory self-description. Although the Hebrew word rendered "oracle" (*n*^{e}*ʾum*; GK 5536) is almost always applied to the Lord in reference to what he solemnly "declares" (cf. 1Sa 2:30), in a few cases it is used of men in prophetic (cf. Balaam son of Beor [Nu 24:3a, 15a]) or wisdom settings (cf. Agur son of Jakeh [Pr 30:1a ("declared")]). Just as the fathers of Balaam and Agur are named in the texts cited, so David is here referred to as "David son of Jesse" (cf. also 1Ch 10:14; 29:26; esp. the editorial note in Ps 72:20: "This concludes the prayers of David son of Jesse"), and just as v.1b is paralleled in v.1c by beginning with the words "the oracle of the man" (*nᵉʾum haggeber*), so are the next lines in the verses cited (Nu 24:3b, 15b ["the oracle of one"]; Pr 30:1b ["This man declared"]).

If in v.1c–e David awards himself three titles that appear grandiose, it is to his credit that two of them give the Lord the glory for David's success. David considers himself to be exalted by the "Most High" (*ʿāl*), an abbreviated divine epithet identified long ago in the Hebrew text (see Notes on 1Sa 2:10; cf. also Hos 7:16; 11:7; Freedman, "Divine Names and Titles," 65, 73, 91; Dahood, "Hebrew-Ugaritic Lexicography III," 324; "The Divine Name *ʿElî* in the Psalms," 452). David represents himself as a man "anointed" (see comments on 5:3; 1Sa 16:13) by the "God of Jacob" (cf. Davidic Pss 20:1; 24:6; also Pss 46:7, 11; 75:9; 76:6; 81:1, 4; 84:8; 94:7; Isa 2:3 = Mic 4:2).

Finally, David declares himself to be "Israel's singer of songs" (*nᵉʿîm zᵉmirôt yiśrāʾēl*, lit., "the pleasant one of the songs of Israel"; cf. Driver, 357, for full discussion). Richardson ("The Last Words of David," 261 and n. 19) asserts that *nʿ(y)m* is "an epithet for heroes and royal persons, as in Ugaritic," and observes that it is "translated 'beloved' by H. L. Ginsberg" (see also NIV note) in *ANET*, 143). But since *nāʿîm* is used in a context of music in Psalm 81:2 (where it is rendered "melodious"), the traditional "singer" is both plausible and defensible. (For a helpful brief summary of the panoramic picture of David that emerges from the seventy-three psalms under the headings "Yahweh According to David," "David's Confessions," "David's Trust," and "David's Portrait," see Tiberius Rata, "David," in *Dictionary of the Old Testament: Wisdom, Poetry, and Writings*, ed. Tremper Longman III and Peter Enns [Downers Grove, IL: InterVarsity Press, 2008], 86–88.)

As for *zᵉmirôt* ("songs"; GK 2369), Theodor H. Gaster ("Notes on 'The Song of the Sea' [Exodus xv.]," *ExpTim* 48 [1936–1937]: 45) suggested long ago that, on the basis of context as well as of cognates in other Semitic languages (including especially Ugaritic), *zimrāt* in Exodus 15:2 (where it is traditionally rendered "song") means "protection" or the like. His proposal and its implications for v.1e have found widespread acceptance over the past half-century (cf. Richardson, "The Last Words of David," 259, 261; Freedman, "Divine Names and Titles," 58; Anderson, 268).

At the same time, however, *zᵉmirôt* is attested frequently in the sense of "song(s)" (cf. Job 35:10; Pss 95:2 ["music and song"]; 119:54; Isa 24:16 ["singing"]). For the entire phrase, Lewis, 52, proposes "the bard of Israel's songs." Although Del Olmo Lete, 416, 425, prefers to render *zᵉmirôt* "Defence" as a divine epithet, he admits that "the possibility of 'word play' cannot be altogether discarded."

2–3ab David's fourfold ascription of divine origin (vv.2–3ab) to the revelation that comes to him (vv.3cd–4) is arranged chiastically. The MT of v.2a has the subject (a construct phrase) first, then the verb (*dibber*), then a prepositional phrase: "The-Spirit-of-the-LORD spoke through-me." The MT of its corresponding line (v.3b) reverses the elements by placing a prepositional phrase first, then the verb (again *dibber*), then the subject (a construct phrase), thus suggesting the following literal translation: "To-me spoke the-Rock-of-Israel." The end result is a tightly crafted inclusio that guarantees the unity of the section (cf. Richardson, "The Last Words of David," 259, 262).

As the "Spirit of God came upon" Balaam and enabled him to utter the "words of God" (Nu 24:2, 4; cf. similarly 1Ch 12:18), so also "the Spirit of the LORD spoke through" David (v.2) and delivered to him the message God wanted him to receive. That David spoke "by the Spirit" on another occasion is affirmed by Jesus himself (Mt 22:43), and David's use of the phrase "spoke through" represents a clear claim to divine inspiration (cf. Hos 1:2; similarly Nu 12:2; 1Ki 22:28). David is conscious of the fact that the "word" of the Lord was on his "tongue" (cf. Davidic Ps 139:4; also the description of the wife of noble character in Pr 31:26) and that the mighty "Rock of Israel" (see comments on 22:3; 1Sa 2:2; cf. esp. Isa 30:29) had spoken to him.

3cd–4 "Qualities of an Ideal King" could well be the caption of the Lord's portrait of royalty mediated through David. The root *mšl* ("rules," v.3) occurs only here in the books of Samuel and was perhaps chosen because of its frequent appearance in OT wisdom literature. "Fear of God," the generic term for "religion, piety" in ancient Israel (cf. similarly Freedman, "Divine Names and Titles," 62), was also a common wisdom motif (see comment on 1Sa 12:14). Thus he who rules in the fear of God rules "in righteousness"—literally, "as a righteous one" (*ṣaddîq*), an epithet that has clear messianic connotations (cf. Jer 23:5; Zec 9:9).

As amply attested by numerous scholarly attempts to translate v.4 (cf. Richardson, "The Last Words of David," 259; David Noel Freedman, "2 Samuel 23:4," *JBL* 90/3 [1971]: 329–30), the terseness of the MT makes its syntax difficult to untangle. The basic outline of the verse is evident, however. The first half compares the rule of the righteous king to the benefits of sunlight, the second half to the fertilizing effects of rain. In so doing it is remarkably similar to Psalm 72, where the ideal ruler, characterized by "righteousness" (72:1–2), will endure as long as the "sun" (72:5) and will be like "rain" that waters the earth (72:6; cf. also Del Olmo Lete, 435–36).

That a king should be compared to the sun, which was originally created to "govern" (*mšl*) the day (Ge 1:16, 18), is not surprising. Indeed, solar language was employed in royal ideology throughout the ancient Near East (cf. the detailed discussion in Hans-Peter Stahli, *Solare Elemente in Jahweglauben des alten Testaments* [OBO 66; Göttingen: Vandenhoeck and Ruprecht, 1985]). The righteous king is like the first "light of morning" (*ʾôr bōqer*, v.4), just after dawn (cf. 17:22 ["daybreak"]; 1Sa 14:36 ["dawn"]; 25:34, 36) on a cloudless day at "sunrise." As Carlson, 257, perceptively observes, "it is thus deeply symbolical that David is punished 'in the sight of the sun'" (see comments on "in broad daylight" in 12:11–12).

The image of "brightness" is continued into the latter half of v.4—now related, however, not to sunshine but to the lightning that accompanies thunderstorms (see 22:13 and comment). It would therefore perhaps be better to translate "brightness associated with rain" (or the like) instead of "brightness after rain" (NIV). As the fructifying influence of rain helps the grass to grow (cf. Dt 32:2), so also the benevolent rule of a righteous king causes his people to flourish (cf. Ps 72:6–7). It may be instructive to observe that news of the death of King Saul evoked from David a curse against the mountains of Gilboa, imploring that they might no longer have dew or "rain" (1:21). If the presence of the ideal king produces health and prosperity, the absence of royal rule—of whatever sort—guarantees famine and drought.

5 Just as the corresponding section is arranged chiastically (see comment on vv.2–3b), so also is the present section (cf. Richardson, "The Last Words of David," 259, 264), which consists of a series of negative rhetorical questions expecting positive answers. The MT begins with *kî-lōʾ* ("Is not"), which is followed by a verb (or verbal adjective), "right/established"; the verse ends with *kî-lōʾ* followed by a verb ("Will he not bring to fruition"). *Kî emphaticum* ("surely" or the like) occurs twice more in the MT of v. 5 and underscores the forcefulness of David's confidence (for other examples of *kî emphaticum* see T. Muraoka, *Emphatic Words and Structures in Biblical Hebrew* [Jerusalem: Magnes], 158–64; Dahood, "Hebrew-Ugaritic Lexicography III," 327; cf. also Anneli Aejmelaeus, "Function and Interpretation of כי in Biblical Hebrew," *JBL* 105/2 [1986]: 195, 208).

Encouraged by the possibilities for righteous leadership implied in the Lord's words, David speaks positively of his "house" (i.e., his family and dynasty; see comment on 7:11b), of the covenant that God had made with him, of the fruition of his salvation, and of the fulfillment of all his desires. He had been convinced that his "house" would be "established" (*kwn*) in God's presence (7:26), as Nathan the prophet had reported to him (cf. 7:11, where, however, "established" renders a different Heb. root), and he is now sure that his "house" is "right with God" (better, "established [*kwn*] in the presence of God").

An enduring dynasty was part of the "everlasting covenant" (*bᵉrîṯ ʿōlām*; GK 1382, 6409) the Lord had made with David (v.5; cf. similar covenants with Noah [Ge 9:16]; Abraham [Ge 17:7]; Israel through Moses at Sinai [Ex 31:16, "lasting covenant"; Lev 24:8]; Aaron [Nu 18:19]; Phinehas [Nu 25:13, "covenant of a lasting (priesthood)"]; the new people of God [Jer 32:40; 50:5; Eze 16:60; 37:26]). Attempts by Freedman ("Divine Names and Titles," 73–74, 92, 100 n. 39) and others (e.g., Richardson, "The Last Words of David," 259, 263–64) to read *ʿôlām* as a divine epithet and translate the clause, "Has not the Eternal made a covenant with me?" founder not only on the frequency of *bᵉrîṯ ʿôlām* as a *terminus technicus* in the OT but also on the common occurrence of its semantic equivalents elsewhere (for details see Weinfeld, 199–201). In addition, "forever" (*ʿad-ʿôlām, lᵉʿôlām*) looms large in ch. 7 (cf. vv.13, 16, 24–26, 29; see comment on 7:13b; see also 22:51 and comment).

After rejoicing in the fact that in every detail the Lord's covenant with him is "arranged" (cf. Job 13:18 ["prepared"]) and "secured" (cf. Dt 7:8 ["kept"], 12 ["keep"]), David expresses his assurance that God will bring his "salvation" to fruition (cf. the Davidic Ps 12:5 ["protect"]; Job 5:4, 11 ["safety"]; see 22:3 and comments) and grant him his "every desire" (as Hiram would later do for David's son Solomon; cf. 1Ki 5:8 ["all you want"], 10; 9:11).

6–7 If in vv.1b–e David speaks in the third person about himself as a man blessed by God, in vv.6–7 by way of contrast he describes the fate of "evil men" (*bᵉlîyaʿal*; see comment on "trouble-makers" in 1Sa 30:22; also Notes on 1Sa 1:16). All of them are to be cast aside like "thorns" (cf. Eze 28:24), whose sharp-pointed branches make them too dangerous to pick up with unprotected hands. Anyone touching them is well-advised to use a tool of "iron" (v.7; see comments on 1Sa 13:19–22) or the "shaft of a spear"—both of which conjure up images of offensive weapons that can be used to kill an enemy (see comments on 1Sa 17:7; see also 2Sa 21:19 and comment). A parallel way of destroying thorns (or enemies) is to burn them up (cf. Ps 118:12; Isa 9:18; 33:12) "where they lie" (*baššāḇeṯ*, felicitously rendered "on the spot, *in situ*" by Johnson, *Sacral Kingship in Ancient Israel*, 17 and n. 8]).

> It would be possible to see here a counter-replica of Jotham's famous apologue (Jdg. ix 7–15), "the trees looking for a king," perhaps the most pungent criticism of the monarchy ever written. In contrast to the attitude of the "thorny shrub" (*ʾāṭāḏ*), the only pretender to kingship who commands everybody to come under this [*sic*] protection ("shadow") and threatens them otherwise with the "fire" that will come out from it, here the "thorn" (*qôṣ*) appears to be unapproachable to any but the unfriendly, and is itself allotted to the "fire" that will eat it up. (Del Olmo Lete, 436–43)

If evil men are "cast aside" (v.6), the anointed of the Lord, God's Messiah, is "exalted" (v.1).

And thus David's "last words" (v.1) come to an end. Along with all of his other poems, they represent a legacy and variety of hymns that are unparalleled elsewhere in Scripture. Israel's ideal king is also, indeed, "Israel's singer of songs," "Israel's beloved singer" (v.1). In the words of the fourth stanza of "Jerusalem, My Happy Home" (Joseph Bromehead, 1795):

There David stands with harp in hand
  As master of the choir:
Ten thousand times that man were blest
  That might this music hear.

"Time has preserved David for us as a poet: the figure of David with a lyre dominates the Western tradition of biblical iconography; the psalmist David is personified daily in the prayers of all Jews and Christians" (Freedman, "The Age of David and Solomon," in Freedman, *History and Religion*, 1:291).

NOTES

6 In *BHS* בְּקוֹץ (*b^eqôṣ*) is a typographical error for כְּקוֹץ (*k^eqôṣ*, "like thorns"; cf. *BH*; cf. Del Olmo Lete, 422 n. 23). The unique form כֻּלָּהַם (*kullāham*, "all of them") is perhaps a combination of the consonants of כֻּלְּהֶם (*kull^ehem*) and the vowels of כֻּלָּם (*kullām*; cf. similarly de Boer, "Texte et traduction," 55).

7 P. de Boer ("Texte et traduction," 55) suggests ("avec de grandes reserves," to be sure) that בַּשָּׁבֶת (*baššābet*, "where they lie"; usually parsed as from ישׁב, *yšb*; see also comment above) derives from the root שׁבת (*šbt*, "cease, rest"), and thus he translates "dans l'air calme"—that is, "in a situation where destruction by fire presents no danger of spreading." Although his proposal is perhaps not as farfetched as it may at first appear, it is surely not an improvement over more traditional renderings. Dahood's "without cessation" fares no better, depending as it does on understanding -בּ (*b-*) in the rare sense of "without" (Dahood, "Hebrew-Ugaritic Lexicography X," 403).

E. David's Mighty Men (23:8–39)

OVERVIEW

Mirroring the account of the memorable deeds of David's heroes in 21:15–22 is the list of his mighty men in 23:8–39, which includes reports of several exploits that heighten the similarities between the two narratives and thus enhance the chiastic structure of chs. 21–24 (see Overview to 21:1–24:25). The section divides naturally into two main segments, the first of which describes adventures experienced by warriors in the highest echelons of David's army (vv.8–23, paralleled in 1Ch 11:11–25) and the second of which provides a list of notable fighting men who were among the "Thirty" (vv.24–39, paralleled in 1Ch 11:26–41a). The first segment consists of three roughly equal parts, each of which summarizes one or more heroic exploits: (1) of the "Three" (vv.8–12); (2) of "three of the thirty chief men" (vv.13–17); (3) of two particularly notable fighters, of whom one was chief of the Three and the other was put in charge of David's bodyguard (vv.18–23).

While it is sometimes assumed that the Three were over the Thirty (cf. Merrill, 282), the precise relationships between the various power blocs in David's military administration remain debatable (for a useful survey see Mazar, "The Military Elite of King David," 310–20). Needless to say, their composition and leadership varied through the years, as even the present section attests.

8These are the names of David's mighty men:
Josheb-Basshebeth, a Tahkemonite, was chief of the Three; he raised his spear against
eight hundred men, whom he killed in one encounter.
9Next to him was Eleazar son of Dodai the Ahohite. As one of the three mighty men, he
was with David when they taunted the Philistines gathered ⌊at Pas Dammim⌋ for battle.
Then the men of Israel retreated, 10but he stood his ground and struck down the Philistines till his hand grew tired and froze to the sword. The LORD brought about a great victory that day. The troops returned to Eleazar, but only to strip the dead.
11Next to him was Shammah son of Agee the Hararite. When the Philistines banded
together at a place where there was a field full of lentils, Israel's troops fled from them.
12But Shammah took his stand in the middle of the field. He defended it and struck the
Philistines down, and the LORD brought about a great victory.
13During harvest time, three of the thirty chief men came down to David at the cave of
Adullam, while a band of Philistines was encamped in the Valley of Rephaim. 14At that time
David was in the stronghold, and the Philistine garrison was at Bethlehem. 15David longed
for water and said, "Oh, that someone would get me a drink of water from the well near the
gate of Bethlehem!" 16So the three mighty men broke through the Philistine lines, drew water
from the well near the gate of Bethlehem and carried it back to David. But he refused to drink
it; instead, he poured it out before the LORD. 17"Far be it from me, O LORD, to do this!" he said. "Is
it not the blood of men who went at the risk of their lives?" And David would not drink it.
Such were the exploits of the three mighty men.
18Abishai the brother of Joab son of Zeruiah was chief of the Three. He raised his spear
against three hundred men, whom he killed, and so he became as famous as the Three.
19Was he not held in greater honor than the Three? He became their commander, even
though he was not included among them.
20Benaiah son of Jehoiada was a valiant fighter from Kabzeel, who performed great
exploits. He struck down two of Moab's best men. He also went down into a pit on a
snowy day and killed a lion. 21And he struck down a huge Egyptian. Although the Egyptian
had a spear in his hand, Benaiah went against him with a club. He snatched the spear from
the Egyptian's hand and killed him with his own spear. 22Such were the exploits of Benaiah
son of Jehoiada; he too was as famous as the three mighty men. 23He was held in greater
honor than any of the Thirty, but he was not included among the Three. And David put
him in charge of his bodyguard.

24Among the Thirty were:
Asahel the brother of Joab,
Elhanan son of Dodo from Bethlehem,

25 Shammah the Harodite,
Elika the Harodite,
26 Helez the Paltite,
Ira son of Ikkesh from Tekoa,
27 Abiezer from Anathoth,
Mebunnai the Hushathite,
28 Zalmon the Ahohite,
Maharai the Netophathite,
29 Heled son of Baanah the Netophathite,
Ithai son of Ribai from Gibeah in Benjamin,
30 Benaiah the Pirathonite,
Hiddai from the ravines of Gaash,
31 Abi-Albon the Arbathite,
Azmaveth the Barhumite,
32 Eliahba the Shaalbonite,
the sons of Jashen,
Jonathan 33 son of Shammah the Hararite,
Ahiam son of Sharar the Hararite,
34 Eliphelet son of Ahasbai the Maacathite,
Eliam son of Ahithophel the Gilonite,
35 Hezro the Carmelite,
Paarai the Arbite,
36 Igal son of Nathan from Zobah,
the son of Hagri,
37 Zelek the Ammonite,
Naharai the Beerothite, the armor-bearer of Joab son of Zeruiah,
38 Ira the Ithrite,
Gareb the Ithrite
39 and Uriah the Hittite.
There were thirty-seven in all.

COMMENTARY

8–12 The parallel in 1 Chronicles is introduced with the statement that David's mighty men and/or their chiefs "gave his kingship strong support to extend it over the whole land" (1Ch 11:10). Since the context in 1 Chronicles is the anointing of David as king over Israel after his seven-year reign in Hebron (1Ch 11:1–3) followed by the conquest of Jerusalem (1Ch 11:4–9), vv.8–39 doubtless represent the organization of David's military command at a time relatively early in his reign over all Israel. Indeed, many of the events in the section should perhaps be dated even earlier in light of the fact that "the appearance of Asahel, brother of Joab, in the list of the heroes [v.24] sets a *terminus ad quem* for the list as a whole, since Asahel was murdered by Abner during the war between Eshbaal and David at the beginning of David's reign at Hebron" (Mazar, "The Military Elite," 318; see comment on 2:23). In most respects the account in vv.8–39 agrees with that in 1 Chronicles 11:11–41a "except that there are a considerable number of errors of the text, more especially in the names, which are frequently corrupt in both texts, so that the true reading cannot be determined with certainty" (K&D, 491).

"These are the names of" (v.8) is a stock introductory formula (cf., e.g., Ex 1:1). *Gibbōrîm*, elsewhere a general term for unusually strong and courageous soldiers (cf. 1Sa 2:4 ["warriors"]; 17:51 ["hero"]), is here translated "mighty men" in a more specific sense, almost always in connection with the number "three" (vv.9, 16–17, 22).

First to be mentioned is Jashobeam (1Ch 11:11; the second element in the variant "Josheb-Basshebeth" in v.8 is probably a scribal error caused by vertical dittography from the end of v.7 [see comment and Notes; for other possibilities see NIV note on v.8]). His patronymic, Tahkemonite (otherwise unknown), is "probably a variant of Hacmonite" (of equally obscure origin) in 1 Chronicles 11:11 (see NIV note; cf. also "Hacmoni" in 1Ch 27:32). Jashobeam, among others during David's long reign (cf., e.g., Abishai [v.18]), was "chief of the Three" (v.8). Since the Hebrew words for "three" (*šlš*, *šlšh*, *šlšt*), "thirty" (*šlšym*), and "officer" (*šlyš*) are similar to each other, they are sometimes miscopied, and it is therefore not always possible to tell which one was intended by the author/compiler (cf. 1Ch 11:11 and NIV note).

Three and thirty are relatively common numbers in the OT, the former "used as a minimum plural" and the latter "to express ... minimum decemplurality" (J. B. Segal, 19). In terms of David's military administration, the regular regiment of four hundred to six hundred men (see comments on 1Sa 22:2; 23:13) "was divided into three units: Two fighting units and one unit to guard the weapons [see comments on 1Sa 25:13; 30:9–10]. This division was most certainly based on ancient tradition. It presumably served as the basis for the emergence of David's three commanding officers or 'champions'" (Mazar, "The Military Elite," 314). As for the number thirty, it is already "found in the premonarchic Israelite tradition, where there is frequent mention of thirty champions, or sons, who were associated with a charismatic personality or with the head of a clan" (Mazar, "The Military Elite," 310; see n. 2, where he cites Jdg 10:4; 12:9; 14:11; 1Sa 9:22; 1Ch 11:42; cf., however, the caveat of McCarter, *II Samuel*, 496–97).

Like Abishai (cf. v.18), the courageous Jashobeam "raised his spear against" a large number of men (v.8), whom he succeeded in killing in a single encounter. Although "eight hundred" may seem an exaggeration, there is no MS evidence that would warrant reducing it to the "three hundred" in the parallel text of 1 Chronicles 11:11, where it probably arose by contamination from the same figure in 1 Chronicles 11:20 (= 2Sa 23:18).

Jashobeam, along with eleven other warriors in vv.9–30 (virtually in sequence), resurfaces in 1 Chronicles 27 as the commander of one of David's twelve army divisions: Jashobeam (v.8; 1Ch 27:2); Dodai (v.9; 1Ch 27:4); Benaiah son of Jehoiada (v.20; 1Ch 27:5); Asahel (v.24; 1Ch 27:7); Shammah/Shammoth/Shamhuth (v.25; 1Ch 27:8); Ira (v.26; 1Ch 27:9); Helez (v.26; 1Ch 27:10); Sibbecai (v.27; 1Ch 27:11); Abiezer (v.27; 1Ch 27:12); Maharai (v.28; 1Ch 27:13); Benaiah the

Pirathonite (v.30; 1Ch 27:14); Heled/Heldai (v.29; 1Ch 27:15).

Next to Jashobeam was Eleazar, the second of the "three mighty men" (v.9). Not to be confused with the man of the same name in 1 Samuel 7:1, Eleazar was the son of Dodai the "Ahohite," the same Benjamite clan (cf. Ahoah [1Ch 8:4]) as that of Zalmon, one of the Thirty (cf. v.28). Unlike other Israelite troops, who "retreated" (lit., "went up/away," v.9; cf. 1Ki 15:19 ["withdraw"]; 2Ki 12:18; Jer 21:2) from a second epic battle against the Philistines near "Pas Dammim" (see NIV note; also comment on Ephes Dammim in 1Sa 17:1, which begins the account of the first battle), Eleazar "stood his ground" (v.10) and joined David as, tit for tat, they "taunted" the enemy (v.9; see comment on 21:21; the same Heb. verb is translated "defy" in 1Sa 17:10, 25–26, 36, 45; see also comments on 1Sa 17:43–47).

Eleazar struck down the Philistines with such fierceness that his hand "froze to the sword" (v.10; for a similar phenomenon in modern times, cf. Kirkpatrick, 216) and thus "grew tired" (cf. Isa 40:30 ["grow ... weary"] and contrast Isa 40:31 ["not grow weary"]). But there was victory nonetheless—a "great victory" that, as in the case of Shammah (cf. v.12), was brought about by the Lord (see comments on 19:2; 1Sa 19:5). Although not participating in the battle itself, the troops who had fled (cf. v.9) returned in order to "strip" the dead (v.10). In so doing, David's men repaid the indignities perpetrated by the Philistines on an earlier occasion (see 1Sa 31:8 and comment).

Third and last of the "three mighty men" (v.9) was "Shammah son of Agee" (v.11), who is not to be identified either with David's third brother (for which see 1Sa 16:9 and comment) or with "Shammah the Harodite" (v.25). Shammah son of Agee was a "Hararite" (a gentilic of unknown derivation) and is mentioned again in v.33 as the father of Jonathan, one of the Thirty (cf. also "Ahiam the Hararite," v.33). As fear of the Philistines had struck panic in the hearts of Israel's troops on other occasions (see comment on v.9), so also the Israelites fled when the Philistines "banded" together (v.11; cf. v.13) in a field full of "lentils" (a staple food crop; see 17:28 and comment). Depending on divine help for victory, however (see comment on v.10), Shammah took his stand in the middle of the field and defeated the enemy.

13–17 Often correlated historically with the events described in 5:17–25 (cf. Tidwell, 198 and n. 33; Brueggemann, *In Man We Trust*, 36), the story of David and the three mighty men at the cave of Adullam is one of the most familiar and best loved in the entire corpus. An act of loyalty and unselfish bravery (v.16a) is matched by an act of gratitude and self-effacing chivalry (vv.16b–17), and the result is an account that highlights the most admirable qualities in all four men.

The "thirty chief men" (v.13) are doubtless to be equated with the "Thirty" (vv.23–24) who were already a part of David's growing military force when he was at Ziklag (cf. 1Ch 12:1, 4; for David's days at Ziklag, see 1Sa 27:6–12; 29:1–30:26). Early on, the Thirty had apparently "formed a kind of supreme command" under the leadership of David (Mazar, "The Military Elite," 310). Three of the thirty had now come "down" to him at the "cave of Adullam" (v.13; see 1Sa 22:1 and comment), while a detachment of Philistines was camped in the "Valley of Rephaim" (see 5:18 and comment). That the "stronghold" (v.14), the "rock" (1Ch 11:15), and the "cave" itself are various ways of referring to the same fortified area cannot be proven (see comments on 5:17; 1Sa 22:4–5; cf. also 1Sa 24:22).

At David's hometown of Bethlehem in Judah (see 1Sa 16:1; 17:12 and comments), the Philistines had established a "garrison" (v.14; cf. 1Sa 14:1, 4, 6, 11, 15 ["outpost"]). His throat parched, David expressed aloud his wistful longing (see comment on 15:4) for a drink of water from the well near Bethlehem's gate (v.15), where as a boy he had doubtless slaked his thirst on many occasions "during harvest time" (v.13). So loyal were David's three "mighty men" that his wish became their command. Heedless to the danger facing them, they marched the twelve miles from Adullam east-northeast to Bethlehem, "broke through" the Philistine lines (v.16; cf. similarly 5:20; Tidwell, 198 n. 33), drew water from the well, and carried it back to David. A modern parallel is noted by Boyd Seevers ("Select Biblical Customs in Light of the Cultural Practices of the Rwala Bedouin Tribe," *Near East Archaeological Society Bulletin* 52 [2007]: 29):

> Just as three of David's mighty men broke through enemy lines to bring their leader water that he particularly craved, so a Rwalan warrior broke into an enemy camp to bring his chief a stud horse that he longed to use to mate with his mare.

The account of David's reaction to the bravery of his men (vv.16b–17) is framed by *wᵉlōʾ ʾābâ lištôtām*: "But he refused to drink it" (v.16b), "And David would not drink it" (v.17). David acts and speaks within the boundaries of the inclusio. Instead of drinking the water, he "poured it out" before the Lord (v.16) as a libation offering (cf. Ge 35:14; Nu 28:7; 2Ki 16:13; Jer 7:18; Hos 9:4; see also 1Sa 7:6 and comment). Instead of quenching his thirst, he solemnly and emphatically denied that he would even think of doing such a thing (v.17; see comments on 20:20; 1Sa 22:15; 24:6) as he declared that the water symbolized the very blood of his men, who had served him "at the risk of" (i.e., "in exchange for," *bêt pretii*; see comment on 14:7; cf. also 3:14 ["for the price of"]) their "lives" (v.17; cf. Nu 16:38 ["at the cost of their lives"]; 1Ki 2:23 ["pay with his life"]; Pr 7:23; cf. esp. La 5:9).

Thus David resisted the temptation to pull rank. "In an act of chivalry he pours the water on the ground, refusing to enjoy what his men have gotten him at great risk. He understands intuitively (and that is his greatness) that such a costly commodity is appropriately used only for a sacramental act ... (note that the central motif is paralleled in John 12:1–8)" (Brueggemann, *In Man We Trust*, 37). And just as the gracious gesture of the woman who poured perfume on Jesus' head would be proclaimed everywhere "in memory of her" (Mt 26:13), so also the exploits (v.17) of the courageous warriors—whose self-denying loyalty prompted David to pour out an oblation to the Lord—would be remembered for all future generations.

18–23 By this point in the Samuel corpus "Abishai the brother of Joab son of Zeruiah" (v.18) is well known to its readers as a brave if impetuous fighting man (see comments on 1Sa 26:6; 2Sa 2:18; 3:30; 16:9; 18:2; 19:21; 21:17). In the light of the overall context of vv.18–19, it is more likely that, like Jashobeam (see comment on v.8), Abishai was chief of the "Three" (v.18) rather than of the "Thirty" (see NIV note for details). Also like Jashobeam (see v.8 and comment), Abishai "raised his spear against" and "killed" a large number of men. His prodigious feat of courage made him as "famous" as the Three themselves (v.18; cf. 8:13 with reference to David) and doubtless contributed to his being "held in greater honor" (cf. the variant "doubly honored" [1Ch 11:21]) than the Three (v.19; see comments on 6:20, 22; 1Sa 9:6; and esp. 1Sa 22:14). Indeed, although he was not included among them, he became their commander.

"Benaiah son of Jehoiada" (v.20) is likewise no stranger to readers of Samuel (see 8:18 and comment). From Kabzeel, a town somewhere in the southern Negev and originally allotted to the tribal territory of Judah (cf. Jos 15:21), he was a "valiant" fighter (like the men of Jabesh Gilead; see 1Sa 31:12 and comment) who performed a number of exploits. Among other notable feats he struck down "Moab's two best men" (not "two of Moab's best men" [NIV], which would be expressed differently in Hebrew) and, in the midst of adverse circumstances, killed a lion (thus emulating his king; see 1Sa 17:34–37 and comment). In the eyes of the narrator, however, the most formidable of Benaiah's accomplishments (if space given to its telling is a reliable index) was apparently his encounter with a "huge" (v.21) Egyptian ("seven and a half feet tall," according to 1Ch 11:23). Armed with only a club, Benaiah snatched the Egyptian's spear from him and killed him with it.

Concluding the first main segment (vv.8–23) of its literary section (see comment on vv.8–39), vv.22–23 echo the terminology of vv.17–19 ("Such were the exploits," vv.17, 22; "as famous as the three/Three," vv.18, 22; "held in greater honor than," vv.19, 23; "not included among them/the Three," vv.19, 23). Since Benaiah was for a while "over the Thirty" (1Ch 27:6)—a position occupied at other times by Ishmaiah the Gibeonite (cf. 1Ch 12:4) and Amasai (cf. 1Ch 12:18)—it is not surprising that he should be held in greater honor than the Thirty were (v.13). King David rewarded Benaiah by putting him in charge of his "bodyguard" (v.23), a position similar to that once occupied by David himself in the days of Saul (see 1Sa 22:14 and comment). The term is perhaps here used in reference to the Kerethites and Pelethites (see 8:18 and comment; see also Notes on 1Sa 30:14).

24–39 A roster of notable warriors (vv.24–39, paralleled in 1Ch 11:26–41a) is the second of the two main segments comprising the literary section that preserves the names and, in a few celebrated cases, the exploits of David's mighty men (vv.8–39). If the first segment (vv.8–23) focuses on the Three, the second concentrates on the Thirty.

The parallel list in Chronicles often varies from that in Samuel, especially in the last few verses. Many of the differences consist of minor spelling or transcription errors, a number of which are recorded in the NIV's footnotes on vv.27–36. The total lack of NIV footnotes on 1 Chronicles 11:26–41 gives the misleading impression that all the scribal slips are in the Samuel list, which is surely not the case. The twelve names in the list that reappear in 1 Chronicles 27 as those of commanders of David's army division have already been noted (see comment on vv.8–12). Reference to them in that role will therefore not be repeated below, nor will every variation between names in the three lists (ch. 23; 1Ch 11; 27), which doubtless derive from different periods in David's reign, be commented on (for a comparison of corresponding names in the MT of the three lists, see Driver, 362–63).

Referred to as *gibbôrê haḥ*ª*yālîm* ("the mighty men") by the Chronicler (1Ch 11:26; the term is used of David in 1Sa 16:18 ["brave man"]; see also comment on 1Sa 9:1), the "Thirty" (v.24) were perhaps "a kind of supreme army council which was largely responsible for framing the internal army regulations, deciding on promotions and appointments, and handling other military matters" (Yadin, 277; see also comment on v.13).

If the "sons of Jashen" (v.32) were only two in number, vv.24–39 enumerate thirty-two men who, together with Jashobeam (v.8), Eleazar (v.9), Shammah (v.11), Abishai (v.18), and Benaiah (v.20), account for the grand total of "thirty-seven" that sums up the whole (v.39). If, however, *bny* ("sons of," v.32) is a dittography of the last three letters of the previous word (*hšʿlbny*, "the Shaalbonite"), and if Jashen's patronymic has dropped out of the text of v.32 (cf. *BHS*; also "the Gizonite" in 1Ch 11:34), then the number of men in vv.24–39 is thirty-one. To bring the total to thirty-seven, an additional name must therefore be sought or implied (perhaps that of Joab, whose inclusion in the list is perhaps self-understood in light of his position "over the [entire] army" [8:16; 20:23]; cf. also the frequent incidental references to Joab in the overall section [vv.18, 24, 37]).

Some of the names in vv.24–39 are very familiar, some are less so, and some are otherwise unknown. Joab's brother Asahel (v.24), who plays a prominent role in ch. 2 (see comment on 2:18), was killed by Abner (cf. 2:23), Saul's cousin (cf. 1Sa 14:50–51). Elhanan son of Dodo (v.24) is not to be confused with the Elhanan who killed Goliath's brother (see 21:19 and comment). Likewise Shammah the Harodite (v.25), who is called "Shammoth" in 1 Chronicles 11:27 and is probably to be identified with Shamhuth in 1 Chronicles 27:8, is not to be confused with other leaders named Shammah (see v.11 and comment).

Another Harodite was Elika (v.25), a name that probably means "God has guarded" (cf. Ran Zadok, "On Five Biblical Names," *ZAW* 89/2 [1977]: 266). The hometown of Shammah and Elika may have been Harod (modern Ein Jalud, nine miles west-northwest of Beth Shan), whose nearby spring proved attractive to Gideon and his army before their battle against the Midianites (cf. Jdg 7:1). Helez (v.26) is a name found also on a recently discovered seal impression (cf. Avigad, 57). Helez the Paltite (v.26) was doubtless from Beth Pelet, a town of unknown location in the Negev in the tribal territory originally allotted to Judah (cf. Jos 15:27).

Ira (v.26) is not the same as the Ira in v.38 (who is perhaps to be equated with Ira the Jairite; see comment and Notes on 20:26). Ira son of Ikkesh ("Crooked," *ʿiqqēš*; see comment on 22:27) was from Tekoa, hometown of the prophet Amos as well as of a notable wise woman (see 14:2 and comment), and Abiezer (v.27) was from Anathoth, hometown of the prophet Jeremiah (cf. Jer 1:1; for its location and pagan associations, see Ronald F. Youngblood, "The Call of Jeremiah," *CTR* 5/1 [1990]: 100–102).

"Mebunnai" (*mbny*, v.27) is better read as "Sibbecai" (*sbky*; see NIV note for details). One of David's heroes mentioned in an earlier chapter, Sibbecai the Hushathite killed Saph, a descendant of Rapha (see 21:18 and comment). Like Eleazar son of Dodai, Zalmon (v.28) was an Ahohite (see v.9 and comment). Maharai (v.28) and Heled/Heleb (see NIV note on v.29) son of Baanah (not to be confused with the Baanah of 4:2) were both from Netophah (a town near Bethlehem [perhaps Ramat Rahel, as suggested by Benjamin Mazar, or "Umm-Tuba, which preserves the ancient name with some corruption" (Gabriel Barkay, "Royal Palace, Royal Portrait?" *BAR* 32/5 [2006]: 43)]; cf. 1Ch 2:54; Ezr 2:22; Ne 7:26; also Ne 12:28).

From Gibeah in Benjamin (Saul's hometown, modern Tell el-Ful [three miles north of Jerusalem; see comment on 1Sa 13:2]), Ithai (*ʾyty* [1Ch 11:31]) should not be confused with Ittai the Gittite (see 15:19 and comment) even though his name is spelled the same way in v.29 (*ʾittay*). Benaiah (v.30; not to be identified with Benaiah son of Jehoiada [v.20]) was from Pirathon, hometown of the judge Abdon "in Ephraim, in the hill country of the Amalekites" (Jdg 12:15). The ancient site is modern Farata, seven miles west-southwest of Shechem.

Hiddai/Hurai (v.30; see NIV note) was from the ravines of Gaash, a mountainous area north of which Joshua was buried at Timnath Serah/Heres (modern Khirbet Timnah, eighteen miles northwest of Jerusalem) in the hill country of Ephraim (cf. Jos 24:30 = Jdg 2:9). Abi-Albon (v.31) was from Beth Arabah, a desert village somewhere on the border between Judah (cf. Jos 15:6, 61) and Benjamin (cf. Jos 18:18, 22), while Azmaveth the Barhumite (v.31) may have been from Bahurim (cf. "Baharumite" in 1Ch 11:33), hometown of the rebel Shimei (see 3:16; 16:5b and comments).

Eliahba (v.32), which means "God conceals (the newborn infant)," is constructed from the same root as Hubba ("Concealed [by God]"), a hypocoristic name found recently on a seal impression (cf. Avigad, 53). The hometown of Eliahba was Shaalabbin/Shaalbim (modern Selbit, nineteen miles southeast of Joppa), a town originally allotted to the tribal territory of Dan (cf. Jos 19:42; Jdg 1:35; 1Ki 4:9). The "son of" (v.33; see first text note in NIV) Shammah the Hararite (one of the Three; see v.11 and comment) was Jonathan (v.32), obviously not to be equated with the famous son of Saul and friend of David. Also a Hararite was Ahiam son of Sharar/Sacar (v.33; see second text note in NIV).

Eliphelet (v.34), clearly not David's son who bore the same name (see 5:16 and comment), was from the Aramean district of Maacah (see 10:6 and comment), whose mercenary troops David decimated in a battle against the Ammonites (cf. ch. 10). Zobah, another kingdom of Aram defeated by David as well as by Saul before him (see comments on 8:3; 10:6; 1Sa 14:47), is mentioned as the homeland of Igal (v.36) son of Nathan (neither the famous prophet [7:2] nor the lesser known son of David [5:14] of the same name).

Especially interesting is the listing of "Eliam son of Ahithophel the Gilonite" (v.34). Father of Bathsheba (see 11:3 and comment), with whom David committed adultery, Eliam was also the son of Ahithophel, David's counselor who defected to Absalom (see 15:12 and comment). Perhaps Ahithophel was inclined to do so because of David's sin against his granddaughter. Hezro (v.35) was from Carmel, a village in the hill country of Judah (see 1Sa 15:12 and comment) that was the hometown of the infamous Nabal (cf. 1Sa 25:2–3). Paarai was an Arbite, perhaps from Arab (also in the hill country of Judah; cf. Jos 15:52), whose modern location is possibly Khirbet er-Rabiya, eight miles southwest of Hebron.

According to 1 Chronicles 11:38, the son of Hagri/Haggadi (v.36; see NIV note) was named Mibhar (*mbḥr*), a word that may have been accidentally omitted from 2 Samuel by haplography with the previous word (*mṣbh*, "from Zobah"). Zelek (v.37) was from Ammon east of the Jordan River, and Naharai, one of Joab's armor-bearers (see 18:15 and comment; David had once been Saul's armor-bearer [cf. 1Sa 16:21]), was from Beeroth in Benjamin (see 4:2 and comment).

Ira (v.38; not the same as the Ira in v.26) was an Ithrite, as was Gareb. Ira the Ithrite is probably to be identified with Ira the Jairite (see Notes on 20:26), who was either David's "priest" or his "royal adviser" (see comment on 20:26). "Ithrite" is perhaps the gentilic of Jattir, a Levitical town located thirteen miles south-southwest of Hebron (see comment on 1Sa 30:27; cf. Olyan, 190).

For reasons unknown, the Chronicler omitted the total of the number of warriors at the conclusion of his list (unlike the "thirty-seven" of v.39) and added another sixteen names (cf. 1Ch 11:41b–47). That vv.24–39 preserve the more original roster is clear from the inclusio formed by its first and last names. If Asahel the brother of Joab (v.24) came to an untimely end at the hands of Abner (cf. 2:23), Uriah the Hittite (v.39) met his tragic death because an adulterous king could find no other way to cover his sinful tracks (see 11:14–17 and comments). None would doubt that in virtually every other respect David, who often genuinely sought to do God's will, was an ideal king (see vv.3cd–4 and comments)—"except in the case of Uriah the Hittite" (1Ki 15:5). "The mention of Uriah the Hittite at the close of ch. 23 prepares us for the outburst of divine anger which the matter of the census provokes against David for his having been seduced by political realities to number an Israel which cannot be numbered" (William J. Dumbrell, *The Faith of Israel* [Grand Rapids: Baker, 1988], 83).

NOTES

8 The abrupt (and ungrammatical) appearance of עדינו העצנו (*ʿdynw hʿṣnw*, "Adino the Eznite," otherwise unknown) in the MT probably arose as a corruption of עורר את־חניתו (*ʿwrr ʾt-ḥnytw*, "raised his spear"; cf. the 1Ch 11:11 parallel; also v.18 = 1Ch 11:20; see NIV note on v.8).

9 Although the *Qere* has the expected definite article (־ה, *h-*) on גִּבֹּרִים (*gibbōrîm*, "mighty men"), the *Kethiv* omits it, perhaps allowing the *h* on the end of the preceding word to perform double duty (cf. Watson, 531).

11 "Banded together" (lit., "came together to/in a band"; לַחַיָּה, *laḥayyâ*) is often read "came together at Lehi" (לֶחְיָה, *leḥyâ*) on the basis of the Lucianic recension of the LXX (ἐπὶ σιάγονα, *epi siagona*, "at a jawbone") as well as of Judges 15:9, 14, 17 (see NIV note), 19 (cf. Driver, 365). In v.13, however, חַיַּת (*ḥayyat*) can only mean something like "group, band" (cf. Ps 68:10 ["people"]), making a revocalization of *laḥayyâ* in v.11 unnecessary.

First Chronicles 11:13 reads "barley" instead of "lentils" and attributes Shammah's feat of courage to Eleazar (and David; cf. 1Ch 11:12–14). Apparently a scribe accidentally omitted from Chronicles the material found in 2 Samuel 23:9b–11a (for details see K&D, *The Books of the Chronicles*, 176–77; also K&D, 495; Driver, 365; Gordon, *I and II Samuel*, 312).

15 The Hebrew word באר (*bʾr*, "well," vv.15–16) is vocalized as though "cistern" (בור, *bwr*) were intended (cf. 1Ch 11:17–18, where *bwr* appears). In any event, the traditional site of "David's Well," half a mile north-northeast of Bethlehem (cf. H. B. Tristram, *Bible Places*, rev. ed. [London: SPCK, 1897], 99), is too far from the city to be the well/cistern mentioned here.

20 "Best men" renders אראל (*ʾrʾl*; 1Ch 11:22 has אריאל, *ʾryʾl*), a word of uncertain meaning. Although it is tempting to connect it with *ʾrʾl* in line 12 of the (Moabite) Mesha inscription, doing so does not assist in elucidating its sense (cf. John C. L. Gibson, *Textbook of Syrian Semitic Inscriptions. Volume I: Hebrew and Moabite Inscriptions* [Oxford: Clarendon, 1971], 80). In the present context it forms a wordplay with אריה (*ʾryh*, "lion"; 1Ch 11:22 has ארי, *ʾry*) later in the verse.

30 The lack of the definite article (־ה, *h-*) on "Pirathonite" is probably due to haplography, since the preceding word (בניה[ו], *bnyh[w]*) ends in *h* (cf. 1Ch 11:31; cf. Watson, 531).

F. The Lord's Wrath against Israel (24:1–25)

OVERVIEW

The books of Samuel close with the account of a plague sent by God against Israel because of David's sin in ordering a census of his troops. Displaying a double inclusio with its literary counterpart in 21:1–14 (see Overview to 21:1–24:25), ch. 24 provides a fitting conclusion to the story of David by calling attention, once more and finally, not only to his ambition and pride, but also to his humility and remorse.

The chapter divides naturally into three approximately equal segments, each of which is constructed within its own inclusio. David's sin is the subject of vv.1–9, in which the command to take a census of "Israel and Judah" (v.1) results in a report of the total number of fighting men "in Israel ... and in Judah" (v.9). David's confession is the subject of vv.10–17, at the beginning of which "David ... said to the LORD, 'I have sinned'" and asked to be relieved of his "guilt" (*ʿăwōn*, v.10) and at the end of which "David ... said to the LORD, 'I am the one who has sinned and done wrong [*heʿĕwêtî*, v.17].'" David's altar is the subject of vv.18–25, in which Gad's command to build "an altar to the LORD on the threshing floor of Araunah the Jebusite" (v.18) results in David's building "an altar to the LORD there" (v.25).

First Chronicles 21:1–6, 7–17, and 18–27 replicate vv.1–9, 10–17, and 18–25 respectively. Differences between the two parallel accounts are not only frequent but also, in a few instances, startling. Only the most important of them will be noted in this commentary.

[1]Again the anger of the LORD burned against Israel, and he incited David against them, saying, "Go and take a census of Israel and Judah."

[2]So the king said to Joab and the army commanders with him, "Go throughout the tribes of Israel from Dan to Beersheba and enroll the fighting men, so that I may know how many there are."

[3]But Joab replied to the king, "May the LORD your God multiply the troops a hundred times over, and may the eyes of my lord the king see it. But why does my lord the king want to do such a thing?"

[4]The king's word, however, overruled Joab and the army commanders; so they left the presence of the king to enroll the fighting men of Israel.

[5]After crossing the Jordan, they camped near Aroer, south of the town in the gorge,
and then went through Gad and on to Jazer. [6]They went to Gilead and the region of
Tahtim Hodshi, and on to Dan Jaan and around toward Sidon. [7]Then they went toward the
fortress of Tyre and all the towns of the Hivites and Canaanites. Finally, they went on to Beersheba in the Negev of Judah.

[8]After they had gone through the entire land, they came back to Jerusalem at the end of nine months and twenty days.

[9]Joab reported the number of the fighting men to the king: In Israel there were eight hundred thousand able-bodied men who could handle a sword, and in Judah five hundred thousand.

[10]David was conscience-stricken after he had counted the fighting men, and he said to the LORD, "I have sinned greatly in what I have done. Now, O LORD, I beg you, take away the guilt of your servant. I have done a very foolish thing."

[11]Before David got up the next morning, the word of the LORD had come to Gad the
prophet, David's seer: [12]"Go and tell David, 'This is what the LORD says: I am giving you three options. Choose one of them for me to carry out against you.'"

[13]So Gad went to David and said to him, "Shall there come upon you three years of famine in your land? Or three months of fleeing from your enemies while they pursue you? Or three days of plague in your land? Now then, think it over and decide how I should answer the one who sent me."

[14]David said to Gad, "I am in deep distress. Let us fall into the hands of the LORD, for his mercy is great; but do not let me fall into the hands of men."

[15]So the LORD sent a plague on Israel from that morning until the end of the time designated, and seventy thousand of the people from Dan to Beersheba died.
[16]When the angel stretched out his hand to destroy Jerusalem, the LORD was grieved because of the calamity and said to the angel who was afflicting the people, "Enough! Withdraw your hand." The angel of the LORD was then at the threshing floor of Araunah the Jebusite.

[17]When David saw the angel who was striking down the people, he said to the LORD, "I am the one who has sinned and done wrong. These are but sheep. What have they done? Let your hand fall upon me and my family."

[18]On that day Gad went to David and said to him, "Go up and build an altar to the LORD on the threshing floor of Araunah the Jebusite."
[19]So David went up, as the LORD had commanded through Gad.
[20]When Araunah looked and saw the king and his men coming toward him, he went out and bowed down before the king with his face to the ground.

[21]Araunah said, "Why has my lord the king come to his servant?"

"To buy your threshing floor," David answered, "so I can build an altar to the LORD, that the plague on the people may be stopped."

[22]Araunah said to David, "Let my lord the king take whatever pleases him and offer it up. Here are oxen for the burnt offering, and here are threshing sledges and ox yokes for the wood.
[23]O king, Araunah gives all this to the king." Araunah also said to him, "May the LORD your God accept you."

[24]But the king replied to Araunah, "No, I insist on paying you for it. I will not sacrifice to the LORD my God burnt offerings that cost me nothing."

So David bought the threshing floor and the oxen and paid fifty shekels of silver for them.
[25]David built an altar to the LORD there and sacrificed burnt offerings and fellowship offerings. Then the LORD answered prayer in behalf of the land, and the plague on Israel was stopped.

COMMENTARY

1–9 Just as the Lord's anger had "burned against" Uzzah because of an irreverent act on his part (6:7), so also the anger of the Lord "burned against" Israel (v.1; cf. also Nu 25:3; 32:13; Jdg 2:14, 20; 3:8; 10:7; 2Ki 13:3), in this case because of an unspecified sin. That it does so "again" suggests from a literary standpoint that it is a reflection on the earlier outbreak of divine wrath that brought about the three-year famine of 21:1.

If the subject of "incited" in v.1 is surely the Lord, it is just as surely *śāṭān* in the parallel text of 1 Chronicles 21:1. A thorough treatment of various attempts to explain the relationship between the two passages is that of John H. Sailhamer ("1 Chronicles 21:1—A Study in Inter-Biblical Interpretation," *TJ* 10 [1989]:33–48), who arranges them "under three headings: harmonistic, redactional, and exegetical" (34). Although harmonistic approaches "all express important theological and biblical insights into the nature of the problem, none of the approaches find support within the immediate text itself. They are, in fact, not so much attempts to explain the difficulty of the text as attempts to explain it away" (36). After dismissing the harmonistic method, Sailhamer quickly (and rightfully) dispenses with the redactional explanation in a single paragraph (37).

But Sailhamer's lengthy exegetical discussion, although stimulating and perceptive in many ways, ultimately fares no better. His rendering of *śāṭān* as "adversary" in 1 Chronicles 21:1 (cf. 19:22; see comment on 1Sa 29:4) in reference to the enemies of Israel (Sailhamer, "1 Chronicles 21:1," 42–44; cf. 1Ki 5:4; 11:23, 25) fails to explain either (1) why the term is not used of Israel's enemies anywhere in Samuel or elsewhere in Chronicles or, especially, (2) how Israel's human "adversary, enemy" could be the subject of "incited" in 1 Chronicles 21:1.

On balance, then, the harmonistic approach remains the best of the available options (for rabbinic alternatives cf. Goldman, 341–42). "The older record [v.1] speaks only of God's permissive action: the later [1Ch 21:1] tells us of the malicious instrumentality of Satan. The case is like that of Job" (Kirkpatrick, 223; cf. Job 1:12; 2:6–7, 10; cf. K&D, 503; Archer, 186–88; Kaiser, *Hard Sayings*, 129–32). The difference between Samuel and Chronicles illustrates "the tendency to associate evil with Satan.... In the second-century (BC) book of Jubilees, for example, the action of God in testing Abraham (Gn. 22:1) is said to have been at the instigation of the Satan-figure 'Mastema' (Jub. 17:15–18:19)" (Gordon, *I and II Samuel*, 317; cf. D. S. Russell, *The Old Testament Pseudepigrapha: Patriarchs and Prophets in Early Judaism* [Philadelphia: Fortress, 1987], 74; Baldwin, 294). However paradoxically, a divinely sent affliction can be called a "messenger of Satan" (2Co 12:7; for discussion cf. Murray J. Harris in *EBC*, 10:396.

Thus the Lord through Satan "incited" David (see 1Sa 26:19 and comment; cf. also Job 2:3; Jer 43:3) against Israel by commanding him to "take a census" of Israel and Judah (v.1). Since census-taking was not sinful in and of itself (cf. Ex 30:11–12; Nu 1:1–2), what was the nature of David's transgression? After a survey of numerous possibilities, Raymond B. Dillard, 104–5, points to

> two passages: (1) Joab's objection in the immediate context (1 Chron 21:3) that even if the count were a hundred times increased, they would all still be David's subjects, and (2) the explicit statement that Joab did not finish the count and did not "take the number of the men twenty years old or less because the Lord had promised to make Israel as numerous as the stars of the sky" (1 Chron 27:23–24). For the Chronicler in particular ... the arena of David's transgression appears to be that taking a census impugns the faithfulness of God in the keeping of His promises—a kind of walking by sight instead of by faith.

Consistent with his tendency to portray David in the best possible light and therefore to revel in his name, the Chronicler frequently substitutes "David" for "the king" as he modifies the Samuel narrative (cf. v.2 with 1Ch 21:2; v.9 with 1Ch 21:5; v.20 with 1Ch 21:21 [2x]; v.24 with 1Ch 21:24 ["King David"]). The king tells Joab (who is "over the army" [8:16; cf. 20:23]) and the army commanders with him to "go" (v.2; cf. v.8), using a verb that means more specifically "go around" (cf.

Nu 11:8), "roam" (cf. Job 1:7; 2:2), in the sense of "range widely." David wants his officers to cover the length and breadth of the land of Israel from north to south, "from Dan to Beersheba" (see comments on 3:10; 17:11; 1Sa 3:20). Concentrating only on the "fighting men" (lit., "people," vv.2–3 ["troops"], 4, 9–10; see comment on "soldiers" in 1Sa 4:3), they are not only to count them but also to "enroll" them (vv.2, 4), an act with purposes more military than statistical (cf. 1Sa 11:8 ["mustered"]; 14:17; cf. esp. Nu 1:2–3, where "take a census of the whole Israelite community" [v.2] is defined more precisely as "number by their divisions all the men in Israel twenty years old or more who are able to serve in the army" [v.3], the verb "number" rendering the same Heb. verb here translated "enroll").

Joab, sensing David's hidden agenda, immediately expresses his reservations. His hope that the Lord will "multiply" (v.3; cf. Dt 1:11 ["increase"]) the troops a hundred times over and that David's eyes will see it is doubtless voiced with reluctance since he wonders how the king could possibly "want" (lit., "be pleased"; cf. 1Sa 28:22; see comment on 1Sa 19:1) to do such a thing. Joab is further convinced that David's precipitous action will "bring guilt on Israel" (1Ch 21:3). But the king is adamant. "Overruled" by David's word (lit., "overpowered," v.4; cf. 3:1; see comments on 10:11; 13:14b ["was stronger than"]), Joab and the army commanders proceed to carry out David's orders.

As the place names in vv.5–7 demonstrate, territories conquered by David are not included in the census. The muster of the militia involves only the "entire land" of Israel and Judah (v.8), and the survey follows its borders in a counterclockwise direction (for an excellent map of the itinerary, see Rasmussen, 119). Not to be confused with the town of the same name to which David sent part of the plunder from his victory over the Amalekites (see 1Sa 30:28 and comment), Aroer (originally allotted to the tribal territory of Reuben; v.5; cf. Jos 13:15–16; 1Ch 5:8) is modern Arair, about fourteen miles east of the Dead Sea on the northern bank of the Arnon River. Its location in the southeastern corner of Israel made it the ideal starting point for the census, which was to include all able-bodied men of military age living within the designated borders. The unnamed (and unknown) "town in the [middle of the] gorge" is invariably mentioned as being in the vicinity of Aroer (cf. Dt 2:36; Jos 13:9, 16).

Continuing northward, Joab's party moves on to Jazer, a Levitical town in the tribal territory of Gad (cf. Nu 32:1, 3, 35; Jos 13:25; 21:39: 1Ch 6:81). The modern site of Jazer is possibly Khirbet es-Sar, located about six miles west of Amman. North of Gad is the region known as Gilead (v.6), which was somewhat larger than Gad at this time (see 1Sa 13:7 and comment). "Tahtim Hodshi" (*tḥtym ḥdšy*), otherwise unmentioned, is a town or region of unknown location somewhere between Gilead and Dan. On the basis of the Lucianic recension of the LXX, the MT is often emended to *hḥtym qdšh*, "[the region of] the Hittites, toward Kedesh [on the Orontes]"—which, however, is about a hundred miles northeast of Dan and is therefore much too distant to serve as the northern boundary of Israel (for discussion see Driver, 374). If the MT's text is corrupt at this point, the most likely solution is that of Patrick Skehan, who suggests *tḥt ḥrmwn* "[the region] below [Mount] Hermon" ("Joab's Census: How Far North [2 Sam 24:6]?" *CBQ* 31/1 [1969]: 45 and nn. 19, 47, 49; cf. similarly Driver, 374; Aharoni, 318 n. 19; McCarter, *II Samuel*, 504–5; cf. Jos 11:3, 17; 13:5).

"[To] Dan Jaan" (*dnh yʿn*), also otherwise unmentioned, may be a village near the town of Dan or a fuller name for Dan itself. It is also possible that the MT is a corruption of *dnh [w]ʿywn*, "to Dan and Ijon," two towns mentioned together also in 1 Kings 15:20 (= 2Ch 16:4). The modern site of ancient Dan is Tell el-Qadi, near the foot of Mount Hermon twenty-five miles north of the Sea of Galilee, and that of Ijon is Tell ed-Dibbin, nine miles north-northwest of Dan on a direct line "toward Sidon" (v.6) on the coast of Lebanon.

Southeast of Sidon the census takers go toward the "fortress of Tyre" (v.7) on the Mediterranean just above the northwestern boundary of Israel (cf. Jos 19:29) in an area inhabited by "Hivites and Canaanites," who were among Israel's perennial enemies (cf. Ex 23:23; Jos 9:1; 12:8). At one time Canaanites had perhaps been ubiquitous in the land (cf. Alan R. Millard, "The Canaanites" [in Wiseman, *Peoples of OT Times*], 36–38), while Hivites were a minor population group of whom nothing is known outside the OT (cf. D. J. Wiseman, "Introduction: Peoples and Nations" [in Wiseman, *Peoples of OT Times*], xv–xvi). Some Hivites, however, may have been Hurrians (cf. Hoffner, "The Hittites and Hurrians" [in Wiseman, *Peoples of OT Times*], 225). In any event, Joshua 11:3 mentions Hivites who lived "below Hermon" (see comment on v.6) in southern Lebanon.

Before returning to Jerusalem (v.8), Joab and his officers travel parallel to the Mediterranean coast and conclude their census at Beersheba in the "Negev of Judah" on Israel's southern border (v.7; see comment on 1Sa 27:10). Modern Beersheba, gateway to and capital of the Negev, is located near the site of its ancient namesake forty-five miles southwest of Jerusalem.

As leader of his team, Joab transmits to David the results of their efforts. He reports the number of "able-bodied men" (v.9; the Heb. idiom implies unusual courage; cf. 11:16 ["strongest defenders"]; 23:20 ["valiant fighter"]; see comment on "valiant men" in 1Sa 31:12) who can "handle a sword" (lit., "draw a sword," as in 1Sa 17:51; 31:4; cf. Jdg 8:10 ["swordsmen"]; 20:2 ["armed with swords"], 15, 17, 25, 35, 46; 2Ki 3:26).

As is well known, the tally of fighting men recorded in Joab's report differs in the parallel accounts. According to v.9, the figures in Israel and Judah are 800,000 and 500,000 respectively, while in 1 Chronicles 21:5 they are 1,100,000 and 470,000 (or, in the LXX, 480,000; cf. *BHS*) respectively. To complicate matters further, "both Josephus and the Lucianic texts of Samuel show 900,000 for Israel and 400,000 for Judah in Samuel" (Dillard, 97), thus raising the possibility that the problem is at least partly text-critical in nature.

In any event, "no theological reason can be suggested for the variation in the numbers; the inflationary glorification so often attributed to the Chronicler is totally absent" (Dillard, 97–98). Indeed, even in the present context the Chronicler's figure for Judah is lower than the corresponding figure in v.9. Nor can one solve the problem by observing that "Joab did not include Levi and Benjamin in the numbering" (1Ch 21:6), since in that case the grand total in Chronicles—not Samuel—should be smaller. How, then, to untie the Gordian knot?

The best solution would seem to lie along lines proposed by J. Barton Payne ("Validity of Numbers in Chronicles," *Near East Archaeological Society Bulletin* 11 [1978]: 5–58), who notes that v.9 refers simply to "Israel" whereas 1 Chronicles 21:5 states that the census covers "all Israel" and that therefore "Chronicles' first sum is greater, perhaps because the regular army of 288,000 (I Chronicles 27:1–15) is included" (p. 16, citing A. M. Renwick in *New Bible Commentary*, 292). As for the difference between the 500,000 men of Judah in v.9 compared to the 470,000 in 1 Chronicles 21:5, it is quite likely that the figure in Samuel is rounded off while that in Chronicles is "more precise" (Payne, "Validity of Numbers," 23).

A second problem relates to the hugeness of the numbers themselves. Although Renwick admits that understanding them literally would "imply a population of at least six million in the small country of Palestine," he nevertheless defends them: "When the intense fertility of the land is considered, such a population is quite reasonable and this view is sustained by the innumerable ruins of cities and villages which still abound" (Renwick, *New Biblc Commetnary*, 292; cf. also Kirkpatrick, 227; K&D, 505–6). Most commentators, however, sense that the numbers are inordinately large when interpreted literally. Payne therefore ("Validity of Numbers," 39) proposes to revocalize *ʾelep* ("thousand"; GK 547) as *ʾallup* ("specially trained warrior") in the light of their description as "able-bodied men who could handle a sword."

But then why it would take almost three hundred days (cf. v.8) to conduct a census of a total of "1,570 outstanding military figures" (J. Barton Payne, *EBC*, 4:407) remains unclear. So it is perhaps best to understand *ʾelep* here in the sense of "military unit" (see comment on 1Sa 4:2), a meaning admirably suited to the present setting (cf. Baldwin, 296; Gordon, *I and II Samuel*, 319; Anderson, 285; McCarter, *II Samuel*, 510).

10–17 Eventually coming to the realization that his command to take a census of Israel's fighting men had been not only "repulsive" to Joab (1Ch 21:6) but also "evil in the sight of God" (1Ch 21:7), David is "conscience-stricken" (v.10; see 1Sa 24:5 and comment). As he had done earlier, so now also he confesses to the Lord: "I have sinned" (see 12:13 and comment)—but this time he adds the word "greatly" (*mᵉʾōd*), perhaps having become more sensitive to the enormity of willful rebellion against God (cf. Ps 19:13).

Not waiting for a prophetic word of absolution this time, David begs the Lord to "take away" his guilt (contrast 12:13). He realizes that he has done a "foolish" thing (*skl*; see comment on 1Sa 13:13)—indeed, it is "very" (*mᵉʾōd*) foolish. "David's confession ... is the ideal repentance of the ideal king.... *skl* ni. is here employed to reveal David's insight into the seriousness of his error in relying on numerical strength instead of on the LORD's power who can 'save by many or few' (1Sa. xiv 6)" (Roth, "A Study of *skl*," 76).

Although David may not have needed a prophet to mediate the assurance of divine forgiveness to him, he apparently does need a prophet to outline for him his future options (v.12; cf. similarly the ministry of the prophetess Huldah to King Josiah in 2Ki 22:11–20). If it is possible to read the verb in v.11b as a pluperfect ("had come"), it is equally possible—and perhaps even more likely—"that Yahweh's word to Gad was given after David had got up" (Alfons Schulz, "Narrative Art in the Books of Samuel," in *Narrative and Novella in Samuel: Studies by Hugo Gressmann and Other Scholars 1906–1923* [JSOTSup 116; Sheffield: Almond, 1991], 128). As the "word of the LORD" had come to the prophets Samuel and Nathan in critical situations (see comments on 7:4; 1Sa 15:10; cf. similarly 1Ki 16:7; 18:1; 2Ki 20:4), so also it comes to the prophet Gad (see 1Sa 22:5 and comment; cf. 1Ch 29:29, where Samuel, Nathan, and Gad are mentioned together as among the chroniclers of David's reign), who is David's "seer" (v.11; cf. 1Ch 29:29; 2Ch 29:25; see comment on 1Sa 9:9 [where, however, "seer" translates a different Heb. word]).

Relayed to David through Gad, the Lord's "three options" (v.12) turn out to be "three punishments" (the MT of v.12 at this point has no noun of any kind in association with "three"): "three years of famine," "three months of fleeing," "three days of plague" (v.13). As the suggested periods decrease in length, the specific punishment linked with each period increases in severity. The choice is David's to make, however. Before Gad can bring back to the Lord an answer from the king, David must "think it over and decide" (lit., "know and see," for which see comments on 1Sa 23:22–23 ["find out"]; 24:11 ["understand and recognize"]).

Since David is forced to choose among the least of three evils, he is in "deep distress" no matter what he does (v.14). But because God's people have always confessed that his "mercy is great" (cf. Ne 9:19, 27, 31; Ps 119:156; Da 9:18), David expresses his desire to fall into the hands of the Lord rather than of human beings. Entirely apart from the fact that he has already experienced famine (cf. 21:1–14) and war (cf. 21:15–22; 23:8–23), therefore, David chooses the three-day plague (v.15):

> War would place the nation at the mercy of its enemies: famine would make it dependent on corn-merchants, who might greatly aggravate the misery of scarcity: only in the pestilence—some form of plague sudden and mysterious in its attack, and baffling the medical knowledge of the time—would the punishment come directly from God, and depend immediately upon His Will. (Kirkpatrick, 228)

Equally instructive is a rabbinic explanation of David's reasoning: "If I choose famine the people will say that I chose something which will affect them and not me, for I shall be well supplied with food; if I choose war, they will say that the king is well protected; let me choose pestilence, before which all are equal" (cited in Goldman, 345).

Divine judgment in the form of a plague was not long in coming. Indeed, it began "that morning" (v.15; cf. v.11). It probably did not continue for three days, however, since an amelioration of "the time designated" might have been effected by the Lord's intervention described in v.16. Furthermore, the Hebrew phrase rendered "until (the end of) the time designated" is understood to mean "until noon" in the LXX and "until the sixth hour" in the Syriac (see *BHS* for details). But however long or short the duration of the plague, "seventy thousand ... died." If David, bent on conquest, had planned the census as a military muster (see comment on v.2), the Lord's response is not unexpected. "Wanting more land and more people to rule, David finds himself with 70,000 fewer subjects" (Dillard, 106).

Who, precisely, are the hapless victims of the plague? The NIV apparently considers them to have been ordinary Israelite "people" (vv.15–17, 21). But since *ʿām* is translated "fighting men, troops" everywhere else in ch. 24 (see comment on v.2), since *ʾîš* (lit., "man") implies "military man" each time it appears in the chapter (vv.9 [3x], 15), and since "from Dan to Beersheba" in v.15 echoes the geographical limits of the military muster ordered by David in v.2, it is preferable to translate *ʿām* as "fighting men" in vv.15–17, 21 as well. The "seventy thousand" who died should thus be understood as "seventy military units" in harmony with the suggested rendering of *ʾelep* in v.9 (see comment).

As in the critical days of Sennacherib's attempted siege of Jerusalem (cf. 2Ki 19:35 = Isa 37:36; cf. 2Ch 32:21), so also in the days of David's extremity the "angel of the LORD" is the instrument of the divinely sent plague (v.16). For centuries the identity of the angel of the Lord has been a subject of vigorous debate. Although many have taught that the angel was Jesus Christ in a preincarnate form (cf. J. Borland, *Christ in the Old Testament* [Chicago: Moody Press, 1978]; Robert L. Reymond, *Jesus, Divine Messiah: The Old Testament Witness* [Ross-shire, Scotland: Christian Focus, 1990], 1), such a view severely weakens (1) the uniqueness of the incarnation and (2) the basic argument of Hebrews 1, which goes to great lengths to point out that Jesus is far superior to all God's angels.

Since the Hebrew word for "angel" also means "messenger," it is perhaps better to understand the angel of the Lord as a special messenger from the court of heaven who bears all the credentials of the King of heaven and can therefore speak and act on his behalf. He can use the first-person pronoun of himself as though he were the sender (cf. Jdg 6:16), or he can use the third-person pronoun in reference to the sender (cf. Jdg 6:12; cf. esp. Jdg 13:3–23 for various titles given to the angel of the Lord: "man of God," "angel of God," "man," "God," "the LORD"). In any case, he symbolizes the presence of the King who sends him. Thus when the angel of the Lord appears, the Lord himself is symbolically present (for discussion cf. Gustav Friedrich Oehler, *Theology of the Old Testament*, 4th ed. [New York: Funk & Wagnalls, 1883], 129–34; Youngblood, *The Book of Genesis*, 166–67). Surely the angel and the Lord are not simply to be equated without further ado. Indeed, in v.16 they are clearly distinguished from each other ("the LORD ... said to the angel"; cf. also the parallel text in 1Ch 21:15, which states that "God sent an angel").

Having already killed a large number of men throughout the rest of the country (v.15), the angel now "stretched out his hand" to destroy the capital city itself (v.16; cf. Ex 9:15; Job 1:11–12 ["lay a finger"]; see 1Sa 6:9 and comment). At this juncture, however, the Lord is "grieved" (*nḥm*; GK 5714) because of the calamity (cf. Ge 6:6–7; Ex 32:12, 14 ["relent"]; Jer 18:8, 10 ["reconsider"]; 26:3, 13, 19; 42:10; Joel 2:13; Jnh 4:2; for discussion of "grieving/relenting/repenting" with God as subject, see comment on 1Sa 15:11). Divine judgment already more than adequate, the Lord says "Enough!" (*rab*; cf. Ge 45:28 ["I'm convinced!"]; Ex 9:28; 1Ki 19:4) and orders the angel to "withdraw" his hand (cf. Ex 4:26 ["let ... alone"]; Dt 4:31 ["abandon"]; 31:6, 8 ["leave"]; Jos 1:5; 10:6; 1Ch 28:20 ["fail"]; Ne 6:3; Ps 138:8).

Visible to David's eyes, the angel and his destructive actions in "striking down" the men (v.17; cf. 1Sa 4:8; 5:6, 9 ["afflicted"]) repulse the king. He again confesses that he has "sinned" (see comment on v.10) and "done wrong" (*ʾānōkî*, emphatic "I," is used with each of the two verbs). The men who are being killed are merely "sheep," who are not guilty and for whom David feels responsible (cf. Jer 23:1–3; Eze 24:5 ["flock"]; 34:2–10; Zec 11:7, 17). David's loving concern for and care of "sheep," whether literal or metaphorical, has characterized him from his first appearance in the books of Samuel (cf. 1Sa 16:11) to his last. Rather than witness the further destruction of his men, he calls the wrath of God down on himself and his own family (cf. Moses' similar plea in Ex 32:32; also Dt 9:26–27).

In preparation for the final pericope in the books of Samuel (vv.18–25), the narrator observes that the angel of the Lord is at the "threshing floor of Araunah the Jebusite" (v.16; for discussion of Jebusites as the pre-Israelite inhabitants of Jerusalem, see comment on 5:6). As will soon become clear in this case, threshing floors in ancient times were often places of sanctity (see comment on 6:6). The Jebusite fortress was on the southeastern hill of Jerusalem (see comment on 5:7), and the threshing floor belonging to Araunah "is usually thought to be north of it, and thus outside the fortified area" (Jones, 126).

Araunah's name is spelled in several different ways in the MT of Samuel and Chronicles: *ʾrwnh* (vv.20–24); *ʾrnyh* (v.18); *ʾrnn* (1Ch 21:15–25; 2Ch 3:1); and, significantly, *hʾwrnh* (*Kethiv*; *hʾrwnh* [*Qere*]), literally, "the Araunah" (v.16). The latter spelling, the first in sequence in ch. 24, opens up the possibility that "Araunah" was a title rather than a proper name, and the MT's accents on *ʾrwnh hmlk* in v.23 lead to the conclusion that the phrase is "to be taken as a unity, indicating that Araunah was given the title *mlk* ['king'], and was in fact the last Jebusite king of the city.... *hmlk* is simply a gloss translating the foreign term into Hebrew for the reader's benefit" (N. Wyatt, "'Araunah the Jebusite' and the Throne of David," *ST* 39 [1985]: 40). Although Wyatt argues at length that Araunah was in fact Uriah the Hittite, his treatment is unconvincing. With respect to the meaning and origin of the word "Araunah,"

> the parallel account in 1 Chronicles 21:14–30, as well as the LXX translation of both accounts [Ορνα, *Orna*], suggests that the M.T. consonants *ʾrwnh* in 2 Samuel 24 have resulted from a transposition of the consonants *ʾwrnh*. The "name" (if it be not rather a title) of this Jebusite was the Hurrian word *ewri-ne* "the lord." The same name (spelled *ʾwrn*) occurs in a text from Ugarit. (Hoffner, "The Hittites and Hurrians" [in Wiseman, *Peoples of OT Times*, 1973], 225)

18–25 In response to David's urgent prayer (v.17), the angel of the Lord (1Ch 21:18) orders the prophet Gad (see comment on v.11) to tell David to "go up" (v.18) to Araunah's threshing floor, which was doubtless located "on an elevated spot exposed to the wind" (G. B. Funderburk, *ZPEB*, 5:739). There David is to "build" (lit., "erect"; cf. 1Ki 16:32 ["set up"]; 2Ki 21:3 = 2Ch 33:3) an altar to the Lord. Prompted by the divine command, David obeys (v.19).

After having "looked" (lit., "looked down," v.20; cf. 1Sa 13:18 ["overlooking"]; La 3:50) and seen David and "his men" (*ʿᵃbādāyw*, lit., "his officials/servants"; see comment on 1Sa 16:15–16) coming over toward him, Araunah leaves the threshing floor (cf. 1Ch 21:21) and pays homage to David, his acknowledged superior ("my lord the king," v.21), by bowing down before him with his "face to the ground" (v.20; cf. 14:4, 22, 33; 18:28; 1Sa 20:41; 25:41; 28:14; see 1Sa 24:8; 25:23 and comments). If Araunah himself had once been the Jebusite king of Jerusalem (see comment on v.18), he is now merely another "servant" of the Israelite king of Jerusalem (v.21; see comment on 1Sa 1:11).

To Araunah's query concerning the purpose of David's visit, the king says that he wants to buy the threshing floor from him as a suitable place where he can "build" an altar to the Lord (the Heb. verb rendered "build" here and in v.25 is not the same as the one used in v.18; see comment). He understands that sacrificing "burnt offerings and fellowship offerings" (v.25) will propitiate the divine wrath (cf. R. de Vaux, *Studies in Old Testament Sacrifice* [Cardiff: University of Wales, 1964], 37–42; Leon Morris, *The Apostolic Preaching of the Cross* [Grand Rapids: Eerdmans, 1956], 129–36) and bring the "plague" (*maggēpâ*) to an end (this term [see 1Sa 6:4 and comment] here and in v.25 is not the same as the Hebrew word translated "plague" in vv.13 and 15). As a similarly devastating plague had been "stopped" in the days of Phinehas son of Eleazar son of Aaron (Nu 25:7–8; Ps 106:30 ["checked"]), so David wants the plague on Israel to cease.

The conversation between David and Araunah is reminiscent of that between Abraham and Ephron (cf. Ge 23:3–15; cf. Youngblood, *The Book of Genesis*, 193–94), and David's situation is just as desperate as Abraham's had been. Like Ephron, Araunah is willing to give whatever is needed (vv.22–23); like Abraham, David insists on paying (v.24a); as in the case of Abraham and Ephron, David and Araunah finally agree on a purchase price (v.24b).

Although they usually toiled as draft animals (cf. 6:6), "oxen" (v.22) were also commonly sacrificed as burnt offerings and fellowship offerings (see 6:13, 17–18 and comments). Ordinarily used to separate heads of grain from husks and chaff (cf. Isa 41:15), "threshing sledges" could also serve as fuel. Commonly employed to guide animals engaged in plowing (cf. 1Ki 19:19), "ox yokes" might also be burned at a barbecue (cf. 1Ki 19:21) or an altar. Although oxen, threshing sledges, and ox yokes constitute the basic trappings of his livelihood, Araunah is prepared to give them to David for a higher purpose. He also expresses his hope that the Lord "your" God (v.23; it would seem that Araunah the Jebusite is deliberately distancing himself from what he considers to be an Israelite deity) will "accept" David (cf. Jer 14:10, 12; Eze 20:40–41; Hos 8:13 ["(be) pleased with"]; cf. esp. Eze 43:27).

To Araunah's gracious (though perhaps not totally disinterested) offer, David replies in characteristic fashion (cf. 23:16b–17), pointedly referring to the Lord as "my" God: "I will not sacrifice to the LORD my God burnt offerings that cost me nothing" (v.24). His emphatic "No" resonates with the sound of authority (see 16:18 and comment) as he insists on paying for the threshing floor (lit., "buying it ... in exchange for [*bêt pretii*; see comments on 14:7; 23:17] a price").

The transaction is finalized as David agrees to pay Araunah "fifty shekels of silver" (see comment on 1Sa 9:8) for the threshing floor and the oxen (v.24), an amount that balloons in the Chronicler's parallel to "six hundred shekels of gold"—a price, however, that doubtless includes the entire "site" (a much larger area, 1Ch 21:25) and that may in fact have involved a subsequent purchase (cf. Kirkpatrick, 232). J. B. Segal, 9, makes the tantalizing but unprovable suggestion that since six hundred is twelve times fifty, "the Chronicler gives this incident a national significance" (encompassing the twelve tribes of Israel).

And so, as Omri king of Israel would later buy the hill of Samaria and build his capital city on it (cf. 1Ki 16:23–24), David king of Israel and Judah buys a threshing floor and builds an altar on it. He then sacrifices "burnt offerings and fellowship offerings" (v.25; see 6:17–18 and comments) as a means of seeking divine favor (see 1Sa 13:9 and comment). The Lord's response? He "answered prayer in behalf of the land" (24:25; for literary significance see Overview to 21:1–24:25). The angel of death having "put his sword back into its sheath" (1Ch 21:27), divine judgment—the plague against Israel—is "stopped" (v.25; see v.21 and comment).

Although David appears content simply to build an altar on the threshing floor of Araunah the Jebusite, his son Solomon will eventually build the temple there (cf. 1Ch 22:1) on the hill called Moriah (cf. 2Ch 3:1; Ge 22:2; cf. Youngblood, *The Book of Genesis*, 187–88).

> At the same site where Abraham once held a knife over his son (Ge 22:1–19), David sees the angel of the Lord with sword ready to plunge into Jerusalem. In both cases death is averted by sacrifice. The temple is established there as the place where Israel was perpetually reminded that without the shedding of blood there is no remission of sin (Heb 9:22). Death for Isaac and for David's Jerusalem was averted because the sword of divine justice would ultimately find its mark in the Son of God (John 19:33). (Dillard, 107)

Small wonder, then, that the NT should begin with "a record of the genealogy of Jesus Christ the son of David, the son of Abraham...."

NOTES

1 In the first two chapters of Job (1:6–9, 12; 2:1–4, 6–7), Satan is called הַשָּׂטָן (*haśśāṭān*; lit., "the Accuser/Adversary [par excellence]"; see NIV note on Job 1:6). By the time of the Chronicler, however, the definite article has been dropped and *śāṭān* has become a proper name (1Ch 21:1).

2 In the context, "Joab and the army commanders" is a better reading than the MT's "Joab the army commander" (for details see NIV note).

12 "Giving" is literally "laying upon" (נטל על, *nṭl ʿl*; cf. La 3:28). The parallel in 1 Chronicles 21:10 reads נטה על (*nṭh ʿl*), literally, "stretching out upon," which would be unique in the sense of "give/offer to" (cf. BDB, 640). Since some Hebrew MSS do in fact read *nṭl ʿl* in 1 Chronicles 21:10 (see *BHS*), *nṭl* is preferable in both passages.

13 That "three years" is a better reading than the "seven years" of the MT is clear not only from the parallel in 1 Chronicles 21:12 and from the LXX evidence (see NIV note) but also from the symmetry of the three punishments themselves (for detailed discussion see Carlson, 204 n. 4). For the significance of the inclusio formed by "a famine for three successive years" (21:1) and "three years of famine" (v.13), see Overview to 21:1–24:25.

14 Instead of "let us fall," the Chronicler reads "let me fall" (1Ch 21:13), perhaps to reflect his perception of David's selflessness and humility. For the literary significance of the use of the rare idiom "fall into/at the hands of" here, see comment on 21:22.

17 Whereas the MT of v.17 reads ואנכי העויתי (*wʾnky hʿwyty*, "and I have done wrong") and that of 1 Chronicles 21:17 reads והרע הרעותי (*whrʿ hrʿwty*, "and I have surely done wickedly"), 4QSamuel[a] offers a text that appears to be more original in that it helps to explain the difference between the parallels in Samuel and Chronicles: ואנכי הרעה הרעתי (*wʾnky hrʿh hrʿty*, "and I, the shepherd, have done wickedly"; cf. Ulrich, 86–87). The antithetical "these are but sheep" favors the Qumran reading as well (cf. Dillard, 97; for "shepherd/flock" as a kind of *Leitmotif* with respect to David, see 1Sa 16:11 and comment).

22 "Burnt offering" (singular) is often used in a collective sense. In the present context, for example, the parallel reads "burnt offerings" (1Ch 21:23), and shortly thereafter the situation is reversed ("burnt offerings," v.24; "burnt offering," 1Ch 21:24).

23 In the MT, the first sentence translates literally as follows: "Everything he-gives Araunah the-king to-the-king." By legitimately rendering "the-king" as a vocative, the NIV reads, "All this Araunah gives, O king, to the king," whence the translation, "O king, Araunah gives all this to the king." In the light of the MT's accents, however, it is more natural to read "Araunah the king gives all this to the king" (see comment on v.16).

1, 2 KINGS

RICHARD D. PATTERSON AND HERMANN J. AUSTEL

Introduction

1. HISTORICAL BACKGROUND

The events of Israel's history from the latter days of King David till the capture of Jerusalem are selectively recounted in the two books of Kings, to which two short footnotes are appended, one concerning an incident in the early days of the exile (2Ki 25:22–26), the other concerning the release of the captured Judean king Jehoiachin after the death of Nebuchadnezzar (25:27–30). The historical details span 971–562 BC.

The involved period moves from the politically powerful and luxurious days at the close of the united kingdom under Solomon to the division of the kingdom under Rehoboam and then traces the fortunes of the northern and southern kingdoms to their demise in 722 BC and 586 BC, respectively. Numerous references to the external political powers and peoples of the times—e.g., the Egyptians, Philistines, Phoenicians, Arameans, Ammonites, Moabites, Edomites, Assyrians, and Chaldeans—are integrated into the inspired record. In particular the Israelites were to experience the Aramean threats and Assyrian pressures of the ninth century BC, the great Assyrian invasions of the eighth century BC, together with the resultant *pax Assyriaca* in the seventh century BC, and the fall of the Neo-Assyrian Empire at the hands of the rising power of the Chaldeans under their brilliant king Nebuchadnezzar II.

Numerous archaeological discoveries have confirmed, illuminated, or supplemented the biblical record, and many of them will be noted in the Commentary and Notes. Particularly important to the understanding of the Bible is the recovered inscriptional material from Assyria and Babylonia. The careful collation of these writings (supplemented by other epigraphic finds) with the biblical narrative has brought greater clarity to the understanding of the Near East during the early and middle segments of the first millennium BC.

Yet Kings is not primarily an account of the political and social history of this period; the work's focus is on Israel's spiritual response to God, who had taken Israel into covenantal relationship with himself (2Ki 17:7–23) and who had bestowed great privileges to the nation through the promise made to David (1Ki 2:2–4). Accordingly, within the pages of Kings is found a detailed summary of the spiritual experiences of a people—particularly its kings, prophets, and priests, whose activities largely point to the need for the advent of the One who would combine the intended ideal of these three offices in himself.

2. UNITY, AUTHORSHIP, AND DATE

The inclusion of the material on but one scroll shows that the Hebrews considered the books of Kings to be one book (see Canonicity). Thematically the continuity of the Elijah narrative (1Ki 17–2Ki 2), itself part of the prophetic section dominating 1 Kings 16:29–2 Kings 9:37, and the recurring phrase "to this day" (1Ki 9:13; 10:12 ["since that day" NIV]; 2Ki 2:22; 10:27; 14:7; 16:6; 17:23, 34, 41; 21:15) clearly indicate that the two books of Kings form a single literary unit.

The problem of the history of the compilation of the book is more pressing. Its author mentions using several source documents, three specifically: (1) "the book of the annals of Solomon" (1Ki 11:41), drawn from biographical, annalistic, and archival material contemporary with the details of 1 Kings 1–11; (2) "the book of the annals of the kings of Israel," mentioned some eighteen times in 1 Kings 14:19–2 Kings 15:31 and drawn largely from the official records of the northern kingdom that were kept by the court recorder (cf. 2Sa 8:16; 20:24; 1Ki 4:3; 2Ki 18:18, 37; 2Ch 34:8); and (3) "the book of the annals of the kings of Judah," mentioned fifteen times (1Ki 14:29–2Ki 24:5), being a record of the events of the reigns of the kings of the southern kingdom from Rehoboam to Jehoiakim.

Other unnamed sources may likewise have been drawn on for the book's final composition, such as the court memoirs of David (1Ki 1:1–2:11), a cycle involving the house of Ahab and the prophets Elijah and Elisha (1Ki 16:29–2Ki 9:37), the records of the prophet Isaiah (Isa 36–39), and two concluding historical abstracts (2Ki 25:22–26, 27–30).

The use of source material and the great time span involved have occasioned numerous suggestions as to the unity, authorship, and date of Kings. Whereas older liberal critical theory tended to find three redactors of Kings, current scholarship focuses on the relation of Kings to the book of Deuteronomy. Kings is seen to be part of a larger work, the Deuteronomistic History, which stretches from Joshua through Kings. Support for this thesis is found in themes and language in Kings that reflect a prevailing Deuteronomistic point of view. Particularly important are the themes of centralization of worship (cf. Dt 12:5), prophetic fulfillment of the Word of God (cf. Dt 18:15–22), and divine retribution for Israel's failure to maintain its cultic orthodoxy (cf. Dt 27; 28:15–68).

Various schemata have been formulated to account for this approach. Some have argued for a single edition of the Deuteronomistic History. Composed in the time of Josiah, it championed the idea that the king's reforms were the means to rectifying the sins of Jeroboam I (cf. 1Ki 13:2; 2Ki 23:15–20).[1] Particularly heinous was Jeroboam's violation of the Deuteronomic law concerning centralized worship. Others

1. For details, see Tremper Longman III and Raymond B. Dillard, *An Introduction to the Old Testament*, 2nd ed. (Grand Rapids: Zondervan, 2006), 172–73.

have decided for a double redaction, the first in the Josianic era and the second during the exile. This second edition was designed to account for the fall of Jerusalem and the conditions of exile.[2]

A great deal of discussion has centered on whether one or more authors were involved in composing the Deuteronomistic History. Martin Noth proposed the idea of a single historian, the "Deuteronomist," who wrote after the capture of Jerusalem in 586 BC in an effort to explain the reasons for the fall of both Israel and Judah.[3] Central to Noth's thesis was the writer's emphasis on such themes as the violation of God's covenant, the importance of centralized worship (in Jerusalem), and the evils of idolatry. Noth believed that Deuteronomy 1:1–4:43 was also the work of the Deuteronomist. Although Noth's theory has gained wide acceptance, many have modified his thesis by finding additional themes that appear to have been important to the Deuteronomic historian.[4]

Others have decided for a multiplicity of authors. Usually this approach proposes a "Deuteronomic School" of writers/editors whose members periodically revised and updated the traditions concerning the united and divided monarchies.[5]

Conservative scholars readily acknowledge the important relationship that Deuteronomy holds to Kings. Thus D. M. Howard observes that "there is a strong 'Deuteronomistic' influence found throughout Joshua–2 Kings, one that is not nearly so visible in Genesis–Numbers."[6] Yet few would be willing to conclude, as liberal scholars often do, that Deuteronomy is a non-Mosaic seventh-century BC document. Quite the contrary, a growing body of evidence supports the time-honored position that Deuteronomy is authentically reflective of its traditional early dating.[7]

Further, even the basic plank in the theory of a late date for Deuteronomy, Deuteronomy 12:5, has been shown to be based on an invalid conclusion. Indeed, G. Wenham points out that rather than being composed to support worship in Jerusalem, this text never really "specifies where 'the place' is."[8] Wenham further notes that such places as Mount Ebal (Dt 27:4–8) and Shechem (Jos 8:30–35; 24; 1Ki 12) were also important shrine centers. J. G. McConville conclusively demonstrates that Deuteronomy 12:5 simply "opposes Yahweh's place of worship to those of *other* gods. It says nothing about the identity of the 'place' that he will choose; the point is simply that *he* will choose it."[9] Indeed this concept antedates Deuteronomy.

2. For details, see ibid., 172–73; see also F. M. Cross, *Canaanite Myth and Hebrew Epic* (Cambridge, Mass.: Harvard Univ. Press, 1973), 274–89; R. D. Nelson, *The Double Redaction of the Deuteronomistic History* (JSOTSup 18; Sheffield: JSOT Press, 1981).
3. Martin Noth, *The Deuteronomistic History* (JSOTSup 15; Sheffield: JSOT Press, 1981).
4. 4. See, for example, H. W. Wolff, "The Kerygma of the Deuteronomic Historical Work," *ZAW* 73 (1961): 171–86; G. von Rad, "The Deuteronomic Theology of History in I and II Kings," in *The Problem of the Hexateuch and Other Essays* (London: Oliver & Boyd, 1966), 205–21; J. G. McConville, "Narrative and Meaning in the Books of Kings," *Bib* 70 (1989): 31–49.
5. See, e.g., A. Lemaire, "Vers l'histoire de la redaction des livres des rois," *ZAW* 98 (1986): 221–36; Gwilym H. Jones, *1 and 2 Kings* (2 vols.; Grand Rapids: Eerdmans, 1984), 1:42–43.
6. D. M. Howard, *An Introduction to the Old Testament Historical Books* (Chicago: Moody Press, 1993), 180–81.
7. See M. Kline, *The Structure of Biblical Authority* (Grand Rapids: Eerdmans, 1972), 131–53; E. Merrill, *Deuteronomy* (NAC; Nashville: Broadman & Holman, 1994), 32–37.
8. Gordon Wenham, "The Date of Deuteronomy: Linch-pin of Old Testament Criticism, Part Two," *Themelios* 11.1 (1985): 15.
9. J. Gordon McConville, *Law and Theology in Deuteronomy* (JSOTSup 33; Sheffield: JSOT Press, 1984), 32.

It is already embedded in the Sinaitic covenant (Ex 20:24). Much the same can be said of the third plank of the proposed Deuteronomistic History—the threat of divine retribution for cultic deviation, which is already present in an extended passage in Leviticus 26:14–39.[10]

Although some conservatives have been willing to concede that the author(s) of Kings also had a hand in the composition of Joshua–Kings,[11] others have called in question the whole construct of a Deuteronomic School. They note that the disagreement among critical scholars as to both the origin and the extent of the "Deuteronomistic History" casts doubt on the validity of the method itself. Indeed the term "Deuteronomistic" is somewhat of a misnomer, for it unwarrantedly assumes that someone associated with the compilation of Deuteronomy was also associated in the production of Kings.

While it is true that there is much in common between Deuteronomy and Joshua–Kings (cf., e.g., Dt 28; Jos 23; 2Ki 17:18–23), W. Kaiser Jr. demonstrates that the basic theological viewpoint of Kings is precisely that which has flowed unswervingly down from Moses.[12] As Kenneth Kitchen remarks, "In fact, a careful reading of the Old Testament at large may simply indicate that much of what is attributed to the Deuteronomic viewpoint is but the common ground of Hebrew mainstream belief (orthodoxy if one will), with rather little that is absolutely distinctive. Hence, 'covenantal' (or, 'mainstream' rather than 'orthodox'?) would be a fairer label than 'Deuteronomic,' if label be needed."[13]

Despite Kings' reflection of mainstream orthodoxy, the point of view and emphases are somewhat different. Whereas Deuteronomy's presentation of the covenantal relationship was prescriptive and narrative, that of Kings is narrative and evaluative. This observation, coupled with differences of internal detail and the newly established evidence for an early dating of Deuteronomy, makes questionable any discussion of a "Deuteronomic School" of history. As R. K. Harrison points out, "There is ... a significant difference of emphasis in the two works, and this fact alone should be sufficient to deter the casual ascription of the epithet 'Deuteronomic' to the work of the author of Kings."[14] Perhaps the most likely conclusion concerning the whole problem is that of D. M. Howard: "The term *Deuteronomistic* can thus be used in a more neutral descriptive way to refer to those books or ideas reflective of the distinctive viewpoints found in Deuteronomy—with no conclusions concerning authorship of Deuteronomy or the other books inherent in the use of the term."[15]

---

10. Admittedly liberal scholars often assign a late date to this text. Yet doing so is unnecessary, for such curses may be found in early Near Eastern treaties as well as law codes that antedate the Mosaic period by centuries. A similar conclusion can be reached with regard to Noth's emphasis on the condemnation of idolatry, for it is found in the first of the Ten Commandments (Ex 20:2–3, 23; cf. 22:20; 32:7–10; Lev 17:7; 26:30).
11. See, for example, Paul R. House, *1, 2 Kings* (NAC; Nashville: Broadman & Holman, 1995), 28–39.
12. W. Kaiser Jr., *Toward an Old Testament Theology* (Grand Rapids: Zondervan, 1978), 63–66.
13. Kenneth Kitchen, "Ancient Orient, 'Deuteronism,' and the Old Testament," in *New Perspectives on the Old Testament*, ed. J. B. Payne (Waco, Tex.: Word, 1970), 17.
14. R. K. Harrison, *Introduction to the Old Testament* (Grand Rapids: Eerdmans, 1969), 732. Harrison notes the difference in focus between the two works: "Whereas in Deuteronomy the blessings of God accrued to those who kept the provisions of the Covenant agreement, in the books of Kings both men and nations alike were evaluated morally and spiritually according to whether or not they had deviated from the Covenant" (222).
15. Howard, *Introduction to the Old Testament Historical Books*, 182.

Everywhere except in the two appendixes, Kings bears the impress of being a unified book expressing the viewpoint of a single author who has woven together his historical data in accordance with a single purpose and with a uniform literary style. Jewish tradition (*b. B. Bat. 15a*) identifies that author as Jeremiah. Since, however, OT narrative literature was usually anonymous, scholars have frequently attributed the authorship of Kings to some prophet who "was nevertheless a man likeminded with Jeremiah and almost certainly a contemporary who lived and wrote under the same influences."[16]

Although little is actually gained by such a position except to avoid the categorical assertion that Jeremiah was the author, yet the author's failure to identify himself as Jeremiah or to use Jeremiah's familiar names for the kings of Judah argues for caution against too readily following the traditional identification of Jeremiah as the author. What can be safely held is that at least the majority of the book bears the impress of being the product of one author, who, as an eyewitness of the Jewish nation's final demise, was concerned to show the divine reasons for that fall. In so doing he utilized many sources, weaving the details together into an integrated whole that graphically portrayed Israel's failure to keep the covenant.

3. ORIGIN, OCCASION, AND PURPOSE

If the conclusions reached in the preceding section are correct, a distinction must be made between the place of origin of the author's sources and that of the book's final edition. Thus some of the sources would have originated in the archives of the royal court (e.g., 1Ki 4; 9–11) or the temple (1Ki 5–8). Edwin Thiele makes a strong case for the records of the separate incidents in the book as being kept in various prophetic centers throughout the northern and southern kingdoms.[17] Such prophetic records are cited as source material for Chronicles (e.g., 1Ch 29:29; 2Ch 9:29; 12:15; 13:22; 26:22). Again, the origin of 2 Kings 18:9–20:19 in the writings of Isaiah (Isa. 36–39) has been well demonstrated by E. J. Young.[18] If all this view is allowed, the author would have had a considerable body of spiritually evaluative material at his disposal. The two exilic appendixes could have originated in Jerusalem or, more probably, in Babylon.

The origin of the basic collection itself would clearly be Jerusalem. The book gives the impression of having been written by an eyewitness to those climactic events closing the checkered histories of Israel and Judah, those dramatic affairs providing the occasion and purpose of the book. Contemplating the tragedy's taking place before his very eyes, the author sets forth an accurate record of the events of his own day and those that had transpired since the glorious days of the Solomonic Era. As such a record, Kings forms a sequel to Samuel.[19]

Kings is, however, more than a chronicle of events. Masterly selecting his sources and utilizing his own experiential knowledge, the author writes to demonstrate conclusively to his readers both the necessity of the believer's keeping his covenantal obligations before God and the history of those people most responsible for leading God's people in their stewardship of the divine economy: Israel's kings and prophets. Hence

16. G. R. Driver, *An Introduction to the Literature of the Old Testament* (Edinburgh: T&T Clark, 1902), 199.

17. Edwin R. Thiele, *The Mysterious Numbers of the Hebrew Kings* (Grand Rapids: Eerdmans, 1965), 174–91.

18. E. J. Young, *The Book of Isaiah* (Grand Rapids: Eerdmans, 1974), 2:556–65.

19. For the relation of Kings to the so-called succession narrative, among the vast literature on the subject see the standard introductions (e.g., Longman and Dillard, *Introduction*, 155) and commentaries (e.g., P. K. McCarter Jr., *II Samuel* [AB; Garden City, N.Y.: Doubleday, 1984], 9–16); see Overview, 1 Kings 1–11.

Kings everywhere bears the twin marks of redemptive history and personal accountability.[20] Key verses include 1 Kings 2:2–5; 8:20, 23–26, 66; 9:4–9; 11:36–39; 2 Kings 8:19; 17:7–23; 21:10–15; 24:1–4, 20. It should be noted, however, that even though the author wrote with a basic philosophy of history, the resultant presentation is not necessarily so interpretative as to diminish the verity of the events and details he narrates. The credibility of the content of both the sources and the author's interpretative use of them are guaranteed by divine inspiration.[21]

4. LITERARY FORM

The nature of the theme and subject matter of Kings makes any discussion of literary style difficult. Nevertheless, certain stylistic features are observable.

The author tended to write thematically and occasionally left his presentation out of chronological order.[22] Notable examples include: (1) Solomon's organization of his kingdom (1Ki 4), which is appended to the discussion of his wisdom in ch. 3 even though the majority of the details belong to a later period; (2) the full details relative to Solomon's building activities (5:1–7:12), which are included before discussing the vessels of the temple and the dedicatory service (7:13–8:66), all of which are recounted before any discussion of the Solomonic politico-socio-economic situation (chs. 9–11); (3) a discussion of later happenings at Jeroboam's newly erected altar (ch. 13), followed by other incidents in Jeroboam's life (14:1–20), immediately after a notice of the building of the rival cult center (12:25–33) but before the author returns to Rehoboam (12:1–24; 14:21–31); (4) the placing together of the bulk of the material relative to the prophetic ministries of Elijah and Elisha into two major groups (1Ki 17–19; 2Ki 1:1–8:15); (5) a discussion of later happenings in Samaria appended to the account of its fall (2Ki 17); (6) the detailing of the most outstanding example of Hezekiah's trust in God (18:7b–19:37) before discussing the details relative to Hezekiah's sickness and recovery and the visit of Merodach-Baladan's embassy (ch. 20); and (7) the details relative to the death of Sennacherib (19:36–37) with the discussion of Sennacherib's western campaign in Judah (18:13–19:36).

When it comes to the presentation of the historical data relative to the history of the divided kingdom, the author rather consistently used the following order: (1) an introductory statement concerning

---

20. Although Chronicles covers much of the same material as Kings, significant differences in perspective are noticeable. Thus the chronicler is more focused on the importance of the Law, with its attendant Levitical procedures and requirements, and worship observances, especially as related to both the history of the southern kingdom and the situation of the new postexilic community. In keeping with this perspective, in some cases events that occur with little or no comment in Kings receive special explanation or comment in Chronicles (e.g., cf. 1Ki 15:23–24 with 2Ch 16:12–14 [cf. vv.7–10]; 2Ki 15:4–7 with 2Ch 26:16–23).

    Significant omissions of material found in Kings may also be noted, such as Solomon's contest for the Davidic throne (1Ki 1–2); Solomon's accruing of foreign wives, with the resultant expansion of idolatry in Israel (1Ki 11); and accounts dealing with Elijah and Elisha, which occupy much of 1 Kings 17–19 and 2 Kings 2–8, 13.

21. See further R. E. Clements, *One Hundred Years of Old Testament Interpretation* (Philadelphia: Westminster, 1976), 47–48; W. Barclay, ed., *The Bible and History* (Nashville: Abingdon, 1968), 13–15.

22. "Author" is used here without the technical distinction between the real and implied author. For details, see G. Osborne, *The Hermeneutical Spiral* (Downers Grove, Ill.: InterVarsity Press, 1991), 154–55.

the accession of the king, normally synchronized with the reign of the corresponding king in the other kingdom; (2) the biographical details—including for the kings of the southern kingdom a statement of the age of the king at his accession, the length of his reign, the name of the queen mother, and a spiritual evaluation of his reign; and involving for the northern kingdom a statement as to the capital city of the king, the length of his reign, and an indication as to his character; (3) a selective record of the king's reign, followed by a concluding formula that mentions a source in which further facts regarding the king's reign may be found, a statement of his death and burial, and an indication of his successor. Outstanding passages exemplifying the full-blown formula are 2 Kings 13:1–9, regarding Jehoahaz of Israel, and 2 Kings 15:1–7, regarding Azariah of Judah.

Arising from the author's attempt to recount the history of the two kingdoms simultaneously, the record is arranged so as to give the full account of one king or dynasty before rehearsing the story of the contemporary activities in the corresponding kingdom. Within this general framework, the author attempts faithfully to relate the facts as he has learned them. In accordance with the source material, however, he often reproduces prophetic pronouncements (with nearly every chapter from 1 Kings 11 to 2 Kings 22 containing prophetic material), poetic utterances (e.g., 1Ki 22:17; 2Ki 19:21–28), and proverbial wisdom (e.g., 1Ki 3:16–28; 20:11; 2Ki 14:9). The total work is marked by a lively style that may best be termed "historical narrative."[23]

Because the author conveys the data in this manner, people who read Kings are well advised to become acquainted with the basic features of narrative genre. This task will involve grasping such distinctions as the narrator (the one who tells the story), the author, whether the real author (the person who wrote the text) or the implied author (the impression the writer leaves of himself through the text), and the reader, whether the implied reader (the person or group the author has in mind in writing the literary piece) or the real reader (the one who actually reads the work). Because the author of Kings freely drew on source material from various places and over a span of several hundred years, he relied heavily on the point of view of individual narrators. The intended effect of the whole is to give readers not only an orderly account of Israel's rise and fall but also the reasons for its checkered history.

Although Kings clearly reports historical information, it also contains prophetic material. Not only are there accounts of the deeds of several prophets but also of many of their oracles.[24] Accordingly, some familiarity with the fine points of prophetic genre is also helpful in understanding Kings.[25]

Important, too, is an understanding of the ways a given account may be structured. This understanding involves recognizing the common signals attendant to unit demarcation within the narrative, such as opening and closing formulae, bracketing, and hinging techniques, as well as the use of distinguishing words, phraseology, or themes to stitch the individual parts of the narrative together. A knowledge of various literary procedures used in providing symmetrical organization within the subunits is also helpful. Walsh calls attention to three prominent types of organization in Kings: (1) two or more parallel sequences

---

23. For a helpful discussion of this term, see Howard, *Introduction to the Old Testament Historical Books*, 23–58.
24. House (*1, 2 Kings*, 57) suggests, "In many ways, it is probably most accurate to call 1, 2 Kings 'prophetic narrative.'"
25. See R. D. Patterson, "Old Testament Prophecy," in *A Complete Literary Guide to the Bible*, ed. L. Ryken and T. Longman III (Grand Rapids: Zondervan, 1993), 296–309; "Prophecy in the Old Testament," in *Dictionary of Biblical Imagery*, ed. L. Ryken, J. C. Wilhoit, and T. Longman III (Downers Grove, Ill.: InterVarsity Press, 1998), 668–70.

(ABCA'B'C'), (2) concentric symmetry (ABCB'A'), and (3) chiastic symmetry (ABCC'B'A').[26] Of still further importance to a literary appreciation of Kings is some knowledge of such narrative features as plot, characterization, and point of view.[27]

Plot usually revolves around conflict and its resolution. "The beginning of a story, with its introduction of conflict, thus pushes us through the middle toward the end, when conflict is resolved."[28] How the author portrays his characters and works them into his overall presentation is significant. In the case of Kings it often underlines the emphasis the author desires to make in a particular pericope. The way the author presents the data of the narrative affects the reader's understanding of the writer's purpose and viewpoint in recording or writing the material. As noted above, the author of Kings has relied a great deal on individual narrators in many places, while assuming the position of narrator himself for events in his own time. "In 1, 2 Kings, as in most Old Testament narratives, the narrator appears to be omniscient.... Readers are thereby offered a vantage point even greater than that enjoyed by the story's characters."[29]

Knowledge of the author's point of view is further gained by noting several stylistic devices that disclose the emphases he intends to make. These devices include repetition of information or speeches, wordplay (such as plays on meaning and sound) intended to give double meaning to verbal expression, and, above all, dialogue. Indeed, the recorded dialogue often becomes the focal point of the author's intention. As Alter remarks, biblical writers are "often less concerned with actions in themselves than with how [an] individual character responds to actions or produces them; and direct speech is made the chief instrument for revealing the varied and at times nuanced relations of the personages to the actions in which they are implicated."[30]

Thus, while long sections of Kings are properly devoted to historical narrative chronicling such elements as wars, political intrigues, and religious and social practices, the author has provided his readers with several means of understanding his (and the Divine Author's) evaluation of them. Accounts of the lives and works of the prophets, as well as special attention to dialogue and the author's stylistic devices, help the reader to appreciate not only the author's point of view and purposes but also encourage the reader to react in a proper and perhaps life-changing manner.

5. THEOLOGICAL VALUES

Because Kings chronicles Israel's spiritual odyssey, it enables us to glean something of the author's theological outlook. The work's main theological interest is the relationship of a sovereign God to a responsible people, Israel. In striking such a balance, the author of Kings draws particular attention to the Mosaic and Davidic covenants (e.g., 1Ki 8:20–26; 2Ki 18:5–6; 23:25). Indeed, the redemptive history and theologi-

---

26. Jerome T. Walsh, *1 Kings* (Berit Olam; Collegeville, Minn.: Liturgical, 1996), xiv; among many helpful sources dealing with narrative style, one may note R. Alter, *The Art of Biblical Narrative* (New York: Basic, 1981); L. Ryken, *Words of Delight* (Grand Rapids: Baker, 1987), 35–156; T. Longman III, "Biblical Narrative," in *Complete Literary Guide*, 69–79; Osborne, *Hermeneutical Spiral*, 153–73; and House, *1, 2 Kings*, 55–68.
27. For a concise discussion of these features, see T. Longman III, *Literary Approaches to Biblical Interpretation* (Grand Rapids: Zondervan, 1987), 87–94.
28. Ibid., 93.
29. House, *1, 2 Kings*, 67.
30. Alter, *Art of Biblical Narrative*, 66.

cal perspective of Kings are largely developed through David and through Israel's appropriation of God's blessing in accordance with her compliance with the standards of the Torah (cf. 1Ki 2:4–5). Important also is the promise of land guaranteed in the Abrahamic and Davidic covenants (e.g., 1Ki 8:22–53; 18:36; 2Ki 13:23; cf. 1Ki 4:20–21, 24).

From the first chapter to the last, God is seen in sovereign control of the world's governments. He alone is the living God (1Ki 8:60; 17:1, 12; 18:15, 39; 22:14; 2Ki 2:6, 14; 5:16; 19:15–19), who is the Creator (2Ki 19:15) and Provider of life (1Ki 17:3–24; 19:1–8). Both transcendent (1Ki 8:27; 2Ki 2:1–12; 19:15) and immanent (1Ki 9:3), he is the omnipresent (1Ki 8:27), omnipotent (1Ki 8:42; 18:38; 2Ki 17:36), and omniscient God (1Ki 3:9, 28; 4:29–34; 5:7, 12; 10:24; 2Ki 19:27), to whom the angels minister (1Ki 13:18; 19:5; 22:19–23; 2Ki 1:15; 19:15) and with whom all the world has to do (1Ki 8:41–43; 2Ki 19:19). A God of love (1Ki 10:9) and goodness (1Ki 8:66; 2Ki 20:19), he is also a God of justice and righteousness (1Ki 2:32–33, 44; 8:31–53; 9:6–9; 10:9; 11:11–13; 13:21–32; 15:29–30; 16:1–4, 12–13, 18–19; 21:19–29; 2Ki 17:18–23; 21:10–15; 24:1–4). The reader of Kings meets God's grace at nearly every turn in its narrative (e.g., 1Ki 11:9–13; 2Ki 20:1–11).[31]

Although human beings are sinners (1Ki 8:46; 11:4; 2Ki 17:14–18), God is the author of redemption (1Ki 8:51) and graciously forgives those who humble themselves before him (1Ki 8:33–40, 46–50; 21:27–29; 2Ki 22:11, 19–20). Moreover, he hears and answers prayer (1Ki 8:28–30, 44–53; 13:6; 17:20–22; 18:36–38; 2Ki 2:14; 4:33–37; 6:17–20; 13:4–5; 19:14–19; 20:2–6) and faithfully keeps his promises (1Ki 8:20, 23–26, 56; 11:12–13, 32, 34; 16:34; 17:14–16; 2Ki 1:17; 7:16–20; 8:19; 9:36–37; 10:10, 17; 13:23; 15:12; 24:13). Human beings ought to worship him (1Ki 3:15; 8:12–66; 9:25; 2Ki 17:28) and follow him completely (1Ki 13:8–26; 2Ki 5:15–16; 11:17; 17:35–39; 20:3). Accordingly, great prominence is given to the temple and its institutions (1Ki 6–8; 2Ki 12:4–16; 21:7; 22:3–7; 23:1–3, 21–23; 24:13; 25:13–17). The believers should make God's inviolable Word and standards (1Ki 16:34; 21:3–4; 2Ki 14:6; 18:12) the center of their lives (1Ki 2:3–4; 6:11–13; 8:58; 9:4; 11:10–11, 38; 2Ki 8:2; 17:37–39; 18:5–6; 21:8; 22:11; 23:1–25) and live so as to be concerned for God's sacred reputation (1Ki 8:60; 2Ki 2:23–25; 5:8; 19:19).

God has revealed himself in many ways (1Ki 3:5–15; 8:10–12; 9:2–9; 11:11–13), but especially to Israel (1Ki 8:51–53, 66; 2Ki 17:35–39; 21:8–9). To that nation he had granted great covenantal promises (2Ki 13:23), especially through David, his servant (1Ki 2:33, 45; 3:6, 14; 6:12–13; 8:20, 23–26, 66; 11:32–39; 15:4–5; 2Ki 8:19; 19:20–37). Although God redeemed Israel (1Ki 8:51; 2Ki 17:7) and patiently guided, cared for, and bore with his people, they rejected him despite his repeated warnings (2Ki 17:7–23; 21:10–15).

Because of Israel's unique relationship to God, the sin of idolatry is severely denounced (1Ki 11:4–2Ki 24:19 *passim*). On the positive side, great place is accorded to prophecy and its fulfillment (1Ki 11:29–39; 12:22–24; 13:1–14:20; 16:1–4, 7, 12–13; 20:22, 28, 35–43; 22:7–38; 2Ki 1:1–2:11, 19–25; 3:11–20; 8:7–15; 9:6–10; 13:14–21; 14:25–27; 17:13, 23; 19:20–37; 20:1–21; 21:10–15; 22:14–20).

Thus Kings does not merely record historical events but represents redemptive and teleological history built around the twin themes of divine sovereignty and human responsibility, particularly as they were operative through God's covenantal people, Israel.

31. J. G. McConville (*Grace in the End* [Grand Rapids: Zondervan, 1993], 134–39) observes that proper "Deuteronomic Theology," rather than being solely based on pure legalism, reaches a climax that may be viewed as "grace in the end."

6. CANONICITY

The canonicity of Kings has never been questioned. From the outset it was regarded by the Hebrews as canonical and, because it was considered to be written by Jeremiah, was placed among the former prophets. Moreover, it was always valued as being foundational for the messages of the canonical prophets.

Due to its length, Kings appears in the LXX as two books called the "Third" and "Fourth" books of "Kingdoms," being the sequel to Samuel, whose books are titled "First" and "Second Kingdoms." The LXX's arrangement was followed by the Latin Vulgate, which titled Kings *Liber Regum Tertius et Quartus*. Josephus's limitation of the Hebrew canon to twenty-four books (*Ag. Ap.* 1.8) would seem to verify the traditional scheme of canonical arrangement, with Lamentations perhaps included with Jeremiah and Ruth with Judges. If so, Kings was clearly recognized as canonical by the first century AD. Its authoritative recognition and employment by Jesus and the NT writers renders out of the question any doubt concerning its canonical status by that time.

7. TEXT

The Hebrew text of Kings has long been of scholarly interest—particularly regarding the relation of the MT to the LXX. It has usually been conceded that while the MT is generally reliable, numerous textual difficulties exist so that the LXX is a valuable tool in ascertaining the correct Hebrew text. The fragments of Kings from Qumran that have thus far been published tend to indicate a text "significantly divergent from the traditional Masoretic Text to suggest that the text of Kings was pluriform in antiquity, just as the text of Samuel has been demonstrated to be."[32] Thus some fragments agree with the LXX, others follow the MT, and still others are unique to Qumran.

8. CHRONOLOGY

Because the OT writers utilized only relative reference points in affixing their time-sequence structure, an absolute dating of a given event on the basis of purely OT data is largely impossible. Moreover, the complexity of methodology and lack of uniformity in determining dated events greatly hampers the quest for precision. Thus in some eras Israel began its new year in the fall; in others, in the spring. In some cases the nonaccession-year system, by which the remaining days of a calendar year in which a king was crowned were counted as that king's first year, was used; in others, the accession-year reckoning was employed, in which case the king's first year would begin with the first day of the calendar year following his inauguration. Still further, an adding of the reign of years of all the Judean kings yields too high a total for the period between Solomon and the fall of Jerusalem.

Accordingly, recourse must be made to secular dates in the ancient Near East that have been established with greater precision. The Canon of Ptolemy (the Greek geographer and astronomer of Egypt, ca. AD 70–161) has been particularly helpful. Ptolemy made a list of the rulers of Babylon from 747 BC until his own day. As well, the discovery of the ancient Assyrian *limmu*, or eponym, lists, by which a given year was named for the person who occupied the office of *limmu*, has also been of great importance. These lists also

32. M. Abegg Jr., P. Flint, and E. Ulrich, *The Dead Sea Scrolls Bible* (San Francisco: Harper, 1999), 260.

often mention important historical or astronomical details, such as an eclipse of the moon or sun. One such solar eclipse has been scientifically computed to have occurred on 15 June 763 BC. The dating of the whole list can therefore be affixed, resulting in a reliable series of dates for the period 892–648 BC. Interestingly, the accession year of Sargon II of Assyria as king over Babylon in both the eponym lists and the Ptolemaic Canon comes out to 709 BC, thus providing a crosscheck on the reliability of these two external sources. Dates for the period before 892 BC must be sought from Mesopotamian data drawn from the various Assyrian and Babylonian lists and synchronous histories (detailing contacts between Assyrian and Babylonian kings) and from Egyptian sources. Dates for the period after 648 BC can be gleaned both from Ptolemy's canon and from the annals of the later Babylonian kings. This latter source, which has been made available through the efforts of D. J. Wiseman, yields a series of precise dates within the period of 626–566 BC.[33]

These sources provide a fairly accurate time sequence for dating the events of the ancient Near East, particularly so for the period represented by Kings (971–566 BC); therefore, where OT events are actually mentioned in external records they may be assigned precise dates. Since several events are common both to Kings and the external sources, the general time framework of much of the period from Solomon to the fall of Jerusalem can be acknowledged as rather well established.

Nevertheless, several problems remain as difficulties that have been resolved in various ways by OT scholars, depending largely on their point of view with regard to harmonizing the biblical dates with the external sources. Some scholars (e.g., Jules Oppert) have attempted to harmonize the Assyrian chronology with the biblical data. Oppert claimed to have discovered a forty-seven-year gap in the Assyrian record that he felt accounted for the variation between the Assyrian and biblical dates. Unfortunately the data he based his claim on have not stood the test of historical verification.

Other scholars have aimed at the harmonization of the biblical events with the established Assyrian dates. This method usually accounts for the seemingly longer period in the OT by assuming a number of coregencies, the overlapping reigns thus reducing considerably the total number of years for the whole series in Kings to a figure that is in line with the Assyrian total. Although this position has generally prevailed among biblical scholars of all theological persuasions, it has yielded varying results; and a number of competing systems have appeared. German scholars have followed largely the system worked out by Begrich as modified by Jepsen, which arrives at its dates by presuming a shift in the month of the new year in Israel and a change from the nonaccession-year scheme to the accession-year system when the Judean states became Assyrian vassals.[34] Andersen (followed with variations by S. Hermann), however, holds that the calendar year always began in the fall, that the nonaccession-year system was consistently employed by both Israel and Judah, and that coregencies and rival kingdoms were not included in reckoning a king's total years.[35]

English writers usually reflect either the system of Edwin R. Thiele or W. F. Albright. The former achieves his dates by a complicated process of calendrical change, variation in the employment of

---

33. D. J. Wiseman, *Chronicles of Chaldaean Kings* (London: British Museum, 1956).

34. Joachim Begrich, *Die Chronologie der Könige von Israel und die Quellen des Rahmens der Königsbucher* (Tübingen: Univ. of Tübingen Press, 1929); A. Jepsen and R. Hanhart, *Untersuchungen zur Israelitischjüdischen Chronologie* (Berlin: de Gruyter, 1964).

35. K. T. Andersen, "Die Chronologie der Könige von Israel und Judah," *ST* 23 (1969): 67–112.

accession-year versus nonaccession-year systems between and within the Judean states, overlapping coregencies, and, where necessary, outright emendation of the biblical text. Albright, who was progressively impressed by the importance of the Lucianic recension of the LXX for determining the chronology of Kings, arrives at his conclusions through still freer use of minor revision of the MT.

Still others (e.g., George Smith) have decided that a correlation between the Assyrian and Hebrew dates is unnecessary, each being viewed as "correct" according to its own system. Smith suggests that there may be errors in the Assyrian annalistic accounts and that often incorrect and needless reconciliations between Assyrian and biblical events have been made.[36] Thus he denies that the Ahabu and Iaua mentioned in the Assyrian records have anything to do with Ahab and Jehu and that Israel had any connection either with the famous Battle of Qarqar (853 BC) or with Assyria at all until the time of Menahem and Tiglath-pileser in the late eighth century BC. Smith's suggestion allows the number of years allotted to a given king in the Hebrew account to be taken more literally, without recourse to any compressed total of years as represented by the coregency theories. But the problem of too many years for the period covered by Kings remains for this theory; and new difficulties arise, such as the need for finding two Hazaels in Syria (if the biblical data are to square with known dates for Syrian kings) and the postulation of errors in the otherwise usually accurate Assyrian records (e.g., in the case of Menahem) in order to deny seemingly obvious historical correlations. The theory has not found many adherents.[37]

The position taken here follows basically that of J. Barton Payne, which, though representing a modification of the coregency theory, maintains a high regard for the MT and refuses to resort to conjectural emendations.[38] Payne affirms that the nonaccession-year dating system was used in the northern kingdom (by which the year of a king's enthronement is considered as both his first year and the last year of his predecessor) and that the new year always began in the spring. The southern kingdom, however, began its year in the fall and used the accession-year system until 848 BC, when, under the influence of Athaliah, Jehoram changed Judah to the nonaccession system. Both kingdoms utilized the accession-year system from the early eighth century BC, probably under the influence of Assyria.

Payne supplies the following guidelines in computing the regnal years of the kings:

> The following interpretative bases concern coregencies ... during the divided kingdom period. (a) The years of coregency are regularly included in the totals for the respective reigns.... (b) The Book of Kings records each ruler in a sequence determined by the beginning of sole reign rather than of coregency.... (c) Coregencies commence with the first rather than accession years.[39]

Admittedly several difficulties remain, notably in the last half of the eighth century BC. On the whole, however, the conclusions reached by Payne seem satisfactory and best able to account for the various his-

---

36. G. A. Smith, *The Assyrian Eponym Canon* (London: Harper & Bros., 1875).
37. For the problem of the identification of Jehu with Iaua, see the objections of P. K. McCarter ("Yaw, Son of Omri: A Philological Note on Israelite Chronology," *BASOR* 216 [1974]: 5–7) and the answers of M. Weippert ("Jau[A] marHumri-Joram odor Jehu von Israel?" *VT* 28 [1978]: 113–18). Note the mediating position of E. R. Thiele ("An Additional Note on 'Yau, Son of Omri,'" *BASOR* 222 [1976]: 19–23).
38. J. Barton Payne, "Chronology of the Old Testament," in *ZPEB*, 1:829–45.
39. Ibid., 1:838.

torical and chronological data, hence it will be followed with but slight modification. The resultant dates for the kings of Israel and Judah follow:

	Northern Kingdom		Southern Kingdom	
First Dynasty	Jeroboam I	931–910	Rehoboam	931–914
	Nadab	910–909	Abijah	913–910
Second Dynasty	Baasha	909–886	Asa	909–868
	Elah	886–885		
	[Zimri]	885		
Third Dynasty	Omri	885–874		
	Ahab	874–853	*Jehoshaphat	872–847
	Ahaziah	853–852	*Jehoram	853–841
	Joram	852–841	Ahaziah	841
			Athaliah	841–835
Fourth Dynasty	Jehu	841–814	Joash	835–796
	Jehoahaz	814–798	*Amaziah	796–767
	*Jehoash	798–782	*Azariah	791–739
	*Jeroboam II	793–753		
	Zechariah	753		
Concluding Kings	Shallum	752	*Jotham	752–736
	Menahem	751–742		
	Pekahiah	741–740	*Ahaz	(743); 736–720
	Pekah	740–732		
	Hoshea	732/1–722	*Hezekiah	729–699
			Manasseh	698–643
			Amon	642–640
			Josiah	640–609
			Jehoahaz	609
			Jehoiakim	609–598
			Jehoiachin	598
			Zedekiah	597–586

* = coregency

For further details see the helpful bibliographies in John H. Hayes and J. Maxwell Miller, eds., *Israelite and Judean History* (London: SCM, 1977), 678–83; Payne, *ZPEB* 1:845; K. A. Kitchen and T. C. Mitchell, "Chronology of the Old Testament," *NBD*, 217–23; S. J. DeVries, "Chronology of the Old Testament," *IDB* 1:580–89.

9. BIBLIOGRAPHY

Commentaries and Histories

Bright, John. *A History of Israel.* 3rd ed. Philadelphia: Westminster, 1981.
Cohn, Robert L. *2 Kings.* Berit Olam. Collegeville, Minn.: Liturgical Press, 2000.
DeVries, Simon J. *1 Kings.* Word Biblical Commentary. Waco, Tex.: Word, 1985.
Dorsey, David A. *The Literary Structure of the Old Testament.* Grand Rapids: Baker, 1999.
Gray, John. *I & II Kings.* 2nd ed. Philadelphia: Westminster, 1970.
Hobbs, T. R. *2 Kings.* Word Biblical Commentary. Waco, Tex.: Word, 1985.
House, Paul R. *1, 2 Kings.* New American Commentary. Nashville: Broadman & Holman, 1995.
Jones, Gwilym H. *1 and 2 Kings.* 2 vols. Grand Rapids: Eerdmans, 1984.
Keil, C. F., and F. Delitzsch. *Biblical Commentary on the Old Testament: The Books of the Kings.* Grand Rapids: Eerdmans, 1954.
Montgomery, James A. *The Books of Kings.* International Critical Commentary. Edinburgh: T&T Clark, 1967.
Walsh, Jerome T. *1 Kings.* Berit Olam. Collegeville, Minn.: Liturgical, 1996.
Wiseman, D. J. *1 & 2 Kings.* Tyndale Old Testament Commentaries. Downers Grove, Ill.: InterVarsity, 1993.

Background Studies and Articles

Aharoni, Y., and M. Avi-Yonah, *The Macmillan Bible Atlas.* New York: Macmillan, 1968.
Alter, Robert. *The Art of Biblical Narrative.* New York: Basic, 1981.
Archer, Gleason. *Encyclopedia of Bible Difficulties.* Grand Rapids: Zondervan, 1982.
Bronner, L. *The Stories of Elijah and Elisha.* Leiden: Brill, 1968.
De Vaux, Roland. *Ancient Israel.* New York: McGraw-Hill, 1961.
Edersheim, Alfred. *Bible History.* 7 volumes. New York: Revell, 1885–1887.
Gordon, Cyrus. *Ugaritic Textbook.* Rome: Pontifical Biblical Institute, 1965.
Hallo, William W. "From Qarqar to Carchemish: Assyria and Israel in the Light of New Discoveries." *Biblical Archaeologist Reader* 2. Edited by D. N. Freedman and E. F. Campbell Jr. Garden City, N.Y.: Doubleday, 1964.
Hallo, William W., and W. K. Simpson. *The Ancient Near East: A History.* New York: Harcourt Brace Jovanovich, 1971.
Howard, D. M., Jr. *An Introduction to the Old Testament Historical Books.* Chicago: Moody Press, 1993.
Kitchen, K. A. *The Third Intermediate Period in Egypt.* Warminster: Aris & Phillips, 1973.
———. "How We Know When Solomon Ruled," *Biblical Archaeology Review* 27 (2001): 32–37, 58.
———. *On the Reliability of the Old Testament.* Grand Rapids: Eerdmans, 2003.
Long, Burke O. "Historical Narrative and the Fictionalizing Imagination." *Vetus Testamentum* 35 (1985): 405–16.
Longman, Tremper III, and Raymond B. Dillard. *An Introduction to the Old Testament.* 2nd ed. Grand Rapids: Zondervan, 2006.
Luckenbill, Daniel David. *Ancient Records of Assyria and Babylonia.* 2 vols. Chicago: University of Chicago Press, 1926–1927.
Stigers, H. G. "Temple." *Zondervan Pictorial Encyclopedia of the Bible* (Grand Rapids: Zondervan, 1976), 5:622–66.
Thiele, Edwin R. *The Mysterious Numbers of the Hebrew Kings.* Grand Rapids: Eerdmans, 1965.
Unger, M. *Archaeology and the Old Testament.* Grand Rapids: Zondervan, 1954.
Ussishkin, David. "King Solomon's Palaces." *Biblical Archaeologist* 36 (1973): 78–105.
Wiseman, D. J. *Chronicles of Chaldaean Kings.* London: British Museum, 1956.
———. "'Is It Peace?'—Covenant and Diplomacy." *Vetus Testamentum* 32 (1982): 311–26.
Wood, Leon J. *Israel's United Monarchy.* Grand Rapids: Baker, 1979.
Young, E. J. *The Book of Isaiah.* 3 vols. Grand Rapids: Eerdmans, 1974.

10. OUTLINE

- I. United Kingdom (1:1–11:43)
  - A. The Rise of Solomon (1:1–2:46)
    - 1. His Accession to the Throne (1:1–2:11)
      - a. Adonijah's plot to seize the crown (1:1–10)
        - i. David's feebleness (1:1–4)
        - ii. Adonijah's attempted coup d'état (1:5–10)
      - b. The counterplan of Nathan (1:11–31)
      - c. Solomon's anointing (1:32–40)
      - d. Adonijah's submission (1:41–53)
      - e. David's charge to Solomon (2:1–11)
    - 2. His Establishment of the Kingdom (2:12–46)
      - a. His assumption to the throne (2:12)
      - b. Adonijah's further scheme and execution (2:13–25)
      - c. The deposition of Abiathar and execution of Joab (2:26–34)
      - d. The elevation of Benaiah and Zadok (2:35)
      - e. The execution of Shimei (2:36–46)
  - B. Solomon's Love for the Lord—God's Approval (3:1–28)
    - 1. The Marriage of Solomon to Pharaoh's Daughter: Her Temporary Residence in the City of David (3:1)
    - 2. Worship at Gibeon (3:2–4)
    - 3. The Appearance of the Lord to Solomon (3:5–15)
      - a. Solomon's prayer for wisdom (3:5–9)
      - b. God's response (3:10–15)
    - 4. Solomon's Wisdom Demonstrated—Public Approval (3:16–28)
  - C. The Glories of Solomon's Reign (4:1–34[4:1–5:14])
    - 1. The Organization of His Kingdom: His Officials (4:1–19)
    - 2. His Royal Splendor (4:20–28[4:20–5:8])
    - 3. His Superior Wisdom (4:29–34[5:9–14])
  - D. Preparations for the Building of the Temple (5:1–18[5:15–32])
    - 1. Solomon's League with Hiram of Tyre (5:1–12[5:15–26])
    - 2. Solomon's Labor Force (5:13–18[5:27–32])
  - E. The Building and Dedication of the Temple (6:1–9:9)
    - 1. The Building of the Temple (6:1–38)
      - a. The outer structure (6:1–14)
      - b. The inner structure (6:15–35)
      - c. The court (6:36)
      - d. The conclusion (6:37–38)
    - 2. Solomon's Other Structures (7:1–12)

- 3. The Vessels of the Temple (7:13–51)
  - a. Hiram the craftsman (7:13–14)
  - b. The two bronze pillars (7:15–22)
  - c. The bronze Sea (7:23–26)
  - d. The ten bronze basins and their stands (7:27–39)
  - e. Summary of Hiram's bronze work (7:40–47)
  - f. The furnishings of the temple (7:48–50)
  - g. The treasures of the temple (7:51)
- 4. The Dedication of the Temple (8:1–66)
  - a. Moving the ark and the tabernacle to the temple (8:1–11)
  - b. Solomon's address (8:12–21)
  - c. Solomon's sevenfold prayer of dedication (8:22–53)
    - i. The theme of the prayer (8:22–30)
    - ii. Seven specific requests (8:31–53)
  - d. Solomon's benediction (8:54–61)
  - e. Solomon's dedicatory sacrifice (8:62–66)
- 5. The Lord's Second Appearance to Solomon (9:1–9)

D'. Events After, but Relating to, the Building of the Temple (9:10–25)
- 1. The Business Relations between Solomon and Hiram (9:10–14)
- 2. Solomon's Labor Force (9:15–23)
- 3. Pharaoh's Daughter Moves to Her Permanent Quarters (9:24)
- 4. Solomon Now Offers Sacrifices at the Temple in Jerusalem (9:25)

C'. The Glories of Solomon's Reign (9:26–10:29)
- 1. Solomon's Commercial Activities (9:26–28)
- 2. The Visit of the Queen of Sheba (10:1–13)
- 3. The Wonders of the Solomonic Era (10:14–29)

B'. Solomon's Love for Pagan Wives—God's Disapproval (11:1–13)
- 1. Solomon's Many Wives (11:1–3)
- 2. Solomon's Turning after Idols (11:4–10)
- 3. God's Announcement of Punishment (11:11–13)

A'. The Decline of Solomon (11:14–43)
- 1. The Rise of Adversaries (11:14–40)
  - a. Hadad the Edomite (11:14–22)
  - b. Rezon of Damascus (11:23–25)
  - c. Jeroboam (11:26–40)
- 2. Solomon's Death and the Accession of Rehoboam (11:41–43)

II. The Divided Kingdom (1Ki 12:1–2Ki 17:41)

A. The Division of the Nation (1Ki 12:1–24)

B. The Reign of Jeroboam in the Northern Kingdom (12:25–14:20)
- 1. The Establishment of Jeroboam's Religion (12:25–32)

2. The Condemnation of Jeroboam's Religion (12:33–13:34)
 a. Jeroboam and the man of god (12:33–13:10)
 b. The man of God and the old prophet (13:11–34)
3. The Consequences of Jeroboam's Religion (14:1–18)
4. Concluding Remarks concerning Jeroboam's Reign (14:19–20)

C. The Early Successors to Rehoboam and Jeroboam (14:21–16:14)
1. The Reign of Rehoboam in the Southern Kingdom (14:21–31)
2. The Reign of Abijah in the Southern Kingdom (15:1–8)
3. The Reign of Asa in the Southern Kingdom (15:9–24)
4. The Reign of Nadab in the Northern Kingdom (15:25–31)
5. The Second Dynasty in Israel (15:32–16:14)
 a. Baasha (15:32–16:7)
 b. Elah (16:8–14)

D. The Era of the Third Dynasty (1Ki 16:15–2Ki 9:37)
1. Interregnum: Zimri and Tibni (1Ki 16:15–22)
2. The Reign of Omri in the Northern Kingdom (16:23–28)
3. The Reign of Ahab in the Northern Kingdom (16:29–22:40)
 a. Ahab's accession (16:29–34)
 b. The prophetic ministry of Elijah (17:1–19:21)
  i. Prologue: Elijah's call (17:1–6)
  ii. Development: Elijah's ministry at Zarephath (17:7–24)
  iii. Resolution: Elijah's contest on Mount Carmel (18:1–46)
   (a) Initiation: Elijah and Obadiah (18:1–15)
   (b) Climax: Elijah and the prophets of Baal (18:16–46)
  iv. Denouement: Elijah's retreat to Horeb (19:1–18)
  v. Epilogue: Elijah and the call of Elisha (19:19–21)
 c. Ahab and the Syro-Israelite campaigns (20:1–43)
  i. The Aramean crisis (20:1–12)
  ii. The Israelite triumph (20:13–34)
  iii. The prophet's rebuke (20:35–43)
 d. Ahab and the conscription of Naboth's vineyard (21:1–29)
 e. Ahab and the campaign for Ramoth Gilead (22:1–40)
  i. Preparations for Ramoth Gilead (22:1–28)
  ii. Closing details concerning Ahab (22:29–40)
4. The Reign of Jehoshaphat in the Southern Kingdom (22:41–50)
5. The Reign of Ahaziah in the Northern Kingdom (1Ki 22:51–2Ki 1:18)
6. The Prophetic Ministry of Elisha in the Era of Jehoram of the Northern Kingdom (2Ki 2:1–9:37)
 a. Prelude: prophetic transition (2:1–25)
 b. Theme: the ministry of Elisha (3:1–8:15)

i. The Moabite campaign (3:1–27)
ii. Various miracles in the northern kingdom (4:1–44)
(a) Elisha and the widow's oil (4:1–7)
(b) Elisha and the lady of Shunem (4:8–37)
(c) Elisha and the supplying of food (4:38–44)
iii. The Aramean crisis (5:1–8:6)
(a) Elisha, Naaman, and Gehazi (5:1–27)
(b) Elisha's further miracle at the Jordan (6:1–7)
(c) The campaign for Samaria (6:8–7:20)
(d) A further note concerning Gehazi (8:1–6)
iv. The anointing of Hazael (8:7–15)
c. Interlude: the reigns of Jehoram and Ahaziah of the southern kingdom (8:16–29)
d. Postlude: the anointing of Jehu and the death of Jehoram of the northern kingdom (9:1–37)
i. Elisha's anointing of Jehu (9:1–10)
ii. Jehu's coup d' état (9:11–37)
E. The Era of the Fourth Dynasty (10:1–15:12)
1. The Reign of Jehu in the Northern Kingdom (10:1–36)
2. The Reign of Athaliah in the Southern Kingdom (11:1–20)
3. The Reign of Joash in the Southern Kingdom (11:21–12:21 [12:1–22])
4. The Reign of Jehoahaz in the Northern Kingdom (13:1–9)
5. The Reign of Jehoash in the Northern Kingdom (13:10–25)
6. The Reign of Amaziah in the Southern Kingdom (14:1–22)
7. The Reign of Jeroboam II in the Northern Kingdom (14:23–29)
8. The Reign of Uzziah in the Southern Kingdom (15:1–7)
9. The Reign of Zechariah in the Northern Kingdom (15:8–12)
F. The Era of the Decline and Fall of the Northern Kingdom (15:13–17:41)
1. The Reign of Shallum in the Northern Kingdom (15:13–15)
2. The Reign of Menahem in the Northern Kingdom (15:16–22)
3. The Reign of Pekahiah in the Northern Kingdom (15:23–26)
4. The Reign of Pekah in the Northern Kingdom (15:27–31)
5. The Reign of Jotham in the Southern Kingdom (15:32–38)
6. The Reign of Ahaz in the Southern Kingdom (16:1–20)
7. The Reign of Hoshea in the Northern Kingdom (17:1–23)
8. The Repopulation of Samaria (17:24–41)
III. The Southern Kingdom (2Ki 18:1–25:30)
A. The Reign of Hezekiah (18:1–20:21)
1. Hezekiah's Accession and Early Deeds (18:1–12)
2. The Assyrian Invasion and Siege of Jerusalem (18:13–37)
3. Prophetic Encouragement amid the Continued Siege (19:1–13)

   4. Hezekiah's Prayer and Isaiah's Prophecy (19:14–37)
   5. Hezekiah's Sickness and Miraculous Recovery (20:1–11)
   6. Hezekiah and Merodach-Baladan's Embassy (20:12–21)

B. The Reign of Manasseh (21:1–18)

C. The Reign of Amon (21:19–26)

D. The Reign of Josiah (22:1–23:30)
   1. Josiah's Accession and Repair of the Temple (22:1–7)
   2. Josiah and the Book of the Law (22:8–20)
   3. Josiah's Further Reforms (23:1–23)
   4. Josiah's Latter Days (23:24–30)

E. The Last Days of Judah (23:31–25:21)
   1. The Reigns of Jehoahaz and Jehoiakim (23:31–24:7)
   2. The Reigns of Jehoiachin and Zedekiah (24:8–25:21)

F. Historical Appendices (25:22–30)
   1. Judah in Exile (25:22–26)
   2. The Later History of Jehoiachin (25:27–30)

Text and Exposition

I. THE UNITED KINGDOM (1:1–11:43)

OVERVIEW

The account of the reign of Solomon in chs. 1–11 demonstrates the faithfulness of God to the Davidic covenant (2Sa 7) in three respects:

1. Solomon as David's son now sits on his father's throne.
2. Solomon, while he follows God wholeheartedly, is greatly blessed, but when he departs from the Lord, God prepares to bring judgment.
3. Solomon builds the house of the Lord that David had wished to build.

Of these three matters, the events surrounding the building of the temple receive the major emphasis, as can be seen from two considerations: (1) The concentric symmetrical structure (shown below) of this section revolves around these events; (2) the amount of space (some two hundred verses) given to the preparation, building, and dedication of the temple, followed by further related comments, is far more than that allotted to any other subject. (Ninety-nine verses are allotted to the succession of Solomon, twenty-nine to his decline, seventy-eight to the glories of his reign [distributed around the account of the building of the temple].)

Solomon himself, on the occasion of his prayer of dedication of the temple (1Ki 8), refers to the faithfulness of God in fulfilling his promise to David by (1) giving him a son to succeed him, (2) allowing him to build the temple, and (3) recognizing the need for faithfulness on the part of David's successors (1Ki 8:17–25).

There have been several previous studies relating to the structure of this section of Kings. They include the following:

- K. I. Parker ("Repetition in 1 Kings 1–11," *JSOT* 42 [1988]: 19–27), who views chs. 1–2 and 11:14–43 as a frame around the two dreams of Solomon.
- M. Brettler ("The Structure of 1 Kings 1–11," *JSOT* 49 [1991]: 87–97) sees the structure as revolving around the pro-Solomon and anti-Solomon sections of 3:3–9:23 and 9:24–11:10, respectively.
- Amos Frisch ("Structure and Its Significance: The Narrative of Solomon's Reign [1 Kings 1–12:24]," *JSOT* 51 [1991]: 3–14) is similar to that suggested here, with the building and dedication of the temple as central; but he includes ch. 12 in his plan.
- Two authors exclude chs. 1–2 in their outline: Y. T. Radday ("Chiasm in Kings," *Linguistica Biblica* 31 [1974]: 52–57) and David A. Dorsey (*Literary Structure*). The former finds the focus in the building of the temple; the latter finds the climax in the dedication of the temple.

The following outline will help the reader visualize the plan of these chapters. The designations A/A', etc., are intended to draw attention to the parallel ideas found in the corresponding sections. The parallel items may be identical or similar in nature, or they may be contrastive. N. W. Lund (*Chiasmus in the New Testament* [Peabody, Mass.:

Hendrickson, 1992], 45–46) states that in a chiastic structure the center is always the turning point and often is the climax of the section. Dorsey, 17–18, points out that in a chiastic structure "the central unit generally functions as the turning point or climax or highlight of the piece."

A. The Rise of Solomon (1:1–2:46)
  B. Solomon's Love for the Lord—God's Approval (3:1–26)
    C. The Glories of Solomon's Reign (4:1–34[4:1–5:14])
      D. Preparations for the Building of the Temple (5:1–18[5:15–32])
        E. The Building and Dedication of the Temple (6:1–9:9)
      D'. Events after, but Related to, the Building of the Temple (9:10–25)
    C'. The Glories of Solomon's Reign (9:26–10:29)
  B'. Solomon's Love for Pagan Wives—God's Disapproval (11:1–13)
A'. The Decline of Solomon (11:14–43)

These chapters revolve around the building and dedication of the temple. It is helpful to note the following correspondences:

A/A': The Rise/Decline of Solomon

i. A: God chooses him; A': God disapproves him

ii. A: God gives him victory over his adversaries; A': God strengthens his adversaries

iii. A: David's charge to Solomon; A': Ahijah's charge to Jeroboam

B/B': Solomon's love for the Lord/Solomon's love for pagan wives

i. B: Right priorities: he loves God; B': Wrong priorities: he loves pagan wives

ii. B: He seeks wisdom from God; B': He participates in the worship of idols

iii. B: God promises blessing; B': God announces punishment

C/C': The glories of Solomon's reign

Both sections demonstrate in different ways his fame, wisdom, honor, and wealth.

D/D': Events related to the building of the temple

i. Hiram's help and remuneration is recounted in both sections

ii. Solomon's conscript labor program is described in both sections

Note that the correspondences may be parallel or contrastive. In the present case the A/A' and B/B' elements are contrastive. The C/C' and D/D' elements are parallel. Though perhaps most commonly in this type of structure the correspondences are of the same kind, either parallel or contrastive, this is not the only instance of a mixture. See, e.g., the structure of Isaiah 40–48 as presented in Dorsey, 226.

Three other correspondences are noteworthy:

1. The two appearances of the Lord to Solomon, first at Gibeon (3:5–14) before the building of the temple, then again in 9:1–9, after the completion of the temple. Note that in 6:11–14 God also spoke to Solomon, apparently through a prophet, because in 11:9 he says that he had appeared twice to Solomon.
2. The two references to the daughter of Pharaoh. In 3:1 he houses her in the city of David until the completion of the temple, his palace, and the wall around the city. In 9:24–25, after the completion of the temple, he moves her into her permanent quarters.
3. In ch. 3 he worships the Lord at the temporary worship site, Gibeon, and 9:25 pointedly recounts his regular worship three times a year at the temple he had built.

A. The Rise of Solomon (1:1–2:46)

1. His Accession to the Throne (1:1–2:11)

a. Adonijah's plot to seize the crown (1:1–10)

OVERVIEW

Solomon is God's choice to be king (2Sa 12:24–25), and though he is opposed by powerful enemies, God establishes him on the throne. God's support of Solomon here to the detriment of his opponents stands in vivid contrast to the way he strengthened Solomon's enemies in ch. 11. God's dealings with Solomon reflect his promise (and warning) in 2 Samuel 7:14–16.

At issue at the outset of the book is the question as to which of David's sons is to succeed him. Two complicating factors are involved: (1) David's feebleness and apparent *laissez-faire* attitude toward government in his later years, and (2) Adonijah's self-willed ambition to succeed his father, based on Adonijah's being the oldest of David's surviving sons. In this ambition he is supported by some influential members of David's government, contrary to David's wishes.

i. David's feebleness (1:1–4)

[1]When King David was old and well advanced in years, he could not keep warm even
when they put covers over him. [2]So his servants said to him, "Let us look for a young virgin
to attend the king and take care of him. She can lie beside him so that our lord the king
may keep warm."

[3]Then they searched throughout Israel for a beautiful girl and found Abishag, a
Shunammite, and brought her to the king. [4]The girl was very beautiful; she took care of the
king and waited on him, but the king had no intimate relations with her.

COMMENTARY

1 This brief account of David's feebleness and apparent inability to act decisively is given as the backdrop to Adonijah's attempted coup. It is somewhat startling to see the once-so-vigorous king now, at scarcely seventy years of age (cf. 2Sa 5:4–5), in such a state of debilitation. Presumably the one thing that did more than anything else to sap David's strength and will to govern decisively in his latter years was the series of disasters let loose on him and his family following his disgraceful act of adultery with Bathsheba and the indirect murder he committed in an attempt to cover up his sin.

This shattering chain of events included Amnon's rape of his half-sister Tamar; Amnon's subsequent murder by Absalom, Tamar's full brother; Absalom's revolt, with its severe disruptions, followed by his death, with its great emotional impact on David (2Sa 18:32–19:8); David's ill-judged census and the resultant plague; and then Sheba's brief revolt. There can be no doubt that these experiences, coupled with his knowledge of moral lapse, though forgiven, did much to rob David of his earlier physical and spiritual elan.

2–4 The point of this paragraph is to show how David's feebleness encouraged Adonijah to believe he could successfully force David's hand in his favor, and why Adonijah's later request to Solomon brought about such severe consequences (see comments at 2:13–25). The woman chosen to minister to David had the status of a concubine, though in actual fact she served David as a nurse. Some have suggested that her role was to attempt to coax David back to sexual vitality, but this purpose is not stated in the text. The narrator states simply that her presence was a means chosen to keep him warm, since his own body did not seem able to generate sufficient heat.

NOTES

1 The first two chapters of 1 Kings are commonly joined with 2 Samuel 9–20 and called the "Succession Narrative." This view was formulated by Leonhard Rost in 1926 (*Die Überlieferung von der Thronnachfolge Davids* [BWANT 3/6; Stuttgart: Kohlhammer, 1926]) and is considered to be one of several previously existing documents utilized by the author of Kings. This theory has ushered in a new approach to the study of source material, namely, focusing on the utilization of historical accounts that cover various parts of Israelite history. The Succession Narrative is considered to be one such unit, having the purpose of justifying the choice of Solomon over his older brothers to reign in David's place, since the latter were found to be unworthy (e.g., R. N. Whybray, *The Succession Narrative: A Study of II Sam. 9–20 and I Kings 1 and 2* [SBT 2/9; London: SCM, 1968], 50–55). There have been many modifications of Rost's original thesis, such as a change in terminology to "Court History," but scholars for the most part have embraced the general thesis.

Some, however, have found fault with this view; they cite such problems as the lack of a definitive starting point, these chapters' lack of a self-contained narrative (P. Ackroyd, "The Succession Narrative (So-Called)," *Int* 35/4 [1981]: 392), and literary differences between the Samuel portion and the Kings portion (J. W. Flanagan, "Court History or Succession Document? A Study of 2 Samuel 9–20 and 1 Kings 1–2," *JBL* 91/2 [1972]: 173–74). P. K. McCarter ("Plots, True or False: The Succession Narrative as Court Apologetic," *Int* 35/4 [1981]: 361) also finds it difficult to reconcile the thematic unity between 1 Kings 1 and 2, where the succession question is so urgent, and 2 Samuel 9–20, where it is not.

Other difficulties are seen in the fact that there are materials in the Samuel portion that have no relation to the Solomonic succession, such as Sheba's revolt (Flanagan, "Court History," 175). The account of David and Bathsheba certainly does nothing to enhance Solomon's status (J. S. Ackerman, "Knowing Good and Evil: A Literary Analysis of the Court History in 2 Samuel 9–20 and 1 Kings 1–2," *JBL* 109/1 [1990]: 55–56). Ackroyd, "Succession Narrative," 392, asks "whether it is justifiable to separate one section (from the larger work) and label it the 'Succession Narrative' rather than see the whole work as in some degree related to the problem of religion and political continuity." McCarter ("Plots," 361) suggests plausibly that the author of Kings utilized the material of Samuel, which preceded the writing of Kings.

Whatever the merits of the hypothetical Succession Narrative might be, it must be recognized that 2 Samuel 7 is the high point of the history of God's relationship with David and that any succession theory must at least include this great promise (cf. G. von Rad, *Old Testament Theology* [New York: Harper & Row, 1962], 311). The Davidic covenant focuses not only on the succession but also on the fact that David's son will build the temple that David longed to build, and that each successive heir to the throne will be responsible to walk in God's ways. Thus it would seem better to view the Solomonic narrative of 1 Kings as a fulfillment of the Davidic covenant, with all three of the major provisions of the covenant being addressed (see the Introduction to chs. 1–11).

With this perspective in mind, it is possible to see 2 Samuel 21–24 not as an intrusion into the narrative but actually as a fitting conclusion to the life of David and as an introduction to 1 Kings. Thus the relevance of 2 Samuel 24 becomes clear: the divine choice of the site for the temple as the place where God is willing to be gracious toward the repentant sinner (see also the expansion in 1Ch 21–29). Even the little note in 2 Samuel 21:15–17 becomes significant in preparing us for the weakness of David recorded in the opening verses of Kings.

2 The expression "to attend" is literally "to stand before" and is used of the activity of a servant or court minister before a master or a king, or of a priest before God (S. Amsler, " עָמַד [*ʿāmad*]," *TDOT*, 2:921).

The fact that David "had no intimate relations" with Abishag, though she was nominally a concubine, is an indication of a lack of virility. Loss of virility was in many cultures considered to be grounds for bringing in a younger king (Jones, 89–90).

The suggestion made by David's staff conforms to a type of diatherapy described by Josephus (*Ant.* 7.343 [14.3]) as a medical prescription. Galen (*Methus medicos* 8.7, cited by Montgomery, 71–72) confirms it as a practice in Greek medicine.

ii. Adonijah's attempted coup d'état (1:5–10)

OVERVIEW

David's feebleness and failure to make his choice of his successor public encouraged Adonijah to force David's hand by presenting him and the people with a *fait accompli*. Adonijah no doubt felt justified in his claim to the throne in that he seems to have been the oldest surviving son (though no normal succession patterns had as yet been established in Israel). However, his ambition was in direct contravention of God's will and David's explicit wishes. He did not wait for prophetic anointing or a royal proclamation. He was like his brother Absalom in being willful and self-centered though a naturally attractive person.

[5]Now Adonijah, whose mother was Haggith, put himself forward and said, "I will be
king." So he got chariots and horses ready, with fifty men to run ahead of him. [6](His father

had never interfered with him by asking, "Why do you behave as you do?" He was also very handsome and was born next after Absalom.)

[7]Adonijah conferred with Joab son of Zeruiah and with Abiathar the priest, and they gave him their support. [8]But Zadok the priest, Benaiah son of Jehoiada, Nathan the prophet, Shimei and Rei and David's special guard did not join Adonijah.

[9]Adonijah then sacrificed sheep, cattle and fattened calves at the Stone of Zoheleth near En Rogel. He invited all his brothers, the king's sons, and all the men of Judah who were royal officials, [10]but he did not invite Nathan the prophet or Benaiah or the special guard or his brother Solomon.

COMMENTARY

5–7 Adonijah's willfulness is attributed in v.6 to David's failure in disciplining him as a boy. Amnon and Absalom showed a similar willfulness.

Joab, the most powerful of Adonijah's supporters, had always been fiercely loyal to David but not necessarily to David's wishes (see comments at 2:5). In supporting Adonijah's pretensions to the throne, Joab was acting characteristically. He was not consciously disloyal to David, but he opposed David's (and God's) choice of Solomon as David's successor and acted on his own inclinations, as he had done so often in the past. Having the support of Joab and the army he controlled seemed practically to guarantee success for Adonijah's cause.

Abiathar, the other named active supporter of Adonijah, had been the only survivor of Saul's massacre of the high priest Ahimelech and his family. Abiathar fled to David at Keilah and brought the ephod with him (1Sa 22:20–22; 23:6, 9). He served as high priest during David's reign and seems to have been senior to Zadok (1Ki 2:26–27; Mk 2:26).

8–10 Adonijah had invited all his brothers (except Solomon) as well as the royal officials. It seems that he had at least their tacit support. There were those, however, who did not support Adonijah. Zadok was the son of Ahitub (2Sa 8:17), a descendant of Eleazar, the third son of Aaron. In 1 Chronicles 12:26–28 Zadok is listed as a warrior of the house of Levi and one of those who came to David at Hebron to offer him the rulership over all Israel.

Benaiah of Kabzeel, son of Jehoiada, was renowned as one of the greatest of David's mighty men (2Sa 23:20–23; 1Ch 11:22–25). David put him in charge of his bodyguard.

Nathan had played an important role in David's reign. He seems to have been particularly close to David. It was to him that David had gone to indicate his desire to build a temple for the Lord, and it was through Nathan that God responded with the Davidic covenant (2Sa 7). Later God sent Nathan to deal with David over the matter of his sin with Bathsheba (2Sa 12). Nathan was also sent by God to David on the occasion of Solomon's birth to declare God's special love for Solomon (2Sa 12:24–25).

Shimei and Rei are otherwise unknown, though Shimei may well be the Shimei, son of Ela (1Ki 4:18), who was appointed by Solomon as one of twelve district governors (4:7).

Also absent was David's "special guard [*gibbôrîm*]" (vv.8, 10). This group was originally comprised of six hundred men who followed David before he was recognized as king. They at some point included the Kerethites and Pelethites. Special mention is made in 2 Samuel 23:8–39 of thirty-seven "mighty men" (officers?) who were renowned for their faithfulness and deeds of valor. Benaiah was their commander (2Sa 23:23). These were not under the authority of Joab and are mentioned in 2 Samuel 15:15–18 as being loyal to David during Absalom's rebellion.

Adonijah's attempted usurpation of the throne began with a ceremonial gathering of his supporters. Absalom had begun his coup in a similar manner (2Sa 15:11–12). The participation of Abiathar and Joab in the ritual sacrifice and communal meal lent an aura of legitimacy to the occasion.

En Rogel (modern Bir Ayyub, "Job's well") was located slightly southeast of Jerusalem, near the confluence of the Hinnom and Kidron valleys. It was somewhat secluded and was thus ideally suited for Adonijah's clandestine gathering of forces before taking public action.

NOTES

5 Despite the assertion of many (DeVries, 21; Alter, 97–100) that it was Solomon and his supporters who were guilty of intrigue, it seems clear that Adonijah was the guilty one. Alter's claim that Bathsheba and Nathan between them succeeded in making a feeble David think that he had made a vow, when in actual fact he had done no such thing, seems to border on specious reasoning. Second Samuel 12:24–25; 1 Chronicles 22:9–10; 28:4–7 clearly show that Solomon was God's choice as well as David's. Adonijah and his followers were fully aware of this choice, as can be seen from the fact that Solomon and his supporters were not invited. Those who see Solomon as the ambitious opportunist can do so only by making the gratuitous assumption that the passages quoted above are an editorial apologetic for Solomon as king. The fact that Solomon was not invited and that Adonijah did not inform David are a strong indications that Adonijah knew full well that he was in the wrong. The clandestine nature of the gathering affords further proof.

The order of David's first four sons was Amnon, Kileab, Absalom, and Adonijah, these four and two others having been born in Hebron (2Sa 3:2–5). Kileab, the second, must have died as a child, for no further mention is made of him. Amnon was slain by Absalom, ostensibly as an act of vengeance for Amnon's rape of Absalom's sister Tamar (2Sa 13:1); but Absalom's later actions make it appear likely that it was his aspirations to the throne, not the desire to avenge his sister, that motivated him in the slaying of his older brother Amnon.

7 First Chronicles 16:39 suggests that Abiathar served as high priest in Jerusalem, where the ark was located. But since Gibeon was the site of the tabernacle and the chief place of worship (1Ki 3:4–15) until such time as the temple should be built, it would seem likely that Zadok was commonly regarded as de facto high priest.

8 Nathan's support for Solomon was rooted in his role of communicating God's forgiveness to David. The very fact that David had named his son "Solomon" ("Peace") was an indication of his awareness that by God's grace the rift between him and God had been healed. To seal the fact of God's full forgiveness, he sent Nathan to add the appellation Jedidiah ("beloved of the Lord") to Solomon (2Sa 12:24–25). The passage clearly implies God's choice of Solomon as David's successor. Keil, 18, notes from 2 Samuel 7:12–16 that God "did not ensure the establishment of the throne to any one of his existing sons, but to him that would come out of his loins (i.e., to Solomon, who was not yet born)."

9 The "Stone of Zoheleth" (אֶבֶן הַזֹּחֶלֶת, *ʾeben hazzōḥelet*) is traditionally thought to mean "serpent's stone," but it is now more commonly thought to mean "sliding stone." DeVries, 14, adopts the plausible view that the term "sliding stone" reflects the fact that this was a place where stones had slid down the steep embankment into the wadi below.

Of interest is the fact that En Rogel was the place where the two messengers who kept in touch with David during Absalom's rebellion stayed as they waited for word from Hushai (2Sa 17:17). DeVries's suggestion that En Rogel was a holy place is, however, debatable.

b. The counterplan of Nathan (1:11–31)

OVERVIEW

When Nathan became aware of the plot, he acted immediately by rousing David to take the steps necessary to ensure the public proclamation of Solomon as king. By so doing Nathan became God's instrument for carrying out the divine purpose. He acted tactfully and judiciously, just as he had done when he reprimanded David for his sin with Bathsheba and Uriah.

11Then Nathan asked Bathsheba, Solomon's mother, "Have you not heard that Adonijah,
the son of Haggith, has become king without our lord David's knowing it? 12Now then, let
me advise you how you can save your own life and the life of your son Solomon. 13Go in to
King David and say to him, 'My lord the king, did you not swear to me your servant: "Surely
Solomon your son shall be king after me, and he will sit on my throne"? Why then has
Adonijah become king?' 14While you are still there talking to the king, I will come in and
confirm what you have said."

15So Bathsheba went to see the aged king in his room, where Abishag the Shunammite
was attending him. 16Bathsheba bowed low and knelt before the king.

"What is it you want?" the king asked.

17She said to him, "My lord, you yourself swore to me your servant by the LORD your God:
'Solomon your son shall be king after me, and he will sit on my throne.' 18But now Adonijah has become king, and you, my lord the king, do not know about it. 19He has sacrificed
great numbers of cattle, fattened calves, and sheep, and has invited all the king's sons,
Abiathar the priest and Joab the commander of the army, but he has not invited Solomon

your servant. [20]My lord the king, the eyes of all Israel are on you, to learn from you who will
sit on the throne of my lord the king after him. [21]Otherwise, as soon as my lord the king is
laid to rest with his fathers, I and my son Solomon will be treated as criminals."
[22]While she was still speaking with the king, Nathan the prophet arrived. [23]And they told
the king, "Nathan the prophet is here." So he went before the king and bowed with his
face to the ground.
[24]Nathan said, "Have you, my lord the king, declared that Adonijah shall be king after
you, and that he will sit on your throne? [25]Today he has gone down and sacrificed great
numbers of cattle, fattened calves, and sheep. He has invited all the king's sons, the commanders of the army and Abiathar the priest. Right now they are eating and drinking with
him and saying, 'Long live King Adonijah!' [26]But me your servant, and Zadok the priest, and
Benaiah son of Jehoiada, and your servant Solomon he did not invite. [27]Is this something
my lord the king has done without letting his servants know who should sit on the throne
of my lord the king after him?"
[28]Then King David said, "Call in Bathsheba." So she came into the king's presence and
stood before him.
[29]The king then took an oath: "As surely as the LORD lives, who has delivered me out of
every trouble, [30]I will surely carry out today what I swore to you by the LORD, the God of
Israel: Solomon your son shall be king after me, and he will sit on my throne in my place."
[31]Then Bathsheba bowed low with her face to the ground and, kneeling before the king,
said, "May my lord King David live forever!"

COMMENTARY

11–31 Nathan sent Bathsheba in first. Her status as favored wife would ensure a quick hearing, and immediate action was indeed necessary. Her role was to rouse David to action by asking him how he could allow Adonijah to become king when he had solemnly sworn that Solomon should reign after him (vv.13, 17). Nathan would then confirm her statements and impress on David the need to act decisively (v.14).

The validity of Solomon's claim to the throne was not in question here. Both Bathsheba and Nathan knew David's disposition in the matter. The danger was that Adonijah would succeed to the throne through David's inaction. Nathan's words, "The eyes of all Israel are on you, to learn from you who will sit on the throne of my lord the king after him" (v.20), prodded David to prompt and vigorous action. He took immediate steps to make his wishes in the matter clear in a public way. The choice of Gihon as the location of the public anointing and proclamation of Solomon as king may well have been dictated by its proximity to En Rogel. By this means David left no doubt in anyone's mind as to his own wishes in the matter. It is clear that this definitive act was received with overwhelming public approval. There was such rejoicing and enthusiasm that the ground shook.

NOTES

12 Nathan's warning reflected reality. The omission of Solomon from the "guest list" was a sure sign that he was marked for death if Adonijah succeeded. The normal practice was for the successful claimant to the throne to execute any unsuccessful rival (see Jdg 9:5; 1Ki 15:29; 2Ki 10:6–14; 11:1).

Jones, 93, is typical of many commentators who, despite the clear intent of the text, see Nathan as engineering a coup d'état by wrongfully bringing Solomon into power. DeVries, 15, correctly rejects Gray's suggestion, 88, that Nathan wanted Bathsheba to convince a senile king by autosuggestion that he had sworn an oath that he in actual fact had not done.

c. Solomon's anointing (1:32–40)

32King David said, "Call in Zadok the priest, Nathan the prophet and Benaiah son of
Jehoiada." When they came before the king, 33he said to them: "Take your lord's servants
with you and set Solomon my son on my own mule and take him down to Gihon. 34There
have Zadok the priest and Nathan the prophet anoint him king over Israel. Blow the
trumpet and shout, 'Long live King Solomon!' 35Then you are to go up with him, and he is
to come and sit on my throne and reign in my place. I have appointed him ruler over Israel
and Judah."
36Benaiah son of Jehoiada answered the king, "Amen! May the LORD, the God of my lord
the king, so declare it. 37As the LORD was with my lord the king, so may he be with Solomon
to make his throne even greater than the throne of my lord King David!"
38So Zadok the priest, Nathan the prophet, Benaiah son of Jehoiada, the Kerethites and
the Pelethites went down and put Solomon on King David's mule and escorted him to
Gihon. 39Zadok the priest took the horn of oil from the sacred tent and anointed Solomon.
Then they sounded the trumpet and all the people shouted, "Long live King Solomon!"
40And all the people went up after him, playing flutes and rejoicing greatly, so that the
ground shook with the sound.

COMMENTARY

32–40 The men that David called to carry out the public anointing of Solomon were Benaiah (v.32), the commander of David's special guard; Zadok (v.34), the priest; and Nathan, the prophet. The servants referred to in v.33 are identified in v.38 as the guard composed of Kerethites and Pelethites.

Gihon (v.33), the site of the anointing, was just outside the city in the Kidron Valley, on the east bank of Ophel. It was at that time Jerusalem's major source of water and was therefore a natural gathering place of the populace.

The fact that Solomon was mounted on David's royal mule demonstrated to the populace that this anointing had David's blessing. The presence of Zadok and Nathan indicated divine approval, and that of Benaiah military approval (House, 93).

NOTES

33 Employment of the mule—פִּרְדָּה (*pirdâ*, "female mule")—was a recent innovation in Israel and seems at this time to have been used primarily by the royal court and the aristocracy. It had to be imported (1Ki 10:25; Eze 27:14) because of the prohibition of Leviticus 19:19 with regard to the crossbreeding of animals. According to 2 Samuel 13:29 (the first mention of mules) they were ridden by David's sons; 18:9 indicates that Absalom was riding a mule at the time of his death. Sometime later, mules seemed to be more common and were used as burden bearers (2Ki 5:17; 1Ch 12:40; Ezr 2:66; see *IDB*, 3:456).

34 The situation described here is that of a coregency. E. Ball ("The Coregency of David and Solomon," *VT* 27 [1977]: 268–79) has shown that there is a strong precedent for such a coregency in Egyptian practice by giving examples from Egypt's sixth through twenty-third dynasties.

35 The correlation of this event with 1 Chronicles 23:1—"When David was old and full of years he made his son Solomon king over Israel"—is not perfectly clear. The suggestion of Edersheim, 7:55–56, and H. L. Ellison (*NBC* [rev. ed.], 382–83) that the statement of 1 Chronicles 23:1 is a compact account of 1 Kings 1:28–40 (esp. vv.38–40) seems likely. The coronation was then further confirmed at the great assembly of leaders as described in 1 Chronicles 28–29. First Chronicles 29:22 describes a second confirmatory anointing as was experienced by Saul and David in 1 Samuel 11:15 and 2 Samuel 2:4; 5:3 (with the latter passage referring to a third anointing, this time to be king over the ten northern tribes as well).

40 It is difficult to understand the claim (Jones, 101) that this text implies that the investiture of Solomon at Gihon was somehow "unconstitutional," as though it were done without public knowledge or consent. The opposite is true. There is no mention of public involvement with Adonijah's (premature) celebration of kingship, but the passage states clearly that the people were enthusiastically present at Solomon's anointing. The whole point of the exercise was to let everyone know whom David had chosen to be the new king.

d. Adonijah's submission (1:41–53)

[41]Adonijah and all the guests who were with him heard it as they were finishing their feast. On hearing the sound of the trumpet, Joab asked, "What's the meaning of all the noise in the city?"

[42]Even as he was speaking, Jonathan son of Abiathar the priest arrived. Adonijah said, "Come in. A worthy man like you must be bringing good news."

[43]"Not at all!" Jonathan answered. "Our lord King David has made Solomon king. [44]The king has sent with him Zadok the priest, Nathan the prophet, Benaiah son of Jehoiada, the Kerethites and the Pelethites, and they have put him on the king's mule, [45]and Zadok the priest and Nathan the prophet have anointed him king at Gihon. From there they have gone up cheering, and the city resounds with it. That's the noise you hear. [46]Moreover, Solomon has taken his seat on the royal throne. [47]Also, the royal officials have come to congratulate our lord King David, saying, 'May your God make Solomon's name more famous than yours and his throne greater than yours!' And the king bowed in worship on his bed [48]and said, 'Praise be to the LORD, the God of Israel, who has allowed my eyes to see a successor on my throne today.'"

[49]At this, all Adonijah's guests rose in alarm and dispersed. [50]But Adonijah, in fear of Solomon, went and took hold of the horns of the altar. [51]Then Solomon was told, "Adonijah is afraid of King Solomon and is clinging to the horns of the altar. He says, 'Let King Solomon swear to me today that he will not put his servant to death with the sword.'"

[52]Solomon replied, "If he shows himself to be a worthy man, not a hair of his head will fall to the ground; but if evil is found in him, he will die." [53]Then King Solomon sent men, and they brought him down from the altar. And Adonijah came and bowed down to King Solomon, and Solomon said, "Go to your home."

COMMENTARY

41–53 The swelling sound of the public's rejoicing and of the instruments reached the ears of Adonijah's supporters at En Rogel (v.41). Their initial puzzlement soon turned to alarm as they learned from Jonathan, son of Abiathar, that Solomon had been publicly proclaimed king and that this news had been received with great enthusiasm (vv.42–48). This development effectively put an end to Adonijah's plot, as its participants quickly scattered (v.49).

The report of David's response to the coronation (vv.47–48) made it clear to all what David's wishes were in the matter. He was profoundly grateful to a gracious and loving God as he saw the people at large accepting his son Solomon as the new king. He would carry out David's wish to build a temple for his God. God's special blessing would be upon him, and with Solomon there would begin the long line of David's descendants who would ultimately lead to the promised Messiah, who was both the son of David and the Son of God.

Adonijah's response to this sudden change of events was to seek asylum by grasping the horns of the altar (v.50). He expected Solomon to execute the rival claimant to the throne, as he himself would have done had he been successful. Solomon was more gracious, however; the new king guaranteed safety for Adonijah as long as he conducted himself properly. To be a "worthy man" (v.52) in this context simply means that Adonijah would renounce any claims to the throne, avoid seditious intrigue, and support Solomon's rights with regard to the kingship over Israel.

NOTES

50 This method of seeking sanctuary was a time-honored custom. In Israel the grasping of the horns of the altar did not provide sanctuary for all types of criminals—only those guilty of the unintentional slaying of another. The horns were the projections at the corners of the altar on which the blood of sacrifice was smeared. To grasp the horns "was to claim the protection of God until the case was judged" (Wiseman, *1 & 2 Kings*, 74).

The location of the altar is not mentioned, though it was most likely in the tent that David had erected in Jerusalem to house the ark of the covenant.

e. David's charge to Solomon (2:1–11)

OVERVIEW

David's last charge to Solomon comes in two parts. The first has to do with Solomon's spiritual life (vv.2–4). David's admonition summarizes the message of Deuteronomy and reminds Solomon of God's promise and exhortation in 2 Samuel 7:12–16. The second gives instruction concerning the disposition of "unfinished business" pertaining to Joab, to the sons of Barzillai, and to Shimei (vv.5–12).

There can be no doubt that much of Solomon's early spiritual vitality and dedication to God may be attributed to David's deep personal relationship to the Lord and desire to honor him. David's legacy to Solomon was thus much more than a great kingdom with secure borders, tributary nations, and considerable wealth and prestige. Far more importantly, he instilled in Solomon a love for God and his Word.

[1]When the time drew near for David to die, he gave a charge to Solomon his son.
[2]"I am about to go the way of all the earth," he said. "So be strong, show yourself
a man, [3]and observe what the LORD your God requires: Walk in his ways, and keep his
decrees and commands, his laws and requirements, as written in the Law of Moses, so
that you may prosper in all you do and wherever you go, [4]and that the LORD may keep
his promise to me: 'If your descendants watch how they live, and if they walk faithfully
before me with all their heart and soul, you will never fail to have a man on the throne of
Israel.'
[5]"Now you yourself know what Joab son of Zeruiah did to me—what he did to the two
commanders of Israel's armies, Abner son of Ner and Amasa son of Jether. He killed them,
shedding their blood in peacetime as if in battle, and with that blood stained the belt
around his waist and the sandals on his feet. [6]Deal with him according to your wisdom,
but do not let his gray head go down to the grave in peace.

[7]"But show kindness to the sons of Barzillai of Gilead and let them be among those who
eat at your table. They stood by me when I fled from your brother Absalom.
[8]"And remember, you have with you Shimei son of Gera, the Benjamite from Bahurim,
who called down bitter curses on me the day I went to Mahanaim. When he came down
to meet me at the Jordan, I swore to him by the LORD: 'I will not put you to death by the
sword.' [9]But now, do not consider him innocent. You are a man of wisdom; you will know
what to do to him. Bring his gray head down to the grave in blood."
[10]Then David rested with his fathers and was buried in the City of David. [11]He had
reigned forty years over Israel — seven years in Hebron and thirty-three in Jerusalem.

COMMENTARY

1–3 See also 1 Chronicles 22:6–14 and 28:9–10, 20 for other admonitions of David to Solomon. His words here echo those of God to Joshua (Jos 1:6–9) as the latter was about to begin in his role as commander of the hosts of Israel (cf. also Dt 31:6–8, 23). The basic injunction for Solomon was that he should conduct himself in his personal life, and in his role as leader of God's people, in accordance with God's Word (cf. also Dt 17:18–20). Solomon was to be strong and show himself to be a man.

The words "strong and courageous" (*ḥᵃzaq weʾᵉmāṣ*, Jos 1:6) encouraged Joshua with respect to the carrying out of his commission to lead Israel into her inheritance in the face of the overwhelming power of the Canaanites. Just so was Solomon as the new leader told to face courageously the challenges that would confront him. For both Joshua and Solomon, courage had its source in God. The manner of their leadership was to be based on God's Word, which would enable them to carry out God's purpose.

4 David reminds his son of his responsibility to be true to the Lord (2Sa 7:12–13). The Davidic covenant was unconditional with respect to its ultimate goal of bringing the Messiah from the line of David, but each individual king must heed God's Word from the heart in order to experience the blessing of God.

5–6 The second part of David's last words left Solomon with some matters that he considered unfinished business. The first had to do with Joab, the commander of David's armies. Joab had been a mixed blessing to David, fiercely loyal but not always faithful in carrying out David's wishes. On the good side it can be said that Joab was an outstanding and courageous general. He never wavered in his loyalty to David's kingship. He also had occasional flashes of spiritual insight, such as his opposition to taking the census (1Ch 21:3–4) that brought grief to David.

On the other hand, Joab had created many problems for David. He had a repeated history of taking matters into his own hands, thereby often creating embarrassing situations for David and forcing his hand. Joab had killed Absalom against David's express command. In 2 Samuel 3:22–27 he killed Abner in an act of treachery.

After the revolt of Absalom, he treacherously rid himself of Amasa, whom David had appointed to replace him. Now once again Joab was trying to force David's hand by supporting Adonijah's attempted usurpation of the succession to the throne.

Why had David not dealt with Joab before? The answer is probably to be found in the fact that David felt under obligation to Joab, and though David was certainly not lacking in courage, he was not able to cope with the mixture of Joab's loyalty and misdeeds. Yet he realized that Joab's murder of Abner and Amasa, at least, must not go unpunished. Solomon was the natural one to deal with the matter, since Joab had been guilty of sedition in attempting to forestall the succession to the throne of the man of David's choice. House, 97, suggests additionally that David might well have been concerned because "Joab [was] ... a powerful, crafty, and dangerous opponent of Solomon's accession to the throne."

7 In the matter of the sons of Barzillai, David was simply asking Solomon to continue to carry out his own promise to Barzillai as a reward for his loyal support during David's brief exile at the time of Absalom's revolt (2Sa 19:31–39).

8–9 The matter of Shimei was more difficult. His actions during David's flight from Absalom (2Sa 16:5–14) were deserving of death, yet on David's return to Jerusalem the gracious king had pardoned Shimei (2Sa 19:18–23). David doubtless made this promise in a moment of profound relief that the kingdom had been restored to him. But he must have realized that Shimei's "repentance" was not sincere and that the man was a potential troublemaker. David now left the matter in Solomon's hands and trusted Solomon's wisdom to deal properly with the situation.

10–11 David had made extensive preparations for a successful reign for his son, particularly with regard to the plans and materials for the temple (see 1Ch 22–29). Now, having ruled a total of forty years (including the first seven years at Hebron over Judah alone), David died, content in the knowledge that the kingdom was in good hands. Just how long the coregency lasted cannot be stated with any degree of certainty. Estimates range from two or three months to several years.

NOTES

2–3 Jones, 107, shows how David's language reflects the book of Deuteronomy and lists sample passages: Deuteronomy 4:29; 6:2, 5; 8:6, 11; 9:5; 10:12, 23; 11:1, 22; 29:8.

10–11 DeVries, 36–37, states: "The tombs of the Judahite kings have been identified on the south slope of Ophel ... on the then-unoccupied southern extremity of the western hill."

2. His Establishment of the Kingdom (2:12–46)

OVERVIEW

During Adonijah's attempt to preempt the throne, Solomon himself did not indulge in plotting to make the throne certain for himself. He exercised remarkable restraint. But once he was formally declared king, he acted firmly and with decisiveness and dispatch.

a. His assumption to the throne (2:12)

[12]So Solomon sat on the throne of his father David, and his rule was firmly established.

COMMENTARY

12 However long or short the coregency was, this verse states that when David died, Solomon's rule was firmly established. There was no question in anyone's mind who was king, and Solomon had firm control over the kingdom.

b. Adonijah's further scheme and execution (2:13–25)

[13]Now Adonijah, the son of Haggith, went to Bathsheba, Solomon's mother. Bathsheba
asked him, "Do you come peacefully?"
He answered, "Yes, peacefully." [14]Then he added, "I have something to say to you."
"You may say it," she replied.
[15]"As you know," he said, "the kingdom was mine. All Israel looked to me as their king.
But things changed, and the kingdom has gone to my brother; for it has come to him from
the LORD. [16]Now I have one request to make of you. Do not refuse me."
"You may make it," she said.
[17]So he continued, "Please ask King Solomon—he will not refuse you—to give me
Abishag the Shunammite as my wife."
[18]"Very well," Bathsheba replied, "I will speak to the king for you."
[19]When Bathsheba went to King Solomon to speak to him for Adonijah, the king stood
up to meet her, bowed down to her and sat down on his throne. He had a throne brought
for the king's mother, and she sat down at his right hand.
[20]"I have one small request to make of you," she said. "Do not refuse me."
The king replied, "Make it, my mother; I will not refuse you."
[21]So she said, "Let Abishag the Shunammite be given in marriage to your brother
Adonijah."
[22]King Solomon answered his mother, "Why do you request Abishag the Shunammite
for Adonijah? You might as well request the kingdom for him—after all, he is my older
brother—yes, for him and for Abiathar the priest and Joab son of Zeruiah!"
[23]Then King Solomon swore by the LORD: "May God deal with me, be it ever so severely,
if Adonijah does not pay with his life for this request! [24]And now, as surely as the LORD

lives—he who has established me securely on the throne of my father David and has founded a dynasty for me as he promised—Adonijah shall be put to death today!" [25]So King Solomon gave orders to Benaiah son of Jehoiada, and he struck down Adonijah and he died.

COMMENTARY

13–17 This section demonstrates that Adonijah was ambitious and not yet finished with his hopes for securing the throne for himself. In asking for the hand of Abishag (v.17), he was almost certainly not pursuing romantic interests but trying to secure for himself a claim to the kingship. De Vaux, 116–17, notes that from some passages it appears that the king's harem, at least in the early days of the monarchy, used to pass to his successor. In 2 Samuel 12:8 Nathan says that it was Yahweh himself who, by establishing David as king of Israel, had given him the wives of his master Saul. Absalom publicly approached the concubines David had left in Jerusalem, which was his way of asserting that he was now king (2Sa 16:21–22). Ishbosheth's anger against Abner, who had taken one of Saul's concubines (2Sa 3:7–8), is readily explained if she had passed by inheritance to Ishbosheth, for Abner's action would imply that he was disputing the power with him.

Although 1:4 states clearly that David had no marital relations with Abishag, her function being a therapeutic one, she was officially regarded as being one of David's wives. As such she would provide an additional argument for Adonijah's royal pretensions. He informed Bathsheba inaccurately that the kingdom had been as good as his and that all Israel had regarded him as king, thus clearly indicating that his aspirations were not really dead.

18–22 Bathsheba agreed to speak for Adonijah, but Solomon saw through the scheme and spoke rather vehemently: "You might as well request the kingdom for him!" (v.22).

It has been suggested that Bathsheba did not naïvely fall into a trap but that she rather wisely and skillfully alerted her son to his brother's aspirations, while at the same time appearing to be sympathetic to Adonijah. The problem is that the text does not indicate what the state of her mind was. It is probably best to assume that she was too naïve to see through Adonijah's scheme and that she felt compassion for him. Solomon's response to her request seems to confirm this.

23–25 Solomon reacted swiftly to Adonijah's ploy and ordered Benaiah to execute him. Though this action may seem harsh, it was clearly necessary, since to leave Adonijah free to continue his machinations would leave a festering sore in the kingdom.

NOTES

18–19 DeVries, 37, suggests, improbably, that Bathseba was using her apparent acquiescence to "get rid of Adonijah."

c. The deposition of Abiathar and execution of Joab (2:26–34)

26To Abiathar the priest the king said, "Go back to your fields in Anathoth. You deserve
to die, but I will not put you to death now, because you carried the ark of the Sovereign
LORD before my father David and shared all my father's hardships." 27So Solomon removed
Abiathar from the priesthood of the LORD, fulfilling the word the LORD had spoken at Shiloh
about the house of Eli.

28When the news reached Joab, who had conspired with Adonijah though not with
Absalom, he fled to the tent of the LORD and took hold of the horns of the altar. 29King
Solomon was told that Joab had fled to the tent of the LORD and was beside the altar. Then
Solomon ordered Benaiah son of Jehoiada, "Go, strike him down!"

30So Benaiah entered the tent of the LORD and said to Joab, "The king says, 'Come out!'"

But he answered, "No, I will die here."

Benaiah reported to the king, "This is how Joab answered me."

31Then the king commanded Benaiah, "Do as he says. Strike him down and bury him,
and so clear me and my father's house of the guilt of the innocent blood that Joab shed.
32The LORD will repay him for the blood he shed, because without the knowledge of my
father David he attacked two men and killed them with the sword. Both of them—Abner
son of Ner, commander of Israel's army, and Amasa son of Jether, commander of Judah's
army—were better men and more upright than he. 33May the guilt of their blood rest
on the head of Joab and his descendants forever. But on David and his descendants, his
house and his throne, may there be the LORD's peace forever."

34So Benaiah son of Jehoiada went up and struck down Joab and killed him, and he was
buried on his own land in the desert.

COMMENTARY

26 Abiathar was banished to his home in Anathoth, about three and one-half miles north of Jerusalem. (The prophet Jeremiah later came from priestly stock at Anathoth.) He deserved to die because he opposed not only David's will but also God's will in the matter of the succession. But since he had served faithfully, having been loyal to David in his hard times and having borne the ark (2Sa 15:24, 29; 1Ch 15:11–15) in his capacity as high priest, Solomon allowed him to live. Notice the words "I will not put you to death now." The reprieve from execution was dependent on continued good behavior.

27 The removal of Abiathar from the active priesthood and the sole tenancy of Zadok as high priest was a fulfillment of God's word to Eli (1Sa 2:30–33).

28–29 Having heard of Solomon's actions with regard to Adonijah and Abiathar, Joab knew that judgment would not be long in coming. In seeking sanctuary by grasping the horns of the altar, he no doubt was thinking only of his involvement with Adonijah's plot. It would be in keeping with Joab's character to have dismissed from his mind any thought of blame, much less punishment, in regard to the two murders. In any case Joab's act of seeking sanctuary would put Solomon's execution order in as bad a light as possible by making him appear to be violating a commonly accepted sanctuary. Solomon would have to contend with strong emotions on the part of many of the people.

30–33 Joab's refusal to leave frustrated Benaiah's mission since Beniah hesitated to touch Joab while he clung to the altar (v.30). When Solomon sent Benaiah back to execute Joab at the altar, Solomon justified the order as an act of justice to remove bloodguiltiness from David and his descendants (v.31). This reasoning was not "specious" (Gray, 109; similarly, Jones 116). Solomon was carrying out David's wishes (v.32). This matter was of great importance to David's conscience and the integrity of his reign because the murders were not a private matter (v.33). One might term Joab's murders as political assassinations. The national interest and conscience were involved.

34 Benaiah carried out Solomon's order, and no public outcry is recorded. On the contrary, the narrator states in the next section that "the kingdom was now firmly established in Solomon's hands" (v.46).

NOTES

28 The horns of the altar provided sanctuary for those guilty of involuntary manslaughter but not for those guilty of premeditated or intentional murder. DeVries, 39, reads "Solomon" for "Absalom" (with the LXX [except for B], as opposed to the MT and Vulgate). This reading makes Solomon out to be acting vindictively. But the context clearly shows that he was carrying out the wishes of his father, David.

d. The elevation of Benaiah and Zadok (2:35)

35The king put Benaiah son of Jehoiada over the army in Joab's position and replaced Abiathar with Zadok the priest.

COMMENTARY

35 Benaiah had been commander of David's personal guard. Now he is commander-in-chief of the whole army. Zadok now becomes the sole high priest, in fulfillment of God's word to Eli in 1 Samuel 2:27–36.

The descendents of Zadok retained the priesthood until 171 BC, when Antiochus conferred it on Menelaus. The Essenes at Qumran were at odds with the priests of the day and awaited the restoration of the Zadokites, whom they looked on as the only legitimate priestly family. Ezekiel restricts the eschatological priesthood to the Zadokites since they alone were innocent of apostasy (Eze 44:15–16).

e. The execution of Shimei (2:36–46)

36Then the king sent for Shimei and said to him, "Build yourself a house in Jerusalem
and live there, but do not go anywhere else. 37The day you leave and cross the Kidron
Valley, you can be sure you will die; your blood will be on your own head."
38Shimei answered the king, "What you say is good. Your servant will do as my lord the
king has said." And Shimei stayed in Jerusalem for a long time.
39But three years later, two of Shimei's slaves ran off to Achish son of Maacah, king of
Gath, and Shimei was told, "Your slaves are in Gath." 40At this, he saddled his donkey and
went to Achish at Gath in search of his slaves. So Shimei went away and brought the
slaves back from Gath.
41When Solomon was told that Shimei had gone from Jerusalem to Gath and had
returned, 42the king summoned Shimei and said to him, "Did I not make you swear by the
LORD and warn you, 'On the day you leave to go anywhere else, you can be sure you will
die'? At that time you said to me, 'What you say is good. I will obey.' 43Why then did you not
keep your oath to the LORD and obey the command I gave you?"
44The king also said to Shimei, "You know in your heart all the wrong you did to my
father David. Now the LORD will repay you for your wrongdoing. 45But King Solomon will be
blessed, and David's throne will remain secure before the LORD forever."
46Then the king gave the order to Benaiah son of Jehoiada, and he went out and struck
Shimei down and killed him.

The kingdom was now firmly established in Solomon's hands.

COMMENTARY

36–40 Shimei was not one of the conspirators with Adonijah, but he had considerable potential for stirring up opposition to the house of David. In a gesture of generosity, David forgave him for his cursing and acts of hatred (2Sa 19:18–23). Yet David sensed the insincerity of Shimei's apology and the probability of a return on Shimei's part to active hostility at the earliest sign of weakness. He also felt that justice had not been served. Shimei was a scoundrel and needed to be dealt with, yet David was powerless because of his promise (v.37).

By forbidding Shimei to leave Jerusalem on pain of death, Solomon kept him "isolated from his kinsmen of Benjamin, who had been the spearhead of the revolt against David under Sheba (2Sa 20)" (Gray, 111). Shimei was forbidden to go anywhere outside Jerusalem, but the Kidron Valley receives particular mention since it is on the direct route toward Bahurim, Shimei's hometown.

For three years Shimei obeyed the restriction of the king (vv.38–39); but when two of his slaves fled to Achish of Gath, he violated his parole and went after his slaves personally (vv.39–40). Had Shimei taken the conditions of his confinement seriously and been an honest man, he would have gone to Solomon and requested either that the latter regain his slaves for him or else allow him to make the trip.

41–46a Solomon called Shimei to account for his breach of an oath to God. He had already been the recipient of a gracious pardon from David. But now Solomon was going to mete out justice on the exact terms of the oath. Shimei had taken grace lightly and demonstrated his unrepentant heart. For these shortcomings he would die in strict accord with the terms of their agreement. He was unworthy of another pardon. With Shimei's execution, justice was fully served, yet in such a way that allowed Shimei to condemn himself.

Solomon's statement that now "King Solomon will be blessed" indicates that the actions he had taken were fully justified and that past injustices had been dealt with, thus enabling him to begin his reign with a clean moral slate.

46b The theme of this statement is picked up again in 4:1. First Kings 3 demonstrates how the statement was confirmed (see comments on ch 3). Chapter 4 and the following chapters relate how Solomon conducted his reign.

NOTES

40 Montgomery, 96ff., gives examples of extradition practices involving fugitives in the second millennium BC. In addition to the Hittite and Akkadian documents pertaining to fugitives, the Aramaic vassal treaties also contain provisions on this matter.

B. Solomon's Love for the Lord—God's Approval (3:1–28)

OVERVIEW

In this section God graciously appears to Solomon and not only affirms his approval of Solomon's kingship but also promises his fullest blessing. This latter promise was contingent on Solomon's continuing to walk in God's ways.

The approval of God in vv.2–15 is bracketed by the approval and recognition of Pharaoh (v.1) and that of his own people at the end of vv.16–18. In other words, Solomon receives approval by God, but also from external (Egypt) and internal (Israel) human sources.

1. The Marriage of Solomon to Pharaoh's Daughter: Her Temporary Residence in the City of David (3:1)

1 Solomon made an alliance with Pharaoh king of Egypt and married his daughter. He brought her to the City of David until he finished building his palace and the temple of the Lord, and the wall around Jerusalem.

COMMENTARY

1 One might wonder at the placement of the announcement of Solomon's marriage to Pharaoh's daughter at this particular point in the narrative. But ch. 3 forms a natural progression to the last statement of ch. 2: "The kingdom was now firmly established in Solomon's hands." This chapter points out (1) the respect with which he was held in Egypt—so much so that Pharaoh gave him his daughter to seal an alliance; (2) God's affirmation and blessing of Solomon and his reign; and (3) the amazement of the people at the unusual wisdom of Solomon in his decision in the case of the disputed baby.

At the same time, however, there is here already an indication that despite Solomon's devotion to the Lord at this time and God's favorable response to his prayer, the seeds of his downfall are already being sown. Many writers, including Edersheim, 5:63, who cites Jewish tradition, feel that Solomon did not violate the law in this marriage; but even though the proscription against marrying foreign wives (i.e., Dt 7:3) referred specifically to Canaanite women, it would seem that the principle holds for pagan wives whatever their origin, unless, of course, they were to convert to the Hebrew faith.

Solomon's marriage to Pharaoh's daughter was the seal of a political alliance with Egypt. That such a marriage came about gives some indication of the importance of the kingdom Solomon inherited from his father as well as the decline of Egyptian power at this time. Formerly, Egyptian pharaohs consistently refused to allow their daughters to marry even the most important and powerful foreign kings. In this instance it appears that Pharaoh felt it to be advantageous to ally himself with Solomon by giving him not only his daughter but also Gezer as a wedding gift. This would assure him clear trade routes through Palestine. Solomon, on his side, could by this means secure his southern border.

The rendering "made an alliance with Pharaoh" reflects accurately the meaning of the Hebrew, "became Pharaoh's son-in-law," which stresses the relationship between father-in-law and bridegroom rather than that between bride and bridegroom. Making alliances through marriage was a common practice as a means of cementing and maintaining international agreements and securing a nation's borders.

The "City of David" was located on the southern portion of the eastern ridge of Jerusalem (cf. Aharoni and Avi-Yonah, map 114). This area lies between the Kidron Valley on the east and the (now nonexistent) Tyropoeon Valley on the west. It slopes down into the Valley of Hinnom at the point where it joins the Kidron Valley. This was the site of Jebusite Jerusalem and David's Jerusalem. Solomon extended the city to the north, where he also built the temple.

Solomon kept Pharaoh's daughter in the older city of David until he had completed his building projects. Then he built a palace for her (1Ki 7:8; 9:24; 2Ch 8:11), presumably as part of his palace complex. The Chronicler indicates that Pharaoh's daughter was not housed in David's palace "because the places the ark of the LORD has entered are holy" (2Ch 8:11).

This note concerning her temporary residence is paralleled by the comment in 9:24 that she moved into the palace built for her. The two references bracket the verses concerning the construction of the temple.

NOTES

1 This marriage was not Solomon's first. Comparing his son Rehoboam's age (forty-one) at the time of his succeeding to the throne (14:21) with the length of Solomon's reign (forty years; cf. 11:42–43), it is clear that he had already married Naamah the Ammonitess before he became king.

It is commonly thought that the Egyptian princess was of the relatively weak Twenty-First Dynasty (cf. Leon Wood, A *Survey of Israel's History* [rev. ed.; Grand Rapids: Zondervan, 1986], 246; Gray, 118–20). A. Malamat ("Aspects of the Foreign Policies of David and Solomon," *JNES* 22 [1963]: 12) identifies this pharaoh as Siamun, second to the last of the Twenty-First Dynasty. K. A. Kitchen ("How We Know When Solomon Ruled," 35–36) agrees with this assessment, as does Wiseman, *1 & 2 Kings*, 82, tentatively. For more on this pharaoh, see Notes on 9:16. To the criticism of some on the basis of the remark of Amenophis III (1386–1349) that from times past no pharaoh's daughter had been given to anyone outside Egypt, Kitchen replies that customs had changed since the reign of Amenophis and cites other examples of royal princesses being given to foreigners in marriage.

2. Worship at Gibeon (3:2–4)

2The people, however, were still sacrificing at the high places, because a temple had not
yet been built for the Name of the LORD. 3Solomon showed his love for the LORD by walking
according to the statutes of his father David, except that he offered sacrifices and burned
incense on the high places.
4The king went to Gibeon to offer sacrifices, for that was the most important high place,
and Solomon offered a thousand burnt offerings on that altar.

COMMENTARY

2 The "however" (*raq*, which also appears in v.3; NIV, "except") is intended to stress the chief area in which conditions were not yet ideal because of the practice of sacrificing at the "high places" (*bāmôt*). These latter were open-air sanctuaries that were found mostly on hilltops (1Ki 11:7; 2Ki 16:4) but also in towns (1Ki 13:32) and valleys (Jer 7:31; Eze 6:3). De Vaux, 284–88, points out that they were mounds or knolls, places of eminence for purposes of worship. The simplest ones had merely an altar, but they might also be more elaborate, as in the case of the one at Gibeon (v.4).

The high places were a constant sore point in Israel, and the prophets of God frequently spoke out against them. There were two basic problems with them: (1) they detracted from the principle of the central sanctuary (Dt 12:1–14); and (2) since worship at high places was a Canaanite custom, syncretism was not only a real danger but an all-too-common occurrence. Israel was specifically forbidden to utilize pagan high places and altars (Dt 12:2–4, 13), and as soon as God had established his people in the Promised Land, they were to worship at a sanctuary in the place appointed by God.

The latter half of the verse gives the reasons for the common use of various "high places" for worship. The temple had not yet been built. Before Eli's time the tabernacle had been at Shiloh; but with the Philistines' capture of the ark, Shiloh lost its significance as the place of God's presence among his people. Even after the ark was returned by the Philistines, it remained for years in the house of Abinadab (1Sa 7:1), until David removed it to Jerusalem (2Sa 6) to a tent he had prepared for it there (v.17). In the meantime the tabernacle was removed from Shiloh after the capture of the ark.

The tabernacle next appears at Nob (1Sa 21), where it remained until Saul massacred the priests there (1Sa 22). At some point after this event it was moved to Gibeon, where it is mentioned in connection with Zadok's high priestly ministry (1Ch 16:39–40). There were then, in effect, two tabernacles during David's reign. The one in Gibeon was without the ark; the one in Jerusalem had the ark but not the original trappings of the tabernacle (2Ch 1:3–5). This state of affairs matched that of the double priesthood of Zadok and Abiathar.

3 Solomon receives high commendation. He loved the Lord and walked in the ways of David. David had loved God from the heart and was deeply aware of the grace of God at work in his life (Pss 18; 31:19, 23; 34:8–10). The very fact that God chose Solomon, the son of Bathsheba, to be David's successor demonstrated the forgiving grace of God. Solomon, as the least likely candidate to be God's choice as king, was certainly fully aware of God's grace.

What seems to be a qualification in respect to Solomon's godliness—"except that he offered sacrifices"—may in actuality not be intended to detract from his character. It may well be that both here and in v.2 the statement concerning worshiping in various high places is an allusion to a state of incompleteness that did not end until the temple was completed. Notice that Samuel brought offerings at various high places (cf. 1Sa 9:11–25). These sacrifices were apparently supplementary to the official services connected with the tabernacle. This practice seems to have been legitimate at this time as long as the high places had no associations with Canaanite religions. After the building of the temple, the high places were no longer legitimate.

4 According to 2 Chronicles 1:2–3, the entire leadership of the nation went with Solomon to Gibeon to bring a great offering to God. That one thousand burnt offerings were brought indicates the special importance of this occasion. Its purpose was clearly to bring thanksgiving for establishing Solomon in the kingdom and also to seek God's blessing on his reign.

NOTES

2–3 There is an alternative opinion with regard to the "except" of v.3, which holds that Solomon's devotion was imperfect because of his worship at the high place at Gibeon (B. Waltke and M. O'Connor, *An Introduction to Biblical Hebrew Syntax* [Winona Lake, Ind.: Eisenbrauns, 1990], 670). This view is in keeping with the usual, negative evaluation of the high places in the remaining references to them in the books of Kings. There is, however, some warrant for the view expressed in the commentary in that the same restrictive adverb רַק (*raq*, "however" [v.2] and "except" [v.3], NIV) occurs in both vv.2 and 3. In v.2 the qualification is explained by the fact that the temple had not yet been built, thus intimating that the same qualification applies to Solomon's practice of worshiping at the high places before the temple was built.

In any case Solomon's worship at Gibeon seems to be justified in that the tabernacle was located there and that there David had installed Zadok the high priest to bring offerings on the altar (1Ch 16:39–43).

3. The Appearance of the Lord to Solomon (3:5–15)

OVERVIEW

This is the first of two personal appearances of God to Solomon (the other is recorded in ch. 9). Here God approves of Solomon's attitude as expressed in his prayer; in the latter passage God approves of the temple Solomon had built but also warns him to continue to remain true to the Lord. That God had in such a remarkable way declared himself willing to pour out his blessing on Solomon and his work makes him all the more culpable in his later apostasy (cf. 1Ki 11:9). With great privilege comes great responsibility.

a. Solomon's prayer for wisdom (3:5–9)

5At Gibeon the LORD appeared to Solomon during the night in a dream, and God said,
"Ask for whatever you want me to give you."
6Solomon answered, "You have shown great kindness to your servant, my father David,
because he was faithful to you and righteous and upright in heart. You have continued
this great kindness to him and have given him a son to sit on his throne this very day.
7"Now, O LORD my God, you have made your servant king in place of my father David.
But I am only a little child and do not know how to carry out my duties. 8Your servant
is here among the people you have chosen, a great people, too numerous to count or
number. 9So give your servant a discerning heart to govern your people and to distinguish
between right and wrong. For who is able to govern this great people of yours?"

COMMENTARY

5 God's appearance to Solomon in a dream was an auspicious beginning for him. God had accepted his sacrifices and indicated his approval. The offer God made to Solomon was as much a test of character as it was a willingness to do for him whatever he wished. It served to demonstrate where Solomon's priorities lay.

6–9 Solomon's response was basically an expression of gratitude for God's kindness in placing David's son on the throne. Though he was correct when he spoke of David's faithful walk before the Lord, the emotion that swept over his heart was an appreciation of the grace of God.

The term "little child," or young lad, relates both to his relative youth and to his inexperience in government. Solomon demonstrated commendable humility, and indeed the task before him was daunting. Only a fool would have entered into the kingship with a carefree and arrogant attitude. The responsibilities facing Solomon were all the greater in that Israel was God's chosen nation. Only if he were armed with wisdom from God would he be able to govern in a manner that would lead his people in God's ways. As king and shepherd (a common designation for a king [Jer 23; Eze 34]), he was responsible for their spiritual welfare as well as for their economic and political well-being.

Another item of thankfulness and praise is added here—the faithfulness of God in respect to the Abrahamic covenant. The words "too numerous to count or number" reflect the words of God to Abraham in Genesis 13:16. God had greatly blessed and increased Abraham's progeny in stature and in numbers.

It is not speculative wisdom that Solomon is concerned about. What he asks for is an understanding or discerning heart so that he might be able to govern God's people justly. This quality of governmental administration, in which truth and justice are paramount and a life lived in the fear of God is at the core, is developed fully in Isaiah 11:2–5. Here Messiah is depicted as the ideal ruler. Solomon represents a type of the Messiah, the Son of David *par excellence*.

NOTES

5 The two personal appearances of the Lord bracket the construction of the temple.

6 The exact meaning of the important word חֶסֶד (*ḥesed*, "kindness") has been much debated. The traditional translation was "lovingkindness" (KJV), "mercy," or "love." The NIV generally translates it as "love." The most frequent word used by the LXX is ἔλεος (*eleos*, "mercy"). The Targums are not perfectly consistent but usually use a derivative of טָב (*ṭāb*, "good"; see H. Stoebe, "חֶסֶד [*ḥesed*]," in *TLOT*, 449–64). Since the publication in 1927 of N. Glueck's doctoral dissertation (translated into English as "Hesed in the Bible"), the prevailing scholarly opinion on the meaning of the word became something like "covenant loyalty." BDB and W. Gesenius and F. Buhl (*Hebräisches und Aramäisches Handwörterbuch über das Alte Testament* [1915; repr., Berlin: Springer, 1954]) have the traditional renderings. But KB (first edition) describes it as the "mutual liability of those ... belonging together." The 1967 edition has moved back toward the more traditional position in those passages addressing God's dealings with human beings: "*Treue, Güte, Hold*," "faithfulness, goodness, grace/favor").

Glueck's view was that *ḥesed* did not basically involve mercy or love but primarily a strict loyalty and faithfulness to covenantal obligations. Katherine Sakenfeld (*The Meaning of Ḥesed in the Hebrew Bible* [Missoula, Mont.: Scholars, 1978]) has modified Glueck's view by seeing the theological usage as (1) deliverance exercised toward the needy who are obedient and (2) forgiveness toward the penitent. This combination of deliverance and forgiveness is an expression of God's faithfulness to his covenantal people.

The translation "kindness," or the like, however, seems to be the best fit for the exegetical requirements of the word's many occurrences. This position has been ably espoused by many recent scholars, such as Stoebe (ibid.); F. Andersen ("Yahweh, the Kind and Sensitive God," in *God Who Is Rich in Mercy*, ed. P. T. O'Brien and D. G. Peterson [Grand Rapids: Baker, 1986], 41–88); and R. L. Harris (*TWOT*, 1:305–7). W. Zimmerli (*TDNT*, 9:381–87) is in substantial agreement.

9 See Psalm 72 for a prayer of Solomon asking for God's blessing on his people and for the ability to govern with compassion and in righteousness.

b. God's response (3:10–15)

10The Lord was pleased that Solomon had asked for this. 11So God said to him, "Since
you have asked for this and not for long life or wealth for yourself, nor have asked for the
death of your enemies but for discernment in administering justice, 12I will do what you
have asked. I will give you a wise and discerning heart, so that there will never have been
anyone like you, nor will there ever be. 13Moreover, I will give you what you have not asked
for—both riches and honor—so that in your lifetime you will have no equal among
kings. 14And if you walk in my ways and obey my statutes and commands as David your
father did, I will give you a long life." 15Then Solomon awoke—and he realized it had been
a dream.

He returned to Jerusalem, stood before the ark of the Lord's covenant and sacrificed burnt offerings and fellowship offerings. Then he gave a feast for all his court.

COMMENTARY

10–13 Solomon bypassed the kind of request most men would commonly make—for prosperity, a long life, and victory over enemies. He sought the more essential thing; as a result, God promised to give him the wisdom he sought in such measure that he would stand alone among men (vv.10–12). In addition God granted him what he had not requested—wealth and honor unequaled in his lifetime (v.13).

Solomon's desire was to be a wise and just shepherd. In granting Solomon "a wise and discerning heart" (*lēb ḥākām wᵉnābôn*; v.12), God gave him the ability to judge and rule well. But here also he went beyond Solomon's request and opened his understanding in areas beyond those having to do with good administration. First Kings 4:29–34 and 10:1–25 sum up his fame and the vast extent of his insight and learning.

14 God's blessing is not automatic. It would depend on Solomon's walk before God. This point comes up frequently in these chapters. God's faithfulness to the Davidic covenant remained fixed; but if Solomon wished to enjoy God's fullest blessing, he would have to walk in accordance with God's will.

15 When Solomon awoke, aware that God had spoken to him in a dream, he returned to Jerusalem and brought burnt offerings and fellowship offerings. By so doing Solomon was expressing his thanks for God's goodness. He brought all his officials together for a feast so that they also might rejoice in thanksgiving at this renewed manifestation of God's grace toward Israel and the house of David.

NOTES

15 Many interpreters take at least part of this verse—"He returned to Jerusalem, stood before the ark of the Lord's covenant"—to be a later addition, either to emphasize the primacy of Jerusalem (Montgomery) or to "redeem the orthodox reputation of the builder of the Temple" (Gray, 126–27). This view is not based on objective evidence and is typical of many similar efforts in various places to distinguish between historical fact and Deuteronomistic insertions (i.e., DeVries, Jones). There is a considerable lack of consistency in the identification of these so-called later insertions because of the subjective nature of these views.

W. S. LaSor (*NBC*, 327) questions the presence of the ark in Jerusalem at this time, but there is no reason to doubt the accuracy of the text (cf. K. A. Kitchen, "Ark" [*NBD*, s.v.]; P. Feinberg, "Tabernacle" [*Wycliffe Bible Commentary* (Chicago: Moody Press, 1975), 1653–54]; and W. Lotz et al., "Ark of the Covenant" [*ISBE* rev., 1:294]).

4. Solomon's Wisdom Demonstrated—Public Approval (3:16–28)

16 Now two prostitutes came to the king and stood before him. 17 One of them said, "My
lord, this woman and I live in the same house. I had a baby while she was there with me.
18 The third day after my child was born, this woman also had a baby. We were alone; there
was no one in the house but the two of us.

19 "During the night this woman's son died because she lay on him. 20 So she got up in
the middle of the night and took my son from my side while I your servant was asleep.
She put him by her breast and put her dead son by my breast. 21 The next morning, I got
up to nurse my son—and he was dead! But when I looked at him closely in the morning
light, I saw that it wasn't the son I had borne."

22 The other woman said, "No! The living one is my son; the dead one is yours."

But the first one insisted, "No! The dead one is yours; the living one is mine." And so
they argued before the king.

23 The king said, "This one says, 'My son is alive and your son is dead,' while that one says,
'No! Your son is dead and mine is alive.'"

24 Then the king said, "Bring me a sword." So they brought a sword for the king. 25 He
then gave an order: "Cut the living child in two and give half to one and half to the other."

[26]The woman whose son was alive was filled with compassion for her son and said to the king, "Please, my lord, give her the living baby! Don't kill him!"

But the other said, "Neither I nor you shall have him. Cut him in two!"

[27]Then the king gave his ruling: "Give the living baby to the first woman. Do not kill him; she is his mother."

[28]When all Israel heard the verdict the king had given, they held the king in awe, because they saw that he had wisdom from God to administer justice.

COMMENTARY

16–28 The incident of the smothered baby is given to illustrate the unusual sagacity of Solomon. Here was a case where there were no witnesses, so it was impossible to prove by conventional means which of the litigants had a just case. Solomon displayed his extraordinary insight into human nature as well as shocking boldness of action in exposing fraud.

The mother of the dead baby wanted a baby of her own. This desire for a baby to mother was stronger than her grief and love for her dead baby. In trying to attach to herself the other woman's baby, she was motivated equally strongly by her envy of the other woman, whose baby was still alive. It was this underlying motive that was the target of Solomon's startling edict: "Cut the living child in two" (v.25). Thus the Gordian knot was cut and true justice was done.

Solomon's verdict and the way it was achieved spread like wildfire, and the people held him in great awe. Here was clear evidence to an unusual degree of a God-given ability to rule with great discernment.

C. The Glories of Solomon's Reign (4:1–34[4:1–5:14])

OVERVIEW

The description of the glories of Solomon's reign is parallel to that recorded in 9:26–10:29. Both descriptions bracket the construction of the temple. They are a fulfillment of 2 Samuel 7:14–15, namely, that God would richly bless the son of David on the condition that he would remain faithful to his God.

1. The Organization of His Kingdom: His Officials (4:1–19)

[1]So King Solomon ruled over all Israel. [2]And these were his chief officials:

Azariah son of Zadok—the priest;

[3]Elihoreph and Ahijah, sons of Shisha—secretaries;
Jehoshaphat son of Ahilud—recorder;
[4]Benaiah son of Jehoiada—commander in chief;
Zadok and Abiathar—priests;
[5]Azariah son of Nathan—in charge of the district officers;
Zabud son of Nathan—a priest and personal adviser to the king;
[6]Ahishar—in charge of the palace;
Adoniram son of Abda—in charge of forced labor.

[7]Solomon also had twelve district governors over all Israel, who supplied provisions for
the king and the royal household. Each one had to provide supplies for one month in the
year. [8]These are their names:

Ben-Hur—in the hill country of Ephraim;
[9]Ben-Deker—in Makaz, Shaalbim, Beth Shemesh and Elon Bethhanan;
[10]Ben-Hesed—in Arubboth (Socoh and all the land of Hepher were his);
[11]Ben-Abinadab—in Naphoth Dor (he was married to Taphath daughter of Solomon);
[12]Baana son of Ahilud—in Taanach and Megiddo, and in all of Beth Shan next to Zarethan below Jezreel, from Beth Shan to Abel Meholah across to Jokmeam;
[13]Ben-Geber—in Ramoth Gilead (the settlements of Jair son of Manasseh in Gilead
were his, as well as the district of Argob in Bashan and its sixty large walled cities with
bronze gate bars);
[14]Ahinadab son of Iddo—in Mahanaim;
[15]Ahimaaz—in Naphtali (he had married Basemath daughter of Solomon);
[16]Baana son of Hushai—in Asher and in Aloth;
[17]Jehoshaphat son of Paruah—in Issachar;
[18]Shimei son of Ela—in Benjamin;
[19]Geber son of Uri—in Gilead (the country of Sihon king of the Amorites and the
country of Og king of Bashan). He was the only governor over the district.

COMMENTARY

1 This verse picks up the theme from 2:46b that the kingdom was now firmly established in Solomon's hand. After showing the threefold manner in which Solomon's reign was confirmed (ch. 3), the narrative now begins to relate Solomon's acts as king.

2a We find here an indication of the organizational development of the kingdom under Solomon. There had already been considerable changes made in Israel during the reigns of the previous two kings. Under Saul the loose confederacy of twelve tribes began to be solidified into a kingdom, but his style of government seems to have been relatively modest and simple. There was no great central bureaucracy and no lavish court, and there is no record of any formal system of taxation.

David developed a kingdom in a truer sense, and he had far greater and more lasting success in defeating Israel's enemies. By the time he died, he had established a great and powerful empire by extending Israel's borders and exercising control over vassal states from the Gulf of Aqaba and the River of Egypt to the northwestern part of the Euphrates. He captured Jerusalem from the Jebusites and made it a strong and permanent capital. David seems to have had some system of internal taxation, and he certainly received tribute from his various vassal states.

Solomon inherited a stable kingdom. He did not expand the empire but did establish a well-organized and strong central government that was much stronger than ever before. He developed a system of taxation and conscript labor to support his great building projects, the foremost being the temple and palace.

The narrator gives us a picture of the organization of the kingdom in vv.2–19. Verses 2–6 list his chief administrators, vv.7–19 his district governors.

2b–6 Various suggestions have been made with regard to Azariah and the office he held. He is often considered to be the son of Zadok (Jones, 134; House, 114), but it would seem from 1 Chronicles 6:8–9 that he was Zadok's grandson. He then became high priest after the death or incapacitation of Zadok. (The designation "son" for "grandson" is common OT usage.) Ahimaaz, Azariah's father, had apparently died or for some reason could not serve. Since Zadok was surely already elderly at the beginning of Solomon's reign, it would not have been long before Azariah replaced him. The expression "the priest" is a common way of designating the high priest (de Vaux, 378; see Notes for alternative suggestions).

The two "secretaries" (*sōpᵉrîm*) served as private secretaries as well as secretaries of state. Their father had served in the same office under David. DeVaux, 131, states that the secretary played a considerable part in public affairs and ranked just below the master of the palace. Jones, 137, suggests that one might have been in charge of internal affairs while the other was responsible for international relations.

The "recorder" (*mazkîr*) was also a high official. De Vaux, 132, calls him the "royal herald." The Hebrew literally means "the one who calls, names, reminds, reports." He was in charge of palace ceremonies, the chief of protocol. He reported public needs to the king and in turn was the king's spokesman (DeVries, 69).

Benaiah, formerly commander of David's special guard, now became the "commander-in-chief" of all the armies.

Zadok, being elderly at Solomon's succession to the throne, probably did not serve long under Solomon. Abiathar was almost immediately deposed, but he would still have continued to carry the honorary title.

Azariah son of Nathan was in charge of the twelve district governors named in vv.7–19.

Zabud was another son of Nathan. His function as priest may have been as a kind of royal chaplain assisting the king in the exercise of his spiritual concerns. Zabud was also called the *rēᶜeh* of David. This seems to have been a title of honor and distinction and indicated one who was a close and trusted personal adviser. Hushai was so designated (2Sa 15:37, trans. "friend").

Ahishar was "in charge of the palace." De Vaux, 129–31, calls him the "master of the palace." Under Solomon Ahishar's functions were apparently restricted to that of chief steward of the palace, but his office gradually gained in importance until it was comparable to the office of the Egyptian vizier, the first minister of state and one empowered to speak for the king. A good example of the importance this office took on is found in Isaiah 22:15–24.

Adoniram was in charge of the forced labor, or corvée. This system was widely practiced in the ancient Near East as a means of carrying out public building projects. Samuel (1Sa 8:12–17) warned that this development would be one of the evils of instituting a monarchy. Its extensive use by Solomon, even though there were lighter demands made on Israelites than on foreign subjects and vassals, eventually created great bitterness and dissatisfaction. This introduction of the corvée was one of the major reasons given by the ten northern tribes for their secession from the kingdom (1Ki 12:4).

7–19 The responsibility of these governors was to provide revenue for Solomon's government and his projects. Each of the twelve had the responsibility for the revenue for one month out of the year. The twelve divisions coincided only in part with the old tribal divisions. In only six instances are tribal names mentioned.

The twelve officers were under the general supervision of Azariah (v.5). De Vaux, 135, holds that though the raising of revenue was the avowed object of this system of district governors, these men held wider responsibilities in the administration of area affairs.

Keil, 46, suggests that the order of the districts is most likely the order in which supplies were to be sent. The territory of Judah is not explicitly mentioned. De Vaux, 135ff., and DeVries, 72, suggest that v.19b should be translated "there was one governor over the land." "The land" would refer to Judah, which had an unnamed governor, perhaps because he was part of the court itself (i.e., perhaps the Azariah of v.5). This view (rejected by Jones, 145, but accepted in the NRSV) is based on the Assyrian custom of referring to the central province of the empire as *mātu*, "the land." The problem with this interpretation is that there would then be thirteen districts instead of the twelve required by v.7.

The rendering of the NIV, NASB, and KJV of v.19—"he [i.e., Geber] was the only governor over the district"—reflects the interpretation that, despite the size of the district governed by Geber, there was only one governor. It would appear that Judah received special privileges, which would tend to foster resentment on the part of the other tribes.

NOTES

2–3 Several views differing from that given in the commentary follow.

(1) The description "priest" refers to Zadok, not to Azariah (so Vul., Syr., KJV). However, to make the sentence say, "Azariah, son of Zadok the priest, (and) Elihoreph and Ahaziah—secretaries" is contrary to the structure of the context: "x son of y—(office)."

(2) The term כֹּהֵן (*kōhēn*, "priest") here refers to a secular office, namely "minister," "privy counselor"; (Keil, 44–45; Karl C. W. F Bahr, *The Books of the Kings* [New York: Scribner, Armstrong, 1872], 47; Edersheim, 5:67 n.l.). This view is based chiefly on 2 Samuel 8:18, where David's sons were "royal advisers" (NIV), "chief rulers" (KJV), "chief ministers" (NASB). *Kōhēn* is regularly translated "priest," and BDB and *HALOT* so understand it. The JB, NEB, NRSV, and NASB also translate "priest" here. S. R. Driver (*Notes on the Hebrew Text and Topography of the Books of Samuel* [Oxford: Clarendon, 1913], 284–85) maintains that the word must be translated "priest," that there is "no trace of any secular office" here.

Seemingly supporting Keil's contention is the fact that the parallel passage in 1 Chronicles 18:17 designates David's sons as "chief officials at the king's side." Notice also that the LXX translates 2 Samuel 8:18 αὐλάρχαι ("chiefs of the court"). The latter passage does afford some difficulty if translated as "priest"; and just in what way David's sons could have functioned as priests is unclear, though de Vaux, 361, cites examples of non-Levites, such as Samuel, who performed certain priestly functions.

(3) Montgomery (112–16; followed by the NEB) emends the text so that the "Elihoreph" of v.3 reads *ʿal-haḥōrep* ("over the autumn"), referring to the beginning of the year. He holds that this expression has reference to the Assyrian *limmu* official by whom the year was designated. There are no valid grounds for such an emendation, which requires yet another to support it: the plural "sons of Shishu" would have to be emended to the singular. Furthermore, it would leave an awkward conjunction "and" before Ahijah—one that would not fit the structural pattern of the rest of the passage. Many writers take the view adopted in the exposition but combine it with the view that the mention of Zadok and Abiathar as priests ought to be deleted (cf. de Vaux, 128; E. W. Heaton, *Solomon's New Men* [New York: Pica, 1974], 50, 184 n. 19).

(4) DeVries, 69, suggests that Azariah is the royal chaplain.

(5) Shisha is listed as David's secretary in 2 Samuel 8:17 (where he is known as "Seraiah") and in 1 Chronicles 18:16 (where he is known as "Shavsha"; see *ISBE* [rev.], 4:455).

19 Most Bible atlases describe these twelve divisions, though the exact boundaries are difficult to determine because of the brief description given here. Apart from the discussion of the inclusion or exclusion of Judah, the chief difficulty is in the question of the relationship of v.19 to v.13. The difficulty is compounded by the fact that the LXX (which has a different verse order in vv.16–19) reads "Gad" instead of "Gilead." Most seem to adopt this rendering, locate Geber's territory in the southernmost portion of the Transjordanian territories, and label the territory of Reuben as now belonging to Gad. B. Beitzel (*Moody Atlas of the Bible* [Chicago: Moody Press, 1985], map 49) locates this territory similarly but retains the name "Reuben" for this territory. In either case the mention of the territories of Sihon and Og is taken to be a general reference to the territories conquered by Moses in Transjordan.

2. His Royal Splendor (4:20–28 [4:20–5:8])

OVERVIEW

These verses are mindful of the Abrahamic covenant and give testimony to God's faithfulness in carrying out his promises. The growth of the nation, numerically and territorially, the prosperity of the people, and their happiness all attest to the blessing of God. The rules of David and Solomon in their broad outlines and at their highest points combine to form a picture of Christ's future victories and reign. David in his passionate love for the Lord, in his victories over the enemies of God's people, and in his establishment of a great kingdom is a type of the coming Messiah. Solomon also is a type, but in a different way—in his wisdom and reign of peace.

[20]The people of Judah and Israel were as numerous as the sand on the seashore; they
ate, they drank and they were happy. [21]And Solomon ruled over all the kingdoms from the
River to the land of the Philistines, as far as the border of Egypt. These countries brought
tribute and were Solomon's subjects all his life.

[22]Solomon's daily provisions were thirty cors of fine flour and sixty cors of meal, [23]ten
head of stall-fed cattle, twenty of pasture-fed cattle and a hundred sheep and goats, as well
as deer, gazelles, roebucks and choice fowl. [24]For he ruled over all the kingdoms west of the
River, from Tiphsah to Gaza, and had peace on all sides. [25]During Solomon's lifetime Judah
and Israel, from Dan to Beersheba, lived in safety, each man under his own vine and fig tree.

[26]Solomon had four thousand stalls for chariot horses, and twelve thousand horses.

[27]The district officers, each in his month, supplied provisions for King Solomon and all
who came to the king's table. They saw to it that nothing was lacking. [28]They also brought
to the proper place their quotas of barley and straw for the chariot horses and the other
horses.

COMMENTARY

20–21[4:20–5:1] The countries David had conquered remained subject to Solomon and brought him tribute throughout his reign. This was certainly a mark of God's blessing. The usual experience of ancient empire builders was that when the old king died, the subject nations would withhold tribute and challenge the new king in mounting a rebellion, thus necessitating repeated punitive expeditions by the new king to reinforce the former king's terms and to prove the ability of the new king to enforce his will. Solomon did not have this problem. God granted him a peaceful reign in which he could focus his energies on the temple and other building projects, as well as on administrative matters and on the building up of extensive and expanding foreign trade. Verses 29–34 attest to achievements that were beyond the normal province of rulers.

4:22–28[5:2–8] This passage gives an indication of the size and splendor of the court of Solomon. This magnificent court, as well as the fabled wisdom of Solomon, stirred great interest throughout the surrounding world (cf. v.34; 10:1–9). The provisions noted here were *daily* requirements.

The "cor" was a large measure of capacity. It was equivalent to the *ḥōmer* ("a donkey load"). Estimates vary considerably as to the exact amount involved and range from 48 gallons to 100 gallons. The daily requirement of fine flour amounted to between 150 and 280 bushels, that of coarse flour or meal, between 300 and 560 bushels. Jones, 146–47, suggests that the number of people who could be fed by this amount of food would amount to anywhere between 14,000 and 32,000 persons. He and others consider these quantities to be exaggerated due to a later attempt to glorify Solomon. Others, however, such as DeVries, 73, more plausibly consider that the amounts are "entirely believable, and (that) there is no reason to doubt that its details are factual." It may well be that the food supported those stationed in the various garrisons as well as those connected with the palace itself.

In addition to the large numbers of domesticated animals, game animals were also brought in. The exact identity of the "choice fowl" (*barbûr*) is not clear. Gray, 143, suggests geese as a possibility, while G. R. Driver (cited in Gray, 143) suggests "young hens," and KB a type of cuckoo.

Solomon's kingdom was a peaceful and prosperous one (v.24). With control over all the kingdoms west of the Euphrates, Solomon was able to provide peace and security for his people. The statement that "each man [sat] under his own vine and fig tree" (v.25) speaks of undisturbed prosperity, and this became a favorite catch phrase used by the prophets to point to the ideal conditions prevailing in Messiah's kingdom (Mic 4:4; Zec 3:10). The fact that a man could enjoy the fruit of the vine and the fig tree meant that the people were able to develop the land without the disruption of war. Apparently, as well, the crop yields were abundant because of God's blessing.

The reading "four thousand" reflects the parallel passage in 2 Chronicles 9:25 and some Greek MSS. The MT reads "forty thousand" and is considered an old copying error. (Because of early systems of numerical abbreviation, transmission errors with numbers were more likely than in other portions of the text.) Keil, 53, holds that the fourteen hundred chariots ascribed to Solomon's court would make four thousand a suitable figure, with two horses per chariot and one in reserve.

The twelve thousand horses (*pārāšîm*) may also indicate horsemen (so the LXX, NRSV, and NASB, with KB showing that either meaning is possible).

3. His Superior Wisdom (4:29–34 [5:9–14])

OVERVIEW

The one attribute most characteristic of Solomon is wisdom. Interest in wisdom (*ḥokmâ*) was widespread in the ancient world. In the Gentile world wisdom was primarily associated with the ability to be successful in a given activity or profession. It was not a speculative discipline but intensely practical. It pertained to all walks of life: priests (in connection with well-performed ritual), magicians (in regard to skill in the practice of their arts), craftsmen of all sorts (with respect to skillful workmanship), and administrators (regarding good management). It did not usually deal with pure moral values. When it was associated with religious activity, its concern had to do with ritual and magical skills.

In the OT *ḥokmâ* is at times used in the broad sense of skill in craftsmanship or administration. An example exists in Exodus 31:3, in which the two craftsmen appointed to make the tabernacle were given wisdom (NIV, "skill") in carrying out their work. This kind of practical wisdom is more commonly applied to life as a whole—the art of being successful, that is, how best to make one's way through life (as reflected in Proverbs). Wise men were those who had unusual insight into human nature and in the problems of life in general. Thus they were sought as advisers to kings and rulers. At the very heart, however, of the concept of wisdom in the OT lies the recognition that God is the author and end of life and that a meaningful or successful life is one that has its focus in God. This finds typical expression in the statement of Job 28:28: "The fear of the Lord—that is wisdom." He who fears the Lord receives wisdom from him, that is, the ability to see things from God's perspective. Thus true wisdom gives discernment in spiritual and moral matters. It also enables human beings to discriminate between that which is helpful and that which is harmful. Every aspect of human endeavor is included: the spiritual, intellectual, secular, and practical. It covers our relationship to God as well as our his relationship to other people.

29God gave Solomon wisdom and very great insight, and a breadth of understanding
as measureless as the sand on the seashore. 30Solomon's wisdom was greater than the
wisdom of all the men of the East, and greater than all the wisdom of Egypt. 31He was
wiser than any other man, including Ethan the Ezrahite—wiser than Heman, Calcol and
Darda, the sons of Mahol. And his fame spread to all the surrounding nations. 32He spoke
three thousand proverbs and his songs numbered a thousand and five. 33He described
plant life, from the cedar of Lebanon to the hyssop that grows out of walls. He also taught
about animals and birds, reptiles and fish. 34Men of all nations came to listen to Solomon's
wisdom, sent by all the kings of the world, who had heard of his wisdom.

COMMENTARY

29–34[5:9–14] The expression "breadth of understanding" refers to a comprehensive understanding and is illustrated by the numerous areas of knowledge in which Solomon was at home (vv.32–33). Egypt and Mesopotamia were noted for their wise men and for the great body of literature they produced. These areas were regarded as major seats of learning and culture, yet Solomon's wisdom and fame exceeded those of the various noted wise men of the nations surrounding Israel.

Solomon's wisdom was recognized to be greater than that of any other man. He is compared in particular with four men noted for their wisdom as expressed in proverbs and songs. The names "Ethan" and "Heman," both Ezrahites, occur in the titles of Psalms 89 and 88, respectively. "Calcol" and "Darda," apart from their appearance with "Ethan" and "Heman" in the genealogical list in 1 Chronicles 2:6, are otherwise unknown. "Mahol" is treated in most translations as a proper name. It may be, however, that the expression "sons of Mahol" is a designation of membership in a guild or profession. "Singers" (*māḥôl*) is literally "dance," but sacred dance and song were closely related.

Solomon was skilled and learned in many areas. He was an astute observer of life and nature. He seems to have had interest in scientific inquiry. Beyond his interest in the realm of nature, however, he was skilled in the interpretation of proverbs and riddles and also in their composition. Many of his proverbs are recorded for us in Scripture. The fact of his later defection is a standing reminder of the importance of the personal application of knowledge.

The name "Solomon" soon became synonymous with a superior wisdom, so much so that kings of distant nations sent representatives to Jerusalem—out of more than simple curiosity. It was a mark of respect and perhaps in many instances a desire to profit from Solomon's wisdom and learning. The account in ch. 10 of the visit of the Queen of Sheba provides a concrete example of this desire and also helps to draw attention to the symmetry of the Solomonic narrative as it is built around the construction of the temple.

NOTES

30[5:10] Gray, 146, notes that *qedem* may denote time as well as place, so that כָּל־בְּנֵי־קֶדֶם (*kol-bᵉnê-qedem*, "all the men of the East") might be translated "all the men of old" (i.e., the ancients). This understanding is unlikely, however, in view of the fact that the other comparison is geographical. Some interpreters think that not Mesopotamia but Edom is meant, since it was the home of Job's comforters.

31[5:11] The relationship between the four wise men named here and those listed in 1 Chronicles 2:6 as sons of Zerah of the tribe of Judah is unclear. Some scholars (e.g., J. B. Payne, "1 Chronicles," *EBC*, 4:334, following K&D), suggest that the mention of these names in the Chronicles passage does not indicate direct lineal descent but later descendants. Others (e.g., Jones, 149), suggest the possibility that the word *Ezrahite* may not be intended to be a patronymic but a word meaning "native") i.e., one of those who lived in the land before the conquest. The names "Heman" and "Ethan" appear in 1 Chronicles 15:17, 19 among the Levitical singers of the family of Korah, thus making the connection to 1 Chronicles 2:6 dubious. If the Ethan and Heman of the Psalm titles are the same men as those named here, then the narrator would obviously be referring to people living after Solomon's time, since Psalm 89 is a Psalm written in times when the kingdom of Judah was at a low ebb. The narrator invokes the Davidic covenant in praying for a revival of the kingdom. See also Marvin E. Tate (*Psalms 51–100* [WBC 20; Dallas: Word, 1990], 395).

D. Preparations for the Building of the Temple (5:1–18 [15–32])

OVERVIEW

The section 5:1–9:9 comprises the central and most important part of the Solomonic history, the construction of the temple. Here Solomon is able to accomplish what David had wanted to do; that accomplishment fulfills God's promise to David that his son would carry out the desire of David's heart. The rest of the narrative is built around this portion in concentric symmetry, as pointed out in the Introduction.

1. Solomon's League with Hiram of Tyre (5:1–12 [15–26])

OVERVIEW

After he had firmly established himself and his administration, Solomon began laying the groundwork for the carrying out of what was the major achievement of his reign—the building of the temple and palace complexes. The planning and oversight of the construction program of a project of such magnitude required considerable managerial skill, and Solomon demonstrated here again the unusual gifts granted to him by God. Assyrian and Babylonian kings prided themselves in large building projects that they considered to be monuments to their wisdom, power, and glory (e.g., Nebuchadnezzar in Da 4:30).

The fact that Solomon's other building projects—his palace, a residence for Pharaoh's daughter, a hall of justice—are mentioned more or less in passing, while the matters concerning the temple receive such extensive treatment, indicate the importance of this project in the author's mind. This is history "with God at its core" (House, 121).

1When Hiram king of Tyre heard that Solomon had been anointed king to succeed
his father David, he sent his envoys to Solomon, because he had always been on friendly
terms with David. 2Solomon sent back this message to Hiram:
3"You know that because of the wars waged against my father David from all sides, he
could not build a temple for the Name of the LORD his God until the LORD put his enemies
under his feet. 4But now the LORD my God has given me rest on every side, and there is
no adversary or disaster. 5I intend, therefore, to build a temple for the Name of the LORD
my God, as the LORD told my father David, when he said, 'Your son whom I will put on the
throne in your place will build the temple for my Name.'
6"So give orders that cedars of Lebanon be cut for me. My men will work with yours, and
I will pay you for your men whatever wages you set. You know that we have no one so
skilled in felling timber as the Sidonians."
7When Hiram heard Solomon's message, he was greatly pleased and said, "Praise be to
the LORD today, for he has given David a wise son to rule over this great nation."
8So Hiram sent word to Solomon:
"I have received the message you sent me and will do all you want in providing the
cedar and pine logs. 9My men will haul them down from Lebanon to the sea , and I will
float them in rafts by sea to the place you specify. There I will separate them and you can
take them away. And you are to grant my wish by providing food for my royal household."
10In this way Hiram kept Solomon supplied with all the cedar and pine logs he wanted,
11and Solomon gave Hiram twenty thousand cors of wheat as food for his household, in
addition to twenty thousand baths of pressed olive oil. Solomon continued to do this
for Hiram year after year. 12The LORD gave Solomon wisdom, just as he had promised him.
There were peaceful relations between Hiram and Solomon, and the two of them made a
treaty.

COMMENTARY

1[15] Hiram of Tyre, who had made peace with David and was a good friend, now sent an embassy to extend his best wishes to Solomon on his accession to the throne. Here is another example of the benefits accruing to Solomon because of his father David. The latter had been on good terms with

Hiram, who now offered Solomon a continuation of friendly relations. The expression Hiram "had always been on friendly terms with David" is literally "Hiram had always loved David." This is correctly understood by most interpreters as an expression of friendly covenantal relations. Some suggest that there may well have been much more here than simply covenantal terminology, that there was genuine friendship and love between the two monarchs.

2[16] Solomon responded in kind and in a preliminary to a trade agreement disclosed to Hiram his intentions with regard to the building project.

3[17] "You know" is a good indication that Hiram's relationship to David was more than one of peaceful coexistence or even of healthy commercial relations. David had let Hiram know what his intentions had been in regard to the building of the temple.

The building of the temple had been a matter very much on David's heart (2Sa 7:1–17; 1Ch 17:1–15). It is one of the outstanding examples of the mentality of this "man after God's own heart." He loved God with all his being and sincerely wanted to honor him. He felt it to be inappropriate that he should live in a fine palace when God's "house" was in reality a tent. Even after he was told that he would not be allowed to build the temple (and was given instead the great promise of the Davidic covenant), he did all he could in the planning and preparation for the temple (1Ch 22; 29) and gave Solomon as much help as possible.

4–5[18–19] God firmly established Solomon in the kingdom. There was peace within the kingdom, and there were no threats from the outside. Solomon was prepared to carry out his father's wishes. David's injunctions to Solomon with regard to the temple are recorded in 1 Chronicles 22:11–16; 28:9–21. Solomon must surely have caught something of David's enthusiasm for this project.

Solomon was aware of his great responsibility both toward God and toward his father, as is made clear by his quoting God's word to David (v.5b). Solomon's speech also evidences his conviction that God would enable him to complete the task: "Your son ... will build the temple for my Name."

6[20] Solomon now asked Hiram for a trade agreement similar to the one that had existed between David and Hiram, but on a much larger scale (cf. 2Sa 5:11; 1Ch 22:4). The cedars of Lebanon were famed for their beauty and were greatly desired by the rulers of Mesopotamia, Egypt, and Syro-Palestine for their building projects. Hiram's work force, skilled in felling and transporting timber, would be supplemented by labor sent by Solomon. The payment for goods and services was to be set by Hiram.

7–9[21–23] On receiving Solomon's message, Hiram responded favorably. Solomon's request would initiate a major trade agreement beneficial to both parties. He agreed to Solomon's proposal and stated that he would be responsible for shipping the timbers by log rafts to the port that Solomon designated. From that point they would be Solomon's responsibility. In return Solomon was to provide Hiram with provisions for his court.

Though Hiram offered to have his own men do the cutting and shipping without the proffered assistance of Solomon's men, in actual fact Solomon did send men to Lebanon to help with the cutting (v.14).

10–11[24–25] There would be an ample supply of timber for Solomon. In return he provided Hiram with wheat and olive oil, commodities not found in abundance in mountainous Phoenicia, whose economy was primarily based on an extensive shipping trade and export of timber.

12[26] The quality of wisdom is once again attributed to Solomon, seen here as a fulfillment of God's promise. The aspect of wisdom referred to here is that of managerial and diplomatic prowess.

NOTES

1[15] "['Hiram'] is an abbreviation for 'Ahiram,' attested for a king of Byblos ca. 1200 B.C." (DeVries, 81).

3[17] Hiram had already assisted David in supplying for him many of the materials he was stockpiling for the future temple (1Ch 22:4). For more on the mutual benefits of the pact between Israel and Tyre, see B. Peckam, "Israel and Phoenicia," in *Magnalia Dei: The Mighty Acts of God* (ed. F. M. Cross, W. E. Lemke, and P. D. Miller Jr.; Garden City, N.Y.: Doubleday, 1976), 231–33.

5[19] On the temple (lit., "house"), see comment on 6:1. The "Name" of God signifies "the active presence in the fullness of (his) revealed character" (Motyer, *NBD*, 863; cf. W. Kaiser, "Name," *ZPEB*, 4:360–66). This expression refers to the fact that God saw fit to identify himself openly and actively with the temple and with Israel.

6[20] "So (give orders)" is literally "so now (give orders)" (וְעַתָּה, *w*[e]*ʿattâ*). This Hebrew expression is used to introduce the main point of the letter (Jones, 155; DeVries, 80). The latter also points out that the וְעַתָּה (*w*[e]*ʿattâ*) of v.4 has the rarer temporal use rather than the more common situational one. In the form in which the letter is given in 2 Chronicles 2, the same expression is used in v.7[6] (translated in the NIV as "[Send me, therefore ..."]). It is of interest to note that in the Aramaic correspondence in Ezra 4–6 there is a corresponding usage, with כְּעַן (*k*[e]*ʿan*) "now" (Ezr 4:13–14; 5:17; 6:6).

The fact that Hiram, king of Tyre, was asked to supply timber and skilled lumbermen indicates that his authority and sphere of influence extended well beyond Tyre (where no cedars grew). Notice that the lumbermen Hiram would use are called "Sidonians," thus indicating Tyrian influence over Sidon (though it is possible that the name "Sidonian" may have been used generally to designate people of what was later called "Phoenicia," since Sidon was the oldest Phoenician city).

7[5:21] DeVries, 82, finds that the expression "this great people" (NIV, "great nation") is unthinkable from the mouth of Hiram and must therefore be a mark of the so-called Deuteronomist (see Introduction). This expression is indeed found in Deuteronomy 4:6–8; in vv.6 and 7 עַם (*ʿam*) is used (as in our passage here). In v.8 גּוֹי (*gôy*) is used, as is also the case in Genesis and Exodus in the restatements of the Abrahamic covenant). However, at this time in history Israel was clearly the more powerful of the two nations—a fact Hiram acknowledged.

As for Hiram's expression of praise to the Lord, Jones, 156, comments that it "need not cause difficulty, as there are many examples of naming another people's deity, both in the Bible (Jdg. 11:21; 2 Kg. 18:25ff) and outside (cf. the Amarna letters and the Moabite Stone)." In Ezra 1:2 Cyrus gives credit for his successes to "the LORD, the God of heaven." (Though the comment might sound as though Cyrus believed in Yahweh, it is known that the king rendered similar obeisance to the gods of other conquered nations.)

8–9[22–23] Montgomery, 135, cites an inscription of Nebuchadnezzar's found in Lebanon: "What no former king had accomplished, I cleaved high mountains, limestone I broke off, I opened. I cut a road for the cedars, and before Marduk my king (I brought) massive, tall, strong cedars, of wonderful beauty, whose dark appearance was impressive, the mighty product of the Lebanon." In a special purchase of wood for Egypt, Wen-Amon (ca. 1000 BC) relates how three hundred men and three hundred oxen were sent to fell the trees, which lay in the forest over the winter; then in the "third month of summer they were dragged to the shore" (ibid.).

11[25] On the unit of capacity, see Note on 4:22.

2. *Solomon's Labor Force (5:13–18 [27–32])*

[13]King Solomon conscripted laborers from all Israel — thirty thousand men. [14]He sent them off to Lebanon in shifts of ten thousand a month, so that they spent one month in Lebanon and two months at home. Adoniram was in charge of the forced labor. [15]Solomon had seventy thousand carriers and eighty thousand stonecutters in the hills, [16]as well as thirty-three hundred foremen who supervised the project and directed the workmen. [17]At the king's command they removed from the quarry large blocks of quality stone to provide a foundation of dressed stone for the temple. [18]The craftsmen of Solomon and Hiram and the men of Gebal cut and prepared the timber and stone for the building of the temple.

COMMENTARY

5:13–14[27–28] The following verses give information on the labor force Solomon raised to carry out the great task of gathering materials and then building the temple. The thirty thousand conscripted laborers were taken from all the tribes of Israel and sent in shifts of ten thousand to help the Phoenicians in the felling and transporting of the timbers from Lebanon. Each shift stayed one month at a time, so that each man worked for Solomon four months per year. The other eight months he worked on his own fields. This method of providing labor (called corvée) for large public projects was common in the ancient world but a fairly recent innovation in Israel. In the list of David's officials, Adoniram is said to be over the forced labor, thus indicating that David used the corvée system to a limited degree; but nothing further is said about it. Solomon, however, used the system extensively. The more splendid the royal court, the greater the demand on the people.

5:15–16[29–30] The seventy thousand carriers and eighty thousand stonecutters were non-Israelites (2Ch 2:17–18). They constituted a permanent "slave labor force" (1Ki 9:21), with the more onerous tasks to perform. Gray, 150, notes that the verb *ḥāṣab*, from which the word "stonecutter" is derived, "denotes the splitting of blocks from the living rock rather than the more skilled operation of hewing or dressing (*pāsal*)." The dressing of the stones was done by Israelite and Phoenician craftsmen. The stone was most likely quarried in Israel, probably much of it in Jerusalem itself. The thirty-three hundred foremen and overseers here were mostly Canaanites, with a smaller group of Israelites acting as higher supervisors.

5:17[31] The "large blocks of quality stone" for the foundation of the temple were squared off so that each stone would fit perfectly. According to 6:7 these large ashlar blocks were cut and squared at the quarry.

5:18[32] Other stones were prepared along with wooden beams by skilled craftsmen, some from Israel but most from Phoenicia. The city Gebal (Byblos) is particularly mentioned as providing a large number of these artisans. Again, according to 6:7, these men performed their craft at a place apart from the building site itself. The logistics required careful planning and measuring, and the system illustrates how well organized the whole program was and how skillfully the work was done.

NOTES

14[28] First Chronicles 29:1–9 describes David's efforts to gather materials for the temple. Mentioned are gold, silver, bronze, iron, wood, onyx, turquoise, various other gems, and marble. These materials were utilized for the finish work, including plating and overlay work, and for the furniture.

13[27] There is a further description of Solomon's labor force in 9:15–23. It consisted of conscript laborers (corvée [מַס, *mas*] here, and מַס־עֹבֵד [*mas-ʿōbēd*, "slave labor force"] in 9:21). The former, Israelites, worked for four months per year and were considered free men, whereas the latter constituted a permanent body of forced laborers. Verses 22–23 describe the kind of obligations required of the Israelites. They were chiefly used in the armed services and in skilled and supervisory positions. See also Jones, 158, and House, 125.

16[30] The numbers of supervisors as given here (3,300) and in 9:23 (550) does not seem to agree with the numbers given in 2 Chronicles 2:18 (3,600) and 2 Chronicles 8:10 (250). Keil, 63–64, following Michaelis, suggests a reasonable solution by noting that the two sets of numbers agree when added: Kings—3,300 + 550 = 3,850; Chronicles—3600 + 250 = 3,850. The differences in the figures arise from the fact that the two authors use a "different method of classification"; that is, Chronicles distinguishes the Canaanite overseers (3,600) from the Israelite (250), while Kings distinguishes between classes of overseers (3,300 lower and 550 higher overseers). Of the latter, 250 were Israelites and 300 Canaanites.

E. The Building and Dedication of the Temple (6:1–9:9)

1. The Building of the Temple (6:1–38)

OVERVIEW

Solomon's major achievement is described in this chapter, an achievement for which he was justly famous. The annals of Mesopotamian kings abound with proud claims of their great building projects, particularly temples to their gods. These projects attested not only to their administrative skills but also to the fact that they had enough wealth and control over their kingdoms that they were able to execute plans that required such vast expenditures of funds and manpower.

The temple is in reality a permanent tabernacle as far as its symbolism and typology are concerned. It is basically the dwelling place of God with his people, but its spiritual and symbolic continuity transcend the structure itself. Whether it be (1) a tent in the wilderness, (2) the splendid, awe-inspiring structure Solomon built, (3) the relatively simple building erected by the returned exiles, (4) the lavish and ornate edifice it became through Herod's efforts, or (5) its future millennial form, it is the house of God, where

God condescends to meet his people. This purpose is seen, for example, in the exchange between David and God in 2 Samuel 7, in which God is described as living among his people in a tent, moving with them from place to place. Later, David's son would build a house for God's Name. From God's perspective there is no essential difference, whether the house be a tent or a splendid structure of stone and cedar.

Perhaps even clearer is Haggai 2:3, 7, 9. Solomon's temple had been destroyed. Now, seventy years later, a new building had been put up—two different buildings, yet in v.3 both together are referred to as "this house." Verse 9 also sees one house, with its "latter glory ... greater than the former" (NASB, versus NIV). God's house had displayed great glory in Solomon's day. In Haggai's time it was physically poor by comparison, but Haggai stated that the time would come when its latter glory would far outshine the former.

When Hebrews 9 compares the earthly sanctuary (v.1) with the perfect, heavenly one (v.11), it is the tabernacle that is discussed in terms of its symbolism and typology. The reason lies in the fact that it is in connection with the tabernacle, for which Moses received specific construction specifications from the Lord, that the proper procedure for sacrifice and worship is given. Since the tabernacle is the forerunner of the temple, the same manner of sacrifice and ritual procedure pertained to both.

Throughout this section the term used for the temple is "house." There is another term that is used throughout the OT in reference to the temple: *hêkāl*. This latter term may also designate a palace and is derived from the Sumerian E.Gal ("big house"), used in Mesopotamia in reference to the largest or most important building in a city. When used in Scripture to designate God's temple, the stress is always on God's administrative activities, whereas the designation "house" has primary reference to its salvific function. The basic plan of the temple proper was the same as that of the tabernacle, except that the dimensions of the sanctuary were doubled. Notice that according to 1 Chronicles 28:11–12, it was David who drew up the plans for the temple as "the Spirit had put in his mind."

Critical orthodoxy has held that the tabernacle was an invention of the priestly school writing during or after the exile. In this view, it was the temple of Solomon that was the original model for the tabernacle rather than the reverse (cf., e.g., de Vaux, 314). But F. M. Cross has defended the priority of the tabernacle in a paper delivered at a colloquium held in Jerusalem on March 14, 1977 (reported by Valerie Fargo in "Temples and High Places: A Colloquium," *BA* 40 [1977]: 55). Cross holds this view because of similarities in the description of the tabernacle to ancient Canaanite descriptions of the tent of the assembly of the gods. Richard Friedman ("The Tabernacle in the Temple," *BA* 40 [1981]: 161–70), a student of Cross, supports the priority of the tabernacle by giving biblical and extrabiblical evidence that it was actually housed in the temple of Solomon. To make the tabernacle a late priestly fabrication is the result of unjustified text-critical assumptions.

a. The outer structure (6:1–14)

[1]In the four hundred and eightieth year after the Israelites had come out of Egypt, in the fourth year of Solomon's reign over Israel, in the month of Ziv, the second month, he began to build the temple of the LORD.

2The temple that King Solomon built for the LORD was sixty cubits long, twenty wide and
thirty high. 3The portico at the front of the main hall of the temple extended the width of
the temple, that is twenty cubits, and projected ten cubits from the front of the temple.
4He made narrow clerestory windows in the temple. 5Against the walls of the main hall
and inner sanctuary he built a structure around the building, in which there were side
rooms. 6The lowest floor was five cubits wide, the middle floor six cubits and the third floor
seven. He made offset ledges around the outside of the temple so that nothing would be
inserted into the temple walls.

7In building the temple, only blocks dressed at the quarry were used, and no hammer,
chisel or any other iron tool was heard at the temple site while it was being built.

8The entrance to the lowest floor was on the south side of the temple; a stairway led up
to the middle level and from there to the third. 9So he built the temple and completed it,
roofing it with beams and cedar planks. 10And he built the side rooms all along the temple.
The height of each was five cubits, and they were attached to the temple by beams of
cedar.

11The word of the LORD came to Solomon: 12"As for this temple you are building, if you
follow my decrees, carry out my regulations and keep all my commands and obey them, I
will fulfill through you the promise I gave to David your father. 13And I will live among the
Israelites and will not abandon my people Israel."

14So Solomon built the temple and completed it.

COMMENTARY

1 Solomon began the actual building of the temple in the fourth year of his reign. Since this event is linked to the exodus of Israel from Egypt, this verse is one of the major pieces of internal evidence for the dating of the exodus. Thiele, 205, believes the ending date for the reign of Solomon to be 931/932 BC, thus putting the beginning of his forty-year reign at 971/970, his fourth year at 967/966, and the date of the exodus at 1447/1446.

Wiseman, *1 & 2 Kings*, 104, gives numerous examples in pointing out that it was common for Mesopotamian kings to date building projects in relation to some national event. Some of the preceding events antedate the new project by as many as 720 years. To relate the building of the temple to the exodus is not surprising, since it marked the fulfillment of the latter part of Moses' song of Exodus 15. This song celebrated the power of God in bringing Israel through the Red Sea and concluded (15:17) with the prophetic statement that God would plant his people on the mountain of his inheritance, the place he had appointed for his dwelling, his sanctuary. This event was indeed one to be celebrated, another landmark event in the history of Israel.

2–10 These verses give the general dimensions of the temple. These dimensions are interior measurements and do not include the thickness of the walls. The temple (lit., "house") is here the main, central structure of the temple complex. Its dimensions were sixty cubits long by twenty wide by thirty high. (The cubit varied somewhat but may for most general purposes be considered approximately eighteen inches in length; see Notes.) It was exactly twice the size of the tabernacle proper.

Many scholars assume that Solomon modeled the temple after existing Canaanite and Syrian tripartite temples, but none have been found that match the measurements of Solomon's structure (Jones, 162). It has also been suggested that Solomon remodeled an existing Jebusite temple (cf. the reference to the study by Konrad Rupprecht in DeVries, 97). But these views tend to be based on the critical assumption that the tabernacle is a late fiction.

There was a portico (or porch, vestibule—*ʾûlām*) attached to the front of the "main hall of the temple" (*hêkāl habbayit; hêkāl* most often refers to a palace or a temple, or, as in this passage, the main room of the temple, distinct from the *dᵉbîr*, "Most Holy Place"). It measured ten by twenty cubits, with its long side going along the breadth of the temple proper.

The description in vv.4–10 includes many technical architectural terms that are no longer perfectly clear today. The "clerestory windows" (*ḥallônê šᵉqupîm*) were probably on the side walls above the side chambers (v.5). The exact nature of the windows is not known. Some interpreters have suggested slatted or latticed windows. Others, following the Targums ("open inside and closed outside") and Aquila ("broad within and narrow without"), suggest windows narrower outside than inside.

Against the outside walls of the temple proper (its main hall and inner sanctuary), Solomon built (vv.5–6) a three-tiered structure divided into an unspecified number of rooms. (Ezekiel's temple [Eze 41:5–11], which also has three tiers of side rooms, has thirty rooms per level.) Verse 10 gives the height of these rooms as five cubits each. At each level of the side rooms, the thickness of the outside of the temple wall was decreased by one cubit so that the floor beam of the side chamber rested on the resulting offset ledge. Thus the width of each successive story increased by one cubit. By this means the beams had supports without being "inserted" or bonded into the inner temple wall. They were not structurally a part of the temple.

It is not necessary to see at v.7, with Gray, 165, and Jones, 165–66, a concession to the "long-standing taboo in the religion of Israel" against using iron in the construction of the altar (Ex 20:25), since iron was indeed used at the quarries. The biblical text does indicate excellent organization and planning. The erection of the temple could go much faster and with far less confusion by utilizing precut and preformed materials. In addition, the relative quiet would be consistent with the sacredness of the undertaking.

The entrance to the side room (v.8) was on the righthand (south) side, probably in the middle (see Notes). Access to the second and third levels is most often understood to have been by means of a spiral staircase (*lûlîm*) that led through the middle story to the third floor.

The first part of v.9 is repeated in v.14, the latter being resumptive, continuing on with the main narrative (DeVries, 95). The information given to us between v.9a and v.14 is the record of (1) the completion of the external structure, and (2) God's message of encouragement to Solomon. Verses 9b–10 record the addition of the roof and the attachment of the side structure. When the narrative begins again in v.14, the following verses relate the finishing of the interior. Verses 11–13 insert the word of encouragement to Solomon after the temple structure had been completed but before the finishing of the interior.

11–13 First Kings 9:2 states that after the dedication of the temple, the Lord appeared to Solomon a second time (the first time having been at Gibeon [1Ki 3]), referring to direct personal appearances of the Lord. In the present passage God evidently spoke to Solomon through a prophet.

These are encouraging words, assuring Solomon of God's blessing on the building of the temple, which was still in progress. God was indeed with Solomon in this massive undertaking, and he would recognize the temple as his dwelling place among his people. There is the reminder, however, that Solomon, if he wished to continue to experience the blessings of the Davidic covenant (see Notes), must exhibit the faith and obedience of David toward the Word of God. The same holds true for succeeding generations of the people Israel. Thus the temple in all its splendor and ritual is by itself not sufficient. God requires obedient hearts. In this matter alone there stands a great gulf between the faith of Israel and the cultic ritual of the surrounding Gentile nations. The call of God issued through Isaiah (Isa 55) was echoed by generations of godly prophets, and Isaiah 55:3 is pertinent to this passage: "Give ear and come to me.... I will make an everlasting covenant with you, my faithful love promised to David."

14 This verse concludes the description of the exterior structure (see comments at v.9). The following verses describe the work done on the interior.

NOTES

1 The view that the 480 years is not to be taken literally is adopted by a great many scholars, including conservatives. They understand this to represent the passing of twelve generations, calculated at forty years each. Since the actual passing of generations is much less, the figure 480 cannot be used in calculating the actual date of the exodus. Some take this figure to be a literary device "setting the building of the Temple exactly halfway between the Exodus and the Exile" (Jones, 162–63). There is, however, nothing in the context to suggest anything other than a literal understanding. The literalness of the 480 years tends to be supported by the practice of Mesopotamian kings mentioned in the commentary.

The site of the building of the temple is not given here, but 2 Chronicles 3:1 states that it was "on Mount Moriah, where the LORD had appeared to his father David. It was on the threshing floor of Araunah the Jebusite, the place provided by David." This was also the site of the (aborted) sacrifice of Isaac by Abraham (Ge 22:2). It lay on the rocky platform just to the north of the city of David on the eastern ridge of Jerusalem, "on an eminence appropriate to its character" (Stigers, 622–66).

On the precise location of the temple, see Stigers (ibid.). A. S. Kaufman ("Where the Ancient Temple of Jerusalem Stood," *BAR* 9 [1983]: 42) suggests that the temple stood approximately 330 feet to the northwest of the present Dome of the Rock, rather than on the site of the Dome itself, as has been usually assumed. However, more recently Leen Ritmeyer (archaeological architect for a number of excavations in Jerusalem) has argued persuasively that Herod's temple, and Solomon's as well, stood over the rock (*al-Sakhra*) over which the Muslim mosque the Dome of the Rock is built. He positions the ark of the covenant on the rock itself ("Locating the Original Temple Mount," *BAR* 18 [1992]: 24–45, 64–65; and "The Ark of the Covenant: Where it Stood in Solomon's Temple" *BAR* 22 [1996]: 46–55, 70–73). Still more recently, D. Jacobson ("Sacred Geometry: Unlocking the Secret of the Temple Mount, Part I," *BAR*

25 [1999]: 42–53, 62–65; and "Sacred Geometry: Unlocking the Secret of the Temple Mount, Part II," *BAR* 25 [1999]: 54–63, 74), using a different methodology, also positions the temple where the Dome of the Rock now stands, but with the difference that it was the middle of the main hall (not the Most Holy Place) of the temple that stood over *al-Sakhra*.

The month Ziv, the second month, corresponds to our April/May.

2 The cubit is the measure of the distance between the elbow and the tip of the middle finger. Since this length varies somewhat from person to person, the exact length had to be standardized for building projects. Bible dictionaries generally give the length of the common cubit to be seventeen and one-half inches. This measurement has been determined by comparing the length of Hezekiah's tunnel (1,749 ft.) with the statement in the Siloam inscription that it was 1,200 cubits long (a round figure?), thus resulting in a cubit length of 17.5 inches. There was also a longer cubit in use, estimated to be about 20.5 inches in length. For a detailed discussion of the various lengths of the medium cubit, see Kaufman, "Ancient Temple," 48–49.

5 The meaning of the word translated "structure"—יָצִיעַ (*yāṣîaᶜ*, Qere), יָצוּעַ, *yāṣûaᶜ* (Kethiv)—is somewhat uncertain. The Hebrew יָצוּעַ (*yāṣûaᶜ*) means "bed, couch." Thus it has been suggested that the rendering here ought to be "foundation" or "platform." Ezekiel 41:8 is cited as bolstering this translation, since in that passage there is clearly a supporting platform built for the three levels of side chambers. Keil, 70, suggests "outwork" (lit., "stratum"), "here, the lower building or outwork erected against the rooms mentioned." Jones, 164–65, after some discussion, agrees that it must refer to a structure built around the temple, a sidewing. The NRSV concurs with the NIV in translating the word as "structure."

7 The stone that was quarried was white limestone and famous for its beauty (called the "royal stone" by the Arabs). It is reduced to lime when exposed to a hot fire. Thus when the temple burned (2Ki 25:9), it was not only the wood that burned; the stones themselves were reduced to powdered lime.

8 The NIV, with other modern versions (NASB, NEB, JB), follows the LXX in reading "the entrance to the lowest [הַתַּחְתֹּנָה, *hattaḥtōnâ*] floor." This attractive possibility enjoys some strong support in the Targums and a similar passage in Ezekiel 41:7. Yet the MT deserves serious consideration. It reads הַתִּיכֹנָה (*hattîkōnâ*, "the middle"). "The middle" then refers to the middle of the wing rather than to the middle floor. In this case the word צֵלָע (*ṣēlāᶜ*, "floor") is not to be understood in the collective sense of "side rooms" but as a single side room. The translation then is, "The entrance was at the middle side chamber on the south wing." The lower floor is not specifically mentioned because it would be the obvious place for the door. The NKJV, NRSV read "middle."

The rendering "spiral staircase" for לוּלִים (*lûlîm*) is suggested by the LXX, Targums, and Vulgate. The remains of such a staircase have been found in a palace of the eighteenth century BC at Achana. Other suggestions have been made such as a series of ladder-like steps, a flying wing, or stairs with landings.

9 Apart from the statement that the roof was constructed of beams and cedar planks, no details are given. Stigers, 5:628, states that the wooden planks formed "a bed on which clay was packed and covered with a pulverized limestone marl, rolled flat, smooth, and hard, providing a cement-like surface which was practically impervious to water."

10 The use to which these side chambers were put is not mentioned, but they were doubtless intended, at least in part, for storage purposes.

12 "I will fulfill through you" is probably better rendered, "I will fulfill with regard to you my promise that I made with David your father" (cf. also NASB, NEB, JB). There is more involved here than the fulfillment of promise in the completion of the temple. There is also the matter of the conditions on which God could bless Solomon.

b. The inner structure (6:15–35)

[15]He lined its interior walls with cedar boards, paneling them from the floor of the
temple to the ceiling, and covered the floor of the temple with planks of pine. [16]He
partitioned off twenty cubits at the rear of the temple with cedar boards from floor to
ceiling to form within the temple an inner sanctuary, the Most Holy Place. [17]The main hall
in front of this room was forty cubits long. [18]The inside of the temple was cedar, carved
with gourds and open flowers. Everything was cedar; no stone was to be seen.

[19]He prepared the inner sanctuary within the temple to set the ark of the covenant of
the LORD there. [20]The inner sanctuary was twenty cubits long, twenty wide and twenty
high. He overlaid the inside with pure gold, and he also overlaid the altar of cedar. [21]Solo-
mon covered the inside of the temple with pure gold, and he extended gold chains
across the front of the inner sanctuary, which was overlaid with gold. [22]So he overlaid the
whole interior with gold. He also overlaid with gold the altar that belonged to the inner
sanctuary.

[23]In the inner sanctuary he made a pair of cherubim of olive wood, each ten cubits high.
[24]One wing of the first cherub was five cubits long, and the other wing five cubits — ten
cubits from wing tip to wing tip. [25]The second cherub also measured ten cubits, for the
two cherubim were identical in size and shape. [26]The height of each cherub was ten
cubits. [27]He placed the cherubim inside the innermost room of the temple, with their
wings spread out. The wing of one cherub touched one wall, while the wing of the other
touched the other wall, and their wings touched each other in the middle of the room.
[28]He overlaid the cherubim with gold.

[29]On the walls all around the temple, in both the inner and outer rooms, he carved
cherubim, palm trees and open flowers. [30]He also covered the floors of both the inner and
outer rooms of the temple with gold.

[31]For the entrance of the inner sanctuary he made doors of olive wood with five-sided
jambs. [32]And on the two olive wood doors he carved cherubim, palm trees and open
flowers, and overlaid the cherubim and palm trees with beaten gold. [33]In the same way
he made four-sided jambs of olive wood for the entrance to the main hall. [34]He also made
two pine doors, each having two leaves that turned in sockets. [35]He carved cherubim,
palm trees and open flowers on them and overlaid them with gold hammered evenly
over the carvings.

COMMENTARY

15–18 When the exterior structure was complete, Solomon lined the interior walls with cedar planks from floor to ceiling. The floors were also covered with wood, in this case pine or fir. Whatever the exact identity of this wood, it was often used together with cedar. The two were highly regarded and became a symbol of luxuriousness and stateliness. From this and the following verses in this chapter, and in ch. 7, it is quite evident that Solomon spared no expense in building the temple; he used the finest and costliest materials available. His prayer in ch. 8 makes it clear that in doing so Solomon was giving expression to his sincere love for, and devotion to, God. Though God could not be enriched, Solomon was demonstrating in a practical way that nothing but the best is owed to God. This is an abiding principle for believers of all ages and ought to find expression in every area of life.

The inner sanctuary, or "Most Holy Place," was partitioned off from the main hall by cedar planks (v.16). No stone was visible anywhere in the temple (v.18). Not only was everything lined with cedar, but also the wood paneling was covered with fine, delicate carvings.

19–22 The inner sanctuary (*d*^{e}*bîr*) was the Most Holy Place, or Holy of Holies, because it housed the ark of the covenant, a symbol of the presence of God. First Samuel 4:4 and 2 Samuel 6:2 speak of God as being enthroned between the cherubim. In Exodus 25:21–22 God said that he would meet with Moses there and give to him all the divine commands for the Israelites. The top of the ark could be called the "mercy seat" or "place of propitiation" in view of the annual sprinkling of the blood of atonement by the high priest. It was from between the cherubim that the glory of the Lord began his departure from the temple in Ezekiel 10:4. Thus the ark in the Most Holy Place is the focal point of the temple and its ritual, not as an object of worship or superstitious awe, but as the place where God manifested his presence in communicating with his people. Thus in this and the following verses everything is designed to express the awesome dignity, splendor, and holiness of God's presence.

The room was a perfect cube, overlaid in its entirety with gold, as was the cedar altar of incense (cf. v.22). This altar was physically placed in the main hall, or Holy Place, directly before the entrance into the Most Holy Place (Ex 30:6); but functionally and symbolically the altar was associated with the Most Holy Place. Thus v.22 notes that it "belonged to the inner sanctuary" (cf. also Heb 9:4). In using this altar, the priest could daily burn incense for the worship of God, who was symbolically enthroned between the cherubim in the inner sanctuary.

Not only the inner sanctuary, but also all the inside walls of the temple were overlaid with gold. The golden chains, stretched across the front of the inner sanctuary, served to strengthen the concept of the inaccessibility of this Most Holy Place.

23–28 Two cherubim made of olive wood and covered with gold were placed in the inner chamber (vv.23, 28). Each had a wingspan of ten cubits (vv.24–26). They were positioned so that they faced the door (2Ch 3:13). Thus their combined wingspan reached from one wall to the other (v.27). (Notice that the two cherubim on the ark faced each other.) These composite figures (cf. Eze 1:4–14) represented the cherubim associated with the throne and government of God (Eze 1:22–28). They also served as the guardians of the way to God (Ge 3:24). The impact on the beholder of these representations of the cherubim would be to impress on that person the awesomeness of God's holiness. Approaching God is not a light or frivolous matter and must be undertaken in the exact way he has prescribed—through the blood of the sacrifice.

29–35 Doors of olive wood were made for the entry to the inner sanctuary, and larger, double-leaved doors of pine or fir were made for the entry to the main hall. Second Chronicles 3:14 does not mention the doors but does mention the veil that was hung between the two chambers. The jambs for both sets of doors were of olive wood. The doors as well as the walls (vv.20–22), and even the floors, were covered with gold (v.30). Gold was also hammered into the carvings on the door (v.32). The covering of the floors with gold has often been scoffed at as being preposterous; yet it is in keeping with Solomon's desire to show forth in the temple, as much as humanly possible, the glory of God. It was his testimony to the greatness of God, and indeed the fame of this temple spread far and wide so that honor and glory accrued to God as a result (10:9).

NOTES

20 The fact that the Most Holy Place was twenty cubits high when the Holy Place or main hall was thirty cubits high has occasioned some discussion. The best evidence suggests that the floor level was the same for both rooms and that there was an attic above the Most Holy Place (Stigers, 5:633).

31 The translation "five-sided jambs" expresses the generally current view of a Hebrew phrase that has occasioned some difficulty. חֲמִשִׁית (*ḥ*ª*mišît*) may be rendered "one-fifth" or "five-sided" (*HALOT*). Gray, 173, suggests that the doorposts together with a gabled lintel, forming a pentagon, may be in view here. Jones, 171–72, noting the appearance of a temple with a five-sided doorway on a coin from Byblos, supports this view.

c. The court (6:36)

[36]And he built the inner courtyard of three courses of dressed stone and one course of trimmed cedar beams.

COMMENTARY

36 An inner court, called in 2 Chronicles 4:9 the court of the priests, was built with three courses of dressed stone and then one layer of trimmed cedar beams. Ezra 6:4 describes the same construction method. This type of construction is well attested at Ras Shamra, Cnossus, Mycenae, and other ancient cities and gave some protection against earthquakes.

Though not stated here, this court contained the bronze altar and the bronze Sea, described in ch 7.

d. The conclusion (6:37–38)

[37]The foundation of the temple of the LORD was laid in the fourth year, in the month of Ziv. [38]In the eleventh year in the month of Bul, the eighth month, the temple was finished in all its details according to its specifications. He had spent seven years building it.

COMMENTARY

37–38 Seven years were required to complete the temple. An enormous amount of labor and a lavish expenditure of funds were involved. All the plans and specifications of David were carried out. It must have been a moment of great satisfaction to Solomon to see the fulfillment of his father's dream; and when God acknowledged the temple by filling it with his glory, Solomon's joy knew no bounds.

2. Solomon's Other Structures (7:1–12)

OVERVIEW

The narrator gives a brief description of the building of Solomon's palace and other structures. The temple was included in this complex along with the palace. Both were enclosed within one courtyard (v.12). This was intended to give visual expression to the fact that the king was to act on behalf of God. He himself was to walk in God's ways and, as shepherd of the people, lead and direct them to God. As such he was a type of Christ, the Son of David, who will rule the earth from Jerusalem and who even now is seated at the right hand of God.

The descriptions of the various parts of the palace are extremely sketchy, so it is difficult to make an accurate reconstruction. No remains of the palace have been found, but the unearthing of two Solomonic "palaces" at Megiddo may furnish some indications of the basic plan. David Ussishkin, 78–105, summarizes the general conclusions that have been drawn from comparative archaeological data. The "palaces" at Megiddo were built on the plan of the *bît-ḥilāni*, an architectural style in use in northern Syria and southern Anatolia. The term was probably originally used to designate a magnificent style of porticoed entry hall, a long room entered on the broad side through a portico with several pillars. Then it came to include the whole complex of rooms served by this entry hall. The throne room was considerably larger than the entry and was also entered on the broad side.

In addition to these two major halls, there were a number of smaller rooms and also apparently one or more courtyards. There was also at least one upper story. The two Megiddo "palaces" follow this plan, as do four *bît-ḥilānis* found in the acropolis of Zinjirli (ancient Samal, an Aramean city of northern Syria). These buildings were constructed in the tenth through the eighth centuries

BC. Verses 6–9 seem to suggest a similar style of construction. These factors may mean that all the buildings except the Palace of the Forest of Lebanon were part of one massive structure, but this is by no means certain. In any case, the Palace of the Forest of Lebanon was a separate building.

The brief treatment given to this section is further testimony that, however grand and imposing the palace complex was, the temple was Solomon's most important achievement, and it is this fact that the narrator wishes to stress. Jones, 174, agrees with this assessment, though he attributes the lack of more information on the magnificent features of the palace complex to the work of the Deuteronomist. Chronicles does not mention the palace construction.

1 It took Solomon thirteen years, however, to complete the construction of his palace.
2 He built the Palace of the Forest of Lebanon a hundred cubits long, fifty wide and
thirty high, with four rows of cedar columns supporting trimmed cedar beams. 3 It was
roofed with cedar above the beams that rested on the columns—forty-five beams,
fifteen to a row. 4 Its windows were placed high in sets of three, facing each other. 5 All the
doorways had rectangular frames; they were in the front part in sets of three, facing each
other.

6 He made a colonnade fifty cubits long and thirty wide. In front of it was a portico, and
in front of that were pillars and an overhanging roof.

7 He built the throne hall, the Hall of Justice, where he was to judge, and he covered it
with cedar from floor to ceiling. 8 And the palace in which he was to live, set farther back,
was similar in design. Solomon also made a palace like this hall for Pharaoh's daughter,
whom he had married.

9 All these structures, from the outside to the great courtyard and from foundation to
eaves, were made of blocks of high-grade stone cut to size and trimmed with a saw on
their inner and outer faces. 10 The foundations were laid with large stones of good quality,
some measuring ten cubits and some eight. 11 Above were high-grade stones, cut to size,
and cedar beams. 12 The great courtyard was surrounded by a wall of three courses of
dressed stone and one course of trimmed cedar beams, as was the inner courtyard of the
temple of the LORD with its portico.

COMMENTARY

1 It took Solomon almost twice as long to build his palace complex as to build the temple. This rather startling statement is commonly thought to reflect negatively on Solomon. But it might be said in his defense that Scripture does not condemn him for the magnificence of his palace complex. The longer construction time might be due to the fact that numerous public and private building units were being constructed, five of which are briefly described in this passage. Also note that in the case of the temple there had been extensive advanced planning and acquisition of materials. Such was not the case with the palace.

2–5 The Palace of the Forest of Lebanon was so named because of its cedar construction. It was an imposing structure one hundred cubits long, fifty cubits wide, and thirty cubits high. Its exact function is not perfectly clear, though it is referred to in 10:17 as the repository of three hundred shields of gold, which might indicate that it was used in part as a treasury. Isaiah 22:8 also speaks of armor placed in the "Palace of the Forest." This latter passage is in a context of warfare, so that it would appear that real weapons, not ceremonial shields, are involved, thus indicating that the building was at least in part an armory, though Wiseman, *1 & 2 Kings*, 111, believes that this was not its essential function.

6–8 The colonnade was a magnificent porticoed entry hall. It is not clear whether this hall was related to the previous building (Jones, 176), was a waiting room for those awaiting hearings in the Hall of Justice (Wiseman, *1 & 2 Kings*, 112), or perhaps was an imposing entry to the latter building.

The throne hall or royal audience chamber also served as the Hall of Justice, where the king personally heard complaints and meted out justice in cases that could not be handled by lesser officials (cf. 3:16–28). The layout of this throne room was most likely similar to that of contemporaneous throne rooms in Syria and Assyria. "Thus, almost certainly it was a rectangular hall with the official entrance in its long side. The throne was placed on a rectangular dais or raised base, constructed at the far side of the hall adjacent to its short wall and centrally placed" (Ussishkin, 90). Usually the throne was placed at the end of the hall, left of the entry. The throne itself is described in 10:18–20.

As to the private residence of Solomon and that for Pharaoh's daughter, nothing is said except that they were similar in design and set away from the public building.

9–12 The stones used in the palace complex were of high quality, precisely cut, and trimmed on both inner and outer faces (v.9). The foundation stones were large, measuring twelve to fifteen feet in length (v.10). Similar ashlar stones have been found above the foundations of the southern "palace" at Megiddo. Burke Long, 178, suggests that the description of the building materials applies to all the Solomonic buildings, including the temple.

The large outer court "enclosed both the Temple and the palace works of Solomon" (Stigers, 5:531). The construction—three layers of stone and one of cedar beams (v.12)—was the same as that of the wall of the inner court. This typically Phoenician construction style is represented at Megiddo in the Solomonic gate as well as in the gate of the court to the southern palace (Ussishkin, 105).

NOTES

1 That the thirteen years are to be understood of the palace alone, apart from the construction of the temple, is seen from 9:10, where twenty years is given as the total building time. House, 130 n. 58, points out that the expression אֶת־כָּל־בֵּיתוֹ (*ʾet-kol-bêtô*; lit., "all his house/palace") implies a joint structure.

3. The Vessels of the Temple (7:13–51)

a. Hiram the craftsman (7:13–14)

[13]King Solomon sent to Tyre and brought Huram, [14]whose mother was a widow from the tribe of Naphtali and whose father was a man of Tyre and a craftsman in bronze. Huram was highly skilled and experienced in all kinds of bronze work. He came to King Solomon and did all the work assigned to him.

COMMENTARY

13–14 Hiram (NIV, "Huram"; so also in 2Ch 2:13; 4:11) was an outstanding master craftsman brought from Tyre. He is obviously to be distinguished from the king of the same name. He was half-Phoenician and half-Israelite, his mother being from the tribe of Naphtali. Our text describes him as being skilled in bronze work. Second Chronicles 2:14 adds that he was likewise skilled in working with gold, silver, iron, stone, wood, and various dyes and fine linen. This description is strongly reminiscent of the skills of Bezalel the craftsman, whom God chose to make the tabernacle (Ex 31:2–3; 35:30–31).

Hiram was "highly skilled and experienced." More literally, "he was filled with wisdom [*ḥokmâ*] and understanding [*tᵉbûnâ*] and knowledge [*daᶜat*] in doing every kind of bronze work." This description illustrates the broad semantic range of the words "wisdom" and "understanding." Hiram's wisdom consisted in his practical skills. Notice that Solomon not only utilized the finest materials, but he also spared no expense in hiring the finest workmen. Since Hiram's skills are so similar to those of Bezalel, who is described in Exodus 31:3 as being especially prepared and enabled by God for the task of building the tabernacle, it is not inappropriate to see in Hiram one also prepared and enabled by God for this special project, though such is not expressly stated. It ought also to be noted that Hiram was the son of a widow—a considerable handicap in the ancient world. That he should achieve such renown in his craftsmanship attests not only to his diligence but also to the grace of God.

NOTES

14 The writer of 2 Chronicles 2:14 records Hiram the king as saying that the mother of Hiram the craftsman was from Dan. This apparent contradiction has a ready solution if one considers that the city of Dan and its territories were by Solomon's time part of the general region of Napthali (cf. Aharoni and Avi-Yonah, map 113). Thus Hiram's mother could easily be of the tribe of Napthali, yet have lived in Dan.

b. The two bronze pillars (7:15–22)

15He cast two bronze pillars, each eighteen cubits high and twelve cubits around, by
line. 16He also made two capitals of cast bronze to set on the tops of the pillars; each
capital was five cubits high. 17A network of interwoven chains festooned the capitals on
top of the pillars, seven for each capital. 18He made pomegranates in two rows encircling
each network to decorate the capitals on top of the pillars. He did the same for each
capital. 19The capitals on top of the pillars in the portico were in the shape of lilies, four
cubits high. 20On the capitals of both pillars, above the bowl-shaped part next to the
network, were the two hundred pomegranates in rows all around. 21He erected the pillars
at the portico of the temple. The pillar to the south he named Jakin and the one to the
north Boaz. 22The capitals on top were in the shape of lilies. And so the work on the pillars
was completed.

COMMENTARY

15–20 These two pillars are the first of the objects made by Hiram/Huram. They were cast of bronze and were large: eighteen cubits high with a circumference of twelve cubits. They were hollow, four fingerbreadths thick (Jer 52:21), and cast in molds (v.46).

The capitals, also bronze, were cast separately and were five cubits in length (v.16). They were bowl shaped (v.42; 2Ch 4:12–13) and adorned with pomegranates, lily petals, and a network of interwoven chains (vv.17–20). D. J. Wiseman and C. J. Davey (*Illustrated Bible Dictionary* [Wheaton, Ill.: Tyndale, 1980], 2:726) suggest that "the capital had four opened and inverted lotus petals [*śûšan*; "lily-work," RSV] four cubits in width ... and above this an inverted bowl [*gullâ*]." This view is based on evidence from the text and from the known examples of the period. If this picture is correct, then the chain network fringed with the two hundred pomegranates encircled the bowl above the inverted lily. (See Wiseman [*NBD*, 593, fig. 116] for a reconstruction of the pillar according to the model suggested above.)

21–22 It is probable that these pillars were freestanding, not structurally a part of the portico. They were placed "at" (l^e) the portico, not "in" (b^e) it (DeVries, 110). Though there are examples of Syrian temples of the same type as Solomon's, in which there were two pillars inside the portico (Tell Tainat [with double pairs of lions] and Ebla [Volkmar Fritz, "Temple Architecture," *BAR* 13 (1987): 38–49]), there also are numerous examples in the ancient Near East—from Egypt, Assyria, Phoenicia, and Cyprus—of similar pairs of freestanding pillars. The fact that they are described here rather than in ch. 6 tends to confirm their structural independence.

The pillar placed on the right hand, or southern, side of the entrance to the portico was named "Jakin." The other, on the left hand or northern side, was named "Boaz." Jones, 182–83, after giving a rather comprehensive list of views, suggests that these pillars "contained oracles confirming the establishment and sustaining of the dynasty by God ... [and] symbolized the covenant between God and his people, and especially between him and the Davidic dynasty."

In practical terms the pillars were to be ever-present reminders to each successive king of the fact that he was ruling by God's appointment and by his grace, and that his strength lay in God.

NOTES

15 Second Chronicles 3:15 states: "In front of the temple he made two pillars, which [together] were thirty-five cubits long." The insertion of the word "together" reflects the view that this figure is the combined length of the shafts of the two columns. "The additional cubit of length most likely was a separate cast base" (Stigers, 5:629). Others (e.g., Keil, 97) hold that the Chronicles passage reflects a scribal error. Second Kings 25:17 and Jeremiah 52:21 both give the length as eighteen cubits.

16 The height of the capitals is given in 2 Kings 25:17 as three cubits. The apparent discrepancy has been explained by some as an error in textual transmission, by others as being due to the fact that the capitals may have been reduced in size during a renovation of the temple during the reign of Joash (2Ki 12:6–14), and by still others as involving a different point of measurement that "would refer to the upper portion of the capital, leaving two cubits for the height of the lily work" (Stigers, 5:629). This last suggestion appears most tenable, particularly since the passage that is largely parallel to 2 Kings 25:17 (i.e., Jer 52:22), reads "five cubits" (thus ruling out the idea of a shortening of the capital).

18 The MT rendered literally is, "he made pillars ... capitals on top of the pomegranates." (Fifty Hebrew manuscripts read "pillars" instead of "pomegranates.") The NIV's rendering reflects a textual change suggested by most commentators. It is assumed that the words "pillars" and "pomegranates" were somehow switched, as seems to be confirmed by v.19. The NASB renders the MT as it stands.

21 R. B. Y. Scott ("The Pillars Jachin and Boaz," *JBL* 58 [1939]: 143–47) has suggested that the names "Jakin" and "Boaz" are the initial words of a dedicatory inscription of the type found on a pillar east of Gudea's temple in Lagash that records Enlil's choice of King Gudea as his high priest. He suggests that the full inscription might have read something like, "He (Yahweh) will establish the throne of David, and his kingdom to his seed forever," and "In the strength of [revocalizing בֹּעַז (*bōʿaz*) to בְּעֹז (*beʿōz*)] Yahweh shall the king rejoice." This suggestion is adopted by Wiseman (*NBD*, 593).

The suggestion of S. Yeivin ("Yachin and Boaz," *PEQ* 91 [1959]: 6–22) that the pillars are reminiscent of the pillars of fire and smoke during the exodus and are thus symbols of the divine presence has been taken up by many who have adopted the view that the pillars were giant incense stands or cressets where the fat of sacrifices was burnt (cf. W. F. Albright, "Two Cressets from Marina and the Pillars of Jachin and Boaz," *BASOR* 85 [1942]: 18–27; H. G. May, "The Two Pillars before the Temple of Solomon," *BASOR* 88 [1942]: 19–27). But there is no indication that these pillars were cressets. The names of the pillars are not appropriate to this suggested symbolism, nor is the archaeological evidence compelling.

c. The bronze Sea (7:23–26)

[23]He made the Sea of cast metal, circular in shape, measuring ten cubits from rim to rim and five cubits high. It took a line of thirty cubits to measure around it. [24]Below the rim, gourds encircled it—ten to a cubit. The gourds were cast in two rows in one piece with the Sea.

[25]The Sea stood on twelve bulls, three facing north, three facing west, three facing south and three facing east. The Sea rested on top of them, and their hindquarters were toward the center. [26]It was a handbreadth in thickness, and its rim was like the rim of a cup, like a lily blossom. It held two thousand baths.

COMMENTARY

23–26 The great Sea, made of cast bronze, was another marvelous example of the superb craftsmanship of Hiram/Huram. It was cast in one piece, including the lily-like rim and the two rows of gourds below the rim (v.24). The bronze bulls were cast separately, since they were later removed by Ahaz and replaced with a stone base (2Ki 16:17). The exact shape is not known. Calculations attempting to determine the exact relationship between the measure of volume, the bath, and the cubit are marred by this lack of information. Some have assumed it to be cylindrical, others, hemispherical in shape. Something approaching a hemisphere is indicated by the fact that it required a support (2Ki 16:17).

The statement regarding the circumference of thirty cubits has been much discussed and criticized, since it yields a value for *pi* of three (rather than 3.14). Various solutions have been suggested involving different means of taking the measurements. The simplest solution is also the most obvious and most likely, that the figures are not intended to be mathematically precise to three or four significant figures, but only to one, yielding a value for *pi* of three. Jones, 184, also adopts this view.

The Sea, together with the ten movable basins, served the same function as the laver had served in the tabernacle—for ceremonial cleansing. Second Chronicles 4:6 informs us that the Sea was used by the priests for their washing, while the basins were used for the rinsing of the burnt offerings. The ceremonial stipulations for the priesthood with regard to the cleansing required in connection with their ministry and approach to God (Ex 30:18–21) were intended to teach a truth that transcends mere ritualism, namely, that he who would approach God and serve him needs to be cleansed from the pollution of the world. In that great passage speaking of the future conversion of Israel (Eze 36:25–28), Ezekiel speaks of the cleansing that God will perform for Israel, removing all filthiness and idolatry from them, giving them a new heart, and causing them to live in the land of God's appointment.

NOTES

25 It has often been claimed that the combination of the bulls and the Sea is related to the pagan myths involving the divine creative activity in overcoming the sea. Actually, the word בָּקָר , *bāqār*, "bull") is the generic term for cattle generally and may indicate oxen as well as cows. The distinctive word for "bull" (שׁוֹר, *šôr*) is not used here. It would have been unthinkable for David and Solomon to try to bring about a syncretization of faith in the Lord with pagan mythology. When occasionally religious forms and terms overlapped with those of the world at large, it was not because biblical revelation adopted pagan superstitions. The terms and forms were clearly defined so there could be no mistaking the uniqueness of God's revelation of himself and of the God-ordained way of humanity's approach to God.

26 The volume of the Sea was 2,000 baths, generally calculated to be about 11,500 gallons. A difficulty arises with reference to the statement in 2 Chronicles 4:5, which says that the value was 3,000 baths (ca. 17,500 gallons). It has been suggested that the discrepancy was occasioned by the type of transmissional error susceptible to numbers given in shorthand form (cf. Keil, 104). The suggestion advanced by G. Goldsworthy (*ZPEB*, 5:318) is the possibility that different standards of measurement were used for the cubit and bath. This seems to be a viable solution since the measure of the bath varied considerably from place to place and time to time. (Compare Jones, 184–85, who cites examples of containers said to measure a bath that have volumes ranging from 22 to 45 liters.)

d. The ten bronze basins and their stands (7:27–39)

27He also made ten movable stands of bronze; each was four cubits long, four wide
and three high. 28This is how the stands were made: They had side panels attached to
uprights. 29On the panels between the uprights were lions, bulls and cherubim—and on
the uprights as well. Above and below the lions and bulls were wreaths of hammered
work. 30Each stand had four bronze wheels with bronze axles, and each had a basin resting
on four supports, cast with wreaths on each side. 31On the inside of the stand there was
an opening that had a circular frame one cubit deep. This opening was round, and with
its basework it measured a cubit and a half. Around its opening there was engraving. The
panels of the stands were square, not round. 32The four wheels were under the panels,
and the axles of the wheels were attached to the stand. The diameter of each wheel was
a cubit and a half. 33The wheels were made like chariot wheels; the axles, rims, spokes and
hubs were all of cast metal.

34Each stand had four handles, one on each corner, projecting from the stand. 35At the
top of the stand there was a circular band half a cubit deep. The supports and panels were
attached to the top of the stand. 36He engraved cherubim, lions and palm trees on the surfaces of the supports and on the panels, in every available space, with wreaths all around.

[37]This is the way he made the ten stands. They were all cast in the same molds and were identical in size and shape.

[38]He then made ten bronze basins, each holding forty baths and measuring four cubits across, one basin to go on each of the ten stands. [39]He placed five of the stands on the south side of the temple and five on the north. He placed the Sea on the south side, at the southeast corner of the temple.

COMMENTARY

27–37 Ten mobile stands were constructed in order to carry the lavers or basins. They were four cubits square and three cubits high. There were lavishly engraved panels all around the stands, every available space being utilized in depicting cherubim, lions, and palm trees (v.36; cf. the picture of a similar bronze cart from Cyprus ca. 1150 BC in *NBD*, fig. 205, 1244). The wheels were like chariot wheels. In v.34 the word "handles" (*kᵉtēpôt*) is probably better rendered "supports," with the NASB and NRSV. The axles went through the bottom of these supports (v.32). These stands were mobile so that the basins could be moved to wherever they were needed.

38–39 The basins were also bronze, each holding forty baths (ca. 230 gallons) and measuring four cubits (ca. six feet). Though they were mobile, their normal placement was in the main hall of the temple, five on the right side and five on the left. Their purpose was to supply water for rinsing the burnt offerings (2 Ch 4:6).

The Sea was placed at the southeastern corner of the temple. Notice that in Ezekiel's temple the river flows from the southeastern corner of the temple (Eze 47:1–2).

e. Summary of Hiram's bronze work (7:40–47)

[40]He also made the basins and shovels and sprinkling bowls.

So Huram finished all the work he had undertaken for King Solomon in the temple of the LORD:

[41]the two pillars;

the two bowl-shaped capitals on top of the pillars;

the two sets of network decorating the two bowl-shaped capitals on top of the pillars;

[42]the four hundred pomegranates for the two sets of network (two rows of pomegranates for each network, decorating the bowl-shaped capitals on top of the pillars);

[43]the ten stands with their ten basins;

[44]the Sea and the twelve bulls under it;
[45]the pots, shovels and sprinkling bowls.
All these objects that Huram made for King Solomon for the temple of the LORD were of burnished bronze. [46]The king had them cast in clay molds in the plain of the Jordan between Succoth and Zarethan. [47]Solomon left all these things unweighed, because there were so many; the weight of the bronze was not determined.

COMMENTARY

40a The small bronze implements are listed starting here. The basins (*kîyōrôt*) are small vessels used for carrying away the ashes from the altar. In 2 Kings 25:14 and 2 Chronicles 4:11 they are called "pots" (*sîrôt*). The shovels were for the actual removal of the ashes from the altar, and the sprinkling bowls (*mizrāqôt*) were large bowls used at the altar of burnt offering, probably for the catching of the blood.

40b–47 The casting of the bronze was done in the lower Jordan Valley. Succoth was on the eastern side of the Jordan on the Jabbok River as it comes into the Jordan Valley. Zarethan is not as certainly located but is placed by Aharoni and Avi-Yonah (map 112) downstream from Zarethan on the Jabbok River, closer to the Jordan, south-by-southwest of Succoth. This general area shows abundant evidence of having been an active center of metallurgy during the period of the Hebrew monarchy. There is an abundance of good clay; and with available wood for charcoal and a prevalent north wind, this area was an ideal center for metalsmiths.

The casting method used by Hiram was the *cire perdue* or lost-wax process, used from 2500 BC in Egypt until the Middle Ages. It is still often used for high-quality sculptures. First a clay core is made, then covered with wax to the desired thickness. The wax is molded according to the intended design, then overlaid with specially prepared clay. The whole mold is then evenly baked for a period of time, possibly several days. During this time the wax is withdrawn through the outer mold through vents. Then molten bronze is poured into the same vents. Huge furnaces must have been used by Hiram and great skill was required to ensure a uniform flow and distribution of molten metal and proper escape of gases (cf. *Encyclopedia Britannica* [1976] 11:1093, 1095–96; 16:430). Only a master craftsman could have successfully carried out so huge an undertaking as was required here.

f. The furnishings of the temple (7:48–50)

[48]Solomon also made all the furnishings that were in the LORD's temple:
the golden altar;
the golden table on which was the bread of the Presence;

49 the lampstands of pure gold (five on the right and five on the left, in front of the inner sanctuary);

the gold floral work and lamps and tongs;

50 the pure gold basins, wick trimmers, sprinkling bowls, dishes and censers;

and the gold sockets for the doors of the innermost room, the Most Holy Place, and also for the doors of the main hall of the temple.

COMMENTARY

48 A list of golden furnishings and implements begins here. On the golden altar, see Exodus 30:1–4. On the table of the bread of the Presence, see Exodus 25:23–30. The present passage does not mention the number of tables, but 2 Chronicles 4:8 informs us that there were ten tables of the Presence. Later, in 2 Chronicles 29:18, after Hezekiah had the temple purified, the priests reported to him that the "table for setting out the consecrated bread, with all its articles" had been purified. It would seem from these accounts that though there were actually ten tables, they were often considered a unit (one table in ten parts, so to speak), which they were as far as their function and symbolism were concerned.

49 On the golden lampstands see Exodus 25:31–40. Here again, as with the table of the Presence, the one lampstand of the tabernacle became ten; yet as far as their function and symbolism were concerned, they were one unit. Note again that the symbolism of the earthly sanctuary as described in Hebrews 9 is based on the OT descriptions of the tabernacle, which served as the basic model for the temple.

50 It is noted that even the sockets of the doors of the Most Holy Place and of the main hall were of gold.

g. The treasures of the temple (7:51)

51 When all the work King Solomon had done for the temple of the LORD was finished, he brought in the things his father David had dedicated — the silver and gold and the furnishings — and he placed them in the treasuries of the LORD's temple.

COMMENTARY

51 With the completion of the temple, Solomon brought into the treasury (possibly the side chambers of ch. 6) the great wealth of gifts David had dedicated to the Lord (1Ch 29). David had, in his great love for the Lord, given freely and gladly his "personal treasures of gold and silver for the temple" of his God, "over and above everything" he had provided for the temple (1Ch 29:3). His love for God and great enthusiasm encouraged his officials to give in a commensurate way. David's infectious joy affected the whole nation. His prayer in 1 Chronicles 29:10–20—a model difficult to surpass—is of joyous thanksgiving for the privilege of being allowed to give to the Lord. His prayer that God would give Solomon wholehearted devotion to keep God's commands and to build the temple has now been answered. One cannot help but feel that just as David's officials caught the joy of giving, so does Solomon catch the enthusiasm of carrying out the great program of building the temple. Thus this passage illustrates well one of the great principles of leadership.

4. The Dedication of the Temple (8:1–66)

OVERVIEW

With the completion of the temple and with all the furniture in place, the crowning event is about to happen: the placement of the ark into its permanent home. For Israel it marks a new era. Now more than ever there is a feeling of permanence. The ark is no longer housed in a temporary shelter in Jerusalem. The dichotomy in the sanctuary, with the ark in Jerusalem and the tabernacle at Gibeon, is ended with the reuniting of the ark and the tabernacle (v.4).

a. Moving the ark and the tabernacle to the temple (8:1–11)

1Then King Solomon summoned into his presence at Jerusalem the elders of Israel, all
the heads of the tribes and the chiefs of the Israelite families, to bring up the ark of the
LORD's covenant from Zion, the City of David. 2All the men of Israel came together to King
Solomon at the time of the festival in the month of Ethanim, the seventh month.
3When all the elders of Israel had arrived, the priests took up the ark, 4and they brought
up the ark of the LORD and the Tent of Meeting and all the sacred furnishings in it. The
priests and Levites carried them up, 5and King Solomon and the entire assembly of Israel
that had gathered about him were before the ark, sacrificing so many sheep and cattle
that they could not be recorded or counted.
6The priests then brought the ark of the LORD's covenant to its place in the inner sanctuary of the temple, the Most Holy Place, and put it beneath the wings of the cherubim.
7The cherubim spread their wings over the place of the ark and overshadowed the ark and
its carrying poles. 8These poles were so long that their ends could be seen from the Holy
Place in front of the inner sanctuary, but not from outside the Holy Place; and they are still
there today. 9There was nothing in the ark except the two stone tablets that Moses had

placed in it at Horeb, where the LORD made a covenant with the Israelites after they came out of Egypt.

[10]When the priests withdrew from the Holy Place, the cloud filled the temple of the LORD. [11]And the priests could not perform their service because of the cloud, for the glory of the LORD filled his temple.

COMMENTARY

1–2 To mark this great occasion with the dignity and solemnity it deserved, Solomon assembled all the elders of Israel along with the tribal and family chiefs. As God's anointed shepherd, he involved all Israel through its elders and chiefs in the moving of the ark and the dedication of the temple. This involved more than mere pomp and ceremony. Solomon was very much in earnest about the spiritual significance of this occasion, and he desired that the heart of all Israel be knit together in this most auspicious occasion, and, more importantly, in the dedication of their hearts to God.

Reference to 6:38, noting the completion of the temple in the eighth month, makes it clear that there was a time lapse between the completion and the dedication of the temple, since the latter was accomplished in the seventh month (the year not being given). The view adopted by Ewald and others that the dedication was held a month before the completion is denied by 7:51, which states that the furnishings were put in place after the completion. The view of Keil, 118, that Solomon waited thirteen years, until his palace was completed, is based on 1 Kings 9:1–2, in which God seems to be responding to Solomon's dedicatory prayer (v.3) after the completion of the palace thirteen years later.

It is difficult, however, to believe that Solomon would wait so long before bringing the ark to the temple. Then, too, the temporal note in 9:1 is most naturally understood to indicate that what is recorded in ch. 9 took place at a time different from the events of ch. 8. Thus most likely Solomon waited eleven months before the dedication. Some have suggested that during this time some of the furnishings might have been completed and installed. But much more to the point is the probability that Solomon waited until the seventh month because of its symbolic importance, for in the seventh month the Feast of Booths was celebrated.

The Feast of Booths was the last in the series of yearly feasts and was also known as the Feast of Ingathering. It was a harvest feast; but more importantly it celebrated the end of the wilderness wanderings and the fact that God had brought his people home to the Land of Promise, that is, that he had given them rest (Dt 12:8–11). Zechariah 14:16–21 singles out this feast as mandatory for surviving Gentiles as well as redeemed Israel in the messianic age. In other words, the Feast of Booths celebrates the fulfillment of God's promise, the establishment of Israel in the land under God's Messiah, which makes it a perfect occasion to complete the temple complex.

For Solomon the completion of the temple betokened the fulfillment of the prophecy of Moses (Ex 15:17), that God would not only establish Israel but also dwell in their midst and be their God (see Rev 21:3 for an eschatological view). Another passage that may have a bearing on Solomon's timing is Deuteronomy 31:10–11, in which God makes provision for a renewal of the covenant every seven years (the year of remission [of debt]) at the time of the Feast of Booths. Though there is no indication in our passage that it takes place during one of those occasions, it is nonetheless of interest that the two stone tablets of the covenant are mentioned as being contained in the ark. It is surely true that Solomon had in his heart and mind the thought of a covenant renewal, a personal and national rededication to God. It is not the ritual that is emphasized but the outpouring of Solomon's heart to God. What could have been merely a ritual dedication is transformed into a genuine expression of praise.

3–5 It was the priests who took up the ark in the prescribed manner. The Levites joined in carrying the tabernacle and its contents. It would have been natural for the tabernacle, the portable and temporary meeting place between God and his people, now to reside in the permanent place prepared by Solomon, though we are not told how or where it was stored.

Before the ark was a great procession of the assembled chiefs and elders led by Solomon. In keeping with the solemnity of the occasion, sheep and cattle were sacrificed in such numbers that no one could keep track. The Hebrew participial form "sacrificing" (*m*[e]*zabb*[e]*ḥîm*; v.5) would indicate that the sacrifices were being made as the ark progressed the short distance from the city of David to the temple. This view is strengthened by the precedent set by David when he brought the ark to Jerusalem (2Sa 6:13). With each six steps taken by the priests carrying the ark, David sacrificed a bull and a fattened calf.

6–8 The priests, who alone were permitted in the temple proper, put the ark in its appointed place, under the outstretched wings of the golden cherubim (v.6), the representations of those highly exalted angelic beings associated with the throne of God and his rule (see comments at 6:23–28). The ark was the focal point of the temple and represented the ruling as well as the atoning presence of God with his people. Though all the other furnishings had been newly made, the ark was still the same as that made while Israel was encamped at Sinai.

The carrying poles of the ark receive special attention here. Exodus 25:15 states that these poles were not to be removed from the ark. Even though the ark was now in its permanent home, the poles remained in place as a reminder of its journeys at the head of God's people.

9 The ark had in it only the two stone tablets from Horeb, the witness of the covenant God had made with his people. It was for this reason that the ark was called the "ark of the covenant of the Lord," as well as the "ark of the testimony." Here was the abiding witness to God's solemn purpose with regard to Israel, to make it a "kingdom of priests and a holy nation" (Ex 19:6).

The ark of the testimony was also a sobering reminder to Israel of her responsibilities before God. With regard to this latter aspect, it must be remembered that were it not for the blood of the atonement, the ark must of necessity be a throne of holy and terrible judgment, for "there is no one righteous, not even one" (Ro 3:10). But by God's gracious provision, the ark became a place of mercy for the one who by faith approached in God's appointed way.

Thus, while the ark was too holy for even the priests to touch, and while it spoke of the awesome holiness and majesty of a sovereign God, it became through the atoning blood a witness to the forgiving, protecting, and comforting presence of God for the believer.

10–11 When the priests had placed the ark in the Most Holy Place and had withdrawn, the cloud of the glory of God descended and filled the temple, just as had been the case at the inauguration of the tabernacle (Ex 40:34–35). God was thereby graciously acknowledging Solomon's handiwork and indicating his intention of dwelling with his people. The glory cloud was the visible manifestation of the presence of God. The rabbinic designation was "the Shekinah glory" ("Shekinah" comes from *škn*, the Heb. root meaning "to dwell"). The concept of the manifested glory of God is a pervasive and important theme in the OT and extends into the NT.

NOTES

2 The "time of the festival" is the Feast of Booths, celebrated for seven days from the fifteenth day of the seventh month. "Ethanim" ("perennial," signifying the onset of the fall or "early" rains) was the older designation for the seventh month. In later times it became known by the Babylonian name "Tishri" ("beginning"—i.e., the start of the civil year), thus moving the author to explain that Ethanim was the seventh month.

4 Jones, 194, deems it to be "most unlikely that the tent and its contents would be brought into the Temple" and considers it to be a late priestly addition. But see R. Friedman ("The Tabernacle in the Temple," *BA* 40 [1981]: 161–70) for evidence of the fact that Solomon's temple contained the Tent of Meeting.

8 The statement that these poles were "so long that their ends could be seen from the Holy Place in front of the inner sanctuary," yet not from outside the Holy Place, is not easy to understand. The ancient rabbinic view was that the tips of the poles touched the veil so as to cause visible protrusions, but it is difficult to understand how they might be visible from the Holy Place but not from the portico. Josephus (*Ant.* 3.136 [6.5]), however, suggests that the ark was placed crosswise to the door, in a north–south alignment, and that the poles, which were extended lengthwise along the ark, were thus also aligned in the same direction, crosswise to the door. This interpretation seems to account best for the statement that the wings of the cherubim, which stretched north to south, overshadowed the ark and its staves (v.7). These carrying poles were so long that the ends could only be seen if one were to look into the Most Holy Place from a place near the opening (i.e., the poles extended considerably beyond the doorway (v.8).

The statement that these poles are "still there today" suggests the use of a historical document and seems to be the author's way of documenting his source (cf. House, 29–30, 139; B. Childs "A Study of the Formula, 'Until This Day,'" *JBL* 82 (1963): 179–92).

9 Hebrews 9:4 says that the ark "contained the gold jar of manna, Aaron's staff that had budded and the stone tablets of the covenant." Although the problem of relating this statement to 1 Kings 8:9 has been addressed in various ways, it may be reasonable to suggest a solution similar to the one applied to the incense altar that is sometimes described as being in the (outer) sanctuary (see comments at 6:22), namely, that this altar was *physically* in the outer sanctuary, just outside the entrance to the inner sanctuary; yet *functionally* it belonged to the latter. Just so the pot of manna and the staff of Aaron, though not actually inside the ark of the testimony, nonetheless formed part of the witness during the days of Moses and perhaps Joshua, thus reminding Israel of their rebellious spirit and lack of trust in God. These events were concrete examples of sinful behavior, but the testimony of the two tablets of stone had a more lasting function.

10 There is a parallel to this event in Acts 2:1–4, in which God marks the inception of the church as the temple of the Holy Spirit by making his presence known through the sound of a mighty rushing wind and by filling those present with the Holy Spirit.

b. Solomon's address (8:12–21)

12Then Solomon said, "The LORD has said that he would dwell in a dark cloud; 13I have
indeed built a magnificent temple for you, a place for you to dwell forever."
14While the whole assembly of Israel was standing there, the king turned around and
blessed them. 15Then he said:
"Praise be to the LORD, the God of Israel, who with his own hand has fulfilled what he
promised with his own mouth to my father David. For he said, 16'Since the day I brought
my people Israel out of Egypt, I have not chosen a city in any tribe of Israel to have a
temple built for my Name to be there, but I have chosen David to rule my people Israel.'
17"My father David had it in his heart to build a temple for the Name of the LORD, the
God of Israel. 18But the LORD said to my father David, 'Because it was in your heart to build
a temple for my Name, you did well to have this in your heart. 19Nevertheless, you are not
the one to build the temple, but your son, who is your own flesh and blood—he is the
one who will build the temple for my Name.'
20"The LORD has kept the promise he made: I have succeeded David my father and now
I sit on the throne of Israel, just as the LORD promised, and I have built the temple for the
Name of the LORD, the God of Israel. 21I have provided a place there for the ark, in which
is the covenant of the LORD that he made with our fathers when he brought them out of
Egypt."

COMMENTARY

12–13 Solomon recognized the glory cloud for what it was and saw in it God's approval and promised presence. His reference to God's dwelling in a dark cloud was based on Exodus 19:9, which speaks of the inapproachability and unknowability of God on the one hand, and on the other hand of God's gracious manifestation of himself in a form that would not bring about the instant destruction of the people (Ex 20:21; Dt 5:22; see also Lev 16:2). Solomon's response to this gracious manifestation is that he has built a "magnificent [lit., 'princely'] temple" for the Lord so that he might sit enthroned in regal splendor as befits his majesty. It is clear from vv.27–28 that Solomon is under no illusions, as though God needs the temple for his own sake. But just as God is enthroned in heaven, so he sees fit to use Solomon's temple as his throne on earth.

14–21 Solomon had been speaking to God. He now turns to the people and blesses them. The blessing takes the form of praise to God for fulfilling his promise to David (v.15; cf. 2Sa 7), not only for providing him with a son to continue the dynasty, but also in providing a permanent resting place for the ark, the symbol of God's presence. The expressions "with his own hand" and "with his own mouth" refer to the sovereign power of God in the fulfilling of his promises. Since the Davidic covenant implied benefit to Israel through God-appointed leadership and ultimately the coming Messiah, God has clearly begun the fulfillment of the covenant; and Israel can expect to receive the bounty of God's blessings if the people walk in his ways.

The blessing begins and ends with the statement that God brought his people (Israel) out of Egypt (vv.16, 21), thus suggesting that the fulfillment of God's promise to David through Solomon is not an end in itself, but serves the larger purpose of providing a permanent resting place for the ark. The prophetic words of Exodus 15:17 are now fulfilled.

c. Solomon's sevenfold prayer of dedication (8:22–53)

i. The theme of the prayer (8:22–30)

OVERVIEW

The theme of Solomon's dedicatory prayer is that as God had seen fit to honor his word up to that time, he will continue to do so, first of all in continuing the line of David, and second, in accepting the prayers of his people and in granting forgiveness. These prayers are seen as being directed to God through the temple. Solomon prays, in effect, that God will always recognize the temple as the way for sinful humanity to approach a holy God.

In the early part of this chapter, one cannot help but sense Solomon's profound feeling of gratitude. His desire is that God might continue to be gracious to David and his successors and to the people Israel. At the same time he recognizes the continued responsibility of king and people to walk in God's ways.

22Then Solomon stood before the altar of the LORD in front of the whole assembly of
Israel, spread out his hands toward heaven 23and said:
"O LORD, God of Israel, there is no God like you in heaven above or on earth below—you
who keep your covenant of love with your servants who continue wholeheartedly in your
way. 24You have kept your promise to your servant David my father; with your mouth you
have promised and with your hand you have fulfilled it—as it is today.
25"Now LORD, God of Israel, keep for your servant David my father the promises you
made to him when you said, 'You shall never fail to have a man to sit before me on the
throne of Israel, if only your sons are careful in all they do to walk before me as you have

done.' [26]And now, O God of Israel, let your word that you promised your servant David my father come true.

[27]"But will God really dwell on earth? The heavens, even the highest heaven, cannot contain you. How much less this temple I have built! [28]Yet give attention to your servant's prayer and his plea for mercy, O LORD my God. Hear the cry and the prayer that your servant is praying in your presence this day. [29]May your eyes be open toward this temple night and day, this place of which you said, 'My Name shall be there,' so that you will hear the prayer your servant prays toward this place. [30]Hear the supplication of your servant and of your people Israel when they pray toward this place. Hear from heaven, your dwelling place, and when you hear, forgive.

COMMENTARY

22 Solomon stands before the entire assembly. Second Chronicles 6:13 notes that he had made a three-cubits-high bronze platform. He stands facing the assembly with his hands outstretched in prayer. The supplicant's standing with outstretched arms and open hands was a common stance for prayer in the ancient world (cf. Isa 1:15). Solomon stands as the representative and shepherd of his people by leading them in public worship and acting as intercessor. His prayer stands as one of the great public prayers of Scripture.

23–24 One of the great dangers in analyzing a prayer such as this one is either to reduce it to its theological bones or to treat it in liturgical terms and thus take the heart out of it by losing its warmth, passion, concern, and love for God. When Solomon opens with that great confession, "O LORD, God of Israel, there is no God like you in heaven above or on earth below" (v.23), it is not liturgy, nor is it merely a statement of theological fact. Solomon is greatly moved on this occasion. It is a day of fulfilled desires and prayers, a day in which God has graciously manifested himself in the glory cloud, a day of bright hope for Israel and the house of David in their covenantal relationship with God. When Solomon extols the greatness and uniqueness of the Lord, it is with a full and overflowing heart. So it was with Israel soon after they experienced the unforgettable crossing of the Red Sea (Ex 15:11). This glad confession is one of the grand themes of the Psalms.

What particularly moves Solomon on this occasion is the faithfulness of God in carrying out his promise (v.24). One of the great self-affirmations of God in the OT is that he is a God of grace (*ḥesed*) and that he is faithful to his word. Two key passages that give expression to these truths are Exodus 34:6–7 and Deuteronomy 7:9–10. *Ḥesed* occurs in both, as does the word "faithfulness" (*ʾᵉmet* in the first passage and *neʾᵉmān* in the second). Exodus 34:6–7 was God's self-revelatory response to Moses after he interceded for a people who had sinned terribly against God. The emphasis is on God's faithful and forgiving love for the repentant sinner. This assurance has its counterpart in the certainty of judgment for the unrepentant.

In Deuteronomy 7:9–10 the situation was different. There was a covenant renewal in progress, and Moses was admonishing Israel to love God and keep his commands. They are to know that

God is faithful to his covenant and to his love for those whose hearts are right toward him. For those who reject him, there is once again the surety of judgment.

Both passages are frequently quoted and alluded to—the first when the need for forgiveness is in the forefront (notable is Nu 14:17–20), the second when people are encouraged to love God and walk in his ways, or when in prayer this attribute of God is the reason for praise or petition. Such is the case in the present passage. (See also Da 9:4, where Daniel confessed the sin of his people, but where the major point of his prayer was to ask God to carry out his promise to bring Israel back to the land.)

In citing God's faithfulness in maintaining his covenant and love, Solomon does not lose sight of human responsibility to respond to God and to love him wholeheartedly. In this way he faithfully reflects the thought of Deuteronomy 7:9–10.

Notice also that Solomon here repeats the thought of v.15, namely, that what God has promised with his mouth, he has fulfilled with his hand. With his sovereign power he is able to fully carry out whatever he has promised.

25–28 Solomon's confidence in praying is bolstered by previously answered prayer. Answered prayer is today also a strong basis for confidence in prayer. A second ground of confidence is God's own promise. His servants frequently claim his promises when they pray, and God honors these requests (cf. Ex 32:13; Da 9:1–19). In making this petition, Solomon recognizes his own responsibility and tacitly rededicates himself to serving God.

The major point, however, of these verses is a plea that God, who has so far been faithful in every way to his covenant with David (as evidenced in the completion of the temple and the rulership of Solomon), might always accept this temple and condescend to dwell there, while receiving those who approach him by way of the temple.

Verse 27 is parenthetical. The request continues in v.28. By means of the rhetorical question, Solomon makes it clear that he is under no illusion as to the significance of the temple, nor is it properly speaking a home for God. It would be utterly impossible to build a house that could even begin to be commensurate with, or adequate to reflect, the majesty of the Lord. God does not need the temple, but the temple needs God! God does not need Israel, but Israel needs God!

Verse 28 continues from v.26. The connection may be rendered: "And let your word ... come true ... in giving attention to your servant's prayer." In making this great request, Solomon realizes that on the actual merits of the case, he has no right to pray as he does were it not for God's own promise given by his grace. The only claim Solomon has on the Lord is God's own word, freely given; but God's Word is a bond that cannot be broken, so Solomon can pray with assurance and confidence. This privilege is the portion of believers of all ages.

29–30 The expression "have the eye fixed on" (NIV, "open toward") an object is a common and graphic way of signifying care and attentiveness (cf. Pss 31:22; 34:15; 101:6). Verse 29 forms the core of the whole prayer. God has condescended to allow a temple to be built for his Name (5:5), and by doing so he has identified himself with his people. Thus through the temple God has provided a place of contact between humanity and God, a way for sinful people to approach a holy God, to have their sins forgiven, and to live in fellowship with him. Solomon prays that God might continue to acknowledge the temple and the one who comes to him by way of the temple, as he has promised.

Solomon next makes a general, practical application of the request of v.29: he anticipates various situations in which a sinful people, suffering calamity because of God's judgment, will repent and pray. Solomon's earnest request is that God will not close his ears to repentant and believing prayer directed to God by way of the temple. God's actual dwelling place, or place of enthronement, is in heaven. The temple, as the place where God's name is enthroned, is the place where sinful people can approach the holy God.

NOTES

22 From 2 Chronicles 6:13 we learn the additional fact that Solomon first stood, then knelt down, still with his arms outstretched and hands open, as is confirmed in 1 Kings 8:54.

ii. Seven specific requests (8:31–53)

OVERVIEW

The background to these verses is found in Leviticus 26 and Deuteronomy 28–30. Both passages begin with the description of the blessing that will be Israel's portion if they walk in God's ways. The bulk of the material describes the curses in the form of various calamities that will befall the people if they do not obey God. Leviticus 26 particularly describes an escalating intensity or seriousness of difficulties, an ever-worsening series of events that will come on a disobedient people. Each calamity is designed to bring them to repentance; but if they still will not repent, then worse will come. In both passages the final blow is exile from the Promised Land. But in Leviticus 26:40–45 and Deuteronomy 30:1–10, God promises that when they are cast out of the land, if they will then take to heart what has befallen them and repent, God will listen to their prayer and restore them to the land.

In asking that God hear the prayers of a repentant people, whatever may have befallen them, Solomon is once again basing his request on the words that God himself has spoken. Thus Solomon can pray with assurance and expectancy.

31"When a man wrongs his neighbor and is required to take an oath and he comes and
swears the oath before your altar in this temple, 32then hear from heaven and act. Judge
between your servants, condemning the guilty and bringing down on his own head what
he has done. Declare the innocent not guilty, and so establish his innocence.
33"When your people Israel have been defeated by an enemy because they have sinned
against you, and when they turn back to you and confess your name, praying and making supplication to you in this temple, 34then hear from heaven and forgive the sin of your
people Israel and bring them back to the land you gave to their fathers.
35"When the heavens are shut up and there is no rain because your people have sinned
against you, and when they pray toward this place and confess your name and turn from

their sin because you have afflicted them, [36]then hear from heaven and forgive the sin of your servants, your people Israel. Teach them the right way to live, and send rain on the land you gave your people for an inheritance.

[37]"When famine or plague comes to the land, or blight or mildew, locusts or grasshoppers, or when an enemy besieges them in any of their cities, whatever disaster or disease may come, [38]and when a prayer or plea is made by any of your people Israel—each one aware of the afflictions of his own heart, and spreading out his hands toward this temple—[39]then hear from heaven, your dwelling place. Forgive and act; deal with each man according to all he does, since you know his heart (for you alone know the hearts of all men), [40]so that they will fear you all the time they live in the land you gave our fathers.

[41]"As for the foreigner who does not belong to your people Israel but has come from a distant land because of your name—[42]for men will hear of your great name and your mighty hand and your outstretched arm—when he comes and prays toward this temple, [43]then hear from heaven, your dwelling place, and do whatever the foreigner asks of you, so that all the peoples of the earth may know your name and fear you, as do your own people Israel, and may know that this house I have built bears your Name.

[44]"When your people go to war against their enemies, wherever you send them, and when they pray to the LORD toward the city you have chosen and the temple I have built for your Name, [45]then hear from heaven their prayer and their plea, and uphold their cause.

[46]"When they sin against you—for there is no one who does not sin—and you become angry with them and give them over to the enemy, who takes them captive to his own land, far away or near; [47]and if they have a change of heart in the land where they are held captive, and repent and plead with you in the land of their conquerors and say, 'We have sinned, we have done wrong, we have acted wickedly'; [48]and if they turn back to you with all their heart and soul in the land of their enemies who took them captive, and pray to you toward the land you gave their fathers, toward the city you have chosen and the temple I have built for your Name; [49]then from heaven, your dwelling place, hear their prayer and their plea, and uphold their cause. [50]And forgive your people, who have sinned against you; forgive all the offenses they have committed against you, and cause their conquerors to show them mercy; [51]for they are your people and your inheritance, whom you brought out of Egypt, out of that iron-smelting furnace.

[52]"May your eyes be open to your servant's plea and to the plea of your people Israel, and may you listen to them whenever they cry out to you. [53]For you singled them out from all the nations of the world to be your own inheritance, just as you declared through your servant Moses when you, O Sovereign LORD, brought our fathers out of Egypt."

COMMENTARY

31–32 Solomon's first request involves cases in which an oath is brought before the Lord in attesting to the truth of a claim (cf. Ex 22:11), cases in which there are no human witnesses (e.g., Ex 22:6–12; Lev 6:1–5). These cases have to do with damage or loss of property entrusted to another person, dispute over lost and found property, or the perpetration of fraud of some sort. Solomon prays that when an oath is brought before the Lord in such a case, he will judge the guilty party and establish the innocence of the other. Solomon's concern here is that God will honor the altar of this temple just as formerly he honored the altar of the tabernacle.

33–34 Solomon's second request involves prayer for forgiveness after a defeat by the enemy (cf. Lev 26:17; Dt 28:25). This defeat is caused by sin and the repeated refusal to listen to God's admonitions. It entails subjugation by the enemy with considerable hardship and the taking of prisoners (not here a mass removal of population). The conditions of restoration are here given as (1) turning back to God (repenting), (2) confessing God's name (i.e., acknowledging his lordship), and (3) prayer in the temple. This last element implies a coming to God in the way prescribed by him. The answer looked for is the forgiveness of sin and restoration of the captives to the land.

35–36 Solomon's third request concerns the drought brought on the land by the sin of the people (cf. Lev 26:19; Dt 28:23). Israel's crops depended on good and well-timed fall and spring rains. The Canaanites thought to ensure for themselves fertility for their land and abundant rains by worshiping Baal, the supposed god of the storm. The Israelites were prone to emulate their neighbors in the licentious worship of this idol. As a consequence God withheld the rain (cf., e.g., chs. 17–18) so that they might realize the Lord alone is the provider of all blessings. This theme is common in the prophets. The pull to worship the Canaanite gods continued to be strong up to the time of the exile.

This passage gives the same three conditions of restoration as v.33. Restoration here involves answered prayer in the forgiveness of sin and the resumption of rain (see Hos 2:5–23). In addition Solomon prays that God might teach Israel how to walk before him so that they can enjoy the fullness of God's blessing.

37–40 Solomon's fourth request deals with famine, various kinds of plagues, and enemy incursions that bring about severe economic disruptions (cf. Lev 26:16, 19–26; Dt 28:22–23, 38, 59–61). The emphasis is on individual recognition and acknowledgment of sin. It puts the stress on personal and individual responsibility before God, first, in that each person recognizes his or her own guilt and responsibility, and second, in that the sinner turns to God in sincere prayer. Notice the emphasis on the heart, that is, one's inner being, rather than on ritual. God, who knows the heart, will respond to a person's prayer in accordance with the reality of his repentance. The object is that people will fear God.

41–43 Solomon's fifth request recognizes God's wider purpose in his dealings with Israel, namely, that as Gentiles see God working in and through Israel, they might desire to know Israel's God. Solomon prays that as foreigners approach God through the temple, God will hear them so that they too will truly come to fear God, as well as to recognize the fact that God's name truly does reside in the temple. It is not a place for empty liturgy.

44–45 Solomon's sixth request involves situations where the people do not have access to the temple because they are in a foreign country. In this instance it involves soldiers sent to battle in distant places. Under these circumstances they are to pray *to the Lord*, toward the temple. It is not the temple per se that rendered prayer effective; it is the Lord, who has seen fit to dwell there, who answers prayer.

46–51 Solomon's seventh request deals with the last in the series of calamities God promised to bring on Israel if they persisted in disobedience (Lev 26:27–39; Dt 28:45–68). But just as God provided hope for a repentant nation in Leviticus 26:40–45 and Deuteronomy 30:1–10, so does Solomon, on the basis of these passages, pray that God will continue to show himself a faithful and forgiving God. A mass deportation of the nation as a whole, with resultant scattering through many nations, would normally spell the end of the nation. In Israel's case, however, God will use calamity and distress to bring her to an awareness of her sin so that she will turn to God and receive forgiveness and be restored. Once again the conditions of restoration are a change of heart, that is, a repentant spirit that leads to confession of sin; a turning back to God from the heart; and a praying toward the land of her fathers and the temple (trusting in God's promise; cf. Da 6:10).

For those who respond as indicated, there will be complete restoration and vindication ("uphold their cause," v.49). God, who loved his people enough and was strong enough to bring them out of the iron-smelting furnace of Egypt, will also bring about his full and sovereign purposes with his people.

Much of the later prophetic message revolved around the hope that God would indeed restore his people from worldwide exile, would lead them to repentance, and would bring them under the glorious reign of the Messiah, the Son of David.

52–53 Here is the conclusion to this magnificent example of believing intercessory prayer. Though throughout his prayer Solomon put great stress on the centrality of the temple, he did not do so for reasons of vainglory, as though the building were his special accomplishment. His basic concern has been for his people: "May you listen to them whenever they cry out to you" (v.52). At the same time he is requesting of God that he will continue to acknowledge the temple as the contact point between God and the people. God has singled them out from all nations to be his special inheritance, and he delivered them from Egypt (v.53). Solomon's prayer is that God will continue to care for his people until the complete fulfillment of his purpose.

NOTES

31 Leviticus 26 and Deuteronomy 28–30 give a preview of Israelite history, including their sinful disobedience, dispersion, and restoration. The restoration from the Babylonian exile is a foreshadowing of Israel's final conversion and restoration as detailed in the Prophets.

42 The arm of God, outstretched or bared, is a frequently used term to signify the unlimited power of God in vanquishing enemies. Thus he redeemed Israel out of Egypt (Dt 4:34; 5:15; see also Isa 52:10). The mighty hand of God has a similar meaning but stresses more the sovereignty of God, his ability to do whatever he sets out to do.

d. Solomon's benediction (8:54–61)

54When Solomon had finished all these prayers and supplications to the LORD, he rose
from before the altar of the LORD, where he had been kneeling with his hands spread
out toward heaven. 55He stood and blessed the whole assembly of Israel in a loud voice,
saying:
56"Praise be to the LORD, who has given rest to his people Israel just as he promised. Not
one word has failed of all the good promises he gave through his servant Moses. 57May
the LORD our God be with us as he was with our fathers; may he never leave us nor forsake
us. 58May he turn our hearts to him, to walk in all his ways and to keep the commands,
decrees and regulations he gave our fathers. 59And may these words of mine, which I have
prayed before the LORD, be near to the LORD our God day and night, that he may uphold
the cause of his servant and the cause of his people Israel according to each day's need,
60so that all the peoples of the earth may know that the LORD is God and that there is no
other. 61But your hearts must be fully committed to the LORD our God, to live by his decrees
and obey his commands, as at this time."

COMMENTARY

54–56 In 2 Chronicles 7:1–3 we find that at the conclusion of Solomon's prayer, "fire came down from heaven and consumed the burnt offering and the sacrifices, and the glory of the LORD filled the temple." This response on God's part was an awe-inspiring and unmistakable confirmation of God's commitment to the temple as his residence among his people.

Solomon rises from his kneeling position and stands before the people to bless them. His heart is filled with praise, and once again he speaks of God's faithfulness in fulfilling all his promises. The key word here is "rest" (v.56), which has important soteriological connotations. In Deuteronomy 12:9–10 "rest" is described as Israel's living in security in the Land of Promise. In the following verses, Israel was told to bring her sacrifices to the place (speaking of the future temple) where God would cause his name to dwell. Then the people would rejoice before the Lord (Dt 12:12). There can be no doubt that Solomon sees the temple as the completion of the picture of rest as portrayed in Deuteronomy 12. Not only is Israel living in peace and security, enjoying the fruitfulness of the land, but also God is formally dwelling in their midst. Solomon's kingdom, with God's "residence" in the center, foreshadows the messianic kingdom with its rest.

57–61 Now Solomon expresses a twofold wish with a twofold purpose. The first wish (vv.57–58) asks that the Lord will always be with his people and never forsake them so that he may turn their hearts to him. The second (vv.59–60) asks the Lord always to remember to uphold the cause of his people so that all peoples may know that the Lord is God. The first speaks of a continued internal working of God to make his people conformable to his will. The second speaks of a continued external working of God to bring about a change in the Gentiles, that they too may come to a saving knowledge of God.

These verses also illustrate the balance between God's work in the human heart and life on the one hand (vv.57, 59) and human beings' responsibility on the other (v.61). Verse 58 recognizes that the ultimate motivation and enabling for a godly life come from God. Verse 61 emphasizes human initiative.

NOTES

54 At the beginning of his prayer (v.22) Solomon was standing. Apparently he sank down to a kneeling position as he began increasingly to feel the urgency of his petitions.

56 The rest enjoyed by Solomon and his generation was not complete, nor was it final. Psalm 95:7b–11 gives sad expression to the fact that Israel had not entered God's true rest because of unbelief and rebellion. Hebrews 3–4 probes this theme and admonishes the Jewish readers not to repeat the mistake of their ancestors but to trust God and his Messiah. "There remains, then, a Sabbath-rest for the people of God" (Heb 4:9). That true and eternal rest is found in Christ and in him alone.

57–58 Verse 57 is more than a request for God's help in times of difficulty. It extends to the desire that God's Spirit may never stop working to bring his people to an obedient walk before the Lord. Verse 58 shows that obeying God's commandments, decrees, and regulations is basically an affair of the heart.

59 עָשָׂה מִשְׁפָּט (*ʿaśâ mišpāṭ*, "uphold the cause") is literally "do or provide justice," which means to do right by someone, to see that a person is fairly treated, and, in some instances, to vindicate someone who has been wronged. In this context it undoubtedly means that God should champion the cause of Israel in the face of all kinds of adversity. It is, of course, self-evident that God's ability to do so depends on the extent to which Israel's cause is in keeping with the will of God.

The expression דְּבַר יוֹם בְּיוֹמוֹ (*dᵉbar yôm bᵉyômô*, "according to each day's need") is reminiscent of other well-loved passages of Scripture, such as:

Exodus 16:16–30: God provided enough manna for each day, no more and no less.
Deuteronomy 33:25: "Your strength will equal your days."
Matthew 6:11: "Give us today our daily bread."
John 1:16: "Of his fullness [i.e., grace] we have all received ... grace upon grace" (NASB), that is, with each new need, God has supplied the needed grace.

61 The expression שָׁלֵם (*šālēm*, "fully committed"; lit., "be complete, whole, entire") means more than just an emotional attachment. It finds expression in an appropriate lifestyle, "to live by his decrees" and "to obey his commands." The words "to live" and "[to] obey" are explanatory infinitives.

The words "as at this time" are a reminder that at the time of the dedication of the temple, enthusiasm was running high. Solomon's prayer was that his people might not slacken in their desire to please God but might continue to walk wholeheartedly in his ways. It is sad that Solomon himself failed in this goal.

e. Solomon's dedicatory sacrifice (8:62–66)

62Then the king and all Israel with him offered sacrifices before the LORD. 63Solomon
offered a sacrifice of fellowship offerings to the LORD: twenty-two thousand cattle and
a hundred and twenty thousand sheep and goats. So the king and all the Israelites
dedicated the temple of the LORD.

64On that same day the king consecrated the middle part of the courtyard in front of
the temple of the LORD, and there he offered burnt offerings, grain offerings and the fat
of the fellowship offerings, because the bronze altar before the LORD was too small to hold
the burnt offerings, the grain offerings and the fat of the fellowship offerings.

65So Solomon observed the festival at that time, and all Israel with him—a vast
assembly, people from Lebo Hamath to the Wadi of Egypt. They celebrated it before the
LORD our God for seven days and seven days more, fourteen days in all. 66On the following
day he sent the people away. They blessed the king and then went home, joyful and glad
in heart for all the good things the LORD had done for his servant David and his people
Israel.

COMMENTARY

62–63 When Solomon had finished his dedicatory prayer, he rejoiced together with all Israel as they celebrated the Feast of Booths. Their celebration was especially meaningful in that the temple was a significant step in Israel's history. There was a new sense of permanence, of having truly arrived in the Land of Promise. The fellowship offerings celebrated this grand occasion. The large number (22,000 cattle and 120,000 sheep and goats) was appropriate both to the occasion and to the number of people present to participate in the fellowship offerings.

For these offerings the fat, the blood, and the entrails belonged to the Lord, and the flesh was eaten by the offerers. They were brought over a period of fourteen days, since according to v.65 the normal period of seven days for the Feast of Tabernacles was extended by another seven days. The fellowship offering was a voluntary act of worship and gave testimony to the fellowship between God and the one whose sin had been forgiven. After those portions belonging to God had been offered, a communal or fellowship meal was held for the offerer and his family and for the Levites.

The verb "dedicate" (*ḥānak*) in v.63 refers to inaugural activities, putting something to the use for which it was intended. This event then marked the beginning of many sacrifices to come.

64–66 To accommodate the large numbers of sacrifices, the whole middle part of the court in front of the temple was consecrated. The large number of sacrifices and the involvement of the people attest to the unity of purpose and the wholeheartedness of the devotion of people and king.

The Feast of Booths was in itself a grand occasion for rejoicing and for an enhanced spirit of community among all Israelites. The dedication of the temple made this occasion all the more joyful and memorable, and the time of celebration was suitably extended. When the people left, they went home rejoicing and fully satisfied in their realization that God's blessing was on the king and on the nation as a whole.

NOTES

63 Solomon consecrated the entire middle courtyard in which the altar stood in order to accommodate the large number of sacrifices. וַיַּחְנְכוּ (*wayyaḥnᵉkû*, "and they dedicated," from חנך, *ḥnk*) refers to inaugural activities such as with a new home (Dt 20:5). It is also the root from which the word Hanukkah (the feast commemorating the rededication of the temple after the desecrations of Antiochus IV Epiphanes) is derived and means basically "to begin, initiate, inaugurate."

5. The Lord's Second Appearance to Solomon (9:1–9)

OVERVIEW

Though this second appearance of the Lord took place thirteen years after the completion of the temple, the author places it here in conjunction with Solomon's dedication of the temple. The reason for doing so is in part to make it clear that God expects Solomon and his successors, as well as the people, to commit themselves wholly to God. Ritual reliance on the temple is not enough—a theme stressed by the prophets (e.g., Isa 1:10–15; Jer 7:1–15). It might well be asked why God did not appear to Solomon until thirteen years after the completion and dedication of the temple. Though it might seem strange that the Lord waited so long, two considerations (besides those discussed in 8:1) make this scenario entirely feasible.

First, God did indeed respond immediately to Solomon's prayer, as signaled by the appearance of the glory cloud and by the consuming of the sacrifices by fire sent from heaven immediately after the king prayed (2Ch 7:1–7). These phenomena must certainly be considered both answers by God and clear endorsements of the temple and of Solomon's dedicatory prayer, too. At this point no other answer was really necessary.

Second, Solomon had come to a spiritual crossroads, as suggested first by the fact that the year in which he completed the palace (his twenty-fourth year, twenty years after he began the temple) is mentioned three times (7:1; 9:1, 10). Apart from the notations on the year that he began (6:1) and finished (6:38) building the temple, this event is the only one linked to his regnal calendar. There were other significant accomplishments (e.g., the fortification of Jerusalem, Hazor, Megiddo, and Gezer; 9:15–19), but they are reported almost in passing.

A second matter that points to a crossroads at this time is the remark in 11:4, that as Solomon grew older he began to follow after other gods, despite God's two appearances to him (11:9). This declension obviously began after his twenty-fourth year, since God does not condemn him in ch. 9. It would be in keeping with the character of God to speak forcefully and urgently to Solomon by warning him against turning from his walk with God (cf. vv.6–9).

[1]When Solomon had finished building the temple of the LORD and the royal palace, and
had achieved all he had desired to do, [2]the LORD appeared to him a second time, as he had
appeared to him at Gibeon. [3]The LORD said to him:
"I have heard the prayer and plea you have made before me; I have consecrated this
temple, which you have built, by putting my Name there forever. My eyes and my heart
will always be there.
[4]"As for you, if you walk before me in integrity of heart and uprightness, as David your
father did, and do all I command and observe my decrees and laws, [5]I will establish your
royal throne over Israel forever, as I promised David your father when I said, 'You shall
never fail to have a man on the throne of Israel.'
[6]"But if you or your sons turn away from me and do not observe the commands and
decrees I have given you and go off to serve other gods and worship them, [7]then I will cut
off Israel from the land I have given them and will reject this temple I have consecrated for
my Name. Israel will then become a byword and an object of ridicule among all peoples.
[8]And though this temple is now imposing, all who pass by will be appalled and will scoff
and say, 'Why has the LORD done such a thing to this land and to this temple?' [9]People will
answer, 'Because they have forsaken the LORD their God, who brought their fathers out of
Egypt, and have embraced other gods, worshiping and serving them — that is why the
LORD brought all this disaster on them.'"

COMMENTARY

1–3 God acknowledged the temple and consecrated it by putting his Name there. Neither the ritual nor the splendor of the building made it the dwelling place of God. It was God's sovereign and gracious choice thus to dwell among his people and to acknowledge them as his own. Solomon had asked (8:29) that God's eyes might be on the temple. God replied that not only his eyes but also his heart would be there. The following verses state the conditions.

4–5 These words reiterate the responsibilities of the Davidic kings. Again, it is emphasized that more than ritual observances are in view. It is the integrity of the heart, the wholehearted walk before God, that he demands. Unfortunately this is the area where Solomon failed later in life. It was not that he rejected God, but his heart became divided in his loyalties (11:4), so that the passion for God that characterized his father and Solomon himself in his younger years was no longer there.

6–9 These verses give dire warning as to the disastrous consequences that result from apostasy. The presence of the temple would not be proof against the judgment of God if king and people turned away from him. (It is at v.6 that the word "you" becomes plural, so that not only Solomon but also his successors and the people are included.) Solomon's history (ch. 11) shows that this warning was needed and particularly at this time in his life. This appearance of God was an act of grace and was intended as an urgent reminder to Solomon to guard his heart.

A second matter of note here is that the consequences of disobedience are far-reaching. As kings, Solomon and his successors were responsible for the whole nation. Failure on the king's part affected all the people. Israel's subsequent history amply illustrates this principle. As the king went, so went the people.

Two interrelated consequences would result from disobedience. One is the exile of the people (v.7), and the other God's rejection of the temple, thus leading to its destruction (vv.8–9). This state of affairs would lead in turn to a twofold reaction on the part of Gentile observers: (1) ridicule of Israel and (2) questions as to the reasons for such a disaster (vv.7, 9).

The seriousness of the threatened disasters is seen from the following considerations. (1) The verb "cut off" (*kārat*; v.7) is frequently used in situations in which a person is cut off or excluded from the fellowship of God's people (e.g., Lev 17:4, 9; Nu 19:20). It is a drastic measure reserved for one who has committed a serious offense against God.

(2) The word "reject" (*šillaḥ*; v.7), used in connection with the temple, is the word used of a man divorcing his wife. As such it speaks of a far more serious matter than the terminating of a business arrangement. Strong emotions and grief are involved. This figure is also used frequently by the prophets in speaking of God as the husband who will put Israel, the unfaithful wife, away.

(3) Israel will become a "byword" (*māšāl*) and an "object of ridicule" (*šᵉnînâ*). These words are "expressive of extraordinary calamity" (Gray, 238) and are found also in Deuteronomy 28:37 (where *māšāl* is rendered "object of scorn" in the NIV) and Jeremiah 24:9. *Māšāl* is usually rendered "a proverb." The second word (*šᵉnînâ*) is related to the word "tooth" (*šēn*) and "make sharp" (*šānan*) and speaks of sharp, cutting taunts (cf. Ps 64:3: "They sharpen their tongues like swords").

NOTES

1 The expression "all he had desired to do" may be rendered more literally, "every deep desire that he wished to carry out." חֵשֶׁק (*ḥēšeq*, "deep desire") involves strong emotional attachment, a passion. The verb is used of a man's strong desire for a woman (Ge 34:8; Dt 21:11), of God's strong love for Israel (Dt 7:7; 10:15), and of a human being's longing for God (Ps 91:14). It speaks here (and in v.19) of the passion with which Solomon carried out his building projects—they were dear to his heart. Second Chronicles 7:11 restricts the object of his desire here to the temple and the palace.

5 On the unconditional aspects of the Davidic covenant, see comments at 2:4.

8 The NIV's "though this temple is now imposing," which is similar in thought to the KJV ("[which] is high") and JB ("as for this exalted Temple"), is an attempt to deal with the Hebrew text without emendations and at the same time take into account the text of 2 Chronicles 7:21. The Hebrew in our passage reads וְהַבַּיִת הַזֶּה יִהְיֶה עֶלְיוֹן (*wᵉhabbayit hazzeh yihyeh ʿelyôn*), which is most naturally rendered "and this house will be high." Second Chronicles 7:21 reads אֲשֶׁר הָיָה עֶלְיוֹן (*ʾašer hāyâ ʿelyôn*), which is normally rendered "which was high." The NIV takes the Chronicles passage to be normative and renders Kings accordingly. Critics generally emend the *ʿelyôn* to either לְעִיִּים (*lᵉʿiyyîm*) or לְאִיִּין (*lᵉʿiyyîn*), so that the translations become "this house will become a ruin" (Kings) and "this house has become a ruin" (Chronicles). The NASB renders: "This house will become a heap of ruins."

Though this rendering fits the general context, it seems to be rather stretching the literal "I will make this house high." The NRSV has the same rendering, following the Syriac and Old Latin. Keil's solution (139), adopted here, is to render Kings as "this house will be high" (i.e., will stand as a high example for all to see) and Chronicles as "this house stands (has become) high" (once again as an example). This approach seems best to fit the demands of the MT and of the context.

D'. Events after, but Relating to, the Building of the Temple (9:10–25)

1. The Business Relations between Solomon and Hiram (9:10–14)

[10]At the end of twenty years, during which Solomon built these two buildings—the
temple of the LORD and the royal palace—[11]King Solomon gave twenty towns in Galilee to
Hiram king of Tyre, because Hiram had supplied him with all the cedar and pine and gold
he wanted. [12]But when Hiram went from Tyre to see the towns that Solomon had given
him, he was not pleased with them. [13]"What kind of towns are these you have given me,
my brother?" he asked. And he called them the Land of Cabul, a name they have to this
day. [14]Now Hiram had sent to the king 120 talents of gold.

COMMENTARY

10–14 This paragraph relates a business transaction between Solomon and Hiram involving the transfer of twenty border towns. These towns were in Galilee in the northwestern part of the territory of Asher, and they bordered Tyre. A town named "Cabul" has been identified in this area.

In the arrangements made in ch. 5, Solomon traded wheat and oil (5:11) for timber. Now we read (vv.11, 14) that Hiram also sent 120 talents of gold (equivalent to about four and one-half tons) to Solomon. Most, if not all, of this gold was used in the construction of the temple. Apparently more payment was required than what Solomon could provide in grain and oil, so he ceded these border towns (v.13). Hiram, after inspecting the area, was not happy with the towns and, according to 2 Chronicles 8:2, returned them to Solomon (presumably in favor of payment of a different kind), who then rebuilt the towns and settled Israelites in them.

The name "Cabul" (v.14) is generally understood to mean "as nothing."

NOTES

13 The Hebrew כָּבוּל (*kābûl*) seems to be derived from כָּ (*kā*, "as") + בַּל (*bal*, "nothing"). The LXX equated the *k* of *kābûl* with *g* and read גְּבוּל (*g*^{e}*bûl*), "border." This transposition is found to occur in the Amarna tablets (*HALOT*, "*Kabul*").

2. Solomon's Labor Force (9:15–23)

15Here is the account of the forced labor King Solomon conscripted to build the
LORD's temple, his own palace, the supporting terraces, the wall of Jerusalem, and Hazor,
Megiddo and Gezer. 16(Pharaoh king of Egypt had attacked and captured Gezer. He had
set it on fire. He killed its Canaanite inhabitants and then gave it as a wedding gift to his
daughter, Solomon's wife. 17And Solomon rebuilt Gezer.) He built up Lower Beth Horon,
18Baalath, and Tadmor in the desert, within his land, 19as well as all his store cities and the
towns for his chariots and for his horses — whatever he desired to build in Jerusalem, in
Lebanon and throughout all the territory he ruled.
20All the people left from the Amorites, Hittites, Perizzites, Hivites and Jebusites (these
peoples were not Israelites), 21that is, their descendants remaining in the land, whom the
Israelites could not exterminate — these Solomon conscripted for his slave labor force,
as it is to this day. 22But Solomon did not make slaves of any of the Israelites; they were
his fighting men, his government officials, his officers, his captains, and the commanders
of his chariots and charioteers. 23They were also the chief officials in charge of Solomon's
projects — 550 officials supervising the men who did the work.

COMMENTARY

15 The description of the forced labor is given in vv.20–23. In the intervening passage there is a brief description of Solomon's various building projects.

"Supporting terraces" (v.15) is generally known by the name "Millo," which is simply a transliteration from the Hebrew *millōʾ*. The nature of the structure involved has been much debated, as has its location. Some have suggested that it refers to a citadel (e.g., NASB note) or tower. Perhaps the most widely held view currently—and that adopted by the NIV—is that it consisted of architectural terracing and buttressing along the northeastern slope of the southeastern ridge known as the City of David.

The purpose would have been to allow the construction of more buildings in the area and, perhaps more importantly, adequate fortifications. Its construction was a major undertaking (cf. 11:27) that ranked in importance with the fortification projects of Jerusalem, Hazor, Megiddo, and Gezer. As to the wall of Jerusalem, the fortifications of Jerusalem would have to be extended considerably so as to include the temple and new palace.

In addition to expanding and strengthening Jerusalem, Solomon selected three key cities for rebuilding (Hazor, Megiddo, and Gezer), or for enlarging and strengthening their fortifications. Archaeological work has demonstrated that these three cities had certain characteristics in common (esp. with regard to their fortifications) attributable to the Solomonic era. Noteworthy are distinctive casemate walls, with the outer wall measuring five feet thick and the inner wall four feet thick. The interior chambers are seven feet wide. Similar walls of the Solomonic era have been found in numerous cities throughout Israel.

Most distinctive are the gate complexes, which are identical in plan and virtually of the same dimensions in all three cities. These gates feature a four-entry, six-chambered inner gate with twin towers at the first entry. Most of the gate extends inward from the casemate wall, with only the twin towers extending out from the wall. At Megiddo, Hazor, and Gezer an outer double-entry gate has been found. At Gezer the entry through the outer gate was from the right at an angle of approximately forty-five degrees. At Megiddo the approach was from the left, the gate being set at approximately seventy-five degrees. The direction and angle of approach was no doubt dictated by the topography.

Hazor was strategically placed in the north (ca. three miles north of the Sea of Galilee), being situated at the juncture of the two major highways approaching from the north. It became Israel's chief bulwark against northern invaders until it was destroyed in the eighth century by Tiglath-Pileser III.

Megiddo was the great fortress that controlled one of the major passes from the Plain of Sharon on the coast into the Valley of Jezreel through the Carmel range. It figures in prophecy as the staging area for the last great battle (Armageddon) in which Christ will defeat the forces of the Antichrist.

16 Gezer, on the road from Joppa to Jerusalem, had been a powerful Canaanite city. Though it was included in the tribal territory of Ephraim, it was not occupied by the Israelites until the time of Solomon, when the king married Pharaoh's daughter and received the town as a wedding gift. Pharaoh had burned the city and killed its inhabitants; he gave it to Solomon to rebuild and populate with Israelites.

17 Upper and Lower Beth Horon were strategically placed for controlling access to the highlands of Judea from the coastal plain through the Valley of Aijalon. The lower city, being about one and one-half miles farther west, was fortified by Solomon to guard against enemy approach from its vulnerable western side.

18 Baalath was the designation of several cities in Canaan. The one in question here is most likely the city also known as Kiriath Jearim, where the ark was kept for some time after its return from the Philistines. This view assumes that the names Baalath and Baalah (by which name Kiriath Jearim was also known) are interchangeable. This city would then be a fortress guarding another of the western approaches to Jerusalem.

Tadmor may be the one instance of conquest ascribed to Solomon (Wood, 292). According to 2 Chronicles 8:3 he first conquered Hamath Zobah, then fortified Tadmor.

19 Solomon built up an extensive network of supply centers and towns to house his chariotry. These places are not specified but certainly included the cities just mentioned, in addition to other strategic locations throughout the kingdom. Though he was a man of peace, Solomon was well prepared militarily to defend his kingdom.

20–24 On the forced labor or corvée, see 4:6 and comments at 5:13–18.

NOTES

15 *Millô᾽* is derived from the root מָלֵא (*mālē᾽*, "to fill"). The Akkadian *tamlu* is a terrace or artificial mound. The term is used in Judges 9:6, 20 in "the house of Millo," apparently a type of fortification. Its principal use, however, is in connection with the fortifications of Jerusalem. T. C. Mitchell (*NBD*, 823) holds to the common view that it is a solid tower or a bastion filling some weak point in the walls (cf. also Wood, 230–31). Aharoni and Avi-Yonah (map 114) shows the Millo to be a fortification between the city of David and Ophel.

The massive structure, now known as the "Stepped-Stone Structure," seems to attest to the view that the term "Millo" refers to supportive terracing. This structure is preserved to a height of 50 feet and may have been as much as 90 feet tall and 130 feet wide at the top (M. Steiner, "Archaeology Proves a Negative," *BAR* 24 [1998]: 29). Though the dating of this structure is in dispute, with views ranging from the tenth century BC (ibid., 29–33, 62) to the twelfth or thirteenth centuries BC (Y. Shiloh, *Excavations at the City of David I, 1978–1982: Interim Report of the First Five Seasons* [*Qedem* 19 (1984): 16], and J. Cahill, "The Archaeological Evidence Proves It" [*BAR* 24 (1998): 34–41, 63]), it seems to fit the criteria of the references in Samuel and Kings. *HALOT* adopts this view (see also W. H. Mare, *The Archaeology of the Jerusalem Area* [Grand Rapids: Baker, 1987], 65; Eliat Mazar, "Excavate King David's Palace" [*BAR* 23 (1997): 50–57]).

A thirteenth- or twelfth-century dating fits well with both the archaeological and biblical data (see J. Cahill, "Archaeological Evidence"). After David took Jerusalem from the Jebusites, we are told in 2 Samuel 5:9 that he built up the area from the "supporting terraces [Millo]" and inward. The Millo would have been constructed by the Jebusites. Solomon then was not the original builder but the one who rebuilt, strengthened, and possibly expanded the existing structure. Later, Hezekiah felt it necessary to strengthen the Millo in anticipation of the siege of Sennacherib. This structure was of great importance, not only for affording more building space in the city of David but also for strategic purposes. The work on this structure was a major undertaking. See comments at v.24.

The walls and gates of these three cities are described in (1) Y. Yadin, *Hazor* (Schweich Lectures 1970; London: Oxford Univ. Press, 1972; see esp. 135–38, 147–61, in the latter section of which Yadin compares the walls and gates of all three cities); (2) Y. Yadin, "New Light on Solomon's Megiddo" (*BA* 23 [1960]: 62–68); (3) William Dever et al., "Further Excavations at Gezer, 1967–71" (*BA* 34 [1971]: 94–132; see esp. the plan of excavated Gezer [96] and 112–16 on the Solomonic gateway); and (4) William Dever, *What Did the Biblical Writers Know, and When Did They Know It?* (Grand Rapids: Eerdmans, 2001), 131–38. On p. 132 Dever notes that similar gates from the same period have also been found at Ashdod and Lachish.

In "Was the 'Solomonic' City Gate at Megiddo Built by King Solomon?" (*BASOR* 239 [1980]: 1–18), D. Ussishkin challenges the identification of the Megiddo gates as Solomonic. Yadin has a rejoinder in the same issue (19–23). The identification of these gates as Solomonic is supported by V. M. Fargo in "Is the Solomonic City Gate at Megiddo Really Solomonic?" (*BAR* 9 [1983]: 16–18) and by Dever in *What Did the Biblical Writers Know, and When Did They Know It?* (132–37).

16 Most identify the pharaoh who defeated Gezer and awarded his daughter to Solomon as Siamun (979–960 BC), of the Twenty-First Dynasty. Kenneth Kitchen ("How We Know When Solomon Ruled," 32–37, 58) agrees and goes on to cite evidence from a victory scene at the temple of Amun (in Tanis) describing Siamun's smiting an enemy with a doubleheaded axe having crescent-shaped blades. Since the depiction of an axe of this type is unique in Egyptian reliefs, Kitchen argues that this one must depict a specific battle. This type of axe comes from the Aegean or the Balkans, so that it most likely shows a battle with a Philistine. The date of Siamun's reign, coupled with this victory scene, links him with Solomon.

3. Pharaoh's Daughter Moves to Her Permanent Quarters (9:24)

[24]After Pharaoh's daughter had come up from the City of David to the palace Solomon had built for her, he constructed the supporting terraces.

COMMENTARY

24 On Pharaoh's daughter, see comments at 3:1. It seems likely that since the work on the Millo, or "supporting terraces," was not begun until after the queen had been moved, the Millo must be located near or in the City of David and the construction activities would have been at or near the site of her temporary home. It also appears likely that existing structures may have been razed to allow the construction over a large area of this buttressing work.

4. Solomon Now Offers Sacrifices at the Temple in Jerusalem (9:25)

[25]Three times a year Solomon sacrificed burnt offerings and fellowship offerings on the altar he had built for the LORD, burning incense before the LORD along with them, and so fulfilled the temple obligations.

COMMENTARY

25 This verse brings to a conclusion Solomon's major achievement. From this point on he worshiped the Lord in the temple, no longer in the various high places. Presumably the people followed suit. As king he led the people, as on the day of dedication, in bringing before the Lord the burnt offerings and peace (or fellowship) offerings on the three great feast days.

The last clause, rendered in the NIV "and so fulfilled the temple obligations," is better rendered literally, with the NASB: "and so he finished the house." This note is intended to close the section on the building of the temple.

NOTE

25 Jones, 218, states that "this note on Solomon's sacrifices is obviously misplaced, and may refer to his sacrifices at David's altar (2Sa 24:25) before the construction of the Temple." But he fails to recognize the deliberate symmetry of the Solomonic account, which contrasts conditions before the building of the temple with the new situation.

C′. The Glories of Solomon's Reign (9:26–10:29)

OVERVIEW

This section corresponds to, and expands on, 4:1–34[4:1–5:14]. Solomon's famed wisdom is now seen as becoming known far beyond Israel's borders and even prompts the Queen of Sheba to visit. His wealth is again described and expanded upon, with emphasis on the external sources of his wealth, both in tribute and in international trade. Many exotic materials and animals are introduced into the kingdom from far-off countries. Precious metals and spices are in abundant supply as a result of Solomon's advantageous commercial activities.

1. Solomon's Commercial Activities (9:26–28)

[26]King Solomon also built ships at Ezion Geber, which is near Elath in Edom, on the
shore of the Red Sea. [27]And Hiram sent his men—sailors who knew the sea—to serve in
the fleet with Solomon's men. [28]They sailed to Ophir and brought back 420 talents of gold,
which they delivered to King Solomon.

COMMENTARY

26–28 A completely new approach to international trade began here as far as Israel was concerned. Phoenicia was the major shipping power in the Mediterranean, while Israel controlled the major inland trade routes in the Levant. With Israel newly exercising control of the Negev as far as the Gulf of Aqaba, new possibilities opened up. Solomon made a treaty with Hiram of Tyre that was mutually beneficial. Both kings would be able to conduct extensive trade throughout the Red Sea area. In this venture Hiram supplied the seamen and shipping and shipbuilding skills, and Solomon gave Tyre access to the Red Sea.

Ophir was fabled for its fine gold (Job 22:24) and as a center for obtaining exotic goods. It provided a rich source of revenue for Solomon and Hiram. Its location is still debated. See 10:11–12 for another reference to this profitable venture.

NOTES

26 Ezion Geber has been identified with Tell el-Kheleifeh, now inland because of changes in the shoreline. It lies between Aqaba and Eilath (Eloth).

28 Some have suggested that Ophir was in East Africa; still others favor Supara near Bombay, India, thus accounting for the length of the voyages. The fact that all the commodities mentioned in 10:22 were well known in ancient India would lend some support to this view. Nevertheless, ancient tradition identifies

Ophir with a location in southwestern Arabia, in which case the three-year journey was due to extensive coastal trade on the way and long layovers as a result of wind and weather conditions. That Ophir was itself a major trading center accounts for the appearance in 10:22 of some commodities (such as apes) that were not indigenous to Arabia but were trade items.

2. The Visit of the Queen of Sheba (10:1–13)

[1]When the queen of Sheba heard about the fame of Solomon and his relation to the name
of the LORD, she came to test him with hard questions. [2]Arriving at Jerusalem with a very great
caravan—with camels carrying spices, large quantities of gold, and precious stones—she
came to Solomon and talked with him about all that she had on her mind. [3]Solomon
answered all her questions; nothing was too hard for the king to explain to her. [4]When the
queen of Sheba saw all the wisdom of Solomon and the palace he had built, [5]the food on his
table, the seating of his officials, the attending servants in their robes, his cupbearers, and the
burnt offerings he made at the temple of the LORD, she was overwhelmed.

[6]She said to the king, "The report I heard in my own country about your achievements
and your wisdom is true. [7]But I did not believe these things until I came and saw with my
own eyes. Indeed, not even half was told me; in wisdom and wealth you have far exceeded
the report I heard. [8]How happy your men must be! How happy your officials, who continually stand before you and hear your wisdom! [9]Praise be to the LORD your God, who has
delighted in you and placed you on the throne of Israel. Because of the LORD's eternal love
for Israel, he has made you king, to maintain justice and righteousness."

[10]And she gave the king 120 talents of gold, large quantities of spices, and precious
stones. Never again were so many spices brought in as those the queen of Sheba gave to
King Solomon.

[11](Hiram's ships brought gold from Ophir; and from there they brought great cargoes
of almugwood and precious stones. [12]The king used the almugwood to make supports for
the temple of the LORD and for the royal palace, and to make harps and lyres for the musicians. So much almugwood has never been imported or seen since that day.)

[13]King Solomon gave the queen of Sheba all she desired and asked for, besides what he
had given her out of his royal bounty. Then she left and returned with her retinue to her
own country.

COMMENTARY

1 To exemplify further the glories of Solomon, the author cites the visit of the queen of Sheba. It illustrates how widespread was his fame. The many legends and highly embellished accounts that have grown around this visit among Arabs, Jews, and Abyssinians attest to the widespread knowledge of the event and to the interest it created.

Sheba was in southwestern Arabia, present-day Yemen. It is the best-watered and most fertile area of Arabia. By employing an extensive irrigation system, it developed a strong agricultural economy. But its chief strength lay in its being a center of trade. Its location kept it fairly secure from the power struggles in the Fertile Crescent and at the same time enabled it to be a convenient trade depot for traffic involving Africa, India, and the Mediterranean countries. It was famous for its trade in perfumes, incense, gold, and gems.

Solomon's fame reached the queen, probably through caravan traders that regularly passed through Israel on their way to Damascus and other points north. What is noteworthy is that his fame was associated with his relationship to the name of the Lord. His fame was a testimony to the greatness of God. House (161 n. 124) notes that the Hebrew construction "makes God the focus for both Solomon's wisdom and his reputation." It has been suggested (e.g., Wiseman, *1 & 2 Kings*, 129) that the real (though unstated) reason for the queen's going to Solomon was for the purpose of making trade agreements. Undoubtedly business was transacted under the polite fiction of an exchange of gifts (cf. vv.2, 10–13). It is clear that she came to see for herself whether or not the glowing reports had been exaggerated.

"Hard questions" (*ḥîdōt*) is generally translated "riddles," which were enigmatic sayings or questions that cloaked a deeper philosophical, practical, or theological truth. Arabic literature abounds in riddles and proverbs. They were a favorite sport and a way to test one's mettle. It would appear from the following verses that the "riddles" or "hard questions" posed by the queen were not merely frivolous tests of mental quickness but a genuine seeking for truths hidden in some of the enigmatic sayings known to her.

2 The queen came with a large caravan of camels carrying the trade goods for which Sheba was noted. Spices (Arabian balm) were native to South Arabia and were highly valued and expensive. Verse 10 mentions the 120 talents (four and one-half tons) of gold and many precious stones, but the spices are singled out for special comment. Never again were so many spices brought in as on that occasion. When she arrived, she put before Solomon all the questions on her mind.

3–5 The reports concerning Solomon's wisdom had not been exaggerated. The queen was not disappointed in his ability or in the wisdom he displayed. Not only his wisdom, but also the splendor of his court and the manner of the temple ceremonies overwhelmed her. This last idea is rendered literally "there was no more spirit left in her," indicating extremely strong emotion. This expression is used in Joshua 2:11 and 5:1 of the dismay and consternation experienced by the Canaanites at the coming of Israel, not because of the strength of Israel's army but because of the evident miraculous working of God in their behalf. "Dismay" would not be correct here, but she was totally undone (NIV, "overwhelmed") with amazement.

6–10 The queen had thought that the reports about Solomon might be exaggerated, that no one person could be as great as he was reputed to be. Yet now she freely confesses that his fame had not even begun to do him justice. "How happy your men must be!" is the word *ʾašrē*, found so often in the Psalms (e.g., Ps 1:1), translated "Blessed!" It stresses the subjective appreciation of a great favor or blessing, an experience to be enjoyed, savored to the fullest.

A wise and good king is a blessing to his subjects, and God's choice of Solomon as king was a mark of his love and favor for Israel.

On v.10, see comments at v.2.

11–13 The wealth of precious materials brought to Solomon from Sheba caused the narrator to insert parenthetically at this point another source of income, namely, the result of Solomon's maritime ventures in conjunction with Hiram (9:26–28). Particular stress is placed on a precious wood that was imported in unheard-of quantities (just as with the spice or balsam that had just come from Sheba). The identity of this almug wood is not known today. Traditionally it has been thought to be a type of sandalwood, but more recently it is considered to be a hard reddish-brown wood (DeVries, 139). It was known and used in Ras Shamra, and it is mentioned in the Alalakh tablets as being used for fine furniture. Solomon used it in the temple and palace and for musical instruments.

Solomon gave the queen all she asked for, perhaps in trade for the items she had brought. In addition he bestowed lavish gifts on her in keeping with his majesty.

NOTES

1 The letter שׁ (*š*) in the word "Sheba" (שְׁבָא, *šᵉbāʾ*) was equivalent to the south Arabic *s*, so that the people were also known as Sabeans. Arab queens from northern Arabia are mentioned in Assyrian records, and Tiglath-Pileser IV lists tribute coming from an Arabian queen.

Keil, 158, suggests that לְשֵׁם יהוה (*lᵉšēm yhwh*, lit., "with regard to the name of the LORD") speaks of "the fame which Solomon had acquired through the name of the Lord, or through the fact that the Lord had so glorified himself in him."

Since Sabean merchants regularly traveled through Israel, certain agreements and financial arrangements were surely already in effect. The fact that Solomon had now put a merchant fleet into the Red Sea and possibly the Indian Ocean might easily have affected Sheba's strong position in the caravan trade. It has therefore been suggested that this possibility was her primary motive in seeing Solomon, especially since the passage is preceded by the account of Solomon's fleet (9:26–28), and since 10:11–12 are brought into the narrative parenthetically. But this view is only speculation. It is possible to explain the whole passage from 9:26 through ch. 10 as an account of the various sources of Solomon's wealth, including Sheba. This is not to say that there was no talk of business (v.13 certainly implies that trading had been done), but it was probably not as a major motive. Compare vv.23–24, which indicate that many others sought an audience with Solomon simply because of his fabled wisdom.

10 The Jewish romantic legend that the queen desired and received a son fathered by Solomon is unsubstantiated, as is the Ethiopic tradition that the royal Abyssinian line was founded by the offspring of Solomon and the queen of Sheba.

11 On the location of Ophir, see Note at 9:28.

12 The word "supports" (מִסְעָד, *misʿād*) is a hapax legomenon, and its meaning is not perfectly clear. Its verbal root has the meaning "to support." In the LXX, Vulgate, and Targums it is translated "buttress." *HALOT* suggests "parapet." The parallel passage in 2 Chronicles 9:11 uses the word מְסִלּוֹת (*mᵉsillôt*), which the LXX and Vulgate translate "stairway."

3. The Wonders of the Solomonic Era (10:14–29)

[14]The weight of the gold that Solomon received yearly was 666 talents, [15]not including
the revenues from merchants and traders and from all the Arabian kings and the
governors of the land.

[16]King Solomon made two hundred large shields of hammered gold; six hundred bekas
of gold went into each shield. [17]He also made three hundred small shields of hammered
gold, with three minas of gold in each shield. The king put them in the Palace of the Forest
of Lebanon.

[18]Then the king made a great throne inlaid with ivory and overlaid with fine gold. [19]The
throne had six steps, and its back had a rounded top. On both sides of the seat were armrests, with a lion standing beside each of them. [20]Twelve lions stood on the six steps, one
at either end of each step. Nothing like it had ever been made for any other kingdom. [21]All
King Solomon's goblets were gold, and all the household articles in the Palace of the Forest of Lebanon were pure gold. Nothing was made of silver, because silver was considered
of little value in Solomon's days. [22]The king had a fleet of trading ships at sea along with
the ships of Hiram. Once every three years it returned, carrying gold, silver and ivory, and
apes and baboons.

[23]King Solomon was greater in riches and wisdom than all the other kings of the earth.
[24]The whole world sought audience with Solomon to hear the wisdom God had put in
his heart. [25]Year after year, everyone who came brought a gift—articles of silver and gold,
robes, weapons and spices, and horses and mules.

[26]Solomon accumulated chariots and horses; he had fourteen hundred chariots and
twelve thousand horses, which he kept in the chariot cities and also with him in Jerusalem.
[27]The king made silver as common in Jerusalem as stones, and cedar as plentiful as
sycamore-fig trees in the foothills. [28]Solomon's horses were imported from Egypt and
from Kue—the royal merchants purchased them from Kue. [29]They imported a chariot
from Egypt for six hundred shekels of silver, and a horse for a hundred and fifty. They also
exported them to all the kings of the Hittites and of the Arameans.

COMMENTARY

14–15 The 666 talents (25 tons) represent Solomon's yearly income in gold from all sources, including commerce and taxes. In addition, there was an unspecified amount of income from tolls or tariffs from the various merchants and business agents who traveled through the land, as well as tribute from conquered kings. The "kings of Arabia" of v.15 were tribal chiefs of miscellaneous peoples living in the desert to the south and to the east. The governors were probably the district governors (4:7–19).

16–17 These verses describe the ceremonial shields that Solomon kept in the Palace of the Forest of Lebanon. "These shields, like all the shields of the ancients, were made of wood or basket-work, and covered with gold plate instead of leather" (Keil, 162). The large shield "was adapted to cover the whole body, being either oval or rectangular like a door. This was carried by the heavy-armed infantry (2 Chronicles 14:8)" (J. Charley, *NBD*, 82). The small shield was carried by archers (2Ch 14:8). Each large shield in this case was covered with six hundred bekas (or half-shekels), the small shield with three minas (= three hundred bekas). The weights per shield were about seven and one-half pounds and three and three-fourths pounds respectively.

18–21 The ivory throne was most likely made of wood and inlaid with ivory (Jones, 227). It is also probable that the non-inlaid parts were the parts overlaid with gold. The throne was a large and imposing object, in keeping with the symbolism of the seat of justice and rulership of a great kingdom. The armrests were flanked by lions, as were each of the six steps (vv.19–20). These lions were probably the symbol of the tribe of Judah (DeVries, 140). Verse 20 illustrates the wealth of Solomon's kingdom.

22 The trading ships are literally "ships of Tarshish." Most likely this name referred to large merchant ships designed to carry ore. They were seaworthy enough to travel long distances under difficult weather conditions. These ships came to be used for other types of cargo as well.

There is abundant evidence of the existence in Solomonic times of copper refineries, though the large installation at Ezion Geber is now recognized to be a fortress and storehouse, not a copper smelter as was first thought (cf. Bright, 211–12). It is likely that refined metals were shipped out of Ezion Geber in return for the exotic items listed in our passage. Compare Ezekiel 27:12, in which Tarshish "exchanged silver, iron, tin and lead for your [i.e., Tyrian] merchandise." In vv.24–25 the ships of Tarshish are described as carrying other kinds of cargo, such as beautiful garments and rugs.

23–25 To the corresponding statement in 4:29–34 extolling the breadth of wisdom and knowledge of Solomon, this passage adds that he was wealthier than any king on earth, and that "the whole world sought audience with Solomon to hear the wisdom God had put in his heart," in accordance with God's promise of 3:13. Those who find this passage misplaced because it is so similar to 4:29–34 have failed to recognize the symmetrical structure of the Solomon account.

26 On the ratio of horses to chariots, Gray, 268, says, "Since three horses (a pair and a led one) were reckoned to a chariot team in Canaan on the evidence of the Ras Shamra texts (UT Krt, 128f), 12,000 horses would number studstock and reserves, as well as horses in breaking and trained animals."

This passage brings to mind the three prohibitions of Deuteronomy 17:16–17 for a future king: (1) He must not acquire great numbers of horses, (2) he must not take numerous wives, and (3) he must not amass for himself great amounts of gold and silver. The Lord takes Solomon to task only for his failure in regard to the second prohibition.

In the matter of horses, there seem to be two concerns: (1) the false reliance on chariotry (the most potent weaponry of the day) as a means of preserving and/or expanding the kingdom, and (2) making Israelites go back to Egypt for the horses. Peter Craigie (*The Book of Deuteronomy* [Grand Rapids: Eerdmans, 1990], 255–56) suggests that this latter concern may have to do with diplomatic or trade relationships, resulting in large-scale importation of horses, or perhaps the trading of men for horses (as mercenaries?—so G. von Rad, *Studies in Deuteronomy* [London: SCM, 1966], 119, who suggests that such trading may account for the Israelite military colony at Elephantine).

Isaiah 31:1–3 warns against going to Egypt for help in reliance on her chariots and horses (cf. also Isa 30:2). This latter passage suggests that in view here is not trade agreements but rather a defense alliance in which Israel put herself under the protective umbrella of Egypt, under her control, thus effectively losing the freedom God had given Israel from Egypt.

On the matter of wealth, one must remember that it was one of the bonuses God had promised to Solomon (3:13). It was God's gift, and he should not be criticized for it. No doubt the prohibition in Deuteronomy has to do with motivation and priorities in which personal gain is the issue. (Compare Jer 22, in which Judah's kings are more concerned for personal luxury than in the welfare of the nation.)

27 Silver, considered a "precious" metal, became a "common" metal because of its abundance. Cedar, which had to be imported from Lebanon, became as common (in buildings) as the indigenous sycamore-fig trees.

28–29 Solomon not only acquired chariots and horses, but he also became a trader in these items. They were imported from Kue (probably Cilicia) and Egypt. The Cilicians had been known for some time as breeders of fine horses. Solomon's agents were active in seeking out the best horses and values available.

NOTES

16–17 The units of weight intended to be understood from the numerical figures associated with the large shields (in both Kings and Chronicles) go unspecified. For example, in saying simply "600," "shekels" would normally be supplied. For the small shield, v.17 specifies "three mina" (= 150 shekels), while Chronicles reads "300" (unspecified). A comparison of the last two figures leads to the conclusion that the unspecified weights are to be understood as *temple* shekels that are one-half the weight of the ordinary shekel. The בֶּקַע (*beqaᶜ*, "split [shekel]") is its equivalent. Thus the NIV's reading of 600 and 300 bekas (temple shekels) is justified.

19 The "rounded top" correctly renders עָגֹל (*ᶜāgōl*). There is no warrant for revocalizing the MT to conform to the LXX's μόσχος (*ᶜēgel*, "calf"), as some suggest. "Archaeological illustrations deny" such a theory (Wiseman, *1 & 2 Kings*, 132). It is possible that the "rounded top" is to be thought of as being similar to the top of the seatback of the throne of King Ahiram of Byblos, as depicted on the latter's sarcophagus (cf. Ussishkin, 91, fig. 7). On this depiction, the top of the throne is folded over the back and downward in an inverted U shape. The top could very well be described as "rounded."

22 For a discussion of the location of Tarshish, see Notes on 22:48–49. תֻּכִּיִּים (*tukkîyîm*, "baboons," NIV) was traditionally rendered "peacocks" (so the KJV, NASB, NRSV). *HALOT*, after weighing all the available evidence, cannot decide between the two options.

28 Since the discovery of the place name "Kue" (קְוֵה, *qᵉwēh*) in the ZKR inscription from Syria (eighth and ninth century BC), the rendering "from Kue" has been accepted as correct. Kue is almost certainly Cilicia. On the substitution of Musri for Egypt, see Notes on 2 Kings 19:24.

B′. Solomon's Love for Pagan Wives—God's Disapproval (11:1–13)

OVERVIEW

This section stands in stark contrast to the statement of 3:3 that Solomon loved the Lord and walked in the ways of his father, David. That fervent love for God is now diluted and even replaced by his love for his pagan wives. God's former approval is now replaced by his disapproval. The former promise to shower Solomon with blessings as long as he remained faithful is now replaced by the announcement of judgment to come. It comes as a shock to the reader to see this giant of a king, with all his God-given abilities, now falling prey to the blandishments of idolatry.

When Solomon became old, he allowed his foreign wives to turn his heart from complete loyalty to the Lord. The syncretism he began to display was a curse that plagued Israel through the years and ultimately led to the destruction of Jerusalem and the temple and to the exile of the people. In later years, Nehemiah, warning the exiles of the dangers of intermarriage with pagan wives, used Solomon as an example (Ne 13:26).

1. Solomon's Many Wives (11:1–3)

[1]King Solomon, however, loved many foreign women besides Pharaoh's
daughter—Moabites, Ammonites, Edomites, Sidonians and Hittites. [2]They were from
nations about which the LORD had told the Israelites, "You must not intermarry with
them, because they will surely turn your hearts after their gods." Nevertheless, Solomon
held fast to them in love. [3]He had seven hundred wives of royal birth and three hundred
concubines, and his wives led him astray.

COMMENTARY

1–3 Solomon not only failed to heed God's prohibition (Dt 17:17) against a king's taking multiple wives, he also disregarded God's injunction against intermarrying with the Canaanites (e.g., Dt 7:3–4). Ignoring this injunction would not only be harmful to the person engaged in such a marriage, but it would also necessarily affect the children. In Solomon's case, his successor, Rehoboam, was the son of an Ammonite woman (14:31). If Solomon was adversely affected by his foreign wives, much more would Rehoboam be influenced by a pagan mother.

Though Solomon may originally have taken foreign wives for the cementing of diplomatic alliances, v.2 states that he "held fast to them in love." This speaks of strong emotional attachment, which is normal and desirable in a husband. But because Solomon was attached to the wrong women, he was led astray. The seven hundred wives and three hundred concubines, though perhaps adding to the splendor of Solomon's kingdom, were his downfall.

In Deuteronomy 10:12; 11:22; 30:20, God admonished Israel to love the Lord and to cling to him. Then they would experience the full blessing of God. Here we read that Solomon loved many foreign wives and clung to them in love. The same words—*ʾāhab* ("love") and *dābaq* ("cling")—are used here and in the Deuteronomy passages. Instead of putting God above all else, as Solomon did earlier in his life (3:3), the king now began to put his wives first.

NOTES

1–3 This passage, with 3:3, forms one of the many correspondences surrounding the building of the temple. The many wives and concubines seem to be far more than necessary for diplomatic purposes and betray in Solomon a desire to display his wealth and grandeur. This necessarily increased the financial burden of his subjects and sowed the seeds of rebellion, which came to fruition when his son became king.

2. Solomon's Turning after Idols (11:4–10)

4As Solomon grew old, his wives turned his heart after other gods, and his heart was
not fully devoted to the LORD his God, as the heart of David his father had been. 5He
followed Ashtoreth the goddess of the Sidonians, and Molech the detestable god of
the Ammonites. 6So Solomon did evil in the eyes of the LORD; he did not follow the LORD
completely, as David his father had done.
7On a hill east of Jerusalem, Solomon built a high place for Chemosh the detestable
god of Moab, and for Molech the detestable god of the Ammonites. 8He did the same for
all his foreign wives, who burned incense and offered sacrifices to their gods.
9The LORD became angry with Solomon because his heart had turned away from the
LORD, the God of Israel, who had appeared to him twice. 10Although he had forbidden
Solomon to follow other gods, Solomon did not keep the LORD's command.

COMMENTARY

4 When Solomon was young, he loved the Lord. When he grew older, he began more and more to turn his affections to his wives, and they turned his heart after other gods—precisely as God said would happen in Deuteronomy 7:3–4 and 17:17. Notice that his love for the Lord is measured by the standard of David, who, with all his faults, loved God fervently throughout his lifetime.

5–8 "Ashtoreth" (v.5) is a deliberate distortion of "Ashtarte," name of the Canaanite fertility goddess. The revocalization is intended to bring to mind the word for "shame" (*bōšet*), because it was a shameful thing to engage in such worship. On "Molech" (or "Milcom," as the MT reads here), see Note on 2 Kings 16:3. The worship of Ashtoreth involved fertility rites. In not only allowing these practices in his own household but even going to the extent of building shrines for these pagan gods, Solomon sinned grievously against the Lord (v.6). The two gods Molek and Chemosh (the Moabite equivalent of the Ammonite Molech or Milcom [vv.7–8]) are particularly mentioned, perhaps because of the extremely abominable practices associated with their worship, including child sacrifice (Lev 18:21; 20:2–5; Jer 32:35).

9–10 Solomon's sin was all the greater because of the special privileges he had enjoyed. God had singled Solomon out by appearing to him twice (see comments at ch. 9). Solomon lacked neither proof nor evidence of God's love and power. He had abundantly tasted God's love (1) by being chosen, contrary to what might have been expected, as David's successor; (2) in being given the special, personal name "Jedidiah" (i.e., "loved by the Lord"); (3) in receiving every benefit imaginable; and (4) in being visited by God twice for encouragement and admonition. He was given success in his endeavors beyond every expectation. These privileges should have created in Solomon a lifelong love and devotion of the deepest kind. But "the miraculously blessed heir of David, leader of the covenant people, has broken the most fundamental command of all: 'You shall have no other gods before me' (Exod 20:3)" (House, 168).

3. God's Announcement of Punishment (11:11–13)

11So the LORD said to Solomon, "Since this is your attitude and you have not kept my
covenant and my decrees, which I commanded you, I will most certainly tear the kingdom
away from you and give it to one of your subordinates. 12Nevertheless, for the sake of
David your father, I will not do it during your lifetime. I will tear it out of the hand of your
son. 13Yet I will not tear the whole kingdom from him, but will give him one tribe for the
sake of David my servant and for the sake of Jerusalem, which I have chosen."

COMMENTARY

11–13 Solomon was king, and he enjoyed the blessing of God because of his relationship to David and the covenant God had made with him. He had not earned God's blessing—he was born into it. He had also been thoroughly instructed and trained by David (and possibly by Nathan) in preparation for the high calling that was his (see comment on 2:2). As much as he could, David had poured into his son his own love and passion for the Lord and his dreams for the house that would reflect the glory of the Lord.

Solomon threw aside all these privileges when he followed after idols. He frittered away the continued joy and fellowship with God that could have been his for life. The punishment would be in accordance with the terms of the covenant with David. Yet even there God exercised mercy for David's sake. The kingdom was not taken from Solomon during his lifetime, nor was the kingdom to be totally removed from the line of David. One tribe would remain to fulfill God's promise to David.

NOTES

13 That one tribe was given to David and ten would be torn away (vv.31, 35) has created some difficulty in understanding. The view represented by Leon Wood ("Simeon, the Tenth Tribe of Israel," *JETS* 19 [1971]: 221–25; see also his *Israel's United Monarchy*, 333) seems best to meet the demands of Scripture. Notice first that according to 12:20 "only the tribe of Judah remained loyal to the house of David." Yet v.21 says that Rehoboam "mustered the whole house of Judah and the tribe of Benjamin." Possibly the contrast between "whole house of Judah" and "the tribe of Benjamin" indicates that Benjamin's loyalties were divided. This possibility is in fact what Wood suggests—that the northern portion of Benjamin, including Bethel, Ramah, and Jericho, became part of the northern nation. Thus, though most of Benjamin joined Judah, it was not counted as a full tribe (i.e., "whole house").

Simeon, which had originally received certain cities scattered throughout Judah as its inheritance, seems to have migrated to the north at some time before the division, since in both 2 Chronicles 15:9 and 34:6 Simeon is listed with Ephraim and Manasseh in such a way that it seems necessary to include it with the north (cf. also J. Oswalt, *ZPEB*, 5:439–40). If this case is correct, then Simeon was counted as part of the northern ten tribes, while Benjamin was not counted as a full tribe. Wiseman, *1 & 2 Kings*, 156, has a similar view, stating that Judah and Benjamin have by now merged.

A'. The Decline of Solomon (11:14–43)

1. The Rise of Adversaries (11:14–40)

OVERVIEW

Before Solomon came to the throne he had powerful adversaries, but God's blessing was on him, and he put them aside in favor of Solomon. Now it is the adversaries who become increasingly powerful as well as worrisome to Solomon. God's blessing is no longer on him as it had been, and after his death his chief adversary took away the larger part of the kingdom from his son.

a. Hadad the Edomite (11:14–22)

14Then the LORD raised up against Solomon an adversary, Hadad the Edomite, from the
royal line of Edom. 15Earlier when David was fighting with Edom, Joab the commander of
the army, who had gone up to bury the dead, had struck down all the men in Edom. 16Joab
and all the Israelites stayed there for six months, until they had destroyed all the men in
Edom. 17But Hadad, still only a boy, fled to Egypt with some Edomite officials who had
served his father. 18They set out from Midian and went to Paran. Then taking men from

Paran with them, they went to Egypt, to Pharaoh king of Egypt, who gave Hadad a house
and land and provided him with food.
[19]Pharaoh was so pleased with Hadad that he gave him a sister of his own wife, Queen
Tahpenes, in marriage. [20]The sister of Tahpenes bore him a son named Genubath, whom
Tahpenes brought up in the royal palace. There Genubath lived with Pharaoh's own
children.
[21]While he was in Egypt, Hadad heard that David rested with his fathers and that Joab
the commander of the army was also dead. Then Hadad said to Pharaoh, "Let me go, that I
may return to my own country."
[22]"What have you lacked here that you want to go back to your own country?" Pharaoh
asked.
"Nothing," Hadad replied, "but do let me go!"

COMMENTARY

14–22 Hadad was the first of three men raised up by God to be adversaries against Solomon. It appears that as his reign drew to a close, these three men became increasingly worrisome to him. Hadad was the only survivor of the royal family of Edom when David's army defeated the Edomites by slaughtering eighteen thousand men (2Sa 8:13–14; 1Ch 18:12–13). This slaughter seems to have taken place over a period of six months, when for some unknown reason Joab sought to destroy the Edomite army (vv.15–16). Hadad managed to escape and found his way to Egypt with a number of servants (v.17). There he was given Pharaoh's sister-in-law as his wife (v.19). He continued in Pharaoh's favor, and Hadad's son was raised with the royal household (v.20).

Hadad, however, continued to harbor strong bitterness against Israel; and the moment the news came that David and Joab had died, Hadad returned to Edom (vv.21–22). There, in some unspecified way, he created trouble for Solomon, presumably not being effective until Solomon's later years.

NOTES

14–16 שָׂטָן (*śāṭān*, "adversary") is the word from which the name of the great adversary of humanity ("Satan") is derived. Second Samuel 8:13–14 naturally attributes the victory to David. Here Joab, as commander-in-chief, receives the credit. In 1 Chronicles 18:12–13 it is Abishai, Joab's brother, who defeats the Edomites. The latter was a high officer and was doubtless in active command of the army when it gained the decisive victory.

19 K. Kitchen ("How We Know When Solomon Ruled," 36–37) provides evidence that it was not at all uncommon after the time of Amenophis III for Egyptian women of royal birth to be given to foreigners as wives (see Notes on 9:16).

b. Rezon of Damascus (11:23–25)

[23]And God raised up against Solomon another adversary, Rezon son of Eliada, who
had fled from his master, Hadadezer king of Zobah. [24]He gathered men around him
and became the leader of a band of rebels when David destroyed the forces of Zobah;
the rebels went to Damascus, where they settled and took control. [25]Rezon was Israel's
adversary as long as Solomon lived, adding to the trouble caused by Hadad. So Rezon
ruled in Aram and was hostile toward Israel.

COMMENTARY

23–25 The second adversary was Rezon, who had served under Hadadezer, king of Zobah. After David defeated Hadadezer (2Sa 8:3–9), Rezon, who had escaped, formed a group of raiders and bandits who ultimately gained control of Damascus (v.24). Since David had thoroughly defeated both Zobah and Damascus, put garrisons in the latter city (2Sa 8:6), and reduced it to a tributary, it seems likely that Rezon's seizing of Damascus did not take place until later in Solomon's reign. At some point, probably after he had finished his palace, Solomon defeated Zobah and Hamath and went as far as Tadmor (2Ch 8:3–4), which he made into a fortified outpost. Thus it is unlikely that Rezon made his move into Damascus until Solomon's declining years. However that may be, he was Solomon's troublemaker in the north, while Hadad caused problems in the south (v.25).

NOTES

23–24 Solomon's only recorded military action is reported here. Hamath and Zobah adjoined one another, and though they had been subjected by David, they seem to have generated considerable unrest, thus requiring Solomon's military attention. Tadmor (known later as Palmyra) was an important oasis on the caravan route between Damascus and Mari on the Euphrates and profited from the trade between Mesopotamia and the Levant.

c. Jeroboam (11:26–40)

[26]Also, Jeroboam son of Nebat rebelled against the king. He was one of Solomon's
officials, an Ephraimite from Zeredah, and his mother was a widow named Zeruah.
[27]Here is the account of how he rebelled against the king: Solomon had built the supporting terraces and had filled in the gap in the wall of the city of David his father. [28]Now

Jeroboam was a man of standing, and when Solomon saw how well the young man did
his work, he put him in charge of the whole labor force of the house of Joseph.
29About that time Jeroboam was going out of Jerusalem, and Ahijah the prophet of
Shiloh met him on the way, wearing a new cloak. The two of them were alone out in the
country, 30and Ahijah took hold of the new cloak he was wearing and tore it into twelve
pieces. 31Then he said to Jeroboam, "Take ten pieces for yourself, for this is what the LORD,
the God of Israel, says: 'See, I am going to tear the kingdom out of Solomon's hand and
give you ten tribes. 32But for the sake of my servant David and the city of Jerusalem, which
I have chosen out of all the tribes of Israel, he will have one tribe. 33I will do this because
they have forsaken me and worshiped Ashtoreth the goddess of the Sidonians, Chemosh
the god of the Moabites, and Molech the god of the Ammonites, and have not walked in
my ways, nor done what is right in my eyes, nor kept my statutes and laws as David, Solomon's father, did.
34"'But I will not take the whole kingdom out of Solomon's hand; I have made him ruler
all the days of his life for the sake of David my servant, whom I chose and who observed
my commands and statutes. 35I will take the kingdom from his son's hands and give you
ten tribes. 36I will give one tribe to his son so that David my servant may always have a
lamp before me in Jerusalem, the city where I chose to put my Name. 37However, as for
you, I will take you, and you will rule over all that your heart desires; you will be king over
Israel. 38If you do whatever I command you and walk in my ways and do what is right in my
eyes by keeping my statutes and commands, as David my servant did, I will be with you. I
will build you a dynasty as enduring as the one I built for David and will give Israel to you.
39I will humble David's descendants because of this, but not forever.'"
40Solomon tried to kill Jeroboam, but Jeroboam fled to Egypt, to Shishak the king, and
stayed there until Solomon's death.

COMMENTARY

26–28 The third and by far most serious problem for Solomon in his latter years was Jeroboam, an Ephraimite of considerable ability and energy. The story of his rebellion starts with v.27. He was part of the Ephraimite labor force working on the Millo (see comments on 9:15) and a breach in the wall of the city of David. Jeroboam did his work so well that he attracted Solomon's attention and was put in charge of the contingent from Ephraim and Manasseh (v.28). He was evidently a charismatic leader.

29–32 About this time, while still overseeing this construction project (which took place sometime after Solomon's twenty-fourth year [9:10–15]), Jeroboam met Ahijah the prophet from Shiloh (v.29). This meeting was, of course, planned on Ahijah's part. When they were alone in the open country, Ahijah symbolically told Jeroboam what

God's plans were for him and Solomon. He tore his own new cloak into twelve pieces (v.30), told Jeroboam to take ten of the pieces (v.31), and then explained the meaning of the prophecy.

33–35 See comments on vv.7–13. This passage also indicates that Solomon was not alone in his defection—the whole leadership was involved.

36 With the words "that David my servant may always have a lamp before me in Jerusalem," God expresses the unconditional aspect of the Davidic covenant: God will at some future time reestablish the throne of David in full glory—in the person of the Messiah, the Anointed One. Keil, 181, notes the recurrence of this expression in 15:4; 2 Kings 8:19; and 2 Chronicles 21:7. He suggests that it is explained in 2 Samuel 21:17, "where David's regal rule is called the light which God's grace had kindled for Israel, and affirms that David was never to want a successor upon the throne." Gray, 297, says that the "light ... symbolizes the living representative of the house of the founder David (cf. 2Sa 14:7)." The symbolism is striking and beautiful. It ought to be noted in addition that not only is the line of David perpetuated as his light is kept burning, but this light is in Jerusalem, the city where God chose to put his Name. There is in view, then, a future for God's city, Jerusalem.

37–38 God gave Jeroboam the grand opportunity of establishing a lasting dynasty. The conditions were the same as those imposed on the sons of David. The standard of the godly walk was once again David. Unfortunately, Jeroboam was an extremely able but unworthy man. He proved to be an ambitious and greedy opportunist. Chapter 12 shows that he had the ability to play on people's emotions to achieve his ends. All his subsequent actions demonstrate the mentality of a man who was determined to achieve his own ends and ignore God and his ways in the process.

39 Here is both a reaffirmation of the enduring nature of God's promise to David and a clear statement to Jeroboam and his successors that the house of David will win in the end. Starting with Rehoboam's loss, first of the ten tribes and then the deprivations of Shishak (ch. 14), Judah became the smaller and the generally weaker kingdom. It was indeed a shock for Rehoboam and the tribe of Judah to be reduced overnight from the most powerful tribe in an illustrious and world-renowned kingdom to a small state that was soon stripped of what wealth it had left. But God said that Judah's plight would not always be thus. There seems to be an implication here, as explicitly stated in the Prophets, that in the future the tribes will all once again be united under the Prince of Judah.

40 At some point after the prophecy of Ahijah, the attempt at rebellion spoken of in v.26 took place. No details are given. It can, however, be reasonably assumed that Jeroboam was busily fanning the flames of dissatisfaction on the part of the northern tribes with the leadership of the house of David and, in particular, the oppressive requirements imposed on them to maintain the splendid style of Solomon's government. Notice the contrast here between Jeroboam and David, both of whom became kings after a disobedient king. David waited on God, but Jeroboam took matters into his own hands.

NOTES

28 "Man of standing" is a possible rendering of גִּבּוֹר חַיִל (*gibbôr ḥayil*); Gray, 273, and House, 171, suggest that Jeroboam may have received a large inheritance from his father, but this understanding is probably not the most accurate in this context. The traditional rendering has been "mighty man of valor" ("valiant warrior," NASB). Gray, 82, says, "Under Saul it comes to mean one able in virtue of his property to equip himself, and possibly also followers, for war." H. Kosmala (*TDOT*, 2:374) takes a more balanced view: "It can mean strength (of a warrior or of military forces), ability (in war or in some vocation), or wealth (possessions), but the meaning must be determined by the context. Thus a *gibbôr ḥayil* can be ... an able man in any aspect, especially with regard to work (Jeroboam I, 1 Kings 11:28)." Kosmala is surely correct, since Jeroboam is further described as an industrious and energetic man. The rendering of the NRSV reflects this understanding: a "very able" man.

29 Ahijah, the prophet from Shiloh, appears again in ch. 14 and is also listed in 2 Chronicles 9:29 as having recorded his prophecy concerning Solomon. House, 172, notes that Ahijah's ministry here heralds the beginning of "the prophets' role as major players in the history of Israel.... In the rest of 1, 2 Kings the prophets act as God's spokespersons, as anointers of new kings, as miracle workers, and as Israel's overall covenant conscience."

30–31 The symbolic tearing of the coat is reminiscent of Samuel's action in 1 Samuel 15:27–31, with a similar significance. The fact that Ahijah tore his coat into twelve pieces, yet gave ten to Jeroboam and one to Solomon's heir (leaving one tribe seemingly unaccounted for), probably indicates that Benjamin was by this time a tribe divided. The northern and smaller portion sided with Jeroboam, while the southern and larger portion sided with Rehoboam and Judah (1Ki 12:21). Thus Benjamin could not be counted as belonging to either side, so that 1 Kings 12:20 says accurately that only Judah remained loyal to the house of David. (See the note at v.13, and Jones, 244, for further discussion.)

2. Solomon's Death and the Accession of Rehoboam (11:41–43)

41 As for the other events of Solomon's reign—all he did and the wisdom he displayed—are they not written in the book of the annals of Solomon? 42 Solomon reigned in Jerusalem over all Israel forty years. 43 Then he rested with his fathers and was buried in the city of David his father. And Rehoboam his son succeeded him as king.

COMMENTARY

41–43 The royal annals of Solomon contained a more complete record of the events surrounding his administration, but the account recorded in Scripture is God's inspired message, given for the instruction and benefit of the reader.

Solomon left a big mark in history. His memory and fame lived on. His name has become synonymous with wisdom. Unfortunately he failed in his latter years to apply that wisdom to his own life. However, he does represent the first stage in the fulfillment of the Davidic covenant; and, despite his faults, he foreshadows the coming Christ, the true Son of David. Christ's victories will far exceed those of David, and the glories of his kingdom will totally outshine those of Solomon. There will be no failure and no end to that kingdom.

II. THE DIVIDED KINGDOM (1KI 12:1–2KI 17:41)

A. The Division of the Nation (12:1–24)

OVERVIEW

Sandwiched between the background (vv.1–3a) and final details (vv.18–24) of 1 Kings 12 are several meetings involving Rehoboam. He meets twice with the northern delegation: once to hear their demands (vv.3b–5), and a second time to deliver his decision (vv.12–17). He also meets twice with his own advisers (vv.6–11).

As the narrative begins, "all the Israelites" (i.e., the various representatives of the northern tribes) were gathered at Shechem for Rehoboam's installation as kingly successor to his father, Solomon. Dramatic tension in the narrative is immediately felt, for Jeroboam (who had earlier fled from Solomon into Egypt [11:40]) had been summoned by the northern delegates to accompany them to Shechem (12:1–3a).

Having heard the request of the northern delegation for a lessening of the burdensome levies on them (vv.3b–5), Rehoboam obtained a three-day waiting period in order to consider this petition. He then consulted with his advisors. Calling in the elder counselors who had served through the difficult Solomonic years, Rehoboam received advice to grant the demands of the delegates so as to gain their loyalty (vv.6–7). Next Rehoboam turned to his own contemporaries for advice (vv.8–9). The young men gave Rehoboam the counsel he wished to hear. They advised him to follow a harsh line (vv.10–11). Was Solomon too hard on them? He would be tougher. His little finger would be thicker than Solomon's loins!

When the prescribed three-day waiting period was over, a second meeting took place, in which the advice of the younger men was delivered to the northern delegation. The news of a hard-line approach occasioned the immediate secession of the northern tribes (vv.12–17). Rehoboam then foolishly decided to test the delegates' resolve by sending Adoniram, his chief tax collector, to gather the taxes; he gathered only stones for his effort. With Adoniram dead and the people gathered into a bitter mob, Rehoboam fled for his life (v.18). There remained only the formal invitation to Jeroboam to become king of the northern tribes, followed by the coronation ceremony before the assembled multitude.

Having failed to acquire the north's willing subservience, Rehoboam decided on an outright invasion of the new kingdom and so gathered a large army (v.21; cf. 2Ch 11:1–4). However, Shemaiah the prophet warned Rehoboam not to attempt to undo what God had decreed (vv.22–24); Rehoboam wisely abandoned the attack.

[1]Rehoboam went to Shechem, for all the Israelites had gone there to make him king.
[2]When Jeroboam son of Nebat heard this (he was still in Egypt, where he had fled from
King Solomon), he returned from Egypt. [3]So they sent for Jeroboam, and he and the whole

assembly of Israel went to Rehoboam and said to him: [4]"Your father put a heavy yoke on us,
but now lighten the harsh labor and the heavy yoke he put on us, and we will serve you."
[5]Rehoboam answered, "Go away for three days and then come back to me." So the
people went away.
[6]Then King Rehoboam consulted the elders who had served his father Solomon during
his lifetime. "How would you advise me to answer these people?" he asked.
[7]They replied, "If today you will be a servant to these people and serve them and give
them a favorable answer, they will always be your servants."
[8]But Rehoboam rejected the advice the elders gave him and consulted the young men
who had grown up with him and were serving him. [9]He asked them, "What is your advice?
How should we answer these people who say to me, 'Lighten the yoke your father put
on us'?"
[10]The young men who had grown up with him replied, "Tell these people who have said
to you, 'Your father put a heavy yoke on us, but make our yoke lighter'—tell them, 'My little finger is thicker than my father's waist. [11]My father laid on you a heavy yoke; I will make
it even heavier. My father scourged you with whips; I will scourge you with scorpions.'"
[12]Three days later Jeroboam and all the people returned to Rehoboam, as the king had
said, "Come back to me in three days." [13]The king answered the people harshly. Rejecting
the advice given him by the elders, [14]he followed the advice of the young men and said,
"My father made your yoke heavy; I will make it even heavier. My father scourged you with
whips; I will scourge you with scorpions." [15]So the king did not listen to the people, for this
turn of events was from the LORD, to fulfill the word the LORD had spoken to Jeroboam son
of Nebat through Ahijah the Shilonite.
[16]When all Israel saw that the king refused to listen to them, they answered the king:

"What share do we have in David,
what part in Jesse's son?
To your tents, O Israel!
Look after your own house, O David!"

So the Israelites went home. [17]But as for the Israelites who were living in the towns of
Judah, Rehoboam still ruled over them.
[18]King Rehoboam sent out Adoniram, who was in charge of forced labor, but all Israel
stoned him to death. King Rehoboam, however, managed to get into his chariot and
escape to Jerusalem. [19]So Israel has been in rebellion against the house of David to this day.
[20]When all the Israelites heard that Jeroboam had returned, they sent and called him to
the assembly and made him king over all Israel. Only the tribe of Judah remained loyal to
the house of David.

[21]When Rehoboam arrived in Jerusalem, he mustered the whole house of Judah and the tribe of Benjamin—a hundred and eighty thousand fighting men—to make war against the house of Israel and to regain the kingdom for Rehoboam son of Solomon.

[22]But this word of God came to Shemaiah the man of God: [23]"Say to Rehoboam son of Solomon king of Judah, to the whole house of Judah and Benjamin, and to the rest of the people, [24]'This is what the LORD says: Do not go up to fight against your brothers, the Israelites. Go home, every one of you, for this is my doing.'" So they obeyed the word of the LORD and went home again, as the LORD had ordered.

COMMENTARY

1–3a It may be that during the years of the united monarchy, the "structure of a double crown, one of Judah and the other of Israel, was maintained," as J. Myers (*II Chronicles* [AB; Garden City, N.Y.: Doubleday, 1965], 65) suggests. Bright, 210, theorizes that Solomon may likewise have gone to Shechem for official recognition by the northern confederacy. Shechem had a long and important history as a political and religious center. It is small wonder, then, that with the death of Solomon and in the midst of troubled times, Shechem would again come into prominence.

The reading of the MT (see Note on v.2) favors the idea that Jeroboam, who was still residing in Egypt since fleeing from the presence of Solomon, first learned of affairs in Shechem when he was summoned by the northern delegates. The alternative reading of the ancient versions and 2 Chronicles 10:2 could imply that Jeroboam himself heard of the proceedings and made himself available to the northern contingent. If the MT is read, it implies that Jeroboam was held in high respect by important factions in the north, hence contact with him continued all the time he was in exile.

3b–5 The petition of the northern group reflects the fact that they were willing enough to recognize Rehoboam as king—provided he would lighten the heavy taxes and social and military levies Solomon had instituted. The emphasis of the MT (see Note on v.4) posits a strong contrast between what Solomon had done and the opportunity that lay before Rehoboam if he would lighten the royal demands.

The proposal for a three-day waiting period for Rehoboam's decision reflects a well-known motif in which the third day becomes the day of special emphasis, decision, and finality (cf. Ex 19:10–16; Est 4:15–16; 2Ki 20:8). Jesus predicted his own resurrection on the third day (e.g., Mt 16:21; 17:23; 20:19), a prophecy that was gloriously fulfilled (Lk 24:21; 1Co 15:4).

6–11 The text gives no hint that the younger advisors whom Rehoboam consulted had any official status in Israel. Their unwise suggested answer to the delegation's demands speaks both of their inexperience and insolence.

Wiseman, *1 & 2 Kings*, 141, may be correct in proposing that the recommended reply of the younger men was a popular proverb (v.10). Scourging with scorpions (v.11) probably refers to a type of whip that produced wounds so painful as to be compared to a scorpion's sting. Perhaps, as often maintained, it was made with spiked barbs or nails.

12–17 Although Rehoboam delivered the harsh ultimatum (vv.13–14), it lacked the crude proverb of v.10 (see Notes). At this point the author of Kings interrupts the narrative (v.15) to point out that the decision of Rehoboam and his counselors was in accordance with a turn of affairs arranged by God's sovereign disposition, as prophesied previously by Ahijah (cf. 1Ki 11:29–39; 2Ch 10:15). While the decision and responsibility for all that took place rested with the human participants, none of it took God by surprise. Indeed, God utilized everything to accomplish his will in judgment against Solomon and the people (cf. 1Ki 11:33).

A carefully composed reply in the note of secession (v.16) indicates that the delegates were prepared for the worst in the negotiations and that reconciliation was now out of the question. All hope for alleviation from their harsh circumstances apparently was lost; therefore, they had no choice but to declare their independence. The narrator adds that although Israelites in the north were severed from Rehoboam's control, those in the south were still under his rule (v.17). This note suggests that no mass exodus of individual Israelites from Rehoboam's jurisdiction occurred.

18–24 Rehoboam's ill-advised attempts to reinstate his sovereignty over Israel first by taxation and then by invasion were unsuccessful. The tax collector was stoned to death and the king's war plans were denounced by the Lord's prophet Shemaiah. The importance of faithful prophets has already been felt in the narrative regarding Solomon's anointing as king (1Ki 1), as well as the prophecy that Jeroboam would one day rule over a large portion of Israel (11:29–39). Prophets and prophecy play a large role in the succeeding narratives (see Introduction: Literary Form).

The narrator interrupts the flow of thought in the passage a third time to point out that up to the time of this account Israel has remained in rebellion against Judah (v.19). This remark indicates that the author's source of information antedates the fall of Samaria in 722 BC.

NOTES

1 G. E. Wright ("Shechem and Tribal League Shrines," *VT* 21 [1971]: 572–603) points out that in the light of historical research it would not be unreasonable "to suggest that ... for 500 years or so (1700–1200 BC) Shechem was a 'Holy City' whose political relations were arranged by compact."

2 The MT's וַיֵּשֶׁב (*wayyēšeb*, "and he dwelt") is read as *wayyāšob* ("and he returned") with A, the Syriac version of the Hexapla, the Vulgate, and 2 Chronicles 10:2 (cf. NLT, NRSV). בְּמִצְרָיִם (*b*[e]*miṣrāyim*, "in Egypt") is to be understood here as "from Egypt," as read in 2 Chronicles 10:2.

It has been suggested that the name Jeroboam ("let the people be great") may be a throne name deliberately chosen to be provocative to Rehoboam; for details, see W. F. Albright, *The Biblical Period from Abraham to Ezra* (New York: Harper & Row, 1963), 30–31. Some (e.g., Bright, 210, and R. W. Klein ["Jeroboam's Rise to Power," *JBL* (1970): 217–18]) suggest that Jeroboam was not personally present at the meeting with Rehoboam but that he returned only after the talks between the north and the south had ended. Perhaps J. Liver's suggestion ("The Book of the Acts of Solomon," *Bib* 46 [1967]: 96ff.) that Jeroboam simply made his influence felt through the delegates is correct.

4 The MT may be understood as saying, "Your father imposed a heavy yoke upon us but you now, lighten [some of] your father's harsh yoke [i.e., compulsory service] ... and we will serve you." Both "your father" and "you now" stand in emphatic position. Walsh, 161, notes the firm resolve in their request, as indicated both by the Hebrew syntax and the paronomasia in the Hebrew *ʾattâ ʿattâ* ("you now").

6–8 M. Weinfeld ("The Counsel of the 'Elders' to Rehoboam and Its Implications," *Maarav* 3 [1982]: 27–53), by subjecting the terminology of v. 7 to a thorough study of both the biblical and extrabiblical evidence, conclusively demonstrates the legal aspects of the northern kingdom's request for exemption from the corvée and the heavy taxes imposed on them. The "young men" were probably Rehoboam's military advisors. For the existence of a council of elders and young arms-bearing men, see "Gilgamesh and Agga," *ANET*, 45; cf. 1 Kings 21:11.

10 קָטָנִּי (*qāṭānnî*, "my littlest part") is usually understood as in the Vulgate: *minimus digitus meus* ("my little finger"). But since the compared member is lesser, *HALOT* may be correct in viewing the phrase euphemistically of the genitals.

18 The NIV's "managed" (*hitʾammēṣ*) means literally "to strengthen oneself, summon all one's strength."

19 The verb translated "rebellion" carries the idea of deliberate sinning, in this case against the will of God.

21 The MT indicates that Rehoboam summoned a crack military force (Heb. "choice fighting men"; cf. GWT, "best soldiers").

22 Shemaiah is associated only with this incident (cf. 2Ch 11:2–4; 12:5–8). He may be identical with the Shemaiah who, with Iddo the seer, wrote a history of the reign of Rehoboam (2Ch 12:15). According to the LXX, Shemaiah was the prophet who figured in the incident of the tearing of Jeroboam's mantle (1Ki 11:29–40), an event that it includes after 12:24. Indeed, at this point the LXX gives an extended discussion of Jeroboam's origin and rise to power.

24 For an interesting study of the political and spiritual implications of Rehoboam's proposed plans to bring the northern kingdom back under his control, see Amos Frisch, "Shemaiah the Prophet versus King Rehoboam: Two Opposed Interpretations of the Schism (1 Kings xii 21–4)," *VT* 38 (1988): 466–68.

B. The Reign of Jeroboam in the Northern Kingdom (12:25–14:20)

OVERVIEW

The narrative of Jeroboam's foundational reign in the northern kingdom proceeds in three episodes: (1) an account of Jeroboam's early activities and reforms (12:25–32); (2) the story of the man of God, to which the narrator adds a stinging evaluation of Jeroboam (12:33–13:34); and (3) the recording of Ahijah's prophecy against the house of Jeroboam, to which is appended a closing evaluative formula covering Jeroboam's reign (1Ki 14:1–20).

The focus in this section centers on Jeroboam's sinful character and actions. The account of his deliberate institution of syncretistic religious programs becomes highlighted by the prophet's denunciation of his apostate altar, as well as the account of the prophet's own death due to his disobedience. Thus the penalty for sin involves the danger of extreme divine punishment for those charged with great responsibilities. Despite these examples of divine justice, Jeroboam remains impenitent (1Ki 13:33–34).

Accordingly, an even greater disaster overtakes Jeroboam's household—the death of a son (1Ki 14:1–18). No record of the king's repentance is appended to the story, however. The father's apostasy has brought tragedy to his household, and his failure heralds the demise of his nation as well.

1. The Establishment of Jeroboam's Religion (12:25–32)

OVERVIEW

The account of Jeroboam's early actions falls into two unequal parts: (1) his building activities (v.25) and (2) his religious innovations (vv.26–32). The greater space devoted to his spiritual "reforms" underscores the king's sinful disposition. Jeroboam's character and its outcome will be the focal points of the author's attention.

25 Then Jeroboam fortified Shechem in the hill country of Ephraim and lived there. From
there he went out and built up Peniel.

26 Jeroboam thought to himself, "The kingdom will now likely revert to the house of
David. 27 If these people go up to offer sacrifices at the temple of the LORD in Jerusalem,
they will again give their allegiance to their lord, Rehoboam king of Judah. They will kill
me and return to King Rehoboam."

28 After seeking advice, the king made two golden calves. He said to the people, "It is too
much for you to go up to Jerusalem. Here are your gods, O Israel, who brought you up out
of Egypt." 29 One he set up in Bethel, and the other in Dan. 30 And this thing became a sin;
the people went even as far as Dan to worship the one there.

31 Jeroboam built shrines on high places and appointed priests from all sorts of people,
even though they were not Levites. 32 He instituted a festival on the fifteenth day of the
eighth month, like the festival held in Judah, and offered sacrifices on the altar. This he did
in Bethel, sacrificing to the calves he had made. And at Bethel he also installed priests at
the high places he had made.

COMMENTARY

25 Jeroboam's plans for the administration of the new kingdom are now detailed. It was imperative that he act wisely, lest the people become dissatisfied and return their allegiance to Rehoboam (vv.26–27). No doubt much of the administrative machinery (minus the hated corvée established by

David and Solomon) was utilized. His years serving Solomon in a responsible position probably aided Jeroboam's leadership in this area. Shechem was refurbished and made the capital. Transjordanian Peniel received his attention also and may have served subsequently as an alternative royal residence (cf. Josephus, *Ant.* 8.225 [8.4]). The fortifying and refurbishing of both sites would provide protection against Aramean advances from the north and northeast.

26–30 The people, however, must be cared for not only administratively but also religiously. Here Jeroboam miscalculated and substituted human wisdom for divine direction. Although God may have allowed the kingdom to be divided politically, he intended no theological schism. Fearing that a continued adherence to the established faith with its center of worship in Jerusalem might return the people's affection to the south, Jeroboam established an alternative and more convenient religious experience. Rather than making the long trip to Jerusalem, the people of the north could now select one of the two more accessible worship centers: Dan, in the northern sector of the northern kingdom, or Bethel, in the extreme south, both of which cities had longstanding traditions as religious centers. Bethel was to be especially prominent throughout the rest of the history of the northern kingdom (cf. Hos 10:5; Am 7:13).

At each cultic center Jeroboam erected a temple, probably to house the sacred image and altar. The golden calves that he caused to be erected (vv.28–29), while striking a traditional chord with the populace (cf. Ex 32:4, 8), were probably not intended to be construed as pagan images per se; rather, they were representations of animals on whose back stood the invisible god, unseen by the eye of the worshiper. Similar practices involving the worship of the Canaanite god Baal Hadad are well documented in the literature and art of Ugarit. It was inevitable that religious confusion and apostasy would soon set in (cf. 14:9; Hos 8:6).

31–32 To further his religious goals, Jeroboam instituted a new religious order drawn from non-Levitical sources (contra Dt 18:1–8). Indeed the Levitical priests refused to have any share in such unscriptural procedures; they chose, instead, to leave their homes and go over to Rehoboam and the southern kingdom, where the true faith was retained (2Ch 11:13–17). In this move they were followed by many other believers from the north.

Completing his religious innovations, Jeroboam instituted an annual feast on the fifteenth day of the eighth month, no doubt rivaling the Feast of Tabernacles in the seventh month in Jerusalem. This practice became a besetting sin condemned repeatedly by the author of Kings; for "each of these actions defied and broke God-given requirements in the law and implied that civil matters were considered more important than religious principle and practice" (Wiseman, *1 & 2 Kings*, 145).

NOTES

25 Based on the repetition of many words and phrases, D. W. Winkle ("Jeroboam's Cultic Innovations and the Man of God from Judah," *VT* 46 [1996]: 101–14) notes the close dependence of the next section on this one. Although he suggests that such repetitions indicate that 12:25–13:34 comprise one literary unit, these may simply function as stitching devices tying the two narratives together.

28 For illustrations of similar cultic practices at Ugarit, see *ANEP*, fig. 500, 501, 522, 534, and 537.

30–31 Jeroboam's "high places" were centers of cult worship that further rivaled the temple in Jerusalem. Excavations at Dan have confirmed the existence of a high place and sacred enclosure. See A. Biran, *Encyclopedia of Excavations in the Holy Land* (Oxford: Oxford Univ. Press, 1977), 1:320. See also J. E. Jennings, "Dan," *The New International Dictionary of Biblical Archaeology*, ed. E. M. Blaiklock and R. K. Harrison (Grand Rapids: Zondervan, 1983), 148–49; H. Shanks, "Avraham Biran—Twenty Years of Digging at Tel Dan," *BAR* 13/4 (1987): 18–21.

The phrase "from all sorts of people" indicates that Jeroboam appointed priests from all levels and segments of society except the Levites.

32 The change of months may have been in keeping with agricultural festival observances—based primarily on calendrical considerations—previously held in Canaan (see J. Morgenstern, "The Festival of Jerobeam I," *JBL* 83 [1964]: 109–17). If so, Jeroboam thereby gave an aura of traditional legitimacy to his bold move for religious independence from the established religion at Jerusalem. On the whole question of Jeroboam's religious reforms, see de Vaux, 97–110.

2. The Condemnation of Jeroboam's Religion (12:33–13:34)

a. Jeroboam and the man of God (12:33–13:10)

OVERVIEW

The condemnation of Jeroboam's religion is told in the form of the story of the man of God. The account is structured in chiastic fashion:

- A Background setting (12:33–13:1)
  - B Pronouncement and sign (13:2–3)
    - C Royal reaction and fulfillment signs (13:4–5)
    - C' Royal reaction and healing (13:6)
  - B' Prophetic declaration (13:7–9)
- A' Conclusion (13:10).

In accordance with his reforms, Jeroboam himself installed the festival on the fifteenth day of the eighth month by personally attending the sacrifice at Bethel. To this event the Lord sent his prophet, who arrived just as Jeroboam was about to make his offering at the altar. Upon his arrival, the prophet denounced the altar and predicted a coming day when a certain Josiah of the house of David would desecrate the altar and bring its apostate offerings to an end. Moreover, the altar itself would split apart and spill its ashes to the ground.

Stretching his hand toward the prophet, the angry king ordered his arrest. Instantly the king's hand became withered and the predicted splitting of the altar took place. The terrified king begged the prophet to entreat God for the restoration of his hand.

When the prophet complied and healing came, Jeroboam invited the man of God to come with him and take sustenance. Jeroboam assured him that he would also receive a gift if he did so. The prophet declined, however, and pointed out that God had commanded him to deliver his denunciation of the altar and go home via a different road from that by which he had come. He was to take no nourishment whatsoever. So it was that the man of God did precisely as he had been instructed.

33 On the fifteenth day of the eighth month, a month of his own choosing, he offered
sacrifices on the altar he had built at Bethel. So he instituted the festival for the Israelites
and went up to the altar to make offerings.
13:1 By the word of the LORD a man of God came from Judah to Bethel, as Jeroboam was
standing by the altar to make an offering. 2 He cried out against the altar by the word of
the LORD: "O altar, altar! This is what the LORD says: 'A son named Josiah will be born to the
house of David. On you he will sacrifice the priests of the high places who now make offerings here, and human bones will be burned on you.'" 3 That same day the man of God gave
a sign: "This is the sign the LORD has declared: The altar will be split apart and the ashes on
it will be poured out."
4 When King Jeroboam heard what the man of God cried out against the altar at Bethel,
he stretched out his hand from the altar and said, "Seize him!" But the hand he stretched
out toward the man shriveled up, so that he could not pull it back. 5 Also, the altar was
split apart and its ashes poured out according to the sign given by the man of God by the
word of the LORD.
6 Then the king said to the man of God, "Intercede with the LORD your God and pray for
me that my hand may be restored." So the man of God interceded with the LORD, and the
king's hand was restored and became as it was before.
7 The king said to the man of God, "Come home with me and have something to eat,
and I will give you a gift."
8 But the man of God answered the king, "Even if you were to give me half your
possessions, I would not go with you, nor would I eat bread or drink water here. 9 For I was
commanded by the word of the LORD: 'You must not eat bread or drink water or return by
the way you came.'" 10 So he took another road and did not return by the way he had come
to Bethel.

COMMENTARY

12:33–13:1 Jeroboam may not have personally offered the sacrifices. He may have simply stood by the altar much as Solomon had done at the dedication of the temple (8:62–64; cf. also Jehu in 2Ki 10:25).

2–3 According to Levitical regulation, the ashes were to be carried off to a clean place for disposal (Lev 1:16; 4:12; 6:10–11). The desecration of the altar and pouring out of its ashes would render the altar and the services unclean.

4–5 The biblical motif of the outstretched hand/arm symbolizes divine omnipotence (Jer 32:17). Although at times it was exercised on behalf of God's people (Ex 6:6), the outstretched hand/arm could also indicate his displeasure, even against his own (Jer 21:5).

6 A prophet was often privileged to intercede for others (e.g., 1Sa 7:8; Am 7:2).

7–9 The prophet's refusal to compromise the terms of his commission stands in bold contrast with the incident in the following verses (vv.11–34) and with the situation of Elisha with his aide, Gehazi (2Ki 5:15–16, 19–27). The implication is clear: God's servant must not make merchandise of the ministry.

NOTES

13:1 אִישׁ אֱלֹהִים (*ʾîš ʾelōhîm*, "man of God") is a general term for a prophet that lays stress on the fact of his divine ministry. Other terms for "prophet" emphasize:

- the person's call: נָבִיא (*nābîʾ*, "prophet")
- reception of the divine communication: רֹאֶה (*rōʾeh*, "seer") and חֹזֶה (*ḥōzeh*, "seer")
- relation between God and the prophet: עֶבֶד יהוה (*ʿebed yhwh*, "servant of Yahweh")
- position before the world as the prophet carried out the God-appointed task: מַלְאַךְ יהוה (*malʾak yhwh*, "the messenger of Yahweh").

If we accept the suggestion of Josephus (*Ant.* 8.240–41 [9.1]) that the prophet's name was "Yadon," the prophet may perhaps be connected with the Iddo mentioned as a chronicler of the events of Abijah's day (2Ch 13:22).

2 Although critical scholars often suggest that the name Josiah is a later insertion by the writer of Kings, and Keil, 202–3, suggests that the name is a mere appellative ("he whom Yahweh supports") that was fulfilled to the very name, there is no a priori reason why God could not record the actual name of the individual involved centuries beforehand (cf. Isa 44:28; 45:1). See also Micah 5:2, where the name of the birthplace of Messiah is given several centuries before Christ's birth.

3 מוֹפֵת (*môpēt*, "sign, wonder") denotes a miracle. The word is used particularly in connection with God's miraculous doings through his messengers in Egypt (Ex 4:21; 7:3, 9; 11:9–10; Dt 4:34; 6:22; 7:19; 26:8; 29:3[2]; 34:11; Pss 78:43; 105:27; 135:9; Jer 32:20–21). It appears frequently in parallel with its synonym אוֹת (*ʾōt*, "sign"; e.g., Ex 7:3; Dt 6:22; Ps 78:43). Whereas the latter term tends to emphasize the intended purpose of God's miraculous doings, the former records the effect the miracle produced on those who beheld it.

b. The man of God and the old prophet (13:11–34)

OVERVIEW

Walsh, 182–83, perceptively points out that this portion of the story of the man of God is told in parallel structure:

A The prophet hears news of the man of God (v.11).
 B He speaks in reaction to the news (v.12).
  C He has his sons saddle his donkey (v.13).
   D He journeys and finds the man of God (vv.14–18).

E He brings the man of God back to eat with him (v.19).

F He subsequently receives and speaks the Lord's message (vv.20–22), which is then fulfilled (vv.23–24).

A' The prophet again hears news with regard to the man of God (v.25).

B' He speaks in reaction to the news (v.26).

C' He has his sons saddle his donkey (v.27).

D' He journeys and finds the body of the man of God (v.28).

E' He brings the body back and honors it (vv.29–30).

F' He then confirms the Lord's message (vv.31–32).

Walsh does not find a parallel for the last element in the first portion of the story (vv.23–24). It may be that the narrator intended the closing remarks of the chapter (vv.33–34) to serve in this capacity, while at the same time forming the conclusion to the whole account concerning the condemnation of Jeroboam's religion.

11Now there was a certain old prophet living in Bethel, whose sons came and told him
all that the man of God had done there that day. They also told their father what he had
said to the king. 12Their father asked them, "Which way did he go?" And his sons showed
him which road the man of God from Judah had taken. 13So he said to his sons, "Saddle
the donkey for me." And when they had saddled the donkey for him, he mounted it 14and
rode after the man of God. He found him sitting under an oak tree and asked, "Are you the
man of God who came from Judah?"

"I am," he replied.

15So the prophet said to him, "Come home with me and eat."

16The man of God said, "I cannot turn back and go with you, nor can I eat bread or drink
water with you in this place. 17I have been told by the word of the LORD: 'You must not eat
bread or drink water there or return by the way you came.'"

18The old prophet answered, "I too am a prophet, as you are. And an angel said to me by
the word of the LORD: 'Bring him back with you to your house so that he may eat bread and
drink water.'" (But he was lying to him.) 19So the man of God returned with him and ate
and drank in his house.

20While they were sitting at the table, the word of the LORD came to the old prophet who
had brought him back. 21He cried out to the man of God who had come from Judah, "This
is what the LORD says: 'You have defied the word of the LORD and have not kept the command the LORD your God gave you. 22You came back and ate bread and drank water in the
place where he told you not to eat or drink. Therefore your body will not be buried in the
tomb of your fathers.'"

23When the man of God had finished eating and drinking, the prophet who had
brought him back saddled his donkey for him. 24As he went on his way, a lion met him on

the road and killed him, and his body was thrown down on the road, with both the donkey and the lion standing beside it. 25Some people who passed by saw the body thrown
down there, with the lion standing beside the body, and they went and reported it in the
city where the old prophet lived.
26When the prophet who had brought him back from his journey heard of it, he said,
"It is the man of God who defied the word of the LORD. The LORD has given him over to the
lion, which has mauled him and killed him, as the word of the LORD had warned him."
27The prophet said to his sons, "Saddle the donkey for me," and they did so. 28Then he
went out and found the body thrown down on the road, with the donkey and the lion
standing beside it. The lion had neither eaten the body nor mauled the donkey. 29So the
prophet picked up the body of the man of God, laid it on the donkey, and brought it back
to his own city to mourn for him and bury him. 30Then he laid the body in his own tomb,
and they mourned over him and said, "Oh, my brother!"
31After burying him, he said to his sons, "When I die, bury me in the grave where the
man of God is buried; lay my bones beside his bones. 32For the message he declared by
the word of the LORD against the altar in Bethel and against all the shrines on the high
places in the towns of Samaria will certainly come true."
33Even after this, Jeroboam did not change his evil ways, but once more appointed
priests for the high places from all sorts of people. Anyone who wanted to become a
priest he consecrated for the high places. 34This was the sin of the house of Jeroboam that
led to its downfall and to its destruction from the face of the earth.

COMMENTARY

11–24 The narrator gives no clues as to the old prophet's motives in pursuing the man of God. Possibly he just wished for fellowship. His deliberate lie, however, casts some doubt on his character. Did he wish to have a share in the man of God's condemnation of Jeroboam's altar by identifying with him? Because he appears to have meant well, perhaps it is best to assume that his desire to support the man of God is an example of intending to do a good service in wrong fashion.

While they are dining, the old prophet receives a message from the Lord. (So important was the message that it is specifically set apart in the Hebrew text.) The Lord's word was a death sentence. Because the man of God disobeyed the terms of his charge, he would face the disgrace of not being buried in his ancestral tomb. He preferred to listen to "good news" rather than God's true word. Despite his earlier victory at Bethel, the later actions of the man of God clearly compromised the will of God. Disobedience to God can only bring defeat (cf. Nu 14:21–23; Dt 11:26–28).

25–32 Having learned the circumstances concerning the man of God's death, the old prophet gave instructions that when he died he should be laid to rest beside the man of God (v.31). So powerful an effect had the whole series of events produced on him, and so assured was he that all the man of God had predicted would surely come to pass, that the old prophet longed, at least in death, to be united with this holy man. The LXX and Old Latin versions curiously suggest that the prophet of Bethel's chief desire was that both his bones and those of the man of God escape the certain doom of the coming judgment on the area. The prophecy was to be fulfilled minutely in the reforms of Josiah (2Ki 23:15–18).

33–34 The narrator brings the whole account of Jeroboam's condemnation to an end by noting that nothing that happened caused Jeroboam to turn from his evil ways; rather, Jeroboam only intensified his apostate religious policy in a program that was to become the ruin of the northern kingdom and for which his name was to live in infamy. Thus it was to be repeatedly said of the wicked kings of the northern kingdom: "He walked in the ways of Jeroboam, the son of Nebat, who made Israel to sin."

NOTES

22 קֶבֶר (*qeber*, "grave") refers here to the family sepulcher, hence the NIV's "the tomb of your fathers." Such tombs, if belonging to the wealthy, could be hewn out of soft limestone and consist of an antechamber and an inner cave where the bodies were laid in niches. A large stone normally guarded the entrance to the sepulchre. For the average person more modest tombs were cut out of the soft limestone in some wadi near the deceased person's home.

32 The mention of the "towns of Samaria" before the founding of the city of Samaria by Omri (16:24) or before the political territory known as Samaria came into being in the Sargonid Period (721–705 BC; 2Ki 17:29) suggests that the words of the old prophet of Bethel have been updated by the author of Kings.

3. The Consequences of Jeroboam's Religion (14:1–18)

OVERVIEW

This section illustrates the grave consequences that will attend the northern kingdom because of Jeroboam's apostate reform policies. The account falls into three main units.

In the first (vv.1–5), the reader is introduced to parallel events in the house of Jeroboam and that of the prophet Ahijah, now well along in years and blind. Jeroboam's son had taken seriously ill. Because he wished to know whether his son would live, Jeroboam sent his wife to Shiloh to inquire of Ahijah, that prophet who once predicted his kingship. Fearing that his reforms might earn an unfavorable reply, Jeroboam told his wife to disguise herself. Ahijah's spiritual sight was not dimmed, however, for the Lord revealed the whole plot to him.

In the second unit (vv.6–16), as soon as Jeroboam's wife arrived, Ahijah announced that he knew her identity. Her disguise did no good, and the Lord had a serious word for Jeroboam: because of his idolatry (vv.7–9), his house and lineage would come to a disastrous end (vv.10–11).

Further, the lad would die as soon as his mother set foot in her own city (vv.12–13). Ahijah concluded his pronouncements by predicting that dynastic change would soon occur in the northern kingdom and eventually the fall of the kingdom itself would come—all a result of Jeroboam's sins (vv.14–16).

The final unit (vv.17–18) records the fulfillment of the dire prophecy. Upon the return of Jeroboam's wife the boy died and was buried.

1At that time Abijah son of Jeroboam became ill, 2and Jeroboam said to his wife, "Go, disguise yourself, so you won't be recognized as the wife of Jeroboam. Then go to Shiloh. Ahijah the prophet is there—the one who told me I would be king over this people. 3Take ten loaves of bread with you, some cakes and a jar of honey, and go to him. He will tell you what will happen to the boy." 4So Jeroboam's wife did what he said and went to Ahijah's house in Shiloh.

Now Ahijah could not see; his sight was gone because of his age. 5But the LORD had told Ahijah, "Jeroboam's wife is coming to ask you about her son, for he is ill, and you are to give her such and such an answer. When she arrives, she will pretend to be someone else."

6So when Ahijah heard the sound of her footsteps at the door, he said, "Come in, wife of Jeroboam. Why this pretense? I have been sent to you with bad news. 7Go, tell Jeroboam that this is what the LORD, the God of Israel, says: 'I raised you up from among the people and made you a leader over my people Israel. 8I tore the kingdom away from the house of David and gave it to you, but you have not been like my servant David, who kept my commands and followed me with all his heart, doing only what was right in my eyes. 9You have done more evil than all who lived before you. You have made for yourself other gods, idols made of metal; you have provoked me to anger and thrust me behind your back.

10"'Because of this, I am going to bring disaster on the house of Jeroboam. I will cut off from Jeroboam every last male in Israel—slave or free. I will burn up the house of Jeroboam as one burns dung, until it is all gone. 11Dogs will eat those belonging to Jeroboam who die in the city, and the birds of the air will feed on those who die in the country. The LORD has spoken!'

12"As for you, go back home. When you set foot in your city, the boy will die. 13All Israel will mourn for him and bury him. He is the only one belonging to Jeroboam who will be buried, because he is the only one in the house of Jeroboam in whom the LORD, the God of Israel, has found anything good.

14"The LORD will raise up for himself a king over Israel who will cut off the family of Jeroboam. This is the day! What? Yes, even now. 15And the LORD will strike Israel, so that it will be like a reed swaying in the water. He will uproot Israel from this good land that he gave to their forefathers and scatter them beyond the River, because they provoked the LORD to anger by making Asherah poles. [16]And he will give Israel up because of the sins Jeroboam has committed and has caused Israel to commit."

[17]Then Jeroboam's wife got up and left and went to Tirzah. As soon as she stepped over the threshold of the house, the boy died. [18]They buried him, and all Israel mourned for him, as the LORD had said through his servant the prophet Ahijah.

COMMENTARY

1–2 Prophets were often consulted on a variety of matters, including the outcome of battle (e.g., 1Ki 22:6–28; 2Ki 3:11–19) or of a sickness (e.g., 2Ki 1:2; 4:22; 5:3–5). Although Shiloh had been previously destroyed by the Philistines (cf. Ps 78:60–64), apparently a small community had grown up there. Jeremiah indicates that the site was desolate again in his day (Jer 7:12, 14; 26:6, 9).

3–4 Gifts were commonly taken to prophets by those seeking an audience (e.g., 1Sa 9:7–8; 2Ki 5:5; 8:8).

5–9 God had intended for Jeroboam to become a genuine spiritual "leader" (*nāgîd*, v.7), but unfortunately Jeroboam's attention to religious matters only led his people into all the evils of gross idolatry.

10–12 Because of Jeroboam's sins, his male descendants would die violent deaths. Once again the potential disgrace of the body's going unburied is sounded (see Note on 13:22).

13 The death of Jeroboam's son may point to God's gracious dealing with young children (cf. 2Sa 12:23). The Talmud, however, assumes that the boy is older and had conducted himself righteously. For he "as crown-prince ... removed the guards set to prevent the faithful going up to Jerusalem where he himself participated in festivals (*b. Mo'ed Qat.* 28b)" (Wiseman, *1 & 2 Kings*, 150).

NOTES

1 Here the LXX departs from the MT and resumes at v.21; the material contained in the MT of vv.1–18 is represented variously in the LXX of 12:24g–n.

2 The LXX identifies Jeroboam's wife as Ano, daughter of Pharaoh Shishak, perhaps confusing the situation with that of Hadad of Edom (cf. 11:14–20). Excavations at Shiloh indicate that the city was destroyed about 1000 BC and remained largely abandoned until the fourth century BC. For details, see H. Vos, *Archaeology in Bible Lands* (Chicago: Moody Press, 1977), 200.

3 For נִקֻּדִים (*niqqudîm*, "[crumbled] bread"), some have suggested a relationship with the Arabic *naqada* ("prick out," hence "cakes with perforations"). Others compare the word with נָקֹד (*nāqōd*, "speckled"; cf. Ge 30:32; cf. also Arab. *naqqaṭa* ["be speckled," II stem]), Ethiopic *naqweṭ* ("point"), and suggest that these were "speckled cakes," like the sweet bread with seeds on a crust still found in the Near East today. The Targum suggests "sweet meats"; the LXX translates it κολλυρία (*kollyria*), "raisin cakes."

בַּקְבֻּק (*baqbuq*, "jar") is onomatopoeic, as it emulates the sound of liquid's being poured out of a jar. דְּבַשׁ (*d*[e]*baš*, "honey") is probably to be retained despite Gray's suggestion (in loc.) that it might be a liquid prepared from grape juice. The two words are properly rendered by the NIV as "jar of honey." Beehive-shaped jugs are well attested in the archaeological artifacts of ancient Palestine; see A. Honeyman, "The Pottery Vessels of the Old Testament," *PEQ* (1939): 76–90; J. Patch, "Honey," *ISBE*, 3:1418–19.

10 The use of לָכֵן הִנְנִי (*lākēn hinnî*, lit., "therefore behold me") followed by the participle is a normal means for introducing a prophetic threat for the imminent future.

מַשְׁתִּין בְּקִיר (*maštîn b*[e]*qîr*, "every last male") means literally "he who urinates against the wall" (cf. KJV). The Hebrew verbal form is doubtless composed with an infixed *t*; note both Akkadian *sianum* and Ugaritic *tyn* ("urinate"). For further examples of "infixed *t*" in Hebrew, see B. W. W. Dombrowski, "Some Remarks on the Hebrew Hithpa'el and Inversative -t in the Semitic Languages," *JNES* 21 (1962): 220–23; M. Dahood, *Psalms* (AB; Garden City, N.Y.: Doubleday, 1965–1970), 3:388–89.

The NIV's rendering is perhaps as reasonable as any of the many attempts to understand עָצוּר וְעָזוּב (*ʿāṣûr w*[e]*ʿāzûb*, "slave or free"), which has become symbolic of "all kinds and classes" (cf. Dt 32:36; 1Ki 21:21; 2Ki 9:8; 14:26).

11 Unlike their counterparts in the West today, dogs were often the scourge of the ancient Near East. Unfed, they became scavengers, always ready to eat anything (cf. 16:4; 21:24; 2Ki 9:36; Pss 22:16; 59:6, 14–15; Jer 15:3). That Ahijah's prophetic threats are presented under the figures of defilement and detested images emphasizes the heinousness of Jeroboam's religion and the awful judgment that results from such practices. Vicious sin begets vigorous judgment. See also Notes on 21:23 and 2 Kings 8:13.

14 The phrase זֶה הַיּוֹם וּמֶה גַּם־עָתָּה {dec63}(*zeh hayyôm ûmeh gam-ʿattâ*, "This is the day! What? Yes, even now") is difficult and has occasioned much discussion. It seems to emphasize what should happen today and immediately afterward. Not only would Jeroboam's son die that very day, but also, because of the king's settled heart condition and predisposition toward sin, God had already set into operation those forces that would ultimately destroy the nation.

15 The אֲשֵׁרִים (*ʾ*[a]*šērîm*, "Asherah poles"), sacred in the worship of the goddess Asherah, became a besetting sin in the northern kingdom and even spread to the south until the reign of Josiah (2Ki 23). This goddess figures prominently in the ancient Canaanite literature and is known from the cultus of other cultures in the ancient Near East as well. Her worship enters the OT in an advanced form in which Asherah has already been fused with other fertility goddesses. The goddess was customarily worshiped in association with sacred trees or poles that were symbolic of life and fertility. For details, see J. C. de Moor (*TDOT*, 1:438–44) and the helpful remarks of A. Lemaire in "Who or What Was Yahweh's Asherah?" (*BAR* 10 [1984]: 42–51).

17 Tirzah, now rather confidently identified with Tell el-Farʿah in the northern portion of Mount Ephraim on the strategic road from Shechem to Bethshan, was noted for its great beauty (SS 6:4). The capital of the northern kingdom was soon to be shifted from Shechem to Tirzah and remained there through the second dynasty. The events of the short-lived reign of Zimri took place in Tirzah (16:15–20). After reigning there for six years, Omri, the founder of the third dynasty, moved the capital to Samaria (16:23–24), which remained the northern capital until its fall in 722 BC.

4. Concluding Remarks concerning Jeroboam's Reign (14:19–20)

[19]The other events of Jeroboam's reign, his wars and how he ruled, are written in the book of the annals of the kings of Israel. [20]He reigned for twenty-two years and then rested with his fathers. And Nadab his son succeeded him as king.

COMMENTARY

19–20 Appended to the record of Jeroboam's rise to the throne, and his reforms, and their consequences is a notice of where further information may be gathered. This literary device, which began with Solomon (11:41–43), is thus continued for the rulers of the divided kingdom.

NOTES

19 For the "book of the annals of the kings of Israel," see Introduction: Unity, Authorship, and Date. Note that hereafter closing formulae will not be specially noted in the commentary unless some distinctive information is contained in them.

C. The Early Successors to Rehoboam and Jeroboam (14:21–16:14)

1. The Reign of Rehoboam in the Southern Kingdom (14:21–31)

OVERVIEW

The short record of Rehoboam's reign focuses on two factors: (1) the spiritual degeneration of God's people in Judah (vv.22–24) and (2) the invasion by the Egyptian pharaoh Shishak (vv.25–28). Opening (v.21) and closing notices (vv.29–31) bracket the details of his reign.

[21]Rehoboam son of Solomon was king in Judah. He was forty-one years old when he became king, and he reigned seventeen years in Jerusalem, the city the LORD had chosen out of all the tribes of Israel in which to put his Name. His mother's name was Naamah; she was an Ammonite.

[22]Judah did evil in the eyes of the LORD. By the sins they committed they stirred up his jealous anger more than their fathers had done. [23]They also set up for themselves high

places, sacred stones and Asherah poles on every high hill and under every spreading
tree. [24]There were even male shrine prostitutes in the land; the people engaged in all the
detestable practices of the nations the LORD had driven out before the Israelites.
[25]In the fifth year of King Rehoboam, Shishak king of Egypt attacked Jerusalem. [26]He
carried off the treasures of the temple of the LORD and the treasures of the royal palace.
He took everything, including all the gold shields Solomon had made. [27]So King Rehoboam made bronze shields to replace them and assigned these to the commanders of
the guard on duty at the entrance to the royal palace. [28]Whenever the king went to the
LORD's temple, the guards bore the shields, and afterward they returned them to the
guardroom.
[29]As for the other events of Rehoboam's reign, and all he did, are they not written in
the book of the annals of the kings of Judah? [30]There was continual warfare between
Rehoboam and Jeroboam. [31]And Rehoboam rested with his fathers and was buried with
them in the City of David. His mother's name was Naamah; she was an Ammonite. And
Abijah his son succeeded him as king.

COMMENTARY

21 With a firm division of the kingdom, the south is hereafter designated Judah. The usual correlation with the northern king is omitted, perhaps because Rehoboam began his reign before the schism or because the narrator simply did not wish to acknowledge the legitimacy of Jeroboam's reign.

22–24 Although the Chronicler reports that Rehoboam began his reign well (2Ch 11:5–17, 23), the king soon abandoned the law of the Lord (2Ch 12:1). Like Jeroboam, he allowed Baal worship centers and pagan fertility practices to spread throughout the land.

25 Shishak had an interesting history. Toward the end of Egypt's weak and divided Twenty-First Dynasty, mention is made of a Lybian who through marriage and favorable dealings with the high priest finally gained control of the government, founding the Twenty-Second Dynasty as Shoshenq I (biblical Shishak). Shoshenq was able to reunify the country and restore a certain amount of stability to the crown. Egypt could now once again look beyond her borders. Having renewed the old ties with Byblos and regained economic supremacy in Nubia, Shoshenq moved northward in an effort to solidify his hold on strategic trade routes.

26–28 The biblical account and the archaeological data from ancient Egypt indicate that Shoshenq swept through much of both Israel and Judah, from which he took heavy spoil (v.26). Shoshenq lists 150 cities he conquered in the campaign.

The Chronicler records that Jerusalem itself was severely looted; only the repentance of Rehoboam and his leaders at God's rebuke through Shemaiah the prophet saved the land and people from total destruction. Significant among the spoils were Solomon's golden shields (v.26; see 10:16–17), kept in the Palace of the Forest of Lebanon (see 7:2). To replace the shields, which were used at state ceremonial functions, Rehoboam had bronze shields made and entrusted them to the commander of his royal bodyguard, who now stored them in the guardhouse (vv.27–28).

29–31 The chapter closes with the additional notice of strained relations between the northern and southern kingdoms throughout Rehoboam's reign (v.30). Since Rehoboam had complied with the divine prohibition against overt warfare (cf. 12:21–24), more than likely the reference is to a "cold war" or to occasional border skirmishes. Rehoboam was succeeded by his son Abijah (v.31).

NOTES

21 Gray, 341–42, suggests that the fact that Rehoboam's mother was an Ammonitess may have political implications, such as an early placating of Ammon by Solomon. The reigning queen mother apparently held an official court status (15:13) and played a powerful role in Judean politics. She is often mentioned alongside the king (Jer 22:26; 29:2) and apparently even wore a crown emblematic of her position (Jer 13:18). The prominence of the position doubtless facilitated Athaliah's usurpation of the royal throne itself (2Ki 11:1–3).

24 קָדֵשׁ (*qādēš*, "[male] shrine prostitute") is used at times as distinct from the feminine form (Dt 23:18). Shrine prostitutes appear among the lists of cultic personnel in ancient Ugarit. See W. F. Albright, *Archaeology and Religion of Israel*, 5th ed. (Garden City, N.Y.: Doubleday, 1969), 153–54. Montgomery, 273, may be correct, however, in suggesting that both sexes are intended (so NIV), the masculine singular being deliberately derogatory and portraying such individuals as little better than beasts. Cultic prostitution was symptomatic of Judah's basic spiritual harlotry, which was to plague the kingdom throughout the years of its existence.

25 Shoshenq's ascendency and triumph were meteoric; Egypt's newfound star, however, fell as quickly as it rose. The pharaoh died suddenly, and the kingdom was left in the hands of those of lesser ability. Egypt's hopes of greatness soon expired.

David Rohl (*Pharaohs and Kings* [New York: Crown, 1995], 149–71, 370–78) presents evidence that convinces him that the biblical Shishak is not to be equated with Shoshenq I but with Ramesses II. He suggests that because Ramesses (unlike Shishak) actually boasts of reaching Salem (= Jerusalem) in his Palestinian campaigning, he is the more likely person to have accomplished what the Bible records. Rohl links known hypocoristic writings of Ramesses II's nomen (or family name), such as *ss*, *ssw*, *ssy*, and *sysw*, to make the equation with biblical Shishak (Heb. *ššq*). Rohl makes much of the fact that the inscription telling of Shoshenq's Palestinian campaign (while incomplete) says nothing concerning Jerusalem.

Detrimental to Rohl's theory is not only the time-honored, accepted Egyptian chronology, but also the fact that Rohl offers no convincing accounting for the *q* in the biblical name. Moreover, the Kethib of 1 Kings 14:25 clearly reads *šwšq* (contra the Qere's *šyšq*, with the manuscript evidence of 2 Chronicles 12:2 being similarly divided), which accords well with the Egyptian "Shoshenq."

It is of interest to note that the biblical record does not necessarily demand that Shishak actually attacked Jerusalem. For whenever the author of Kings speaks of actual fighting against a place he regularly uses phraseology made up of compound verbs (i.e., עָלָה [*ʿālâ*, "come up against"] plus some added Hebrew verb with meanings such as "fought against" [1Ki 12:24; 20:26; 2Ki 3:21; 12:18; 16:5; cf. 1Ki 22:29–30], "besieged" [with subsequent hostilities; 1Ki 16:17; 2Ki 6:24; 17:5; 18:9; 24:10], "smote" [2Ki 15:14], "captured" [1Ki 9:16], or "seized" [2Ki 16:9; 18:13]). No such phraseology is used here in 1 Kings 14:25

(cf. 2Ch 12:2). All that is required by the context is that Shishak deployed his troops in menacing fashion toward Jerusalem, thus achieving his purposes without actually having to fight against or even reach the city. Indeed, the Chronicler points out that the Lord's promise guaranteed that Jerusalem would not fall to Shishak, though his people would become subject to the Egyptian king.

Still another dissenting voice with regard to the Shishak/Rehoboam connection is that of F. Clancy ("Shishak/Shoshenq's Travels," *JSOT* 86 [1999]: 3–23). For Clancy, Shoshenq did not conduct a comprehensive sweep of Palestine but a series of forays into the Negev and Judean Shephelah. Clancy, 20, discounts the historicity of the biblical record, viewing 1 Kings 14 as a late literary piece "created as part of a theme foreshadowing the destruction of Jerusalem."

The biblical text is defensible, however, even according to Clancy's scenario. Thus Shoshenq's strong presence and advance toward the Judean Shephelah may have been sufficient cause for Rehoboam to buy him off with lavish gifts. For excellent studies of Shishak and his Palestinian campaign, see J. Currid, *Ancient Egypt and the Old Testament* (Grand Rapids: Baker, 1997), 172–202; K. Kitchen, *Third Intermediate Period*, 85–88, 109–16, 287–302. For a discussion of the Egyptian nomen, see A. H. Gardiner, *Egyptian Grammar* (London: Oxford Univ. Press, 1957), 71–76.

26 According to the LXX, the weapons David had dedicated as a result of his campaign against the Aramean Hadadezer (cf. 2Sa 8:7) were all carried away. See Note on 2 Kings 11:10.

28 The term רָצִים (*rāṣîm*, "guards") refers to an ancient and well-known class of professional soldiers. The name means literally "runners" and was used of a class of royal escorts who ran before the king (2Sa 15:1; 1Ki 1:5; cf. Akkad. *rēdû*, "runner"; see the remarks of G. R. Driver and J. C. Miles, *The Babylonian Laws* [Oxford: Clarendon, 1960], 2:161). The term also designates the royal bodyguard that constantly protected the king and assisted him in crucial matters (1Sa 22:17; 2Ki 10:25). Here it appears that their duties also included keeping watch over the various portions of the palace and temple complex.

31 The information that Rehoboam was buried with his fathers is omitted from 2 Chronicles 12:16, the Chronicler possibly viewing Rehoboam as unworthy of being mentioned alongside David and Solomon. He also makes no reference to Rehoboam's pagan mother.

"Abijam" is read by the MT. At least ten MSS and the Hebrew edition of Kennicott and DeRossi read "Abijah" (cf. LXX, Αβιου, *Abiou*). Montgomery, 273, suggests that Abijam was a popular designation of the king, the *am* being hypocoristic, as in the case of the name found at Tell Taᶜannak—"Ahiyami"; see also Gordon, 349. Doubtless the king's name was Abijah ("Yahweh is my father"), as befitting a king of the southern kingdom.

2. The Reign of Abijah in the Southern Kingdom (15:1–8)

OVERVIEW

The short account of Abijah's reign is structured in standard format: accession statement (vv.1–2) with spiritual evaluation (vv.3–5), historical note (v.6), and closing formula (vv.7–8).

[1]In the eighteenth year of the reign of Jeroboam son of Nebat, Abijah became king of
Judah, [2]and he reigned in Jerusalem three years. His mother's name was Maacah daughter
of Abishalom.
[3]He committed all the sins his father had done before him; his heart was not fully
devoted to the LORD his God, as the heart of David his forefather had been. [4]Neverthe-
less, for David's sake the LORD his God gave him a lamp in Jerusalem by raising up a son to
succeed him and by making Jerusalem strong. [5]For David had done what was right in the
eyes of the LORD and had not failed to keep any of the LORD's commands all the days of his
life—except in the case of Uriah the Hittite.
[6]There was war between Rehoboam and Jeroboam throughout Abijah's lifetime. [7]As for
the other events of Abijah's reign, and all he did, are they not written in the book of the annals
of the kings of Judah? There was war between Abijah and Jeroboam. [8]And Abijah rested with
his fathers and was buried in the City of David. And Asa his son succeeded him as king.

COMMENTARY

1–5 Attention is focused on the short-lived reign of Abijah (v.1) in but few details: (1) the continuing prominence of the dowager queen Maacah (v.2); (2) the continuance of apostasy in the southern kingdom (v.3); and (3) the continuing war with the north (v.6). Maacah (v.2) was apparently the daughter of Uriel of Gibeah (2Ch 13:2) and Tamar (2Sa 14:27), hence the granddaughter of Absalom, David's rebellious son. The favorite of Rehoboam's eighteen wives, she was the mother of Abijah and the grandmother of Asa (vv.9–10). Her continued prominence testifies to her strong personality.

Although Abijah was a poor representative of the house of David (cf. 11:4), God, who remains faithful (2Ti 2:13), would honor the man after his own heart in preserving his heir (cf. 1Sa 13:14; Ps 89:19–29; Ac 13:22). Further, God was to take responsibility for turning around the religious situation in Judah—he would raise up a godly son to its throne.

6–8 Abijah inherited his father's continued friction with Jeroboam and the northern kingdom, only now it took the form of open warfare between the two Hebrew states. Fortunately for Judah, Abijah's underlying faith could rise to the surface in times of crisis. Second Chronicles 13:3–22 relates one such instance. In a major battle between the two antagonists, Abijah and his few troops were delivered from certain defeat when the Lord intervened for them in response to Abijah's prayer.

NOTES

2 "Three years" is the correct reading here, not the six years of the LXX. As Rehoboam was already forty-one years old at his ascension and reigned twenty-seven years, Abijah was probably himself of mature years when he ascended the throne. It is little wonder, then, that it could be said of him that he had known nothing but war in his lifetime (v.6).

3 שָׁלֵם (*šālēm*, "fully devoted") connotes the thoughts of "be whole, be at peace with." Here David is called אָבִיו (*ʾābîw*, "his father"), the term, as with other biblical terms for relationship (e.g., "son"), being used in its extended sense. The NIV is correct in translating "his forefather."

4 נִיר (*nîr*, "lamp") is used figuratively in the OT of human posterity. A man's life and work were not extinguished if he had progeny (11:36 [see Note]; 2Ki 8:19; 2Ch 21:7).

3. The Reign of Asa in the Southern Kingdom (15:9–24)

OVERVIEW

Between the standard formulae of accession notice (vv.9–10) and closing formula (vv.23–24), rather full information is given concerning Asa's spiritual condition (vv.11–15) and details of events during his long reign (vv.16–22). As for the former, Asa used his first ten years of peace (cf. 2Ch 14:1) to expunge idolatry and enforce the observance of true religion. In all these efforts he "did what was right in the eyes of the LORD" (v.11). As for the latter, the narrator reports the outbreak and continuance of hostilities between the northern and southern kingdoms after Baasha became king of Israel.

[9]In the twentieth year of Jeroboam king of Israel, Asa became king of Judah, [10]and he
reigned in Jerusalem forty-one years. His grandmother's name was Maacah daughter of
Abishalom.
[11]Asa did what was right in the eyes of the LORD, as his father David had done. [12]He
expelled the male shrine prostitutes from the land and got rid of all the idols his fathers
had made. [13]He even deposed his grandmother Maacah from her position as queen
mother, because she had made a repulsive Asherah pole. Asa cut the pole down and
burned it in the Kidron Valley. [14]Although he did not remove the high places, Asa's heart
was fully committed to the LORD all his life. [15]He brought into the temple of the LORD the
silver and gold and the articles that he and his father had dedicated.
[16]There was war between Asa and Baasha king of Israel throughout their reigns.
[17]Baasha king of Israel went up against Judah and fortified Ramah to prevent anyone from
leaving or entering the territory of Asa king of Judah.
[18]Asa then took all the silver and gold that was left in the treasuries of the LORD's temple
and of his own palace. He entrusted it to his officials and sent them to Ben-Hadad son of
Tabrimmon, the son of Hezion, the king of Aram, who was ruling in Damascus. [19]"Let there
be a treaty between me and you," he said, "as there was between my father and your
father. See, I am sending you a gift of silver and gold. Now break your treaty with Baasha
king of Israel so he will withdraw from me."

[20]Ben-Hadad agreed with King Asa and sent the commanders of his forces against the
towns of Israel. He conquered Ijon, Dan, Abel Beth Maacah and all Kinnereth in addition to
Naphtali. [21]When Baasha heard this, he stopped building Ramah and withdrew to Tirzah.
[22]Then King Asa issued an order to all Judah — no one was exempt — and they carried
away from Ramah the stones and timber Baasha had been using there. With them King
Asa built up Geba in Benjamin, and also Mizpah.
[23]As for all the other events of Asa's reign, all his achievements, all he did and the cities
he built, are they not written in the book of the annals of the kings of Judah? In his old
age, however, his feet became diseased. [24]Then Asa rested with his fathers and was buried
with them in the city of his father David. And Jehoshaphat his son succeeded him as king.

COMMENTARY

9–10 When Asa assumed the kingly office in the twentieth year of Jeroboam's reign (910 BC), the influence of Maacah, his grandmother and the dowager queen, was still pronounced (vv.9–10). Although Asa's long, forty-one year reign was to be eventful, during his first ten years he enjoyed a time of peace (cf. 2Ch 14:1), perhaps the benefit of Abijah's victory over the north.

11–15 The Chronicler provides further information on Asa's spiritual reforms. In the third month of the fifteenth year of his reign, Asa, encouraged by the prophet Azariah (2Ch 15:1–7), convened an assembly in which all true Israelites were invited to renew the covenant with the Lord. The meeting was attended with great praise and joy (2Ch 15:9–15). At the same time Asa instituted stringent spiritual reforms aimed at removing the remaining vestiges of idolatry and fertility rites (2Ch 15:8). Even the politically and religiously powerful Maacah was disposed of once and for all (v.13). No doubt she had used the outbreak of the war as an occasion to reintroduce the public worship of Asherah (v.13; cf. 2Ch 15:16). While Asa stopped short of a total cleansing of the land, he was a God-fearing man, who led the way for his people in public dedication to God (vv.14–15; cf. 2Ch 15:17–18).

16 The Chronicler records that before the outbreak of hostilities between Baasha and Asa, Asa faced and defeated an invasion led by Zerah the Ethiopian (2Ch 14:9–15). Zerah was probably a commander in the forces of the Egyptian pharaoh Osorkon I (914–874 BC).

17 After the deaths of Jeroboam and his son Nadab (vv.25–32), a new dynasty began with Baasha. Baasha's accession year was the third year of Asa's reign. Baasha apparently was initially occupied with securing the throne and other internal affairs. But with a victorious and strengthened Judah, whose renewed vitality had succeeded even in drawing away many of his citizens, Baasha could no longer remain inactive.

Moving swiftly into Judah, Baasha seized Ramah, only four miles north of Jerusalem itself (v.17). This action not only stopped the further drawing away of Baasha's subjects but also cut off the main road north out of Jerusalem, thus shutting down all communications between Judah and Israel and giving Baasha control of the trade routes.

18–19 Asa's reaction to Baasha's advance in sending a delegation to the Aramean king Ben-Hadad was rebuked by God's prophet Hanani (16:1). Asa reacted by throwing Hanani into prison. Thus began a long and checkered history of the persecution of God's prophets (2Ch 16:7–10; cf. 2Ki 17:13–14).

Although Ben-Hadad first appears here in the biblical record, he was to play a major role in Near Eastern affairs in subsequent years. A longstanding hostility had existed between the Arameans and the Hebrews. David had subdued the chief Aramean tribes occupying the main area of Syria itself (cf. 2Sa 8:3–12; 1Ch 18:3–11); and although these regions largely remained subservient to Solomon, already in Solomon's day Rezon ben Eliada had managed to establish himself in Damascus; he remained "Israel's adversary as long as Solomon lived" (11:23–25). Despite the fact of any treaty arrangement that Ben-Hadad may have had with Baasha, he was lured away by Asa's all-too-generous payment.

20–22 The swift strikes of Ben-Hadad against Baasha's northern section not only gained for him access to the international caravan routes leading from Egypt through Phoenicia and on to Damascus but also gave Asa the desired relief in Judah (v.20). In order to meet the new emergency on his northern flank, Baasha was forced to abandon his operations at Ramah (v.21).

Asa, for his part, quickly mobilized Judah's forces, retook Ramah, dismantled Baasha's fortifications, and used the building material to fortify Mizpah and Geba (v.22), thus providing strongholds for his reestablished control in Benjamin.

23–24 The parting notices concerning Asa deal with the loathsome disease in his feet (v.23) that served only to harden his heart. For his funerary observance Asa had the air filled with sweet spices (2Ch 16:12–14); but no amount of manmade perfume can hide the noxious stench of the life of a believer alienated from God!

NOTES

10 Since the MT calls Maacah Asa's mother, some scholars have suggested that Abijah and Asa were brothers. Others have suggested that Maacah was the name of two different women, one of whom bore Abijah and the other Asa. The NIV takes the simpler view that the mother of Abijah and Asa's grandmother were one and the same person. This interpretation seems the obvious intent of the passage.

Other notable dowagers include the biblical queen Athaliah (2Ki 11), the Egyptian queen Hatshepsut (1504–1483 BC), Nabonidus's mother Adad-guppi, and the Assyrian queen Sammuramat (811–806 BC), perhaps the original queen behind the legendary Greek Semiramis. On the importance and position of the dowager, see the comments of Gray, 106 (see also S. W. Baur, "Queen Mother," *ISBE*, 4:25:13–14).

12 The author of Kings has telescoped Asa's early and later religious reforms into one summary account. For details as to the chronology of events of Asa's reign, see Thiele, 59–62; Kitchen, *Third Intermediate Period*, 309.

It has been suggested that etymologically גִּלֻּלִים (*gillulîm*," idols") means "forms in the round," whether sculptured or objects in the natural world. In the OT it is used synonymously with שִׁקּוּצִים (*šiqqûṣîm*, "detested thing, idol") and in collocation with טָמֵא (*ṭāmēʾ*, "be unclean"). Some have suggested a relationship with גֵּל (*gēl*, "dung pellet"), hence "filthy thing, idol." Still others suggest a relationship to the Arabic *galil* ("venerated object"). At any rate, throughout the OT it is always used disdainfully (e.g., Lev 26:30). See further *TDOT*, 3:1–5.

13 The Kidron Valley, the deep depression east of Jerusalem between the temple heights and the Mount of Olives, became from Asa's time onward the place where reforming kings destroyed all idolatrous cultic objects (cf. 2Ki 23:4–15; 2Ch 29:16; 30:14).

15 The dedicated articles may have included material from the local shrines outside Jerusalem, spoils from the war with Zerah, or even Rehoboam's bronze shields made to replace the golden shields taken by Sheshonq.

17 Ramah is to be identified with the present-day Arab village of Ar-ram, five and one-half miles north of Jerusalem. It lay on the main north-south commercial artery and was of strategic military importance since it controlled access to the foothills of Ephraim and the Mediterranean coast.

19 Was Asa's referral to an existing treaty between Judah and Damascus a fact or a manufactured wish? Gray, 352, opts for the former idea and suggests that this possibility may explain why Abijah was so successful against Jeroboam. The simplest solution seems to be that Asa suggested that a treaty had tacitly existed since the days of the united monarchy. The phrase "between my father and your father" need indicate nothing more than a general reference to existing relations between these Aramean and Jewish heads of state. Asa appears to be finding legal grounds for Ben-Hadad to justify his violation of the Aramean treaty with Israel.

23 Various suggestions have been made as to the nature of Asa's diseased feet. The Talmud decides for gout, and Montgomery, 278, for dropsy. Others have suggested that "feet" is a euphemism for the reproductive organ; hence, Asa had venereal disease. Wiseman, *1 & 2 Kings*, 157, however, cautions that "this [disease] has not yet been identified in the Old Testament period."

4. The Reign of Nadab in the Northern Kingdom (15:25–31)

25 Nadab son of Jeroboam became king of Israel in the second year of Asa king of
Judah, and he reigned over Israel two years. 26 He did evil in the eyes of the LORD, walking in
the ways of his father and in his sin, which he had caused Israel to commit.
27 Baasha son of Ahijah of the house of Issachar plotted against him, and he struck
him down at Gibbethon, a Philistine town, while Nadab and all Israel were besieging
it. 28 Baasha killed Nadab in the third year of Asa king of Judah and succeeded him as
king.
29 As soon as he began to reign, he killed Jeroboam's whole family. He did not leave
Jeroboam anyone that breathed, but destroyed them all, according to the word of the
LORD given through his servant Ahijah the Shilonite — 30 because of the sins Jeroboam had
committed and had caused Israel to commit, and because he provoked the LORD, the God
of Israel, to anger.
31 As for the other events of Nadab's reign, and all he did, are they not written in the
book of the annals of the kings of Israel? 32 There was war between Asa and Baasha king of
Israel throughout their reigns.

COMMENTARY

25–32 Jeroboam's son Nadab succeeded him and reigned in Tirzah (v.25). In his second year Nadab attempted to capture the important Philistine city of Gibbethon (cf. 16:15–17). However, in the midst of the siege he was assassinated by Baasha (probably one of his military officers), who seized the throne (vv.27–28). Baasha immediately killed all members of the royal house (v.29), thus confirming Ahijah's prediction that God would judge the sins of the house of Jeroboam (v.30).

NOTES

27 Baasha's father is named Ahijah, as was the prophet who predicted the doom of the house of Jeroboam (cf. 14:9–16). Though they are not the same individual, the identical names provide a touch of irony to the whole episode.

30 The narrator's observation concerning the liquidation of the line of Jeroboam I (cf. v.26) indicates that Nadab was as apostate as his father.

5. The Second Dynasty in Israel (15:32–16:14)

a. Baasha (15:32–16:7)

OVERVIEW

Baasha's reign is told in standard format: accession statement with spiritual evaluation (vv.33–34), historical details (16:1–4), and closing formula, to which are added statements reinforcing the opening spiritual evaluation (vv.5–7). Because this literary arrangement is so commonly employed in Kings, hereafter attention will be drawn in the Overview only where distinctive details are related.

33In the third year of Asa king of Judah, Baasha son of Ahijah became king of all Israel
in Tirzah, and he reigned twenty-four years. 34He did evil in the eyes of the LORD, walking in
the ways of Jeroboam and in his sin, which he had caused Israel to commit.
16:1Then the word of the LORD came to Jehu son of Hanani against Baasha: 2"I lifted you
up from the dust and made you leader of my people Israel, but you walked in the ways of
Jeroboam and caused my people Israel to sin and to provoke me to anger by their sins.
3So I am about to consume Baasha and his house, and I will make your house like that of
Jeroboam son of Nebat. 4Dogs will eat those belonging to Baasha who die in the city, and
the birds of the air will feed on those who die in the country."

[5]As for the other events of Baasha's reign, what he did and his achievements, are they not written in the book of the annals of the kings of Israel? [6]Baasha rested with his fathers and was buried in Tirzah. And Elah his son succeeded him as king.

[7]Moreover, the word of the LORD came through the prophet Jehu son of Hanani
to Baasha and his house, because of all the evil he had done in the eyes of the
LORD, provoking him to anger by the things he did, and becoming like the house of
Jeroboam — and also because he destroyed it.

COMMENTARY

15:33–16:6 Jehu ben Hanani's denunciation of Baasha indicates that dynastic change did not signal spiritual improvement. Walsh, 214, perceptively points out that Jehu's condemnation of Baasha is structured with the same three elements as that of Ahijah in his condemnation of Jeroboam: Yahweh's deeds in behalf of the king (v.2a; cf. 14:7b), the king's sins nevertheless (v.2b; cf. 14:16b), and the Lord's warning of dire judgment to come (v.3; cf. 14:10b–11).

7 Many have questioned God's fairness in raising up Baasha to bring an end to the first dynasty. Central to the discussion is the phrase "and also because he destroyed it." Two problems arise: (1) the antecedent of "it" and (2) the precise translation of the Hebrew particle rendered "because" in the NIV. As for the former problem, most English translations render the Hebrew pronoun "it" and understand the antecedent to be "the house of Jeroboam." On the whole this solution is the simplest.

In the latter case the particle translated "because" suggests that God condemned Baasha for becoming an imitator of Jeroboam's sinful house and did so in spite of the fact that he had himself been raised up of God to put an end to Jeroboam and his line. Implicit in the statement is the condemnation of Baasha's murder of Jeroboam's line. It is one thing to displace a rival; it is another thing to use God's commission as an excuse for carrying out selfish ambition. Baasha's perpetuation of Jeroboam's sins betrays his improper motivations. Although he had raised up Baasha in spite of his murderous intention, God in no way condoned Baasha's deeds.

NOTES

1 Jehu son of Hanani (cf. 2Ch 20:34) is known also as the author of a history that was included in "the book of the kings of Israel" (see Introduction: Literary Form). He was also to be active in the reign of Jehoshaphat of Judah (cf. 2Ch 19:2–3). For additional details on the reign of Baasha, see Josephus (*Ant.* 8.298–308 [12.3–4]).

2 The words "lifted you up from the dust" emphasize the lowly origin of Baasha. Note God's tender reminder that Israel was yet "my people." The term was used again and again by the prophets of the eighth century in delivering God's pleadings to an unrepentant Israel.

b. Elah (16:8–14)

[8]In the twenty-sixth year of Asa king of Judah, Elah son of Baasha became king of Israel,
and he reigned in Tirzah two years.
[9]Zimri, one of his officials, who had command of half his chariots, plotted against him.
Elah was in Tirzah at the time, getting drunk in the home of Arza, the man in charge of the
palace at Tirzah. [10]Zimri came in, struck him down and killed him in the twenty-seventh
year of Asa king of Judah. Then he succeeded him as king.
[11]As soon as he began to reign and was seated on the throne, he killed off Baasha's
whole family. He did not spare a single male, whether relative or friend. [12]So Zimri
destroyed the whole family of Baasha, in accordance with the word of the LORD spoken
against Baasha through the prophet Jehu— [13]because of all the sins Baasha and his son
Elah had committed and had caused Israel to commit, so that they provoked the LORD, the
God of Israel, to anger by their worthless idols.
[14]As for the other events of Elah's reign, and all he did, are they not written in the book
of the annals of the kings of Israel?

COMMENTARY

8–14 As in the case of Jeroboam's son Nadab, so Baasha's son Elah reigned but two years (v.8) and was also assassinated. In Elah's case also, a conspiracy apparently existed, an assassination was carried out, and the leader of the conspiracy—here Zimri—took the throne and executed the family of the previous king and any possible heirs. Unlike Nadab's assassin, however, Zimri did not found a new dynasty.

NOTES

8 For "the twenty-sixth year," 2 Chronicles 16:1 has "the thirty-sixth year," which is probably a copyist's error (see Archer, 225–26).

11 For מַשְׁתִּין (*maštîn*, "a single male"), see Note on 14:10. The גֹּאֲלָיו (*gōʾ*^{a}*lāyw*, lit., "his relatives") were those charged with restoring the dead man's property and avenging his death (cf. Jos 20:3; 2Sa 14:11; see also *TDOT*, 2:350–52).

D. The Era of the Third Dynasty (1Ki 16:15–2Ki 9:37)

1. Interregnum: Zimri and Tibni (16:15–22)

[15]In the twenty-seventh year of Asa king of Judah, Zimri reigned in Tirzah seven days.
The army was encamped near Gibbethon, a Philistine town. [16]When the Israelites in the

camp heard that Zimri had plotted against the king and murdered him, they proclaimed
Omri, the commander of the army, king over Israel that very day there in the camp. [17]Then
Omri and all the Israelites with him withdrew from Gibbethon and laid siege to Tirzah.
[18]When Zimri saw that the city was taken, he went into the citadel of the royal palace and
set the palace on fire around him. So he died, [19]because of the sins he had committed,
doing evil in the eyes of the LORD and walking in the ways of Jeroboam and in the sin he
had committed and had caused Israel to commit.

[20]As for the other events of Zimri's reign, and the rebellion he carried out, are they not
written in the book of the annals of the kings of Israel?

[21]Then the people of Israel were split into two factions; half supported Tibni son of
Ginath for king, and the other half supported Omri. [22]But Omri's followers proved stronger
than those of Tibni son of Ginath. So Tibni died and Omri became king.

COMMENTARY

15–20 Zimri's fiery ambitions were to go up in flames. As soon as the encamped army at Gibbethon heard of the coup d'état, they proclaimed their commander, Omri, king and marched on Tirzah (vv.15–17). Unlike his predecessor, who was assassinated while getting drunk at a friend's house (vv.9–10), Zimri saw that his bid for the throne would fail at the hands of Omri and the military, so he committed suicide by torching the royal palace around him.

21–22 The narrator treats the short period of divided loyalties between Tibni and Omri with a terse statement: "Tibni died and Omri became king."

NOTES

21 Tibni, son of Ginath, is otherwise unknown in the OT. The name itself may be paralleled in the Akkadian "Tabni-Ea" ("may Ea give a son") and the Phoenician "Tabnit." The LXX and Josephus render his name "Tamni." "Ginath" could indicate a place name. Gina is mentioned in the Amarna Tablets, possibly the OT En Gannim (Jos 19:21), modern Jenin on the southern edge of the Plain of Esdraelon. The LXX reports that Tamni was aided by his brother Joram, and Josephus (*Ant.* 8.311 [12.5]) says that Omri's followers killed Tamni.

Montgomery, 290, suggests that Omri's name is of Arabic origin (cf. "Omar"), being frequently attested in South Arabia. It seems possible that Omri may have been a foreigner who had risen to prominence in the military. The close relationship of the third dynasty with Phoenicia may point to his Canaanite extraction, while the choice of Jezreel may indicate Omri's affinity with the tribe of Issachar.

Although the Scriptures dispose of Omri's accomplishments in a few verses (see also Mic 6:16, which indicates that Omri enacted some statutes of lasting spiritual damage), secular history indicates that Omri was a man of international importance. The Moabite Stone (*ANET*, 320–21) relates that Omri had conquered the fertile and strategic Moabite plains north of the Arnon River. His stature is further attested by the fact that the Assyrian kings uniformly designate Israel by the name *Bit Ḫumria* ("House of Omri"). In accordance with common custom, it may be that he arranged the marriage of his son Ahab to Jezebel, the Phoenician princess, possibly for economic benefits and to offset the rising power of Ben-Hadad of Damascus, whom Ahab was to face throughout his reign.

2. The Reign of Omri in the Northern Kingdom (16:23–28)

[23]In the thirty-first year of Asa king of Judah, Omri became king of Israel, and he reigned
twelve years, six of them in Tirzah. [24]He bought the hill of Samaria from Shemer for two
talents of silver and built a city on the hill, calling it Samaria, after Shemer, the name of the
former owner of the hill.

[25]But Omri did evil in the eyes of the LORD and sinned more than all those before him.
[26]He walked in all the ways of Jeroboam son of Nebat and in his sin, which he had caused
Israel to commit, so that they provoked the LORD, the God of Israel, to anger by their worthless idols.

[27]As for the other events of Omri's reign, what he did and the things he achieved, are
they not written in the book of the annals of the kings of Israel? [28]Omri rested with his
fathers and was buried in Samaria. And Ahab his son succeeded him as king.

COMMENTARY

23 Because Omri is credited with a twelve-year reign, even though his son Ahab succeeds him a scant seven years later (v.29), it seems apparent that the narrator credits to Omri's rule the four-year period of interregnum.

24 The chief event of Omri's reign was the building of a new capital. The choice of Samaria had a double benefit: it lay in neutral territory in terms of tribal affiliation, and it was defensible—a benefit that would be tested later (cf. 20:1–21; 2Ki 6:24; 18:9–10).

25–28 The narrator's spiritual evaluation of Omri is even worse than that of his predecessors. Not only did he perpetuate the spiritual sins of Jeroboam, but also his ties with Phoenicia subjected Israel to its pagan social and religious practices.

NOTES

24 Samaria was situated on a hill overlooking the chief commercial route of the Esdraelon Plain. Excavations there confirm the biblical indications that Omri was its first builder.

3. The Reign of Ahab in the Northern Kingdom (16:29–22:40)

OVERVIEW

In the broad scheme of the author's arrangement of the details concerning the life and times of Ahab, 16:29–34 serves as more than an accession statement. It provides the setting for the stories about the lives of Ahab and Elijah. In depicting the desperate spiritual depths of the northern kingdom, wicked Ahab will serve as the antagonist to God's servant Elijah.

Before the closing formula (22:39–40), the narratives concerning these two men are told in two clusters. The first centers on Elijah (chs. 17–19), while the second features Ahab and his interaction with God's prophets, including Elijah (20:1–22:40). Within the latter group of narratives we are also exposed to the complex nature of Ahab's character through four distinct episodes. Three of them deal with Syro-Israelite hostilities (chs. 20–22) and one with Ahab's coveting of Naboth's vineyard (ch. 21).

The reader is also introduced to one of the chief literary foils in the accounts that comprise the later events detailed in this section—an even more wicked Jezebel. Indeed, Ahab's debased spiritual conduct finds its nurturing in relation to his wife, Jezebel, who, as the narratives will show, is more ruthless than he.

a. Ahab's accession (16:29–34)

29In the thirty-eighth year of Asa king of Judah, Ahab son of Omri became king of Israel,
and he reigned in Samaria over Israel twenty-two years. 30Ahab son of Omri did more evil
in the eyes of the LORD than any of those before him. 31He not only considered it trivial
to commit the sins of Jeroboam son of Nebat, but he also married Jezebel daughter of
Ethbaal king of the Sidonians, and began to serve Baal and worship him. 32He set up an
altar for Baal in the temple of Baal that he built in Samaria. 33Ahab also made an Asherah
pole and did more to provoke the LORD, the God of Israel, to anger than did all the kings of
Israel before him.

34In Ahab's time, Hiel of Bethel rebuilt Jericho. He laid its foundations at the cost of his
firstborn son Abiram, and he set up its gates at the cost of his youngest son Segub, in
accordance with the word of the LORD spoken by Joshua son of Nun.

COMMENTARY

29–30 No more notorious husband-and-wife team than Ahab and Jezebel is known in all the sacred Scriptures (cf. 21:25–26). Ahab built on his father's foundation, not only in bringing Israel into the arena of international conflict, but also in causing it to serve and worship Baal (v.30).

31–32 Ahab was a man of complex character. The remainder of this chapter makes it clear that he was unconcerned with true, vital faith (cf. 21:20). Not only did he participate personally in the sins of Jeroboam, but having willingly married Jezebel, he also followed her in the worship of Baal-Melqart, thus officially instituting and propagating Baal worship throughout his kingdom.

34 An example of his spiritual infidelity is seen in that he allowed Hiel of Bethel to rebuild Jericho as a fortified town, despite Joshua's longstanding curse on it. The undertaking was to cost Hiel the lives of his eldest and youngest sons, in accordance with Joshua's prophetic pronouncement (Jos 6:26).

The subsequent chapters of 1 Kings show that Ahab was selfish and sullen (20:43; 21:4–5), cruel (22:27), morally weak (21:1–16), and concerned with luxuries of this world (22:39). Though he could display real bravery (ch. 20; 22:1–39) and at times even heeded God's Word (18:16–46; 20:13–17, 22, 28–30; 21:27–29; 22:30), nevertheless he was basically a compromiser as far as the will of God was concerned (20:31–34, 42–43; 22:8, 18, 26–28). The divine estimation of his character stands as a tragic epitaph: "There was never a man like Ahab, who sold himself to do evil in the eyes of the LORD" (21:25; cf. 16:33; 21:20; see also the note on 2Ki 10:18).

NOTES

31 Although Montgomery, 291, disallows it, the name אִיזֶבֶל (*ʾîzebel*, "Jezebel") is probably derived from the Semitic *ʾayya zebul* ("Where [is] the prince?"). Names with *ayya* are common enough (cf. *ʾayya ʾabu*, "Job," i.e., "Where is the father?"; see H. B. Huffmon, *Amorite Personal Names in the Mari Texts* [Baltimore: Johns Hopkins Univ. Press, 1965], 102–3, 161), and *zebul* was a standard title for Baal at Ugarit. Indeed the separate parts of the name were actually recited in the cultic ceremony: "Where is Baal the Mighty, Where is the Prince, Lord of the Earth?" (Gordon, 49). A relation to the old East Semitic deity *ʾAyya* (see J. J. M. Roberts, *The Earliest Semitic Pantheon* [Baltimore: Johns Hopkins Univ. Press, 1976], 19–21) is unlikely. It is possible that the scribes saw in the name an obvious pun, since אִי (*ʾî*) can under certain conditions be understood as "no" (hence, "no prince"), or *zebul* can be read *zibl* ("dung"; hence "Where is the dung?"). See further the note on 2 Kings 1:2.

Ethbaal, Jezebel's father, was not only king of the Sidonians but, according to Josephus (*Ag. Ap.* 1.123 [18]), was also a priest of Astarte when he gained the throne by murdering the last of the descendants of Hiram I of Tyre. Ethbaal's dynasty endured for at least a century. Thus, as Josephus (*Ant.* 8.317 [13.1]) reports, he was king of Tyre and Sidon. The fact that Ben-Hadad I erected a stele to Baal-Melqart may well indicate that a treaty existed between Phoenicia and Israel.

32 Ahab's altar in the temple in Samaria doubtless was patterned after its prototype in Tyre, which Hiram had built and in which he set a golden pillar (Josephus, *Ant.* 8.145 [5.3]).

34 While it is true that Joshua appointed Jericho to the territory of Benjamin (Jos 18:12), there is evidence of habitation there subsequent to Joshua's curse and prior to Hiel's rebuilding activities (cf. Jdg 3:13; 2Sa 10:5; 1Ch 19:5). There is neither scriptural nor archaeological indication, however, of any building of a permanently fortified place. Whether Hiel deliberately sacrificed his sons as foundation offerings (as the Targum explains)—a practice well documented in the ancient Near East (see R. A. Macalister, *The Excavations of Gezer* [London: Murray, 1912], 2:428; but see Montgomery, 287–88)—or whether his building activities were attended by the accidental deaths of his two sons, Joshua's predictive curse was completely fulfilled.

Ahab himself was possibly behind the building activities, considering Jericho important to his military problems with Moab (cf. 22:39; 2Ki 1:1; 3:5 with the Moabite Stone, lines 6–9; *ANET*, 320). For a discussion of Jericho, see W. Dumbrell, "Jericho," *Major Cities of the Biblical World*, ed. R. K. Harrison (Nashville: Nelson, 1985), 130–38. For suggestions as to the complex textual history linking Joshua 6:26 and 1 Kings 16:34, see Lea Mazor, "The Origin and Evolution of the Curse upon the Rebuilder of Jericho—A Contribution of Textual Criticism to Biblical Historiography," *Text* 14 (1988): 1–26.

b. The prophetic ministry of Elijah (17:1–19:21)

OVERVIEW

Chapters 17–19 comprise a collection of stories concerning Elijah's prophetic ministry. They fall into four basic groups. First, 17:1–6 provides an introduction to the overall plot dealing with one period of Elijah's spiritual odyssey. Here we meet not only the prophet himself but also two of the chief characters who will play such a prominent role in his ministry: Ahab and, above all, God. The underlying problem is Israel's fascination with Baal, the Canaanite storm god. So it is that God's prophet confronts Ahab, who has become a royal sponsor of Baalism. Here, too, we see God's provision and protection of his prophet at the Kerith Ravine while Elijah gains preparatory assurance of God's empowerment for the future struggle.

The story develops as Elijah is led to Zarephath, where both he and a needy widow are cared for by the Lord's miraculous provision. This period of Elijah's spiritual odyssey gave the prophet further assurance of God's power and intention to go before his prophet when the climactic day of the contest with Baal would take place (17:7–24).

The resolution to the problem of Israel's infidelity and flirtation with Baal is told in two stages. First, Elijah met one of God's faithful servants, Obadiah. Obadiah was also a highly trusted official for Ahab. Through him Elijah arranged a contest with Baal's prophets at Mount Carmel (18:1–15). Second, the actual contest was joined in which the Lord miraculously burned Elijah's water-soaked sacrifice, while Baal failed to respond to his prophets. Elijah was shown to be the true prophet, while Baal's prophets were put to death (18:16–46).

Although the following account is at first seemingly unrelated to the drought, sober reflection clarifies that it serves as a denouement to the whole narrative. Because Jezebel was furious over Baal's defeat on Mount Carmel, she frightened Elijah into fleeing. Eventually he was divinely directed to Mount Horeb. There the Lord reassured, reinstated, and commissioned his prophet anew (19:1–18). Serving as an epilogue to the whole section, 19:19–21 tells of Elijah's carrying out a portion of his renewed commission in seeing to the call of Elisha to prophetic service.

Several features give the section cohesive literary unity. Robert L. Cohn ("The Literary Logic of 1 Kings 17–19," *JBL* 101 [1982]: 343–49) notes in each chapter an announcement (17:1; 18:1; 19:2), a journey (17:2–5; 18:2; 19:3–4), two encounters (17:6–7, 8–16; 18:7–16, 17–20; 19:5–6, 7), a miracle (17:7–23; 18:21–38; 19:7–18), and a conversion (17:24; 18:41–19:1; 19:19–21).

i. Prologue: Elijah's call (17:1–6)

[1]Now Elijah the Tishbite, from Tishbe in Gilead, said to Ahab, "As the LORD, the God of
Israel, lives, whom I serve, there will be neither dew nor rain in the next few years except at
my word."
[2]Then the word of the LORD came to Elijah: [3]"Leave here, turn eastward and hide in the
Kerith Ravine, east of the Jordan. [4]You will drink from the brook, and I have ordered the
ravens to feed you there."
[5]So he did what the LORD had told him. He went to the Kerith Ravine, east of the Jordan,
and stayed there. [6]The ravens brought him bread and meat in the morning and bread and
meat in the evening, and he drank from the brook.

COMMENTARY

1 Verse 1 connects with the previous section by including King Ahab in the details. In meeting Elijah, the Lord's prophet, and hearing his denunciation, Ahab must have realized that the Lord was bringing condemnation of his state sponsorship of Baal, the Canaanite god of fertility and rain.

The phrase "neither dew nor rain" is reminiscent of David's lament over Saul and Jonathan (2Sa 1:21). The importance of these words to the reputation of Baal can be seen in Dan'el's lament over Aqhat in the Ugaritic literature (see *ANET*, 153).

By "rain" was meant the regular early and latter rain of October/November and March/April. Their loss would be a mark of God's disfavor (see *EBC*, 2:253–54). The dew (often falling as heavy as drizzle in some regions of Palestine) was also a sign of God's favor to his covenantal people (Dt 33:28; Pr 19:12). However, it could be withdrawn from a thankless and apostate people (Hag 1:10). How good and pleasant it is when a grateful and obedient people willingly serve God in oneness of heart. Such service becomes as refreshing to God as the dew (Pss 110:3; 133:1, 3).

2–6 The location of the brook (or wadi) Kerith is uncertain. The Jordan River basin has many such narrow gorges. Implicit in the story is Elijah's compliance with the Lord's command. Such obedience is a necessary element in experiencing God's guidance and protection (1Sa 15:22–23; Ps 119:1–4; Da 9:4).

NOTES

1 The name Elijah means "Yah is my God." The designation "the Tishbite" is uncertain. The NIV, following the RSV (cf. LXX), interprets it as a place name in Gilead. Since Byzantine times Listib, eight miles north of the Jabbok River in the area of the shore of Mar Ilyas, has been suggested as Elijah's hometown.

A Thisbe/Tisbeh in Naphtali is known from the apocryphal story of Tobit. This latter identification seems more likely since the MT (followed by the Vulgate) literally reads that Elijah was merely one of the "settlers" in Gilead; therefore, Elijah had probably come from Tisbeh in Naphtali and had taken up residence among the settlers in Gilead. It is also plausible to suggest that Elijah's family had been displaced to Gilead during the Aramean wars of Baasha's time.

ii. Development: Elijah's ministry at Zarephath (17:7–24)

OVERVIEW

The story of Elijah's miraculous deeds at Zarephath falls into two sections. In the first (vv.7–16), the lack of rain has caused the brook Kerith to dry up (v.7). Accordingly, God sends Elijah to a widow at Zarephath in order that both his prophet and she might be cared for during the severe drought (vv.8–10). Upon his arrival, Elijah puts a difficult test before her (vv.11–14). If she would first bake a small loaf for Elijah before seeing to her family's needs, God would honor her faith with a supply of flour and oil so long as the drought should last. Taking the prophet at his word, she obeys, and everything comes to pass as he has promised (vv.15–16).

The second portion (vv.17–24) is structured in chiastic symmetry.

A When the widow's son falls gravely ill and dies, she blames Elijah for causing the development so as to bring up her sin before her (vv.17–18).

B Elijah takes the child from his mother (v.19).

C Having pled with God for the boy's life, through God's enablement he is able to effect the lad's resuscitation (vv.20–22).

B' Elijah takes the boy back to his mother and announces his recovery (v.23).

A' The mother now praises Elijah and acknowledges his prophetic status (v.24).

[7]Some time later the brook dried up because there had been no rain in the land.
[8]Then the word of the LORD came to him: [9]"Go at once to Zarephath of Sidon and stay
there. I have commanded a widow in that place to supply you with food." [10]So he went to
Zarephath. When he came to the town gate, a widow was there gathering sticks. He called
to her and asked, "Would you bring me a little water in a jar so I may have a drink?" [11]As
she was going to get it, he called, "And bring me, please, a piece of bread."

[12]"As surely as the LORD your God lives," she replied, "I don't have any bread—only a
handful of flour in a jar and a little oil in a jug. I am gathering a few sticks to take home
and make a meal for myself and my son, that we may eat it—and die."

[13]Elijah said to her, "Don't be afraid. Go home and do as you have said. But first make
a small cake of bread for me from what you have and bring it to me, and then make

something for yourself and your son. [14]For this is what the LORD, the God of Israel, says:'The
jar of flour will not be used up and the jug of oil will not run dry until the day the LORD
gives rain on the land.'"
[15]She went away and did as Elijah had told her. So there was food every day for Elijah
and for the woman and her family. [16]For the jar of flour was not used up and the jug of oil
did not run dry, in keeping with the word of the LORD spoken by Elijah.
[17]Some time later the son of the woman who owned the house became ill. He grew
worse and worse, and finally stopped breathing. [18]She said to Elijah, "What do you have
against me, man of God? Did you come to remind me of my sin and kill my son?"
[19]"Give me your son," Elijah replied. He took him from her arms, carried him to the upper
room where he was staying, and laid him on his bed. [20]Then he cried out to the LORD, "O
LORD my God, have you brought tragedy also upon this widow I am staying with, by causing her son to die?" [21]Then he stretched himself out on the boy three times and cried to
the LORD, "O LORD my God, let this boy's life return to him!"
[22]The LORD heard Elijah's cry, and the boy's life returned to him, and he lived. [23]Elijah
picked up the child and carried him down from the room into the house. He gave him to
his mother and said, "Look, your son is alive!"
[24]Then the woman said to Elijah, "Now I know that you are a man of God and that the
word of the LORD from your mouth is the truth."

COMMENTARY

7–16 Two aspects of the setting are significant. The first is the location where the events occurred. Zarephath was situated in Phoenician territory, Jezebel's homeland and the heartland of Baal. Because the city lay in enemy territory, it might be overlooked for some time in Ahab's search for Elijah (cf. 18:10).

The second is the growing severity of the drought. Once again the theme of command and compliance is featured. At Elijah's instructions the widow puts Elijah's needs ahead of her own. It proves to be a wise decision, for her meager rations continue to be adequate for each day's needs (cf. Mt 6:11). Thus both Elijah and the widow learn to put their continued faith and trust in the Provider rather than in the provision.

Not only the Lord's daily supplying of their needs, but also the fact that God does so in the very area where Baal is counted on to provide the rains needed for the land's fertility will further prepare the prophet for the contest with Baal's prophets that lies ahead. This incident and that which follows are reminders of God's love and concern for all who respond to him in genuine faith (cf. Lk 4:24–26).

17 As in the previous episode (v.7), the narrator reports the passing of a period of some time. The absence of breath indicated that the lad has died from his illness. Rather than his experiencing a mere "temporary suspension of animation or deprivation of the faculties" (Gray, 382), both the mother and Elijah attest to the boy's death (vv.18–20, 23).

18 The mother feels that some forgotten sin on her part must have occasioned her son's death. She believes that such sin cannot go unrequited in the presence of a man in whom the Spirit of God is abiding (cf. Mk 1:24; Lk 5:8).

The term "man of God" could be used of a prophet (e.g., Dt 33:1; 1Sa 9:6). It was used previously of the prophet from Bethel who condemned Jeroboam's altar (1Ki 13:1) and appears later to refer to Elisha (2Ki 6:15). In the NT Paul challenged Timothy with similar phraseology (1Ti 6:11).

19 Elijah stayed in a room (or temporary shelter) on the roof, which was accessible from outside the house. Such structures were common in the Near East. This arrangement allowed the widow not only her needed privacy but also guarded her reputation.

20–21 There is no certain indication that Elijah used the same technique that Elisha would later use with the Shunammite's lad (cf. 2Ki 4:34), though that possibility exists. Paul was prepared to perform a similar symbolic act in the case of Eutychus (Ac 20:10; cf. 9:36–43).

24 The woman's testimony to Elijah expresses more than admiration for the prophet. She acknowledges that truth is to be found in his God-given words. Thus the chapter ends as it began, by testifying to the efficacy of the prophetic word.

NOTES

9 Zarephath (cf. Akkad. *ṣarpitu*, Egyp. *ḏarp̄ata*, Gr. *sarepta*) is modern Ras Sarafand, seven miles south of Sidon. The widow's position was most precarious. Widows such as this one were largely dependent on charity and very poor. For Elijah to seem to make himself dependent on such a one would provoke a dramatic test of faith in God's provision. See R. Patterson, "The Widow, the Orphan and the Poor," *BSac* 130 (1973): 223–34.

12 מָעוֹג (*māʿôg*, "cake, bread") is usually derived from the Arabic *ʾawaju* ("curved," hence "round cake/bread"). It differs from the more usual word עֻגָה (*ʿugâ*, "cake of [bread]") found in v.13. Note that the denominative verb עוּג (*ʿûg*, "bake [a cake]") was used of baking on stones (cf. 19:6) heated with dry dung rather than charcoal for fuel (cf. Eze 4:12).

18 For the expression "What do you have against me?" see the note on 2 Kings 3:13 (cf. Jdg 11:12; 2Sa 16:10; Jn 2:4).

24 The Syrian translation, followed by Jerome, that the lad was the prophet Jonah is totally unsatisfactory and historically impossible (cf. 2Ki 14:25).

iii. Resolution: Elijah's contest on Mount Carmel (18:1–46)

OVERVIEW

Chapter 18 provides the resolution both to the problem of the terrible drought and the underlying question of whether Yahweh or Baal is God. It proceeds in two sections: an initial movement featuring Elijah and Obadiah (vv.1–15), and a climactic second account of Elijah's contest with the prophets of Baal (vv.16–46).

(a) Initiation: Elijah and Obadiah (18:1–15)

OVERVIEW

This opening pericope is structured in chiastic symmetry.

A God commands Elijah to present himself before Ahab. He, not Baal, will send rain on the land (vv.1–2a).

B Meanwhile, we learn that Ahab and his trusted official, Obadiah (who was also a believer in Yahweh), have left on a sweep of the land searching for fodder for the royal animals (vv.2b–6).

C As Obadiah proceeds on his assignment, he meets Elijah, who instructs him to inform Ahab that he is back and desires an audience with the king (vv.7–8).

B' Obadiah protests. Because Ahab had sought Elijah everywhere, if Obadiah should report to Ahab that he had found Elijah but God suddenly sent his prophet elsewhere, Obadiah's life could be in danger (vv.9–14).

A' Elijah assures Obadiah that he will present himself to Ahab (v.15).

[1]After a long time, in the third year, the word of the LORD came to Elijah: "Go and present yourself to Ahab, and I will send rain on the land." [2]So Elijah went to present himself to Ahab.

Now the famine was severe in Samaria, [3]and Ahab had summoned Obadiah, who was in charge of his palace. (Obadiah was a devout believer in the LORD. [4]While Jezebel was killing off the LORD's prophets, Obadiah had taken a hundred prophets and hidden them in two caves, fifty in each, and had supplied them with food and water.) [5]Ahab had said to Obadiah, "Go through the land to all the springs and valleys. Maybe we can find some grass to keep the horses and mules alive so we will not have to kill any of our animals." [6]So they divided the land they were to cover, Ahab going in one direction and Obadiah in another.

[7]As Obadiah was walking along, Elijah met him. Obadiah recognized him, bowed down to the ground, and said, "Is it really you, my lord Elijah?"

[8]"Yes," he replied. "Go tell your master, 'Elijah is here.'"

[9]"What have I done wrong," asked Obadiah, "that you are handing your servant over to Ahab to be put to death? [10]As surely as the LORD your God lives, there is not a nation or kingdom where my master has not sent someone to look for you. And whenever a nation or kingdom claimed you were not there, he made them swear they could not find you. [11]But now you tell me to go to my master and say, 'Elijah is here.' [12]I don't know where the Spirit of the LORD may carry you when I leave you. If I go and tell Ahab and he doesn't find you, he will kill me. Yet I your servant have worshiped the LORD since my youth. [13]Haven't

you heard, my lord, what I did while Jezebel was killing the prophets of the LORD? I hid a hundred of the LORD's prophets in two caves, fifty in each, and supplied them with food and water. [14]And now you tell me to go to my master and say, 'Elijah is here.' He will kill me!"

[15]Elijah said, "As the LORD Almighty lives, whom I serve, I will surely present myself to Ahab today."

COMMENTARY

1 According to the NT the drought lasted three and one-half years (Lk 4:25; Jas 5:17). If the three-and-one-half-year period is not conventional language for a particular period of tribulation (cf. Da 7:25; 12:7, 11; Rev 11:3), the three years of the MT may be taken either as an approximate period of time or as a standard motif for a time of spiritual activity. The difference may, of course, be a matter of how the time involved is calculated.

3 The title עַל הַבַּיִת (*ʿal habbayit*, "in charge of the palace") is a technical term designating the king's chief officer (cf. Arza, 16:9; see comments on 4:6). Obadiah serves as a literary foil to contrast the ungodly character of Ahab. While Ahab's concern for fodder for the royal animals goes unrequited, Obadiah manages to supply food for the Lord's prophets.

4–6 Fifty constituted a standard company, whether for military purposes (2Ki 1:9, 12–13) or others (2Ki 2:7).

7–8 Obadiah's recognition of Elijah may be due to the fact that the prophet was well known or because of his strange attire (2Ki 1:8). So also was the case of the one who came in the spirit of Elijah (Mt 3:4).

9–15 Obadiah saw Elijah's command as a virtual death sentence unless the prophet actually appeared before Ahab. Elijah's assurance not only comforted Obadiah but also gave testimony to his obedience to the divine commission (in contrast to Jonah).

NOTES

3 Obadiah (which means "servant of the LORD") has been identified in Jewish tradition with the minor prophet of the same name, but such an identification is unlikely. His office apparently involved being the king's personal representative and the bearer of the royal seal.

4 For this association of prophets that met and possibly lived together for study, prophesying and spiritual edification, and service, see 1 Samuel 10:5; 2 Kings 2:3–7; 6:1–2. LaSor (*NBC* [rev. ed.], 343) wisely cautions against ascribing too much prominence to the school of prophets, as is sometimes done (cf., e.g., C. F. Whitley, *The Prophetic Achievement* [Leiden: Brill, 1963], 3–4; R. B. Y. Scott, *The Relevance of the Prophets* [rev. ed.; New York: MacMillan, 1968], 45–47). Certainly the OT says little about them. That Obadiah would have little difficulty in finding caves for the sons of the prophets can be seen in that over two thousand caves have been counted in the Mount Carmel area. The NIV's "fifty in each" is probably the correct understanding, as read in thirteen Hebrew MSS and as comparison with v.13 indicates. The LXX reads "by fifties" (cf. RSV, NASB). One "fifty" seems to have been omitted in the transmission of the MT here.

5 The importance of horses to Ahab is reflected in the records of Shalmaneser III of Assyria (859–824 BC), who mentioned that two thousand chariots were furnished by Ahab to the Syrian coalition that opposed him at Qarqar (see *ANET*, 279).

15 The NIV correctly translates יהוה צְבָאוֹת (*yhwh ṣ^ebā'ôt*, "Yahweh of hosts") as "LORD Almighty," discerning that the divine name cannot stand in the construct state. Accordingly Byzantine and medieval writers preferred to translate the term by κύριος παντοκράτωρ (*kyrios pantokratōr*, "Lord Almighty"), found frequently in the LXX (cf. 2Co 6:18). The form is probably an abbreviation of some longer term, such as "The Lord YHWH, the God of hosts" (Am 3:13). Theologically it signifies that the Lord stands as a mighty ruler at the head of a vast retinue of heavenly powers ready to act at his command. See further G. Vos, *Biblical Theology* (Grand Rapids: Eerdmans, 1954), 258–63; C. K. Lehman, *Biblical Theology* (Scottdale, Penn.: Herald, 1971), 1:222–30.

(b) Climax: Elijah and the prophets of Baal (18:16–46)

OVERVIEW

The whole affair concerning the drought reaches its climax in the contest on Mount Carmel. The account is structured in four units, the first and last forming an inclusio featuring dialogue between Elijah and Ahab.

1. Obadiah carries out Elijah's instructions to report to Ahab his return. Elijah then instructs Ahab to summon the prophets of Baal to Mount Carmel for a contest as to who represents true deity (vv.16–19).
2. When all are present on Mount Carmel, Elijah addresses the people and presents a challenge to follow either God or Baal. He then prepares the format of the contest, to which all agree (vv.20–24).
3. In the course of the contest Baal's prophets are unsuccessful in getting their god to answer their petition to accept their sacrifice. However, Yahweh does answer Elijah's plea with a heaven-sent consuming fire, even though the sacrifice has been doused with water. The people are convinced by the miraculous deed, and at Elijah's command the prophets of Baal are executed (vv.25–40).
4. True to Elijah's warning to Ahab, a huge storm comes, thus signaling the end of the drought. The whole episode concludes with Elijah's running ahead of Ahab's chariot as the king makes his way to Jezreel (vv.41–46).

[16]So Obadiah went to meet Ahab and told him, and Ahab went to meet Elijah. [17]When he saw Elijah, he said to him, "Is that you, you troubler of Israel?"

[18]"I have not made trouble for Israel," Elijah replied. "But you and your father's family have. You have abandoned the LORD's commands and have followed the Baals. [19]Now
summon the people from all over Israel to meet me on Mount Carmel. And bring the four
hundred and fifty prophets of Baal and the four hundred prophets of Asherah, who eat at
Jezebel's table."

[20]So Ahab sent word throughout all Israel and assembled the prophets on Mount
Carmel. [21]Elijah went before the people and said, "How long will you waver between two
opinions? If the LORD is God, follow him; but if Baal is God, follow him."

But the people said nothing.

[22]Then Elijah said to them, "I am the only one of the LORD's prophets left, but Baal has
four hundred and fifty prophets. [23]Get two bulls for us. Let them choose one for themselves, and let them cut it into pieces and put it on the wood but not set fire to it. I will
prepare the other bull and put it on the wood but not set fire to it. [24]Then you call on
the name of your god, and I will call on the name of the LORD. The god who answers by
fire — he is God."

Then all the people said, "What you say is good."

[25]Elijah said to the prophets of Baal, "Choose one of the bulls and prepare it first, since
there are so many of you. Call on the name of your god, but do not light the fire." [26]So they
took the bull given them and prepared it.

Then they called on the name of Baal from morning till noon. "O Baal, answer us!" they
shouted. But there was no response; no one answered. And they danced around the altar
they had made.

[27]At noon Elijah began to taunt them. "Shout louder!" he said. "Surely he is a god! Perhaps he is deep in thought, or busy, or traveling. Maybe he is sleeping and must be awakened." [28]So they shouted louder and slashed themselves with swords and spears, as was
their custom, until their blood flowed. [29]Midday passed, and they continued their frantic
prophesying until the time for the evening sacrifice. But there was no response, no one
answered, no one paid attention.

[30]Then Elijah said to all the people, "Come here to me." They came to him, and he
repaired the altar of the LORD, which was in ruins. [31]Elijah took twelve stones, one for each
of the tribes descended from Jacob, to whom the word of the LORD had come, saying,
"Your name shall be Israel." [32]With the stones he built an altar in the name of the LORD,
and he dug a trench around it large enough to hold two seahs of seed. [33]He arranged the
wood, cut the bull into pieces and laid it on the wood. Then he said to them, "Fill four
large jars with water and pour it on the offering and on the wood."

[34]"Do it again," he said, and they did it again.

"Do it a third time," he ordered, and they did it the third time. [35]The water ran down
around the altar and even filled the trench.

36At the time of sacrifice, the prophet Elijah stepped forward and prayed: "O LORD, God
of Abraham, Isaac and Israel, let it be known today that you are God in Israel and that I
am your servant and have done all these things at your command. 37Answer me, O LORD,
answer me, so these people will know that you, O LORD, are God, and that you are turning
their hearts back again."
38Then the fire of the LORD fell and burned up the sacrifice, the wood, the stones and the
soil, and also licked up the water in the trench.
39When all the people saw this, they fell prostrate and cried, "The LORD — he is God! The
LORD — he is God!"
40Then Elijah commanded them, "Seize the prophets of Baal. Don't let anyone get
away!" They seized them, and Elijah had them brought down to the Kishon Valley and
slaughtered there.
41And Elijah said to Ahab, "Go, eat and drink, for there is the sound of a heavy rain." 42So
Ahab went off to eat and drink, but Elijah climbed to the top of Carmel, bent down to the
ground and put his face between his knees.
43"Go and look toward the sea," he told his servant. And he went up and looked.
"There is nothing there," he said.
Seven times Elijah said, "Go back."
44The seventh time the servant reported, "A cloud as small as a man's hand is rising from
the sea."
So Elijah said, "Go and tell Ahab, 'Hitch up your chariot and go down before the rain
stops you.'"
45Meanwhile, the sky grew black with clouds, the wind rose, a heavy rain came on and
Ahab rode off to Jezreel. 46The power of the LORD came upon Elijah and, tucking his cloak
into his belt, he ran ahead of Ahab all the way to Jezreel.

COMMENTARY

17–18 Ahab calls Elijah the "troubler of Israel." Indirectly, at least, Ahab feels that the famine has been all Elijah's fault; because of Elijah's hostile attitude, Baal has been angered and so has withheld rain for the past three years. Elijah's reply is particularly instructive. Not he, but Ahab and his family are the real troublers, for they have made Baal worship the state religion (v.18). The plural "Baals" indicates that Baal was worshiped under various titles at different locations.

19 Mount Carmel is part of the Carmel Ridge, which divides the coastal plain of Palestine into the Plain of Acco to the north and the plains of Sharon and Philistia to the south. To this day a Carmelite monastery, dedicated to the remembrance of Elijah, exists at the end of the northwestern part of the mountain. The actual scene of Elijah's contest, however, may well be sought on the eastern side among Carmel's taller peaks at El Muhraqa.

Note that the four hundred prophets of Asherah, included in Elijah's challenge, are not present for the contest (cf. vv.22, 40).

20–21 Elijah confronts the people who have gathered on the mountain with the same challenge that Joshua had issued so long ago: Serve God or serve another (cf. Mt 6:24). Unlike Joshua's people, Elijah's audience holds its peace.

22–29 Elijah proposes a test in accordance with the scriptural precedent established by Aaron (Lev 9). As the contest stretches on, Elijah mocks the prophets of Baal. See Note on v.27.

30–35 The availability of a fallen altar to Yahweh makes Mount Carmel an ideal place for the contest. The altar's disarray is a visible reminder of the people's broken spiritual condition. Further, the twelve stones will remind them of the Lord's proper claim on his people as descendents of Jacob/Israel.

36–37 The verb translated "stepped forward" is the same as that translated "come here" in v.30. Thus the narrator implies that the people, who are now far away from God spiritually, need to draw near to God's appointed means of worship. "Israel" here replaces "Jacob" in the familiar motif of "the God of Abraham, Isaac, and Jacob." The change is doubtless deliberate. Much as their ancestor Jacob achieved success by clinging to Yahweh, so the people must abandon Baal and return to the God of their covenant.

38–40 God's answer to Elijah's prayer stands in stark contrast to Baal's dead silence at his prophets' ecstatic frenzy (cf. v.29). G. E. Saint-Laurant ("Light from Ras Shamra on Elijah's Ordeal upon Mount Carmel," in *Scripture in Context*, ed. C. E. Evans, W. W. Hallo, and J. B. White [Pittsburgh, Penn.: Pickwick, 1980], 135) concludes that "the biblical author has deliberately emphasized those dimensions of the story which most sharply contrast the powerful dominion of Yahweh with the impotence of Baal."

41–43 The excitement of these dramatic events is heightened by a Hebrew word (*hāmôn*, "sound") that signals the rumbling thunder announcing the fast approaching storm. Rain is on the way, though Elijah also needs to pray for it (cf. Jas 5:18).

44–46 The Hebrew word for "cloud" (*ʿāb*) refers to a thick, dark, rainy cloud mass (cf. Jdg 5:4; 2Sa 23:4). Ahab's need for haste in the face of the oncoming cloudburst can be appreciated when one realizes that his chariot must travel seventeen miles through the accumulating mud and across the quickly swelling dry wadis.

NOTES

21 The verb פָּסַח (*pāsaḥ*, "waver") means literally "be lame" (cf. Akkad. *pessû*, "lame"). In the Piel it means "limp," as in the case of Mephibosheth (2Sa 9:13). Elijah obviously intends a wordplay comparing the people's indecision with the frenzied ritualistic dancing of the prophets of Baal. See R. de Vaux, "The Prophets of Baal on Mt. Carmel," in *The Bible and the Ancient Near East* (Garden City, N.Y.: Doubleday, 1971), 240–43.

27 Elijah's irony borders on sarcasm (cf. 22:15). שִׂיחַ (*śîaḥ*, "deep in thought") and שִׂיג (*śîg*, "busy"; probably a biform of סִיג/סוּג [*sûg/sîg*, "move, turn back"]). De Vaux ("The Prophets of Baal on Mount Carmel," 243–46) suggests that they are synonymous and typical of Baal-Melqart's commercial activities. G. R. Driver ("Problems of Interpretation in the Heptateuch," *Mélanges bibliques rédiges en l'honneur de André Robert* [Paris: Bloud & Gay, 1957], 66–68) likewise considers them synonymous and equates the former word with *śîaḥ/śûaḥ*, "to defecate"). He concludes that the whole phrase is euphemistic. See also G. Rendsburg, "The Mock of Baal in 1 Kings 18:27," *CBQ* 50 (1988): 414–17.

On the whole it may be safest to follow the NIV here in separating all three ideas of the verse and relating them to the known activities of the great gods of the ancient Near East.

29 The time of the evening sacrifice, when the chief daily service would be observed (Josephus, *Ant.* 14.65 [4.3]) was about 3:00 p.m. (see Alfred Edersheim, *The Temple* [Grand Rapids: Eerdmans, 1972], 143). On the question of Baal's resting, see the interesting study by H. Jackson, "Elijah's Sleeping Baal" (*Bib* 79 [1998]: 413); he finds parallels with the Egyptian literature dealing with arousing a sleeping god, and contrasts with the Mesopotamian Atraḫasis Epic, in which Enlil's loss of sleep is due to humankind's noisy activities.

37–38 For a similar figure, see the comments on Joel 2:12–14. For the "fire of the LORD/God," see Leviticus 9:24; Numbers 11:1–3; 2 Kings 1:10–12; 1 Chronicles 21:26; 2 Chronicles 7:1. Fire was a symbol of the divine presence (Ex 3:2; 19:17–18; Dt 5:4), especially in God's purifying and sanctifying influences (Eze 1:13; Mal 3:2–3).

Several scholars have suggested that the "fire" was a lightning stroke; if so, it heralded the onset of the soon-coming storm. L. Bronner, 54–77, demonstrates that Yahweh's command over fire, water, and rain is a deliberate repudiation of Baal, who was assumed to have command over these elements.

46 Jezreel, modern Zenʾin, lay at the foot of Mount Gilboa, midway between Megiddo and Bethshan. Elijah's running ahead of Ahab's chariot contains several points of interest. (1) While Elijah's strength for such a long run was due to divine enablement (cf. Isa 40:31), even on a natural basis it would not be impossible. Montgomery, 307, points out that Arab runners can easily cover one hundred miles in two days.

(2) The position as an outrunner for the king was a privileged one in the ancient Near East (see the "Barrakab Inscription," *ANET*, 655; cf. Est 6:9, 11).

(3) Elijah may have been concerned for spiritual progress in Israel. What would happen when Ahab faced Jezebel with the news of the events of this day? Would Israel follow God or Baal (cf. v.21)? Elijah himself would come to wicked Jezebel as a herald of the truth (cf. Jnh 1:2; 3:2; 1Ti 2:7; 2Ti 1:11; 2Pe 2:5).

(4) The motif of the "outstretched hand of God" in behalf of his own is a familiar one in the OT (see, e.g., Ex 6:6–7; 7:5; Dt 5:15; 26:5–9; Jer 32:16–22). The prophets used it also to remind Israel and Judah that that same divine hand could be stretched out in judgment against his own when sinful disobedience entered their lives (Isa 5:25–26; 9:12–17; 10:4; Jer 21:5; Eze 14:13; 16:27).

iv. Denouement: Elijah's retreat to Horeb (19:1–18)

OVERVIEW

The first portion of ch. 19 proceeds in a series of three short scenes. In the first (vv.1–4a), Jezebel's threats against Elijah's life cause him to flee southward to the desert beyond Beersheba. There the discouraged prophet wishes for death but is sustained by an angel, who instructs him to go further southward (vv.4b–8). Reaching Mount Horeb he finds shelter in a cave, where the Lord patiently but firmly first reproves, then restores and commissions his servant anew (vv.9–18).

1Now Ahab told Jezebel everything Elijah had done and how he had killed all the
prophets with the sword. 2So Jezebel sent a messenger to Elijah to say, "May the gods deal
with me, be it ever so severely, if by this time tomorrow I do not make your life like that of
one of them."
3Elijah was afraid and ran for his life. When he came to Beersheba in Judah, he left his
servant there, 4while he himself went a day's journey into the desert. He came to a broom
tree, sat down under it and prayed that he might die. "I have had enough, LORD," he said.
"Take my life; I am no better than my ancestors." 5Then he lay down under the tree and fell
asleep.
All at once an angel touched him and said, "Get up and eat." 6He looked around, and
there by his head was a cake of bread baked over hot coals, and a jar of water. He ate and
drank and then lay down again.
7The angel of the LORD came back a second time and touched him and said, "Get up and
eat, for the journey is too much for you." 8So he got up and ate and drank. Strengthened
by that food, he traveled forty days and forty nights until he reached Horeb, the mountain
of God. 9There he went into a cave and spent the night.
And the word of the LORD came to him: "What are you doing here, Elijah?"
10He replied, "I have been very zealous for the LORD God Almighty. The Israelites have
rejected your covenant, broken down your altars, and put your prophets to death with the
sword. I am the only one left, and now they are trying to kill me too."
11The LORD said, "Go out and stand on the mountain in the presence of the LORD, for the
LORD is about to pass by."
Then a great and powerful wind tore the mountains apart and shattered the rocks
before the LORD, but the LORD was not in the wind. After the wind there was an earthquake,
but the LORD was not in the earthquake. 12After the earthquake came a fire, but the LORD
was not in the fire. And after the fire came a gentle whisper. 13When Elijah heard it, he
pulled his cloak over his face and went out and stood at the mouth of the cave.
Then a voice said to him, "What are you doing here, Elijah?"
14He replied, "I have been very zealous for the LORD God Almighty. The Israelites have
rejected your covenant, broken down your altars, and put your prophets to death with the
sword. I am the only one left, and now they are trying to kill me too."
15The LORD said to him, "Go back the way you came, and go to the Desert of Damascus.
When you get there, anoint Hazael king over Aram. 16Also, anoint Jehu son of Nimshi
king over Israel, and anoint Elisha son of Shaphat from Abel Meholah to succeed you as
prophet. 17Jehu will put to death any who escape the sword of Hazael, and Elisha will put

to death any who escape the sword of Jehu. [18]Yet I reserve seven thousand in Israel—all whose knees have not bowed down to Baal and all whose mouths have not kissed him."

COMMENTARY

1 Jezebel was of royal blood and every bit a queen. She could be ruthless in pursuing her goals (21:11–15). Her personality was so forceful that even Ahab feared her and was corrupted by her (16:31; 21:25). Both the northern kingdom (16:32–33) and the southern kingdom, through the marriage of her step-daughter Athaliah into the royal house of Judah (2Ki 8:16–19; 11:1–20; 2Ch 21:5–7), experienced moral degradation and spiritual degeneracy through her corrupting influence.

2–3 Probably Elijah played into Jezebel's hand. Had she really wanted him dead, she could have seized him without warning and slain him. The great prophet's flight betrayed a notable spiritual flaw, as God's subsequent dealing with Elijah displays. His God-given successes had fostered an inordinate pride (cf. vv.4, 10, 14), which had made him take his own importance too seriously. Moreover, Elijah had come to bask in the glow of the spectacular. He may have fully expected that because of what had been accomplished at Mount Carmel, Jezebel would capitulate and pagan worship would come to an end in Israel—all through his influence!

What Elijah needed to learn, God would soon show him (vv.11–12). God does not always move in the realm of the extraordinary. To live always seeking one "high experience" after another is to have a misdirected zeal. The majority of life's service is in quiet, routine, humble obedience to God's will.

4 Elijah's request for death indicates the depth of his disillusionment and despair. The scene is reminiscent of Jonah's great disappointment at God's sparing of Nineveh (Jnh 4:3).

5–7 Elijah should have recognized God's concern for his prophet in the angel's supplying his need for nourishment for the journey that lay ahead. The narrator expects the reader to make the connection between the Kerith Ravine incident (17:2–6) and the miraculous supply at the widow of Zarephath's home (17:13–16). In the latter case the correlation is unmistakable, for the Hebrew words used for "the cake of bread" and "jar" are those used previously in 17:13–14.

8 Horeb (i.e., Mount Sinai) is called "the mountain of God" (see Ex 3:1; see also Ex 4:27; 18:5; Dt 5:2; for the significance of Sinai, see *TWOT*, 2:622–23). Elijah's forty-day journey is not without significance. Indeed, a straight trip from Beersheba would require little more than a quarter of that time; therefore, the period is designedly symbolic. As the children of Israel had a notable spiritual failure and so had to wander forty years in the wilderness, so a defeated Elijah was to spend forty days in the desert (cf. Nu 14:26–35). As Moses had spent forty days on the mountain without bread and water, sustained only by God while he awaited a new phase of service (Ex 34:28), so Elijah was to spend forty days thrown on the divine enablement as he prepared for a new charge by God (cf. Mt 4:1–2). As Moses was to see the presence of God (Ex 33:12–23), so Elijah was to find God, though in a different way from that which he could ever imagine.

9–10 Ironically, before the contest on Mount Carmel Obadiah had quartered one hundred prophets in two separate caves to hide them from Ahab's wrath. Now it is Elijah who finds himself in a cave. He may have been in a spot more sacred than he realized. The Hebrew text says, "He came there to *the* cave," possibly the very "cleft in the rock" where God had placed Moses as his glory passed by (Ex 33:21–23).

At length the word of the Lord aroused Elijah. The penetrating interrogation called for minute self-evaluation (v.9b; cf. Ge 3:9). Did Elijah yet understand his failure and God's gracious guidance in bringing him to this place? Elijah's reply indicated that he did not. Like Phineas of old, he alone had been zealous for the Lord in the midst of gross idolatry (v.10; cf. Nu 25:7–13). In his self-pity Elijah apparently forgot the faithful prophets whom Obadiah had previously hidden. Unlike Jonah, who was disappointed in God's graciousness to the people of Nineveh when they repented at Jonah's preaching (Jnh 4:1–2), Elijah was disappointed that his spectacular victory was at best short-lived.

11–12 Wind, earthquake, and fire are all natural phenomena that often heralded God's presence or appearance (Ex 19:16–18; Dt 5:23–26; Jdg 5:4–5; 2Sa 22:8–16; Pss 18:7–15; 68:8; Heb 12:18). Elijah's recognition of God's voice in the "gentle whisper" (cf. NRSV, "sound of sheer silence") should have been a lesson for Elijah. Even God did not always operate in the realm of the spectacular.

13–14 Because Elijah knew he could not look at God and live, like Moses before him he covered his face (cf. Ex 33:20–22). The repetition of the Lord's question, "What are you doing here?" may be understood in several ways. (1) It may be an emphatic reiteration of the original question (v.9) as to why he is there rather than about his prophetic commission. (2) It may be an advance on the first question, asking whether Elijah understood (a) the significance of this holy place and (b) why he was brought there. Perhaps all these possibilities are involved. In any case, Elijah's answer indicates that either he does not understand the interrogation or stubbornly refuses to admit its implications.

15–18 God again deals graciously with his prophet. He must go back to the northern kingdom (v.15), the place where he had veered off the track with God in his spiritual life (cf. Abram, Ge 13:3–4; John Mark, Ac 15:39). Elijah still has work to accomplish for God. That task is threefold: (1) in the realm of international politics, he is to anoint Hazael to succeed Ben-Hadad, Israel's perennial adversary in Damascus; (2) in national affairs, Jehu is to be anointed as the next king (v.16); and (3) in the spiritual realm, Elisha is to be commissioned as his successor (cf. God's instruction to Moses in Nu 27:18–23).

The threefold commission is singularly interrelated (v.17). Jehu's work will supplement that of Hazael; that is, those people in Israel who escape Hazael's purge will be dealt with by Jehu. In turn, those who survive Jehu's slaughter must face the spiritual judgment of Elisha. To encourage his restored prophet further, God sets the record straight: there are yet seven thousand true believers in Israel who have not embraced Baal (v.18).

It is to Elijah's credit that he does respond favorably to God's dealing with him. No such certainty was forthcoming in the case of Jonah.

NOTES

3 Most modern commentaries and versions follow the lead of the ancient versions in pointing the Hebrew phrase וַיִּרָא (*wayyirā*ʾ, "and he was afraid") rather than reading the MT's וַיַּרְא (*wayyar*ʾ, "and he saw"). R. B. Allen, however ("Elijah the Broken Prophet." *JETS* 22 [1979]: 202), demonstrates the defensibility of the MT. He contends that Elijah fled not in fear but as a prophet broken by Jezebel's unrepentant paganism and continuing power over the nation and its destiny.

4 The "broom tree" is a shrub found in abundance in southern Palestine. It has long slender branches with small leaves and fragrant, delicate blossoms. Common among the wadis, they often reach a height of ten feet (cf. *Fauna and Flora of the Old Testament* [London: United Bible Societies, 1972], 100–101).

7 For "the angel of the LORD," see Notes on 2 Kings 1:3.

15 For Hazael see the comment on 2 Kings 8:8; for Jehu, see 2 Kings 9–10.

16 Abel Meholah was situated in the Jordan Valley south of Bethshan. Famous for Gideon's victory over the Midianites (Jdg 7:22), it will now be the scene of Elisha's submission to the Lord's call to prophetic ministry. Although kings or priests were anointed for office, this place is the only one where a prophet is so designated.

v. Epilogue: Elijah and the call of Elisha (19:19–21)

[19]So Elijah went from there and found Elisha son of Shaphat. He was plowing with twelve yoke of oxen, and he himself was driving the twelfth pair. Elijah went up to him and threw his cloak around him. [20]Elisha then left his oxen and ran after Elijah. "Let me kiss my father and mother good-by," he said, "and then I will come with you."

"Go back," Elijah replied. "What have I done to you?"

[21]So Elisha left him and went back. He took his yoke of oxen and slaughtered them. He burned the plowing equipment to cook the meat and gave it to the people, and they ate. Then he set out to follow Elijah and became his attendant.

COMMENTARY

19–21 The number of oxen plowing signifies that Elisha comes from a family of some means. A surrender to ministry would mean counting the cost.

Elijah took the same mantle with which he had covered his face and threw it over Elisha as an act of investiture. Elisha responded without hesitation. Taking his leave of Elijah, Elisha returned home to enjoy a farewell meal with his family and friends. The meat was cooked over Elisha's own plowing equipment. Thus he had burned his past behind him. Henceforth he would serve God. Doing so, however, meant first learning more of him through being Elijah's assistant.

Walsh, 279–80, points out the finality of Elisha's break with the past. He notes that the verb translated "slaughtered" (Heb. *zābaḥ*) is customarily used of killing an animal for sacrifice. As well, the phrase used in the act of boiling the animal is significant in that it "evokes the notion of a *šlm*, or communion sacrifice, in which a person offers an animal to Yahweh in thanksgiving for divine blessings and uses the sacrificial meat to host a meal for family and friends."

NOTES

21 Elisha's genuine break with the past stands in bold contrast with those false disciples who wished only to appear pious before Jesus (Mt 8:18–22; Lk 9:57–62). Elisha begins a period of humble service and training at the side of the master prophet, much as Joshua served under Moses (cf. Ex 24:13–18; Nu 27:18–23; Dt 1:38; 3:21–22, 27–28; 31:7–23; 34:9).

c. Ahab and the Syro-Israelite campaigns (20:1–43)

i. The Aramean crisis (20:1–12)

OVERVIEW

This section is comprised of three units structured in chiastic symmetry.

A An introductory narrative statement dealing with the Aramean invasion provides the background for the whole narrative concerning the Syro-Israelite conflict (v.1).

B A series of three diplomatic exchanges (vv.2–4, 5–9, 10–11) highlights the growing political crisis.

A' A narrative statement (v.12) brings closure to the section, while also providing the setting for the account of the two military confrontations that follow (vv.13–34).

[1]Now Ben-Hadad king of Aram mustered his entire army. Accompanied by thirty-two
kings with their horses and chariots, he went up and besieged Samaria and attacked it.
[2]He sent messengers into the city to Ahab king of Israel, saying, "This is what Ben-Hadad
says: [3]'Your silver and gold are mine, and the best of your wives and children are mine.'"
[4]The king of Israel answered, "Just as you say, my lord the king. I and all I have are yours."
[5]The messengers came again and said, "This is what Ben-Hadad says: 'I sent to demand
your silver and gold, your wives and your children. [6]But about this time tomorrow I am
going to send my officials to search your palace and the houses of your officials. They will
seize everything you value and carry it away.'"
[7]The king of Israel summoned all the elders of the land and said to them, "See how this
man is looking for trouble! When he sent for my wives and my children, my silver and my
gold, I did not refuse him."
[8]The elders and the people all answered, "Don't listen to him or agree to his demands."
[9]So he replied to Ben-Hadad's messengers, "Tell my lord the king, 'Your servant will do
all you demanded the first time, but this demand I cannot meet.'" They left and took the
answer back to Ben-Hadad.

[10]Then Ben-Hadad sent another message to Ahab:"May the gods deal with me, be it ever so severely, if enough dust remains in Samaria to give each of my men a handful."

[11]The king of Israel answered, "Tell him:'One who puts on his armor should not boast like one who takes it off.'"

[12]Ben-Hadad heard this message while he and the kings were drinking in their tents, and he ordered his men:"Prepare to attack." So they prepared to attack the city.

COMMENTARY

1 The identity of Ben-Hadad (possibly a dynastic throne name) has been the subject of much scholarly debate. Some scholars (e.g., Albright, Bright, House, Montgomery, Unger) decide that this king is still Ben-Hadad I, assigning to him a reign that spanned most of the ninth century. Others (e.g., Edwards, Keil, Kitchen, Malamat, Wiseman, Wood), on the basis of v.34, which appears to differentiate the king of this chapter from the one who invaded the northern kingdom previously in the days of Baasha, suggest that Ben-Hadad I died somewhere about 860 BC and that he was succeeded by his son Ben-Hadad II (ca. 860–843 BC).

On the whole the second interpretation seems to fit the historical details adequately and allows the most natural interpretation of v.34. The Annals of Shalmaneser III of Assyria (858–824 BC) give his name as (H)adad-Ezer, possibly a throne name. Accordingly, the identity and dates of the Aramean kings adopted here are as follows:

Ben-Hadad I (ca. 885–860 BC), son of Tabrimmon (1Ki 15:18)
Ben-Hadad II (ca. 860–842 BC)
Hazael (ca. 841–802 BC)
Ben-Hadad III (ca. 802–780? BC)

Confederations of kings were common in the ancient Near East. Shalmaneser III mentions that this same Hadad-Ezer was part of a coalition of twelve kings that withstood him at the Battle of Qarqar. The Zakir Stele mentions a coalition of seven kings headed by Ben-Hadad III (see *ANET*, 655–56).

Ben-Hadad may have had several motives for attacking Ahab late in his reign. Perhaps Ben-Hadad wanted Ahab to join his anti-Assyrian coalition (as Ahab later did). Perhaps it was due to the longstanding commercial rivalry and political enmity that had festered since Baasha's days, coupled with the fear that Ahab might become an ally of the Assyrian king. At any rate, the effects of the drought and famine had created an opportunity to eliminate further difficulty from his southern frontier. Gathering a coalition of thirty-two local rulers, he swept southward and put Samaria itself under siege.

2–6 Ben-Hadad's terms were a virtual call for Ahab to be reduced to vassal status. His second set of demands was extreme; they amounted to the right of unlimited search and seizure not only of the palace but also the homes of Ahab's officials. The ultimatum, almost certain to be refused, served as a pretext for war.

7–9 As Rehoboam before him had done (12:6–7), Ahab assembled the elder officials for consultation.

10–11 Ben-Hadad's bombastic claim threatened Samaria with so thorough a destruction that there would not be enough of it left to make a handful of dust for each of his men. Such propaganda was often utilized in wartime situations (cf. 1Sa 17:43) as part of typical psychological warfare.

Ahab's reply is a classic illustration of Near Eastern colloquial wisdom. "Let not him who girds [his armor] boast like him who takes it off" (cf. NASB) might be approximated well in colloquial Western parlance: "Let not one who puts on his uniform boast like one who takes it off." In other words, Ahab is hinting that Ben-Hadad and his forces may well be like those who die with their boots on. Note the colorful rendering of the NLT (1996): "A warrior still dressing for battle should not boast like a warrior who has already won."

12 Walsh, 299, appropriately remarks, "Ben-hadad has his battle plans laid all along and is simply waiting for a sufficient excuse to put them in action."

NOTES

1 For an interesting literary analysis of ch. 20, see Long, 405–16. F. M. Cross ("The Stele Dedicated to Melcarth by Ben-Hadad of Damascus," *BASOR* 205 [1972]: 36–42) postulates four kings named Ben-Hadad: I (885–870); II (870–842); III (845–842); and IV (806–770), the latter being the son of Hazael (841–806). For an evaluation and criticism of Cross's view and the whole problem, see W. Shea, "The Kings of the Melqart Stela," *Maarav* 1 (1979): 159–76. See further Note on 2 Kings 13:3.

A less satisfactory solution is offered by W. T. Pitard, "Arameans," in *Peoples of the Old Testament World*, ed. A. J. Hoerth, G. L. Mattingly, and E. M. Yamauchi (Grand Rapids: Baker, 1994), 217–20. See also his *A Historical Study of the Syrian City State from Earliest Times Until Its Fall to the Assyrians in 732 B.C.* (Winona Lake, Ind.: Eisenbrauns, 1987), 125–38.

3 Ben-Hadad's initial request is reminiscent of Xerxes' later demands for submission on the part of the Greeks by presenting the token demands of earth and water (Herodotus, *Persian Wars* 5.17ff., 73; 7.133, 174). The fact that Ahab willingly acquiesced to Ben-Hadad's initial demands indicates Israel's desperate condition.

10 Aquila's text of the LXX renders Ben-Hadad's boast even more dramatically by declaring that his soldiers would not find enough of the destroyed city to carry away the dust "by pinches." Another Greek variant suggests that there would not be enough dust left to make a foxhole. Wiseman, *1 & 2 Kings*, 176, notes similar usage of proverbs in diplomatic exchanges in the ancient Akkadian and Egyptian literature. For a scriptural example of psychological warfare, see 2 Kings 18:19–35.

ii. The Israelite triumph (20:13–34)

OVERVIEW

This section contains two distinct narratives. The first tells of the battle for Samaria (vv.13–25) and the second of the battle at Aphek (vv.26–34). The central characters in both accounts are the kings Ahab and Ben-Hadad together with their counselors.

The two battle reports proceed in quasiparallel fashion.

A Before the first battle, the Lord's prophet assures Ahab that the Lord will give him the victory and counsels him to attack the Aramean forces (vv.13–14).

  B Ahab musters his army while Ben-Hadad and his chiefs are getting drunk in their tents (vv.15–16).

    C The Israelite attack is successful; it inflicts heavy losses on the Arameans and puts the survivors to flight (vv.17–20a).

      D Ben-Hadad manages to escape while the Israelites are inflicting heavy losses on the enemy forces (vv.20b–21).

        E After the battle both kings receive advice from their counselors. The Lord's prophet warns Ahab that Ben-Hadad will return; Ben-Hadad's officers advise him to select a battle site in the plains where Israel's "mountain god" will be ineffective (22–25).

A' In the second battle, both kings muster their forces at Aphek (vv.26–27).

  B' Ahab is advised that the Lord will once more give him the victory (v.28).

    C' When the battle is joined the Israelites are again successful (vv.29–30a).

      D' Ben-Hadad manages to escape and hides in Aphek (v.30b).

        E' Ben-Hadad's officials advise him to seek Ahab's mercy—a strategy that proves more successful than they could have hoped (vv.31–34).

[13]Meanwhile a prophet came to Ahab king of Israel and announced, "This is what the
LORD says: 'Do you see this vast army? I will give it into your hand today, and then you will
know that I am the LORD.'"

[14]"But who will do this?" asked Ahab.

The prophet replied, "This is what the LORD says: 'The young officers of the provincial
commanders will do it.'"

"And who will start the battle?" he asked.

The prophet answered, "You will."

[15]So Ahab summoned the young officers of the provincial commanders, 232 men. Then
he assembled the rest of the Israelites, 7,000 in all. [16]They set out at noon while Ben-Hadad
and the 32 kings allied with him were in their tents getting drunk. [17]The young officers of
the provincial commanders went out first.

Now Ben-Hadad had dispatched scouts, who reported, "Men are advancing from
Samaria."

[18]He said, "If they have come out for peace, take them alive; if they have come out for
war, take them alive."

[19]The young officers of the provincial commanders marched out of the city with the
army behind them [20]and each one struck down his opponent. At that, the Arameans fled,

with the Israelites in pursuit. But Ben-Hadad king of Aram escaped on horseback with some of his horsemen. 21The king of Israel advanced and overpowered the horses and chariots and inflicted heavy losses on the Arameans.

22Afterward, the prophet came to the king of Israel and said, "Strengthen your position and see what must be done, because next spring the king of Aram will attack you again."

23Meanwhile, the officials of the king of Aram advised him, "Their gods are gods of the hills. That is why they were too strong for us. But if we fight them on the plains, surely we will be stronger than they. 24Do this: Remove all the kings from their commands and replace them with other officers. 25You must also raise an army like the one you lost — horse for horse and chariot for chariot — so we can fight Israel on the plains. Then surely we will be stronger than they." He agreed with them and acted accordingly.

26The next spring Ben-Hadad mustered the Arameans and went up to Aphek to fight against Israel. 27When the Israelites were also mustered and given provisions, they marched out to meet them. The Israelites camped opposite them like two small flocks of goats, while the Arameans covered the countryside.

28The man of God came up and told the king of Israel, "This is what the LORD says: 'Because the Arameans think the LORD is a god of the hills and not a god of the valleys, I will deliver this vast army into your hands, and you will know that I am the LORD.'"

29For seven days they camped opposite each other, and on the seventh day the battle was joined. The Israelites inflicted a hundred thousand casualties on the Aramean foot soldiers in one day. 30The rest of them escaped to the city of Aphek, where the wall collapsed on twenty-seven thousand of them. And Ben-Hadad fled to the city and hid in an inner room.

31His officials said to him, "Look, we have heard that the kings of the house of Israel are merciful. Let us go to the king of Israel with sackcloth around our waists and ropes around our heads. Perhaps he will spare your life."

32Wearing sackcloth around their waists and ropes around their heads, they went to the king of Israel and said, "Your servant Ben-Hadad says: 'Please let me live.'"

The king answered, "Is he still alive? He is my brother."

33The men took this as a good sign and were quick to pick up his word. "Yes, your brother Ben-Hadad!" they said.

"Go and get him," the king said. When Ben-Hadad came out, Ahab had him come up into his chariot.

34"I will return the cities my father took from your father," Ben-Hadad offered. "You may set up your own market areas in Damascus, as my father did in Samaria."

Ahab said, "On the basis of a treaty I will set you free." So he made a treaty with him, and let him go.

COMMENTARY

14–16 Both the personnel and the timing of the attack were unusual. Attacks were not ordinarily launched at noon. This tactic together with the sending out of 232 specially selected young men may have caught the Arameans completely off guard.

17–21 The battle strategy appears to have been to send out the small but well-trained advance party, who could perhaps draw near to the Syrians without arousing too much alarm, and then, at a given signal, initiate a charge. In conjunction with Ahab's main striking force, this process would both catch the drunken Arameans off guard and throw them into confusion. The plan was more successful than Ahab dared to imagine.

22 Late spring into early summer was one of two regular seasons for military expedition, when grass was readily available for the cattle.

23–31 For the second campaign the counselors advised Ben-Hadad to dispense with the calling of individual units that left him with an army of heterogeneous parts and to form an integrated whole that would comprise a disciplined fighting force.

Undisciplined, noncohesive units can easily quit fighting in the midst of the battle's heat (cf. Antony's difficulties in Greece in his fighting with Octavian) or get sidetracked by stopping for plunder (as did the army of Thutmose III before Megiddo).

32–34 Ahab and Ben-Hadad were apparently rearranging the terms of a previously existing treaty, perhaps enacted as a result of the action detailed in 15:18–20. Here, of course, the stipulations are somewhat reversed: the lost Israelite districts are restored and the trade concessions in Damascus previously held by Ben-Hadad in Samaria are granted to Ahab.

The reason for Ahab's leniency toward Ben-Hadad may lie in his appraisal of the troublesome political situation of those days. Already Shalmaneser III was on the move against the Aramean tribes. Ahab doubtless preferred to have a restored and friendly Ben-Hadad, with his ability to deliver a sizeable force of chariots and infantry between himself and Shalmaneser.

Indeed, the two allies, along with several other Aramean kings, were soon to face Shalmaneser head-on in the famous Battle of Qarqar (853 BC). In so doing Ahab was trusting in his own appraisal of his needs and the world situation rather than in God, who had given him the miraculous victory. In a touch of irony the author uses a form of the same verb (*šlḥ*) for the sending away of Ahab (NIV, "let him go") that was utilized previously of Ben-Hadad's sending of messengers to Ahab (vv.2, 5–7, 9–10).

NOTES

14–15 The נְעָרִים (*naʿ^{a}rîm*, "young officers") probably comprised a mobile unit of professional soldiers. Like the following term—שָׂרֵי הַמְּדִינוֹת (*śārê hamm^{e}dînôt*, "provincial commanders"; cf. Est 1:3)—it is a technical military designation. See further B. Cutler and J. MacDonald, "The Identification of the NAʿAR in the Ugaritic Texts," *UF* 8 (1976): 27–35.

31 For חֶסֶד (*ḥesed*, "merciful"), see Note on 3:6. While Ben-Hadad's counselors undoubtedly hoped for generosity from Ahab, Gray, 429, may be correct in suggesting that the Syrians were counting on the Israelites' known reputation for being covenant makers and keepers.

Just as the counsel given after the first battle (v.23) set the background for the second, so the successful counsel of Ben-Hadad's officials after the second campaign provides the backdrop for the prophetic condemnation of Ahab to follow (vv.35–43). The chapter thus displays fine structural and thematic unity.

32 The counselors' sackcloth was symbolic of mourning and penitence. The rope around the head was a sign of supplication, the figure being that of the porter at the wheel of the victor's chariot. Thus on his third campaign Sennacherib uses the figure of holding the yoke as a metaphor for vassalage in reporting conditions after his victory at Ashkelon (see *ANET*, 287).

33 The force of the verbal aspect of נָחַשׁ (*nāḥaś*, "take as a good sign") indicates that Ben-Hadad's embassy came looking for a favorable omen in Ahab's speech or attitude. Accordingly, Ahab's use of the term "my brother" (v.32) appeared to be an exceptionally good sign.

34 For details of similar treaty stipulations, see the vassal treaties of Matiʾilu of Arpad with the Assyrian king Ashurnirari V (*ANET*, 532–33) and with Bargaʾyah of *Ktk* (see *ANET*, 659–61). One may wonder whether in accordance with ancient precedent Ben-Hadad came and put his shoulder to Ahab's chariot, thereby giving a symbolic act of submission (see the Barrakab Inscription [*ANET*, 655]).

For details of Shalmaneser's campaigning against Aram and Israel, see M. Elat, "The Campaigns of Shalmaneser III against Aram and Israel," *IEJ* 25 (1975): 25–35. For the battle of Qarqar, see Hallo, 158–61.

iii. The prophet's rebuke (20:35–43)

OVERVIEW

Ahab's self-trust and his leniency toward Ben-Hadad were not to go without divine rebuke. God again raised up a prophet to deal with Ahab. While this incident has its own self-contained story line, it takes its setting from Ahab's failure to deal properly with his defeated foe Ben-Hadad. As the account unfolds, we learn that a prophet of the Lord asked one of the prophet's companions to smite the seer (v.35). Because the second prophet refused to obey the divine direction, he was immediately killed by a lion (v.36). The first prophet then got another man to strike him (v.37). Thus wounded, he waited in a disguise for Ahab (v.38). When the king passed by, the prophet represented himself as a soldier who had been wounded in battle and had been assigned a prisoner to guard on penalty of his life or the payment of a large sum of money (v.39). Unfortunately, he had inadvertently allowed his prisoner to escape (v.40a).

Merciless Ahab confirmed the death sentence (v.40b). At that point the prophet revealed himself to the king (v.41). The prophet's action had been symbolic. Ahab was that one who had allowed the prisoner to escape; therefore, as he himself had judged to be right, the king would pay with his life and Israel would suffer loss (v.42). It was a sullen and angry Ahab who returned in triumph from the battle to his palace in Samaria (v.43).

[35]By the word of the LORD one of the sons of the prophets said to his companion, "Strike me with your weapon," but the man refused.

[36]So the prophet said, "Because you have not obeyed the LORD, as soon as you leave me a lion will kill you." And after the man went away, a lion found him and killed him.

[37]The prophet found another man and said, "Strike me, please." So the man struck him and wounded him. [38]Then the prophet went and stood by the road waiting for the king. He disguised himself with his headband down over his eyes. [39]As the king passed by, the prophet called out to him, "Your servant went into the thick of the battle, and someone came to me with a captive and said, 'Guard this man. If he is missing, it will be your life for his life, or you must pay a talent of silver.' [40]While your servant was busy here and there, the man disappeared."

"That is your sentence," the king of Israel said. "You have pronounced it yourself."

[41]Then the prophet quickly removed the headband from his eyes, and the king of Israel recognized him as one of the prophets. [42]He said to the king, "This is what the LORD says: 'You have set free a man I had determined should die. Therefore it is your life for his life, your people for his people.'" [43]Sullen and angry, the king of Israel went to his palace in Samaria.

COMMENTARY

35 Although mention has been made previously of Obadiah's hiding of groups of fifty prophets (18:4), here is the first mention in Kings of "the sons of the prophets" (cf. 2Ki 2:3–7, 15; 4:1, 38; 5:22; 6:1; 9:1).

36–43 The principle of making payment or restitution for the loss of an entrusted item was already established in the law (cf. Ex 22:7–15). The silver payment, however, was an exorbitant one—one hundred times more than the price of a slave (Ex 21:32).

As a spoil of holy warfare in which God clearly had given the victory, Ben-Hadad should have been devoted to destruction (cf. Lev 27:29; Jos 6:17–21; 1Sa 15:7–10, 18–23). Like David before him (2Sa 12:1–10), Ahab has determined his own fate.

NOTES

43 סַר (*sar*, "sullen") comes from the root *sārar* ("be stubborn"; cf. Akkad. *sarāru*, "be unstable, obstinate"). It often portrays Israel, which, like Ahab, walked in its own stubborn way (cf. Ne 9:29; Ps 78:8; Isa 1:23; 65:2; Jer 5:23; 6:28; Zec 7:11).

The word translated by the NIV as "angry" (Heb. *zāʿēp*) may also be viewed as deriving from a second homographic root meaning "look pitiful/wretched." In either case, Ahab did not return to Samaria in the best of spirits! For details, see *NIDOTTE*, 1:1129–31.

d. Ahab and the conscription of Naboth's vineyard (21:1–29)

OVERVIEW

The narrative concerning Ahab's taking of Naboth's vineyard falls into two sections. The first is structured in chiastic symmetry.

A Ahab covets Naboth's vineyard. Unfortunately for the king, he fails in his attempt to buy it. He goes home "sullen and angry."

B When Jezebel finds Ahab pouting in his chamber and learns of the reason for it, she assures him that she will get the property for him (vv.4b–7).

C Jezebel conspires with city officials and leading citizens to denounce Naboth as a blasphemous traitor to the crown (vv.8–10).

C' The plot is duly carried out and results in Naboth's execution (vv.11–14).

B' Jezebel informs Ahab of Naboth's death and the availability of his vineyard (v.15).

A' Ahab takes possession of the property (v.16).

Moreover, as Walsh, 317, points out, the parallel series share common elements such as location (A and A'), dialogue between Ahab and Jezebel (B and B'), and characters (C and C'), thus tying the units more closely together.

The second section is developed in concentric symmetry.

A The Lord instructs Elijah to go to meet Ahab in Naboth's vineyard and denounce him for his deed (vv.17–19).

B Elijah does so and condemns both Ahab and Jezebel (vv.20–24).

C The account is interrupted by the narrator's own evaluation of the evils of the royal couple (vv.25–26).

B' Ahab reacts to Elijah's rebuke with apparently genuine contrition (v.27).

A' The Lord promises to postpone parts of the threatened judgment until the days of Ahab's son (vv.28–29).

Unity of plot is achieved by featuring the Lord himself in the first and last portions of this unit, and Elijah in the second and fourth. The narrator's denunciation of the royal couple is thus allowed to be of central importance. His evaluation adds cumulative evidence for the divine rebuke, while the whole episode has been chosen under inspiration to illustrate their corrupt character.

[1]Some time later there was an incident involving a vineyard belonging to Naboth the Jezreelite. The vineyard was in Jezreel, close to the palace of Ahab king of Samaria. [2]Ahab

said to Naboth, "Let me have your vineyard to use for a vegetable garden, since it is close to my palace. In exchange I will give you a better vineyard or, if you prefer, I will pay you whatever it is worth."

3But Naboth replied, "The LORD forbid that I should give you the inheritance of my fathers."

4So Ahab went home, sullen and angry because Naboth the Jezreelite had said, "I will not give you the inheritance of my fathers." He lay on his bed sulking and refused to eat.

5His wife Jezebel came in and asked him, "Why are you so sullen? Why won't you eat?"

6He answered her, "Because I said to Naboth the Jezreelite, 'Sell me your vineyard; or if you prefer, I will give you another vineyard in its place.' But he said, 'I will not give you my vineyard.'"

7Jezebel his wife said, "Is this how you act as king over Israel? Get up and eat! Cheer up. I'll get you the vineyard of Naboth the Jezreelite."

8So she wrote letters in Ahab's name, placed his seal on them, and sent them to the elders and nobles who lived in Naboth's city with him. 9In those letters she wrote:

"Proclaim a day of fasting and seat Naboth in a prominent place among the people. 10But seat two scoundrels opposite him and have them testify that he has cursed both God and the king. Then take him out and stone him to death."

11So the elders and nobles who lived in Naboth's city did as Jezebel directed in the letters she had written to them. 12They proclaimed a fast and seated Naboth in a prominent place among the people. 13Then two scoundrels came and sat opposite him and brought charges against Naboth before the people, saying, "Naboth has cursed both God and the king." So they took him outside the city and stoned him to death. 14Then they sent word to Jezebel: "Naboth has been stoned and is dead."

15As soon as Jezebel heard that Naboth had been stoned to death, she said to Ahab, "Get up and take possession of the vineyard of Naboth the Jezreelite that he refused to sell you. He is no longer alive, but dead." 16When Ahab heard that Naboth was dead, he got up and went down to take possession of Naboth's vineyard.

17Then the word of the LORD came to Elijah the Tishbite: 18"Go down to meet Ahab king of Israel, who rules in Samaria. He is now in Naboth's vineyard, where he has gone to take possession of it. 19Say to him, 'This is what the LORD says: Have you not murdered a man and seized his property?' Then say to him, 'This is what the LORD says: In the place where dogs licked up Naboth's blood, dogs will lick up your blood — yes, yours!'"

20Ahab said to Elijah, "So you have found me, my enemy!"

"I have found you," he answered, "because you have sold yourself to do evil in the eyes of the LORD. 21'I am going to bring disaster on you. I will consume your descendants and cut off from Ahab every last male in Israel — slave or free. 22I will make your house like that of Jeroboam son of Nebat and that of Baasha son of Ahijah, because you have provoked me to anger and have caused Israel to sin.'

[23]"And also concerning Jezebel the LORD says:'Dogs will devour Jezebel by the wall of Jezreel.'

[24]"Dogs will eat those belonging to Ahab who die in the city, and the birds of the air will feed on those who die in the country."

[25](There was never a man like Ahab, who sold himself to do evil in the eyes of the LORD, urged on by Jezebel his wife. [26]He behaved in the vilest manner by going after idols, like the Amorites the LORD drove out before Israel.)

[27]When Ahab heard these words, he tore his clothes, put on sackcloth and fasted. He lay in sackcloth and went around meekly.

[28]Then the word of the LORD came to Elijah the Tishbite: [29]"Have you noticed how Ahab has humbled himself before me? Because he has humbled himself, I will not bring this disaster in his day, but I will bring it on his house in the days of his son."

COMMENTARY

1–8 Just as Ahab had gone home "sullen and angry" in 20:43, so he goes home "sullen and angry"(same two Heb. words) after Naboth's refusal to sell his property. This circumstance may account for the placement of ch. 21 after ch. 20. Although land was considered as belonging to God and entrusted to people as tenants, Naboth's refusal indicates that the course of action proposed by Jezebel would be profane in the eyes of God, since it is expressly forbidden in the law (Lev 25:23–28; Nu 36:7–12).

9–13 On a given day the elders and nobles, who comprised a sort of local senate (cf. Dt 16:18), were to call an assembly for solemn fasting (v.9), as though the city had committed some great sin (cf. 1Sa 7:6) whose penalty needed averting (cf. Lev 4:13–21; Dt 21:1–9; 2Ch 20:2–4; Joel 1:14–15). Should the person who was the cause of God's judgment against the city be found out, he would be sorely punished (cf. Jos 7:16–26; 1Sa 14:40–45).

Naboth was to be given a conspicuous place so that the two accusers could easily single him out (v.10; cf. Nu 35:30; Dt 17:6; 19:15; cf. Mt 18:16; 26:60; 2Co 13:1). It may be that Naboth was an influential person anyway, so his prominent position at the meeting would not arouse suspicion.

The charge against Naboth was twofold: he had blasphemed both God and the king. The penalty for such action was death by stoning (Dt 13:10–11; 17:5) outside the city (Lev 24:14; Dt 22:24). Proper procedure called for at least two witnesses (Dt 17:6; 19:15). They were to lay their hands on the accused (Lev 24:14) and cast the first stones (cf. Jn 8:7). Since death by stoning was the responsibility of the whole community, the rest of the people were to take up the stoning.

14–24 According to 2 Kings 9:26, Naboth's sons were also put to death at the same time. Ahab used the pretext that since there was no male heir and because the crime was a capital offense, the crown could lay a claim against the property. Such confiscation was clearly against the spirit of the law (Dt 13:12–16; 17:17).

25–26 The narrator's evaluation reinforces the divine estimation of Ahab: Ahab was the vilest of all the Israelite kings. Completely under the domination of his wicked, pagan wife, he was unmatched in evil and spiritual harlotry in Israel. Thus the confiscation of Naboth's vineyard was very much in line with the character and record of the royal couple.

27–29 The rending of garments was a common expression of grief or terror in the face of great personal or national calamity (Ge 37:29, 34; 44:13; Nu 14:6; Jos 7:6; Jdg 11:35; 2Sa 1:2; 3:31; 2Ki 5:7–8; 11:14; 19:1; 22:11; Ezr 9:3; Est 4:1; Job 2:12). The Lord then mitigated his words of judgment against Ahab.

NOTES

1 The phrase "some time later" is omitted in the LXX, since it inverts chs. 20 and 21. הֵיכָל (*hêkāl*, "palace") first occurs here in Kings in this sense. Previously it was used of Solomon's temple (6:3, 5, 17, 33; 7:21, 50). Both meanings are allowable. The word is of Mesopotamian origin (see Overview to 6:1–38; see Sumerian É.GAL; Akkad. *êkallu*, "big house, palace"; cf. also Egyp. *pr-ʾꜥ*, "big house," and only later "Pharaoh"; see A. Gardiner, *Egyptian Grammar* [3rd ed.; London: Oxford Univ. Press, 1957], 75).

The title "king of Samaria" (cf. 2Ki 1:3) locates the base of power for the Omride dynasty.

7 The independent personal pronoun "you," in an emphatic position in the MT, probably indicates a touch of sarcasm: "*Are you not* the one who exercises kingship over Israel?"

8 Written by a royal scribe, an ancient letter was chiefly in the form of a scroll written in columns (occasionally on both sides) and sealed in clay or wax imprinted with the sender's personal sign. Many such seals have been found in the excavations of the Holy Land (cf. *TWOT*, 2:632–34).

10 The two witnesses are called literally "sons of Belial" (i.e., "sons of worthlessness"; cf. Pr 19:28). The term is used of utter reprobates (hence the NIV's "scoundrels"; cf. Jdg 19:22; 1Sa 10:27) and came to be applied by Jewish writers and the writers of the NT to Satan (cf. 2Co 6:15).

F. I. Andersen ("The Socio-Juridical Background of the Naboth Incident," *JBL* 85 [1966]: 46–55) suggests that the charge against Naboth was that he defaulted on his promise to sell his land to the king, a charge that would provide grounds for Ahab's seizure of Naboth's property in accordance with the legal codes of the ancient Near East. If, in addition, he had taken a formal oath in the presence of God and king as to his rightful ownership of the property or as to his refusal to sell, and he was convicted of wrongdoing, such blasphemous conduct would demand his death.

15 D. J. Wiseman ("Mesopotamian Gardens," *Anatolian Studies* 33 [1983]: 139) mentions royal confiscation of land in the case of a man found guilty and executed for treachery in ancient Syria.

19 R. Jamieson (R. Jamieson, A. R. Fausset, and D. Brown, *A Commentary, Critical and Explanatory, on the Old and New Testaments* [Hartford: Scranton, 1870], 2:365) points out that since dogs were allowed to run wild in packs in the ancient world, it was common to speak of giving the carcass of an enemy or a scoundrel to the dogs (cf. Ps 68:23 and Achilles' treatment of Hector in Homer's *Iliad*, Book 22). The fact that the prophecy was not literally fulfilled is conditioned by vv.27–29; the modified prophecy was fulfilled in Jehu's slaughter of Ahab's sons (2Ki 9:26) and in the licking of Ahab's blood by dogs at the pool in Samaria (1Ki 22:37–38).

23 The fact that 2 Kings 9:10, 36–37 uses the phrase "the plot of ground at Jezreel" need not mean that one must insert it here in v.23 as do the Vulgate, Syriac, Targum, and nine Hebrew MSS, which corrected v.23 in accordance with the later fulfillment statement in 2 Kings 9:36.

27–29 M. White ("Naboth's Vineyard and Jehu's Coup: The Legitimation of a Dynastic Extermination," *VT* 44 [1994]: 66–76) suggests that these verses provide the basic point to the whole narrative.

e. Ahab and the campaign for Ramoth Gilead (22:1–40)

OVERVIEW

With this chapter the narrator brings the account of Ahab's life to its close. Although a great deal of attention is devoted to the battle and its preparations, the underlying reason for it all is also divulged. Indeed, this battle is seen as merely the surface account of the deeper structure of Ahab's life and its termination. For this king, with whom God had been so patient and forgiving, the battle was God's means of bringing closure to one whose legacy was multiplied evil (cf. 16:30–34; 21:25–26).

Understood in this manner, the first forty verses of ch. 22 may be viewed as written in straightforward narrative: (1) Ahab's plans for occupying Ramoth Gilead (vv.1–6); (2) God's plans for Ahab's demise (vv.7–28); (3) Ahab's death at Ramoth Gilead (vv.29–38); and (4) closing notices concerning Ahab (vv.39–40). For convenience these verses will be considered in two parts: (1) preparations for Ramoth Gilead (vv.1–28), and (2) closing details concerning Ahab (vv.29–40).

i. Preparations for Ramoth Gilead (22:1–28)

1For three years there was no war between Aram and Israel. 2But in the third year Jehoshaphat king of Judah went down to see the king of Israel. 3The king of Israel had said
to his officials, "Don't you know that Ramoth Gilead belongs to us and yet we are doing
nothing to retake it from the king of Aram?"
4So he asked Jehoshaphat, "Will you go with me to fight against Ramoth Gilead?"
Jehoshaphat replied to the king of Israel, "I am as you are, my people as your people,
my horses as your horses." 5But Jehoshaphat also said to the king of Israel, "First seek the
counsel of the LORD."
6So the king of Israel brought together the prophets—about four hundred men—and
asked them, "Shall I go to war against Ramoth Gilead, or shall I refrain?"
"Go," they answered, "for the Lord will give it into the king's hand."
7But Jehoshaphat asked, "Is there not a prophet of the LORD here whom we can inquire of?"
8The king of Israel answered Jehoshaphat, "There is still one man through whom we
can inquire of the LORD, but I hate him because he never prophesies anything good about
me, but always bad. He is Micaiah son of Imlah."
"The king should not say that," Jehoshaphat replied.

9So the king of Israel called one of his officials and said, "Bring Micaiah son of Imlah at
once."
10Dressed in their royal robes, the king of Israel and Jehoshaphat king of Judah were sitting on their thrones at the threshing floor by the entrance of the gate of Samaria, with all
the prophets prophesying before them. 11Now Zedekiah son of Kenaanah had made iron
horns and he declared, "This is what the LORD says: 'With these you will gore the Arameans
until they are destroyed.'"
12All the other prophets were prophesying the same thing. "Attack Ramoth Gilead and
be victorious," they said, "for the LORD will give it into the king's hand."
13The messenger who had gone to summon Micaiah said to him, "Look, as one man the
other prophets are predicting success for the king. Let your word agree with theirs, and
speak favorably."
14But Micaiah said, "As surely as the LORD lives, I can tell him only what the LORD tells me."
15When he arrived, the king asked him, "Micaiah, shall we go to war against Ramoth
Gilead, or shall I refrain?"
"Attack and be victorious," he answered, "for the LORD will give it into the king's hand."
16The king said to him, "How many times must I make you swear to tell me nothing but
the truth in the name of the LORD?"
17Then Micaiah answered, "I saw all Israel scattered on the hills like sheep without a shepherd, and the LORD said, 'These people have no master. Let each one go home in peace.'"
18The king of Israel said to Jehoshaphat, "Didn't I tell you that he never prophesies anything good about me, but only bad?"
19Micaiah continued, "Therefore hear the word of the LORD: I saw the LORD sitting on his
throne with all the host of heaven standing around him on his right and on his left. 20And the
LORD said, 'Who will entice Ahab into attacking Ramoth Gilead and going to his death there?'
"One suggested this, and another that. 21Finally, a spirit came forward, stood before the
LORD and said, 'I will entice him.'
22"'By what means?' the LORD asked.
"'I will go out and be a lying spirit in the mouths of all his prophets,' he said.
"'You will succeed in enticing him,' said the LORD. 'Go and do it.'
23"So now the LORD has put a lying spirit in the mouths of all these prophets of yours.
The LORD has decreed disaster for you."
24Then Zedekiah son of Kenaanah went up and slapped Micaiah in the face. "Which way
did the spirit from the LORD go when he went from me to speak to you?" he asked.
25Micaiah replied, "You will find out on the day you go to hide in an inner room."
26The king of Israel then ordered, "Take Micaiah and send him back to Amon the ruler of
the city and to Joash the king's son 27and say, 'This is what the king says: Put this fellow in
prison and give him nothing but bread and water until I return safely.'"

[28]Micaiah declared, "If you ever return safely, the LORD has not spoken through me." Then he added, "Mark my words, all you people!"

COMMENTARY

1–4 Some three years after the last Syrian war (1Ki 20), probably late in the same year that the combined Aramean and Hebrew forces had withstood Shalmaneser III at Qarqar (853 BC), Ahab became concerned for the recovery of Ramoth Gilead to the east of the Jordan. Although the territory had been ceded over to Israel by Ben-Hadad in his submission to Ahab (cf. 15:20; 20:34), the affair with Assyria had probably kept the Israelites from reoccupying the territory. With the threat of hostilities somewhat relaxed, however, and with Ben-Hadad once again flexing his military muscle, the strategic importance of Ramoth Gilead, with its key fortress at the eastern end of the Plain of Jezreel barring access to the very heart of Israel, became all too apparent.

Having consulted his officials, Ahab sought the help of Jehoshaphat. Jehoshaphat's reply is a classic piece of idiomatic Hebrew: "Like me, like you; like my people, like your people; like my horses, like your horses." Thus Jehoshaphat puts himself and his forces, both infantry and chariots, at Ahab's disposal.

5–14 In keeping with ancient Near Eastern protocol, divine counsel was sought before battle (see Note on v.5). Jehoshaphat asked for the Lord's will in the matter. Ahab, however, called in his own prophets, who could be counted on to give the king his desired answer. Their initial reply appears somewhat vague in that Yahweh is not specifically mentioned, nor is the victorious king identified. The later speech of Zedekiah ben Kenaanah (v.11), however, makes it clear that the advice of Ahab's prophets intended that Israel's God would give Ahab the victory. Moreover, as the prophet Micaiah is summoned (v.9), much against Ahab's wishes (v.8), he is warned that his reply had better be in line with that of Zedekiah and the state prophets. Micaiah's reply reflects his true status as the Lord's prophet. He can repeat only what the Lord gives him.

15–23 Micaiah's two visions indicate that Israel will be defeated at Ramoth Gilead (v.17). The second reinforces the first with the added feature that God intends the battle to be the means by which Ahab will lose his life (vv.20–23).

The troublesome lying spirit that God sanctions here is best understood as a parabolic vision, indicating that God sovereignly will use the advice of Ahab's prophets to bring about the king's demise. Like several other instances in the OT, the ploy may be seen as a *ruse de guerre* (e.g., Jos 2:1–7; 8:1–28; Jdg 3:15–25; 5:24–27; 7:20; 2Ki 6:15–20; 7:6–7).

24–28 Micaiah's visions are met with two reactions, to each of which the prophet gives a reply. To Zedekiah's slapping of his face, Micaiah predicts that the false prophet will learn the truth when he is forced to hide on the day of invasion. This prophecy was probably fulfilled when Jehu seized the palace. To Ahab's sentencing of him to prison on minimum rations until the king should return, Micaiah replied that if Ahab returned at all, the Lord had not spoken through his prophet. Micaiah's reply amounts to a virtual announcement of the king's certain death.

NOTES

1 The exact location of Ramoth Gilead is debated, with at least three sites being strong possibilities. Famed as a key administrative center in the Solomonic era (1Ki 4:13), the city was lost to Israel when Ben-Hadad took it from Omri (cf. Josephus, *Ant.* 8.398–99 [15.3]). It was to figure greatly in the fall of the Omride dynasty (cf. 2Ki 9:1–15; 2Ch 22:2–6).

That Ahab's daughter was married to Jehoshaphat's son probably indicates that at least a loose alliance existed between the two kingdoms. By "horses" Jehoshaphat probably meant his war chariots (cf. Ex 15:19). The parallel account in 2 Chronicles 18:3 does not read these words but does give Jehoshaphat's promise to join Ahab in war.

2 Jehoshaphat's "going down" to see Ahab reflects the prominence of Jerusalem. Traditionally one "goes down" from or "comes up" to Jerusalem, which is situated high in the Judean hill country.

5 The kings of the ancient Near East commonly sought the will of their god(s) before entering into battle. See, for example, the Zakir Inscription (*ANET*, 655) and the Moabite Stone (*ANET*, 320–21). The Assyrian kings regularly consulted an oracle before battle (see the various annalistic reports in *ANET*, 274–301). For consulting the Lord before battle, see Judges 20:27–28; 1 Samuel 23:2–4; 30:8; 2 Samuel 5:19–25.

6 Cyrus Gordon (*The Ancient Near East* [3rd rev. ed.; Newcastle: Norton, 1965], 202) calls such false prophets "a variety of court flatterers."

9 סָרִיס (*sārîs*, "[court] official") comes from the Akkadian *ša rēšii* (*šarri*) ("the one of the [king's] head"). Its frequent translation by "eunuch" comes from the ancient practice of using such men in key positions in the court (cf. Est 2:3–15; 4:4–5; see further *TWOT*, 2:634–35).

10 Threshing floors were often used as places of important assemblies. At times the site also held spiritual significance (cf. Jdg 6:36–40). Thus Joseph mourned for Jacob at a threshing floor (Ge 50:10), and David built an altar and Solomon the temple at the famous threshing floor of Araunah (2Sa 24:18–25; 1Ch 21:15–22:1; 2Ch 3:1). In Canaanite tradition the threshing floor became the scene where court was held at a place near the city gate (see *ANET*, 144–45, 151, 153). Gordon, 381, compares the word to the Akkadian *maqrattu* found at Nuzu, which depicts a place where a court of justice was held.

11 For the image of the goring horn, see Daniel 8; Micah 4:13; Zechariah 1:18–19. Sennacherib, on his fifth campaign, reported that he led his men like a wild ox (see R. Borger, *Babylonisch-Assyrische Lesestücke* [Rome: Pontifical Biblical Institute, 1963], 3:47). Ashurbanipal reported that his enemies were gored by the goddess Ninlil's horns (see *ANET*, 300). Pharaoh could also be represented as a goring bull, as already on the Narmer Palette (see Seton Lloyd, *The Art of the Ancient Near East* [New York: Praeger, 1961], 32–33, ill. 14).

12–16 Ahab apparently sensed the sarcasm in Micaiah's voice. God's prophets were not above using sarcasm when the situation demanded it (e.g., 1Ki 18:27; cf. Job 12:1–2).

17 The motif of the shepherd and the sheep is a familiar one. God himself was shepherd to Israel, his flock (Isa 40:11; Jer 31:10; Eze 34:12; cf. Ge 48:15; 49:24; Pss 23:1; 80:1). Israel's leaders were charged with caring for the people as a shepherd watched over his flock (Nu 27:17). The later prophets were to address Israel's leaders as false shepherds (Jer 2:8; 10:21; 23; 25:32–38; Eze 34; Zec 10:2–3; 11:4–17). Ultimately the Messiah would be the great (Heb 13:20) and good shepherd, who lays down his life for his sheep (Zec 13:7; Jn 10:11–18; 1Pe 2:25). For the smitten shepherd and the scattered sheep, see Zechariah 13:7; Matthew 26:31; Mark 14:27.

19 For the use of trickery in the OT, see R. D. Patterson, "The Old Testament Use of an Archetype: The Trickster," *JETS* 42 (1999): 385–94.

That the angels do form a heavenly assemblage is stated elsewhere in the Scriptures (Job 1:6; 2:1; Pss 82:1; 89:6–7; 103:19–20; 148:1–2; Zec 6:5–8; cf. 1Ti 5:21; Heb 1:6; 12:22; Rev 5:11–12; 7:11–12; 14:10), though their doing so in no way need be construed that they meet to counsel God or to intercede for those on earth.

20 The "lying spirit" is, as Keil, 276–77, and Montgomery, 339, correctly maintain, the personified spirit of prophecy (cf. 1Sa 10:10–12; 19:23–24; Zec 13:2; 1Jn 4:6) that works in accordance with the sovereign will of God. That the prophets were under evil influence is true; but their delusive prophecies only fed the king's own self-destructive ends. The Lord used all these conditions to effect his will in the situation.

26 The "king's son" probably refers here to an important state official who was of royal blood. See A. F. Rainey, "The Prince and the Pauper," *UF* 7 (1975): 427–32.

ii. Closing details concerning Ahab (22:29–40)

OVERVIEW

These verses tell of the battle for Ramoth Gilead and Ahab's personal strategy for the battle (vv.29–31), Ahab's death in the battle (vv.32–36), and final notices concerning his death and accomplishments (vv.37–40). Through it all the reader is to remember that the exciting details concerning the flow of battle and the Israelite defeat are but the means for carrying out God's will with regard to Ahab.

[29]So the king of Israel and Jehoshaphat king of Judah went up to Ramoth Gilead. [30]The
king of Israel said to Jehoshaphat, "I will enter the battle in disguise, but you wear your
royal robes." So the king of Israel disguised himself and went into battle.
[31]Now the king of Aram had ordered his thirty-two chariot commanders, "Do not fight
with anyone, small or great, except the king of Israel." [32]When the chariot commanders
saw Jehoshaphat, they thought, "Surely this is the king of Israel." So they turned to attack
him, but when Jehoshaphat cried out, [33]the chariot commanders saw that he was not the
king of Israel and stopped pursuing him.
[34]But someone drew his bow at random and hit the king of Israel between the sections
of his armor. The king told his chariot driver, "Wheel around and get me out of the fighting. I've been wounded." [35]All day long the battle raged, and the king was propped up
in his chariot facing the Arameans. The blood from his wound ran onto the floor of the

chariot, and that evening he died. [36]As the sun was setting, a cry spread through the army:
"Every man to his town; everyone to his land!"
[37]So the king died and was brought to Samaria, and they buried him there. [38]They
washed the chariot at a pool in Samaria (where the prostitutes bathed), and the dogs
licked up his blood, as the word of the LORD had declared.
[39]As for the other events of Ahab's reign, including all he did, the palace he built and
inlaid with ivory, and the cities he fortified, are they not written in the book of the annals
of the kings of Israel? [40]Ahab rested with his fathers. And Ahaziah his son succeeded him
as king.

COMMENTARY

29–31 Two battle strategies are noted here. The king of Aram directed his men to seek out Ahab in the fray. Thus he would repay Ahab's leniency (cf. 1Ki 20:34, 42). Ahab, on his part, entered the battle disguised as a common soldier but told Jehoshaphat to wear his royal robes. Seeking out the enemy leader was a common battle tactic, for doing so could both disrupt the opposition's battle plans and demoralize its troops.

32–36 The Aramean king's plan nearly cost Jehoshaphat his life. Ahab's plan backfired when an Aramean bowman randomly shot him between one of the strips of armor, made with moveable joints that attached the solid breastplate to the lower armor. Although Ahab gave orders to his chariot driver to remove him from the raging battle, apparently the fighting was so intense that the driver could not dislodge the chariot from the fray. Whether or not the wound was a mortal one, Ahab bled to death in his chariot.

37–38 True to previous prophecy (1Ki 21:19), dogs lapped up Ahab's blood at a pool in Samaria where prostitutes bathed.

39–40 Ahab's palace (cf. Am 3:15), unearthed in the excavations at Samaria, could be described as an "ivory house" for two reasons: (1) the outside of the building was covered with a polished white limestone that would give an ivory-like appearance in the gleaming sun, and (2) many articles of ivory decorated the inside of the palace.

NOTES

29 The Chronicler (2Ch 19:1–3) reports that God's prophet denounced Jehoshaphat's involvement at Ramoth Gilead.

32 For אָמְרוּ (*ʾāmᵉrû*, "they thought"), see Note on 2 Kings 5:11.

34 Wiseman, *1 & 2 Kings*, 189, remarks, "Armour made up of linked small metal plate segments from this period has been found at Lachish and at Nuzi and Nimrud in Iraq ... the shot appears to have struck between the chain mail ... and the breastplate." The NIV follows the LXX here in translating "out of the fighting"; the MT reads "out of the camp."

38 The alternative reading of the NIV, "cleaned the weapons," depends on changing זֹנוֹת (*zōnôt*, "harlots") to זְיָנוֹת (z^e*yānôt*), from the Aramaic sense of "armor" (cf. KJV; Syr., "they cleaned his armor"). The reference to harlots is not without its point. That pool where Ahab's blood flowed may have been a sacred one erected for the lustration rites of the priestesses of the very cult Ahab and Jezebel introduced into Israel. Such "priestesses" are called by the sacred writer for what they were: "harlots." The LXX is emphatic: "The swine and the dogs licked up the blood and the harlots bathed in the blood."

4. The Reign of Jehoshaphat in the Southern Kingdom (22:41–50)

[41]Jehoshaphat son of Asa became king of Judah in the fourth year of Ahab king of
Israel. [42]Jehoshaphat was thirty-five years old when he became king, and he reigned
in Jerusalem twenty-five years. His mother's name was Azubah daughter of Shilhi. [43]In
everything he walked in the ways of his father Asa and did not stray from them; he did
what was right in the eyes of the LORD. The high places, however, were not removed, and
the people continued to offer sacrifices and burn incense there. [44]Jehoshaphat was also at
peace with the king of Israel.
[45]As for the other events of Jehoshaphat's reign, the things he achieved and his military
exploits, are they not written in the book of the annals of the kings of Judah? [46]He rid the
land of the rest of the male shrine prostitutes who remained there even after the reign of
his father Asa. [47]There was then no king in Edom; a deputy ruled.
[48]Now Jehoshaphat built a fleet of trading ships to go to Ophir for gold, but they never
set sail — they were wrecked at Ezion Geber. [49]At that time Ahaziah son of Ahab said to
Jehoshaphat, "Let my men sail with your men," but Jehoshaphat refused.
[50]Then Jehoshaphat rested with his fathers and was buried with them in the city of
David his father. And Jehoram his son succeeded him.

COMMENTARY

41–42 Jehoshaphat, who had ruled three years as coregent with his father, Asa, came into independent rule in the fourth year of Ahab of Israel (874–853 BC, i.e., 870 BC; v.41). His total reign was some twenty-five years (873–848 BC; v.42). The record of Jehoshaphat's reign is greatly abbreviated by the author of Kings; it contains only a short sketch of his lengthy reign, a brief evaluation of his spiritual condition and activities, and a few notices of international events before recording his death. A fuller discussion of the events of Jehoshaphat's reign can be found in 2 Chronicles 17:1–21:1.

43–46 Jehoshaphat's spiritual condition was basically sound and largely commended by God (v.43a; cf. 2Ch 17:3–4; 19:4–7; 20:3–13, 32). His concern for spiritual things (2Ch 17:7–9) manifested itself in religious and social reforms (v.46;

cf. 2Ch 17:6; 19:3–11). Accordingly, God blessed his reign (2Ch 17:1–6, 12–18:1) and gave him respite and respect from all the lands round about (v.44; 2Ch 17:10–11; 20:28–30). He did, however, stop short of a full purging of idolatry (v.43b; 2Ch 20:33); and the marriage of his son Jehoram to Athaliah, Ahab's daughter, was to bring about a tragic condition in Judah (2Ki 8:18–19; 11:1–3; 2Ch 21:6–7, 11).

Three other tragic areas are singled out in the divine record: (1) Jehoshaphat went with Ahab to the battle of Ramoth Gilead, despite Micaiah's warning (22:1–40; cf. 2Ch 18:28–19:3); (2) he subsequently entered into an ill-fated commercial venture with Ahaziah (vv.48–49; 2Ch 20:35–37); (3) still later, he went with Jehoram on his expedition into Transjordan (2Ki 3:6–27).

47–49 The historical notice in v.47 is probably intended to explain how it was that Jehoshaphat could have renewed commercial activities in Ezion Geber. The Edomite weakness may be attributable to Jehoshaphat's victory over the Transjordanian coalition, as detailed in 2 Chronicles 20. Jehoshaphat's commercial alliance with Ahaziah (v.48) was denounced by the Lord through his prophet Eliezer (2Ch 20:36–37). Because Ahaziah was an apostate, God sent a storm to destroy the fleet before it could set sail. Evidently Jehoshaphat was wise enough to refuse a second trading proposal put forward by Ahaziah (v.49).

50 The notice of Jehoshaphat's passing is amplified by the fact that his further life and history were recorded in the historical records of Jehu son of Hanani (cf. 2Ch 20:34).

NOTES

45 Jehoshaphat's exploits and military achievements included the strengthening of his border by establishing permanent garrison cities along the northern frontier (2Ch 17:1–2, 12), the training and equipping of a sizeable army (2Ch 17:14–19) that was able to quell a Transjordanian invasion (2Ch 20:1–30), and the placing of Edom under the power of Judah, which thereby controlled the important caravan route to the south (2Ki 3:8–27; 2Ch 20:36). His political successes inaugurated an era of peace and cooperation with Israel, with which Judah had been constantly at war (v.44; 2Ki 3; 2Ch 18:1–19:3). Jehoshaphat was also an able administrator who effected important judicial (2Ch 19:5–11) and religious reforms (2Ch 17:3–9).

46 For male shrine-prostitutes, see Note on 14:24.

47 Edom's continued dependence on Judah can be seen in the fact that it joined with Israel and Judah in their later expedition to Moab (2Ki 3:9–27).

48–49 The phrase "trading ships" can also be translated "ships of Tarshish" (cf. NIV note; see comment on 10:22). The original location of Tarshish has not been established with absolute certainty. Some have linked it with Tartessus in Spain (BDB, 1076) or with Numidian Africa (Young, 1:128). The inscriptions of Esarhaddon of Assyria (681–668 BC) equate Tarshish with a Phoenician land at the western end of the Mediterranean Sea (cf. Jnh 1:3), and an inscription from Nora on Sardinia links that Phoenician trading center with Tarshish (see Unger, 225–26). Isaiah 23:1 perhaps connects Tarshish with Greek maritime activity (cf. Ge 10:4; Isa 66:19). W. F. Albright ("New Light on the Early History of Phoenician Colonization," *BASOR* 83 [1941]: 21) points out the relation of Tarshish with Akkadian *taršišu* ("smelting plant, refinery") and suggests that Jehoshaphat's ships of Tarshish were a refinery fleet that transported smelted ore.

While Tarshish apparently lay in the western Mediterranean, possibly on Sardinia, it could be reached via Ezion Geber (10:22; 2Ch 20:36). Accordingly, Cyrus Gordon (*Before Columbus* [New York: Crown, 1971], 113–14, 136–37) boldly suggests an Atlantic port, possibly even a new world site, such as Mexico!

Not only metal ores, but also various precious and exotic commodities are tied in with Tarshish fleets (e.g., gold, silver, iron, tin, lead, ivory products, and peacocks; cf. 10:22; 2Ch 9:21; Jer 10:9; Eze 27:12). The trade in these luxury items from distant lands may have transferred the original significance into a general term for a distant and exotic land reached by "Tarshish ships."

5. The Reign of Ahaziah in the Northern Kingdom (1Ki 22:51–2Ki 1:18)

OVERVIEW

The short account of Ahaziah of Israel's kingship is structured in chiastic symmetry:

- A Notice of accession (1Ki 22:51–53)
  - B Ahaziah falls and then sends messengers to Ekron (2Ki 1:1–2).
    - C An angel instructs Elijah to meet the messengers (vv.3–4).
      - D The messengers report back to Ahaziah (vv.5–8).
      - D' Ahaziah thrice sends soldiers to bring Elijah to Samaria (vv.9–14).
    - C' An angel instructs Elijah to accompany the third contingent of soldiers with God's message (vv.15–16).
  - B' Ahaziah dies as a result of his fall (v.17).
- A' Closing notice (v.18)

Thus this section focuses not so much on Ahaziah's reign but on God. At issue is God's position in the royal house of the northern kingdom. Elijah's amazing power should have been enough to convince all concerned as to who truly is God—Yahweh or Baal.

[51]Ahaziah son of Ahab became king of Israel in Samaria in the seventeenth year of
Jehoshaphat king of Judah, and he reigned over Israel two years. [52]He did evil in the eyes
of the LORD, because he walked in the ways of his father and mother and in the ways of
Jeroboam son of Nebat, who caused Israel to sin. [53]He served and worshiped Baal and
provoked the LORD, the God of Israel, to anger, just as his father had done.
[2Ki 1:1]After Ahab's death, Moab rebelled against Israel. [2]Now Ahaziah had fallen through
the lattice of his upper room in Samaria and injured himself. So he sent messengers, saying to them, "Go and consult Baal-Zebub, the god of Ekron, to see if I will recover from this injury."

[3]But the angel of the LORD said to Elijah the Tishbite, "Go up and meet the messengers of the king of Samaria and ask them, 'Is it because there is no God in Israel that you are going off to consult Baal-Zebub, the god of Ekron?' [4]Therefore this is what the LORD says: 'You will not leave the bed you are lying on. You will certainly die!'" So Elijah went.

[5]When the messengers returned to the king, he asked them, "Why have you come back?"

[6]"A man came to meet us," they replied. "And he said to us, 'Go back to the king who sent you and tell him, "This is what the LORD says: Is it because there is no God in Israel that you are sending men to consult Baal-Zebub, the god of Ekron? Therefore you will not leave the bed you are lying on. You will certainly die!"'"

[7]The king asked them, "What kind of man was it who came to meet you and told you this?"

[8]They replied, "He was a man with a garment of hair and with a leather belt around his waist."

The king said, "That was Elijah the Tishbite."

[9]Then he sent to Elijah a captain with his company of fifty men. The captain went up to Elijah, who was sitting on the top of a hill, and said to him, "Man of God, the king says, 'Come down!'"

[10]Elijah answered the captain, "If I am a man of God, may fire come down from heaven and consume you and your fifty men!" Then fire fell from heaven and consumed the captain and his men.

[11]At this the king sent to Elijah another captain with his fifty men. The captain said to him, "Man of God, this is what the king says, 'Come down at once!'"

[12]"If I am a man of God," Elijah replied, "may fire come down from heaven and consume you and your fifty men!" Then the fire of God fell from heaven and consumed him and his fifty men.

[13]So the king sent a third captain with his fifty men. This third captain went up and fell on his knees before Elijah. "Man of God," he begged, "please have respect for my life and the lives of these fifty men, your servants! [14]See, fire has fallen from heaven and consumed the first two captains and all their men. But now have respect for my life!"

[15]The angel of the LORD said to Elijah, "Go down with him; do not be afraid of him." So Elijah got up and went down with him to the king.

[16]He told the king, "This is what the LORD says: Is it because there is no God in Israel for you to consult that you have sent messengers to consult Baal-Zebub, the god of Ekron? Because you have done this, you will never leave the bed you are lying on. You will certainly die!" [17]So he died, according to the word of the LORD that Elijah had spoken.

Because Ahaziah had no son, Joram succeeded him as king in the second year of Jehoram son of Jehoshaphat king of Judah. [18]As for all the other events of Ahaziah's reign, and what he did, are they not written in the book of the annals of the kings of Israel?

COMMENTARY

1–2 Ahab's son Ahaziah (853–852 BC), who perpetuated his father's wickedness, incurred God's judicial anger (1Ki 22:51–53). The divine judgment took numerous forms:

1. Politically, Moab found in the death of Ahab occasion to rebel against Israel (v.1).
2. Economically, God thwarted Ahaziah's attempted commercial enterprise with Jehoshaphat (1Ki 22:47–48; 2Ch 20:36–37).
3. Personally, the circumstances of Ahaziah's life were allowed to proceed in such a way that Israel's new king suffered a seriously injurious fall through the latticework of the upper chamber to the courtyard below (2Ki 1:2).

Ahaziah was aware of the seriousness of his physical condition. In such circumstances a person's basic spiritual temperament will often surface. Immersed in the Baalism of his father, Ahaziah sent messengers to inquire of the oracle at Ekron whether he would recover from his injuries (v.2). The question naturally arises as to why Ahaziah should send away to foreign soil to inquire of Baal, since Baalism permeated the Israelite kingdom. The answer may be threefold.

1. Politically, the young king may well have had his political rivals and enemies, as was so often true in Israel and the ancient Near East.
2. Religiously, Baal seems to have been particularly the cult god of Ekron (e.g., as opposed to Dagon at Ashdod). Moreover, the Philistines and possibly the Baal of Ekron had a well-known reputation for divination and soothsaying (1Sa 6:2; Isa 2:6).
3. Geographically, Ekron, being located just a few miles from the confluence of Israel's southwestern border with Judah and Philistia, lay near at hand.

3–4 Previously, angels have played an important role in Elijah's ministry (cf. 1Ki 19:5, 7); as then, so now (cf. vv.15–16) an angel twice deals with Elijah. The term "the angel of the LORD" occurs in Kings only in this setting (cf. v.15) and in 1 Kings 19:7 and 2 Kings 19:35. In none of these cases does the term appear to refer to a Christophany. Both here and in 1 Kings 19 (note esp. v.5), the angel in question is Yahweh's messenger (angel) in contradistinction to that of the wicked royalty. In 2 Kings 19:35 God's death angel is in view.

The title "king of Samaria" reflects a frequent biblical custom of designating a king by his capital city (cf. 1Ki 21:1; Jnh 3:6) and is by no means a mark of a late editor, as is often charged. Prophetic use of sarcasm has already been seen in Elijah's mocking of Baal (1Ki 18:27) and Micaiah's parroting of the false prophets' words to Ahab (see Note on 1Ki 22:15–16).

5–8 The fearful appearance and awful message caused the messengers to return instantly to the king (v.5), where they reported to Ahaziah the whole episode (v.6). The king recognized at once that the stern rebuke was from none other than Elijah the Tishbite (v.8). The secret mission and hidden desires of the royal chambers were not unknown to the true King of the universe. Did Ahaziah understand this truth? If so, the scriptural record contains no hint that Ahaziah repented in the least; rather, all that follows speaks of an obdurate and sinful heart.

9–14 In contrast to the arrogance of the first two commanders of fifty soldiers—an insolence that brought them and their men instant divine judgment—the third commander approached Elijah with respect. With tact he asked God's prophet to accompany them to Samaria. No indication exists that Elijah acted out of personal vindictiveness or vengeance; rather, the arrogance of the first two officers was as much directed toward God as Elijah. For as God's authoritative prophet, Elijah was defending the sacred reputation of God and the authority of his word. Once again fire symbolized the awesome presence of God (cf. 1Ki 18:38).

Threefold repetition is a favorite authorial device in Kings, which has used it a number of times previously (1Ki 18:33–35; 20:2–11; cf. also 11:9–13).

15–18 The account closes with elements found near its beginning. Once again an angel gives directions to God's prophet. As a final note the narrator reports that Ahaziah's fall ended in his death. His demise, however, was due as much to his stubborn disbelief and settled wickedness as the fall itself. Ahaziah's brother succeeded the childless king in what was the second year of the reign of Jehoshaphat's son, also named Jehoram (852 BC), of the southern kingdom (v.17).

NOTES

1:1 The notice concerning the Moabite rebellion provides the historical framework for events after the passing of Ahab. The author will return to the Moabite problem again in ch. 3.

2 On the upper room see Note on 9:30. The typical Syrian upper balcony was enclosed with a jointed wooden latticework that, while suitable for privacy, could easily be broken. For legislation concerning protective parapets to minimize the danger of someone's falling from domestic houses, see Deuteronomy 22:8.

The exact name and distinct nature of בַּעַל זְבוּב (*ba^cal z^ebûb*, "Baal Zebub"), the local god of Ekron, have been much discussed (cf. Mt 12:24). The more original cognate may be "Baal Zebul" ("Baal is prince"; see Note on 1Ki 16:31).

Although Hebrew scribes may have, with pejorative intent, deliberately perpetuated the inherent confusion in the names, so that "Baal Zebul" ("prince Baal") became "Baal Zebel" ("lord of dung") and "Baal Zebub" ("lord of flies"), here the present form "Baal Zebub," reflected fully in the Syrian and Vulgate traditions, may indicate a more originally positive designation. The existence in Ugaritic of the cognate term *il ḏbb* (*ANET*, 137) may, as J. J. M. Roberts (*The Earliest Semitic Pantheon* [Baltimore: Johns Hopkins Univ. Press, 1972], 119) suggests, make it "impossible to simply dismiss *zebub* as a vulgarization for *zebul*." Moreover, the uncertainties inherent in Ugaritic *ḏ* (see *UT*, 26–27) complicate the entire picture so that perhaps the original signification will never be known.

3 The Hebrew verb דָּרַשׁ (*dāraš*, "consult") is frequently used for consulting a deity. The particular construction employed here is often used when a false deity is involved (cf. 1Sa 28:7; 1Ch 10:13). This episode is the second of four instances in the books of Kings in which a dying king sends messengers to inquire as to his chances of recovery (cf. 1Ki 14:1–18; 2Ki 8:7–15; 20:1–11). This incident is unique in that the king does not send his messengers to Yahweh. Nevertheless, in all four cases the Lord's word proves effective: Jeroboam, Ahaziah, and Ben-Hadad all die; Hezekiah is healed as a result of his soul-searching pleading with God. See further R. Cohn, "Convention and Creativity in the Book of Kings: The Case of the Dying Monarch," *CBQ* 47 (1985): 603–16.

8 בַּעַל שֵׂעָר (*ba^cal śē^cār*, lit., "possessor of hair") has been understood in two ways: (1) "a hairy man" (so the ancient versions, KJV, NASB), and (2) "a garment of hair" (so the NIV, RSV, and the majority of modern commentators). Not only the syntax, which stresses the appearance of Elijah as one who wore a hairy garment girded at the waist with a leather belt, but also the prophetic garb itself (cf. Zec 13:4) and the typical role of Elijah ascribed to John the Baptist (Mt 3:4) favor the latter view.

9 The term "captain of fifty" indicates something of the organization of Israel's standing army (see further de Vaux, 214–28). The similar title occurs in the Akkadian *rab ḫamšû*. The hill on which Elijah sat has been identified by many as one of the peaks of the Carmel mountain range.

17 The chronological note with regard to Jehoram of Israel's ascending to the throne takes its point of departure as the second year of Jehoram of Judah insofar as Jehoram would rule Judah for the greater part of the time that Israel's Jehoram was ruling in the north.

	Israel	Judah
2 Kings 1:17	Jehoram's first year	= Jehoram's second year (cf. his coregency) = 852 BC
2 Kings 3:1	Jehoram's first year	= Jehoshaphat's eighteenth year (since his independent reign, which began in 870/869) = 852 BC
2 Kings 8:16	Jehoram's fifth year	= Jehoram's first year (of independent rule) = 848 BC

So Jehoram of the northern kingdom reigned 852–841 BC; Jehoram of the southern kingdom, 853 (coregent)/848 (full power)–841 BC; and Jehoshaphat, southern kingdom, 872 (coregent)/870/869 (full power)–848/847 BC. See further Archer, 204–5.

6. The Prophetic Ministry of Elisha in the Era of Jehoram of the Northern Kingdom (2:1–9:37)

OVERVIEW

At first sight this section appears to present a myriad of diverse details rather loosely related to one another only by the mention of Elisha in each chapter. Indeed, many scholars have decided that especially chs. 2–8 represent various stages of editorial collection. Conservatives have reacted to such suggestions in many ways—from ignoring the problem altogether to finding intricate subsurface thematic interconnections between the various portions. (See the excellent bibliography in Phillip E. Satterthwaite, "The Elisha Narratives and the Coherence of 2 Kings 2–8," *TynBul* 49 [1998]: 1–28.)

The study presented here keeps two basic tenets in focus: (1) Kings contains a great deal of material that is best termed "prophetic narrative," and (2) the ancients applied well-known methods of composition and compilation (see Introduction: Literary Form). The careful application of these principles provides a rationale for the canonical arrangement of the material in these chapters and their placement after ch. 1.

Thus ch. 2 provides a hinge to both the first and third chapters, for the Samaria mentioned in 1:1 is seen again at the conclusion of Elisha's journeying at the end of ch. 2. Likewise ch. 3 begins with the mention of Samaria and deals with the Moabite problem already noted in 1:1. Chapter 3 ends with the Israelite soldiers' (and Elisha's) returning to the northern kingdom. Accordingly, Elisha's early miracles in the northern kingdom are the subject of ch. 4. Moreover, various themes connect the miracles of ch. 4, such as the common theme of food (4:2–8, 38–41, 42–44), the concern of mothers for their families (4:1, 8–37), and terms such as the "sons of the prophets" (4:1, 38) and "[holy] man of God" (4:7, 9, 21–22, 25, 27, 40, 42). Further connections are noted in the Overview to ch. 4.

The section 5:1–8:6 details Elisha's further life-giving miracles during the Aramean crisis. We also learn more about Elisha's servant Gehazi, whom we first meet in ch. 4 (vv.27–31). He figures prominently in the dealings between Elisha and the Aramean commander Naaman and is present in the concluding episode of 8:1–6. Thus matters concerning Gehazi are placed strategically to form an inner inclusio.

Nor are connections between the various units of this section wanting. Elisha's instructions to Naaman to bathe in the Jordan River in ch. 5 provide a setting for Elisha's miracle at the Jordan in 6:1–7. The problem of the Aramean crisis detailed in 6:8–23 provides the background for the events that occur in 6:24–7:20. The famine of this latter unit in turn supplies the occasion for the account of the return of the Shunammite's land in 8:1–6. Thus matters concerning Aram, Samaria, and Elisha largely highlight the entire section.

In a brief interlude the narrator resumes his practice of tracing events in the kingdom parallel to the one under consideration (8:16–29). He then completes his treatment of the events of Elisha's ministry with a discussion of the prophet's part in the anointing of Jehu and Jehu's subsequent coup d'état (9:1–37).

Several other words and thematic associations are discernable in these chapters, but enough has been shown to demonstrate that the material in them is not haphazardly brought together. Indeed, they need to be accounted for in no other way than the careful forethought of the author/narrator.

a. Prelude: prophetic transition (2:1–25)

OVERVIEW

Chapter 2 sketches the prophetic succession from Elijah to Elisha. Central to the narrative is Elisha's witnessing of Elijah's translation to heaven (vv.9–12). The account is told in chiastic symmetry:

A Elijah and Elisha depart for Bethel (vv.1–2)
  B Elijah and Elisha at Bethel (vv.3–4)
    C Elijah and Elisha at Jericho (vv.5–6)
      D The sons of the prophets watch as Elijah and Elisha cross the Jordan (vv.7–8)
        E Elisha's request and the translation of Elijah (vv.9–12)
      D' The sons of the prophets watch as Elisha crosses the Jordan (vv.13–18)
    C' Elisha at Jericho (vv.19–22)
  B' Elisha at Bethel (vv.23–24)
A' Elisha departs from Bethel (v.25)

The overall pattern of the chapter thus displays the form of the journey from Bethel to and back from the Jordan River. It also contains strong elements of a quest motif, for Elisha is aware of Elijah's impending passing and is determined not only to be with him when it happens but also to receive Elijah's final blessing. He also desires empowerment as Elijah's successor. Having accomplished that goal, he retraces his steps and on the way performs miraculous deeds both in Jericho and Bethel. He then moves on to Samaria via Mount Carmel. The movement to Samaria provides the hook to the next narrative, which begins with the mention of Joram's becoming king in Samaria (3:1).

[1]When the LORD was about to take Elijah up to heaven in a whirlwind, Elijah and Elisha
were on their way from Gilgal. [2]Elijah said to Elisha, "Stay here; the LORD has sent me to
Bethel."
But Elisha said, "As surely as the LORD lives and as you live, I will not leave you." So they
went down to Bethel.
[3]The company of the prophets at Bethel came out to Elisha and asked, "Do you know
that the LORD is going to take your master from you today?"
"Yes, I know," Elisha replied, "but do not speak of it."
[4]Then Elijah said to him, "Stay here, Elisha; the LORD has sent me to Jericho."
And he replied, "As surely as the LORD lives and as you live, I will not leave you." So they
went to Jericho.
[5]The company of the prophets at Jericho went up to Elisha and asked him, "Do you
know that the LORD is going to take your master from you today?"
"Yes, I know," he replied, "but do not speak of it."
[6]Then Elijah said to him, "Stay here; the LORD has sent me to the Jordan."
And he replied, "As surely as the LORD lives and as you live, I will not leave you." So the
two of them walked on.
[7]Fifty men of the company of the prophets went and stood at a distance, facing the
place where Elijah and Elisha had stopped at the Jordan. [8]Elijah took his cloak, rolled it up
and struck the water with it. The water divided to the right and to the left, and the two of
them crossed over on dry ground.
[9]When they had crossed, Elijah said to Elisha, "Tell me, what can I do for you before I am
taken from you?"
"Let me inherit a double portion of your spirit," Elisha replied.
[10]"You have asked a difficult thing," Elijah said, "yet if you see me when I am taken from
you, it will be yours—otherwise not."
[11]As they were walking along and talking together, suddenly a chariot of fire and horses of
fire appeared and separated the two of them, and Elijah went up to heaven in a whirlwind.
[12]Elisha saw this and cried out, "My father! My father! The chariots and horsemen of Israel!"
And Elisha saw him no more. Then he took hold of his own clothes and tore them apart.

13He picked up the cloak that had fallen from Elijah and went back and stood on the
bank of the Jordan. 14Then he took the cloak that had fallen from him and struck the water
with it."Where now is the LORD, the God of Elijah?" he asked. When he struck the water, it
divided to the right and to the left, and he crossed over.
15The company of the prophets from Jericho, who were watching, said, "The spirit of
Elijah is resting on Elisha." And they went to meet him and bowed to the ground before
him. 16"Look," they said, "we your servants have fifty able men. Let them go and look for
your master. Perhaps the Spirit of the LORD has picked him up and set him down on some
mountain or in some valley."
"No," Elisha replied, "do not send them."
17But they persisted until he was too ashamed to refuse. So he said, "Send them."
And they sent fifty men, who searched for three days but did not find him. 18When they
returned to Elisha, who was staying in Jericho, he said to them, "Didn't I tell you not
to go?"
19The men of the city said to Elisha, "Look, our lord, this town is well situated, as you can
see, but the water is bad and the land is unproductive."
20"Bring me a new bowl," he said, "and put salt in it." So they brought it to him.
21Then he went out to the spring and threw the salt into it, saying, "This is what the LORD
says:'I have healed this water. Never again will it cause death or make the land unproductive.'" 22And the water has remained wholesome to this day, according to the word Elisha
had spoken.
23From there Elisha went up to Bethel. As he was walking along the road, some youths
came out of the town and jeered at him."Go on up, you baldhead!" they said."Go on up,
you baldhead!" 24He turned around, looked at them and called down a curse on them in
the name of the LORD. Then two bears came out of the woods and mauled forty-two of the
youths. 25And he went on to Mount Carmel and from there returned to Samaria.

COMMENTARY

1–6 On the journey from Gilgal to the Jordan River Elijah urges Elisha to remain behind on three different occasions. Three times Elisha refuses to leave his prophetic master. Once again, threefold repetition figures strongly in the telling of the story (see comments on 1:9–14). The phrase translated by the NIV as "stay here" is cast in a polite form. Rather than indicating that Elijah is prohibiting Elisha from accompanying him first to Bethel, then to Jericho, and then finally to the Jordan, it suggests that Elijah is testing Elisha as to whether he will remain with him to the end.

It would appear from the narrative that Elijah had disclosed to his various students that his ministry is nearing a close and that someday soon he will pass by for the last time. Elisha either knows from separate divine communication or strongly suspected that this day might be Elijah's last. Strongly desirous of God's will for his life and concerned to succeed Elijah as the Lord's prophet to Israel, Elisha is determined to be with his tutor until the end. It is instructive to note that even though Elijah knows this day will be his last on earth, his concern is that the Lord's work will continue after his passing; so he wants to assure himself of the progress of his "seminary students."

7 Fifty prophetical students are privileged to witness the great miracle of Elijah's translation into heaven and the passing of the prophet's mantle to Elisha. What a contrast these fifty spiritually concerned young men form with the squads of fifty that Ahaziah had recently sent to Elijah (cf. ch. 1)!

8 The young students behold a grand scene. The two great prophets, master and successor, stand on the banks of the Jordan. Taking his prophet's mantle and rolling it up rod-like—as did Moses of old at the Red Sea (cf. Ex 14:16–28)—Elijah smites the river. Immediately the waters to the north pile up in a heap, with the waters on the south continuing to run toward the Dead Sea. As happened so long ago, the waters of the Jordan again part; the two men pass through on dry ground (cf. Ex 14:21–22; 15:8; Jos 2:10; 3:14–17; 4:22–24; Ps 114:3–5).

But here they go in the opposite direction. Whereas Israel had crossed into Canaan to take possession of its God-appointed earthly heritage—and Elisha, too, must return there to the place of his appointment—Elijah passes out of Canaan through the boundary waters of the Jordan to his heavenly service, there to await a future earthly appearance (cf. Mal 4:5; Mt 17:4; Mk 9:5; Lk 9:33; Rev 11:6). In this regard his ministry anticipates that of his Messiah, who came incarnately to an earthly service (Jn 1:14) and subsequently, as resurrected Savior, ascended again into heaven, there to await his triumphant, glorious second advent (cf. Zec 14:3, 9; Mt 24:30; Ac 1:9–11; 1Ti 3:16; Rev 19:11–17).

9 When Elisha requested a double portion of Elijah's spirit, he may not have asked simply for the privilege of being Elijah's successor in terms of the Deuteronomic legislation concerning the eldest son's inheritance (Dt 21:17), for both he and Elijah knew that Elisha was to be Elijah's successor-heir (cf. 1Ki 19:16–21). Nor was the request simply to give some confirmatory sign to Elisha, for doing so would scarcely be "a difficult thing" (v.10). Rather, the enormity of the loss of Elijah must have so gripped the humble Elisha that, claiming his position as heir, he asked for the firstborn's "double portion"—that is, for specially granted spiritual power far beyond his own capabilities to meet the responsibilities of the awesome task that lay before him. He wished, virtually, that Elijah's mighty prowess might continue to live through him.

10 The request lay beyond Elijah's power to grant. Nonetheless Elijah told Elisha that if God chose to allow Elisha to see Elijah's translation, then (and only then) would the full force of Elisha's request be granted. The sign would indicate to Elisha that God, who alone could grant such a request (cf. Jn 3:34; 1Jn 3:24; 4:13), had in fact done so.

11–12 Elijah was taken up to heaven in the whirlwind, not in the chariot and horses of fire as so often taught. Nor is the account of Elijah's translation drawn from mythological sources (contra Jones, 385–86), such as those depicting a god moving across the sky (e.g., the Egyptian god Re).

13–15 Elijah's fallen mantle lay at Elisha's feet. The younger prophet had once had that mantle symbolically laid on his shoulders (1Ki 19:19); now it would rest there permanently. All he needed to do was to pick it up. Once again the presence of those who witnessed the entire spectacle is mentioned. What they had seen convinced them that the Spirit who once rested upon Elijah was now in control of Elisha's prophetic ministry.

16–18 The failure to locate Elijah gave assurance to the sons of the prophets that they truly had seen him go up into heaven and that Elijah's departure was permanent. Doubtless Elijah's reputation for disappearing and reappearing suddenly (cf. 1Ki 18:12) may have lain behind their concern. In any case, Elisha was surely now the acknowledged leading prophet in Israel.

19–22 Although Jericho had been rebuilt (with difficulty) in the days of Ahab (1Ki 16:34), it had remained unproductive. Apparently the water still lay under Joshua's curse (cf. Jos 6:26), so that both citizenry and land suffered greatly (v.19). Elisha's miracle fully removed the age-old judgment, thus allowing a new era to dawn on this area (vv.20–22). The use of a previously unused bowl (cf. Dt 21:3) of salt (cf. Nu 18:19) probably symbolized the Lord of the covenant's (cf. 2Ch 13:5) cleansing of the water and its permanent purity.

23–25 The public insult against Elisha was aimed ultimately at the God he represented. Elisha's prophetic ministry was in jeopardy; so the taunt had to be dwelt with decisively. With these two miracles Elisha's position as God's chief prophetic successor to Elijah was assured.

NOTES

1 The MT reads literally "in the whirlwind," probably emphasizing the well-known whirlwind by which Elijah was translated into heaven without dying.

2 Whether the Gilgal mentioned here is the city near Jericho or the Gilgal that lay north of Bethel is uncertain. If the narratives in 4:38–44 and 6:1–7 take place at the Gilgal near Jericho, perhaps that site is the location here also. Sadly, Gilgal and Bethel were to be condemned by prophets in the next century as centers of pagan idolatry (Hos 4:15; 9:15; 12:11; Am 4:4; 5:5).

The mention of fifty prophets from Jericho in v.7 does not, as F. W. Meyer (*Elijah and the Secret of His Power* [Chicago: Moody Press, 1976], 154) maintains, demand that the schools were always formed into groups of fifty young men (cf., e.g., 4:43); rather, the mention merely indicates that fifty of their number were present. Doubtless the three prophetic schools were in some way dependent on Elijah's leadership.

3 The Hebrew verb used here is also used of Enoch's translation (Ge 5:24).

9 The "double portion" has been widely discussed. The position taken here avoids the extremes of holding that nothing more than the right of succession is requested by Elisha (Montgomery) and the view that Elisha is asking for a double measure of Elijah's Holy Spirit (Luther), an idea often fortified by noting that Elisha performed "double" the miracles that Elijah had done (see e.g., J. P. Free, *Archaeology and Bible History* [Wheaton, Ill.: Scripture, 1962], 184–85).

Spiritual comparisons between Elijah and Christ are abundant. Certainly the desire of each to prepare his disciples adequately for events after his departure is most evident (cf. Lk 24:44–48; Jn 14–16; see also the apostles' concern for their readers [2Ti 4:18; 2Pe 1:12–15]).

11 Isaiah (Isa 66:15–16) utilizes the figure of fire and chariots like a whirlwind to depict God's coming in judicial anger against sinful humanity. Much of that imagery was probably drawn from texts portraying God as present in intense thunderstorms (e.g., Pss 18:9–15; 29:3–9).

12 Elisha's cry is one of tribute to Elijah. The translated prophet had been a spiritual father to Israel and as such, spiritually, her foremost defense. Elisha would doubtless be pleased at the same testimony given to him at his death (2Ki 13:14). The cry is one of personal sorrow and loss as well, as his rending of his clothes indicates (cf. Joel 2:13; see Note on 1Ki 21:27).

14 The LXX inserts before Elisha's question, "and it was not divided." The translators may have deduced that the waters remained undivided before Elisha's question and until the second mention of his striking of the waters.

20 For the use of salt in ritual purification, see Leviticus 2:13; Numbers 18:19; Ezekiel 43:24.

23 Baldness, regarded as a disgrace, was here an epithet of scorn (cf. Isa 3:17, 24).

24 Montgomery, 366, notes that bears were common enough in ancient Israel. The *Ursus Syriacus* was noted for its ferocity. The awfulness of the sentence has caused many to brand the account as incompatible with genuine piety. The youths' taunting "Go on up" was doubtless a mocking caricature of Elijah's own "going up" into heaven. The name and sacred reputation of God himself was at stake both in Elijah's translation and the reception of Elisha's prophetic ministry (cf. Dt 18:15). It should be pointed out that the Hebrew phrase translated "youth" (NIV) is best understood as young lads or young men. As W. C. Kaiser Jr. (*Hard Sayings of the Old Testament* [Downers Grove, Ill.: InterVarsity Press, 1988], 123) remarks, "From numerous examples where ages are specified in the Old Testament, we know that these were boys from twelve to thirty years old."

Accounts such as this one and the execution of the Canaanites, while difficult to understand from the purely human ethical standpoint, must be left ultimately to divine sovereignty and the justice of an all-righteous God, who does not act capriciously. Certainly in each case the vileness and corruption of the Canaanite religion and its danger to Israel are to be underscored.

That Elisha visits Mount Carmel (cf. 1Ki 18) and Samaria (cf. 2Ki 1) demonstrated further that he now is serving as Elijah's successor.

b. Theme: The ministry of Elisha (3:1–8:15)

i. The Moabite campaign (3:1–27)

OVERVIEW

With this chapter the ministry of Elisha reaches national proportions. For the narrator, both the reigns of Joram in the northern kingdom and the historical event of this chapter, the Moabite campaign, are opportunities to inform readers of Elisha's growing prowess and mighty deeds.

After the customary accession notice (vv.1–3), the chapter returns (cf. 1:1) to the subject of the Moabite rebellion by detailing Joram's reaction to it. The details of the campaign against Moab are given in straight narrative: (1) occasion of the campaign (vv.4–6); (2) preparations for the campaign (vv.7–9a); (3) the stalled campaign and the appeal to Elisha (vv.9b–15a); (4) Elisha's prophecy of victory (vv.15b–19); (5) the fulfillment of Elisha's prophecy in the campaign (vv.20–25); (6) the close of the campaign (vv.26–27).

[1]Joram son of Ahab became king of Israel in Samaria in the eighteenth year of
Jehoshaphat king of Judah, and he reigned twelve years. [2]He did evil in the eyes of the
LORD, but not as his father and mother had done. He got rid of the sacred stone of Baal that
his father had made. [3]Nevertheless he clung to the sins of Jeroboam son of Nebat, which
he had caused Israel to commit; he did not turn away from them.

[4]Now Mesha king of Moab raised sheep, and he had to supply the king of Israel with a
hundred thousand lambs and with the wool of a hundred thousand rams. [5]But after Ahab
died, the king of Moab rebelled against the king of Israel. [6]So at that time King Joram set
out from Samaria and mobilized all Israel. [7]He also sent this message to Jehoshaphat king
of Judah: "The king of Moab has rebelled against me. Will you go with me to fight against
Moab?"

"I will go with you," he replied. "I am as you are, my people as your people, my horses as your horses."

[8]"By what route shall we attack?" he asked.

"Through the Desert of Edom," he answered.

[9]So the king of Israel set out with the king of Judah and the king of Edom. After a
roundabout march of seven days, the army had no more water for themselves or for the
animals with them.

[10]"What!" exclaimed the king of Israel. "Has the LORD called us three kings together only
to hand us over to Moab?"

[11]But Jehoshaphat asked, "Is there no prophet of the LORD here, that we may inquire of
the LORD through him?"

An officer of the king of Israel answered, "Elisha son of Shaphat is here. He used to pour water on the hands of Elijah."

[12]Jehoshaphat said, "The word of the LORD is with him." So the king of Israel and Jehoshaphat and the king of Edom went down to him.

[13]Elisha said to the king of Israel, "What do we have to do with each other? Go to the
prophets of your father and the prophets of your mother."

"No," the king of Israel answered, "because it was the LORD who called us three kings together to hand us over to Moab."

[14]Elisha said, "As surely as the LORD Almighty lives, whom I serve, if I did not have respect
for the presence of Jehoshaphat king of Judah, I would not look at you or even notice
you. [15]But now bring me a harpist."

While the harpist was playing, the hand of the LORD came upon Elisha [16]and he said,
"This is what the LORD says: Make this valley full of ditches. [17]For this is what the LORD says:
You will see neither wind nor rain, yet this valley will be filled with water, and you, your
cattle and your other animals will drink. [18]This is an easy thing in the eyes of the LORD; he
will also hand Moab over to you. [19]You will overthrow every fortified city and every major

town. You will cut down every good tree, stop up all the springs, and ruin every good field
with stones."
[20]The next morning, about the time for offering the sacrifice, there it was—water flowing from the direction of Edom! And the land was filled with water.
[21]Now all the Moabites had heard that the kings had come to fight against them; so
every man, young and old, who could bear arms was called up and stationed on the
border. [22]When they got up early in the morning, the sun was shining on the water. To the
Moabites across the way, the water looked red—like blood. [23]"That's blood!" they said.
"Those kings must have fought and slaughtered each other. Now to the plunder, Moab!"
[24]But when the Moabites came to the camp of Israel, the Israelites rose up and fought
them until they fled. And the Israelites invaded the land and slaughtered the Moabites.
[25]They destroyed the towns, and each man threw a stone on every good field until it was
covered. They stopped up all the springs and cut down every good tree. Only Kir Hareseth
was left with its stones in place, but men armed with slings surrounded it and attacked it
as well.
[26]When the king of Moab saw that the battle had gone against him, he took with him
seven hundred swordsmen to break through to the king of Edom, but they failed. [27]Then
he took his firstborn son, who was to succeed him as king, and offered him as a sacrifice
on the city wall. The fury against Israel was great; they withdrew and returned to their
own land.

COMMENTARY

1–3 Joram's accession notice includes mention of his tearing down of the stele to Baal that Ahab had established. Although erection of this stele is not mentioned in the earlier records of Ahab's activities, Ahab's having done so would scarcely be out of character for the royal couple. The location of the stele is uncertain, but similar stones had existed since the days of Jeroboam I (1Ki 14:23) and were still in evidence at the time of the later purge of Jehu (2Ki 10:26–27). In addition, Joram is condemned for perpetuating Jeroboam's state religion and thus leading Israel into continued apostasy.

4–6 The narrator describes Moab's rebellion in terms of withholding the required annual tribute. These verses resume and flesh out the historical notice of 1:1. The discovery of the Moabite Stone of King Mesha brings the affairs of Israel's Omride dynasty into close relationship with Moab (cf. Note on 1Ki 16:21; see *ANET*, 320–21).

While the precise historical details and correspondences are difficult to trace, apparently Omri had defeated northern Moab (with southern Moab seeming to have remained free of Israelite domination; cf. 2Ch 20)—a subjugation that was to continue for some forty years, that is, throughout Omri's reign (885–874 BC) and those of Ahab (874–853 BC) and Ahaziah (853–852 BC), and also the first part of Jehoram's (852–841 BC). The domination of Moab would thus be by Omri and Ahab, with the insurrection against Israel occurring after the death of Ahab (1:1; 3:5) and partially through the reign of Omri's grandson J(eh)oram.

The Moabite Stone also tells of King Mesha's systematic victories, which enabled him to drive Israel out of his territory. Apparently his campaigning brought the entire northern portion of the country under his control, thus making any Israelite attempt to retaliate via the area east of Jericho extremely risky at best. In the face of the emergency, Joram mobilized "all Israel," which "probably included the local militia as well as the regular army" (Hobbs, 35).

7–9a Once again Jehoshaphat joins an Israelite king on a military mission (cf. 1Ki 22:1–40). No doubt because the launching of an attack on Moab's northern sector was dangerous, Jehoshaphat proposed a campaign route through Edom. The narrator mentions that the king of Edom also joined the venture. Because 1 Kings 22:47 relates that at this time there was no king in Edom, and 2 Kings 8:22 records that in the time of Jehoshaphat's son Jehoram "Edom rebelled against Judah and set up its own king," the Edomite "king" was apparently a client-ruler for Jehoshaphat; so a route through Judean-controlled Edom seemed the logical, though less direct, choice.

9b–15a When the lengthy trek proved to be so arduous and long that the water supply failed, Joram and Jehoshaphat became worried as to the outcome of the campaign. Having learned of Elisha's presence and something of his relation to Elijah, the two kings sought him out. Because Elisha knew of Jehoshaphat's concern for spiritual matters, he assured the kings that he would seek God's mind in the situation.

Elisha's call for a harpist probably indicates the need for creating a proper mood for receiving God's message in the midst of the prevailing turmoil and despair. Although 1 Samuel 10:5–6 is often put forward as setting a precedent for normal prophetic activity, such a precedent is scarcely demonstrable; for the "prophesying" there was assuredly in the sense of proclaiming and praising the person and work of God.

15b–19 The prophecy of an ample water supply was accompanied by the need for human response. The kings' men were to dig ditches; for though they would see no storm, yet the Lord would send water in abundance.

Likewise the word of the Lord included instructions for the proposed invasion. If carried out explicitly, victory would certainly follow.

20–25 God's miraculous sending of water fulfilled the first part of Elisha's prophecy to the kings. It accomplished more than expected, for the Moabites wrongly assumed from the red appearance of the water that the former antagonists had had a falling out that led them to mutual destruction (cf. similarly, 2Ch 20:22–23). Wiseman, *1 & 2 Kings*, 201, suggests that they misread the effect of "the red stone of the Wadi Hesa reflecting on the water."

To bring the reader to this point in the account the narrator steps back to note that the approach of the allies was not unknown to the Moabites. Accordingly, they had mobilized "every man, young and old, who could bear arms," and deployed them along the Wadi Ḥesa, which formed the border between Moab and Edom.

The Moabites' mistake turned the tide of war and led to the allied invasion of Moab itself. Moab was soundly defeated, with the allies effecting near total destruction on city and countryside in accordance with Elisha's prophecy. The allies failed to appropriate the full provisions of the prophecy, however, during the siege of Kir Hareseth.

27 The narrator reports that because of the Moabite king's sacrifice of his firstborn, "the fury against Israel was great." The precise meaning of this great fury is unclear. The same Hebrew phrase occurs elsewhere five times (Dt 29:28; Jer 21:5; 32:37; Zec 1:15; 7:12). In every case except Zechariah 1:15, the Lord's fury is against Israel for violating God's covenant. Here, however, it is Moab that has sinned. Perhaps the great fury wells up because Israel's assault has driven the Moabite king to desperate lengths. Some scholars have suggested that the fury is Israel's own, brought on by their disgust at the gruesome spectacle of human sacrifice.

NOTES

4 נֹקֵד (*nōqēd*, lit., "sheepmaster") is a term also applied to Amos (1:1). Gray, 484–85, suggests that since the term is also applied to one of the chief priests at Ugarit and is related to an Akkadian verbal cognate used in divination through animal livers, Mesha himself may have been a hepatoscopist. Although there can be no certainty in the matter, support for this view may arise from the reported "revelations" to Mesha and in the sacrifice of his own son to accomplish the deliverance of Moab.

7 Jehoshaphat remained a relative of Jehoram of Israel, for his son (and coregent), also named Jehoram, had married Athaliah, the daughter of Ahab (and perhaps Jezebel; see Note on 8:26) and hence a sister of Jehoram of Israel. Thus, Jehoram of Judah was a nephew by marriage of Jehoram of Israel.

9 The chronological relation of the campaigns of 2 Kings 3 and 2 Chronicles 20:1–29 is variously understood. If the events detailed in Chronicles took place prior to those in 2 Kings 3, the choice of a route through Edom is even more understandable. If as seems more likely, however, 2 Chronicles tells of a later invasion, the memory of the Judahite participation in the earlier invasion of Moab may have inspired a strengthened Moabite king to even the score. For the Kings–Chronicles relation, see M. J. Selman, *2 Chronicles* (TOTC; Downers Grove, Ill.: InterVarsity Press, 1994), 421–22.

12 Elisha's own reputation and past relationship with Elijah are evidently well known to Jehoshaphat. Whether Elisha was by divine direction traveling with the army, as diviner-prophets often did in the ancient Near East (cf. C. F. Jean, *Archives royales de Mari*, ed. A. Parrot and G. Dossin [Paris: Imprimerie Nationale, 1950ff.], 2, letter 22, lines 28–31), or simply was ministering in the area is uncertain.

13 The Hebrew idiom מַה לִּי וָלָךְ (*mâ-lî wālāk*, "What do we have to do with each other?") is commonly used to express emphatic denial (cf. 2Sa 16:10) or differences of opinion between the persons involved (cf. Jn 2:4).

15 Elisha's call for a minstrel has often been cited as evidence that Israel's prophets were ecstatics. But as Leon Wood (*The Holy Spirit in the Old Testament* [Grand Rapids: Zondervan, 1976], 118) points out, "It is more likely amid these calamitous circumstances Elisha simply wanted soothing music played so that he might be quieted before God and thus to be brought to a mood conducive for God to reveal to him his will."

16 Miraculous deeds and prophecies associated with the prophets often included instructions for human participation and response, perhaps as encouragement to faith (cf. 1Ki 17:13–16; 2Ki 2:20; 4:3–6; 5:10; 13:14–19; 20:7).

19 The wartime measures depicted here are severe and, in the case of the despoiling of the fruit trees, even beyond the normal limitations of battle (cf. Dt 20:19–20). The biblical indication of Moab's numerous fortified cities has been demonstrated to be accurate by archaeological investigations in the area. For conditions in ancient Moab, including Moab's numerous fortifications, see Nelson Glueck, "Explorations in Eastern Palestine," AASOR 18–19 (1939): esp. pp. 60-113; and AASOR 25–28 (1951): esp. pp. 371ff.

20 Flash flooding in otherwise dry wadis is common enough in arid portions of the world. Not only the timing of the heaven-sent waters, but also the total effect of their arrival bespeak the miraculous fulfillment of Elisha's prophetic message. Seemingly barren and harmless riverbeds can become perilous places for those unfortunate enough to become trapped there in torrential waters born from distant storm-soaked mountains.

21 The Moabite Stone mentions Mesha's campaigning on the southern border (lines 32–33). For text and translation of the inscription itself, see J. C. L. Gibson, *Textbook of Syrian Semitic Inscriptions* (Oxford: Clarendon, 1975), 1:71–83. For text and commentary see H. Donner and W. Röllig, *Kanaanäische und Aramäische Inschriften* (Wiesbaden: Otto Harrassowitz, 1964), 1:33; 2:168–79. For the suggestion that the term "House of David" occurs in line 31 of the inscription, see A. Lemaire, "'House of David' Restored in Moabite Inscription," *BAR* 20/3 (1994): 30–37.

23 That disaffection between allied kings can develop may be illustrated by the case of the Graeco-Egyptian campaign against the Persian holdings in Phoenicia in 360 BC (see A. H. Gardner, *Egypt of the Pharaohs* [Oxford: Clarendon, 1961], 376; Diodorus 15.90ff.).

26 Although the Hebrew may be understood as the king of Moab's attempting to "break through to" the Edomite lines (i.e., for support as a result of the Edomites' defecting to the Moabite forces), more than likely the meaning is "break out against" (i.e., because the Edomites offered the least amount of force). No evidence exists for the conjecture to read "Aram" for "Edom" and so see the Moabite king as attempting to make his way in safety to friendly Aramean territory.

27 The account of Mesha's sacrifice of his firstborn son is a case of Scripture providing supplementary information to details of secular history. Montgomery, 363, reports that Mesha's desperate action of human sacrifice is amply paralleled in the literature of the ancient Near East.

ii. Various miracles in the northern kingdom (4:1–44)

OVERVIEW

Chapter 4 continues the presentation of Elisha's ministry by narrating four miraculous deeds after his return from the Jordan. Although the narratives record separate incidents, they are bound together by many common threads. Thus the term "man of God" to refer to Elisha is found in all four stories (vv.7, 9, 21–22, 25, 27, 40, 42). Also in all four stories occur prophetic instruction (vv.3, 7, 29, 38, 41, 43) and a concern for food/sustenance (vv.2–8, 38, 42). Attention to servants is noted in the last three of the accounts (vv.12, 14, 16, 22, 24–25, 27, 29, 31, 38, 43).

Other threads stitching the sections together include: for the first and second units, "shut the door" (vv.4–5, 21, 33), "what to do?" (vv.2, 13), and a mother's concern for her family; for the first and third, "sons/company of the prophets" (vv.1, 38) and "pour out" (vv.4–5, 40–41). As noted below, the second narrative concerning Elisha and the Shunammite woman also displays close inner thematic parallelism and verbal repetition at the scenes of some subunits.

Together all these features argue for careful authorial composition and editing. For convenience the chapter will be considered in three segments: Elisha and the widow's oil (vv.1–7), Elisha and the lady of Shunem (vv.8–37), and Elisha and the supply of food (vv.38–44).

(a) Elisha and the widow's oil (4:1–7)

OVERVIEW

This story is told in a familiar format: (1) a widow goes to Elisha with a problem; (2) Elisha gives her instructions; (3) Elisha's instructions are carried out; and (4) the widow goes to Elisha, who provides the solution to her problem.

[1]The wife of a man from the company of the prophets cried out to Elisha, "Your servant
my husband is dead, and you know that he revered the LORD. But now his creditor is
coming to take my two boys as his slaves."
[2]Elisha replied to her, "How can I help you? Tell me, what do you have in your house?"
"Your servant has nothing there at all," she said, "except a little oil."
[3]Elisha said, "Go around and ask all your neighbors for empty jars. Don't ask for just a
few. [4]Then go inside and shut the door behind you and your sons. Pour oil into all the jars,
and as each is filled, put it to one side."
[5]She left him and afterward shut the door behind her and her sons. They brought the
jars to her and she kept pouring. [6]When all the jars were full, she said to her son, "Bring me
another one."
But he replied, "There is not a jar left." Then the oil stopped flowing.
[7]She went and told the man of God, and he said, "Go, sell the oil and pay your debts.
You and your sons can live on what is left."

COMMENTARY

1 A widow's indebtedness had brought about her creditor's insistence that her two children be taken as slaves to work off the debt. However inhumane this might seem, the creditor was within his rights, for Mosaic law allowed him to enslave the debtor and his children until the next Year of Jubilee to work off the debt (Ex 21:2–4; Lev 25:39; Ne 5:5; Isa 50:1; Am 2:6; 8:6; cf. Mt 18:25).

2–4 Once again the prophet's instructions involved human response and participation. Elisha's instructions meant that the quantity of oil would be limited only by the amount of empty jars she would be able to gather. The command to fill the jars behind closed doors prevented the miracle from becoming a mere spectacle. Hers was a private need privately met by a sovereign and loving God (cf. Mt 6:6). This incident is reminiscent of Elijah's helping the widow of Zarephath (1Ki 17:7–16).

5–6 The woman's response in faith was rewarded. The fact that Elisha would not be there when the miracle took place was intended to display the power of God alone and thus encourage the widow to still greater faith. Devout obedience can produce great spiritual blessing!

7 God's meeting of the needs of both the widow and Elisha is in keeping with his concern for the downtrodden of society, such as widows, orphans, and the poor (Dt 10:18–19; Ps 82:3–4; Isa 1:23; Jas 1:27).

NOTES

1 Josephus (*Ant.* 9.47 [4.2]) and some rabbis speculate that the widow's husband was the righteous Obadiah, who had aided the persecuted prophets during Ahab's reign (1Ki 18:4)—a work carried on by the widow herself after his demise, but to her financial ruin. Support for this suggestion has been found in the widow's plea that her husband, like Obadiah, was one who revered the Lord (cf. 1Ki 18:12).

2 The enslavement of family members in lieu of payment of debt was widely practiced in the ancient Near East (cf. Code of Hammurabi, par. 117, 119, 213).

7 For this motif, see my comments in "The Widow, the Orphan and the Poor," *BSac* 130 (1973): 223–34.

(b) Elisha and the lady of Shunem (4:8–37)

OVERVIEW

This narrative falls into two distinct but somewhat parallel sections. The first (vv.8–20) largely forms the setting for the miraculous deed in the second (vv.21–37). Each of these subunits in the first section is introduced by the phrase "one day" (vv.8, 11, 18). While the second section bears no such distinguishing mark, its three subunits greatly reflect those of the first section. The passage may be outlined in parallel sections as follows:

First section

A Preparation to receive Elisha (vv.8–10)
B Elisha and the woman (vv.11–17)
C Death of the son (vv.18–20)

Second section

A' Preparation for going to Elisha (vv.21–26)
B' The woman and Elisha (vv.27–30)
C' Revival of the son (vv.31–37)

[8]One day Elisha went to Shunem. And a well-to-do woman was there, who urged him
to stay for a meal. So whenever he came by, he stopped there to eat. [9]She said to her

husband, "I know that this man who often comes our way is a holy man of God. 10Let's
make a small room on the roof and put in it a bed and a table, a chair and a lamp for him.
Then he can stay there whenever he comes to us."

11One day when Elisha came, he went up to his room and lay down there. 12He said to
his servant Gehazi, "Call the Shunammite." So he called her, and she stood before him.
13Elisha said to him, "Tell her, 'You have gone to all this trouble for us. Now what can be
done for you? Can we speak on your behalf to the king or the commander of the army?'"

She replied, "I have a home among my own people."

14"What can be done for her?" Elisha asked.

Gehazi said, "Well, she has no son and her husband is old."

15Then Elisha said, "Call her." So he called her, and she stood in the doorway. 16"About
this time next year," Elisha said, "you will hold a son in your arms."

"No, my lord," she objected. "Don't mislead your servant, O man of God!"

17But the woman became pregnant, and the next year about that same time she gave
birth to a son, just as Elisha had told her.

18The child grew, and one day he went out to his father, who was with the reapers. 19"My
head! My head!" he said to his father.

His father told a servant, "Carry him to his mother." 20After the servant had lifted him up
and carried him to his mother, the boy sat on her lap until noon, and then he died. 21She
went up and laid him on the bed of the man of God, then shut the door and went out.

22She called her husband and said, "Please send me one of the servants and a donkey
so I can go to the man of God quickly and return."

23"Why go to him today?" he asked. "It's not the New Moon or the Sabbath."

"It's all right," she said.

24She saddled the donkey and said to her servant, "Lead on; don't slow down for me
unless I tell you." 25So she set out and came to the man of God at Mount Carmel.

When he saw her in the distance, the man of God said to his servant Gehazi, "Look!
There's the Shunammite! 26Run to meet her and ask her, 'Are you all right? Is your husband
all right? Is your child all right?'"

"Everything is all right," she said.

27When she reached the man of God at the mountain, she took hold of his feet. Gehazi
came over to push her away, but the man of God said, "Leave her alone! She is in bitter
distress, but the Lord has hidden it from me and has not told me why."

28"Did I ask you for a son, my lord?" she said. "Didn't I tell you, 'Don't raise my hopes'?"

29Elisha said to Gehazi, "Tuck your cloak into your belt, take my staff in your hand and
run. If you meet anyone, do not greet him, and if anyone greets you, do not answer. Lay my
staff on the boy's face."

30But the child's mother said, "As surely as the Lord lives and as you live, I will not leave
you." So he got up and followed her.

[31]Gehazi went on ahead and laid the staff on the boy's face, but there was no sound or response. So Gehazi went back to meet Elisha and told him, "The boy has not awakened."
[32]When Elisha reached the house, there was the boy lying dead on his couch. [33]He went in, shut the door on the two of them and prayed to the LORD. [34]Then he got on the bed and lay upon the boy, mouth to mouth, eyes to eyes, hands to hands. As he stretched himself out upon him, the boy's body grew warm. [35]Elisha turned away and walked back and forth in the room and then got on the bed and stretched out upon him once more. The boy sneezed seven times and opened his eyes.
[36]Elisha summoned Gehazi and said, "Call the Shunammite." And he did. When she came, he said, "Take your son." [37]She came in, fell at his feet and bowed to the ground. Then she took her son and went out.

COMMENTARY

8–10 Shunem lay seven kilometers north of Jezreel and thirty-two kilometers east of Mount Carmel. An ancient site, it is mentioned in the annals of the Egyptian pharaoh Thutmosis III (fifteenth century BC) and Shishak (tenth century BC), as well as in the Amarna letters.

The Shunammite woman is termed a "great woman." Her wealth and social prominence would necessitate no formal favors from the prophet. Being a pious woman, her concern for Elisha was purely spontaneous and bears the imprint of a genuine, godly sense of hospitality. The provision of a permanent room on the roof for Elisha "indicates something of the respect in which he was held by the woman" (Hobbs, 51).

11–17 A second "one day" takes the reader to Elisha's desire to repay the woman in some way. Unlike in his earlier question to the widow as to what help he could be (v.2), Elisha now speaks through Gehazi, as the prophet does throughout the early portions of the narrative (vv.11–13, 15, 25, 29), doubtless to avoid any semblance of impropriety.

18–20 The third "one day" reverses the anticipated joy of "holding a son" (cf. v.16) to the agony of witnessing the death of the promised son. The cause of the lad's death is generally considered to be sunstroke, although uncertainly so.

21–25a The "greatness" of the woman is shown in her decisive actions both in taking the child to Elisha's room and in her instant resolve to take the matter to the prophet who had promised a son to her. The woman's request to her husband for a servant to provide transportation so that she could go to Elisha elicits from him no reaction regarding the health of the sick lad. Some interpreters suggest that the husband appears less than concerned for his wife and sick boy; however, her reply, "It's all right," may hint at some anxiety in the tone of his voice.

His question as to why she would wish to see Elisha when it was neither the New Moon nor the Sabbath may point to the prophet's practice of receiving people on holy days, perhaps for worship or teaching. The husband may not have offered to accompany her because the day was undoubtedly a work day, not a holy day when he would be free to go.

25b–30 The Shunammite's reply is deliberately ambiguous. It may be taken as a polite greeting or simply as her resolve to deal with no one other than Elisha. The mother's deep bitterness of sorrow is shown in her pointed rhetorical question. She had not asked for a son; it was Elisha that had promised one to her. Was now her great gift from God to be snatched from her and so leave her in a worse state than before? It would have been better never to have had a son than to have such joy taken away so quickly!

Elisha's command to Gehazi to greet no one on the way underscores the urgency of the situation. His mission must not be slowed down with idle greetings or compromised with common business (cf. Lk 10:4).

Although the author of Kings assigns no reason for Elisha's instructions and actions, Elisha surely did not send Gehazi on a hopeless mission. Because he was young, Gehazi could cover the distance to Shunem quickly; and it was imperative that a representative of God arrive there as soon as possible. Very likely Gehazi's task was preparatory and symbolic of the imminent arrival of Elisha himself.

The woman's greatness and forcefulness are further revealed in her dealing with Elisha and his servant. She would entrust neither herself nor the final disposition of her son to Gehazi but rather stayed with Elisha until he could reach Shunem. Her faith and concern for her son's cure were totally centered in God's approved prophet. The woman's declaration must have struck a familiar chord for Elisha, for he himself had steadfastly thrice vowed to Elijah that he would not leave him, using the same words (2Ki 2:2, 4, 6).

33 The command to "shut the door" echoes Elisha's earlier instructions to the widow (v.4). In these two cases the prophet's miracle working was not for public display but intended to provide for individuals' needs and the increasing of their faith.

34 Although Elisha's attempt to revive the dead lad bears similarities to that of his teacher Elijah (cf. 1Ki 17:19–21), the two events show pronounced differences. While Elijah stretched himself over the boy, Elisha placed himself above him and matched eyes, mouth, and hands with those of the lad. Although Elijah's lad revived instantly, Elisha needed a second time to stretch himself out on the lad to effect the desired result.

37 Whereas the woman fell at Elisha's feet earlier in desperation and grief, she now does so in heartfelt gratitude and praise. Unlike her earlier exit from Elisha's room, when she left a dead son behind a closed door, she now takes him out with her, alive and well.

NOTES

12 Gehazi is called Elisha's נַעַר (*naʿar*, "lad, servant"). For the same word as a social/military term, see Note on 1 Kings 20:14–15. For the use of the word to connote special concern, see H. Bariligo, "The Case of the *neʿārin*," *Beth Mikra* 27 (1981–82): 151–80. Gehazi may be the unnamed chief attendant in v.43. The term שָׁרַת (*šārat*, "serve, attend") was used of Elisha's own relation to Elijah (1Ki 19:21). Later Gehazi referred to himself simply as Elisha's "servant" or "slave" (cf. 2Ki 5:25).

Gehazi is portrayed in a less-than-satisfactory light in several places in the narrative. His lack of solid spiritual fiber surfaces in ch. 5. Later Jewish tradition is strongly condemnatory of Gehazi.

27 For the grasping of the feet in humiliation and veneration, see Matthew 28:9.

29 Bronner, 105, suggests that placing Elisha's staff on the boy's body would prevent its premature burial. Perhaps the staff as the symbol of God-given prophetic power (cf. Ex 4:1–4; 17:8–13) signified Elisha's faith that God would stay further physical degeneration until he could come.

32–35 Elisha's faith was evidenced not only by his fervent prayer but also in his carrying out of known prophetic symbolism (cf. 1Ki 17:21; Ac 20:9–10; for NT raisings of the dead, see Mk 5:39–42; Lk 7:13–15; Jn 11:43–44; Ac 9:36–43).

(c) Elisha and the supplying of food (4:38–44)

OVERVIEW

The chapter closes with two incidents involving the supply of food. In the first (vv.38–41), Elisha gives instructions to prepare a stew for the sons of the prophets at Gilgal. As a consequence one student gathers fruit from a wild vine. When the fruit is suspected to be poisonous, the students' outcry brings Elisha's instructions to put some flour in the pot of stew. Upon doing so, the stew is now edible. The story moves in the familiar ABA' pattern, with Elisha's instructions bracketing the narrative (vv.38, 41).

The second incident involves the multiplication of some small loaves of freshly baked barley bread and some ears of new grain. Elisha's instruction to his servant to set this unexpected blessing before the gathered group is met with hesitation. Humanly speaking, the gift is insufficient to feed everyone (v.43); nevertheless, Elisha orders their distribution and tells his servant that there will surely be sufficient food for all—in fact, some of it will be left over. And so it comes to pass.

Both accounts are told in a manner typical of prophetic miracle working: background/setting (vv.38–39, 42); a problem arises (vv.40, 43a); the prophet's instructions are carried out and the problem is solved (vv.41, 43b–44).

38Elisha returned to Gilgal and there was a famine in that region. While the company of the prophets was meeting with him, he said to his servant, "Put on the large pot and cook some stew for these men."

39One of them went out into the fields to gather herbs and found a wild vine. He gathered some of its gourds and filled the fold of his cloak. When he returned, he cut them up into the pot of stew, though no one knew what they were.
40The stew was poured out for the men, but as they began to eat it, they cried out, "O man of God, there is death in the pot!" And they could not eat it.

41Elisha said, "Get some flour." He put it into the pot and said, "Serve it to the people to eat." And there was nothing harmful in the pot.

[42]A man came from Baal Shalishah, bringing the man of God twenty loaves of barley bread baked from the first ripe grain, along with some heads of new grain. "Give it to the people to eat," Elisha said.

[43]"How can I set this before a hundred men?" his servant asked.

But Elisha answered, "Give it to the people to eat. For this is what the LORD says: 'They will eat and have some left over.'" [44]Then he set it before them, and they ate and had some left over, according to the word of the LORD.

COMMENTARY

38–40 Elisha, as titular head of the prophets, duly acted as host at the communal meal. In this role he anticipated the divine Host, who so often freely and abundantly provided for his disciples (cf. Mt 15:29–39; Mk 14:12–25; Lk 24:28–31; Jn 6:1–13; 21:9–13; 1Co 11:23–25). Elisha's servant is not identified by name in this story or the next but is commonly assumed to be Gehazi in both.

41 As had been the case with Elijah his teacher, Elisha used flour to demonstrate the concern of God for people's daily provisions (cf. 1Ki 17:14–16).

42–43a The small loaves of fresh barley bread and ears of new grain were brought to Elisha as firstfruits. Normally these portions were reserved for God (Lev 23:20) and the Levitical priests (Nu 18:13; Dt 18:4–5). Because the religion in the northern kingdom was apostate, the owner of the portions brought them to someone (Elisha) whom he considered to be the true repository of godly religion in Israel.

43b–44 Elisha's faith lay in the living God for supplying ample food. The prophet's example applies today (cf. Mt 6:11). The multiplication of the loaves in accordance with the word of the Lord through his prophet anticipates the messianic ministry of the living Word himself (cf. Mt 14:16–20; 15:36–37; Jn 6:11–13). Like Elisha's servant, Jesus' followers could also show skepticism about the sufficiency of the food supply (Mt 14:17; 15:33; Jn 6:7–9).

NOTES

38 For the problem of the location of Gilgal, see Note on 2:2.

42 Baal Shalishah is probably to be identified with Khirbet al Marjamah in the Sharon Plain. Saul went there in search of his father's donkeys (1Sa 9:3–4). For the significance of Sharon, see my remarks in *NIDOTTE*, 4:1212–13.

43b–44 C. S. Lewis (*Miracles* [New York: MacMillan, 1953], 16–17) calls such cases "miracles of the old creation" involving "miracles of fertility"—that is, those in which humans see in extraordinary fashion that which God alone has produced customarily in nature. While far beyond human ability to accomplish, they are routine for the Lord of the impossible.

iii. The Aramean crisis (5:1–8:6)

(a) Elisha, Naaman, and Gehazi (5:1–27)

OVERVIEW

The telling of Elisha's miraculous deeds continues with the account of an Aramean army commander named Naaman, who was afflicted with a serious skin ailment. The story is told in straightforward narrative. (1) In the opening section Naaman learns, through his wife's servant (an Israelite maiden who had been taken captive in an earlier Aramean raid into Israelite territory), of the existence of a miracle-working Israelite prophet. Naaman, having received his king's permission, departs for Samaria carrying letters of transit to the king of Israel, as well as gifts for Elisha. When he arrives at Elisha's house, the prophet, rather than receiving him, sends him away to wash in the Jordan River. Naaman departs disappointed and angry.

(2) Upon considering the advice of one of his servants, Naaman decides to follow Elisha's instructions. On doing so he is healed and returns to the Israelite prophet to thank and reward him for the cure. When Elisha refuses any gift, Naaman leaves and takes with him some Israelite soil, apparently on which to kneel when worshiping the God of Israel (vv.13–19a).

(3) Elisha's servant Gehazi decides to gain for himself some of the gifts that Naaman was carrying. He goes to Naaman with a fabricated story of a sudden need that had arisen back at Elisha's house. Gehazi returns with the gifts and hides them (vv.19b–24).

(4) When Gehazi appears before his master Elisha, he is confronted with his misdeed. Elisha condemns him to being afflicted with Naaman's ailment (vv.25–27).

Thematic symmetry is achieved by focusing on the opening and closing sections dealing with the bothersome skin ailment, while the middle two portions revolve around the matter of whether gifts should be received for performing the Lord's service. Several of the other literary threads, which knit together the fabric of the account, will be noted in the commentary that follows.

[1]Now Naaman was commander of the army of the king of Aram. He was a great man
in the sight of his master and highly regarded, because through him the LORD had given
victory to Aram. He was a valiant soldier, but he had leprosy.
[2]Now bands from Aram had gone out and had taken captive a young girl from Israel,
and she served Naaman's wife. [3]She said to her mistress, "If only my master would see the
prophet who is in Samaria! He would cure him of his leprosy."
[4]Naaman went to his master and told him what the girl from Israel had said. [5]"By all
means, go," the king of Aram replied. "I will send a letter to the king of Israel." So Naaman
left, taking with him ten talents of silver, six thousand shekels of gold and ten sets of cloth-

ing. 6The letter that he took to the king of Israel read: "With this letter I am sending my
servant Naaman to you so that you may cure him of his leprosy."

7As soon as the king of Israel read the letter, he tore his robes and said, "Am I God? Can
I kill and bring back to life? Why does this fellow send someone to me to be cured of his
leprosy? See how he is trying to pick a quarrel with me!"

8When Elisha the man of God heard that the king of Israel had torn his robes, he sent
him this message: "Why have you torn your robes? Have the man come to me and he will
know that there is a prophet in Israel." 9So Naaman went with his horses and chariots
and stopped at the door of Elisha's house. 10Elisha sent a messenger to say to him, "Go,
wash yourself seven times in the Jordan, and your flesh will be restored and you will be
cleansed."

11But Naaman went away angry and said, "I thought that he would surely come out to
me and stand and call on the name of the LORD his God, wave his hand over the spot and
cure me of my leprosy. 12Are not Abana and Pharpar, the rivers of Damascus, better than
any of the waters of Israel? Couldn't I wash in them and be cleansed?" So he turned and
went off in a rage.

13Naaman's servants went to him and said, "My father, if the prophet had told you to
do some great thing, would you not have done it? How much more, then, when he tells
you, 'Wash and be cleansed'!" 14So he went down and dipped himself in the Jordan seven
times, as the man of God had told him, and his flesh was restored and became clean like
that of a young boy.

15Then Naaman and all his attendants went back to the man of God. He stood before
him and said, "Now I know that there is no God in all the world except in Israel. Please
accept now a gift from your servant."

16The prophet answered, "As surely as the LORD lives, whom I serve, I will not accept a
thing." And even though Naaman urged him, he refused.

17"If you will not," said Naaman, "please let me, your servant, be given as much earth as a
pair of mules can carry, for your servant will never again make burnt offerings and sacrifices to any other god but the LORD. 18But may the LORD forgive your servant for this one
thing: When my master enters the temple of Rimmon to bow down and he is leaning on
my arm and I bow there also — when I bow down in the temple of Rimmon, may the LORD
forgive your servant for this."

19"Go in peace," Elisha said.

After Naaman had traveled some distance, 20Gehazi, the servant of Elisha the man of
God, said to himself, "My master was too easy on Naaman, this Aramean, by not accepting
from him what he brought. As surely as the LORD lives, I will run after him and get something from him."

21So Gehazi hurried after Naaman. When Naaman saw him running toward him, he got
down from the chariot to meet him. "Is everything all right?" he asked.

[22]"Everything is all right," Gehazi answered. "My master sent me to say, 'Two young men
from the company of the prophets have just come to me from the hill country of Ephraim.
Please give them a talent of silver and two sets of clothing.'"
[23]"By all means, take two talents," said Naaman. He urged Gehazi to accept them, and
then tied up the two talents of silver in two bags, with two sets of clothing. He gave them
to two of his servants, and they carried them ahead of Gehazi. [24]When Gehazi came to the
hill, he took the things from the servants and put them away in the house. He sent the
men away and they left. [25]Then he went in and stood before his master Elisha.
"Where have you been, Gehazi?" Elisha asked.
"Your servant didn't go anywhere," Gehazi answered.
[26]But Elisha said to him, "Was not my spirit with you when the man got down from
his chariot to meet you? Is this the time to take money, or to accept clothes, olive groves,
vineyards, flocks, herds, or menservants and maidservants? [27]Naaman's leprosy will cling
to you and to your descendants forever." Then Gehazi went from Elisha's presence and he
was leprous, as white as snow.

COMMENTARY

1–2 The latter days of the reign of Israel's king Jehoram were marked by hostilities with the Aramean king Ben-Hadad II. Probably because of Israel's failure to participate in the continued Syro-Assyrian confrontation that marked most of the sixth decade of the ninth century BC, the Arameans continually chastened the northern kingdom with systematic raids (cf. 6:8), culminating in an all-out military excursion into Israel (cf. 6:24–7:20). Apparently during the course of one such raid, an Israelite maiden had fallen into the hands of Ben-Hadad's field marshall, Naaman.

3 Elisha was called by the internationally known term "prophet." But Elisha was more; he was the prophet par excellence of Israel. Samaria, as the chief and capital city, may denote Israel as such or may indicate that Elisha had a residence there (cf. 6:32).

4–6 Letters concerning medical courtesy and the giving of gifts in connection with the situation are attested in several ancient Near Eastern archives. Naaman's gifts, however, were exceptionally large.

7 Jehoram's reaction to what he considered a letter of provocation is reminiscent of the comments between the Hyksos king Apophis and the Egyptian pharaoh Seqnen-Re at Thebes (*ANET*, 231–32). For a biblical example, see 1 Kings 20:1–11; cf. 2 Kings 14:8–10.

8–9 Elisha may have still been at Gilgal when news reached him of the king's consternation (so Hobbs, 64). A Gilgal location would fit well with Elisha's instructions to Naaman to bathe in the Jordan River. It would also explain the canonical placement of ch. 5 after ch. 4, which closed with Elisha at Gilgal, and before 6:1–7, which again places Elisha at the Jordan. If so, the maid's remark (v.3) may point to Elisha's normal home in Samaria.

10 Elisha's instructions to Naaman reflect the general procedure for healing leprosy (Lev 14:7–9), although the specific details are different.

The command for Naaman to bathe seven times in the Jordan River may approximate the sevenfold sprinkling administered by the priest. The number seven occurs frequently in the regulations in Leviticus 13–14, probably symbolizing the wholeness and completeness of the healing process.

11–12 Naaman expected to be received with respect and that some distinctive act of healing would be performed, rather than his being sent to an Israelite river. After all, the great rivers of Damascus were available back home. The Abana is usually idenified with the modern Barada River, which originates in the Anti-Lebanon mountains. The Pharphar is uncertain though often identified with the ᶜAwaj, south of Damascus.

15–16 Naaman could in no sense be allowed to think that God's favor was to be purchased or that the prophet served God only for the desire of personal gain. Indeed Elisha was responsible to a higher authority. The narrator captures the force of Elisha's commitment by a play on the word for "standing." While Naaman stood before Elisha (v.15), Elisha stood before Yahweh (v.16; so KJV, NKJV, NASB; cf. NIV's "whom I serve").

Moreover, a soul for whom God was concerned was at stake. God's blessing had been designed for Naaman's response in repentance and faith (cf. Ro 2:4), Gentile though he was (cf. Lk 4:27).

17–18 The narrator reports without approval or condemnation Naaman's request for two loads of dirt to be carried back home. This report may indicate that although Naaman's public duties as the king's "right-hand man" might cause him to bow down to the state god, he wanted to build a personal altar to Yahweh.

20–21 The story next focuses on Gehazi, who saw an opportunity to gain some of the proffered commodities for himself (v.20). Slipping away stealthily, he overtook the Syrian general (v.21). What a contrast can be seen in the meeting between Naaman and Gehazi! Naaman's descent from his chariot to meet Elisha's servant is a mark of his being a changed man. No longer a proud, arrogant person (vv.9–12), the grateful (v.15), reverent (v.17), and humble (v.18) Aramean came down from his honored place to meet a prophet's servant. He who had been a fallen, hopeless sinner displayed the true believer's grace. Contrariwise Gehazi, who had enjoyed all the privileges of his master's grace, was about to abuse them and fall from that favor.

A further contrast in spiritual attitudes may be seen in Gehazi's oath (v.20) as compared with that of Elisha (v.16). Although Elisha's oath displays his servant's heart before God, Gehazi's borders on a blasphemous taking of the Lord's name in vain (Ex 20:7).

23–24 Unlike Elisha (vv.15–16), greedy Gehazi gladly accepts Naaman's generous offer of gifts. Naaman even supplies two servants to assist Gehazi in carrying them. Naaman's servants must surely have been perplexed by Gehazi's subsequent actions in dismissing them without taking the gifts directly to Elisha.

The exact understanding of "the hill" (*hāᶜōpel*) is uncertain. Because it cannot refer to its most common designation as a district in Jerusalem (e.g., 2Ch 27:3), the meaning of the term must be related to the place where Elisha was now residing. If Samaria, it could refer to some well-known ascent or citadel (Gray, 510). If Gilgal, it could refer to some vantage point where Gehazi could carry out his deed in presumed concealment from Elisha's view. In this regard the LXX (cf. Vul.) translates "the darkness" (probably transposing the Heb. consonants *ᶜpl* to *ʾpl*), while the Targum reads "a hidden place."

25–27 Gehazi attempts to steal back to Elisha's house unnoticed—only to be confronted by the prophet (v.25). His master knows all that has transpired (v.26)! Gehazi's lies only worsen the situation (v.25). Previously Naaman stood before Elisha in humble gratitude (v.15). Gehazi stands before him in attempted deception. He apparently does not appreciate that as Elisha's attendant his is a privileged position of spiritual responsibility.

Accordingly, Elisha announces Gehazi's punishment: Naaman's condition will become Gehazi's. Elisha's privileged aide is banished in disgrace, for he has misused his favored position in an attempt to acquire wealth for himself. Gehazi needs to learn that the ministry has no place for those who will make merchandise of it.

NOTES

1 While the term "commander of the army" is not the only one used of an army's highest-ranking officer, such is its clear intention in the case of Phicol (Ge 21:22), Sisera (1Sa 12:9), and Joab (1Ch 27:34; cf. also the theophany in Jos 5:14–15). Doubtless Naaman held such an honor with the Aramean king, who must have been Ben-Hadad II.

Naaman's epithets are instructive: אִישׁ גָּדוֹל (*ʾîš gādôl*, "a great man"), a man of high social standing and importance whose influence reached to the king himself (cf. the lady from Shunem, 4:8); נְשֻׂא פָנִים (*n*ᵉ*śuʾpānîm*, "highly regarded," lit., "lifted up of face"), a term reminiscent of his being dubbed with the king's scepter (cf. Est 8:3–4); גִּבּוֹר חַיִל (*gibbôr ḥayil*, "valiant soldier"), that is, a man of landed property whose wealth, bearing, and personal valor destined him for high military service.

Because מְצֹרָע (*m*ᵉ*ṣōrā*ʿ, "leper") was translated in the LXX by words in the word group λέπρα (*lepra*, "leprosy"; true leprosy, however, was normally designated by ἐλεφαντίασις [*elephantiasis*]), ancient (e.g., Vul., *leprosus*, "leprous"; Peshitta, *g*ᵉ*rēb*, "leper") and modern translations have followed its lead. Contemporary scholarship, however, prefers "skin disease" (cf. GWT). See further the comments of G. J. Wenham, *The Book of Leviticus* (NICOT; Grand Rapids: Eerdmans, 1979), 189–214.

3 For the various OT terms for prophet, see Note on 1 Kings 13:1. The maiden's confident assertion that Elisha could "cure him [Naaman] of his leprosy" is reminiscent of Miriam, who also was received back into the camp after her healing from leprosy. The Hebrew verb is the same in both cases: אָסַף (*ʾāsap*, "gather, receive"; here, "take away, remove").

5–6 Examples of letters concerning medical matters are known from the Hittite, Mari, and Assyrian archives. For details, see D. J. Wiseman, "Medicine in the Old Testament World," in *Medicine and the Bible*, ed. B. Palmer (Exeter: Paternoster, 1986), 32. For Egyptian examples see J. Breasted, *Ancient Records of Egypt* (London: Histories & Mysteries of Man, 1988), 4:34–37.

Letters of introduction such as that sent by the Aramean king were, of course, common (cf. 2Co 3:1). For correspondence in the ancient Near East, see H. W. F. Saggs, *The Greatness That Was Babylon* (New York: Hawthorne, 1962), 244–47; A. L. Oppenheim, *Letters from Mesopotamia* (Chicago: Univ. of Chicago Press, 1967).

8 For the tearing of robes in grief and agitation, see Note on 11:14. For the problem of the location of Gilgal, see Notes on 2:2 and 4:38.

10 For the wide use of the number seven symbolically in the OT and the ancient Near East, see J. J. Davis, *Biblical Numerology* (Grand Rapids: Baker, 1968), 115–19. For the number seven, see *NIDOTTE*, 4:34–37.

11 אָמַר (*ʾāmar*) is normally used of "speaking," but occasionally some of the wider usages attested in this common Semitic root (e.g., Akkad. "see"; Geez "show"; Tigre "know") are at times felt in the OT. The Hebrew idiom "to say in one's heart" (i.e., "think") is a kindred idea (Dt 8:17; 1Ki 12:26), so that the use of the verb independently with a similar nuance is a natural development (cf. Ge 20:11; 26:9; Ru 4:4; 1Sa 20:26; 2Sa 5:6; 12:22; 1Ki 22:32). See further *TDOT*, 1:328–45.

The position of the prepositional phrase "unto me" (*ʾēlay*) is emphatic: "(I thought)—unto me he would surely come out!" Naaman was incensed.

12 For the MT's "Abana" (cf. LXX, Vul.) the Qere and Syriac read "Amana." The Amana/Abana valley is noted for its natural loveliness.

13–14 The servant called his master "father." The term may indicate the respect he felt for Naaman (cf. 2:12; 6:21). Suggested emendations are unnecessary. For washing and cleansing, see Psalm 51:2; Isaiah 1:16. The story of Naaman's cleansing remained well known into NT times (Lk 4:27).

17–18 Montgomery, 377, reports that the transporting of holy soil was a widespread custom. The name of the Aramean god Rimmon probably contains a scribal parody of the Syrian storm god Hadad, whom the Assyrians called *Ramman* ("the thunderer"). The father of Ben-Hadad I was named Tabrimmon (1Ki 15:18); so the equation of Rimmon with Hadad as the god of the royal house of Damascus seems certain. Both gods are often integrated with the Canaanite Baal. In typical Jewish fashion the Aramean god is given a new vowel pointing, here that of the Hebrew word for pomegranate.

20 כִּי אִם רַצְתִּי (*kî-ʾim-raṣtî*, "I will run") contains an extremely emphatic resolve (cf. 1Sa 25:34). Gehazi will most certainly correct Elisha's light treatment of this foreigner by going after him and relieving him of some of the "blessing." Naaman's greeting and Gehazi's reply are those of Gehazi's question and the Shunammite's reply in the previous chapter (4:26). Both replies involve deception, although with different emphases. The verbal repetition provides further reason for the canonical placement of ch. 5 after ch. 4.

23–24 The Hebrew word for Naaman's urging of Gehazi (*prṣ*) is a conscious play on that used of his earlier urging of Elisha (*pṣr*; v.16). The latter is a common verb for urging an action on someone (e.g., Jacob's urging of Esau to accept his gift; Ge 33:11). The former is frequently used of breaking through something (e.g., a city wall; 2Ki 14:13). It can also imply the bursting of a new situation upon someone/something, whether in blessing (Ge 30:30, 43) or judgment (2Sa 6:8). Here Naaman presumes that, like Elisha previously, his servant might need added pressure to accept the gifts, even though they have been requested. The deliberate play on the verbs illustrates Naaman's generous spirit as opposed to Gehazi's callous avarice. For the two verbs involved, see *NIDOTTE*, 3:656–57, 691–94.

That the MT's *hāʿōpel* is the proper reading, whatever its understanding, is certain not only from uniform manuscript attestation but also from the Syriac reading, which, while apparently influenced by the LXX, yet retains the usual Hebrew meaning for the term *ʿōpel*. Thus we get the conflated reading, "a hidden/secret place of a hill/mountain." Wherever the location of Gehazi's nefarious deed was, any mound just large enough to accomplish the task was all that was necessary.

(b) Elisha's further miracle at the Jordan (6:1–7)

OVERVIEW

This story proceeds like the two miracle accounts that precede the Naaman narrative. After the background/setting (vv.1–4a), a problem arises (vv.4b–5), and the prophet involves the participant in solving the problem (vv.6–7).

[1]The company of the prophets said to Elisha, "Look, the place where we meet with you is too small for us. [2]Let us go to the Jordan, where each of us can get a pole; and let us build a place there for us to live."

And he said, "Go."

[3]Then one of them said, "Won't you please come with your servants?"

"I will," Elisha replied. [4]And he went with them.

They went to the Jordan and began to cut down trees. [5]As one of them was cutting down a tree, the iron axhead fell into the water. "Oh, my lord," he cried out, "it was borrowed!"

[6]The man of God asked, "Where did it fall?" When he showed him the place, Elisha cut a stick and threw it there, and made the iron float. [7]"Lift it out," he said. Then the man reached out his hand and took it.

COMMENTARY

1–4 Whether this company of prophets was quartered at Jericho or nearby Gilgal is uncertain. Either location is possible, since the request is to go to the Jordan River for lumber. Although this area of the Jordan Valley was not noted for its supply of wood, the narrator takes it for granted that a sufficient source was available.

5–7 The narrator simply describes the miracle without further comment. As in two previous miracle accounts, throwing something is part of the healing process (cf. 2:21; 4:41). Attempts to explain how iron could float are futile, as are rationalistic explanations (e.g., Jones, 422).

(c) The campaign for Samaria (6:8–7:20)

OVERVIEW

The account of the Aramean campaign for Samaria proceeds in two broad movements. The first (vv.8–23) is written in chiastic symmetry.

A Elisha has the ability to know the Aramean king's raiding strategies and can thus repeatedly deliver the Israelites from possible danger (vv.8–10).

B When the Aramean king learns of Elisha's capabilities, he dispatches troops to Dothan to capture him (vv.11–14).

C When Elisha's servant sees the enemy forces, he is greatly alarmed; therefore, in accordance with Elisha's prayer, the Lord opens the servant's eyes to behold God's angelic forces protecting the city (vv.15–17).

C' Next, through Elisha's prayer the Aramean troops are so blinded that Elisha is able to lead them to Samaria. After their eyes are opened, they find that they are trapped inside Israel's capital city (vv.18–20).

B' When the Israelite king wishes to kill the Arameans, Elisha advises that a better course is to treat them well and release them (vv.21–22).

A' Having received kind treatment the Arameans return home, and Israel is delivered from further Aramean raids (v.23).

The second account (6:24–7:20) records a later Aramean strike that placed Samaria under siege. It is told in two phases, each written in similar fashion.

A The Aramean king's siege of Samaria results in a severe *famine* (6:24–29).

B Blaming Elisha, God's prophet, for the terrible conditions, which had reduced the city to cannibalism, the king vows to have him killed. Instead, *Elisha gives a prophecy* of sure relief from the siege and its famine (6:30–7:2).

A' Due to the *famine* four lepers go to the Aramean camp and find it deserted, for the Lord has tricked the Arameans into fleeing in such haste that they have left their goods behind. The lepers' report to the king that the siege has been lifted is eventually confirmed (vv.3–16).

B' The details of *Elisha's prophecy* are minutely fulfilled (vv.17–20).

[8]Now the king of Aram was at war with Israel. After conferring with his officers, he said,
"I will set up my camp in such and such a place."
[9]The man of God sent word to the king of Israel: "Beware of passing that place, because
the Arameans are going down there." [10]So the king of Israel checked on the place indicated by the man of God. Time and again Elisha warned the king, so that he was on his
guard in such places.
[11]This enraged the king of Aram. He summoned his officers and demanded of them,
"Will you not tell me which of us is on the side of the king of Israel?"
[12]"None of us, my lord the king," said one of his officers, "but Elisha, the prophet who is
in Israel, tells the king of Israel the very words you speak in your bedroom."
[13]"Go, find out where he is," the king ordered, "so I can send men and capture him." The
report came back: "He is in Dothan." [14]Then he sent horses and chariots and a strong force
there. They went by night and surrounded the city.

[15]When the servant of the man of God got up and went out early the next morning, an
army with horses and chariots had surrounded the city. "Oh, my lord, what shall we do?"
the servant asked.
[16]"Don't be afraid," the prophet answered. "Those who are with us are more than those
who are with them."
[17]And Elisha prayed, "O LORD, open his eyes so he may see." Then the LORD opened the
servant's eyes, and he looked and saw the hills full of horses and chariots of fire all around
Elisha.
[18]As the enemy came down toward him, Elisha prayed to the LORD, "Strike these people
with blindness." So he struck them with blindness, as Elisha had asked.
[19]Elisha told them, "This is not the road and this is not the city. Follow me, and I will lead
you to the man you are looking for." And he led them to Samaria.
[20]After they entered the city, Elisha said, "LORD, open the eyes of these men so they can
see." Then the LORD opened their eyes and they looked, and there they were, inside Samaria.
[21]When the king of Israel saw them, he asked Elisha, "Shall I kill them, my father? Shall I
kill them?"
[22]"Do not kill them," he answered. "Would you kill men you have captured with your
own sword or bow? Set food and water before them so that they may eat and drink and
then go back to their master." [23]So he prepared a great feast for them, and after they had
finished eating and drinking, he sent them away, and they returned to their master. So the
bands from Aram stopped raiding Israel's territory.
[24]Some time later, Ben-Hadad king of Aram mobilized his entire army and marched up
and laid siege to Samaria. [25]There was a great famine in the city; the siege lasted so long
that a donkey's head sold for eighty shekels of silver, and a quarter of a cab of seed pods
for five shekels.
[26]As the king of Israel was passing by on the wall, a woman cried to him, "Help me, my
lord the king!"
[27]The king replied, "If the LORD does not help you, where can I get help for you? From the
threshing floor? From the winepress?" [28]Then he asked her, "What's the matter?"
She answered, "This woman said to me, 'Give up your son so we may eat him today, and
tomorrow we'll eat my son.' [29]So we cooked my son and ate him. The next day I said to her,
'Give up your son so we may eat him,' but she had hidden him."
[30]When the king heard the woman's words, he tore his robes. As he went along the wall,
the people looked, and there, underneath, he had sackcloth on his body. [31]He said, "May
God deal with me, be it ever so severely, if the head of Elisha son of Shaphat remains on
his shoulders today!"
[32]Now Elisha was sitting in his house, and the elders were sitting with him. The king
sent a messenger ahead, but before he arrived, Elisha said to the elders, "Don't you see

how this murderer is sending someone to cut off my head? Look, when the messenger
comes, shut the door and hold it shut against him. Is not the sound of his master's footsteps behind him?"
[33]While he was still talking to them, the messenger came down to him. And the king
said, "This disaster is from the LORD. Why should I wait for the LORD any longer?"
[7:1]Elisha said, "Hear the word of the LORD. This is what the LORD says: About this time
tomorrow, a seah of flour will sell for a shekel and two seahs of barley for a shekel at the
gate of Samaria."
[2]The officer on whose arm the king was leaning said to the man of God, "Look, even if
the LORD should open the floodgates of the heavens, could this happen?"
"You will see it with your own eyes," answered Elisha, "but you will not eat any of it!"
[3]Now there were four men with leprosy at the entrance of the city gate. They said to
each other, "Why stay here until we die? [4]If we say, 'We'll go into the city'—the famine is
there, and we will die. And if we stay here, we will die. So let's go over to the camp of the
Arameans and surrender. If they spare us, we live; if they kill us, then we die."
[5]At dusk they got up and went to the camp of the Arameans. When they reached the
edge of the camp, not a man was there, [6]for the Lord had caused the Arameans to hear the
sound of chariots and horses and a great army, so that they said to one another, "Look, the
king of Israel has hired the Hittite and Egyptian kings to attack us!" [7]So they got up and
fled in the dusk and abandoned their tents and their horses and donkeys. They left the
camp as it was and ran for their lives.
[8]The men who had leprosy reached the edge of the camp and entered one of the tents.
They ate and drank, and carried away silver, gold and clothes, and went off and hid them.
They returned and entered another tent and took some things from it and hid them also.
[9]Then they said to each other, "We're not doing right. This is a day of good news and we
are keeping it to ourselves. If we wait until daylight, punishment will overtake us. Let's go
at once and report this to the royal palace."
[10]So they went and called out to the city gatekeepers and told them, "We went into the
Aramean camp and not a man was there—not a sound of anyone—only tethered horses
and donkeys, and the tents left just as they were." [11]The gatekeepers shouted the news,
and it was reported within the palace.
[12]The king got up in the night and said to his officers, "I will tell you what the Arameans
have done to us. They know we are starving; so they have left the camp to hide in the
countryside, thinking, 'They will surely come out, and then we will take them alive and get
into the city.'"
[13]One of his officers answered, "Have some men take five of the horses that are left in
the city. Their plight will be like that of all the Israelites left here—yes, they will only be
like all these Israelites who are doomed. So let us send them to find out what happened."

[14]So they selected two chariots with their horses, and the king sent them after the
Aramean army. He commanded the drivers, "Go and find out what has happened." [15]They
followed them as far as the Jordan, and they found the whole road strewn with the clothing and equipment the Arameans had thrown away in their headlong flight. So the messengers returned and reported to the king. [16]Then the people went out and plundered the
camp of the Arameans. So a seah of flour sold for a shekel, and two seahs of barley sold for
a shekel, as the LORD had said.

[17]Now the king had put the officer on whose arm he leaned in charge of the gate, and
the people trampled him in the gateway, and he died, just as the man of God had foretold
when the king came down to his house. [18]It happened as the man of God had said to the
king: "About this time tomorrow, a seah of flour will sell for a shekel and two seahs of barley for a shekel at the gate of Samaria."

[19]The officer had said to the man of God, "Look, even if the LORD should open the
floodgates of the heavens, could this happen?" The man of God had replied, "You will see
it with your own eyes, but you will not eat any of it!" [20]And that is exactly what happened
to him, for the people trampled him in the gateway, and he died.

COMMENTARY

8–13 The MT indicates that the Aramean incursions were carried out frequently. Apparently the Aramean king hoped to catch Joram at some point, perhaps during his travels or hunting trips. The repeated occasions of such raids and Elisha's timely warnings are further indicated by the Hebrew idiom "not once or twice" (v.10; "time and again," NIV). As in the situation with Naaman (5:8–10), Elisha is seemingly on good terms with Joram.

14 The Aramean king dispatched an unusually large force to capture one man. Perhaps he reasoned that this was necessary so as to be sure that Elisha could not escape from Dothan.

15–16 The perspective of the siege changes to that of the viewers from within Dothan. The narrator notes that Elisha's servant "rose early." It is often reported that the Lord's servants rose early, especially to worship God (e.g., Ge 28:16–22; Ex 24:4–8; 1Sa 1:19; 2Ch 29:20–35; Job 1:5). Such a practice is also recorded of Jesus (Mk 1:35). The psalmists often commend the morning hour for spiritual exercise (e.g., Pss 59:16; 88:13; 92:2; 143:8). No indication is found here that Elisha's servant was praying (although such might be assumed); rather, he saw only overwhelming danger.

17 The spectacle that the servant was permitted to see is reminiscent of the earlier scene at Elijah's translation (2:11).

18–23 The opening of the blinded Arameans' eyes parallels the opening of Elisha's servant's eyes, which had previously been blind to unseen spiritual realities. Because the soldiers would have to follow Elisha for some distance in order to get to Samaria, Hobbs, 78, and Keil, 326, may be correct in suggesting that the blindness was more mental delirium or deception than physical loss of sight. A similar conclusion with regard to the only other occurrence of the noun involved (Ge 19:11) is less certain and therefore suggests caution in interpreting both contexts.

24 At a later date war broke out again between Ben-Hadad II and Joram (v.24). Perhaps the miraculously arranged temporary lull had been divinely designed to teach Israel God's abiding love and concern for his people, to whom he had sent his duly authenticated prophet, Elisha. But with no evidence of repentance by Israel, God withdrew his protective hand; and Israel faced a full-scale Syrian invasion. The Arameans were eminently successful—they penetrated to the gates of Samaria itself and put the city under a dire siege.

25–30 The lengthy siege evoked a severe famine that, in turn, produced highly inflated prices for the humblest commodities. So scarce had food become that one day, as the king was on a tour about the embattled city's wall, he stumbled upon a case of cannibalism (v.26).

31 The king blamed Elisha for the terrible siege and famine. He apparently reasoned that it was Elisha whom Ben-Hadad had been after all along. Moreover, Elisha's humiliation of the Aramean troops sent to capture him had further infuriated their king. Indeed, the very troops whom Elisha had talked the king into releasing were probably even now part of the besieging force!

32 The narrator's recording of the verb "sitting" brings a note of calmness to the prevailing chaos of the situation. The reader is thus prepared for a change of conditions in the existing circumstances. Elisha in fact is as aware of the Israelite king's intentions as he was of the Aramean king (6:12). Thus he knew why the king's messenger was coming and that the king himself would soon arrive to see whether the deed had been accomplished. Elisha's instructions to "shut and secure the door" would perhaps forestall the messenger's murderous attempt until Elisha could deliver an encouraging word to the king.

33 Just who is speaking is somewhat ambiguous in the MT (so also the KJV, the ancient versions, and modern foreign language versions). Is it the messenger, Elisha, or the king, as suggested by many commentators and modern English translations (emending the text; e.g., NIV, NLT, NKJV, NRSV, REB)? Following the MT, the choice appears to be either Elisha (Hobbs) or the messenger (GWT). If the former is the case, Elisha is perhaps indicating that the siege and famine have served their divine purpose, and it is time for a change of conditions. If the latter, the messenger is delivering the king's own sentiment of the hopelessness of the situation. If the messenger's word is essentially the king's, no emendation is required. Elisha's following pronouncement (7:1), as well as the syntax, would appear to favor taking the words as those of the king through his messenger.

7:1–2 In contrast to the previous note of despair, Elisha prophesies that by the next day conditions will so improve that good products will be available again in substantial quantity. When Joram's chief aide finds such a statement preposterous, Elisha assures him that not only will the prophecy come true, the officer will see it fulfilled with his own eyes, but he will not partake of it! His faithless incredulity will cause him to miss God's blessing on the people.

3–4 Like the previous episode, this one begins with seated men (cf. "stay," NIV). This time it is four lepers whose situation is desperate. They faced starvation and death where they are. Accordingly, they have nothing to lose by deserting to the Arameans.

5–7 Once again the Lord uses a *ruse de guerre* to accomplish his mysterious purposes. The Arameans feared a coalition of Hittite and Egyptian kings coming against them. By Hittite is meant the Neo-Hittite remnants of the once mighty Hittite nation of Anatolia now living in northern Syria. The

Egyptians would be part of the gradually weakening Twenty-Second Dynasty.

8–12 The lepers' happy despoiling of the abandoned Aramean camp soon turns to caution. Whether stricken by moral conviction, feelings of guilt, or the realization of possible reprisal, they determine to share the good news with their fellow Israelites in Samaria. When the news reaches the king, however, he suspects an Aramean trick. Withdrawal in feigned retreat so as to set up an ambush was a common military tactic (cf. Jos 8:3–23).

13–16 Once again a servant gives a high official sound advice or information (cf. 3:11; 5:13; 6:12). The seeming incongruity of selecting five horses but sending two chariots has been approached in a variety of ways. Perhaps it is simplest to suggest that there were five men who made a selection from the horses but that they either rode in two chariots, or some of the men rode horses while others went in two chariots. In any case, the king follows the advice and sends out a detail of men to investigate the lepers' report. With the Arameans' flight confirmed, great booty is taken from their camp—so much booty that Elisha's prophecy comes true.

17–20 The narrative closes with an affirmation of the complete fulfillment of Elisha's prophecy, including the death of the king's trusted aide, who had scoffed at Elisha's prediction. The incident once again underscores the nature of Kings as both historic and prophetic narrative.

NOTES

6:14 Dothan was situated about fourteen kilometers north of Samaria.

15 שָׁכֵם (*šākēm*, "rise early") occurs idiomatically in Jeremiah (eleven times) to depict God's repeated efforts at reaching his disobedient people. Zephaniah (Zep 3:7) utilizes the verb to describe Judah's punishment for acting "corruptly in all they did."

16 Elisha's word of assurance to this servant has become a source of comfort to many subsequent servants of God who have faced seemingly overwhelming adversity.

17 The spectacular sight that the servant is enabled to see is like the double army of angels encamped around Jacob (Ge 32:1–2). The Lord's promise to "encamp around those who fear him" (Ps 34:7; cf. 55:18; 91:11–12) has become a visible reality to Elisha's servant. The whole episode underscores the power of prayer (cf. Jas 5:16). For divine revelation to men and for the activities of the unseen world, see Ezekiel 10–11; Daniel 10 (cf. Nu 12:6).

19 Keil, 326, correctly explains Elisha's deception as a *ruse de guerre*. Yet in a sense his words will prove true in that the city where Elisha will ultimately be found is Samaria, not Dothan.

21–22 The records of the ancient Near East are uneven as to the treatment of captured people. For example, in some cases the Assyrian king Ashurbanipal carried them off as slaves (see Luckenbill, 2:296), while in others he executed them on the spot (ibid., 2:304). In still other cases the citizens of some cities were variously treated. Thus in Ashurbanipal's capture of Elamite Bit-Imbi some were carried off alive, while others were killed and their heads cut off (ibid., 2:306).

Similarly, David executed two-thirds of the captured Moabites, while the rest were allowed to live as vassals (2Sa 8:2). A still different scenario may be seen in Sennacherib's treatment of the people of Ekron.

Although he killed its leading citizens, he took others as prisoners of war, while still others were released (Luckenbill, 2:120).

25 The written consonants of the MT's חרייונים have been divided in some translations into חֲרֵי יוֹנִים (*ḥărê yônîm*, "dove's dung"; so NASB, KJV, RSV). The NIV apparently follows Gray, 518, and others in adopting an often-suggested emendation to חֲרוּבִים (*ḥarûbîm*, "[carob] seed pods"). The pointing of the MT הִרְיוֹנִים (*ḥiryyônîm*) comes from the reading of a few MSS and the Qere: דִּבְיוֹנִים (*dibyônîm*, "doves'/pigeons' droppings"). If dove's dung is not the popular name for some common food or was not simply to be used as fuel for fire or as a substitute for salt (so Josephus, *Ant.* 9.62 [4.4]), the reduction of the people to eating dung may be paralleled by a similar incident at the siege of Jerusalem (see Josephus, *J.W.* 5.571 [13.7]).

For ancient Near Eastern parallels to conditions in time of siege, see J. C. Greenfield, "Doves' Dung and the Price of Food: The Topoi of II Kings 6:24–7:2," in *Storia e tradizioni di Israele: Scritti in onore di J. Alberto Soggin*, ed. D. Garrone and F. Israel (Brescia: Paideia, 1991), 121–26.

26–29 Cannibalism in time of siege was the prophetic threat for Israel's disobedience (Lev 26:29; Dt 28:53, 57; Eze 5:10). It was to befall Jerusalem both in OT times (La 2:20; 4:10) and in NT times (cf. Josephus, *J.W.* 6.201–13 [3.4]). For extrabiblical cases see A. Leo Oppenheim, "Siege Documents from Nippur," *Iraq* 17 (1955): 68–89.

7:1 Public business was carried on at the gate of the city (cf. Ge 19:1; Ru 4:1; 2Sa 15:1–5). The rare Hebrew expression כָּעֵת מָחָר (*kāʿēt māḥār*, "by this time tomorrow") emphasizes the certainty of Elisha's prediction.

2 Hebrew שָׁלִישׁ (*šālîš*, "officer") has been variously understood. Because it is related to the Hebrew word for "three," it is commonly assumed to designate originally the third man in a war chariot, who acted as an armor bearer, and later some trusted official. Such an understanding appears justified by the use of the term in 9:25. Hobbs, 89, however, points out that it appears in both military and nonmilitary contexts to designate choice officials serving in important capacities. In any case, this officer is Joram's chief aide, as was the situation with Naaman (5:18).

6 Since Egypt was in decline at this time, some scholars have suggested that a Cilician kingdom known as Muṣri, whose spelling in Semitic would have been the same first three consonants (*mṣr*) as the Hebrew word for "Egypt," was intended (see Gray, 524–25; Montgomery, 387). But since the Akkadian spelling for "Egypt" was uniformly *muṣir* throughout the first millennium BC, there can be little doubt that the MT intends Egypt. See further the note on 19:24.

9 עָוֹן (*ʿāwôn*) means primarily "iniquity," then the "guilt" that stems from iniquity, and thus the consequences of it all—"punishment." Accordingly, what the lepers feared was not that the Arameans might return and do them in but that a greedy failure to share in the available bounty would make them culpable and hence deserving of divine punishment.

13 The verse is a well-known crux, with the MT being generally regarded as corrupt (see Gray, 525). Certainly the redundant phraseology makes the syntax awkward at best. But the report of impassioned speech with its broken diction makes an accurate recording difficult. The NIV has paraphrased well the intent of the MT. The whole emphasizes the seemingly hopeless situation in which Israel found itself.

(d) A further note concerning Gehazi (8:1–6)

OVERVIEW

This short narrative completes the major portion of stories concerning God's miracle-working prophet. Though Elisha is not part of the story, his presence is felt in the details. Indeed, the fourfold testimony to his miraculous efforts in raising the Shunammite lady's son is the focus of the account. We meet again not only the Shunammite but also Gehazi, who is now in a position both to aid the lady's cause and to testify of Elisha's miracle in her behalf. Thus the story forms an addendum to that of 4:8–37.

[1]Now Elisha had said to the woman whose son he had restored to life, "Go away with
your family and stay for a while wherever you can, because the LORD has decreed a famine
in the land that will last seven years." [2]The woman proceeded to do as the man of God
said. She and her family went away and stayed in the land of the Philistines seven years.
[3]At the end of the seven years she came back from the land of the Philistines and went
to the king to beg for her house and land. [4]The king was talking to Gehazi, the servant of
the man of God, and had said, "Tell me about all the great things Elisha has done." [5]Just as
Gehazi was telling the king how Elisha had restored the dead to life, the woman whose
son Elisha had brought back to life came to beg the king for her house and land.

Gehazi said, "This is the woman, my lord the king, and this is her son whom Elisha
restored to life." [6]The king asked the woman about it, and she told him.

Then he assigned an official to her case and said to him, "Give back everything that belonged to her, including all the income from her land from the day she left the country until now."

COMMENTARY

1–2 The Shunammite woman, who previously had confidently told Elisha that she had no particular needs (4:13), had learned through the death and raising of her son to depend on God's prophet and his judgment; therefore, she had taken his warning seriously and left her house and lands for the duration of the seven-year famine. Gray, 527, suggests that her older husband had probably died by this time and the family estate was being "held in trust by the crown." Her return within seven years may have aided her legal claim to her property (cf. Ex 21:2; 23:10–11; Lev 25:1–7; Dt 15:1–6; Ru 1:1, 22; 4:3–4).

3 The woman's intention to appeal ("beg," NIV) to the king was likely more in the nature of lodging a formal complaint. Although she had come to depend on Elisha's judgment, she was yet a woman of firm resolve.

4–5 The narrator switches from past background to the present situation. The king who once sought Elisha's life (6:30–33) now desires to hear more about the wonder-working Elisha, whose prophecy concerning the end of the famine has come true.

Apparently either Gehazi's "leprosy" has been cured or, like Naaman, his affliction of the skin did not keep him from normal activities, including even an audience with the king. The story hints at the possibility that Gehazi has repented of his sins and has been restored to a place of usefulness for God. The Gehazi who was ineffective in his previous context with the Shunammite is now a source of help to her.

6 In contrast to his father, Ahab, whose greed caused him to appropriate another's property (1Ki 21), Joram not only restores the woman's property but also the back income owed to her.

NOTES

1–3 Seven-year famines were not unknown in the ancient Near East (cf. Ge 41:29–32; see also *ANET*, 31). The verb translated "stay for awhile" (NIV) indicates that the Shunammite woman was only to become a resident alien in a foreign land, with full intention of returning to her own land.

6 For סָרִיס (*sārîs*, "official") see Notes on 1 Kings 22:9 and 2 Kings 18:17.

iv. The anointing of Hazael (8:7–15)

OVERVIEW

The account of dynastic succession in Damascus is told in the familiar chiastic pattern.

A Ben-Hadad sends Hazael to Elisha to inquire as to his chances of recovery (vv.7–8).

B Elisha gives Hazael a message that both addresses the fate of the king and includes a prophecy concerning himself (vv.9–13).

A' Hazael reports back to Ben-Hadad and subsequently assassinates him (vv.14–15).

As so often in biblical narrative, dialogue becomes the chief focus of the account.

7Elisha went to Damascus, and Ben-Hadad king of Aram was ill. When the king was told, "The man of God has come all the way up here," 8he said to Hazael, "Take a gift with you and go to meet the man of God. Consult the LORD through him; ask him, 'Will I recover from this illness?'"

9Hazael went to meet Elisha, taking with him as a gift forty camel-loads of all the finest wares of Damascus. He went in and stood before him, and said, "Your son Ben-Hadad king of Aram has sent me to ask, 'Will I recover from this illness?'"

10Elisha answered, "Go and say to him, 'You will certainly recover'; but the LORD has
revealed to me that he will in fact die." 11He stared at him with a fixed gaze until Hazael felt
ashamed. Then the man of God began to weep.
12"Why is my lord weeping?" asked Hazael.
"Because I know the harm you will do to the Israelites," he answered. "You will set fire to
their fortified places, kill their young men with the sword, dash their little children to the
ground, and rip open their pregnant women."
13Hazael said, "How could your servant, a mere dog, accomplish such a feat?"
"The LORD has shown me that you will become king of Aram," answered Elisha.
14Then Hazael left Elisha and returned to his master. When Ben-Hadad asked, "What did
Elisha say to you?" Hazael replied, "He told me that you would certainly recover." 15But the
next day he took a thick cloth, soaked it in water and spread it over the king's face, so that
he died. Then Hazael succeeded him as king.

COMMENTARY

7–8 The next incident from the Elisha cycle both closes the wars with Ben-Hadad II and initiates the critical circumstances that will culminate in the crucial events of 841 BC (see ch. 9). Ben-Hadad II, the Aramean king (860–842 BC), lay ill. Apparently he was sick enough to fear that his illness might be terminal. Under such circumstances a person will often reach out to unusual sources for help. Ben-Hadad knew all too well of Elisha's prowess (cf. 6:12–23), so he sent an inquiry to his former antagonist expecting an honest reply.

Once again we see the motif of a ruler's sending to inquire as to his chances of survival (cf. 1:2). The fact that Elisha was in Damascus and able to move about freely attests to the high respect in which God's prophet was held. The presence of Elisha in Aramean Damascus would also enable him to fulfill Elijah's assignment to anoint Hazael as king (1Ki 19:15), though no formal anointing would take place.

9 The exorbitant amount of gifts that Hazael took with him in gaining an audience with Elisha testifies further to Elisha's importance, as does his portraying of Ben-Hadad as Elisha's "son." Granted Elisha's earlier rejection of Naaman's extraordinary offer (5:15–16, 26), it may be assumed that these gifts were likewise refused.

10 Although the Kethiv of the MT clearly reports Elisha as saying that Ben-Hadad would not (*lōʾ*) live, the ancient versions and modern translations uniformly follow the Qere by reading "[say] to him" (*lô*; see Notes). If the Qere is read, Elisha is saying that although Ben-Hadad's illness is not terminal, he will certainly die; therefore, Hazael's subsequent report to his master is the truth—but not the whole truth (v.14).

11–13 While Elisha's stare eventually brings embarrassment to Hazael (so the NIV, but see Notes), Elisha himself breaks down and weeps at what he knows Hazael will someday do. Hazael's denial will prove to have a hollow ring, for subsequent Scripture records that he often oppressed God's people (8:28; 9:14–15; 10:32–33; 12:17–18; 13:3, 22).

14–15 Elisha's assurances to Hazael that he would be the next king of Damascus may have given to him the pretext that he had a mandate to be carried out. The next day brought the opportunity to carry out the nefarious deed. Having smothered the king, he assumed the throne.

The instrument of death appears to have been either a thick cloth (NIV) or a sieve-like covering that could be used as a mosquito net, which "when dipped in water would act as a cooler for the person in bed" (Hobbs, 102).

NOTES

10 For the writing of לֹא (*lōʾ*) where לוֹ (*lô*) is intended, see GKC, par. 103g. The fact that the focus of attention in these verses is dialogue rather than narrative illustrates well Robert Alter's contention, 65–66, that in Hebrew narrative the authors were often more concerned with how the characters in the story reacted to the situation than the flow of action.

11 The MT is unclear as to who did the staring and who was ashamed. The NIV is probably correct in assuming a change of subject. Since Elisha is the subject of v.10, it is likely that the staring is his and that it caused Hazael to become embarrassed.

Alternatively, either Elisha or Hazael could be the subject of both actions. If Elisha, his steady gaze finally brought him such a sense of shame at what Hazael would someday do that he broke into tears. If Hazael, he stared at the prophet, in whose presence he was already uncomfortable, until the realization of what Elisha was hinting at made him embarrassed.

12 For the barbaric picture described here, see Note on 15:16.

13 For the dog as a figure of abasement, see Note on 1 Kings 14:11.

15 Hazael is often mentioned in the records of Shalmaneser III. Hazael's usurpation is duly noted in that Hazael is called "son of a nobody." See further Luckenbill, 1:246; Wiseman, *1 & 2 Kings*, 214. Gray, 528, 532, denies that any assassination took place. He suggests that Ben-Hadad died in his sleep and that his death was discovered when an attendant came in to change the netted covering the next morning. Such an interpretation, however, not only leaves Elisha's prophecy unfulfilled but also has Elisha telling Hazael to deliver a lie to Ben-Hadad.

c. Interlude: The reigns of Jehoram and Ahaziah of the southern kingdom (8:16–29)

OVERVIEW

Before completing the major section detailing Elisha's ministry, the narrator shifts attention to two contemporary kings in the southern kingdom. The section divides naturally into two straightforward narratives, the first dealing with Jehoram (vv.16–24) and the second with Ahaziah (vv.25–29). Both units proceed in standard fashion: accession notice with spiritual evaluation (vv.16–19, 25–27), historical note (vv.20–22, 28–29), and closing formula (vv.23–24). No closing formula is included for Ahaziah because his demise is taken up in the next chapter (9:27–29).

The historical note in each case deals with wartime events. Jehoram unsuccessfully attempted to quell an Edomite rebellion (vv.20–22); Ahaziah went to visit Joram, king of Israel, who had been wounded in renewed Aramean-Israelite hostilities at Ramoth Gilead (vv.28–29). These verses in turn provide the setting for the following account (9:1–37).

[16]In the fifth year of Joram son of Ahab king of Israel, when Jehoshaphat was king of Judah, Jehoram son of Jehoshaphat began his reign as king of Judah. [17]He was thirty-two years old when he became king, and he reigned in Jerusalem eight years. [18]He walked in the ways of the kings of Israel, as the house of Ahab had done, for he married a daughter of Ahab. He did evil in the eyes of the LORD. [19]Nevertheless, for the sake of his servant David, the LORD was not willing to destroy Judah. He had promised to maintain a lamp for David and his descendants forever.

[20]In the time of Jehoram, Edom rebelled against Judah and set up its own king. [21]So Jehoram went to Zair with all his chariots. The Edomites surrounded him and his chariot commanders, but he rose up and broke through by night; his army, however, fled back home. [22]To this day Edom has been in rebellion against Judah. Libnah revolted at the same time.

[23]As for the other events of Jehoram's reign, and all he did, are they not written in the book of the annals of the kings of Judah? [24]Jehoram rested with his fathers and was buried with them in the City of David. And Ahaziah his son succeeded him as king.

[25]In the twelfth year of Joram son of Ahab king of Israel, Ahaziah son of Jehoram king of Judah began to reign. [26]Ahaziah was twenty-two years old when he became king, and he reigned in Jerusalem one year. His mother's name was Athaliah, a granddaughter of Omri king of Israel. [27]He walked in the ways of the house of Ahab and did evil in the eyes of the LORD, as the house of Ahab had done, for he was related by marriage to Ahab's family.

[28]Ahaziah went with Joram son of Ahab to war against Hazael king of Aram at Ramoth Gilead. The Arameans wounded Joram; [29]so King Joram returned to Jezreel to recover from the wounds the Arameans had inflicted on him at Ramoth in his battle with Hazael king of Aram.

Then Ahaziah son of Jehoram king of Judah went down to Jezreel to see Joram son of Ahab, because he had been wounded.

COMMENTARY

16–19 The synchronism of v.16 records the year of Jehoram's assumption of full power of state (see the Note on 1:17). Jehoram's ungodly character is noted along with the primary factor in the spiritual apostasy: his marriage to Ahab's daughter (v.18; cf. ch. 11). Indeed, the royal marriage of the two houses of Israel and Judah was to spell catastrophe for Judah. Already Athaliah's influence was felt in Jehoram's murder of the royal house (cf. 2Ch 21:4) and the subsequent introduction of Baal worship (1Ki 16:29–33; 2Ki 11:17–18; 2Ch 24:7). Both Jehoram and Ahab, his father-in-law, were dominated by strong willed *femmes fatales*, by whom they would fall both spiritually and physically (cf. 1Ki 21:25–26; see Josephus, *Ant.* 9.96 [5.1]).

The Chronicler (2Ch 21:11) adds that Jehoram "caused the people of Jerusalem to prostitute themselves and ... led Judah astray" according to the religion of the Canaanites. Further, he notes that after his father's death Jehoram slew all his brothers and any possible claimant to the throne (2Ch 21:2–4). Despite Jehoram's spiritual and moral bankruptcy, God honored the covenant with the house of David (v.19; cf. 2Ch 21:7) and did not destroy the kingdoms.

God's promise to David is a testimony to divine faithfulness. Although some members of the Davidic line might abrogate the benefits of the Davidic covenant (cf. 2Sa 7:11b–16 with Ps 89:19–37), God's promise will continue. The full terms in that covenant are to be realized in the new covenant centered in the Greater David (Ps 110; Jer 31:31–37; 33:15–16; Eze 37:21–28; Mt 27:64; Ac 2:29–36; Rev 11:15, etc.).

20–22 The narrator reports the results of Jehoram's folly in the form of two military engagements, to which the Chronicler adds a third. (1) Edom revolted successfully in a rebellion that nearly cost Jehoram his life while attempting to suppress it (vv.20–22a; cf. 2Ch 21:8–10a). (2) Simultaneously Libnah revolted (v.22b; cf. 2Ch 21:10b). (3) The Philistines and Arabians launched a massive attack that reached Jerusalem itself and cost the king all his sons except Ahaziah (cf. 2Ch 21:16–17 with 22:1).

The location of Zair (v.21) is uncertain, though the context dictates that it was either on the border between Judah and Edom or not far from it. The Hebrew verb translated "crossed over" ("went," NIV) suggests an Edomite locale. Libnah was situated in southwestern Judah (Jos 15:42) close to Lachish and the Philistine border (2Ki 19:8).

Due to the economic importance of established trade routes, Judah's clashes with Edom usually triggered Philistine and Arabian military activities with Judah (2Ch 21:16; 26:6–7; 28:17–19; cf. Joel 3:4–8, 19; Am 1:6–8; Ob 11–14). It is not certain whether the Philistine-Arab attack of 2 Chronicles 21:16–17 occurred precisely at the time of Libnah's revolt, but the two events most certainly were related to each other and to the Edomite rebellion.

23–24 The closing formula makes no mention of Jehoram's death from an incurable disease in the bowels (cf. 2Ch 21:15, 18–19). Nor does it note that although he was buried in the City of David, he was excluded from the royal sepulcher (2Ch 21:20b).

25–26a Ahaziah succeeded his father, Jehoram, in the critical year 841 BC. He was not to survive the momentous waves of political events that were to inundate the ancient Near East in that year. Indeed in 841 BC Shalmaneser III of Assyria (859–824 BC) at last was able to break the coalition of western allies with whom he had previously fought a long series of battles (853, 848, 845). While all these complex details were part of God's teleological processes in the government of the nations and his dealing with Israel, doubtless the longstanding controversy and the growing specter of Assyrian power could be felt in the political intrigues that brought about the death of Ben-Hadad II of Damascus and the downfall of the

Omride dynasty in Israel. Before 841 had ended Hazael would be master of Damascus (where Shalmaneser had set him up after having defeated him in battle), the pro-Assyrian Jehu would initiate the fourth dynasty in Israel (chs. 9–10), and the wicked Athaliah would sit as usurper on the throne of Judah (ch. 11).

26b–29 Ahaziah, too, was under the paganistic spell of wicked Athaliah (v.26b; cf. 2Ch 22:3–5) and perpetuated the Baalism that his father had fostered (v.27). Likewise, at the first opportunity he joined with Ahab's son Joram in renewed hostilities with the Arameans in Ramoth Gilead (v.28; 1Ki 22:1–40). Once more the battle went badly for Israel and Judah, for in that battle King Joram was sorely wounded and returned to Jezreel for rest and recovery from his wounds (v.29; cf. 9:14–16). The chapter ends with a concerned Ahaziah on his way to visit Joram in Jezreel. He would not return to Jerusalem alive (cf. 9:16, 24–29).

The mention of Joram and Ahaziah at Jezreel recalls Ahab's sin there in the matter of Naboth's vineyard and Elijah's denunciation of the royal house (1Ki 21:1–24). It also provides the setting for the carrying out of Elijah's prophecy detailed in the next chapter.

NOTES

18 Jehoram is the first king of Judah to be cited as walking "in the ways of the kings of Israel." His son Ahaziah (vv.26–27) would be similarly condemned. In both cases the link with Ahab through Jehoram's marriage to Athaliah is put forward as a primary cause of their evil spiritual deportment.

22 Although Amaziah later attacked Edom (14:7), it was never again under Judah's control.

23 Second Chronicles 21:12–15 records a letter of divine judgment from Elijah the prophet to King Jehoram. Archer, 225–26, argues persuasively that Elijah may actually not have been yet translated into heaven before the accession of Jehoram of Judah. See also M. J. Selman, *2 Chronicles* (TOTC; Downers Grove, Ill.: InterVarsity Press, 1994), 435–36.

25 For details as to political relations between Shalmaneser III of Assyria and Syro-Palestine, see Hallo, 157–62; Michael C. Astour, "841 BC: The First Assyrian Invasion of Israel," *JAOS* 91 (1971): 383–89; A. R. Green, "Sua and Jehu, The Boundaries of Shalmaneser's Conquest," *PEQ* (1979): 35–39. See also comments on 10:32–33.

26 Ahaziah doubtless was twenty-two when he began to reign, not forty-two as 2 Chronicles 22:2 affirms in a reading that preserves an ancient scribal slip. Note the similar problem in 2 Kings 24:8 (cf. 2Ch 36:9–10).

The NIV correctly translates בַּת עָמְרִי (*bat ʿomrî*) as "the granddaughter of Omri" (cf. v.18), her patrilineage being traced back to the founder of Israel's third dynasty. The Hebrew words for "son" and "daughter" often have nuances such as "grandson" (e.g., Ge 31:28) and "granddaughter" (as here). See further the discussion in *TDOT*, 2:149–53, 333–36. The precise relationship of Athaliah to Ahab and Jezebel has been variously debated by scholars, with differing conclusions being drawn, such as Athaliah's being (1) the daughter of Omri (Gray), (2) the daughter of Ahab and Jezebel (Keil), or (3) simply the daughter of Ahab (but not of Jezebel; Bright). For details, see Jones, 446–47.

d. Postlude: the anointing of Jehu and the death of Joram of the northern kingdom (9:1–37)

OVERVIEW

The account of the transition from the third to the fourth dynasties in the northern kingdom also brings to a conclusion the major narrative concerning Elisha's great ministry (see Note on v.1). The two are inextricably bound together.

This chapter begins with Elisha's delegating a member of the prophetic band to carry out Elijah's divine commission to anoint Jehu as Israel's king (see 1Ki 19:16). This delegate is instructed to go to Ramoth Gilead to perform the task. (It should be noted that the mention of Ramoth Gilead links this narrative to the preceding one [cf. 8:28].) Apparently also the younger prophet was to deliver the full ramifications of Elijah's assignment (cf. 1Ki 19:17) and then to flee immediately (2Ki 9:1–10).

The rest of ch. 9 (vv.11–37) tells of Jehu's carrying out of that assignment. It proceeds in three phases. (1) Jehu's men learn that he has been anointed as Israel's king, and they duly crown him as such (vv.11–15). (2) The means of Jehu's taking kingly power are then detailed in the second phase. Jehu not only puts Joram to death but also pursues and wounds Ahaziah, the king of Judah (vv.16–29). (3) The final unit recounts the execution and demise of Jezebel (vv.30–37). All three sections are linked together by the Hebrew *haššālôm*, "Is it well/peace?" (vv.11, 17–19, 22, 31)—a question that takes on an increasingly dramatic tone.

i. Elisha's anointing of Jehu (9:1–10)

1The prophet Elisha summoned a man from the company of the prophets and said
to him, "Tuck your cloak into your belt, take this flask of oil with you and go to Ramoth
Gilead. 2When you get there, look for Jehu son of Jehoshaphat, the son of Nimshi. Go to
him, get him away from his companions and take him into an inner room. 3Then take the
flask and pour the oil on his head and declare, 'This is what the LORD says: I anoint you king
over Israel.' Then open the door and run; don't delay!"
4So the young man, the prophet, went to Ramoth Gilead. 5When he arrived, he found
the army officers sitting together. "I have a message for you, commander," he said.
"For which of us?" asked Jehu.
"For you, commander," he replied.
6Jehu got up and went into the house. Then the prophet poured the oil on Jehu's head
and declared, "This is what the LORD, the God of Israel, says: 'I anoint you king over the
LORD's people Israel. 7You are to destroy the house of Ahab your master, and I will avenge
the blood of my servants the prophets and the blood of all the LORD's servants shed by
Jezebel. 8The whole house of Ahab will perish. I will cut off from Ahab every last male in

Israel—slave or free. [9]I will make the house of Ahab like the house of Jeroboam son of Nebat and like the house of Baasha son of Ahijah. [10]As for Jezebel, dogs will devour her on the plot of ground at Jezreel, and no one will bury her.'" Then he opened the door and ran.

COMMENTARY

1 The scene of Jehu's anointing would be that same Ramoth Gilead where the Israelite troops remained stationed in prolonged confrontation with the Damascene Arameans.

2–5 Much as Moses' work was carried on by Joshua, so Elijah's tasks were carried on by Elisha. As Elisha, who had been Elijah's assistant, carried out his commission, so Elisha in turn sends a fellow from the sons of the prophets to complete the assignment. The full details of Elisha's charge are omitted here but are probably reflected in the speech of the young prophet (vv.6–10).

6–10 As the first two dynasties were brought to an end by divine judgment (cf. 1Ki 14:10–11; 15:29–30; 16:3, 7–8, 11–12; 19:17; 21:21–24), so would the third. The speech of the prophet is not a mere editorial insertion as some suggest; rather, it provides further information as to the charge Elisha gave to him.

NOTES

1 Chapters 9 and 10 are commonly taken as comprising one unit describing Jehu's seizure of power and the establishment of the fourth dynasty. For example, in an interesting study F. O. Garcia-Treto ("The Fall of the House: A Carnivalesque Reading of 2 Kings 9 and 10," *JSOT* 46 (1990): 47–65) points out the presence of the word "house" (eighteen times) as a leitmotif depicting not only the crowning of Jehu but also alluding negatively to the house of David.

However, I have chosen to link ch. 9 to the ministry of Elisha for several reasons. (1) Jehu's anointing is ultimately a carrying out of the divine commission to his tutor Elijah. (2) Chapter 9 records the end of the third dynasty and its reigning king, Joram, during whose time Elisha ministered. (3) Verses 14b–15a provides a distinct flashback to 8:28–29a. (4) Geographically the events of ch. 9 begin where ch. 8 concluded. Understood in this way, the story of Jehu's coup d'état again displays characteristics of both historical and prophetic narrative.

Admittedly ch. 9 has affinities with ch. 10, but it also has strong links with ch. 8. Arguably ch. 9 could be termed a hinge chapter—one that both looks backward to what has preceded and forward to what lies ahead. In this regard it functions much like Jeremiah 25. For details, see my remarks in "Of Bookends, Hinges, and Hooks: Literary Clues to the Arrangement of Jeremiah's Prophecies," *WTJ* 51 (1989): 109–31.

5 The fact that Jehu and his officers were "sitting together" (NIV) has been taken by some (Gray, 540; Jones, 455–56) to indicate that they were already plotting Joram's overthrow.

ii. Jehu's coup d'état (9:11–37)

[11]When Jehu went out to his fellow officers, one of them asked him, "Is everything all
right? Why did this madman come to you?"

"You know the man and the sort of things he says," Jehu replied.

[12]"That's not true!" they said. "Tell us."

Jehu said, "Here is what he told me: 'This is what the LORD says: I anoint you king over
Israel.'"

[13]They hurried and took their cloaks and spread them under him on the bare steps.
Then they blew the trumpet and shouted, "Jehu is king!"

[14]So Jehu son of Jehoshaphat, the son of Nimshi, conspired against Joram. (Now Joram
and all Israel had been defending Ramoth Gilead against Hazael king of Aram, [15]but King
Joram had returned to Jezreel to recover from the wounds the Arameans had inflicted on
him in the battle with Hazael king of Aram.) Jehu said, "If this is the way you feel, don't let
anyone slip out of the city to go and tell the news in Jezreel." [16]Then he got into his chariot
and rode to Jezreel, because Joram was resting there and Ahaziah king of Judah had gone
down to see him.

[17]When the lookout standing on the tower in Jezreel saw Jehu's troops approaching, he
called out, "I see some troops coming."

"Get a horseman," Joram ordered. "Send him to meet them and ask, 'Do you come in
peace?'"

[18]The horseman rode off to meet Jehu and said, "This is what the king says: 'Do you
come in peace?'"

"What do you have to do with peace?" Jehu replied. "Fall in behind me."

The lookout reported, "The messenger has reached them, but he isn't coming back."

[19]So the king sent out a second horseman. When he came to them he said, "This is what
the king says: 'Do you come in peace?'"

Jehu replied, "What do you have to do with peace? Fall in behind me."

[20]The lookout reported, "He has reached them, but he isn't coming back either. The
driving is like that of Jehu son of Nimshi — he drives like a madman."

[21]"Hitch up my chariot," Joram ordered. And when it was hitched up, Joram king of
Israel and Ahaziah king of Judah rode out, each in his own chariot, to meet Jehu. They met
him at the plot of ground that had belonged to Naboth the Jezreelite. [22]When Joram saw
Jehu he asked, "Have you come in peace, Jehu?"

"How can there be peace," Jehu replied, "as long as all the idolatry and witchcraft of
your mother Jezebel abound?"

[23]Joram turned about and fled, calling out to Ahaziah, "Treachery, Ahaziah!"

[24]Then Jehu drew his bow and shot Joram between the shoulders. The arrow pierced
his heart and he slumped down in his chariot. [25]Jehu said to Bidkar, his chariot officer, "Pick

him up and throw him on the field that belonged to Naboth the Jezreelite. Remember
how you and I were riding together in chariots behind Ahab his father when the LORD
made this prophecy about him: 26'Yesterday I saw the blood of Naboth and the blood
of his sons, declares the LORD, and I will surely make you pay for it on this plot of ground,
declares the LORD.' Now then, pick him up and throw him on that plot, in accordance with
the word of the LORD."
27When Ahaziah king of Judah saw what had happened, he fled up the road to Beth
Haggan. Jehu chased him, shouting, "Kill him too!" They wounded him in his chariot on
the way up to Gur near Ibleam, but he escaped to Megiddo and died there. 28His servants
took him by chariot to Jerusalem and buried him with his fathers in his tomb in the City of
David. 29(In the eleventh year of Joram son of Ahab, Ahaziah had become king of Judah.)
30Then Jehu went to Jezreel. When Jezebel heard about it, she painted her eyes,
arranged her hair and looked out of a window. 31As Jehu entered the gate, she asked,
"Have you come in peace, Zimri, you murderer of your master?"
32He looked up at the window and called out, "Who is on my side? Who?" Two or three
eunuchs looked down at him. 33"Throw her down!" Jehu said. So they threw her down, and
some of her blood spattered the wall and the horses as they trampled her underfoot.
34Jehu went in and ate and drank. "Take care of that cursed woman," he said, "and bury
her, for she was a king's daughter." 35But when they went out to bury her, they found
nothing except her skull, her feet and her hands. 36They went back and told Jehu, who
said, "This is the word of the LORD that he spoke through his servant Elijah the Tishbite:
On the plot of ground at Jezreel dogs will devour Jezebel's flesh. 37Jezebel's body will be
like refuse on the ground in the plot at Jezreel, so that no one will be able to say, 'This is
Jezebel.'"

COMMENTARY

11 The word translated "madman" is a strong one used of madness in general (Dt 28:34) and of David's feigned madness at Gath (1Sa 21:12–15). As in the case of Shemaiah's contempt for Jeremiah (Jer 29:24–28), so here the word displays the disdain in which God's faithful prophets were often held (Hos 9:7).

12–13 The officers' cloaks were laid for Jehu, the steps of the house probably serving as a makeshift throne, with Jehu probably sitting on the top ones. The strewing of garments was a mark of homage or respect. In this way a greater King was welcomed with strewn garments upon his entering Jerusalem (Mt 21:8). Even a dead king could be shown respect by the use of a cloak: Alexander wrapped the fallen body of his enemy Darius in his own cloak before sending it to Persepolis for burial (see W. W. Tarn, *Alexander the Great* [Boston: Beacon, 1979], 58–59).

14–16 The mention of Ahaziah's visiting of Joram at Jezreel not only reminds us of the existing situation (cf. 8:29b) but also provides a link with the succeeding narrative (vv.30–37).

17–20 Although the narrator reports Joram's response to the approach of Jehu and his troops, what happens outside Jezreel is largely seen through the eyes of the lookout and the dialogue between Jehu and Joram's messengers.

21 The meeting between Jehu, Joram, and Ahaziah on the land that once belonged to Naboth provides a touch of dramatic irony. The reader is thus prepared for the fulfillment of prophecy concerning the house of Ahab.

22–24 The third recording of the question as to whether Jehu had come in peace provides another example of the narrator's use of threefold repetition (see comments on 3:9–14). The royal query was greeted in a still rougher manner than the two preceding questions. Joram's espousal of the idolatry and witchcraft instituted by Jezebel had rendered impossible any talk of "peace." Joram realized Jehu's reply meant that a coup d'état was taking place. Having warned Ahaziah of the treachery, Joram attempted to flee but was struck dead in his chariot by Jehu's well-aimed arrow. Joram, the final king of the third dynasty, comes to an end similar to that of his infamous father, Ahab (1Ki 22:34–35).

25–26 In fulfillment of Elijah's prophetic threat (cf. 1Ki 21:19–24), which apparently Jehu and his chariot officers had heard, Jehu instructed his aide to throw Joram's fallen body onto Naboth's field. The variance between Jehu's words and 1 Kings 21:19, 21–24 may be accounted for by noting that Jehu was merely repeating the substance of Elijah's words in such a way as to accredit himself as God's avenging agent. Since apparently Jehu was close enough to hear these words, he must have enjoyed a close relationship with the throne that lasted after Ahab's death, so he was left in charge of the Israelite forces after Joram was wounded.

27–29 The circumstances of Ahaziah's flight, capture, death, and burial have been much discussed. Taken at face value, the account in 2 Kings reports that Ahaziah was wounded on the ascent to Gur and died in Megiddo, from where his body was taken to Jerusalem for burial. Second Chronicles 22:8–9 seems to indicate that Ahaziah was overtaken in Samaria, where he had sought refuge with relatives, and was brought to Jehu and executed, his body being interred with honor by Jehu's men.

One way of reconciling the problem is to suggest that although Ahaziah was wounded at the ascent to Gur, he was apprehended by Jehu's men in Samaria (where he lay recovering from his wounds) and then taken to Megiddo, where he was put to death. His body was then given to his servants, who took it to Jerusalem for burial in the royal tomb (v.28; cf. 2Ch 22:9). Whereas the author of Kings emphasized Ahaziah's flight and eventual execution in Megiddo, the Chronicler laid stress on his arrest. The accounts, therefore, are supplementary, not contradictory.

30–31 Jezebel mockingly greeted Jehu with the same question that had been used by Joram and his messengers: "Is it well?" ("Have you come in peace?" NIV). Doubtless the queen had received the full details of what had happened. The question, therefore, drips with sarcasm as her reference to Jehu as "Zimri" (a traiterous usurper) shows. The mention of Zimri may also mask her suggestion that Jehu's usurpation will also be short-lived.

32–34 After Jezebel's death and with cold disdain, Jehu dined in Jezebel's own house while her body lay trampled under horses' hoofs in the street. Jehu's callous treatment of Jezebel is later tempered by Jehu's reminding himself that she was a king's daughter. As such she deserved a proper burial. He failed to recognize her as Israel's queen, however, for he considered her the idolatrous root of Israel's apostasy (cf. v.22).

35–37 Elijah's prophecy of Jezebel's demise is told in all its grisly horror. As in the former instance (vv.24–26), so once again Jehu expands the report of Elijah's words. Like Ahab (1Ki 22:38), dogs were actively involved in denigrating Jezebel's abandoned corpse.

NOTES

11 As Gray, 542, points out, this passage is often cited along with such passages as Jeremiah 29:26 to show that ecstasy was an essential feature of Hebrew prophecy. This theory is sometimes utilized to reduce the OT prophets to the level of the wicked excesses of heathen diviners. For criticism of this theory, see Leon Wood, *The Prophets of Israel* (Grand Rapids: Baker, 1979), 37–56; see also Notes on 3:15.

12 The word translated "that's not true" intends a deliberate lie. Here, however, it was probably used hyperbolically and in good sport by Jehu's fellow officers who, though having little use for God or his prophets, nonetheless wanted to know what had really happened. One is reminded of the question put to Alexander after his consultation with the oracle at Siwah (see U. Wilken, *Alexander the Great* [New York: Norton, 1967], 121–29).

13 The word translated "bare steps" denotes an otherwise unknown architectural term. Some suggest that it may mean a landing on the steps (Gray, 543; Cohn, 67). For the blowing of the trumpet and the shouting of "Long live the king," see 1 Kings 1:34 (cf. 2Ki 11:12).

14b–15a Although these words are set off as a separate paragraph in the MT, there is no need to treat them as a redactor's intrusion. Nor should they be viewed as the original introduction to the reign of Jehu, which, though omitted at 9:1, was adapted by the editor from 8:28–29a and subsequently reintroduced here presumably to "account for the absence of Joram" (Gray, 543). Rather, the narrator here reminds his readers of the circumstances that necessitated Jehu's swift move against Jezreel.

18 D. J. Wiseman ("'Is It Peace?'" 319–21) suggests that the whole incident from Elisha's anointing to Joram's questions reflects terminology drawn from international protocol and negotiations. If so, for Joram the negotiations failed.

20 "Like a madman" is derived from the same root as the word used for madness in v.11. The phrase has caused great problems so that the versions have rendered it variously. The LXX uses the term with the idea of a peculiar alternating motion, the Vulgate with a word meaning an (hostile) approach, and the Peshitta with a word meaning "hastily." Interestingly, the Targum translates it "quietly" (a concept found also in Josephus, *Ant.* 9.117 [6.3]), hence "marched slowly and in good order."

22 זְנוּנִים (*zᵉnûnîm*, "idolatry"; lit., "harlotries") and כְּשָׁפִים (*kᵉšāpîm*, "witchcraft, sorceries"; cf. Akkad. *kišpu* ["witchcraft, sorcery"] from *kašāpu* ["to bewitch, cast a spell"]) designate the heinous nature of Jezebel's reign. Spiritual whoredom had allured Israel's religious devotees into demonic practices.

29 For the apparent discrepancy in the details relative to Ahaziah's accession to the throne, see Note on 8:26 and the remarks of Archer, 206.

30 Jezebel's adornment may have been intended to create a queenly appearance in the face of impending death and served as a royal burial preparation. Jezebel was in her "upper chamber," with the whole upper story probably forming the royal quarters, much in the style of the Syrian *bit ḫillāni* ("house with windows"), which had attached balconies with latticework screens (see Note on 1:2; also Note on 1Ki 17:19). For the figure of the woman at the window, cf. Judges 5:28; see also Aharoni and Avi-Yonah, 85; R. Patterson, "The Song of Deborah," *Tradition and Testament*, ed. John and Paul Feinberg (Chicago: Moody Press, 1981), 141.

34 Jehu sat at the king's table, not "as if nothing untoward had happened" (Montgomery, 403), but as attesting his right to the royal domain and as a mark of communion between the local officials and the new king.

E. The Era of the Fourth Dynasty (10:1–15:12)

1. The Reign of Jehu in the Northern Kingdom (10:1–36)

OVERVIEW

The account of Jehu's reign is given in three broad movements. In place of the usual accession statement we are exposed to the bloody details of his ruthless extermination of all potential rivals to his newly gained throne (vv.1–17). This section contains details of three bloody purges: the killing of seventy of Ahab's sons (vv.1–11), that of forty-two relatives of the Judahite king Ahaziah (vv.12–14), and that of the remainder of Ahab's relatives (vv.15–17).

The central portion of the chapter gives details of Jehu's deceitful murdering of the priests of Baal and the destruction of the temple of Baal in Samaria (vv.18–27). A final section (vv.28–36) contains three short units dealing with the character of Jehu's religion (vv.28–31), his difficulties with the Aramean Hazael (vv.32–33), and the usual final notices concerning his reign (vv.34–36). Thematic links between the first two units may be seen in Jehu's murderous activities and the appearance of Jehonadab ben Recab. The second unit links with the third in Jehu's attention to Baalism.

[1]Now there were in Samaria seventy sons of the house of Ahab. So Jehu wrote letters
and sent them to Samaria: to the officials of Jezreel, to the elders and to the guardians of
Ahab's children. He said, [2]"As soon as this letter reaches you, since your master's sons are
with you and you have chariots and horses, a fortified city and weapons, [3]choose the best
and most worthy of your master's sons and set him on his father's throne. Then fight for
your master's house."

[4]But they were terrified and said, "If two kings could not resist him, how can we?"

[5]So the palace administrator, the city governor, the elders and the guardians sent this
message to Jehu: "We are your servants and we will do anything you say. We will not
appoint anyone as king; you do whatever you think best."

[6]Then Jehu wrote them a second letter, saying, "If you are on my side and will obey me,
take the heads of your master's sons and come to me in Jezreel by this time tomorrow."

Now the royal princes, seventy of them, were with the leading men of the city, who
were rearing them. 7When the letter arrived, these men took the princes and slaughtered
all seventy of them. They put their heads in baskets and sent them to Jehu in Jezreel.
8When the messenger arrived, he told Jehu, "They have brought the heads of the princes."

Then Jehu ordered, "Put them in two piles at the entrance of the city gate until
morning."

9The next morning Jehu went out. He stood before all the people and said, "You are
innocent. It was I who conspired against my master and killed him, but who killed all
these? 10Know then, that not a word the LORD has spoken against the house of Ahab will
fail. The LORD has done what he promised through his servant Elijah." 11So Jehu killed
everyone in Jezreel who remained of the house of Ahab, as well as all his chief men, his
close friends and his priests, leaving him no survivor.

12Jehu then set out and went toward Samaria. At Beth Eked of the Shepherds, 13he met
some relatives of Ahaziah king of Judah and asked, "Who are you?"

They said, "We are relatives of Ahaziah, and we have come down to greet the families of
the king and of the queen mother."

14"Take them alive!" he ordered. So they took them alive and slaughtered them by the
well of Beth Eked — forty-two men. He left no survivor.

15After he left there, he came upon Jehonadab son of Recab, who was on his way to
meet him. Jehu greeted him and said, "Are you in accord with me, as I am with you?"

"I am," Jehonadab answered.

"If so," said Jehu, "give me your hand." So he did, and Jehu helped him up into the
chariot. 16Jehu said, "Come with me and see my zeal for the LORD." Then he had him ride
along in his chariot.

17When Jehu came to Samaria, he killed all who were left there of Ahab's family; he
destroyed them, according to the word of the LORD spoken to Elijah.

18Then Jehu brought all the people together and said to them, "Ahab served Baal a
little; Jehu will serve him much. 19Now summon all the prophets of Baal, all his ministers
and all his priests. See that no one is missing, because I am going to hold a great sacrifice
for Baal. Anyone who fails to come will no longer live." But Jehu was acting deceptively in
order to destroy the ministers of Baal.

20Jehu said, "Call an assembly in honor of Baal." So they proclaimed it. 21Then he sent
word throughout Israel, and all the ministers of Baal came; not one stayed away. They
crowded into the temple of Baal until it was full from one end to the other. 22And Jehu said
to the keeper of the wardrobe, "Bring robes for all the ministers of Baal." So he brought
out robes for them.

23Then Jehu and Jehonadab son of Recab went into the temple of Baal. Jehu said to
the ministers of Baal, "Look around and see that no servants of the LORD are here with
you — only ministers of Baal." 24So they went in to make sacrifices and burnt offerings.

Now Jehu had posted eighty men outside with this warning:"If one of you lets any of the
men I am placing in your hands escape, it will be your life for his life."
[25]As soon as Jehu had finished making the burnt offering, he ordered the guards and
officers:"Go in and kill them; let no one escape." So they cut them down with the sword.
The guards and officers threw the bodies out and then entered the inner shrine of the
temple of Baal. [26]They brought the sacred stone out of the temple of Baal and burned it.
[27]They demolished the sacred stone of Baal and tore down the temple of Baal, and people
have used it for a latrine to this day.
[28]So Jehu destroyed Baal worship in Israel. [29]However, he did not turn away from the
sins of Jeroboam son of Nebat, which he had caused Israel to commit—the worship of
the golden calves at Bethel and Dan.
[30]The LORD said to Jehu, "Because you have done well in accomplishing what is right in
my eyes and have done to the house of Ahab all I had in mind to do, your descendants will
sit on the throne of Israel to the fourth generation." [31]Yet Jehu was not careful to keep the
law of the LORD, the God of Israel, with all his heart. He did not turn away from the sins of
Jeroboam, which he had caused Israel to commit.
[32]In those days the LORD began to reduce the size of Israel. Hazael overpowered the Israelites throughout their territory [33]east of the Jordan in all the land of Gilead (the region of
Gad, Reuben and Manasseh), from Aroer by the Arnon Gorge through Gilead to Bashan.
[34]As for the other events of Jehu's reign, all he did, and all his achievements, are they
not written in the book of the annals of the kings of Israel?
[35]Jehu rested with his fathers and was buried in Samaria. And Jehoahaz his son
succeeded him as king. [36]The time that Jehu reigned over Israel in Samaria was twenty-
eight years.

COMMENTARY

1–5 Jehu's official letters appear in typical ancient Near Eastern form: (1) addressee (the city officials, the elders or civic leaders, and the guardians charged with the custody of the royal family), and (2) main body of the letter, introduced by the phrase "he says." Jehu's message was clearly a challenge to support him or fight. Cohn, 71, suggests that the officials submitted to Jehu because of "their fear to stand against the assassin of two kings."

6–8 The excessive demands of Jehu's second letter were also met by the cowardly leaders of Samaria. The piling up of the severed heads of captives at the city gate as a warning against opposing the conqueror is often attested in Assyrian records. Thus, for example, Shalmaneser III reports in his famous Monolith Inscription:

> From Hubushkia I departed [to] Sugunia, the royal city of Arame, the Urartian (Armenian), I drew near. The city I stormed (and) captured. Multitudes of his warriors I slew. His booty I carried off. A pyramid (pillar) of heads I reared in front of his city. (Luckenbill, 1:213)

Such grisly acts knew no bounds. On one occasion Ashurbanipal severed the head of his fallen enemy and reported:

> I did not give his body to be buried. I made him more dead than he was before. I cut off his head and hung it on the back of Nabû-kâtâ-sabat, (his) twin brother (?). (Luckenbill, 2:312)

Ashur-nasir-pal was particularly vicious in his treatment of the captured enemy. The events of one occasion form a macabre parallel to the account here in 2 Kings:

> To the city of Suru of Bit-Halupê I drew near, and the terror of the splendor of Assur, my lord, overwhelmed them. The chief men and the elders of the city, to save their lives, came forth into my presence and embraced my feet, saying: "If it is thy pleasure, slay! If it is thy pleasure, let live! That which thy heart desireth, do!" Ahiababa the son of nobody, whom they had brought from Bit-Adini, I took captive. In the valor of my heart and with the fury of my weapons I stormed the city. All the rebels they seized and delivered them up. Azi-ilu I set over them as my own governor. I built a pillar over against his city gate, and I flayed all the chief men who had revolted, and I covered the pillar with their skins; some I walled up within the pillar, some I impaled upon the pillar on the stakes, and others I bound to stakes round about the pillar; many within the border of my own land I flayed, and I spread their skins upon the walls and I cut off the limbs of the officers, of the royal officers who had rebelled. Ahiababa I took to Nineveh, I flayed him, I spread his skin upon the wall of Nineveh. My power and might I established over the land of Lake. (Luckenbill, 1:144–45)

9–11 Jehu uses duplicity and deception in spreading the responsibility for the execution of Ahab's sons over the whole populace. Yet he tries to absolve all concerned. He affirms that what he and they have done has the divine sanction of carrying out Elijah's prophecy against the house of Ahab. For good measure he then orders the seizure and execution of any who might yet remain of Ahab's descendants in Jezreel, as well as any of Jehoram's officials, aides, and friends (v.11). Even the state priests who served them are put to death.

12–14 The term translated "relatives" customarily means "brothers." Since the brothers of Ahaziah had been carried off and killed in the days of Jehoram (2Ch 21:17), however, the term must be used in its extended sense of Ahaziah's relatives (stepbrothers, nephews, cousins, etc.).

This traveling band appears to have come up the coast and turned eastward to the road that led from Jezreel to Jenin. Since Beth Eked lay east-northeast of Jenin, they must have left the main road, which went on to Samaria, and would have needed to turn southward to reach the Israelite capital. Hobbs, 128, suggests that these forty-two men were really soldiers who were traveling "by an inconspicuous route, to avenge the death of their king and his cousins." If the traditional understanding is followed, however, the circumlocutious route may have been taken to avoid meeting Jehu. If so, their worst fears were about to be realized.

15–17 On leaving yet another bloody scene, Jehu encountered a mysterious figure, one Jehonadab the Recabite, who, having heard of Jehu's anti-Baal crusade, had apparently come to meet the new Israelite king. Jeremiah (Jer 35) records that Jehonadab was the leader of an ascetic group who lived an austere, nomadic life in the desert, drinking no wine and depending solely on the Lord for their sustenance. Separatist to the core and strong patriots, they lived in protest against the materialism and religious compromise rampant in Israel. Accordingly, Jehonadab may have seen in Jehu's reputed desire to purge the nation of its heathenism a hope of national repentance and longing for Yahweh. Thus it may be that Jehonadab and the Recabites had probably been greatly influenced by the ministry of Elisha with Elijah's words being dramatically fulfilled before their eyes. Like John the Baptist of the NT, Jehonadab had a kind of kingdom hope that in Jehu the fortunes of Israel would soon be restored.

18–24 Jehu's speech to the assembled populace is filled with deception. Did Ahab serve Baal a little? Jehu would serve him more. While this a fortiori statement does show some accuracy in that Ahab did build a temple for Baal (1Ki 16:32), he could repent when challenged by divine rebuke (1Ki 21:28–29). Further, he gave to his children names containing elements coupled with "Yahweh."

In order to "serve" Baal, Jehu orders a "great sacrifice." The irony in this remark is that only too late will the devotees of Baal learn that they are the ones to be sacrificed!

25–27 Although the NIV implies that Jehu himself offered the heathen sacrifice, he may simply have seen to its accomplishment by the proper priests, much as Solomon did at the dedication of the temple (1Ki 8:62–63). The extermination of the priests of Baal is followed by the destruction of his temple. Leaving the bodies of the worshipers in the open and turning the temple ruins into a latrine is reminiscent of the fate of Jezebel, whose body was likewise left on the ground "like refuse" (2Ki 9:37).

28–33 Jehu had exterminated the worship of Baal in Israel (v.28). For this the Lord commended him and promised to him a royal succession to the fourth generation (v.30). Yet Jehu was to prove a disappointment to God, for his reform was soon seen to be political and selfish rather than born of any deep concern for God (v.31). Not only did he fail to keep the law in his heart, he also perpetuated the state cult of the golden calf established by Jeroboam I (v.29). Jehu is commended and rewarded for his faithfulness in carrying out Elijah's prophecies against Ahab's wicked house. God's promise was literally kept; Jehu's descendants—Jehoahaz, Joash, Jeroboam II, and Zechariah—succeeded him in turn in Israel's fourth dynasty.

Yet while there is acceptance of the effects of the deed, the man and his motives did not necessarily win divine approval. Jehu's true heart may be seen in his halfhearted observance of the law, his espousal of Jeroboam's apostate state religion, and his manipulation of any and all circumstances for his desired, selfish ends. The latter point is amply illustrated by his submission to Shalmaneser III, as recorded by the Assyrian king on his famous Black Obelisk: "The tribute of Jehu, son of Omri; I received" (*ANET*, 280). Accordingly there is no contradiction in the Lord's condemnation of Jehu as delivered by Hosea (Hos 1:4).

It is small wonder, therefore, that God allowed Hazael systematically to plunder and reduce the size of Israel. Although defeated by Shalmaneser III of Assyria in 841 BC, this Aramean king managed to retain his independence, and since his former ally Israel was now ruled by a pro-Assyrian king, he looked menacingly southward. Hazael took advantage of Shalmaneser's primary occupation with affairs in the east during the years 839–828 BC and final six years of revolt at home (827–822) to afflict Jehu (841–814) and his son Jehoahaz (814–798) severely. Not only was Israelite Transjordan lost to Hazael's forces, but the Aramean king, on the death of Jehu, was also able to march unchecked into Israel and Judah (cf. 12:18). How appropriately Elisha had wept (8:11–12)! Only the appearance of a new, strong Assyrian king (Adad-Nirari III, 841–783 BC) would check Hazael's relentless surge (see Note on 13:4–5).

34–36 Whatever other "achievements" Jehu may have accomplished are passed over in silence by the narrator, who moves quickly to a typical presentation of final details concerning the end of the king's reign.

NOTES

1 Retaining the "officials of Jezreel" read by the MT could indicate that before Jehu had come from Megiddo to Jezreel, those officials in Jezreel entrusted with the care of the royal children had taken their wards and fled to Samaria. The letters thus addressed per se to "the officials of Jezreel" (i.e., the place where they often served and from which they had just come) would be intended for all the officials of Samaria (cf. v.5). Such an address would make the leaders of Samaria aware that Jehu meant business and yet indicate that their lives were not in jeopardy—Jehu simply wanted the royal survivors. Thus construed, "Jezreel" would not necessarily be viewed as a textual error (cf. Keil, 346).

More usually, however, "Jezreel" is emended to "Israel"; or the phrase is altered so as to read "to the officials of the city, to the elders, etc." This latter suggestion has the support of some ancient MSS and versions and appears to be demanded by the reply in v.5. The difficulty of preserving the sense of the MT may argue for the alternative reading. Moreover, those addressed in v.1 are those who reply in v.5.

The problem is further complicated by the word סְפָרִים (*s^e^pārîm*, "letters"). While one may argue for the sending of just one letter (the *m* of the MT being viewed as an enclitic *m*, as with Montgomery, 408; cf. LXX), most versions follow the MT in reading "letters." Josephus (*Ant.* 9.125 [6.5]) suggests that Jehu wrote two letters, one to those who cared for the children and one to the officials of Samaria.

2 וְעַתָּה (*w^eᶜattâ*, "and now") is the usual means in ancient correspondence for introducing the demands or decision of the writer. Obviously the contents of the letter are greatly abbreviated. The author of Kings records only the barest essential data necessary to his account. Accordingly, the elaborate attempts of A. Alt ("Der Stadtstaat Samaria," in *Kleine Schriften zum Geschichte des Volkes Israel* [Munich: Beck, 1959], 3:285–88; see further G. Buccellati, *Cities and Nations of Ancient Syria* [Rome: Universita di Roma, 1966], 187–91), who relies heavily on the three diplomatic letters of exchange here to detect a distinction between the city-state and the kingdom of Israel with the capital at Jezreel, is at best tentative. For representative examples of ancient Near Eastern correspondence, see A. Leo Oppenheim, *Letters from Mesopotamia* (Chicago: Univ. of Chicago Press, 1967).

8 Josephus (*Ant.* 9.127 [6.5]) suggests that the men bearing the severed heads arrived while Jehu and his friends were eating supper! If so, one is reminded of the Assyrian relief showing the king feasting with his queen while the head of his vanquished enemy hangs in a nearby tree (*ANEP*, 156, pl. 451).

15 The term "son of Recab" became a tribal designation for the ascetically minded Recabites (Jer 35:1–16). So faithful had the later Recabites been to the precepts laid down by Jehonadab that Jeremiah could announce their exemption from the coming Chaldean invasion (Jer 35:17–19).

According to 1 Chronicles 2:55, Recab came from a Kenite clan. Because Hobab, the father-in-law of Moses, was also a Kenite (Nu 10:29), Keil, 349, suggested that "the Recabites were probably descendants of Hobab, since the Kenites the sons of Hobab had gone with the Israelites from the Arabian desert to Canaan, and had there carried on their nomad life (Judg. i. 16, iv. 11, 1 Sam xv. 6)." F. S. Frick ("The Rechabites Reconsidered," *JBL* 90 [1971]: 279–87) suggests that the term רכב (*rkb*) was associated with chariots. Accordingly, Jehu was especially happy to have the backing of such a man.

Based on strictly biblical information, however, traditional scholarship has held that the Recabites were people noted not only for their abilities in metalworking and crafts but also for their orthodoxy.

As craftsmen and tradesmen, the nomadic Kenites were known in the period of the monarchy to have lived extensively in southern Judah, though the events in Judges 4–5 demonstrate that some of them had previously migrated northwest into Galilee—a fact that authenticates Jehonadab's more northerly connections.

25 For רָצִים (*rāṣîm*, "guards"; lit., "runners") and שָׁלִשִׁים (*šālišîm*, "officers"), see Note on 1 Kings 14:28.

2. The Reign of Athaliah in the Southern Kingdom (11:1–20)

OVERVIEW

The account of Athaliah's usurpation and brief reign is told in straightforward narrative. (1) Athaliah seizes the throne and puts to death all possible known rivals. Meanwhile, godly Jehosheba, the wife of the high priest Jehoiada, rescues one prince, the boy Joash (vv.1–3). (2) In the seventh year Jehoiada lays careful plans to replace the usurper with the rightful boy king (vv.4–8). (3) The plot is successful, and Joash is crowned and anointed king (vv.9–12). (4) Too late Athaliah learns of the plot and is seized and put to death (vv.13–16). (5) Jehoiada leads the people in covenantal renewal and the purging of Baalism, and Joash is duly installed on the throne of Judah (vv.17–20).

[1]When Athaliah the mother of Ahaziah saw that her son was dead, she proceeded to
destroy the whole royal family. [2]But Jehosheba, the daughter of King Jehoram and sister of
Ahaziah, took Joash son of Ahaziah and stole him away from among the royal princes, who
were about to be murdered. She put him and his nurse in a bedroom to hide him from
Athaliah; so he was not killed. [3]He remained hidden with his nurse at the temple of the
LORD for six years while Athaliah ruled the land.

[4]In the seventh year Jehoiada sent for the commanders of units of a hundred, the
Carites and the guards and had them brought to him at the temple of the LORD. He made a
covenant with them and put them under oath at the temple of the LORD. Then he showed
them the king's son. [5]He commanded them, saying, "This is what you are to do: You who
are in the three companies that are going on duty on the Sabbath—a third of you guarding the royal palace, [6]a third at the Sur Gate, and a third at the gate behind the guard, who
take turns guarding the temple—[7]and you who are in the other two companies that
normally go off Sabbath duty are all to guard the temple for the king. [8]Station yourselves
around the king, each man with his weapon in his hand. Anyone who approaches your
ranks must be put to death. Stay close to the king wherever he goes."

[9]The commanders of units of a hundred did just as Jehoiada the priest ordered. Each
one took his men—those who were going on duty on the Sabbath and those who

were going off duty—and came to Jehoiada the priest. [10]Then he gave the commanders the spears and shields that had belonged to King David and that were in the temple
of the LORD. [11]The guards, each with his weapon in his hand, stationed themselves around
the king—near the altar and the temple, from the south side to the north side of the
temple.

[12]Jehoiada brought out the king's son and put the crown on him; he presented him
with a copy of the covenant and proclaimed him king. They anointed him, and the people
clapped their hands and shouted, "Long live the king!"

[13]When Athaliah heard the noise made by the guards and the people, she went to the
people at the temple of the LORD. [14]She looked and there was the king, standing by the
pillar, as the custom was. The officers and the trumpeters were beside the king, and all the
people of the land were rejoicing and blowing trumpets. Then Athaliah tore her robes and
called out, "Treason! Treason!"

[15]Jehoiada the priest ordered the commanders of units of a hundred, who were in
charge of the troops: "Bring her out between the ranks and put to the sword anyone who
follows her." For the priest had said, "She must not be put to death in the temple of the
LORD." [16]So they seized her as she reached the place where the horses enter the palace
grounds, and there she was put to death.

[17]Jehoiada then made a covenant between the LORD and the king and people that
they would be the LORD's people. He also made a covenant between the king and the
people. [18]All the people of the land went to the temple of Baal and tore it down. They
smashed the altars and idols to pieces and killed Mattan the priest of Baal in front of the
altars.

Then Jehoiada the priest posted guards at the temple of the LORD. [19]He took with him
the commanders of hundreds, the Carites, the guards and all the people of the land, and
together they brought the king down from the temple of the LORD and went into the
palace, entering by way of the gate of the guards. The king then took his place on the
royal throne, [20]and all the people of the land rejoiced. And the city was quiet, because
Athaliah had been slain with the sword at the palace.

COMMENTARY

1–3 As in other desperate times, a righteous woman would be used by God to stem the tide of apostasy. This ninth-century "Jochebed" (the mother of Moses) was named Jehosheba. A princess in her own right—being the daughter of Jehoram and sister of Ahaziah—she was also the wife of the high priest Jehoiada (2Ch 22:11). Conspiring with her nurse (and doubtless the high priest as well), Jehosheba hid the baby, at first in one of the palace chambers, then subsequently smuggled him into her temple quarters, where she managed to conceal him for six full years.

4 The Chronicler (2Ch 23:1–2) lists the names of the officers whom Jehoiada took into his confidence concerning the existence of the rightful king and with whom he entered into covenant to unseat Athaliah. The Chronicler also adds that these men gathered the Levites and family heads and brought them to Jerusalem.

Several differences in detail are observable between 2 Chronicles 23 and 2 Kings 11 in accordance with the goals of the authors. More than likely, both accounts are merely summary statements of the essential details, the account in Kings emphasizing the part played by the military in defense of the king and palace, and that in Chronicles, the role of the Levites in making the temple secure. The two, then, are supplementary, not contradictory.

The "Carites" are mentioned only here and in 2 Samuel 20:23, where they are associated with the Pelethites, who appear as bodyguards of the king. In that passage the LXX reads "Kerethites," the more usual term associated with the Pelethites (cf. 1Ki 1:38). Both terms are connected with the Aegean world, the former with Crete, the latter more specifically with the Philistines. While some scholars see a distinction in origin between the Carites (Silicia) and Kerethites (Crete), the alternations between the two in 2 Samuel 20:23 may argue that they are the same.

5–11 Though details of Jehoiada's plan of action are somewhat difficult to trace, the following steps appear to have been taken. (1) The royal bodyguard that was relieved from duty at the beginning of the Sabbath went to the temple, where the high priest provided them with the weapons stored in the sanctuary. (2) The men then formed two groups so as to surround the rightful king. (3) The bodyguard that came on duty subdivided into three groups, who stood guard at (a) the palace, (b) the Sur Gate (or "Foundation Gate"; 2Ch 23:5), and (c) the "gate behind the guard" (cf. the "gate of the guards"; 2Ki 11:19).

According to 2 Chronicles 23:7, the Levites formed a further circle around the king that was especially charged with the security of the temple. As Edersheim, 7:18, remarks:

> This division of Levites was to form an outer circle not only around the king, but also around his military guard. This also explains the difference in the directions given in 2 Kings 11:8 to the military guards to kill those who penetrated their "ranks," and in 2 Chronicles 23:7 to the Levites, to kill those who penetrated into the Temple. In other words, the Levites were to stand beyond the guards, and to prevent a hostile entrance into the Temple buildings; and if any gained their way through them to the ranks of the military, they were to be cut down by the guards. Thus the king was really surrounded by a double cordon—the military occupying the inner court around his person, while the Levites held the outer court and the gates.

12 With everyone in place, Jehoiada led the king to the appointed spot, perhaps in the innermost court between the temple and the altar, and anointed him as king, to the shouts of acclamation of the gathered throng. The "copy of the covenant" refers not only to the Ten Commandments (Ex 31:18), but also the whole law of God (Ps 119:88). Although the situation is not without difficulty, according to Deuteronomy 17:18 a copy of the law was to be made by the king himself from one given to him by the priests and was to be kept with the king always so that it became the rule for all his life. Thus by putting the crown on the young king's head and a copy of the law in his hand, Jehoiada was acting in accordance with the ancient scriptural precedent—a move calculated to strengthen the hand of the supporters of the rightful king of the people.

13–16 The narrator now shifts scenes to the palace where Athaliah has heard the clamor. Rushing to the source of the jubilation, she beholds the newly crowned king standing on the royal dais at the eastern gate of the inner court to the temple. He is surrounded by high officials from the religious order and the military. She shrieks out her condemnation: "Treason!" But her cry will have as little effect as that of Israel's Joram to Athaliah's son Ahaziah (9:23). At Jehoiada's command she is seized, escorted to the gate used for the palace horses, and put to death by the sword. Thus Athaliah, the most infamous queen of Judah, dies at the hands of executioners much as did her mother, Jezebel, queen of Israel (9:27–37).

17–20 The people needed to return to true worship and a life of service to God. This was particularly necessary after the ungodly reign of Athaliah. The covenantal renewal testified of the king's relation to the Lord as heir to the Davidic covenant. Purging the land of Baalism and reinstituting proper Levitical leadership accompanied the people's pledge to serve the king and the Lord (cf. 2Ch 23:17–19).

The fire of spiritual reform had been ignited and was to burn brightly for a time. Yet in the dependence of the king on others could be seen a flicker that would one day cause the fiery zeal for the Lord to flicker in the chilling winds of apostasy. This same Joash and many of the same officials would, on another day, pull Judah down to the dregs of the degraded Canaanite religion they had just rendered dormant. Merely programmed religion is perilous; genuine faith must be personal.

NOTES

2 According to Josephus (*Ant.* 9.141 [7.1]), Jehosheba (Jehoshabeath; 2Ch 22:11) was Ahaziah's half sister, born to Jehoram by another woman. The same may also have been true of the royal infant Joash, whose mother was one Zibiah of Beersheba (2Ch 24:1). If so, his parentage could explain the reason the infant was missed in Athaliah's massacre; perhaps even his birth was unnoticed by the queen mother. Interestingly Jehoiada had his young ward, Joash, take two wives (2Ch 24:3), to whom were born sons and daughters.

6 The Talmud identifies the Sur Gate as the temple court's eastern gate. Here unclean animals would be turned away.

7 Although scholars disagree as to the precise reconstruction of the details, it is generally conceded that the Sabbath changeover provided an ideal time for Jehoiada to utilize all the guards in effecting his plan. See further Jones, 478–80, and G. Robinson, "Is II Kings XI:6 a Gloss?" *VT* 27 (1977): 56–61.

10 These weapons were originally dedicated by David from his campaign against the Aramean Hadadezer (2Sa 8:7). According to the LXX on 1 Kings 14:26, these weapons were carried away in Shishak's campaign, though the MT does not specifically say so. This passage may indicate that David's weapons were not surrendered at that time together with "all the treasures," or simply that the replaced weaponry continued to be known as "King David's."

12 The Hebrew noun עֵדוּת (*ʿēdût*, "precept, statute") is also a treaty term (cf. the related Akkad. *adu*, "formal agreement"), being used in contexts dealing with covenants, especially with the Davidic covenant (see M. Weinfeld, "בְּרִית," *TDOT*, 2:257, 259). Not only because of ancient scriptural warrant, then, but also in affirmation of obedience to God's covenant with David, Jehoiada proclaimed this renewal of the promise given to the house of David, thus giving further support for the deposing of Athaliah. The NIV's "copy of the covenant" is, therefore, doubly meaningful. The copy of the law in his hand would be a visible symbol of the pledge to live so as to make the promise of God's covenant granted to David and his house fully applicable to Joash's reign. T. N. D. Mettinger (*King and Messiah* [Lund: Gleerup, 1977], 287) puts forward the unlikely suggestion that here the noun refers to a dedicatory plaque.

14 The NIV follows the usual understanding of הָעַמּוּד (*hāʿammûd*) as "the pillar," as do the LXX, Syriac, and most modern versions and commentaries. The word can also signify a raised platform. The Vulgate translates the noun as "tribunal" (cf. 2Ch 23:13, *gradum*, "step"), a reading followed by the French *La Sainte Bible* ("l'estrade"), the Italian *La Sacra Biblia* ("palco"), and the NJB ("dais").

In the parallel account in 2 Chronicles 23:13, the LXX reads "in his place," a translation certainly allowable for the MT there and in the similar circumstances regarding Josiah (2Ch 34:31). Keil, 362, suggests that the king's platform was placed "at the eastern gate of the inner court ... and it was most probably identical with the brazen scaffold ... mentioned in 2 Chronicles vi.13."

17 For further instances of the instituting of covenantal renewal, see Deuteronomy 31:9–13; Joshua 24; 2 Samuel 7:8–16; 2 Kings 23:1–3. The Scriptures do not record the existence of a temple to Baal. Josephus (*Ant.* 11.154 [7.4]) maintains that Athaliah and her husband, Joram, had seen to its erection.

The name Mattan, the priest of Baal, is reminiscent of the original name of Judah's last king, Zedekiah (2Ki 24:17). The name is also attested elsewhere in the OT (cf. 1Ch 25:4, 16; Ne 11:17, 22) and on a seal found at Lachish.

20 No need exists for viewing the statement as a variant priestly account of the earlier popular one (e.g., Gray, 381–82). The NIV correctly translates the Hebrew verb here as "had been slain" (i.e., at the time mentioned in v.16).

4. The Reign of Joash in the Southern Kingdom (11:21–12:21 [12:1–22])

OVERVIEW

Between the accession statement, with its spiritual evaluation (11:21–12:3), and the closing notice of Joash's reign (12:19–21), the narrator largely deals with the king's desire to repair the temple.

That subject is dealt with in three phases. (1) Joash instructs the priests concerning the collection of funds needed to make the necessary repairs (vv.4–5). (2) When the whole program lags for over two decades, the king orders that a new program be put into operation. Accordingly, the restoration work on the temple is able to proceed (vv.6–16). (3) The happy account of temple repairs, however, has an unhappy ending. When Aramean expansion under Hazael reaches Jerusalem, Joash buys him off by stripping the temple of its treasures (vv.17–18). Nor does Joash come to a happy end, for conspirators rise up and assassinate him (vv.19–21).

21 Joash was seven years old when he began to reign.

12:1 In the seventh year of Jehu, Joash became king, and he reigned in Jerusalem forty years. His mother's name was Zibiah; she was from Beersheba. 2 Joash did what was right in the eyes of the LORD all the years Jehoiada the priest instructed him. 3 The high places, however, were not removed; the people continued to offer sacrifices and burn incense there.

4 Joash said to the priests, "Collect all the money that is brought as sacred offerings to the temple of the LORD — the money collected in the census, the money received from personal vows and the money brought voluntarily to the temple. 5 Let every priest receive the money from one of the treasurers, and let it be used to repair whatever damage is found in the temple."

6 But by the twenty-third year of King Joash the priests still had not repaired the temple. 7 Therefore King Joash summoned Jehoiada the priest and the other priests and asked them, "Why aren't you repairing the damage done to the temple? Take no more money from your treasurers, but hand it over for repairing the temple." 8 The priests agreed that they would not collect any more money from the people and that they would not repair the temple themselves.

9 Jehoiada the priest took a chest and bored a hole in its lid. He placed it beside the altar, on the right side as one enters the temple of the LORD. The priests who guarded the entrance put into the chest all the money that was brought to the temple of the LORD. 10 Whenever they saw that there was a large amount of money in the chest, the royal secretary and the high priest came, counted the money that had been brought into the temple of the LORD and put it into bags. 11 When the amount had been determined, they gave the money to the men appointed to supervise the work on the temple. With it they paid those who worked on the temple of the LORD — the carpenters and builders, 12 the masons and stonecutters. They purchased timber and dressed stone for the repair of the temple of the LORD, and met all the other expenses of restoring the temple.

13 The money brought into the temple was not spent for making silver basins, wick trimmers, sprinkling bowls, trumpets or any other articles of gold or silver for the temple of the LORD; 14 it was paid to the workmen, who used it to repair the temple. 15 They did not require an accounting from those to whom they gave the money to pay the workers, because they acted with complete honesty. 16 The money from the guilt offerings and sin offerings was not brought into the temple of the LORD; it belonged to the priests.

17 About this time Hazael king of Aram went up and attacked Gath and captured it. Then he turned to attack Jerusalem. 18 But Joash king of Judah took all the sacred objects dedicated by his fathers — Jehoshaphat, Jehoram and Ahaziah, the kings of Judah — and the gifts he himself had dedicated and all the gold found in the treasuries of the temple of the LORD and of the royal palace, and he sent them to Hazael king of Aram, who then withdrew from Jerusalem.

[19]As for the other events of the reign of Joash, and all he did, are they not written in
the book of the annals of the kings of Judah? [20]His officials conspired against him and
assassinated him at Beth Millo, on the road down to Silla. [21]The officials who murdered him
were Jozabad son of Shimeath and Jehozabad son of Shomer. He died and was buried
with his fathers in the City of David. And Amaziah his son succeeded him as king.

COMMENTARY

11:21–12:3 [12:1–4] The spiritual evaluation of Joash is qualifiedly favorable. The notice that Joash conducted himself circumspectly while Jehoiada was still alive is ominous in tone (cf. 2Ch 24:17–22) and a reminder of the need for personal faith.

4–5 [5–6] Joash's first edict concerning preparations for the repairing of the temple (doubtless made early in his reign; cf. 2Ch 24:5) called for the setting aside of money collected as payment of special religious taxes and voluntary offerings. The Chronicler adds that the Levites were to gather such funds personally from the cities of Judah.

6–8 [7–9] Though all haste was bidden in the matter, yet by the twenty-third year the work had not yet begun (2Ch 24:5). No formal reasons are cited for this seeming lack of effort by the Levites. But whatever the problem was, the system was not working. So the king took away the priests' supervision of the task, and the prestige of the royal office was lent to the project.

9–16 [10–17] Joash decreed that a chest be set outside the wall to the inner court at the southern gate on the righthand side of the entrance to the temple, so that everyone who passed through might cast a contribution in for the temple's repair (v.9; cf. 2Ch 24:8). Joash also had a proclamation read throughout Judah concerning the need and the intent of the box; in the proclamation he urged all citizens to participate willingly, in accordance with Moses' ancient institution (cf. Ex 25:2–3; 30:12–16; Lev 27:2–8 with 2Ch 24:9). The response was tremendous (v.10; cf. 2Ch 24:10).

When there was ample money to begin the repairs, the workmen were commissioned (vv.11–12; cf. 2Ch 24:11–13). A comparison of v.13 with 2 Chronicles 24:14 indicates that no monies were used for making the sacred vessels so long as the repairs of the temple proceeded. So successful was the king's program and so responsibly did all concerned carry out their duties that there was even money left over for the provision of sacred vessels for the sanctuary service (2Ch 24:14).

17–21 [18–22] The date of the Aramean invasion mentioned here probably occurred soon after the death of Samsi-Adad V of Assyria in 811 BC, for the death of a king in the ancient Near East customarily signaled an occasion for military activity; moreover, for the first few years after Samsi-Adad's death, Queen Semiramis ruled Assyria as regent for the young Adad-Nirari III (811–783 BC). Accordingly, Hazael seized the opportunity to march inland against the recently crowned Joash; Hazael followed up this march with a full strike into Philistia and Judea. His victorious moves brought him much booty and left many dead; even Joash was wounded in the campaign.

This fact need not imply, however, that Joash was assassinated as he lay recovering from his wounds, as some scholars have suggested. Actually the details of the Aramean campaign and Joash's death may be separated by nearly a decade, with Joash's death not coming until 796 BC. In the OT details are often telescoped, with events of cause and effect brought together though chronologically separated by many years and other events.

The Chronicler (2Ch 24:15–18) reports that after the death of Jehoiada, Joash fell under the influence of godless advisors, who turned his heart to Canaanite practices. It was to no avail that God sent his prophets to warn against this apostatizing. Even Jehoiada's son Zechariah was stoned to death for delivering God's message (2Ch 24:20–22).

Apparently the citizens could no longer tolerate this situation, so they put Joash to death. As the bed had become the scene of Ben-Hadad's death at the hands of Hazael (2Ki 8:15), so it was for Joash (2Ch 24:25); conspirators assassinated him "in Beth Millo" (2Ki 12:20).

NOTES

11:21 [12:1] Joash became king at age seven (11:21), coincidently, in the seventh year of Jehu's reign. Likewise, Athaliah was overthrown in her seventh year (11:4).

5 [6] The noun מַכָּר (*makkār*, "treasurers" [NIV]; lit., "his assessor") comes from the Semitic root that means "do business" (so, e.g., Akkad.; cf. Heb. מָכַר [*mākar* "sell"]; hence, e.g., Akkad. *makkāru*, "trader"; Ugar. *mkr*, "merchant"; cf. Egyp. *mkr*, "merchant"). Here the term must refer to a type of temple personnel who, perhaps, as Gray, 586, suggests, assisted the priests with the evaluation of sacrifices and offerings brought to the temple. The term is also used of the temple personnel and of tax assessors at Ugarit. Both earlier and recent translators have struggled with the noun. The KJV translated it "acquaintance" (cf. NJB), while the NKJV renders it "constituency." The NRSV and GWT give it as "donors," while the REB has "treasurer."

6 [7] By the "twenty-third year" of King Joash is meant the twenty-third year of his reign. The king is now thirty.

9 [10] At first sight a discrepancy seems to exist between the details in Kings and those in Chronicles. Whereas this verse locates Joash's chest "beside the altar, on the right side" (cf. Josephus, *Ant.* 9.163 [8.2]), 2 Chronicles 24:8 places it without, "at the gate of the temple." Actually the chest could not have been placed beside the altar per se, for this would contravene Levitical stipulation. The intent of the text of Kings is simply that the chest was set against the wall of the altar at the entrance that lay to the righthand side of the altar, or the southern entrance to the middle court. So understood, the texts of Kings and Chronicles are in natural agreement.

10–16 [11–17] The accounts in Kings and 2 Chronicles 24:9–14 are supplementary. The officers who collected the money from the full chest were two: (1) the royal secretary and (2) the high priest's designated official. Having been brought to the royal office, the money would be weighed and then distributed to the supervisors of the building operations. The men involved were so trustworthy that no accounting was demanded of them.

Because coinage is first mentioned in postexilic times (Ezr 2:69), Wiseman, *1 & 2 Kings*, 237, is perhaps correct in suggesting that what was collected was silver, which "when melted down into ingots was readily available for payments."

20 [21] For "Millo," see Note on 1 Kings 9:15. The identification of the descent of Silla is uncertain. As Edersheim, 7:33, observes, it "probably marks a locality, but it is difficult of explanation." The royal bed often became a deathbed in the ancient Near East (cf., e.g., the account of the assassination of the Egyptian king Amenemhet [*ANET*, 418–19]).

21 [22] The variation of "Zabad" in 2 Chronicles 24:26 and "Jozabad" here may simply be one of a shortened form, much like that between Joash and Jehoash.

The variation between Jehozabad's apparent mother Shomer (Kings) and Shimrith (Chronicles) may be accounted for in terms of the difference between feminine names ending in *ah* (here shortened further in MT) and *t*. It is also possible that the Shomer of Kings was the father of Shimrith (Chronicles), mother of Jehozabad. It is singularly strange that both men may have had the same name and both mothers were from Transjordan.

4. The Reign of Jehoahaz in the Northern Kingdom (13:1–9)

1In the twenty-third year of Joash son of Ahaziah king of Judah, Jehoahaz son of Jehu
became king of Israel in Samaria, and he reigned seventeen years. 2He did evil in the eyes
of the LORD by following the sins of Jeroboam son of Nebat, which he had caused Israel to
commit, and he did not turn away from them. 3So the LORD's anger burned against Israel,
and for a long time he kept them under the power of Hazael king of Aram and Ben-Hadad
his son.

4Then Jehoahaz sought the LORD's favor, and the LORD listened to him, for he saw how
severely the king of Aram was oppressing Israel. 5The LORD provided a deliverer for Israel,
and they escaped from the power of Aram. So the Israelites lived in their own homes as
they had before. 6But they did not turn away from the sins of the house of Jeroboam,
which he had caused Israel to commit; they continued in them. Also, the Asherah pole
remained standing in Samaria.

7Nothing had been left of the army of Jehoahaz except fifty horsemen, ten chariots and
ten thousand foot soldiers, for the king of Aram had destroyed the rest and made them
like the dust at threshing time.

8As for the other events of the reign of Jehoahaz, all he did and his achievements, are
they not written in the book of the annals of the kings of Israel? 9Jehoahaz rested with his
fathers and was buried in Samaria. And Jehoash his son succeeded him as king.

COMMENTARY

1–3 Jehoahaz's reign began in the same year that Joash launched his campaign to repair the temple (12:6). The negative spiritual evaluation of his reign is accompanied by the statement that God allowed the Aramean king Hazael to afflict the northern kingdom repeatedly.

4–9 The chronological understanding of the details of vv.4–7 (cf. vv.22–24) turns on two items: (1) a comparison of the details of the scriptural account with the recorded history of the ancient Near East, and (2) a recognition that Ben-Hadad is not here called king but merely the son of Hazael. With regard to the latter point, Keil, 375–76, is probably correct in suggesting that Ben-Hadad's activity lay in his service as a commanding officer in his father's army. As to the former point, it seems clear that Hazael's chief military activity fell in the early periods surrounding the death of Samsi-Adad V in 811 BC, specifically, during the five years that followed while Semiramis was regent for the young Adad-Nirari III (811–783 BC; see Note on 12:17).

Aramean fortunes were always linked to the Assyrians, who traditionally sought an access route to the Mediterranean. Accordingly, Hazael's ability to move effectively against Israel-Judah was contingent on Assyria's intervention. Thus when Adad-Nirari III was at last able to rule in his own right, he turned his attention immediately to the Aramean problem in a series of western thrusts (805–802 BC), the last of which saw the capture of Damascus and the submission of the western states.

The strong position of Assyria after 805 would seem to call for the attack described here to have occurred between the period 814–806, before the revived Assyrian presence in great power in the west. Afterward Israel had respite from the Aramean menace; therefore, it is likely that Adad-Nirari III was Israel's deliverer sent in answer to Jehoahaz's seeking of the Lord's favor. Unfortunately, while Jehoahaz's repentance appeared to be genuine, he allowed the state religion of the golden calves and the cult associated with the Asherah pole in Samaria to continue. A gracious and compassionate God displayed his concern for these latter-day recipients of the benefits of the covenant made with the patriarchs by preserving the northern kingdom, though in a severely weakened state (cf. vv.22–23).

NOTES

3 The Hebrew expression "all the days" appears to be a general term for "a long time" (NIV). Hazael is known to have been on the throne as late as 805 BC. Adad-Nirari III mentions his siege of Damascus and the carrying off of booty at that time (Luckenbill, 1:261, 263). In the inscription Hazael is simply designated "Lord," perhaps a shortened form from Arslan Tash (ancient *Ḥadatu*, the Assyrian provincial capital of the west) reading "Belonging to our Lord, Hazael."

Since nothing is heard of Hazael beyond the fall of Damascus and since shortly after that Ben-Hadad III is known to be occupying the throne (though in a much reduced capacity), we may provisionally assign the date of these two Aramean kings as follows: Hazael, ca. 841–802; Ben-Hadad III, 802–780.

4–5 The "deliverer" has been variously identified as Zakir of Hamath (E. Yamauchi, "Documents from Old Testament Times: A Survey of Recent Discoveries," *WTJ* 41 [1978]: 26–27; S. Cook, CAH, 3:363), Jehoash and Jeroboam II of the northern kingdom (Keil, 375), Elisha (Gray, 595), and Adad-Nirari III of Assyria (J. B. Payne, *The Theology of the Older Testament* [Grand Rapids: Zondervan, 1962], 132). In the light of the historical records noted above, this last suggestion is perhaps the simplest, with Adad-Nirari III being Israel's "savior-deliverer" much as Cyrus would later be God's "shepherd" (Isa 44:28–45:1).

5. The Reign of Jehoash in the Northern Kingdom (13:10–25)

OVERVIEW

The juxtaposition of the accession statement plus spiritual evaluation (vv.10–11) with the closing notices (vv.12–13) is unique. The usual attention to historical details is thus allowed to form the climax of the narrative (vv.14–25). Here we learn that even on his deathbed Elisha is able to give the king a prediction of a series of victories over the hated Arameans (vv.14–19). But before telling of the fulfillment of that prophecy (vv.22–25), the narrator inserts an interesting note concerning a later miracle in association with the remains of Elisha's dead body (vv.20–21).

10 In the thirty-seventh year of Joash king of Judah, Jehoash son of Jehoahaz became king of Israel in Samaria, and he reigned sixteen years. 11 He did evil in the eyes of the LORD and did not turn away from any of the sins of Jeroboam son of Nebat, which he had caused Israel to commit; he continued in them.

12 As for the other events of the reign of Jehoash, all he did and his achievements, including his war against Amaziah king of Judah, are they not written in the book of the annals of the kings of Israel? 13 Jehoash rested with his fathers, and Jeroboam succeeded him on the throne. Jehoash was buried in Samaria with the kings of Israel.

14 Now Elisha was suffering from the illness from which he died. Jehoash king of Israel went down to see him and wept over him. "My father! My father!" he cried. "The chariots and horsemen of Israel!"

15 Elisha said, "Get a bow and some arrows," and he did so. 16 "Take the bow in your hands," he said to the king of Israel. When he had taken it, Elisha put his hands on the king's hands.

17 "Open the east window," he said, and he opened it. "Shoot!" Elisha said, and he shot. "The LORD's arrow of victory, the arrow of victory over Aram!" Elisha declared. "You will completely destroy the Arameans at Aphek."

18 Then he said, "Take the arrows," and the king took them. Elisha told him, "Strike the ground." He struck it three times and stopped. 19 The man of God was angry with him and said, "You should have struck the ground five or six times; then you would have defeated Aram and completely destroyed it. But now you will defeat it only three times."

20 Elisha died and was buried.

Now Moabite raiders used to enter the country every spring. 21 Once while some Israelites were burying a man, suddenly they saw a band of raiders; so they threw the man's body into Elisha's tomb. When the body touched Elisha's bones, the man came to life and stood up on his feet.

22Hazael king of Aram oppressed Israel throughout the reign of Jehoahaz. 23But the LORD was gracious to them and had compassion and showed concern for them because of his covenant with Abraham, Isaac and Jacob. To this day he has been unwilling to destroy them or banish them from his presence.

24Hazael king of Aram died, and Ben-Hadad his son succeeded him as king. 25Then Jehoash son of Jehoahaz recaptured from Ben-Hadad son of Hazael the towns he had taken in battle from his father Jehoahaz. Three times Jehoash defeated him, and so he recovered the Israelite towns.

COMMENTARY

10–13 The notice that Jehoash succeeded to Israel's throne in the thirty-seventh year of Joash of Judah's reign appears to be at variance with the data in 13:1, which indicates that Jehoahaz became king in Joash's twenty-third year. Because Jehoahaz reigned seventeen years, one would expect something like the thirty-ninth year of Joash's reign to be the point of correlation. Indeed some manuscripts of the LXX (cf. NEB) contain such a reading.

Alternatively, one may suggest either that Jehoash had a two-year coregency with his father Jehoahaz (Wiseman, *1 & 2 Kings*, 241) or that beginning here the narrator switches from the nonaccession year system to the accession year system for the kings of the northern kingdom (Thiele, 72). In either case the reading of the MT can be allowed to stand.

14 Jehoash addressed Elisha with words reminiscent of the venerable prophet's own testimony at Elijah's translation (cf. 2:12 and Note). Because Jehoash came to Elisha and addressed him courteously, the Lord used the occasion to increase Jehoash's slim faith.

15–19 Elisha's placing of his hands on those of the king is reminisicent of his earlier act in raising the Shunammite's son. The act was full of symbolism, with God himself assuring the king of Israel's victory. The fact that Jehoash failed to shoot all the arrows at his disposal would limit the number of battles that he would win. Final victory would elude Jehoash; the deed would be accomplished only later by Jeroboam II (14:25–28).

20–21 Because Elisha's bones are mentioned, it is assumed that this miracle must have occurred much later. If "bones" is a synecdoche for the whole body, however, such an assumption need not be made. As a figure of speech, "bones" may have been selected because of its use as representing the seat of one's health (Pr 15:30; Isa 58:11) and that which is said to live again (Isa 66:14). National revival could also be symbolized by the coming to life of dead bones (Eze 37:1–14).

At any rate, more than the resuscitation of the dead man is surely intended here. Indeed, the juxtaposition of this event with the preceding account makes it clear that herein was another divinely intended sign. God was the God of the living, not the dead (cf. Lk 20:38), not only for the man who had been restored to life but for Israel as well. The nation could yet "live" if it would but appropriate the eternally living God as its own. The entire episode was a further corroborative sign that what Elisha had prophesied would certainly come to pass.

22–25 The chapter closes with some historical notices concerning the strained Aramean-Israelite relations during the reign of Jehoahaz and Jehoash. Conditions improved during Jehoash's reign as the Israelite king; in accordance with Elisha's prophecy, he defeated the Aramean king Ben-Hadad III, son of Hazael, three times. This record is a further indication of the inviolability of God's Word and God's continued faithfulness to the basic covenant made with the patriarchs.

NOTES

16 The prophet offered Jehoash the opportunity to assume a position of spiritual leadership. But the king failed to do so; his faith was scant, and the divine evaluation of his character (v.11) is not favorable.

20 The planned war campaigns in the ancient Near East could take place any time between April and the late fall (see de Vaux, 251). The type of razzia, or plundering foray, envisioned here, however, need not be structured quite so closely, though the text indicates that the Moabite raids were regularly carried out about the same time each year.

22–25 For the historical reconstruction of the period of Israelite-Aramean relations, see the Note on 13:3. An early eighth-century BC inscription of Adad-Nirari III at tell Er Rimah mentions the tribute of "Iuʾasu (Jehoash) the Samaritan." The growing preoccupation of Adad-Nirari III with the affairs in the east and Jehoash's treaty link with him, along with the growing weakness of Aram in the days of Ben-Hadad III (who was being pressed by Zakir of Hamath and Luash), provided the historical framework for the outworking of Elisha's prophecy. See further A. Malmat, "The Arameans," in D. J. Wiseman, ed., *Peoples of Old Testament Times* (Oxford: Clarendon, 1973), 145–46, 152–53; D. W. Thomas, *Documents from Old Testament Times* (New York: Harper & Row, 1961), 242–50.

6. The Reign of Amaziah in the Southern Kingdom (14:1–22)

OVERVIEW

The usual accession statement gives Amaziah a positive evaluation qualified only by his allowing the high places and the sacrifices performed there to continue (vv.1–4). The historical notices concerning his reign focus on three areas of activity: (1) his execution of his father's assassins (vv.5–6); (2) his defeat of Edom (v.7); and (3) his foolish confrontation with Jehoash of the northern kingdom (vv.8–14).

The section comprising the closing notice is unusual. It begins by repeating the closing notice with regard to Jehoash's life (vv.15–16; cf. 13:12–13). The effect is twofold. It not only reminds the reader of how greatly Amaziah's reign is tied to that of Jehoash, but it also provides a transition to the reign of Jeroboam II that follows. The concluding rehearsal of Amaziah's passing gives details both of his rebuilding of Elath and his death due to a broad-based conspiracy against him (vv.17–21).

[1]In the second year of Jehoash son of Jehoahaz king of Israel, Amaziah son of Joash king of Judah began to reign. [2]He was twenty-five years old when he became king, and he reigned in Jerusalem twenty-nine years. His mother's name was Jehoaddin; she was from Jerusalem. [3]He did what was right in the eyes of the LORD, but not as his father David had done. In everything he followed the example of his father Joash. [4]The high places, however, were not removed; the people continued to offer sacrifices and burn incense there.

[5]After the kingdom was firmly in his grasp, he executed the officials who had murdered his father the king. [6]Yet he did not put the sons of the assassins to death, in accordance with what is written in the Book of the Law of Moses where the LORD commanded: "Fathers shall not be put to death for their children, nor children put to death for their fathers; each is to die for his own sins."

[7]He was the one who defeated ten thousand Edomites in the Valley of Salt and captured Sela in battle, calling it Joktheel, the name it has to this day.

[8]Then Amaziah sent messengers to Jehoash son of Jehoahaz, the son of Jehu, king of Israel, with the challenge: "Come, meet me face to face."

[9]But Jehoash king of Israel replied to Amaziah king of Judah: "A thistle in Lebanon sent a message to a cedar in Lebanon, 'Give your daughter to my son in marriage.' Then a wild beast in Lebanon came along and trampled the thistle underfoot. [10]You have indeed defeated Edom and now you are arrogant. Glory in your victory, but stay at home! Why ask for trouble and cause your own downfall and that of Judah also?"

[11]Amaziah, however, would not listen, so Jehoash king of Israel attacked. He and Amaziah king of Judah faced each other at Beth Shemesh in Judah. [12]Judah was routed by Israel, and every man fled to his home. [13]Jehoash king of Israel captured Amaziah king of Judah, the son of Joash, the son of Ahaziah, at Beth Shemesh. Then Jehoash went to Jerusalem and broke down the wall of Jerusalem from the Ephraim Gate to the Corner Gate — a section about six hundred feet long. [14]He took all the gold and silver and all the articles found in the temple of the LORD and in the treasuries of the royal palace. He also took hostages and returned to Samaria.

[15]As for the other events of the reign of Jehoash, what he did and his achievements, including his war against Amaziah king of Judah, are they not written in the book of the annals of the kings of Israel? [16]Jehoash rested with his fathers and was buried in Samaria with the kings of Israel. And Jeroboam his son succeeded him as king.

[17]Amaziah son of Joash king of Judah lived for fifteen years after the death of Jehoash son of Jehoahaz king of Israel. [18]As for the other events of Amaziah's reign, are they not written in the book of the annals of the kings of Judah?

[19]They conspired against him in Jerusalem, and he fled to Lachish, but they sent men after him to Lachish and killed him there. [20]He was brought back by horse and was buried in Jerusalem with his fathers, in the City of David.

[21]Then all the people of Judah took Azariah, who was sixteen years old, and made him king in place of his father Amaziah. [22]He was the one who rebuilt Elath and restored it to Judah after Amaziah rested with his fathers.

COMMENTARY

1–4 Like David, the founder of the dynasty, Amaziah did that which was right except in one particular matter (cf. 1Ki 15:5). His failure to do away with worship at the high places is illuminated by the Chronicler's report that Amaziah did not serve God "wholeheartedly" (2Ch 25:2).

5–7 In accordance with prevailing ancient Near Eastern practice, when Amaziah felt secure on the throne, he executed his father's murderers. He did not follow the usual custom of killing their children, however. Both the narrator here and the Chronicler (2Ch 25:4) point out that this behavior harmonized with the stipulations of Deuteronomy 24:16.

Although the narrator dismisses Amaziah's victory over Edom with a single verse, the affair receives expanded treatment in 2 Chronicles 25:5–15. According to the Chronicler, Amaziah laid careful plans for the reconquest of Edom (lost in the days of Jehoram; 8:20–22). He began with a general census and conscription of able-bodied men twenty years of age and older (2Ch 25:5). He added to the three-thousand-man army by raising another one hundred thousand mercenaries from Israel (2Ch 25:6), which he subsequently dismissed when rebuked by one of the Lord's prophets (2Ch 25:7–10, 13). Thus encouraged that his cause was just and that God would give him the victory, Amaziah invaded Edom and inflicted a crushing defeat. The narrator of Kings reports an overwhelming victory in the Valley of Salt and the capture of Sela (see Notes). Success in Edom did not result in permanent occupation of the area, however (see Note on 8:22).

Life's successes are not always the victories they seem to be. A notable defeat for Amaziah occurred here (2Ch 25:14–16). Having vanquished Edom and carried off booty and captives, he foolishly worshiped their captive gods. For this the man of God again rebuked Amaziah. This time Amaziah rejected the Lord's warning. He threatened the prophet and sent him away. Yet before he left, that prophet announced Amaziah's doom for his spiritual callousness and self-will.

8–11 The motive behind Amaziah's proud challenge to Jehoash is not difficult to suggest. Amaziah was doubtless buoyed by his recent success in Edom and perhaps seeking vengeance for the pillaging rampage against the cities of Judah by the dismissed Israelite mercenaries (2Ch 25:13). Jehoash's attempt to dissuade Amaziah fell on deaf ears. Neither the fable nor Jehoash's stern warning was sufficient to prevent Amaziah's ill-advised attack. True to the prophetic warning (2Ch 25:16), Amaziah was set on a course of self-destruction.

12–16 Jehoash not only routed Amaziah's army (2Ch 25:22) but also took Judah's king captive. Jehoash followed up his triumph with a thrust against Jerusalem that resulted in the loss of some six hundred feet of city wall, the confiscation of the temple furnishings and palace treasures, and the taking of many prisoners of war. Amaziah's lesson in self-will had cost his nation dearly. The Chronicler (2Ch 25:20) reports that behind it all lay the wise hand of divine providence arranging the details of the lives of all concerned to teach Amaziah and Judah the folly of trusting in foreign gods.

As for the two gates mentioned here, the Ephraim Gate apparently was situated in the northern wall close to the modern Damascus Gate, while the Corner Gate was farther west (cf. 2Ch 26:9). The northwestern section of the wall was Jerusalem's most vulnerable spot.

17–18 Some uncertainty exists concerning the details of Amaziah's later life. Many build on the Chronicler's report (2Ch 25:23–24) that Jehoash took Amaziah captive to suggest that Jehoash kept him in captivity for ten years. At Jehoash's death he was released and returned to Judah, where he ruled jointly with his son Azariah for fifteen years. The uprising that led to Amaziah's death appears to have been widespread. His apostasy and defeat may have brought him many adversaries.

19–20 The return of Amaziah's body by horse-drawn chariot may point to a stately funeral cortege. Or it could mean that the very royal chariot by which Amaziah thought to make his escape was used to carry his dead body back to Jerusalem, or perhaps that his own chariot formed the hearse for the procession. The scriptural presentation (cf. 15:3; 2Ch 25:27) does not always cast Amaziah in a particularly good light. Indeed, the narrator presents his entire reign as an aspect of the era of Jehoash of Israel (13:10–14:16). Even his final fifteen years are discussed in relation to Jehoash's death (14:17–22).

21–22 The mention of Azariah's (Uzziah's) restoration of Edomite Elath marks the first significant act of his independent rule and largely sets a historical peg for the entrance of the king into his period of greatness (cf. 2Ch 26:3–15).

NOTES

7 Although Wiseman, *1 & 2 Kings*, 244, and A. F. Rainey ("Sela [of Edom]," *IDBSup*, 800) disallow it, Sela has usually been identified with the site near modern Petra. If this identification is correct, the seizure of Sela was a remarkable feat, for it lay amid the seemingly impregnable rocks and cliffs of the Wadi Musa. There the Nabataean stronghold of Petra would one day be erected. See further J. Lawlor, *The Nabataeans in Historical Perspective* (Grand Rapids: Baker, 1974), 127–39, and A. Negey, "Petra," *Encyclopedia of Archaeological Excavations in the Holy Land*, ed. M. Avi Yonah (Englewood Cliffs, N.J.: Prentice-Hall, 1975), 4:943–58.

According to 2 Chronicles 25:11–12, the capture of Sela was preceded by an overwhelming victory in the Valley of Salt below, in which ten thousand Edomites lost their lives and an equal number were subsequently cast from one of Sela's heights to the jagged valley below. Such a valley was located south of the Dead Sea (see Aharoni and Avi-Yonah, 89).

9 With this fable compare that of Jotham in Judges 9:7–15. For the Hebrew fable itself, see R. J. Williams, "The Fable in the Ancient Near East," in *A Stubborn Faith*, ed. E. C. Hobbs (Dallas: Southern Methodist Univ. Press, 1956), 3–26.

11 The Beth Shemesh mentioned here as the location of battle was situated west of Jerusalem (cf. 1Sa 6:9), as opposed to other sites with the same name in Lower Galilee (Jos 19:22, 38).

13 The rehearsal of Amaziah's patrilineage here is unusual. It may be a reminder of the legitimacy of his claim to the Judean crown, even in exile.

17 For a suggested chronological reconstruction of Amaziah's later years, see Thiele (83–87). For a discussion of the chronological problems of chs. 13–15, see the helpful excursus of Hobbs, 184–85.

19 Lachish would again play a vital role in the latter days of Hezekiah and in Judah's final demise (Jer 34:7), as attested by the famous Lachish Letters (see Note on 25:22).

21 If Azariah's age at the time of his coregency with his father is in view, the preposition תַּחַת (*taḥat*) is to be translated "beside" or "under the authority of" (i.e., his father; cf. 15:1–2; 2Ch 26:1–3). For this use of the preposition, see Genesis 41:35; Numbers 5:19. For the use of the *waw*-consecutive construction as a pluperfect, see *IBHS*, 552–53.

22 For a more radical reconstruction of the chronological problems in ch. 14, see M. Naor, "Who Built Eilat and Restored It to Judah (2 Kgs 14:22)?" *Beth Mikra* 23 (1978): 285–91.

7. The Reign of Jeroboam II in the Northern Kingdom (14:23–29)

[23]In the fifteenth year of Amaziah son of Joash king of Judah, Jeroboam son of Jehoash
king of Israel became king in Samaria, and he reigned forty-one years. [24]He did evil in the
eyes of the LORD and did not turn away from any of the sins of Jeroboam son of Nebat,
which he had caused Israel to commit. [25]He was the one who restored the boundaries of
Israel from Lebo Hamath to the Sea of the Arabah, in accordance with the word of the
LORD, the God of Israel, spoken through his servant Jonah son of Amittai, the prophet from
Gath Hepher.

[26]The LORD had seen how bitterly everyone in Israel, whether slave or free, was suffering;
there was no one to help them. [27]And since the LORD had not said he would blot out the
name of Israel from under heaven, he saved them by the hand of Jeroboam son of Jehoash.

[28]As for the other events of Jeroboam's reign, all he did, and his military achievements,
including how he recovered for Israel both Damascus and Hamath, which had belonged
to Yaudi, are they not written in the book of the annals of the kings of Israel? [29]Jeroboam
rested with his fathers, the kings of Israel. And Zechariah his son succeeded him as king.

COMMENTARY

23–29 The chapter closes with a brief notice of the forty-one year reign of Jeroboam II (793–752 BC). The era of Jeroboam (northern kingdom) and Azariah (southern kingdom) would mark a significant change in the fortunes of God's people. These days would be marked by unparalleled prosperity for the twin kingdoms, both economically and politically. Indeed together they would acquire nearly the same territorial dimensions as in the days of the united monarchy (v.25).

But God's blessings are too often taken for granted, and so it proved to be in Israel and Judah in the eighth century BC (cf. Hos 13:6; Am 6:1–6). Spiritually, the lives of God's people degenerated into open sin in the northern kingdom (cf. Hosea, Amos) and into empty formalism in the south (cf. Joel). In such an era God therefore raised up the great writing prophets, one of whom, Jonah, is mentioned here (v.25).

Great responsibility for Israel's spiritual problem lay with her leadership. Jeroboam II, while a capable administrator and military leader, had no concern for vital religion (v.24; cf. Hos 5:1–7; 6:1–7). He simply carried out the ritual of the standard state religion begun by Jeroboam I.

Nonetheless, Jeroboam's external accomplishments were many. In accordance with an unrecorded prophecy of Jonah, Jeroboam restored fully the borders of Israel so that they extended from the entrance of Hamath (or Lebo Hamath; see Note on v.25), in the great Beqaʾ Valley amid the Lebanese Mountains, to the Sea of Arabah (or Dead Sea). Apparently even Hamath and Damascus came under Israelite superiority (v.28). Amos (Am 6:13–14) indicates that the Transjordanian territories were probably also recovered at this time.

In all these developments the faithfulness of God, despite Israel's unfaithfulness (cf. Hos 2:2–3:5; 11:1–11; 14:4–8; Am 3:1–15), is evident. Because Israel had fallen into such desperate spiritual conditions (vv.26–27), a merciful God had acted in behalf of his people. As he had granted them deliverance from external pressures by sending Adad-Nirari III of Assyria against the Arameans (cf. 13:5), thus initiating a period of recovery under Jehoash (13:25), so now in a grander way he culminated that deliverance with full victory over the Arameans—one that included Israel's recovery of its former boundaries (vv.27–28).

When Jeroboam II died in 752 BC, he left behind a strong kingdom but, unfortunately, one whose core foundation was so spiritually rotten that the edifice of state would not long withstand the rising tides of international intrigue and pressure.

NOTES

23 Jeroboam II's assumption of power in the fifteenth year of Amaziah (782–781 BC) indicates the time of his independent rule. His forty-one year reign reckons from 793, the time of his appointment as coregent with his father, Jehoash.

25 The Hebrew phrase translated "Lebo Hamath" (NIV) refers to a location known from the Assyrian records of Tiglath-Pileser III (see Luckenbill, 1:294). Alternatively, it may be translated "entrance to Hamath."

The Sea of the Arabah may well be equated with "the valley of the Arabah" of Amos 6:14, which, in turn, may be the same as Isaiah's (Isa 15:7) "Ravine of the Poplars" at the southern end of the Dead Sea across the Jordan. If so, Jeroboam's Transjordanian conquest was total. It would appear that Uzziah and Jeroboam and the twin kingdoms lived in essential harmony and cooperation.

For the relation of the mention of Jonah here to the occasion of Jonah's prophecy, see Richard D. Patterson and Andrew E. Hill, *Minor Prophets* (Cornerstone Biblical Commentary; Carol Stream, Ill.: Tyndale, 2008), 285.

26 For the phrase "slave or free," see Notes on 1 Kings 14:10.

28 Among the "other events" of Jeroboam II was his attention to the economy and the agricultural needs of the country. Verification of Israel's prosperity comes from the recovery of the famous Samaria

Ostraca, dating from this general period. These ostraca are bills of lading for delivery of fine oil and barley sent to Samaria from the royal estates. For the texts themselves, see J. Gibson, *Syrian Semitic Inscriptions* (Oxford: Clarendon, 1973), 5–15. On the great inner corruption of Israelite society in the eighth century BC, see Bright, 241–48.

The NIV (cf. Montgomery, 446), sensing the difficulty of retaining the MT's לִיהוּדָה (*lîhûdâ*, "for Judah") in the light of the known history of the era, repoints the MT to read "to Yaudi." So construed it reflects the name of an ancient city in northern Syria (cf. *ANET*, 654), better known in the Assyrian inscriptions as Samal (see W. Beyerlin, *Near Eastern Religious Texts Relating to the Old Testament* [Philadelphia: Westminster, 1975], 260).

The pointing of the MT can be maintained, however, if one understands it to indicate that Jeroboam restored Damascus and Hamath to Judah (together) with Israel. This understanding would imply that Uzziah had allied himself with Jeroboam in the enterprise. A similar approach is taken by Manahem Haran ("The Rise and Decline of the Empire of Jeroboam ben Joash," *VT* 17 [1967]: 296). Note, however, that Haran emends the Hebrew text by reading w^e ("and") instead of b^e ("in") before Israel. For uses of the Hebrew preposition b^e meaning "in, with," see *IBHS*, 196–97.

The preposition b^e is known to interchange with other prepositions in parallel structure in northwest Semitic languages (see *UT*, 92–93), including Hebrew. Examples include b^e with *taḥat* ("under"; Isa 57:5), with *min* ("from"; Ps 18:8[9], and with l^e ("at, in"; Ge 49:27; Ecc 11:6). The fluctuation in the meaning of b^e may suggest that in parallel with l^e here the phrase may be translated "to Judah (and) to Israel."

The distinction between "the entrance to Hamath" (or Lebo Hamath; v.25) and Hamath and Damascus here is an accurate one. "Damascus" and "Hamath" must refer to the kingdoms represented by the capital cities. Hamath lay outside the boundaries of ideal Israel (cf. Nu 34:8; cf. 2Sa 8:9–12) and never was captured by David as such.

The Assyrian Adad-Nirari III captured Damascus shortly before (802 BC). Though Adad-Nirari's weak successors campaigned in the area five times from 773–754 BC, they were largely occupied with matters to the east and south; therefore, the Assyrians were not really in a position to oppose Jeroboam's expansion northward. For light on these events and campaigns during this period in Syria from the Assyrian annals of the eighth century BC, see Luckenbill, 2:260–68; Hallo, 44; E. Merrill, *Kingdom of Priests* (Grand Rapids: Baker, 1987), 374–75.

8. The Reign of Uzziah in the Southern Kingdom (15:1–7)

[1]In the twenty-seventh year of Jeroboam king of Israel, Azariah son of Amaziah king of Judah began to reign. [2]He was sixteen years old when he became king, and he reigned in Jerusalem fifty-two years. His mother's name was Jecoliah; she was from Jerusalem. [3]He did what was right in the eyes of the LORD, just as his father Amaziah had done. [4]The high places, however, were not removed; the people continued to offer sacrifices and burn incense there.

5The LORD afflicted the king with leprosy until the day he died, and he lived in a separate
house. Jotham the king's son had charge of the palace and governed the people of the land.
6As for the other events of Azariah's reign, and all he did, are they not written in the
book of the annals of the kings of Judah? 7Azariah rested with his fathers and was buried
near them in the City of David. And Jotham his son succeeded him as king.

COMMENTARY

1–4 Judah's tenth king was Azariah ("Yahweh has helped"), known also as Uzziah (vv.13, 30, 32, 34, "Yahweh is my strength"), the latter name possibly being assumed on the occasion of his independent reign (v.1). Uzziah was made coregent at the time of Amaziah's ill-conceived campaign against Jehoash (14:8–14; 2Ch 25:17–24). After Amaziah's assassination in 767, Uzziah took the throne in his own right and ruled until 740. Thus, counting his coregencies, Uzziah ruled some fifty-two years.

Several reasons may be found for such a lengthy reign besides the longevity of the king. First, Israel's perennial enemy, Assyria, was in a state of severe decline. After the death of the vigorous king Adad-Nirari III (810–783), Assyria was ruled by three weak kings—Shalmaneser IV (782–774), Assur-Dan III (773–756), and Assur-Nirari V (755–746)—who strove desperately to maintain themselves against the advance of their hostile northern neighbor, Urartu. Other campaigns took them mainly to the south and east. Moreover, Assyria was rocked internally by plagues in 765 and 759 and by internal revolts from 763 to 759.

Second, relations between Jeroboam II of Israel and Uzziah remained cordial, so that together the two nations were able eventually to acquire nearly the same territorial dimensions as in the days of the united monarchy. Indeed the Chronicler makes it clear that the era of the early eighth century BC was one of great expansion militarily, administratively, commercially, and economically—a period whose prosperity was second only to that of Solomon (2Ch 26:1–15).

Third, and more basically, Uzziah was noted as a man who began well because of the spiritual heritage he had received from his father (v.3; cf. 2Ch 26:4–5). Accordingly, God's abundant blessing was shed on him (2Ch 26:6–15) so that his fame spread throughout the Near Eastern world (2Ch 26:8, 15).

The mention of the continued worship at the "high places" indicates a state policy of noninterference with competing religious forms that had been in force since at least the time of Joash (cf. 12:3; 14:3–4). The apparent compromise is indicative of a basic spiritual shallowness that was to surface in the prophecies of the great writing prophets of the eighth century BC.

5 Great earthly success is often difficult to manage to spiritual benefit. As with Solomon before him, Uzziah's successes proved to be his undoing. His great power fostered such pride and haughtiness that about 750 BC he sought to add to his vast power by usurping the prerogatives of the sacred priesthood. Challenged to his face by the priests as he attempted to make an offering at the altar of incense, he was also instantaneously judged by God, who smote him with leprosy (or a serious skin disease). Driven from the temple forever, Uzziah thereafter remained a leper, dwelling in isolation until his death (2Ch 26:16–21). During Uzziah's last decade, due to his condition, his son Jotham was made coregent and public officiator, though probably Uzziah remained the real power behind the throne.

6–7 Although Uzziah was buried in the city of David and in the royal burial field, his body was excluded from the royal tombs (cf. 2Ch 26:22–23).

An ossuary was discovered by E. L. Sukenik ("Funerary Tablet of Uzziah, King of Judah," *PEQ* 63 [1931]: 217–21) with the Aramaic inscription, "Hitherto were brought the bones of Uzziah, king of Judah. Do not open."

NOTES

5 Uzziah's "separate house" (בֵּית־הַחָפְשִׁית, *bêt-haḥāpšît*) involves the king's occupying a place where he was free from the routine responsibilities of royalty (cf. the Heb. of 1Sa 17:25). The term is a difficult one and receives varying treatment in the ancient versions; the Peshitta renders it, "in a house hidden away," and the Vulgate, "in a free house, separately." The LXX simply transliterates the term (αφφουσωθ). A. Guillaume ("Hebrew and Arabic Lexicography, A Comparative Study," *AbrN* 4 [1965]: 6) suggests a relation with the Arabic *ḥaffaša* ("he stayed in his tent," i.e., "he dwelt in his house without leaving it"). W. Rudolph ("Ussias 'Haus der Freiheit,'" *ZAW* 89 [1977]: 418–20) suggests that the Hebrew term is a euphemism for formal isolation.

That Uzziah remained the dominant figure behind the throne would be certain if he could be identified with that "Azriau" mentioned as the leader of a coalition that opposed Tiglath-Pileser III in his first western campaign. For details, see Thiele, 93–94; D. Luckenbill, "Azariah of Judah," *AJSL* 41 (1925): 217–32; contrariwise, see Montgomery, 446–47. Many scholars, however, maintain that the reference must be to the king of Iauda in northern Syria (see Montgomery, 446–47; Hobbs, 194).

Jotham's title עַל־הַבָּיִת (*ʿal-habbayit*, "over the palace"; lit., "over the house") doubtless deals with the management of the myriad of complex details relative to the smooth functioning of palace life. The title was previously ascribed to Solomon's chamberlain Ahishar (1Ki 4:6) and later was to be held by Eliakim, Hezekiah's official (2Ki 18:18; Isa 36:3). The title is known from a clay seal impression from Lachish bearing the name "Gedaliah," probably the one whom the Babylonians appointed governor after the fall of Jerusalem (25:22).

Josephus (*Ant.* 9.225 [10.4]) connects the events of Uzziah's condition with the earthquake recorded in Amos 1:1. For a discussion of "leprosy" in the Bible, see Note on 5:1.

6 For Uzziah's "other events" and general conditions in the eighth century BC, see my remarks concerning the background to Joel (see *EBC*, vol. 7).

9. The Reign of Zechariah in the Northern Kingdom (15:8–12)

[8]In the thirty-eighth year of Azariah king of Judah, Zechariah son of Jeroboam became
king of Israel in Samaria, and he reigned six months. [9]He did evil in the eyes of the LORD, as
his fathers had done. He did not turn away from the sins of Jeroboam son of Nebat, which
he had caused Israel to commit.

[10]Shallum son of Jabesh conspired against Zechariah. He attacked him in front of the people, assassinated him and succeeded him as king. [11]The other events of Zechariah's reign are written in the book of the annals of the kings of Israel. [12]So the word of the LORD spoken to Jehu was fulfilled: "Your descendants will sit on the throne of Israel to the fourth generation."

COMMENTARY

8–12 Little is recorded of Zechariah, the fourth descendant of Jehu to assume the throne of Israel, except the familiar evaluation that he did evil in perpetuating the idolatrous sins of Jeroboam I and that he died in an assassination plot. With the passing of Zechariah, the Lord's prophetic promise to Jehu (10:30) stood fulfilled (cf: Am 7:9).

The shortness of Zechariah's reign and that of Shallum, his murderous successor, points up the great contrast in their abilities with those of Jeroboam II and underscores the weakness of the northern kingdom. The openness of Shallum's deed is expressive of Israel's social degradation. If "son of Jabesh" points to Shallum's place of origin, it would indicate that he was a Transjordanian Gileadite. A later Gileadite plot would take the life of King Pekahiah (v.25).

NOTES

10 The MT's difficult reading קָבָל־עָם (*qābāl-ʿām*, "in front of the people" [NIV], i.e., in public view) is emended in the Lucianic recension of the LXX to read "In Ibleʿam" (cf. NIV note), thus making Zechariah's death near where Jehu had massacred Judah's royal house (9:27; 10:12–14)—perhaps a touch of poetic justice.

F. The Era of the Decline and Fall of the Northern Kingdom (15:13–17:41)

1. The Reign of Shallum in the Northern Kingdom (15:13–15)

[13]Shallum son of Jabesh became king in the thirty-ninth year of Uzziah king of Judah, and he reigned in Samaria one month. [14]Then Menahem son of Gadi went from Tirzah up to Samaria. He attacked Shallum son of Jabesh in Samaria, assassinated him and succeeded him as king.

[15]The other events of Shallum's reign, and the conspiracy he led, are written in the book of the annals of the kings of Israel.

COMMENTARY

13–15 Shallum's minimal reign of but one month was terminated by a retaliatory raid by Menahem, who, in turn, usurped the throne. Menahem, who may have been a military commander under Zechariah, brought his forces from Tirzah against Shallum in Samaria. Tirzah was an ancient Canaanite city important for its strategic commercial location and noted for its surpassing beauty (SS 6:4). The city had served as a royal retreat (1Ki 14:17) and a national capital (1Ki 16:8–10) and had remained important.

NOTES

14 The name "Menahem" (meaning "comforting") may indicate that the new king's parents were well advanced in years or that his parents found comfort in his birth as a result of the death of an earlier child. The name of his father, "Gadi," is a shortened form of "Gaddiyahu," found in an ostracon from Samaria (*ANET*, 321).

2. The Reign of Menahem in the Northern Kingdom (15:16–22)

16At that time Menahem, starting out from Tirzah, attacked Tiphsah and everyone in
the city and its vicinity, because they refused to open their gates. He sacked Tiphsah and
ripped open all the pregnant women.
17In the thirty-ninth year of Azariah king of Judah, Menahem son of Gadi became king
of Israel, and he reigned in Samaria ten years. 18He did evil in the eyes of the LORD. During
his entire reign he did not turn away from the sins of Jeroboam son of Nebat, which he
had caused Israel to commit.
19Then Pul king of Assyria invaded the land, and Menahem gave him a thousand talents of
silver to gain his support and strengthen his own hold on the kingdom. 20Menahem exacted
this money from Israel. Every wealthy man had to contribute fifty shekels of silver to be given
to the king of Assyria. So the king of Assyria withdrew and stayed in the land no longer.
21As for the other events of Menahem's reign, and all he did, are they not written in the
book of the annals of the kings of Israel? 22Menahem rested with his fathers. And Pekahiah
his son succeeded him as king.

COMMENTARY

16 Menahem's raid against Tiphsah is set off in a separate paragraph in the MT. The narrator thus indicates that this military action took place before he became king (cf. Josephus, *Ant.* 9.230–31). Was Menahem on a "march of terror" (Cohn, 107) or, being an army commander, was he on a mission ordered by Zechariāh (Hobbs, 196–97)? If the latter scenario is the case, it would indicate that his absence with the armed forces may have provided Shallum with the opportunity for his coup.

Complicating the picture is the problem of the identity of Tiphsah. Tiphsah was situated on the Euphrates (1Ki 4:24). The supposed unlikelihood that this far northern location was intended has caused some commentators to suggest an emendation to Tappuah. Such a reading is found in the Lucianic recension of the LXX (cf. NJB, NLT, REB). Tappuah has the advantage of lying in nearby Ephraim (Jos 16:8). Nevertheless, the seven-day hold that Shallum had on Samaria may indicate that it took a week for news of the coup to reach Menahem at Tiphsah and for him to return. In any case, whether Menahem was still at Tiphsah or had already returned to Tirzah, he went to Samaria to deal with Shallum. Having done so, he seized the throne for himself (v.14).

17–22 Menahem's decade of rule is characterized as one of total sinfulness. In addition to further prostituting Israel's religious experience, he compromised its independence by becoming a vassal to Pul (or, more properly, Tiglath-Pileser III, 745–727 BC) of Assyria. His motive in doing so was not one of patriotic concern for Israel's survival; rather, he hoped that the Assyrian alliance would solidify his hold on the throne of Israel, possibly against a potential rival such as Pekah (vv.27–31).

In order to gain the Assyrian king's backing, he levied a tax of fifty shekels of silver on the wealthy men of the realm so that the assessed levy of one thousand talents of silver might be gathered. Since a talent then weighed about seventy-five pounds, this total was obviously a tremendous sum. Nevertheless the sum was fully met, and Tiglath-Pileser "withdrew and stayed in the land no longer" (v.20).

While Menahem thus bought the crown for himself and respite from Assyria, the stiff stipulations were to cause further internal friction that was to ignite the fires of insurrection soon after his son Pekahiah succeeded him. Although Menahem had thought to buy time—perhaps even Israel's independence—his policy was to spell the beginning of the end. A totally apostate Israel was to reap the harvest of her spiritual wickedness at the hands of the very ones whom Menahem had trusted for deliverance.

To understand the complex events of the late eighth century BC, a word must be said concerning the Assyrians. After nearly a half century of decline, Assyria reawakened with the usurpation of the throne by Tiglath-Pileser III in 745 BC (Pul in v.19). Indeed he and his successors in the Neo-Assyrian Empire were to effect a drastic change in the balance of power in the ancient Near East. Having solidified the kingdom in the east, Tiglath-Pileser turned his attention to the west in 743. Although the exact course of his western campaign is difficult to follow, it seems clear that all Syro-Palestine submitted to the Assyrian yoke. Among those nations and kings whose tribute is recorded in his annals is the name "Menahem of Israel," thus confirming the biblical account.

NOTES

16 Identified with Tell el Farʿah, Tirzah remains one of the most striking confirmations of biblical details turned up by the archaeologist's spade. See G. E. Wright, "The Excavation of Tell el Farʿah," *BA* 12 (1949): 66–68. For examples of the heinous foreign practice of "ripping open" expectant mothers, see 2 Kings 8:12; Hosea 13:16; Amos 1:13.

19–20 Pul and the Assyrian Tiglath-Pileser III are one and the same individual (cf. 1Ch 5:26). Assyrian kings frequently had two names, a throne name for Assyria and one for Babylonia. Thus the Tiglath-Pileser of Assyria was known as Pul(u) in Babylon much as Shalmaneser V was known as Ululaia. For information regarding Tiglath-pileser III's western campaign, see CAH, 3:33–35; Hallo, 169–71.

Hobbs, 198–200, argues at length that Tiglath-Pileser III did not invade Israel but instead came to Menahem's aid against a third party. The fifty shekels of silver were thus paid to Assyrian mercenaries. Hobbs's unlikely suggestion founders on at least two points. (1) His objection to גִּבּוֹרֵי הַחַיִל (*gibbôrê haḥayil*, lit., "the men of wealth") as referring to the wealthy overlords overlooks the fact that the lady from Shunem was described by the feminine equivalent to this phrase. (2) Hobbs fails to account for the raising of such a sum by an army commander.

Possible reference to these events in Menahem's dealings with Tiglath-Pileser III may be reflected in Hosea's oracle (Hos 8:7–10), though J. B. Payne (*Encyclopedia of Biblical Prophecy* [New York: Harper & Row, 1973], 404) prefers to associate Hosea's warning with the events of that Assyrian king's second western campaign.

3. The Reign of Pekahiah in the Northern Kingdom (15:23–26)

[23]In the fiftieth year of Azariah king of Judah, Pekahiah son of Menahem became king of
Israel in Samaria, and he reigned two years. [24]Pekahiah did evil in the eyes of the LORD. He
did not turn away from the sins of Jeroboam son of Nebat, which he had caused Israel to
commit. [25]One of his chief officers, Pekah son of Remaliah, conspired against him. Taking
fifty men of Gilead with him, he assassinated Pekahiah, along with Argob and Arieh, in the
citadel of the royal palace at Samaria. So Pekah killed Pekahiah and succeeded him as king.
[26]The other events of Pekahiah's reign, and all he did, are written in the book of the
annals of the kings of Israel.

COMMENTARY

23–26 Few details are recorded of the two-year reign of Menahem's son Pekahiah except the notice of his evil spiritual condition and the coup d'état that took his life. Pekah, his assassin and successor, was one of Pekahiah's chief officers. The report that fifty men accompanied him indicates that Pekah was a military commander.

The notice of a twenty-year reign for Pekah (v.27) would seem to indicate that this Gileadite strong man had laid claim to the crown some twelve years earlier. Apparently he had been prevented from taking the throne only by Menahem's swift action in the unsettled times during Shallum's conspiracy. Pekahiah's appointment of Pekah to be a chief officer may have been an attempt to placate a rival party. The usurpation and troubled times that followed may suggest that there was an anti-Assyrian party that remained submerged during the rule of the fiery Menahem.

NOTES

25 The NIV takes the enigmatic "Argob and Arieh" (lit., "eagle and lion") to be personal names. Alternatively, they might refer to place names. M. J. Geller ("A New Translation for 2 Kings XV 25," *VT* 26 [1976]: 374–77) takes the two names as a compound phrase referring to a sphinxlike statue that symbolically guarded the gate, much as the colossal *aladlammu* figures that protected the gates of the Neo-Assyrian kings.

4. The Reign of Pekah in the Northern Kingdom (15:27–31)

27In the fifty-second year of Azariah king of Judah, Pekah son of Remaliah became king of
Israel in Samaria, and he reigned twenty years. 28He did evil in the eyes of the LORD. He did not
turn away from the sins of Jeroboam son of Nebat, which he had caused Israel to commit.
29In the time of Pekah king of Israel, Tiglath-Pileser king of Assyria came and took Ijon,
Abel Beth Maacah, Janoah, Kedesh and Hazor. He took Gilead and Galilee, including all the
land of Naphtali, and deported the people to Assyria. 30Then Hoshea son of Elah conspired
against Pekah son of Remaliah. He attacked and assassinated him, and then succeeded
him as king in the twentieth year of Jotham son of Uzziah.
31As for the other events of Pekah's reign, and all he did, are they not written in the book
of the annals of the kings of Israel?

COMMENTARY

27–31 The chronology of Pekah's time is beset with serious problems. To Pekah is attributed a twenty-year reign, beginning with the end of the fifty-two-year reign of Azariah of Judah. Further, v.30 indicates that his reign was terminated by Hoshea's conspiracy in the twentieth year of Jotham's rule. Verse 33, however, indicates that Jotham reigned but sixteen years. Moreover, v.32 notes that Jotham himself began to rule in Pekah's second year. Further synchronisms occur in v.8, where the thirty-eighth year of Uzziah is marked as Zechariah's accession year; in 16:1, where the seventeenth year of Pekah and the accession year of Ahaz are equated; and in 17:1, where the twelfth year of Ahaz is given as the first of Hoshea's nine years.

Because, on the basis of both biblical and secular history, the fall of Samaria can be assigned confidently to 722 BC, and because Azariah's fifty-second year can be shown to be 740 BC, it would appear that there is no room for a twenty-year reign by Pekah. Further, due allowance must be made for the reigns of Zechariah (six months), Shallum (one month), Menahem (ten years), Pekahiah (two years), and Hoshea (nine years) in the same interval of time.

The resolution of these data, while difficult, is not impossible. Probably because Pekah carried out a consistent anti-Assyrian policy, the chronicles of the southern kingdom gave full credit to Pekah's regnal claims. It would seem that already at the death of Zechariah in 752 BC, Pekah had claimed the kingship and was recognized as king in Transjordanian Gilead; however, the swift action of the Israelite military forces through Menahem prevented Pekah from furthering his aspirations for the next decade. In 742, when the powerful Menahem died, the problem of Pekah again surfaced, with Pekahiah solving the problem by bringing Pekah into a position of prominence. After two years, Pekah was able to find an opportunity to dispose of Pekahiah and rule in his own right over all Israel until the troublesome international events associated with Tiglath-Pileser III's second western campaign (734–732) forced his demise at the hands of a pro-Assyrian faction led by Hoshea (732).

Allowing for the differing accession systems in Israel and Judah, the various dates and data can be harmonized as follows:

753/752 BC: Uzziah's thirty-eighth year (including coregency), the year of Shallum's usurpation and of Menahem's seizing the throne of Israel, the year of Pekah's "rule" in Gilead

742 BC: The death of Menahem, the accession of Pekahiah

740/739 BC: The assassination of Pekahiah and the accession of Pekah, the death of Uzziah in Judah and the accession of Jotham (already a coregent since 752/751) in the "second year" of Pekah's independent rule

736 BC: The year Jotham gave the reigns of government over to Ahaz (= Pekah's "seventeenth year")

732/731 BC: Hoshea seizes power (= Pekah's "twentieth year" and the twelfth year of Ahaz (who apparently had been appointed crown prince and heir designate by his father in the crisis during Tiglath-Pileser III's first western campaign in 744)

732/731 BC: Jotham's twentieth year (Jotham had apparently lived for four years beyond the relinquishment of his throne to Ahaz)

Pekah's stormy beginning was to characterize his short independent rule. In 734 BC Tiglath-Pileser III swept out of Assyria on a second western campaign that was to break the anti-Assyrian coalition headed by the Aramean king Rezin and Pekah of Israel. By 732 the alliance was thoroughly broken and Damascus had fallen. All the western Fertile Crescent, from the Taurus Mountains on the north to the border of Egypt on the south, lay in Assyrian hands. The Syrian states were divided into five provinces, Israel into three.

The battle against Israel centered in Galilee: Ijon, Abel Beth Maacah, Janoah, Kedesh, and Hazor—all known Galilean cities. The text also adds significantly that Tiglath-Pileser III penetrated into Pekah's center of power, Gilead. Because the cities lay in a general north-south direction, the biblical account may well preserve the Assyrian king's line of march. The mention of Janoah may indicate that after the victory over Kadesh, Tiglath-Pileser divided his forces, half proceeding southward against Hazor and on to Gilead, and the other half moving southwest to Janoah and then on to Phoenicia.

With the loss of Galilee and Gilead and with the presence of Assyrian troops all along Israel's western frontier, it seemed evident that Pekah's anti-Assyrian policy had brought Israel to the point of extinction. Accordingly, while Tiglath-Pileser was concluding the siege of Damascus in 732 BC, Hoshea succeeded in defeating and displacing Pekah. That insurrection cost the controversial Gileadite his life. With the dispatching of Pekah and submission to Tiglath-Pileser, the ultimate demise of Israel was postponed for a decade. But its end was sure, for its corruption was total, having permeated all levels of society.

NOTES

27 For details relative to the intricate chronological problems of this period, see H. Stigers, "Pekah," *ZPEB*, 4:669–71; H. Tadmor, "The Campaigns of Sargon II of Ashur: A Chronological-Historical Study," *JCS* 12 (1958): 22–40, 77–100; Thiele, 77–140; Payne, *ZPEB*, 1:839–42; Hobbs, 204–5.

29 For information relative to Tiglath-Pileser III's second western campaign, see Hallo, 171–74; Aharoni and Avi-Yonah, 94–95. It is, of course, possible that the biblical record simply summarizes the account of Tiglath-Pileser III's campaign against Israel, with no conclusions drawn as to the order of his plan of attack. Bright, 217, suggests a coastal attack in 734 BC, the Syro-Israelite thrust in 733, and the taking of Damascus in 732. For the Assyrian text, see *ANET*, 283–84.

30 Tiglath-Pileser III claims that the Israelites "overthrew their king Pekah and I placed Hoshea as king over them" (*ANET*, 284). He goes on to record Israel's tribute to him. Evidently by submitting to Tiglath-Pileser, the pro-Assyrian party in Israel sought immediate recognition of its government and confirmation of Hoshea as king (see also Note on 17:1).

Hobbs, 203, points out that "the name 'Hoshea' contains an ironic twist. It is derived from the root ישׁע 'to save' and contrasts vividly with the activities of the promised מוֹשִׁיעַ 'savior' mentioned in 13:5."

5. The Reign of Jotham in the Southern Kingdom (15:32–38)

[32]In the second year of Pekah son of Remaliah king of Israel, Jotham son of Uzziah king
of Judah began to reign. [33]He was twenty-five years old when he became king, and he
reigned in Jerusalem sixteen years. His mother's name was Jerusha daughter of Zadok.
[34]He did what was right in the eyes of the LORD, just as his father Uzziah had done. [35]The
high places, however, were not removed; the people continued to offer sacrifices and burn
incense there. Jotham rebuilt the Upper Gate of the temple of the LORD.

[36]As for the other events of Jotham's reign, and what he did, are they not written in the
book of the annals of the kings of Judah? [37](In those days the LORD began to send Rezin
king of Aram and Pekah son of Remaliah against Judah.) [38]Jotham rested with his fathers
and was buried with them in the City of David, the city of his father. And Ahaz his son
succeeded him as king.

COMMENTARY

32–33 Already coregent for at least a decade, during Jotham's reign political and religious conditions remained largely as they were in Uzziah's time. The country's prosperity continued as well (2Ch 27:1–4). Regrettably that prosperity was to lead, as it so often does, to spiritual neglect (cf. Isa 1–5)—a condition that was to make Judah ripe for open apostasy in Ahaz's day.

34–35 Jotham turned his attention to his country's internal needs. He rebuilt the Upper Gate at the northern entrance of the temple. From the Chronicler (2Ch 27) we learn much more. Thus Jotham extended the wall of Ophel (2Ch 27:3; cf. 26:9). He also turned his attention to urban planning, constructing cities in the highlands of Judah that, together with a system of towers and fortifications in the wooded areas, could serve both economic and military purposes.

At the onset of his reign the Ammonites, from whom Uzziah had exacted tribute (2Ch 26:8), refused to acknowledge Jotham's overlordship, thus occasioning successful campaigns against the Ammonites so that they once again paid their tribute (2Ch 27:5). The notice that this tribute continued into the second and third year may correlate with the probability that about the year 736 BC Jotham had turned over the reigns of government to his coregent son, Ahaz, possibly due to some failure in health or to rising international tensions.

36–38 Toward the end of Jotham's reign, political storm clouds began to appear on the international horizon. The Chronicler speaks of "all his wars" (2Ch 27:7); and the narrator of Kings notes that Rezin, the Aramean king, and Pekah, Israel's king, began their incursions into Judah. The issue was designed by the Lord to test the young Ahaz in spiritual things (cf. Isa 7:1–8:10), but there would be no repentance forthcoming.

NOTES

35 For archaeological light on Jotham's building activities, see E. Oren, "Ziqlag—A Biblical City on the Edge of the Negev," *BA* 45 (1982): 177–78.

6. The Reign of Ahaz in the Southern Kingdom (16:1–20)

OVERVIEW

Between the accession statement, with its unusually strong negative spiritual evaluation (vv.1–4), and the brief closing notice (vv.19–20), the narrator focuses on two areas of concern. (1) In the political realm he provides details of a Syro-Israelite incursion (vv.5–6), to which Ahaz reacted by bribing the Assyrian king to act as his rescuer (vv.7–9). (2) He also catalogs Ahaz's temple innovations, which took the form of a new Damascene type of altar (vv.10–11) and the religious services there (vv.12–16). Further modifications included changes in the temple furnishings (vv.17–18). All these developments in Ahaz's reign are presented as commentary illustrating the fact that Ahaz "did not do whata was right in the eyes of the LORD his God" (v.2).

[1]In the seventeenth year of Pekah son of Remaliah, Ahaz son of Jotham king of Judah began to reign. [2]Ahaz was twenty years old when he became king, and he reigned in

Jerusalem sixteen years. Unlike David his father, he did not do what was right in the eyes
of the LORD his God. 3He walked in the ways of the kings of Israel and even sacrificed his
son in the fire, following the detestable ways of the nations the LORD had driven out before
the Israelites. 4He offered sacrifices and burned incense at the high places, on the hilltops
and under every spreading tree.

5Then Rezin king of Aram and Pekah son of Remaliah king of Israel marched up to fight
against Jerusalem and besieged Ahaz, but they could not overpower him. 6At that time,
Rezin king of Aram recovered Elath for Aram by driving out the men of Judah. Edomites
then moved into Elath and have lived there to this day.

7Ahaz sent messengers to say to Tiglath-Pileser king of Assyria, "I am your servant and
vassal. Come up and save me out of the hand of the king of Aram and of the king of Israel,
who are attacking me." 8And Ahaz took the silver and gold found in the temple of the LORD
and in the treasuries of the royal palace and sent it as a gift to the king of Assyria. 9The
king of Assyria complied by attacking Damascus and capturing it. He deported its inhabitants to Kir and put Rezin to death.

10Then King Ahaz went to Damascus to meet Tiglath-Pileser king of Assyria. He saw an
altar in Damascus and sent to Uriah the priest a sketch of the altar, with detailed plans for
its construction. 11So Uriah the priest built an altar in accordance with all the plans that
King Ahaz had sent from Damascus and finished it before King Ahaz returned. 12When
the king came back from Damascus and saw the altar, he approached it and presented
offerings on it. 13He offered up his burnt offering and grain offering, poured out his drink
offering, and sprinkled the blood of his fellowship offerings on the altar. 14The bronze altar
that stood before the LORD he brought from the front of the temple — from between the
new altar and the temple of the LORD — and put it on the north side of the new altar.

15King Ahaz then gave these orders to Uriah the priest: "On the large new altar, offer the
morning burnt offering and the evening grain offering, the king's burnt offering and his
grain offering, and the burnt offering of all the people of the land, and their grain offering and their drink offering. Sprinkle on the altar all the blood of the burnt offerings and
sacrifices. But I will use the bronze altar for seeking guidance." 16And Uriah the priest did
just as King Ahaz had ordered.

17King Ahaz took away the side panels and removed the basins from the movable
stands. He removed the Sea from the bronze bulls that supported it and set it on a
stone base. 18He took away the Sabbath canopy that had been built at the temple and
removed the royal entryway outside the temple of the LORD, in deference to the king of
Assyria.

19As for the other events of the reign of Ahaz, and what he did, are they not written
in the book of the annals of the kings of Judah? 20Ahaz rested with his fathers and was
buried with them in the City of David. And Hezekiah his son succeeded him as king.

COMMENTARY

1–2 The name "Ahaz" is a shortened form of "Jehoahaz" (cf. the similar name "Ahaziah"). Ahaz's name appears in its fuller form in the tribute lists of Tiglath-Pileser III (Luckenbill, 1:287).

The notice that Ahaz was but twenty years old at his accession and that he ruled sixteen years has occasioned no little difficulty, particularly since, according to 2 Chronicles 29:1, his son Hezekiah was already twenty-five when he succeeded his father. Some manuscripts of the ancient Greek and Syriac versions at 2 Chronicles 28:1 record Ahaz's age at his accession as twenty-five. While this reading would have the advantage of making Ahaz appreciably older at the time of his son's birth, the MT's lower figure is not impossible in the light of ancient Near Eastern marriage practices.

If a sixteen-year independent reign (732–716 BC) for Ahaz is not primarily in view here, the answer to this knotty problem is to be sought in the tangled chronology of the late eighth century BC. Ahaz may have lived four years after handing over the reigns of government to Hezekiah in 720 BC, an event that may be related to the Assyrian-Philistine wars of 720 and 716 BC. Accordingly, the Chronicler's note as to Hezekiah's accession is reckoned from the sole reign of Hezekiah in 716 BC. In that case, Ahaz would have been born in 756 and died in 716, while Hezekiah was born in 741–740, when Ahaz was fifteen or sixteen. Such a scenario may account for the reading of the Greek and Syriac texts for 2 Chronicles 28:1 that Ahaz was "twenty years old when he began to reign."

3–4 Not content to continue the standing state policies of limited religious compromise, Ahaz transgressed the bounds of propriety by imitating the idolatrous heathen practices of Israel. Most nefarious of all was his participation in the debased Molech rites (see Notes). He went so far as to send his own son through the sacrificial fires (v.3; cf. Lev 18:21; 20:1–5; Dt 12:31; 2Ki 21:6). According to the scriptural data, these rites took place at the confluence of the Hinnom and Kidron valleys in a sacred enclosure known as Topheth (cf. 23:10; Isa 30:33; Jer 7:31).

The exact nature of the sacrifices and the divinities involved has been the subject of much discussion. The same type of sacred place with the same name has been found in the transplanted Phoenician colony of Carthage. That the sacrificial offering was called by a name made up of the same Semitic consonants (*mlk*) contained in the name "Molech" would seem to argue that the god involved was the old Canaanite deity Baal, with human sacrifice made to him called *mlk* (cf. Jer 19:5; 32:35). The rites were heinous and a total defilement of the God-ordained sacrificial service. The later spiritual reformation of Josiah was to bring an end to these sinister proceedings, a judgment Jeremiah utilized in picturing God's coming judgment on his sinful people (Jer 2:23; 7:30–33; 19:5–6).

The valley's reputation for extreme wickedness gave rise to the employment of its name as a term for the eschatological place of punishment of the wicked (*1 En.* 27:1ff.; 54:1ff.; 56:3–4; 90:26), a designation confirmed by Christ himself (Mt 5:22, 29–30; 10:28; 18:9; 23:15, 33; 25:41).

5–6 The full details of the complex international situation must be gleaned not only from 2 Kings 16 but also from 15:37; 2 Chronicles 28; and Isaiah 7:1–16. These sources show that the Syro-Israelite alliance had been operative against Judah already in Jotham's day (2Ki 15:37). The allied attack against Judah was two-pronged. Rezin came along the eastern portion of Judah, drove down to the key seaport of Elath, and took it (v.6; 2Ch 28:5). Pekah launched an effective general campaign against northern Judah that resulted in the death of thousands of its citizens and the capture of hundreds of others (though the captives were later granted their freedom and returned to Jericho through the intercession of the prophet Obed; cf. 2Ch 28:6–15).

Moreover, the newly liberated Edom took the opportunity to strike back and carried away some Judahites to captivity (2Ch 28:17). As well, the Philistines found the time ripe to make renewed incursions into the western Shephelah and take captive certain cities in southern Judah.

An attack aimed at taking Jerusalem and installing a new king on the throne is described in Isaiah 7:2–6. Surrounded by hostile enemies on all sides, Ahaz received God's prophet Isaiah. He assured Ahaz that the enemy would fail; God himself would see to that. Ahaz could request any confirmatory sign that he wished, and it would be granted (Isa 7:7–11). Ahaz, with a flare of piety, refused Isaiah's offer (Isa 7:12); he preferred to rely on his own resourcefulness. God nevertheless gave Ahaz a sign, the prophecy that Matthew associates with the virgin birth of the Messiah (Isa 7:13–16; cf. Mt 1:22–23).

God was superintending the whole complex undertaking. He would deal with apostate Israel (cf. 2Ki 17:5–18; 18:11–12), thwart the plans of Rezin and Pekah by bringing defeat to them (Isa 7:5–16), and chastise spiritually bankrupt Ahaz (2Ch 28:5, 19).

7–9 Ahaz's request to Tiglath-Pileser III was couched in diplomatic language that displayed his respect and submission to him. The narrator thus shows that rather than trusting in the Lord (cf. Isa 7:10–16), Ahaz put forward a "persuasive effort to draw the Assyrian king into Ahaz's war, to protect him as a father would a son" (Cohn, 113). Tiglath-Pileser complied all too readily, eventually thoroughly subduing the Arameans, taking Damascus and deporting its inhabitants, and executing Rezin (v.9). Israel was spared only through Hoshea's coup d'état and swift submission to Assyria—a takeover that cost Pekah his life (15:29–30).

10–11 According to the records of Tiglath-Pileser III, the Assyrian king called for a meeting of his new vassals in Damascus. Ahaz was impressed with the type of altar in use there and sent back instructions to Uriah the priest for its construction. The text gives no hint that Uriah objected to Ahaz's command; rather, the altar's construction was completed and ready for use by the time the king arrived back in Jerusalem.

12–13 When Ahaz returned he had his daily offerings presented on this new altar, thereby dedicating the altar's use to the Lord. The offerings that were made were all of the sweet-savor type, expressing the maintenance of the believer's communion with God. The burnt and meal offerings symbolized dedication and service, the fellowship (peace) offering symbolized fellowship, and the drink offering emphasized the joy of life poured out to God in Spirit-led obedience (v.13). What a parody of piety! He who knew nothing of genuine godliness would feign his devotion to God—and that via an alien altar!

14–16 The following verses catalog Ahaz's further religious innovations, all of which speak of his deepening apostasy. The prescribed brazen altar was transferred from facing the sanctuary entrance to the northern side. Accordingly, all future offerings would be made on the recently dedicated Damascene altar. Ahaz would henceforth use the brazen altar in connection with his divination practices, thus indicating Ahaz's involvement in Assyrian pagan rites.

17 Ahaz went even further. He appropriated the high stands holding the altar for their brass. Likewise he lowered the molten Sea by taking away the bronze bulls that supported it and placed it on a low stone pedestal. The narrator assigns no reason for these actions. Perhaps Ahaz needed the brass for future payment of tribute, or it was simply a matter of streamlining the temple furnishings.

18 Not content with these "reforms" in the matter of ceremonial furnishings, Ahaz went still further. The covered structure that opened to the inner court, together with the king's private entrance to that place, were removed "in deference to the king of Assyria." The exact impact of these words is difficult to ascertain. Whether Tiglath-Pileser wanted less prestige to be held by his new vassal or felt that such a special royal place might indicate too close a tie to an established religion that might later foster a spirit of independence against Assyria is uncertain. At any rate, the wholesale changes were either made at the Assyrian king's suggestion or were done to gain his pleasure.

19–20 Ahaz went yet further in his apostasy. According to the Chronicler (2Ch 28:24–25; cf. 29:7), he went so far as to desecrate the temple furniture and close the temple itself so that the services within the Holy Place were discontinued. "Worship services" would henceforth be held only in connection with the new altar or at one of the several altars erected throughout Jerusalem or at the high places dedicated to the various gods established throughout Judah by royal edict (28:24–25). All his innovations speak volumes as to Ahaz's depraved spiritual condition. It is small wonder, then, that the Chronicler reports that Ahaz provoked the Lord's anger (28:25). When Ahaz died, he was not accorded proper burial in the royal tombs. He who was "unlike David" in his relation to the Lord (2Ki 16:2; 2Ch 28:1) was not laid to rest beside him.

NOTES

3 The Molech problem is a complex one. That literal human sacrifice was involved (contra N. H. Snaith, "The Cult of Molech," *VT* 16 [1966]: 123–24) is abundantly shown in the Canaanite literary texts and is elsewhere implied or stated in the OT.

In some cases "Molech" appears to refer to a personal god (e.g., possibly but not certainly Lev 20:1–5), though opinions vary as to the deity's identity. Some scholars suggest Milcolm, the national god of Ammon (1Ki 11:7), whose name itself is a deliberate scribal misvocalization of the name based on the Semitic word *mlk*. (For discussion of the nature and function of Milcolm, see W. H. Shea, "Milkom as the Architect of Rabbath-Ammon's Natural Defences in the Ammon Citadel Inscription," *PEQ* 111 [1978]: 17–25.) But 2 Kings 23:10, 13 appears to differentiate between the worship of Milcolm and Molech. (Some scholars suggest that "Molech" likewise is a scribal corruption, with the vowels for the consonants *mlk* being supplied from the Hebrew *bōšet*, "shame.") Others interpreters consider Molech to be Melek Athtar, a well-known astral deity in the ancient Near East of whom several deities (e.g., Milcolm and Chemosh) are local expressions (see J. Gray, "Molech, Moloch," *IDB* 3:422–23; cf. Am 5:26–27; Ac 7:43).

The name Molech more than likely originates in the ancient Semitic term *mālik*, being the absolute state of a noun meaning "king." Thus the word was at first an epithet of a deity. Significantly the first reference to God as "king" comes from the mouth of the pagan diviner Balaam (Nu 23:21), as R. B. Allen ("The Theology of the Balaam Oracles," in *Tradition and Testament*, ed. John and Paul Feinberg [Chicago: Moody Press, 1981], 103, 118) aptly points out. J. J. M. Roberts (*The Earliest Semitic Pantheon* [Baltimore: Johns Hopkins Univ. Press, 1972], 42–43, 105–6) decides that Dagan was the original deity with whom the term was combined. In time the term split off and became used independently. As this independent unit, the name was utilized throughout the Semitic world. (See further J. Ebach, "ADRMLK, Moloch und BAʾALADR: Eine Notiz zum Problem der Moloch-Verehrung im alten Israel," *UF* 11 [1979]: 211–26.)

Though the evidence renders certain that the term *mālik* enjoyed widespread use as a divine name, however, the issue is whether an independent deity by that name is intended in the OT and more specifically in eighth/seventh-century Judah. Although George C. Heider (*The Cult of Molek* [Sheffield: JSOT Press, 1985]) argues forcibly for a chthonic deity whose worship was especially observed in Jerusalem, the linguistic and archaeological data as harmonized with the biblical data (cf. 23:10 with Jer 7:31; 19:5–6; 32:35) would appear to favor the idea that *mlk* refers to a type of sacrifice made to Baal in a sacred enclosure known as a "tophet." (Notice, however, that in Syrian "tophet" means "fire pit.") For further details see B. H. Warmington, *Carthage* (Baltimore: Penguin, 1964), 158–60; L. E. Stager and S. R. Wolff, "Child Sacrifice at Carthage," *BAR* 10 (1984): 30–47.

10 For Tiglath-Pileser III's inscription listing Ahaz, see *ANET*, 282. The prototype of Ahaz's new altar has been often disputed, with some deciding for an Assyrian-style altar (e.g., Cohn, Gray, Gressman, Kittel, Montgomery, T. H. Robinson) and others (e.g., de Vaux) favoring an Aramean one. The latter position appears to be in harmony with the Chronicler's report that Ahaz was influenced by the "gods of the kings of Aram" (2Ch 28:23).

דְּמוּת (*dᵉmût*, "likeness") and תַּבְנִית (*tabnît*, "shape, pattern") are well rendered by the NIV's "sketch" and "detailed plans." The former word gives the altar's outward appearance and may indicate an artist's sketch; the latter suggests an architect's drawing.

12–13 Whether Ahaz personally offered sacrifices on the new altar or simply supervised Uriah's actions is uncertain (cf. Solomon, 1Ki 8:62–64; Jeroboam, 12:33–13:1; Jehu, 2Ki 10:25).

15 The Hebrew verb translated "for seeking guidance" (NIV) bears many nuances. Whether Ahaz intended to use the altar as a place for seeking the Lord's guidance through prayer (cf. Ps 27:4) or for some aspect of syncrestic divination is uncertain.

17 For the Solomonic basins and movable stands and the molten Sea, see 1 Kings 7:23, 27. They are mentioned among the several items that were carried away in the later Babylonian despoiling of Jerusalem (25:13–14; Jer 27:19–20; 52:17–23).

The Hebrew translated "stone base" (NIV; cf. LXX) refers not to the stone pavement of the court as the Vulgate suggests, but, as Keil, 407, decides, to a pedestal made of stones.

7. The Reign of Hoshea in the Northern Kingdom (17:1–23)

OVERVIEW

Because of its subject matter, this section is uniquely structured. Although it begins with the usual accession statement plus spiritual evaluation (vv.1–2), which is followed by the customary historical notices (vv.3–6), the rest of the unit largely comprises a theological explanation for the defeat and exile of God's people in the northern kingdom (vv.7–23). Here are catalogued the sins of Israel (vv.7–17) for which God's judgment must necessarily have been imposed (vv.18–20). A final summary of the charges against the northern kingdom closes the section (vv.21–23).

[1]In the twelfth year of Ahaz king of Judah, Hoshea son of Elah became king of Israel
in Samaria, and he reigned nine years. [2]He did evil in the eyes of the LORD, but not like the
kings of Israel who preceded him.
[3]Shalmaneser king of Assyria came up to attack Hoshea, who had been Shalmaneser's
vassal and had paid him tribute. [4]But the king of Assyria discovered that Hoshea was a traitor, for he had sent envoys to So king of Egypt, and he no longer paid tribute to the king
of Assyria, as he had done year by year. Therefore Shalmaneser seized him and put him
in prison. [5]The king of Assyria invaded the entire land, marched against Samaria and laid
siege to it for three years. [6]In the ninth year of Hoshea, the king of Assyria captured Samaria and deported the Israelites to Assyria. He settled them in Halah, in Gozan on the Habor
River and in the towns of the Medes.
[7]All this took place because the Israelites had sinned against the LORD their God, who
had brought them up out of Egypt from under the power of Pharaoh king of Egypt.
They worshiped other gods [8]and followed the practices of the nations the LORD had
driven out before them, as well as the practices that the kings of Israel had introduced.
[9]The Israelites secretly did things against the LORD their God that were not right. From
watchtower to fortified city they built themselves high places in all their towns. [10]They
set up sacred stones and Asherah poles on every high hill and under every spreading tree. [11]At every high place they burned incense, as the nations whom the LORD had
driven out before them had done. They did wicked things that provoked the LORD to
anger. [12]They worshiped idols, though the LORD had said, "You shall not do this." [13]The
LORD warned Israel and Judah through all his prophets and seers: "Turn from your evil
ways. Observe my commands and decrees, in accordance with the entire Law that I
commanded your fathers to obey and that I delivered to you through my servants the
prophets."
[14]But they would not listen and were as stiff-necked as their fathers, who did not trust in
the LORD their God. [15]They rejected his decrees and the covenant he had made with their
fathers and the warnings he had given them. They followed worthless idols and themselves became worthless. They imitated the nations around them although the LORD had
ordered them, "Do not do as they do," and they did the things the LORD had forbidden
them to do.
[16]They forsook all the commands of the LORD their God and made for themselves two
idols cast in the shape of calves, and an Asherah pole. They bowed down to all the starry
hosts, and they worshiped Baal. [17]They sacrificed their sons and daughters in the fire. They

practiced divination and sorcery and sold themselves to do evil in the eyes of the LORD,
provoking him to anger.
18So the LORD was very angry with Israel and removed them from his presence. Only the
tribe of Judah was left, 19and even Judah did not keep the commands of the LORD their
God. They followed the practices Israel had introduced. 20Therefore the LORD rejected all
the people of Israel; he afflicted them and gave them into the hands of plunderers, until
he thrust them from his presence.
21When he tore Israel away from the house of David, they made Jeroboam son of Nebat
their king. Jeroboam enticed Israel away from following the LORD and caused them to
commit a great sin. 22The Israelites persisted in all the sins of Jeroboam and did not turn
away from them 23until the LORD removed them from his presence, as he had warned
through all his servants the prophets. So the people of Israel were taken from their
homeland into exile in Assyria, and they are still there.

COMMENTARY

1–6 Shalmaneser V succeeded Tiglath-Pileser III in 727 BC and reigned until 722 BC, when he in turn was succeeded by Sargon II (721–705 BC). Dynastic succession was often a time for vassal states to attempt to liberate themselves. Apparently Hoshea found in the situation opportunity to rebel against Assyria. He hoped to find ready support from the king of Egypt.

The mention of "So king of Egypt" in v.4 has occasioned a good deal of controversy, for there is no known Egyptian king by that name. Attempts have been made to identify this "So" with Osorkon of the Twenty-Third Dynasty, with Shabako of the Twenty-Fifth Dynasty, with a Saite (Twenty-Sixth) Dynasty king, or to assign to him merely a field commander's status. Two theories have found the most favor with scholars. (1) H. Goedicke ("The End of So, King of Egypt," *BASOR* 171 [1963]: 64–66) maintained that Sais (lit., *saʾw*), the Egyptian capital of the Twenty-Fourth Dynasty, would be pronounced *sā* in Akkadian (the lingua franca of the ancient Near East) but *sô* in Hebrew. Thus understood, v.4 would read, "he had sent envoys to Sais (even unto) the king of Egypt" (see NIV note).

(2) More recently A. R. Green ("The Identity of King So of Egypt—An Alternative Interpretation," *JNES* 52 [1993]: 99–108) has made a strong case for identifying So with the Twenty-Fifth Dynasty pharaoh Piankhy. He suggests that Piankhy's Horus name *Simaʾ Tawy* would have been taken over in Hebrew as *Siwaʾ* (סוא, *swʾ*), which would have been written and pronounced *Sô*. He notes a similar case in which the Persian month Simanu was taken over as Siwan in Hebrew (Est 8:9).

In the quest for power in Egypt Tef Nekht, the founder of the Twenty-Fourth Dynasty, had brought an end to the decadent Twenty-Second Dynasty, while Piankhy had dispatched the Twenty-Third. The two rivals met in 727 BC, with Piankhy emerging as the winner. Such a victor might have appealed to Hoshea as one who would be able to support him in his defection.

Because of the natural confusion that often arose when a new king took office, it sometimes took several years for him to put matters back in order. Just such a situation is known to have occurred in Assyria (see L. Levine, *Two Neo-Assyrian Stelae from Iran* [Toronto: Royal Ontario Museum, 1972], 39–41). Thus it would not be unusual for Shalmaneser to be delayed until 725 BC before being able to deal with Hoshea. After a three-year siege Samaria fell, and a huge number of people were deported and resettled in various places in the Assyrian empire.

Although the Babylonian chronicler credits Shalmaneser with the capture of Samaria, Sargon II claims that it was he who captured it (see Luckenbill, 2:2, 26–27; V. H. Matthews and D. C. Benjamin, *Old Testament Parallels* [New York: Paulist, 1991], 127–29). Perhaps the campaign was launched by Shalmaneser and completed by Sargon.

7–17 The narrator rehearses the causes that necessitated the divine punishment. His indictment of Israel begins with a reminder that God alone had released the Israelites from their oppression and bondage in Egypt and had brought them to the Promised Land. Their historical foundation was essentially a spiritual one. Having brought Israel from bondage to glorious freedom, God had every right to expect them to walk in newness of life, as befitting a redeemed people (cf. Dt 5–6; 10:12–11:32).

The opposite, however, proved to be the case. The shameful record of Israel's spiritual harlotry is catalogued (cf. Isa 5; Mic 6:3–5, 9–16). Against the clear prohibitions of God (Ex 20:2–6; Lev 18:4–5, 26; 20:22–23; Dt 5:6–10), the people entered into the patterns of worship practiced by the pagan nations God had driven out of the land. Israel's own kings formally initiated this apostasy, and all Israel followed their devious plan to pretend to worship God in the official state religion.

Matters grew even worse. The external rites became more openly false. Israel's worship included setting up sacred shrines and Asherah poles, the following of pagan incense customs, worshiping at cultic high places, and even open idolatry. Although God had driven the nations that practiced these abominations out of the land, Israel continued to corrupt itself with them. Despite the fact that God had sent prophets to warn the people to turn from this wickedness, Israel kept associating itself with the abominations of the Canaanites. It also appropriated their punishment. Just as God had driven out the Canaanites, so he would drive Israel out (vv.18–20, 23), into exile (v.23).

The warning proved futile. Obdurately set in their ways, the Israelites refused to acknowledge God's commands and warnings. Like the surrounding nations, they followed worthless idols and became useless to God. They tried every sort of idolatry, from that involving the calves of Jeroboam to the poles of Asherah, from the worship of the heavenly hosts to that of Baal, and the loathsome practice of human sacrifice. Divination and deliberate sorcery had further corrupted their spiritual experience. Most basic of all, they had not only denied God's covenant with them, but they had also refused the God of the covenant by rejecting his rightful sovereignty over them.

18–23 The inevitable result was that Israel aroused God's righteous wrath (vv.18–19). In accordance with the set terms of the inviolable covenant, God must punish his nation. And so he did, by allowing Israel to fall into the hands of the Assyrian invader (vv.20–23). Judah was left to ponder its own spiritual condition before God. Unfortunately, Judah would fail to learn from the lesson of Israel.

NOTES

4 Among other sources dealing with the identity of King So, the following deserve special mention: D. B. Redford, "A Note on II Kings 17, 4," *Journal of the Society for the Study of Egyptian Antiquities* 11 (1981): 75–76; D. L. Christensen, "The Identity of 'King So' in Egypt (2 Kings xvii 4)," *VT* 39 (1989): 140–53; and J. Day, "The Problem of 'So, King of Egypt' in 2 Kings xvii 4," *VT* 42 (1992): 289–301.

10 For "Asherah poles," see Note on 1 Kings 14:15.

12 For "idols" (or "images in the round"), see Note on 1 Kings 15:12.

14 The "stiff-necked ... fathers" were disbelieving Israelites in Moses' day (cf. Dt 10:16). Their descendants also had not trusted God. The verb אָמַן (*ʾāman*, "be firm"), used here in the Hiphil stem, connotes the idea of a belief that brings true reliance (i.e., genuine biblical faith; cf. Isa 53:1). The derived noun אֱמוּנָה (*ʾemûnâ*, "faithfulness") lays stress on outward conduct that gives full attestation to an inward reality (cf. Isa 7:9; see also *TDOT*, 1:293–309; *NIDOTTE*, 1:427–33; and my remarks in *Nahum, Habakkuk, Zephaniah* [Chicago: Moody Press, 1991], 219–23).

16–17 For the passing of children through fire, see Note on 16:3. The origin of astral worship in Israel is obscure. Although it was condemned in the Torah (Dt 4:19; 17:3), it is attested as early as the eighth century BC (Am 5:26). It may have gained official sanction in the northern kingdom through the subjection of Menahem and Hoshea to Assyria and then been introduced into Judah under similar conditions by Ahaz (cf. 23:12). The practice thrived in the days of Manasseh (21:5) but was abolished by Josiah (23:4–5, 12).

18–20 The syntax of the MT here is most expressive. The writer proceeds asyndetically, exclaiming poignantly, "Only the tribe of Judah was left." Yet even they did not keep the Lord's commands but walked in the practices that Israel had observed. Knowing the outcome of Judah's history, the writer was so overcome that he had to add these words parenthetically to Israel's history.

21–23 The rehearsal of Israel's sin in following the perversity of Jeroboam closes with a note that Israel was yet in exile in the days of the author of Kings, thus making any proposed postexilic date for this section of Kings most problematic.

8. The Repopulation of Samaria (17:24–41)

[24]The king of Assyria brought people from Babylon, Cuthah, Avva, Hamath and Sepharvaim and settled them in the towns of Samaria to replace the Israelites. They took over Samaria and lived in its towns. [25]When they first lived there, they did not worship the LORD; so he sent lions among them and they killed some of the people. [26]It was reported to the king of Assyria: "The people you deported and resettled in the towns of Samaria do not know what the god of that country requires. He has sent lions among them, which are killing them off, because the people do not know what he requires."

[27]Then the king of Assyria gave this order: "Have one of the priests you took captive from Samaria go back to live there and teach the people what the god of the land
requires." [28]So one of the priests who had been exiled from Samaria came to live in Bethel
and taught them how to worship the LORD.
[29]Nevertheless, each national group made its own gods in the several towns where they
settled, and set them up in the shrines the people of Samaria had made at the high places.
[30]The men from Babylon made Succoth Benoth, the men from Cuthah made Nergal, and
the men from Hamath made Ashima; [31]the Avvites made Nibhaz and Tartak, and the Sep-
harvites burned their children in the fire as sacrifices to Adrammelech and Anammelech,
the gods of Sepharvaim. [32]They worshiped the LORD, but they also appointed all sorts of
their own people to officiate for them as priests in the shrines at the high places. [33]They
worshiped the LORD, but they also served their own gods in accordance with the customs
of the nations from which they had been brought.
[34]To this day they persist in their former practices. They neither worship the LORD nor
adhere to the decrees and ordinances, the laws and commands that the LORD gave the
descendants of Jacob, whom he named Israel. [35]When the LORD made a covenant with the
Israelites, he commanded them: "Do not worship any other gods or bow down to them,
serve them or sacrifice to them. [36]But the LORD, who brought you up out of Egypt with
mighty power and outstretched arm, is the one you must worship. To him you shall bow
down and to him offer sacrifices. [37]You must always be careful to keep the decrees and
ordinances, the laws and commands he wrote for you. Do not worship other gods. [38]Do
not forget the covenant I have made with you, and do not worship other gods. [39]Rather,
worship the LORD your God; it is he who will deliver you from the hand of all your enemies."
[40]They would not listen, however, but persisted in their former practices. [41]Even while
these people were worshiping the LORD, they were serving their idols. To this day their
children and grandchildren continue to do as their fathers did.

COMMENTARY

24 To the demise of Israel and her indictment, a historical note is appended. In accordance with the deportation system used so fully by Tiglath-Pileser III and followed by his successors, a vast transplantation of populaces occurred. Israelites were sent to Mesopotamia and even beyond; Babylonians and Arameans were transferred to Israel. Not only did the Assyrian monarchs hope to make the repopulated and reconstituted districts more manageable, they also hoped to train and encourage the citizenry to transfer their loyalties to the Assyrian Empire.

The order in which the cities are mentioned may indicate the sequence of making up the train of relocated personnel; up from Babylon, past Cuthah, westward along the Euphrates River to Hamath, and then southward through Syria and Phoenicia into Israel. (For the Assyrian practice of deportation, see the remarks in CAH, 3:41–42.) Notice that Samaria now names the new Assyrian province, the name being drawn from Tiglath-Pileser III's former designation of Israel as "Samerina" (see Luckenbill, 1:276, 279; 2:134).

The time of the deportees' arrival has been much discussed. Since Sargon records the quellings of a revolt in southern Mesopotamia in his first year and the deporting of people to "Hatti Land" (i.e., Palestine) and speaks of suppressing similar revolts in Syria and Arabia in his second and seventh years, doubtless the repopulation of Samaria began almost immediately (see Luckenbill, 2:3, 6–8). Later Assyrian kings added substantially to Samaria's members (Ezr 4:2, 9–10).

25–27 When the new settlers faced the menace of lions roaming freely through the area, they immediately suspected that "the god of the land" was punishing them because of their failure to worship him. As Hobbs, 237, observes, "A belief in the relationship between the correct worship of a local god and the fortunes of the local inhabitants is a widespread belief in the ancient Near East." There was some truth to their evaluation of the situation. Although God had sent his people into exile because of their failure to live up to the stipulations of the covenant with God, he would not leave the land without any witness to himself. The lions were a reminder of the broken covenant and of God's claim on the land (Lev 18:24–30; 26:21–22).

28–31 The Israelite priest sent back to the northern kingdom would teach the false worship instituted by Jeroboam. The result was a mixture of truth combined with the corrupted experience of Israel (now deepened by two centuries of growing apostasy) and the pagan rites brought by the new settlers.

Moreover, the various immigrants continued the worship of their own gods in the places where they settled (v.29). Those from Babylonia worshiped "Succoth Benoth" (v.30), possibly a deliberate scribal pun on the Babylonian *Sarpanitu*, the name of Marduk's wife (see Notes). Those from Cuth continued their worship of "Nergal," the chthonic deity and god of pestilence.

Those from Syrian backgrounds worshiped the deities associated with their cults. The Syrian gods that are recorded here are likely all deliberate misspellings. "Ashima" may be an abbreviated name for the goddess Malkat Shemayin or the Canaanite Asherah (cf. Am 8:14 [NIV text note]). Some scholars have suggested its connection with the late Syrian goddess Sima or with the well-known Phoenician god Eshmun. "Nibhaz" (v.31) is otherwise unknown. "Tartak" is possibly a miswriting of "Attargatis," name of the familiar west Semitic goddess. "Adrammelech" and "Anammelech" are similar corrupt names perhaps representing Canaanite forms related to the Mesopotamian deities Ishtar/Astarte and Anu.

32–41 Thus from the onset this Samarian worship was syncretistic. While the various people observed the worship of the Lord (in its corrupt, Jeroboamic form), they also continued their own religious practices (vv.32–33). The author of Kings evaluates the situation as being one of total confusion (v.34). Above all he makes it clear that the new Samarian worship did not represent the true faith; for it was syncretistic (vv.34, 40–41), and it violated the clear commands and stipulations contained in Israel's covenant with God (vv.34–40).

With this summation the divine case against Israel has been made. Despite everything the great Redeemer had done for his people, their thankless, hardened, and apostate hearts had led them into spiritual, moral, and social corruption and thus to their own demise (cf. Hos 13:4–9). Israel's checkered history should have provided a lesson for Judah; it remains an example for the church (cf. 1Co 10:11–13).

NOTES

26–27 Lions have been reported in the area not only in biblical times (1Ki 13:24; 20:36; Am 3:12) but also in modern times. Interestingly, God likens himself to a lion both as a judge of Israel (Hos 5:14–15) and as a lion roaring for its young to come to him (Hos 11:10). That Sargon would have sent such a priest to deal with an internal religious problem can no longer be doubted. See S. M. Paul, "Sargon's Administrative Dictum in 2 Kings 17:17," *JBL* 88 (1969): 73–74.

30 As pointed in the MT, "Succoth Benoth" (סֻכּוֹת בְּנוֹת) means "booth of girls," a nonsensical form. The precise Babylonian deity involved is difficult to ascertain. Hebrew scribes frequently altered the names of pagan deities, thereby refusing to acknowledge their existence (e.g., the "Babylonian" names of the three Hebrew friends of Daniel [Da 1:7; cf. Mt 12:24–27]). Similarly the names of the Syrian deities of v.31 are likely all deliberate misspellings.

31 For other possible identifications of Adrammelech, see W. F. Albright, *Archaeology and the Religion of Israel*, 5th ed. (Garden City, N.Y.: Doubleday, 1969), 162–64; J. Gray, "The Desert God 'Attar,'" *JNES* 8 (1949): 78–80; S. Kaufman, "The Enigmatic Adad-Milki," *JNES* 37 (1978): 101–9.

41 Some Samarians, however, worshiped the true God (cf. 2Ch 30:10–19). For the later features of the Samaritan religion and the Jewish hatred of the Samaritans, see John 4:9; 8:48; A. Edersheim, *History of the Jewish Nations* (Grand Rapids: Baker, n.d.), 249; idem, *Life and Times of Jesus the Messiah* (Grand Rapids: Eerdmans, 1943), 1:396–403.

III. THE SOUTHERN KINGDOM (18:1–25:30)

A. The Reign of Hezekiah (18:1–20:21)

OVERVIEW

The narrator now turns his attention to one of the two exemplary kings of Judah, the sole surviving member of the twin kingdoms. The account proceeds in straight narrative form, although not necessarily in strict chronological order.

The opening accession statement with its glowing praise of Hezekiah's faith and early, God-empowered accomplishments (18:1–8) is followed by a short historical notice linking his reign with that of Hoshea and the fall of Samaria (18:9–12). Thereafter the narrator moves to a lengthy rehearsal of Sennacherib's siege of Jerusalem and the city's miraculous deliverance (18:13–19:37). That account focuses on three main areas: (1) The Assyrian invasion of Judah and siege of Jerusalem (18:13–17); (2) Hezekiah's reaction to this development together with Isaiah's prophetic encouragement and the continual Assyrian psychological warfare during the siege (19:1–13); and (3) Hezekiah's prayer and the fulfillment of Isaiah's prophecy of Jerusalem's deliverance (19:14–37).

The narrator closes his presentation of events in Hezekiah's reign with two important incidents. The first one centers on Hezekiah's life-threating sickness and miraculous recovery (20:1–11). The second stems from the first. Merodach-Baladan, the Chaldean king of Babylon, hears of Hezekiah's miraculous cure and sends ambassadors to congratulate him on his recovery. When Hezekiah foolishly shows to them evidence of his wealth, Isaiah rebukes him (20:12–19). To this is appended the usual closing notices heralding the king's accomplishments (20:20–21).

Unity in the total narrative is achieved by means of subject matter and *dramatis personae*. Thus the first four sections (chs. 18–19) share in common the theme of the Assyrian presence in the Holy Land, while the second, third, and fourth sections deal with the Assyrian invasion of Jerusalem (18:13–19:37). Further unity is achieved for the account of Sennacherib's siege of Jerusalem by means of establishing a verbal inclusio. Thus in describing Sennacherib's retreat (19:36), the narrator reverses the order of the action in the sequence of verbs used to tell of his advance (18:17). Hezekiah is not the only featured character throughout these three chapters, for the prophet Isaiah (cf. Isa 36–39) also plays a key role (chs. 19–20). The result is a carefully crafted narrative dealing with a king unequaled in his trust of the Lord (18:5).

1. Hezekiah's Accession and Early Deeds (18:1–12)

1In the third year of Hoshea son of Elah king of Israel, Hezekiah son of Ahaz king
of Judah began to reign. 2He was twenty-five years old when he became king, and he
reigned in Jerusalem twenty-nine years. His mother's name was Abijah daughter of
Zechariah. 3He did what was right in the eyes of the LORD, just as his father David had done.
4He removed the high places, smashed the sacred stones and cut down the Asherah poles.
He broke into pieces the bronze snake Moses had made, for up to that time the Israelites
had been burning incense to it. (It was called Nehushtan.)

5Hezekiah trusted in the LORD, the God of Israel. There was no one like him among all
the kings of Judah, either before him or after him. 6He held fast to the LORD and did not
cease to follow him; he kept the commands the LORD had given Moses. 7And the LORD was
with him; he was successful in whatever he undertook. He rebelled against the king of
Assyria and did not serve him. 8From watchtower to fortified city, he defeated the Philistines, as far as Gaza and its territory.

9In King Hezekiah's fourth year, which was the seventh year of Hoshea son of Elah king
of Israel, Shalmaneser king of Assyria marched against Samaria and laid siege to it. 10At the
end of three years the Assyrians took it. So Samaria was captured in Hezekiah's sixth year,
which was the ninth year of Hoshea king of Israel. 11The king of Assyria deported Israel to
Assyria and settled them in Halah, in Gozan on the Habor River and in towns of the Medes.
12This happened because they had not obeyed the LORD their God, but had violated his
covenant—all that Moses the servant of the LORD commanded. They neither listened to
the commands nor carried them out.

COMMENTARY

1–2 Perhaps the knottiest of all chronological problems in the Scriptures occurs in this chapter. The data are as follows: the third year of Hoshea is the accession year of Hezekiah's twenty-nine-year reign (cf. v.1 with 2Ch 29:1); v.9 equates Hoshea's seventh year with Hezekiah's fourth year, and v.10 places Hoshea's ninth year in juxtaposition with Hezekiah's sixth year. Thus, the dating of the early years of Hezekiah's reign is inextricably tied with Hoshea's rule. Since Hoshea came to the throne in 732/731 BC, Hezekiah would appear to have begun his rule in 729/728.

Verse 13, however, records the invasion of Sennacherib that led to the famous Battle of El Tekeh as being in Hezekiah's fourteenth year. Since that date can be accurately determined as being 701 BC, this verse would seem to place Hezekiah's accession date at 716/715 (cf. Isa 36:1). Adding to the difficulties is the scriptural notice in 16:1–2 that Ahaz reigned for sixteen years after Pekah's seventeenth year (736/735), thus making Ahaz's final date to be 720/719.

Despite the many ingenious attempts to resolve these difficulties, the harmonization of these data remains a thorny problem. Obviously we are not yet able to grasp fully the details and principles employed by the Hebrew writers in making these chronological correlations. While definite resolution of the details cannot be made presently, it may be simplest to view 729/728 as Hezekiah's first year as coregent with Ahaz, a joint rule he was to share until 720/719. After Ahaz's death in 716, Hezekiah would then have ruled independently from 715 onward, or fourteen years before the Assyrian campaign of 701. If the commencement of Hezekiah's independent rule began only in 715 and Ahaz's reign terminated in 720/719, the actual reins of government would have passed to Hezekiah some three or four years before Ahaz's death, much as Jotham may have lived until 732 after committing governmental control to Ahaz in 736 (see Note on 16:2).

3–4 Hezekiah's godly character is sketched at the onset. He was concerned about the things of God and followed in the footsteps of David his forefather in performing righteous deeds (v.3). Early in Hezekiah's reign this interest took the form of a thorough reformation of the idolatrous practices of Ahaz (v.4). In addition to taking away the high places and destroying the cultic stone pillars and Asherah poles, Hezekiah's iconoclastic purge singled out Moses' bronze serpent (cf. Nu 21), which had become an object of veneration.

5–6 The divine evaluation is a favorable one: (1) There was none who equaled Hezekiah in his trust of the Lord (v.5); (2) he followed the Lord faithfully (v.6a); and (3) he obeyed implicitly the law of God (v.6b). Hence God was with him and blessed him with success (v.7). Hezekiah's character stands as a reminder that living for God's glory is for the believer's good also (cf. v.7 with 2Ch 31:20–21).

Although the writer of Kings concentrates on the political events of Hezekiah's reign, the author of Chronicles gives supplemental information as to Hezekiah's continuing reformation. Hezekiah's spiritual concern brought about a cleansing of the temple, thus undoing the evil deeds of Ahaz (29:3–19). The cleansing was followed by a reconstruction and rededication of the temple (29:20–36), accomplished with proper sacrifices (29:20–24), sincere worship (29:25–30), and glad service to God (29:31–36). Hezekiah's further reforms included the reinstitution of the Passover (2Ch 30), observed after careful forethought (30:1–12) in accordance with the divine command, tempered with mercy (30:13–22), and with protracted festivity (30:23–27).

The author of Chronicles tells of still later iconoclastic purges in which all the people of Israel participated (2Ch 31:1) and of Hezekiah's further attention to spiritual details and provisions (31:2–19). He closes with the notice that Hezekiah characteristically lived out his life in utter devotion to God and so was successful in everything he did (31:20–21).

7–12 Hezekiah's godly concern brought him good success. The narrator points out that Hezekiah rebelled against the king of Assyria; he also moved against "the great king's" vassal, Philistia, and defeated it from one end to the other.

The time of Hezekiah's rebellion and occupation of Philistia must lie late in his reign, probably near the middle of the last quarter of the eighth century BC. Hezekiah's early years were doubtless devoted to religion and internal affairs. Indeed, Sargon's western expeditions in 717/716 and again in 712, the latter of which centered on Philistia and involved military action against Egypt and Transjordania, would make any military move by Hezekiah most unlikely until much later. But Sargon's last half-decade (710–705) was occupied with troubles nearer to home. Restless Arameans applied constant pressure in southern Mesopotamia; there was also the ever-present menace of Merodach-Baladan (cf. 20:12–13), the perennial king of Bit-Yakin and claimant to the throne of Babylon. Accordingly, Hezekiah's growing boldness and military operations must fall within Sargon's last years, or at his death in 705—the usual occasion for such actions (cf. Hobbs, 253; House, 352–53).

Verses 9–11 provide a summary of matters narrated in 17:1–6, while v.12 applies the general condemnation of Israel begun in 17:7 to the specific case of the northern kingdom. The narrator has inserted these details here to highlight the significant difference between Hoshea, the last king of the northern kingdom, and Hezekiah, his younger contemporary in the southern kingdom. While Hezekiah's actions produced dangerous results, Hezekiah's trust in the Lord brought God's blessing even in the political realm.

NOTES

1 Because of the close correspondences between 2 Kings 18–20 and Isaiah 36–39, interpreters have attempted to determine which of the two passages depends on the other. E. J. Young, 2:556, observes, "By far the greater number of modern critics hold that the original narrative is found in 2 Kings and not in Isaiah." Young, however, ably defends the priority of Isaiah in a lengthy appendix. See further J. N. Oswalt, *The Book of Isaiah* (NICOT; Grand Rapids: Eerdmans, 1998), 1:700–701; K&D, *The Prophecies of Isaiah*, 2:80–84.

4 The worship and bringing of incense associated with the bronze serpent, the ancient symbol of personal deliverance, may have been connected with the Asherah cult. Grammatically the name Nehushtan may indicate a play on words, נְחַשׁ הַנְּחֹשֶׁת (*n*[e]*ḥaš hann*[e]*ḥōšet*, "the bronze serpent") contemptuously being called by Hezekiah נְחֻשְׁתָּן (*n*[e]*ḥuštān*, "thing of brass"), or it may be understood as the name given by the devotees to the cult object.

Such a brazen serpent reportedly was found in R. Macalister's excavations at Gezer. See K. Kitchen, "Serpent, Brazen," *NBD*, 1165–66. For the prevelance of serpents in the religious symbolism of the ancient Near East, see H.-J. Fabry, *TDOT*, 9:361–63. See also R. C. Stallman, *NIDOTTE*, 3:84–88.

2. The Assyrian Invasion and Siege of Jerusalem (18:13–37)

[13]In the fourteenth year of King Hezekiah's reign, Sennacherib king of Assyria attacked all the fortified cities of Judah and captured them. [14]So Hezekiah king of Judah sent this message to the king of Assyria at Lachish: "I have done wrong. Withdraw from me, and I will pay whatever you demand of me." The king of Assyria exacted from Hezekiah king of Judah three hundred talents of silver and thirty talents of gold. [15]So Hezekiah gave him all the silver that was found in the temple of the LORD and in the treasuries of the royal palace.

[16]At this time Hezekiah king of Judah stripped off the gold with which he had covered the doors and doorposts of the temple of the LORD, and gave it to the king of Assyria.

[17]The king of Assyria sent his supreme commander, his chief officer and his field commander with a large army, from Lachish to King Hezekiah at Jerusalem. They came up to Jerusalem and stopped at the aqueduct of the Upper Pool, on the road to the Washerman's Field. [18]They called for the king; and Eliakim son of Hilkiah the palace administrator, Shebna the secretary, and Joah son of Asaph the recorder went out to them.

[19]The field commander said to them, "Tell Hezekiah:

"'This is what the great king, the king of Assyria, says: On what are you basing this confidence of yours? [20]You say you have strategy and military strength — but you speak only empty words. On whom are you depending, that you rebel against me? [21]Look now, you are depending on Egypt, that splintered reed of a staff, which pierces a man's hand and wounds him if he leans on it! Such is Pharaoh king of Egypt to all who depend on him. [22]And if you say to me, "We are depending on the LORD our God" — isn't he the one whose high places and altars Hezekiah removed, saying to Judah and Jerusalem, "You must worship before this altar in Jerusalem"?

[23]"'Come now, make a bargain with my master, the king of Assyria: I will give you two thousand horses — if you can put riders on them! [24]How can you repulse one officer of the least of my master's officials, even though you are depending on Egypt for chariots and horsemen ? [25]Furthermore, have I come to attack and destroy this place without word from the LORD? The LORD himself told me to march against this country and destroy it.'"

[26]Then Eliakim son of Hilkiah, and Shebna and Joah said to the field commander, "Please speak to your servants in Aramaic, since we understand it. Don't speak to us in Hebrew in the hearing of the people on the wall."

[27]But the commander replied, "Was it only to your master and you that my master sent me to say these things, and not to the men sitting on the wall — who, like you, will have to eat their own filth and drink their own urine?"

[28]Then the commander stood and called out in Hebrew: "Hear the word of the great king, the king of Assyria! [29]This is what the king says: Do not let Hezekiah deceive you. He cannot deliver you from my hand. [30]Do not let Hezekiah persuade you to trust in the LORD

when he says, 'The LORD will surely deliver us; this city will not be given into the hand of the
king of Assyria.'
31"Do not listen to Hezekiah. This is what the king of Assyria says: Make peace with me
and come out to me. Then every one of you will eat from his own vine and fig tree and
drink water from his own cistern, 32until I come and take you to a land like your own, a
land of grain and new wine, a land of bread and vineyards, a land of olive trees and honey.
Choose life and not death!
"Do not listen to Hezekiah, for he is misleading you when he says, 'The LORD will deliver
us.' 33Has the god of any nation ever delivered his land from the hand of the king of
Assyria? 34Where are the gods of Hamath and Arpad? Where are the gods of Sepharvaim,
Hena and Ivvah? Have they rescued Samaria from my hand? 35Who of all the gods of these
countries has been able to save his land from me? How then can the LORD deliver Jerusalem from my hand?"
36But the people remained silent and said nothing in reply, because the king had commanded, "Do not answer him."
37Then Eliakim son of Hilkiah the palace administrator, Shebna the secretary and Joah
son of Asaph the recorder went to Hezekiah, with their clothes torn, and told him what the
field commander had said.

COMMENTARY

13 The date of Sennacherib's campaign must be calculated from the time of Hezekiah's independent rule in 715 BC, a date that harmonizes well with the data from Assyrian sources. Sennacherib (705–681) was at first occupied with affairs close to home and so was not free to deal with Hezekiah. His first two campaigns were launched against the nearer menace, the continuing presence of Merodach-Baladan and the pesky Arameans—problems he inherited from his father. But having secured the situation in the south and east, Sennacherib was free to deal with the west, against which he launched his famous third campaign.

His annals (see Luckenbill, 2:118–21) record the might of his all-out attack. Swooping down from the north, Sennacherib quickly dispatched the Phoenician cities and then unleashed his fury against Philistia. He notes that the citizens of Ekron had thrown in their lot with the Egyptians and Hezekiah of Judah and even went so far as to deliver their king (and Sennacherib's vassal) into the hands of Hezekiah for confinement. Apparently bypassing Ekron for the moment, Sennacherib marched down the Philistine coast as far as Ashkelon. Having secured the submission of that key city and having deported its king to Assyria, Sennacherib turned his attention inland in a thrust that would not only secure the key city of Lachish but would also effectively cut off the remaining Philistines and Judahites from Egyptian help.

14–16 Verse 14 joins Sennacherib's campaign at this point. Sennacherib has taken Lachish and is busily engaged in mopping up the nearby fortified cities of Judah. With Phoenicia and most of

Philistia laid waste, and with Sennacherib's forces already in the land, Hezekiah sensed the enormity of his impending doom. Overwhelmed by a sense of certain tragedy, he acted out of human propriety and sent a letter of submission to Sennacherib, indicating that he would agree to whatever terms of tribute Sennacherib would demand. In meeting Sennacherib's levy, Hezekiah emptied the coffers of both temple and palace and stripped the gold from the doors and doorposts of the temple.

The Chronicler's report (2Ch 32:2–8) hints that Hezekiah must have quickly sensed that Sennacherib was not to be dissuaded in his quest for Jerusalem. So Hezekiah made serious defensive preparations in view of the anticipated Assyrian siege. He also addressed the people with traditional words that encouraged trust in the Lord (32:7; cf. Jos 1:6–9; 1Ch 22:13; 28:20).

17–18 The seriousness of Sennacherib's intentions can be seen in his sending of high-ranking officers and a great force to the city. The names associated with the Assyrian delegation are known Assyrian military and administrative titles.

The nouns involved are not personal names, as implied in the KJV, but known Assyrian military titles. The first term—תַּרְתָּן (*tartān*, "supreme commander")—stands for the Assyrian *turtannu* ("second in command," i.e., to the king, or "supreme field commander"; cf. Isa 20:1). The second term—רַב־סָרִיס (*rab-sārîs*, "chief officer"; lit., "chief eunuch")—is the title of a senior military officer and is taken by some to be the equivalent of the Assyrian *rab ša-rēši* ("chief of the head"). In either case the idea is given properly in the NIV (cf. Jer 39:3, 13). The third officer—רַב־שָׁקֵה (*rab-šāqēh*, "chief aide")—is the Akkadian *rab šaqu* ("chief cupbearer, commandant"), a high administrative office.

In proper diplomatic exchange Hezekiah sent three of his high-ranking officials: Eliakim, son of Hilkiah, the palace administrator (cf. Isa 22:20–21); Shebna, the scribe; and Joash, son of Asaph, the king's herald. The location of the meeting place of the two delegations has been much discussed. Similarly, the precise identification of the various pools mentioned in connection with the Assyrian menace (cf. 20:20; 2Ch 32:4, 30; Isa 22:9, 11; 36:2) and Hezekiah's plans for the defense of Jerusalem (2Ch 32:1–8; Isa 22:8–11) have been subjects of much controversy.

The available data for the location of the meeting place seem to point to northwestern Jerusalem at a spot where the enemy might easily enjoy a commanding view of the city. Confirmation of this understanding may be forthcoming from Josephus (*J.W.* 5.303 [7.3]; 5.504 [12.2]), who speaks of this area as "the camp of the Assyrians." If this conclusion is correct, the Upper Pool of v.17 and the pool of 20:20 (cf. 2Ch 32:30; Isa 7:3; 22:9–11) are to be differentiated. Certainly Hezekiah would have taken steps to ensure the security of both pools, as well as the cutting off of all water sources available to Sennacherib's army (cf. 2Ch 32:3–4; Isa 22:9–12).

Further evidence for differentiation between the pools of v.17 and 20:20 comes from the scriptural indication that, prior to Hezekiah's siege preparations, the area was in use—as the scene of Isaiah's earlier meeting with Ahaz. What a contrast in circumstances this spot was witnessing! Here Isaiah had carried the encouraging message of the God of the universe to a godless king; now the emissaries of "the great king" bore a distressing dispatch to the God-fearing Hezekiah.

19–21 The Assyrian spokesman's message to Hezekiah was couched in terms of psychological warfare. The Assyrians were rather well informed of developments in Jerusalem, for Hezekiah's reputation for trust (*bṭḥ*) becomes the focal point of his argument. Although rendered differently by the NIV in accordance with English language conventions, this same Hebrew verbal root occurs seven times in these verses. In pointing out the utter folly of relying on Egypt for military aid, he employs the verb five times. What kind of trust can they hope to place in such a splintered reed?

The figure of Egypt as a splintered reed is appropriate. The Nile River was rich in the reeds that were so important to Egyptian life. In this respect Sennacherib's evaluation of Egypt harmonized with the prophecies of Isaiah (Isa 20; 30:3–5; 31:1–3). How seldom does humanity learn the lessons of history! Ezekiel was to deliver a similar oracle in the days of the neo-Babylonian crisis (Eze 29:6–7).

22–25 The Rabshakeh next considers the religious basis of Judah's trust. Did they trust in Yahweh? Hezekiah has misled them in tearing down their places of worship. Instead he has forced them to worship at altars of royal choice (v.22). The Rabshakeh then concludes his opening speech by way of a challenging summation. Militarily, neither tiny Judah nor trusted friend Egypt could stand against the Assyrian king. Even if he supplied the horses, the combined allies would not have enough riders for them! Religiously they were misguided, for it was Yahweh himself who had sent Sennacherib to attack Judah.

26–27 The reply of Hezekiah's delegation aimed at switching the speech to diplomatic language rather than continuing in the language of Judah. The present use of Hebrew could be discouraging to the people. Aramaic became the diplomatic lingua franca of the Near East in the neo-Assyrian period. That a well-educated member of Sennacherib's staff could speak both Hebrew and Aramaic as well as Akkadian need no longer be doubted. H. W. F. Saggs (*Assyriology and the Study of the Old Testament* [Cardiff: Univ. of Wales Press, 1969], 17–18) notes that the Assyrians frequently sent a token contingent to effect the surrender of a city and brought in a full striking force only after a refusal. Saggs also points out a close parallel between the conduct of the Assyrian officers at Jerusalem with that of certain officers who sent a report to the Assyrian king during the siege of Babylon. There the officers, hoping to draw support over to the Assyrians, also addressed their remarks to the native populace.

28–30 Scorning the Hebrew delegation's request, the Rabshakeh shouted all the louder. He began his second speech (still in Hebrew) with a renewed denunciation of Hezekiah's efforts to get the people to trust in Yahweh for deliverance.

31–35 The Rabshakeh's argument again focuses on two main areas. In the first he promises that deportation would mean a life of productive tranquility rather than hardship. Why face certain death in an Assyrian assault? In the second argument he applies logic to his former points concerning their religious orientation: No other great god has been able to save its venerators from the Assyrian forces.

36–37 The first episode concerning the siege closes on a somber note. Although the people obediently follow the king's directive of silence, the king's officials report to him with torn clothes. The tearing of clothes here was perhaps a sign of both grief and shame that God's name had been blasphemed (cf. 19:4).

NOTES

13 Second Kings 18:13, 17–20:19 is closely reproduced in Isaiah 36:1–38:8; 39:1–8. The writer of 2 Chronicles 32:9–19 has restructured and stylized the material of 2 Kings 18:19–38; 19:10–13. Jenkins's suggestion ("Hezekiah's Fourteenth Year," *VT* 26 [1976]: 284–98) that the details of this section are to be connected with Sargon's suppression of the revolt headed by Ashdod in 714–712 BC but later reinterpreted in the light of Sennacherib's campaign of 701 is foundationless.

Sennacherib claims the capture of forty-six fortified cities of Judah as well as many forts and villages. Although his annals do not mention a campaign against Lachish, excavations there, as well as palace reliefs from Nineveh depicting details of the siege, confirm the biblical account (see Alfred Hoerth, *Archaeology and the Old Testament* [Grand Rapids: Baker, 1998], 350–51). An inscription on a relic in the British Museum indicates that Sennacherib did indeed take the city, along with much booty.

14 Hezekiah's "confession" employs known diplomatic parlance. From an Assyrian point of view, a "sin" against the crown meant any offense that involved the failure to recognize Assyrian sovereignty. The king of Lydia makes a similar plea to Ashurbanipal after a frightful Cimmerian invasion. "Your father cursed my father and so evil came upon him. As for me, I am your slave who fears you. Be gracious unto me and I will pull your yoke" (N. J. Lau and S. Langdon, *The Annals of Ashurbanipal* [Leiden: Brill, 1903], plate 8, lines 124–25). Although Hezekiah might not have intended subservience to Sennacherib, the incident breathes the air of diplomatic negotiations. See D. J. Wiseman, "'Is It Peace?'" 316–17. Hezekiah's tribute is strikingly confirmed by Sennacherib's own account (see Luckenbill, 2:120–21).

17 For further details as to the problem of the location of this consultation and of the Jerusalemite pools mentioned in connection with Hezekiah, see Gray, 679–82, 703–4; for a brief discussion of Jerusalem's water supply, see Yigal Shiloh, "The Rediscovery of Warren's Shaft," *BAR* 7 (1981): 24–39; idem, "The City of David Archaeological Project: The Third Season–1980," *BA* 44 (1981): 161–71; and I. W. J. Hopkins, *Jerusalem: A Study in Urban Geography* (Grand Rapids: Baker, 1970), 45–47. For Hezekiah's siege preparations, see B. Mazar and G. Cornfield, *The Mountain of the Lord* (Garden City, N.Y.: Doubleday, 1975), 175–77. For a consideration of the accurate recording of the Rabshakeh's speech, see H. Wildberger, "Die Rede des Rabsake vor Jerusalem," *TZ* 35 (1979): 35–47. For the precise understanding of the Rabshakeh's title, see H. Tadmor, "Rab-saris and Rab-shakeh in 2 Kings 18," in *The Word of the Lord Shall Go Forth*, ed. C. L. Meyers and M. O'Connor (Winona Lake, Ind.: Eisenbrauns, 1983), 279–85.

18 Eliakim and Shebna are mentioned also in Isaiah 22, where Shebna was yet the royal chamberlain. Isaiah prophesied that Shebna would be replaced by Eliakim. This development had apparently come to pass, but Shebna still held the important post of secretary.

19 The Rabshakeh's pious words reflect normal diplomatic speech both in form and content. A relief from Khorsabad depicts an Assyrian officer standing on a siege machine addressing a city's defenders while reading from a scroll (Wiseman, *1 & 2 Kings*, 277).

"The great king" was the standard designation appropriated by all the neo-Assyrian kings and followed by the neo-Babylonian and Persian monarchs. In time past it was reserved for those kings who had achieved international recognition as heads of "super powers." Thus the Hittite king Hattushilish III chided the Assyrian king Adad-Nirari I in his bid for the right to bear this title and to call himself Hattushilish's "brother" (a title implying equal rank). Although Adad-Nirari had achieved great things, he had not yet achieved "brotherhood." For details, see CAH, 3:258–59, 278; G. Beckman, *Hittite Diplomatic Texts*, 2nd ed. (Atlanta: Scholars Press, 1999, 146–47). It is interesting to note that throughout his orations the Rabshakeh accords royal status to the Assyrian king while simply mentioning Hezekiah by name.

22 Cohn, 130, suggests that here the Rabshakeh's words were probably meant to appeal to those citizens who were opposed to Hezekiah's reforms.

27 For the words "dung" and "urine," the Masoretes euphemistically substituted "their going forth" and "the water of their feet." The written text, however, preserves the Assyrian language of the street, words no doubt chosen to dramatize the horror of the coming siege. The Assyrians were not above the use of crude speech for dramatic effect. Thus Sennacherib reports in his eighth campaign that the terrified enemy charioteers "passed hot urine and left their excrement in their chariots" (my translation from the original Assyrian; cf. R. Borger, *Babylonisch-Assyrische Lesestücke* [vol. 3; Rome: Pontifical Biblical Institute, 1963], table 50).

31 The vine and fig tree were well-known symbols for God's blessing of his people (cf. Joel 1:7), and "water from the well" ("water from his own cistern," NIV) signified refreshment and abundance of life.

32 The verb יַסִּית (*yassît*, "he is misleading")—as opposed to the synonymous פִּתָּה (*pittâ*, "deceive")—carries the idea of cunning. The Rabshakeh suggests that Hezekiah is deceitful: although he encourages the people with talk of divine intervention, he really knows better.

3. Prophetic Encouragement amid the Continued Siege (19:1–13)

[1]When King Hezekiah heard this, he tore his clothes and put on sackcloth and went into
the temple of the LORD. [2]He sent Eliakim the palace administrator, Shebna the secretary
and the leading priests, all wearing sackcloth, to the prophet Isaiah son of Amoz. [3]They
told him, "This is what Hezekiah says: This day is a day of distress and rebuke and disgrace,
as when children come to the point of birth and there is no strength to deliver them. [4]It
may be that the LORD your God will hear all the words of the field commander, whom his
master, the king of Assyria, has sent to ridicule the living God, and that he will rebuke
him for the words the LORD your God has heard. Therefore pray for the remnant that still
survives."
[5]When King Hezekiah's officials came to Isaiah, [6]Isaiah said to them, "Tell your master,
'This is what the LORD says: Do not be afraid of what you have heard—those words with
which the underlings of the king of Assyria have blasphemed me. [7]Listen! I am going to
put such a spirit in him that when he hears a certain report, he will return to his own country, and there I will have him cut down with the sword.'"
[8]When the field commander heard that the king of Assyria had left Lachish, he withdrew and found the king fighting against Libnah.
[9]Now Sennacherib received a report that Tirhakah, the Cushite king of Egypt, was
marching out to fight against him. So he again sent messengers to Hezekiah with this
word: [10]"Say to Hezekiah king of Judah: Do not let the god you depend on deceive you
when he says, 'Jerusalem will not be handed over to the king of Assyria.' [11]Surely you
have heard what the kings of Assyria have done to all the countries, destroying them

completely. And will you be delivered? [12]Did the gods of the nations that were destroyed by my forefathers deliver them: the gods of Gozan, Haran, Rezeph and the people of Eden who were in Tel Assar? [13]Where is the king of Hamath, the king of Arpad, the king of the city of Sepharvaim, or of Hena or Ivvah?"

COMMENTARY

1–2 The narrator stitches this section to the last one by noting Hezekiah's tearing his clothes and donning sackcloth (traditional symbols of mourning; cf. Est 4:1–3; Joel 1:13). The king took two further steps: (1) He went with heavy heart to the temple to pour out his soul before God; and (2) he sent Eliakim, Shebna, and the leading priests, all dressed in sackcloth, to meet with Isaiah so that he might hear God's word through his prophet (v.2; cf. Dt 18:18).

3 In briefing Isaiah as to the present emergency, the king's delegation also explained Hezekiah's deep concern in the matter. It was a day of "distress." The word connotes not only the idea of trouble because of the Assyrian menace, but also the anguish of heart that every true Israelite must have felt. Furthermore, it was a day of rebuke and correction; Hezekiah sensed that the Lord was even now chastising his people (cf. Hos 5:9–15). As well it was a day of disgrace or contempt; perhaps God was even now about to reject and cast off his people completely (cf. Dt 32:18–43; Jer 14:12; La 2:6).

4–11 As trust was featured in the previous section, "hearing" is particularly emphasized in this one. Hezekiah *heard* the report (v.1). God *heard* the blasphemous taunts of the Rabshakeh (v.4). Hezekiah is not to fear the Assyrian officer's words (v.6). Sennacherib will *hear* a report that will cause him to return home (v.7). The Rabshakeh *hears* that Sennacherib has moved on from Lachish to Libnah and reports to him there (v.8). Sennacherib's message to Hezekiah challenges him with the fact that he has *heard* what the Assyrians have done to other countries (v.11). The cumulative effect of this repetition is to leave the reader with the impression that all parties involved are or will be cognizant of what is happening.

5–7 Hezekiah's message to Isaiah stressed the prophet's close relation to Yahweh by calling the Lord "your [Isaiah's] God." Isaiah's message to the king's emissaries terms Hezekiah "your [the emissaries'] master." Isaiah assures the king that not only will Sennacherib hear a disturbing report and depart for his own country, but also he will later (though not necessarily immediately) be killed.

The report that Sennacherib was to hear probably does not refer to the news of the destruction of his army (v.35), for Sennacherib himself would be at Jerusalem at that time. Nor could it refer to the report of Tirhakah's advance (v.9), for he responded with force to that move. Instead, it must refer to upsetting news from the Assyrian homeland. Coupled with the God-implanted spirit of fear and the destruction of his army (vv.35–36), it would be sufficient to send Sennacherib rushing home.

8–9 When a report came to Sennacherib concerning an Egyptian advance against him, he sent a messenger to Jerusalem with an official letter for Hezekiah. A space break extending from before v.8 to the middle of v.9 calls attention to events contemporaneous with Isaiah's words to Hezekiah. The latter half of v.9 returns to matters concerning Jerusalem.

While reconciliation of the details of Sennacherib's campaign with the data of 2 Kings 18:13–19:37 remains difficult, it is by no means impossible. Some scholars see in the scriptural passage two parallel accounts of Sennacherib's delegations to Hezekiah: (1) 18:13–19:7 and (2) 19:8–37. They are divided, however, as to whether 19:36–37 belongs to the second account or the first and as to whether 19:8–9a belongs with the second account or forms a bridge between the two. Actually there is no need to see any parallel account in 19:8–37 at all, the latter portion's being a continuance of the psychological warfare already initiated. Moreover, it chiefly relates details that are not contained in the earlier portion.

Some scholars who maintain the integrity of the MT argue that a harmonization between the scriptural record and Sennacherib's annals can be made only by postulating that after the Battle of El Tekeh (reflected in 18:13–16), Sennacherib returned many years later to fight a second campaign against Jerusalem (18:17–19:37). The mention of the coming of Tirhakah to do battle with Sennacherib seems to support the idea that this section of the text must refer to a second campaign, unmentioned in Sennacherib's annals, that took place between the onset of Tirhakah's reign in 690 BC and the death of Sennacherib in 681. Certain studies by Egyptologists purported to show that Tirhakah was only nine or ten years old in 701 and hence could not have been at El Tekeh.

Several data tell against the two-campaign hypothesis. While Sennacherib mentioned five other subsequent campaigns, he makes no mention of any renewed engagement in the west or with Judah. This seems strange if indeed he had fought a subsequent campaign against Jerusalem. The mention of Tirhakah as being Pharaoh, when at El Tekeh he would not yet have been the king, is a simple example of an author's writing after the event and proleptically giving to an individual his eventual title. It is of interest to note that Tirhakah's own stele does precisely the same thing: "His Majesty [Tirhakah] was in Nubia, as a goodly youth ... amidst the goodly youths whom His Majesty King Shebitku had summoned from Nubia" (K. A. Kitchen, *Ancient Orient and Old Testament* [Chicago: InterVarsity Press, 1966], 82–83). Recent studies (see Notes, v.9) have demonstrated that Tirhakah was at least twenty or twenty-one years old in 701 BC and possibly even older, hence well able to lead his brother Shebitku's forces.

Finally, it is questionable whether Hezekiah actually lived into the second decade of the seventh century BC as necessitated by the thesis of two campaigns. In sum, Sennacherib's single recorded campaign harmonizes well with the biblical account. It is better to accept the primacy of the scriptural order of events than the boasts of Sennacherib, whose report is laid out geographically and thematically in his annals.

10–13 Though Sennacherib's message to Hezekiah gives polite recognition to his royal title, it is also full of biting sarcasm. Because Hezekiah is noted for his trust in Yahweh, the Lord's ability to deliver Jerusalem is the central issue. The point of Sennacherib's rhetorical question is that no one else's god has been successful in opposing the Assyrian monarch, and neither will Hezekiah's.

NOTES

3 The latter part of the verse evidently contains a well-known proverb that emphasized the need for superior strength to intervene in a time of overwhelming danger (cf. Hos 13:13).

6 The word נַעַר (*na*ʿ*ar*, "underling" [NIV]) is usually translated "lad" or "servant." However, J. MacDonald ("The Status and Roll of the *NA*ʿ*AR* in Israelite Society," *JNES* 35 [1976]: 147–70) has argued forcefully that in military contexts those designated by this term are young men of good birth who spend their lives in the service of the king. MacDonald prefers the term "squire." If that meaning is correct, the Lord's words need not be taken in so derogatory a fashion as usually assumed but may be a reflection of their social status. These men are merely professional officials carrying out the words of the king. There is here, however, a greater King, who will deal personally and finally with "the great king" of Assyria.

9 For a thorough presentation of the two-campaign hypothesis, see Bright, 282–87. See also C. Begg, "Sennacherib's Second Palestinian Campaign: An Additional Indication," *JBL* 106 (1987): 685–86. For details relative to Tirhakah, see S. Horn, "The Chronology of King Hezekiah's Reign," *AUSS* 2 (1964): 153–64; Kitchen, *Third Intermediate Period*, 154–72, 383–86; A. F. Rainey, "Taharqa and Syntax," *TA* 3 (1976): 38–41.

B. Geiger ("2 Kings XVIII 14–16 and the Annals of Sennacherib," *VT* 21 [1971]: 604–6) has demonstrated that it is impossible to harmonize the details of 18:14–16 with the account of Sennacherib's third campaign as required by the two-campaign theorists. See further N. Naʾaman, "Sennacherib's 'Letter to God' on His Campaigns to Judah," *BASOR* 214 (1974): 25–39 (cf. his "Sennacherib's Campaign to Judah and the Date of the *LMLK* Stamps," *VT* 29 [1979]: 61–86).

4. Hezekiah's Prayer and Isaiah's Prophecy (19:14–37)

OVERVIEW

The remainder of ch. 19 contains three major sections. In the first (vv.14–19) Hezekiah takes Sennacherib's letter to the temple, spreads it out before the Lord, and prays. The prayer contains typical elements of lament and prayer psalms (cf. Ps 44). Thus it contains an opening statement of praise to God (v.15) before petitioning God to note Sennacherib's taunts (v.16). In the closing portion (vv.17–19) Hezekiah acknowledges Sennacherib's accomplishments against other nations and their gods and pleads with the Lord to deliver Jerusalem.

The second section falls into two units: (1) a denunciation of Sennacherib from Isaiah (vv.20–28) and (2) a prophecy for Hezekiah. (1) In the case of Sennacherib, the Lord is aware of the Assyrian king's blasphemous taunts (vv.21–23a) and his bombastic boasting (vv.23b–24). Addressing these matters in inverse order the Lord answers that he will judge the Assyrian king for his braggadocio. He needs to realize that he owes all his success to Yahweh, the true world ruler (vv.25–26). Because of his blasphemy against Yahweh, he will be turned back at Jerusalem without achieving its capture (vv.27–28).

(2) A second unit features Isaiah's prophetic words to Hezekiah. The king is assured that a remnant will survive the Assyrian threat and will prosper nicely (vv.29–31). Indeed, the Lord will defend the city and deliver it (vv.32–34).

The chapter closes with a twofold historical notice: (1) the Assyrians suffer a staggering loss before the walls of Jerusalem and return home (vv.35–36); and (2) much later Sennacherib is assassinated by his own sons—ironically while he is worshiping a god that is powerless to save him (v.37).

14 Hezekiah received the letter from the messengers and read it. Then he went up to
the temple of the LORD and spread it out before the LORD. 15 And Hezekiah prayed to the
LORD: "O LORD, God of Israel, enthroned between the cherubim, you alone are God over all
the kingdoms of the earth. You have made heaven and earth. 16 Give ear, O LORD, and hear;
open your eyes, O LORD, and see; listen to the words Sennacherib has sent to insult the
living God.

17 "It is true, O LORD, that the Assyrian kings have laid waste these nations and their lands.
18 They have thrown their gods into the fire and destroyed them, for they were not gods
but only wood and stone, fashioned by men's hands. 19 Now, O LORD our God, deliver us
from his hand, so that all kingdoms on earth may know that you alone, O LORD, are God."

20 Then Isaiah son of Amoz sent a message to Hezekiah: "This is what the LORD, the God of
Israel, says: I have heard your prayer concerning Sennacherib king of Assyria. 21 This is the
word that the LORD has spoken against him:

"'The Virgin Daughter of Zion
    despises you and mocks you.
The Daughter of Jerusalem
    tosses her head as you flee.
22 Who is it you have insulted and blasphemed?
    Against whom have you raised your voice
and lifted your eyes in pride?
    Against the Holy One of Israel!
23 By your messengers
    you have heaped insults on the Lord.
And you have said,
    "With my many chariots
I have ascended the heights of the mountains,
    the utmost heights of Lebanon.
I have cut down its tallest cedars,
    the choicest of its pines.
I have reached its remotest parts,
the finest of its forests.
24 I have dug wells in foreign lands
and drunk the water there.
With the soles of my feet
    I have dried up all the streams of Egypt."

25 "'Have you not heard?
    Long ago I ordained it.

In days of old I planned it;
now I have brought it to pass,
that you have turned fortified cities
into piles of stone.
26 Their people, drained of power,
are dismayed and put to shame.
They are like plants in the field,
like tender green shoots,
like grass sprouting on the roof,
scorched before it grows up.

27 "'But I know where you stay
and when you come and go
and how you rage against me.
28 Because you rage against me
and your insolence has reached my ears,
I will put my hook in your nose
and my bit in your mouth,
and I will make you return
by the way you came.'

29 "This will be the sign for you, O Hezekiah:

"This year you will eat what grows by itself,
and the second year what springs from that.
But in the third year sow and reap,
plant vineyards and eat their fruit.
30 Once more a remnant of the house of Judah
will take root below and bear fruit above.
31 For out of Jerusalem will come a remnant,
and out of Mount Zion a band of survivors.

The zeal of the LORD Almighty will accomplish this.

32 "Therefore this is what the LORD says concerning the king of Assyria:

"He will not enter this city
or shoot an arrow here.
He will not come before it with shield
or build a siege ramp against it.
33 By the way that he came he will return;
he will not enter this city,
declares the LORD.

[34]I will defend this city and save it,
for my sake and for the sake of David my servant."

[35]That night the angel of the LORD went out and put to death a hundred and eighty-five thousand men in the Assyrian camp. When the people got up the next morning—there were all the dead bodies! [36]So Sennacherib king of Assyria broke camp and withdrew. He returned to Nineveh and stayed there.

[37]One day, while he was worshiping in the temple of his god Nisroch, his sons Adrammelech and Sharezer cut him down with the sword, and they escaped to the land of Ararat. And Esarhaddon his son succeeded him as king.

COMMENTARY

14–19 The recorded prayer is likely a summation of Hezekiah's words. The opening praise (v.15) clearly sets Hezekiah's theological perspective at variance with that of Sennacherib (v.16; cf. v.12). Unlike the so-called gods, the Lord is the sole ruler of all and Creator of heaven and earth. Sennacherib's success against other nations and their gods misses the point. Because Yahweh is the living God, Hezekiah can petition him to note Sennacherib's boasts and to redeem his people. Then all nations will know that Yahweh alone is God (Dt 6:4). Hezekiah's prayer implies that the Lord's reputation is at stake (cf. 1Sa 17:46; 1Ki 18:37; Ps 79:1–10).

20 Hezekiah's plea for deliverance has made two points in connection with Sennacherib's letter (vv.14–19): (1) Sennacherib's bombastic boasting and (2) his blasphemy against the Lord. Through Isaiah, God deals with both points as well as Hezekiah's petition for deliverance.

21–23a The Lord's reply through his prophet treats Hezekiah's complaints against the Assyrian king in inverse order. Sennacherib's blasphemy is dealt with first in an opening taunt song. The Rabshakeh had taunted the citizens of Jerusalem previously (18:23–25); now the Jerusalemites will be able to return the favor. They are pictured as saying a mocking good-bye to Sennacherib. Already, then, there is a strong hint of Sennacherib's failure. He will fail because he has dared to cast insults against the Holy One of Israel.

23b–24 Sennacherib's boasting is considered next. The language here is figurative, the point being that in Sennacherib's mind no obstacle of human beings or nature was sufficient to withstand him. The words repeat Sennacherib's inner musings, ideas known only to himself—or so he thought. But God knows the innermost intents of all people (Ps 7:9; 44:21), and his word penetrates their deepest being (Heb 4:12). The revelation of these hidden desires ought to have struck terror into Sennacherib's heart and convinced him that Yahweh is truly God (cf. Da 2:47).

On his second campaign Sennacherib had scaled hitherto inaccessible mountain passes and would do so again in his subsequent campaign. The other deeds had been accomplished only in his own mind. Like the greatest of Mesopotamian kings, he would penetrate Lebanon to secure its cedar. He saw himself drinking water from the wells he would dig in arid places (see Note on v.24). Contrariwise, he would dry up Egypt's delta by the soles of his feet. Sennacherib's plans of conquest probably included Egypt, to which the western nations of the Fertile Crescent looked for support. But that goal was not to be reached by an Assyrian king until the days of Esarhaddon (671 BC) and Ashurbanipal (667, 663). Interestingly the floodwaters of the Nile would serve as a veritable fortress for the late Egyptian pharaoh Nectanebo I (378–361 BC) in his defense against the invading Persians in 373 BC.

25–28 God next deals with Sennacherib's elevated self-image. In reality, whatever he has accomplished is in accordance with God's governing of the nations (vv.25–26). Sennacherib's blasphemous disposition is well known to God. His every thought and action is open to the Lord. God will judge Sennacherib with the result that he and his forces will return to Assyria without capturing Jerusalem (vv.27–28).

29–31 The Lord's message to Hezekiah is one of encouragement. First he gives the king a reassuring sign. The sign will be one of extreme importance to besieged Jerusalem. In what remained of the present year, there will be food enough from that which has been spilled accidentally in the sowing and has sprung up by itself as an aftergrowth.

Since military campaigns were regularly planned to coincide with the harvest so that the armies might live off the land, and since Israel's year began in early fall, there would be little left of "this year." Accordingly as the new year dawned, because of the extent of the devastation the surviving remnant of Jerusalem and Judah would again largely depend on grain that came up of its own accord in random fashion.

For the third year, however, there was a direct divine command: "Sow and reap, plant vineyards and eat fruit." Here was direct assurance that the people might resume normal agricultural activities with the full expectation of eating the fruits of their labor. When in the harvest of the third year the people ate in abundance, they would know assuredly that God had been in the entire crisis.

30–31 Hobbs, 281, points out that the OT's teaching on the theme of the remnant often blends together the thought of historical and eschatological survivors.

32–34 God closed his message to Hezekiah with a final word concerning the Assyrian king. Sennacherib would not only not enter Jerusalem but would not even lay a full-scale siege against it (v.32). No arrow would fall into the city; neither shield nor siege ramp would appear before it. Quite the contrary, Sennacherib would turn around and go home (v.33). For God himself was defending and would deliver Jerusalem for his own name's sake (vv.4, 19) and on the basis of his standing promise to David (v.34; cf. 2Sa 7; 1Ki 11:13, 34–39; 2Ki 8:19).

That Sennacherib failed in his attempt to take Jerusalem is apparent from the annals of his third campaign. Although he claimed the capture and despoiling of some forty-six Judean cities, when it came to Jerusalem he could only report: "Himself [Hezekiah] I made a prisoner in Jerusalem, his royal residence, like a bird in a cage" (*ANET*, 288). Sennacherib's face-saving words have their sole validity in his having surrounded Jerusalem during his protracted campaigning in Judah and Philistia.

The previous attempt to unseat illegally the house of David in the days of Hezekiah's father, Ahaz, had been overruled by God (Isa 7:1–16). Sennacherib's efforts to unseat the godly Hezekiah would fare no better. When it was time for a sinful Jerusalem to fall, it would happen at divine direction (2Ch 36:14–17), and even then the house of David would be sovereignly sustained until the coming of the Messiah (Isa 7:1–9:7; Mt 1; Lk 1:26–37, 67–69; 2:4–11).

35–36 According to Josephus (*Ant.* 10:21–22 [1.5]), when Sennacherib saw the decimation of his troops at Jerusalem, he feared for the safety of the rest of his army and fled to Nineveh. Though he would conduct five more campaigns, no mention of another return to Judah is given. The Israelites' God was the living God (cf. v.16)!

In describing Sennacherib's retreat the narrator reverses the order of action utilized in the sequence of verbs describing his advance. Thus the "went up, came, and stood" of 18:17 becomes "departed, went, and sat/dwelled" here in 19:36.

37 Twenty years later (681 BC) two of Sennacherib's own sons assassinated him and successfully escaped to Urartu. Another son, Esarhaddon (681–686), succeeded Sennacherib as king. The last vestige of the divine prophecy stood complete. While God's program may seem to tarry (cf. 2Pe 3:4–9), it will be accomplished. The mills of God grind slowly but exceedingly finely.

NOTES

14 Hezekiah's spreading out of Sennacherib's letter may be illustrated by comparison with contemporary Mesopotamian practice. Wiseman, *1 & 2 Kings*, 281, reports that at times letters were placed "in the temple to be read by the god." Josephus's suggestion (*Ant.* 10:16 [1.4]) that Hezekiah "rolled up the epistle and laid it up within the temple" appears to miss the point.

16 Such anthropomorphic ascriptions to God are common in the OT (cf. Pss 17:2, 6; 34:15; Hab 1:2, 13). See W. J. Dumbrell, "Anthropomorphisms," *NIDOTTE*, 4:391–99.

21 For the use of the taunt song in the ancient Near East, see P. C. Craigie, "The Song of Deborah and the Epic of Tukultininurta," *JBL* 88 (1969): 161–62; "Taunt," in *Dictionary of Biblical Imagery*, ed. L. Ryken, J. C. Wilholt, and T. Longman III (Downers Grove, Ill.: InterVarsity Press, 1998), 841–42. For the shaking/tossing of the head in scorn or derision, see Job 16:4; Psalm 22:7; 109:25; and Jeremiah 18:16.

The term (בַּת) בְּתוּלַת (*b*[e]*tûlat* [*bat*]) "virgin (daughter) of" is a stereotyped phrase with civil or national emphasis; for example virgin (daughter) of Sidon (Isa 23:12), Zion (Isa 37:22; La 2:13), Babylon (Isa 47:1), Egypt (Jer 46:11), Judah (La 1:15), Israel (Jer 18:13; 31:21; Am 5:2), my people (Jer 14:17). This emphasis may be one feature in Isaiah's selection of a different Hebrew word (עַלְמָה, *ʿalmâ*) for "virgin" in Isaiah 7:14. The use here suggests the image of a chaste mother (Jerusalem) who will not be violated by her attacker (Sennacherib).

23 For Sennacherib's mountain campaign, see Luckenbill, 2:161–62. The penetration of Lebanon's forest is a frequent boast of the Mesopotamian kings from Gilgamesh onward; see A. Heidel, *The Gilgamesh Epic and Old Testament Parallels* (Chicago: Univ. of Chicago Press, 1963), 6–7.

24 The digging of wells was common in the ancient Near East and extremely important (e.g., Ge 26:18–22). Sennacherib often reported his concern with water, especially in association with the traditional Mesopotamian royal duty of the digging of canals (e.g., Luckenbill, 2:149–50). Although Sennacherib's traversing of formidable streams is frequently reported (ibid., 2:123, 144), the Assyrian did not reach the Nile River in Egypt. Some have suggested, however, that Sennacherib's boast may have pictured his diverting of the waters of the streams of Egypt much as the Chaldeans did later at Nineveh. For discussion of the Chaldean attack, see my remarks in *Nahum, Habakkuk, Zephaniah* (Chicago: Moody Press, 1991), 106–7.

יְאֹרֵי מָצוֹר (*y*ᵉʾ*ōrêmāṣôr*, "streams of Egypt") is literally "the rivers of besieged/fortified places" (cf. KJV). The noun *māṣôr* is commonly used in martial contexts. Note that besiegers' diversion of the water supplies of protected cities was a common battle tactic; see Cyrus's actions at Babylon as recorded by Herodotus (*Persian Wars* 1.190–91). In some places (e.g., Isa 19:6; 37:25; Mic 7:12), however, it has been taken as an alternative spelling for Egypt (cf. Akkad. *muṣur/muṣri*, "Egypt"; see Luckenbill, 2:298). The NIV reflects this idea here, but it is by no means certain. Of the four contexts mentioned, Ezekiel 27:7 rests purely on a conjectural emendation. Micah 7:12 can be understood as "fortified cities" (cf. KJV), though the text at this point is difficult and some wordplay seems clearly demanded. Moreover, the parallel with "Assyria" seems to call for a place name, hence Egypt (though "Tyre" could conceivably be read). In Isaiah 19:6 there is no warrant for reading "streams of Egypt" since the usual spelling for Egypt occurs in the context, unless it be that the combination with יְאֹר (*y*ᵉʾ*ōr*, "river"), as here and in Isaiah 37:25, has become a stereotyped phrase meaning "streams of Egypt."

Others scholars have suggested a still different solution to the problem, namely, that there was a land called by the Assyrians *muṣur/muṣri*, presumably located north of the Taurus Mountains in Asia Minor (see Luckenbill, 1:223; cf. Gray, 268–69). Accordingly, some have suggested that the normal spelling for Egypt—מִצְרַיִם (*miṣrayim*)—can at times be confused with *muṣri* (proposed examples include 1Ki 10:28–29; 2Ki 7:6, but neither case is at all certain). On the problem of *muṣur/muṣri*, see H. Tadmor, "Que and Musri," *IEJ* 11 (1961): 423–32.

Hayim Tawil ("The Historicity of 2 Kings 19:24 [= Isa 37:25]: The Problem of *Yeʾore Maṣor*," *JNES* 41 [1982]: 195–206) has conjectured that the much-debated term refers to the streams of (Mount) Musri (modern Jebel Bashiqah), whose headwaters were used by Sennacherib to bring water to Nineveh in 702 and 609 BC. (Tawil argues for the latter date, thus siding with those who favor a second western campaign for Sennacherib.) While he makes an admirable case for such an identification here, his proposal to read *muṣri* twice in Micah 7:12 struggles a great deal more and fails completely in Isaiah 19:6.

25 Sennacherib often boasted of his thorough devastation of enemy cities; see Luckenbill, 2:117.

26 Grass growing out of mud roofs quickly perishes as a result of lack of depth for its roots (for the scriptural representation of humankind as grass, see Pss 37:2; 90:5–6; 103:15–16; Isa 40:6–8; 1Pe 1:24). The image of the sirocco, suggested here, is made explicit in the Dead Sea Isaiah Scroll, which reads in Isaiah 37:27: "scorched by the east wind." For English translation, see *The Dead Sea Scrolls Bible*, ed. M. Abegg Jr., P. Flint, and E. Ulrich (San Francisco: Harper San Francisco, 1999), 328.

28 The figures of the hook in the nose and the bit in the mouth are used in the OT of restraining animals (e.g., Ps 32:9; Eze 19:4). Used in reference to Sennacherib's activities, the figures are doubly fitting. For Sennacherib needed to be restrained like a wild animal (cf. Isa 30:28), and it would be done to him in this same manner frequently employed by the Assyrians in treating their captured prisoners (see Luckenbill, 2:314–15, 319). Royal Assyrian drawings often depict the leading of bound prisoners of war (cf. Pritchard, *ANEP*, vol. 1, fig. 121).

29 In the regulations for the sabbatical year (Lev 25:5, 11), סָפִיחַ (*sāpîaḥ*, "what grows by itself"; e.g., grain that grows from seed spilled unintentionally in the sowing) designated grain left untouched by plowing that grew up of its own accord. Hence some interpreters have suggested that 701 BC was a sabbatical year, and the next year would be a fiftieth or jubilee year, in which no sowing could take place (Lev

25:11–12). While this theory could suggest divine timing to stimulate trust in God, unfortunately it cannot be proven conclusively. The text itself gives no such indication, and the Chronicler may hint that such observances had not been regularly observed (2Ch 36:21). סָחִישׁ (*sāḥîš*, lit., "random growth") is probably a by-form of שָׁחִיס (*šāḥîs*, "random growth").

The possibility of divine superintendence even in timing these events to concur with the sabbatical year and the Year of Jubilee, followed by a third year of newness of life's activities, may perhaps take on a different nuance. This possibility depends on whether the concurrence can be shown to be related to the use of the numeral three in specialized contexts. The motif of the third day/year (etc.) can be employed to: (1) emphasize decisiveness of action or the resolution of problems (Ge 34:25; 40:18–20; 42:18; 1Sa 20:12; 1Ki 12:12; Est 5:1); (2) set aside a day of specialized activity (Ex 19:1, 15; Nu 19:12, 19; 31:19; 2Ki 20:5, 8); (3) do spiritual service for God (Ezr 6:15); and (4) observe spiritual sacrifice and communion in newness of walk with God (Lev 7:17; Lk 13:32; 24:5b–7, 21, 44–49; Ac 10:40; 1Co 15:4; see comments on 1Ki 12:3b–5).

31 For the remnant see G. F. Hasel, *The Remnant* (Berrien Springs, Mich.: Andrews Univ. Press, 1972).

32 A parallel to Sennacherib's boast can be found in the well-known Apology of the Hittite king Hattusilis III, who reports that the goddess Ishtar shut up his nephew and rival Urhitesupas in the city of Samuhas "like a pig in a sty" (E. H. Sturtevant and G. Bechtel, *A Hittite Chrestomathy* [Philadelphia: Linguistic Society of America, 1935], 81).

35 For the destroying angel of the Lord, see Exodus 12:12–13, 23; 2 Samuel 24:15–16; for the angelic destruction of armies, see Revelation 9:13–18; for the divine deliverance of Israel, see Isaiah 26:20–21; Joel 3:16–17; Zechariah 12:6–9; 13:8–9.

Herodotus (*Persian Wars* 2.141) preserves an Egyptian tradition that in answer to the prayers of Sethos, the god Vulcan delivered the Egyptians from Sennacherib at Pelusium by sending field mice through the Assyrian camp to eat up the Assyrians' quivers and bow strings and the leather straps on their shields. Weaponless, the major portion of the Assyrian army barely escaped with its life.

37 "Nisroch" is an intentional scribal corruption, probably of "Marduk." For "Adrammelech" see comments and Note on 17:31. "Sharezer" is a hypocoristic form (cf. "Belshazzar" [Da 5:1] and Daniel's "Babylonian" name "Belteshazzar" [Da 1:7]).

5. Hezekiah's Sickness and Miraculous Recovery (20:1–11)

[1]In those days Hezekiah became ill and was at the point of death. The prophet Isaiah son of Amoz went to him and said, "This is what the LORD says: Put your house in order, because you are going to die; you will not recover."

[2]Hezekiah turned his face to the wall and prayed to the LORD, [3]"Remember, O LORD, how I have walked before you faithfully and with wholehearted devotion and have done what is good in your eyes." And Hezekiah wept bitterly.

[4]Before Isaiah had left the middle court, the word of the LORD came to him: [5]"Go back
and tell Hezekiah, the leader of my people, 'This is what the LORD, the God of your father
David, says: I have heard your prayer and seen your tears; I will heal you. On the third day
from now you will go up to the temple of the LORD. [6]I will add fifteen years to your life. And
I will deliver you and this city from the hand of the king of Assyria. I will defend this city for
my sake and for the sake of my servant David.'"

[7]Then Isaiah said, "Prepare a poultice of figs." They did so and applied it to the boil, and
he recovered.

[8]Hezekiah had asked Isaiah, "What will be the sign that the LORD will heal me and that I
will go up to the temple of the LORD on the third day from now?"

[9]Isaiah answered, "This is the LORD's sign to you that the LORD will do what he has promised: Shall the shadow go forward ten steps, or shall it go back ten steps?"

[10]"It is a simple matter for the shadow to go forward ten steps," said Hezekiah. "Rather,
have it go back ten steps."

[11]Then the prophet Isaiah called upon the LORD, and the LORD made the shadow go back
the ten steps it had gone down on the stairway of Ahaz.

COMMENTARY

1 Taken at face value, the opening phrase—"in those days" (v.1)—seems to place the events of this chapter near the time of Sennacherib's invasion in 701 BC. Several data need to be considered, however, before adopting such a position.

First, because Hezekiah was granted fifteen additional years of life, his years would extend beyond the accession date of his son Manasseh in 698. While a coregency is possible, and there is the option that Hezekiah gave the crown to Manasseh, neither alternative commends itself, especially in the light of Manasseh's demonstrated wickedness (cf. ch. 21). It is possible, of course, that Manasseh's ungodly character only surfaced after his father's death, much as Nero was at his worst only after the death of his teacher, Seneca.

Second, Hezekiah's sickness must be coordinated with Merodach-Baladan's embassy (v.12). Merodach-Baladan enjoyed two periods of rule in Babylon that coincide with Hezekiah's reign: 721–710 BC, a period ending when Sargon drove him back to his tribal position in Bit Yakin, and a short period in 703, when Merodach-Baladan succeeded in retaking the throne of Babylon from the popular favorite, Marduk-zakir-shumi. This short-lived latter rule was terminated when Sennacherib invaded Babylon, thus sending the wily Merodach-Baladan scurrying for safety once more.

Scholars have argued at least four positions as to the events of 20:1–11. (1) Thiele, 159, 465, holds that Hezekiah's sickness and Merodach-Baladan's embassy came after the Battle of El Tekeh and subsequent to the withdrawal of Sennacherib in 701 BC. According to this theory Merodach-Baladan, who was reduced to fighting guerrilla warfare in his exiled status, hoped to find in Hezekiah a new ally for a renewed bid for a wide-ranging anti-Assyrian coalition.

(2) Many scholars hold that the events of ch. 20 took place in 701 BC before the fall of Jerusalem. This position appears to gain strength from a literary perspective. For not only are the events of ch. 20 placed canonically after the invasion of Jerusalem both here and in Isaiah and 2 Chronicles (32:24–26), but this placement also makes Hezekiah's recovery from sickness a sign of Jerusalem's deliverance from Sennacherib (Cohn, 142). The statement of the text (vv.5–6) is that God will not only extend Hezekiah's life by fifteen years but also deliver the city. Both actions are to be taken for the sake of God's reputation (cf. 19:16–19) and because Hezekiah is David's heir.

The difficulties facing both this view and Thiele's are twofold. On the one hand, Merodach-Baladan does not appear to be in any position to have sent an embassy to Hezekiah after 703 BC, for Sennacherib hunted him unmercifully at that time. On the other hand, it must be asked how Hezekiah could have shown Merodach-Baladan's embassy much in the treasury (vv.13, 15) since he had already previously stripped away everything in order to give tribute to Sennacherib (18:14–16).

(3) Another view places the events of ch. 20 around 703 BC (Bright, 267; cf. Wiseman, *1 & 2 Kings*, 285–86). This position has the advantage of being compatible with details of Merodach-Baladan's life and being closely related to the Assyrian crisis associated with Hezekiah's defection from Assyria and expansionist activities (18:7–8). The main difficulty for this view is one of chronology. The additional fifteen years granted to Hezekiah would take his reign well beyond the inauguration of Manasseh's kingship. A coregency between righteous Hezekiah and wicked Manasseh seems unlikely.

(4) A fourth view holds to a still earlier date for these events. Proceeding from a 698/97 BC date for Hezekiah's death, Hezekiah's illness and fifteen added years of recovery would be placed at 713/12 BC, with Merodach-Baladan's embassy arriving shortly afterwards. Indeed, a later date for Hezekiah's death appears to be extremely difficult to harmonize with the data concerning historical events at the time of the beginning of his twenty-nine-year reign (cf. 18:1, 10).

The facts of Babylonian history accord well with this view. Because Merodach-Baladan had lived at peace with Sargon since 721 BC, the news of the renewed Babylonian intrigue could have given occasion for Sargon's attack against him in 710. These data may also tie in with Sargon's campaign against the Egyptian and Philistine alliance, leading to the battle for Ashdod in 712, and may indicate something of the general nature of the anti-Assyrian international intrigues. Sargon mentions that Judah was invited by the allies to join them in the rebellion.

The shortness of Merodach-Baladan's later rule appears to be telling against the other three views. The main objection to this position is that it makes the prophesied deliverance of Jerusalem somewhat distant from Sennacherib's attack. Yet the elapse of time allows full weight for the scriptural indication of Hezekiah's successes (2Ch 32:27–30) and Isaiah's assurances to him (2Ki 20:6, 19) to be felt. It would also help to explain Hezekiah's growing boldness after the death of Sargon in 705 BC (2Ki 18:7–8).

The problem of harmonizing the biblical chronological data with the known facts of external history poses problems for each one of the above views. On the whole, the easiest course may be taking the phrase "in those days" as a general statement referring to some time in the reign of Hezekiah. If this interpretation is correct, the events of ch. 20 (cf. Isa 38–39) probably belong chronologically before those of 18:7b–19:37, these latter verses being recorded beforehand simply as the example par excellence of Hezekiah's trust in God (cf. 18:7a). If Young (2:457–58, 507, 556–65) is correct that Isaiah's prophecy in chs. 36–39 forms the basis for the text in Kings and that the events of Isaiah 36–37 (cf. 2Ki 18:7b–19:37), though occurring later, are given first to round off his discussion dealing with the Assyrian period of his ministry before moving on to the Babylonian period (Isa 40–66, introduced by chs. 38–39), then the author of Kings may be following the thematic order of Isaiah. If so, the present order in Kings, like that of Isaiah, is more logical than chronological.

2–3 Hezekiah's turning of his face to the wall can be understood in a negative (cf. Ahab, 1Ki 21:4; see Hobbs, 290) or positive sense (Gray, 696; House, 373). Because Hezekiah is noted for his trust in the Lord (2Ki 18:5), and since he pleads with God on the basis of a wholehearted devotion to the Lord, it is perhaps best to give him the benefit of any doubt. The fact that God did answer his prayer instantly and Hezekiah praised God after his recovery (Isa 38:9–20) attest to Hezekiah's proper attitude of heart. Indeed, selfish, misdirected prayer (Jas 4:3) and petitions that are contrary to God's will are not granted (Dt 3:23–26; 2Co 12:8; cf. 2Ch 7:14; Jn 15:7).

4 The middle court (so Qere; Kethiv, "middle city") was situated between the palace and temple (cf. 1Ki 7:7–8).

5–6 Once again the third element in the sequence ("on the third day") becomes the occasion of a new beginning (see Note on 19:29). The promise of an additional fifteen years of life and divine protection was both a blessing and a caution for Hezekiah. Although God would defend the city, both for the honor of his name and the covenant with David, Hezekiah now had a specified amount of time in which to serve the Lord and his country. The mention of David as Hezekiah's "father" was a reminder to the king that he was David's spiritual heir. Accordingly, he was to be a man of similar persuasion of heart (cf. 1Ki 11:4; 14:8).

7 Although contemporary medical procedures were followed in treating Hezekiah's ailment, the real healing came from God himself. The use of figs to draw an ulcerated sore is an ancient practice, being attested as early as the Ras Shamra Tablets (*UT* 55:28; 56:3). Pliny (*Natural History* 22:7) also mentions such a remedy.

8 Hezekiah asked Isaiah for a confirmatory sign that all that he had said was true. How different was his attitude from that of Ahaz, who refused any divine sign (Isa 7:12)!

9–11 The word "steps" has been variously understood. Some interpreters have suggested that by the term "steps of Ahaz" is meant both a sundial and the degrees of shadow registered on it (so Targ., Jerome, Symmachus; cf. KJV; Keil, 464). Current scholarship tends to take the phrase literally of a flight of stairs by which time was told in accordance with the sun's shadow cast on it apparently by some physical object. Young (2:515 n.) has perhaps the best suggestion:

> It is thought that the device consisted of two sets of steps each facing a wall whose shadow fell upon the steps. As the sun rose, the eastern steps would be in the wall's shadow, which as the day advanced, would grow shorter. On the other hand, during the afternoon, the steps facing west would more and more be in the shadow. According to IQ, the steps were of the *ʿlwt* (upper chamber) of Ahaz. Possibly it was midday when Isaiah spoke. The shadow had just descended the eastern steps and now was ready to ascend the western steps. Instead, however, the shadow again ascended the eastern steps ("Behold, I am causing to return [i.e., to ascend] the shadow of the steps which dawn [during the morning] on the steps of Ahaz, namely, the sun, etc.").

By whatever means the deed was accomplished, it was a miracle effected by the sovereign power of God alone and intended to be a sign to Hezekiah that he would recover and serve yet another fifteen years.

NOTES

1 For data relative to the earlier date for Hezekiah's illness and Merodach-Baladan's embassy, see J. B. Payne, *ZPEB*, 1:843–44; J. Oswalt, *The Book of Isaiah* (NICOT; 2 vols.; Grand Rapids: Eerdmans, 1986), 1:672–75.

3 Hezekiah's concern stands in contrast to the sentiment found in the inscription of the Eshmunʾazar Sarcophagus: "I have been snatched away before my time, the son of a number of restricted days." For the translation see *ANET*, 662; for commentary see H. Donner and W. Röllig, *Kanaanäische und Aramäische Inschriften* (Wiesbaden: Harrassowitz, 1964), 2:21. Interesting parallels occur (1) in the inscription of Agbar the priest and (2) in the Apology of Hattusilis:

> (1) Because of my righteousness before him, he gave me a good name and prolonged my days (*ANET*, 661).
>
> (2) For Hattusilis, the years (are) short.... Now give him to me and let him be my priest. Then he (shall be) alive (E. H. Sturtevant and G. Bechtel, *A Hittite Chrestomathy* [Philadelphia: Univ. of Pennsylvania Press, 1935], 66).

7 Similar measures for healing are widely attested in the ancient world. For details see R. K. Harrison, "Medicine," *IDB*, 3:331–34; Keil, 462–63. The nature of Hezekiah's sickness is unknown. Possibly it was a melanoma. S. Levin ("Hezekiah's Boil," *Judaism* 42 [1993]: 214–19) suggests a possible tuberculosis rash (scrafula).

9–11 The miracle has been much debated. Certainly there is no need to postulate any reversal of the earth's rotation or receding of the sun. The fact that the miracle was felt only "in the land" (i.e., Judah; cf. 2Ch 32:31) makes such solutions most dubious. Similarly, reports of a supposed lost astronomical day rest on specious grounds. A simple localized refraction of the sun's rays would be sufficient to account for the phenomenon. Keil, 465, reports that such a case was noted in AD 1703. J. C. Whitcomb (*Solomon to the Exile* [Grand Rapids: Baker, 1971], 127–29) is probably correct in calling it a "geographically localized miracle."

6. Hezekiah and Merodach-Baladan's Embassy (20:12–21)

12 At that time Merodach-Baladan son of Baladan king of Babylon sent Hezekiah letters
and a gift, because he had heard of Hezekiah's illness. 13 Hezekiah received the messengers
and showed them all that was in his storehouses—the silver, the gold, the spices and the
fine oil—his armory and everything found among his treasures. There was nothing in his
palace or in all his kingdom that Hezekiah did not show them.

14 Then Isaiah the prophet went to King Hezekiah and asked, "What did those men say,
and where did they come from?"

"From a distant land," Hezekiah replied. "They came from Babylon."

15 The prophet asked, "What did they see in your palace?"
"They saw everything in my palace," Hezekiah said. "There is nothing among my treasures that I did not show them."
16 Then Isaiah said to Hezekiah, "Hear the word of the LORD: 17 The time will surely come
when everything in your palace, and all that your fathers have stored up until this day, will
be carried off to Babylon. Nothing will be left, says the LORD. 18 And some of your descendants, your own flesh and blood, that will be born to you, will be taken away, and they will
become eunuchs in the palace of the king of Babylon."
19 "The word of the LORD you have spoken is good," Hezekiah replied. For he thought,
"Will there not be peace and security in my lifetime?"
20 As for the other events of Hezekiah's reign, all his achievements and how he made
the pool and the tunnel by which he brought water into the city, are they not written
in the book of the annals of the kings of Judah? 21 Hezekiah rested with his fathers. And
Manasseh his son succeeded him as king.

COMMENTARY

12 While Merodach-Baladan's sending of diplomatic correspondence and a gift were probably in the manner of a courteous communication of his congratulations and well wishes for Hezekiah, he may have had more political purposes in mind. Thus, Josephus (*Ant.* 10.30–35 [2.2]) hints behind all this courtsey lay his hopes of securing Hezekiah as an ally in an anti-Assyrian coalition.

13 Although unwise under the circumstances, Hezekiah's actions were common protocol to impress important foreign visitors, especially potential allies (cf. 1Ki 10:6–7; see C. T. Begg, "Hezekiah's Display (2 Kgs 20, 12–19)," *BN* 38/39 [1987]: 14–18).

14–18 Isaiah confronted the king concerning his all-too-ready reception and disclosures to the Babylonian embassy (cf. Isa 39:5). Hezekiah had been foolish. Not only would the extent of Jerusalem's wealth now be known and desired by all, but also one day this same Babylon would invade the land and carry off its populace and all its treasures (v.17). Even Hezekiah's own descendants would be taken captive and employed in the service of a Babylonian king (v.18; cf. 24:12–16; 2Ch 33:11; Da 1:3–5). Quite out of keeping with his righteous character, Hezekiah's folly would prove to be a contributing factor in the fulfillment of the ancient prophecies (Lev 26:33; Dt 28:64–67; 30:3). Hezekiah's experience remains a stern warning to all people concerning the perils of pride (cf. Pr 16:5, 18; 28:25–26; 29:23).

19 Hezekiah's response has been variously understood. Some interpreters view it as a callous regard for his own safety (e.g., Cohn, 144). Others consider it an acknowledgment of God's grace and goodness (e.g., Keil, 468). The Chronicler reports that Hezekiah, having been rebuked for his pride, humbled himself. Although he would face danger in his day, the Babylonian threat would not materialize until later (2Ch 32:25–26). The canonical commendation of Hezekiah as a man of trust tends to indicate that Hezekiah accepts the Lord's rebuke through Isaiah and is grateful that God's final judgment of Judah will not come immediately.

20–21 The customary closing notice of Hezekiah's reign concludes not only this section but also the entire account of Hezekiah's reign. The mention of the making of "the pool and tunnel" in this context may point to Hezekiah's later preparations for Sennacherib's siege of Jerusalem.

The extent of his success is expanded by the Chronicler, from whom we also learn that the water conduit mentioned in 2 Kings tapped the waters of Gihon (2Ch 32:27–31). These waters were directed within Jerusalem's walls via a specially constructed tunnel leading to a reservoir known as the Pool of Siloam. The completion of this 1,777-foot tunnel made the waters of Gihon inaccessible to an enemy but readily available to inhabitants within the besieged city.

Archaeological confirmation of Hezekiah's architectural feat came with the recovery of the Siloam inscription, which recorded the excitement of Hezekiah's work crews, who completed the tunnel when they met within the rock-hewn conduit after beginning at the opposite ends of Gihon and Siloam (see *ANET*, 321; Keil, 435; Hobbs, 295–96).

The Chronicler (2Ch 32:33) reports that Hezekiah was buried with full honors by the citizens of Jerusalem in the upper section of the tombs of the sons of David.

NOTES

12 The MT's "Berodach-Baladan" should be read as in Isaiah 39:1, "Merodach-Baladan." The name is a Hebraic representation of the Akkadian "Marduk-apal-iddina" ("Marduk has given a son").

13 These spices were widely used as fragrances, in cosmetics, and in worship and funerary rites. Highly prized, they were included in the presents brought by the queen of Sheba to Solomon (1Ki 10:2, 10). Probably frankincense and myrrh made up the chief spices. For the commercial importance of spices, see G.W. Van Beek, "Frankincense and Myrrh," *BA* 23 (1960): 69–95. By the "armory" is probably meant "the Palace of the Forest of Lebanon" (cf. 1Ki 7:2–5; Isa 22:8).

17 Although Isaiah's prophecy began to be fulfilled already in the days of Hezekiah's son, Manasseh (2Ch 33:11), its full realization came only with the fall of Jerusalem in 586 BC (2Ch 36:18), more than a full century later. The mention of Jerusalem's fall to Babylon at a time when Assyria was the dominant power and immediate threat is clear evidence of the inspiration of Scripture and the trustworthiness of biblical prophecy (cf. Isa 41:21–23; 44:7–8; Rev 1:1, 19).

B. The Reign of Manasseh (21:1–18)

[1]Manasseh was twelve years old when he became king, and he reigned in Jerusalem
fifty-five years. His mother's name was Hephzibah. [2]He did evil in the eyes of the LORD,
following the detestable practices of the nations the LORD had driven out before the
Israelites. [3]He rebuilt the high places his father Hezekiah had destroyed; he also erected

altars to Baal and made an Asherah pole, as Ahab king of Israel had done. He bowed down
to all the starry hosts and worshiped them. 4He built altars in the temple of the LORD, of
which the LORD had said, "In Jerusalem I will put my Name." 5In both courts of the temple
of the LORD, he built altars to all the starry hosts. 6He sacrificed his own son in the fire,
practiced sorcery and divination, and consulted mediums and spiritists. He did much evil
in the eyes of the LORD, provoking him to anger.

7He took the carved Asherah pole he had made and put it in the temple, of which the
LORD had said to David and to his son Solomon, "In this temple and in Jerusalem, which I
have chosen out of all the tribes of Israel, I will put my Name forever. 8I will not again make
the feet of the Israelites wander from the land I gave their forefathers, if only they will be
careful to do everything I commanded them and will keep the whole Law that my servant
Moses gave them." 9But the people did not listen. Manasseh led them astray, so that they
did more evil than the nations the LORD had destroyed before the Israelites.

10The LORD said through his servants the prophets: 11"Manasseh king of Judah has committed these detestable sins. He has done more evil than the Amorites who preceded
him and has led Judah into sin with his idols. 12Therefore this is what the LORD, the God
of Israel, says: I am going to bring such disaster on Jerusalem and Judah that the ears of
everyone who hears of it will tingle. 13I will stretch out over Jerusalem the measuring line
used against Samaria and the plumb line used against the house of Ahab. I will wipe out
Jerusalem as one wipes a dish, wiping it and turning it upside down. 14I will forsake the
remnant of my inheritance and hand them over to their enemies. They will be looted and
plundered by all their foes, 15because they have done evil in my eyes and have provoked
me to anger from the day their forefathers came out of Egypt until this day."

16Moreover, Manasseh also shed so much innocent blood that he filled Jerusalem from
end to end — besides the sin that he had caused Judah to commit, so that they did evil in
the eyes of the LORD.

17As for the other events of Manasseh's reign, and all he did, including the sin he
committed, are they not written in the book of the annals of the kings of Judah?
18Manasseh rested with his fathers and was buried in his palace garden, the garden of
Uzza. And Amon his son succeeded him as king.

COMMENTARY

1 The usual accession statement plus spiritual evaluation is lengthened by a rehearsal of the sins for which Manasseh is condemned as one of Judah's most wicked kings. The author of Kings has nothing good to say about Manasseh despite his later repentance, reforms, and accomplishments (2Ch 33:12–19). By his early sins, all Judah was influenced toward a settled apostasy that would one day spell disaster for the southern kingdom (2Ki 21:9; cf. 24:3–4). From a literary perspective, Manasseh and his son Amon serve as foils to Hezekiah (v.3) and Josiah (22:2; 23:25).

2–9 The charges against Manasseh are recounted (cf. 2Ch 33:2–9). They are introduced as a reproducing of the practices that the pre-Israelite settlers had followed and for which God had dispossesed them. In this way Manasseh emulates his apostate grandfather King Ahaz (2Ki 16:2–4) and the wicked King Ahab of Israel (1Ki 16:32–33). These apostasies include rebuilding of the high places, erecting altars to Baal and the stellar deities, and making of Asherah poles (vv.3–4), which he eventually places in the temple (v.7). His participation in the loathsome Molech rites (cf. 16:3)—sorcery, divination, and various types of spiritism (v.6)—were forbidden by Mosaic law (Lev 19:26; Dt 18:9–14). The sins enumerated here are reminiscent of the activities for which the northern kingdom fell and its people sent into exile (17:7–17). Thus this evil son reverses the worship standards of his father, Hezekiah (v.3).

10–11 With v.10 the divine indictment and judgment begins. Manasseh's evil practices exceed those of the pre-Israelite inhabitants of Canaan (cf. v.2). The king's example and sponsorship of such rites have led the people into sin.

12–13 God therefore sets in motion those forces that will bring destruction on Jerusalem and Judah (cf. Jer 15:1–4). In rehearsing the coming judgment, God uses three well-known literary figures: (1) the tingling ears, (2) the measuring and plumb lines, and (3) the dish wiped clean. The first figure emphasized the severity of the judgment: it will be of such untold dimension that it will strike terror into the hearts of all who hear of its execution (cf. 1Sa 3:11; Jer 19:3–9).

In the second God uses a figure often associated with building (cf. Zec 1:16) but employed also of the measuring of destruction (Isa 34:11; Am 7:7–9). Just as God had taken the measure of Samaria so as to destroy it, so Jerusalem will fall. Even as the Lord had plumbed the house of Ahab in order to exterminate it, so the people of Jerusalem will be executed.

The third figure emphasizes the complete destruction of Jerusalem. As one wipes a dish clean by turning it over so that no drop is left, so Jerusalem's destruction will be total. None will remain.

14–15 The sins of God's people will bring about their inevitable destruction (cf. Dt 28:49–68; Isa 42:22; Jer 30:16; Hab 1:5–11; Zep 3:1–7). The Lord's condemnation and sentence culminate with the observation of his people's long-checkered history of spiritual disobedience, which spelled their doom.

16 The charges (vv.2–9) and judgment (vv.10–15) concerning Manasseh and Judah are framed by a final summation, which carries an additional charge of murder. Jewish legend accuses Manasseh of the murder of the prophets, one of whom was Isaiah (see Josephus, *Ant.* 10.37 [3.1]; J. H. Charlesworth, ed., *The Old Testament Pseudepigrapha* [Garden City, N.Y.: Doubleday, 1985], 2:385; cf. Heb 11:37).

17–18 The writer of Kings brings Manasseh's history to a close by indicating further source material for the details of his infamous life and noting that at his death he was buried in his private garden, called "the garden of Uzza." The picture thus presented by our author is bleak; it portrays the dominant themes of the vast majority of Manasseh's long reign. This critical evaluation is a proper one. Manasseh's personal example and leadership in sin were to have a permanent effect by bringing on Judah's demise despite the temporary reforms of Josiah.

The Chronicler records that the Lord humbled Manasseh by allowing him to fall into the hands of the king of Assyria, an event that brought about Manasseh's repentance and a short period of religious reformation (2Ch 33:11–17). Although the time of Manasseh's capture, release, and repentance is nowhere indicated, the fact that Kings presents such a uniform description of Manasseh's bad character tends to suggest that this experience must have occurred late in his reign. The widespread revolts during the reign of Ashurbanipal, which occurred from 652–648 BC, may provide the occasion for Manasseh's summons to Babylon and imprisonment. If so, his subsequent release and reform were apparently far too late to have much of an effect on the obdurately backslidden populace.

NOTES

1 The era of the reigns of Manasseh and Amon (698/97–640 BC) was to be eventful. When Sennacherib died, he left an Assyrian kingdom that comprised nearly all the ancient Fertile Crescent, exclusive of Egypt. It was a strong kingdom, one ruled through a well established bureaucracy that had inherited and built on the time-honored techniques of Mesopotamian administrative procedure.

Accordingly, though the annals of Esarhaddon (681–668 BC) and Ashurbanipal (668–626) record numerous campaigns that advanced Assyrian territory from Persia and Arabia on the east and south to Egypt as far up the Nile as Thebes on the southwest, still, the times were largely peaceful and prosperous. They are often designated the *Pax Assyriaca*. Thus Esarhaddon and Ashurbanipal were largely able to enjoy the fruits of the earlier Sargonid kings' labor and could turn their attention to great building projects, religious pursuits, and the cultivation of the Assyrian *beaux arts* and *belles lettres*. Layard's discovery of the library of Ashurbanipal at Nineveh calls attention to the Assyrian king's concern to cultivate the Mesopotamian literary tradition.

3 Manasseh's renewed introduction of astral worship ran counter to scriptural injunctions (Dt 4:19; 17:2–7). Such practices had already been condemned by the eighth-century prophets (e.g., Isa 47:13; Am 5:26). The effects of Manasseh's evil were to continue beyond his days, as the denunciations of the seventh-century prophets testify (e.g., Jer 8:2; 19:13; Zep 1:5).

7–8 For the Asherah pole see comments on 1 Kings 14:15. God's promises in the Mosaic covenant were conditioned on human compliance (Dt 28). Likewise, although the provisions in the Davidic covenant were unconditional, individuals could act so as to forfeit its benefits for themselves (Ps 89:3–4, 20–37).

11 For details concerning the wide-ranging movements of the Amorites, see A. H. Sayce and J. A. Soggin, "Amorites," *ISBE*, 1:13–14. For a preliminary study of the northwest Semitic language known as Amorite, see I. Gelb, "La Lingua degli Amoriti," *Acadamia Nazionale dei Lincei* 8/13, fasicles 3–4 (1958): 173–264.

17–18 Additional source material for information on Manasseh is included in 2 Chronicles 33:18–19. Some scholars suggest that Manasseh's captivity occurred during the reign of Esarhaddon (681–668 BC), who mentioned the summoning of Manasseh along with other rulers to Nineveh (see *ANET*, 291). It is true that Esarhaddon had many vassals (for details see D. J. Wiseman, "The Vassal Treaties of Esarhaddon," *Iraq* 20 [1958]: 1–99). Yet although Esarhaddon did often summon his vassals to himself, his time seems much too early to be harmonized with the scriptural record.

Moreover, the Bible indicates that Manasseh was called to Babylon, not Nineveh. Babylon became virtually a second capital of the realm in Ashurbanipal's day. Ashurbanipal also mentioned Manasseh among the kings who accompanied him on his first Egyptian campaign in 668 BC (see *ANET*, 294), but here (as in the case of Esarhaddon's inscription) Manasseh did not seem to be in the king's disfavor.

In favor of a later date (ca. 650–648 BC) is the fact that the revolts of that time involved sizeable opposition in the west, including such time-honored Judahite allies as Phoenicia and Egypt. The whole affair revolved around Ashurbanipal's seditious brother Shamash-shum-ukin and the city of Babylon. Since Ashurbanipal himself then occupied the throne of Babylon for a year (648–647), it would afford a logical time for Manasseh's summons to Babylon in order to determine his degree of participation in the revolt. Manasseh's eventual acquittal and return to Judah would allow little time for his newly found faith to have a permanent effect.

The otherwise unknown garden of Uzza must have been in the palace grounds, for the Chronicler (2Ch 33:20) reports that Manasseh was buried "in his palace."

C. The Reign of Amon (21:19–26)

[19]Amon was twenty-two years old when he became king, and he reigned in Jerusalem
two years. His mother's name was Meshullemeth daughter of Haruz; she was from Jotbah.
[20]He did evil in the eyes of the LORD, as his father Manasseh had done. [21]He walked in all the
ways of his father; he worshiped the idols his father had worshiped, and bowed down to
them. [22]He forsook the LORD, the God of his fathers, and did not walk in the way of the LORD.

[23]Amon's officials conspired against him and assassinated the king in his palace. [24]Then
the people of the land killed all who had plotted against King Amon, and they made
Josiah his son king in his place.

[25]As for the other events of Amon's reign, and what he did, are they not written in the
book of the annals of the kings of Judah? [26]He was buried in his grave in the garden of
Uzza. And Josiah his son succeeded him as king.

COMMENTARY

19–22 The short reign of Amon was a replay of the earlier period of his father, Manasseh. The author of Kings notes simply that he was as evil as his father and so perpetuated every aspect of Manasseh's earlier idolatry (vv.20–21). The Chronicler (2Ch 33:21–23) adds that Amon failed to humble himself; rather, he "increased his guilt."

23–26 In 640 BC, wicked Amon was assassinated by his own officials, who in turn were executed by the populace (vv.23–24). Just as the people of the land put an end to wicked Athaliah and installed young Joash as king (11:18–21), so Amon's son Josiah was established as the next king (v.26).

Although the Scriptures give no reason for the conspiracy, its cause may lie within the tangled web of revolts that Ashurbanipal suppressed from 642–639 BC and that caused him to turn his attention to the west. Certainly his menacing advance took him as far as Phoenicia. At this time, too, he may have resettled newly deported elements in Samaria (cf. Ezr 4:9–10). Amon's death may thus reflect a power struggle between those who wished to remain loyal to the Assyrian crown and those who aspired to link Judah's fortunes to the rising star of Psammetik I (664–609) of Egypt's Twenty-Sixth Dynasty.

NOTES

23 For background details and suggestions as to the reasons for Amon's assassination, see A. Malamat, "The Historical Background of the Assassination of Amon," *IEJ* 3 (1953): 82–102; and "The Twilight of Judah in the Egyptian-Babylonian Maelstrom," *Congress Volume: Edinburgh, 1974* (VTSup 28; Leiden: Brill, 1975), 123–45.

D. The Reign of Josiah (22:1–23:30)

OVERVIEW

Between the customary accession statement plus spiritual evaluation (22:1–2) and the closing notice (23:28–30) the narrator focuses on those details of Josiah's reign that illustrate the king's unwavering dedication to the Lord. Beginning with Josiah's eighteenth regnal year, he tells of the king's order for the repair of the temple (vv.3–7). When in the course of the work "the Book of the Law" is found, its contents are duly reported to the king (vv.8–10). Upon hearing the words of the scroll, Josiah is immediately concerned to learn from the Lord the implications for God's people of what he has heard (vv.11–13). Accordingly, a delegation of high-ranking religious and civil officials go to the prophetess Huldah, who warns them that the Lord's judgment will soon fall on the southern kingdom, although not until after the king's death (vv.14–20).

The Lord's warning through Huldah leads Josiah to put into effect a number of religious reforms. Three areas of action are detailed: (1) covenantal renewal (23:1–3), (2) cultic cleansing (vv.4–20), and (3) the celebration of the Passover (vv.21–23). Thus Josiah begins with convening the people and publicly reading the scroll. Afterwards the king leads the people in a ceremony of covenantal renewal in which all present pledge their allegiance to the Lord and the precepts and obligations they have heard (23:1–3).

Next the king launches a vigorous campaign of reforms aimed at purging any semblance of false worship. The reforms are thoroughgoing. Beginning with the places of worship in Judah and Jerusalem, he removes the pagan priests and destroys their images and equipment (vv.4–7). Having removed the priests who served at the various high places in Judah, he desecrates the shrines and the pagan symbols and sites throughout the southern kingdom (vv.8–14).

Not content with reforms in the southern kingdom, Josiah orders the destruction of the altar at Bethel—and even goes so far as to exhume the bones of the dead and burn them on the altar. Thus the place would be defiled forever. Only the remains of the man of God who denounced the altar when Jeroboam dedicated it are spared. The purging of paganism accomplished at Bethel is then followed by similar actions throughout the northern kingdom (vv.15–20).

Afterward, at the proper time the king orders the celebration of the Passover in Jerusalem. It is observed in accordance with strict adherence to the covenant unparalleled since ancient times (vv.21–23).

The narrator then approaches final matters concerning Josiah's reign. He notes that although the king conducted a thorough cleansing of paganism throughout Judah and Jerusalem, it was too late to turn aside the Lord's final judgment (vv.24–27). Noting the death of Josiah as he opposed Pharaoh Neco at Megiddo (vv.28–30) augments the customary closing notice.

Thematic unity in these fifty verses is accomplished by emphasizing Josiah's total dedication to the Lord and the standards of his Word (22:2, 19–20; 23:1–3, 21–25). Likewise, the threat of the Lord's inevitable judgment (22:13–20; 23:26–27) lurks in the background despite Josiah's strong efforts at reform. This theme in turn prepares the reader for the narrating of events that follow swiftly in the remainder of the book.

1. Josiah's Accession and Repair of the Temple (22:1–7)

[1]Josiah was eight years old when he became king, and he reigned in Jerusalem thirty-
one years. His mother's name was Jedidah daughter of Adaiah; she was from Bozkath. [2]He
did what was right in the eyes of the LORD and walked in all the ways of his father David,
not turning aside to the right or to the left.

[3]In the eighteenth year of his reign, King Josiah sent the secretary, Shaphan son of
Azaliah, the son of Meshullam, to the temple of the LORD. He said: [4]"Go up to Hilkiah the
high priest and have him get ready the money that has been brought into the temple of
the LORD, which the doorkeepers have collected from the people. [5]Have them entrust it
to the men appointed to supervise the work on the temple. And have these men pay the
workers who repair the temple of the LORD—[6]the carpenters, the builders and the masons.
Also have them purchase timber and dressed stone to repair the temple. [7]But they need
not account for the money entrusted to them, because they are acting faithfully."

COMMENTARY

1–2 Like Joash before him, Josiah is a mere lad when he assumes the throne (cf. 11:21). Josiah is noted for his piety, his devotion to the Lord, and a commitment to the law of Moses (cf. 23:25). The description of Josiah as "not turning aside to the right or to the left" from the standards of God for human beings is apparently drawn from Deuteronomy 17:11, 20; 28:14. The right hand/left hand motif, which frequently expresses completeness or full participation on the part of the persons involved (cf. Eze 39:3; Da 12:7; Jnh 4:11; 2Co 6:7), here stresses Josiah's singlehearted devotion to God's approved course of conduct for his life.

3–7 Although the narrator begins his account of Josiah's pious actions in the king's eighteenth regnal year, the Chronicler calls attention to Josiah's earlier activities (2Ch 34:3–7). He reports that already in Josiah's eighth year of reign the young king "began to seek the God of his father David." This course was followed by an initial purging of idolatrous practices in Judah and Jerusalem four years later. From the details supplied by the Chronicler it would seem that the reforms instituted by Josiah began already in the twelfth year of his reign.

However, the many similarities that exist between the Chronicler's account and those of the narrator of Kings appear at first glance to present a contradiction in details. Several theories have been advanced to account for the relation of the material in Kings and Chronicles. M. Selman (*2 Chronicles* [TOTC; Downers Grove, Ill.: InterVarsity Press, 1994], 529–30) may be correct in observing that "it would not be surprising if some events in the reformation were repeated, since no previous attempt to eradicate Canaanite religion ever proved entirely successful."

Josiah's choice of Shaphan to head the royal commission was a wise one; for his godly influence was to be felt not only in his own time but also in that of his sons Ahikam (Jer 26:24), Elasah (Jer 29:3), and Gemariah (Jer 36:10, 25), and his grandson Gedaliah (2Ki 25:22; Jer 39:14; 40:7). The steps taken by Josiah appear to follow those undertaken by Joash previously (12:4–16). They probably included placing a chest at the entrance of the temple for receiving the people's freewill offerings. According to 2 Chronicles 34:9, this money was contributed even by believing Israelites who resided in the northern kingdom.

NOTES

3 For suggestions as to the reasons for the Chronicler's chronology of events in Josiah's reign, see H. G. M. Williamson, *1 and 2 Chronicles* (NCBC; Grand Rapids: Eerdmans, 1982), 396–98. J. M. Myers (*II Chronicles* [AB; Garden City, N.Y.: Doubleday, 1965], 205) perceptively adds, "If the preaching of Zephaniah is connected with events between 630–25 BC, Josiah's early piety ... is quite credible." Decaying conditions in Assyria in the last years before Ashurbanipal's death in 626 BC may have allowed Josiah's reform policies to spill into the north.

4 Second Chronicles 34:8 mentions two other men who made up the king's commission: Maaseiah and Joah, son of Joahaz, the royal herald. It was an important task; accordingly, Josiah sent trusted officials to see to it.

2. Josiah and the Book of the Law (22:8–20)

8Hilkiah the high priest said to Shaphan the secretary, "I have found the Book of the Law in the temple of the LORD." He gave it to Shaphan, who read it. 9Then Shaphan the secretary went to the king and reported to him: "Your officials have paid out the money that was in the temple of the LORD and have entrusted it to the workers and supervisors at

the temple." [10]Then Shaphan the secretary informed the king, "Hilkiah the priest has given
me a book." And Shaphan read from it in the presence of the king.
[11]When the king heard the words of the Book of the Law, he tore his robes. [12]He gave
these orders to Hilkiah the priest, Ahikam son of Shaphan, Acbor son of Micaiah, Shaphan
the secretary and Asaiah the king's attendant: [13]"Go and inquire of the Lord for me and for
the people and for all Judah about what is written in this book that has been found. Great
is the Lord's anger that burns against us because our fathers have not obeyed the words of
this book; they have not acted in accordance with all that is written there concerning us."
[14]Hilkiah the priest, Ahikam, Acbor, Shaphan and Asaiah went to speak to the prophetess Huldah, who was the wife of Shallum son of Tikvah, the son of Harhas, keeper of the
wardrobe. She lived in Jerusalem, in the Second District.
[15]She said to them, "This is what the Lord, the God of Israel, says: Tell the man who sent
you to me, [16]'This is what the Lord says: I am going to bring disaster on this place and its
people, according to everything written in the book the king of Judah has read. [17]Because
they have forsaken me and burned incense to other gods and provoked me to anger by
all the idols their hands have made, my anger will burn against this place and will not be
quenched.' [18]Tell the king of Judah, who sent you to inquire of the Lord, 'This is what the
Lord, the God of Israel, says concerning the words you heard: [19]Because your heart was
responsive and you humbled yourself before the Lord when you heard what I have spoken against this place and its people, that they would become accursed and laid waste,
and because you tore your robes and wept in my presence, I have heard you, declares the
Lord. [20]Therefore I will gather you to your fathers, and you will be buried in peace. Your
eyes will not see all the disaster I am going to bring on this place.'"
So they took her answer back to the king.

COMMENTARY

8–10 Scholars have often argued as to the contents of the scroll (see Notes). The king's later reaction when he heard the Law read (vv.11–13) and the subsequent further reforms (23:4–20) and religious observances (2Ch 35:1–19) indicate that it included at least key portions, if not the whole, of Deuteronomy (e.g., Dt 28–30).

The importance of the scroll is underscored in the sentence order of the MT (lit.): "A scroll of the Torah (Law) I have found in the house of the Lord." The urgency of the situation is expressed by the haste with which the narrator reports the giving of the scroll to Shaphan and its speedy delivery to the king. Here again the narrator emphasizes the scroll by saying, "Hilkiah the priest has given me a [scroll]" (v.10).

11–13 The king's reaction at the reading of the newly found scroll stands in stark contrast with that of his son Jehoiakim at the reading of Jeremiah's scroll (Jer 36:24). Josiah's ordering of an official inquiry to the Lord indicates his strong reaction to that portion of the scroll that was read to him. Josiah's asking for God's understanding in what appeared to be a crisis situation may be compared with that of Hezekiah (20:2–3) and contrasted with that of King Ahaziah, who sought a pagan deity (1:2).

12–13 Joining Shaphan and his son Ahikam on the commission were Asaiah and Achbor. Achbor (called Abdon in 2Ch 34:20) was the father of Elnathan, one of Jehoiachin's advisers (Jer 26:22; 36:25). According to 2 Chronicles 34:21, Josiah's concern was for Israel as well as for Judah.

14 Huldah the prophetess is otherwise unknown in the OT. The fact that Zephaniah was not consulted may indicate that his prophetic ministry had ceased by this time. Although Jeremiah had certainly begun prophesying (cf. Jer 1:1), it may be that his early ministry (Jer 1–6) had been completed and, having contributed to Josiah's early spiritual concern he was presently at Anathoth. It has been suggested that Huldah's husband, Shallum (son of Tokhath, son of Hasrah [2Ch 34:22]), may have been related to Jeremiah (Jer 32:7–12), but this relation is not certain.

The second district (or quarter; Zep 1:10) was so named because it formed the first addition to the old city. Its location is probably to be sought west of the temple complex in the upper Tyropoeon Valley, in the commercial quarter (Gray, 159). Such a location might indicate the humble circumstances of the faithful prophetess and her husband.

15–20 Huldah's word to the delegation contains two messages. As the scroll indicates, Jerusalem is doomed as a result of its idolatry (vv.15–17). The king, however, will not live to see the city's demise (vv.18–20). In this latter message Josiah's future is like that of Hezekiah before him (20:16–19).

At first sight this promise seems to be at variance with the fact that Josiah died in battle (23:29–30). However, though the words in v.20 might be understood as indicating a peaceful death, such an interpretation need not be required. The phrase "be gathered to one's fathers" simply points to the fact that men die and are buried, not to the manner of their death (cf. Ge 25:8, 17; 35:29; 49:29, 33; Nu 20:24–29; 27:13; 31:2; Dt 32:50, Jdg 2:10; Job 27:19; Jer 8:2; 25:33).

NOTES

8 The precise contents of the scroll have long been debated. Among those scholars who argue for the entire book of Deuteronomy, some suggest that it was written in Josiah's time to justify his reforms. Others view it as a product of priests who fled the northern kingdom and subsequently placed it in the temple. Still others contend that it was written down in earlier times but was lost or misplaced for some time before the reign of Josiah. Yet others suggest that the newly found scroll was a testimonium of covenantal material. Keil, 478, opts for the whole Pentateuch deposited by the side of the ark of the covenant.

For details, see Unity, Authorship, and Date in the Introduction. See also my comments in "The Divided Monarchy," in *Giving the Sense: Understanding and Using Old Testament Historical Texts*, ed. David M. Howard, Jr. and Michael A. Grisanti (Grand Rapids: Kregel, 2003), 183–86, and the standard OT introductions and commentaries on Kings and Deuteronomy. For a critical treatment postulating a seventh-century BC date for Deuteronomy but as a continuation of earlier (perhaps even Mosaic) material, see E. W. Nicholson, *Deuteronomy and Tradition* (Oxford: Blackwells, 1962), 1–17, 119–24.

9 The names of the trusted officials who supervised the repair project are recorded in 2 Chronicles 34:12.

20 P. S. F. Van Keulen ("The Meaning of the Phrase *wnʾspt ʾl qbrtyk bšlwm* in 2 Kings xxii 20," *VT* 46 [1996]: 256–60) suggests that although Josiah would be buried in peaceful conditions, his death would be a violent one. However, the phrase may simply reflect Josiah's state of well-being with God. The phrase is drawn from ancient diplomatic parlance, as shown by Wiseman, "'Is It Peace,'" 323–25.

"To be gathered to one's fathers" may also contain an underlying hint of an OT hope for life after death. That the reality of a conscious afterlife existed in OT times may be seen from Genesis 22:5; Job 14:14–15; 19:25–27; Psalm 16:9–11; 22:22–24; 49:14–15; 73:23–26; Isaiah 25:8; 26:19; Daniel 12:2–3; Hosea 13:14.

3. Josiah's Further Reforms (23:1–23)

1Then the king called together all the elders of Judah and Jerusalem. 2He went up to
the temple of the LORD with the men of Judah, the people of Jerusalem, the priests and
the prophets—all the people from the least to the greatest. He read in their hearing
all the words of the Book of the Covenant, which had been found in the temple of the
LORD. 3The king stood by the pillar and renewed the covenant in the presence of the
LORD—to follow the LORD and keep his commands, regulations and decrees with all his
heart and all his soul, thus confirming the words of the covenant written in this book.
Then all the people pledged themselves to the covenant.

4The king ordered Hilkiah the high priest, the priests next in rank and the doorkeepers to remove from the temple of the LORD all the articles made for Baal and Asherah and
all the starry hosts. He burned them outside Jerusalem in the fields of the Kidron Valley
and took the ashes to Bethel. 5He did away with the pagan priests appointed by the kings
of Judah to burn incense on the high places of the towns of Judah and on those around
Jerusalem—those who burned incense to Baal, to the sun and moon, to the constella-
tions and to all the starry hosts. 6He took the Asherah pole from the temple of the LORD
to the Kidron Valley outside Jerusalem and burned it there. He ground it to powder and
scattered the dust over the graves of the common people. 7He also tore down the quarters
of the male shrine prostitutes, which were in the temple of the LORD and where women
did weaving for Asherah.

8Josiah brought all the priests from the towns of Judah and desecrated the high places,
from Geba to Beersheba, where the priests had burned incense. He broke down the
shrines at the gates—at the entrance to the Gate of Joshua, the city governor, which is on
the left of the city gate. 9Although the priests of the high places did not serve at the altar
of the LORD in Jerusalem, they ate unleavened bread with their fellow priests.

10He desecrated Topheth, which was in the Valley of Ben Hinnom, so no one could use
it to sacrifice his son or daughter in the fire to Molech. 11He removed from the entrance to

the temple of the LORD the horses that the kings of Judah had dedicated to the sun. They were in the court near the room of an official named Nathan-Melech. Josiah then burned the chariots dedicated to the sun.

12He pulled down the altars the kings of Judah had erected on the roof near the upper room of Ahaz, and the altars Manasseh had built in the two courts of the temple of the LORD. He removed them from there, smashed them to pieces and threw the rubble into the Kidron Valley. 13The king also desecrated the high places that were east of Jerusalem on the south of the Hill of Corruption—the ones Solomon king of Israel had built for Ashtoreth the vile goddess of the Sidonians, for Chemosh the vile god of Moab, and for Molech the detestable god of the people of Ammon. 14Josiah smashed the sacred stones and cut down the Asherah poles and covered the sites with human bones.

15Even the altar at Bethel, the high place made by Jeroboam son of Nebat, who had caused Israel to sin—even that altar and high place he demolished. He burned the high place and ground it to powder, and burned the Asherah pole also. 16Then Josiah looked around, and when he saw the tombs that were there on the hillside, he had the bones removed from them and burned on the altar to defile it, in accordance with the word of the LORD proclaimed by the man of God who foretold these things.

17The king asked, "What is that tombstone I see?"

The men of the city said, "It marks the tomb of the man of God who came from Judah and pronounced against the altar of Bethel the very things you have done to it."

18"Leave it alone," he said. "Don't let anyone disturb his bones." So they spared his bones and those of the prophet who had come from Samaria.

19Just as he had done at Bethel, Josiah removed and defiled all the shrines at the high places that the kings of Israel had built in the towns of Samaria that had provoked the LORD to anger. 20Josiah slaughtered all the priests of those high places on the altars and burned human bones on them. Then he went back to Jerusalem.

21The king gave this order to all the people: "Celebrate the Passover to the LORD your God, as it is written in this Book of the Covenant." 22Not since the days of the judges who led Israel, nor throughout the days of the kings of Israel and the kings of Judah, had any such Passover been observed. 23But in the eighteenth year of King Josiah, this Passover was celebrated to the LORD in Jerusalem.

COMMENTARY

1–3 Josiah's godly concern manifests itself in his active role in leading his people in covenantal renewal. As Joshua before him (Jos 24:1–27), he delivered the Lord's words to the assembled throng. As the Israelites of that earlier day, the people "pledged themselves to the covenant." As Joash before him (2Ki 11:14), Josiah stood by "the pillar" (or on a raised platform).

4–7 Following the ceremony the pagan cultic articles were taken outside Jerusalem to the Kidron Valley and burned; subsequently, their ashes were taken to Bethel, where paganism first had its official sanction in Israel (v.4). In taking the detested pagan abominations to the Kidron (v.6), Josiah followed the lead of the earlier royal reformers Asa (1Ki 15:13) and Hezekiah (2Ch 29:16; 30:14).

The phrase "the fields of the Kidron Valley" is strikingly similar to Jeremiah 31:40, where in describing the extent of the restored Jerusalem the words "all the terraces out to the Kidron Valley" are met. Since Jeremiah's designation of the renewed city appears to circumscribe it—going from northeast to northwest, then down the west and across from southwest to southeast, then up the east side to the Horse Gate—the fields would appear to lie in the lower portion of the Kidron Valley. Jeremiah indicates that dead bodies were cast there and that ashes of various types were taken there. Probably the sweepings of the temple and the refuse of the city were carried there as well. Situated near the detested and loathsome place known as Tophet in the Valley of Hinnom (cf. v.10; Jer 7:31; 19:5–6), the whole area was one of defilement. It just may be that Kings and Jeremiah refer to the same area and yield an apt description of the isolated and defiled place to which Josiah consigned the detestable and defiling cultic objects.

The carrying of the ashes to Bethel constituted a public desecration of this place where pagan worship received state sponsorship (1Ki 12:28–29).

8–9 The precise understanding of "the shrines [or high places] at the gates" is uncertain. J. A. Emerton ("The 'High Places of the Gates' in 2 Kings xxiii 8," *VT* 44 [1994]: 455–57) points out that the available evidence suggests such shrines were located at Israelite and Canaanite city gates. The previous service of the Levitical priests at the various high places throughout Judah rendered them ineligible to officiate in the temple services (v.9); hence they were put on a status with those priests who had bodily defects (Lev 21:17–23).

10–12 The wickedness associated with the abominable Molech rites in the Valley of Ben Hinnom, as well as the utilization of the area as a dump for burning refuse, gave rise to the use of the name *gê ḥinnōm* ("Valley of Hinnom") for the place of final punishment, which in the Greek NT gets transliterated as *gehenna* (Mt 5:22, 29–30; 10:28; Jas 3:6; cf. Rev 19:20; 20:14–15).

The utilization of the horse in the solar cultus was widespread in the ancient Near East, being attested particularly in Assyrian and Aramean inscriptional and artifactual sources. Ezekiel reports that devotees of solar worship practiced their ritual within the inner court at the entrance to the temple, between the porch and the altar. Such worship probably came into Judah's religious experience with the abominations that Ahaz introduced (16:10–16) and were later restored by Manasseh (21:3). The narrator had previously reported Manasseh's placing of "altars to all the starry hosts" in the two courts of the temple (21:3–5).

13–14 The pagan altars near Jerusalem were built by Solomon and stemmed from his many politically motivated marriages to foreign women (1Ki 11:5, 7, 33). The covering of the desecrated sites of pagan worship with human bones would defile them forever (cf. Nu 19:16).

15–18 It appears that Josiah's authority extended at least into the southern portions of the former northern kingdom. The growing weakness of the Assyrian empire probably allowed Josiah to advance his control northward (cf. v.19).

Josiah's actions at Bethel fulfilled the words of the unknown prophet of earlier days (1Ki 13:2–3). The unknown prophet and the older prophet from Samaria were buried in the latter's family tomb at Bethel (1Ki 13:31).

19–20 Josiah's further acts of reform could be construed as a defiling of the altars near Bethel (i.e., in the southern portions of the northern kingdom). However, the Chronicler (2Ch 34:6) indicates that Josiah's actions reached much farther northward, thus constituting a thorough cleansing "throughout Israel" (34:7).

21–23 Once again the importance of the "Book of the Covenant" is emphasized (cf. vv.2–3). Unlike Hezekiah's Passover, which was observed in accordance with certain restricted conditions (2Ch 30:1–4, 13) and innovations (30:23–27), Josiah's celebration followed the strict requirements of the law. The importance of this Passover is stressed by the Chronicler, who devotes nineteen verses to describing it (2Ch 35). He notes participation by those present from "all Judah and Israel ... and the people of Jerusalem" (35:18). The ratification of the covenant (2Ki 23:1–3) thus reaches a climactic and positive note. Like the first Passover participants (Ex 12:24–28), the believers of Josiah's day affirmed their loyalty to the Lord.

NOTES

2 By the term "the Book of the Covenant" may be intended that Josiah had those portions of the law read that dealt with Israel's basic covenant with God (e.g., Lev 26; Dt 28; see Note on 1Ki 8:31).

4–6 For a comparison of Josiah's godly leadership with that of Moses, see C. A. Klein, "Moses and Josiah, A Rabbi's Experience with His Congregation," *Dor le Dor* (1986/87): 199–201.

Jeremiah 26:23 confirms that in the Kidron Valley was a burial ground for the common people. The scattering of the ashes of the objects of heathen idolatry may indicate that the burials there were likewise idolatrous.

7 Although הַקְּדֵשִׁים (*haqqᵉdēšîm*) denotes "the male shrine prostitutes," probably the term is used generically for prostitutes of both sexes who were employed in the heinous Canaanite fertility rites (cf. Dt 23:17–18).

8 Y. Yadin's suggestion ("Beersheba: The High Place Destroyed by King Josiah," *BASOR* 222 [1976]: 5–17) that the high places in question were at Beersheba rather than Jerusalem is unlikely. So also is Gray's proposal (230) to read "shrines of the gate genii" or "gatekeepers."

10 For Topheth and Molech, see Note on 16:3.

11 Recent excavations at Jerusalem have uncovered a sacred shrine that included images of horses. פַּרְוָר (*parwār*, "court") is a *hapax legomenon*, unless it is to be equated with פַּרְבָּר (*parbār*, lit., "pavilion"; 1Ch 26:18). Unfortunately the exact meaning of this latter word is also uncertain. The NIV's "court" reflects a meaning well known in late Hebrew. The sense of the passage here seems to demand a roofed area over the courtyard that was used for stabling the horses and chariots employed in the solar cultus.

12 The "upper room" was probably located in one of those buildings near the gate (cf. Jer 35:4). The OT attests to the use of the roof for astral worship (Jer 19:13; Zep 1:5) and also for Baal worship (Jer 32:29). The latter case finds a parallel in the legend of King KRT (*ANET*, 143–44).

16 The REB follows the longer LXX text in adding a statement proclaiming Josiah's action as "fulfilling the word of the Lord announced by the man of God when Jeroboam stood by the altar at the feast."

4. Josiah's Latter Days (23:24–30)

[24]Furthermore, Josiah got rid of the mediums and spiritists, the household gods, the
idols and all the other detestable things seen in Judah and Jerusalem. This he did to fulfill
the requirements of the law written in the book that Hilkiah the priest had discovered
in the temple of the LORD. [25]Neither before nor after Josiah was there a king like him who
turned to the LORD as he did—with all his heart and with all his soul and with all his
strength, in accordance with all the Law of Moses.

[26]Nevertheless, the LORD did not turn away from the heat of his fierce anger, which
burned against Judah because of all that Manasseh had done to provoke him to anger.
[27]So the LORD said, "I will remove Judah also from my presence as I removed Israel, and I
will reject Jerusalem, the city I chose, and this temple, about which I said, 'There shall my
Name be.'"

[28]As for the other events of Josiah's reign, and all he did, are they not written in the
book of the annals of the kings of Judah?

[29]While Josiah was king, Pharaoh Neco king of Egypt went up to the Euphrates River
to help the king of Assyria. King Josiah marched out to meet him in battle, but Neco
faced him and killed him at Megiddo. [30]Josiah's servants brought his body in a chariot
from Megiddo to Jerusalem and buried him in his own tomb. And the people of the
land took Jehoahaz son of Josiah and anointed him and made him king in place of his
father.

COMMENTARY

24–25 As Josiah had meticulously fulfilled the requirements of the law relative to Israel's ceremonial worship with his many reforms, his repair of the temple, and his reinstitution of the Passover, so he put away the evils of false personal religion. This included both people who dealt in spiritism and all sorts of objects of detestable idolatry. In summary, it could be said of Josiah that none of the kings of Israel and Judah was his equal in zeal for the law (v.25). As Moses was unequaled among the early prophets (Dt 34:10–12), as David was noted for his heart devotion to God (1Ki 9:4), and as Hezekiah was noted for his faith (18:5), so Josiah knew no rival in uncompromising adherence to the law of Moses. The statement in v.25 forms an inclusio with 22:2, thus framing the entire picture of Josiah's righteous life.

26–27 The account of Josiah's godly life ends on a note of sadness. Despite all that he had done to remove Judah's idolatry, the effects of Manasseh's gross spiritual wickedness had had a permanent effect (v.26). Although Judah's outward worship experience was set in order, the people's confession had been a mere externality. With the passing of

Josiah, the internal condition of their obdurately apostate heart quickly surfaced (cf. Jer 5). Accordingly, God's just wrath would yet reach his sinful people. If the prophets and righteous Josiah had not been able to turn the people from their wicked ways, only God's judgment could have the desired effect.

28–30 Although the closing notices concerning Josiah's life are brief, they hint at the nature of the complex international events of the last quarter of the seventh century BC. With the death of Ashurbanipal in 626 BC, the already decaying Neo-Assyrian Empire began to crumble quickly away. By 625 the Chaldean king Nabopolassar was able to achieve independence for Babylon. From that point on throughout the course of the next two decades, the Assyrian territory was systematically reduced, especially as Nabopolassar found common cause against Assyria, first with the Medes (616) and later with the Ummanmanda (possibly a designation for the Scythians). In 614 the time-honored capital of Assyria, Asshur, fell to the Medes. In 612 Nineveh itself fell to the coalition of Chaldeans, Medes, and Ummanmanda, with the surviving Assyrian forces under Ashur-uballit fleeing to Haran.

In those critical times concerned with the rising power of the new Mesopotamian coalition, Egypt's Pharaoh Neco, of the Twenty-Sixth Dynasty, honored the previous diplomatic ties with Assyria. As Neco's predecessor, Psammetik I, had come to the aid of Assyria in 616 BC, so Neco moved to join the surviving Assyrian forces under Ashur-uballit. It was to prevent this movement of Egyptian aid that Josiah deployed his forces in the Valley of Megiddo in 609. That action cost Josiah his life, though it did delay the Egyptian forces from linking with their Assyrian allies before Haran fell to the Chaldeans and Medes. A subsequent attempt to retake Haran failed completely. The best Egypt could give the doomed Assyrians was a four-year standoff, with the opposing armies facing each other at Carchemish on the western Euphrates.

The Chronicler (2Ch 35:20–25) reports that Josiah had refused Neco's attempts to avoid the affair at Megiddo and rather, having disguised himself, had personally fought against the Egyptians until he was mortally wounded. At that point Josiah was rushed back to Jerusalem, where he was buried in his own tomb. Quite understandably all the people, including the prophet Jeremiah, lamented him. Thus passed one of God's choicest saints and one of Judah's finest kings. Josiah's determined action had brought about his tragic death, but he was thereby spared the greater tragedy of seeing the ultimate death of his nation a scant twenty-three years later.

NOTES

29–30 For further details as to political developments in the last quarter of the seventh century BC, see Wiseman, *Chronicles of Chaldaean Kings*, 5–31; A. Parrot, *Babylon* (New York: Philosophical Library, 1956), 80–88; idem, *Nineveh and the Old Testament* (New York: Philosophical Library, 1955), 76–87; and CAH, 3:126–31, 206–12. A seal bearing the name of Pharaoh Psammetik I has been found in the excavations of Jerusalem; see G. Garner, "Diggings," *Buried History* 16 (1980): 9.

E. The Last Days of Judah (23:31–25:21)

OVERVIEW

The account of the last four kings of Judah builds on the warning that despite the efforts of Josiah to purge the land of paganism, Judah was doomed (23:25–27). Josiah's own death at the hands of a foreign power virtually served as a harbinger of that of his nation (23:29–30). The narrator moves swiftly through the sad story of the events of the next twenty-three years in straightforward narrative fashion.

Nevertheless, the structure of his account displays a careful blending of historical fact with literary artistry. Thus the reigns of Jehoahaz (three months) and Jehoiakim (eleven years; 23:31–24:7) are set in loose parallel with those of Jehoiachin (three months) and Zedekiah (eleven years; 24:8–25:21). Similarities can be pointed out in comparing the two sections. Both Jehoahaz and Jehoiachin were taken captive after three months of reign and eventually died in exile. Both Jehoiakim and Zedekiah led rebellions against their former overlords. Despite their youth at their accession, all four kings are condemned for their wickedness. All four were embroiled in a series of foreign invasions culminating in the final demise of Judah, which the narrator had foreshadowed earlier (17:18–20).

Also to be noted are the levying of tribute against Jerusalem, the looting of the city (23:33, 35; 24:13; 25:13–17), and the exiling of its citizenry (24:14–16; 25:11, 21). While the inclusion of much of this information may be attributed to the details of history, "still the correspondence of a number of significant details suggests purposeful arrangement by the writer" (Cohn, 164).

1. The Reigns of Jehoahaz and Jehoiakim (23:31–24:7)

31 Jehoahaz was twenty-three years old when he became king, and he reigned in
Jerusalem three months. His mother's name was Hamutal daughter of Jeremiah; she was
from Libnah. 32 He did evil in the eyes of the LORD, just as his fathers had done. 33 Pharaoh
Neco put him in chains at Riblah in the land of Hamath so that he might not reign in
Jerusalem, and he imposed on Judah a levy of a hundred talents of silver and a talent of
gold. 34 Pharaoh Neco made Eliakim son of Josiah king in place of his father Josiah and
changed Eliakim's name to Jehoiakim. But he took Jehoahaz and carried him off to Egypt,
and there he died. 35 Jehoiakim paid Pharaoh Neco the silver and gold he demanded. In
order to do so, he taxed the land and exacted the silver and gold from the people of the
land according to their assessments.

36 Jehoiakim was twenty-five years old when he became king, and he reigned in Jerusalem eleven years. His mother's name was Zebidah daughter of Pedaiah; she was from
Rumah. 37 And he did evil in the eyes of the LORD, just as his fathers had done.

24:1During Jehoiakim's reign, Nebuchadnezzar king of Babylon invaded the land, and
Jehoiakim became his vassal for three years. But then he changed his mind and rebelled
against Nebuchadnezzar. 2The LORD sent Babylonian, Aramean, Moabite and Ammonite
raiders against him. He sent them to destroy Judah, in accordance with the word of the
LORD proclaimed by his servants the prophets. 3Surely these things happened to Judah
according to the LORD's command, in order to remove them from his presence because of
the sins of Manasseh and all he had done, 4including the shedding of innocent blood. For
he had filled Jerusalem with innocent blood, and the LORD was not willing to forgive.
5As for the other events of Jehoiakim's reign, and all he did, are they not written in the
book of the annals of the kings of Judah? 6Jehoiakim rested with his fathers. And Jehoiachin his son succeeded him as king.
7The king of Egypt did not march out from his own country again, because the king of
Babylon had taken all his territory, from the Wadi of Egypt to the Euphrates River.

COMMENTARY

31 The selection of Jehoahaz by the people of the land (v.30b; cf. 14:21; 21:24) is beset with problems. According to 1 Chronicles 3:15, Johanan, not Jehoahaz (or Shallum), was Josiah's eldest son. Because nothing further is known of Johanan, we may justifiably surmise that he had died much earlier. Jehoiakim, the next eldest son, was passed over and the kingship conferred on Jehoahaz, who was two years younger (cf. 2Ki 23: 36).

Why Jehoahaz was selected instead of Jehoiakim is not certain. The reason may lie in his pro-Babylonian sentiments or in the fact that Jehoahaz was Josiah's son by Hamutal, whereas Jehoiakim's mother was Zebudah. Perhaps Hamutal enjoyed a favored status. Libnah's traditional dislike of Judah (cf. 8:22) may also have played a part in the selection of Jehoahaz. Indeed, Josiah's marriage to a girl from Libnah may have been politically motivated. Thus by selecting the son whose mother came from a district that was often hostile to the political center at Jerusalem, the people may have hoped that the new king would be more acceptable to the Egyptian crown than Jehoiakim, his older brother, whose mother came from Rumah (cf. v.36).

32–35 The people evidently misjudged the situation, however. For Pharaoh Neco soon found fault with Jehoahaz, deposed him, and carried him away in chains to Egypt. This time the Egyptian king chose the next king of Judah. Jehoiakim's raising of the tribute money levied on Judah is narrated ahead of the statements concerning his accession to the throne (v.36).

Neco (609–594 BC) was the second pharaoh of Egypt's Twenty-Sixth or Saite Dynasty (663–625), so named for the traditional home of its dynastic rulers in the Nile Delta. After the withdrawal of the Assyrians in 663, Psammetik I (663–609), the founder of the dynasty, was soon able to reunite the country. During those years when Ashurbanipal of Assyria became increasingly preoccupied with affairs closer to home, Psammetik was able to restore much of Egypt's fortunes.

Noted for a cultural renaissance that emphasized a conscious reproduction of Egypt's traditional intellectual and artistic achievements, the Saite Dynasty was nevertheless forward-looking in its political outlook. Indeed, it was to display an inner solidarity that would render it a force to be reckoned with by the competing powers of the late seventh and early sixth centuries BC. Its fall to the Persians in 525 would mark the passing of Egypt's last prestigious dynasty. Although Egypt would know moments of independence later in her Twenty-Eighth, Twenty-Ninth, and Thirtieth dynasties (434–341 BC), a native dynasty would never again know greatness in the ancient Near Eastern world.

36–37 Jehoiakim's rule was like that of the wicked kings who preceded Josiah (cf. 2Ch 36:5, 8). Jeremiah (Jer 22:17; 36:31) represents him as a monster who despoiled his own people (Jer 22:13–14); opposed the Lord's servants (Jer 26:20–23; 36:21–23); filled the land with violence, apostasy, and degradation (Jer 18:18–20; cf. 11:19); and led his people into open apostasy and degradation (Jer 8:4–12; 8:18–9:16; 10:1–9; 11:1–17; 12:10–12; 13:1–11; 17:21–23; 19:3–5; 23:1–2, 9–40; 25:1–7).

24:1 Jehoiakim and Judah were soon to change masters. After the final defeat of the combined Assyrian and Egyptian forces at Carchemish, Nebuchadnezzar overtook the remaining Egyptian forces at Hamath. Those Egyptian troops that managed to escape fled to Egypt (cf. Jer 46:2). Nebuchadnezzar boasted that he thus took "the whole land of Hatti" (i.e., Syro-Palestine); doubtless our text is therefore correct in reading that Judah and Jehoiakim became his vassal. This switch is further corroborated in Nebuchadnezzar's own chronicles, where, after reporting his succession to the kingship in 605 BC, he records for the following year the submission and tribute of "all the kings of Hatti."

The record in 2 Chronicles that lists Nebuchadnezzar's looting of articles from the temple in Jerusalem and his placing of Jehoiakim in bonds so as to take him to Babylon (2Ch 36:6–7; cf. Da 1:1–2) may harmonize with the present text in Kings. Whether or not Jehoiakim was actually taken to Babylon is uncertain. At any rate, Jehoiakim submitted to Nebuchadnezzar and served him for the next three years.

However, Jehoiakim apparently awaited an opportunity to throw off the Babylonian yoke. When in 601 BC Neco turned back Nebuchadnezzar's forces at the Egyptian border, Jehoiakim assumed his moment had arrived and so rebelled. Once again Judah would lean on the "broken reed" that was Egypt.

2–4 War had cost both the Chaldeans and the Egyptians dearly; therefore, Nebuchadnezzar was unable to mobilize the troops and equipment to deal with impudent Judah, now newly allied with his Egyptian adversary, Neco. Nebuchadnezzar spent the next few years rebuilding his armed might in anticipation of the time when he could deal with the insurgents. Meanwhile, he moved against the Arameans and Arabians, thus strengthening his hold on Judah's Egyptian flank (v.2). This strategy also positioned him to utilize the Transjordanian tribes to send raiding parties into Judah (Hobbs, 349). The narrator of Kings reports that that harassment found its ultimate origin in God's command to bring judgment on wicked Judah, which followed the trail of Manasseh's evil deeds. The prophets had repeatedly warned of impending judgment (vv.3–4; cf., e.g., Jer 15:1–9; Hab 1:2–6; Zep 1:4–13; 3:1–7), but their warning remained unheeded.

5–7 In 598 BC Nebuchadnezzar was ready. Gathering his huge force, he set out for Jerusalem and the impenitent Jehoiakim. Josephus (*Ant.* 10 [7.1]) claims that Nebuchadnezzar executed the Judahite king personally. It may be, however, that even as he set out for Judah, Jehoiakim lay dead, being succeeded by his son Jehoiachin (but see Note on 24:11). It is of interest to note that of the last four kings of Judah only Jehoiakim was said to "rest with his fathers." Yet Bright, 327, suggests that Jehoiakim was assassinated. Such an understanding may accord well with Jeremiah's prophecy that Jehoiakim would not have a proper burial (see Note on v.6); rather, his body would be thrown out and dragged "outside the gates of Jerusalem" (Jer 22:18–19; 36:30). The Chronicler takes no notice of his burial.

NOTES

31 That Shallum/Jehoahaz was Josiah's third son, not his fourth as in the order in 1 Chronicles 3:15, is certain, for Zedekiah, who is listed third, was only twenty-one years old when he became king in 597 BC (24:18). Zedekiah would thus be only ten years old in 609, the year of Jehoahaz's accession at twenty-three years of age. The names of Zedekiah and Jehoahaz occurred together probably because they were from the same mother, with Zedekiah's name being listed before Jehoahaz's in deference to his longer reign. Since Jehoiakim preceded Zedekiah as king, Jehoahaz's name was listed last.

33–35 For details as to the Saite Dynasty, see Kitchen, *Third Intermediate Period*, 399–408; J. H. Breasted, *History of Egypt* (New York: Bantam, 1964), 470–85. Riblah was situated on the Orontes River. Fortified by the Egyptians, it served as their staging area for operations against the Assyrians. Later Nebuchadnezzar would make Riblah his headquarters for his western campaigns (25:6, 20).

36 Since Jehoiakim was twenty-five at his accession, he was older than both Jehoahaz, who preceded him (v.31), and Zedekiah, who succeeded him eleven years later at the age of twenty-one.

24:1 For further details on Nebuchadnezzar's victory at Carchemish and the subsequent events, see Jeremiah 46:1–12; Wiseman, *Chronicles of Chaldaean Kings*, 23–29; Thiele, 163–66. Daniel and his three friends were among those deported to Babylon during this first movement of Nebuchadnezzar into Judah in 605/604 BC (Da 1:1).

2 The term כַּשְׂדִּים (*kaśdîm*, "Babylonians, Chaldeans") designates the inhabitants of a region in southern Babylonia. Beginning with Nabopolassar it is applied to the "Neo-Babylonian" kingdom. After Nebuchadnezzar's subsequent subjugation of the Near East, "Chaldea" and "Chaldean" soon replaced "Babylonia" and "Babylonian" as the names of the country and populace who ruled the ancient Near Eastern world from their splendorous capital at Babylon. After the fall of the Chaldean (or Neo-Babylonian) dynasty, the term "Chaldean" survived chiefly in the older, more specialized technical sense of "soothsayer."

6 The cause of Jehoiakim's death is not given (see Notes on 24:11). Perhaps those who wished to placate Nebuchadnezzar assassinated him. See R. Green, "The Fate of Jehoiakim," *AUSS* 20 (1982): 103–9. A violent end for Jehoiakim seems probable on the basis of Jeremiah 22:18–19; 36:30–31. Though the various texts of the MT do not support the idea of a proper burial for Jehoiakim, some manuscripts of the LXX report his burial "in the garden of Uzzah."

7 Traditionally the Wadi of Egypt has been identified with Wadi el Arish, though N. Naʾaman ("The Brook of Egypt and Assyrian Policy on the Border of Egypt," *TA* 6 [1979]: 68–90) has argued convincingly for Nahal Besar.

2. The Reigns of Jehoiachin and Zedekiah (24:8–25:21)

[8]Jehoiachin was eighteen years old when he became king, and he reigned in Jerusalem three months. His mother's name was Nehushta daughter of Elnathan; she was from Jerusalem. [9]He did evil in the eyes of the LORD, just as his father had done.

[10]At that time the officers of Nebuchadnezzar king of Babylon advanced on Jerusalem and laid siege to it, [11]and Nebuchadnezzar himself came up to the city while his officers were besieging it. [12]Jehoiachin king of Judah, his mother, his attendants, his nobles and his officials all surrendered to him.

In the eighth year of the reign of the king of Babylon, he took Jehoiachin prisoner. [13]As the LORD had declared, Nebuchadnezzar removed all the treasures from the temple of the LORD and from the royal palace, and took away all the gold articles that Solomon king of Israel had made for the temple of the LORD. [14]He carried into exile all Jerusalem: all the officers and fighting men, and all the craftsmen and artisans — a total of ten thousand. Only the poorest people of the land were left.

[15]Nebuchadnezzar took Jehoiachin captive to Babylon. He also took from Jerusalem to Babylon the king's mother, his wives, his officials and the leading men of the land. [16]The king of Babylon also deported to Babylon the entire force of seven thousand fighting men, strong and fit for war, and a thousand craftsmen and artisans. [17]He made Mattaniah, Jehoiachin's uncle, king in his place and changed his name to Zedekiah.

[18]Zedekiah was twenty-one years old when he became king, and he reigned in Jerusalem eleven years. His mother's name was Hamutal daughter of Jeremiah; she was from Libnah. [19]He did evil in the eyes of the LORD, just as Jehoiakim had done. [20]It was because of the LORD's anger that all this happened to Jerusalem and Judah, and in the end he thrust them from his presence.

Now Zedekiah rebelled against the king of Babylon.

[25:1]So in the ninth year of Zedekiah's reign, on the tenth day of the tenth month, Nebuchadnezzar king of Babylon marched against Jerusalem with his whole army. He encamped outside the city and built siege works all around it. [2]The city was kept under siege until the eleventh year of King Zedekiah. [3]By the ninth day of the fourth month the famine in the city had become so severe that there was no food for the people to eat. [4]Then the city wall was broken through, and the whole army fled at night through the gate between the two walls near the king's garden, though the Babylonians were surrounding the city. They fled toward the Arabah, [5]but the Babylonian army pursued the king and overtook him in the plains of Jericho. All his soldiers were separated from him and scattered, [6]and he was captured. He was taken to the king of Babylon at Riblah, where sentence was pronounced on him. [7]They killed the sons of Zedekiah before his

eyes. Then they put out his eyes, bound him with bronze shackles and took him to
Babylon.
[8]On the seventh day of the fifth month, in the nineteenth year of Nebuchadnezzar
king of Babylon, Nebuzaradan commander of the imperial guard, an official of the king of
Babylon, came to Jerusalem. [9]He set fire to the temple of the LORD, the royal palace and all
the houses of Jerusalem. Every important building he burned down. [10]The whole Babylonian army, under the commander of the imperial guard, broke down the walls around
Jerusalem. [11]Nebuzaradan the commander of the guard carried into exile the people who
remained in the city, along with the rest of the populace and those who had gone over to
the king of Babylon. [12]But the commander left behind some of the poorest people of the
land to work the vineyards and fields.
[13]The Babylonians broke up the bronze pillars, the movable stands and the bronze Sea
that were at the temple of the LORD and they carried the bronze to Babylon. [14]They also
took away the pots, shovels, wick trimmers, dishes and all the bronze articles used in the
temple service. [15]The commander of the imperial guard took away the censers and sprinkling bowls—all that were made of pure gold or silver.
[16]The bronze from the two pillars, the Sea and the movable stands, which Solomon
had made for the temple of the LORD, was more than could be weighed. [17]Each pillar was
twenty-seven feet high. The bronze capital on top of one pillar was four and a half feet
high and was decorated with a network and pomegranates of bronze all around. The
other pillar, with its network, was similar.
[18]The commander of the guard took as prisoners Seraiah the chief priest, Zephaniah the
priest next in rank and the three doorkeepers. [19]Of those still in the city, he took the officer
in charge of the fighting men and five royal advisers. He also took the secretary who was
chief officer in charge of conscripting the people of the land and sixty of his men who
were found in the city. [20]Nebuzaradan the commander took them all and brought them to
the king of Babylon at Riblah. [21]There at Riblah, in the land of Hamath, the king had them
executed.
So Judah went into captivity, away from her land.

COMMENTARY

8–9 The customary accession statement records Jehoiachin's age as eighteen. In 2 Chronicles 36:9 Jehoiachin's age is given as eight. Because Jehoiachin was married, it seems better to view that reading as a scribal slip, to follow the age recorded here in v.8, and to read in the ancient versions "eighteen." Even a few Hebrew manuscripts read "eighteen" in the Chronicles passage.

Since Jehoiachin's name (cf. "Yo-Yakin" [Eze 1:2]) is entered as "Jeconiah" in the genealogies

(1Ch 3:16–17), it was probably his original name. This conclusion harmonizes with the fact that Jeremiah, who at times used the personal names of the kings (e.g., Shallum, Jehoahaz [Jer 22:11]), usually rendered his name as "Jeconiah" (Jer 24:1; 27:20; 28:4; 29:2), while sometimes shortening it to "Coniah" (Jer 22:24, 28; 37:1). Jeconiah probably took the name "Jehoiachin" as his throne name, much as Shallum took the name "Jehoahaz," Eliakim was given the throne name "Jehoiakim," and Mattaniah was given the name "Zedekiah."

The narrator supplies no details to illustrate his negative spiritual evaluation of Jehoiachin, which does, however, harmonize with the picture presented by Jeremiah (Jer 22:28–30) and Ezekiel (Eze 17:16–21).

10–12 Hobbs, 351, remarks that "the quick surrender has been rightfully interpreted as reason for the Babylonians' remarkably lenient treatment of the king and his officials."

The seeming discrepancy between the date of Jehoiachin's imprisonment, given here as the eighth year of Nebuchadnezzar's reign and in Jeremiah 52:28 as his seventh year, is to be accounted for on the basis of the differing calendars used by the authors. The Jewish system is utilized here and the Babylonian in Jeremiah (see further Thiele, 167–72).

13 According to the Chronicler, Nebuchadnezzar had previously taken part of Jerusalem's smaller treasures (2Ch 36:7; cf. Da 1:2). This time his despoilment was a major one, with only a few smaller gold and silver items left behind (cf. 25:15), along with the larger brass vessels (cf. 25:13–17; Jer 27:18–22).

14–16 The statement as to the deportation of "all Jerusalem" begins with a general notice of the removal of the men in accordance with their military potential, followed by a further cataloging of Jerusalem's citizenry according to their social status: the king, the dowager, the king's wives, the royal officials, the active military, the craftsmen, and the artisans.

The craftsmen and artisans were important to both the economic and the military needs of the community. Their loss would have manifold ramifications for the city, for both its economy and its defense. Only those who lacked status or professional skill were left behind.

Jeremiah had prophesied the capture of Jehoiachin (Jer 22:24–27). According to Ezekiel 1:1; 3:21, the prophet Ezekiel was also taken into captivity at this time.

The difference between the figures given in vv.14 and 16, as well as those in Jeremiah 52:28, have been accounted for in various ways. (1) The 10,000 of v.14 may be a round figure including the 7,000 fighting men and 1,000 craftsmen and artisans of v.16, plus 3,023 others (Jer 52:28).

(2) The 10,000 (v.14) may be a round figure representing the total number of deportees, some of which came from Judah (v.16) and others from Jerusalem (Jer 52:28).

(3) Hobbs, 353–54, postulates that the 10,000 of v.14 constituted military personnel as well as craftsmen and artisans. Those mentioned in v.16 were made up of 7,000 from the royal household and staff, as well as military personnel, plus another group of 1,000 craftsmen and artisans. Hobbs suggests further that these latter groups were construction engineers especially skilled in erecting various siege works.

(4) F. B. Huey Jr. (*Jeremiah, Lamentations* [NAC; Nashville: Broadman, 1993], 438) argues that the total number of deportees was 18,000 (vv.14, 16), of which 3,023 (Jer 52:28) were men.

(5) T. Latesch (*Bible Commentary: Jeremiah* [St. Louis, Mo.: Concordia, 1952], 370), however, maintains that the group mentioned in Jeremiah 52:28 refers to those who were carried away at

Jehoiakim's death, while those mentioned in Kings were a different group, taken captive in Jehoiachin's reign.

17 Mattaniah (renamed Zedekiah) was the third son of Josiah. Nebuchadnezzar claims that he himself appointed Mattaniah as king (Wiseman, *Chronicles of Chaldaean Kings*, 72–73).

18–20 The narrator likens Zedekiah's evil character to that of Jehoiakim. Both kings foolishly rebelled against Nebuchadnezzar (24:1, 20), thus endangering their nation's existence. Like Jehoiakim, Zedekiah was condemned for being insensitive and unresponsive to God's warnings through Jeremiah (Jer 21:1–10; 34:1–3, 17–22; 37:1–2, 6–10; for Jehoiakim, see comment on 23:37). As it was under Jehoiakim's reign (24:2–4), so now Judah's settled apostasy would occasion God's judgment. This time it would constitute the *coup mortel.*

Zedekiah's rebellion appears to stem from a renewed confidence in Egypt that brought him into a strange alliance with former enemies as well as friends, including Edom, Moab, Ammon, Tyre, and Sidon (cf. Jer 27:1–11). The anti-Assyrian alliance may have arisen at a time when a new pharaoh acceded to the throne and Nebuchadnezzar faced rebellions at home.

In Egypt, after the death of Neco in 594 BC, his son Psammetik II reigned for six years and left behind many monuments that attest to the vitality of his short-lived rule. In 589/588 his son Apries succeeded him to the throne with grandiose schemes of glory. Soon after his accession he appears to have influenced Zedekiah to revolt against Babylon (cf. Eze 17:15–18).

Zedekiah's confidence was ill-placed, however, for not only was Apries's help insufficient, but neither did his strength or sagacity merit such trust. His own life was to be marked by a series of difficulties, ending in a coup d'état and death in battle during a vain attempt to regain his throne.

25:1–3 Helpful supplemental details to the narrator's report come from Jeremiah's record of events. By combining this information the following general picture emerges. Nebuchadnezzar set up his headquarters in Riblah. Located along the banks of the Orontes River in the Hamath district, Riblah lay on the main route along the western corridor of the Fertile Crescent. Because ample provisions could be found nearby, the site was, logistically speaking, ideally situated as a field headquarters for military expeditionary forces. Neco had used it thus (cf. 23:33), as had Nebuchadnezzar in his campaign against the Egyptians in 605/604 BC. Nebuchadnezzar then systematically reduced the towns of Judah in a campaign that culminated in the capture of Lachish and Azekah (Jer 34:7). Finally he placed Jerusalem under a total siege (Jer 39:1; 52:4; cf. Eze 24:2).

When Nebuchadnezzar's troops were forced to withdraw momentarily to deal with an Egyptian relief column led by Apries (Jer 37:5), the misguided Jerusalemites prematurely assumed that they had been delivered from the siege (Jer 37:6–10). Nonetheless, Jerusalem's beleaguered defenders were kept enclosed by the Chaldeans almost continuously until July of 586 BC (v.2). Finally, when strength and provisions were completely exhausted (v.3; cf. Jer 52:6; La 4:9–10; cf. Dt 28:53–55), the Neo-Babylonian troops breached the walls and poured into the city (v.4; cf. Jer 39:2–3). The prophesied tragedy had occurred (cf. Jer 19–20; 27–28; 37:8–10, 17; 38:17–23).

4–5 The two walls near the king's garden between which Zedekiah and his army slipped out of Jerusalem probably lay at the extreme southeastern corner of the city, which gave direct access to the Kidron Valley (cf. Ne 3:15). The NIV is probably correct in reading "toward the Arabah" (i.e., with the definite article). "The Arabah" commonly designated the great Jordan Rift Valley, which extends the entire length of the Holy Land from the Sea of Galilee to the Gulf of Aqabah. Zedekiah's apprehension in the plains that lay south of Jericho (v.5) confirms this identification. As prophesied, the flight failed (Jer 32:3–5; 34:1–3).

6–7 The details of Zedekiah's punishment harmonize with Ezekiel's prophecy (Eze 12:10–14). Zedekiah eventually died in captivity in Babylon (cf. Jer 34:4–5; 52:10–11).

8–12 About one month later, Nebuzaradan, the commander of Nebuchadnezzar's own imperial guard, arrived in Jerusalem to oversee its despoilation and destruction (v.8). The Babylonians first set fire to all Jerusalem's prominent buildings, including the temple and palace (cf. Jer 52:13). Then they demolished the city's walls (vv.9–10). Next followed the deportation of key individuals of the citizenry of Jerusalem and the populace of the surrounding countryside. Some of these people apparently willingly defected to the invaders (v.11; cf. Jer 39:9; 52:15). Only the poorest of the people were left; they were to work the nearby fields and vineyards so that a stratum of inhabitants unlikely to cause further insurrection might be left to care for the basic needs of the remaining people of the land (v.12; cf. Jer 39:10).

13–17 Particular notice is given to the temple furniture and furnishings that the Babylonians carried away as spoils of war. Primary focus is on those heavy bronze items that had to be broken into smaller pieces to be removed: the pillars, the movable stands, and the Sea (v.13). The bronze gained from those items—together with the bronze bulls under the brazen Sea (cf. Jer 52:20)—was incalculable (v.16). A comparison of this account with the fuller inventory in Jeremiah 52:17–23 reveals a thorough looting of all the gold, silver, and bronze temple utensils.

18–21 The disposition of the chief religious, military, and governmental officials as well as sixty of the notable men is given next. Among these men were the high priest Seraiah, the next-ranking priest Zephaniah, the commander-in-chief of Jerusalem's fighting men, and the secretary for the mobilization of Judah's citizenry (vv.18–19). All these prominent officials and people were taken to Riblah and executed (vv.20–21). Nebuchadnezzar would brook no further interference with the established order that Nebuzaradan had left behind. With the officialdom and leadership either put to death or taken captive into exile, it could be expected that the remaining populace would passively submit to their Babylonian overlords.

NOTES

8 For light on Jehoiachin's age when he came to the throne, see Archer, 214–15.

11 Josephus (*Ant.* 10:99–102 [7.1]) gives an interesting account of Nebuchadnezzar's movements in 597 BC. Josephus claims that Nebuchadnezzar personally had Jehoiakim executed, while placing Jehoiachin on the throne. Having left Jerusalem, it occurred to him that Jehoiachin might be a source of trouble to him because he had killed the young king's father. Accordingly, he sent his army back to Jerusalem to take Jehoiachin and the elite of Jerusalem captive and installed Zedekiah on the throne.

Although Josephus's theory has the advantage of being easily reconciled with 2 Chronicles 36:6, 10, it squares neither with the facts of Nebuchadnezzar's chronicles nor with the biblical record here in vv.5–17.

Nor would it be logical, for the very reasons suggested by Josephus, for Nebuchadnezzar to have made Jehoiachin king rather than Zedekiah.

17 Nebuchadnezzar's records concerning his military movements after this Judean campaign in his seventh year are spotty at best. Thereafter, only a skirmish in northern Syria in his eighth year, a movement to the Tigris in the following year (including his mention of suppressing a rebel), followed by a trip to Syria are recorded. The main Chaldean chronicles then end, having stated only that Nebuchadnezzar, in his eleventh year, mustered his army for an expedition to Syria. Unfortunately, no Babylonian record of the campaign of 586 BC is extant.

One more glimpse of Nebuchadnezzar's further campaigning is afforded in one or two of the tablets that indicate he invaded Egypt in his thirty-seventh year (568/567 BC; cf. Jer 43:8–10; see Wiseman, *Chronicles of Chaldaean Kings*, 94–95).

25:1 Lachish Letter IV (*ANET*, 322) confirms Nebuchadnezzar's advance: "We are watching for the signals of Lachish ... for we cannot see Azekah."

דָּיֵק (*dāyēq*, "siege work"; cf. Jer 52:4) has been variously identified as a wall of circumvallation (Gray, 764) or a siege tower (Keil, 511–12; cf. GKC, 197–98). Sennacherib mentions the use of earthen ramps in his siege of Jerusalem, and the Assyrian kings often depicted the use of siege towers so that the attackers might fight on the same level as the defenders on the walls. The Hebrew term here probably signifies a tower that has been called into place atop the siege mound. For the similar mention of earthen ramps and siege towers, see Ezekiel 21:22.

2 Details of Nebuchadnezzar's systematic reduction of the countryside are confirmed in the Lachish Letters, which graphically portray the movement of the Babylonian forces in Judah (see *ANET*, 321–22). Evidence for the fall of Azekah (Letter IV), written soon after Jeremiah 34:7, is particularly revealing (see previous Note). As well the report of Judah's sending of a high army official to Egypt (Letter III) and of the unrest in Jerusalem (Letter VI) are illuminating, as is the mention of "the prophet" (= Jeremiah? Letter VI).

7 The Assyrian Annals attest the practice of putting out the eyes of prisoners (see A. Parrot, *Babylon* [New York: Philosophical Library, 1956], 97; cf. Jdg 16:21).

18 From Ezra 7:1 we learn that Ezra the scribe would descend from Seriah. Interestingly, Seriah's sons were not executed but merely deported (1Ch 6:15). Zephaniah may be that same son of Maaseiah whom Jeremiah (Jer 21:1; 29:25) mentioned as a notable priest. The three "doorkeepers" were seemingly priests whose special duty was to superintend the security of the temple; hence, they were important officials.

19 The exact function of the royal advisors is unclear. The Hebrew text describes them as "five men from those who saw the king's face." Jeremiah (Jer 52:25) gives their number as seven. Both sources indicate that this was not the complete total of royal advisors but merely those "who were found in the city" (i.e., had not been able to make their escape).

21 Excavations in Judah and Jerusalem confirm the biblical indication of the complete destruction wrought by the Babylonian invaders. For details see Unger, 291–92.

F. Historical Appendices (25:22–30)

1. Judah in Exile (25:22–26)

22Nebuchadnezzar king of Babylon appointed Gedaliah son of Ahikam, the son of
Shaphan, to be over the people he had left behind in Judah. 23When all the army officers
and their men heard that the king of Babylon had appointed Gedaliah as governor, they
came to Gedaliah at Mizpah — Ishmael son of Nethaniah, Johanan son of Kareah, Seraiah
son of Tanhumeth the Netophathite, Jaazaniah the son of the Maacathite, and their
men. 24Gedaliah took an oath to reassure them and their men. "Do not be afraid of the
Babylonian officials," he said. "Settle down in the land and serve the king of Babylon, and it
will go well with you."

25In the seventh month, however, Ishmael son of Nethaniah, the son of Elishama, who
was of royal blood, came with ten men and assassinated Gedaliah and also the men of
Judah and the Babylonians who were with him at Mizpah. 26At this, all the people from
the least to the greatest, together with the army officers, fled to Egypt for fear of the
Babylonians.

COMMENTARY

22–24 The captivity of God's disobedient people, begun in 605/604 BC, was completed. Seventy years would go by until the exiled Judeans would again see their homeland (2Ch 36:15–21). Although the prominent men of Jerusalem were largely deported, Jeremiah and Gedaliah were left behind (v.22; cf. Jer 39:11–14).

Jeremiah's stand on the Babylonian issue was doubtless well known. Gedaliah's attitude was probably that of Ahikam, his father and a noted official (2Ch 34:20), who had supported Jeremiah (Jer 26:24). The choice of Gedaliah as governor over the newly formed district was a popular one. At first things went well (cf. Jer 40:1–12). Because of their confidence in Gedaliah, many of the surviving little guerrilla bands made their way back to Jerusalem to lay down their arms and take up residence there (vv.23–24), as did many of the Judeans who had fled to the Transjordanian lands (cf. Jer 40:11–12). Even Jeremiah at first went to Mizpah to lend his assistance to Gedaliah (Jer 40:6).

25–26 Although Gedaliah was warned that Baalis, the Ammonite king, had sent Ishmael to assassinate him, Gedaliah trusted him (Jer 40:13–16). Ishmael came from a prominent family. His grandfather Elishama had served as Jehoiakim's secretary of state (Jer 36:12).

Supplemental details of Ishmael's dastardly crime are reported in Jeremiah. There we learn that following the assassination, Johanan ben Kareah caught up with Ishmael near the great pool in Gibeon and freed those whom Ishmael and his forces had captured. Ishmael, however, made good his escape to Ammon (Jer 41:11–15). Because the refugees feared reprisal for Gedaliah's murder, Johanan led a large contingent of them into Egypt, where the anti-Babylonian Pharaoh Apries was on the throne. The fleeing Jews took Jeremiah along with them despite his counsels and warnings (Jer 41:16–43:7).

NOTES

22 Confirmation of the existence and importance of Gedaliah comes from a clay seal impression from Lachish that reads, "Belonging to Gedaliah, who is over the house." See J. M. Ward, "Gedaliah," *IDB*, 3:360.

23 Seriah is to be distinguished from the high priest who was taken into exile (v.18). The names of Ishmael and Jaazaniah have been recovered from excavations in Israel and appear in many nonbiblical sources (for details, see Hobbs, 366).

26 The existence of the Jews in Egypt in the fifth century BC is now illustrated by the Elephantine Papyri. See B. Porten, *Archives from Elephantine* (Berkeley: Univ. of California Press, 1968).

2. The Later History of Jehoiachin (25:27–30)

[27]In the thirty-seventh year of the exile of Jehoiachin king of Judah, in the year Evil-
Merodach became king of Babylon, he released Jehoiachin from prison on the twenty-
seventh day of the twelfth month. [28]He spoke kindly to him and gave him a seat of honor
higher than those of the other kings who were with him in Babylon. [29]So Jehoiachin put
aside his prison clothes and for the rest of his life ate regularly at the king's table. [30]Day by
day the king gave Jehoiachin a regular allowance as long as he lived.

COMMENTARY

27–30 Evil-Merodach's (561–560 BC) release of the Judean king from prison and Jehoiachin's good treatment by the subsequent Babylonian kings (cf. Jer 52:31–34) finds confirmation from the recovery of ration tablets from the reign of Nabonidus listing among the recipients "Yaukin, king of the land of Yahud [Judah]." Thus, Jehoiachin was considered the rightful king of Judah even by the Babylonians.

Here the final curtain falls on the drama of the divided monarchy. The light of God's gracious concern for his people illuminates what had been a note of dark despair. Although God's people had been judged, as they must, yet God would be with them even in the midst of their sentence. Jehoiachin's release and renewed enjoyment of life thus stands as a harbinger of the further release and return of the entire nation, in accordance with God's promises (cf. Jer 31:18; La 5:21). Spiritually minded believers can perhaps see in this incident an assurance of God's greater redemption from bondage of those who look forward to him who gives release and eternal refreshment to all who love his appearing.

NOTES

28–30 Jehoiachin's renewed royal recognition harmonizes with the esteem in which he continued to be held in Judah. Jar handles found at Tell Beit Mirsim and Beth Shemesh bearing the stamp "Eliakim, steward of Yaukin" (= Jehoiachin) testify to the populace's continued recognition of Jehoiachin as the rightful king of Judah. For details of this inscription and Jehoiachin's name on the ration tablets from Nabonidus's reign, see Unger, 293, 296–97.

J. J. Granowski ("Jehoiachin at the King's Table: A Reading of the Ending of the Second Book of Kings," in *Reading between Texts*, ed. D. N. Fewell [Louisville: Westminster, 1992], 173–88) finds an interesting parallel between Jehoiachin's good treatment in Babylon and that of Mephibosheth by David (2Sa 9). In so doing he sees notes of both pessimism and optimism. Although Kings records the ending of an era, the fact that Jehoiachin lived on in friendly circumstances offered hope for Israel's new beginning. R. D. Nelson (*First and Second Kings* [IBC; Atlanta: John Knox, 1987], 267) suggests that Jehoiachin's fate was "richly ambiguous rather than merely negative."

We want to hear from you. Please send your comments about this book to us in care of zreview@zondervan.com. Thank you.